International Directory of COMPANY HISTORIES

International Directory of COMPANY HISTORIES

VOLUME 32

Editor

Jay P. Pederson

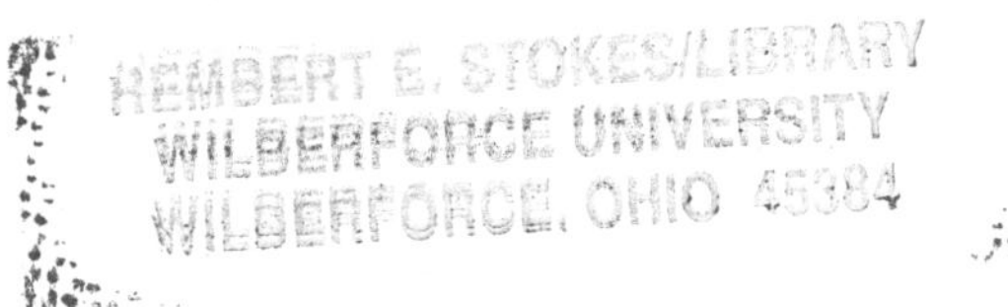

ST. JAMES PRESS

AN IMPRINT OF THE GALE GROUP

DETROIT • NEW YORK • SAN FRANCISCO
LONDON • BOSTON • WOODBRIDGE, CT

STAFF

Laura Standley Berger, Joann Cerrito, David J. Collins, Steve Cusack,
Nicolet V. Elert, Jamie C. FitzGerald, Kristin Hart, Laura S. Kryhoski,
Margaret Mazurkiewicz, Michael J. Tyrkus, *St. James Press Editorial Staff*

Peter M. Gareffa, *Managing Editor, St. James Press*

Library of Congress Catalog Number: 89-190943

British Library Cataloguing in Publication Data

International directory of company histories. Vol. 32
I. Jay P. Pederson
338.7409

ISBN 1-55862-391-4

Printed in the United States of America
Published simultaneously in the United Kingdom

St. James Press is an imprint of The Gale Group

Cover photograph: Trading floor of the Chicago Mercantile Exchange
(courtesy Chicago Mercantile Exchange)

10 9 8 7 6 5 4 3 2 1

CONTENTS

Company Histories

PREFACE

The St. James Press series *The International Directory of Company Histories (IDCH)* is intended for reference use by students, business people, librarians, historians, economists, investors, job candidates, and others who seek to learn more about the historical development of the world's most important companies. To date, *IDCH* has covered over 4,500 companies in 32 volumes.

Inclusion Criteria

Most companies chosen for inclusion in *IDCH* have achieved a minimum of US$50 million in annual sales and are leading influences in their industries or geographical locations. Companies may be publicly held, private, or nonprofit. State-owned companies that are important in their industries and that may operate much like public or private companies also are included. Wholly owned subsidiaries and divisions are profiled if they meet the requirements for inclusion. Entries on companies that have had major changes since they were last profiled may be selected for updating.

The *IDCH* series highlights 10% private and nonprofit companies, and features updated entries on approximately 45 companies per volume.

Entry Format

Each entry begins with the company's legal name, the address of its headquarters, its telephone, toll-free, and fax numbers, and its web site. A statement of public, private, state, or parent ownership follows. A company with a legal name in both English and the language of its headquarters country is listed by the English name, with the native-language name in parentheses.

The company's founding or earliest incorporation date, the number of employees, and the most recent available sales figures follow. Sales figures are given in local currencies with equivalents in U.S. dollars. For some private companies, sales figures are estimates and indicated by the abbreviation *est.* The entry lists the exchanges on which a company's stock is traded and its ticker symbol, as well as the company's NAIC codes.

Entries generally contain a *Company Perspectives* box which provides a short summary of the company's mission, goals, and ideals, a *Key Dates* box highlighting milestones in the company's history, lists of *Principal Subsidiaries, Principal Divisions, Principal Operating Units, Principal Competitors,* and articles for *Further Reading.*

American spelling is used throughout *IDCH*, and the word ''billion'' is used in its U.S. sense of one thousand million.

Sources

Entries have been compiled from publicly accessible sources both in print and on the Internet such as general and academic periodicals, books, annual reports, and material supplied by the companies themselves.

Cumulative Indexes

IDCH contains two indexes: the **Index to Companies**, which provides an alphabetical index to companies discussed in the text as well as to companies profiled, and the **Index to Industries**, which allows researchers to locate companies by their principal industry. Both indexes are cumulative and specific instructions for using them are found immediately preceding each index.

Suggestions Welcome

Comments and suggestions from users of *IDCH* on any aspect of the product as well as suggestions for companies to be included or updated are cordially invited. Please write:

The Editor
International Directory of Company Histories
St. James Press
27500 Drake Rd.
Farmington Hills, Michigan 48331-3535

ABBREVIATIONS FOR FORMS OF COMPANY INCORPORATION

A.B.	Aktiebolaget (Sweden)
A.G.	Aktiengesellschaft (Germany, Switzerland)
A.S.	Atieselskab (Denmark)
A.S.	Aksjeselskap (Denmark, Norway)
A.Ş.	Anomin Şirket (Turkey)
B.V.	Besloten Vennootschap met beperkte, Aansprakelijkheid (The Netherlands)
Co.	Company (United Kingdom, United States)
Corp.	Corporation (United States)
G.I.E.	Groupement d'Intérêt Economique (France)
GmbH	Gesellschaft mit beschränkter Haftung (Germany)
H.B.	Handelsbolaget (Sweden)
Inc.	Incorporated (United States)
KGaA	Kommanditgesellschaft auf Aktien (Germany)
K.K.	Kabushiki Kaisha (Japan)
LLC	Limited Liability Company (Middle East)
Ltd.	Limited (Canada, Japan, United Kingdom, United States)
N.V.	Naamloze Vennootschap (The Netherlands)
OY	Osakeyhtiöt (Finland)
PLC	Public Limited Company (United Kingdom)
PTY.	Proprietary (Australia, Hong Kong, South Africa)
S.A.	Société Anonyme (Belgium, France, Switzerland)
SpA	Società per Azioni (Italy)

ABBREVIATIONS FOR CURRENCY

DA	Algerian dinar
A$	Australian dollar
Sch	Austrian schilling
BFr	Belgian franc
Cr	Brazilian cruzado
C$	Canadian dollar
RMB	Chinese renminbi
DKr	Danish krone
E£	Egyptian pound
EUR	Euro Dollars
Fmk	Finnish markka
FFr	French franc
DM	German mark
HK$	Hong Kong dollar
HUF	Hungarian forint
Rs	Indian rupee
Rp	Indonesian rupiah
IR£	Irish pound
L	Italian lira
¥	Japanese yen
W	Korean won
KD	Kuwaiti dinar
LuxFr	Luxembourgian franc
M$	Malaysian ringgit
Dfl	Netherlands florin
Nfl	Netherlands florin
NZ$	New Zealand dollar
N	Nigerian naira
NKr	Norwegian krone
RO	Omani rial
P	Philippine peso
Esc	Portuguese escudo
Ru	Russian ruble
SRls	Saudi Arabian riyal
S$	Singapore dollar
R	South African rand
W	South Korean won
Pta	Spanish peseta
SKr	Swedish krona
SFr	Swiss franc
NT$	Taiwanese dollar
B	Thai baht
£	United Kingdom pound
$	United States dollar
B	Venezuelan bolivar
K	Zambian kwacha

International Directory of

COMPANY HISTORIES

A&E Television Networks

235 East 45th Street
New York, New York 10017
U.S.A.
Telephone: (212) 210-1400
Fax: (212) 983-4370
Web site: http://www.AandE.com

Private Company
Incorporated: 1984
Sales: $322 million (1997)
NAIC: 513210 Cable Television Networks; 512110 Video Production; 511120 Magazine Publishers

A&E Television Networks began modestly in 1984 with one cable channel, The Arts & Entertainment Network, which presented a variety of cultural programming, much of it British. By adding original programming and developing a strong franchise through its popular ''Biography'' series, the network succeeded in attracting more viewers as well as launching new cable channels, including The History Channel, The Biography Channel, and History Channel International. By 1999 the A&E Network reached more than 78 million cable subscribers, while The History Channel was seen by more than 70 million households in more than 50 countries.

Focusing on Cultural Programming: 1984–87

The Arts & Entertainment Network (A&E) was formed in 1984 by four partners: American Broadcasting Co. Inc. (ABC), the Hearst Corporation, National Broadcasting Co. Inc. (NBC), and the Rockefeller Group. Its predecessors were two failed cable ventures, the ARTS cable service, which was a joint venture of Hearst and ABC, and The Entertainment Channel, which was co-owned by The Rockefeller Group and RCA, then the parent of NBC. The Entertainment Channel had been launched as a premium channel that required subscribers to pay an extra monthly fee. Herb Granath, head of ABC Video Enterprises, recruited Nickolas Davatzes from Warner Amex Cable Communications to serve as chief executive.

A&E was established as a cultural cable channel, but unlike its non-cable competitor Public Broadcasting Service (PBS), it was expected to turn a profit. In order to persuade cable systems to carry the new channel, A&E offered to set up video libraries of its tapes in local libraries. Known as the National Cable Library Project, this tactic won favor for A&E in hundreds of communities that were wired for cable.

When it began broadcasting on February 1, 1984, the Arts & Entertainment Network went to 1,500 cable systems with nine million subscribers. The network had one sponsor, and its principal asset was an agreement with the British Broadcasting Corporation (BBC) that gave it first rights to a range of British programming. In its first year, two-thirds of A&E's programming came from the BBC.

By mid-1986, A&E was carried on more than 2,200 cable systems in the United States and Canada and reached nearly 20 million cable subscribers. About 40 percent of programming came from the BBC, including a ten-part miniseries on the Borgias and a six-part miniseries on Sigmund Freud. The network's programming, acquired at bargain prices, was predominantly cultural and included jazz performances, operas, dramas based on literary classics, symphonic concerts, classic movies, celebrity interviews, and a variety of documentaries. It also broadcast reruns of series acquired from the broadcast networks to fill its 20-hour broadcast day.

As A&E approached its third anniversary, *TV Guide* offered this appraisal: ''Clearly, A&E is delivering some of the very best of the world's television. It has more actors, dancers, singers, and musicians on a daily basis than any network, and a range of arts programming never before done by an advertiser-supported TV network.''

A Broader Range of Programming: 1987–92

In 1987 A&E made an important decision to acquire the rights to the ''Biography'' series, which initially aired once a week in the fall of 1987 and later became a key franchise for A&E in the 1990s. For its first three years, all of the episodes were acquired and nearly all were about historical figures.

The network turned its first profit in 1987, and in 1988 revenues surpassed $50 million, with an operating profit estimated at a modest $4 million. The network was reaching 37

Company Perspectives:

A&E Television Networks, a joint venture of The Hearst Corporation, ABC, Inc., and NBC, is an award-wining, international media company offering consumers a diverse communications environment including television programming, magazine publishing, web sites, music and home videos, as well as supporting nationwide initiatives.

million cable subscribers. From 1987 to 1997, it would enjoy an average growth of more than 30 percent per year in profits and revenues.

While A&E was still the home of fine arts programming, it had also added historical documentaries and several off-network sitcoms to its lineup. Such shows were cited as part of a trend away from ''narrowcasting'' and were in fact an attempt to broaden the network's appeal. Its core audience at this time was upscale and over the age of 25. New programs, such as ''Living Dangerously,'' which profiled people who liked to take risks, the weekly stand-up comedy series ''An Evening at the Improv,'' and a 19-week variety show called ''Good Time Café'' were designed to attract viewers between the ages of 18 and 25, and possibly even younger. A&E's broadcast of straight news footage of the Kennedy assassination in 1988 resulted in the network's highest ratings to date.

In 1990 A&E began commissioning original episodes of ''Biography,'' after it acquired the ''Biography'' library and trademark from the owner of the original series, which was broadcast in the early 1960s with Mike Wallace as host. New episodes covered contemporary political leaders and celebrities in addition to historical figures.

In 1991 A&E had four major programming categories: performing arts, drama, documentary, and comedy. Its daytime programming was filled with classic one-hour dramas such as ''The Fugitive,'' ''The Avengers,'' and ''The Rockford Files.'' During the year it began publishing the magazine *A&E Monthly,* which served as a program guide.

A Boost for Original Programming: 1993–94

A&E achieved its best rating to date in February 1993 with a varied mix of comedy, drama, documentary, and performing arts. It registered a 0.9 average audience rating, representing 532,000 households during prime time, according to A.C. Nielsen Co. A&E's president and CEO, Nickolas Davatzes, noted that the programming budget was the network's single largest expenditure. During the past year the network had boosted domestic production, producing three comedy series—''An Evening at the Improv,'' ''Caroline's Comedy Hour,'' and ''Comedy on the Road''—as well as such new series as ''Charlton Heston Presents the Bible'' and ''The American West.'' A&E also continued to maintain strong ties with international co-production partners, such as the BBC, with whom it did more co-productions than with any other partner.

Expansion plans outside the United States were limited to North America. A&E was reaching four million of the 6.5 million cable households in Canada and was in the developmental stages of expanding into Mexican households.

In June 1993 The Rockefeller Group sold its 12.5 percent interest to its three partners, Hearst, ABC, and NBC. The Rockefeller Group was the only partner without other television interests, and the company decided to sell its interest in A&E because it did not fit with its core business of real estate. The transaction left ABC and Hearst each owning 37.5 percent of A&E, with NBC owning the remaining 25 percent. The three remaining partners agreed to continue their agreement for an additional 50 years.

In December 1993 it was announced that News Production would produce 22 original episodes of ''The Twentieth Century'' for A&E starting in September 1994, with CBS news correspondent Mike Wallace as the host. The show was an update of a series that originally aired between 1957 and 1966 on CBS with Walter Cronkite as the host.

Ad revenues for 1993 increased by 30 percent to approximately $105 million. Profits rose 47 percent, although specific figures were not released, and total revenues were estimated at $147 million, a 27 percent increase over 1992. Davatzes termed 1993 ''an absolutely defining year'' for A&E.

A&E celebrated its tenth anniversary in 1994. It officially changed its name from Arts and Entertainment to A&E and redefined its range of programming, announcing that it would focus on three themes: original biographies, mysteries, and specials. Mysteries would include several whodunit-type series, and ''specials'' included miniseries and original movies. ''Biography,'' which was expanded from one night a week to five, continued to draw some of the network's highest ratings.

Biography and History, Growing in Importance: 1995–97

Plans for a separate history channel were announced in early 1993, and a new production unit was established in June of that year. Start-up costs were not revealed, but were expected to be less than the $100 million it cost USA Networks to launch the Sci-Fi Channel. In preparing for the launch, A&E acquired a documentary library from Lou Reda Productions and also bought long-term rights for a substantial archive of documentaries from Hearst Entertainment, a subsidiary of one of its parent companies.

The History Channel finally premiered on January 1, 1995. The company expected between 500,000 and one million subscribers at launch. Initial programming included four prime-time series: ''Year by Year,'' featuring documentary newsreels; ''History Alive,'' with original and exclusive historical documentaries; ''Movies in Time,'' including miniseries and movies such as ''Shogun'' and *Gandhi;* and both new and classic episodes of the documentary series ''Our Century.'' Approximately 30 percent of the channel's programming would be original. The History Channel was also perceived as being able to drive the company's expansion overseas. Many of A&E's international co-productions left it without international rights for those programs.

A&E added 18 percent more original programming in 1994 and 1995, creating several original specials based on its most

Key Dates:

1984: Arts and Entertainment Network is formed and begins broadcasting on February 1.
1987: ''Biography'' is introduced in the fall as a once-a-week prime-time series.
1990: The network begins commissioning original episodes of ''Biography.''
1993: The Rockefeller Group sells its interest in A&E to the three remaining partners: Hearst Corporation, ABC, and NBC.
1994: ''Biography'' is expanded to five nights a week. A&E celebrates its tenth anniversary by changing its name from Arts and Entertainment to A&E.
1995: The History Channel premieres on January 1. The History Channel U.K. is introduced on November 1.
1997: *Biography* magazine is launched.
1998: A&E launches its first digital channels, The Biography Channel and History Channel International, in November.

popular series, ''Biography'' and ''Investigative Reports with Bill Kurtis.'' For the 1994–95 season, A&E commissioned more than 100 hours of ''Biography'' regular programming. Other key prime-time series included ''A&E Stage,'' ''American Justice,'' ''Civil War Journal,'' and ''20th Century.'' Altogether, A&E ordered more than 640 hours of first-run material for its 1994–95 season, up from 520 hours for 1993–94 and 447 hours for 1992–93. The network planned to stick to its principal genres: biographies, mysteries, and documentaries, plus a variety of specials. Its fourth quarter 1994 ratings were the highest in its history, up some 38 percent over the previous year. A&E's average prime-time audience was pegged at 636,000 households by A.C. Nielsen.

The History Channel U.K. was introduced on November 1, 1995, with three-hour blocks scheduled at 4–7 p.m. weekdays. It was A&E's first international venture, in partnership with British Sky Broadcasting, a U.K. pay-TV direct-to-home operator. A&E planned to make the channel a full-time network once its digital transponder was launched in 1996 or 1997. Filling the three-hour block were ''History Alive,'' ''Our Century,'' and ''Biography,'' which was tailored for British audiences and featured a British host.

For 1995 A&E's prime-time ratings were flat, and there was a significant drop in daytime ratings, with the network losing daytime viewers to CNN and Court Television broadcasts of the O. J. Simpson trial.

By 1996 A&E's programming was 85 percent original, with only four out of 21 weekly prime-time hours not being original programming. January 1996 was the network's highest-rated month ever, due in large part to the success of the six-hour British miniseries ''Pride and Prejudice,'' based on the 19th-century novel of the same name by Jane Austen. The series garnered a prestigious Peabody Award for the network. As a result, A&E planned to sign up more literary specials for the coming year.

For the 1995–96 season, a sixth night of ''Biography'' was added, called ''Biography This Week'' and featuring a profile of someone who had made news during the past seven days. In some cases existing episodes were updated, but in other cases A&E rushed to produce a new episode, as it did for Yitzak Rabin, George Burns, and Gene Kelly.

Following a six-month trial period, Barnes & Noble agreed to install A&E's ''Biography'' line of $19.95 videos in its superstores, which would number about 400 in 1996. Trade sources estimated A&E Home Video's revenues at $14 million, most of which came from direct response sales. About four to six new videocassettes were released each quarter, and the network had a catalog of some 100 video titles.

The History Channel proved to be very successful. It began its second full year with eight million subscribers, a figure that doubled to 16 million by April 1996. It was the number one station that cable operators planned to add, mainly because of its superior programming quality, according to a survey by Myers Communications. In May 1996 the *New York Times* called The History Channel ''one of the most remarkable success stories in cable television.'' THC's strongest audience was male viewers between the ages of 35 and 64, and they tended to be more educated and affluent than the average television viewer.

The History Channel also led A&E's international expansion. In April 1996 Brazil's TVA, a pay-television service reaching 800,000 homes, signed a deal with The History Channel to launch a Brazilian version, to be called Canal Historia. In the United Kingdom, The History Channel U.K. surpassed the one million mark in subscribers in 1996, after Bell Cablemedia and Cable Tel began carrying it. THC was now being carried by five of the seven largest U.K. cable systems, giving it a 75 percent market penetration less than one year after being launched. In 1997 The History Channel expanded into the Nordic and Baltic regions of Europe, through an agreement with Modern Times Group, and also debuted in Canada. AETN International was the global division responsible for marketing THC outside the United States.

THC also expanded into radio and video in 1996. ''From the Archives of the History Channel'' debuted in September on ABC Radio Networks. The short features consisted of 60-second segments highlighting events and milestones that occurred on that date. Starting September 1, 1996, Borders Books and Music began offering THC videos in a dedicated space entitled, ''Bring History Home.''

By the end of 1996 THC had more than 35 million subscribers, adding 19.2 million subscribers during 1996 and projecting a total of more than 40 million subscribers by the end of 1997. It was carried in 70 of the top 100 markets and seen in almost every major American city.

A&E also continued to develop and expand its flagship series, ''Biography,'' and to introduce related products. The ''Biography'' web site (www.biography.com) was launched in July 1996, a version of the series for children premiered in fall 1996, and a line of ''Biography'' audio tapes was slated for 1997. Original ''Biography'' made-for-television movies were also in the works. A&E was commissioning more than 130 hours of original ''Biography'' episodes per season, and its library included episodes dating back to 1961.

In 1997 A&E partnered with publisher Random House to publish short biographies of about 200 pages each. The first four "Biography" books, published in the fall of 1997, covered Muhammad Ali, Jacqueline Kennedy Onassis, Ronald Reagan, and Pope John Paul II. The trade paperbacks were published by Crown, a subsidiary of Random House.

Now in its tenth year, "Biography" was one of cable television's most respected programs, as well as being A&E's strongest brand. When it was first launched, it was a form of programming that no other network was doing, and the franchise continued breaking new ground. In April 1997 A&E launched *Biography* magazine, with an initial circulation of 100,000 and content that was created independently of the TV program. *Biography* replaced the eight-year-old *A&E Monthly,* a general entertainment magazine that doubled as a program guide. *Biography* benefited from the distribution clout of The Hearst Corporation, one of A&E's parent companies. By mid-1998, circulation had reached 367,000.

The year 1997 was A&E's most profitable and highest-rated in its 13-year history. It had an average 1.4 rating in prime time for the 1996–97 season, up from 1.3 for 1995–96. The network projected operating cash for 1997 would be $129 million, against total revenues of $322 million. The network reached more than 70 million cable subscribers.

Building on Strengths: 1998–99

A&E expanded its programming in biography, mystery, and documentaries for the 1998–99 and 1999–2000 seasons. There were about 130 original "Biography" premieres each season, and "Biography Movies" offered extended looks at P.T. Barnum, Lillian Hellman, and Dashiell Hammett, among others. Original mysteries were produced for A&E's "Mysteries to Die For" series, and different documentary series were shown each weeknight at 9 p.m. following "Biography: American Justice" and "Investigative Reports," both hosted by Bill Kurtis; "L.A. Detectives" and "Inside Stories," two new series; and "The Unexplained," which also featured Kurtis as the host.

THC announced that it would team with Mayflower Tours to promote tours to U.S. landmarks as part of a growing interest in historic travel. A special web site, www.historytravel.com, was launched, and trips were scheduled to Alcatraz and to Northeast seaports on a vintage rumrunner. A quarterly history travel magazine was also planned. These efforts were tied in to THC's Saturday morning series "History Channel Traveler."

By January 1998 it was clear that THC could become as successful as A&E. THC's success was attributed to several factors: a strong parent in A&E, which has helped promote the network; high-quality programming; few direct competitors; and an audience eager for history programming. As THC grew, it relied less on archive shows from A&E's library, many of them on military themes, and began to produce original programming. At the beginning of 1998 it had about 40 percent original programming, and it expected to have about 75 percent original programming for the 1998–99 season.

In October 1998 THC teamed with Madison Square Garden Network to develop several short-form programs to be called "This Moment in New York Sports History." MSGN planned to air the 30-second shorts during its coverage of New York sports events and its nightly SportsDesk news show.

In November 1998 A&E launched its first digital channels, The Biography Channel and History Channel International. The channels would be carried on Tele-Communications Inc.'s digital Headend in the Sky system. The commitment to digital format required A&E to spend up to $10 million annually to reformat programming from A&E and The History Channel for digital distribution and to rent transponder space.

In February 1999 The History Channel premiered its new slogan, "The official network of every millennium." In August THC posted its highest-rated prime time to date with an average 0.8 universe rating, equal to 500,000 households. Shows broadcast during the month included the premier of THC's original miniseries "The History of Sex." In September THC reported that it passed the 60 million mark in subscribers, making it one of the fastest-growing cable services.

A&E also continued to build its "Biography" franchise in 1999. Circulation of "Biography" magazine for the first half of 1999 reached 528,000, an increase of 44 percent over the previous year. Magazine advertising revenues for the first seven months of 1999 were up 250 percent, to about $5 million.

In the spring of 1999 promotion of four two-hour TV movies in the Horatio Hornblower series included cross-promotions by the American Library Association, Barnes & Noble, publisher Little Brown, and software maker Strategy First.

Original Programming, a Continuing Strength

A&E realized that its strength resided in the quality of its original programming. Since the A&E Network was formed in 1984, it had won numerous Emmy Awards and 88 Cable ACE Awards. After only five years, The History Channel was reaching nearly as many cable subscribers as A&E and was the second fastest growing television network in U.S. history. The company's two other channels, The Biography Channel and History Channel International, were positioned to grow once the cable industry and the viewing public switched to a greater acceptance of digital television.

Principal Divisions

The History Channel; The Biography Channel; History Channel International; AETN Enterprises; AETN International.

Principal Competitors

The Discovery Channel; Public Broadcasting Service.

Further Reading

"A&E Breaks 70 Million," *Broadcasting & Cable,* October 13, 1997, p. 49.

"A&E Networks," *Mediaweek,* February 8, 1999, p. 12.

"A&E Powers Up," *Broadcasting & Cable,* May 10, 1993, p. 38.

"A&E Spin-Off Network The History Channel Will Debut on Jan. 1, 1995," *Broadcasting & Cable,* May 30, 1994, p. 26.

"Behind the Scenes," *Broadcasting & Cable,* March 10, 1997, p. S10.

" 'Biography' at 10," *Broadcasting & Cable,* March 10, 1997, p. S1.

"The Bio on 'Biography,' " *Mediaweek,* June 20, 1994, p. 4.

Block, Valerie, "Cable Spinoff Magazine Has Life of Its Own," *Crain's New York Business,* September 13, 1999, p. 16.

Brown, Rich, "Arts & Entertainment," *Broadcasting & Cable,* February 20, 1995, p. 23.

——, "Arts & Entertainment to Make History," *Broadcasting & Cable,* April 19, 1993, p. 27.

——, "Biography Channel in Works; A&E Also Plans to Capitalize on Popular Series with Audiocassettes," *Broadcasting & Cable,* June 17, 1996, p. 58.

——, "New Networks Jockey for Channel Position," *Broadcasting & Cable,* May 23, 1994, p. 42.

——, "Programming Investment Provides Boost for A&E," *Broadcasting & Cable,* March 1, 1993, p. 24.

Burgi, Michael, "A&E Networks," *Mediaweek,* June 17, 1996, p. 12.

——, "A&E: Ten Years After; With a New Name, Image and World View," *Mediaweek,* February 7, 1994, p. 9.

——, "Arts & Entertainment Revamps Format," *Adweek Eastern Edition,* February 7, 1994, p. 12.

——, "Cable's Menu Expands with Original Fare," *Mediaweek,* April 11, 1994, p. 24.

"Cable Networks Set Their Fall Slates," *Broadcasting,* May 4, 1992, p. 42.

Carter, Bill, "For History on Cable, the Time Has Arrived," *New York Times,* May 20, 1996, p. C1.

Coates, Colby, "At A&E, Some of the Best New Shows Are the Old Shows," *Mediaweek,* July 20, 1992, p.12.

Cooper, Jim, "The History Channel," *Mediaweek,* September 6, 1999, p. 16.

——, "History Channel Plays Ball," *Mediaweek,* October 19, 1998, p. 16.

Dempsey, John, "Cablers Strike up the Band," *Variety,* June 22, 1998, p. 1.

——, "TV Rewrites Rerun Rules," *Variety,* January 11, 1999, p. 1.

"Docs on Tap for A&E," *Broadcasting & Cable,* June 1, 1998, p. 36.

"Expanding on a Theme," *Broadcasting & Cable,* March 10, 1997, p. S16.

Flinn, John, "It's All History Now," *Adweek Eastern Edition,* April 29, 1996, p. S6.

Goldstein, Seth, "Biography Adds Life to Barnes & Noble," *Billboard,* March 16, 1996, p. 91.

——, "Borders Gets Vid Exclusive," *Billboard,* August 31, 1996, p. 6.

——, "Two Cable Networks Move into Retail," *Billboard,* May 27, 1995, p. 7.

"Hairy-Chested History," *New York Times,* April 21, 1999, p. B7.

Hickey, Neil, "Just What Cable Didn't Need—Another Cultural Network," *TV Guide,* August 2, 1986, p. 34.

"History Channel Adds Production Unit," *Broadcasting & Cable,* June 7, 1993, p. 26.

"History Channel Opens World to 'Traveler,' " *Broadcasting & Cable,* November 10, 1997, p. 66.

"History for the Ages," *Broadcasting & Cable,* February 15, 1999, p. 70.

Hovey, Susan, "A Biography Worth Reading," *Folio,* April 1, 1997, p. 36.

"Interest in Cable Network Is Sold to 3 Other Parties," *Wall Street Journal,* June 16, 1993, p. B8.

Johnson, Debra, "A&E Is Home Sweet Home to British Drama," *Broadcasting & Cable,* January 13, 1997, p. 92.

Johnson, Debra, and Nicole McCormick, "History Tops 1 Million Subs," *Broadcasting & Cable,* October 21, 1996, p. 50.

Katz, Michael, "A&E and MTG Pair for History," *Broadcasting & Cable,* August 25, 1997, p. 39.

——, "A&E Buys Mundo Ole Stake," *Broadcasting & Cable,* September 29, 1997, p. 69.

Kleinfield, N.R., "A&E: A Cable Success Story," *New York Times,* April 16, 1989, p. H31.

"Look at Him," *Broadcasting & Cable,* June 1, 1998, p. 15.

McAvoy, Kim, "Prime Time for Documentaries," *Broadcasting & Cable,* June 29, 1998, p. 34.

McClellan, Steve, "Making History at A&E," *Broadcasting & Cable,* March 10, 1997, p. 55.

McConville, Jim, "Arts & Entertainment," *Broadcasting & Cable,* February 19, 1996, p. 34.

——, "History Channel to Launch in London," *Broadcasting & Cable,* October 9, 1995, p. 60.

"New 'Century,' " *Broadcasting & Cable,* December 13, 1993, p. 30.

Newman, Melinda, "A&E Requests More of Bennett's 'Live,' " *Billboard,* April 11, 1998, p. 14.

O'Connor, John J., "Revered or Reviled in the Name of Biography," *New York Times,* March 20, 1997, p. B1.

Petrozzello, Donna, "A&E Unveils Digital Networks," *Broadcasting & Cable,* November 16, 1998, p. 56.

——, "History Channel Makes History," *Broadcasting & Cable,* March 2, 1998, p. 37.

——, "Launch Links ABC, History Channel," *Broadcasting & Cable,* August 5, 1993, p. 41.

——, "Making Cable Artful and Entertaining," *Broadcasting & Cable,* November 23, 1998, p. 69.

——, "Making History," *Broadcasting & Cable,* April 27, 1998, p. 44.

——, "Secrets and Lives: A&E Will Offer Mystery and Biography Feature-Length Films," *Broadcasting & Cable,* May 4, 1998, p. 102.

Richmond, Ray. "Dramatic Strategy Puts A&E at Home," *Variety,* May 5, 1997, p. 221.

"The Rockefeller Group Has Relinquished Its 12.5% Interest in the A&E Network," *Broadcasting & Cable,* June 21, 1993, p. 76.

Rosenblum, Trudi M., "A&E Television Network Launches A&E Audiobooks," *Publishers Weekly,* May 5, 1997, p. 38.

Schlosser, Joe, "A&E Taking 'Biography' to the Movies," *Broadcasting & Cable,* May 5, 1997, p. 62.

——, "Cable's Class of 1995," *Broadcasting & Cable,* March 17, 1997, p. 65.

Schneider, Steve, "A&E Aims to Woo Younger Viewers," *New York Times,* February 22, 1987, p. H30.

——, "A&E Is Trying to Broaden Its Image," *New York Times,* October 19, 1986, p. H29.

"Several Cable Networks," *Mediaweek,* April 1, 1996, p. 16.

Shepherd, Lloyd, "Discovery in, A&E out at BBC," *Broadcasting & Cable,* July 14, 1997, p. 18.

Stanley, T.L., "A&E Assembles Literary Armada to Help Buoy Hornblower Films," *Brandweek,* March 1, 1999, p. 6.

Stephens, Francine, "A&E's 'Biography' Finally Gets Booked," *Publishers Weekly,* May 26, 1997, p. 24.

Torpey-Kemph, Anne, "History Channel Hits 60 Mil Mark," *Mediaweek,* September 13, 1999, p. 30.

Worrell, Kris, "The Past Is Present on History," *Broadcasting & Cable,* May 4, 1998, p. 72.

—David P. Bianco

Activision, Inc.

3100 Ocean Park Boulevard
Santa Monica, California 90405
U.S.A.
Telephone: (310) 255-2000
Fax: (310) 255-2100
Web site: http://www.activision.com

Public Company
Incorporated: 1979
Employees: 800
Sales: $436.5 million (1999)
Stock Exchanges: NASDAQ
Ticker Symbol: ATVI
NAIC: 51121 Software Publishers

Headquartered in Santa Monica, with five domestic and ten international offices, Activision, Inc. is a leading designer, publisher, and distributor of interactive entertainment software. Although the company's mainstay is electronic games for PlayStation, Nintendo, and Sega system consoles, Activision also sells lifestyle CDs and a broad range of PC games (*Earthworm Jim, Muppet Treasure Island, Battletech, Spycraft*) appealing to all ages. From the notorious *Quake* and *Cabela's Big Game Hunter* series to *Star Trek* and Disney title franchises, Activision has seen its revenues jump to nearly half a billion dollars in the last few years. Led by Robert Kotick and Brian Kelly, its under-40 wunderkinds, Activision is poised for the new century with a myriad of software titles, from value-based to top-of-the-line graphics, and several exclusive distribution agreements with the industry's top game designers.

Birth of Electronic Gaming in the 1970s and 1980s

Activision's story begins in 1979, just a year after the first compact disc (CD) was developed by the Philips Consumer Electronics company based in The Netherlands. Video arcade games had been in existence since Bruce Bushnell founded Atari and created *Pong* in 1972, launching what became the electronic gaming industry. As a result of Bushnell's achievements, northern California-based Activision put out its shingle as the first independent developer and distributor of entertainment software. The fledgling company's aim was to enter the embryonic gaming market and capture a healthy chunk before competitors realized the industry's true potential. In 1980, following the introduction of the Atari 2600 home video console, Activision debuted its first series of titles for the Atari 2600 called *Pitfall!* While Atari designed and sold its own games, including *Centipede* and *Missile Command,* Activision countered with *Kaboom!* in 1981 and *River Raid* in 1982. Activision's titles went on to sell millions and put the company on the map; Atari reaped billions and then fell into disarray from poor management.

Although Atari was acquired, split up, and able to reemerge many years later, it had lost its edge in the 1980s. Activision and several other start-ups picked up the slack and ran. One of Activision's major competitors, Infocom, introduced the adventure game *Zork* in 1982. *Zork,* like the *Pitfall!* series, was a phenomenal success and spawned four sequels and two spinoffs (*Enchanter* and *Sorcerer*), which eventually became part of the Activision brand lineup.

In 1983 Activision capitalized on its recognition by going public. Yet trouble, similar to the fate suffered by Atari, was down the road. Following the old adage of beating the competition by joining it, Activision acquired Infocom in 1987. The newer, bigger Activision's vision for the future included not only changing its name to Mediagenic in 1988, but expanding its product line beyond gaming software to include business applications programs as well. In retrospect, this was a miscalculation—the Activision name and brand recognition were quite strong and taking its core business beyond electronic entertainment was a mistake. Yet Mediagenic did leave its mark on the industry by producing the first CD-ROM interactive entertainment game, *The Manhole,* and by having the prescience to open an office in Japan, a technological hotbed of the industry.

Interactive Games Boom: 1990s

By the dawn of the 1990s, the Activision name was about to be resurrected. The executive management of the BHK Corporation, Robert A. Kotick and Brian G. Kelly, bought a control-

> **Company Perspectives:**
>
> *Every day, the employees of Activision work hard to provide audiences around the world with compelling interactive entertainment. The company is recognized as a leading publisher, developer and distributor of quality innovative software and is affiliated with some of the most important brands in entertainment, including Disney/Pixar's* Toy Story 2 *and* A Bug's Life, *Disney's* Tarzan, *LucasArt's* Star Wars: Episode 1 The Phantom Menace*; Marvel Comic's* X-MEN *and* Spider-Man *and Paramount's* Star Trek.

ling interest in Mediagenic in 1991, a year in which Mediagenic lost $26.8 million on revenues of $28.8 million. The following year, after merging the Disc Company into Mediagenic, the company was restructured, changed its name back to Activision, and moved to a new headquarters in Santa Monica. Kotick was chairman and CEO, and Kelly was president and COO of the rechristened company. The same year, 1992, the company continued global expansion by opening its first office in Australia and another in the United Kingdom in 1993.

By 1994 Activision needed funds to keep up its aggressive production schedule for new and improved game titles and to maintain its share of the North American entertainment software market, which had reached sales of $930 million. The company raised some $40 million to further these needs, as the average cost to produce an exciting, well-developed electronic game ran upwards of $200,000, and the company needed to sell around 40,000 copies to break even. But Activision was doing something right; by fiscal 1995 (March 31) revenues reached $57.8 million and the following year brought a healthy climb to $86.6 million, with earnings jumping from $1.9 million in 1995 to $5.9 million for 1996.

For Activision, 1997 was a heady year. Not only did the company buy worldwide interactive rights to the popular *Heavy Gear* robot role-playing games (a successor to the *Mech Warrior 2* product line) and the best-selling *Quake II,* but it teamed up with Hollywood action movie heavyweight Bruce Willis on the PlayStation game *Apocalypse.* This marked the debut of any creative property or game designed specifically for a well-known personality. In addition, Activision made several significant acquisitions, including that of game developer Raven Software Corporation (maker of the popular *Heretic* series of titles), a German marketing firm, and two interactive software distributors (CentreSoft Ltd. of the United Kingdom and NBG EDV Handels & Verlag GmbH, based in Germany). The company finished its fiscal year with revenues of $189.2 million, a stunning 119 percent increase over the previous year's $86.6 million.

Continuing with its international expansion efforts, Activision opened an office in France in 1998. On the domestic front came the purchase of Head Game Publishing, the Minnesota-based software distributor of sporting games, such as the best-selling *Cabela* hunting series, and the worldwide rights to the next installment of the ever popular *Quake* series from Id Software, called *Quake III Arena.* The company also inked several development deals with corporate giants: with Marvel Comics, to develop PlayStation games featuring perennial cartoon and comic book favorites Spiderman and the X-Men; with Disney Interactive, to create tie-in games from its popular animated films, including *Tarzan, Toy Story 2,* and *A Bug's Life*; and with Viacom Consumer Products, to design and distribute games based on the Star Trek franchise, which included the original *Star Trek* television series and its successors *Star Trek: The Next Generation, Star Trek: Deep Space Nine,* and *Star Trek: Voyager.* The Viacom deal also included the nine *Star Trek* feature films. Yet another coup came when Activision and LucasArts Entertainment Company (founded by George Lucas of *Star Wars* fame) entered into an exclusive two-year publishing and distribution partnership in the United Kingdom and 45 other countries to distribute all forthcoming LucasArts games for computers and PlayStation consoles.

Each of the aforementioned agreements put Activision in an incredibly strong position for the next few years. This was backed up by its fiscal 1998 numbers, which were restated to include revenues from acquisitions, and reached nearly $312.1 million. On the management front, Kelly was named co-chairman with Kotick, and was replaced as president and COO by former Con-Agra snack foods president Ron Doornink.

Trouble in Mind: 1998 and 1999

Despite Activision's growth through acquisitions and exclusivity agreements, the company also was affected by major changes in the industry itself. The phenomenal success of electronic gaming, which increased by more than 40 percent to $5.5 billion in 1998 (sales came close to rivaling movie box office receipts at $6.9 billion), brought greater visibility. With this visibility came the worst kind of scrutiny after the teenage shooting sprees in Colorado, Kentucky, and Washington. Belatedly, parents became concerned about the games their children were playing and the possible effects of violence and blood-spattered screens. For their part, game developers, Activision included, toned down the blood and gore in some of the more popular games played by younger kids, while labeling games with age indicators (''E'' for everyone, ''T'' for teens, ''M'' for mature, ''A'' for adults only). If the labels were not enforced by retailers or renting establishments, however, they did little good. Some legislators proposed making it a crime to sell ''mature'' or ''adults only'' games to minors; the gaming industry proposed electronic tagging for adult or mature games, which alerted cashiers during scanning to require identification if the purchaser was not an adult. Regardless of these or other measures, however, many violent games were downloaded from the Internet, for which there was no regulation.

Caught in the maelstrom was Activision. Several of its games were known for explicit graphics, including the best-selling *Quake* series the company distributed for Id Software. Activision was also the target of a Seattle advocacy group called Mothers Against Violence when a member's son saw an advertisement for *Vigilante 8* featuring an armed school bus and an expelled misfit named Molo who sought retribution through violent acts. In a May *Wall Street Journal* article, Doug Lowenstein, president of the Interactive Digital Software Association (IDSA), a lobbying group for electronic game developers and distributors, stated that though there was little research, this much could be said: about 57 percent of all electronic games

Key Dates:

1979: Activision is founded.
1980: Designs and sells its first Atari 2600 game series, *Pitfall!*
1983: Company goes public.
1988: Activision becomes Mediagenic.
1991: Robert Kotick and Brian Kelly acquire Mediagenic.
1992: Company is restructured, reincorporated, and again named Activision.
1997: Revenues hit $189.2 million, 119 percent over previous year's $86.6 million.
1998: Revenues snowball to $312.1 million.
1999: Revenues top $436.5 million; income increases by 193 percent to $15.3 million.

were played by adults, and converted board games such as Life and Monopoly were among the market's fastest-growing products. Further, in the past five years, of the 5,000 games put into the rating system, more than two-thirds were deemed appropriate for all ages to play. Quoted in a May *New York Times* article, Lowenstein was determined to put the issue to rest once and for all: "The evidence does not exist to support a link between playing violent video games and community mass murder. Video games don't teach people to hate. Video games don't teach people to become Nazis." Yet for legislators and parents, the issue was far from over.

Although legislation controlling video game content had not been passed, Activision and several other developers independently scaled back the graphic gore in some of the historical warfare or "god-games." Activision's popular *Civilization: Call to Power* was among the toned down games, and less brutal versions from both Microsoft (*Age of Empires II*) and Electronic Arts (*Alpha Centauri*) were released as well. Although the violence question was not settled and would not be for some time, Activision carried on business as usual in 1999. The company continued its trend of exclusive distribution agreements with three more deals: the first with the Liverpool-based Psygnosis, for the company to sell and distribute all of Psygnosis's PlayStation and CD entertainment software titles (including the multimillion-selling *Formula One, Destruction Derby,* and *Colony Wars* series) in North America; the second with Fox Sports, for international territories including Europe, Asia, India, the Middle East, and South Africa; and the third with Codemasters Limited, to become its exclusive North American affiliate label.

Activision's next move, a merger/acquisition, hinged on its desire to provide customers with a wide-ranging product line. Expert Software, Inc., a Florida-based mass market developer and distributor of value-priced leisure software, was merged into Activision's holdings and marked its segue into the burgeoning lower-priced software market segment. This was followed by the purchase of another Florida-based developer, Elsinore Multimedia, which had created the *Cabela's Big Game Hunter* series for Head Games (acquired by Activision in 1997), which had become a huge best-seller because of what Johnny Wilson, editor-in-chief of *Computer Gaming World,* considered the "Bubba factor," that is, low-cost games sold through discount chains such as Wal-Mart. Then came another software developer, the Los Angeles-based Neversoft Entertainment, designers of the successful *Tony Hawk Pro Skater* titles.

In the late 1990s game designers and distributors, Activision included, were experiencing a substantial shift away from PC games to consoles. The introduction of Sega's Dreamcast system provided another jolt to the trend in the fall of 1999. Although Activision rolled with the punches by creating games for Dreamcast systems, just as it did for PlayStation and Nintendo 64, it soon became a question of how many dollars to allocate to developing new PC games if consumers were abandoning them in favor of the much more realistic console games. As the competition grew more intense, rising development costs (running as much as $2 million per game) and retail space (usually for from 50 to 75 titles, when nearly 4,000 were released annually) were serious threats. Statistics quoted in the *Wall Street Journal* found that the consoles were eating away at the PC market share, which was 40 percent of the gaming market in 1997 and down to 34 percent in 1998. The trend was due to continue after Dreamcast's heavily touted debut and new Nintendo and PlayStation consoles due out in 2000.

For fiscal year 1999, Activision was on a roll with year-end revenues rocketing 40 percent to $436.5 million, with net income leaping to $15.3 million from the previous year's $5.1 million, a whopping 197 percent increase. North American operations in 1999 increased from the previous fiscal year's 24 percent to 34 percent of revenues, while international revenues fell slightly from 1998's 71 percent to 1999's 66 percent. Yet both segments experienced significant growth, with domestic operations rising 66 percent and international operations climbing 29 percent for 1999. To keep up with expanding operations, Activision's top three, Kotick, Kelly, and Doornick, added two new executive vice-presidents to the fold—Michael Rowe and Kathy Vrabeck—to oversee human resources and global brand management, respectively.

PCs, Consoles, and Beyond: 2000 Forward

As the turn of the century approached, Activision was well positioned to maintain its status as a leading interactive entertainment company with publishing and development operations in the United States, Canada, the United Kingdom, France, Germany, Japan, and Australia and distributing arms in Belgium, Germany, The Netherlands, and the United Kingdom. With the company's extensive domestic distribution network, upwards of 11,000 retail locations in North America, Activision hedged its bets by designing and distributing games for a variety of platforms, from PCs to the consoles, including PlayStation, Nintendo 64, Dreamcast, and even Nintendo's handheld Gameboy. With increased exposure through motion picture tie-ins, both from movies to games (*A Bug's Life* and *Toy Story 2*), and from games to movies (*Interstate 76, Spycraft,* and *Zork*), Activision continued to support its current franchise titles and was actively seeking new properties with proven potential.

Principal Divisions

Activision Merchandising TDC; Activision Publishing; Activision Studios.

Principal Competitors

Electronic Arts, Inc.; Nintendo Company; GT Interactive Software Corporation; Eidos Interactive Inc.; Microsoft Corporation; Sony Corporation.

Further Reading

Pollack, Andrew, "*Star Trek* Set to Become Video Games," *New York Times,* September 28, 1998.

Takahashi, Dean, "*Deer Hunter* Hit Shoots Down Computer-Game Snobs," *Wall Street Journal,* October 1, 1998, n.p.

——, "Entertainment + Technology: You've Played the Game . . . Now See the Movie, Or So Hollywood Hopes," *Wall Street Journal,* March 14, 1999, p. R14.

——, "Game Makers, Taking Hits, Try to Shield Kids," *Wall Street Journal,* May 25, 1999, p. B1.

——, "New Video Games Will Challenge PCs," *Wall Street Journal,* September 2, 1999, p. B6.

——, "Three New Games Let You Build Civilizations, But This Time Play Nice," *Wall Street Journal,* August 5, 1999, p. B1.

——, "Video-Game Makers See Soaring Sales Now—and Lots of Trouble Ahead," *Wall Street Journal,* June 15, 1998, p. R10.

—Nelson Rhodes

AFC Enterprises, Inc.

Six Concourse Parkway
Suite 1700
Atlanta, Georgia 30328-5352
U.S.A.
Telephone: (770) 391-9500
Toll Free: (800) 222-5857
Fax: (770) 353-3074
Web site: http://www.afc-online.com

Private Company
Incorporated: 1992 as America's Favorite Chicken Company, Inc.
Employees: 17,359
Sales: $609.1 million (1998)
NAIC: 722211 Limited-Service Restaurants; 722213 Snack & Nonalcoholic Beverage Bars; 311920 Coffee & Tea Manufacturing; 422490 Other Grocery & Related Products Wholesalers

AFC Enterprises, Inc., through its ownership of the Popeyes Chicken and Biscuits and Churchs Chicken chains, holds the number two position in the U.S. fast-food chicken sector, trailing only KFC, which is owned by TRICON Global Restaurants, Inc. The Popeyes chain, specializing in a Cajun-style fried chicken that is spicier than most conventional recipes, consists of 1,325 units, 1,152 of which are franchised. Total sales for the Popeyes system of franchises were $954 million in 1998. Churchs, which features a Southern-style menu, numbers 1,450 units, 948 of which are franchised. The Churchs system recorded sales of more than $755 million in 1998. AFC also owns the Cinnabon chain of 370 cinnamon roll bakeries, which are located in 39 states, Canada, and Mexico; 171 of these outlets are franchised. The company's Seattle Coffee Company subsidiary is a maker and wholesaler of specialty coffees and owns and franchises 75 Seattle's Best Coffee and 18 Torrefazione Italia coffeehouses. Overall, of the company's more than 3,300 restaurants, bakeries, and cafes, nearly 550 of them are located outside of the United States, in about two dozen foreign countries. The Ultrafryer Systems unit of AFC Enterprises makes gas fryers and other restaurant equipment, which it sells to its own restaurants and to other restaurant operators. AFC Enterprises is privately held. Major shareholders include investment company Freeman Spogli & Co., with a 54 percent stake; Canadian Imperial Bank of Commerce, 16 percent; and Frank Belatti, the company's chairman and CEO, eight percent.

Popeyes Early Years

The first Popeyes was opened by Al Copeland in June 1972. Copeland's success with Popeyes is a classic rags-to-riches tale. A native of New Orleans, Copeland dropped out of tenth grade at age 16 to help support his ailing mother and, after working for some time as a soda jerk, was hired by his older brother who ran a chain of donut shops. At 18, Copeland sold his car for capital to open his own one-man donut operation, thereby becoming his brother's first franchisee. He quickly turned the shop into the chain's biggest moneymaker and went on to spend ten modestly successful years in the donut business. The opening of a Kentucky Fried Chicken store in New Orleans in 1966, however, caught Copeland's eye when he saw that KFC—with a shorter workday—was making about four times as much money per week as his donut shop. Inspired by KFC's success, Copeland used his donut profits to open a restaurant in 1971 named Chicken on the Run.

After six months of operation, Chicken on the Run was grossing only $1,100 a week—$900 short of the break-even point—which prompted Copeland to close the store and begin planning for another donut shop. In a last-ditch effort at success in the chicken business, however, he chose a spicier Louisiana Cajun-style recipe and reopened the restaurant under the name Popeyes Mighty Good Fried Chicken, after Popeye Doyle, Gene Hackman's character in the film *The French Connection.* In its third week of operation, Copeland's revived chicken restaurant brought in $2,100 of receipts, breaking the profit barrier for the first time.

Copeland opened his second Popeyes in New Orleans about a year later, by which time the original location was selling more than $5,000 worth of chicken a week. By the end of 1974, there were 15 Popeyes in operation, and within only two years

Company Perspectives:

''We believe we have an obligation to create economic opportunity in the communities we serve—an obligation both to those communities and to our business. If we can stimulate genuine economic expansion and opportunity in a community, then in all likelihood we can enhance our own position in that market and make ourselves stronger in the process. To that end, we manage this company under a philosophy that requires us to ask ourselves constantly whether we are doing the most effective job possible of deploying our corporate resources not only to generate a fair return on current investments, but to create economic and human opportunity in the markets we are privileged to serve.'' —Frank Belatti, chairman and CEO

of opening the second Popeyes the number had grown to 24. Unable to find a bank willing to finance the chain's early expansion, Copeland relied upon the company's own cash flow. In 1975, what would become the company's most popular advertising campaign was launched, featuring the ''Love That Chicken'' jingle performed by local musician Dr. John. The jingle became wildly popular in New Orleans, so much so that it was once spontaneously sung in unison by the Superdome crowd at a New Orleans Saints football game.

Copeland began franchising Popeyes in 1977 and brought in his brother Bill to handle the expansion program. At the time, there were already about 50 company-owned stores in the chain. Although the Popeyes system increased its sales in 1977 to $21.5 million—about $5 million more than the previous year—the company recorded a $391,381 net loss. In 1978 the company nearly folded when the chain's rapid expansion led to overextended credit. Rather than scale back the pace of growth, however, Copeland continued his aggressive marketing tactics and proceeded with developing a strong territorial franchising system. By mid-1978, Popeyes restaurants were located in 28 cities, for a total of 125 units ranging geographically from El Paso to Miami to Detroit. That same year, company-owned stores averaged more than $12,000 in sales per week, while franchised units brought in roughly $9,000. Popeyes' advertising continued to emphasize the company's New Orleans roots, featuring local landmarks and the jazz music of Louisiana-based artists. Popeyes' menu included, along with its trademark spicy chicken, homemade onion rings, corn on the cob, deep-fried clams, and Louisiana Dirty Rice dressing.

Expansionary 1980s

By the early 1980s, Popeyes was the third largest fast-food chicken chain, behind KFC and Churchs. Under Popeyes' corporate structure, company-owned stores—which numbered 76 in November 1982—were held by Al Copeland Enterprises, Inc., while the 239 outside-owned franchises were overseen by a subsidiary of Al Copeland Enterprises named Popeyes Famous Fried Chicken and Biscuits. In the Popeyes system, stores were franchised five at a time; buyers paid $25,000 for the first unit and $10,000 each for options on the other four. Franchisees typically operated 15 to 20 restaurants in an area for which they were licensed. By late 1982, Popeyes restaurants were located in five countries, with a roughly half-and-half mix between urban and suburban sites. Copeland Enterprises' sales for 1982 were about $185 million, about $20 million higher than in 1981. New menu items included chicken tacos, barbecued beans, red beans and rice, and, most important, a new biscuit. The biscuit alone was responsible for a more than 20 percent unit-sales increase. To ensure consistent product quality, all mid-level managers were required to participate in a two- to three-day training course in biscuit preparation at company headquarters.

In 1983 Popeyes began test-marketing breakfast items, including grits, eggs, and fried potatoes, and sandwiches made with Popeyes' popular biscuit. Beer and wine were also tested in some stores. In 1984 Copeland Enterprises launched a chain of more upscale full-service Cajun-American restaurants, appropriately named Copeland's. Debuting in New Orleans, Copeland's featured a 100-item menu overseen personally by its owner. The same year, the Popeyes chain consisted of about 400 outlets in 35 states and five foreign countries, generating sales of $250 million and earnings of $6 million. Sales slumped somewhat, however, in part as a result of McDonald's newly introduced Chicken McNuggets, which brought in about $1 billion. Popeyes was slow to counter with its own version, because of Al Copeland's dissatisfaction with the quality control of his company's entry into that market.

By the mid-1980s, with a personal fortune of close to $100 million, Copeland had become a noted celebrity around New Orleans. His hobbies included racing 50-foot powerboats, touring New Orleans in Rolls Royces and Lamborghinis, and outfitting his Lake Pontchartrain home with lavish Christmas decorations, including half a million lights and a three-story-tall snowman. Copeland's wealth was derived primarily from his 100 percent ownership of Copeland Enterprises and his 95 percent interest in the Popeyes franchising arm. By 1985, Copeland Enterprises operated about 100 company-owned Popeyes outlets, approximately half of them in the New Orleans area. The chain's total of more than 500 stores included locations in Puerto Rico, Panama, and Kuwait. Popeyes' most visible advertising campaign in 1985, produced by its new agency, Doyle Dane Bernbach of New York, depicted eating spicy Cajun-style chicken as a ''hair-raising experience.'' Customers eating the chicken were shown with their hair literally standing on end after tasting the product. The spots continued to use the ten-year-old ''Love That Chicken'' slogan. In 1985 the Popeyes system spent three percent of gross sales for advertising expenditures, a relatively low figure for the industry. The following year, Popeyes separated from its agency and began producing its commercials in-house.

In 1986 sales for the entire Popeyes system reached $420 million. That same year, Popeyes began to test-market Cajun popcorn shrimp in nearly 100 Chicago and New Orleans stores, as well as home delivery in New Orleans and Houston. In New Orleans, where four of 50 company units were involved in the experimental home delivery program, a central computer relayed orders to the appropriate Popeyes outlet. The program was discontinued in 1987, however, as its high costs resulted in a $4.7 million loss for Copeland Enterprises, leaving the company in the red for the year. Also in 1987, Popeyes introduced 39-cent miniature chicken sandwiches called Little Chickadees,

Key Dates:

1952: Churchs Fried Chicken to Go is founded by George W. Church, Sr., in San Antonio.
1972: First Popeyes is opened by Al Copeland in New Orleans.
1975: "Love That Chicken" jingle first appeared in Popeyes advertising.
1977: Copeland begins franchising Popeyes.
1985: Popeyes chain totals more than 500 units.
1989: Parent company of Popeyes—Al Copeland Enterprises, Inc.—buys Churchs Chicken chain.
1991: Copeland Enterprises files for bankruptcy.
1992: America's Favorite Chicken Company, Inc. is created as new parent company to Popeyes and Churchs.
1996: Company changes name to AFC Enterprises, Inc.
1997: AFC acquires Chesapeake Bagel Bakery.
1998: Seattle Coffee Company and Cinnabon International Inc. are acquired.
1999: Chesapeake Bagel Bakery is sold to New World Coffee-Manhattan Bagel, Inc.

consisting of a Cajun-spiced one-ounce square chicken patty, pickles, and a mayonnaise-based sauce all on a toasted bun. The sandwiches were a response to plans by KFC to launch a similar product. Popeyes advertising budget for 1987—between $12 million and $17 million—was spent, in large part, on a new campaign showing Popeyes as the clear winner in side-by-side taste tests with KFC and Churchs.

Popeyes grew to 700 units by 1988. For the first time, Copeland realized that Copeland Enterprises had outgrown its management structure, and that he needed to delegate some of his responsibilities. As a result, he created the positions of president, chief financial officer, and executive vice-president of operations. Copeland then recruited a pair of executives from Churchs in a move that brought about accusations of company secrets being given away by defectors. Later in the year, Copeland made a play for control of Churchs with an unsolicited $296 million bid. (The Churchs Chicken chain had been founded in 1952 in San Antonio, Texas, by George W. Church, Sr., under the name Churchs Fried Chicken to Go; the company went public in 1969 as Churchs Fried Chicken, Inc., a chain approaching 100 units in size.) The move came on the heels of a 1987 takeover attempt by Churchs' former president, Richard Sherman, whose $12.25-a-share buyout offer was declined by company management.

In February 1989, Churchs agreed to be acquired by Al Copeland Enterprises, Inc. for $392 million. Under the terms of the agreement, $11 per share was paid for the first 86.5 percent of Churchs' stock, and the remaining shares were swapped for .44 shares of newly created preferred stock in the merged company. The new company, named Al Copeland Enterprises, Inc., controlled about 17 percent of the $10 billion fried chicken market, but together the two chains were still only about one-third the size of KFC. Within a couple months of the takeover, Copeland fired 12 percent of Churchs' staff, including Ernest Renaud, the company's president and chief executive. Copeland himself replaced Renaud as CEO and also became chairman of Churchs' board, while James Flynn, president of Copeland Enterprises, became Churchs' president.

The acquisition of Churchs soon proved to be lethal to Copeland Enterprises. To finance the acquisition, Copeland Enterprises borrowed about $450 million from a group of lending institutions led by the Canadian Imperial Bank of Commerce (CIBC) and Merrill Lynch and Company. This move, however, created interest costs of at least $100,000 a day and could not be covered by Churchs' revenues, which had been declining since 1985 to the point of a $14.5 million loss in 1988. Since a far higher percentage of Churchs outlets were company-owned than Popeyes, Copeland Enterprises began selling Churchs franchises to their managers in an effort to raise money. The drive brought in only $21 million, however, and in 1989 Copeland Enterprises reported a net loss of $35.9 million on revenue of $415 million—a loss due in large part to interest payments of $55.6 million to CIBC and Merrill Lynch.

Early 1990s: Emerging from Bankruptcy

In November 1990, Copeland Enterprises announced itself in default on $391 million in debts and that it was in danger of bankruptcy if payment was demanded by one of its lenders. The company, operating at a net loss of more than $11 million for the first three quarters of the year, failed to make payments due in September of $3.3 million in bridge-loan interest and $4.2 million on principal. By that time, Popeyes had overtaken the struggling Churchs chain for the number two spot in market share, garnering 11.4 percent on sales of $547 million at 783 stores, to Churchs 10.7 percent on sales of $514 million at 1,163 outlets.

Copeland Enterprises filed for bankruptcy law protection in April 1991 when attempts to restructure its debts failed. During the summer, a settlement plan appeared imminent that would have resulted in Merrill Lynch owning about 85 percent of the company. The tentative agreement also called for Al Copeland to relinquish ownership of the company and his secret recipe and to receive $31 million in cash, five Popeyes stores, and a company jet. In return, Copeland would have a $3 million personal debt to the company forgiven and would retain a contract to supply the chain with spices. When Merrill Lynch began to withdraw its support for this plan, however, the court invited CIBC (which was acting as an agent for a syndicate of former Copeland Enterprises lending institutions), Copeland Enterprises, and Copeland himself to submit individual reorganization plans. The plan submitted by CIBC called for full ownership of the company to be given to CIBC, for Merrill Lynch to come up empty-handed, and for Copeland to continue receiving royalties for his ownership of the Popeyes recipe. Under the plan entered by Copeland, Copeland would retain ownership of the company while creditors would receive reduced debt payments after the company emerged from bankruptcy.

In October 1992, Judge Frank Monroe chose the CIBC reorganization plan, modified to give Merrill Lynch a small stake, and shortly thereafter America's Favorite Chicken Company, Inc. (AFC) was created as the new parent company to Popeyes and Churchs. Having established headquarters in Atlanta, AFC also assumed control of Copeland Enterprises subsidiary Far West Products, a manufacturer of foodservice equipment such as refrigerators, freezers, and fryers under the Ultrafryer Systems brand. Named AFC chairman and chief executive was Frank J. Belatti, former president of Arby's Inc., the fast-food roast beef sandwich chain that Belatti had led through a turnaround in his stint there from 1985 to 1991, during which time the chain doubled its number of units and increased its annual sales from $750 million to $1.2 billion.

Mid-to-Late 1990s: Revitalized and Diversified for the 21st Century

In November 1992 Belatti announced a 100-day action plan for Popeyes and Churchs. The plan, which was launched in 1993, included programs to enhance the system's image, to improve employee and franchise relations, and to upgrade operational efficiency and quality. The reimaging program, which involved the remodeling of hundreds of Churchs and Popeyes restaurants at the cost of millions of dollars, helped boost same-unit sales. The Churchs chain, which was seriously neglected during its short period of ownership by Copeland Enterprises, gained its first new units in years. It also gained near autonomy from the Popeyes chain, as AFC divided its two chains into two completely separate groups, with competition between the two actively encouraged. During 1993 AFC also entered into an agreement with Canada-based Cara Operations, Ltd., under which Cara added Churchs menu items to more than 160 Harvey's restaurants and committed to opening more than 50 stand-alone Churchs restaurants throughout Canada.

Under Belatti's leadership the Popeyes and Churchs chains grew even stronger in 1994 and 1995 when AFC opened more than 440 new restaurants. Systemwide sales for 1995 hit $1.39 billion, a marked increase over the $1.12 billion of 1992. Dick Holbrook, who like Belatti had previously worked at Arby's, was named president of AFC during 1995. The following year, Los Angeles-based investment company Freeman Spogli & Co. gained a 58 percent interest in AFC for about $320 million, as well as several seats on the company board. CIBC's stake in the company was thereby reduced to about 18 percent. The infusion of capital from Freeman Spogli helped AFC reduce the heavy debt burden it had been carrying since its formation. Also during 1996, a year in which the firm showed its first profit in its short existence, America's Favorite Chicken changed its name to AFC Enterprises, Inc.

The name change was precipitated by a repositioning of the company, through which AFC aimed to expand beyond fast-food chicken outlets. Dubbing itself the "Franchisor of Choice," AFC envisioned itself as a holder of a portfolio of brands, each of which would be highly sought after by franchisees. By keeping franchisees profitable, happy, and thereby loyal, AFC hoped that its franchisees would choose to buy another AFC franchise when they were ready to expand. The company, therefore, set out on the acquisition trail, with its first purchase coming in May 1997 when it spent $11.8 million for the 165-unit Chesapeake Bagel Bakery chain. Added during 1998 were Seattle Coffee Company, for $68.8 million, and Cinnabon International Inc., for about $64 million. Seattle Coffee was a maker, wholesaler, and retailer of specialty coffee under the Seattle's Best Coffee and Torrefazione Italia brands, and it ran coffee shop chains under both brand names, with about 50 of the former and 15 of the latter. Seattle-based Cinnabon ran a chain of bakeries featuring rich, oversized cinnamon rolls, with most of the 214 company-owned and 144 franchised outlets located in malls. Following these additions, AFC Enterprises pared back its brand portfolio in 1999, selling Chesapeake Bagel Bakery to New World Coffee-Manhattan Bagel, Inc., thereby exiting from the increasingly crowded bagel shop sector.

In addition to diversifying its portfolio of franchisable brands, AFC Enterprises also expanded aggressively overseas during the second half of the 1990s. Faced with the powerful Starbucks Corporation in the United States, AFC concentrated on international growth for the Seattle's Best Coffee chain, signing development agreements for 225 new units in the Middle East, Japan, Taiwan, and Indonesia. During 1999 AFC signed its first Asian development agreement for the Cinnabon chain, with 42 units slated to open in Thailand, Singapore, and Vietnam by 2004; AFC also reached agreements to franchise 107 Cinnabons in the Middle East and 15 Cinnabons in Venezuela. By decade's-end the company had approximately 550 of its various branded outlets outside the United States, nearly triple the 192 such units that existed at the time AFC was formed in 1992. The company also initiated a minority advancement program called "The New Age of Opportunity," which recruited, trained, and assisted minority franchisees and suppliers. Community-minded, Belatti was credited as the visionary behind "The New Age" program as well as AFC Enterprises' large-scale support of Habitat for Humanity, a charity building low-priced houses for poor families. From 1992 through 1999 AFC helped construct more than 200 such homes.

Although AFC's Franchisor of Choice era was in its infancy, the early results were encouraging. Corporate revenue for 1998 was $609.1 million, a 26 percent increase over the $483.8 million of 1997. Systemwide sales increased 13 percent in 1998, reaching $1.8 billion. AFC already had more than 3,300 restaurants overall at the end of the century, with commitments for more than 1,700 new outlets worldwide. The company also had managed to erase the last of the debt that had been carried over from the bankruptcy of Copeland Enterprises. As it moved into the 21st century, AFC Enterprises was likely to continue to seek additional brands to purchase for its portfolio and to attempt to fund at least some of this growth through a long anticipated IPO.

Principal Subsidiaries

AFC Properties; Seattle Coffee Company; Cinnabon International, Inc.

Principal Competitors

Boston Chicken, Inc.; Burger King Corporation; Chick-fil-A Inc.; CKE Restaurants, Inc.; International Dairy Queen, Inc.; KFC; McDonald's Corporation; New World Coffee-Manhattan Bagel, Inc.; Schlotzsky's, Inc.; Starbucks Corporation; Subway; TRICON Global Restaurants, Inc.; Wendy's International Inc.

Further Reading

Alva, Marylin, "Popeyes Pops Hard-Sell Ads," *Nation's Restaurant News,* July 20, 1987.

——, ''Popeyes Rolls Little Chickadees As KFC Readies Sandwich Blitz,'' *Nation's Restaurant News,* June 22, 1987.

Andrews, Nina, ''Fried-Chicken Merger Creates No. 2 Concern,'' *New York Times,* February 17, 1989.

Barrier, Michael, ''Chicken That Packs a Punch,'' *Nation's Business,* July 1989.

Blumenthal, Karen, ''Churchs Agrees to Be Acquired by Copeland Unit,'' *Wall Street Journal,* February 16, 1989.

——, ''Copeland Says It's in Default on $391 Million,'' *Wall Street Journal,* November 7, 1990.

Brooks, Steve, ''A Boost Up the Ladder,'' *Restaurant Business,* December 10, 1996, pp. 43–44.

Bruno, Karen, ''Copeland Makes Churchs Bid,'' *Nation's Restaurant News,* November 7, 1988.

Cebrzynski, Gregg, ''Barbara Timm-Brock: Individual Success Comes Through Team Success for AFC Enterprises' New Chief Product Officer,'' *Nation's Restaurant News,* January 1999, pp. 36, 40.

Charlier, Marj, ''Spicy Cajun,'' *Wall Street Journal,* March 22, 1989.

Donovan, Sharon, ''Popeyes Strums Cajun Theme in Chicken,'' *Advertising Age,* July 15, 1985.

Fadiman, Mark T., ''The Popeye Challenge,'' *Forbes,* February 13, 1984.

Fisher, Christy, ''Popeyes Touts New Orleans,'' *Advertising Age,* March 4, 1991.

Hamstra, Mark, ''AFC Brews Export Plan for Coffee-Shop Brands,'' *Nation's Restaurant News,* February 9, 1998, pp. 1, 74.

——, ''AFC Buys Chesapeake, Taps Luther As Popeyes Prexy,'' *Nation's Restaurant News,* March 10, 1997, pp. 6, 159.

——, ''AFC Enterprises: An Ongoing Evolution,'' *Nation's Restaurant News,* August 4, 1997, pp. 51+.

——, ''AFC Set to Gobble Up Cinnabon Chain,'' *Nation's Restaurant News,* August 31, 1998, pp. 1, 139.

——, ''Frank J. Belatti: Expanding AFC's Horizons by Shooting for the Moon,'' *Nation's Restaurant News,* October 6, 1997, pp. 146, 148, 236–37.

Hayes, Jack, ''AFC Unveils New Brands,'' *Nation's Restaurant News,* June 13, 1994, p. 1.

Kramer, Louise, ''Holbrook Eyes New Ideas, Expansion at AFC,'' *Nation's Restaurant News,* September 4, 1995, p. 3.

Liesse, Julie, ''Popeyes Muscles In,'' *Restaurants and Institutions,* January 1, 1983.

Marshall, Christy, ''Popeyes Fights Off KFC with Fast, Spicy Chicken,'' *Advertising Age,* July 10, 1978.

Ortega, Bob, ''Copeland Emerges from Bankruptcy Minus Its Founder,'' *Wall Street Journal,* October 21, 1992.

Papiernik, Richard, ''AFC Isn't Chicken About Positioning Company for an IPO,'' *Nation's Restaurant News,* March 15, 1999, pp. 11, 80.

Romeo, Peter, ''Copeland Ousts Renaud, Lays Off 12% at Churchs,'' *Nation's Restaurant News,* April 10, 1989.

——, ''Is It Fixed Yet?,'' *Restaurant Business,* February 10, 1994, p. 56.

——, ''Popeyes Abandons Home-Delivery Test,'' *Nation's Restaurant News,* March 30, 1987.

Schoifet, Mark, ''Copeland Beefs Up Popeyes,'' *Nation's Restaurant News,* July 8, 1985.

——, ''Popeyes Tests Delivery at 17 Southern Outlets,'' *Nation's Restaurant News,* May 26, 1986.

—Robert R. Jacobson
—updated by David E. Salamie

A.G. Edwards
INVESTMENTS SINCE 1887

A.G. Edwards, Inc.

One North Jefferson Avenue
St. Louis, Missouri 63103
U.S.A.
Telephone: (314) 955-3000
Fax: (314) 955-5402
Web site: http://www.agedwards.com

Public Company
Incorporated: 1967 as A.G. Edwards & Sons, Inc.
Employees: 15,500
Sales: $2.24 billion (1999)
Stock Exchanges: New York
Ticker Symbol: AGE
NAIC: 52312 Securities Brokerage; 52311 Investment Banking and Securities Dealing; 52321 Securities and Commodity Exchanges; 52392 Portfolio Management (pt); 52393 Investment Advice; 551112 Offices of Other Holding Companies; 52592 Trusts, Estates, and Agency Accounts

A.G. Edwards, Inc. is a holding company whose subsidiaries provide a full range of retail brokerage services, including securities and commodities brokerage, asset management, mutual funds, investment banking, insurance, trust, and real estate. Subsidiary A.G. Edwards & Sons, Inc., is one of the largest retail brokerage firms in the United States, with more than 650 offices throughout the nation to serve both individual and institutional investors. A.G. Edwards is known for its conservative investment approach, and the company is a traditional commission-based brokerage.

Early History and Political Roots: 1800s

Albert Gallatin Edwards, the founder of A.G. Edwards, was the son of Governor Ninian W. Edwards, an important figure in the early history of the state of Illinois. Born October 15, 1812, Albert Gallatin Edwards was named (with remarkable prescience, as events proved) after U.S. Secretary of the Treasury Albert Gallatin, an influential advocate of fiscal conservatism in Washington, D.C. Young Edwards was born in Kentucky and grew up in Illinois, of which his father was territorial governor and later state governor and senator after its admission to the Union in 1818. After graduating from West Point in 1832, A.G. Edwards served briefly with the U.S. Army's first permanent cavalry unit, based south of St. Louis. There he met and in 1835 married Louise Cabanne, a member of one of the oldest St. Louis families. He subsequently resigned from the Army to work for the local wholesaling firm of William L. Ewing.

With ties to leading families in Missouri, Illinois, and Kentucky, Edwards, not surprisingly, prospered in the world of trade. William Ewing specialized in the supply of goods to stores throughout the southwestern United States, a role for which its St. Louis location rendered the company well suited. Albert Edwards brought to the firm a number of important political connections, most notably with a rising Illinois attorney named Abraham Lincoln. Edwards's older brother, Ninian Wirt Edwards, had followed his father into Illinois politics, where he enjoyed little success but became a fixture in the capital city's social and political circles. Ninian's wife, Elizabeth, was a member of the powerful Todd family of Kentucky, and her cousin, John Todd Stuart, became the law partner of Abraham Lincoln in 1839. The Edwardses were soon close friends of Lincoln—so close, in fact, that the future president married the sister of Elizabeth Todd in the home of Ninian Edwards in 1842. Whether Mary Todd was a good love match for Abe Lincoln has long been a subject of debate, but she was certainly a political asset, as Lincoln would later be of great help economically to the Edwards family.

When the Civil War erupted in 1861, Albert G. Edwards proved loyal to the party of his in-law President Lincoln, staunchly defending the Union cause in a state torn between factions of both parties. Edwards was involved in the defeat of Confederate troops at St. Louis early in the war, and in 1861 he was made a brigadier general in the Missouri State Militia and later bank examiner for the state of Missouri. On April 9, 1865, Edwards was appointed assistant Secretary of the Treasury by Lincoln, who was assassinated six days later. Edwards's job was to oversee the Sub-Treasury Bank in St. Louis, a regional depository similar to today's Federal Reserve Banks. He would

Company Perspectives:

At A.G. Edwards, our ultimate objective is caring for our clients' investments and financial futures. We focus on listening to gain an understanding of our clients' goals, on providing explanations for what are often complex financial issues, and on being there for our clients when they need us—in good times and bad.

continue as assistant secretary throughout the administrations of four subsequent presidents, retiring in 1887 at the age of 75 with a solid reputation in the financial community of St. Louis.

Founding of a Brokerage Firm in the Late 1800s

Edwards's retirement was brief, however. Less than two months later he formed a partnership with his eldest son, Benjamin Franklin Edwards, to buy and sell stocks, bonds, and similar investment instruments. Because banks were then among the heaviest traders in securities, Albert Edwards's strong ties with the St. Louis banking community would be invaluable to the new brokerage house of A.G. Edwards & Sons (AGE). The company soon announced that it would become the first St. Louis broker to handle transactions on the New York Stock Exchange (NYSE) for local banks. By thus allying itself more closely with banking interests and the NYSE, AGE escaped involvement with the briefly fashionable St. Louis Mining and Stock Exchange, where heavily leveraged mining stocks were traded like poker chips until the markets' sudden collapse in the early 1890s. When the Exchange closed for good during the depression of 1893, it took with it many local brokerage companies, but AGE suffered only minor losses. This was the first of many occasions on which AGE's conservative investment policy would save it from the worst of the markets' cyclical downturns.

Albert G. Edwards died in 1892 at age 80, leaving the brokerage business in the hands of George Lane Edwards, the founder's second son, who was born in 1869. George Edwards would serve as managing partner of the firm from 1891 to 1919, at which time his brother Albert Ninian Edwards took over. With the recovery of the St. Louis economy in the late 1890s, AGE increased its trading on the NYSE, buying a seat on the exchange for $29,500 in 1898 and two years later opening its first New York office. A year later, AGE was instrumental in the creation of the St. Louis Stock Exchange, which enjoyed immediate popularity; trade volume reached a peak in 1902 of $44 million that would not be exceeded until the salad days of the late 1920s. Federal regulation of the wilder financial schemes cooled market activity in the intervening years, during which time AGE built on its blue chip reputation and quietly prospered.

Changing Times in the 1920s and 1930s

The nature of the investment business changed radically after World War I. The widespread sale during the war of government ''Liberty Bonds'' introduced the concept of financial markets to millions of private citizens who had no alternative to leaving their savings in bank accounts or holding it as hard cash. In the booming 1920s this trend was greatly accelerated and brokers like AGE adjusted accordingly, shifting an increasing amount of their attention from banks and wealthy investors to the mass retail market of small investors. Under the direction of managing partner Albert N. Edwards, the company added its first brokers devoted solely to the soliciting of new individual investors, of whom the firm gained countless numbers as the bull market of the 1920s roared toward its catastrophic conclusion. Stock speculation became a hobby and passion for millions of Americans who ten years before did not know Wall Street from Main Street, many of them trading stocks for which they paid margins as low as ten percent of the current price.

Fortunately for AGE, St. Louis brokerage houses kept their margin requirements higher than the New York firms, thus softening the pain of October 24, 1929, when the stock market crash wiped out many investors and began ten years of national depression. AGE came through the crisis of 1929 in relatively good condition, its largest single loss only $5,000 (on an account of $1 million), but the years following were bleak. Not only had the great crash soured a whole generation of Americans on the notion of stock investments, it brought the entire securities industry under a cloud of suspicion for its role in the calamity. Again, the brunt of this criticism was felt in New York, while regional firms such as AGE were correctly perceived as having acted more responsibly toward their customers. Indeed, when the NYSE reorganized its governing body in the late 1930s in an effort to convince the U.S. Securities and Exchange Commission (SEC) that it had addressed past regulatory lapses, it named AGE's own William McChesney Martin, Jr., as its first paid president. Martin was AGE's first floor broker and only 31 at the time, but his status as an outsider and a man of integrity combined to make him the ideal candidate. He remained president of the Exchange until 1941, when he joined the Army.

In St. Louis, meanwhile, AGE was now led by Presley W. Edwards, son of Benjamin Edwards and grandson of founder Albert Edwards. This latest Edwards faced a brutal business environment in the 1930s—''Every day you went home exhausted from doing nothing,'' he was quoted as saying in AGE's official company history—but the lean years forced AGE to adopt the thrift and assiduity that later made the company's fortunes. Presley Edwards foresaw that AGE's future lay in the direction of small branch offices, but his plans were blocked by the United States' entry into World War II in 1941. A boon for most American businesses, the war only continued the Depression's long freeze in the securities markets, and AGE's retail expansion did not get underway until the 1950s.

Expansion in the 1950s and 1960s

Renewed investor confidence and the strong postwar economy allowed AGE to increase its number of branch offices to 11 in five states by 1957, which jumped to 19 by 1960 and then quickly to 44 only five years later. AGE had been the first brokerage house outside New York to install a computer back in the 1950s, and its sophisticated approach to data management helped the company coordinate the activities of its widely scattered and generally small branch offices. At the head of this 300-person brokerage force was Benjamin Franklin Edwards III, who joined his great-grandfather's company in 1956 and ten

Key Dates:

1887: Albert Gallatin Edwards forms A.G. Edwards & Son Stock and Bond Traders with his son Benjamin Franklin Edwards.
1898: A.G. Edwards buys a seat on the New York Stock Exchange.
1900: A New York branch office is established.
1917: Company sells "Liberty Bonds," thus introducing financial savings alternatives to small investors.
1966: Benjamin F. Edwards III, great grandson of founder, is appointed managing partner.
1967: A.G. Edwards incorporates, and Benjamin F. Edwards is named CEO and chairman.
1971: A.G. Edwards becomes a publicly traded company.
1987: Company celebrates its 100th anniversary.
1996: A.G. Edwards launches web site.

years later was its president at the age of 33. Rather surprisingly, the combined handicaps of youth, great responsibility, and family expectations did not deter Benjamin Edwards III; as of 1999 he remained the CEO of a company far larger than his forebears would have thought possible and was cited numerous times as one of the outstanding CEOs in the securities business.

When Benjamin Edwards took over the top spot at AGE in 1965, the nation's economy was booming and brokerage houses were expanding on every front. The question for AGE was not whether to expand but in what direction; as a mid-sized regional player in the securities industry the company could have embarked on any number of different paths. Edwards and his staff conducted a two-year study of AGE's strengths and weaknesses relative to the emerging marketplace, concluding in 1968 that they should continue what they were already doing but on a larger scale. As Benjamin Edwards later described in *Investor's Daily:* "We ended up with a model that called for the delivery of financial services of value to a 'mass/class' market through a network of retail branches acting as agents of the customer. [The brokers'] allegiance was to clients, not to us."

Central to Edwards's declaration are the terms "mass/class" and "allegiance." By "mass/class" Edwards meant that his brokerage force would concentrate its energies on the mass of individual investors, the "little people" of middle America, and only incidentally pursue the wealthy, "class" investor. That meant continuing to open more retail offices in small communities around the country—from 44 in the mid-1960s to 450 in 1992—and staffing them with a higher proportion of brokers than the average Wall Street outlet. It also meant largely ignoring the big-money deal-making that came to be known on Wall Street as investment banking. AGE has always done its share of stock underwriting, but it did not get caught up in the exotic corporate deals of the 1980s simply because its clients were not corporations and because Benjamin Edwards maintained a healthy skepticism toward get-rich-quick schemes of all kinds.

The second key term of Edwards's statement quoted in *Investor's Daily,* "allegiance," is harder to define but probably more fundamental to AGE's success. All brokers claimed to be acting on behalf of their clients, and it would be easy to dismiss Edwards's statement as routine puffery if not for the fact that AGE's history appeared to confirm its truth. AGE had long made it a policy not to trade stocks on its own account, just as it did not market its own investment packages to clients. Either step could easily divide the "allegiance" of a broker between the welfare of his customers and the making of money for the corporation, eventually destroying the relationship of trust between client and broker on which AGE had built its reputation. For the same reason, AGE refused to lure top brokers away from other firms with bonuses and high salaries and encouraged its own brokers to maintain annual sales figures about 30 percent lower than the industry average. Freed from the pressure to earn high commissions, AGE brokers were more likely to consider the interests of their clients instead of looking to make the maximum number of trades possible in every eight-hour day. As compensation, AGE let the brokers keep approximately ten percent more in commission than was standard in the industry.

Continued Growth Through the 1980s

The result of AGE's "goody two-shoes" philosophy, as Edwards humorously characterized it in the *New York Times,* was a tradition of loyalty from customers and employees alike. When the company suffered large losses in the industry shake-out of the early 1970s, AGE employees responded to management's frank call for help by working five-day weeks for four-days pay and cutting overall costs by 17 percent in a matter of months. Brokers tended to stay at AGE for its low-pressure approach to sales and closely knit, supportive environment. "There's less politicking here and more teamwork," commented one senior broker when interviewed for the company's profile in *The 100 Best Companies to Work for in America,* which appeared in 1983.

Customer loyalty was tested severely in the period following the SEC's 1975 decision to deregulate commission rates. Soon "discount houses" appeared in the securities business, offering to transact trades at prices substantially lower than those charged by full-service houses like AGE. Such discounters appealed directly to small investors from whom AGE earned the bulk of its revenues and should have taken a significant piece of market share; but it appeared that the discounters did not adversely affect AGE's business, even though the latter refused to lower its commission rates. Indeed, the period from 1975 to 1990 saw the greatest expansion in AGE history, offices increasing from 100 to more than 400 and employees from 2,000 to over 8,000. Clearly, the company's several hundred thousand customers valued the knowledge and experience of AGE brokers more than the dollars they would have saved by using a discounter, which typically offered no client counseling. AGE's success in the face of such direct competition confirmed the company's long-held belief that when it comes to money handling, customers desire above all a broker whom they know and trust.

The most dramatic demonstration of AGE's independence from Wall Street fashions—and the strength derived from such independence—was provided by the market crash in October 1987, the year AGE celebrated its 100th anniversary. The 1980s had seen a phenomenal rise in the deal-making power of investment bankers, many of whom earned enormous fees for engineering mergers, acquisitions, and leveraged buyouts that were often undercapitalized and sometimes fraudulent, as in the cases of Michael Milken and Ivan Boesky. The market crash destroyed this glitter-and-greed atmosphere, and in its wake about 18 percent of the industry's employees had lost their jobs by 1991. By contrast, AGE, since it did not trade its own account, sustained minor losses in the crash and in the following years *increased* its workforce by 33 percent.

Remaining True to Tradition Amid Industry Changes in the 1990s

The 1990s enjoyed a strong economy that gave rise to increased activity and changes in the financial sector. Entering the 1990s, AGE experienced tremendous growth in every category, bottom-line earnings that made its competitors green with envy, and, most remarkable for a company expanding so quickly, virtually no long-term debt. AGE was not, however, without trials; as the market turned toward discounting and fee-based services rather than commissions, it became more challenging for AGE to remain committed to its traditional and conservative approach to investing. Edwards was vocal about his opinions regarding the economic climate and was steadfast regarding AGE's loyalty to clients. In his letter to shareholders in AGE's 1993 annual report, for instance, Edwards denounced the increasingly popular fee system, noting that the industry had turned toward charging fees for any number of services. Edwards was also vocal about the battle between fees and commissions. He believed the commission system held brokers accountable to clients, while fees did not and could be detrimental to customer accounts. Edwards explained in an interview in *Securities Industry Management* in 1994, "The tie that binds should be between the broker and the client. This whole business of trying to tie the client to the house and immobilize the broker is bad news for our industry." Apparently AGE's workforce agreed with Edwards; according to *The Loyalty Effect*, AGE's broker retention rate, at 92 percent in the mid-1990s, was well above the industry average of 80 to 85 percent.

AGE's status as traditional and conservative did not mean the company was not progressive. AGE had long been open to new technology, having installed its first computer system in 1949. In 1990 the firm spent $25 million to upgrade and expand its computer system, adding a satellite-based communications system that allowed the St. Louis headquarters and branch offices to transmit data and voice messages. Four years later a computerized bond processing and inventory management system was put into operation, as well as the Edwards Information Network, a satellite-based audio communications network that disseminated timely information to brokers. Also that year brokers were introduced to the Broker Workstation, an interactive computer system designed to provide news updates to investment brokers. Though AGE was against online trading, the company launched its own web site in 1996, providing clients with access to account and investment information.

Profitability continued, but in order to remain competitive in the rapidly changing, high-pressure investment industry, AGE was forced to change with the times. Despite its contention that clients seldom invested wisely when allowed to trade on their own money, in 1997 the company began to offer clients that very option. AGE also opened a branch office in New York City that year, something the company had avoided for a century. A year later AGE introduced a program that allowed clients to purchase no-load funds. AGE's program was innovative in that it offered broker advice concerning no-load funds, which were typically purchased by do-it-yourself investors.

In 1999 AGE announced it would allow clients to make online trades, but only with the approval of a broker and a commission. The company refused to offer discounts, although rival brokerages had started discounting to compete with Internet discount firms, which allowed customers to make trades for a minimal fee. Despite AGE's online plans, Edwards remained firm in his beliefs that online trading was not the wave of the future and that eventually clients would return to full-service brokerages. Edwards told the *Grand Rapids Press*, "When you trade your own money, fear and greed come in."

AGE's revenues rose steadily, as did the company itself. While competitors succumbed to new pressures such as online trading, AGE grew primarily through traditional avenues, such as opening additional branches, increasing its workforce, upgrading computer systems, and searching for strategic acquisitions. In 1991 the company had 442 offices and 4,317 brokers; by the end of fiscal year 1999, which ended February 28, AGE had 639 offices and more than 6,500 financial consultants. In fiscal 1999 alone, AGE added 45 offices and nearly 500 employees. The company expanded its headquarters in St. Louis with a 405,000-square-foot addition and received a thrift charter, allowing AGE to nationally expand its trust services. Fiscal 1999 also saw AGE's fourth consecutive record year in both revenue and net earnings.

The reputation of excellence that AGE had built up over the centuries continued into the 1990s. Not only was AGE selected as one of "The 100 Best Companies to Work for in America" in *Fortune* magazine's annual survey for a fourth time in 1998, but the company also received recognition and top honors in publications including *SmartMoney, Worth,* and *Kiplinger's.* As AGE approached yet another new millennium, it looked toward the future rather than to the past. Though the firm planned to keep pace with industry changes, it also planned to remain true to the company's mission and focus on the client. "The pace of change in our industry continues to accelerate," Edwards noted in a prepared statement. He continued: "Our guiding beacon remains the benefit of our clients. Our efforts toward the future are focused on being of value to our clients and building and strengthening client relationships."

Principal Subsidiaries

A.G. Edwards & Sons, Inc.; Gull-AGE Capital Group, Inc.; A.G. Edwards Trust Company FSB; AGE Commodity Clearing Corp.; Edwards Development Corp.; A.G. Edwards Life Insurance Company; AGE Properties, Inc.; AGE Investments, Inc.; A.G. Edwards Investment Management Consulting Services, Inc.; A.G. Edwards Capital, Inc.

Principal Competitors

Paine Webber Group Inc.; Merrill Lynch & Co., Inc.; The Jones Financial Companies, L.P., LLP; Morgan Stanley Dean Witter & Co.; The Charles Schwab Corporation; E*TRADE Group, Inc.

Further Reading

A.G. Edwards: A Heritage of Serving Investors, St. Louis, Mo.: A.G. Edwards & Sons, Inc., 1991, revised edition, 1998.

''And the Winners Are . . . ,'' *Worth,* July/August 1999.

Branch, Shelly, ''The 100 Best Companies to Work for in America,'' *Fortune,* January 11, 1999.

Forbat, Pamela Savage, ''A.G. Edwards: Business As Usual,'' *Registered Representative,* March 1996.

Friedman, Amy, ''Positive Prospects,'' *Financial Services Weekly,* June 11, 1990.

Gallagher, Jim, ''Sitting Pretty: Being 'Out in the Sticks' Saved Edwards,'' *St. Louis Post-Dispatch,* April 1, 1991.

Hanford, Desiree J., ''A.G. Edwards Sticks with Its Traditions,'' *Wall Street Journal,* May 26, 1998, p. B13.

Leblanc, Sydney, ''Interview: Benjamin F. Edwards III,'' *Securities Industry Management,* August/September 1994.

Levering, Robert, Milton Moskowitz, and Michael Katz, *The 100 Best Companies to Work for in America,* Reading, Mass.: Addison-Wesley, 1983.

Reichheld, Frederick F. and Thomas Teal, *The Loyalty Effect,* Boston, Mass.: Harvard Business School Press, 1996, 323 p.

Rogers, Doug, ''A.G. Edwards Matches Profit with Stock Price Performance,'' *Investor's Daily,* June 6, 1991.

Santoli, Michael, ''A.G. Edwards Praised and Criticized for Low-Risk Way,'' *Austin American-Statesman,* October 26, 1996, p. 4.

Scott, Mac, ''Edwards Quietly Climbs Ranks of Wall Street,'' *St. Louis Business Journal,* January 6–12, 1992.

Wayne, Leslie, ''Where the Brokers Are Still Smiling,'' *New York Times,* November 26, 1989.

Wells, Garrison, ''Brokerage Lags in Web Trading–On Purpose,'' *Grand Rapids Press,* September 10, 1999, p. A12.

—Jonathan Martin
—updated by Mariko Fujinaka

Akorn, Inc.

2500 Millbrook Drive
Buffalo Grove, Illinois 60089-4694
U.S.A.
Telephone: (847) 279-6100
Toll Free (800) 535-7155
Fax: (847) 279-6123
Web site: http://www.akorn.com

Public Company
Incorporated: 1971
Employees: 313
Sales: $56.7 million (1998)
Stock Exchanges: NASDAQ
Ticker Symbol: AKRN
NAIC: 334517 Irradiation Apparatus Manufacturing; 339112 Surgical and Medical Instrument Manufacturing; 325412 Pharmaceutical Preparation Manufacturing; 339115 Ophthalmic Goods Manufacturing; 42221 Drugs and Druggists' Sundries Wholesalers

Akorn, Inc. is a niche pharmaceutical market leader in the United States, focusing on the manufacture and marketing of a variety of products, including diagnostic and therapeutic pharmaceuticals in the ophthalmology, rheumatology, anesthesia, and antidote sectors. More than 300 companies worldwide compete with Akorn in the ophthalmic marketplace alone, including Montgomery, Alabama-based Blount International Inc. and Thornwood, New York-based Carl Zeiss Inc. The company's ophthalmic division manufactures and markets an extensive line of diagnostic and therapeutic pharmaceuticals, in addition to surgical instruments and related supplies. Diagnostic products, primarily used in the office setting, include mydriatics and cycloplegics, anesthetics, topical stains, gonioscopic solutions, and angiography dyes. Therapeutic products include antibiotics, anti-infectives, steroids, steroid combinations, glaucoma medications, decongestants/antihistamines, and anti-edema medications. Surgical products include surgical knives and other surgical instruments, balanced salt solution, post-operative kits, surgical tapes, eye shields, anti-ultraviolet goggles, facial drape supports, and other supplies. Non-pharmaceutical products include various artificial tear solutions, lubricating ointments, lid cleansers, vitamin supplements, and contact lens accessories.

The company sells its products throughout the United States to physicians, optometrists, wholesalers, group purchasing organizations, and pharmacies. Additionally, the company markets generic brand, small-volume niche pharmaceuticals and anesthesia products used in the treatment of specialty indications, including rheumatoid arthritis and pain management, and provides contract manufacturing services through its injectable division, Taylor Pharmaceuticals, headquartered in Decatur, Illinois. Top competitors in the various pharmaceutical and ophthalmic segments include Merck & Co., Novartis AG, Bristol-Myers Squibb Company, Glaxo Wellcome PLC, Alcon Laboratories, Bausch & Lomb, and Allergan.

A Company Formed by Circumstance: 1969–71

Joe Yazbeck, the founder, started the company in 1969, as he traveled throughout Louisiana selling ophthalmic pharmaceuticals out of the trunk of his car. As he went, Yazbeck created a catalog from which his customers could order products from him. In addition to selling products, Yazbeck sold small blocks of stock in the company to anyone who would listen to him and, eventually, the company was forced under Securities Exchange Commission guidelines to go public. Thus, Yazbeck incorporated Akorn, Inc. in Louisiana in 1971, placing its headquarters in the small town of Abita Springs, near New Orleans.

The company grew slowly over the next decade and a half, but truly began gaining mass in the late 1980s, as other companies were acquired. In January 1988, Akorn acquired Spectrum Scientific Pharmaceuticals, Inc. for more than 187,000 shares of common stock. Less than a year later, in September 1989, the company acquired Norbrook America, Inc. for one million shares of common stock. The acquisition was merged into subsidiary Walnut Pharmaceuticals, Inc. in May 1990 which, in turn, was sold by Akorn in July 1993. In July 1990 the company acquired certain assets of Optometric Pharmaceuticals Inc. for some $355,000, merging the acquisition into subsidiary Spectrum Scientific Pharmaceuticals, Inc.

Company Perspectives:

Akorn, Inc. is a vertically integrated specialty pharmaceutical company, focusing on niche markets such as ophthalmology, anesthesia, antidotes, and rheumatology. The Company has internal resources devoted to research and development, manufacturing, distribution and sales and marketing. Akorn's growth strategy relies on internal product development as well as acquisition and licensing of specialty products from others.

New Leadership: 1991–98

In 1991, Dr. John N. Kapoor, a Bombay-born, American-educated, Chicago-based venture capitalist who had a track record working with pharmaceutical, medical, and biomedical companies, took the helm at Akorn. Kapoor immigrated to the United States in 1964 to obtain his doctorate in medicinal chemistry. By 1977, he was working at Invenex Laboratories, in charge of research and development for the pharmaceutical manufacturer, but was bored with his job. Stone Container Corp., which had purchased a company called LyphoMed (founded in 1969 in Chicago) to "freeze-dry drugs, such as antibiotics, too unstable to store in liquid form," according to Christine Donahue in *Forbes*, hired Kapoor to be LyphoMed's general manager. His job was to bolster the struggling pharmaceutical division, which was racking up losses of $75,000 a month. Kapoor negotiated to buy the division from Stone for $2.7 million, and dramatically turned the company around, with revenue growing from $6 million in 1981 to $159 million in 1989, eventually selling the firm to Japan-based Fujisawa Pharmaceutical Company.

Wealthy from the sale but not quite ready to retire, Kapoor went on to purchase a two-thirds stake in Chico, California-based O.P.T.I.O.N. Care Inc., approximately the fourth largest provider of home intravenous therapy at the time, from Sutter Health for $18 million in 1990. Serving as chairman of the company, Kapoor also would go on to hold that position for NeoPharm, Inc., a company which manufactured drugs for diagnosis and treatment of cancer.

When he finally took the helm at Akorn, Kapoor immediately began to change the direction of the company, moving away from catalog-based distribution and creating a full-scale manufacturing company. In January 1992, the company acquired Taylor Pharmaceuticals, a manufacturer of specialty injectable pharmaceutical products, for more than 926,000 shares of stock. The acquisition significantly bolstered the company's manufacturing abilities. In July 1994, the company acquired the intraocular lens segment of Azusa, California-based Optical Radiation Corp.'s ophthalmic products division for 5.25 million shares of stock. The rest of Optical Radiation was acquired by Benson Eyecare Corp. of Rye, New York.

Acquisition seemed to be the key word in the industry as, in March 1995, two of Akorn's top British competitors, Glaxo Holdings and Wellcome, merged to form Glaxo Wellcome PLC. In 1995, the company reported total sales of $30 million. Akorn continued to forge ahead, acquiring, in May 1996, San Clemente, California-based Pasadena Research Laboratories, Inc. (PRL), a distributor and marketer of injectable products. The Taylor Pharmaceutical Division was formed with PRL and Taylor as the base, thrusting the company into the injectable pharmaceutical market.

Also that month, the company's AK-T-Caine PF (tetracine HCl) product was given approval by the U.S. Federal Drug Administration (FDA) to be used as a topical anesthetic for use in ophthalmic surgery. A study by Dr. Eric J. Rothchild of the Rothchild Eye Institute in Del Ray Beach, Florida, highly touted the new product, saying that "eyes treated with preservative-free tetracaine were again visibly smoother, and there was less disruption of the epithelium" and that the eyes healed faster with this product.

In July 1996, the company acquired the rights to distribute an injectable product line in the anesthesia/analgesia market from Belgium-based Janssen Pharmaceutica NV, for $1.6 million. That year, the combined company's total revenue jumped 13 percent to $33.9 million. Acquisitions continued in April 1997, as the company agreed to purchase a number of products from Becton-Dickinson and Company. Later that year, the company made plans to acquire Socoloff Health Supply Co. (a.k.a. Solos Ophthalmology), for undisclosed terms. The acquisition of the Norcross, Georgia-based company, which manufactured and distributed hand-held ophthalmic instruments and disposable operating room devices, was called off in December of that year. In 1997, Akorn's total revenue climbed again, to $42 million, an increase of 23.9 percent over the previous year.

In 1998, the company continued to grow, as Akorn acquired Advanced Remedies, Inc. (ARI), an ophthalmic manufacturing and research and development facility, in July from New Jersey-based Sidmak Laboratories Inc. In September, the company moved its principal executive offices to its new location in Buffalo Grove, Illinois. During 1998, the company engaged in clinical trials for its new potential migraine-relieving product, called TP-1000. That year the company also released, through its ARI acquisition, a generic form of cromolyn sodium 4%, a drug used to treat allergies of the eye. The new product was created to compete with Allergan's Opticrom and Bausch & Lomb's Crolom (which dominated the U.S. market in 1997, with a market share of ten percent and sales of $11 million).

Changing of the Guard: 1998

Near the end of 1998, at the annual meeting of The American Academy of Ophthalmology, Akorn launched its corporate web site. That year, the company's total revenues climbed again, by 35 percent, rising to $56.7 million, and the company had five Abbreviated New Drug Applications (ANDAs) approved by the FDA. The growth was attributed by Akorn's new president and CEO, Floyd Benjamin, as coming from "strength in the base business of diagnostics, antidotes and anesthesia as well as growth from products acquired in 1998." Benjamin, formerly the president of the company's Taylor Pharmaceuticals division, replaced Kapoor in November 1998, as the latter stepped out of day-to-day operations, but retained his position as chairman of the board.

With an ongoing strategy of key acquisitions and new product introduction (as of September 1999, the company had eight

Key Dates:

1969: Company is founded by Joe Yazbeck.
1971: Business incorporates in Louisiana.
1991: Dr. John Kapoor becomes president of Akorn.
1992: Company acquires specialty manufacturer Taylor Pharmaceuticals.
1998: Akorn releases eyecare product that competes with products manufactured by Allergan and Bausch & Lomb; Floyd Benjamin replaces Kapoor as president.

ANDAs and three NDAs awaiting approval at the FDA, and, since January 1996, the company has acquired or licensed 14 branded specialty pharmaceutical products from Allergan Inc., ALZA Corp., and Janssen Pharmaceutical), Akorn's sales continued to rise slowly but steadily, promising to propel the company past the $100 million mark in the early 21st century.

Principal Subsidiaries

Taylor Pharmaceuticals Inc.

Principal Divisions

Ophthalmic Products; Injectable Products.

Principal Competitors

Blount International Inc.; Carl Zeiss Inc.; Merck & Co.; Novartis AG; Bristol-Myers Squibb Company; Glaxo Wellcome PLC; Alcon Laboratories, Inc.; Bausch & Lomb Incorporated; Allergan, Inc.

Further Reading

''Akorn Announces Purchase Plan,'' *Chicago Tribune*, November 18, 1997.
''Akorn Cancels Acquisition,'' *Chicago Tribune*, December 12, 1997.
''Akorn, Inc. Reports Second Quarter Results; Discusses 1999 Outlook Sales Up 15 Percent; Gross Profit Up 19 Percent,'' *PR Newswire*, July 20, 1999, p. 4941.
''Akorn Launches Cromolyn Sodium, Anti Allergic Eye Drug,'' *Business Wire*, May 8, 1998.
''Benson Eyecare Corp.; Definitive Agreement Set to Buy Optical Radiation,'' *Wall Street Journal*, July 5, 1994.
Donahue, Christine, ''Micronutrients and Macrodollars,'' *Forbes*, February 27, 1984, p. 96.
''New Product Newswire: Rx: AK-T-Caine PF,'' *Drug Topics*, May 20, 1996.
Pulley, Mike, ''Sale by Sutter Health Frees Chico Firm to Chase Growth,'' *Business Journal Serving Greater Sacramento*, October 29, 1990, p. 2.
''The Red Chip Review: Discovering Tomorrow's Blue Chips Today,'' *PR Newswire*, June 17, 1999.
Rothchild, Eric J., ''Preservative-Free Tetracaine Promotes Quicker, Better Corneal Wound Healing,'' *Ocular Surgery News*, August 1997.

—Daryl F. Mallett

Alamo Group Inc.

1502 E. Walnut Street
Seguin, Texas 78155
U.S.A.
Telephone: (830) 379-1480
Fax: (830) 372-9679
Web site: http://www.alamo-group.com

Public Company
Incorporated: 1969 as Terrain King
Employees: 1,342
Sales: $200.5 million (1998)
Stock Exchanges: New York
Ticker Symbol: ALG
NAIC: 333112 Lawn and Garden Tractor and Home Lawn and Garden Equipment Manufacturing; 333111 Farm Machinery and Equipment Manufacturing

Taking its name from the famous Texas landmark, Alamo Group Inc. of Seguin, Texas, has been building a solid reputation since 1969. Manufacturing and selling a wide range of agricultural and industrial mowing and maintenance equipment under trademarked brand names (Alamo Industrial, Herschel-Adams, Bomford, McConnel, M&W, Rhino, SMA, Tiger), Alamo's products have proven both reliable and cost effective for customers worldwide. From maintaining federal and state highways throughout the United States, to manicuring the complex beauty of the Palace of Versailles' gardens, to turf care at the Dallas-Fort Worth airport and Nolan Ryan's Texas ranch, Alamo equipment has been getting the job done efficiently and professionally for the last 30 years.

In the Beginning: 1950s–70s

It could be said that the evolution of Alamo Group began back in the 1800s with several scientific breakthroughs, components of a larger whole none could foresee at the time. Inventors were experimenting with power in its myriad forms from Alexander Volta's electric battery in 1800, Richard Trevithick's steam railway locomotive in 1804, and Samuel Brown's gas-powered car in 1826. Another like-minded inventor, Edward Budding, was working on a cutting implement to control the growth of grass. In 1830 Budding perfected his newfangled invention, the lawnmower—while a blacksmith named John Deere tinkered in his one-man shop pursuing similar technology. Both Budding and Deere were aimed in the same direction, one leading to the varied holdings of both the Alamo Group and Deere & Company, and what became the multibillion-dollar agricultural machinery industry of today.

In the early 1900s, several companies began cropping up around the globe, to maintain turf and vegetation in both commercial and residential settings. In 1903, the British company Bomford Turner, Limited was founded, producing tractor-mounted hedge and turf mowing equipment for farmers, ranchers, and governmental agencies throughout the United Kingdom. Another British company, McConnel, was founded in 1936, manufacturing and selling growth maintenance equipment, using hydraulically powered attachments. In 1939 a tractor company, Servis-Rhino, began manufacturing and selling a rugged line of agricultural equipment, and within in a few years Signalisation Moderne Autoroutière (SMA), and its subsidiaries of Orléans, France, began working with the French government to maintain highways and roadsides. The destinies of Bomford, McConnel, Rhino, and SMA all collided in the last decades of the 20th century as they became part of a relatively unknown Texas corporation intent on becoming a global leader in the agricultural and industrial vegetation maintenance market.

Though Donald J. Douglass was not even born when Bomford Turner was established, by the time he was in his mid-20s he had graduated from the University of Texas in 1954 and gone on to a three-year stint as a Navy fighter pilot. He then worked for a chemical manufacturer as well as a Houston-based venture capital company before earning an M.B.A. from Stanford University. His experiences led him to realize there were thousands of quiet, unexciting companies making millions of dollars. These were the companies without flashy advertising campaigns and well known products, but they were nonetheless selling items necessary for everyday industrial, agricultural, or corporate life. Unheralded though they might be, these companies had cornered their markets and were returning solid profits

Company Perspectives:

Alamo Group Inc. is the world leader in the design, manufacture and distribution of rugged, high-quality, tractor-mounted mowing and other vegetation maintenance equipment.

year after year for their stockholders. Douglass took his cues from the lesser known giants and began his entrepreneurial climb with turf maintenance, mowing in particular. He started by selling rotary-based mowing equipment in 1955. By 1969 Douglass knew enough about the market to buy the Engler Manufacturing Company of Houston, creator of the popular Terrain King wide-cutting mowers, for $2.1 million. To capitalize on Engler's brand recognition, Douglass renamed his company Terrain King. Within months Douglass was on the move again, this time securing the patented Slopemower product line, which boasted another mowing breakthrough, a patented telescoping boom mower. By 1970, Terrain King was an official success, with $3 million in sales and $80,000 in earnings.

Douglass continued to expand Terrain King in the early 1970s with the purchase of D&D Bumper Works in 1971. D&D Bumper Works had perfected a line of pickup truck accessories, useful to Terrain King's burgeoning business. With D&D came that company's 75,000-square-foot manufacturing facility, located in Seguin, Texas. This acquisition was a harbinger of the future, as Seguin later became Terrain King's North American headquarters, after the company began moving production of its mowing equipment into the plant in 1973.

Another major force in Terrain King's future arrived when Oran F. Logan, an engineer with a degree in accounting, was hired as vice-president in 1972. Logan installed the company's first computerized manufacturing system. By 1974 Terrain King was gaining momentum and reached $5 million in annual revenues; the following year came the relocation from Houston to Seguin. The new headquarters was then expanded by another 125,000 square feet, just as the company began to gain a foothold in the governmental and industrial mowing and maintenance markets. To concentrate more fully on its core business, mowing, Terrain King sold off the truck accessories line to create more manufacturing space for its increasing highway mowing operations in 1977. On the heels of this decision came the acquisition of a large right-of-way mowing product line in 1978, and allocating funds for the research and development of more such equipment.

New Decade, New Focus: 1980s

With the new decade of the 1980s, Terrain King made another shift in business—away from road maintenance and focusing more on agricultural and governmental mowing. The move seemed precipitous, as the company celebrated a milestone in 1981 with sales surpassing the $10 million mark, reaching $11.1 million. In its efforts to continue to stay head-and-shoulders above the competition, Terrain King bought and installed its first CAD/CAM system in 1982 and began acquiring selected businesses again the following year. Mott Corporation, purchased in 1983, brought advanced and very profitable flail mowing technology to Terrain King, along with a 96,000-square-foot manufacturing facility. Through Mott's varied distributors, Terrain King took its first foray into the international mowing marketplace.

Yet 1983 was most significant for the company's move away from the Terrain King name in favor of the Alamo Group Inc. The new name reflected a parent company with several successful brand names (Terrain King, Slopemower, Mott) and the new directions Douglass and Logan foresaw in its future. Not only did the management team see increased exposure in Europe, but in North America as well with additional complementary product lines. One such development was the 1984 purchase of the Triumph Machinery Corporation of New Jersey, which designed and produced hydraulic sickle-bar mowing equipment. Alamo reached another milestone in 1984, climbing above the $20 million mark, with year-end revenues hitting nearly $25 million.

In the mid-1980s Logan was promoted to president and COO of the company, as well as a director, with Douglass remaining CEO and chairman. Further acquisitions came too, with both Servis-Rhino and the Kansas-based BMB Company in 1986. The former brought the heavy-duty Rhino agricultural line; the latter brought light-duty mowers and a 150,000-square-foot manufacturing facility, which the ever expanding company needed to maintain its growth. In 1987 Alamo reincorporated in Delaware, added onto its Kansas facility, and celebrated tremendous year-end numbers with $48.4 million in revenues, almost double its revenues of just three years earlier.

Blade Warriors: 1990s

By the dawn of the 1990s, Alamo had outgrown its skin several times and accommodated this growth by finding and acquiring companies with similar or needed technology. Using both acquired manufacturing facilities and adding onto its own several times, Alamo had succeeded beyond both Douglass and Logan's expectations. Yet in 1990 came the first, although very slight, downturn in the company's sales to $53.7 million from 1989's $54 million. Though few viewed this with much alarm, certainly not the nation's 7,600 agricultural dealers who relied heavily on Alamo's brand names, it halted the company's breakneck pace of the previous several years.

In 1991 the company turned its attentions to building an international presence as strong as its base operations in the United States. A major step in this direction was its announcement to acquire McConnel, a U.K. manufacturer of vegetation maintenance equipment; and to come to the rescue of the Adams Hard-Facing Company and AHF Corporation, which were operating under Chapter 11 federal bankruptcy laws. Alamo bought the Adams name and product line for $3.6 million, which consisted of new and replacement parts for tillage and construction equipment, sold throughout North America. By the end of the year, in November, Alamo had purchased all outstanding stock of McConnel and completed its acquisition.

With 1992, Alamo leapt out of its two-year slowdown and was again on a roll. The year's revenues, after 1991's sedentary $58 million, brought a whopping 35 percent increase in sales to $78.1 million, due in large part to its increased European pres-

Key Dates:

1955: Company predecessor is founded by Donald J. Douglass.
1969: Douglass buys Engler Manufacturing Company and changes name to Terrain King.
1983: Terrain King becomes Alamo Group Inc.
1987: Alamo Group Inc. is reincorporated in Delaware.
1993: Alamo becomes publicly traded.
1995: Company issues a second public offering.
1998: Shareholders vote to be acquired/merged with subsidiaries of Woods Equipment Company of Illinois for $180 million.
1999: Acquisition/merger is called off in February; Douglass and Logan resign as CEO and COO, but remain as chairman and board member, respectively; Ronald Robinson takes over as president and CEO.

ence. The next year proved as heady, with the company's first-quarter initial public offering (IPO) of 1.6 million shares, which sold at $11.50 per share. The IPO raised some $16 million to fuel Alamo's continuing acquisitions, or what the company referred to as ''potential inductees'' into its growing family of brands. One such inductee was Bomford Turner, Limited of Salford Priors, England, in the fourth quarter. Bomford Turner's clients were primarily European, with heavy concentration in the United Kingdom, as well as Germany, France, Scandinavia, Australia, the Far East, and North America. With the Bomford acquisition, Alamo made its European headquarters in Salford Priors, near Birmingham.

By the end of 1993, though Alamo's business still rested primarily in U.S. agricultural sales (51 percent) and its stalwart governmental contracts (36 percent), European revenues had increased to 13 percent, though Douglass and Logan hoped to raise this figure to 25 percent over the next few years. To maintain its client base and attract new customers, Alamo had introduced some 21 new or improved products, many of which bolstered the Rhino brand of heavy equipment. While overall agricultural dealers declined by nearly 15 percent from 1990 to 1993, Rhino dealerships mushroomed nearly 27 percent in the same three-year period. Alamo's revenues for 1993 rose to $88.5 million, while net income increased by 23 percent to $7.8 million.

In 1994 Alamo was again on the move, purchasing France's SMA in March. The SMA family of products, combined with the earlier acquisitions of Bomford and McConnel, made Alamo the largest manufacturer of heavy-duty agricultural equipment in Europe. To continue its successful expansion outside North America, Alamo's management turned its attentions to Asia, Mexico, and Central and South America for future possibilities, while adding to its presence in industrial and governmental markets with the acquisition of Tiger Corp. in the last quarter. Year-end sales surged to $120 million, a 35 percent jump over the previous year's figures, with income following suit to reach nearly $9.2 million (an increase of 18 percent over 1993).

Alamo's stock was listed on the New York Stock Exchange (ticker symbol ALG) and the company made a second public offering of two million shares at $17.50 each in July 1995. Proceeds of more than $33 million once again bolstered the company's bottom line by lowering debt, and strengthened its position for further acquisitions. Throughout the year, Alamo pursued five acquisitions, beginning in April with M&W Gear Company, which took the company into hay-making equipment; May's Rhino International, Inc., a Chinese manufacturer and distributor of tractors (not related to Alamo's other Rhino line), and Certified Power Train Specialists, Inc. The remaining two acquisitions were NJM Dabekausen Beheer BV, a distributor for Bomford products in the Netherlands and Germany, which was integrated into Bomford in June, and the November acquisition of the Herschel Corporation, a leading manufacturer of farm equipment replacement parts, which was combined with the Adams product line and collectively referred to as Herschel-Adams. Alamo finished the year with sales of nearly $164 million, a robust 37 percent increase over 1994.

A Bumpy Road: 1996–99

Alamo's near nonstop growth began to catch up with it in 1996. Though sales rose 12 percent over the previous year, fueled mostly by 1995 acquisitions, net income was affected by a series of concerns that plagued the company for several years to come. Severe weather, including drought conditions in the Southwest, snowstorms in the Northeast, and excess rain in Midwestern states, caused a fall in agricultural sales; charges related to its major growth spurt in 1995 also weighed heavily on profits for the year. A sizeable thorn was the recently acquired Rhino International, affected by floods in China, which required costly and extensive improvements, and a lawsuit filed by Rhino's former owner. Alamo's management, however, continued to strive for longer term goals and increased its research allocations to $1.7 million for new product development. Additionally, Douglass and Logan's 1993 projection for the European market, to bring in a quarter of the company's revenues within a few years, was realized with 26 percent of sales in 1996, and helped along by the acquisition of Forges Gorce in France in the last quarter. Yet Europe was not the only hot spot for Alamo, as sales in Asia had gained a foothold and the company had plans to open a new office in Thailand the next year.

Alamo's strategies appeared to be paying off with another bumper year in 1997, with overall revenue hitting $203.1 million and income leaping to $13.6 million after 1996's disappointing $8.8 million. European sales were strong until the fourth quarter when they tapered off, yet this downturn was offset by solid returns in the United States. There were no acquisitions during the year and stock prices held steady in the $18 per share range, with a high of over $23 in the third quarter. Alamo was poised for a promising year in 1998 and caught the attention of the Woods Equipment Company and two of its own subsidiaries, the WEC Company and the AGI Acquisition Corp. Woods turned the tables on Douglass and Logan with an offer to buy Alamo and merge it into the Illinois-based company's holdings. The privately held Woods made an offer of $180 million to buy Alamo in August.

By November 1998, a special stockholder meeting convened and approved the terms to merge Alamo with WEC Company and AGI Corp. Yet internal problems began to take their toll on Alamo, as its ongoing troubles with Rhino International had led management to close the embattled manufacturer. The termination of Rhino International's operations began to cost the company millions, along with several lawsuits filed by Rhino customers. In addition to the company's vexations with Rhino International, weather conditions again brought down core agricultural sales while farming conditions and currency problems plagued European sales, which tumbled over 11 percent from 1997. Fourth quarter earnings were significantly down, and stock value fell 19 percent with a low of only $10 per share, compared to the previous year's $19 per share. Alamo's poor showing at the end of 1998 fueled a falling out with Woods Equipment Company and its subsidiaries, and the proposed and approved acquisition/merger was called off in February 1999. Neither participant had been able to agree on certain closing conditions, and Alamo's poor year-end results became a major stumbling block. According to a *Wall Street Journal* article about the merger's cancellation, Paul Wood, chairman of WEC, had declared that ''Alamo's condition, prospects and value are materially worse than a year ago and materially worse than the projections and forecasts made before and since the time of the merger agreement.''

The troubles continued in the first and second quarters of 1999. A pervasive drought throughout much of the United States and a continuing worldwide agricultural recession besieged Alamo from within and without. For the first six months of 1999 net sales were down 14.5 percent to $93.3 million from the previous year's $109.1 million and net income fell for the first two quarters as well. The numbers reflected the downswing in agricultural sales, which were 51 percent of Alamo's sales for the first six months in 1998 and fell to 42 percent in 1999, yet with upswings in both industrial (35 vs. 30 percent) and European sales (23 vs. 20 percent). Yet the most remarkable fallout of 1999 came in July with the resignation of founder Douglass as CEO, a post he had held since 1969. Logan also stepped down as COO, after 18 years in the position. Taking their places was Ronald A. Robinson (formerly president of Svedala Industries Inc.) as CEO and president, though Douglass remained Alamo's chairman and Logan remained a board member.

The new Alamo, with Robinson at the helm, believed the worst times were behind. With the approach of a new century came a wiser, leaner Alamo, with Rhino's disposal complete, and what the company had termed ''cyclical'' drought giving way to what all hoped was a bountiful year ahead for both domestic and European operations. From its first sale through late 1999, Alamo had concentrated on several key factors to further its business: geographic expansion, new product development, acquisitions, and customer satisfaction. It remained to be seen whether the same game plan would work in the years to come.

Principal Divisions

Alamo Industrial; Rhino; M&W; McConnel; Bomford; SMA; Tiger; and Herschel-Adams product lines.

Principal Competitors

Allied Products Corporation; Deere & Company; The Toro Company.

Further Reading

Bass, Frank, ''Following a Rough Year, the Grass Looks Greener for Alamo Group,'' *Wall Street Journal,* June 18, 1997.

Hardy, Eric S., ''No Rust Here,'' *Forbes,* December 30, 1996.

Opdyke, Jeff D., ''Turning the Tide: Small Stocks Look Ready to Stage a Comeback,'' *Texas Journal,* January 22, 1997.

Schifrin, Matthew, ''Watching the Grass Grow,'' *Forbes,* October 21, 1996, p.182.

—Nelson Rhodes

American Crystal Sugar Company

101 North Third Street
Moorhead, Minnesota 56560
U.S.A.
Telephone: (218) 236-4400
Fax: (218) 236-4422
Web site: http://www.crystalsugar.com

Cooperative
Incorporated: 1973
Employees: 1,263
Sales: $676.6 million (1998)
NAIC: 311313 Beet Sugar Manufacturing; 311221 Wet Corn Milling

American Crystal Sugar Company is a 2,800-member agricultural cooperative based in the Red River Valley region of northwestern Minnesota and northeastern North Dakota, a region sometimes referred to in the sugarbeet industry as the nation's ''sugar bowl.'' American Crystal is the largest U.S. processor of beet sugar, with sugar plants located in East Grand Forks, Crookston, and Moorhead, Minnesota; and Drayton and Hillsboro, North Dakota. Its position as a top competitor in sugar production was strengthened in 1993 through the formation of Bloomington, Minnesota-based United Sugars Corporation. A marketing company formed in partnership with Southern Minnesota Beet Sugar Cooperative of Renville, Minnesota, and Minn-Dak Farmers Cooperative of Wahpeton, North Dakota (the upper Midwest's two other major sugarbeet growing co-ops), United Sugars ranks as the nation's top beet sugar supplier and holds about 25 percent of the entire domestic sugar market; it offers a full line of consumer sugar products under the Crystal and Pillsbury Best brands as well as private labels, in addition to supplying sugar to commercial clients, such as Kraft General Foods, Hershey Foods Corp., and Mars Inc. American Crystal's history goes back to 1899, and the company has been a pioneering force in the industry, particularly since 1973, when a group of growers assumed both ownership and management of the originally family-controlled concern. American Crystal is also a partner with Minn-Dak and Southern Minnesota in Midwest Agri-Commodities Company, which markets sugarbeets, sugarbeet molasses, and other specialty commodities. Moreover, it holds a 46 percent interest in ProGold Limited Liability Company, which is active in the corn sweetener market through a wet corn milling plant.

Early History

During the late 19th century, sugarbeets were still little more than an experimental crop in the Red River Valley. By then beet sugar was, however, a major commodity in Europe, outpacing in tonnage that of imported cane sugar. A German chemist named Andreas Marggraf had experimented with sugar extraction from the *Beta vulgaris* as early as 1747, and, in 1802, the first German sugarbeet factory was built. Another stimulus to the industry came in 1811, when Napoleon sought to outflank a British blockade of France's chief raw sugar source, the West Indies. Under Napoleon, some 40 sugarbeet processing factories were soon established in France. For countries and regions with colder climates, sugarbeets offered the possibility of a huge new source of income, a crop that could directly compete in quality with sugarcane, which is limited to tropical and subtropical growing areas.

According to Walter Ebeling in *The Fruited Plain,* ''the first successful beet-sugar factory in the United States was established in California in 1879.'' California, in fact, would prove a key growing region for sugarbeets for roughly the next hundred years; Ebeling noted that as late as 1975 the state led the country in production, followed by Idaho, Colorado, and Washington. The American Beet Sugar Company, owned by the Oxnard family and based in Denver, was one of the first sugarbeet producers, having been formed in 1899. Through the early decades of the 20th century, American Beet developed into a six-plant operation over three states: Colorado, California, and Nebraska.

At the same time, a beet-processing plant owned by the Minnesota Sugar Company had sprung up in Chaska, southwest of Minneapolis and St. Paul. By 1919, Red River Valley farmers were experiencing success with sugarbeet growing and had begun shipping their harvest to the Chaska plant. Minnesota Sugar, in

Company Perspectives:

American Crystal Sugar Company is a world-class agricultural cooperative that specializes in sugar and sugar-based products and by-products.

Our mission is to simultaneously maximize shareholder returns and customer satisfaction through innovative farming practices, low-cost production methods and sales and marketing leadership.

turn, commenced "large scale experiments in the Valley," according to *50 Years in the Valley,* an American Crystal retrospective. Closely affiliated with Minnesota Sugar was the Northern Sugar Company of Mason City, Iowa, which also figured largely in the early development of the Red River Valley.

In 1922, a crisis was at hand for Colorado's American Beet Sugar Company, which was fast becoming a neglected and vulnerable family business. Following a board meeting convened in April of that year, a special committee was formed to investigate and redirect the company. Then, in June, three successive events—the resignation of second American Beet president Robert Oxnard; the death of original company president Henry Oxnard; and the resignation of chairperson and appointed president H. Rieman Duval—threw the already beleaguered company into a tailspin. Although Duval's resignation was at first rejected, he was eventually replaced by R. Walter Leigh.

By 1924, with Leigh at the helm, the Colorado company was facing the possibility of dissolution. Only three of its six plants were still operating, and only one of these three, the Oxnard, California, plant, was considered sufficient to handle present operations without costly renovation. Leigh recommended that American Beet, if it intended to survive, should seek out new territories and either acquire or form a coalition with other successful beet operations. Both American Beet's chief chemist and vice-president ventured to Minnesota that year to explore the Red River territory and the possibility of an alignment, if not merger, with Northern Sugar and Minnesota Sugar.

During this time, the Commercial Clubs of Grand Forks, North Dakota, and East Grand Forks, Minnesota, had been negotiating with Minnesota Sugar over the construction of what would be the Valley's first sugarbeet processing plant. H.A. Douglas, president of both Minnesota and Northern Sugar, had announced the prior year that his Chaska-based company would commit $1 million toward the construction of the proposed plant, provided the area's farmers and business leaders raised an additional $500,000. The completion of the deal appeared a foregone conclusion—considering the high interest of all parties involved—until a conference with Douglas at the behest of American Beet was held in Chicago in September 1924. During that meeting, American Beet representatives indicated the company's interest in entering new locations while possibly relocating its idle factories or acquiring existing factories. Following another conference in October, during which a purchase price for both Northern and Minnesota Sugar was discussed, American Beet completed negotiations in November, acquiring Minnesota Sugar for $1.97 million and Northern for $2.45 million. The deal included the property involved in the East Grand Forks development but did not obligate American Beet to build a factory there.

Rumors and speculation abounded among Valley growers and civic leaders through the spring of 1925, when the acquisition was finalized. Shortly thereafter, American Beet officials cleared the air. The construction of a plant would be postponed and a local in-progress sale of stock in the East Grand Forks development, named the Red River Sugar Company, would need to be rescinded. Fortunately for the beet farmers, the wait for a new plant was not long. In 1926, American Beet erected a 2,000-tons-per-day capacity plant in East Grand Forks. Early that same year, the farmers established the Red River Valley Beet Growers Association, which would work in cooperation with American Beet on a number of matters, including acreage allotment. An early indication of the venture's success was the negotiated expansion from 10,500 acres planted in 1926 to 20,000 acres in 1927.

By 1934, American Beet had changed its name to American Crystal Sugar Company and had come to depend heavily on the Red River Valley for its prosperity. That year was a particularly devastating one for the sugarbeet industry, however, due not only to the nation's crippled economy but also to an outbreak of "curly top," an insect-transmitted virus that ruined over 85 percent of the sugarbeet crop across the country. The East Grand Forks operation was the only American Crystal unit to post a profit. All told, the company lost $1.3 million in 1934. Both it and the sugarbeet industry as a whole rebounded over the next several years, however, thanks to the work of plant breeders who developed superior beet hybrids that were more resistant to "curly top" and other viruses.

According to *50 Years in the Valley:* "East Grand Forks and the Valley beet industry flourished during World War II, just as it had during the Great Depression and other times of economic strife. It made consistent profits while many of the Company's other plants faltered. The consistent high quality of Valley sugarbeets contrasted with those produced in other parts of the country because of the Valley's fertile soils, productive farmers and comparatively better moisture conditions. Certainly there were bad years in the Valley, but its overall consistency made it a sugarbeet mecca."

1946–81: Expansion and Cooperative Formation

Following the war, American Crystal readied for expansion, purchasing land for two additional plants in 1946. Two years later, the company completed construction of what was essentially the first new factory in the industry in almost two decades. This plant was located in Moorhead, Minnesota, about 70 miles south of East Grand Forks. Completion of the other plant, in Crookston, Minnesota, followed in 1954. In 1965, a fourth American Crystal plant was brought into operation, this time in Drayton, North Dakota.

By then the American sugar industry was beginning to undergo changes, prompted by Fidel Castro's coup in Cuba. Cuba, a historically large supplier of sugar to the United States, was penalized by an amendment to the Sugar Act that redistributed the country's quota and ultimately benefited U.S. sugar

Key Dates:

1899: The American Beet Sugar Company is formed as one of the first sugarbeet producers.
1925: American Beet acquires Minnesota Sugar and Northern Sugar.
1926: Company constructs sugarbeet processing plant in East Grand Forks, North Dakota.
1934: American Beet changes its name to American Crystal Sugar Company.
1948: Moorhead, Minnesota, processing plant is completed.
1954: Third processing plant is built in Crookston, Minnesota.
1965: Fourth American Crystal plant begins operations in Drayton, North Dakota.
1972: Two Midwestern sugarbeet cooperatives are formed: Minn-Dak Farmers Cooperative and Southern Minnesota Beet Sugar Cooperative (SMBSC).
1973: American Crystal is transformed into a grower-owned cooperative.
1975: The Red River Valley Cooperative and its processing plant in Hillsboro, North Dakota, is absorbed by American Crystal.
1982: American Crystal, Minn-Dak, and SMBSC form a joint venture, Midwest Agri-Commodities Company, to market beet byproducts.
1993: American Crystal, Minn-Dak, and SMBSC form second joint venture, United Sugars Corporation, the largest beet sugar marketing company in the United States.
1995: American Crystal, Minn-Dak, and Golden Growers Cooperative form ProGold Limited Liability Company to build and operate a wet corn milling plant.
1997: United States Sugar Corporation joins the United Sugars alliance, creating a nationwide sugar marketer; United Sugars begins a national rollout of Pillsbury Best Sugar.
1999: American Crystal increases its sugarbeet acreage to 500,000.

producers. Although Congressional support for the U.S. sugar industry would become increasingly important in later years, the Cuban situation had only a limited effect on domestic sugar production. With the early 1970s came cutbacks in planted acres for American Crystal. In 1973, amidst depressed conditions in the industry, Red River Valley acreage was at 150,000 and trending downward. The company was then operating only six of its 11 plants (four of which had become mainstays of the Red River Valley economy) and had curtailed any plans for future development. As Steve Brandt wrote in *Corporate Report Minnesota:* ''American Crystal Sugar was a moribund Denver-based company, held by a trust that was content to reap company profits for philanthropic activities that had been laid down by the firm's founding family. Management seemed bent on restricting operations.''

Members of the Beet Growers Association had for some time recognized the gravity of the situation, and—hoping to capitalize on possibilities for the future, if plant improvements and other actions were undertaken—had already made plans in late 1971 to acquire a nine percent interest in American Crystal that was up for sale. The association was headed by Executive Secretary Aldrich Bloomquist, who in a letter to Crystal executives proposed at the same time an ambitious alternative plan: the sale of the entire company to the growers. By February 1973, the $66 million deal was sealed, with approximately one-third of the money to come from area farmers (through $100 per acre equity stakes) and the remaining two-thirds through long-term financing from the Bank for Cooperatives in St. Paul.

In 1974, its first full year as a farmer-owned cooperative, American Crystal announced plans for a new $40 million plant, to be built adjacent to the original East Grand Forks factory, which would be renovated at the same time. Together, the improvements would allow the company to expand acreage by up to 14 percent, a growth-oriented move the Growers Association had fought for repeatedly, and increasingly unsuccessfully, during the latter years of outside ownership. The company also grew in 1975 by absorbing the Red River Valley Cooperative, which was proceeding with the construction of a factory in Hillsboro, North Dakota. Meanwhile, two additional Midwestern sugarbeet co-ops were chartered, both in 1972. One was a North Dakota group called Minn-Dak Farmers Cooperative (Minn-Dak), which formed in the Wahpeton area and proceeded to dedicate a plant there before the 1974 harvest. The other was Southern Minnesota Beet Sugar Cooperative (SMBSC), which was established after that area's Growers Association received word in 1971 that the Chaska plant was due to close forever at the end of the season. SMBSC began construction of their $60 million plant, located east of Renville in southern Minnesota, in early 1973. In an early sign of partnership, American Crystal managed the plant until 1978, when SMBSC took control.

The timing of all of this heady growth in the ''sugar bowl'' could hardly have been more fortunate, for sugar prices were just about to skyrocket. Although U.S. farmers were typically prevented from suffering, or benefiting, from volatility in sugar prices, a new farm bill completed in 1973 contained no such stipulation. Egerstrom summarized the unusual situation: ''American farmers produce about half the sugar consumed annually in the United States. The rest is surplus from other sugar countries that sell most of their exports under contracts at fixed prices. There weren't surpluses of anything during the early 1970s. Sugar crops around the world that were spared drought were raked by hurricanes and other natural problems. American Crystal and the Red River Valley beet growers were in for a windfall. World sugar prices shot up from about 15 cents a pound to as high as 70 cents.'' As Bloomquist remarked: ''We had farmers who recovered their entire investment in the co-op that first year.'' Of course, sooner or later the opposite scenario would occur, as in 1977 when a worldwide sugar surplus developed. American Crystal and its fellow co-ops have since successfully lobbied for a strong national sugar support program, despite occasional opposition from consumer groups and food processors.

1982 and Beyond: Cooperating Cooperatives

In 1982 American Crystal joined Minn-Dak and SMBSC as a partner in Midwest Agri-Commodities Company. Headquartered in Corte Madera, California, near San Francisco, Midwest was established to market beet byproducts, namely molasses and pellet-sized pulp, which was used principally as feed for dairy cattle. In 1993 Japanese buyers represented Midwest's largest customer base, purchasing some 63 percent of the pulp produced by Midwest, a figure that in turn represented more than 60 percent of all beet pulp imported by Japan. European markets were also a key destination for the three co-ops' byproducts.

In June 1991 American Crystal announced plans to construct a $31 million molasses desugarization plant at its East Grand Forks site in order to increase the co-op's production capacity. Desugarization involves extracting approximately 86 percent of the sugar contained in the molasses produced as a byproduct during sugar production. The facility was expected to produce some 130 million more pounds of sugar from the same tonnage of beets then being processed. Due to delays involving the Minnesota Pollution Control Agency, the plant was not completed until just prior to the 1993–94 processing campaign. Meantime, in March 1992 Joseph P. Famalette was hired as president and CEO of American Crystal to replace the retiring Al Bloomquist. Famalette was a former executive with Minnesota-based processor International Multifoods Corporation.

In 1993 American Crystal's position as a top competitor in sugar production was strengthened through the formation of Bloomington, Minnesota-based United Sugars Corporation, another jointly owned venture with SMBSC and Minn-Dak. United Sugars immediately ranked as the nation's top beet sugar marketer. By this time, American Crystal had invested, as a cooperative, over $200 million in plants, equipment, improvements, and research designed to enhance efficiency and increase profitability for its members. By almost all accounts the money had been well spent. Not only did the cooperative generate an estimated $1 billion annually to the economy of the Red River Valley, but it also continued to set high industry standards for quality while simultaneously setting new records for sugar production (1.9 billion pounds of sugar in 1993), total net beet payment ($284 million), and sugar sales (1.8 billion pounds). In addition, while more than 80 percent of the co-op's sugar was purchased by food processors, including General Mills, Sara Lee, Nestlé, Hershey, and Kraft, the company's namesake brand of packaged sugar ranked number one among retailers in the upper Midwest.

In the fall of 1994 American Crystal raised more than $28 million and increased its sugarbeet production through a public stock offering. For each share of stock purchased, buyers were required to grow one acre of sugarbeets for the co-op. The following spring American Crystal finalized a deal that expanded its operations into wet corn milling and the corn sweetener field, as part of a planned diversification. The co-op invested $48 million to take a 49 percent stake (later reduced to 46 percent) in a new joint venture, ProGold Limited Liability Company, whose other owners were Minn-Dak and Golden Growers Cooperative. ProGold planned to build a $261 million wet corn milling plant in Wahpeton, North Dakota, to produce high fructose corn syrup, corn starch, corn oil, ethanol, and various byproducts.

In April 1995 Famalette resigned to take a position with a California co-op. Mark Richardson was named interim president before Dan McCarty took over as president and CEO. In the fall of 1996 American Crystal completed another public offering of about 20,500 preferred shares, which translated into a like number of additional sugarbeet acreage, and increased the co-op's total acreage to more than 435,000.

Just a few months after the ProGold facility began production of corn sweeteners in October 1996, the bottom dropped out of that market due to excess supply. As a result, American Crystal delayed a planned expansion of its East Grand Forks molasses desugarization operation. It also turned over operation of the ProGold facility in Wahpeton to corn sweetener rival Cargill Inc., with Cargill sharing the profits with the co-op owners. During 1997 American Crystal also completed a study of future growth opportunities, which concluded that diversification should be abandoned in favor of a recommitment to the sugar industry. That year the co-op made two significant sugar-related moves: it entered into an alliance with U.S. Sugar Corporation, the largest grower of sugar cane in Florida, which made United Sugars the first nationwide producer and distributor of refined sugar, with a 25 percent market share; and it began rolling out the industry's first premium national brand—Pillsbury Best Sugar. The use of the Pillsbury name had been gained through a licensing agreement with Minneapolis-based Pillsbury Company, a unit of U.K.-based Grand Metropolitan PLC (which soon merged with Guinness PLC to form Diageo plc). Meantime, 1997 also saw American Crystal produce a record amount of sugar despite the heavy blizzards and a 500-year flood that visited the Red River Valley that year.

In 1998 American Crystal completed the largest beet-slicing expansion in its history through expansion of its East Grand Forks and Hillsboro facilities, which work cost $57 million. The co-op was also constructing a molasses desugarization facility at its Hillsboro location which would be capable of processing about 200,000 tons of molasses. Slated to be operational in 2000, this project was being completed by Crystech L.L.C., a 50–50 joint venture of American Crystal and Toronto-based Newcourt Credit Group Inc. At a total cost of $96 million, it represented the largest capital expenditure in American Crystal history. By 1999 the co-op had increased its sugarbeet acres to 500,000 thanks to the sale of stock in the fall of 1997 representing 61,500 acres of additional land. Under the leadership of new president and CEO James J. Horvath, the co-op was also investigating the addition of organically grown sugar to its product line. With all of these expansionary moves, American Crystal moved toward the 21st century on the upswing, with 100 years in the sugar business and 25 years as a cooperative behind it.

Principal Subsidiaries

Crystech L.L.C. (50%); Midwest Agri-Commodities Company (33.3%); ProGold Limited Liability Company (46%); United Sugars Corporation (33.3%).

Principal Competitors

Alberto-Culver Company; Christian Hansen; Cumberland Packing Corp.; Imperial Sugar Company; Monsanto Company; Sugar Foods; Tate & Lyle PLC.

Further Reading

Alster, Norm, "Getting the Middleman's Share," *Forbes,* July 4, 1994, pp. 108–9.

"American Crystal Delays Plant Project Expansion," *Minneapolis Star Tribune,* March 12, 1997, p. 3D.

Brandt, Steve, "Poor Prices Put Crystal on Spot with Beet Farmers," *Minneapolis Tribune,* March 29, 1982, pp. B3, B4.

——, "Sweet Deal," *Corporate Report Minnesota,* January 1986, pp. 91–96.

Bueno, Jacqueline, "U.S. Sugar Joins Midwest Co-op, Paving Way for a National Brand," *Wall Street Journal,* July 30, 1997, p. B4.

Campbell, Erin, "Crystal to Stick to Sugar," *Grand Forks (N.D.) Herald,* December 5, 1997, p. 1A.

"Cereal Investigation Doesn't Concern Beet Fiber Producer," *Minneapolis Star Tribune,* July 9, 1989, p. 4B.

"Company News," *Minneapolis Star Tribune,* June 26, 1991, p. 2D.

"Cooperatives Pool Beet Production," *Minneapolis Star Tribune,* December 27, 1984.

Ebeling, Walter, *The Fruited Plain: The Story of American Agriculture,* Berkeley: University of California Press, 1979, 433 p.

Egerstrom, Lee, "Sweet Profits: Red River Valley's Sugar Beet Goes on with Savory Sales for American Crystal," *St. Paul Pioneer Press,* December 10, 1984, pp. 1, 9–10.

50 Years in the Valley, Moorhead, Minn.: American Crystal Sugar Company, 1976.

Henderson, Julie, "American Crystal Sugar Considers Growing Sugar Organically," *Grand Forks (N.D.) Herald,* July 8, 1998.

Johnson, Rona K., "Red River Valley Beet Harvest Set to Start," *Agweek,* August 29, 1994, p. 29.

Jones, Jim, "Growers Soured by Sugar Bill Loss," *Minneapolis Star,* October 25, 1978.

Kennedy, Tony, "American Crystal Sugar Exec Leaving," *Minneapolis Star Tribune,* April 27, 1995, p. 3D.

——, "Crystal Sugar's New CEO Happy to Run Own Show," *Minneapolis Star Tribune,* February 10, 1992, p. 2D.

Phelps, David, "Organized, Well-Financed Lobby Effort Helps Make Life Sweet for Sugar Growers," *Minneapolis Star Tribune,* March 19, 1987, p. 10A.

"President of Crystal Sugar Co. Beats Ouster Bid, Then Resigns," *Minneapolis Star Tribune,* January 21, 1986, p. 11B.

Rustebakke, Brian, "American Crystal Celebrates 25 Years As Co-op," *Grand Forks (N.D.) Herald,* December 4, 1998, p. 1B.

——, "Crystal Opts to Harvest It All," *Grand Forks (N.D.) Herald,* October 9, 1999, p. 1A.

Schmickle, Sharon, "Red River's Beet Boom Means a Bust for Belize," *Minneapolis Star Tribune,* April 16, 1989, p. 25A.

Shoptaugh, Terry L., *Roots of Success: History of the Red River Valley Sugarbeet Growers,* Fargo, N.D.: Institute for Regional Studies, 1997, 270 p.

Struck, Myron, "American Crystal Is Top State PAC," *Minneapolis Star Tribune,* July 11, 1988, p. 4D.

"Sugar Firms to Combine Marketing Operations," *Minneapolis Star Tribune,* July 30, 1997, p. 3D.

"Sugar Glut May Lead to Sales Quotas," *Minneapolis Star Tribune,* April 7, 1993, p. 3D.

"3 Sugar Beet Co-Ops Sign Merger Deal," *Minneapolis Star Tribune,* November 3, 1993, p. 3D.

"Three Sugar Co-Ops Are Planning to Join Forces," *Minneapolis Star Tribune,* March 15, 1993, p. 1B.

—Jay P. Pederson
—updated by David E. Salamie

American Lawyer Media Holdings, Inc.

345 Park Avenue South
New York, New York 10010
U.S.A.
Telephone: (212) 779-9200
Fax: (212) 696-4514
Web site: http://www.lawnewsnetwork.com

Private Company
Incorporated: 1997
Employees: 870
Sales: $121.5 million (1998)
NAIC: 51112 Periodical Publishers; 51113 Book Publishers

American Lawyer Media Holdings, Inc., a holding company formed in 1997, is a leading publisher for the legal profession. It publishes 21 periodicals, including the *American Lawyer*; an award-winning monthly magazine; the *National Law Journal,* the nation's major national newspaper for lawyers; the *New York Law Journal* and other regional publications; and several specialized newsletters and periodicals. It also publishes over 100 law books, operates several web sites on national and regional legal topics, and offers a wide variety of seminars and conferences for lawyers and other professionals. The holding company thus continues to make major contributions to legal journalism, a field founded by its predecessor firms. By describing law firm finances, management, and other legal trends and events, its writers shed light on a profession that historically wanted little if any publicity.

Origins of Predecessor Companies

Although law firms began growing in the late 1800s to meet the needs of expanding corporations and continued to recruit more and more attorneys in the 20th century, the legal profession remained for all practical purposes a secret society guided by its own rules of professional conduct. In 1908 and 1975, for example, the profession adopted rules prohibiting cooperation with journalists, writers, and other outsiders. The goal was to prevent any public discussion of lawyers' success and their clients, which was seen as self-promotion or advertising. Some law firms even refused to tell outsiders how many attorneys they employed. Although courts relied on historical judicial precedents, the legal profession wanted nobody to know its own history.

That all changed rather dramatically in the late 1970s. The U.S. Supreme Court in Bates v. State Bar of Arizona (1977) struck down professional barriers against advertising, and about the same time the new field of legal journalism began. Because of these developments, "A few years later the interested reader could find an abundance of information about firm organization, finances, relations to clients, office politics, and so forth," wrote law professors Marc Galanter and Thomas Palay in their 1991 book detailing the transformation of big law firms.

Two competing publications made the difference. In 1978 James A. Finkelstein began publishing the *National Law Journal*, a weekly newspaper for attorneys. First handed out at the 1978 annual meeting of the American Bar Association in New York City, the newspaper in August began to be published weekly. In 1978 Finkelstein began the paper's annual survey of the nation's 200 largest law firms, which he called in the September 19, 1983 issue "our most widely requested feature by readers."

Finkelstein admitted that at first he was uncertain that lawyers would buy his newspaper. However, he stated in the September 24, 1984 issue that "we have been extremely pleased with the reaction of the profession. When we began, it was unusual for attorneys to talk openly about their work; now it is common for them to feel they can speak with us and trust us. . . ."

The *National Law Journal*'s readership steadily increased in the 1980s, from 160,000 in 1983 to 250,000 in 1988. In addition, their survey expanded in 1983 to cover the nation's 250 largest law firms.

Meanwhile, Steven Brill, "who revolutionized legal coverage," according to the February 24, 1992 *New York Times*, began his contributions to legal journalism. Brill was born in 1950 in New York City. After graduating from Yale Law School in 1975, he began his career as a journalist instead of practicing law. His 1978 book *The Teamsters* was a bestseller. Writing an *Esquire* column on lawyers led him to consider

Key Dates:

1978: James A. Finkelstein begins publishing the *National Law Journal.*
1979: Steven Brill begins publishing the *American Lawyer* in February.
1985: Brill persuades his British corporate backers to buy nine regional legal newspapers.
1991: Court Television is started in July by Brill to broadcast trials live.
1993: Brill starts Counsel Connect, an electronic bulletin board service, and launches *Law Technology News.*
1994: *Corporate Counsel* is started by Brill.
1995: Court TV receives high Nielsen ratings from broadcasting the O.J. Simpson murder trial.
1995: *IP Worldwide* is first published by Brill.
1996: *AmLaw Tech* is founded.
1997: The newly formed holding company acquires American Lawyer Media, L.P. and National Law Publishing Company, Inc.
1998: A company subsidiary purchases Corporate Presentations, Inc.; Legal Communications, Ltd.; and the *Delaware Law Monthly*; the *American Lawyer* and *Legal Business* publish their first survey of the world's largest law firms; the firm hires William L. Pollak as its president/CEO for a five-year period; company ends Counsel Connect and replaces it with Law News Network, a national Internet site.
1999: The firm expands its Internet presence with new web sites and begins the *Daily Deal* newspaper.

starting a new magazine about lawyers. In 1978 Brill and his business associate Jay Kriegel, encouraged by *Esquire* editor Clay Felker, met with the British conglomerate Associated Newspapers Ltd., the *Esquire*'s financial supporters. Associated Newspapers agreed to invest the first $3 million in the magazine, which raised a total of $35 million to get started.

In February 1979 the first issue of the *American Lawyer* featured Brill's article on Joseph Flom, who had led Skadden Arps Slate Meagher and Flom into the ranks of the most prosperous U.S. law firms and also served as chairman of the board of editors of the *National Law Journal*. In this article Brill emphasized law firm finances, a topic usually not discussed by most lawyers. In these early years Brill both managed the magazine and wrote the lead articles. Well known for his unrelenting demand for accuracy, Brill took the unusual step of printing errors and the names of responsible reporters in his magazine.

Brill soon began publishing his ranking of the nation's top 100 law firms. Unlike the *National Law Journal*'s rankings by number of attorneys, Brill ranked firms by their annual revenues. Although some initially considered the *American Lawyer* no more than a gossipy lightweight magazine, in the 1980s some law firms sought to be included in Brill's publication. Former U.S. Supreme Court Chief Justice Warren Berger said in the August 12, 1991 *New York* that, ''*American Lawyer* routinely revealed information–revenues, partners' salaries, and fees–that had always been closely guarded by firms. Brill also looked at the business ethics of individual firms, and how they treated young associates, which turned his magazine into a bible among law-school graduates.''

By 1984 Associated Newspapers followed Brill's advice by acquiring nine regional legal newspapers, including *New Jersey Law Journal* and Washington, D.C's *Legal Times*. By then Jay Kriegel had left, and Brill was both editor and publisher. Brill hoped the addition of the new regional newspapers would solve his firm's financial problems, but the firm kept losing money. In 1989 *Manhattan Lawyer* failed.

The kind of information provided by Brill and Finkelstein's periodicals influenced the process of lateral hiring of experienced attorneys from rival law firms. Such hiring had long been done, but most attorneys previously remained lifelong members of their firms. Some critics argued that the new business orientation of law firms hurt the profession by decreasing firm collegiality and creating a dog-eat-dog atmosphere. Mass defections of entire departments and mergers between firms became more common.

In any case, the new legal journalism influenced the American legal profession as it grew rapidly in the 1980s. In 1985, 508 law firms employed at least 51 lawyers, compared to only 38 firms that had more than 50 lawyers in the late 1950s. The largest law firm in the United States in 1968 had 169 attorneys. In 1988 the largest firm employed 962 attorneys.

Other trends that Brill, Finkelstein, and the other legal journalists wrote about included the hiring of more women and minority attorneys, increased specialization of legal practice, and the many mergers and acquisitions of the 1980s. In addition, they looked at entire new legal fields resulting from new industries such as biotechnology and software.

Developments in the 1990s

In 1991 Brill started Court Television, a $40 million joint venture involving Time Warner, NBC, and Cablevision Systems Corporation. Later NBC bought out Cablevision's share, and Liberty Media became a Court TV partner. Court TV had some initial success, broadcasting well known trials of William Kennedy Smith, John Wayne Bobbitt, and the Menendez Brothers. Showing the long murder trial of O.J. Simpson brought Court TV into 30 million homes, up from just 2.5 million in 1991.

On May 1, 1993 Brill started Counsel Connect to provide inexpensive legal advice and research on common legal questions as one way to reduce expensive legal services. The electronic bulletin board service (BBS) by October had signed 600 clients, including 80 of the nation's 100 largest law firms and also the legal department of General Electric and other corporations. Originally offered at $975 per month plus 65 cents a minute, Counsel Connect's price for small firms dropped by October to just $6 a month and 65 cents a minute to access the database.

Brill in 1996 acknowledged that many thought that the *American Lawyer* and particularly its annual rankings of the top U.S. 100 law firms had ruined the legal profession. In the magazine's July/August 1996 issue, he cited a Boston attorney who had stated on Counsel Connect that, ''When the *American Lawyer* brought the bottom line out of the closet, it became okay, among other things, to chuck 'low productivity partners.' What could be more destructive of collegiality?''

In response, Brill defended his publication for providing ''real market information to lawyers and their customers'' and that it had ''made and will continue to make the profession stronger in every way in the next century than it would have been.''

Meanwhile, changes occurred in the ownership of Brill's rival, the National Law Publishing Company, Inc. On December 1, 1995 Boston Ventures, through a wholly owned subsidiary, NLPC Acquisitions, acquired about 94.3 percent of National for about $142 million. At the same time, NLPC Acquisitions was merged into National, with National remaining the surviving company.

The Creation of American Lawyer Media Holdings, Inc.: 1997

In early 1997 Steven Brill sold his share in the companies he founded, American Lawyer Media and its affiliate Courtroom Television Network Inc. to Time Warner, mainly because of Time Warner's new vice-chairman, Ted Turner. Brill repeatedly had tried to buy out Court TV's three owners, NBC, Time Warner, and Liberty Media, claiming in the August 1997 *Vanity Fair* that the three ''really hated each other'' and had different goals. Brill claimed that Time Warner agreed with his plan, but Turner did not. Brill received $20 million in this transaction and soon started *Brill's Content*, a magazine about the media.

Time Warner Cable Programming's President Thayer Bigelow took over management of Court TV and also considered a Brill plan to start regional court channels in conjunction with the regional legal newspapers, but that concept never materialized due to decreased audience interest. Court TV's ratings had plummeted by early 1997. Meanwhile, Time Warner decided to offer the *American Lawyer*, Counsel Connect, and nine regional legal newspapers to interested buyers.

At that point Bruce Wasserstein entered the picture. He had graduated with honors from the University of Michigan, Harvard Business School, and Harvard Law School. He began practicing law in 1972 at New York City's Cravath, Swaine & Moore before joining The First Boston Corporation in 1977. In 1988 Wasserstein and Joseph Perella left First Boston to found the Wasserstein Perella Group, Inc. (WPG). Wasserstein served as WPG's chairman, president, and CEO.

On August 1, 1997 Cranberry Partners LLC was created as a limited liability company in Delaware. Cranberry then started ALM Holdings, LLC in Delaware. ALM Holdings in turn formed three companies, including two wholly owned subsidiaries, ALM, LLC as a New York limited liability company and Counsel Connect, LLC, a Delaware limited liability company, and a 99 percent-owned subsidiary called ALM IP, LLC, a Delaware firm.

On August 27, 1997 Cranberry closed its acquisition of American Lawyer Media, L.P. for $63 million. When this acquisition closed, Cranberry was held by W.P. Management Partners, LLC on behalf of U.S. Equity Partners, L.P. and some of its affiliates. WP Management Partners was the merchant banking entity of Wasserstein Perella Group, Inc. Wasserstein's firms were based in New York City.

The next step occurred on November 26, 1997, when Cranberry merged with the Delaware firm of ALM Capital Corporation, which at the same time was renamed American Lawyer Media Holdings, Inc. On the same day, ALM Holdings, LLC merged into ALM Capital Corp. II, which was renamed American Lawyer Media, Inc., a subsidiary of American Lawyer Media Holdings, Inc.

Bruce Wasserstein, the board chairman of American Lawyer Media Holdings, Inc., also wrote a 1998 book about mergers and acquisitions. *Big Deal: The Battle for Control of America's Leading Corporations* was described in the spring 1999 *Directors & Boards* as ''valuable as a basic or intermediate introduction to the world of M&A.''

After investments from its stockholders Wasserstein & Co., Inc.; U.S. Equity Partners L.P.; and U.S. Equity Partners (Offshore) L.P., the holding company through its subsidiary acquired all outstanding stock of National Law Publishing Company, Inc. from Boston Ventures and James A. Finkelstein for about $203 million. This acquisition completed the joining of the two former rival publishers of legal periodicals, American Lawyer Media and National Law Publishing. James Finkelstein stayed on as a director of the holding company, National Law Publishing Company's president/CEO, and as vice-chairman of American Lawyer Group, reporting to Chairman Wasserstein.

On March 3, 1998 the holding company through a subsidiary purchased Corporate Presentations, Inc., the owner of LegalTech, followed by the March 31 acquisition of Legal Communications, Ltd. In October the firm acquired the *Delaware Law Monthly*. In December 1998 it also began the Law News Network, described in its 1998 10-K annual report as ''the Internet's most extensive daily national legal newsource.'' The network's web site (www.lawnewsnetwork.com) provided current legal news and material from the holding company's periodicals, plus some original content and links to other web legal sites.

In 1998 advertising provided about 56 percent of the holding company's net revenues of $121.5 million. Other revenues came from subscriptions (19 percent), ancillary products and services (23 percent), and Internet services (two percent).

In 1999 American Lawyer Media Holdings started new publications and web sites and also formed joint ventures to promote its products and services. For example, in February it worked with the American Bar Association to put on the Chicago Techshow '99 and also started *California Law Week*. In March the holding company announced a strategic partnership with Compuserve. On September 14, 1999, American Lawyer Media Holdings launched the *Daily Deal*, a new periodical printed and distributed by Presspoint. It also joined with Martindale-Hubbell to start Newslinks, a web service to help law firm marketing.

These and other ventures indicated the holding company and its various subsidiaries were pressing ahead to stay competitive in the rapidly changing legal publishing field. An increasing number of law firms used the Internet to share professional papers and articles on general and specialized areas of the law.

Such decentralization was a major trend in the Information Age or what author Alvin Toffler called the Third Wave. Dealing with such general changes was one of American Lawyer Media Holdings' major challenges as it prepared to enter the new century and millennium.

Principal Subsidiaries

American Lawyer Media, Inc.; National Law Publishing Company, Inc.; Professional On Line, Inc.; The New York Law Publishing Company; NLP IP Company; PPC Publishing Corporation.

Principal Competitors

Harcourt General, Inc.; Reed International PLC; Thomson Corporation.

Further Reading

''Brill, Steven,'' *Current Biography Yearbook 1997,* New York: H.W. Wilson Company, pp. 42–44.

Brill, Steven, '' 'Ruining' the Profession,'' *American Lawyer*, July/August 1996, pp. 5–6.

Brown, Rich, and Steve McClellan, ''Court TV's Steve Brill: Witness for a Nation,'' *Broadcasting & Cable*, February 6, 1995, p. 43.

Burgi, Michael, and Jeff Gremillion, ''In Test of Will, Ted Beats Brill; Court TV Founder Steps Aside As Turner Nixes Buyback Plan,'' *MEDIAWEEK*, February 24, 1997, p. 6.

Calabresi, Massimo, ''Swaying the Home Jury [the Menendez Brothers' Trial],'' *Time*, January 10, 1994, p. 56.

Carmody, Deirdre, ''A Magazine's Trials, Now on Home Video,'' *New York Times*, February 24, 1992, p. D8 (late edition).

Cole, Lewis, ''Court TV,'' *Nation*, February 21, 1994, p. 243.

Conant, Jennet, ''Don't Mess with Steve Brill,'' *Vanity Fair*, August 1997, pp. 62, 64, 66, 69, 73–74.

Finkelstein, James A., ''Publisher's Letter,'' *National Law Journal*, September 19, 1983, p. 12; September 24, 1984, p. 12; and September 26, 1988, p. 12.

Frum, David, ''Lawyers in Cyberspace,'' *Forbes*, October 25, 1993, p. 56.

Galanter, Marc, and Thomas Palay, *Tournament of Lawyers: The Transformation of the Big Law Firm,* Chicago: University of Chicago Press, 1991.

Gremillion, Jeff, ''Publishing Top Lawman,'' *MEDIAWEEK*, November 10, 1997, p. 26.

Kaback, Hoffer, ''Behind the Art of M&A with Bruce Wasserstein,'' *Directors & Boards*, Spring 1999, p. 16.

Minerbrook, Scott, ''It's Court Time,'' *U.S. News & World Report*, July 15, 1991, p. 16.

Morris, John E., ''The Global 50,'' *American Lawyer*, November 1998, pp. 45–49.

Mullich, Joe, ''Jury in for Extended Net: Counsel Connect Services 40,000 Lawyers Looking to Confer with Co-Counsel, Clients,'' *PC Week*, July 14, 1997, p. 25.

Schlosser, Joe, ''Bigelow in for Brill: Interim Court TV CEO Says He's Considering Many Options,'' *Broadcasting & Cable*, March 17, 1997, p. 16.

Schrage, Michael, ''Steve Brill,'' *MEDIAWEEK*, November 20, 1995, p. IQ14.

Turner, Richard, ''Sudden Exit of a Would-Be Mogul: Tough Editor Steven Brill Gives Up the American Lawyer and Court TV,'' *Newsweek*, March 10, 1997, p. 74.

—David M. Walden

Andrew Corporation

10500 West 153rd Street
Orland Park, Illinois 60462
U.S.A.
Telephone: (708) 349-3300
Toll Free: (800) 232-6767
Fax: (708) 349-5410
Web site: http://www.andrew.com

Public Company
Incorporated: 1947
Employees: 4,572
Sales: $791.8 million (1999)
Stock Exchanges: NASDAQ Chicago
Ticker Symbol: ANDW
NAIC: 334210 Telephone Apparatus Manufacturing; 334220 Radio and Television Broadcasting and Wireless Communications Equipment Manufacturing; 334417 Electronic Connector Manufacturing; 334511 Search, Detection, Navigation, Guidance, Aeronautical, and Nautical System and Instrument Manufacturing; 335929 Other Communication and Energy Wire Manufacturing

Andrew Corporation is an international supplier of communications equipment, systems, and services. Among the company's principal products are coaxial cable, connectors, and systems used in various telecommunications systems; a variety of antennas and antenna systems, including microwave antenna systems and special application antennas used in cellular systems, navigation, FM and television broadcasting, multipoint distribution services, instructional television, radar systems, and surveillance systems; and wireless accessories, including portable antennas, batteries, battery chargers, paging accessories, and hands-free kits. About 57 percent of revenues are generated in the area of coaxial cable systems and bulk cables. Andrew has eight manufacturing plants in the United States and additional factories in Canada, Australia, Scotland, Brazil, China, and India; nearly half of revenues stem from products exported from the United States or manufactured abroad.

1937–49: From Consulting to Manufacturing

The company was founded as a sole proprietorship in 1937, when 34-year-old engineer Victor J. Andrew began to manufacture equipment for the directional antennas used by AM radio broadcasters. Andrew received a Ph.D. from the University of Chicago in 1932, and then worked at the Army Signal Corps Laboratories in Fort Monmouth, New Jersey, and at Westinghouse in Chicopee Falls, Massachusetts. Andrew soon returned to Chicago to go into business for himself, renting a bungalow on the city's southwest side where he installed a modest array of tools and equipment. His first sales were for custom designed phasing, tuning, and transmission line equipment for AM radio, though Andrew also offered his services as an engineering consultant to broadcast antenna users. Andrew had intended to make consulting the major part of his business, but World War II brought with it a ban on new broadcast station construction, and so he had little consulting work to do. Andrew concentrated instead on manufacturing, developing a number of new products and achieving significant sales of phasing and tuning equipment and of coaxial cables and rigid coaxial lines.

A strong demand for broadcast products spurred the company's initial growth, and the company moved to new quarters in the same Chicago neighborhood several times in its first ten years. During World War II, Andrew received large orders from the military for coaxial cables and later for dry air pumps which the Air Force used to pressurize airborne radar pods. After the war, Andrew continued its ties to the military, supplying coaxial transmission line which was used to monitor nuclear blast testing both above and below ground. In 1947 the company was incorporated as Andrew Corporation, with Victor Andrew installed as board chairman and CEO, and his wife Aileen named president. That same year, Andrew bought 430 acres of undeveloped land in the Chicago suburb of Orland Park—the clear land being necessary for outdoor testing of antennas—and eventually the company built its manufacturing and management facilities there as well.

1949–69: Microwave Antennas, HELIAX, and International Expansion

Andrew Corporation began making and marketing microwave antennas for both civilian and military communications in 1949, and Cold War demand for Andrew's products during the 1950s

Company Perspectives:

Andrew Corporation is a leading global supplier of equipment, systems and services for communications markets. To achieve long-term growth, the company will continue building on its key strengths: market leadership, customer orientation, breadth of product line, global presence, financial strength, and productivity.

kept the company busy. Andrew made switching devices, waveguides, and high-powered coaxial lines that were used in military radar systems. Its HELIAX continuous, semi-flexible coaxial cable came on the market in 1953 and became an important part of company growth. Coaxial cable, including HELIAX and RADIAX slotted coaxial cable, continued to make up the bulk of the company's business into the 21st century.

As demand for Andrew's products grew, the company opened new offices in the United States and abroad. In 1951 the company incorporated a branch, Andrew California Corporation, in order to take advantage of the growing West Coast electronics industry. Two years later, the firm opened a Canadian affiliate because Andrew had had substantial export sales to Canada. The Whitby, Ontario, affiliate immediately did well for itself, supplying other British Commonwealth markets and opening up new opportunities for Andrew abroad. Meantime, net sales exceeded $2 million in 1954.

Andrew Corporation had been actively scouting European markets since 1958, and in 1966 the company was offered a large microwave antenna system contract in England, with the proviso that a portion of the equipment had to be manufactured in Australia. Due to the clause, Andrew entered both the British and Australian markets at once, founding Andrew Antennas Proprietary Limited in Australia and Andrew Antenna Systems Limited in the United Kingdom the same year. The Australian division took on a contract for the installation of microwave equipment along a 1,500-mile route from Adelaide to Perth. The company experienced many initial difficulties caused by the long distance between the U.S. design team and the Australian affiliate, but despite many costly setbacks, the project was completed satisfactorily, and the Australian branch eventually became one of Andrew's most successful foreign operations.

Early 1970s to Mid-1980s: Shift to Private Microwave Antenna Systems

In the early 1970s, Andrew's market began to change from government and military contracts to private sector applications. In the United States, companies were allowed to compete with AT&T in long-distance communication beginning in 1972, and these so-called Other Common Carriers (OCCs) utilized microwave antennas for their telephone service. Andrew was an acknowledged world leader in microwave technology, and its business grew appreciably as the OCCs such as MCI and Sprint undertook large-scale construction projects. Andrew's growth in the microwave antenna business was at times as much as 25 percent a year between 1972 and 1984. The company held around 60 percent of the world market share in microwave antenna systems, with higher percentages in its top markets in the United States, Canada, and Australia.

The company had unparalleled technical expertise and had been in the market longer than any of its competitors, and in the early 1980s Andrew's dominance was unchallenged. Sales in 1980 reached $89 million, with two-thirds coming from domestic markets. That year Andrew went public, though the Andrew family retained a substantial portion of the stock.

When the U.S. Justice Department broke up AT&T in 1982, Andrew grew even more rapidly. AT&T itself was one of the company's top customers, and with the breakup it and the OCCs demanded still more Andrew microwave transmission technology. The company experienced record sales, with revenues for 1984 exceeding $200 million for the first time. But sales declined abruptly in 1985 when fiber optics began to supersede microwave technology in some areas. Fiber optic cables were found to transmit voice and data faster than microwave systems and with less distortion. Andrew management had had some signs that this might happen, but had anticipated more time to prepare for the new technology.

Late 1980s to Early 1990s: Seeking New Markets

Floyd L. English, who became president and CEO of Andrew in 1983, had worried for years that the company was too narrowly focused. As soon as Andrew's sales began to slacken, English took measures to shift the company into other markets. The company began acquiring smaller firms that would help Andrew open new markets. Andrew was particularly interested in cellular telephone technology and in reentering government work with intelligence gathering communications systems. Andrew bought two small military communications manufacturers, Scientific Communications, Inc., and Kintec Corp., in 1986. With these acquisitions, Andrew was able to secure U.S. Army and Navy and international contracts for antenna receivers and optical tracking equipment, and by 1987 sales in the company's government products division had climbed by 88 percent.

However, while sales increased, earnings did not, and the defense electronics business experienced difficulty because of cost overruns and technical problems. Andrew's government division operated at a $3.9 million loss in 1988. In 1991 DRAGON FIX radio transmission interceptors manufactured by Andrew were used in the Persian Gulf War, but the government division still did not turn a profit.

In the late 1980s, the company predicted that corporations would continue to need enhanced communications between distant computer workstations, and Andrew planned to become a major player in the computer networking market. Andrew bought two companies involved in computer linking technology, Scott Communications, Inc. and Local Data, Inc., in 1987. In 1990 it spent $15 million on a similar company, Emerald Technology, Inc. These acquisitions formed the core of what became a major business area for Andrew. By 1993, computer interconnect technology made up about 15 percent of Andrew's total sales.

Andrew also expanded its mobile communications business rapidly, developing an innovative slotted coaxial cable called RADIAX that eliminated problems with cellular phone use in tunnels, subways, and buildings. The company won a contract to wire the new English Channel rail tunnel with a distributed

Key Dates:

1937: Victor J. Andrew begins making equipment for the directional antennas used by AM radio broadcasters.
1947: Company is incorporated as Andrew Corporation.
1949: Company begins making microwave antennas for both civilian and military communications.
1971: Company founder Andrew dies; C. Russell Cox is named CEO.
1972: Inauguration of U.S. long-distance telephone competition leads to company shift to private microwave antenna systems.
1980: Andrew goes public.
1983: Floyd L. English is named president and CEO.
1984: Sales exceed $200 million for the first time.
1986: Scientific Communications, Inc., and Kintec Corp., makers of military communications equipment, are acquired.
1996: The Antenna Company, maker of wireless antennas and accessories, is acquired; revenues of $869.5 million are recorded.
1997: Major restructuring includes disposal of network products business.
1999: As part of another major restructuring, 880 members of the workforce are cut.

communications system utilizing the company's RADIAX cable, and subsequently worked on many subway projects, particularly in Europe and Russia. Andrew entered joint ventures in Russia to build fiber optic communication systems in subways in Moscow and St. Petersburg and then created another joint venture to build and operate a 400-mile fiber optic network between Moscow and St. Petersburg. The Andrew network gave callers from these metropolitan areas clearer signals and access to international communications links. This was especially important to Western companies operating in Russia, who had not had effective communication with home offices. In 1994 Andrew worked on in-building communication systems for the new Denver International Airport and in one of the world's largest office buildings, the USAA building in San Antonio, Texas.

By 1992, Andrew had completely recovered from the decline in its U.S. microwave telecommunications business. Sales that year were a record $442 million, with nearly half coming from overseas (an area that had been just ten percent of profits in 1990). Earnings were also strong, and the company's stock performed well. The computer networking business turned only a modest profit, but the government division finally turned a profit in 1992. While this area had lost $1.9 million in 1991, the next year profits were $5.6 million on sales of $66 million.

Though the U.S. cellular market showed signs of maturing, Andrew had hopes for continued growth abroad. Andrew had been a major supplier to a consortium led by its longtime customers AT&T and GTE, and their Argentina contract was worth an estimated $35 million. In 1994 Andrew took on a $5.6 million job for subway communications in Hong Kong and had many new orders in Eastern Europe. In addition, Andrew's involvement in Russia offered the promise of substantial growth because the country averaged ten telephones per 100 inhabitants.

Mid-1990s and Beyond

In 1995 Andrew received the largest order in its history, a $48.6 million contract to expand the cellular telephone and paging systems in the Hong Kong Metro. In December 1995 the company purchased 51 percent interests in two Brazilian firms, Mapra Industria e Comercio Ltda. and Gerbo Telecommunicacoes e Servicos Ltda., that manufactured and distributed antennas, waveguides, and towers as well as providing installation services. With Mapra and Gerbo, Andrew formed a cable manufacturing company in which Andrew held a 70 percent stake. In 1997 the company increased its stakes in Mapra and Gerbo themselves to 70 percent.

In March 1996 Andrew acquired the Antenna Company , a maker and marketer of wireless telephone antennas and wireless accessories, including batteries, battery chargers, and hands-free kits. The company also increased its presence in South Africa that year through the purchase of an 80 percent interest in the Satcom Group of Companies for $3.2 million. Revenues surged by 20 percent in 1996 in large part because of the emergence of personal communication systems (PCS), which functioned as a phone, pager, answering machine, and voice-mail system, while also delivering crisper sound and more security than analog cellular phone technology. After the Federal Communication Commission held its PCS auction in early 1995, the winners scrambled to set up PCS infrastructure—towers and microwave antennas—with many of them contracting with Andrew for the work.

In the late 1990s Andrew was hurt by a slowdown in the expansion of the U.S. wireless market—particularly that of PCS—as well as by the global economic crisis that affected the company's international operations, particularly its major undertakings in Russia and Brazil. Revenues peaked at $869.5 million in 1997 (an increase of 9.6 percent over the previous year), before declining to $852.9 million in 1998 and $791.8 million in 1999. During this period Andrew launched two separate restructuring efforts to jettison underperforming businesses and focus more sharply on core areas. In mid-1997 the company disposed of its network products business and its fiber optic sensors and global messaging development activities, and also significantly restructured its wireless products operation in Europe. Andrew recorded a $22.8 million after-tax charge in fiscal 1997 in relation to this restructuring. In March 1999 the company announced its second major restructuring in less than two years. Initiatives this time included the phasing out of its line of AVS small aperture earth station products, the divestment of its SciComm government electronics business, a shift to the outsourcing of telecommunication tower manufacturing, and the transfer of wireless accessories manufacturing from Addison, Illinois, to Mexico and China. Approximately 600 permanent employees and 280 temporary and contract workers lost their positions as a result, and Andrew recorded an after-tax charge of $28.1 million during fiscal 1999.

In addition to the second restructuring, Andrew also made a number of purchases to beef up its core businesses in 1999. It purchased the remaining 20 percent of Satcom and acquired

Maine-based Passive Power Products, Inc., the largest supplier of digital television filters in the world. In October 1999 Andrew announced that it had acquired Chesapeake Microwave Technologies, Inc. , a maker of radio frequency and microwave amplifiers and assemblies used in wireless communications systems.

In the late 1990s Andrew set a long-term goal of generating $500 million in annual revenue from new businesses by 2002. The company identified three main markets for this growth: wireless, Internet access, and broadcast. The wireless sector, although its growth had slowed, still had tremendous potential as only eight percent of the world population used wireless services as of 1999. In addition, the Strategis Group forecasted subscriber growth of more than 20 percent per year through 2003. In the Internet sector, Andrew was focusing on the emerging market for broadband wireless Internet access. By late 1999 the company had received two major orders for local multipoint distribution services (LMDS) antennas; LMDS was designed to provide high-speed Internet access and two-way, broadband, wireless transmission of data, voice, and video. In the broadcast sector, Andrew was involved in another emerging technology, that of digital television, and was manufacturing digital TV antennas, filters, and combiners. Andrew's involvement in these various cutting-edge technologies positioned the company for a new period of rapid growth, although much would depend on the speed with which consumers adopted the new products.

Principal Subsidiaries

Andrew A.B. (Sweden); Andrew AG (Switzerland); Andrew AO (Russia); Andrew Canada, Inc.; Andrew Communications Oy (Finland); Andrew Corporation (Mexico) S.A. de C.V.; Andrew España, S.A. (Spain); Andrew Financial Services Corporation; Andrew GmbH (Germany); Andrew Industria e Comercio, Ltda. (Brazil; 70%); Andrew International Corporation; Andrew Kommunikationssysteme AG (Switzerland); Andrew Passive Power Products, Inc.; Andrew Satcom Africa (Pty.) Ltd. (South Africa); Andrew S.A.R.L. (France); Andrew S.R.L. (Italy); Andrew Systems Inc.; Andrew Telecom, Inc.; Andrew Telecommunications India Pvt. Ltd.; Andrew Telecommunications (Suzhou) Co. Ltd. (China).

Principal Competitors

ADC Telecommunications, Inc.; Alcatel; Allen Telecom Inc.; Allgon AB; Amphenol Corporation; Belden Inc.; Brightpoint, Inc.; Cablerie D'Eupen S.A.; CellStar Corporation; CommScope, Inc.; Cubic Corporation; Dielectric Communications; Fiberbond; Gabriel Electronics Inc.; Gemini Industries Inc.; Hughes Electronics Corporation; Kathrein-Werke AG; Lucent Technologies Inc.; Matsushita Communication Industrial Co., Ltd.; Motorola, Inc.; Nera ASA; Nokia Corporation; Nortel Networks Corporation; Raychem Corporation; RFS; ROHN Industries, Inc.; RSI Wireless; Scientific-Atlanta, Inc.; Showa Electric Wire & Cable Co., Ltd.; Superior Cellular Products; Tadiran Limited; Telefonaktiebolaget LM Ericsson; Vertex Communications Corporation; Watkins-Johnson Company.

Further Reading

''Andrew Corporation Investors Brief,'' *Wall Street Transcript,* September 12, 1988.

''Andrew Corporation Presentation,'' *Wall Street Transcript,* April 19, 1982.

Autry, Ret, ''Companies to Watch: Andrew,'' *Fortune,* June 17, 1991, p. 70.

Berss, Marcia, ''Crossed Signals?'' *Forbes,* December 21, 1992, p. 344.

Byrne, Harlan S., ''Andrew Corp.: High-Tech Products, Global Ambitions,'' *Barron's,* March 29, 1993, pp. 42–44.

——, ''Strong Signal: Andrew Corp. Helps Build Information Superhighway,'' *Barron's,* December 19, 1994, p. 13.

Cahill, Joseph B., ''Andrew Corp. Gets Zapped,'' *Crain's Chicago Business,* July 28, 1997, p. 3.

Cleaver, Joanne, ''Antennas Fading Out, Andrew Corp. Eyes Its Also-Ran Markets,'' *Crain's Chicago Business,* February 14, 1985, p. 3.

Cox, Russell, *Andrew, 1937–1987: A Half Century in Communications,* Orland Park, Ill.: Andrew Corp., 1987.

Ditlev-Simonsen, Cecilie, ''Technology and Tradition: Andrew Corp. Hews to Traditions,'' *Chicago Tribune,* June 29, 1987, Sec. 4, p. 1.

Dugan, I. Jeanne, and Greg Burns, ''Stars You May Never Have Heard Of,'' *Business Week,* March 24, 1997, p. 85.

Goodman, JoEllen, ''Ailing Andrew Spurns Recapitalization Plan,'' *Crain's Chicago Business,* August 18, 1986, p. 55.

——, ''Andrew Takes Aim at Military Market with Acquisition,'' *Crain's Chicago Business,* December 1, 1986, p. 3.

Gorak, David A., ''Andrew Set to Dial up Sales in Non-Telephone-Related Biz,'' *Crain's Chicago Business,* February 17, 1986, p. 20.

——, ''Earthbound Microwave Unit a Drag on Andrew's Growth,'' *Crain's Chicago Business,* February 16, 1987, p. 24.

Lashinsky, Adam, ''Andrew Corp. Answers Russian Telecom Calls,'' *Crain's Chicago Business,* September 18, 1995, p. 15.

Marcial, Gene G., ''A Phone-Gear Star Named Andrew,'' *Business Week,* August 2, 1999, p. 109.

Murphy, H. Lee, ''Adaptable Manufacturer Andrew Undaunted by Defense Cutbacks,'' *Crain's Chicago Business,* March 5, 1990, p. 30.

——, ''Andrew Catches a Wave As Earnings, Stock Swell,'' *Crain's Chicago Business,* December 21, 1992, p. 4.

——, ''Andrew, Rivals Tussle for Wireless Market,'' *Crain's Chicago Business,* February 22, 1999, p. 9.

——, ''Andrew Sets Sights Overseas for Growth,'' *Crain's Chicago Business,* February 14, 1994, p. 52.

——, ''Andrew's Military Campaign Becoming Obstacle Course,'' *Crain's Chicago Business,* February 27, 1989, p. 58.

——, ''Cooling Andrew on Comeback Trail,'' *Crain's Chicago Business,* March 9, 1998, p. 55.

——, ''Ex-Military Topsider Adds Macho to Andrew Offensive,'' *Crain's Chicago Business,* February 22, 1988, p. 49.

——, ''PCS Plans Pump up Andrew's Prospects,'' *Crain's Chicago Business,* February 26, 1996, p. 9.

——, ''Wireless Surge Lifts Andrew's Outlook,'' *Crain's Chicago Business,* February 24, 1997, p. 12.

Wolinsky, Howard, ''Declining Profit Leads Andrew to Trim Jobs,'' *Chicago Sun-Times,* July 17, 1997, p. 49.

——, ''Slumping Wireless Sales Force Job Cuts,'' *Chicago Sun-Times,* March 9, 1999, p. 41.

Young, David, ''Wiring Russia: Andrew Installing Fiber-Optics System,'' *Chicago Tribune,* December 18, 1992, Sec. 3, pp. 1–3.

—A. Woodward
—updated by David E. Salamie

Apache Corporation

One Post Oak Central
2000 Post Oak Boulevard, Suite 100
Houston, Texas 77056-4400
U.S.A.
Telephone: (713) 296-6000
Fax: (713) 296-6480
Web site: http://www.apachecorp.com

Public Company
Incorporated: 1954
Employees: 1,281
Sales: $876.4 million (1998)
Stock Exchanges: New York Chicago
Ticker Symbol: APA
NAIC: 211111 Crude Petroleum and Natural Gas Extraction

Apache Corporation is one of the leading independent crude oil and natural gas producers in the United States. The company, which has proven reserves of 613 million barrels of oil equivalent, maintains exploration and production efforts in the United States, Canada, Egypt, Australia, Poland, the People's Republic of China, and the Ivory Coast. Apache has had particular success in increasing the production at properties it has acquired from other companies.

Early History

Longtime chairman and CEO Raymond Plank, more than any other individual, is credited with creating and building Apache. Plank's first foray into the business world occurred at age nine, in 1931, when he started making and selling cider from his family's Minnesota orchard. "It drove my mother crazy," mused Plank in the January 3, 1994 issue of *Forbes,* "But I was a gleaner." Indeed, his unceasing entrepreneurial penchant was his earmark throughout most of his life.

Plank served as a bomber pilot during World War II before completing his education at Yale University in 1946. He and fellow alum and roommate W. Brooks Field, who was also a World War II veteran and Minneapolis native, headed back to their hometown with grandiose dreams of starting a business. They planned to begin publishing a magazine for Midwestern readers that would be patterned after *Time* or the *Atlantic Monthly.* It was this loosely formed plan that would lead to the creation of one of the nation's most prosperous independent oil companies.

After returning to Minnesota in their $400 army surplus jeep, Fields and Plank found that the printing house they had counted on to help finance and print their publication had just been purchased by a new owner. They quickly decided to start an accounting and tax assistance service, instead. Despite an absolute dearth of experience in their newly chosen profession, Plank and Fields opened Northwest Business Service in downtown Minneapolis. The partners' surplus jeep became the company car, and their first employee carried her own typewriter to work. After a rough start, Plank and Fields were able to pay themselves a meager monthly salary of $20. Of this early venture, Plank recalls, "Failure back then was never a thought."

Fields soon left the company to enter the grain brokerage business. Replacing him was Plank's childhood friend Charles Arnao, Jr., and Truman E. Anderson, a young and successful insurance salesman. Although its accounting and bookkeeping business continued to prosper in the early 1950s, the team formed a partnership called APA (for Anderson, Plank, and Arnao), a subsidiary meant to investigate new ventures. Through APA the partners discovered a lucrative, though risky, niche in investing in oil and gas exploration. Excited by the possibilities offered by the emerging industry, Plank and his friends decided to concentrate solely on oil and gas operations.

The three partners founded Apache Oil Corporation in 1954 to arrange and participate in investments related to oil and gas exploration. Three original principles continued to guide the company throughout most of the 20th century. First, rather than investing through a (potentially corrupt) third-party promoter, as was the common practice in Minneapolis, Apache would ensure that the drillers worked directly for the investors. Second, Apache would ensure that a professional staff managed the drilling and financial operations of each venture. Finally, Apache would spread its investors' resources over several drill-

Key Dates:

1954: Apache Oil Corporation is founded in Minneapolis, Minnesota.
1955: The company's first well in Cushing, Oklahoma, produces seven barrels of oil per day.
1963: Cofounder Raymond Plank gains full management control of the company.
1967: Apache discovers the Recluse, Wyoming, field, which eventually yields 2,800 barrels per day.
1981: Apache Petroleum Company, the first publicly traded master limited partnership, is created as an investment vehicle.
1982: Company purchases oil and gas properties from Dow Chemical for $402 million.
1986: Apache purchases oil and gas properties from Occidental Petroleum for $440 million; company suffers first full-year loss as a result of plummeting oil prices and the enactment of the Tax Reform Act of 1986, which eliminates most limited partnership tax advantages.
1987: Plank begins to change the entire focus of the company from an organizer of limited partnerships and investment vehicles to a conventional exploration and production company; company relocates its headquarters to Denver.
1991: Apache purchases oil and gas properties, which include 111 million barrels of reserves, from Amoco Production Company for $546 million.
1992: Company moves its headquarters to Houston.
1993: Company ventures outside of North America for the first time with the acquisition of Hadson Energy Resources, in Western Australia.
1994: Apache acquires 315 oil and gas fields from Texaco for $571 million, and acquires Calgary-based DEKALB Energy Company for $285 million.
1997: Apache and its partners in the Khalda Concession in Egypt enter into a 25-year, $1.2 billion contract to supply gas to the Egyptian General Petroleum Corporation.
1999: Company purchases assets in the Gulf of Mexico from Shell Exploration & Production Company for $746 million, and properties in western Canada from Shell Canada Limited for $517 million.

ing ventures, thus reducing their risk of losing all or most of their money from a single failed endeavor.

Apache Oil Corporation finished its first producing oil well in 1955 in Cushing, Oklahoma. Although the well only churned out a paltry seven barrels per day, Apache's second attempt resulted in a well that generated more than 30 barrels an hour. Plank and friends, who were sweating it out in a ramshackle Minneapolis office, were relieved—up to that point, the venture had been on very shaky ground. As a result of a few successful drilling ventures, the company was able to report a net profit of $12,535 in 1955 from sales of $190,000.

After surviving its first year—the company was even able to replace its card table and chairs with some real office furniture—Apache basked in a string of successes. The company generated revenues of $630,000 in 1956, wowing its investors with solid returns. By 1959 the enterprise had expanded into 23 states and two Canadian provinces. Its base of shareholders quickly grew from 1,000 in 1959 to more than 4,000 by the early 1960s. Furthermore, the company formed a second investment subsidiary, First Apache Realty Program (later named Apache Realty Corp.). It was formed as a limited partnership to invest in commercial real estate. Apache's first project was a 50-store shopping plaza in Minneapolis.

Apache's entrance into real estate was largely the result of Anderson's efforts. Anderson and Plank—Arnao left the company to form his own business—both agreed that increasing government regulation of the oil and gas exploration industry threatened to virtually extinguish their company. More diversification was needed in ventures such as telephone companies and steel. Plank, however, did not share Anderson's enthusiasm for emphasizing real estate investments. An escalating rift between the cofounders climaxed in 1963. Anderson, in a startling move, called a board meeting and asked its members to fire Plank because he was showing signs of "overwork." At the same meeting, the board accepted Anderson's resignation and transferred all management responsibilities to Plank.

With Plank solely in charge after ten years of operation, Apache posted 1964 sales of $9.2 million, net income of $661,000, and $9.3 million in new drilling capital from its investors. Confirming its commitment to continued growth through risk and innovation, Apache issued a corporate objective on its tenth anniversary. Written by Plank, it included these words: "the capacity of the individual is infinite. Limitations are largely of habit, convention, acceptance of things as they are, fear, or lack of self confidence."

Although other limitations, namely government price caps and regulation, battered its competitors, Apache remained profitable during the 1960s as the number of oil industry participants plummeted from 30,000 to 13,000. Besides its diversification into other businesses and its acquisition of several struggling competitors, Apache benefited from one of its most successful oil finds. In 1967 Apache drilled a well in the tiny town of Recluse, Wyoming, which immediately began delivering 50 barrels per hour. After drilling 11 more wells nearby, Apache was getting 2,800 barrels of oil each day from its Recluse operations. Analysts credited Apache's skilled management team with allowing the company to successfully exploit a sudden strike of that magnitude.

Late 1960s and 1970s: Diversifying, Then Refocusing on Petroleum

Despite this fortuitous discovery, Apache continued to diversify through acquisition during the late 1960s and early 1970s in an effort to minimize the effects of oil industry woes. By 1970, in fact, the company had established a network of 24 subsidiary firms ranging from engineering and electronics companies to farming and water supply operations. It continued to expand its holdings during the 1970s, evolving into a large conglomerate. Important contributors to Apache's success during that period included Jaye Dyer, John Black, John D. Hansen, Roland E. Menk, and John A. Kocur. In addition, Plank invited his old roommate Fields to join the company's board in 1973—Fields and Plank had remained good friends throughout the years. "Who can turn down an invitation like that," said Fields.

Recognizing a trend toward higher oil prices, which would hurt its non-oil and non-gas producing subsidiaries, Apache began formulating plans during the mid-1970s to sell many of its diversified holdings. In 1977 the company established a timetable for the sale of most of Apache's remaining subsidiaries, a move that would also increase funding for oil and gas development. Although Apache had received much criticism for its widespread diversification, company management credited its external investments with helping the company survive the 1960s and early 1970s.

Apache lost a large portion of its oil and gas operations in 1977 when it sold its Apexco subsidiary. Apexco had been created to handle Apache's energy endeavors. But Apache re-emphasized its expertise in the gas and oil business in the late 1970s, and by the early 1980s had again established itself as a major player in the industry. Even by 1978 Apache was recognized as one of the leading deep drilling companies in the United States. Almost as though it was signaling an end to Apache's oil and gas adversity, the era of the late 1970s and early 1980s was punctuated by the largest blowout (oil well explosion) in the history of the petroleum industry. An Apache well in Texas erupted in a blaze that took 16 months and $42 million to extinguish.

1980s: Transition to Conventional Exploration and Production Company

After achieving notable success with its oil and gas ventures in the late 1970s, Apache formed the Apache Petroleum Company (APC) in 1981. APC, the first publicly traded master limited partnership to appear on the board of the New York Stock Exchange, was created as an innovative investment vehicle that would take advantage of favorable tax laws. As industry drilling activity vaulted to post-1950s highs in the early 1980s, APC attracted nearly 60,000 limited partners and Apache sales leapt to $221 million by 1984. Plank ranked the creation of APC as the most significant development in the company's history. Indeed, APC spawned an entirely new industry of publicly traded master limited partnerships (MLPs). The early 1980s were also marked by Apache's 1982 acquisition of oil and gas properties from Dow Chemical for $402 million.

Apache realized record income levels during the early and mid-1980s; net income fluctuated around $22 million during the early 1980s before slipping to a still healthy $9.4 million in 1985. In 1986, however, the oil and gas industries spiraled into a down cycle. After declining slowly throughout the early 1980s, prices, particularly for oil, plummeted in 1986 as the market became glutted. The downturn was magnified for Apache by the Tax Reform Act of 1986 (TRA), which Congress passed. The TRA effectively eliminated the tax advantages associated with limited partnerships, crushing one of the most lucrative sides of Apache's business. The company recorded its first full-year loss, of $10.9 million, in 1986. That year also saw Apache make another large acquisition of oil and gas fields, through a $440 million deal with Occidental Petroleum.

Undaunted by analyst's predictions of doom for Apache and its industry peers, Plank and his management team immediately began plotting a strategy for the future. In 1986, in fact, the company went out on a limb by investing a large portion of its available resources in new oil and gas reserves, which were selling at record low prices. Moreover, demonstrating his ability to adapt to change, Plank pioneered a complete reorganization of the company in 1987 and 1988. Surprising analysts, Plank changed the entire focus of the company from an organizer of limited partnerships and investment vehicles to a conventional exploration and production company relying on internal cash flow to fund operations.

Evidencing the significance of the change was the 1987 movement of company headquarters from Minneapolis to Denver, and a significant reduction of the Apache workforce. Distressed by both Apache's rapid transition out of its core business and its negative earnings—in 1987 Apache posted a $71 million net loss—investors registered their concerns on Wall Street. The company's stock price declined in 1988 as Apache continued to buy up new reserves, increase its debt burden, and restructure. "Given what was happening in our industry, that wasn't surprising," said Plank in the October 16, 1989, issue of the *Denver Business Journal.* "We were changing our whole basis of doing business, so it's understandable that the market got a little pessimistic."

Plank's arrival on the Denver business scene underscored the aggressive, no-holds-barred management style that had made Apache so successful in the past. Plank was irritated by both a lack of an intelligible U.S. energy policy and government intervention in the oil and gas industry, and he had been prodding his Denver peers to get organized and take action since 1985, when he invested in locally owned drilling operations. Not surprisingly, he clashed with many of the local industry elites. "Frankly, they're entitled to their opinion, and I don't happen to care what it is," stated Plank in the May 1989 issue of *Corporate Report Minnesota.* "I was getting pretty tough on the independent sector of our industry, and I have no regrets whatever. They sat there and watched their butts melt and themselves go broke."

Just as it had weathered the industry fallout of the 1960s, Apache began to emerge from its predicament in 1988, when it posted a positive net income of $9 million. Furthermore, after increasing its exploration and development expenditures to $45 million in 1988, it planned to more than double that figure to $92 million in 1989. Apache was conducting its oil and gas reserve acquisition and development program with the help of industry veteran Mick Merelli, who joined the Apache team in 1987 as president and chief operating officer. Apache's new strategy allowed it to discredit its detractors as sales shot up 74 percent in 1989, to $247 million, and net income lurched to $22.1 million. In 1990, moreover, sales and income reached a record $273 million and $40.3 million.

Steady 1990s Growth Through Acquisition

Despite his company's remarkable recovery and restored reputation, the 68-year-old Plank had no intention of slowing down going into the 1990s. Adhering to its strategy of growth through acquisition and development of oil and gas reserves, Apache doubled its reserves between 1990 and 1993 to more than 225 million barrels. A majority of this increase resulted from perhaps the most significant investment in the company's 37-year history. In 1991, Apache purchased oil and gas properties, which included 111 million barrels of reserves, from Amoco Production Company for $546 million. "Shortly afterward, a cow leaned against one of the plugged wells and knocked out the plug," jested Plank in the January 3, 1994, issue of *Forbes*. "When crude flowed out, Apache put the well back into production and drilled more wells around it."

Apache complemented its Amoco deal with an additional $350 million in acquisitions during 1992 and 1993, including its first outside of North America, the $98 million purchase of Hadson Energy Resources Corporation, which managed fields in Western Australia. As prices for oil stabilized and those for natural gas began a slow recovery, Apache continued to boost its production. Total output rose steadily from 17 million barrels of oil equivalent (MMboe), a measure that also applies to gas production, in 1989 to 31 MMboe in 1993. As a result, Apache's revenues grew from $247 million to $467 million during the same period, reflecting a jump of 90 percent. Net income hovered in the $35 million to $45 million range throughout the early 1990s. Importantly, despite its intense acquisition efforts, Apache had succeeded in reducing its ratio of debt-to-equity from 53 percent in 1991 to a healthier 37 percent in 1993. Meanwhile, the company relocated its headquarters again, this time settling in Houston, a city centrally located in relation to Apache's U.S. properties.

Augmenting rapid domestic expansion during the early 1990s were Apache operations overseas. Although they represented a negligible share of company receipts, foreign drilling ventures were becoming an increasingly important component of Apache's growth strategy. Western Australia represented the core of its international operations. In 1994, however, Apache agreed to purchase a one-third interest in an exploratory offshore venture in eastern China's Bohai Bay. The following year the company began selling oil in Egypt after discoveries were made in the Qarun Concession in the Western Desert, which was estimated to contain 70 million barrels of oil. Back in North America, Apache in late 1994 acquired the oil and gas production assets of Crystal Oil Co.—which were principally located along the Arkansas-Louisiana border and in southern Louisiana—for $101 million. In early 1995 Apache made its largest purchase to date, the $571 million acquisition from Texaco, Inc. of 315 oil and gas fields in Texas, Louisiana, and the Rocky Mountains. Also in early 1995 the company bought out Calgary-based DEKALB Energy Company in a $285 million stock swap. Through its early 1990s acquisitions spree, Apache increased its proven reserve base from 106.1 MMboe at the beginning of 1991 to 420.6 MMboe at the end of 1995.

In addition to its business exploits during the early 1990s, Apache—guided by Plank's affection for outdoor sports—was notable for its environmental awareness. This was reflected in efforts to restrict development of 20,000 acres of foothill grazing lands in Wyoming. In 1992 and 1993, moreover, Apache's Australian division received the West Australian "Environmental Excellence" award for conducting drilling and pipeline rehabilitation operations with minimal disruption to sensitive wildlife habitats. "The degree to which we're defiling this planet, it's a greater threat than nuclear annihilation," Plank observed in the May 1989 issue of *Corporate Report Minnesota*.

Apache's overseas expansion continued in 1996 and 1997. The company became the largest independent oil operator in Egypt with the acquisition of the Phoenix Resource Companies in 1996. The following year, Apache and its partners in the Khalda Concession entered into a 25-year, $1.2 billion contract to supply natural gas to the Egyptian General Petroleum Corporation. China was also proving fertile for Apache, with a well in Bohai Bay delivering 15,400 barrels of oil per day in a 1997 test, making it China's largest discovery well. Apache obtained its first operations in Poland in April 1997 when it gained operatorship and a 50 percent interest in more than 5.5 million acres near Lublin, southeast of Warsaw.

Plank's decades-long experience with the boom-and-bust cycles of the petroleum industry was in evidence in the late 1990s. The Asian economic crisis, which began in 1997, was a major factor—along with the virtual collapse of OPEC—in an oil glut that forced down the price of a barrel of crude by late 1998 to about $11. When inflation was factored in, this was the cheapest price in history; just one year earlier, the price had been about $23. Plank had anticipated in mid-1997 that the industry was headed for another downturn (although not one as severe as actually took place), and began to take measures to survive the coming storm. He cut spending, reduced the company's debt load, and sold off nearly $200 million in assets. In 1998 Apache was also forced to take an after-tax charge of $158 million to write down the value of its U.S. assets. This led to a net loss of $129.4 million in 1998, a year in which revenues fell to $876.4 million, a 26 percent decline from the 1997 figure of $1.18 billion.

As he had done in the past, Plank next proceeded back to the acquisitions arena, before the industry had made a full recovery, making two large purchases in 1999. In May, Apache completed a $746 million cash-and-stock deal to obtain 22 oil and gas fields in the Gulf of Mexico from Shell Exploration & Production Company, a unit of Shell Oil Company. These properties had proven reserves of 127.3 MMboe. In early 1999 they were producing an average of 29,000 barrels of oil and 125 million cubic feet of gas per day, which translated into a significant increase from Apache's 1998 daily average of 73,000 barrels of oil and 590 million cubic feet of gas. In December Apache completed a purchase of oil and gas properties in the Canadian provinces of Alberta, British Columbia, and Saskatchewan from Shell Canada Limited for C$761 million (US$517 million). The properties had proven reserves of 87.5 MMboe and were producing about 12,500 barrels of oil and 64.8 million cubic feet of gas per day.

Apache's contrarian approach left it in a strong position at the end of the 20th century, despite intensifying industry competition and consolidation. In fact, the megamergers of the late 1990s—for example, the creation of Exxon Mobil Corporation from the merger of two industry giants—were welcomed by Plank. He told the *Wall Street Journal* in late 1999 that the top oil companies "[are] always going to need someone to take their second-hand clothes." Apache had built its large reserve base by acquiring "second-hand" properties, mainly during industry downturns when prices were low. It was then able to profitably exploit these supposedly inferior properties by boosting output through the drilling of additional wells. Apache was clearly one of the shrewdest competitors in the oil industry, with a proven knack for adapting to and exploiting its ups and downs.

Principal Subsidiaries

Apache Foundation; Apache Gathering Company; Apache Holdings, Inc.; Apache International, Inc.; Apache Overseas, Inc.; Nagasco, Inc.; Apache Oil Corporation; Burns Manufacturing Company; Apache Energy Limited (Australia); Apache West Australia Holdings Limited (Island of Guernsey); DEK Energy Company; Phoenix Exploration Resources, Ltd.; Apache Khalda Corporation LDC (Cayman Islands); Apache Qarun Exploration Company LDC (Cayman Islands); Apache North America, Inc.

Principal Competitors

Adams Resources & Energy, Inc.; Amerada Hess Corporation; Anadarko Petroleum Corporation; Atlantic Richfield Company; BP Amoco p.l.c.; Burlington Resources Inc.; Chesapeake Energy Corporation; Chevron Corporation; Conoco Inc.; Cross Timbers Oil Company; Devon Energy Corporation; EEX Corporation; El Paso Energy Corporation; EOG Resources, Inc.; Exxon Mobil Corporation; Forcenergy Inc.; Forest Oil Corporation; Helmerich & Payne, Inc.; HS Resources, Inc.; KCS Energy, Inc.; Kerr-McGee Corporation; Murphy Oil Corporation; Noble Affiliates, Inc.; Nuevo Energy Company; Ocean Energy, Inc.; Phillips Petroleum Company; Pioneer Natural Resources Company; Royal Dutch/Shell Group; Santos Ltd; Shell Oil Company; Texaco Inc.; TransTexas Gas Corporation; Ultramar Diamond Shamrock Corporation; Union Pacific Resources Group Inc.; Unocal Corporation.

Further Reading

''Apache Corp.: Timely Major Expansion Program,'' *Oil and Gas Investor,* April 1996, pp. 12–13.

Brown, Robert M., *Journey into Risk Country: The First Thirty Years of Apache Corporation,* Minneapolis: Apache Corp., 1985, 88 p.

Byrne, Harlan S., ''Apache,'' *Barron's,* September 20, 1993.

——, ''Apache Corp.: Acquire and Exploit,'' *Barron's,* June 28, 1999, p. 24.

——, ''Apache Corp.: Well-Oiled,'' *Barron's,* September 9, 1996, p. 20.

David, Gregory E., ''Apache Corp.: Bargain Basement Buyer,'' *Financial World,* July 20, 1993.

——, ''Maverick: Apache's Septuagenarian Boss Thinks Everyone in the Oil and Gas Industry Has It Wrong,'' *Financial World,* February 28, 1995, pp. 44–45.

Even, Beth, ''Whatever Happened to Ray Plank?'' *Corporate Report Minnesota,* May 1989.

Fisher, Daniel, ''Dry Powder: Unlike Many of Its Competitors, Apache Saw Lower Oil Prices Coming, Cut Its Spending, and Sold Assets,'' *Forbes,* December 14, 1998, p. 214.

Knott, David, ''Apache Hunts Gas for Regulated Markets,'' *Oil and Gas Journal,* November 24, 1997, p. 40.

Liesman, Steve, Carlos Tejada, and Christopher Cooper, ''Major Minors: As Big Oil Gets Bigger, Its Leftovers Provide Feast for Independents,'' *Wall Street Journal,* July 1, 1999, pp. A1+.

Mack, Toni, ''Energy,'' *Forbes,* January 3, 1994.

Percefull, Gary, ''Denver Independent Most Active Driller in Oklahoma,'' *Tulsa World,* August 27, 1989.

Rudnitsky, Howard, ''Hedging,'' *Forbes,* September 28, 1992.

——, ''When Others Sell, It's Time to Buy,'' *Forbes,* April 10, 1995, p. 62.

Sample, James D., ''Apache Investors Like What They See in Revamped Company,'' *Denver Business Journal,* October 16, 1989.

Snow, Nick, ''Apache Buying Shell's Shallow Gulf Properties,'' *Oil and Gas Investor,* June 1999, p. 69.

Solomon, Caleb, ''Apache Set to Buy Texaco Properties for $600 Million,'' *Wall Street Journal,* November 30, 1994, p. A8.

''U.S. Drilling: Industry Needs to Think Positive,'' *World Oil,* February 1994.

—Dave Mote
—updated by David E. Salamie

Applied Power Inc.

13000 W. Silver Spring Dr.
Butler, WI 53007
U.S.A.
Telephone: (262) 783-9279
Fax: (262) 783-9790
Web site: http://www.apw-inc.com

Public Company
Incorporated: 1910 as American Grinder and Manufacturing Company
Employees: 11,200
Sales: $1.75 billion (1999)
Stock Exchanges: New York
Ticker Symbol: APW
NAIC: 326199 All Other Plastics Product Manufacturing; 332439 Other Metal Container Manufacturing; 332999 All Other Miscellaneous Fabricated Metal Product Manufacturing; 335999 All Other Miscellaneous Electrical Equipment and Component Manufacturing; 337214 Office Furniture (Except Wood) Manufacturing; 326291 Rubber Product Manufacturing for Mechanical Use; 332912 Fluid Power Valve and Hose Fitting Manufacturing; 333995 Fluid Power Cylinder and Actuator Manufacturing; 333996 Fluid Power Pump and Motor Manufacturing; 336399 All Other Motor Vehicle Parts Manufacturing; 336413 Other Aircraft Parts and Auxiliary Equipment Manufacturing

Applied Power Inc. is a global manufacturer with two principal segments: APW Electronics and APW Industrial. APW Electronics, which the company rapidly built up through late 1990s acquisitions, is a leading global maker of electronic enclosure systems. These systems organize and configure electronic components, and house, protect, and insulate the resulting electronic systems in such areas as computer networking, semiconductors, and telecommunications. In conjunction with its enclosure systems, APW Electronics also makes power supplies, thermal management products, racks and subracks, and ergonomic work environment furniture for computer operations, engineers, scientists, and manufacturing personnel. APW Industrial makes a wide range of niche consumer and industrial products related particularly to hydraulics, electromechanics, rubber/elastomer molding, and magnetic and electronic controls. In October 1999 Applied Power announced that it was exploring a sale of APW Industrial in order to concentrate on its rapidly growing APW Electronics segment.

Early History: From Hand Grinders to Hydraulic Products

Applied Power was founded in 1910 in Milwaukee, Wisconsin. The company got its start as American Grinder and Manufacturing Company, a producer of hand grinders that sharpened tools used in agriculture and other fields. The company's advertisements claimed that its products were suitable for use in ''Ship Yards, Construction Work, Lumber Camps, Mining and Engineering, Signal and Line Repair Work, Machine Shops, Garages, etc.'' When the United States entered World War I, American Grinder began to manufacture water and oil pumps for use in engines that powered trucks and other military vehicles. At the end of the war, the company decided to continue its manufacture of these products, offering them to the general automotive market that was then beginning to take root and grow.

By the end of its first decade, American Grinder had expanded its line to include hand tools as well as pumps, a move made at the behest of the company's distributor. For this new line, American Grinder chose the trade name ''Blackhawk,'' in reference to the Blackhawk Army Division, which had fought with distinction in World War I. The line's logo featured an arrowhead with the silhouette of an Indian and the slogan ''Service, Quality, Finish.'' Many of the tools sold, such as sets of socket wrenches in different sizes, were designed for use in automobile repairs.

After American Grinder chose to call its engine pumps and mechanic's tools Blackhawk, this trade name began to establish a reputation in the automotive field. In 1925 American Grinder officially changed its company name to Blackhawk, and, shortly thereafter, the company sold off its line of tool grinders, as it

Company Perspectives:

We believe that size is the enemy of our entrepreneurial spirit. We plan to fight size with the quality of our team members and the quality of their relationships one to the other. Our goal is to endure and flourish long term.

reoriented itself towards the automobile industry. Eventually, however, Blackhawk water pumps were made obsolete, as car manufacturers began to include this equipment in their vehicles as a matter of course. After discontinuing its pump operations, Blackhawk sought out a replacement business. In 1927 the company purchased a small hydraulic jack manufacturer, the Hydraulic Tool Company, in Los Angeles, California, which fit the bill. After acquiring these operations, Blackhawk marketed the Hydraulic Tool Company's products under the Blackhawk trade name.

As Blackhawk grew, its products gained a wider reputation, and its trade name became known across the country. In the late 1920s, Blackhawk expanded its line further when a snowplow manufacturer asked the company to help it develop a hydraulic pump to replace the hand winch then used to raise and lower the plow. In response to this request, Blackhawk developed a hydraulic system, made up of a hand pump, a long bending hose, and a hydraulic cylinder, which it marketed under the name Power-Packer. This line was soon expanded to include other remote-control hydraulic systems for use in different kinds of equipment. By the end of the 1920s, the company's logo—placed on its expanded line of products—had evolved to feature an Indian's profile in a large feathered headdress, placed inside an abstract representation of an arrowhead.

In the mid-1930s Blackhawk further expanded its product offerings when it used the technology developed for use in snow plows to make products for the collision repair market. Calling this line "Porto-Power," Blackhawk marketed hydraulic tools to be used in repairing auto bodies. The Porto-Power line featured a set of pumps and cylinders, with a variety of attachments that could be used to perform different pulling, pushing, and straightening tasks to fix damaged cars. In the late 1930s, Blackhawk marketed its Porto-Power line of products to a wider pool of customers, offering them for use in industrial and construction fields, through various distributors. The company tailored its products to different tasks and industries, creating special pumps and cylinders that could be used as building blocks for different applications.

International Expansion in the Postwar Era

In 1955 Blackhawk sold off its original line of hand tools, as its business evolved away from that area into more complicated systems. Late in that decade, the company decided to further restructure itself to provide more definition for each of its different parts. The two lines of products, Blackhawk and Power-Packer, became separate business units within the company. In 1960 the company's industrial and construction lines were set apart and given the name Enerpac in an effort to strengthen their identity within their respective markets.

Also in 1960, Blackhawk began an effort to expand its markets beyond the borders of the United States. Although its products had long been sold in other countries through importers and distributors, Blackhawk began to set up its own direct overseas operations, to both sell and manufacture goods. Its first targets for growth were the United Kingdom and continental Europe.

In 1961 Blackhawk changed its corporate name to Applied Power Industries, Inc. in an effort to better reflect the different aspects of its operations. In the 1960s, the company expanded through acquisitions of other companies in its field. In January 1966, it bought Rivett, Inc., and two years later, Applied Power purchased Branick Manufacturing, Inc. In 1969 the company acquired the Big Four division of the Studebacker Company. In May 1970, Applied Power added the operations of the Bear Manufacturing Company, and later that year, the company added another business unit to its corporate profile, taking over the Marquette Corporation. This company was a maker of diagnostic systems and service equipment, including products designed especially for use with batteries, for automobiles.

Also in 1970, Applied Power increased its geographical scope further when it opened a subsidiary in the Netherlands. This trend continued the following year, when Applied Power made a number of purchases that increased its international holdings. The company acquired Bear Equipment & Services, Ltd., of Scarborough, Canada, and renamed it Applied Power Automotive Canada, Ltd. In addition, Applied Power bought 80 percent of two French companies, Matairco, which eventually became a separate business unit of its parent company, and Société-Hydro-Air S.a.r.L. Three years later, Applied Power completed its acquisition of these properties, increasing its stake in them to 100 percent. In January 1973, Applied Power Industries became Applied Power Inc.

Following the simplification of its name, Applied Power also streamlined its corporate structure. In the mid-1970s, the company fine-tuned its operations, shedding businesses that did not fit with its larger corporate identity, or that were not as profitable as others. In 1975 the company sold Hydralique Gury S.A. to a group of French investors for $2.1 million. Five years later, the company divested itself of its Bear Wheel Service and Marquette Engine Diagnostic Equipment Product Lines, reaping $8 million.

In 1981 Applied Power added the last of its major brand groups when it purchased Electro-Flo, Inc. This company supplemented Applied Power's Power-Packer unit in providing specialized hydraulic products for use in the manufacture of other kinds of heavy equipment. Electro-Flo used electronic controls of hydraulic systems to enable precise movement and positioning of machinery. Electro-Flo technology, which included microprocessors, flow control valves, and electronic sensors, was used in the precise laying of asphalt by road-reconditioning equipment and in the movement of booms on materials-handling machinery.

Mid-1980s Through Mid-1990s: Acquisitions and Restructuring

By 1985, Applied Power's 75th year in business, the company had become a solid operation closely held by the members

Key Dates:

1910: American Grinder and Manufacturing Company is founded in Milwaukee.
1925: Company changes its name to Blackhawk.
1927: Hydraulic Tool Company, a maker of hydraulic jacks, is purchased.
1955: Company sells its original line of hand tools.
1960: Foreign expansion is stepped up with the establishment of the first direct overseas operations; Europe is the first area targeted for growth.
1961: Company changes its name to Applied Power Industries, Inc.
1973: Company changes its name to Applied Power Inc.
1985: Richard G. Sim, a former General Electric Company executive, is brought in as president and CEO; revenues reach $100 million.
1986: The Blackhawk automotive division is sold to Hein-Werner Company.
1987: Company goes public through an IPO, with a listing on the NASDAQ.
1989: Company engineers a $147 million hostile takeover of Barry Wright Corporation, maker of electronic control equipment; revenues increase to $245 million.
1992: In a recessionary environment, company reports loss of $24.4 million.
1993: Stock begins trading on the New York Stock Exchange.
1995: Revenues surpass $500 million for the first time.
1998: Company acquires VERO Group plc for $191.7 million, ZERO Corporation for $386 million, and Rubicon Group plc for $371 million; revenues surpass $1 billion for the first time.
1999: A restructuring organizes the company's operations into two segments: APW Electronics and APW Industrial; company announces in September that it is seeking to sell APW Industrial to focus on its fast-growing enclosures business.

of its founding family. Lacking new blood, however, the company had begun to stagnate. While its operations returned a steady profit, the company had ceased growing. In an effort to remedy this situation and increase Applied Power's financial returns, company leaders brought an outside executive aboard, hiring Richard G. Sim, a former General Electric Company executive, as president and CEO.

Among the first steps taken in the mid-1980s were a series of acquisitions. The company bought half of the Toyo Hydraulic Equipment Company, of which it already owned the other half, and also added Electro-Hydraulic Controls, Inc., for which it paid $2.6 million in cash. In 1986 Applied Power divested itself of one of its core businesses—and the line of products with the longest heritage of any made by the company—when it sold its Blackhawk automotive division to the Hein-Werner Company for $9.3 million. One year later, in August 1987, the newly defined Applied Power offered stock to the public for the first time, tendering 1.8 million shares, which traded on the NASDAQ. With the proceeds from this sale, the company moved to reduce part of the debt it had amassed through its long string of acquisitions. At the end of 1987, Applied Power reported a loss of $1.6 million.

In 1988 Applied Power returned to its roots, reentering the field that had launched the company decades before, when it purchased a manufacturer of hand tools, Garner-Bender, Inc., for $31.4 million. This company was subsequently renamed GB Electrical, Inc. The next year, Applied Power made its most ambitious purchase to date, when it engineered the hostile takeover of the Barry Wright Corporation for $147 million. This purchase doubled the size of Allied Power and increased its debt sixfold. Barry Wright, an ailing manufacturer based in Watertown, Massachusetts, made equipment for use in computer rooms and devices that controlled vibration. The company's earnings had dropped in the previous year from $8.4 million to $1.3 million as its sales stagnated. Applied Power's executives hoped that their acquisition could come to dominate certain niche markets profitably. Such previous successes helped Applied Power notch sales of $245 million in 1989, up from $100 million just four years earlier.

In integrating Barry Wright with the rest of its operations, Applied Power faced a challenging task—it sought to streamline Barry Wright's product line and cut its manufacturing costs. The first of the new acquisition's units to face the ax was Barry Wright's Wright Line division, a maker of furnishings and enclosures for technical environments. Applied Power attempted to sell this business in 1992, taking a $25 million write-down charge, but ended up selling only portions of it. These developments followed a year of lackluster results in 1991, when earnings fell to $12 million, hurt by the overall high costs of absorbing the Barry Wright operations and by a general recession. As a maker of tools for use in construction, Applied Power was hurt in particular by the slump in that industry. While its GB Electrical unit and its Enerpac operations continued to contribute strongly, another company unit, Apitech, which had been recently inaugurated to develop high-tech valves and other equipment to improve automobile suspensions, continued to eat up millions of dollars in research and development costs.

This trend continued in 1992, as Applied Power reported a loss of $24.4 million. In an effort to strengthen its positions, Applied Power reorganized certain aspects of its operations, altering the structure of its Barry Controls division in California and changing the nature of its Power-Packer operations in Europe. In addition, the company moved forward aggressively in foreign markets, purchasing the remaining portions of its joint venture operations in Mexico and Germany. Anticipating dramatic growth in Asia, Applied Power hired a new executive to run its Asian operations in Korea and Japan, with the intention of intensifying marketing efforts in those countries.

This thrust toward foreign markets continued in 1993, as Applied Power entered into a joint project with the Detec Design and Industrie Company in Germany to manufacture hydraulic products. That year the company's stock moved from the NASDAQ to the New York Stock Exchange. Applied Power began recovering from its early 1990s doldrums in 1994, when it posted profits of $16.6 million, its best year since 1990. The following year, revenues surpassed the $500 million mark for the first time, and the company began pursuing larger acquisitions again. San Diego-based Vision Plastics Manufacturing Co. was acquired that year for $21.5 million. Vision was a producer of plastic cable ties which GB Electrical distributed. In early 1996 Applied Power spent about $10 million to acquire CalTerm Inc., a supplier of electrical products for do-it-yourself automotive repairs, based in El Cajon, California. Like Vision, CalTerm fit in well alongside the GB Electrical unit.

Late 1990s and Beyond: The Rise of Electronic Enclosures

The late 1990s were marked by Applied Power's rapid acquisition-led expansion into the electronic enclosure products and systems sector. Unlike many of the company's other businesses—including Enerpac, Barry Controls, and Power-Packer—which were cyclical in nature, the enclosures business was growth-oriented, expanding at an annual rate of 35 percent in the late 1990s. The enclosures sector also offered higher margins than other Applied Power sectors, and was a highly fragmented industry, rife for consolidation. Applied Power set out to be *the* enclosure consolidator.

Ironically, given that the company had attempted to sell it in 1992, Wright Line was Applied Power's entrance into this sector. By the mid-1990s Wright Line had sales of $95 million, representing about 18 percent of overall sales, and was one of Applied Power's fastest growing and most profitable units. The company then made a number of acquisitions in the late 1990s, most of which were enclosure-related. In September 1996 Applied Power completed its largest purchase since 1989 when it spent $52 million for Everest Electronic Equipment, Inc., a maker of custom and standard electronic enclosures based in Anaheim, California. For the fiscal year ending in August 1997, Applied Power posted revenues of $672.3 million, 28 percent of which was generated by the company's enclosure products and systems unit.

Applied Power acquired Racine, Wisconsin-based Versa Technologies, Inc. (Versa/Tek) in October 1997 for $141 million. Versa/Tek included several businesses, some of which fit in with Applied Power's engineered solutions unit, which included Barry Controls and Power-Packer. These were Power Gear, maker of hydraulic leveling systems for the recreational vehicle market; and Mox-Med, which made silicone rubber products for medical equipment. Other Versa/Tek units included Milwaukee Cylinder, a maker of hydraulic cylinders that fit alongside Enerpac and the company's tools and supplies division; and Eder Industries, a maker of electronic control systems for a variety of industries. Eder Industries had synergies with both the engineered solutions and the enclosures segments, but was initially placed within engineered solutions.

Applied Power next acquired VERO Group plc in June 1998 for $191.7 million (fending off a competing bid by Pentair, Inc.) and ZERO Corporation the following month in a merger valued at $386 million. Based in the United Kingdom, VERO manufactured electronic enclosures and related products, including racks, backplanes, and power supplies. VERO, which in 1997 had sales of $170 million and earnings of $17 million, helped Applied Power broaden its line of products in the European market. ZERO, which was based in Los Angeles and had 1997 revenues of $260 million, was also active in the electronic enclosures market; its system packaging, thermal management, and engineered cases served the telecommunication, instrumentation, and data processing markets. These major acquisitions helped increase Applied Power's fiscal 1998 revenues to $1.23 billion, an increase of 37 percent over 1997 results. The company's enclosure products segment was now its largest segment, accounting for 39 percent of overall sales. Net income for 1998 was reduced to $26.7 million because of a $52.6 million charge relating to acquisition costs, plant consolidations, and other restructuring costs.

In September 1998 Applied Power completed its third major enclosure acquisition in the span of four months, with the $371.5 million purchase of U.K.-based Rubicon Group plc , one of the leading manufacturers of electronic enclosures in Europe. Rubicon brought to Applied Power a new segment of the enclosure market, that of automated teller machines, and it manufactured safes, the surrounding enclosure, and other ATM component parts as well as providing assembly services. With this latest acquisition, Applied Power was now the number one worldwide supplier of custom electronic enclosures, a position it had attained in an astonishingly short period.

In early 1999 the company received another boost when it landed a ten-year, $200 million contract to supply electronic enclosure systems for wireless base station equipment to Sweden-based Telefonaktiebolaget LM Ericsson. Applied Power announced a restructuring of its operations in May of that year, which involved the organizing of its operations into two segments: APW Electronics and APW Industrial. The former included all of the enclosure products and systems businesses along with McLean Thermal Management and Eder Industries. Applied Power's remaining operations, including most of its engineered solutions and tools and supplies units were grouped within APW Industrial. For the fiscal year ending in August 1999, APW Electronics generated $1.06 billion in revenues (60 percent of overall revenues), while APW Industrial contributed $696 million. Overall profits reached a record $79.4 million. With the company's future clearly resting with its fast-growing enclosures operations, Applied Power announced in September 1999 that it was seeking a buyer for APW Industrial so it could focus solely on APW Electronics. The completion of this divestment would mark the culmination of a dramatic—and remarkable rapid—transformation of Applied Power from manufacturer of a wide range of tools and industrial products and systems to a focused, global leader of a single industry segment, a segment it had entered only in 1989 and had only a small presence in as late as August 1996.

Principal Subsidiaries

Air Cargo Equipment Corporation; Airspeed LLC; Ancor Products, Inc.; Applied Power Credit Corporation; Applied Power International Ltd.; Applied Power Investments II Inc.; APW Enclosure Systems, Inc.; APW Enclosure Systems, LLC; APW Enclosure Systems, LP; APW Investments, Inc.; APW Tools and Supplies, Inc.; Aspen Motion Technologies, Inc.; Barry Controls Corporation; Barry Wright Corporation; Calterm Taiwan, Inc.; Cambridge Aeroflo, Inc.; Columbus Manufacturing Company L.L.C.; DCW Holding, Inc.; Del City Wire, Inc.; Eder Industries, Inc.; Electronic Solutions; HSP USA Inc.; Innovative Metal Fabrication; McLean Midwest Corporation; McLean West Inc.; Milwaukee Cylinder Company; Mox-Med, Inc.; New England Controls, Inc.; Nielsen Hardware Corporation; Precision Fabrication Technologies, Inc.; Rubicon USA Inc.; VERO Electronics Inc.; Versa Technologies, Inc.; WL International, Inc.; Wright Line Inc.; ZERO Corporation; ZERO Enclosures, Inc.; ZERO International, Inc.; ZERO-East Division, ZERO Corporation; AIC (Hong Kong) Ltd. (49%); Air Cargo Equipment (U.K.); AP International Corporation (Barbados); Applied Power Distribution GmbH (Germany); Applied Power Asia Pte, Ltd. (Singapore); Applied Power Australia Limited; Applied Power Canada Ltd.; Applied Power do Brasil Equipamente Ltda. (Brazil); Applied Power Europa B.V. (Netherlands); Applied Power Europe S.A. (France); Applied Power Export Corp. (U.S. Virgin Islands); Applied Power (Far East) Ltd. (Japan); Applied Power Finance B.V. (Netherlands); Applied Power GmbH (Germany); Applied Power Holding GmbH (Germany); Applied Power Hytec (M) Sdn. Bhd. (Malaysia); Applied Power International, S.A. (France); Applied Power International, S.A. (Switzerland); Applied Power Italiana S.p.A. (Italy); Applied Power Japan Ltd.; Applied Power Korea Ltd. (South Korea); Applied Power Limited (U.K.); Applied Power (Mexico) S. de R.L. de C.V.; Applied Power Moscow (Russia); Applied Power New Zealand Limited; APW Enclosures Ltd. (Ireland); APW Finance Limited (U.K.); APW Enclosure Products and Systems Limited (U.K.); APW Enclosure Systems Holdings Limited (U.K.); APW Enclosure Systems Limited (Rubicon) (U.K.); Barry Controls GmbH (Germany); Barry Controls U.K. Ltd.; C-Fab Manufacturing Ltd. (Ireland); C-Fab Developments Ltd. (Ireland); Danica Supply A/S (Denmark); Danica Supply UK Limited; Enerpac Asia Pte. Ltd. (Singapore); Enerpac Canada Ltd.; Enerpac Nederland B.V. (Netherlands); Enerpac Hydraulic Technology (India) Pte. Ltd.; Enerpac Ltd. (U.K.); Enerpac S.A. (France); Hormann Electronics Ltd. (Ireland); Norelem S.A. (France); Power-Packer do Brasil Ltd. (Brazil); Power-Packer Espana, S.A. (Spain); Power-Packer Europa B.V. (Netherlands); Power-Packer France S.A.; Productos Aereos, S.A. (Mexico); Samuel Groves & Co. Limited (U.K.); Shanghai Blackhawk Machinery Co. Ltd. (China); VERO Electronics AB (Sweden); VERO Electronics GmbH (Germany); VERO Electronics Limited (U.K.); VERO Electronics Overseas Investments Limited (U.K.); VERO Electronics SA (France); VERO Electronics SrL (Italy); Wright Line Europe, B.V. (Netherlands); ZERO FSC Corp. (U.S. Virgin Islands); ZERO McLean Europe Ltd. (U.K.).

Principal Operating Units

APW Electronics; APW Industrial.

Principal Competitors

ASCET, Inc.; Banner Aerospace, Inc.; Commercial Intertech Corp.; Cooper Industries, Inc.; Dolby Laboratories Inc.; Dover Corporation; Eaton Corporation; Fluke Corporation; Haworth, Inc.; Herman Miller, Inc.; Maval Manufacturing Inc.; NCT Group, Inc.; Parker Hannifin Corporation; Pentair, Inc.; The Stanley Works; Steelcase Inc.; Twin Disc, Incorporated; Williams Controls, Inc.

Further Reading

Byrne, Harlan S., ''Applied Power: Struggling Past a Big Acquisition,'' *Barron's,* October 12, 1992.

Daykin, Tom, ''Applied Power Sells New Headquarters,'' *Milwaukee Journal Sentinel,* December 1, 1999, p. 2.

——, ''Applied Power to Buy British Company: Butler-Based Company to Pay $347.8 Million for One of Europe's Largest Manufacturers of Electronic Enclosures,'' *Milwaukee Journal Sentinel,* September 2, 1998, p. 1.

——, ''Applied Power Has Value, Growth Potential, Analyst Says,'' *Milwaukee Journal Sentinel,* October 5, 1998, p. 10.

Gallun, Alby, ''Airline Business Propels Applied Power,'' *Business Journal-Milwaukee,* September 19, 1997, p. 1.

——, ''Applied Power Continues Binge of Acquisitions,'' *Business Journal-Milwaukee,* December 12, 1997, p. 9.

——, ''Applied Power to Take $52.6 Million Charge,'' *Business Journal-Milwaukee,* October 2, 1998, p. 3.

Hawkins, Lee, Jr., ''Applied Power Lands 10-Year Deal Worth More Than $200 Million,'' *Milwaukee Journal Sentinel,* February 25, 1999, p. 7.

Holley, Paul, ''A Selective Applied Power Goes on the Prowl Again,'' *Business Journal-Milwaukee,* May 4, 1996, p. 5.

Kirchen, Rich, ''Applied's Mathematics: Manufacturer Figures to Be 'On Way Back,' '' *Business Journal-Milwaukee,* July 9, 1994, p. 1.

Savage, Mark, ''Applied Power Boosts Bid for British Company,'' *Milwaukee Journal Sentinel,* May 13, 1998, p. 1.

——, ''Applied Power Deal Lures Competitor,'' *Milwaukee Journal Sentinel,* May 6, 1998, p. 1.

——, ''Applied Power Sets $52 Million Deal,'' *Milwaukee Journal Sentinel,* August 29, 1996, p. 1.

——, ''Applied Power to Buy ZERO Corp.,'' *Milwaukee Journal Sentinel,* April 7, 1998, p. 1.

Sharma-Jensen, Geeta, ''Applied Power Agrees to Deal,'' *Milwaukee Journal Sentinel,* September 4, 1997, p. 1.

—Elizabeth Rourke
—updated by David E. Salamie

Aqua Alliance Inc.

30 Harvard Mill Square
Wakefield, Massachusetts 01880
U.S.A.
Telephone: (781) 246-5200
Fax: (781) 245-6293
Web site: http://www.aquaalliance.com

Public Subsidiary of Vivendi
Incorporated: 1987 as R-C Acquisitions, Inc.
Employees: 2,500
Sales: $445.1 million (1998)
Stock Exchanges: American
Ticker Symbol: AAI
NAIC: 221310 Water Supply and Irrigation Systems; 221320 Sewage Treatment Facilities; 325314 Fertilizer (Mixing Only) Manufacturing; 541330 Engineering Services; 541620 Environmental Consulting Services; 561990 All Other Support Services; 562211 Hazardous Water Treatment and Disposal; 562212 Solid Waste Landfill; 562910 Remediation Services

Formerly known as Air & Water Technologies Corporation, Aqua Alliance Inc. (AAI) is a leading provider of water, wastewater, and hazardous waste services. Among other activities, the company operates, maintains, and manages water and wastewater treatment facilities; designs and constructs water and wastewater facilities; and provides for the remediation of hazardous waste. AAI's customers are mainly governmental, including municipalities and state and federal agencies; the company is at the forefront of the emerging trend toward the privatization of municipal water and wastewater systems. AAI operates and manages the water and wastewater systems for the Commonwealth of Puerto Rico. Among the other water treatment facilities it operates are those in Brockton and Lynn, Massachusetts, as well as in Alamogordo, New Mexico. It manages wastewater treatment facilities in Oklahoma City; Cranston, Rhode Island; Taunton, Massachusetts; West Haven, Connecticut; and Kenner, Louisiana. A public company, Aqua Alliance is an 83 percent owned subsidiary of Vivendi, a French conglomerate which is the largest water company in the world.

Origins in the Late 1980s

R-C Acquisitions, Inc., was formed in 1987 by Eckardt C. Beck with the help of Odyssey Partners, Allen & Company Incorporated, and some affiliates of First Chicago Corporation as a means of acquiring Research-Cottrell, Inc., an engineering and construction company, through a leveraged buyout. After the acquisition, the company retained the name Research-Cottrell but changed its focus to environmental treatment. The following year, it acquired Zecco, Inc., a Northboro, Massachusetts, firm specializing in hazardous waste cleanup. Shortly afterward, Zecco was merged with another of Research-Cottrell's subsidiaries, Metcalf & Eddy, Inc.—which dealt with water and sewage treatment and industrial waste problems—to form Metcalf & Eddy Companies, Inc. (MECI).

Toward the end of 1988, Research-Cottrell made yet another acquisition through another of its subsidiaries, Power Applications & Manufacturing Company (PAMCO), Inc. This time the prize was Waukesha Engine Servicenter and Waukesha Engine Servicenter of Arizona—collectively known as WESI—companies involved in the sale of generating sets, pumping equipment, and compressors. WESI had customers in many different areas, including wastewater treatment and the gas and oil industry.

In June 1989 Research-Cottrell changed its name to Air & Water Technologies Corporation (AWT). AWT continued its program of acquisitions in the environmental control field, with the same month's purchase—through the Metcalf & Eddy subsidiary—of various assets of the hazardous waste firms H.G. Anderson Equipment Corporation and Anderson Testing Company, Inc. A few months later, again through Metcalf & Eddy, Air & Water Technologies acquired certain assets of YWC (formerly known as York Wastewater Consultants) Inc.'s operation and maintenance service division and also the outstanding common stock of YWC Northeast. The YWC companies provided wastewater treatment services to cities in the northeastern United States.

Key Dates:

1987: R-C Acquisitions, Inc. is formed, acquires Research-Cottrell, Inc., and adopts the Research-Cottrell name.
1989: Company changes its name to Air & Water Technologies Corporation (AWT).
1990: Compagnie Generale des Eaux (CGE) purchases a 16 percent stake in AWT for $100 million.
1994: CGE ups its stake in AWT to 40 percent.
1996: CEO Claudio Elia is killed in the Balkans trade mission plane crash, which also took the life of U.S. Commerce Secretary Ron Brown; Robert B. Sheh is brought in as the new chairman and CEO.
1997: AWT nears bankruptcy and is rescued by CGE, which increases its stake to 83 percent.
1998: CGE changes its name to Vivendi; AWT divests major portion of Research-Cottrell; company changes its name to Aqua Alliance Inc. (AAI); headquarters moves to Massachusetts and four operating regions are established: Chicago, Atlanta, Wakefield, and San Diego.
1999: Divestment of Research-Cottrell is completed.

Early 1990s Difficulties

AWT acquisitions in 1990 included Petrolgroup, Inc., and Regenerative Environmental Equipment Company, Inc. (REECO). The latter company, based in Morris Plains, New Jersey, produced incineration technology used in the destruction of volatile organic compounds (VOCs) and other toxic substances found in polluted air. The REECO acquisition was part of the AWT's strategy to take advantage of the stricter air pollution controls put into effect by the passage of the 1990 Clean Air Act Amendments. The company also entered a joint venture in plastic recycling with Hammers Plastic Recycling of Iowa Falls, Iowa. As part of the project, AWT bought a ten percent share in Hammers. That same year, the France-based Compagnie Generale des Eaux (CGE)—the world's largest water company, providing water for 33 million customers throughout Europe—purchased 16 percent of AWT for a price of $100 million.

Also in 1990, Air & Water Technologies sued the Puerto Rican Aqueduct and Sewer Authority, or PRASA, for $31 million in delinquent payments. PRASA, however, fought back. A government affiliate of PRASA performed an audit of the disputed contract, questioning "up to $39,988,200 of billings for possible technical violations of equipment procurement procedures." Though the U.S. Court of Appeals for the First Circuit dismissed PRASA's appeal, PRASA asked the U.S. Supreme Court to review that dismissal, and their request was granted.

Despite troubles with PRASA and a few other projects, at the beginning of the 1990s it appeared that Air & Water Technologies was ready to put most of its expansion expenditures behind it and concentrate on gaining profitable clients. By this time the company comprised three major subsidiaries: Research-Cottrell, Metcalf & Eddy, and Residuals Management. Research-Cottrell focused on air and thermal pollution issues and provided services in the areas of regulatory assistance, consulting, permitting, and research and development. Metcalf & Eddy served as the water and solid waste department of AWT. Like Research-Cottrell, it provided regulatory assistance, consulting, and permitting services to its clients. Metcalf & Eddy also performed waste minimization, sludge management, solid waste management, as well as groundwater and hazardous waste remediation. Residuals Management produced recycled plastic products from industrial and consumer sources and handled asbestos and lead removal, disposal, and abatement.

In addition to working through its three major subsidiaries, AWT at this time served its customers through five regional centers in the United States—Central, East, New England, South, and West—and a separate division devoted to its clients in the federal government. In 1991, approximately 44 percent of the AWT's revenues came from contracts with federal, state, and municipal government agencies. The company's international division provided services in 44 countries in Europe, Asia, the Middle East, and Canada. It saw particular growth in the European market during the early 1990s due to the fall of communist governments in Eastern Europe. Also during the early 1990s, CGE gradually increased its stake in AWT to 24.5 percent.

Mid-1990s and Beyond

By 1994 AWT was floundering. It was in severe financial straits because it remained burdened by the hefty debt load Beck had taken on in the 1987 LBO. Beck had counted on customers snapping up pollution control systems in order to comply with new government regulations, but many utilities and firms came up with cheaper ways to reach compliance, such as shutting down high-polluting plants, switching to cleaner coal, or purchasing emissions allowances. AWT's foray into the asbestos abatement business had also turned into a mistake as asbestos removal proved to be a crowded, low margin sector. After failing to find a buyer, AWT liquidated Residuals Management in mid-1994, taking a $35 million charge to do so. Overall, from 1991 to 1993, AWT lost a total of $41.4 million.

In June 1994, with no end in sight to the company's red ink, AWT was rescued by CGE, which injected an additional $65 million into the ailing firm, increasing its stake to 40 percent and gaining the right to appoint a new management team. Claudio Elia, who was the head of CGE's U.S. holding company, replaced Beck as chairman and CEO of AWT. Along with the increased stake, the transaction also involved the transfer to AWT of a CGE subsidiary, Houston-based Professional Services Group, Inc. (PSG), the largest manager of water and wastewater treatment facilities in the United States. Metcalf & Eddy was involved in this sector in a much smaller way, and its operations in this area were merged into PSG. To this time, the privatization of municipal water and wastewater systems had been growing at a rather slow pace, but CGE was convinced that it was poised to take off.

Air & Water Technologies showed major improvement in 1995, when it posted an operating gain of $16.8 million (but a net loss of $8 million), compared to an operating loss of $182.5 million for the previous year (when it had a net loss of $261.8 million). The company continued to be dogged by difficulties, however. In April 1996 Elia was one of about a dozen U.S.

senior corporate executives who accompanied U.S. Commerce Secretary Ron Brown on a trade mission to the Balkans which ended in a fatal plane crash. After CGE executives took over management of AWT on an interim basis, Robert B. Sheh was brought in as the new chairman and CEO. Sheh had been CEO of International Technology Corp. In December 1996 the CEO of Professional Services Group resigned, a few months after being placed on paid leave while AWT investigated allegations that PSG officials made improper payments to members of the Houston City Council and others in connection with the possible privatization of Houston's water system. The AWT probe uncovered some questionable financial transactions, and the company turned this information over to the U.S. Department of Justice, which had already initiated its own investigation and was continuing to look into the matter as of late 1999.

Sheh was unable to turn the company's fortunes around, and AWT was near bankruptcy by September 1997. Once again, CGE came to the rescue. The French conglomerate reached an agreement with AWT on a recapitalization plan whereby it invested approximately $200 million to increase its stake to 83 percent. This enabled Air & Water Technologies to finally bring its debt level under control; long-term debt was reduced from $307.8 million at the end of fiscal 1997 to $119.4 million the following year. AWT's board asked for Sheh's resignation so two CGE executives could take charge. Named to the chairmanship was William Kriegel, who was also chairman and CEO of Sithe Energies Inc., a New York-based independent power producer which was also a majority-owned subsidiary of CGE, as well as chairman and CEO of CGE's U.S. holding company, Anjou International Co. The new president and CEO was Thierry Mallet, who had helped turn around Sociedad Mediterranea de Aguas, CGE's water and wastewater unit in Spain.

The new leadership immediately embarked on an ambitious program of reorganization and streamlining, the highlight of which was the focusing of the company on water. To this end, AWT announced in December 1997 that it would sell off Research-Cottrell, its original company. In 1998 AWT sold a major part of the business, then completed the divestment in January 1999 with the sale of REECO. These moves left the company with a much narrower focus, with water, wastewater, and hazardous waste services comprising the bulk of operations. The year 1998 was also marked by name changes. Compagnie Generale des Eaux was transformed into Vivendi, while Air & Water Technologies adopted the name Aqua Alliance Inc. (AAI) in October. According to a company document, the new name was selected because "it clearly states the company's two greatest strengths: its dedication to the water business and the relationship formed with its clients." Also in October 1998, AAI moved its headquarters from Branchburg, New Jersey, to Wakefield, Massachusetts; and it began merging its two main units, Metcalf & Eddy and Professional Services Group, as part of a restructuring of operations into four regions operating from Chicago, Atlanta, Wakefield, and San Diego.

Principal Subsidiaries

AWT Air & Water Technologies Canada, Limited; AWT Capital, Inc.; Chesapeake Sunrise Marketing Corporation; EnviroSolutions, LLC; Falcon Associates, Inc.; Flex-Kleen Corp.; Lerman Design Corp.; M&E Auburn, Inc.; M&E II, Inc.; M&E Pacific, Inc.; M&E Services, Inc.; MEPAC Services, Inc.; Merscot Inc.; Merscot II, Inc.; Metcalf & Eddy, Inc.; Metcalf & Eddy of Canada Ltd.; Metcalf & Eddy de Puerto Rico, Inc.; Metcalf & Eddy International, Inc.; Metcalf & Eddy Management, P.C.; Metcalf & Eddy of Massachusetts, Inc.; Metcalf & Eddy of Michigan, Inc.; Metcalf & Eddy of New York, Inc.; Metcalf & Eddy of Ohio, Inc.; Metcalf & Eddy Services, Inc.; Metcalf & Eddy Technologies, Inc.; PIECO, Inc.; Power Application & Mfg. Co.; PQ Energy, Inc.; Production Rentals, Inc.; Professional Services Group, Inc.; PSG of Puerto Rico, Inc.; Rental Tools, Inc.; Thermal Transfer Corporation; Utility Services Group Inc.; 2815869 Canada, Inc.; Vee-Six, Inc.

Principal Competitors

American Water Works Company, Inc.; Bechtel Group, Inc.; United Water Resources; United States Filter Corporation; Waste Management, Inc.

Further Reading

"Air & Water Says CEO of Subsidiary Resigned As Probe Continues," *Wall Street Journal,* December 6, 1996.
"Air & Water's Claudio Elia Among Victims of Plane Crash in Croatia," *Waste Business,* April 10, 1996, p. 1.
"Air & Water's Sheh Is Asked by Board to Resign Positions," *Wall Street Journal,* October 28, 1997, p. B12.
Browning, E.S., "Two Big French Environmental Firms Expand in the U.S. Through Mergers," *Wall Street Journal,* April 6, 1994, p. A8.
"CGE Insiders Take Over AWT," *Engineering News Record,* November 17, 1997, p. 15.
"French Firm Rescues Ailing AWT," *Engineering News Record,* October 6, 1997, p. 19.
"Industry Giants Change Spots to Be Profitable and Competitive," *Engineering News Record,* October 19, 1998, p. 14.
"Industry Veteran Bob Sheh Expected to Head AWT," *Engineering News Record,* November 18, 1996, p. 16.
Jones, Terril Yue, "Water, Water Everywhere: Your Tap Water May Not Taste Like Perrier, but It May Just Be Just as French," *Forbes,* November 30, 1998, p. 323.
Lang, Steven, "AWT to Liquidate Asbestos Abatement Business after Failing to Find Buyer," *Hazardous Waste Business,* June 1, 1994, p. 1.
Lubove, Seth, "The Bureaucrat As Businessman," *Forbes,* August 15, 1994, p. 64.
"Plastic Recycling Joint Venture," *Chemical Week,* February 21, 1990.
"Research Cottrell Buys REECO," *Chemical Week,* November 14, 1990.
Roberts, Johnnie L., "Cottrell Agrees to Buyout Bid of $43 a Share," *Wall Street Journal,* June 9, 1987.
Rubin, Debra K., "French Twist for a U.S. Firm," *Engineering News Record,* June 20, 1994, p. 16.
——, "French 'Mr. Fix-It' to Jump-Start Air & Water Technologies," *Engineering News Record,* December 22, 1997, p. 14.
Toy, Stewart, "France's Water Giant Takes a Gulp of New Business," *Business Week,* July 30, 1990.

—Elizabeth Wenning
—updated by David E. Salamie

Archer-Daniels-Midland Company

4666 East Faries Parkway
P.O. Box 1470
Decatur, Illinois 62525
U.S.A.
Telephone: (217) 424-5200
Fax: (217) 424-5839
Web site: http://www.admworld.com

Public Company
Incorporated: 1923
Employees: 23,603
Sales: $14.28 billion (1999)
Stock Exchanges: New York Chicago Tokyo Frankfurt Swiss
Ticker Symbol: ADM
NAIC: 111419 Other Food Crops Grown Under Cover; 112511 Finfish Farming and Fish Hatcheries; 311119 Other Animal Feed Manufacturing; 311211 Flour Milling; 311212 Rice Milling; 311213 Malt Manufacturing; 311221 Wet Corn Milling; 311222 Soybean Processing; 311223 Other Oilseed Processing; 311312 Cane Sugar Refining; 311320 Chocolate and Confectionery Manufacturing from Cacao Beans; 311823 Dry Pasta Manufacturing; 311830 Tortilla Manufacturing; 311999 All Other Miscellaneous Food Manufacturing; 312140 Distilleries; 325193 Ethyl Alcohol Manufacturing; 325411 Medicinal and Botanical Manufacturing; 422510 Grain and Field Bean Wholesalers; 493130 Farm Product Warehousing and Storage; 522110 Commercial Banking; 523130 Commodity Contracts Dealing

Archer-Daniels-Midland Company (ADM) is one of the world's leading processors and distributors of agricultural products for food and animal feed, with additional operations in transportation and storage of such products. Its principal operations are in the processing of soybeans, corn, and wheat, the three largest crops in the United States. ADM also processes cocoa beans, milo, oats, barley, and peanuts. The company's feed products are sold to farmers, feed dealers, and livestock producers, while its food products are sold to food and beverage manufacturers. Among ADM's better-known products are NutriSoy, a soy protein; Novasoy Isoflavones, an ingredient used in dietary supplements; xanthan gum, a thickening agent used in food products such as salad dressings; citric acid and lactic acid, both used as food additives in food and beverage products to increase their acidity; natural vitamin E; and ethanol, an additive made from corn that is added to gasoline to improve the fuel efficiency of vehicles. With 247 processing plants (including those owned, leased, or operated in joint ventures) in the United States and 121 overseas, Archer-Daniels-Midland calls itself the "Supermarket to the World." For most of its history, ADM was quiet and conservative; however, in the mid-1990s the company hurtled into the headlines through its involvement in price-fixing schemes involving citric acid and the livestock feed additive lysine.

Early History

John W. Daniels began crushing flaxseed to make linseed oil in Ohio in 1878, and in 1902 he moved to Minneapolis, Minnesota, to organize the Daniels Linseed Company. The company consisted of a flax crushing plant that made three products: raw linseed oil, boiled linseed oil, and linseed cake or meal. In 1903 George A. Archer joined the firm, and in a few years it became the Archer-Daniels Linseed Company. Archer also brought experience to the firm, as his family had been in the business of crushing flaxseed since the 1830s. Archer and Daniels then hired a young bookkeeper by the name of Samuel Mairs, who eventually became the company's chairperson.

These three men had a common goal of "year-round production at low margins," a goal that continued to direct the company into the 21st century. Archer and Daniels used hydraulic presses to process flaxseed, and their linseed oil was essentially the same as that used by the ancient Egyptians. In the early years, profits were low, but Archer-Daniels Linseed never finished a year in debt. They also grew slowly, buying the stock of the Toledo Seed & Oil Company as well as the Dellwood Elevator Company, a grain elevator firm.

In 1923 the company purchased the Midland Linseed Products Company and then incorporated as the Archer-Daniels-

Company Perspectives:

We think of ourselves as a global company because we produce a truly global product: food.

It isn't subject to trends, and the demand never decreases. It transcends all languages, all boundaries, all social classes. Kings and presidents need it as much as the people they serve.

Food is the common element of humanity. And in an increasingly urban world, the job of growing, producing, and distributing food falls upon a relatively small group of individuals and entities.

ADM is one of those entities. Using a production and distribution network with points at strategic locations around the world, we're taking the farmer's bounty and making it accessible to everyone. And because we're a global company, each one of those locations feels like home.

Midland Company. The 1920s also brought other significant changes. Archer, Daniels, and Mairs began the scientific exploration of methods to alter the chemical structure of linseed oil. This project initiated the company's successful research and development program. Research and development allocations were not commonplace for companies at that time, and the market took note of the company's slogan: "Creating New Values from America's Harvests."

Throughout the 1920s the company made steady purchases of oil processing companies in the Midwest while engaging in other agricultural activities. It built elevators on Minneapolis loading docks to store grain awaiting shipment down the Mississippi to other ports. Then, in 1930, Archer-Daniels-Midland purchased the Commander-Larabee Company, a major flour miller with plants in Minnesota, Kansas, and Missouri. Commander-Larabee was capable of producing 32,000 barrels per day. The purchase of Commander-Larabee had two additional advantages: it allowed ADM to coordinate its oil byproduct business with Commander-Larabee's feedstuff byproduct business, and the mutual sales effort lowered overhead. During this time, the company also discovered how to extract lecithin from soybean oil, reducing the price of lecithin from ten dollars to one dollar per pound. (Lecithin was widely used as an emulsifier in the food and confectionery industries.) As a result of Archer-Daniels-Midland's growth strategies and research activities, the company had $22.5 million in assets by 1938.

As a linseed oil manufacturer, Archer-Daniels-Midland interacted with more than just the food market. The paint product industry used drying oils—namely, linseed, tung, and perilla—in the manufacture of various products to add critical gloss and hardness properties to paint finishes. The demand for drying oil in the paint industry fluctuated widely because it depended heavily on construction, as well as on the availability and price of imported oils, since most oils were imported from the Far East and South America. Sales and profits also fluctuated due to the quality and size of each year's harvest. Despite these challenges and the onset of the Great Depression, the company continued to turn a profit, in part because Archer-Daniels-Midland had been working to adapt oils to new markets, including soaps, drugs, brake fluids, lubricants, petroleum, and chemicals.

Since Archer-Daniels-Midland knew the value of its research department, it appropriated 70 percent of its earnings ($1–$2 million annually) back into the business for development and expansion. One result was a process whereby the usable fibers (the tow) of flax straw (a waste product up to then) could be used in the manufacture of flax papers. World War II made it impossible for the company to increase its facilities as much as it wished; nevertheless, ADM's capacities grew significantly from 1930 to 1945. From a 1929 processing capacity of 20 million bushels of flaxseed per day, the company could process 36.6 million bushels per day by 1945. Wheat flour capacity went from zero to 30 million bushels per day. Grain storage capacity increased from 7.5 million to 50.4 million bushels per day.

Postwar Growth

The immediate postwar years from 1946 through 1949 showed dramatic growth: sales increased 287 percent, and net income increased 346 percent. In 1949 sales were $277 million, with a $12 million net profit. Archer-Daniels-Midland was well positioned in several market areas because it supplied basic ingredients to a wide range of industries. The company was the leading U.S. processor of linseed oil, the fourth largest flour miller, and the largest soybean processor. It also served the paint, leather, printing, gasoline, paper, cosmetics, pharmaceuticals, rubber, ceramics, munitions, and insecticides industries.

A conservative management style had consistently safeguarded the company's success. For instance, whenever possible, Archer-Daniels-Midland hedged its purchases of raw products by sales in the futures markets or by forward sales of the completed products. By the end of fiscal year 1949, the company had no bank debt, and it had paid a dividend every year from 1927 onward. All plants were kept at a high state of operating efficiency, using modern, streamlined methods. There had also been a change in the processing level. The company began to put its products through advanced physical processing instead of selling them in a raw or semi-finished state, thereby increasing profit margins. Overall, management estimated that 40 percent of its increase in sales from 1939 to 1949 was due to new products and methods.

Because the company supplied core oils used in foundry industries, the outbreak of the Korean War increased demands on production through the early 1950s. The company was also increasing its outlay for whale oil procurement, which it had begun in the 1930s, and began increasing its production of protein concentrates, marketing them extensively for stockfeeding purposes.

When President Thomas L. Daniels (son of the founder) and Chairperson Samuel Mairs celebrated Archer-Daniels-Midland's 50th anniversary in 1952, the company was manufacturing over 700 standard products and had extended its operations overseas. More foreign expansion followed in Peru, Mexico, the Netherlands, and Belgium. In these ventures, the company specialized in partnerships with local interests. President Daniels expressed the company's attitude toward foreign involvement

Key Dates:

1878: John W. Daniels begins crushing flaxseed to make linseed oil in Ohio.
1902: Daniels moves to Minneapolis to organize the Daniels Linseed Company.
1903: George A. Archer joins the firm, which is renamed the Archer-Daniels Linseed Company within a few years.
1923: Company purchases the Midland Linseed Products Company, then incorporates as the Archer-Daniels-Midland Company.
1930: Commander-Larabee Company, a major flour miller, is acquired.
1966: Dwayne O. Andreas purchases a block of stock, gaining seats on the company board and the executive committee.
1970: Andreas is named CEO.
1971: Company purchases Corn Sweeteners, Inc., producer of high-fructose syrups, glutens, oil, and caramel color.
1972: Andreas is elected chairman.
1981: The Columbian Peanut Company is acquired.
1986: Company forms grain marketing joint venture with Growmark.
1996: Company pleads guilty to two counts of fixing prices of lysine and citric acid and pays $100 million in criminal fines.
1997: Company acquires W.R. Grace's cocoa business, marking its entry into that sector; G. Allen Andreas is named CEO.
1998: Three former company executives, including Michael D. Andreas, are convicted by a federal jury of price fixing.
1999: Dwayne Andreas retires as chairman; CEO Allen Andreas is named to the additional post of chairman; Michael Andreas begins serving two-year prison sentence.

in the late 1950s when he said: ''ADM looks with particular favor on Western Europe as an area of great chemical producers. . . . All industry there is expanding rapidly, both for local consumption and for export to other parts of the world.''

Archer-Daniels-Midland had weathered the Great Depression and World War II, but ran into trouble during the 1960s. Although it made several grain production and storage purchases in the early 1960s, unstable commodities prices and the company's chemicals operations were causing losses. Net earnings were $75 million in 1963 and then declined to about $60 million in 1964, dropping even further to $50 million the following year. By 1965, the company could not cover its dividend. At this time, John Daniels, president and grandson of one of the founders, and Shreve M. Archer, Jr., a company director, recruited Dwayne O. Andreas to the leadership team. Andreas gradually took control of the company, gaining seats on the board and the executive committee in 1966, being named CEO in 1970, and being elected chairman in 1972. Andreas revolutionized Archer-Daniels-Midland.

Mid-1960s Through 1980s: Andreas the ''Soybean King''

Andreas's low profile appealed to the company management, as did his background in the production of farm products. One of the first things Andreas did was eliminate a 27-person public relations department. Eschewing the advice of analysts and often declining to talk to reporters, Andreas was a unique executive. His political views were often in opposition to those of the larger business community; for example, he advocated increases in the corporate income tax rate.

Andreas believed that one specific product—soybeans—could do a great deal to turn the company around. Andreas recalled, ''I knew that ADM was a dozen years ahead of everyone else in textured vegetable protein research, and I believed that was where important action was going to be.'' Whereas scientists advocated an almost pure protein product derived from the soybean, Andreas encouraged the development of textured vegetable protein, a 50 percent protein soy product that was far more economical to produce. His increasing power in the company (by 1968 he was chair of the executive committee) made his plans a reality. Andreas described his actions thus: ''One of the first things I did was to take the edible soy out of the lab and construct a plant in Decatur (Illinois) to make all the grades of edible soy protein in 1969.'' He expected to exceed the plant's capacity by 1976. However, by 1973, with doubled production, the plant was already short of demand. Textured vegetable protein was widely used in foodstuffs, and soybean oil later became the number one food and cooking oil in use.

The company also sold its troublesome chemical properties to Ashland Oil & Refining Company for $35 million in 1967. That year, it acquired the Fleischmann Malting Company, which would become a very profitable producer of malts for the food and beverage industry. Andreas proved expert at maintaining a good profit margin on soybeans, too. Two or three cents shaved off costs made large differences on this item, which carried slender profit margins. Andreas's management rules of efficiency and profitability echoed the founders' practices.

With unprofitable operations sold, profitable ones newly acquired, and the increasing success of the soybean, the company entered another major area of operations. In 1971 it purchased Corn Sweeteners, Inc., producer of high-fructose syrups, glutens, oil, and caramel color. Corn Sweeteners brought good returns for Archer-Daniels-Midland and increased the company's finished-food capabilities.

Throughout the 1970s, the company built textured vegetable protein plants in Europe and South America. In addition, Dwayne Andreas brought several other members of his family into Archer-Daniels-Midland as the company expanded. (In fact, a 1988 treatment in *Financial World* characterized ADM as the Andreas ''family dynasty.'') Three Andreas family members became heads of various divisions, although the company continued to retain one Archer and one Daniels in high-ranking positions into the 1990s.

From the net low of $50 million in earnings in 1965, net earnings were near $117 million in 1973. This increase paralleled the upward swing in U.S. soybean production and exports from 700 million bushels per day in 1965 to 1.3 billion in 1973.

That growth continued through the 1970s and into the 1980s. During this time, Archer-Daniels-Midland had several major subdivisions, the largest of which was the Oilseed Processing Division. In this division, soy products soon outstripped linseed and all others, earning Andreas the nickname ''Soybean King.'' The next largest, the Corn Sweeteners Division, produced ethanol in addition to high-fructose products. In fact, the Decatur, Illinois, plant was the single largest source of ethanol in the United States. Archer-Daniels-Midland Milling Company processed the company's grains, and in 1986 the milling division became even larger when ADM entered into a grain marketing joint venture with Growmark Inc., a large Midwestern grain merchandising and river terminal cooperative. The venture was called ADM/Growmark.

Another division, the Columbian Peanut Company, acquired in 1981, produced oil and peanut products, and Archer-Daniels-Midland was the leading domestic peanut sheller. Gooch Foods, Inc., was the company's market name for a line of pasta products, which increased in demand after the advent of microwave pasta dishes. Other divisions of Archer-Daniels-Midland included Southern Cotton Oil Company, Fleischmann Malting Company, Inc., American River Transportation Company, Supreme Sugar Company, and the British Arkady Co., Ltd., which was a supplier of specialty products to the bakery industry.

1990s and Beyond

ADM made its first-ever foray into consumer food products with the characteristically low-profile launch of its Harvest Burger brand soy-based meat substitute in the early 1990s. The product's reduced fat, calories, and cholesterol attracted American consumers, many of whom sought out the product even before it had advertising support. In 1993 the Pillsbury Company assumed responsibility for supermarket retailing of Harvest Burgers. For the hungry of the world, the soy product was an inexpensive source of protein with a longer shelf life than traditional sources such as meat and milk. As CEO Andreas pointed out in a 1993 interview with *Direct Marketing* magazine, ''You can feed 20 times as many people off of an acre of land by raising soy alone, than growing soy and feeding it to an animal and then eating that animal.'' Andreas called the development of the meatlike soy product ''the most important food development of this century.''

During the second half of the 1990s, ADM experienced significant growth, with revenues increasing from $12.56 billion to $16.11 billion from fiscal 1995 to fiscal 1998 before falling to $14.28 billion in 1999. Net earnings declined throughout this period, however, falling from the record level of $795.9 million in 1995 to $266 million in 1999. ADM blamed the declining results of the late 1990s largely on two coinciding phenomena: the Asian economic crisis, which later spread to Russia and Latin America, and record crop harvests. The economic downturn significantly dampened demand for protein and vegetable oils in the affected areas, while at the same time prices for farm commodities fell to their lowest levels in more than a decade.

The squeeze on profit margins led to increasing competition and consolidation in the food industry. Archer-Daniels-Midland was heavily involved in this consolidation and spent about $4.6 billion in the second half of the 1990s building new plants, expanding existing ones, and making numerous acquisitions. In mid-1997 ADM paid $470 million for the cocoa business of W.R. Grace & Co., thereby entering the chocolate and cocoa industry. The company quickly added six additional cocoa-processing plants purchased from E D & F Main Group PLC for $223 million. ADM organized these operations as its ADM Cocoa Division, which by the end of the 1990s was grinding 450,000 metric tons of cocoa beans per year, about 20 percent of the world crop. Also in 1997 the company acquired Quincy, Illinois-based soybean processor Moorman Manufacturing Co. for $296 million; purchased a 42 percent stake in United Grain Growers of Canada, a firm involved in grain merchandising and other agricultural activities; acquired a 30 percent stake in Minnesota Corn Processors, operator of wet corn milling plants in Minnesota and Nebraska; and spent $258 million for a 22 percent interest in Mexico-based Gruma S.A. de C.V., the world's largest producer and marketer of corn flour and tortillas. During this period ADM also formed a number of joint ventures, including International Malting Company, 40 percent owned by ADM and 60 percent by the LeSaffre Company, which operated barley malting plants in the United States, Australia, Canada, and France; ADM-Riceland Partnership, a 50–50 venture with Riceland Foods Inc., which processed rice and rice products; and a joint venture with Gruma, 40 percent owned by ADM, that operated seven wheat flour mills in Mexico. The most significant divestments during the later 1990s were those of Supreme Sugar and British Arkady.

Many of these deals occurred after G. Allen Andreas, nephew of Dwayne Andreas, was named CEO in April 1997. Allen Andreas's path to the top was cleared following the downfall of Michael D. Andreas, Dwayne's son and heir-apparent, in a highly publicized price-fixing scheme. The scheme first came to light in 1995 when Mark E. Whitacre, a whistleblower for the FBI, was fired by ADM from his position as head of its BioProducts division for allegedly embezzling millions of dollars from the company. Whitacre had been secretly acting as an informant to the FBI, providing the bureau with documentation, including audio- and videotapes, of alleged price-fixing schemes involving three products derived from corn: lysine, high-fructose corn syrup, and citric acid. At the center of the collusion were two top ADM executives: Vice-Chairman Michael Andreas and Terrance S. Wilson, head of the company's Corn Processing division. In late 1996, following guilty pleas by its partners in price fixing (including Ajinomoto Co. and Kyowa Hakko Kogyo, both of Japan), Archer-Daniels-Midland pleaded guilty to two counts of fixing prices for lysine, a hot-selling livestock feed additive, and for citric acid, and agreed to pay $100 million in fines, by far the largest criminal antitrust settlement in history. By late 1998 the company had paid nearly another $100 million to settle lawsuits brought by customers and investors. Whitacre in 1998 was sentenced to nine years in prison for swindling $9.5 million from ADM; the following year he was sentenced to an additional 20 months for his role in price-fixing at ADM (he had originally been given immunity in the price-fixing case but it was stripped after prosecutors learned of the embezzlement). Wilson retired from ADM in 1996 and Michael Andreas went on an indefinite leave of absence. They both were convicted by a federal jury of price fixing in 1998, and began serving two-year sentences in October 1999. In addition, they were each fined $350,000.

Archer-Daniels-Midland's legal difficulties were far from over. The company faced a number of class-action civil antitrust lawsuits, the largest of which involved purchasers of high-fructose corn syrup—including beverage giants PepsiCo, Inc., and the Coca-Cola Company—which could cost ADM and other defendants hundreds of millions of dollars. ADM was also the subject of government investigations in Europe and Mexico. At the end of the 20th century, Archer-Daniels-Midland faced the challenge of overcoming the huge amounts of negative publicity that had resulted from the various price-fixing probes and suits. It appeared that it would take years before the aura of scandal would be removed from the ADM name.

Principal Subsidiaries

ADM Agri-Industries Ltd. (Canada); ADM Europe BV (Netherlands); ADM Europoort BV (Netherlands); ADM/Growmark River Systems, Inc.; ADM Beteiligungs GmbH (Germany); ADM International Ltd. (U.K.); ADM Investor Services, Inc.; ADM Ireland Holdings Ltd.; ADM Milling Co.; ADM Oelmuhlen GmbH & Co. KG (Germany); ADM Ringaskiddy (Ireland); ADM Transportation Co.; ADMIC Investments NV (Netherlands Antilles); Agrinational Insurance Company; Agrinational Ltd. (Cayman Islands); Alfred C. Toepfer International (Germany; 50%); American River Transportation Co.; Ardanco, Inc. (Guam); Collingwood Grain, Inc.; Compagnie Industrielle Et Financiere (CIP) (Luxembourg; 42%); Consolidated Nutrition, L.C. (50%); Erith Oil Works Ltd. (U.K.); Fleischmann Malting Company, Inc.; Gruma S.A. de C.V. (Mexico; 22%); Hickory Point Bank & Trust Co.; Midland Stars, Inc.; Oelmuhle Hamburg AG (Germany; 95%); Premiere Agri Technologies Inc.; Tabor Grain Co.

Principal Divisions

ADM North American Oilseed Processing Division; ADM South American Oilseed Processing Division; ADM Cocoa Division; ADM BioProducts Division; ADM Animal Health and Nutrition Division; ADM Food Additives Division; ADM Nutraceutical Division; ADM Protein Specialties Division; ADM Transportation Division; ADM Research Division.

Principal Competitors

Ag Processing Inc; Agribrands International, Inc.; Ajinomoto Co., Inc.; The Andersons, Inc.; Bartlett and Company; Cargill, Incorporated; Cenex Harvest States Cooperatives; ConAgra, Inc.; ContiGroup Companies, Inc.; Corn Products International, Inc.; Eridania Beghin-Say; Farmland Industries, Inc.; GROWMARK Inc.; Pioneer Hi-Bred International, Inc.; Riceland Foods, Inc.; The Scoular Company; Southern States Cooperative, Incorporated; Tate & Lyle PLC; Universal Corporation.

Further Reading

Brinkman, Paul, "ADM Execs Report to Federal Prison," *Decatur (Ill.) Herald & Review,* October 6, 1999.

——, "ADM Focuses on Ethics in Wake of Price-Fixing Case," *Decatur (Ill.) Herald & Review,* July 11, 1999.

Burton, Thomas M., et al., "Corn Plot: Investigators Suspect a Global Conspiracy in Archer-Daniels Case," *Wall Street Journal,* July 28, 1995, pp. A1+.

Henkoff, Ronald, "The ADM Tale Gets Even Stranger," *Fortune,* May 13, 1996, pp. 113–14, 116, 118, 120.

——, "Betrayal," *Fortune,* February 3, 1997, pp. 82–85, 87.

Kahn, E.J., Jr., *Supermarketer to the World: The Story of Dwayne Andreas, CEO of Archer Daniels Midland,* New York: Warner, 1991, 320 p.

Kilman, Scott, "ADM Ex-Officials Get 2 Years in Jail in Sign of Tougher Antitrust Penalties," *Wall Street Journal,* July 12, 1999, p. A4.

——, "ADM Warns Grain Suppliers to Start Segregating Genetically Altered Crops," *Wall Street Journal,* September 2, 1999, p. A2.

——, "Jury Convicts Ex-Executives in ADM Case," *Wall Street Journal,* September 18, 1998, p. A3.

——, "Mark Whitacre Is Sentenced to 9 Years for Swindling $9.5 Million from ADM," *Wall Street Journal,* March 5, 1998, p. B5.

Kilman, Scott, and Thomas M. Burton, "Three Ex-ADM Executives Are Indicted: Wilson, Michael Andreas, and Informant Whitacre Cited in Antitrust Case," *Wall Street Journal,* December 4, 1996, p. A3.

Kilman, Scott, Bruce Ingersoll, and Jill Abramson, "Risk Averse: How Dwayne Andreas Rules Archer-Daniels by Hedging His Bets," *Wall Street Journal,* October 27, 1995, pp. A1+.

Lieber, James B., *Rats in the Grain: The Dirty Tricks of the "Supermarket to the World," Archer Daniels Midland,* New York: Four Walls Eight Windows, 1999.

Melcher, Richard A., "All Roads Lead to ADM," *Business Week,* September 23, 1996, p. 42.

——, "Into the Harsh Glare at Archer Daniels," *Business Week,* October 23, 1995, pp. 34–35.

Melcher, Richard A. Greg Burns, and Douglas Harbrecht, "It Isn't Dwayne's World Anymore," *Business Week,* November 18, 1996, pp. 82, 84.

Neal, Mollie, "Reaping the Rewards of Skillful Marketing While Helping Humanity," *Direct Marketing,* September 1993, pp. 24–26.

Noah, Timothy, "EPA Came Through for Archer-Daniels-Midland Soon After Andreas's Role at Presidential Dinner," *Wall Street Journal,* July 6, 1994, p. A20.

Sachar, Laura, "Top Seed," *Financial World,* May 3, 1988, pp. 2–28.

Upbin, Bruce, "Vindication," *Forbes,* November 17, 1997, pp. 52+.

Whitacre, Mark, "My Life As a Corporate Mole for the FBI," *Fortune,* September 4, 1995, pp. 52+.

—April Dougal Gasbarre
—updated by David E. Salamie

Arthur Murray International, Inc.

1077 Ponce De Leon Blvd.
Coral Gables, Florida 33134
U.S.A.
Telephone: (305) 445-9645
Fax: (305) 445-0451
Web site: http://www.arthurmurray.com

Private Company
Incorporated: 1946
Employees: 30
Sales: $50 million (1998 est.)
NAIC: 611610 Dance Studios

Arthur Murray International, Inc. is a private dance instructional company best known for its ''footprints'' style of teaching dance. The company consists of approximately 275 franchised studios in eight countries including the United States, Australia, Canada, Germany, Israel, Japan, Italy, and South Africa. Former staff members who have worked their way up in the company own and operate the franchised studios. These owners typically began their careers with Arthur Murray as dance instructors, realized the opportunity of operating a studio, and reached executive level. Arthur Murray staff members were eligible to become franchisees within just a few years of beginning as teachers. Sales for Arthur Murray International during the late 1990s amounted to an estimated $50 million.

The company was designed to teach people to dance in the simplest fashion in order for them to build confidence and poise, find a fun way to exercise, and meet new people. The program was structured with four basic movements, from which combinations were derived. The first lesson was free and, thereafter, lessons averaged about $40 and ranged in skill from introductory to competition-level programs. Not only did Arthur Murray offer basic dance programs based on skill level, the company also offered extended curriculums covering virtually the entire spectrum of dance.

Early 1900s: Murray Teichman's New Career

Arthur Murray International, Inc. was founded by an ambitious man named Murray Teichman who, in 1912 decided to teach dance in the evenings at New York City's Grand Central Palace in order to make some extra money while working in an architectural office during the day. He did this for two years until he accepted a position as a full-time dance instructor for G. Hepburn Wilson, the first instructor to offer individual dance lessons as opposed to class lessons. It was around this time, in 1914, that Murray Teichman met the Baroness de Kuttleson. She convinced him to change his name to Arthur Murray and worked with him as his dance partner in Asheville, North Carolina, in a resort called the Battery Park Hotel.

In 1919 Arthur Murray enrolled at Georgia Tech for business administration and taught dance in his spare time at the Grill Room of the resort hotel, the Georgian Terrace. He had over 1,000 children enrolled in his dance lessons, all varying in age groups and social levels. Clients included people such as famed golfer Bobby Jones and the Chandler twins of the Coca-Cola estate. Murray earned $15,000 per year teaching dance in this manner, a major achievement at that time.

The first time dance music was broadcast live on the radio was on March 27, 1920, and was credited to Arthur Murray. He arranged the event using Georgia Tech students and transmitted the music from the radio station, which was only just a few miles away from the Georgia Tech affair. The novel event received national coverage.

1920s–30s: First Losses, Then Gains, Then Franchising

At about this same time in 1920, Murray began a mail-order business headlined, ''Learn to Dance at Home'' using a new ''kinetoscope'' technology which included a toy moving-picture device. He ordered 1,000 kinetoscopes and placed ads with coupons. He had an abundance of replies so he placed more ads. However, the kinetoscope manufacturer went bankrupt and Murray did not get his money back. This was the first decline Murray felt since he had begun profiting in dance instruction.

Due to the difficulty he was experiencing with the mail-order business, Murray then came up with the idea of the ''footprints'' style of teaching dance, now an Arthur Murray trademark. Since he was able to outline the dance steps and formulate a proposal, he obtained a loan and began a new mail-

Company Perspectives:

Dancing can lead to romantic situations or can simply be an enjoyable, friendly interaction between two people . . . the choice being a mutual one by both partners. At Arthur Murray, dancing is a social pursuit. Dance partners cannot help but take an interest in the person in their arms. Naturally, on the dance floor there are many introductions and new friendships begin when the music stops. Through dancing, many people experience personal improvements in other areas too—hair styles and general appearance. Consequently, a positive personality can be developed through exposure to a dance environment such as that found at the Arthur Murray Franchised Dance studios.

order business. Murray created a dance instruction book using the footprints diagrams and placed a few newspaper ads. He decided that people would not accept the latest dance trends from Georgia and he moved his office to Fifth Avenue in New York and hired a secretary to handle the responses to the ads and the mail orders. The courses sold for $10, however business was slow and Murray suffered financially.

Murray then decided to leave Atlanta and move to New York in 1923. He placed an ad entitled ''How I Became Popular Overnight'' in a national magazine. He received 37,000 replies. Then he ran the same ad in the *New York Times* Book Section. He enjoyed similar success and business started to pick up again. By the spring of 1925, when Murray married Kathryn, his mail-order business was six years old, netting $35,000 per year, and more than five million Americans had learned to dance through the mail. After that, when advertising costs increased, Murray abandoned the mail-order business and returned to personal dance instruction.

The 1920s were difficult for business, especially during the stock market crash of 1929. The Arthur Murray studio was located at 11 East 43rd Street in New York. Before the crash, it was utilizing six floors for its sessions. However, the studio survived the Depression with only two floors remaining active.

After the Depression, Murray used health concerns as a means to promote dance lessons. He developed an organizational magazine called the *Murray-Go-Round,* which still exists today. It was in the magazine and the advertisements that Murray conveyed the idea of dance as a way to develop confidence, exercise, and become popular.

In 1937, Arthur Murray developed the Big Apple dance with given ''call'' names such as ''Peel the Apple'' and ''Cut the Apple.'' Just one year later, John Hennesey, general manager of the Statler Hotels, requested that Murray send his instructors to the Statler chain of hotels. Murray did, but with a business deal that the teachers send a percentage of what they made to him and keep the rest. This began the Arthur Murray franchise system and, in 1938, the first franchised Arthur Murray school opened in Minneapolis. By 1946, there were 72 franchised studios grossing almost $20 million per year and Arthur Murray was incorporated. At that time, students were paying for lessons at $4 to $10 per hour.

1950s: Arthur Murray and Television

Arthur Murray began his venture into the world of television by buying five 15-minute spots on CBS in July 1950. He also convinced his wife, Kathryn, to teach for the show. Before producing the third show, Murray bought a half-hour series on ABC for the summer and called the show the ''Arthur Murray Dance Party.'' Two years later, by the summer of 1952, the ''Arthur Murray Dance Party'' had broadcast 100 shows and had signed its first sponsor, General Foods. During this time, new student enrollments averaged at about 2,000 per week. Finally, from April 1957 through 1961, Murray included famous stars in his dance competitions on the ''Arthur Murray Dance Party.'' Numbering among the studio's famous student clientele were Johnny Carson, Mr. & Mrs. Merv Griffin, Bob Hope, Katherine Hepburn, Ed Sullivan, Don Ameche, Helen Hays, Joey Bishop, Jane Fonda, and Kris Kristofferson.

1960s: Style and Management Changes

The 1960s brought dance style changes. The Twist in 1961 replaced romantic, social dances. For Arthur Murray, this meant a decline in business for a couple of years. In 1964, Arthur and Kathryn Murray retired from active participation in Arthur Murray International, Inc. George B. Theiss, along with Phillip Masters, Samuel Costello, and other investors, bought the company. Theiss became president and Masters took the position of chairman. Theiss began his career with Arthur Murray as a teacher, first learning the Arthur Murray Magic Step method in Madison, Wisconsin. He became a franchise owner and manager in 24 cities and one of the major franchisees of the company. Masters also became a teacher, and later, a franchise owner. He was named Zone Supervisor of the Arthur Murray studios in the Northeast.

With new leadership, Arthur Murray evinced a fresh vitality and approach to teaching dance. In 1967, Theiss coined the phrase ''Touch Dancing'' to refer to social or partnership dancing. From about 1968 onward, Touch Dancing remained popular in conjunction with such Latin dances as the Mambo, Merengue, and Tango.

1970s and 1980s: Disco and Touch Dancing

In December 1977, *Saturday Night Fever* was released. This marked a substantial increase in people taking lessons at the Arthur Murray studios. By 1978, everyone wanted to learn the Hustle and by mid-1979, the Fox Trot, Rumba, and Cha-Cha, all Touch Dances, were popular. During this time, Arthur Murray also hosted the first world championship competition to be held in the United States, in New York City.

Finally, while on a trip with his wife in Paris, Theiss found the Lambada. He brought it back to the United States and introduced it to the Arthur Murray Dance Board. Arthur Murray became the first dance school to teach the Lambada in the United States.

1990s and The New Millennium: The Health Concern

The 1990s brought tremendous change for both the Arthur Murray organization and American culture as a whole. Arthur

Key Dates:

1912: Murray Teichman begins teaching dance as a second job in the evenings.
1914: Teichman becomes the dance partner to the Baroness de Kuttleson, who also convinces him to change his name to Arthur Murray.
1920: Murray coordinates the world's first radio broadcast of live dance music for a group of Georgia Tech students.
1920: Murray begins his mail-order business, ''Learn to Dance at Home,'' which leads to his footprints style of teaching dance.
1923: Arthur Murray writes the ad headlined ''How I Became Popular Overnight.''
1925: Mail-order business nets $35,000 per year with more than five million Americans having learned to dance by mail; Arthur Murray returns to personal dance instruction.
1930: Arthur Murray starts an organizational magazine called the Murray-Go-Round.
1937: Arthur Murray develops the Big Apple dance given ''call'' names, such as ''Peel the Apple'' and ''Cut the Apple.''
1938: First official opening of a franchised school occurs in Minneapolis.
1946: Arthur Murray International incorporates; company has 72 franchised studios grossing nearly $20 million annually.
1950: Arthur Murray buys a half-hour show from ABC called the ''Arthur Murray Dance Party''; Murray's wife, Kathryn, teaches dance on the show.
1952: ''Arthur Murray Dance Party'' signs with their first sponsor, General Foods.
1964: Arthur Murray retires from active participation in the organization and George B. Theiss, along with Phillip Master, Samuel Costello, and other investors, buy the company.
1968: George B. Theiss coins the phrase ''Touch Dancing,'' popular among the Latin dances.
1991: Arthur Murray dies.
1995: Samuel Costello dies.
1999: Kathryn Murray dies.

Murray died in 1991. The company celebrated its 80th year in May 1993. Samuel Costello died in 1995. During that same year in November, Arthur Murray International invited presidential hopefuls to a Presidential Dance-Off, scheduled for February 1996. The idea came after the film *An American President* was released. In the movie, Michael Douglas told Annette Bening that he danced well because he took six lessons at Arthur Murray.

In terms of dance, people turned to a variety of line dances. Some lasted only a couple of months, while others, like the Macarena, lasted a couple of years. By 1996, Latin dances were extremely popular. Ballroom and competitive dancing was on the rise as it came to be known as ''Dance Sport.'' Along with this trend of ''Sport Dancing,'' came the introduction of competitive dance in the future Olympics.

The idea of dance as a sport seemingly paralleled the nation's concern with health in the 1990s. During this time, an increasing number of Americans exercised, dieted, and looked after their physical and psychological health. Indeed, health became of paramount interest for many people in the 1990s due to mounting job pressures and life stressors.

Proven to be a health benefit, dance instruction from Arthur Murray was now being used for physical therapy in hospitals such as Walter Reed in Washington, D.C. The medical profession had helped the Arthur Murray business by recognizing dance as both a physical and psychological benefit, making dance one of the ideal exercises. Dance, a light aerobic workout, was a stress and tension reducer and could even help people lose weight. Dance exercise became fun because lessons were taught as part of an enjoyable social event. Studies concluded dance to be one of the top five physical activities out of 60 choices. Due to all these benefits, physicians and psychiatrists were recommending dance as a means to healthier physicality and mentality.

All these factors benefited the Arthur Murray studios, and the company continued to promote a healthy well-being as part of the benefits of taking lessons. ''Ballroom dance is a rigorous activity that uses the larger muscle groups, and is usually done over the course of an hour, or an entire evening,'' said Theiss. ''It's most frequently compared to ice dancing, and no one would question the athletic ability of an ice skater. Since we work without gliding across the ice, it's possible that a competitive ballroom dancer might even be in better shape than a figure skater.'' Firmly rooted as one of the founding forces in the dance instruction field, Arthur Murray International could well be expected to maintain its prominence, no matter the changing trends and lifestyles of its constituency, for years and years to come.

Principal Subsidiaries

Arthur Murray Studios.

Principal Competitors

Dance America; Fred Astaire; YWCA.

Further Reading

Murray, Kathryn, and Betty Hannah Hoffman, *My Husband, Arthur Murray,* New York: Simon and Schuster, 1960.

—Kimbally A. Medeiros

Artisan Entertainment Inc.

2700 Colorado Avenue; Second Floor
Santa Monica, California 90404
U.S.A.
Telephone: (310) 449-9200
Fax: (310) 255-3940
Web site: http://www.artisanent.com

Private Company
Incorporated: 1984 as International Video Entertainment
Employees: 160
Sales: $180 million (1998 est.)
NAIC: 512110 Video Production and Distribution

Artisan Entertainment Inc. produces, distributes, and markets motion pictures. Specializing in independent films, Artisan has had box office triumphs with movies such as *The Blair Witch Project.* However, the bulk of Artisan's revenues are derived from its home video distribution arm, which controls the licenses to a library of over 2,000 movies including *Terminator 2: Judgment Day, Dirty Dancing,* and *Reservoir Dogs.* Artisan's library enables the company to remain independent in an era when most other formerly unaffiliated production companies (often referred to as "indies") have been purchased by major studios. Artisan also operates a division that produces, acquires, and distributes programming for cable and pay-per-view television. Owned by an investor group headed by Bain Capital, Artisan has undergone several changes in ownership and management. Founded in 1981 as Family Home Video, the company's name was changed first to International Video Entertainment (I'VE), later to LIVE Entertainment Cos., and finally in 1998 to Artisan.

Formation of Original Company: 1981

Noel C. Bloom founded Family Home Entertainment in 1981. Bloom, who had initially entered the video business as a distributor of pornographic videos, recognized the growth potential of the fledgling home video industry. Although videocassette recorders were still a novelty at the time, Bloom forged relationships with several film production companies which provided Family Home Entertainment with the license to manufacture and distribute video copies of films. Family Home Entertainment concentrated mostly on children's titles.

In 1984, Bloom incorporated his enterprise as International Video Entertainment (I'VE), which included the Family Home Entertainment label, as well as USA Home Video, Monterey Video, and Thrillervideo. By 1986, video distribution had become such a lucrative operation that companies such as I'VE were able to help underwrite the costs of movies in exchange for their video rights. Securing the rights to even a single popular title could be a boon for a company. As Bloom commented to the *San Diego Union-Tribune* in 1984, for example, distributing Bo Derek's film *Bolero* was like "shipping gold."

Under the Leadership of Carolco: 1987–93

Despite its early successes, however, I'VE fell deeply into debt during its expansion. At the close of 1986, I'VE posted a net loss of $20 million, despite an infusion of cash resulting from the purchase of 25 percent of the company by Carolco Pictures Inc.—an independent film company responsible for the phenomenally popular "Rambo" movies. "I'VE was a mess, probably on the verge of bankruptcy," a securities analyst told the *Los Angeles Times* in 1986. "Carolco bought . . . in the hope and belief they could turn it around." By January 1987, Carolco had completed its acquisition of I'VE, and the video distributor became a subsidiary of Carolco.

Faced with I'VE's outstanding potential–and at the same time its substantial problems—Carolco appointed Jose Menendez, a well-respected former executive at RCA, to head up its new subsidiary. Menendez immediately returned I'VE to profitability by aggressively seeking video distribution contracts with independent producers. Relying on his strong Hollywood connections, Menendez sealed up deals with Ed Pressman (the producer of Oliver Stone's hit film *Wall Street*), as well as with action-picture star Sylvester Stallone. "Menendez . . . took a second-rate home video supplier and made a business out of it," an analyst told the *Los Angeles Daily News* on August 26, 1990.

In June 1987, Menendez oversaw I'VE's acquisition of Lieberman Enterprises, the second largest U.S. distributor of

Company Perspectives:

Artisan Entertainment is not afraid to step up and assume the mantle of the industry's number one full-service independent film studio. With its aggressive decision-making style, filmmaker-friendly approach, diverse holdings, and combined industry experience, Artisan's ascension is firmly on course.

music and home videos. With this purchase, I'VE could tap into Lieberman's substantial mass market distribution network to stores such as Wal-Mart in the Midwest. Menendez instituted additional changes when he cut I'VE's employees from 550 down to 167. The following year, I'VE was rechristened LIVE Entertainment. Profits for 1988 soared to $16 million, as LIVE released a number of hit rental titles such as *Teenage Mutant Ninja Turtles* and *Rambo III.*

The year 1989 brought further changes to LIVE. The company moved its headquarters from Thousand Oaks to Van Nuys, California. It also made its initial foray into the retail sector of the market in June of that year with its acquisition of BeckZack Corp., which controlled an 81-store chain of audio and home video retail stores called Strawberries. However, the year would prove more memorable because of Menendez's tragic death. Both he and his wife were shot repeatedly at close range in their Beverly Hills home, fueling rumors in the media of LIVE's supposed mob connections. Newspapers pondered whether Menendez's death was connected to I'VE's seedy roots (the California Attorney General had issued a report on organized crime in 1986 which fingered Bloom as a ''major distributor of X-rated movies,'' according to the August 25, 1989, *Wall Street Journal*). However, all such suppositions of a link between LIVE, organized crime, and Menendez's death were eventually refuted when Menendez's own sons—Lyle and Eric—were convicted of their father's heinous murder.

Shaken by the fallout, the company conducted an extensive search to find Menendez's successor. Finally, in 1990, Wayne Patterson, a former chairman of Pace Membership Warehouse, was named LIVE's chairman and chief executive officer. The company's troubles did not end, however. LIVE's parent company, Carolco, fell prey to a host of financial problems. As the *Los Angeles Times* explained on January 21, 1991, ''Carolco ha[d] long been known for its big budget movies and lavish spending, even by Hollywood standards.'' The studio's free-wheeling ways racked up debt, which forced it to cut back on production. Since nearly one-third of LIVE's revenues were derived from sales of videotapes of Carolco films, Carolco's troubles directly impacted LIVE. Moreover, LIVE's chain of retail stores began to report heavy losses.

LIVE's resources were further taxed by the company's decision to enter into strategic partnerships with several movie companies. In 1990 alone, LIVE signed long-term pre-production deals to distribute videos from a slew of movie companies, including Miramax Films, New Visions Pictures, Avenue Pictures, Gladden Entertainment, Scotti Brothers Films, and Working Title Films. The same year, LIVE bought Munich-based VCL, the leading home video distributor in Germany. This was an important transaction because it marked LIVE's first effort to establish for itself an international presence. LIVE also acquired Navarre Corp., a music and PC software distributor that LIVE integrated into its Lieberman operations. Adding to this spate of acquisitions, LIVE's Strawberries division purchased Waxie Maxie, a 33-store chain of audio and video products. But LIVE was not finished. In 1991, it completed a deal that had been nearly a year in the making, when it spent over $60 million to bring Vestron, Inc. into its fold. This new property was a video distributor and movie maker that had been faltering ever since the tremendous success of its 1987 release *Dirty Dancing.* However, this purchase made sense for LIVE because Vestron's video library included such profitable titles as *Platoon* and the ''National Geographic'' series, as well as the ever popular *Dirty Dancing.*

LIVE and Carolco proposed merging in 1991. Late in the year, however, both companies' stock prices dropped precipitously, forestalling any future discussion of unification—the spotlight focused on both companies only illuminated the financial difficulties each faced. In an effort to pare its operations, LIVE sold Lieberman Enterprises to Handleman Co. Further shaking up the company, CEO Patterson resigned in December 1991, and was replaced by David Mount, formerly the head of LIVE's Home Video Division.

Financial Collapse in 1993

Although LIVE took in a significant amount of money on the strength of its 1991 video release of *Terminator 2: Judgment Day,* the company reported losses of $107 million on earnings of $361 million. LIVE scored some commercial success in 1992 with its release on video of the Academy Award-winning film *The Crying Game,* as well as *Basic Instinct.* Even more noteworthy was LIVE's entrance into movie production in 1992 with *Reservoir Dogs* and *Light Sleeper.* Nevertheless, saddled particularly by the albatross of its retail division, LIVE lost $14.8 million in 1992, and total revenue for the year had dropped 19 percent. By the close of 1992, LIVE was ''[c]onstrained by debt and a lack of capital, and in danger of defaulting on its bonds,'' according to the January 11, 1994, *Los Angeles Times.* As a result of its dire financial situation, the company filed a ''prepackaged'' bankruptcy petition in February 1993.

LIVE's time in bankruptcy proceedings was mercifully short. The company emerged in March 1993, with court approval to issue new notes and preferred stock in order to retire its old debt. Carolco survived its own restructuring, and surrendered its share of LIVE to a group of major investors, led by Pioneer Electronic Corporation.

Charting a New Course: 1994

In 1994, Roger Burlage took the helm at LIVE. His influence as CEO was profound. As the *Hollywood Reporter* explained on April 21, 1997, Burlage was ''instrumental in transforming LIVE from being essentially an acquirer and supplier of home video product into a diversified entertainment company that compete[d] with major Hollywood studios.'' One of his first actions was to shed LIVE's foundering and unprofitable retail division. After selling Strawberries and Waxie Maxie, he turned

Key Dates:

1981: Family Home Entertainment is formed.
1982: Company changes name to International Video Entertainment (I'VE).
1984: I'VE is incorporated.
1986: I'VE is acquired by Carolco Pictures Inc.
1988: I'VE is renamed LIVE Entertainment.
1989: LIVE acquires Strawberries, an East Coast chain of retail audio and video stores.
1991: LIVE purchases most assets of video distributor and movie maker Vestron, Inc.
1992: LIVE begins producing movies.
1997: LIVE is acquired by Bain Capital and converted to a private corporation.
1998: LIVE is renamed Artisan Entertainment and relocates to Santa Monica, California.

his attention to diversifying the company. To this end, Burlage launched a domestic television production unit and steered the company toward devoting more energy to producing and distributing its own original films. Nevertheless, LIVE did not abandon its primary focus on video distribution. In 1994 the company released the Academy Award-winning *The Piano,* followed the next year by the hit movie *Stargate.* After LIVE returned to profitability in 1995, the company debuted five films for theatrical release, including *The Substitute, The Arrival,* and *Trees Lounge.*

New Ownership, New Direction: 1997

Despite Burlage's efforts to transform LIVE into a new sort of company—one rooted in movie production as well as home video distribution—his freedom to operate was constrained by pressure from LIVE's shareholders, particularly after the publicly traded company lost $3.4 million in 1996. ''His hands have been tied by the market,'' an analyst noted to the Hollywood Reporter. In April 1997, this situation changed dramatically, when LIVE agreed to be acquired for $150 million in cash by an investor group led by Bain Capital of Boston and Richland Gordon & Co. Not only did this transaction provide LIVE with the $49 million it needed to pay off long-term debt, but it also made LIVE a private company, no longer dependent on the whims of the market. After settling a shareholder suit in July related to the buyout, LIVE's new owners quickly took action to streamline the company. In August, 40 of LIVE's 166 jobs were cut, and it was widely speculated that LIVE's investors wanted to strip down the company and sell it in a few months, or else abandon film production altogether.

LIVE's new management was perfectly frank about their goals for the company. As the *Los Angeles Times* explained on July 27, 1998, the three leading voices at LIVE ''loudly vowed to turn it into the preeminent independent motion picture studio.'' Although Burlage was initially retained as LIVE's chairman, new executives Bill Block, Mark Curcio, and Amir Malin strove to craft a new image for LIVE, as well as a new purpose. Block, a former ICM agent, and Malin, once a partner at October Films, were installed as LIVE's co-presidents, and began to plot LIVE's creative course. Curcio, who had been a financial consultant at Bain Capital, oversaw financial matters.

Block, Malin, and Curcio sought to explore LIVE's potential as an independent film producer. Other prominent indies, such as Miramax, New Line, Orion, and October Films, had recently been subsumed into larger movie studios. But LIVE afforded unique opportunities. Unlike almost all other independent studios, LIVE controlled one of the largest home video libraries in the country. ''From both a management and shareholder perspective, we saw tremendous value in LIVE's video library,'' Malin told *Video Business.* ''It's very difficult for companies to survive without a library that offsets the vagaries of the box office.'' The steady stream of revenue that LIVE's home video distribution provided could carry the company steadily through the financial turbulence of independent film production.

Soon after the management trio took control of LIVE, the company rereleased the 1987 hit film *Dirty Dancing* (whose rights it had acquired in the Vestron deal) to theaters nationwide. In September 1997, LIVE debuted a home-grown product, director Wes Craven's horror film *Wishmaster,* which opened in 2,500 U.S. theaters. In October 1997, LIVE broke new ground again when it signed a long-term contract with Showtime Networks Inc., in which Showtime (a premium cable television channel) received exclusive television rights for all LIVE films released at theaters between September 1, 1997, and December 31, 2000.

Birth of Artisan Entertainment

After these accomplishments, LIVE focused on polishing its image. ''We are tarnished by the past,'' Curcio confided in the *Los Angeles Times* on July 27, 1998, referring to the Menendez scandal, as well as to some mediocre films LIVE had created. To emphasize a break with the past, the company changed its name to Artisan Entertainment in April 1998. ''We decided Artisan best described our drive and dedication in bringing quality entertainment to audiences worldwide,'' Curcio said in a press release explaining the company's new moniker. At the same time, Artisan moved its corporate headquarters from the San Fernando Valley to Santa Monica, and into a facility that could not only house all of the company's growing divisions, but was also closer to the Hollywood pulse. Artisan also moved into a new loft space in New York's Tribeca district to shore up the company's East Coast and international connections. Even more important to Artisan's reinvention were the relationships it formed with top filmmakers. With acclaimed directors such as Steven Soderburgh, Artisan sought only financial stakes and did not meddle in creative decisions. The strategy paid off. In 1998, Artisan released to theaters *Pi, Permanent Midnight, Ringmaster,* and *The Cruise. Pi*—whose rights Artisan had procured at the Sundance Film Festival—won both critical and commercial acclaim.

While Artisan broke into independent film production, the company continued to develop the most revenue-generating portion of its business. In 1997 and 1998, Artisan acquired three home video catalogues. After purchasing the distribution rights to Hallmark Home Entertainment (including Hallmark Hall of Fame television movies) and Cabin Fever, Artisan acquired the Republic Entertainment division of Spelling Entertainment Group Inc. With the Spelling deal, Artisan obtained the rights to distribute such classic films as *It's a Wonderful Life* and *High Noon,* as well as modern movies and the home video releases of television shows including *Twin Peaks.*

Although 1998 proved overall to be a mediocre year for Artisan's theatrical releases, the company hit a gold mine in 1999 when it bought the distribution rights to *The Blair Witch Project* at the 1999 Sundance Film Festival. This edgy film about three college students who set off into the woods to explore local legends about witchcraft cost only $35,000 to make. Artisan concentrated its marketing on the Internet, both in an effort to keep costs down and to reach young adult consumers. In its first weekend at theaters, *Blair Witch* earned $29.2 million, which *Red Herring* termed "an unheard-of amount for a film with no big stars, no high-powered directors. . . ."

Despite the vicissitudes of the film market, Artisan's future prospects looked bright. The company controlled a video library of over 6,600 titles. Curcio told the July 26, 1999, *Wall Street Journal* that Artisan's 1998 revenues had topped $180 million, and the company had earned a net profit of $5 million. Moreover, he anticipated 1999 revenue to exceed $300 million, and net income to break $7 million. Artisan pledged not to overextend itself in its nascent role as an indie film studio. The company set the goal of making (or acquiring as it did with *Blair Witch* and *Pi*) eight to ten films per year.

Principal Competitors

DreamWorks SKG; Trimark Holdings, Inc.; GoodTimes Entertainment; Viacom Inc.; Sony Pictures Entertainment; Metro-Goldwyn-Mayer Inc.; Time Warner Inc.

Further Reading

Apodaca, Patrice, "Video Firm Expected to Reduce Size Distribution," *Los Angeles Times,* January 21, 1992.

"The Bain Trust Behind Artisan," *Video Business,* July 27, 1998.

"Bolero Red Hot," *San Diego Union-Tribune,* October 25, 1984.

Creply, Michael, "Slain Entertainment Executive Jose Menendez's Conflict and Controversy," *Los Angeles Times,* August 25, 1989.

Daniels, Jeffrey, "LIVE Sold for $150 Million," *Hollywood Reporter,* April 27, 1997.

Hughes, Kathleen, and John Emschwiller, "Fuzzy Picture: Beverly Hills Murder of Executive and Wife Haunts a Video Firm," *Wall Street Journal,* August 25, 1989.

Orwall, Bruce, "Movies: Small Studio Brews a Success Mixing the Web and Edgy Film," *Wall Street Journal,* July 26, 1999.

Pendleton, Jennifer, "LIVE Entertainment Survives Tragedy Stronger Than Ever," *Los Angeles Daily News,* August 26, 1990.

Perkins, Anthony, "Tinseltown and the Incumbent Fallacy," *Red Herring,* October, 1999.

Wallace, Amy, "A Studio That Says, 'Roll 'Em' Movies," *Los Angeles Times,* July 27, 1998.

—Rebecca Stanfel

Aurora Foods Inc.

456 Montgomery Street
Suite 2200
San Francisco, California 94104
U.S.A.
Telephone: (415) 982-3019
Fax: (415) 982-3023
Web site: http://www.aurorafoods.com

Public Company
Incorporated: 1996 as Aurora Foods Holdings Inc.
Employees: 1,311
Sales: $789.2 million (1998)
Stock Exchanges: New York
Ticker Symbol: AOR
NAIC: 42242 Packaged Frozen Food Wholesalers; 42249 Other Grocery and Related Products Wholesalers

Aurora Foods Inc. produces and markets branded food products that have already been developed and established by other companies. These products have generally been in existence for some time and have achieved strong name recognition and good market position, but have been designated as non-core lines by their previous owners. Aurora's brands fall into two main categories: dry grocery and frozen foods. Through its dry grocery division, the company markets Duncan Hines baking mix products and Mrs. Butterworth's and Log Cabin syrup products. Its frozen foods division includes Van de Kamp's and Mrs. Paul's seafood products, Aunt Jemima frozen breakfast products, Celeste frozen pizzas, Chef's Choice frozen skillet meals, and Lender's Bagels. Aurora owns and operates its own frozen food manufacturing facilities, which are located in Jackson, Tennessee; Erie, Pennsylvania; and Yuba City, California. The company's dry grocery products, however, are produced by third-party manufacturing and packaging companies.

1995–97: Buying "Orphan" Brands

Aurora Foods' portfolio of branded products began when a San Francisco-based investment firm organized a group of private investors to acquire the Van de Kamp's frozen seafood line from Pillsbury. The investment firm behind the deal—Dartford Partnership L.L.C.—was headed by Ian Wilson, a long-term veteran of the food and beverage industry. Wilson, whose earlier background included a stint as president of Coca-Cola's Pacific Group and as CEO of Dole Food Co., had been buying and selling grain-based food businesses for more than ten years. When he organized the Van de Kamp's purchase, he planned to use it as a starting point for further brand purchases. Wilson's goal was to purchase product lines that had good brand equity and market position but that had been designated as non-core by their owners and were therefore being undermarketed and undermanaged. He believed that by nurturing and developing these neglected, "orphan" brands he could revitalize and grow them.

The Van de Kamp's line fit Wilson's profile of an "orphan" brand perfectly. With a history dating back to 1915, it was a market leader in the frozen seafood business but had been designated by Pillsbury as a non-core brand. Receiving little attention or marketing from Pillsbury, the line's revenues were gradually diminishing. In September 1995, Dartford Partnership purchased the Van de Kamp's business for $190 million. In addition to the seafood products, the acquisition included a small frozen dessert line.

In May 1996, Wilson made another branded product acquisition, purchasing the Mrs. Paul's frozen seafood line from the Campbell Soup Company. Mrs. Paul's was added to Van de Kamp's, Inc., the company Dartford had formed to acquire the Van de Kamp's line. Two more product lines joined the growing portfolio in July: Aunt Jemima frozen breakfasts and Celeste frozen pizzas. Both businesses, which were acquired from the Quaker Oats Company, were suffering from declining sales when Aurora purchased them.

Meanwhile, Dartford Partnership was putting together another acquisition. In December 1996, Dartford and two other investment groups—Fenway Partners, Inc. and McCown De Leeuw & Co., Inc.—banded together to purchase the Mrs. Butterworth's brand of syrups and pancake mixes. Forming a holding company called Aurora Foods Holdings, the investors acquired the syrup business from Unilever United States, Inc. for a purchase price of $114.1 million. Just a few months later,

Company Perspectives:

We aspire to be the leader in restoring and revitalizing well-known packaged food brands. As part of this mission we aim to: Build long term shareholder value; Develop and energize our employees; Form partnerships with our suppliers and customers; Exceed consumer expectations.

Aurora Foods made its second acquisition, purchasing the Log Cabin brand of syrups from Kraft Foods, Inc. for $222 million. Together, Mrs. Butterworth's and Log Cabin held the top position in the syrup market, with a combined share of 34 percent.

Early 1998: Van de Kamp's and Aurora Foods Merge

Aurora Foods kicked off 1998 with its largest acquisition to date. In January, the company purchased the Duncan Hines line of baking mixes from Procter & Gamble for $445 million. Duncan Hines had a 26 percent market share in cake and cupcake mixes and annual sales of approximately $250 million, but no longer fit with Procter & Gamble's growth strategy. Aurora, which had 1997 sales of around $200 million, more than doubled its size with the Duncan Hines purchase.

Under the terms of the acquisition, Aurora purchased the Duncan Hines production equipment, which was located at a plant in Jackson, Tennessee. The company then signed a five-year outsourcing agreement with Gilster-Mary Lee Corporation for production of Duncan Hines products. Aurora estimated that this outsourcing would result in a cost savings of $12.4 million.

Although Aurora Foods and Van de Kamp's were both owned by the same investment firms and were both formed to acquire and market branded products, the investors' original plan had been to keep the two companies separate. In the spring of 1998, however, it was decided that they should join forces in order to benefit from economies of scale. The newly formed company, Aurora Foods, Inc., was headquartered in San Francisco and had almost $1 billion in sales. Its chairman and CEO was Ian Wilson. Three other Dartford partners joined Wilson as vice-chairman, executive vice-president, and CFO of the newly formed company. A few months after the merger was complete, in June 1998, Aurora went public in an initial offering of 14.5 million shares priced at $21 each.

While Aurora worked to merge its operations and positioned itself for further growth, it simultaneously worked to revitalize its existing brands. The company's strategy for doing so was straightforward and formulaic. It consisted of reducing operating costs and then investing the operating savings in marketing programs and product innovation.

The cost reduction side of the formula was achieved largely by consolidation of operations, outsourcing, and maintaining an extremely low administrative overhead. For example, Aurora combined and streamlined its frozen seafood business by moving the Mrs. Paul's operation into the Van de Kamp's facilities. It cut costs by outsourcing the production of its Log Cabin and Mrs. Butterworth's syrups and Duncan Hines mixes. It also maintained an unusually small corporate staff, aggressively cutting out administrative redundancies. The results of the company's expense trimming added up to an annual savings of approximately $66 million and resulted in a lower cost of goods sold, and a higher gross profit margin.

The savings Aurora realized from its cost-reduction measures were poured into reinvigorating and marketing its brands. Wilson explained the company's strategy in a 1998 interview with *Milling & Baking News*. "In being non-core, none of these brands has had anything done to it," he said, adding "The attention has gone elsewhere. There's no new products, there's no new packaging, there's no media spending. The product gets managed for cash flow, and the first thing that gets taken away is the media spending and the consumer advertising. We add that back in, and take the brand back up to where it was before."

Aurora's first step toward breathing new life into its brands was to refocus consumers' attention on them. The company invested heavily in this effort, spending between 23 and 30 percent of its total sales on marketing and advertising as opposed to the industry average of 20 to 25 percent. This level of marketing was a substantial increase for all of Aurora's brands; for example, Duncan Hines' consumer advertising immediately doubled when it became an Aurora brand.

The development of new advertising campaigns was an important part of Aurora's marketing expense. In 1998, the company aired television advertising for its Log Cabin brand for the first time in five years, using a newly created slogan: "In the heart of every home, there's a little Log Cabin." Aurora also launched a new print and television ad campaign for Duncan Hines, featuring the tagline "You're why I bake a Duncan Hines cake." Aunt Jemima's, too, got new exposure through a series of print ads and television spots geared to kids on the popular Nickelodeon TV network.

Aurora did not rely solely on a beefed-up ad budget to boost sales. A second key component of the strategy was the introduction of new products. From its formation in 1995 to the middle of 1998, the company introduced more than 20 new products that built on its existing branded lines. The majority of the new products were premium seafood items rolled out under the Van de Kamp's and Mrs. Paul's names—such as teriyaki tuna, grilled lemon pepper and herb fish fillets, and salmon with dill sauce. Aurora also expanded the Celeste pizza line by adding the Mama Celeste Fresh Baked Rising Crust pizza in November 1997.

In addition to adding completely new products to its lines, Aurora reformulated several of its existing products, to make them more appealing to consumers. In 1998, the company reformulated its Duncan Hines brownie mixes to incorporate better chocolate flavoring systems. It also introduced a sugar-free version of its Log Cabin syrup. Aurora also developed new packaging for several of its brands. Aunt Jemima's packaging, which had been white, was redesigned in a bright red—to make it stand out in the freezer case. The standard, generic Log Cabin syrup bottle was replaced with a container in the shape of a log cabin, making it automatically more identifiable. The company also began producing a gallon jug of Mrs. Butterworth's syrup specifically designed to appeal to club stores.

Key Dates:

1995: Dartford Partnership organizes purchase of Van de Kamp's brand from Pillsbury.
1996: Van de Kamp's, Inc. acquires Mrs. Paul's, Aunt Jemima, and Celeste brands; Dartford Partnership and other investors form Aurora Foods Holdings Inc. to purchase Mrs. Butterworth's brand of syrups.
1997: Aurora Foods Holdings acquires Log Cabin brand of syrups.
1998: Aurora Foods Holdings acquires Duncan Hines brand; Van de Kamp's, Inc. and Aurora Foods Holdings merge to form Aurora Foods Inc.; newly formed Aurora Foods Inc. goes public.
1999: Aurora acquires Chef's Choice and Lender's Bagels brands.

Aurora's well-defined approach was proving successful. All of its brands had been on a downward trajectory when Aurora acquired them—and each one showed significantly improved sales growth within one year of acquisition. The most dramatic example of this was Celeste pizza. Prior to being acquired by Aurora, Celeste's sales had diminished by approximately 17 percent over two years. Under Aurora's management, however, the downward slide was reversed; Celeste's sales grew by 31 percent during the first two years after its acquisition. Sales of Mrs. Paul's, Aunt Jemima, and Duncan Hines products also showed notable improvement almost immediately.

1999 and Beyond

Having established a formula that worked, Aurora continued to employ it in 1999. In January and February, the company rolled out several new products—including Aunt Jemima mini-pancakes and french toast sticks, Van de Kamp's and Mrs. Paul's Seafood Tenders and Seafood Selects, and a series of Mrs. Butterworth's syrups in different flavors. Also in February, Aurora began airing new advertising campaigns for several of its brands.

In April 1999, Aurora made its first acquisition in more than a year, purchasing the Chef's Choice brand from Seattle-based Sea Coast Foods, Inc. for $50 million. Chef's Choice was a line of ten skillet meals—entire meals that could be prepared in a single skillet in under 15 minutes. Skillet meals were a rapidly growing segment of the grocery industry, with industrywide sales growing from $35 million in 1997 to $125 million in 1998. Chef's Choice itself had seen rapid growth; its sales had increased from $27 million in 1997 to $57 million in 1998.

Another acquisition followed a few months later. In September 1999, Aurora announced that it had agreed to purchase the Lender's Bagel line from Kellogg Company for $275 million. Lender's was an easy market leader, with a 77 percent share of the frozen bagel market and a 69 percent share of the refrigerated segment. The acquisition, which was completed in November, boosted Aurora's total sales by approximately $200 million.

Meanwhile, the company continued to improve and expand upon its existing products. Early in 1999, it unveiled new, vertical package designs for its entire Van de Kamp's and Mrs. Paul's lines. The new packages freed up shelf space, which was a benefit to retailers. Moreover, because no other frozen seafood brand had vertical packaging, the new design was easier for consumers to spot. Aurora also made some modifications to its Aunt Jemima waffles, giving them a new round shape and increasing the waffle count per box.

Aurora's goals for the future were ambitious. The company aimed for annual revenue growth of eight to ten percent and operating profit growth of more than 15 percent. To attain its goals, Aurora planned to continue keeping operating expenses low and marketing budgets high. More product line extensions, reformulations, and package redesigns were in the works. The company also planned to broaden its distribution to include more restaurants, club stores, and mass merchandisers.

Acquisition of new brands was another likely avenue of growth. In its 1998 annual report, Aurora indicated that it continued to seek new ''orphan'' brands that met with its criteria—strong market position, good brand equity, and potential for growth.

Principal Divisions

Dry Grocery Division; Frozen Food Division.

Principal Competitors

Bestfoods; ConAgra, Inc.; The Earthgrains Company; General Mills, Inc.; Interstate Bakeries Corporation; Kellogg Company; Kraft Foods, Inc.; The Pillsbury Company; The Quaker Oats Company; Unilever PLC; Vlasic Foods International Inc.

Further Reading

Barron, Kelly, ''Brand Orphanage,'' *Forbes*, November 15, 1999, p. 100.
Davidson, Gordon, ''Growing Orphan Brands at Aurora Foods,'' *Milling & Baking News*, 1998.
Kennedy, Tony, ''Pillsbury Says It Has a Buyer for Van de Kamp's: Investors Would Pay $190 Million for Seafood Brand,'' *Minneapolis Star Tribune*, July 13, 1995, p. 1D.
Much, Marilyn, ''Food Drive: Aurora Becomes Foster Parent to Familiar 'Orphan' Brands,'' *Investor's Business Daily*, January 14, 1999.
''Procter & Gamble Sells Duncan Hines Baking Mixes to Another Ohio Firm,'' *Minneapolis Star Tribune*, December 9, 1997, p. 3D.

—Shawna Brynildssen

Balance Bar Company

1015 Mark Avenue
Carpinteria, California 93013
U.S.A.
Telephone: (805) 566-0234
Fax: (805) 566-0235
Web site: http://www.balance.com

Public Company
Incorporated: 1992 as Bio Foods Inc.
Employees: 80
Sales: $81.7 million (1998)
Stock Exchanges: NASDAQ
Ticker Symbol: BBAR
NAIC: 422480 Health Foods Wholesaling; 42249 Other Grocery and Related Product Wholesaling

Balance Bar Company is a leader in the nutritional foods and natural products industry. Natural products contain no artificial colors, flavors, chemicals, or preservatives. The firm develops and distributes popular lines of nutritional bars and drinks manufactured by another company. All Balance Bar products have 40 percent calories from carbohydrates, 30 percent from protein, and 30 percent from dietary fats. Competing firms also make products based on this controversial 40-30-30 Zone Diet, popularized by a 1995 best-selling book that recommended it as a way to lose weight. The firm distributes its products mainly through health food stores but also sells them in grocery stores, health clubs, drugstores, and mass merchandisers. Like many other firms, Balance Bar Company appeals to busy professionals who may not have time for a balanced meal or may need a nutritious snack. In the late 1990s the company added more products and fortified them with vitamins and herbs. A number of celebrity trainers and athletes use or endorse the firm's products. For example, the Los Angeles Lakers chose Balance Bar as the teams official bar.

Origins

The Balance Bar story begins with a California native named Barry Sears, who majored in chemistry at Occidental College in Los Angeles and then completed his Ph.D. in biochemistry at Indiana University. He continued his study of nutrition at Boston University and Massachusetts Institute of Technology. After his 53-year-old father died in 1972 and Sears himself was hospitalized with a heart problem in 1984, he focused on the role of fats in heart disease.

By the late 1980s Sears adopted what was known as the Zone Diet that called for 40 percent of daily caloric intake from carbohydrates and 30 percent each from fats and proteins. Most doctors considered this controversial diet to have far more fat and protein than needed. It also was similar to earlier diets promoted in the 1960s and 1970s by Dr. Robert Atkins and others.

In any case, Barry Sears began teaching others his nutritional concepts. For example, Garret Giemont, the Los Angeles Rams' former strength coach, in 1989 began encouraging team members to adopt Sears's diet. The Los Angeles Raiders, the Stanford University's men and women's swimming teams, and other athletes and trainers also embraced the Zone Diet.

Meanwhile, Sears and various family members and associates became entangled in what could be called ''bar wars'' that resulted in the formation of different companies, including the predecessor of the Balance Bar Company. In 1989 Barry Sears's sister Sheri fell in love with Bill Logue, a 55-year-old used car salesman who wanted to invest in her brother's Biosyn bars made under his direction by a Canadian firm. In 1990 she moved to San Diego, where she and Logue ran a firm distributing Biosyn bars. Logue invested his life savings in his company and asked Barry Sears to guarantee an ongoing supply of the Biosyn bars, but Sears had other plans.

In the early 1990s Barry Sears began a business relationship with Dick Lamb, a Biosyn bars consumer who had been a windsurfing champion, an Olympic judge, and the founder of a Santa Barbara sporting-goods manufacturer. Their lawyers were drawing up a contract to start a new company when the deal fell apart, due in part to Sears's past debt problems.

''In backing out of his deal with Lamb, Sears appears to have made a grievous business error,'' wrote Jessica Seigel in the February 1997 *Los Angeles Magazine*. Lamb said that Sears had told him a patent was pending on the nutrition bars, but the

Key Dates:

1992: Four entrepreneurs found Bio Foods Inc. in April.
1995: First major wholesale customer is obtained; Barry Sears publishes *The Zone.*
1997: Firm introduces Balance Drink Mix and begins expanding into grocery and other outlets.
1997: TV advertising is started.
1998: *Inc.* magazine ranks the firm as the nation's 14th fastest growing private company; IPO is completed and company changes name to Balance Bar Company in June.
1999: *Health Supplement Retailer* names Balance Bar as the "Best Selling Energy Bar" for the second year in a row.

lack of a patent allowed Lamb and his investors to contract directly with the Canadian manufacturer that controlled the formulas. Thus in 1992 Lamb, Tom Davidson, and two others founded Bio Foods Inc. in Santa Barbara, California, to distribute Balance Bars made by Bariatrix of Canada. Chairman Tom Davidson owned 45 percent of the firm, while Executive Vice-President Dick Lamb owned 11 percent.

Meanwhile, Sheri Sears and Bill Logue started their own company to sell a competing line of 40-30-30 nutrition bars. Based in San Diego, PR* Nutrition, Inc. employed 50 workers by early 1997 and in 1998 was acquired by Twinlab Corporation.

Barry Sears then worked out a deal to start another Balance Bar competitor. He teamed up in 1993 with New Hampshire businessman Matt Freese to form a company selling BioZone bars and other products using multilevel marketing.

Sears in June 1995 published his book *The Zone* about his controversial nutritional concepts. By the following June Sears's book had sold over 400,000 hardcover copies, gone through 32 printings, and enjoyed 12 weeks on the *New York Times* bestseller list. About the same time, other authors published books advocating high levels of protein, including *Protein Power* by physicians Michael R. Eades and Mary Dan Eades and also a revised edition of *Dr. Atkins Diet Revolution.*

Expansion and New Challenges in the 1990s

In 1995 Bio Foods, marketer of Balance Bar products, named James Wolfe as its new chief executive officer, and two years later he became president. A Buffalo native, Wolfe graduated from the University of Buffalo with a B.S. in business administration and did graduate studies at New York University. He served as a senior manager at 7-Up Foods, Coca-Cola USA, and Welch's, and from 1986 to 1995 was president of Wolfe Marketing, a consulting firm in Santa Barbara.

With many years in the food and beverage industry, Wolfe led Bio Foods as it introduced new products and expanded its distribution and marketing methods. In 1995 the firm's Chocolate Balance Bar won the National Nutritional Foods Association's "People's Choice" Award, and the following year the company introduced Mocha, Cranberry, Banana Coconut, and Almond Brownie Balance Bar flavors. It also changed packaging of its Balance Bars.

In addition, in 1995 Bio Foods signed its first national natural foods distributor and by the following year had in place a number of nationwide natural foods brokers and distributors. In 1997 and 1998 the firm diversified its distribution by selling its products in grocery, convenience, drug, sports, club, and mass merchandising outlets. In 1997 the company increased its Balance Bar flavors from seven to ten and also introduced a new 40-30-30 product called Balance Drink Mix in five flavors in canister and single-serving options.

In 1998 Bio Foods changed its name to the Balance Bar Company as it became a public corporation with its shares under the BBAR ticker traded on the NASDAQ exchange. When the last episode of the popular TV sitcom *Seinfeld* aired, the company was prepared to capitalize on the marketing opportunity, reportedly spending almost ten percent of its ad budget at the time for a commercial designed to gain national prominence for its namesake brand.

The company in September 1998 added another product for consumers, again based on the 40-30-30 formula. The three flavors of the new Balance + Bars featured additional nutrients compared to the regular Balance Bars. Honey Peanut had ginseng; Yogurt Berry had *Ginkgo biloba*; and the Chocolate Covered Banana Bars had rose hips and antioxidants.

Balance Bar Company in March 1999 introduced four flavors of a new nutritional beverage called Total Balance. With this product, the firm "entered the estimated $1 billion ready-to-drink nutritional category," stated the firm's summer 1999 newsletter. Fortified with 22 vitamins and minerals, Total Balance was available in 9.5 ounce cans in chocolate, mocha, strawberry, and vanilla flavors.

About the same time, Balance Bar launched a $15 million advertising campaign run by the Suissa Miller ad agency. The campaign, featuring TV, radio, and print ads, was started "soon after the company's most popular bar, Balance Bar Honey Peanut, outsold the nearest competitor's bar by $1 million, becoming the number 1 selling energy/nutrition bar in the country," according to the summer 1999 newsletter.

In June 1999 the firm introduced its trademarked Balance Outdoor line of nutritional bars available in four flavors. A press release stated the Balance Outdoor Crunchy Peanut Bar had "50 percent more protein and 40 percent less sugar than the leading competitor," the PowerBar Performance Peanut Butter flavored bar. CEO/President Jim Wolfe stated that "because the bars are uncoated, whether you are rock climbing in the desert sun or hiking through the forest, we have a product that will stand up to the elements and deliver great-tasting nutrition to keep you going."

As part of the firm's introduction of Balance Outdoor Bars, it also announced a partnership with American Forests in which sales of the new bar would help support the Global ReLeaf campaign to plant trees in the USA. "Our consumers are environmentally conscious on both the local and national level," said Jim Wolfe in his firm's summer 1999 newsletter. "The efforts of the Global ReLeaf campaign extend to every part of the country . . . providing the ideal partner for Balance Bar Company to help preserve the great outdoors.''

In October 1999 the Balance Bar Company announced a new strategic alliance with Jenny Craig, Inc. to formulate and market five flavors of Jenny Craig diet bars intended mainly for women. In the fall/winter 1999 *In Balance* newsletter, the firm stated, ''This is the first time a Jenny Craig product will be seen on retail shelves.''

In 1999 the three athletes of Team Balance Bar represented the company in a ten-event competition called the Hi-Tec Adventure Racing Series. The athletes won more races than any other team. This contest, which included kayaking, trail runs, and mountain biking, was good publicity for the firm, for it was shown on Fit TV, The Outdoor Life Network, and Fox Sports Net.

With the introduction of several new products and expanded distribution outlets, Balance Bar's sales increased rapidly. From $1.3 million sales in 1995, the firm's sales grew to $10.5 million in 1996, $39.6 million in 1997, and $81.7 million in 1998. Balance Bar in 1998 recorded net income of $5.2 million, a 213 percent increase from 1997. The firm gained about 40 percent of its 1998 sales from natural foods distributors and retailers, and customers in the United States accounted for about 98 percent of its sales.

The growing popularity of Balance Bar products was documented by ACNielsen ScanTrack and SPINS NaturalTrack. For example, they found that in 1997 Honey Peanut Balance Bar was the best-selling bar in grocery stores, and in 1998 the firm's products gained the number one market share in mass merchandising outlets.

The firm's growth was accompanied by various legal challenges. For example, in 1997 Barbara and Joseph Flanagan sued both the manufacturer and distributor of Balance Bars for not listing peanuts on the wrapper. The Flanagans believed peanuts in a Balance Bar caused their son to die from an allergic reaction. Because of this case, the U.S. Food and Drug Administration started a thorough investigation of Balance Bars. However, the FDA's compliance officer in Irvine, California, said her agency found no evidence of any nuts in the various Balance Bar flavors.

Rival firm PowerBar asked the National Advertising Division (NAD) of the Council of Better Business Bureaus to investigate the accuracy of ads promoting Balance Bars. After examining Balance Bar endorsements, American Heart Association statements, FDA regulations, the company's consumer surveys, and medical studies, the NAD in February 1998 concluded that the Balance Bar ads generally were ''substantiated, but the NAD suggested it lacked 'sufficient testing, scientific/medical support and research to support' certain performance claims, weight-loss claims, and taste claims,'' according to the April 1998 *Consumers' Research Magazine*. Balance Bar disagreed with the NAD report but voluntarily modified the challenged advertising.

As the century ended, Balance Bar Company enjoyed considerable consumer demand for its nutritional bars and drinks. However, in 1999 its stock price slumped, in part from stiff competition from many companies. Its main competitor was PowerBar Inc. based in Berkeley, California. The 1990s saw the entry of numerous firms into the energy bar and drink industry, so hungry consumers enjoyed numerous choices at grocery stores or health food stores or other outlets. Some shoppers spent the time to compare ingredients, but others selected items on just flavor and price. Some bought similar items through multilevel marketing and thus avoided stores altogether. In any case, this intense competition indicated that the Balance Bar Company needed to be quite innovative to remain successful in the 21st century.

Principal Competitors

PowerBar Inc.; PR* Nutrition, Inc.; Clif Bar Inc.; The ProZone Company; BioZone; Weider Nutrition International; Abbott Labs; Mannatech; Met-Rx Engineered Nutrition; NSA International; Rexall Sundown; Slim-Fast; Worldwide Sport Nutritional Supplements; Odwalla.

Further Reading

Gower, Timothy, ''Protein Pushers,'' *Esquire*, August 1996, p. 40.

Gregory, Stephen, ''Small Business: Balance Bar Savors Record Sales for Quarter: The Company's Growth Plan Is on Track As Sales Top $20 Million for the Period, up 86% Over Last Year,'' *Los Angeles Times*, July 22, 1998, p. 6.

In Balance (company newsletter), Summer, Fall, and Winter 1999 editions.

Kass, Jeff, ''Suit Claims Health Bar Caused Boy's Death: Joey Flanagan, 12, Died Last Year Because of Reaction to Ingredient Not Listed on Label, Parents Say,'' *Los Angeles Times*, August 16, 1997, p. 4.

Kruger, Renee M., ''The Herb Garden Grows,'' *Discount Merchandiser*, December 1998, pp. 45–47.

Marston, Wendy, ''The New Diet Food,'' *Health*, September 1996, p. 98.

Moore, Brenda L., ''Fans Say Changing Dietary Habits Sweeten Prospects for Balance Bar,'' *Wall Street Journal*, March 17, 1999, p. CA2 (eastern edition).

Sears, Barry, and Bill Lawren, *The Zone: A Dietary Road Map*, New York: HarperCollins, 1995.

Seigel, Jessica, ''Zoned Out,'' *Los Angeles Magazine*, February 1997, pp. 34–43.

Spencer, Peter, ''Calling All Consumers: Advertising Battles,'' *Consumers' Research Magazine*, April 1998, p. 43.

Tresniowski, Alex, and Stephen Sawicki, ''Into the Zone,'' *People Weekly*, June 17, 1996, p. 171.

—David M. Walden

Banta Corporation

225 Main Street
Box 8003
Menasha, Wisconsin 54952-8003
U.S.A.
Telephone: (920) 751-7777
Fax: (920) 751-7790
Web site: http://www.banta.com

Public Company
Incorporated: 1901 as George Banta Printing Company
Employees: 7,000
Sales: $1.34 billion (1998)
Stock Exchanges: New York
Ticker Symbol: BN
NAIC: 323110 Commercial Lithographic Printing; 323115 Digital Printing; 323117 Book Printing; 323122 Prepress Services; 339110 Medical Equipment and Supplies Manufacturing; 541430 Graphic Design Services; 541511 Custom Computer Programming Services

Banta Corporation, one of the nation's largest printing and digital imaging companies, literally started in a small-town Wisconsin dining room in 1886. From its humble beginnings, Banta grew to become a technologically advanced, multifaceted reproducer of a wide variety of information, from small-run periodicals to educational and popular books to catalogs and direct marketing materials, with these activities conducted by Banta's Book, Catalog, Direct Marketing, Information Services, and Publications Groups. Among the products and services offered by the company's Digital Services Group are software and services for managing digital content, online publishing, electronic commerce, and web site hosting and maintenance. The Global Turnkey Group is involved in comprehensive supply chain management, from document printing through delivery to the end user, mainly for U.S. and European manufacturers of computer hardware and software. The Healthcare Products Group makes and distributes single-use healthcare products, such as examination gowns and dental bibs, and foodservice products, such as table covers and disposable bibs. By the late 1990s, Banta had acquired a diverse array of printing and digital imaging companies, reported sales of more than $1.3 billion, and maintained 33 production facilities in the United States and five in Europe located in Ireland, Scotland, and the Netherlands.

From Humble Beginnings to Pioneering Printer

In the 1880s, company founder George Banta was a traveling agent for Phoenix Fire Insurance, based in Menasha, Wisconsin, some 80 miles north of Milwaukee. Banta was also a printing buff and, much to the distress of his new bride, Nellie, he brought a printing press into the only room in their house big enough to accommodate it. Two years, one house, and one baby later, Nellie Banta insisted on evicting the press to a shed built in the backyard. George bought a noisy gasoline engine to run the press and also hired one full-time worker for the tiny operation whose main business consisted of printing his insurance forms.

After a fire in 1901 burned down the shed, Banta moved his equipment to a Main Street store front, added a platen job press, and incorporated the business as George Banta Printing Company, with the purpose of "engaging in the business of job and newspaper printing, bookbinding, and manufacture of books and pamphlets." Two years later the corporation was renamed George Banta Publishing Company. The strain of running the shop along with his insurance job took its toll on George Banta, who had a history of malaria and lung problems. In 1904 his doctors ordered him West to recuperate. To save their business, Nellie stayed behind in Menasha and took over as manager. She proved a determined and effective entrepreneur. Meanwhile, George, who had been a Phi Delta Theta member at Indiana University and remained active in the fraternity's national organization, landed a contract to print the Phi Delta magazine, and in time also signed up a number of other fraternities and sororities.

George's educational contacts—his father was dean of the Indiana University law school—helped the company win orders for university catalogs and annuals, as well as some textbooks and magazines. Thus, Banta Publishing grew mainly as a specialist in book and periodical printing. Not that it turned away commercial customers; in its early days, it regularly printed

Company Perspectives:

Succeeding in the Information Age requires more than keeping pace. The most successful companies look to the future and apply cutting-edge technologies that put them a step ahead. Banta Corporation offers an extraordinary suite of innovative, world-class capabilities that streamline the capture, management and distribution of print and digital information. We improve clients' competitiveness by providing solutions that help them deliver information in a variety of print and electronic formats, at ever-faster speeds and at lower costs.

large-volume promotional booklets for Quaker Oats. In 1910 Banta was ready for its own building, a two-story plant just across the Fox River. These facilities, vastly enlarged over the decades, remained the site of Banta Company's offices, the largest division of Banta Corporation, and a complex of printing facilities into the late 1990s.

In 1911, 18-year-old George Banta, Jr., dropped out of college and assumed charge of the office. The replacement of Nellie was somewhat brusque, wrote *Appleton Post-Crescent* contributor Kay Roberts, but while the ''Founder's wife'' reminisced that she ''missed the five dollars a week she earned,'' she also maintained she had much to attend to at home and ''left with few regrets.'' George, Sr., while periodically bothered by health problems, continued to be a major sales contributor and retained overall leadership as president until his death in 1935 at age 76. Nellie then assumed the presidency until she died in her 86th year in 1951.

The company continued to grow, with emphasis on the educational market. As a historical review in the 1990 annual report noted, Banta was emphatic on keeping ''pace with technological change.'' However, ''rather than attempting to serve many markets, the company focused initially on ones in which it could build special strengths and capabilities.'' Even though the company consistently ranked among the top five U.S. printers in the 1980s and 1990s, Banta liked to concentrate on numerous niche businesses and sought to be the leader or a strong contender in each market it entered.

By the onset of World War I, Banta was printing 184 scholarly, technical, and educational journals. The war years brought a harsher climate which lasted into the early 1920s, but then, as the decade progressed, Banta benefited from an ''explosion in education.'' By the end of the decade, Banta found itself in the right place for an innovative concept. One of George, Jr.'s brothers-in-law, Russell Sharp, wrote an elementary school workbook and turned to Banta to produce it. The company soon became the leader in printing workbooks as these softcover scholastic aids became a major educational tool from first grade right up through graduate school. Eventually this expertise helped make Banta a leader in softcover books for the professional market as well as for ''trade'' books (general interest books sold through bookstores).

Always technically progressive, Banta acquired its first web offset press in 1940. In the early days, the prevailing state of the art in paper, platemaking, ink, and other printing supplies limited the jobs considered suitable for offset. Banta became a pioneer in pushing development of improved supplies as well as speedier and higher-quality presses. As web offset developed into the printing method of choice for many applications, the expanding Banta Company established itself as a major player in the industry.

In 1946 Banta expanded beyond its home complex with the 42,000-square-foot Midway plant, built halfway between downtown Menasha and nearby Appleton. Even as it kept expanding its printing business, the company contracted its name, dropping the ''Publishing'' to become George Banta Company, Inc. in 1954. The streamlined name also eliminated possible confusion about Banta's role: it did the production work for books and periodicals, while publishers (who create and market books) were its customers.

Late 1960s Through 1980s: Pressing Forward Via Acquisitions

Banta, which did barely $3.5 million in business at the end of World War II and $10 million in the mid-1950s, attained $33 million in sales by 1968. Family leadership had been interrupted in 1961 when John H. Wilterding, who had started at Banta in 1923, succeeded George Banta, Jr., as president. On Wilterding's retirement in 1965, however, George Banta III, the son of George, Jr., took over. Conglomeration had become the fashion throughout American enterprise, and the printing industry was no exception. George III related: ''We had many beautiful offers to sell out . . . but we decided to remain independent.'' Banta set out to prepare itself for the new order. In 1968 it brought in Menasha-born Kimberly Clark executive William H. Fieweger as president, with George Banta III as chairman, a post he retained until his retirement in 1983.

Within a year, the Banta-Fieweger team had the company's first long-range expansion plan ready, based on the recognition that the industry was ''becoming increasingly capital intensive'' and hence required ''larger economic units.'' The Banta plan aimed to: continue internal growth, ''notably from educational sources''; acquire selected small firms to promote expansion; and encourage technological advancement not just by buying new equipment, but by innovating new methods and directions. The acquisition program began in 1969 with the $2.4 million purchase of Daniels Packaging of Rhinelander, Wisconsin, which specialized in producing foil and flexible film wrap for food and other grocery products. Somewhat ironically, this first acquisition also became the first major unit disposed of by Banta; in 1989 the greatly expanded Daniels was sold for an after-tax gain of $9.6 million.

In 1970, Banta added periodicals printer Hart Press of Minnesota and Menasha neighbor Northwestern Engraving, which prepared color separations for printers and for whom Banta had been a major customer. These acquisitions along with internal growth boosted Banta sales volume above $50 million for the first time. In March 1971 Banta was ready to go public, selling 455,000 shares (a 29 percent interest) at $12.50 per share. Over the next two-and-a-half decades, the share value multiplied more than 25-fold.

Key Dates:

1901: George Banta incorporates his printing business as George Banta Printing Company.
1903: Company is renamed George Banta Publishing Company.
1910: A two-story plant is completed in Menasha.
1940: Company purchases its first web offset press.
1946: 42,000-square-foot Midway Plant is completed, located midway between Menasha and Appleton.
1954: Company's name is changed to George Banta Company, Inc.
1969: Acquisition program begins with purchase of Daniels Packaging.
1970: Sales reach $50 million.
1971: Company goes public through a $5.7 million initial public offering.
1989: Revenues surpass the half-billion mark; company name is streamlined to Banta Corporation.
1995: Company acquires Cork, Ireland-based BG Turnkey Services Ltd.; revenues top the $1 billion mark for the first time.
1998: Company's stock moves from the NASDAQ to the New York Stock Exchange.
1999: A restructuring is initiated, resulting in the elimination of 650 jobs and the closure of three facilities.

Acquisitions continued through the 1970s and 1980s. Ling Products of Neenah, Wisconsin, acquired in 1973, made disposable products for the health and foodservice industries, such as examination gowns, table covers, and bibs. KCS Industries of Milwaukee, purchased in 1975, produced point-of-sale displays. Moreover, R.J. Carroll of Harrisonburg, Virginia, bought in 1976 and later named Banta Harrisonburg, provided Eastern production facilities for Banta's basic education-oriented business. Banta's most important acquisition came in 1988, under the leadership of chairman and CEO Harry W. Earle, when Minnesota-based Beddor Companies joined the fold. The move increased Banta's size by about two-thirds and put it into consumer catalogs and direct mail materials, among the fastest growing segments of retail merchandising. It also added to Banta's softcover capacity through printer Viking Press of Minneapolis (no relation to the well-known New York publisher Viking). The merger pushed sales above the half-billion mark in 1989 and brought Banta into the *Fortune* 500. At the same time, Banta further streamlined its corporate name to Banta Corporation.

1990s and Beyond

Acquisitions of ''high-quality'' companies remained high on the Banta agenda in the 1990s. Thus, in 1994, Banta added Danbury Printing and Litho of Connecticut, augmenting its capabilities in the direct marketing industry with a strategic manufacturing facility in the Northeast. Another 1994 acquisition was United Graphics of Kent, Washington, which gave Banta a second western printing plant to complement its Utah facility, Bushman Press, acquired in 1991. Through the United Graphics purchase, Banta also added software giant Microsoft Corporation to its already broad roster of top-level computer industry customers. Donald D. Belcher came to Banta as president in the fall of 1994 from office supplier Avery Dennison and took over the chairmanship and CEO position from retiring Calvin Aurand, Jr., in 1995.

All told, Banta added 23 companies during the first quarter century of its acquisition policy. Banta succeeded in obtaining strong growth from companies following their acquisition, which meshed into its overall plan for ''aggressive and profitable growth'' from internally developed new products and services.

Banta organized its many acquisitions into several product groups that operated as largely autonomous enterprises, an approach the company believed would make them ''quicker, more nimble, and better able to respond to customer needs.'' The three largest groups in the mid-1990s, each with a little over one-fifth of total volume, were the Book, Catalog, and Direct Marketing units. The Banta Book Group handled both educational and general books, and also produced instructional games such as ''Trivial Pursuit,'' a game wildly popular in the mid-1980s.

The Publications Group, which accounted for about one-eighth of total volume, put out more than 500 educational, trade, religious, and fraternal magazines with circulation mostly in the 15,000-to-350,000 range. Niche-conscious Banta specialized in this type of periodical rather than large-scale consumer magazines ''because they are less subject to cyclical variation in number of advertising pages; also because regular planned growth is easier to achieve, since each new periodical adds only modestly to sales.'' Smaller groups were the Banta Digital Group, Information Services, and the more specialized KCS (signs, displays, etc.) and Ling (single-use products) units.

Banta planned to stay strong in the 1990s, noted Belcher, by ''investing ahead of the curve in new technologies.'' Between 1990 and 1994, Banta reinvested $265 million in its operations, $87 million in 1994 alone. Such a figure represented around ten percent of revenues, more than double the industry average. Capital acquired in the early 1990s included a $20 million printing press whose wide web permitted the printing of 50 percent more pages across the web of paper while running at nearly 50 percent greater speed. In another plant, a Xeikon full-color digital system printed entirely from digital information, requiring no film or plates. Other electronic and optical systems, often enhanced by proprietary software programs, sped prepress preparation and after-printing processing (addressing and distribution), enabling Banta to offer fast turnaround and highly customized service, such as catalogs or direct mail pieces with content tailored for specific recipients. Similarly, college texts could be custom-bound to match a professor's specific course curriculum.

Chairman Belcher expected Banta's core business to remain ''imaging on paper,'' even as the design, production, and distribution processes which turned out these familiar print products were being ''revolutionized by digital technologies.'' In addition, he predicted that a broad array of nonprint products, including CD-ROMs and ''image archiving,'' would show proportionally faster growth than print. An example of the new kinds of jobs that were being taken on by Banta was an electronic catalog for a major business-to-business cataloger that was essentially a CD-ROM version of its printed catalog. For computer industry customers, Banta not only printed instruction manuals but provided on-demand electronic printing, duplication of floppies, diskettes, and CD-ROMs, and assembly of software kits.

Though Banta had long expressed interest in the global market, foreign expansion had barely begun in the 1990s. In 1994 Banta established a software documentation unit in the Netherlands, which enabled domestic customers to download data for printing and distribution overseas. The following year came a much larger purchase, that of Cork, Ireland-based BG Turnkey Services Ltd. The Cork, Ireland-based company had annual sales of about $160 million and provided services to European computer industry customers similar to those offered by Banta's existing U.S. operations, including manual and promotional item printing, disk and CD-ROM duplication, software package assembly, and fulfillment. BG became part of the Banta Global Turnkey Group. Also in 1995, Banta moved into the burgeoning world of the Internet with the acquisition of New Frontiers Information Corp., a Cambridge, Massachusetts, software company specializing in the creation of online catalogs and ordering systems. Revenues for 1995 topped $1 billion for the first time.

Acquisitions continued in the late 1990s. In September 1997 Banta paid about $50.7 million in cash for the Omnia Group, a Troy, Michigan, supplier of single-use medical and dental products. The Omnia operation was merged into Banta's existing single-use products unit, which by this time was known as the Banta Healthcare Group. In October 1997 Banta acquired Greenfield Printing & Publishing Company—a printer of special interest and trade magazines based in Greenfield, Ohio—for about $21.3 million. Also in late 1997 Banta initiated a restructuring program, which entailed a $13.5 million charge and was completed in 1998. The company sold most of its KCS unit, including its point-of-purchase sign and display business; its interactive video operation; and three Banta Global Turnkey facilities in Sacramento and Irvine, California, and in Provo, Utah.

During 1998 Banta expanded into the Latin American market for the first time through the acquisition of a 30 percent interest in Morgan Impresores S.A., one of the largest printers in Chile with annual sales of about $45 million. Continuing to seek opportunities outside the United States, Banta in mid-1999 formed a joint venture with Grupo Imagen, a Queretaro, Mexico-based sheet-fed printer. During 1998 Banta made its first release of B*z*media, a digital content management system for storing, archiving, retrieving, and "repurposing" digital information for print or electronic distribution. In early 1999 leading educational publisher Houghton Mifflin Company selected Banta to develop two online education pilot programs to test Internet-based delivery of customized educational materials, as well as to begin development of a B*z*media system for the publisher that would encompass both textbook and Internet output. The company was also developing a B*z*commerce electronic-commerce product which enabled Banta customers to sell and distribute their products through a web site.

Meanwhile, in January 1999 Banta signed a $100 million contract with IDG Books Worldwide, publisher of the bestselling "For Dummies" series and other trade titles. Banta committed to printing a variety of books for IDG, and also agreed to provide inventory management, order fulfillment, distribution, and returns processing. The company built a 250,000-square-foot distribution center in Harrisburg, Virginia, which had a storage capacity for about 16 million books and was slated to be used exclusively for IDG products.

In April 1999 Banta announced a restructuring program aimed at generating annual savings of $18–$20 million by 2000. Underperforming facilities in Kent, Washington; Charlotte, North Carolina; and Berkeley, Illinois, were slated for closure, and 650 workers, representing about nine percent of the overall workforce, lost their jobs. The restructuring, which resulted in a fiscal 1999 charge of about $50 million, was part of a three-part program to position Banta for the early 21st century, with the second and third parts both being partially funded through the restructuring savings. The company planned to step up its acquisitions program, as outlined by Belcher: "Recent acquisitions have boosted our technology and value-added service capabilities, and we are now accelerating our acquisition activities with the goal of aggressively growing our most profitable core print sectors and our healthcare business." The third part of the program was to continue the company's aggressive development of digital technology products, such as B*z*media and B*z*commerce.

Principal Subsidiaries

Banta Direct Marketing, Inc.; Banta Europe Corp. (Ireland); Banta Healthcare Products, Inc.; Banta Security Printing, Inc.; Banta Global Turnkey B.V. (Netherlands); Banta Global Turnkey France; Banta Global Turnkey Limited (Ireland); Banta Global Turnkey Limited (Scotland); Banta Packaging & Fulfillment, Inc.; Banta Software Services International, Inc.; Banta Specialty Converting, Inc.; Danbury Printing & Litho, Inc.; KnowledgeSet Corporation; New Frontiers Information Corporation; One Pass Network, Inc.; United Graphics Inc.; Wrapper, Inc.; Banta Publications-Greenfield, Inc.; Cidex International, Inc.; Banta Direct Marketing-Berkeley, Inc.; Omnia I, Inc.; Tidi Products, Inc.; Meadows Information Systems, Inc.; Greenfield Holdings Corp.; Banta Cayman Islands Corp. (Cayman Islands); Type Designs, Inc.; Ad Run Around, Inc.; Banta Ireland Corp.; Turnkey Services Holding Corp.; Banta Holding Corp.

Principal Operating Units

Book Group; Catalog Group; Digital Group; Direct Marketing Group; Global Turnkey Group; Healthcare Group; Information Services Group; Publications Group.

Principal Competitors

Anderson Lithograph Company; Berlin Industries Inc.; Big Flower Holdings, Inc.; Champion Industries, Inc.; Consolidated Graphics, Inc.; Courier Corporation; Dai Nippon Printing Co., Ltd.; Hart Graphics, Inc.; Mail-Well, Inc.; Quad/Graphics, Inc.; Quebecor Printing Inc.; R.R. Donnelley & Sons Company; Tufco Technologies, Inc.

Further Reading

"Banta to Restructure in a Four-Part Plan," *Graphic Arts Monthly*, November 1997, p. 26.

Belcher, Donald D., Presentation on Banta Corporation to the New York Society of Security Analysts, company document, March 6, 1995.

Byrne, Harlan S., ''Banta Corp. Acquisition Doubles Sales, Moves It into Fast-Growing Field,'' *Barron's,* May 29, 1989.

——, ''Banta Corp.: A Power of the Press,'' *Barron's,* March 20, 1995, p. 24.

Hawkins, Lee, Jr., ''Banta Shedding Parts of KCS: Firm to Close Printing Operation at Milwaukee Plant, Sell Display Business As Part of Restructuring Plan,'' *Milwaukee Journal Sentinel,* September 27, 1997.

——, ''Menasha-Based Banta Corp. Lands $100 Million Publishing Contract,'' *Milwaukee Journal Sentinel,* January 28, 1999.

——, ''Menasha, Wis.-Based Printing Firm Banta Corp. to Lay Off 650 Workers,'' *Milwaukee Journal Sentinel,* April 13, 1999.

Joshi, Pradnya, ''Banta Acquires Software Company,'' *Milwaukee Journal Sentinel,* October 10, 1995.

Olson, Jon, ''Banta Corp. Makes Move into Europe,'' *Milwaukee Journal Sentinel,* August 29, 1995, p. D1.

——, ''Banta Is Making an Imprint on Wall Street,'' *Milwaukee Journal Sentinel,* September 16, 1995.

Roberts, Kay, ''The Founder's Wife,'' *Appleton (Wisc.) Post-Crescent,* February 4, 1979.

''Short and Sweet: Banta Digital Services Uses Digital Press Technology to Develop the On-Demand Print Market,'' *American Printer,* September 1995, pp. 36–38.

Stapel, Jeff, and Lorrie Potash, ''Banta—90 Years of Growth,'' *Banta Company Magazine,* 1991, pp. 18–20.

—Henry R. Hecht
—updated by David E. Salamie

BILL BLASS

Bill Blass Ltd.

550 Seventh Avenue
New York, New York 10018
U.S.A.
Telephone: (212) 221-6660
Fax: (212) 302-5166

Private Company
Incorporated: 1968 as Bill Blass Inc.
Employees: 40
Sales: $50 million (1998 est.)
NAIC: 315222 Men and Boys' Cut and Sew Suit, Coat and Overcoat Manufacturing; 315233 Women's and Girls' Cut and Sew Dress Manufacturing; 315234 Women's and Girls' Cut and Sew Suit, Coat, Tailored Jacket and Skirt Manufacturing; 54149 Other Speicalized Design Services

Bill Blass Ltd. produces clothing collections by the designer Bill Blass and licenses an array of products that bear his name or initials. Blass's fashions have long been a favorite of wealthy and prominent women, including several presidents' wives. His clothes ''are rarely thought of as artistic or trendsetting or remarkable,'' according to Susan Orlean of the *New Yorker;* rather, writes Holly Haber of *WWD,* he is ''the quintessential designer for 'ladies who lunch.' '' Bill Blass Ltd., which is also prominent in menswear and men's accessories (accounting for about 40 percent of its revenue) and licenses products that include fragrances and furniture, ranked as the fourth most recognized American designer in a 1999 survey. The 77-year-old Blass sold his business in 1999.

''Overnight'' Stardom in the 1960s

Born in 1922 in Fort Wayne, Indiana (which he told Leila E.B. Hadley of the *Saturday Evening Post* was ''a miserable place to grow up in''), Blass knew he wanted to design clothing at a very early age, and in his teens he was already selling sketches to firms in Manhattan's Seventh Avenue garment district. He left for New York City immediately after graduation from high school, soon finding a job as a $35-a-week sketch artist for a sportswear firm. After service in World War II, he became a designer for the Manhattan firm of Anna Miller and Co., Ltd. In the late 1950s Anna Miller merged her company with her brother's firm, Maurice Rentner Ltd.

Rentner, a manufacturer of high-priced clothing, was noted for catering to the ''amply proportioned'' woman. ''Our 1959 collection was quite a shock to the buyers,'' Rentner's chairman recalled when later interviewed for the *New York Times* by Nora Ephron. ''They came in looking for matronly stuff and we gave them Bill's young look. . . . They ate it up.'' Blass quickly rose in the firm to head designer, vice-president, and partner.

By 1963 Blass was a celebrated designer, having received the Coty American Fashion Critics' Award for the second time. His designs were known for quality fabric, simple lines, mix-and-match combinations of fabrics and patterns, impeccable tailoring, and brilliant colors. His customers included Jacqueline Kennedy, Happy Rockefeller, and Marilyn Monroe. The beige chantilly-lace dress in which he clad model Jean Shrimpton for a Revlon lipstick ad proved a sensation. Put into production by instant demand, it achieved unprecedented sales in such stores as Bonwit Teller, Lord and Taylor, and Neiman-Marcus. Blass was also designing furs, swimsuits, rainwear, and children's wear for other companies, plus accessories such as shoes, hosiery, scarves, gloves, luggage, jewelry, and wristwatches. He was even asked to design a tire. The designer established a Rentner licensing and franchising subsidiary, Bill Blass Inc., in 1968.

Blass claimed to be the first American designer of women's apparel to enter the menswear field. He told Barbaralee Diamonstein that he designed for the man over 35 who wanted to look ''with it, but not ridiculous. . . . It was a terribly silly period. Grown men looked like their own sons, with long sideburns and bell-bottomed pants and body jewelry.'' Pincus Brothers-Maxwell began manufacturing, distributing, and marketing Bill Blass menswear, including suits, shirts, ties, shoes—and even a kilt—in 1967. A *Life* article called the line ''a blend of Damon Runyon and the Duke of Windsor.'' ''The man over 40 needs help,'' Blass explained to the magazine. ''My [suit] jackets are more fitted and cut higher in the arm hole to make

Key Dates:

1960: Blass becomes chief designer of Maurice Rentner Ltd.
1968: Bill Blass Inc. becomes a Rentner subsidiary for the designer's licensed products, including a menswear line.
1970: Blass buys out his Rentner partners and renames the company Bill Blass Ltd.
1980: Annual sales of Blass-labeled goods reach $200 million.
1993: Bill Blass Ltd. is licensing 56 products.
1999: Blass sells the company.

him look thinner and stay thinner.'' The designer was a recipient of the first Coty Award for Menswear in 1968.

Essentially traditional in taste, Blass, despite his commercial and critical success, also found designing women's apparel to be a challenge in this decade. ''The single most difficult period for me was the 'sixties,' '' he recalled for a 1981 *Vogue* article by Edith Law Gross. ''For the first time, clothes came from the street. . . . Overnight, you had to make clothes that were cut off to here, that were amusing, bizarre, but above all young. I survived by making crisp, attractive clothes that my customer also could relate to.'' In 1970 Blass won a third Coty American Fashion Critics' Award and, with it, lifetime membership in the Coty Hall of Fame. Also in 1970, he bought out his Rentner partners and renamed the company Bill Blass Ltd.

The 1960s were the first time that fashion designers became celebrities in their own right, worthy of hobnobbing with their wealthy and socially prominent customers. Before, Blass told Diamonstein, ''The designers were anonymous, they weren't interviewed. They never talked to the press, and they rarely saw the buyers.'' A handsome and charming bachelor, the sophisticated Blass was perfectly placed to profit from the decade's relaxed social mores. He advanced his career by cultivating the right women, establishing precedent by inviting them to his shows and seating them in the front row. He was not, Cathy Horyn of the *New York Times* wrote in 1999, ''at the intersection of American fashion and society. He was the intersection.''

Blass was also making public appearances around the country, averaging more than 30,000 miles of travel a year, with models wearing his designs in tow. A fashion editor described him to Ephron as ''a super-businessman [who] . . . can sell the eyelashes off a hog.'' But he also knew when *not* to sell, having learned, he later told Gross, ''one key thing: never sell anybody anything that isn't attractive on her.''

Tending to Business: 1970–90

The mainstay of Blass's clothing for women in the 1970s was the blazer. Trousers were prominent, and were dressed up with fur-trimmed wrap coats and cardigan sweaters. The designer introduced his Blassport ready-to-wear sportswear division in 1972. Three years later he revived the cocktail dress and, in 1978, added a signature perfume.

The total volume of Bill Blass sales by all licensees reached the $200-million level in 1980. By the early 1980s Blass's roster of licensees came to 30 in the United States alone. His name was now on perfumes and colognes, bed linen, towels, glassware, eyeglasses, Lincoln Continental automobiles, and even backgammon sets and a box of chocolates. Jeans were added in 1987, and the total worldwide sales volume of Blass-labeled goods reached $450 million in 1989. But Blass was taking great care to make sure his name was not being used inappropriately, vetoing such propositions as Blass-designed stoves, refrigerators, orthodontic braces, and fabric-lined coffins.

The licensed revenues depended ultimately on the prestige of Bill Blass Ltd.'s own collections, whether these expensive productions made money or not. Blass's strength, he told Gross, was ''making the sketch, and then I'm best at fitting. Because then I can spot absolutely what I want and what's wrong. . . . I'll tell you the secret of a great dress: it looks as though human hands hadn't touched it.'' Blass expanded his list of celebrity clients, which now included politically prominent women such as Nancy Reagan, Barbara Bush, Nancy Kissinger, and Pamela Harriman; media presences such as Katharine Graham and Barbara Walters; and performers such as Candice Bergen, Anjelica Huston, Mary Tyler Moore, Jessye Norman, and Barbra Streisand.

In keeping with the decade, Blass's designs for the 1980s were more ornate and luxurious than those of the past. He employed such materials as panne velvet, satin, taffeta, cashmere, and sable, and he beaded sashes, skirts, blouses, and evening jackets. Blazers were replaced by jackets typically mixed, in suits, with different materials. Twin cashmere sweater sets were paired with long matching skirts of silk satin or lace bouffant. Beaded and embroidered evening dresses, at $5,000, were among his best sellers in the early to mid-1980s. Asked by Daimonstein why his clothes were so expensive, Blass replied, ''I'm an avid believer that we have to have clothes made in this country. Therefore we pay more money. . . . [The] cost of labor and fabrication is what makes the clothing expensive.''

Closing Time: The 1990s

Although now over 70, the indefatigable Blass was out on the road as always in 1993, when his couture ''trunk show'' traveled to 24 cities, with Blass himself accompanying it to Atlanta, Chicago, Nashville, Philadelphia, San Francisco, Washington, and Troy, Michigan. At Saks Fifth Avenue in New York City, he set a record for American designers by selling more than $500,000 worth of dresses. At this time Bill Blass Ltd. was licensing 56 products, including window shades. Bill Blass USA, a bridge line (between couture and ready-to-wear) was launched in 1995 and licensed to Augustus Clothiers.

Pennsylvania House introduced a Bill Blass furniture collection of 50 pieces in 1997. The following year Blass, who had been licensing fragrances to Revlon for almost 30 years, bought out his contract and assigned it to Five Star Fragrances. The women's jeans license was awarded to The Resource Club Ltd., a private-label manufacturer. The Bill Blass USA line closed and was replaced by a better-than-bridge suit collection to be made and marketed by Zaralo.

Pared to 42, the Bill Blass licensees generated about $760 million in annual sales in 1998, and the designer collection was bringing in another $20 million to $25 million in retail. Blass hired George Ackerman, a former Donna Karan executive, to replace him as chief executive officer in March 1998. Shortly before year's end, however, Ackerman left the company for reasons that were not disclosed, and Blass, who had recently suffered a minor stroke, resumed his former duties. He announced in February 1999 that he was planning to sell his firm.

Blass, in October 1999, concluded an agreement to sell his company to Haresh T. Tharani, chairman of The Resource Club, the firm's largest licensee, and Michael Groveman, the firm's chief financial officer, with the former becoming chairman and the latter chief executive officer. The purchase price was to be paid by issuing investment-grade bonds self-liquidating over ten years, based on the Blass trademarks, brand equity, and licensing revenues. The designer committed himself to maintaining an active role in the company through a long-term contract "with financial interest." A new company, called Tharanco, was to be established to own and operate Bill Blass Ltd.

CAK Universal Credit Corp. financed the purchase by lending the new owners the money to buy the company. The loan was secured by the company's trademarks and licenses, which were placed into an entity that would receive all the cash from the licenses. Robert D'Loren, cofounder of CAK, described the transaction as an alternative to going public, telling Lisa Lockwood of *WWD* that since the cyclical nature of the apparel business made Bill Blass Ltd. below investment-grade creditworthiness, "What we do is structure a loan so credit becomes investment grade—triple B or better. . . . By creating investment grade asset-backed bonds, we have forged a vehicle that enables apparel industry leaders to leverage their assets at favorable terms, while allowing large financial institutions, which have strict investment requirements, to invest in these assets."

Principal Competitors

Calvin Klein Inc.; Polo/Ralph Lauren Corporation; Tommy Hilfiger Corporation.

Further Reading

Diamonstein, Barbaralee, *Fashion: The Inside Story,* New York: Rizzoli, 1985, pp. 46–52.

Ephron, Nora, "The Man in the Bill Blass Suit," *New York Times Magazine,* December 8, 1968, pp. 52, 182, 184–85, 187, 191–92, 195.

"The Fairchild 100," *WWD/Women's Wear Daily,* November 1999, pp. 60, 75–76.

Friedman, Arthur, "Ackerman Is 1st Blass CEO," *WWD/Women's Wear Daily,* April 2, 1998, p. 20.

Gross, Edith Law, "Bill Blass and Women: An American Affair," *Vogue,* March 1981, pp. 339, 360–61.

Haber, Holly, "Bill Blass Gets Set to Call It a Career at the Millennium," *WWD/Women's Wear Daily,* February 16, 1999, p. 1ff.

Hadley, Leila E.B., "Man a la Mode," *Saturday Evening Post,* April 6, 1968, pp. 30–31.

Horyn, Cathy, "Blass: An American Original, Seen Only in Silhouette," *New York Times,* August 24, 1999, p. B12.

Lockwood, Lisa, "Bill Blass Goes the Bond Route," *WWD/Women's Wear Daily,* October 28, 1999, p. 1ff.

"The Man Who Made the 'Scarsdale Mafia' Suit," *Life,* June 13, 1969, p. 67.

Martin, Richard, *Contemporary Fashion,* Detroit: St. James Press, 1994, pp. 62–63.

Milbank, Caroline Rennolds, *New York Fashion,* New York: Abrams, 1989, pp. 218–19.

Orlean, Susan, "King of the Road," *New Yorker,* December 20, 1993, pp. 86–92.

Reed, Julia, "Million Dollar Bill," *Vogue,* January 1990, pp. 200–07, 241.

Sherrod, Patricia, "Models of Taste," *Chicago Tribune,* September 14, 1997, Sec. 15, pp. 1, 8.

Wilson, Eric, "Ackerman Quits Blass," *WWD/Women's Wear Daily,* December 22, 1998, p. 6.

—Robert Halasz

The Boeing Company

7755 East Marginal Way South
Seattle, Washington 98108
U.S.A.
Telephone: (206) 655-2121
Fax: (206) 655-9391
Web site: http://www.boeing.com

Public Company
Incorporated: 1934 as Boeing Airplane Company
Employees: 227,000
Sales: $56.15 billion (1998)
Stock Exchanges: New York Amsterdam Brussels London Tokyo Pacific Boston Cincinnati Midwest Philadelphia
Ticker Symbol: BA
NAIC: 336411 Aircraft Manufacturing; 336413 Other Aircraft Parts and Auxiliary Equipment Manufacturing; 336414 Guided Missile and Space Vehicle Manufacturing; 336415 Guided Missile and Space Vehicle Propulsion Unit and Propulsion Unit Parts Manufacturing; 336419 Other Guided Missile and Space Vehicle Parts and Auxiliary Equipment Manufacturing; 334511 Search, Detection, Navigation, Guidance, Aeronautical, and Nautical System and Instruments Manufacturing; 334290 Other Communications Equipment Manufacturing

The Boeing Company is the largest aerospace company in the world, thanks to its 1997 merger with McDonnell Douglas Corporation and its 1996 purchase of the defense and space units of Rockwell International Corporation. The corporation is the world's number one maker of commercial jetliners and military aircraft. Boeing has more than 9,000 commercial aircraft in service worldwide, including the 717 through 777 families of jets and the MD-80, MD-90, and MD-11. In the defense sector, the company makes military aircraft, including fighter, transport, and attack aircraft; helicopters; and missiles. In addition to its position as the nation's top NASA contractor—and the leader of the U.S. industry team for the International Space Station—Boeing is also involved in commercial space projects such as satellite networks and a sea-based satellite launch platform.

Beginnings, Early 20th Century

Founder William Boeing was raised in Michigan, where his father operated a lucrative forestry business. While he was in San Diego, California, in 1910, Boeing met a French stunt pilot named Louis Paulhan who was performing at the International Air Meet. When Paulhan took Boeing for an airplane ride, it marked the beginning of Boeing's fascination with aviation.

After two years of study at Yale's Sheffield School of Science, Boeing returned to Michigan to work for his father. He was sent first to Wisconsin and later to the state of Washington to acquire more timber properties for the family business. In Seattle he met a navy engineer named Conrad Westerveldt who shared his fascination with aviation. A barnstormer named Terah Maroney gave the two men a ride over Puget Sound in his seaplane. Later Boeing went to Los Angeles to purchase his own seaplane, thinking it would be useful for fishing trips. The man who sold him the plane and taught him how to fly was Glenn Martin, who later founded Martin Marietta.

While in Seattle, Boeing and Westerveldt made a hobby of building their own seaplanes on the backwaters of Puget Sound. It became more than a hobby when a mechanic named Herb Munter and a number of other carpenters and craftsmen became involved. In May 1916, Boeing flew the first ''B&W'' seaplane. The next month he incorporated his company as the Pacific Aero Products Company. The company's first customer was the government of New Zealand, which employed the plane for mail delivery and pilot training. In 1917 the company's name was changed to Boeing Airplane Company.

Boeing and his partners anticipated government interest in their company when the United States became involved in World War I. They discovered their hunch was correct when the company was asked to train flight instructors for the army. After the war, Boeing sold a number of airplanes to Edward Hubbard, whose Hubbard Air Transport is regarded as the world's first airline. The company shuttled mail between Seattle and the trans-

Company Perspectives:

The Boeing Company, after its merger in 1997 with McDonnell Douglas and acquisition in 1996 of the defense and space units of Rockwell International, became the largest aerospace company in the world. Its history mirrors the history of aviation. Boeing is the world's largest manufacturer of commercial jetliners, military aircraft and the nation's largest NASA contractor.

pacific mailboat that called at Victoria, British Columbia. Later, when the post office invited bids for various airmail routes, Hubbard tried to convince Boeing to apply for the Chicago to San Francisco contract. Boeing mentioned the idea to his wife, who thought the opportunity looked promising. In the prospect, he and Hubbard created a new airline named the Boeing Air Transport Company. They submitted a bid and were awarded the contract.

To meet the demands of their new business Boeing and his engineers developed an extremely versatile and popular airplane called the Model 40. Fitted with a Pratt & Whitney air-cooled Wasp engine, it could carry 1,000 pounds of mail and a complete flight crew, and still have room enough for freight or passengers. The Kelly Airmail Act of 1925 opened the way for private airmail delivery on a much wider scale. As a result, a number of airline companies were formed with the intention of procuring the stable and lucrative airmail contracts. One of these companies was Vernon Gorst's Pacific Air Transport, which won various routes along the Pacific Coast. Boeing purchased this company and then ordered a young employee named William Patterson to purchase its outstanding stock. Boeing also purchased Varney Airlines, which began operation in 1925 and won almost every mail contract it applied for until it became overextended and had financial difficulties.

1929–34: "United" Era

With the addition of National Air Transport, Boeing's airline holdings formed the original United Air Lines. In 1928 all these companies were organized under a holding company called the Boeing Aircraft and Transportation Company. In 1929 a larger holding company was formed, the United Aircraft and Transportation Company. Included in this group were the "United" airlines and Stout Airlines; Pratt & Whitney (engines); Boeing, Sikorsky, Northrop, and Stearman (manufacturers); and Standard Steel Prop and Hamilton Aero Manufacturing (propellers). Boeing was made chairman of the company and Fred Rentschler of Pratt & Whitney was named president.

Boeing and Rentschler became extremely wealthy in this reorganization by exchanging stock with the holding company in a method similar to J.P. Morgan's controversial capital manipulation. They multiplied their original investments by a factor of as much as 200,000 times. It was, however, entirely legal at the time. In 1933 the government conducted an investigation of fraud and other illegal practices in the airline industry. Boeing was called upon to testify and explain his windfall profits before a Senate investigating committee. Under examination he admitted to making $12 million in stock flotations.

Boeing was so infuriated with the investigation that he retired from the company (at age 52) and sold all his aviation stocks. Upon Boeing's departure the company's production manager, Phil Johnson, was named the new president. But William Boeing was not forgotten by the aircraft industry. In 1934 he was recognized for his innovation in aeronautical research and development with the award of the Daniel Guggenheim medal, "for successful pioneering and achievement in aircraft manufacturing and air transport."

1934–52: Breakup and Military Aircraft

In 1934 a government investigation of collusion in the airmail business led to a suspension of all contracts awarded. As a result, the U.S. Congress declared that airline companies and manufacturers could not be part of the same business concern. This led to the break-up of the three aeronautic conglomerates: Boeing's United, the Aviation Corporation of the Americas, and North American Aviation. All of the Boeing company's aeronautic properties east of the Mississippi became part of a new company, United Aircraft (later renamed United Technologies), operated by Fred Rentschler. The western properties, principally the Boeing Airplane Company, remained in Seattle exclusively manufacturing airframes. Pat Patterson was put in charge of the commercial air carriers, which retained the name of United Air Lines and based their operations at Chicago's Old Orchard (later O'Hare) airport.

In the years leading up to World War II Boeing led the way in developing single-wing airplanes. They were constructed completely of metal to make them stronger and faster; more efficient aerodynamic designs were emphasized; retractable landing gear and better wings were developed, along with multiple "power plant" technology; and, finally, directional radios were installed which enabled better navigation and night flying. Boeing had established itself as the leading manufacturer of airplanes.

When the United States launched its wartime militarization program, Boeing was called upon to produce hundreds of its B-17 "Flying Fortresses" for the U.S. Army. During the war the B-17 became an indispensable instrument for the U.S. Air Corps. In June 1944, when production was at its peak, Boeing's Seattle facility turned out 16 of these airplanes every 24 hours. By this time the company was also producing an improved bomber called the B-29 "Super Fortress." It was this airplane that dropped the atomic bombs on Hiroshima and Nagasaki in August 1945.

Boeing's president, Phil Johnson, died unexpectedly during the war. He was replaced with the company's chief lawyer, William M. Allen, on the last day of the war. Under Allen's leadership, Boeing produced a number of new bombers, including the B-47, B-50, and the B-52. Boeing's B-307 Stratoliner, a B-17 converted for transporting passengers, was succeeded by the B-377 Stratocruiser in 1952. The Stratocruiser was a very popular double-deck transport, most widely used by Northwest Orient. It was also Boeing's only airplane built for the commercial airline market since before the war.

1953–69: Jets, Missiles, and Rockets

In the spring of 1953 Bill Allen persuaded the secretary of the U.S. Air Force, Harold Talbot, to allow Boeing the use of

Key Dates:

1917: Founder William Boeing incorporates Pacific Aero Products Company, involved in plane making, mail delivery, and pilot training.
1918: Company changes its name to Boeing Airplane Company.
1929: United Aircraft and Transportation Company is formed as a holding company for Boeing-controlled airlines and makers of airplanes, engines, and propellers.
1934: Government investigation of airmail business leads to break-up of United, with Seattle-based Boeing Airplane Company emerging with a sole focus on manufacturing.
1944: In peak wartime production, 16 B-17s are produced every 24 hours.
1954: The Boeing 707 jet makes its first flight.
1960: Philadelphia-based Vertol Aircraft Corporation, a maker of military helicopters, is acquired.
1961: Company changes its name to The Boeing Company; completes first test launch of a Minuteman missile at Cape Canaveral, Florida.
1964: The three-engine 727 passenger jet is introduced.
1966: Company launches first Lunar Orbiter, which sends photos of the moon back to Earth.
1967: The shorter-route 737 jet makes its first commercial flight.
1968: Apollo 8, which takes the first astronauts around the moon, is launched in December boosted by a Saturn V rocket, for which Boeing had built the first stage.
1970: The 747, the first of the ''jumbo jets,'' makes its first commercial flight.
1971: Strict austerity measures, including the layoff of 43,200 employees, save the company from bankruptcy.
1976: First air-launched cruise missile is test-fired from a B-52.
1981: The first NATO AWACS is delivered to West Germany; the 767 makes its first flight.
1982: The 757 makes its first flight.
1993: NASA names the company the prime contractor for the International Space Station.
1995: First 777-200 is delivered to United Airlines.
1996: The aerospace and defense units of Rockwell International are acquired.
1997: McDonnell Douglas, number one in military aircraft and number three in commercial aircraft worldwide, is acquired, making Boeing the largest aerospace company in the world.
1999: Company-led consortium successfully launches a commercial satellite from a floating platform at sea.

the government-owned B-52 construction facilities for the development of a new civilian/military jet. Boeing invested $16 million in the project, which was intended to put the company ahead of the Douglas Aircraft Company. Douglas had dominated the commercial airplane market for years with its popular propeller-driven DC series.

This new jet, the B-707, first rolled off the assembly line in 1957. American Airlines, a loyal Douglas customer, was the first to order the new jet. Their defection so alarmed Douglas that the company accelerated development of its nearly identical DC-8 passenger jetliner. The government later took delivery of Boeing's military version of the jet, the KC-135 tanker, alternately known as the ''missing 717.'' Meanwhile, Boeing expanded its involvement in the defense market through the 1960 acquisition of Philadelphia-based Vertol Aircraft Corporation, a maker of military helicopters. During the Vietnam War, Boeing Chinook and Sea Knight helicopters were heavily utilized by American forces.

Boeing, which changed its name to The Boeing Company in 1961, enjoyed a large degree of success and profitability with the 707. The company devoted its resources to the development of a number of other passenger jet models, including the 720 (a modified 707) and the 727, which was introduced in 1964. The 727 was Boeing's response to a successful French model called the Caravelle. The Caravelle's engines were located in the rear of the fuselage, uncluttering the wings and reducing cabin noise. Boeing adopted this design for its three-engine 727, which carried 143 passengers. Douglas, unwilling to be passed by, introduced a similar two-engine model called the DC-9 in 1965.

During this time the company also recognized a demand for a smaller 100-passenger jetliner for shorter routes. As a result, Boeing developed the 737 model. The 737 seemed to run counter to the general trend at Boeing of building larger, more technologically advanced jetliners, but it did have a place in the market and made a profit.

Boeing's next engineering accomplishment was the creation of a very large passenger transport designated the 747. This new jetliner was capable of carrying twice as many passengers as any other airplane. Its huge dimensions and powerful four-engine configuration made it the first of a new class of ''jumbo jets,'' later joined by McDonnell Douglas's DC-10 and Lockheed's 1011 Tri-Star. The first 747 was produced in 1968, and it made its first commercial voyage in January 1970 on a Pan American flight from New York to London.

The 1960s also saw Boeing active in the defense and NASA contracting sectors. As the Cold War continued, Boeing was selected to develop the Minuteman intercontinental ballistic missile system. The company completed the first test launch of a Minuteman missile at Cape Canaveral, Florida, in February 1961. The Minuteman II and Minuteman III followed later in the decade. In 1966 Boeing was selected to design, develop, and test the short-range attack missile (SRAM); by the early 1970s the company had produced 1,000 SRAMs.

As far back as 1959 Boeing had developed a prototype manned, reusable space vehicle similar to the Space Shuttle of two decades later. Called Dyna-Soar, the project was canceled in 1963. Boeing was heavily involved in NASA's Apollo project of the 1960s, beginning with its production of several Lunar Orbiters, the first of which was launched in 1966. The Orbiters circled the moon, sending photographs of the moon back to Earth, which helped NASA select safe landing sites for the Apollo missions. Boeing was also responsible for the first stage of the Saturn V Apollo rocket, which launched *Apollo 8* in

December 1968, the mission that took the first astronauts around the moon. (The second stage of the Saturn V was built by Rockwell's aerospace unit and the third by McDonnell Douglas—two entities that would be acquired by Boeing late in the 20th century.) In 1969 Boeing began building the Lunar Roving Vehicle, which was used to explore the moon in the early 1970s on the final three Apollo missions.

1970–82: Averting Bankruptcy; Diversification; the 757 and 767

Boeing had seemingly ended the 1960s on high notes. On July 20, 1969, the first human being walked on the moon, with Boeing having played its key role in the *Apollo 11* mission. By the time the 747 was first delivered in 1969, 160 orders had been placed for the jetliner. Boeing was counting on increased sales of commercial aircraft to make up for the revenue shortfall engendered by the winding down of the Apollo program. But the aviation industry was hit by a recession just as the 747 was beginning production, leading to an 18-month period when the company received not one new order from a domestic carrier. Aggravating the situation for a new jet that had not yet established itself in the market were higher than expected startup costs and initial delivery problems. A further blow came when development was halted on the 2707, a supersonic transport better known as the ''SST.'' Boeing and Lockheed had been selected to design the SST back in 1964, but progress on this aircraft was slow and costly. Despite the support of Senator Henry Jackson, the U.S. Congress in 1971 voted not to fund further development of the SST. Shortly thereafter Boeing abandoned the project altogether. Boeing's situation was so dire that the company was close to bankruptcy. In 1969 a new chief executive, Thornton Wilson, was appointed to head the organization. Faced with an impending disaster, Wilson pared the workforce down from 80,400 to 37,200 between early 1970 and October 1971. The layoffs at Boeing had a profound effect on the local economy, as unemployment in Seattle rose to 14 percent.

Wilson's austerity measures paid off quickly. Soon Boeing's jets were rolling off the tarmac, and employees were called back to work. After the company's initial recovery, it received a deluge of commercial airplane orders and military contracts. Boeing had been selected as the prime contractor for the airborne warning and control system (AWACS) aircraft. First test-flown in 1972, the AWACS was a modified version of a 707 used by the military as an airborne early warning system. The first NATO AWACS was delivered to West Germany in 1981. Another key defense contract won by Boeing was for the air-launched cruise missile (ALCM), which was first test-launched from a B-52 in 1976. Under a $4 billion defense department contract, construction began on an assembly facility for the ALCM program in July 1980 in Kent, Washington. In the space sector Boeing built the *Mariner 10* spacecraft, which was launched in November 1973 and completed a flyby of Mercury in March 1975. Three years later the company won a contract with NASA to construct the inertial upper stage rocket used to boost the Space Shuttle.

In 1978 Boeing started development of two new passenger jet models—the 757 and the wide-body 767—intended to take the company into the 21st century. The 767 made its first flight in 1981 while the 757 did likewise one year later. Utilizing advanced technology and improved engines, these jetliners were Boeing's response to McDonnell Douglas's MD series and the European Airbus consortium's 300 series. They also were more fuel-efficient than previous models, in response to the oil shortages of the 1970s, and quieter—the latter a nod to growing concern over aircraft noise. For airlines, the 757 and 767 also had added benefits: they required smaller crews and their shared design led the Federal Aviation Administration to declare in 1983 that any pilot qualified to fly one model was automatically qualified to fly the other. Besides the 757 and 767, Boeing offered an updated 737 for the shorter-range rural ''puddle-jumper'' market and modified 747s capable of greater range and passenger capacity.

During this period of prosperity with commercial jetliners, Boeing made several attempts to diversify its business. Not all of them were successful. In the 1970s Boeing entered the metro-rail business, manufacturing mass transit systems for Boston, San Francisco, and Morgantown, West Virginia. The systems were modern, computerized, and efficient. They were also prone to frequent breakdowns. After fulfilling its obligation to rectify the systems (at great cost), Boeing decided to discontinue its ground transport business. Other short-lived ventures were the management of a housing project for the U.S. Department of Housing and Urban Development, the building of a desalinization plant in the Virgin Islands, the construction of three huge wind turbines in the Columbia River gorge, and the irrigation of a 6,000-acre farm in an eastern Oregon desert.

Mid-1980s to Mid-1990s: The 777 and Another Industry Downturn

Boeing established an ''Advanced Products Group'' in the later years of the 1980s to oversee the company's more futuristic aircraft and keep it at the technological vanguard. Boeing's twin-engine wide-body 777, originally scheduled to be introduced with the 757 and 767, attracted little interest and was temporarily shelved. The development of the fuel-efficient, 150-passenger 777 was also delayed when declining fuel costs and rising research and development expenses reduced demand. By 1990 the 777 had made a comeback: an initial order of 34 airplanes and 34 options placed by United Airlines put the new jet, which carried 350 passengers, into official production. The first 777-200 was delivered to United in 1995.

Frank Shrontz advanced to Boeing's chief executive office in 1986, at the start of the world's largest aircraft order binge in history, and led the manufacturer from sales of $16.3 billion in 1986 to $29.31 billion in 1991. Although Boeing remained profitable, its earnings declined steadily in the mid-1980s and its stock dropped 20 points in October 1987. Boeing jets were involved in four fatal air accidents from December 1988 to March 1989, and the company missed its first delivery deadline in two decades when the 747-400 experienced production delays. These internal problems were exacerbated by increased competition from Airbus, which was heavily subsidized by a consortium of European companies and governments.

Nevertheless, in 1990 Boeing chalked up record sales and net profits of $27.6 billion and $1.4 billion, respectively, and ended the year with a $97 billion backlog. But after its experiences of the 1980s, and due to CEO Shrontz's vigilance, Boeing

Boise Cascade Corporation

111 West Jefferson Street
.O. Box 50
oise, Idaho 83728-0001
S.A.
lephone: (208) 384-6161
: (208) 384-7224
b site: http://www.bc.com

lic Company
rporated: 1931 as Boise Payette Lumber Company
oyees: 23,039
$6.16 billion (1998)
Exchanges: New York Midwest
Symbol: BCC
113110 Timber Tract Operations; 113310
ging; 321113 Sawmills; 321210 Veneer, Plywood,
Engineered Wood Product Manufacturing; 322100
, Paper, and Paperboard Mills; 322211 Corru-
d and Solid Fiber Box Manufacturing; 322230
onery Product Manufacturing; 421310 Lumber,
ood, Millwork, and Wood Panel Wholesalers;
0 Roofing, Siding, and Insulation Material
salers; 421390 Other Construction Material
salers; 453210 Office Supplies and Stationery
454110 Electronic Shopping and Mail-Order
; 454390 Other Direct Selling Establishments

cade Corporation has grown from a small local
ny into a major manufacturer of wood products,
per products and a major distributor of building
se Cascade Office Products Corporation, a pub-
mpany 81.2 percent owned by Boise Cascade
a leading wholesaler of office products, includ-
mputer consumables, furniture, and paper. The
more than two million acres of timberland in
and holds long-term leases or licenses on an
00 acres.

Lumber Beginnings

established under the name Boise Cascade
57 through the merger of the Boise Payette Lumber Company and the Cascade Lumber Company of Yakima, Washington. Boise Payette had been one of Idaho's top lumber producers since its formation in 1931; however, the building boom following World War II had seriously depleted its timberlands. The Cascade Lumber Company had been in operation since 1902, when it was founded by George S. Rankin, the owner of several other businesses in the Yakima Valley. Rankin had been joined in this new venture by a business associate, Fred V. Pennington, and other individuals experienced in lumber operations in the Midwest. Initially, Cascade owned timberland at the headwaters of the Yakima River, which it had purchased for $100,000, and also operated several retail lumberyards in the area in addition to its Yakima mill. These yards were closed in 1914 and consolidated into one lumberyard at the Yakima sawmill, which continued operating even after the merger with Boise Payette.

Robert V. Hansberger, who had joined Boise Payette in 1956 as president, saw the merger of the two companies as an opportunity for Boise Payette to replenish its timber supply. More importantly, combining the resources of the two firms would enable the resulting company to build a base of raw materials large enough to allow it to expand beyond lumber production into the manufacture of paper and pulp products.

In 1958 the company, now known as Boise Cascade, built a kraft pulp and paper mill in Wallula, Washington, and corrugated container plants at both Wallula and Burley, Idaho. The paper and pulp area grew rapidly over the next five years with further expansion of the company's paper and wood production capacity. In spite of this success, Hansberger and his management team recognized how vulnerable the company was because of the cyclical nature of the wood and paper industries. They decided to diversify into other areas as a hedge against possible downturns in demand for its forest products.

Late 1960s: Diversification

Since joining the company, Hansberger had filled the company's top management ranks with graduates of the country's leading business schools. He permitted these executives to operate independently and expand the company's operating divisions as they saw fit. In 1964 Boise Cascade entered the office

began to institute retrenchment moves. Although the manufacturer experienced three years of rising sales and earnings from 1989 to 1992, prospects for the future of the company—and the industry—were not bright. Worldwide orders of all aircraft declined from 1,662 in 1989 to 439 in 1991, and cancellations from the besieged airlines diminished expected delivery figures even more. The commercial airline industry's downturn started in 1990, heralding brutal price wars and canceled aircraft orders. Around the same time, the Cold War was winding down and Pentagon spending on military systems went into a sharp decline as well, buffeting Boeing's defense unit. By the fall of 1992, Boeing's stock suffered on Wall Street, selling for about $35 per share, down from a high of nearly $62 in 1990.

Shrontz moved to reduce Boeing's cost structure by 20 to 30 percent by 1997, even though his firm was the world's lowest-cost aircraft producer. Production cuts soon led to layoffs. Boeing's workforce declined each year from 1989 to 1993, for a total of 40,000 jobs lost. Early in 1994, Shrontz announced that about 30,000 jobs—one-fourth of the company's remaining workforce—would be eliminated over the course of the year. Sales for 1993 declined to $25.44 billion from 1992's $30.18 billion, and net earnings slid from $1.55 billion to $1.24 billion. Additional workforce reductions came in 1994 and 1995, years in which revenue and earnings declined still further, dropping to $19.52 billion and $393 million, respectively, by 1995.

Meanwhile, in 1993 NASA selected Boeing as the prime contractor for the International Space Station, which was called the largest international science and technology endeavor ever undertaken, and which was scheduled for completion in the early 21st century. In addition, the company was also becoming increasingly involved in commercial space projects, most notably Sea Launch, a consortium 40 percent owned by Boeing with partners from Russia, the Ukraine, and Norway. In December 1995 this venture received its first order: ten commercial space satellite launches from Hughes Space and Communication Co. In October 1999 Sea Launch successfully made the first launch of a commercial satellite from a floating platform at sea. In the military contracting sector, in late 1996 Boeing was selected as one of two finalists, along with Lockheed Martin, to build and test two variants of the Joint Strike Fighter, a multiservice aircraft slated to be deployed in the 21st century by the U.S. Air Force, Marine Corps, and Navy, along with the U.K. Royal Navy. The project carried the potential for a massive $160 billion contract. Also in 1996 Philip Condit was named CEO of Boeing; Condit became chairman as well in early 1997.

Late 1990s and Beyond: Major Acquisitions and the 747-x Stretch

The industrywide difficulties in the aerospace and defense fields in the first half of the 1990s led to a wave of consolidation through mergers and acquisitions. Preoccupied with straightening out its own house, Boeing watched from the sidelines—that is, until the company completed two major acquisitions within an eight-month period. In December 1996 Boeing paid $3.2 billion for the aerospace and defense holdings of Rockwell International. Gained in the transaction were Rockwell's contracts for the Space Shuttle and the International Space Station, as well as activities in launch systems, rocket engines, missiles, satellites, military airplanes, and guidance and navigation systems. In August 1997 Boeing completed a $14 billion acquisition of McDonnell Douglas, vaulting Boeing into the number one position worldwide in the aerospace industry. McDonnell had been the world's number three maker of commercial aircraft, with its MD series of jets; the acquisition therefore increased Boeing's share of the world market for large commercial jetliners to more than 60 percent—and it left Boeing with just one major competitor in that sector: the European Airbus consortium, which held about one-third of the world market. As the market for commercial planes was once again on the upswing at the time, Boeing particularly coveted the added production capacity the acquisition brought. Another key attraction—and perhaps even more important—was the opportunity to further bolster the company's defense and space operations, which it hoped would provide a counterbalance to the boom-and-bust cycle of commercial jets. McDonnell was number two among U.S. defense contractors and was the number one maker of military aircraft worldwide. Among the military aircraft were the F/A-18, which formed the core of the U.S. Navy's jet fleet, and the F-15, which was the U.S. Air Force's top fighter aircraft. Following the McDonnell acquisition, Condit remained chairman and CEO of Boeing, while Harry Stonecipher, McDonnell's CEO, was named president and chief operating officer.

Unfortunately, 1997 turned disastrous for Boeing for reasons wholly unrelated to its acquisition spree. Attempting to take advantage of the upswing in airplane orders, which was in part caused by the aging of the airliners' fleets, Boeing committed to doubling its production over an 18-month period. Various snafus led to production delays, including the wholesale shutdown of some production units while out-of-sequence work was brought back into line. The company took pretax charges in 1997 totaling a whopping $3 billion plus, more than half of which stemmed from the production difficulties. Boeing also took a $1.4 billion charge related to its decision to phase out production of the MD-80 and MD-90 jets by early 2000. These charges led the company to record its first loss in 50 years, a net loss of $178 million on revenues of $45.8 billion. Additional charges were taken during 1998, but the company managed to post net income of $1.12 billion on sales of $56.15 billion thanks to the strong performance of its defense and space operations. It also managed to increase the number of aircraft it produced from the 374 of 1997 to more than 550 in 1998. The company was in the midst of a major cost-containment effort, with its workforce expected to be reduced from its peak of 238,000 at year-end 1997 to between 185,000 and 195,000 by the end of 2000.

As it prepared for the 21st century, Boeing's defense and space operations appeared to be healthy despite such setbacks as the August 1998 explosion of a Delta III rocket making its maiden voyage, with a satellite in tow, and the delays in the development of the International Space Station because of economic turmoil in Russia. In October 1998 the Air Force awarded Boeing a $1.38 billion contract to launch a new generation of rockets, and Boeing in 1999 also won a $4.5 billion contract to develop spy satellites for the CIA and others. If anything was clouding Boeing's future it was the commercial aircraft sector, where Airbus was developing into a formidable adversary. In late 1999 Aerospatiale SA of France merged with the aerospace unit of DaimlerChrysler AG to form European Aeronautic Defense & Space Co., which now held 80 percent of Airbus, with the other 20 percent owned by British Aerospace plc. This streamlining of the ownership structure brought closer the long-anticipated transformation of Airbus into a publicly traded, focused corporation; should that occur, no longer could Boeing dismiss Airbus as a clumsy consortium propped up by government subsidies. In fact, the battle lines appeared to have been drawn by the two rivals at the end of the 20th century in the development of the next generation of super jumbo jets. Airbus had in the planning stages a brand-new jet, the A-3XX, envisioned as the largest jetliner ever, featuring four engines, double decks running the length of the fuselage, a range of 8,800 miles, and passenger capacity of 555 to 655. The project was estimated to cost $12 billion. Boeing had in mind producing a bigger, longer-range version of its 747 jet, dubbed the 747-x Stretch, with seating capacity of 500 to 520, a range of 8,625 miles, and a projected cost of just $2–$3 billion. An intense competition for contracts with airliners was expected in the early 21st century as the super jumbos began to take shape.

Principal Subsidiaries

757UA, Inc.; 767ER, Inc.; Aileron Inc.; Akash, Inc.; Aldford-1 Corporation; ARGOsystems Inc.; Astro Limited; Astro-II, Inc.; Autonetics, Inc.; Bahasa Aircraft Corporation; BCS Richland, Inc.; Beaufoy-1 Corporation; Boeing Aerospace Ltd.; Boeing Aerospace Operations Inc.; Boeing Agri-Industrial Company; Boeing Commercial Information and Communication Company; Boeing Commercial Space Company; Boeing Constructors, Inc.; Boeing Domestic Sales Corporation; Boeing Enterprises, Inc.; Boeing Financial Corporation; Boeing Global Services, Inc.; Boeing Information Services, Inc.; Boeing International Corporation; Boeing International Logistics Spares, Inc.; Boeing International Sales Corporation; Boeing Investment Company, Inc.; Boeing Leasing Company; Boeing Logistics Spares, Inc.; Boeing Middle East Limited; Boeing North American, Inc.; Boeing Offset Company, Inc.; Boeing Operations International, Incorporated; Boeing Overseas, Inc.; Boeing Precision Gear, Inc.; Boeing Space Operations Company; Boeing Support Services, Inc.; Boeing Technology International, Inc.; Boeing Travel Management Company; Canard Holdings, Inc.; CBSA Leasing II, Inc.; CBSA Leasing, Inc.; Cougar, Ltd.; Dillon, Inc.; Gaucho-1 Inc.; GAUCHO-2 Inc.; Hanway Corporation; Longacres Park, Inc.; Longbow Golf Club Corporation; McDonnell Douglas Corporation; Montana Aviation Research Company; North American Aviation, Inc.; Rainier Aircraft Leasing Inc.; Rocketdyne Technical Services Company; Rocketdyne, Inc.; Sunshine Leasing Company - 1; Taiko Leasing, Inc.; Thayer Leasing Company - 1; VC-X 757, Inc.; Wingspan, Inc.

Principal Competitors

Aerospatiale Matra; Airbus Industrie; The BFGoodrich Company; Bombardier Inc.; British Aerospace plc; Cordant Technologies Inc.; DaimlerChrysler AG; Dassault Aviation SA; Kaman Corporation; Lockheed Martin Corporation; Northrop Grumman Corporation; Raytheon Company; Sextant Avionique; Textron Inc.; Thomson S.A.; United Technologies Corporation.

Further Reading

Banks, Howard, "Moment of Truth," *Forbes,* May 22, 1995, p. 51.

Bauer, Eugene E., *Boeing in Peace and War,* Enumclaw, Wash.: Taba Publishing, 1990, 364 p.

Bernstein, Aaron, Andy Reinhardt, and Seanna Browder, "Lost in Space at Boeing: Post-Merger Clashes Throw the Aerospace Giant Off-Course," *Business Week,* April 27, 1998, p. 42.

Biddle, Frederic M., "Boeing Is Placing Its Bets on Smaller, Cheaper Airliners," *Wall Street Journal,* July 6, 1998, p. A22.

——, "Boeing Is Still Waiting for Merger Results to Take Off," *Wall Street Journal,* March 2, 1998, p. B6.

——, "Boeing's Effort to Cushion Itself from Cycles Backfires," *Wall Street Journal,* October 24, 1997, p. B4.

Biddle, Frederic M., and John Helyar, "Behind Boeing's Woes: Clunky Assembly Line, Price War with Airbus," *Wall Street Journal,* April 24, 1998, p. A1.

Bilstein, Roger E., *Flight in America, 1900–1983: From the Wrights to the Astronauts,* Baltimore: Johns Hopkins University Press, 1984, 356 p.

Bowers, Peter M., *Boeing Aircraft Since 1916,* Annapolis, Md.: Naval Institute Press, 1989, 668 p.

Browder, Seanna, "Getting Boeing to Fly Right," *Business Week,* September 27, 1999, p. 104.

Cloud, David S., "McDonnell Douglas, Chinese Trading Firm Are Indicted by U.S.," *Wall Street Journal,* October 20, 1999, p. A4.

Cole, Jeff, "Airbus Prepares to 'Bet the Company' As It Builds a Huge New Jet: It Could Seat Nearly 1,000; Meanwhile, Boeing Opts to Simply Retool Its 747," *Wall Street Journal,* November 3, 1999, pp. A1, A10.

——, "Air Power: Boeing Plan to Acquire McDonnell Douglas Bolsters Consolidation," *Wall Street Journal,* December 16, 1996, p. A1.

——, "Boeing, in a Strategic Shift, to Develop Its Own Satellite Systems and Services," *Wall Street Journal,* June 14, 1999, p. A3.

——, "Boeing to Proceed with Bigger 747 Jet," *Wall Street Journal,* September 20, 1999, pp. A2, A4.

——, "Shrontz Turns Over Controls at Boeing As Rivals Rev Up," *Wall Street Journal,* April 29, 1996, p. B4.

——, "Sleepless in Seattle: Onslaught of Orders Has Boeing Scrambling to Build Jets Faster," *Wall Street Journal,* July 24, 1996, p. A1.

Cole, Jeff, and Charles Goldsmith, "Rivalry Between Boeing, Airbus Takes New Direction," *Wall Street Journal,* April 30, 1997, p. B4.

Cole, Jeff, and Steven Lipin, "Boeing Deal Will Strengthen Company: Acquisition of Rockwell's Aerospace and Defense Operations Is Announced," *Wall Street Journal,* August 2, 1996, p. A3.

Edmondson, Gail, Janet Rae-Dupree, and Kerry Capell, "How Airbus Could Rule the Skies," *Business Week,* August 2, 1999, p. 54.

Holmes, Stanley, "Boeing Thinks Small, Airbus Thinks Big in Demand for Aircraft in Next 20 Years," *Seattle Times,* June 16, 1999.

Ingells, Douglas J., *747: The Story of the Boeing Super Jet,* Fallbrook, Calif.: Aero Publishers, 1970.

Irving, Clive, *Wide-Body: The Triumph of the 747,* New York: Morrow, 1993, 384 p.

Kuter, Lawrence S., *The Great Gamble: The Boeing 747,* University of Alabama Press, 1973, 134 p.

Lubove, Seth, "Destroying the Old Hierarchies," *Forbes,* June 3, 1996, p. 62.

Lynn, Matthew, *Birds of Prey: Boeing Vs. Airbus: A Battle for the Skies,* rev. ed., New York: Four Walls Eight Windows, 1997, 244 p.

Mansfield, Harold, *Billion Dollar Battle: The Story Behind the "Impossible" 727 Project,* edited by James Gilbert, New York: Ayer, 1965.

——, *Vision: A Saga of the Sky,* New York: Ayer, 1965.

Osterland, Andrew, "Philip M. Condit of the Boeing Company (CEO of the Year)," *Financial World,* April 15, 1997, p. 66.

Pasztor, Andy, "Boeing 777s Face Curbs from FAA," *Wall Street Journal,* October 28, 1999, pp. A3, A5.

Pasztor, Andy, and Jeff Cole, "Boeing Discloses Defect, Delays Jet Deliveries," *Wall Street Journal,* November 3, 1999, pp. A2, A10.

Rae-Dupree, Janet, "Can Boeing Get Lean Enough?," *Business Week,* August 30, 1999, p. 182.

Redding, Robert, and Bill Yenne, *Boeing: Planemaker to the World,* London: Arms and Armour Press, 1983; rev. ed., San Diego: Thunder Bay Press, 1997, 256 p.

Reinhardt, Andy, and Seanna Browder, "Fly, Damn It, Fly: A New Boeing Crew Tries to Navigate a Turnaround," *Business Week,* November 9, 1998, p. 150.

Reinhardt, Andy, Seanna Browder, and Ron Stodghill II, "Three Huge Hours in Seattle: How Boeing and McDonnell Cut the Biggest Deal in Aviation History," *Business Week,* December 30, 1996, p. 38.

Rodgers, Eugene, *Flying High: The Story of Boeing and the Rise of the Jetliner Industry,* New York: Atlantic Monthly Press, 1996, 502 p.

Sabbagh, Karl, *Twenty-First Century Jet: The Making and Marketir the Boeing 777,* New York: Scribner, 1996, 366 p.

Serling, Robert J., *Legend and Legacy: The Story of Boeing a People,* New York: St. Martin's Press, 1992, 480 p.

Squeo, Anne Marie, "Boeing, Raytheon Successfully Test Inte for National Missile System," *Wall Street Journal,* Oc 1999, p. A4.

Taylor, Alex, III, "Boeing: Sleepy in Seattle," *Fortune,* 1995, p. 92.

Wilhelm, Steve, "Boeing Aims Higher in Satellite Busin *Sound Business Journal,* October 4, 1999.

—April Doug

—updated by David

Boise Ca lumber comp paper, and pa materials. Boi licly traded c Corporation, is ing supplies, c company owns North America additional 330,0

The firm was Corporation in 19

began to institute retrenchment moves. Although the manufacturer experienced three years of rising sales and earnings from 1989 to 1992, prospects for the future of the company—and the industry—were not bright. Worldwide orders of all aircraft declined from 1,662 in 1989 to 439 in 1991, and cancellations from the besieged airlines diminished expected delivery figures even more. The commercial airline industry's downturn started in 1990, heralding brutal price wars and canceled aircraft orders. Around the same time, the Cold War was winding down and Pentagon spending on military systems went into a sharp decline as well, buffeting Boeing's defense unit. By the fall of 1992, Boeing's stock suffered on Wall Street, selling for about $35 per share, down from a high of nearly $62 in 1990.

Shrontz moved to reduce Boeing's cost structure by 20 to 30 percent by 1997, even though his firm was the world's lowest-cost aircraft producer. Production cuts soon led to layoffs. Boeing's workforce declined each year from 1989 to 1993, for a total of 40,000 jobs lost. Early in 1994, Shrontz announced that about 30,000 jobs—one-fourth of the company's remaining workforce—would be eliminated over the course of the year. Sales for 1993 declined to $25.44 billion from 1992's $30.18 billion, and net earnings slid from $1.55 billion to $1.24 billion. Additional workforce reductions came in 1994 and 1995, years in which revenue and earnings declined still further, dropping to $19.52 billion and $393 million, respectively, by 1995.

Meanwhile, in 1993 NASA selected Boeing as the prime contractor for the International Space Station, which was called the largest international science and technology endeavor ever undertaken, and which was scheduled for completion in the early 21st century. In addition, the company was also becoming increasingly involved in commercial space projects, most notably Sea Launch, a consortium 40 percent owned by Boeing with partners from Russia, the Ukraine, and Norway. In December 1995 this venture received its first order: ten commercial space satellite launches from Hughes Space and Communication Co. In October 1999 Sea Launch successfully made the first launch of a commercial satellite from a floating platform at sea. In the military contracting sector, in late 1996 Boeing was selected as one of two finalists, along with Lockheed Martin, to build and test two variants of the Joint Strike Fighter, a multiservice aircraft slated to be deployed in the 21st century by the U.S. Air Force, Marine Corps, and Navy, along with the U.K. Royal Navy. The project carried the potential for a massive $160 billion contract. Also in 1996 Philip Condit was named CEO of Boeing; Condit became chairman as well in early 1997.

Late 1990s and Beyond: Major Acquisitions and the 747-x Stretch

The industrywide difficulties in the aerospace and defense fields in the first half of the 1990s led to a wave of consolidation through mergers and acquisitions. Preoccupied with straightening out its own house, Boeing watched from the sidelines—that is, until the company completed two major acquisitions within an eight-month period. In December 1996 Boeing paid $3.2 billion for the aerospace and defense holdings of Rockwell International. Gained in the transaction were Rockwell's contracts for the Space Shuttle and the International Space Station, as well as activities in launch systems, rocket engines, missiles, satellites, military airplanes, and guidance and navigation systems. In August 1997 Boeing completed a $14 billion acquisition of McDonnell Douglas, vaulting Boeing into the number one position worldwide in the aerospace industry. McDonnell had been the world's number three maker of commercial aircraft, with its MD series of jets; the acquisition therefore increased Boeing's share of the world market for large commercial jetliners to more than 60 percent—and it left Boeing with just one major competitor in that sector: the European Airbus consortium, which held about one-third of the world market. As the market for commercial planes was once again on the upswing at the time, Boeing particularly coveted the added production capacity the acquisition brought. Another key attraction—and perhaps even more important—was the opportunity to further bolster the company's defense and space operations, which it hoped would provide a counterbalance to the boom-and-bust cycle of commercial jets. McDonnell was number two among U.S. defense contractors and was the number one maker of military aircraft worldwide. Among the military aircraft were the F/A-18, which formed the core of the U.S. Navy's jet fleet, and the F-15, which was the U.S. Air Force's top fighter aircraft. Following the McDonnell acquisition, Condit remained chairman and CEO of Boeing, while Harry Stonecipher, McDonnell's CEO, was named president and chief operating officer.

Unfortunately, 1997 turned disastrous for Boeing for reasons wholly unrelated to its acquisition spree. Attempting to take advantage of the upswing in airplane orders, which was in part caused by the aging of the airliners' fleets, Boeing committed to doubling its production over an 18-month period. Various snafus led to production delays, including the wholesale shutdown of some production units while out-of-sequence work was brought back into line. The company took pretax charges in 1997 totaling a whopping $3 billion plus, more than half of which stemmed from the production difficulties. Boeing also took a $1.4 billion charge related to its decision to phase out production of the MD-80 and MD-90 jets by early 2000. These charges led the company to record its first loss in 50 years, a net loss of $178 million on revenues of $45.8 billion. Additional charges were taken during 1998, but the company managed to post net income of $1.12 billion on sales of $56.15 billion thanks to the strong performance of its defense and space operations. It also managed to increase the number of aircraft it produced from the 374 of 1997 to more than 550 in 1998. The company was in the midst of a major cost-containment effort, with its workforce expected to be reduced from its peak of 238,000 at year-end 1997 to between 185,000 and 195,000 by the end of 2000.

As it prepared for the 21st century, Boeing's defense and space operations appeared to be healthy despite such setbacks as the August 1998 explosion of a Delta III rocket making its maiden voyage, with a satellite in tow, and the delays in the development of the International Space Station because of economic turmoil in Russia. In October 1998 the Air Force awarded Boeing a $1.38 billion contract to launch a new generation of rockets, and Boeing in 1999 also won a $4.5 billion contract to develop spy satellites for the CIA and others. If anything was clouding Boeing's future it was the commercial aircraft sector, where Airbus was developing into a formidable adversary. In late 1999 Aerospatiale SA of France merged with the aerospace unit of DaimlerChrysler AG to form European Aeronautic Defense & Space Co., which now held 80 percent of Airbus, with the other 20 percent owned by British Aerospace plc. This streamlining of the ownership structure brought closer the long-anticipated transformation of Airbus into a publicly traded, focused corporation; should that occur, no longer could Boeing dismiss Airbus as a clumsy consortium propped up by government subsidies. In fact, the battle lines appeared to have been drawn by the two rivals at the end of the 20th century in the development of the next generation of super jumbo jets. Airbus had in the planning stages a brand-new jet, the A-3XX, envisioned as the largest jetliner ever, featuring four engines, double decks running the length of the fuselage, a range of 8,800 miles, and passenger capacity of 555 to 655. The project was estimated to cost $12 billion. Boeing had in mind producing a bigger, longer-range version of its 747 jet, dubbed the 747-x Stretch, with seating capacity of 500 to 520, a range of 8,625 miles, and a projected cost of just $2–$3 billion. An intense competition for contracts with airliners was expected in the early 21st century as the super jumbos began to take shape.

Principal Subsidiaries

757UA, Inc.; 767ER, Inc.; Aileron Inc.; Akash, Inc.; Aldford-1 Corporation; ARGOsystems Inc.; Astro Limited; Astro-II, Inc.; Autonetics, Inc.; Bahasa Aircraft Corporation; BCS Richland, Inc.; Beaufoy-1 Corporation; Boeing Aerospace Ltd.; Boeing Aerospace Operations Inc.; Boeing Agri-Industrial Company; Boeing Commercial Information and Communication Company; Boeing Commercial Space Company; Boeing Constructors, Inc.; Boeing Domestic Sales Corporation; Boeing Enterprises, Inc.; Boeing Financial Corporation; Boeing Global Services, Inc.; Boeing Information Services, Inc.; Boeing International Corporation; Boeing International Logistics Spares, Inc.; Boeing International Sales Corporation; Boeing Investment Company, Inc.; Boeing Leasing Company; Boeing Logistics Spares, Inc.; Boeing Middle East Limited; Boeing North American, Inc.; Boeing Offset Company, Inc.; Boeing Operations International, Incorporated; Boeing Overseas, Inc.; Boeing Precision Gear, Inc.; Boeing Space Operations Company; Boeing Support Services, Inc.; Boeing Technology International, Inc.; Boeing Travel Management Company; Canard Holdings, Inc.; CBSA Leasing II, Inc.; CBSA Leasing, Inc.; Cougar, Ltd.; Dillon, Inc.; Gaucho-1 Inc.; GAUCHO-2 Inc.; Hanway Corporation; Longacres Park, Inc.; Longbow Golf Club Corporation; McDonnell Douglas Corporation; Montana Aviation Research Company; North American Aviation, Inc.; Rainier Aircraft Leasing Inc.; Rocketdyne Technical Services Company; Rocketdyne, Inc.; Sunshine Leasing Company - 1; Taiko Leasing, Inc.; Thayer Leasing Company - 1; VC-X 757, Inc.; Wingspan, Inc.

Principal Competitors

Aerospatiale Matra; Airbus Industrie; The BFGoodrich Company; Bombardier Inc.; British Aerospace plc; Cordant Technologies Inc.; DaimlerChrysler AG; Dassault Aviation SA; Kaman Corporation; Lockheed Martin Corporation; Northrop Grumman Corporation; Raytheon Company; Sextant Avionique; Textron Inc.; Thomson S.A.; United Technologies Corporation.

Further Reading

Banks, Howard, ''Moment of Truth,'' *Forbes,* May 22, 1995, p. 51.

Bauer, Eugene E., *Boeing in Peace and War,* Enumclaw, Wash.: Taba Publishing, 1990, 364 p.

Bernstein, Aaron, Andy Reinhardt, and Seanna Browder, ''Lost in Space at Boeing: Post-Merger Clashes Throw the Aerospace Giant Off-Course,'' *Business Week,* April 27, 1998, p. 42.

Biddle, Frederic M., ''Boeing Is Placing Its Bets on Smaller, Cheaper Airliners,'' *Wall Street Journal,* July 6, 1998, p. A22.

——, ''Boeing Is Still Waiting for Merger Results to Take Off,'' *Wall Street Journal,* March 2, 1998, p. B6.

——, ''Boeing's Effort to Cushion Itself from Cycles Backfires,'' *Wall Street Journal,* October 24, 1997, p. B4.

Biddle, Frederic M., and John Helyar, ''Behind Boeing's Woes: Clunky Assembly Line, Price War with Airbus,'' *Wall Street Journal,* April 24, 1998, p. A1.

Bilstein, Roger E., *Flight in America, 1900–1983: From the Wrights to the Astronauts,* Baltimore: Johns Hopkins University Press, 1984, 356 p.

Bowers, Peter M., *Boeing Aircraft Since 1916,* Annapolis, Md.: Naval Institute Press, 1989, 668 p.

Browder, Seanna, ''Getting Boeing to Fly Right,'' *Business Week,* September 27, 1999, p. 104.

Cloud, David S., ''McDonnell Douglas, Chinese Trading Firm Are Indicted by U.S.,'' *Wall Street Journal,* October 20, 1999, p. A4.

Cole, Jeff, ''Airbus Prepares to 'Bet the Company' As It Builds a Huge New Jet: It Could Seat Nearly 1,000; Meanwhile, Boeing Opts to Simply Retool Its 747,'' *Wall Street Journal,* November 3, 1999, pp. A1, A10.

——, ''Air Power: Boeing Plan to Acquire McDonnell Douglas Bolsters Consolidation,'' *Wall Street Journal,* December 16, 1996, p. A1.

——, ''Boeing, in a Strategic Shift, to Develop Its Own Satellite Systems and Services,'' *Wall Street Journal,* June 14, 1999, p. A3.

——, ''Boeing to Proceed with Bigger 747 Jet,'' *Wall Street Journal,* September 20, 1999, pp. A2, A4.

——, ''Shrontz Turns Over Controls at Boeing As Rivals Rev Up,'' *Wall Street Journal,* April 29, 1996, p. B4.

——, ''Sleepless in Seattle: Onslaught of Orders Has Boeing Scrambling to Build Jets Faster,'' *Wall Street Journal,* July 24, 1996, p. A1.

Cole, Jeff, and Charles Goldsmith, ''Rivalry Between Boeing, Airbus Takes New Direction,'' *Wall Street Journal,* April 30, 1997, p. B4.

Cole, Jeff, and Steven Lipin, ''Boeing Deal Will Strengthen Company: Acquisition of Rockwell's Aerospace and Defense Operations Is Announced,'' *Wall Street Journal,* August 2, 1996, p. A3.

Edmondson, Gail, Janet Rae-Dupree, and Kerry Capell, ''How Airbus Could Rule the Skies,'' *Business Week,* August 2, 1999, p. 54.

Holmes, Stanley, ''Boeing Thinks Small, Airbus Thinks Big in Demand for Aircraft in Next 20 Years,'' *Seattle Times,* June 16, 1999.

Ingells, Douglas J., *747: The Story of the Boeing Super Jet,* Fallbrook, Calif.: Aero Publishers, 1970.

Irving, Clive, *Wide-Body: The Triumph of the 747,* New York: Morrow, 1993, 384 p.

Kuter, Lawrence S., *The Great Gamble: The Boeing 747,* University of Alabama Press, 1973, 134 p.

Lubove, Seth, ''Destroying the Old Hierarchies,'' *Forbes,* June 3, 1996, p. 62.

Lynn, Matthew, *Birds of Prey: Boeing Vs. Airbus: A Battle for the Skies,* rev. ed., New York: Four Walls Eight Windows, 1997, 244 p.

Mansfield, Harold, *Billion Dollar Battle: The Story Behind the ''Impossible'' 727 Project,* edited by James Gilbert, New York: Ayer, 1965.

——, *Vision: A Saga of the Sky,* New York: Ayer, 1965.

Osterland, Andrew, ''Philip M. Condit of the Boeing Company (CEO of the Year),'' *Financial World,* April 15, 1997, p. 66.

Pasztor, Andy, ''Boeing 777s Face Curbs from FAA,'' *Wall Street Journal,* October 28, 1999, pp. A3, A5.

Pasztor, Andy, and Jeff Cole, ''Boeing Discloses Defect, Delays Jet Deliveries,'' *Wall Street Journal,* November 3, 1999, pp. A2, A10.

Rae-Dupree, Janet, "Can Boeing Get Lean Enough?," *Business Week,* August 30, 1999, p. 182.

Redding, Robert, and Bill Yenne, *Boeing: Planemaker to the World,* London: Arms and Armour Press, 1983; rev. ed., San Diego: Thunder Bay Press, 1997, 256 p.

Reinhardt, Andy, and Seanna Browder, "Fly, Damn It, Fly: A New Boeing Crew Tries to Navigate a Turnaround," *Business Week,* November 9, 1998, p. 150.

Reinhardt, Andy, Seanna Browder, and Ron Stodghill II, "Three Huge Hours in Seattle: How Boeing and McDonnell Cut the Biggest Deal in Aviation History," *Business Week,* December 30, 1996, p. 38.

Rodgers, Eugene, *Flying High: The Story of Boeing and the Rise of the Jetliner Industry,* New York: Atlantic Monthly Press, 1996, 502 p.

Sabbagh, Karl, *Twenty-First Century Jet: The Making and Marketing of the Boeing 777,* New York: Scribner, 1996, 366 p.

Serling, Robert J., *Legend and Legacy: The Story of Boeing and Its People,* New York: St. Martin's Press, 1992, 480 p.

Squeo, Anne Marie, "Boeing, Raytheon Successfully Test Interceptor for National Missile System," *Wall Street Journal,* October 4, 1999, p. A4.

Taylor, Alex, III, "Boeing: Sleepy in Seattle," *Fortune,* August 7, 1995, p. 92.

Wilhelm, Steve, "Boeing Aims Higher in Satellite Business," *Puget Sound Business Journal,* October 4, 1999.

—April Dougal Gasbarre
—updated by David E. Salamie

Boise Cascade Corporation

1111 West Jefferson Street
P.O. Box 50
Boise, Idaho 83728-0001
U.S.A.
Telephone: (208) 384-6161
Fax: (208) 384-7224
Web site: http://www.bc.com

Public Company
Incorporated: 1931 as Boise Payette Lumber Company
Employees: 23,039
Sales: $6.16 billion (1998)
Stock Exchanges: New York Midwest
Ticker Symbol: BCC
NAIC: 113110 Timber Tract Operations; 113310 Logging; 321113 Sawmills; 321210 Veneer, Plywood, and Engineered Wood Product Manufacturing; 322100 Pulp, Paper, and Paperboard Mills; 322211 Corrugated and Solid Fiber Box Manufacturing; 322230 Stationery Product Manufacturing; 421310 Lumber, Plywood, Millwork, and Wood Panel Wholesalers; 421330 Roofing, Siding, and Insulation Material Wholesalers; 421390 Other Construction Material Wholesalers; 453210 Office Supplies and Stationery Stores; 454110 Electronic Shopping and Mail-Order Houses; 454390 Other Direct Selling Establishments

Boise Cascade Corporation has grown from a small local lumber company into a major manufacturer of wood products, paper, and paper products and a major distributor of building materials. Boise Cascade Office Products Corporation, a publicly traded company 81.2 percent owned by Boise Cascade Corporation, is a leading wholesaler of office products, including supplies, computer consumables, furniture, and paper. The company owns more than two million acres of timberland in North America and holds long-term leases or licenses on an additional 330,000 acres.

Lumber Beginnings

The firm was established under the name Boise Cascade Corporation in 1957 through the merger of the Boise Payette Lumber Company and the Cascade Lumber Company of Yakima, Washington. Boise Payette had been one of Idaho's top lumber producers since its formation in 1931; however, the building boom following World War II had seriously depleted its timberlands. The Cascade Lumber Company had been in operation since 1902, when it was founded by George S. Rankin, the owner of several other businesses in the Yakima Valley. Rankin had been joined in this new venture by a business associate, Fred V. Pennington, and other individuals experienced in lumber operations in the Midwest. Initially, Cascade owned timberland at the headwaters of the Yakima River, which it had purchased for $100,000, and also operated several retail lumberyards in the area in addition to its Yakima mill. These yards were closed in 1914 and consolidated into one lumberyard at the Yakima sawmill, which continued operating even after the merger with Boise Payette.

Robert V. Hansberger, who had joined Boise Payette in 1956 as president, saw the merger of the two companies as an opportunity for Boise Payette to replenish its timber supply. More importantly, combining the resources of the two firms would enable the resulting company to build a base of raw materials large enough to allow it to expand beyond lumber production into the manufacture of paper and pulp products.

In 1958 the company, now known as Boise Cascade, built a kraft pulp and paper mill in Wallula, Washington, and corrugated container plants at both Wallula and Burley, Idaho. The paper and pulp area grew rapidly over the next five years with further expansion of the company's paper and wood production capacity. In spite of this success, Hansberger and his management team recognized how vulnerable the company was because of the cyclical nature of the wood and paper industries. They decided to diversify into other areas as a hedge against possible downturns in demand for its forest products.

Late 1960s: Diversification

Since joining the company, Hansberger had filled the company's top management ranks with graduates of the country's leading business schools. He permitted these executives to operate independently and expand the company's operating divisions as they saw fit. In 1964 Boise Cascade entered the office

Company Perspectives:

Our three core values say best who we are and how we do business at Boise Cascade: safety, integrity, and Total Quality.

Our safety record is one of the best in the forest products industry . . . and in the United States. We're regularly recognized by our industry associations for safety excellence.

Our integrity shows in the relationships we've built with our customers. It's reflected in our efforts to study and protect wildlife in our forests. And it's conveyed in the communities where our employees' volunteer efforts help support hundreds of projects.

Total Quality is a commitment by each of us to always strive for excellence, to continuously improve the company's performance, and to consistently meet the expectations of our customers, employees, and shareholders. In short, Total Quality is the way we do business.

Our employees' commitment to our core values and their quest to give you the quality products and services you expect are why we're a leader in the building, paper, and office products industries.

products distribution business. By 1969 Boise Cascade had completed over 30 mergers and acquisitions and had become the third largest forest products company in the United States. Its operations now encompassed such diverse activities as residential and mobile home construction, recreational vehicle production, publishing, and cruise management.

One of the company's major interests during the mid-1960s was the field of real estate speculation and recreational land development. In 1967 alone, Boise Cascade acquired U.S. Land Company, Lake Arrowhead Development Company, and Pacific Cascade Land Company, and amassed real estate holdings of 126,000 acres in more than 12 states, with the majority of the land in California. Hoping to sell this property to large investors, the company met with little success and was forced to revise its strategy and develop the land itself into residential and recreational areas.

Although the company experienced greater success with this approach and sales were brisk, the new business division encountered several unanticipated problems. For example, Boise Cascade became a prime target for a growing ecological movement, particularly on the West Coast, which was concerned about the impact of the company's plans on the environment. Activist groups often hampered the company's efforts to gain approval for its developments from local planning agencies. Another major setback resulted from a series of lawsuits brought against Boise Cascade by the California attorney general. These legal actions were filed in response to complaints from prospective buyers about the tactics used by the company's salesmen, many of whom had been inherited in the course of the company's acquisitions of realty projects. The suits were eventually settled at a cost of $59 million.

In addition to these problems, Boise Cascade also experienced serious cash-flow difficulties related to its land development business. In this industry, the developer was responsible for paying the costs of constructing a community's sewer and water systems. These costs, typically, were high and had to be paid immediately, yet the developer was unable to collect its revenues until up to seven years after its sales were made. In an attempt to infuse the firm with fresh capital to fund the land development business on an ongoing basis, Boise Cascade acquired Ebasco in 1969. Ebasco and its subsidiaries were in the engineering and construction business and provided engineering services to major utilities. It was particularly attractive to Boise Cascade because it was rich with cash. It held millions of dollars worth of Latin American bonds, payable in U.S. dollars, that had been gained through the sale of Ebasco's utility operations in Argentina, Brazil, Chile, Colombia, and Costa Rica. By 1970 it was clear the company's land development business was in serious trouble, accumulating losses that placed the entire organization in jeopardy.

Upon the 1968 purchase of Princess Cruises, the company shifted its marketing efforts away from independent travel agencies, which had originally spurred the growth of the cruise line. Instead, it instituted a direct-mail campaign that was developed internally and proved less effective in generating business. As a result, the cruise line went from profits to losses within a matter of months.

1970s and 1980s: Divestments and Restructuring

In an attempt to reverse its losses, Boise Cascade wrote off a significant portion of its real estate holdings and divested its residential housing operation, along with other assets judged to be inadequate performers or lying too far outside the company's core business areas. In light of the lead-development reversals, Robert Hansberger, the architect of the company's rapid growth, resigned in 1972 and was replaced as president and chief executive officer by John Fery. Fery had been hired as Hansberger's assistant in 1957 and had ascended to executive vice-president and director within ten years.

After taking the helm, Fery immediately placed tighter controls on the company's internal management structure. He began selling off additional subsidiaries, including several Latin American investments gained in the Ebasco purchase, in order to reduce debt and refocus the firm's energies on forest products. As a result of these measures, Boise Cascade moved from a $171 million net loss to a $142 million net profit in just one year. Fery also instituted a five-year, billion-dollar capital spending program that was intended to help reduce the company's dependence on areas with correlating demand cycles, such as lumber and plywood, in favor of businesses with higher and more consistent growth potential. Fery's strategy placed greater emphasis on the manufacture of products for the construction industry and on paper products that could be marketed directly to end users in business form printing, data processing, and publishing.

This initiative propelled Boise Cascade into the 1980s as a specialized and efficient manufacturer of forest products and owner of timberland. By 1982 the company encountered sluggish demand for its products on two key fronts. The housing industry was badly depressed, reducing the demand for building products. The company's pulp and paper operation, intended to help Boise Cascade weather downturns in its other markets, experienced similar problems as industrial firms cut back ex-

Key Dates:

1902: Cascade Lumber Company of Yakima, Washington, is founded.
1931: Boise Payette Lumber Company is founded.
1957: Boise Cascade Corporation is created through the merger of Boise Payette Lumber and Cascade Lumber.
1958: The company's first pulp and paper mill and first corrugated container plants are built.
1964: Boise Cascade enters the office products distribution business.
1969: Diversification program results in various activities, including land development, recreational vehicle production, and cruise management.
1972: John Fery takes the helm, focusing the company on core areas: paper, building products, and office products distribution.
1987: Company sells its consumer packaging division.
1990: Recession hits Boise Cascade hard.
1992: Wholesale segment of office products distribution business is sold.
1994: Paper division begins three-year refocusing, with five paper mills sold or shut down.
1995: Company sells minority stake in Boise Cascade Office Product Corporation, retaining an 82.7 percent interest.
1999: Billerica, Massachusetts-based Furman Lumber, Inc., is acquired and merged into the company's wholesale building products unit.

penditures in response to the weakening economy. Over the next two years, the firm closed a number of inefficient or unprofitable mills and consolidated its marketing operations. In 1987 Boise Cascade sold its consumer packaging division, which had manufactured containers for various products, and a chain of retail building materials centers that had been acquired from Edwards Industries in 1979. Labor contracts with union employees were renegotiated in an attempt to reduce the company's overall cost structure.

At this time, the Federal Trade Commission accused Boise Cascade of violating the Robinson-Patman Act and the Federal Trade Commission (FTC) Act. In its suit, filed in 1980, the FTC claimed that the company had purchased office products for resale to commercial users and retailers at prices below those available to competitors. The FTC subsequently issued a cease and desist order to the firm in 1986. In 1988, however, an appeals court reversed this directive, determining that the FTC had not effectively substantiated its claim that the company's purchasing practices had adversely affected competition. The case was reargued before the FTC, resulting in a renewed finding of violation.

Early 1990s Recession

When the paper industry rebounded in 1986, Boise Cascade and other manufacturers began construction to increase both production and capacity to meet the demand. By 1990, however, this response to the market upswing resulted in an oversupply of paper and excess industry capacity that caused prices and profits to drop. Boise Cascade again found itself vulnerable to the peaks and valleys of another cyclical industry.

Although periods of recession were not new to Boise Cascade, the severity of this economic slump, coupled with the company's large investment in facility renovation and expansion, presented formidable challenges unrivaled in the company's history. Within the paper industry, the grades of paper most severely affected by the recession were newsprint and uncoated business and printing papers—the two grade categories in which Boise Cascade was most heavily committed. To make matters worse, preservation limits on the harvesting of timber in the Pacific Northwest, where the company maintained a greater presence than its competitors, reduced the supply of timber and consequently negatively affected operating costs. Expansion costs, especially the company's $550 million modernization program at its International Falls, Minnesota, paper mill, which was funded by borrowed money, raised its debt level, adding to the economic woes of the company. Boise Cascade's office products division also felt the brunt of the recession, suffering substantial losses in sales and profits.

To mitigate losses during the downturn, Boise Cascade formulated a business plan in 1990 to respond to the debilitating economic situation. The company decided to retain only those mills that could be upgraded to compete on a worldwide basis, to lessen its dependence on timber in the Pacific Northwest, and to sell assets that did not fit within its new strategic plan.

By the following year, the nation was still mired in a recession, and the paper industry continued to suffer from an oversupply of paper. Conditions at Boise Cascade were not much better. Facing its most difficult year ever, Boise experienced a drop in sales from 1990 levels; operating costs continued to rise due to timber supply reductions in the Pacific Northwest. The company, however, continued to invest heavily toward the expansion and modernization of its facilities, spending $2.2 billion on such programs over a three-year period. The combination of lower prices, increased operating costs, and the high interest payments stemming from capital investment projects resulted in a net loss of over $79 million, a considerable drop from a profit of $267 million two years earlier. In an effort to streamline the company, Boise Cascade announced the sale of $250 million of assets it no longer deemed strategically prudent to own. In July 1991, Boise Cascade sold its 50 percent interest in Durapack AG, a corrugated container manufacturer in Europe, for $50 million. Also in 1991, the company sold 29,500 acres of timberland in western Oregon and by January 1992 had sold the wholesale segment of its office products distribution business.

Despite its efforts to recover from the downturn, Boise Cascade suffered even greater losses in 1992. Sales dropped to $3.7 billion from nearly $4 billion in 1991, and the company recorded a net loss of $227 million. Still plagued by the same problems that had affected the company since the beginning of the recession in 1989, Boise Cascade responded by expanding its production of specialized papers and increasing the breadth of its office products distribution business. After divesting its wholesale operations, the company expanded its commercial distribution channels by opening new facilities in South Carolina and Florida, and acquired an existing office products distribution business in Minnesota. A year earlier, Boise Cascade had attempted to tap into the growing trend for recycled products by converting its Vancouver, Washington, mill into a recycled white paper facility. But none of these endeavors could wrest Boise Cascade from the grip of the recession.

Mid-to-Late 1990s and Beyond

Boise Cascade continued to be troubled into 1994, suffering from the prolonged slump in paper prices and burdened by a $2 billion debt load. The company paid down some of the debt by issuing almost $500 million in preferred stock in 1992 and 1993. Overall sales were on the rise in 1993 and 1994, growing to $3.96 billion and $4.14 billion, respectively, but Boise Cascade continued in the red, posting net losses of $77 million in 1993 and $63 million in 1994. In April 1994 Fery retired from his position as CEO, remaining chairman, with George J. Harad, who had been president and chief operating officer, moving into the CEO slot. Harad soon took on the chairmanship as well.

During 1995 Boise Cascade rode a sharp increase in paper prices to record sales of $5.07 billion and net income of $352 million, which resulted in the company's first profitable year since 1990. That year the company was also in the midst of a three-year restructuring of its paper division, in which five paper mills were sold or shuttered and the division shifted to a primary focus on office, printing and converting, packaging, and value-added uncoated white papers. In 1995 the company sold its remaining stake in its Canadian newsprint unit, Rainy River Forest Products Inc. During the following year came the sale of a coated-paper mill in Rumford, Maine, and 667,000 acres of woodlands to Mead Corporation for about $650 million. Meanwhile, in April 1995 Boise Cascade also sold 17.3 percent of its office products subsidiary, Boise Cascade Office Products (BCOP), to the public in an initial public offering of 10.6 million shares at $12.50 per share. Immune to the ups and downs of the paper industry, BCOP had been a consistent bright spot for Boise Cascade since it exited from the wholesale sector in 1992. Revenues for BCOP increased from $672 million in 1992 to $1.99 billion in 1996 while net income increased from $19 million to $102 million during the same period.

Boise Cascade faced additional challenges in its wood products manufacturing unit, as prices for lumber were flat at the same time that timber sales from federal lands were dwindling, driving up production costs. Unable to operate them at acceptable levels of profitability, the company closed sawmills in Horseshoe Bend, Idaho, and Fisher, Louisiana, during 1998 and a sawmill in Elgin, Oregon, in 1999. A plywood plant in Yakima, Washington, had also been slated for closure but remained open following a major fire in September 1998 at the company's plywood plant in Medford, Oregon. In October 1999 Boise Cascade also sold 56,000 acres of timberland in central Washington to U.S. Timberlands Yakima, L.L.C. for about $60 million.

In September 1999 Boise Cascade completed the acquisition of Furman Lumber, Inc., based in Billerica, Massachusetts. The purchase added 12 regional building materials distribution centers in the East, Midwest, and South to the company's wholesale building products unit, which already boasted 16 such centers, most of which were located in the West. Boise Cascade thereby became a national distributor of various commodity and value-added building products. Furman had recorded fiscal 1999 sales of $574 million, while the company's building products distribution unit had posted sales of $861 million in 1998.

Boise Cascade did not fare as well with an attempted bid for Le Groupe Forex Inc., Canada's leading maker of oriented strand board, a product similar to plywood in strength but cheaper to produce. In a battle with Louisiana-Pacific Corporation waged in the summer of 1999, Boise Cascade lost a bidding war despite making two separate offers for Forex, of $470 million and $500 million.

Through the first nine months of 1999, Boise Cascade appeared headed for a possible turnaround year, with sales of $5.08 billion, an increase of almost ten percent over the same period during 1998, and net income of $124.3 million, a vast improvement over the net loss of $25.9 million recorded in 1998. In a period of consolidation brought about by industry-wide excess production, Boise Cascade—despite its improved performance—appeared vulnerable to a takeover by a larger forest products rival. In addition to Louisiana-Pacific's takeover of Forex, International Paper Company acquired Union Camp Corporation, and Weyerhaeuser Company took over MacMillan Bloedel Ltd. Potential suitors of Boise Cascade could view the company's stake in Boise Cascade Office Products as a potential post-takeover cash-raising divestment, increasing the likelihood of a takeover.

Principal Subsidiaries

Boise Cascade Office Products Corporation (81.2%); Boise Southern Company; Minidoka Paper Company.

Principal Competitors

Bowater Inc.; Champion International Corporation; Georgia-Pacific Corporation; International Paper Company; Fort James Corporation; Louisiana-Pacific Corporation; The Mead Corporation; Potlatch Corporation; Smurfit-Stone Container Corporation; Temple-Inland Inc.; Westvaco Corporation; Weyerhaeuser Company; Willamette Industries Inc.; Corporate Express Inc.; Office Depot Inc.; Office Max Inc.; Staples Inc.; US Office Products Company.

Further Reading

Anderson, Steven, ''Price Slump, Market Woes Prompt Boise Cascade Cuts,'' *Idaho Business Review,* January 4, 1999, p. 9.

Bary, Andrew, ''No Paper Tiger,'' *Barron's,* January 29, 1996, pp. 20–21.

Benoit, Ellen, ''Late Bloomer in the Forest,'' *Financial World,* September 8, 1987.

''Boise Cascade Shifts Toward Tighter Control,'' *Business Week,* May 15, 1971.

Carlton, Jim, ''Boise Cascade Bids About $470 Million for Timber Firm,'' *Wall Street Journal,* July 29, 1999, p. A6.

——, ''Boise Cascade Bows out of Bidding War for Forex After Rival Increases Offer,'' *Wall Street Journal,* August 16, 1999, p. B12.

Chipello, Christopher J., ''Stone-Consolidated Offers to Acquire Rainy River Forest for $552 Million,'' *Wall Street Journal,* August 18, 1995, p. A5.

''Cinderella,'' *Forbes,* November 15, 1972.

Downs, Tim, ''New Uncoated Free-Sheet Capacity Starts up at Boise's I-Falls Mill,'' *Pulp & Paper,* May 1991, p. 98.

Fischl, Jennifer, ''Mead and Boise: The Long and the Short,'' *Financial World,* November 18, 1996, p. 24.

Gonzalez, Jason, ''Boise, L-P Battle It out for Groupe Forex,'' *National Home Center News,* August 9, 1999, pp. 9, 278.

Heiman, Grover, ''Getting Back to Basics,'' *Nation's Business,* January 1983.

Narisetti, Raju, ''Mead to Buy Coated-Paper Mill, Woods from Boise Cascade for $650 Million,'' *Wall Street Journal,* October 1, 1996, p. A4.

Richards, Bill, ''Boise Cascade May Be out of the Woods in First Period,'' *Wall Street Journal,* April 12, 1993, p. B4.

Taylor, John H., ''Fery on the Defensive,'' *Forbes,* November 12, 1990, pp. 52–58.

Tucker, John, ''Wood Products Companies Contemplating Their Futures: Boise Cascade, TJI Face Choices As Consolidation Comes to Industry,'' *Idaho Statesman,* June 27, 1999, p. 1D.

Valentin, Erhard K., ''Anatomy of a Fatal Business Strategy,'' *Journal of Management Studies,* May 1994, pp. 359ff.

''Will Quality Tell?,'' *Forbes,* July 15, 1970.

Yang, Dori Jones, and Phillip L. Zweig, ''Boise Has a Lot of Paper Work to Do,'' *Business Week,* May 9, 1994, pp. 78–79.

—Sandy Schusteff and Jeffrey L. Covell
—updated by David E. Salamie

BorgWarner Automotive.

Borg-Warner Automotive, Inc.

200 South Michigan Avenue
Chicago, Illinois 60604
U.S.A.
Telephone: (312) 322-8500
Fax: (312) 461-0507
Web site: http://www.bwauto.com

Public Company
Incorporated: 1987
Employees: 10,100
Sales: $1.84 billion (1998)
Stock Exchanges: New York
Ticker Symbol: BWA
NAIC: 336350 Motor Vehicle Transmission and Power Train Parts Manufacturing; 336310 Motor Vehicle Gasoline Engine and Engine Parts Manufacturing; 336399 All Other Motor Vehicle Parts Manufacturing

Not to be confused with its former parent (Borg-Warner Corporation) or ex-sibling (Borg-Warner Security Corporation), Borg-Warner Automotive, Inc. is one of the world's leading developers and suppliers of automotive parts and systems found in passenger cars, sport utility vehicles, and light trucks. The company maintains 20 operations in the United States and about a dozen more elsewhere, including Canada, China, France, Germany, India, Italy, Japan, Korea, Mexico, Taiwan, and Wales. Known primarily for supplying powertrain components, including transfer cases and automatic transmissions, to major automakers in North America, Europe, and Asia, Borg-Warner Automotive also makes chain and chain systems, such as timing chain systems; air/fluid systems, such as intake manifolds, air pumps, and vapor recovery systems; and turbochargers. The company has undergone significant changes over the years, but Borg-Warner Automotive's manufacturing skill and reputation have allowed it to not only weather the breakup of its corporate family, but to triumph first as a private, then as a newly public, independent company in 1993.

Early History

Borg-Warner's history is as complex and interesting as one of its powertrain assemblies: a cluster of components (in this case, small, specialized auto parts manufacturers) harmoniously working to power a highly successful industrial giant. To tell the story of Borg-Warner Automotive, one must trace the formation of several disparate manufacturers in the United States and abroad. The first of these was Morse Equalizing Spring Company of New York, founded in 1880, which patented the rocker joint. In 1901 Warner Gear of Muncie, Indiana, was formed, and the next year, Marvel-Schebler Carburetor Company began operations in Flint, Michigan. A fourth company, Long Manufacturing, came on line in Chicago to manufacture automobile radiators, while a fifth company, Borg & Beck, was organized in 1904. All of these companies figured in the development of Borg-Warner Automotive.

By 1906 Morse manufactured a line of automobile chains that were soon licensed for sale in England and Germany. Then came the production of automotive timing chains, followed quickly by Warner Gear's development of the industry's first manual transmission. In 1910 Long Manufacturing moved from Chicago to Detroit while a sixth rookie in the auto game, Mechanics Machine Company of Rockford, Illinois, began producing transmissions in 1911. Over the next several years, Morse built a new facility in England as Warner Gear fashioned a growing reputation for quality.

By the 1920s, Borg & Beck's sturdy yet inexpensive clutch was mass-produced in millions of cars while Mechanics Machine Co. developed a universal joint with continuous lubrication, an innovation that rendered the former model (which had to be greased every 500 miles) obsolete. At the same time, Warner Gear standardized its manual transmissions and introduced the T64, at nearly half the cost of its predecessors. In the young yet burgeoning auto industry, each of the aforementioned companies was busy developing a specialized product line, unaware that they would be united under the banner of Borg-Warner in a sweeping merger in 1928. Borg & Beck, Marvel Carburetor, Mechanics Universal Joint (renamed from Mechanics Machine in 1925), and Warner Gear became the Borg-Warner Corporation. The follow-

Company Perspectives:

The accelerating pace of change in powertrain technology is driving growth at Borg-Warner Automotive. Change sets the stage for joint development with our automaker customers of new engines, automated transmissions and four-wheel drive systems. Our customers gain innovative and cost-effective solutions while we increase BWA content in each vehicle they produce. Our job is to stay ahead of the curve. The pursuit of product leadership drives our growth. At BWA–driven is a state of mind.

ing year, Morse Chain (an auto timing and industrial chain producer at this time) and Long Manufacturing joined the new company at the same time that the Norge firm (including its Detroit Gear subsidiary) was acquired.

1930–50: Firsts and Innovations

The next decade brought several technological firsts for both Borg-Warner and the industry: Warner Gear pioneered the ''synchronizer,'' a device that made a manual transmission's gear teeth mesh together with ease for smooth shifting; Morse Chain brought out its first roller chain; and Borg-Warner's self-contained overdrive transmission was introduced to immediate success as Chrysler and 11 other automakers quickly placed orders. Borg-Warner Automotive Service Parts Division was also launched in the 1930s, and in 1936, to emphasize Borg-Warner's commitment to and enthusiasm for auto racing, the company commissioned a sterling silver trophy for the Indianapolis 500 (the first was presented to Louis Meyer). As the decade neared its close, Stieber Rollkupplung GmbH (the predecessor to Borg-Warner GmbH) was founded in Munich in 1937.

In the prewar 1940s Borg-Warner created its Spring Division (to supply automatic transmission parts), began working on transfer cases, and soon directed its attention to World War II production needs. Among its contributions were Morse Chain's drives for Navy tug boats and jeeps built with Warner Gear's transmissions. After the war, Warner Gear's technology briefly lent itself to the medical field in 1949, producing iron lungs. It then returned to auto parts in 1950 with three revolutionary developments—the torque converter, a three-speed automatic transmission (the ''Ford-O-Matic''), and a newfangled clutch that would become one of the company's biggest sellers worldwide. Automotive sales for the company reached over $200 million. Among the first automakers to jump at Borg-Warner's newest innovations were Studebaker and Ford. The latter was so enamored of Borg-Warner's transmissions that it signed a five-year exclusive contract with Borg-Warner in 1951 for the production of automatic transmissions.

1950s–70s: Expansion and Diversification

As the 1950s continued, Borg-Warner expanded its operations in several new directions. Not only did the company venture into South America, creating Borg & Beck do Brasil, but it also built new facilities in Simcoe, Ontario, and Letchworth, England. The English facility was soon producing Warner Gear's overdrive units and the Model D.G. automatic transmission. In 1956 the T10 four-speed high performance manual transmission was introduced in the Chevrolet Corvette to wide acclaim. As Marvel-Schebler tinkered with a fuel injection system, Borg-Warner built (and patented) the first retractable seat belt restraint system and developed a line of paper-related wet friction components.

To broaden its international operations, Borg-Warner acquired Coote & Jurgenson, an Australian transmission producer for autos and tractors in 1957. Three years later, Brummer Seal Company was merged into Borg-Warner's Spring Division. The next year, 1961, was the beginning of a new era—though few recognized it as such—as James F. Bere joined the company as head of the Borg & Beck subsidiary. In 1962 Borg-Warner expanded into Mexico, and into Asia in 1964 and 1965 with two Japanese joint ventures (NSK-Warner and Tsubakimoto-Morse).

As the company's varied units continued to devise new product innovations (the ''Hy-Vo'' chain, Flex-Bands, and the aluminum Model 35 automatic transmission), Bere nimbly climbed the corporate ladder and was named as group vice-president at age 42. Yet he ruffled feathers the following year when he openly discussed, in detail, the financial data of each of the company's ten divisions, a practice not done before at decentralized Borg-Warner. As a result, insiders were shocked when Chairman Robert S. Ingersoll announced Bere as his new president in 1968, promoting him over four company veterans. Instead of being fired for his boldness, Bere had begun a trend: rather than keep profits and losses shrouded in a need-to-know fog, he had been open and honest about company performance. Yet with Bere's frankness came bleak consequences: the closure of underperforming subsidiaries to relieve and strengthen assets that had been forced to carry their weight. Though Borg-Warner diversified into chemicals, plastics, industrial products, financial assistance, and eventually even into security and armored car services, its automotive division had remained a constant, usually contributing upwards of 50 percent of Borg-Warner's total revenue.

In 1969 Aisin-Warner was formed as another joint venture with Japan to build automatic transmissions, including the advanced Model 35, which was now distributed to 30 automakers for use in over 100 vehicles ranging from Nissans to Jaguars. The following year Borg-Warner acquired the Massachusetts-based Nu-Era Gear and improved on its automatic transmission by developing the Model 45, which was soon manufactured in new facilities in Australia and South Wales. Marvel-Schebler expanded by merging with Tillotson Carburetor in 1971, the same year that Borg & Beck christened a new plant in Michigan.

In 1972, just four years after his surprise appointment as president, Bere became CEO when Ingersoll left the company and the United States to become an ambassador to Japan. The next year, Borg-Warner introduced its full-time, four-wheel drive (4WD) transfer cases using Hy-Vo drive chains, while its newest manufacturing operation opened in Ireland. Over the next several years came two new major innovations (the Model T50 five-speed transmission and continuously variable transmission for commercial vehicles); further expansion (new plants in Arkansas and New York and renovation of Warner

Key Dates:

1928: Borg-Warner Corporation is formed.
1929: Company acquires Morse Chain.
1950: A three-speed automatic transmission, the "Ford-O-Matic," is introduced.
1956: The T10 four-speed high performance manual transmission is introduced in the Chevrolet Corvette.
1973: Company introduces full-time, four-wheel drive transfer cases using Hy-Vo drive chains.
1987: Company is taken private through a $4.4 billion leveraged buyout.
1993: Borg-Warner Automotive, Inc. is spun off from Borg-Warner Security Corporation.
1994: The "Torque-on-Demand" four-wheel drive transfer case debuts.
1996: Company acquires three automotive businesses from Coltec Industries.
1997: Borg-Warner enters turbocharger market through purchase of majority interest in German firm.

Gear's Indiana facility); the issuance of two million common shares of Borg-Warner stock; and Bere's election as chairman of the board in 1975.

Surviving the Tumultuous 1980s

When Borg-Warner celebrated its 50th anniversary in 1978, its automotive profits had reached $98 million. The next year, overall sales topped $2.7 billion as the company headed into the tumultuous 1980s. Although U.S. auto production fell by 25 percent in 1980, Borg-Warner kept its losses to a respectable 16 percent decline, a good amount below the national average. This was due in part to its continuing improvement of the T4 and T5 manual transmissions and its production of new, lightweight transfer cases. Yet transfer cases took a giant technological leap in the 1980s with the introduction of sport utility vehicles and light trucks such as the Ford Ranger.

Buoyed by steady sales of transmissions and transfer cases, the company experimented with electronic sensors, silicon technology, and non-asbestos friction materials. Borg-Warner also tightened its focus by selling Morse Industrial and its automotive service parts divisions in 1981. Three years later, the company consolidated its many automotive operations under the umbrella of Borg-Warner Automotive, Inc., setting up international headquarters in Troy, Michigan. Sales for the newly named automotive conglomerate topped $1 billion in 1984. By 1985 Borg-Warner Automotive employed 10,000 people and began using high volume laser-cutting in its Frankfort, Illinois, plant. It also produced its one-millionth T5 manual transmission that year, while continuing its consolidation. During this time, Warner Gear was renamed Transmission Systems, Borg & Beck was renamed Clutch Systems, and Marvel-Schebler became known as Control Systems.

In 1986 Borg-Warner experienced a changing of the guard; after 25 years of service, Bere stepped down as CEO (remaining chairman of the board) and was succeeded by Richard J. Doyle as president and CEO. Doyle's first year at the helm was marked by several highs, including an exclusive contract to manufacture its new Model 1356 transfer cases for all of Ford's light trucks and sport utility vehicles. Additionally, the company opened sales offices in Frankfurt, Sao Paulo, Seoul, and Tokyo and signed a licensing agreement with Nanjing Motor Works of Beijing, boosting international sales to a record high of 30 percent of its $3.4 billion in revenue.

1987–93: Private Company Era

Yet for all of Borg-Warner Automotive's success, there was a steep price—the interest of corporate raiders Irwin Jacobs and Samuel Heyman in the fast-and-loose leveraged buyout (LBO) haven of the 1980s. After spending $680 million, Jacobs and Heyman each possessed ten percent of the company, to the shock and dismay of Borg-Warner's board. Determined to squelch not only Jacobs' and Heyman's takeover attempt but any future opportunists as well, Borg-Warner's brass decided to take the company private. Turning to Merrill Lynch Capital Partners, an LBO fund, Borg-Warner's board was supposed to offer stockholders $43 per share. Instead, the directors decided to wait, hoping Jacobs and Heyman would lose interest.

However, in March 1987 Heyman bought Jacobs' holdings and offered stockholders $46 a share in a hostile takeover bid. Borg-Warner again turned to Merrill Lynch, but Heyman's offer had upped the ante to a buyout valued at over 20 times the company's earnings. In May, Merrill Lynch completed one of the ten biggest LBOs of the decade for $4.4 billion ($3.4 billion from banks and $1 billion from junk bond sales), establishing 51 percent ownership in the now private Borg-Warner.

The 65-year-old Bere assumed the CEO role again to oversee the company's breakup. The already daunting task was made more difficult by the onset of Black Monday, a dramatic plunge in the stock market. The drop substantially affected the sales of the chemical and plastics division (sold to General Electric for $2.3 billion) and Borg-Warner Acceptance Corp. (sold to TransAmerica for $782.5 million). What was left were Borg-Warner Security ($1.3 billion in revenue for 1989), and its subsidiary, Borg-Warner Automotive (BWA), with sales of $958 million in 1989 and earnings of $93 million. Sales fell to $920 million in 1990 as a result of an industry slump.

Around this time, transfer case technology branched into heavy duty and all-wheel drive for several models from General Motors. BWA also developed the new 1354 model for Ford Explorers and Ranger trucks, while the "touch drive" model was installed in all F-series trucks. This year also marked the appointment of Donald C. Trauscht, a 23-year company veteran, as president of BWA, and by 1991 over one million model 1354 transfer cases had been installed in F-series trucks along with Borg-Warner's automatic locking hubs, which became the industry standard.

1993 and Beyond: Public Again

In the early 1990s BWA offered the industry's first three-year/36,000-mile warranty on transfer cases and debuted in 1994 its latest technological breakthrough: the "Torque-on-

Demand'' transfer case capable of automatically shifting from two- to four-wheel drive when necessary. This innovation led to another sole-source agreement with Ford for the rest of the decade. Also debuting in 1994 was the Morse Gemini Chain System. Meanwhile, the T56 six-speed manual transmission became standard in Chrysler's Viper sportscar and new Ford Mustangs, and international operations were expanded in Japan and China. The year 1993 saw the appointment of Siegfried P. Adler as president of BWA, as Trauscht was elevated to president and CEO of the unit's parent company, Borg-Warner Security. That year Borg-Warner Automotive, Inc. was spun off into an independent company with J. Gordon Amedee as chairman and CEO.

Closing the year with $985.4 million in sales (and a net loss of $97.1 million due to spinoff accounting charges), up from 1992's $926 million (and a net loss of $12 million), BWA pointed to a number of milestones as evidence of its continued vitality: production of its three-millionth T5 manual transmission and four-millionth transfer case for Ford; the signing of a ''life of the product'' pact with General Motors for its advanced ''Maji-Band'' brake band assembly for automatic transmissions; and a new five-year contract with SsangYong Motor Company for manual transmissions and transfer cases.

In July 1994, John Fiedler was named president and CEO of Borg-Warner Automotive after serving Goodyear's North American Tire division for 30 years. The company, poised for a renaissance as the automotive industry boomed, was now comprised of four subsidiaries: Automatic Transmission Systems, Control Systems, Morse TEC (Chain Systems), and Powertrain Systems. The latter unit, propelled by transfer cases—the darling of the sport utility vehicle and light truck industry—grew by over 12 percent to account for 40 percent ($550.7 million) of 1994's total $1.2 billion in revenues.

When Fiedler came on board, one of his first pronouncements was his intention to double BWA's revenues by the end of the 1990s, implement a slew of cost reductions, improve productivity, increase foreign investments, and form more joint ventures both in and out of North America. Fiedler also hinted that he and BWA's directors were in an acquisitive mood: ''We're in an excellent position to grow and we're going to raise some eyebrows,'' he told *Barron*'s in August 1994, after posting an impressive 25 percent sales gain for the first half of the year, way over the industry's 11 percent overall increase. The company finished 1994 with sales of $1.22 billion and a net profit of $64.4 million.

With the exception of the effects of a significant strike at General Motors in 1998, sales grew steadily in the mid-to-late 1990s thanks to a booming U.S. economy, the growing popularity of light trucks and sport utility vehicles, and a series of significant acquisitions. In June 1996 Borg-Warner Automotive acquired three automotive operations—Holley Automotive, Coltec Automotive, and Performance Friction Products—from Coltec Industries Inc. for $283 million, thereby bolstering its air/fluid systems unit and enabling it to develop integrated air-management systems for vehicles. The acquired businesses were manufacturers of a range of products, including air induction systems, throttle bodies, electric air pumps, and oil pumps. In December 1996 Borg-Warner sold its unprofitable North American manual transmission business to Mexico-based Transmisiones y Equipos Mecanicos S.A. de C.V. The company took an after-tax charge of $35 million in connection with the sale, which caused net earnings to fall from $74.2 million in 1995 to $41.8 million in 1996, even while net sales were increasing from $1.33 billion to $1.54 billion, a 16 percent jump.

In October 1997 BWA entered a new market segment, that of turbochargers, through the purchase of a controlling 63 percent stake in AG Kühnle, Kopp & Kausch, a German maker of turbochargers and turbomachinery, for $42.4 million. One year later, the company purchased full control of AG Kühnle's turbocharger business for $95.7 million, then renamed it 3K-Warner Turbosystems GmbH. With emission standards becoming increasingly stringent in Europe, automakers were expanding their use of turbodiesel engines, which were cleaner and more fuel efficient than conventional gasoline engines. The turbochargers required in the turbodiesel engines were a key to their fuel efficiency, and BWA viewed turbochargers as a clear area of future growth. In March 1999 Borg-Warner substantially increased its turbocharger business with the purchase of Savannah, Georgia-based Kuhlman Corporation for $693 million. Kuhlman consisted of three main businesses, two of which were sold off later in 1999: Kuhlman Electric, a maker of transformers for the utility industry, and Coleman Cable, a manufacturer of wire and cable for utilities and other industries. The third unit was Schwitzer, Inc., a maker of turbochargers for diesel engines, heavy-duty steel fuel tanks, and fan drives. The addition of Schwitzer's turbocharger business to that of 3K-Warner propelled Borg-Warner Automotive into the number two position worldwide in turbochargers, with a 27 percent market share, trailing only AlliedSignal Inc.'s Garrett Turbocharger Systems unit, which held a 50 percent share.

In October 1999 BWA completed another large acquisition, this one a $310 million purchase of the fluid power division of Eaton Corporation. Borg-Warner combined the acquired cooling systems operations with its existing cooling systems business to form Borg-Warner Automotive Cooling Systems.

With sales nearing $2 billion by the late 1990s, Fiedler set a new goal of doubling sales to $4 billion by the early 21st century. He also aimed to maintain profit margins of between 14 and 16 percent before interest and taxes—which was the best in the industry. At the close of the decade, two of the company's divisions—those specializing in chain systems and automatic transmission systems—held more than 50 percent of the global market, while the turbo systems and powertrain systems units were both number two in the world. Borg-Warner Automotive appeared to be well positioned for the future with a variety of leading positions in the automotive parts and systems industry.

Principal Subsidiaries

Borg-Warner Automotive Powertrain Systems Corporation; Borg-Warner Automotive Air/Fluid Systems Corporation; Borg Warner Automotive Morse TEC Corporation; Borg-Warner Automotive Foreign Sales Corporation; Borg-Warner Automotive Automatic Transmission Systems Corporation; Kuhlman Corporation; EMTEC Products Corporation; Schwitzer, Inc.

Principal Competitors

AlliedSignal Inc.; Dana Corporation; Eaton Corporation; Intermet Corporation; New Venture Gear, Inc.; Robert Bosch GmbH; Siemens AG; Simpson Industries, Inc.; SPX Corporation; TRW Inc.; Tsubakimoto Precision Products Co., Ltd.; Valeo S.A.

Further Reading

Bautz, Mark, "Wall Street Newsletter," *Money,* June 1995, pp. 68–72.
Benoit, Ellen, "A Survivor," *Forbes,* April 21, 1986, pp. 100, 104.
Bere, James F., "The Director As Servant and Leader," *Directors & Boards,* Spring 1991, pp. 7-8.
Borss, Marcia, "A Debtor with Options," *Forbes,* November 26, 1990, p. 64.
Byrne, Harlan S., "Lean Machine," *Barron's,* August 15, 1994, p. 19.
"CEO Interview: Borg-Warner Automotive," *Wall Street Transcript,* May 31, 1999.
Crown, Judith, "Borg-Warner Faces Life After CEO Bere," *Crain's Chicago Business,* January 13, 1992, pp. 1, 29.
Flaherty, Robert J., "Now the Real Test Begins," *Forbes,* February 18, 1980, pp. 134, 138.
"Follow-Through," *Forbes,* March 3, 1980, p. 12.
"Four-Firm Merger in '28 Formed Borg-Warner," *Automotive News,* April 24, 1996, p. 90.
Gornstein, Leslie, "Open Road for Borg-Warner Exec," *Crain's Chicago Business,* July 11, 1994, pp. 22–23.
Jewett, Dale, "Borg-Warner Chief Maps Future: Transmissions Will Continue to Drive Company's Growth," *Detroit News,* April 13, 1999, p. B3.
Lowe, Frederick H., "He's a Big Sports Fan," *Chicago Sun Times,* January 29, 1995.
Miller, James P., "Borg-Warner Automotive Agrees to Buy Three Coltec Lines for $283 Million," *Wall Street Journal,* April 29, 1996, p. B7E.
Nathans, Leah, "Hot for Glory," *Business Month,* January 1989, pp. 55–59.
Oursler, Will, *From Ox Carts to Jets: Roy Ingersoll and the Borg-Warner Story,* Englewood Cliffs, N.J.: Prentice-Hall, 1959, 346 p.
Quintanilla, Carl, "Borg-Warner to Buy Kuhlman Corp. in Bid to Increase Diesel Market Share," *Wall Street Journal,* December 21, 1998, p. B5.
Saxon, Wolfgang, "James F. Bere, 69, A Chicago Leader and Corporate Chief," *New York Times,* January 4, 1992, p. 27.
Sherefkin, Robert, "Borg-Warner Takes High Road to Growth," *Automotive News,* April 5, 1999, p. 20.
Spragins, Ellyn, "Healthy Smokestacks," *Forbes,* August 15, 1983, pp. 58–59.
Taninecz, George, "America's Best Plants: Borg-Warner Automotive," *Industry Week,* October 19, 1998, pp. 44–46.

—Taryn Benbow-Pfalzgraf
—updated by David E. Salamie

Brooks Sports Inc.

11720 North Creek Parkway
Bothell, Washington 98011
U.S.A.
Telephone: (425) 488-3131
Fax: (425) 483-8181
Web site: http://www.brookssports.com

Private Company
Incorporated: 1914
Employees: 75
Sales: $60 million (1998 est.)
NAIC: 316219 Other Footwear Manufacturing

Brooks Sports Inc. is a small yet well-recognized athletic footwear and apparel manufacturer, best known for its running shoes, which ranked as one of the top three brands in the United States during the late 1970s. Success during the late 1970s sent the company reeling during the 1980s, as it failed to sustain its market leadership and floundered. A refocused market strategy during the 1990s, targeted toward serious runners in the 35- to 54-year-old age bracket, reinvigorated Brooks, prompting diversification into apparel in 1997. The company designs and manufactures a full range of running and fitness footwear and apparel, maintaining a global presence in the athletic market.

Origins

Founded in 1914, Brooks began business as a maker of ice skates and cleated sports shoes, but the company did not distinguish itself until more than 60 years later, when it thrived as a manufacturer of running shoes. During the 1970s, the popularity of jogging swept across the United States, carrying with it the popularity of Brooks footwear. Led by its signature Vantage brand, Brooks rose to dizzying heights in the fast-growing athletic footwear industry, securing a large share of the ever increasing revenues and profits that helped transform an upstart rival named Nike into a multibillion-dollar business empire. Like Nike, Brooks emerged as a favorite among the burgeoning ranks of running enthusiasts who embraced the sport from coast to coast. By the late 1970s, Brooks ranked as one of the top three running shoe brands in the country, seemingly bound for the same size of fortune that the much younger Nike would later claim. The comparisons between Nike and Brooks ended shortly after the late 1970s, however; to the chagrin of Brooks's management, Nike was able to sustain the momentum generated during the late 1970s and develop a sprawling business with a domineering presence in the athletic market. Brooks, meanwhile, faltered quickly, tripped up by the confidence instilled during its meteoric rise into the industry's elite during the late 1970s. Industry pundits later theorized that the cause of Brooks's sudden collapse came from the company's errant attempts to ape the strategy used by Nike. Ironically, Nike, albeit indirectly, later intervened as Brooks's savior, but during the intervening period separating Brooks's collapse and its resurrection, the company teetered precariously on the brink of insolvency. Although the company was founded at the start of World War I, the story of its success truly began in the wake of the disaster that followed its late 1970s rise to prominence.

Caught up in the fervor created by the running craze during the late 1970s, Brooks overextended itself and quickly paid the price for its zeal. The company expanded into other athletic footwear markets, using its success in the running shoe market as the basis for diversifying into an array of footwear markets, including basketball, aerobics, and baseball. As Brooks diversified, it also entered the expensive realm of securing celebrity endorsements from well-recognized, professional athletes. Signing big-name athletes was a marketing strategy employed by Nike, and Brooks, eager to keep pace with the rising giant of the industry, followed suit, signing athletes such as football quarterback Dan Marino and basketball star James Worthy to endorse the company's $70 shoes. Problems began to surface when Brooks's business began to slacken, leaving the company overexposed to the business downturn and unable to operate efficiently or effectively. In response to the financial difficulties that subsequently beset Brooks, the company trimmed operating costs by using cheaper materials for its footwear. In a further bid to stanch the mounting financial losses, the company slashed prices and began distributing more and more of its merchandise to deep discount chains such as Kmart, where Brooks footwear retailed for as low as $20. Consequently, the brand lost credibility, its image tarnished by inferior products

Company Perspectives:

If your feet aren't happy, you're not happy. If you're not happy, we're not happy. So what do we do? We simply make the most comfortable running shoes imaginable.

and a marketing strategy that repelled the company's original customers, joggers.

Behind the scenes, Brooks had a parent company that endured the perennial losses posted by its subsidiary. Rockford, Michigan-based Wolverine World Wide Inc., best known for its brand of Hush Puppies shoes, acquired Brooks in 1982, operating the company as a subsidiary named Brooks Shoe Inc. During the 1980s, Wolverine World Wide felt the sting of Brooks's pervasive problems, guilty itself of perpetuating the problems by supporting Brooks with what critics described as weak marketing. During Wolverine World Wide's decade of ownership, Brooks racked up $60 million in losses, recording eight consecutive years of unprofitability. By the early 1990s, Wolverine World Wide was ready to unload the burdensome drag on its earnings, and in early 1993 the company found a willing buyer. Ownership of Brooks changed hands in February 1993, marking the beginning of a new era for the troubled shoe manufacturer. To Brooks's new parent company fell the difficult task of injecting the 79-year-old concern with the vitality it had lost during the 1980s.

New Ownership for the 1990s

Brooks's new parent company was the Rokke Group (later Aker RGI), a privately held Norwegian investment group with interests in shipping, real estate, commercial fishing, and sporting goods. Led and founded by Bjorn Gjelsten and Kjell Rokke, the investment firm paid $21 million for Brooks, a deal that included Brooks's U.S. operations and its worldwide licensing and distribution network. Following its acquisition by the Rokke Group, the company was renamed Brooks Sports Inc. and relocated near the Rokke Group's U.S. headquarters in Seattle. Brooks's international headquarters in Grand Rapids, Michigan, and its domestic headquarters in Hanover, Pennsylvania, were consolidated in Bothell, Washington, a Seattle suburb, as were the finance and accounting office in Michigan and the company's sourcing office in Taiwan. At the time of the acquisition, Brooks was generating roughly $100 million in annual, worldwide sales, although company officials would later contend that the financial figures reported by Wolverine World Wide were inflated. What was beyond argument, however, was the anemic domestic performance of Brooks. Sales in the United States had plateaued at approximately $25 million annually. Further, the eight years of consecutive financial losses were compounded by the deteriorated strength of the Brooks brand name. The company that had once ranked as one of the top three brands in the United States had plummeted to 25th place by 1993, when Brooks controlled 0.4 percent of the domestic market.

Profound changes were clearly needed, but in the midst of the reorganization and consolidation that occupied the company's attention throughout much of 1993, there were few signs that sweeping reforms were underway. In fact, the company appeared to be regressing rather than pressing forward with a restorative plan, as the launch of a new shoe dubbed "The Truth" fell victim to numerous delays and the lack of a marketing campaign. The problems stemmed from Brooks's senior management, which was in disarray following the Rokke Group's acquisition of the company, thereby delaying the implementation of any program designed to cure Brooks's ills. The cloud hanging over Brooks's managerial ranks was cleared away substantially in August 1993, when three of the company's senior executives—including the president—departed, each leaving the company, according to various, contradictory accounts, either after being fired or after voluntarily stepping aside. With the departure of what the July 1, 1994 *Puget Sound Business Journal* described as "a faltering management team," stewardship of the company devolved to Rokke Group's chairman and CEO, Bjorn Gjelsten. Gjelsten's leadership of Brooks was a temporary solution to the company's most pressing problem. Gjelsten assumed day-to-day control over the company while he searched for a permanent replacement. By the end of 1993, he had found such a person, a well-regarded executive named Helen Rockey, who at the time was working for Nike.

Raised in Seattle, Rockey graduated from the University of Washington with a bachelor's degree in economics in 1978, ending her academic career two years later, after she had earned her master's degree in business administration. Rockey joined a production management training program at a plywood and sawmill in Oregon, spent one year working as vice-president of marketing for a Tacoma, Washington, company called Big Toys Inc., and then found a lasting position at Nike. Nike hired Rockey in 1984 as a special sales manager of the company's then small apparel division. She quickly distinguished herself at Nike, ultimately earning promotion to the position of general manager of the company's sport graphics and accessories divisions, which marketed merchandise such as hats, T-shirts, and water bottles. Rockey spearheaded tremendous growth at the divisions, highlighted by a four-year period in which she increased sales from $8 million to $500 million. Gjelsten was impressed, convinced that Rockey was capable of marshaling Brooks towards profitability and restoring the company's brand image to its former luster. In January 1994, Rockey was named president of Brooks, becoming the first female to head a major athletic shoe company in the United States.

Comeback Beginning in 1994

Upon assuming control over Brooks, Rockey implemented sweeping changes, announcing her intention to increase sales and profits by 25 percent during the ensuing three to five years. Her plan centered on reengineering Brooks's products rather than restructuring the company itself, an approach that focused the company's attention on serious runners—the core of the company's traditional success. Other sports categories were discontinued, eliminating any traces of Brooks's attempts to present itself as a "mini-Nike." After sharpening the company's focus on the running shoe market, Rockey turned to redesigning Brooks's footwear, as she desperately sought to distance her regime from the company that sold its cheaply made products in Kmart stores for as little as $20.

By June 1994, Rockey had delivered "The Truth" to retailers, a back-to-basics running shoe that retailed for $109. Concur-

Key Dates:

1914: Brooks is formed.
1982: Wolverine World Wide acquires Brooks.
1993: Norwegian investment firm The Rokke Group purchases Brooks.
1994: Former Nike executive Helen Rockey is appointed president.
1997: Brooks introduces a full line of apparel in the spring.
1998: J.H. Whitney & Co. acquires controlling interest in Brooks.
1999: Bruce Pettet is named president and CEO after Rockey's departure.

rently, Rockey began circuiting the country's retail establishments, concentrating on the specialty running stores that had always served as Brooks's strongest distribution channel. In trying to restore confidence in the Brooks name, Rockey articulated three corporate objectives that assuaged retailers' fears of dealing with the Brooks brand. First, she preached product excellence, promising revamped products with a drastically reduced defect rate. She stressed operational execution, promising on time delivery of the company's merchandise. Lastly, she promised better sell-through support, detailing plans to provide marketing support that incorporated individual retail establishments. Part of the program involving closer ties between Brooks and retailers included the sponsorship of athletes—in the new Rockey era, expensive celebrity endorsement deals were eliminated. Instead, Brooks began building a stable of 200 runners grouped into four sponsorship categories: world class, national, regional, and local. Sponsorship deals in many cases were restricted to free gear, rather than cash payments, and required the athletes to forge a relationship with their local retailer by making promotional appearances and conducting running clinics at particular stores. Because of the company's policy to eschew celebrity endorsement deals, Brooks gave up its chase of the hotly pursued youth markets, in which success was heavily dependent on the fame of the athlete who endorsed a particular shoe. Instead, Brooks concentrated on 35- to 54-year-old customers, the strongest market niche of serious runners.

The changes implemented by Rockey created a more focused, leaner company. Profitability, conspicuously absent during the eight years preceding Rockey's appointment as president, was restored after her first year of stewardship, putting the company on firm footing. Initially, the aim was to strip down the company and narrow its focus, eliminating all expenditures that did not address Rockey's three objectives. Once profitability had been restored and the Brooks brand name began to exude some of its former strength, Rockey could assume a more aggressive posture. Accordingly, the full effect of her influence did not materialize until Brooks's exited the mid-1990s and began building on its distribution base of specialty running stores.

Sales during the late 1990s rose energetically, driven upward by the palmy mood pervading Brooks's Bothell headquarters. Having re-established the brand in specialty running stores, Rockey endeavored to win back the business of regional sporting goods stores and department stores, and registered quick success. In 1996, for instance, Nordstrom Inc. carried Brooks footwear at just one store, but a year later, the department store chain carried the company's shoes at 30 locations. As the number of retail locations stocking the company's footwear increased, sales increased as well, particularly in the United States, where the company had incurred its greatest damage prior to Rockey's arrival. Against the backdrop of a 48 percent increase in domestic sales in 1996, Rockey unveiled her next plan of attack, announcing in mid-1996 that Brooks would enter the apparel business. The company introduced a full-line of technical running and fitness apparel for women and men in the spring of 1997, adding a substantial revenue stream to Brooks's business. After a 29 percent increase in apparel sales in 1998, the company's apparel business accounted for 15 percent of total sales by the end of the decade.

Despite the undeniable resurgence of Brooks, Aker RGI—Brooks's parent company—decided to cut its ties to the footwear and apparel manufacturer. In November 1998, the Norwegian holding company sold controlling interest in Brooks to Stamford, Connecticut, venture capital firm J.H. Whitney & Co. for $40 million. Aker RGI, which had decided to pay more attention to its commercial fishing and real estate holdings, retained a 20 percent stake in Brooks, selling 60 percent to J.H. Whitney. The remaining 20 percent interest in Brooks was purchased by Rockey and 70 other Brooks employees, giving management a substantial stake in what promised to be a promising future. In early 1999, orders from specialty running shops were up 84 percent, punctuating the strident success of the company during the latter half of the 1990s. Between 1995 and 1999, sales increased an average of 30 percent annually, fueling confidence that Rockey, who now had a substantial, vested interest in Brooks's success, would spearhead commensurate growth as the company entered the 21st century. In March 1999, such expectations were shattered when Rockey made a startling announcement.

In March 1999, Rockey announced she was leaving Brooks to join Birmingham, Alabama-based retailer Just For Feet Inc. as president and CEO. Insiders and outsiders were shocked by the news, coming a few short months after Rockey had led an employee buyout of the company. Rockey saw her chance to join a higher profile company, and took it, leaving Vice-President of Sales and Marketing Bruce Pettet, a Brooks executive since 1995, in charge of running the company. Pettet took over the titles of president and CEO from Rockey, promising a continuation of the policies and strategies developed and pursued by his predecessor. In November 1999, Pettet presided over the acquisition of Total Quality Apparel Resource Inc., a National City, California, company that had previously served as an independent apparel contractor for Brooks. The acquisition, organized as a subsidiary of Brooks, strengthened the company's presence in apparel, which company officials projected to be a 25 percent contributor to the company's overall sales. With the change in leadership and consistently strong financial performance behind it, Brooks prepared for the decade ahead, resurrected by the Rockey era and confident that Pettet's tenure of leadership would engender further success in the 21st century.

Principal Subsidiaries

Total Quality Apparel Resource Inc.

Principal Competitors

Nike, Inc.; adidas-Salomon AG; Reebok International Ltd.; Fila Holding S.p.A.

Further Reading

''Brooks's New Looks,'' *WWD,* August 22, 1996, p. 9.

Butler, Simon, ''Just For Feet Names Helen Rockey President, COO—New Chief to Use Her Marketing Skills to Establish the Firm's National Presence,'' *Footwear News,* March 22, 1999, p. 1.

——, ''Employees Now Navigating the Waters at Brooks Sports,'' *Footwear News,* November 2, 1998, p. 8.

Carr, Debra, ''Brooks Buys R-T-W Maker,'' *Footwear News,* November 1, 1999, p. 4.

Gaffney, Andrew, ''Helen Rockey,'' *Sporting Goods Business,* September 1994, p. 56.

Gallagher, Leigh, ''Runner's World,'' *Forbes,* February 22, 1999, p. 96.

Jung, Helen, ''Brooks Shoe Chief Wants to Run Up Profits, Reputation,'' *Knight-Ridder/Tribune Business News,* January 31, 1994, p. 01310069.

Kim, Nancy J., ''Brooks Quickens the Pace in Running Shoes,'' *Puget Sound Business Journal,* July 5, 1996, p. 1.

——, ''Brooks Sprints to Record Shoe Sales,'' *Puget Sound Business Journal,* July 4, 1997, p. 1.

——, ''Brooks Sports Sprints Ahead in Sales Race,'' *Puget Sound Business Journal,* February 6, 1998, p. 7.

——,''The Race of Her Life,'' *Business Journal-Portland,* July 19, 1996, p. 12.

McAllister, Robert, ''Brooks' New Owners Hope to Lure Runners,'' *Footwear News,* September 6, 1993, p. 24.

Sather, Jeanne, ''Shoemaker Brooks Takes Its First Steps on Comeback Trail,'' *Puget Sound Business Journal,* July 1, 1994, p. 6.

——, ''Brooks Loses Ground in Shoe Race,'' *Puget Sound Business Journal,* December 17, 1993, p. 1.

Silverman, Dick, ''Brooks Will Focus Marketing on Running,'' *Footwear News,* February 15, 1993, p. 7.

Tedeschi, Mark, ''It's a Rockey Future for Just For Feet,'' *Sporting Goods Business,* April 16, 1999, p. 10.

Webster, Nancy Coltun, ''Books: Bruce Pettet,'' *Advertising Age,* June 28, 1999, p. S33.

—Jeffrey L. Covell

·Buffets, Inc.·

Buffets, Inc.

10260 Viking Drive
Eden Prairie, Minnesota 55344-7229
U.S.A.
Telephone: (612) 942-9760
Fax: (612) 903-1356
Web site: http://www.buffet.com

Public Company
Incorporated: 1983
Employees: 24,350
Sales: $868.9 million (1998)
Stock Exchanges: NASDAQ
Ticker Symbol: BOCB
NAIC: 722211 Limited-Service Restaurants; 722110 Full-Service Restaurants

Buffets, Inc. is one of the most successful businesses in the restaurant industry, owning and operating 388 eating establishments in 36 states and franchising another 24 in ten states. The vast majority of the units are operated under one of two names: Old Country Buffet (a total of 258) or HomeTown Buffet (140). These buffet-style restaurants feature a "scatter system" with several separate food islands or counters rather than the straight-line system typical of most buffets. The company's remaining units are divided among two formats: Country Roadhouse Buffet and Grill, which combines a buffet with display cooking of grilled foods; and Original Roadhouse Grill, a nonbuffet menu-format steakhouse also with display preparation of grilled entrees. Buffets also holds an 80 percent stake in Tahoe Joe's, Inc., which operates two Tahoe Joe's Famous Steakhouses in California.

Instantly Successful Beginnings

Buffets was founded by Roe Hatlen in 1983. Hatlen, a veteran of the restaurant industry, had spent nine years with International King's Table, Inc., an Oregon-based chain whose revenues were boosted to an annual $40 million with Hatlen's help. In 1982, Hatlen moved to Minnesota, where he took an executive position at the publicly held Pizza Ventures chain of restaurants. After only eight months at Pizza Ventures, however, he was let go when the company was acquired and reorganized by Godfather's Pizza.

During this time, Hatlen contacted his friend and former colleague at King's Table, C. Dennis Scott, an experienced restaurant operator responsible for running 22 King's Table restaurants. Hatlen persuaded Scott to leave the financial security of King's Table to pursue a new restaurant venture.

Hatlen and Scott decided to open a buffet style operation, which they expected to prove economical both for themselves and their customers. Without wait staff and bartenders, the buffet would necessitate a lower payroll than more formal operations and might appeal to customers who preferred not to pay gratuities.

The partners divided responsibilities along the lines of their expertise, with Hatlen handling financial matters and Scott overseeing the details of restaurant management. Hatlen was able to purchase Pizza Ventures' discarded computer system for five cents on the dollar and tapped his network of acquaintances in the restaurant business for investment capital, amassing about $750,000 by the time Buffets, Inc. was incorporated on October 13, 1983.

Scott planned the restaurant's offerings, designing a series of menus that centered on typical U.S. favorites, such as fried chicken, baked fish, and hamburgers. With particular attention to the value-conscious diner, he made sure that each meal included salad and dessert. Also featured were pasta dishes and other fare that could be prepared fresh in small batches throughout the day by cooks rather than by highly trained and expensive chefs.

With a staff of 29, Old Country Buffet opened in March 1984 in a small strip mall on the outskirts of Minneapolis. There, customers encountered a plain but comfortable decor, a buffet station with lines at either end, affording the customer a view of all food items, and a generous and varied menu. Customers prepaid the fixed rate before lining up at the buffet.

The restaurant was an instant success. Hatlen's and Scott's initially cautious projections for sales of $1 million during its

Company Perspectives:

Our food quality, friendly service and cleanliness will exceed your expectations.

first year were doubled by the end of 1984. By October 1985, nine Old Country Buffet restaurants were in operation around Wisconsin, Illinois, and Minnesota, requiring a total of 687 employees and netting sales of $59.5 million. Moreover, several investors were encouraging Buffets, Inc. to go public, which it did that year with an initial offering of 525,000 shares.

Rapid Expansion: Mid-1980s to Early 1990s

The cash flow generated by the offering allowed the company to expand over the next few years. By 1987, the Old Country Buffet chain had grown to include 11 restaurants in Minnesota, seven in Wisconsin, four in Illinois, and the remainder in new territories, including Missouri, Nebraska, Pennsylvania, and Oklahoma.

Public recognition of Old Country Buffets steadily increased. Moreover, *Restaurants and Institutions,* a food industry trade magazine, praised the buffets as ''shipshape'' and ''financially responsible.'' The reviewer also observed that buffets were beginning to offer strong competition to the country's cafeterias.

While buffets and cafeterias offered similar menus, the buffet featured a fixed rate policy, which proved less costly to the customer than the pay-per-item policy common in cafeterias. Moreover, buffets began to offer an alternative to the standard straight-line cafeteria layout. In 1989 Old Country Buffet restaurants adopted a new ''scatter system'' layout that featured individual food islands throughout, a system that hastened the self-service process and thereby allowed each restaurant to accommodate more customers. The number of restaurants in the chain rose to 70 by the beginning of 1990.

Buffets also became known for providing employment opportunities in the early 1990s, when economic recession led to high unemployment rates on a national level. During this time, Buffets placed a series of newspaper advertisements targeting potential managers seeking long-term employment. Emphasizing the rapid growth and continued success of Buffets, the copy received widespread attention and garnered the company the *Personnel Journal*'s Vantage Award for 1989.

In an effort to maintain employees knowledgeable in food production and personnel management, and to help curb its high employee turnover rate, Buffets opened a training center for managers at their Eden Prairie headquarters in Minnesota. There, employees underwent five weeks of seminars and three weeks of hands-on training in the headquarters restaurant.

Though at least 75 percent of Buffets employees were on part-time schedules in the early 1990s, graduates of the eight-week program helped established a solid managerial framework in almost all Old Country Buffets. Each restaurant retained two managers: one associate manager and one general manager in charge of operations. To maximize the profitability of each unit, the company based 50 percent of the general manager's annual salary on the profitability of his or her establishment.

In addition to enhancing the company's workforce, founder Hatlen also focused on procuring new restaurant locations left by unsuccessful retailers, whose incomplete leases gave him considerable negotiating power with desperate landlords. These cheaper rents helped make 1990 the seventh record year for earnings; sales soared 26 percent to $145.2 million, up from 1989's total of $115.4 million.

By 1991, Buffets operated a total of 110 restaurants, including those under the direction of two new subsidiaries. Gateway Buffets, acquired in 1989, came with a purchase price of $1.9 million. Evergreen Buffets was purchased for $1.7 million from C. Dennis Scott, who had left the company in 1990.

Firmly established as a leader in the restaurant industry, the company earned its fifth accolade from *Forbes* magazine as one of the 200 best small companies in the United States in 1992. Buffets' gross sales for 1992 reached $247.5 million, a figure that was bolstered one year later when the company discontinued its policy of serving free meals to employees. Charging employees $2 per meal, Buffets' added $300,000 to the sales total. Overall sales reached $334.9 million in 1993, an increase of 35 percent over 1992.

Mid- to Late 1990s: HomeTown Acquisition and New Formats

Buffets entered the mid-1990s as a 180-unit strong chain, with plans for continuing rapid expansion. By mid-1996 there were more than 250 Old Country Buffet restaurants. There was also a significant challenger to Buffets in the form of HomeTown Buffet Inc. of San Diego, which had been founded by C. Dennis Scott in 1991. By mid-1996 Scott's company operated 74 HomeTown Buffets, a format that used the scatter system pioneered by Buffets, and two Original Roadhouse Grills (steakhouses where entrees were ordered from a menu and prepared at an ''on-display'' grill); and franchised 19 HomeTown Buffets. For 1995, HomeTown reported earnings of $6.6 million on revenues of $152.4 million.

In June 1996, then, Buffets announced that it would acquire HomeTown Buffet, in a stock and debt transaction valued at about $190 million when it was consummated in September 1996. The merger made good geographic sense, as the strongest markets for Old Country Buffet were in the Midwest and Southeast while HomeTown had the majority of its units on the West Coast. The deal also reunited the cofounders of Buffets, with Hatlen continuing as chairman and CEO and Scott serving as vice-chairman. Buffets' headquarters remained in Eden Prairie. At year-end 1996, Buffets owned or franchised a total of 270 restaurants.

The acquisition resulted in some difficulties for Buffets as merger costs were larger than expected and merger savings did not materialize as fast as anticipated. Despite impressive revenues of $750.7 million for 1996, Buffets suffered a net loss of $7.2 million as a result of asset impairment and site closing costs and merger charges totaling $49.6 million. Weak performances at 38 units led to the asset impairment costs and the

Key Dates:

1983: Buffets, Inc. is founded by Roe Hatlen.
1985: Company goes public.
1989: "Scatter system" buffet format is introduced.
1996: HomeTown Buffet is acquired.
1999: Company purchases 80 percent stake in Tahoe Joe's, Inc.

closing of three restaurants, while the merger charges stemmed in part from the shuttering of five units because of their proximity to other units and from the closure of the San Diego headquarters of HomeTown Buffet. In another follow-up to the merger, during 1997 Buffets converted more than two dozen Old Country Buffets to HomeTown Buffets; such conversions were said to increase sales at stagnating units.

Buffets was back on track in the late 1990s, posting net income of $28.6 million in 1997 and $39.4 million in 1998, on revenues of $808.5 million and $868.9 million, respectively. In 1998 the company increased the number of company-owned restaurants from 360 to 386. Part of this increase came from the acquisition of 11 eating establishments from Country Harvest Buffet Restaurants, Inc. for $5.6 million. Ten of these units were subsequently converted to the company's buffet format with one of them converted to an Original Roadhouse Grill. Buffets also began testing two new restaurant formats, both of which were buffets with a twist. The PizzaPlay format offered Italian food and pizza served buffet style along with nonfood entertainment, including big screen televisions for sporting events, televisions showing children's cartoons, and a game area. This format was received lukewarmly by customers, and was abandoned during 1999. The second test format was called Country Roadhouse Buffet and Grill and its feature attraction was a display grill as part of its buffet. Both the Original Roadhouse Grill and the Country Roadhouse Buffet and Grill formats were performing well enough to be slated for expansion in 2000. In April 1999 Buffets purchased an 80 percent stake in Tahoe Joe's, Inc., the operator of two Tahoe Joe's Famous Steakhouses in California, thereby moving further into the nonbuffet sector.

The company broke ground in late 1998 on a new headquarters to be located in Eagan, Minnesota. As it entered 2000, Buffets was planning steady expansion of its buffet concepts primarily in existing markets but also extending into new territories such as Florida and Nevada. The Original Roadhouse Grill chain was performing well, with a dozen units in operation and with newer units averaging more than $3 million in sales per year. The company also had plenty of cash on hand to fund further expansion, acquisitions, and testing of new concepts.

Principal Subsidiaries

Dinertainment, Inc.; Distinctive Dining, Inc.; HomeTown Buffet, Inc.; HomeTown Development and Construction, Inc.; OCB Restaurant Co.; OCB Realty Co.; OCB Purchasing Co.; OCB Property Co.; Restaurant Innovations, Inc.

Principal Competitors

Advantica Restaurant Group, Inc.; Applebee's International, Inc.; Bob Evans Farms, Inc.; Carlson Restaurants Worldwide Inc.; CBRL Group, Inc.; FRD Acquisition Co.; Fresh Choice, Inc.; Furr's/Bishop's, Incorporated; Investors Management Corp.; Luby's, Inc.; Metromedia Company; Pancho's Mexican Buffet, Inc.; Piccadilly Cafeterias, Inc.; The Restaurant Co.; Ryan's Family Steak Houses, Inc.; Shoney's, Inc.; Star Buffet, Inc.; VICORP Restaurants, Inc.

Further Reading

Brumback, Nancy, "Buffeted by Change," *Restaurant Business,* January 1, 1997, pp. 53–54+.

"Buffets, Inc. Planning Its Biggest Expansion Ever During 1991," *Wall Street Journal,* November 16, 1990.

"Buffets Inc. Profits Jump Despite Slowed Economy," *Nation's Restaurant News,* September 9, 1991.

Carlino, Bill, "Buffets Inc. Purchases Rival HomeTown Buffet," *Nation's Restaurant News,* June 17, 1996, p. 1.

"Corporate Performance: Buffets," *Fortune,* February 12, 1990, p. 118.

Crecca, Donna Hood, "C. Dennis Scott," *Nation's Restaurant News,* January 1997, pp. 194, 196.

Dunnavant, Keith, "End of the Line," *Restaurant Business,* February 10, 1992, p. 44.

Fiedler, Terry, "Really Cookin'," *Minnesota Business Journal,* March 1986, p. 20.

Marcial, Gene G., "Buffets to Make Your Mouth Water," *Business Week,* July 1, 1996, p. 91.

Martin, Richard, "Old Country Buffet Parent Loses Recipe Lawsuit," *Nation's Restaurant News,* October 24, 1994, p. 3.

Meeks, Fleming, and R. Lee Sullivan, "If at First You Don't Succeed," *Forbes,* November 9, 1992, p. 172.

"Old Country Buffet Plans to Sell 525,000 Shares," *Nation's Restaurant News,* October 7, 1985.

Papiernik, Richard L., "Buffets Eyes Two Test Concepts to Replace Tired Units," *Nation's Restaurant News,* March 9, 1998, pp. 6, 11, 52.

——, "Buffets Hones Margins and Marketing into a Profitable Edge," *Nation's Restaurant News,* August 24, 1998, pp. 11, 22, 24.

——, "Buffets Inc. Engine Is Back on Track, Pulling Its Load," *Nation's Restaurant News,* March 1, 1999, pp. 11, 81.

Peterson, Susan E., "Buffets, HomeTown to Merge," *Minneapolis Star Tribune,* June 5, 1996, p. 1D.

Phelps, David, "A 'More Knowledgeable' Buffets Turns Optimistic," *Minneapolis Star Tribune,* June 23, 1997, p. 1D.

"Recruitment: Ads with Flair," *Personnel Journal,* October 1989, p. 50.

Schafer, Lee, "Salad Days: Buffets Inc. Is Ten Years Old, but Still Fresh Under CEO Roe Hatlen," *Corporate Report Minnesota,* June 1, 1994, p. 32.

Weleczi, Ruth, "Buffets, Inc.," *Minneapolis-St. Paul City Business,* June 24, 1991, p. 31.

—Gillian Wolf
—updated by David E. Salamie

Cablevision Electronic Instruments, Inc.

200 Menlo Park Drive
Edison, New Jersey 08837
U.S.A.
Telephone: (732) 650-3400
Toll Free: (800) 253-0186
Fax: (732) 650-3892
Web site: http://www.thewiz.com

Wholly Owned Subsidiary of CSC Holdings, Inc.
Founded: 1976
Employees: 4,000
Sales: $464.4 million (1998)
NAIC: 443112 Radio, Television & Other Electronic Stores; 44312 Computer & Software Stores

Cablevision Electronic Instruments, Inc. operates The Wiz, one of the largest retailers of consumer electronics in the United States. Its main products are video and audio equipment, home office equipment, compact discs and other prerecorded music, digital video discs, and videocassettes. A subsidiary of Cablevision Systems Corporation's CSC Holdings, Inc. subsidiary, Cablevision Electronic operates about 40 Wiz stores, all in the New York City metropolitan area. The Wiz accommodates the parent organization by selling Cablevision's telephone, online, and Internet access services; tickets to the two New York City professional sports teams the company owns (the New York Knicks and the New York Rangers); and tickets to other events at Cablevision-owned Madison Square Garden or events at Radio City Music Hall, which Cablevision leases and manages.

Two Decades of Growth: 1976–95

Norman Jemal, aided by his four sons, started Nobody Beats the Wiz when he opened a store in 1976 on Fulton Street in downtown Brooklyn. Little is known of the reclusive founder or the early years of his business; indeed, the Wiz introduced a Founder's Day sale in 1993 without ever mentioning his name. Employees—and even former employees—were reluctant to say anything to reporters about the Jemals. One staffer would not even give his name in order to say that the company had nothing to say about the Jemals. A former company executive who apparently chose to remain anonymous despite having nothing bad to impart, told James T. Madore of *Newsday* in 1998, "They are good people to work for because they treat you like family. They also take secrecy to the extreme."

By 1986 Nobody Beats the Wiz had 11 stores and was doing an estimated $200 million in annual sales. The chain entered New Jersey and Long Island that year by purchasing six Lafayette Electronics/Circuit City stores. It opened its first superstore in 1987, in Scarsdale, New York, and in 1991 introduced even larger stores, the first of them in Lake Grove, Long Island. Nobody Beats the Wiz was a heavy advertiser, reportedly running some 180 radio and television commercials on any given day. Such superstar athletes as football Hall of Famer Joe Namath, New York Giants quarterback Phil Simms, and New York Knicks center Patrick Ewing plugged its wares.

During the late 1980s and early 1990s several players in the New York metropolitan area's intensively competitive consumer electronics field went bankrupt, including Crazy Eddie Inc., Newmark & Lewis Inc., 47th Street Photo Inc., and Trader Horn. Nobody Beats the Wiz took full advantage of the opportunity, having opened, by mid-1992, 14 stores since 1988, for a total of 36, including five in Connecticut and a 25,000-square-foot superstore at Broadway and Eighth Street in Manhattan. The company spent $45.6 million on advertising in 1992. A survey found the Wiz first in market share among metropolitan area consumer electronics customers, with 17 percent.

In 1994 Nobody Beats the Wiz began selling personal computers and allied products in order to counter competitors such as Computer City and CompUSA, who were entering the New York market. It also established a home-shopping and business-to-business division that year to boost sales still further. Wiz booths at concert venues such as the 25th-anniversary Woodstock Festival sold compact discs. The chain's sales level rose from an estimated $500 million in 1993 to about $775 million in 1994.

In 1995 Nobody Beats the Wiz moved into the Philadelphia area, Holyoke, Massachusetts, and upstate New York as far north as Albany. There were signs, however, that the chain was

Key Dates:

1976: Norman Jemal opens the first Wiz store in Brooklyn.
1986: Nobody Beats the Wiz chain consists of 11 stores.
1993: Sales reach $500 million.
1994: Nobody Beats the Wiz begins selling personal computers.
1996: Chain reaches peak, with about 67 stores and over $1 billion in annual sales.
1997: Nobody Beats the Wiz files for bankruptcy protection, following a period of overspending and industry downturn.
1998: Cablevision buys the chain for $101 million.

beginning to lose impetus for the first time, as Circuit City Stores Inc. and Best Buy Co. began moving into its territory. In October 1995 suppliers and competitors announced that nine of the 13 Wiz music outlets in Washington, D.C., had closed or were in the process of closing. Even so, company sales rose to about $950 million that year, and it was the nation's third largest consumer electronics retailer.

Overexpansion Leads to Bankruptcy: 1996–97

Nobody Beats the Wiz entered the Boston metropolitan area in 1996 with glitzy displays and advertising promising deep discounts. The chain's 62 stores rang up at least $1 billion in sales that year and earned $30 million in net income. Shortly before the end of the year the company, which had always devised its own ads, hired Bozell Worldwide to introduce a more sophisticated approach. ''The days are gone when you can scream and yell at consumers,'' a Bozell executive told Harry Berkowitz of *Newsday.* He said that the agency would focus more of the company's advertising budget on television and target fewer but ''better quality'' customers. Nobody Beats the Wiz had spent $87 million on advertising in 1995.

Nobody Beats the Wiz kept up with the times by introducing Internet access at its New Jersey stores in 1996 and adding custom-built personal computers to its line of products the following year. It also opened a large store on midtown Manhattan's Fifth Avenue. By 1997, however, the chain was in financial trouble because of increased competition, general weakness in the nation's consumer electronics sector, overspending on advertising, and perhaps an overgenerous policy on returns. Vendors were receiving late payments or no payment at all, and some ceased making shipments. A realtor told Judith Messina of *Crain's New York Business,* ''In the past two years, they've expanded very rapidly, opening up extremely large 50,000-square-foot stores. Those units are expensive and, in some markets, maybe not necessary.'' The Wiz reached its maximum size of about 67 stores at this time, but some were in bad locations, not easily seen by motorists.

Nobody Beats the Wiz's weakest link was New England, where commercials by such New York sports stars as Derek Jeter of the Yankees had little appeal and ''slam-bang, push-it-in-your face promotion'' was distasteful, a Boston marketing professor told Madore and Randi Feigenbaum of *Newsday.* Prodded by its principal lender, Congress Financial Corp., the chain announced in July that it would close stores in Framingham, Holyoke, and Saugus, Massachusetts, and Meriden and Newington, Connecticut, to focus on business in its core New York metropolitan area. But as the Christmas season approached, the Wiz's financial situation was so dire that it sold 30 percent of the firm to Paragon Capital L.L.C. for $27 million in order to be able to fill the stores with merchandise through the end of the year.

This measure failed to buy enough time for Nobody Beats the Wiz, which soon faced numerous lawsuits from unpaid landlords and equipment suppliers. The company filed for Chapter 11 bankruptcy protection in December 1997, closed 17 of its roughly 50 remaining stores, and received court permission to draw on a $150 million line of credit in order to pay $132 million worth of debt. Only secured creditors could expect payment, however, because the company owed $354.6 million.

Cablevision to the Rescue: 1998–99

Nobody Beats the Wiz seemed doomed for dissolution at this point, since no major electronics retailer filing for bankruptcy in the New York area had emerged from Chapter 11 in more than a decade. But in February 1998 the company was sold for $101 million to Cablevision Systems Corporation James Dolan, chief executive officer for the giant cable-TV, sports, and entertainment company, said outlets like the Wiz were valuable marketing tools for selling Cablevision's wares, such as cable modems and advanced digital set-up boxes. Cablevision also owned Madison Square Garden as well as the Knicks and Rangers sports franchises. It also was providing cable television with much sports and entertainment programming and had taken a 25-year lease on Rockefeller Center's Radio City Music Hall.

Cablevision moved quickly to restore the chain—renamed The Wiz—to health. By May 1998 it had persuaded many vendors to resume shipment of goods. An interim management team, recruited from the retailing consultant Carl Marks Group, hired The Lord Group advertising agency to produce a new campaign. The Wiz signed a three-year agreement to offer Bell Atlantic Mobile service to any customer buying a mobile phone. In-store kiosks sought to sell Cablevision's Optimum Online Internet access to purchasers of Wiz-stocked cable modems. The parent company signed a $1 billion deal in 1999 to have Sony Corporation build digital set-top boxes for its cable customers, with Wiz stores as distribution sites.

Bill Marginson, founder of a Dallas-based chain of appliance and furniture stores, assumed the position of president and CEO in December 1998. The chain moved its headquarters from Carteret, New Jersey, to Edison, New Jersey, consolidated warehouses, and dropped marginal merchandise such as toys, sunglasses, and watches. A fall 1998 survey found that 16 percent of all Long Island residents had visited a Wiz store within the last three months, ranking the chain second in its field only to P.C. Richard & Son.

Although The Wiz resumed heavy print and television advertising, the emphasis changed from price discounting to product features, custom service, warranties, and in-store financing, according to an April 1999 *Newsday* story. Dolan said that Cablevision service centers were being established in the stores and that better light and interactive displays were in the works. Renovations were planned for 15 stores in 1999. ''You can expect us to further invest in the retail area on behalf of The Wiz,'' he told Madore. ''We think it's there, and now that we have stabilized the business we'll begin to take advantage of the synergies.''

Some retail observers questioned whether The Wiz could flourish except as a deep discounter. A trade journal editor told Madore, ''They are a big chain, not an upscale boutique. . . . The Wiz has to offer entry level products at low prices and to respond to what Circuit City, P.C. Richard and others are doing.'' He said that a focus on consumer service required better-quality sales clerks and added, ''there still needs to be improvements on the store level.'' In addition, a research analyst wrote that ''This shift in strategy is negatively affecting near-term revenues.''

The Wiz chain consisted, at the end of 1998, of a warehouse and 40 retail stores. Revenue from the date of acquisition came to $464.4 million in that year, of which audio equipment accounted for 39 percent, video equipment for 24 percent, and home office equipment for 20 percent. The remaining 17 percent came from compact discs and other prerecorded music, digital video discs, VHS video and other prerecorded movies, and warranty and service contracts. Cablevision Electronic sustained a loss of $24.5 million. *Newsday* reported in October 1999 that The Wiz might end the year with losses of $20 million because of problems in converting to a new inventory system and the chain's deemphasis on price competition. Earlier in the year, Cablevision executives had been hopeful that The Wiz would return to profitability in 1999.

There were 39 Wiz stores in late 1999: 17 in New York City, 13 in New Jersey, six on Long Island, and one each in Westchester County, New York; Rockland County, New York; and Connecticut. As many as 25 were planned for the future. Three new ''concept'' stores designed to better market Cablevision goods and services were due to open in the near future; one of the three, a 25,000-square-foot outlet in Bay Shore, Long Island, was scheduled for completion in November 1999.

Principal Competitors

Best Buy Co.; Circuit Stores Inc.; P.C. Richard & Son Corp.; Tops Appliance City, Inc.

Further Reading

Anastasi, Nick, ''Wiz to Expand As Cablevision Corp. Preps Digital Push,'' *Long Island Business News,* September 24, 1999, p. 1A.

Berkowitz, Harry, ''Wiz Bucks Old Ways, Opts to Hire Ad Agency,'' *Newsday,* December 20, 1996, pp. A83–A84.

Birger, Jon, and Lisa Sanders, ''Wiz Uses Cash Rapidly, Needs Buyer, Investor,'' *Crain's New York Business,* December 22, 1997, pp. 1, 19.

''Cablevision's Growing Empire,'' *Newsday,* February 8, 1999, pp. C14–C15.

Elliott, Stuart, ''Electronics Chain Plays Coy About Identity of Founder, Who Is Pictured in Splashy Promotion,'' *New York Times,* April 29, 1993, p. D29.

Furman, Phyllis, ''Survey: Nobody Beating the Wiz in Sales,'' *Crain's New York Business,* June 29, 1992, p. 17.

Gerena-Morales, Rafael, ''Wiz Shifts Focus to N.J.-N.Y.,'' *Bergen Record,* July 8, 1997, p. B1.

McCabe, Kathy, ''Electronics Retailer Pulls Plug in N.E.,'' *Boston Globe,* July 5, 1997, pp. D1, D3.

——, ''The Wiz Heads North,'' *Boston Globe,* March 1, 1996, p. 65.

Madore, James T., ''Cablevision Not Yet Able to Turn Around The Wiz,'' *Newsday,* October 14, 1999, p. A55.

——, ''New CEO Takes Helm at The Wiz,'' *Newsday,* December 2, 1994, p. A64.

——, ''Wiz Plugs into New Approach,'' *Newsday,* April 29, 1999, p. A71.

Madore, James T., and Randi Feigenbaum, ''What Beat the Wiz,'' *Newsday,* February 16, 1998, pp. C8–C10.

Messina, Judith, ''The Wiz Buffeted by Cash Crunch,'' *Crain's New York Business,* January 13, 1997, pp. 1, 47.

Ravo, Nick, ''Wiz Is Latest Chain to Fall in Tough Electronics Market,'' *New York Times,* December 21, 1997, Sec. 1, p. 43.

Walsh, Sharon, and Kirstin Downey Grimsley, ''Wiz Music Chain Closing Nine of Its 13 Area Stores,'' *Washington Post,* October 21, 1995, pp. D1–D2.

—Robert Halasz

CADWALADER

Cadwalader, Wickersham & Taft

Cadwalader, Wickersham & Taft

100 Maiden Lane
New York, New York 10038
U.S.A.
Telephone: (212) 504-6000
Fax: (212) 504-6666
Web site: http://www.cadwalader.com

Partnership
Founded: 1792
Employees: 650
Sales: $175 million (1998 est.)
NAIC: 54111 Offices of Lawyers

Cadwalader, Wickersham & Taft claims the distinction of being the United States' oldest law firm, tracing its roots to 1792. For decades it was one of the top New York City law firms, but in the late 20th century it slipped as many other law firms aggressively gained more clients. However, in the 1990s Cadwalader updated its business practices and regained a position as one of the city's top 25 law firms. Like other law firms, its practice in the 1990s involved traditional corporate clients, such as banks, insurance companies, and utility firms, but also has expanded into relatively new areas such as environmental, intellectual property, and healthcare law.

The Early Decades: 1792–1878

When the United States back in 1792 consisted of just four million persons and New York had about 33,000 residents, the New York Supreme Court admitted 22-year-old John Wells as an attorney. Wells had graduated from Princeton and then moved to the city. His early practice probably involved real estate, debt collections, and other commercial claims. In 1804 he represented James Cheetham, the editor of the *American Citizen,* in Cheetham v. Smith. Although his client lost the case, Wells soon became well-known among his fellow attorneys.

In 1818 Wells organized a partnership with George Washington Strong, who graduated from Yale and in 1805 began his legal career. Unlike Wells, Strong early in his career was quite busy with at least 100 cases of commercial and maritime law every year. After the 1807 Embargo Act shut down the port, Strong worked on many cases to collect debts from those who had lost their jobs or on real estate foreclosures. His business clients included Union Bank, the New York Sugar Refining Company, and the Columbian, American, and New York Fire Insurance Companies. In 1816 Strong helped found the Bank for Savings in the City of New York. He also served prominent families and individuals, such as the Vanderbilts and John Jacob Astor.

When Wells died in 1823, Strong brought George Griffin, another Yale graduate, into the partnership that continued to prosper as New York City expanded, especially after the 1825 completion of the Erie Canal that connected the heartland to the nation's largest port. The partnership moved in 1830 to Wall Street, where it remained until 1985.

In 1835 Strong replaced Griffin with Marshall S. Bidwell, his new partner and former member of the Canadian Parliament. Bidwell became a well-known litigator, representing clients such as author James Fenimore Cooper in a libel suit. Strong's son George Templeton Strong joined the law firm in 1838. The Strong, Bidwell & Strong partnership served business clients such as the Bank of America, the Merchants' Exchange Company, the Seamen's Bank for Savings, and the Neptune Insurance Company, and gained more real estate and mortgage work as the city grew. For example, Manhattan's first tenements were built in the 1840s as more Irish and other European immigrants poured into the city. The firm also represented bankruptcy clients following the panics of 1837 and 1857.

In 1855 George Washington Strong died. Although the partnership was renamed Bidwell & Strong, George Templeton Strong became the most prominent partner through the 1860s, especially due to his extensive civic involvement. Strong was an officer or leader of the Philharmonic Society, Trinity Church, and the U.S. Sanitary Commission, which had been established to improve the health of Union soldiers during the Civil War. In the 1850s Strong helped create Columbia College's law school, recognizing that the apprenticeship system was outdated.

In the 1870s Strong died and Charles E. Strong, his first cousin, kept the firm going. New clients in that decade included

Key Dates:

1792: John Wells begins practicing law in New York.
1818: The partnership of Wells & Strong is formed.
1873: Charles E. Strong begins a solo practice.
1878: Strong & Cadwalader is formed.
1914: Cadwalader, Wickersham & Taft is organized.
1980s: The firm starts practices in consumer products, healthcare, and environmental law.
1988: Los Angeles office opens.
1996: Firm starts its branch office in Charlotte, North Carolina.
1997: London office opens.
1998: Firm closes its Los Angeles office.

Wells Fargo, Western Union Telegraph Company, the founders of the New York Medical College & Hospital for Women and Children, and also Steinway & Sons, New York's famous piano maker. In the law firm's bicentennial history, Charles E. Strong was said to "represent the transition [from small generalist law firms to large specialized firms]: he was concerned with 'family law' in the management and advice he provided to his trusts and estates clients, but also undertook the legal work for the firm's major business clients."

New Era of Corporate Law Starting in the Late 1800s

With corporate America booming after the Civil War, the law firm in 1878 hired John L. Cadwalader, who previously had graduated from Princeton College and Harvard Law School and served as the nation's Assistant Secretary of State. In 1878 Strong & Cadwalader with its six lawyers and four staff members was one of the nation's larger law firms. They used the newly invented typewriter (1868) and telephone (1876) to run their business and also adopted the "Cravath system" in which law firms hired top law school graduates as associates, instead of training unpaid law clerks in the apprenticeship system. About the same time, the law firm gained new clients, such as the Title Guaranty & Trust Company, Manhattan Trust Company, the Real Estate Exchange, and the Real Estate Trust.

In the years before World War I, the law firm represented other corporate clients, including United States Steel; the Aluminum Company of America; Allis-Chalmers Company; Phelps, Dodge; London's S. Pearson & Son; National Railways of Mexico; Seattle Lighting Company; Chase National Bank; and the Mutual Life Insurance Company of New York. Some of the firm's clients literally built New York City's infrastructure, including its subways, railroad tunnels, and the Grand Central Terminal.

In the Progressive Era, the law firm represented not only corporate clients, but also those not so prosperous. Since its formation in 1848, the New York Association for Improving the Condition of the Poor had used the law firm's assistance.

In 1914 George Wickersham and Henry W. Taft joined the law firm that adopted its permanent name of Cadwalader, Wickersham & Taft, with a total of eight partners, 15 associates, and 29 other staff employees. President Taft's former attorney general, Wickersham chaired President Hoover's commission on law enforcement that advised continuing Prohibition. He also chaired the Council on Foreign Relations founded in 1921. Taft, an expert in antitrust law, represented several railroads, including the New York, New Haven & Hartford Railroad and the St. Louis & San Francisco Railroad.

During the Great Depression, Cadwalader held its own, largely due to foreclosure and bankruptcy work. It also gained media attention when it represented a member of the famous Vanderbilt family and also helped Margaret Mitchell successfully defend herself in a landmark copyright lawsuit that had accused her of plagiarizing when she wrote *Gone with the Wind*.

During World War II, Cadwalader lost 35 lawyers and staff when they joined the military, a typical development for many law firms at that time. To compensate, the firm hired more women, including in 1942 its first woman partner, Catherine Noyes Lee, "the first woman to hold such a position in a major Wall Street law firm," according to the firm's history.

Post-World War II Developments

With the U.S. economy growing after the war, Cadwalader also recovered. By 1952 the firm had 47 lawyers, and in 1965 that number had grown to 76 lawyers. From the 1950s through the 1970s Cadwalader was one of the nation's major law firms involved in financing transactions for the shipping industry. In the 1970s, for example, the firm helped write a $1 billion contract for constructing liquid natural gas ships and also wrote a unique lease that allowed ships to be built with private funding that were then leased to the government's Military Sealift Command. During the heyday of the firm's shipping practice, it represented clients' interests in Europe, Asia, and the Middle East. But the industry declined in the early 1980s, so Cadwalader represented creditors that foreclosed on 12 ships of the United States Lines, the largest shipping bankruptcy in U.S. history.

In the 1970s and 1980s Cadwalader participated in the litigation explosion in U.S. society. In the 1970s it won court cases against the Internal Revenue Service that "established the principle that the government, 'the Sovereign,' could be sued and held liable for lease contracts," according to its 1994 history. In the early 1980s Cadwalader represented William Tavoulareas in his defamation lawsuit against the *Washington Post*, a case that helped expand the firm's practice in media, communications, and First Amendment law.

Cadwalader also defended Diamond Shamrock, a manufacturer of Agent Orange, when it was sued by over two million Vietnam veterans in a class-action lawsuit settled out of court in 1984. The firm's work in this case led it into toxic waste lawsuits involving asbestos and chromium producers. In 1989 the law firm gained a $2.5 billion settlement for 300,000 women who had sued for damages from the Dalkon Shield birth control device made by the A.H. Robins Company.

In the 1980s Cadwalader also won a major case against Arthur Anderson & Company in what was the largest judgment against an accounting firm. Other Cadwalader financial litigation concerned the Hunt brothers' silver market scheme, the

Lombard Wall bankruptcy, and Ivan Boesky's involvement with Drexel Burnham.

Practice in the 1990s

In the early 1990s Cadwalader suffered an economic decline, as did many other law firms as part of an overall national downturn. Consequently, in 1994 a firm committee voted to end the unprofitable Palm Beach office and terminate some of its partners. James W. Beasley, Jr., then sued the firm. A Florida judge in 1996 ruled in Beasley's favor, awarding him $2.5 million, based on the fact that Cadwalader's outdated partnership agreement lacked a means to expel a partner.

This case represented some general trends. For example, Leslie Corwin, an attorney specializing in partnership law, estimated that about half the firms he had worked with had obsolete charters, the basic reason several terminated partners have sued their former law firms. It seemed ironic that some law firms helped their clients in the fast-paced Information Age yet neglected their own operating rules.

It should be emphasized that Cadwalader in the 1990s became more business-oriented, a step necessary to survive as a firm. In the process it adopted methods unheard of in earlier decades, such as using direct mail to gain clients, as reported in the book *Malice Aforethought.*

Cadwalader represented some major clients involved in Latin American project finance deals in the late 1990s. Several involved privatization of formerly state-controlled facilities. For example, the firm advised the Puerto Rican government in the $365 million privatization of the North Coast Super Aqueduct; Doe Run Resources in the $1 billion privatization of a Peruvian mine; the government of Paraguay in the $8 billion privatization of the Yacyreta hydroelectric facility owned jointly by Paraguay and Argentina; UBS Securities in the $1.5 billion privatization of the Argentina Airport System; and the Bank of America in the $500 million privatization of a Guatemalan distribution firm called EEGSA. The law firm also counseled NationsBank in two transactions, one to finance a $1 billion Mexican fiber optic system run by Alestra and also to privatize Light Rio, a distribution company in Rio de Janeiro.

In 1996 Cadwalader opened a new branch office in Charlotte, North Carolina with eight attorneys. By late August 1998, the office had grown to 30 attorneys and was relocating to a larger office in the city's Carillon Building. According to a firm press release on August 31, 1998, Cadwalader was the "first major Wall Street law firm to open a North Carolina office," and Charlotte was described as "the country's second largest financial center."

By March 1999 Cadwalader had added about 100 lawyers in little over a year. With a total of 400 lawyers, it was ranked as the 22nd largest law firm based in New York City. The firm in early 1999 received considerable attention in the legal press when it gave its first-year associates a huge pay raise after lagging behind rival firms in years past. Starting January 1, 1999, the first-year associates had a salary and guaranteed bonus totaling $107,000. With many associates leaving their initial law firms for greener pastures, Cadwalader also began offering associates paid one-month sabbaticals after their fifth year.

Rival firms often grew from mergers with other law firms. According to the *National Law Journal*'s 1998 survey of the nation's 250 largest firms, 29 law firm mergers in 1998 added 840 attorneys, compared with 20 firms that added 387 lawyers through mergers in 1997. However, Cadwalader's managing partner Robert O. Link, Jr., in the *National Law Journal* of November 16, 1998 said, "We've never merged with a firm, and I don't see it happening within the foreseeable future." Cadwalader relied on recruiting associates and lateral hires (i.e., organic growth) to expand.

In spite of Cadwalader's overall growth, it closed its Los Angeles branch office in late 1998, since the firm and its clients concluded that Los Angeles had not become a major financial center. The Los Angeles branch had reached a total of 30 lawyers, but some partners there either returned to New York City or joined other Los Angeles law firms.

In its third century of practice, Cadwalader faced new challenges and opportunities, from the introduction of the "euro," the new currency of the European Community, to the North American Free Trade Agreement approved during the Clinton administration, to the booming frontiers of the new electronic economy.

Principal Competitors

Baker & McKenzie; Skadden, Arps, Slate, Meagher & Flom; Stroock & Stroock.

Further Reading

Barrett, Paul M., "A Once-Stodgy Firm Makes a Flashy Return, But at What Cost?" *Wall Street Journal*, August 17, 1998, p. A1.

Cherovsky, Erwin, "Cadwalader, Wickersham & Taft," *The Guide to New York Law Firms,* New York: St. Martin's Press, 1991, pp. 41–44.

Friedman, Thomas L., *The Lexus and the Olive Tree,* New York: Farrar, Straus and Giroux, 1999.

Gardner, Deborah S., *Cadwalader, Wickersham & Taft: A Bicentennial History 1792–1992,* New York: Cadwalader, Wickersham & Taft, 1994.

Shepherd, Ritchenya, "Firms Get Urge to Merge," *National Law Journal*, November 16, 1998, p. A1.

Snider, Anna, "Cadwalader Leapfrogs Firms in Setting Associate Salaries," *New York Law Journal*, March 18, 1999, pp. 1, 8.

Starkman, Dean, "New York Firm's Expelled Partner Is Awarded $2.5 Million by Judge," *Wall Street Journal*, July 26, 1996, p. B2 (eastern edition).

—David M. Walden

The Coca-Cola Company

The Coca-Cola Company

One Coca-Cola Plaza
Atlanta, Georgia 30313
U.S.A.
Telephone: (404) 676-2121
Toll Free: (800) 468-7856
Fax: (404) 676-6792
Web site: http://www.cocacola.com

Public Company
Incorporated: 1892
Employees: 28,600
Sales: $18.81 billion (1998)
Stock Exchanges: New York Boston Cincinnati Midwest Pacific Philadelphia Frankfurt Zurich
Ticker Symbol: KO
NAIC: 312111 Soft Drink Manufacturing; 311930 Flavoring Syrup and Concentrate Manufacturing; 311411 Frozen Fruit, Juice, and Vegetable Manufacturing; 312112 Bottled Water Manufacturing

The Coca-Cola Company is the world's number one maker of soft drinks, holding 51 percent of the global market. Coca-Cola's red and white trademark is probably the best-known brand symbol in the world. Headquartered since its founding in Atlanta, Coca-Cola makes two of the top three soft drinks in the world, Coca-Cola Classic at number one and Diet Coke at number three. The company also operates one of the world's most pervasive distribution systems, offering its more than 160 beverage products in nearly 200 countries worldwide. Nearly two-thirds of sales are generated outside North America, with revenues breaking down as follows: North America, 37 percent; Greater Europe (which includes parts of Eurasia, such as Russia), 26 percent; Middle and Far East, 21 percent; Latin America (including Mexico), 12 percent; Africa, three percent; and other regions, one percent. Among the company's products are a variety of carbonated beverages, sports drinks, juices, teas, coffees, and bottled water, under such brands as Fanta, Sprite, Mr. PiBB, Mello Yello, TAB, Surge, Citra, POWERaDE, Fruitopia, Saryusaisai, Aquarius, Bonaqa, and Dasani. Coca-Cola owns the Minute Maid Company, a leading North American maker of juices and other beverages, including Hi-C fruit drinks, Five Alive citrus drinks, Bright & Early breakfast beverages, and Bacardi mixers. Moreover, the company, through its Schweppes Beverages unit, also holds the rights to such brands as Schweppes, Canada Dry, Dr Pepper, and Crush in 157 countries, primarily located outside North America and Europe. Coca-Cola's development into one of the most powerful and admired firms in the world has been credited to proficiency in four basic areas: consumer marketing, infrastructure (production and distribution), product packaging, and customer (or vendor) marketing.

Creation of a Brand Legend

The inventor of Coca-Cola, Dr. John Styth Pemberton, came to Atlanta from Columbus, Georgia, in 1869. In 1885 he set up a chemical laboratory in Atlanta and went into the patent medicine business. Pemberton invented such products as Indian Queen hair dye, Gingerine, and Triplex liver pills. In 1886 he concocted a mixture of sugar, water, and extracts of the coca leaf and the kola nut. He added caffeine to the resulting syrup so that it could be marketed as a headache remedy. Through his research Pemberton arrived at the conclusion that this medication was capable of relieving indigestion and exhaustion in addition to being refreshing and exhilarating.

The pharmacist and his business partners could not decide whether to market the mixture as a medicine or to extol its flavor for its own sake, so they did both. In *Coca-Cola: An Illustrated History,* Pat Watters cited a Coca-Cola label from 1887 which stated that the drink, "makes not only a delicious . . . and invigorating beverage . . . but a valuable Brain Tonic and a cure for all nervous affections." The label also claimed that "the peculiar flavor of Coca-Cola delights every palate; it is dispensed from the soda fountain in the same manner as any fruit syrup." The first newspaper advertisement for Coca-Cola appeared exactly three weeks after the first batch of syrup was produced, and the famous trademark, white Spenserian script on a red background, made its debut at about the same time.

Coca-Cola was not, however, immediately successful. During the product's first year in existence, Pemberton and his

Company Perspectives:

As the world's largest beverage company, we refresh the world. We do this by developing superior soft drinks, both carbonated and noncarbonated, and profitable nonalcoholic beverage systems that create value for our Company, our bottling partners, our customers, our share owners and communities in which we do business. In creating value, we succeed or fail based on our ability to perform as worthy stewards of several key assets: (1) Coca-Cola, the world's most recognized trademark, and other highly valued trademarks; (2) The world's most effective and pervasive distribution system; (3) Satisfied customers, who make a good profit selling our products; (4) Our people, who are ultimately responsible for building this enterprise; (5) Our abundant resources, which must be intelligently allocated; (6) Our strong global leadership in the beverage industry in particular and in the business world in general.

partners spent around $74 in advertising their unique beverage and made only $50 in sales. The combined pressures of poor business and ill health led Pemberton to sell two-thirds of his business in early 1888. By 1891, a successful druggist named Asa G. Candler owned the entire enterprise. It had cost him $2,300. Dr. Pemberton, who died three years earlier, was never to know the enormous success his invention would have in the coming century.

Candler, a religious man with excellent business sense, infused the enterprise with his personality. Candler became a notable philanthropist, associating the name of Coca-Cola with social awareness in the process. He was also an integral part of Atlanta both as a citizen and as a leader. Candler endowed Emory University and its Wesley Memorial Hospital with more than $8 million. Indeed, the university could not have come into existence without his aid. In 1907 he prevented a real estate panic in Atlanta by purchasing $1 million worth of homes and reselling them to people of moderate income at affordable prices. During World War I, Candler helped to avert a cotton crisis by using his growing wealth to stabilize the market. After he stepped down as the president of Coca-Cola, he became the mayor of Atlanta and introduced such reforms as motorizing the fire department and augmenting the water system with his private funds.

1891–1919: Rapid Growth Under the Candlers

Under Candler's leadership, which spanned a 26-year period, the Coca-Cola Company grew quickly. Between 1888 and 1907, the factory and offices of the business were moved to eight different buildings in order to keep up with the company's growth and expansion. As head of the company, Candler was most concerned with the quality and promotion of his product. He was particularly concerned with production of the syrup, which was boiled in kettles over a furnace and stirred by hand with large wooden paddles. He improved Pemberton's formula with the help of a chemist, a pharmacist, and a prescriptionist. In 1901, responding to complaints about the presence of minute amounts of cocaine in the Coca-Cola syrup, Candler devised the means to remove all traces of the substance. By 1905, the syrup was completely free of cocaine.

In 1892, the newly incorporated Coca-Cola Company allocated $11,401 for advertising its drink. Advertising materials included signs, free sample tickets, and premiums such as ornate soda fountain urns, clocks, and stained-glass lampshades, all with the words "Coca-Cola" engraved upon them. These early advertising strategies initiated the most extensive promotional campaign for one product in history. Salesmen traveled the entire country selling the company's syrup, and by 1895 Coca-Cola was being sold and consumed in every state in the nation. Soon it was available in some Canadian cities and in Honolulu, and plans were underway for its introduction into Mexico. By the time Asa Candler left the company in 1916, Coke had also been sold in Cuba, Jamaica, Germany, Bermuda, Puerto Rico, the Philippines, France, and England.

An event that had an enormous impact on the future and very nature of the company was the 1899 agreement made between Candler and two young lawyers that allowed them to bottle and sell Coca-Cola throughout the United States: the first bottling franchise had been established. Five years later, in 1904, the one-millionth gallon of Coca-Cola syrup had been sold. In 1916 the now universally recognized, uniquely contour-shaped Coke bottle was invented. The management of all company advertising was assigned to the D'Arcy Advertising Agency, and the advertising budget had ballooned to $1 million by 1911. During this time, all claims for the medicinal properties of Coca-Cola were quietly dropped from its advertisements.

World War I and the ensuing sugar rationing measures slowed the growth of the company, but the pressure of coal rations led Candler's son, Charles Howard, to invent a process whereby the sugar and water could be mixed without using heat. This process saved the cost of fuel, relieved the company of the need for a boiler, and saved a great amount of time since there was no need for the syrup to go through a cooling period. The company continued to use this method of mixing into the 1990s.

Although Candler was fond of his company, he became disillusioned with it in 1916 and retired. One of the reasons for this decision was the new tax laws which, in Candler's words, did not allow for "the accumulation of surplus in excess of the amount necessary for profitable and safe conduct of our particular business." (It has also been suggested that Candler refused to implement the modernization of company facilities.)

1919–55: The Woodruff Era

Robert Winship Woodruff became president of the company in 1923 at the age of 33. His father, Ernest Woodruff, along with an investor group, had purchased it from the Candler family in 1919 for $25 million, and the company went public in the same year at $40 a share. After leaving college before graduation, Woodruff held various jobs, eventually becoming the Atlanta branch manager and then the vice-president of an Atlanta motor company, before becoming the president of Coca-Cola.

Having entered the company at a time when its affairs were quite tumultuous, Woodruff worked rapidly to improve Coca-Cola's financial condition. In addition to low sales figures in 1922, he had to face the problem of animosity toward the

Key Dates:

1886: Pemberton concocts Coca-Cola, a mixture of sugar, water, caffeine, and extracts of the coca leaf and the kola nut.
1891: Candler, a druggist, gains complete control of Pemberton's enterprise.
1892: Candler incorporates The Coca-Cola Company.
1899: The first bottling franchise is established.
1905: Coca-Cola syrup is completely free of cocaine.
1916: The unique, contour-shaped Coke bottle is introduced.
1919: Robert Winship Woodruff and an investor group buy the company for $25 million; the company goes public at $40 per share.
1923: Robert Winship becomes president of the firm.
1943: Coca-Cola plants are set up near fighting fronts in North Africa and Europe, helping boost American GI spirits and introduce Coke to the world market.
1961: Sprite makes its debut.
1981: Roberto Goizueta becomes chairman.
1982: Columbia Pictures is acquired for $750 million; Diet Coke is introduced to the market.
1985: Coca-Cola is reformulated; New Coke is rejected by consumers, and the company brings back the original formula, calling it Coca-Cola Classic.
1987: Company sells its entertainment business to Tri-Star Pictures.
1990: Sales surpass the $10 billion mark for the first time.
1997: Douglas succeeds Goizueta as chairman and CEO.
1999: Company acquires the rights to sell Schweppes, Canada Dry, Dr Pepper, and Crush brands in 157 countries, not including the United States, Canada, Mexico, and most of Europe.
2000: Coca-Cola announces that Ivester will step down as CEO, to be replaced by COO Douglas N. Daft.

company on the part of the bottlers as a result of an imprudent sugar purchase that management had made. This raised the price of the syrup and angered the bottlers. Woodruff was aided in particular by two men, Harrison Jones and Harold Hirsch, who were adept at maintaining good relations between the company and its bottling franchises.

Woodruff set to work improving the sales department; he emphasized quality control, and began advertising and promotional campaigns that were far more sophisticated than those of the past. He established a research department that became a pioneering market research agency. He also worked hard to provide his customers with the latest in technological developments that would facilitate their selling Coca-Cola to the public, and he labored to increase efficiency at every step of the production process so as to raise the percentage of profit from every sale of Coca-Cola syrup.

Through the 1920s and 1930s such developments as the six-pack carton of Coke, which encouraged shoppers to purchase the drink for home consumption, coin-operated vending machines in the workplace, and the cooler designed by John Stanton expanded the domestic market considerably. Also, by the end of 1930, as a result of the company's quality control efforts, Coca-Cola tasted exactly the same everywhere.

Considered slightly eccentric, Woodruff was a fair employer and an admired philanthropist. In 1937, he donated $50,000 to Emory University for a cancer diagnosis and treatment center, and over the years gave more than $100 million to the clinic. He donated $8 million for the construction of the Atlanta Memorial Arts Center. Under his leadership the Coca-Cola Company pioneered such company benefits as group life insurance and group accident and health policies, and in 1948 introduced a retirement program.

Woodruff was to see the Coca-Cola Company through an era marked by important and varied events. Even during the Great Depression the company did not suffer thanks to Woodruff's cost-cutting measures. When Prohibition was repealed, Coca-Cola continued to experience rising sales. It was World War II, however, that catapulted Coca-Cola into the world market and made it one of America's first multinational companies.

Woodruff and Archie Lee of the D'Arcy Advertising Agency worked to equate Coca-Cola with the American way of life. Advertisements had, in Candler's era, been targeted at the wealthy population. In Woodruff's time the advertising was aimed at all Americans. By early 1950, African Americans were featured in advertisements, and by the mid-1950s there was an increase in advertising targeted at other minority groups. Advertising never reflected the problems of the world, only the good and happy life. Radio advertising began in 1927, and through the years Coca-Cola sponsored many musical programs. During World War II, Woodruff announced that every man in uniform would be able to get a bottle of Coke for five cents no matter what the cost to the company. This was an extremely successful marketing maneuver and provided Coke with good publicity. In 1943, at the request of General Eisenhower, Coca-Cola plants were set up near the fighting fronts in North Africa and eventually throughout Europe in order to help increase the morale of U.S. soldiers. Thus, Coca-Cola was introduced to the world.

Coke was available in Germany prior to the war, but its survival there during the war years was due to a man named Max Keith who kept the company going even when there was little Coca-Cola syrup available. Keith developed his own soft drink, using ingredients available to him, and called his beverage Fanta. By selling this beverage he kept the enterprise intact until after the war. When the war was over the company continued to market Fanta. By 1944, the Coca-Cola company had sold one billion gallons of syrup, by 1953 two billion gallons had been sold, and by 1969 the company had sold six billion gallons.

1955–81: Diversification, New Products, and Foreign Expansion

The years from the end of World War II to the early 1980s were years of extensive and rapid change. Although Woodruff stepped down officially in 1955, he still exerted a great amount of influence on the company over the coming years. There were a series of chairmen and presidents to follow before the next major figure, J. Paul Austin, took the helm in 1970; he was followed by Roberto Goizueta in 1981. In 1956, after 50 years with the D'Arcy Advertising Agency, the Coca-Cola Company turned its accounts over to McCann-Erickson and began enormous promotional campaigns. The decade of the 1950s was a time of the greatest European expansion for the company. During this decade Coca-Cola opened approximately 15 to 20 plants a year throughout the world.

The company also began to diversify extensively, beginning in 1960, when the Minute Maid Corporation, maker of fruit juices and Hi-C fruit drinks, was acquired by Coca-Cola. Four years later the Duncan Foods Corporation also merged with the company. In 1969 Coca-Cola acquired the Belmont Springs Water Company, Inc., which produced natural spring water and processed water for commercial and home use. The following year the company purchased Aqua-Chem, Inc., producers of desalting machines and other such equipment, and in 1977 Coca-Cola acquired the Taylor Wines Company and other wineries. These last two companies were sold later under Goizueta's leadership.

In addition to its diversification program, the Coca-Cola Company also expanded its product line. Fanta became available in the United States during 1960 and was followed by the introduction of Sprite (1961), TAB (1963), and Fresca (1966), along with diet versions of these drinks. One reason that Coca-Cola began to introduce new beverages during the 1960s was competition from Pepsi Cola, sold by PepsiCo, Inc. Pepsi's success also motivated the Coca-Cola Company to promote its beverage with the slogan "It's the Real Thing," a subtle, comparative form of advertising that the company had never before employed.

Things did not always run smoothly for Coca-Cola. When Coke was first introduced to France, the Communist party, as well as conservative vineyard owners, did what they could to get the product removed from the country. They were unsuccessful. Swiss breweries also felt threatened, and spread rumors about the caffeine content of the drink. More consequential was the Arab boycott in 1967 which significantly hindered the company's relations with Israel. In 1970 the company was involved in a scandal in the United States when an NBC documentary reported on the bad housing and working conditions of Minute Maid farm laborers in Florida. In response, the company established a program that improved the workers' situation. In 1977 it was discovered that Coca-Cola, for various reasons, had made $1.3 million in illegal payments over a period of six years, mostly to executives and government officials in foreign countries.

During the 1970s, under the direction of Chairman J. Paul Austin and President J. Lucian Smith, Coca-Cola was introduced in Russia as well as in China. To enter the Chinese market, the company sponsored five scholarships for Chinese students at the Harvard Business School, and supported China's soccer and table-tennis teams. The beverage also became available in Egypt in 1979, after an absence there of 12 years. Austin strongly believed in free trade and opposed boycotts. He felt that business, in terms of international relations, should be used to improve national economies, and could be a strong deterrent to war. Under Austin, Coca-Cola also started technological and educational programs in the Third World countries in which it conducted business, introducing clean water technology and sponsoring sports programs in countries too poor to provide these benefits for themselves.

Austin's emphasis was on foreign expansion. Furthermore, under Austin's management the company became more specialized. Where Woodruff was aware of all facets of the company, Austin would delegate authority to various departments. For instance, he would give general approval to an advertising scheme, but would not review it personally. Smith was responsible for the everyday operations of the company, and Austin would, among other things, set policies, negotiate with foreign countries, and direct the company's relations with the U.S. government.

1981–97: The Goizueta Era

Roberto Goizueta became chairman in 1981, replacing Austin. The Cuban immigrant immediately shook up what had become a risk-averse, tradition-obsessed, barely profitable company. Less than a year after becoming chairman, he made two controversial decisions. First, he acquired Columbia Pictures for about $750 million in 1982. Goizueta thought that the entertainment field had good growth prospects, and that it would benefit from Coca-Cola's expertise in market research. Secondly, without much consumer research, Goizueta introduced Diet Coke to the public, risking the well-guarded trademark that until then had stood only for the original formula. Something had to be done about the sluggish domestic sales of Coca-Cola and the intense competition presented by Pepsi. In 1950, Coke had outsold Pepsi by more than five to one, but by 1984 Pepsi had a 22.8 percent share of the market while Coke had a 21.6 percent share. Goizueta's second 1982 gamble paid off handsomely when Diet Coke went on to become the most successful consumer product launch of the 1980s, and eventually the number three soft drink in the entire world.

In 1985 Goizueta took another chance. Based on information gathered from blind taste tests, Goizueta decided to reformulate the 99-year-old drink in the hope of combating Pepsi's growing popularity. The change to New Coke was not enthusiastically greeted by the U.S. public. Apparently Goizueta did not take into account the public's emotional attachment to the name "Coca-Cola" and all that it stood for: stability, memories, and the idea of a "golden America." Within less than a year the company brought back the "old" Coke, calling it Coca-Cola Classic. New Coke was universally considered the biggest consumer product blunder of the 1980s, but it was also viewed in a longer term perspective as a positive thing, because of the massive amount of free publicity that the Coke brand received from the debacle.

In September 1987, Coca-Cola agreed to sell its entertainment business to TriStar Pictures, 30 percent of which was owned by Coca-Cola. In return, Coca-Cola's interest in TriStar was increased to 80 percent. Coca-Cola's holding in TriStar was gradually distributed as a special dividend to Coca-Cola shareholders until the company's interest was reduced to a minority, when TriStar changed its name to Columbia Pictures Entertainment and sought its own listing on the New York Stock Exchange. Although the company's flirtation with entertainment appeared to be ill-advised, Coca-Cola ended up with $1 billion in profits from its short-term venture.

In a 1984 article in the *New York Times,* Goizueta stated that he saw Coca-Cola's challenge as "continuing the growth in profits of highly successful main businesses, and [those] it may choose to enter, at a rate substantially in excess of inflation, in order to give shareholders an above average total return on their investment." Goizueta projected that by 1990 his new strategy would nearly double the company's net income to $1 billion. His prediction came true in 1988. Two years later revenues surpassed the $10 billion mark.

In the mid-1980s, Coca-Cola reentered the bottling business, which had long been dominated by family-operated independents. Coca-Cola began repurchasing interests in bottlers worldwide with a view toward providing those bottlers with financial and managerial strength, improving operating efficiencies, and promoting expansion into emerging international markets. The trend started domestically, when the parent company formed Coca-Cola Enterprises Inc. through the acquisition and consolidation of two large bottlers in the South and West in 1986. The parent company acquired more than 30 bottlers worldwide from 1983 to 1993. By then, the market value of the company's publicly traded bottlers exceeded the company's book value by $1.5 billion.

Called "one of the world's most sophisticated and powerful marketing organizations," the company's schemes for the 1990s included the 1993 global launch of the "Always Coca-Cola" advertising theme. The new campaign was formulated by Creative Artists Agency, which took over much of the brand's business in 1992 from longtime agency McCann-Erickson Worldwide. In addition to the new campaign, a 32-page catalog of about 400 licensed garments, toys, and gift items featuring Coke slogans or advertising themes was released. The 1994 introduction of a PET plastic bottle in the brand's distinctive, contour shape resulted from corporate marketing research indicating that an overwhelming 84 percent of consumers would choose the trademarked bottle over a generic straight-walled bottle. But the company's primary challenge for the last decade of the 20th century came in the diet segment, where top-ranking Diet Coke was losing share to ready-to-drink teas, bottled waters, and other "New Age" beverages, which were perceived as healthier and more natural than traditional soft drinks. Coca-Cola fought back by introducing its own new alternative drinks, including POWERaDE (1990), the company's first sports drink, and the Fruitopia line (1994). In 1992 the company and Nestlé S.A. of Switzerland formed a 50–50 joint venture, Coca-Cola Nestlé Refreshment Company, to produce ready-to-drink tea and coffee beverages under the Nestea and Nescafé brand names. Also during this time, Coca-Cola purchased Barq's, a maker of root beer and other soft drinks.

Goizueta died of lung cancer in October 1997, having revitalized and awakened what had been a sleeping giant. Goizueta had turned the company into one of the most admired companies in the world, racking up an impressive list of accomplishments during his 16-year tenure. Coca-Cola's share of the global soft drink market was approaching 50 percent, while in the United States Coke had increased its share to 42 percent, overtaking and far surpassing Pepsi's 31 percent. Revenues increased from $4.8 billion in 1981 to $18.55 billion in 1996; net income grew from $500 million to $3.49 billion over the same period. Perhaps Goizueta's most important—and influential—contribution to the storied history of Coca-Cola was his relentless focus on the company's shareholders. The numbers clearly showed that he delivered for his company's owners: return on equity increased from 20 percent to 60 percent, while the market value of the Coca-Cola Company made a tremendous increase, from $4.3 billion to $147 billion. Perhaps most telling, a $1,000 investment in Coca-Cola in 1981 was worth, assuming that dividends were reinvested, $62,000 by the time of Goizueta's death.

Late 1990s and Beyond

Goizueta's right-hand man, Douglas Ivester, was given the unenviable task of succeeding perhaps the most admired chief executive in the United States; it turned out that the first few years of Ivester's reign would prove more than challenging. Although Coca-Cola remained steadily profitable, it was beset by one problem after another in the late 1990s. Having restructured its worldwide bottling operations under Goizueta, the firm moved into a new phase of growth based on the acquisition of other companies' brands. Its already dominant market share and a sometimes arrogant and aggressive approach to acquisition led some countries, particularly in Europe, to take a hard line toward the company. In late 1997, for example, Coca-Cola announced it would acquire the Orangina brand in France from Paris-based Pernod Ricard for about $890 million. French authorities, who had fined Coca-Cola for anti-competitive practices earlier that year, blocked the purchase. In December 1998 Coca-Cola announced that it would purchase several soft drink brands—including Schweppes, Dr Pepper, Canada Dry, and Crush—outside the United States, France, and South Africa from Cadbury Schweppes plc for $1.85 billion. After encountering regulatory resistance in Europe, Australia, Mexico, and Canada, the two companies in July 1999 received regulatory approval for a new scaled-down deal valued at about $700 million, which included 155 countries but not the United States, Norway, Switzerland, and the member states of the European Union with the exception of the United Kingdom, Ireland, and Greece. Later in 1999 separate agreements were reached that gave Coca-Cola the Schweppes brands in South Africa and New Zealand.

With nearly two-thirds of sales originating outside North America, Coca-Cola was hit particularly hard by the global economic crisis of the late 1990s, which moved from Asia to Russia to Latin America. In Russia, where the company had invested $750 million from 1991 through the end of the decade, sales fell about 60 percent from August 1998, when the value of the ruble crashed, to September 1999. Rather than retreating from the world stage, however, Ivester viewed the downturn as an opportunity to make additional foreign investments at bargain prices, essentially sacrificing the short term for potentially huge long-term gains. While the economic crisis was still wreaking havoc, Coca-Cola was faced with another crisis in June 1998 when several dozen Belgian schoolchildren became ill after drinking Coke that had been made with contaminated carbon dioxide. Soon, 14 million cases of Coca-Cola products were recalled in five European countries, and France and Belgium placed a temporary ban on the company's products. The crisis, though short-lived, was a public relations disaster because company officials appeared to wait too long to take the situation seriously, admit that there had been a manufacturing error, and apologize to its customers. Meanwhile, around this same time, four current and former employees had filed a racial discrimination suit against the firm in the United States.

Despite the seemingly endless string of challenges the company faced in the late 1990s, Coca-Cola was also moving forward with new initiatives. In February 1999 the company announced plans to launch its first bottled water brand in North America. Dasani was described as a "purified, non-carbonated water enhanced with minerals." In October 1999 the company announced that it would redesign the look of its Coca-Cola Classic brand in 2000 in an attempt to revitalize the flagship's stagnant sales. Labels would continue to feature the iconic contour bottle but with a cap popped off and soda fizzing out. In addition, the Coke Classic slogan "Always," which had been used since 1993, would be replaced with the tagline "Enjoy," which had been used on Coke bottles periodically for decades. The company also planned to increase the appearances of the eight-ounce contour bottle, in a particularly nostalgic move. The renewed emphasis on this classic brand icon and the resurrection of the "Enjoy" slogan seemed to be a fitting way for a U.S.—if not global—institution to launch itself into the new millennium.

Principal Subsidiaries

The Minute Maid Company; The Coca-Cola Export Corporation; Coca-Cola Financial Corporation; Coca-Cola Interamerican Corp.; Coca-Cola G.m.b.H. (Germany); Coca-Cola Industries Ltda. (Brazil); Coca-Cola Southern Africa Ltd. (South Africa); Coca-Cola Enterprises Inc. (40%); Coca-Cola Beverages plc (U.K.; 50.5%); Thai Pure Drinks Limited (Thailand; 49%); Embotelladoras Coca-Cola Polar S.A. (Chile; 29%); Coca-Cola Nordic Beverages (Norway; 49%); Coca-Cola Amatil Limited (Australia; 43%); Panamerican Beverages, Inc. (Panama; 24%); Coca-Cola FEMSA, S.A. de C.V. (Mexico; 30%).

Principal Operating Units

Africa Group; Greater Europe Group; Latin America Group; Middle & Far East Group; North America Group.

Principal Competitors

PepsiCo, Inc.; Cadbury Schweppes plc; Dr Pepper/Seven Up, Inc.; Ferolito, Vultaggio & Sons; National Beverage Corp.; Ocean Spray Cranberries, Inc.; Philip Morris Companies Inc.; The Procter & Gamble Company; The Quaker Oats Company; Triarc Companies, Inc.; Unilever plc; Virgin Group Ltd.

Further Reading

Allen, Frederick, *Secret Formula: How Brilliant Marketing and Relentless Salesmanship Made Coca-Cola the Best-Known Product in the World,* New York: HarperBusiness, 1994, 500 p.

Applegate, Howard L., *Coca-Cola: A History in Photographs, 1930 through 1969,* Osceola, Wisc.: Iconografix, 1996, 126 p.

Beatty, Sally, and Nikhil Deogun, "Coke Revisits Its Emotional Ads of the '70s," *Wall Street Journal,* July 8, 1998, p. B8.

Candler, Charles Howard, *Asa Griggs Candler,* Atlanta: Emory University, 1950, 502 p.

The Chronicle of Coca-Cola, Since 1886, Atlanta: Coca-Cola Company, [n.d.].

The Coca-Cola Company: An Illustrated Profile of a Worldwide Company, Atlanta: Coca-Cola Company, 1974.

Cowell, Alan, "The Coke Stomach Ache Heard Round the World," *New York Times,* June 25, 1999, p. C1.

Deogun, Nikhil, "Aggressive Push Abroad Dilutes Coke's Strength As Big Markets Stumble," *Wall Street Journal,* February 8, 1999, pp. A1+.

——, "Can Coke Rise to the Global Challenge?," *Wall Street Journal,* September 24, 1998, p. C1.

Deogun, Nikhil, et al., "Anatomy of a Recall: How Coke's Controls Fizzled Out in Europe," *Wall Street Journal,* June 29, 1999, pp. A1+.

Echikson, William, "Have a Coke and a Smile—Please," *Business Week,* August 30, 1999, p. 214A.

Enrico, Roger, and Jesse Kornbluth, *The Other Guy Blinked: And Other Dispatches from the Cola Wars,* New York: Bantam, 1988, 280 p.

Graham, Elizabeth C., and Ralph Roberts, *The Real Ones: Four Generations of the First Family of Coca-Cola,* New York: Barricade Books, 1992, 344 p.

Greisling, David, *I'd Like the World to Buy a Coke: The Life and Leadership of Roberto Goizueta,* New York: Wiley, 1998, 334 p.

Hagerty, James R., and Amy Barrett, "Can Douglas Ivester End Coke's Crisis?," *Wall Street Journal,* June 18, 1999, p. B1.

Harrison, DeSales, *"Footprints on the Sands of Time": A History of Two Men and the Fulfillment of a Dream,* New York: Newcomen Society in North America, 1969, 24 p.

Hays, Constance L., "A Sputter in the Coke Machine: When Its Customers Fell Ill, a Master Marketer Faltered," *New York Times,* June 30, 1999, p. C1.

Huey, John, "In Search of Roberto's Secret Formula," *Fortune,* December 29, 1997, pp. 230–32, 234.

Kahn, Ely Jacques, *The Big Drink: The Story of Coca-Cola,* New York: Random House, 1960, 174 p.

Laing, Jonathan R., "Is Coke Still It?," *Barron's,* May 9, 1994, pp. 29–33.

McKay, Betsy, "Coke Faces the Return of Recycling Issue," *Wall Street Journal,* September 13, 1999, p. B8.

——, "Cola on the Rocks, Coke Plans a 'Classic' Redesign," *Wall Street Journal,* October 13, 1999, pp. B1, B4.

Morris, Betsy, "Doug Is It," *Fortune,* May 25, 1998, pp. 70–74, 78, 80, 82, 84.

Oliver, Thomas, *The Real Coke: The Real Story,* New York: Viking Penguin, 1987, 195 p.

Pendergrast, Mark, *For God, Country and Coca-Cola: The Unauthorized History of the Great American Soft Drink and the Company That Makes It,* New York: Macmillan, 1993, 556 p.

Santoli, Michael, "Coke Is No Longer It," *Barron's,* April 5, 1999, p. 15.

——, "How Coke Is Kicking Pepsi's Can," *Fortune,* October 28, 1996, pp. 70–73+.

Watters, Pat, *Coca-Cola,* New York: Doubleday, 1978, 288 p.

Yazijian, Harvey Z., and J.C. Louis, *The Cola Wars,* New York: Everett House, 1980, 386 p.

—April Dougal Gasbarre
—updated by David E. Salamie

COHU, inc.

Cohu, Inc.

5755 Kearny Villa Road
San Diego, California 92123-1111
U.S.A.
Telephone: (858) 541-5194
Fax: (858) 277-0221
Web site: http://www.cohu.com

Public Company
Incorporated: 1947 as Kalbfell Laboratories, Inc.
Employees: 900
Sales: $171.5 million (1998)
Stock Exchanges: New York
Ticker Symbol: COHU
NAIC: 333298 All Other Industrial Machinery Manufacturing; 333999 All Other Miscellaneous General Purpose Machinery; 33422 Radio and Television Broadcasting and Wireless Communications Equipment Manufacturing; 334419 Other Electronic Component Manufacturing; 334515 Instrument Manufacturing for Measuring and Testing Electricity and Electrical Signals; 334519 Other Measuring and Controlling Device Manufacturing

Cohu, Inc. is the largest U.S.-based supplier of test handling equipment used by semiconductor manufacturers in final test operations. Its subsidiaries Delta Design and Daymarc design, manufacture, market, and service a broad range of test handlers for the semiconductor industry. The company's second segment comprises television and other equipment manufacture and marketing, including electronic products used in electronic imaging, surveillance, detection, closed circuit television, metal detection, and microwave communication. The company's Cohu Inc. Electronics Division, the original core of the company, has been a designer, manufacturer, and seller of television cameras, closed circuit television cameras, camera control systems, test equipment, lenses, monitors, and other accessories to support its camera lines, for over 40 years. The customer base for these products is broadly distributed between machine vision, scientific imaging, and security/surveillance markets. A third segment, the company's Fisher Research Laboratory, Inc. subsidiary (''the world's oldest and proudest name in metal detectors,'' according to the company), supplies metal detectors, cable fault location devices, and related equipment to the utility and construction industries for use primarily in locating or tracing buried pipes and cables. Fisher also manufactures a line of portable metal detectors used by hobbyists and treasure hunters, including the Gemini-3, a lightweight unit for the hobbyists or prospectors to find ore veins, and the Aquanaut, an underwater detector used by sport divers, salvagers, and professional treasure hunters. Finally, Broadcast Microwave Services, Inc. (BMS) serves as a manufacturer of microwave radios, antenna systems, and support equipment used to transmit television video and audio signals.

Kalbfell Laboratories: 1947

Cohu, Inc. is the result of an evolution from a tiny laboratory partnership created in 1945. One of the partners was Dr. David Kalbfell and the partnership, called Kalbfell Laboratories, Inc., was created to build machinery such as precision voltage standards. The company eventually moved into the manufacture of solid state test equipment, including voltmeters and ohmmeters. In 1947 the company was incorporated in California under the same name and commenced active operations that year. In September 1954, the company name was changed to Kay Lab. In June 1956, the company issued 400,000 shares in its first public financing, and the name Kintel Electronics was adopted. In 1957, Kintel Electronics and the remnants of Kay Lab were liquidated, and all of the assets and liabilities of the company were acquired by Lamott T. Cohu and other investors; the company was reincorporated in Delaware as Cohu Electronics Inc. Cohu went public, and the current name, Cohu, Inc., was adopted in 1972.

After selling his company to Cohu, Dr. Kalbfell went on to purchase Instruments, Inc. The San Diego, California-based company, founded in 1941, had been in the electronics manufacturing business since 1962. Management of the company was eventually turned over to Kalbfell's son Ken, who oversaw its surge to the forefront of technology in the area of high power solid state amplifiers for over 30 years through its manufacture

Company Perspectives:

Cohu's long established role in advanced technology is based on a continuing commitment to quality, product performance and competitiveness.

of both linear and switching amplifiers used in sonar and low frequency radio transmitters. The linear amplifiers became the de facto standard for every sonar transducer manufacturer in the country. The switching amplifiers, likewise, became the preferred choice for most of the U.S. Navy's submarines. The units were best known for their reliability and the limited amount of damage caused when a failure occurred. Kalbfell also served in several positions in IEEE before his son.

The core of Kalbfell's original company was recreated as Cohu Inc. Electronics Division in 1957, following the sale of the company. Recognized worldwide as a leading U.S. manufacturer of high-performance closed-circuit television cameras and systems, the Cohu Electronics Division earned its reputation through the development and production of advanced designs, reliable products, and a firm commitment to customer service for over 40 years. The company continued to expand through sales and new geographical areas covered. However, its greatest growth came from the acquisition of other companies and diversification into new industries.

Key Acquisitions: 1960s-80s

In the late 1920s, Dr. Gerhard Fisher, a German immigrant who had studied electronics at the University of Dresden, relocated from New Jersey to Palo Alto, California, to work for the Federal Telegraph Corporation. There, Fisher served as an assistant to Frederick Kloster, who had developed an electronic direction finder for the Navy during World War I, and who, after the war, had come to Federal Telegraph to develop this technology for commercial shipping applications. In 1929, Fisher developed airborne navigation aids for Western Air Express, that improved on designs from Kloster's radio direction finder and was awarded some of the first patents issued in the field of airborne direction finding by means of radio. In the course of his work he encountered some strange errors and, once he solved these problems, he had the foresight to apply the solution to a completely unrelated field, that of metal and mineral detection.

Fisher Research Laboratory got its start in Fisher's garage, located at 1505 Byron Street in Palo Alto in 1931. There, with four employees, Fisher began manufacturing a device he called the "Metallascope." Laboring at the new technology, the tiny group filed and received patents on the metallascope, and drew some notoriety along the way, as Dr. Albert Einstein was one of the people who came to the tiny garage to visit. Fisher would later recall their historic meeting: "He [Einstein] didn't think my Metallascope was very useful." Apparently Einstein was wrong.

By 1936 the "M-Scope," as it had been nicknamed, became a better known and more widely used product when it was found helpful in locating buried metal such as coins, jewelry, ore veins, and relics. Sales increased, and suddenly the garage was no longer large enough to contain the fledgling company, which also began manufacturing a variety of electronics products, including radio telephones and marine radios.

Fisher Research Laboratory moved to a small building at 745 Emerson Street in Palo Alto. In 1939, just prior to World War II, Fisher Research Laboratory moved to a larger building on University Avenue in Palo Alto. The company continued to bounce around, looking for more space and better facilities. Among other moves, in 1961 Fisher adopted a larger production facility in Belmont, California; in 1974, the company moved about 90 miles southeast to a building on I Street in Los Banos; and, in 1990, Fisher built its present plant in the Los Banos Industrial Park.

During World War II and the Korean War, Fisher Research was called upon to contribute its technical competence to the war efforts. While doing so, and because the company was busy with the call to national security, Fisher patents began expiring and competitors sprang up and began building similar products. Over the years, Fisher had also manufactured Geiger counters, radio communications systems, voltage detectors, and cable fault locators. Dr. Fisher retired in 1967, when the company was acquired by Cohu, and died in 1981. A new line of security products was released in the 1990s, such as walk-through metal detectors and hand-scanning devices, giving the division entry to a new market segment.

Delta Design, Inc. was founded in 1957 to manufacture environmental and ambient high-speed component test handlers for semiconductor devices, environmental test chambers, life-aging and burn-in chambers, and systems and programmers. The environmental and high-speed component test handlers are used by the electronics industry in the testing of integrated circuits. The temperature devices are used by laboratories to control temperature of isolated environments. The rate-step programmer is used with a temperature control chamber to control the rate of change of the temperature within the chamber. Products are sold to the semiconductor industry. Delta Design was acquired by Cohu in 1983.

Daymarc Corporation was founded in 1959. The privately held company was among the first to manufacture gravity-feed, fully-automatic semiconductor test handling equipment. Acquired by Cohu in June 1994, Daymarc, with four lines of test handlers—the 717 Series, 3000 Series and 4000 Series of gravity handlers, and the Enterprise test-in-tray handlers—was a complimentary company to the pick-and-place test handling equipment manufactured by Delta Design.

Broadcast Microwave Services, Inc. was founded in 1982 by a group of former Tayburn, Inc. employees to develop and market microwave products for video transmission. Two years later, the company was purchased by and became a wholly owned subsidiary of Cohu Inc. Since then, BMS developed an extensive product line for television broadcasting providing connections between studios and transmitters (STL, TSL, ICR), electronic news gathering (ENG) capabilities for mobile vans, fixed wing and helicopter aircraft, and portable applications. An extensive capability was developed for military and law enforcement applications for unmanned vehicle video, data and control, test range instrumentation and advanced ground &

Key Dates:

1931: Fisher Research Laboratory is founded.
1947: Kalbfell Laboratories is founded.
1957: Lamott T. Cohu buys the company, which reincorporates as Cohu Electronics Inc.; Delta Design is founded.
1959: Daymarc Corporation is founded.
1967: Cohu acquires Fisher Research.
1982: Broadcast Microwave Services is founded.
1983: Cohu acquires Delta Design.
1984: Cohu acquires Broadcast Microwave.
1994: Cohu acquires Daymarc.

aerial surveillance. BMS completed an extensive product improvement program in 1996, updating the product line to surface mount technology.

Changes: 1990s

In 1997, a difficult year for the semiconductor equipment industry hit. As a result, Cohu entered 1998 with a strong backlog, but order rates declined during the first quarter and, by mid-year, had fallen to less than 50 percent of earlier year levels. In response to these conditions and, like most companies in the industry, the company reduced its workforce and production rates significantly throughout the year. However, the company continued to fund product development at record levels, since a continuous stream of new products remained vital to its long-term success. Despite the tough conditions in the industry, the company performed well, increasing net sales to $187.8 million, and increasing net income to $29.2 million, and Delta Design won its second straight Supplier Excellence Award from Texas Instruments.

In 1998, the company was again impacted by the worldwide slowdown in demand for semiconductor equipment. As a result, net sales decreased nine percent to $171.5 million, and net income slipped to $11.7 million. However, in May of that year, the Cohu Semiconductor Equipment Group (SEG) was formed ''to provide a strategic focus and organizational structure for continued growth,'' said company President and CEO Charles A. Schwan in a press release. The SEG encompassed Cohu's Delta Design subsidiary, Daymarc, and the Asian operations of both companies.

Numerous changes took place at the highest levels in 1998 and 1999. In July 1998, C. Kenneth Gray joined Cohu's semiconductor equipment group as vice-president of sales and marketing. A year later, William S. Ivans, who had been with the company since 1957 and served as the company's president and CEO from 1965 to 1983 and chairman of the board since 1983, was killed in a glider plane accident. He was replaced by Schwan, who gave up his title of president. Shortly thereafter, in October of that year, the company named James A. Donahue, who had joined Delta Design in 1978, as president and COO.

Aside from changes in management, the company was doing well in 1999. Schwan, in the company's second quarter report, said that the company ''benefited from the improved business conditions in the semiconductor equipment industry and strong demand for our new pick and place test handlers.'' The company also increased its workforce to compensate for increased demand. A two-for-one stock split in August reflected just how well the company was performing. The third quarter continued apace, with record sales of $61.7 million and net income of $7.5 million as sales of the company's ''Castle and Summit handlers . . . resulted in record orders for the quarter,'' said Schwan. ''We believe our strong balance sheet and global market presence place the company in a position to benefit from the positive long-term outlook of the semiconductor and semiconductor equipment industries.''

Principal Subsidiaries

Broadcast Microwave Services, Inc.; Cohu Inc. Electronics Division; Daymarc Corp.; Delta Design, Inc.; Fisher Research Laboratory Inc.

Principal Competitors

Ultrak Inc.; Adaptive Broadband.

Further Reading

Brammer, Rhonda, ''A 40%-Off Sale: Sizing up Small Caps,'' *Barron's*, December 23, 1996, p. 23.
——, ''Semi Recovery,'' *Barron's*, May 26, 1997, p. 19.
''Cohu's Loss,'' *Electronic News (1991)*, July 19, 1999, p. 4.
''Cohu Inc.,'' *Electronic News (1991)*, July 6, 1998, p. 14.
''Cohu Inc.,'' *San Diego Business Journal*, November 17, 1986, p. 22.
''Cohu Inc.,'' *San Diego Business Journal*, September 28, 1998, p. 39.
''Cohu Inc.,'' *Wall Street Journal*, July 16, 1999, p. B5(W).
''Cohu Inc.,'' *Wall Street Journal*, October 18, 1999, p. B14.

—Daryl F. Mallett

The Copps Corporation

2828 Wayne Street
Stevens Point, Wisconsin 54481
U.S.A.
Telephone: (715) 344-5900
Fax: (715) 344-5925
Web site: http://www.copps.com

Private Company
Incorporated: 1892 as E.M. Copps and Company
Employees: 4,625
Sales: $560 million (1999 est.)
NAIC: 445110 Grocery Stores; 422410 Groceries, General Line, Wholesaling

The Copps Corporation is one of Wisconsin's largest privately held businesses. It owns and operates 18 supermarkets and is a wholesale distributor to more than 50 supermarkets throughout Wisconsin. The company's stores operate under the names Copps IGA, Duke's Finer Foods, and Copps Food Centers. In addition to traditional grocery fare, Copps Food Centers feature floral departments, fresh-squeezed vegetable and fruit juices, in-store bakeries, nutritional foods departments, liquor stores, video rental departments, and delicatessens. Copps is also testing a meal solutions center, which combines IGA (Independent Grocers Association) and Kraft products in different weekly recipes. The company sets aside as much as 1,400 square feet per store to stock organically grown produce. Copps is owned by fourth generation members of the founding Copps family, and is ranked number 422 in *Forbes* magazines Private 500 listing.

Post Civil War-Era Entrepreneur

Egbert Morton (E. M.) Copps founded the Copps Corporation in 1892. Prior to starting the business, E.M. served as an Army captain, having risen from the rank of enlisted private. In 1865 he was offered a commission as a major if he remained in the Army. E.M. refused the offer, writing that he was "anxious to get home for work on the farm or to go into business." He returned to Chateauguay, New York, the town of his birth, but soon went west, in search of fresh opportunities. He settled approximately 900 miles away in Marinette, Wisconsin, where he used the remainder of his Army pay to build a lumber mill on the banks of the Menominee River. He also purchased a stand of timber a few miles away, near Peshtigo. E.M. and his wife, Florence, a Green Bay school teacher, traveled to Peshtigo on the night of October 8, 1871, the night that would become known for "The Great Peshtigo Fire." Alerted to the conflagration, the young couple fled to the river, and managed to survive by remaining in the water until daybreak, haunted by the screams of the 1,200 residents who lost their lives that night. Coincidentally, The Great Chicago Fire (which claimed 300 lives) happened on the same night, overshadowing the tragedy in Peshtigo. The rest of the country heard nothing of the Peshtigo fire until two days later because the telegraph lines had been destroyed.

Plagued by fire a second time, E.M.'s Marinette timber mill burned to the ground two years later. He and his wife decided to move to a new location, trying their luck with another mill along the Wisconsin River near downtown Stevens Point. Within the next 12 years, two more fires struck their businesses, and in 1877 his uninsured lumber yard burned, taking both his lumber and that of his customers. Company records state that "Tenacity was certainly E.M.'s virtue. In July 1885, a fire was caused by two lads throwing fire crackers into a pile of sawdust. E.M. faced losses many times greater than the insurance coverage. Yet, he rebuilt the mill, profitably sold it and moved to Tomahawk to manage a sawmill and planing mill." Before long the couple had seven children to feed. They wanted to return to Stevens Point where they had left so many friends behind. The couple agreed that owning another sawmill was out of the question, but they decided that the agricultural town was growing and in need of a wholesaler for basic supplies including coal, salt, seeds, feed, flour, hay, and grain. At the age of 52, E.M. opened the doors to his grocery business, E.M. Copps & Company. The business supplied the local loggers, river men, farmers, and neighbors.

The couple's second son, Alfred, joined the business five years later. In 1897, young Alfred took it upon himself to sell a rail car of molasses to area retailers. Successful at that, he was soon delivering other grocery items, until it became necessary for the family to build a second warehouse across the street. When the Spanish-American War was declared in 1898, Alfred was one of the first to volunteer, satisfied to do his part for the country, returning to the business in the following year. As E.M.

Company Perspectives:

Copps people have delivered the goods since 1892.

approached the age of 70, another son, Clinton, joined the firm as a full-time salesman, freeing Alfred to take on more of the management responsibilities. Alfred was operating as buyer for the business and recognized an opportunity in selling potatoes—Portage County was Wisconsin's potato growing capital. He profited by some large-scale potato deals, entering negotiations with another potato dealer, Len Starks, who had been asked by the Soo Line Railroad to build a warehouse for storage. Starks, in turn, convinced Alfred that he should build and own the building for storing both his (Starks's) and Copps's potatoes. Alfred's memoirs explained that "At the time we were storing our grocery items in three warehouses. This was overly expensive, so Stark's idea was sound, but we did not have the $30,000 needed for construction." He continued, "But, Starks had instant access to the money through his Chicago bank. So within days we had a 30-year property lease with the Soo Line and this 30-year agreement with Starks."

Marketing Under the Deerwood Label: Post World War I

During this period the company name was changed to The Copps Company. In need of a larger sales force Alfred recruited his brother Clinton, who, it was said, "could sell icicles to an Eskimo." Items that were outside the line of groceries, such as feed grains and seeds, were dropped. The retail coal business was retained and taken over by C.G. Fletcher and Len Starks took over all the warehouses and the entire potato business as an even trade for the amount of the potato loan. Copps then became recognized as a wholesale grocery house. Clinton decided that private labels would be a lucrative venture, selling coffee as the first of many "Deerwood" products. He showed grocers how to freshly grind and roast the coffee at each of their stores. Premium quality eggs, peanuts, and a limited array of items were sold under the Deerwood label. Total assets at this time (1918) amounted to approximately $108,000. In the post-World War I years, cash was scarce. Copps needed about $25,000 for the purchase of grocery stock to be sold over the winter months. The family was unable to obtain a bank loan because conditions in the money market were so bad that E.M.'s bank, where he served as a trustee, refused to loan them money. Alfred told the Copps salesmen that they would have to do more to ensure that customers paid more promptly, an effort that quickly made a difference. The brothers then switched to another bank in town for financing, and were given the needed funds.

Alfred served as company president after the death of his father. He constructed a two-story addition to the main building. During Prohibition the company was faced with difficult ethical decisions. As dealers of cane sugar, they were overwhelmed by the large volumes of sugar requested by some of their customers. Aware that the sugar would probably be put to use for the production of illegal alcohol, the Copps brothers refused sales to "suspicious looking bag men laying stacks of bills on our counter. . .". Alfred commented, "I didn't want to spend 20 years in the Federal Pen." Despite refusals of such profitable opportunities, the business had accumulated assets in the range of $300,000 by 1930.

Alfred realized that grocery retailing would be a great business for the future. He enlisted the help of his son, Chandler, who had worked in Washington, D.C., with an A&P store following his graduation from Ohio State University. Alfred hoped that Chandler could contribute what he had learned about retailing in the urban grocery industry. Clinton's son, Don, also began working for the business, specializing in the produce department. Alfred joined the United Buyers group of wholesalers, becoming a board member and serving until 1944. After Chandler's death in 1942, Don's other brother, Gordon, took over in the sales department. When business was slowing down, Gordon and Don became impatient and went to Chicago to discuss possibilities with members of the then new Independent Grocers Association. They learned that they should be able to cut costs from the 10 to 11 percent they were operating with, to nearly four percent, by signing up 90 retailers with Copps wholesaling compared to the 560 they were dealing with. The plethora of very small independent retailers was dropped since they were too small to order the minimum $275 weekly that would make business lucrative for Copps. In addition to selling dry goods to the qualifying retailers, the company would also sell fresh fruits and vegetables. Copps did manage to bring the costs down to the four to five percent goal. Gordon Copps also established a subsidiary company, utilizing a cash and carry policy in order to continue supplying to many of the smaller retailers within proximity to the Stevens Point Warehouse.

1960: Building a Forerunner to Superstores

Copps finally entered into the retail business when it purchased a store in Black River Falls through another small subsidiary company, the Central Wisconsin Company. Copps acquired several other retail stores before building the first "Foodliner," the East Side IGA, in Stevens Point—the forerunner to the Superstore creations of the 1980s.

By 1964, Copps was operating 12 foodliners in nine cities. A 93,600-square-foot warehouse was built on Stevens Point's south side to accommodate the wholesaling operation. With Gordon in charge of warehousing, the latest warehouse had 20-foot ceilings to enable high vertical stacking with forklifts. The office was fitted with an IBM computer system, with automatic billing and other mechanical and technological conveniences. Several smaller buildings were also acquired for storing frozen food items. By then the company had 137 employees and wholesale revenues of $20 million.

Gordon and Don, serving as chairman and president, respectively, saw innovation as the ticket to success. They envisioned one-stop shopping and experimented with several combinations of food and discount department stores in both the wholesale and retail markets. Following Gordon's death in an automobile accident, Don took over as chairman until his retirement in the 1980s. The sons of Don (Michael and Lucky [Don, Jr.]) and Gordon (Tim, Fred, and Tom) stepped in when needed, and after Don's retirement his son Michael took over as chairman, while Lucky served as executive vice-president. Gordon's sons took over as president, executive vice-president, and vice-president. The new team—the fourth generation of grocery managers—decided to quit the general merchandise discount stores,

Key Dates:

1892: Company is founded in central Wisconsin, supplying the basic necessities.
1923: E.M. Copps dies.
1944: Copps aligns with IGA.
1960: Copps builds first "foodliner," the East Side IGA, in Stevens Point.
1970: Company experiments with combination food and discount department stores.
1984: Prototype Superstore opens in Oshkosh, Wisconsin.
1992: Company celebrates 100 years in business.

focusing on wholesaling and retailing grocery products. They began thinking in terms of Superstores. The prototype Superstore, with 60,000 square feet of shopping space, was opened in 1984, in Oshkosh, Wisconsin. Other Superstores soon opened in Manitowoc, Appleton, Green Bay, Stevens Point, and Fond du Lac. The produce section was highlighted and positioned as the first stop for shoppers. Engineers designed spotlighting, dark ceilings, and wooden bulk bins in an attempt to highlight the polished products and downplay fixtures. Some of Copps' stores housed banks, travel agencies, post offices, complete service desks, and floral and natural foods departments.

The 1990s: Helping People Make Healthy Choices

The company set up consumer boards for each store, made up of frequent shoppers who met regularly to discuss the pros and cons of shopping at Copps. The company continued to pride itself on giving customers what they wanted. With the growth in awareness concerning healthy diets, Copps made every effort to inform consumers about the choices available to them. It started using "Nutri-Guide" product labels to simplify shopping for customers with special dietary needs. The Copps Consumer Affairs department started a Food for Life program, helping shoppers choose groceries for healthy eating with free recipes and pamphlets.

Still very active in the wholesale business, Copps built another Stevens Point warehouse for $5 million in 1991 to house perishable and dry goods. The company also sponsored a Silent Partner program, providing financing help to smaller independents who could not borrow funds at the same lower rate that Copps could borrow at. The company also sponsored financial planning seminars for independents, in addition to an employee training program.

Since the scale of the Superstores (sometimes as large as 80,000 square feet) was overkill for many smaller Wisconsin communities, the company experimented in the early 1990s with scaled-down models (around 44,000 square feet). In smaller towns like Wautoma, that had year-round populations of 1,500, an even smaller store was constructed. Copps management realized that people from outlying areas would shop at these stores, bringing the customer base in Wautoma, for example, closer to 5,000. Mass merchandiser Wal-Mart asked Copps to share its shopping center in Stevens Point, thinking that Copps would be an added traffic draw. The Copps family worried that if they refused the invitation, Wal-Mart would ask one of Copps's competitors. Since Stevens Point was the company headquarters, Copps wanted to maintain its dominant status there, and accepted the offer, replacing one of two Copps Food Centers already operating in the town. The 450-item produce department was labeled the "Garden of Eden." A simulated tree trunk reached from the floor to an artificial skylight that dominated the department's ceiling space. Artificial leafy branches and banners promoting healthy eating hung from the skylight. Periodically, a soundtrack of rain and thunder, reinforced by a misting of the produce—and flickering lights simulating a lightning effect—attracted the attention of customers.

To remain competitive, Copps implemented a natural foods strategy to attract the growing numbers of nutrition-conscious customers. It hired people who had already integrated natural foods into their lifestyles, and who were knowledgeable about the products. The company's Madison store was its best natural foods market, and when Whole Foods revealed plans to enter that market, Copps company directors encouraged department heads to travel to Chicago to see what the competition had to offer at their stores. The director of the Copps natural foods department in Madison explained that "This way, when Whole Foods does open up, the impact would be felt less because consumers would see us as providing alternatives to Whole Foods," according to Lisa Saxton of *Supermarket News.* The company offered 75 bulk items, including a wide variety of bulk spices. Emphasis was placed on the freshness and quality of its products, and competitive prices. The fastest-growing natural foods category at Copps was its frozen foods, featuring five doors worth of easy-to-prepare items. Copps offered a large five-sided juice and melon bar with an open center where employees squeezed the fresh juice for the weekly juice program and prepared "watermelon boats," watermelon halves stuffed to the brim with other fruits. Some stores also offered a Muro citrus peeler, which peeled, cored, and segmented citrus fruits.

In a company document, Tom Copps, executive vice-president for public affairs stated that: "In this business, you have to grow or die. You can't sit idle." Apparently, in the Copps family, "sitting idle" simply was not in the genes.

Principal Competitors

Cub Foods; Sam's Club; Piggly Wiggly Southern, Inc.; Whole Foods Market, Inc.

Further Reading

Alaimo, Dan, "Copps, K-VA-T Enter Shared Transaction Fee Program Arena," *Supermarket News,* May 13, 1996, p. 53.

Bennett, Stephen, "Acid Test," *Progressive Grocer,* December 1993, p. 36.

Ingram, Bob, "A New Beat in the Heartland," *Supermarket Business,* August, 1995, p. 35.

Saxton, Lisa, "Natural Cause: Copps Corporation Is Hoping a Stepped-Up Emphasis on Natural Foods Will Stave Off Inroads from Specialty Competition," *Supermarket News,* October 16, 1995, p. 35.

Stickel, Amy I., "Rising Self-Service: The Bakery Department in Copps," *Supermarket News,* July 24, 1995, p. 48.

—Terri Mozzone

CROWN CORK & SEAL

Crown Cork & Seal Company, Inc.

One Crown Way
Philadelphia, Pennsylvania 19154-4599
U.S.A.
Telephone: (215) 698-5100
Toll Free: (800) 523-3644
Fax: (215) 698-5201
Web site: http://www.crowncork.com

Public Company
Incorporated: 1927
Employees: 38,459
Sales: $8.30 billion (1998)
Stock Exchanges: New York Paris
Ticker Symbol: CCK
NAIC: 322214 Fiber Can, Tube, Drum, and Similar Products Manufacturing; 326160 Plastics Bottle Manufacturing; 326199 All Other Plastics Product Manufacturing; 332115 Crown and Closure Manufacturing; 332116 Metal Stamping; 332431 Metal Can Manufacturing; 332439 Other Metal Container Manufacturing; 333510 Metalworking Machinery Manufacturing

Crown Cork & Seal Company, Inc. is one of the world's leading packaging manufacturers, making one out of every five beverage cans used in the world and one out of every three food cans used in North America and Europe. In addition to making metal food and beverage cans, Crown Cork also produces other metal packaging, including aerosol cans, specialty packaging, can ends, and closures and crowns. The company also makes plastic containers for beverages, food, household and industrial products, personal care products, cosmetics and fragrances, and medical and pharmaceutical products; composite packaging, such as that used for frozen juice concentrate; and can making equipment. With 223 plants located in 49 countries, Crown Cork derives about 60 percent of its revenues from outside the United States, with almost three-fourths of non-U.S. revenues derived in Europe. The company's position as a global packaging powerhouse was largely gained through an aggressive program of acquisition launched in 1989, which increased net sales from $1.9 billion to $8.3 billion by the late 1990s.

Early History: From Crowns to Cans

The company traces its origins to 1892 when William Painter invented the "crown cork," a metal crown used to package soft drinks and beer in bottles. Painter soon started the Crown Cork & Seal Company of Baltimore. He quickly expanded the company overseas and by the time of his death in 1906 the company had manufacturing operations in Germany, France, the United Kingdom, Japan, and Brazil. After recovering from the disruptions of World War I, Crown Cork survived the Prohibition era by shifting its production from beer to soft drinks.

In 1927 the company was incorporated in New York City as Crown Cork & Seal Company, Inc. following its merger with New Process Cork Company Inc. and New York Improved Patents Corporation. The following year the company formed the Crown Cork International Corporation as a holding company for subsidiaries engaged in bottle crown and other cork business outside the United States. Crown Cork's early entry into the foreign market gave Crown Cork an advantage over its competitors in the container and closure fields.

Crown Cork did not even venture into the can making business until 1936 when it purchased the Acme Can Company and began building its first large can plant in Philadelphia under the name Crown Can. While the middle of the Great Depression would seem to be the worst possible time to enter a capital-intensive industry, Crown's can operation was successful right from the start. Processed canning was quickly taking the place of home canning as the preferred way to preserve and store perishable goods. For this reason the container industry—for most of the 20th century—remained immune to the economic cycles that plagued most other types of businesses, industrial or otherwise.

Late 1950s: Connelly and the Turnaround

Crown Cork & Seal was an enigma within the container business because it had achieved financial results that contradicted industry logic. Profit margins in can manufacturing had been small and shrinking for decades, and can makers like

Company Perspectives:

We owe our success to a legacy of leadership and invention that began in 1892 when our founder, William Painter, invented a better way to package soft drinks and beer. Painter's vision revolutionized the bottling industry. His ingenuity, and the leadership of those who came after him, helped to build Crown Cork & Seal into the world-class company it is today.

American and Continental had been relying on diversification and economies of scale to create profits. Crown Cork & Seal, on the other hand, had neither expanded into noncontainer fields nor sought to augment its own can making program by purchasing other small can operations. Yet it managed to maintain an earnings growth rate of 20 percent a year. How did it do this?

The answer can be traced back to 1957, when John F. Connelly, an Irishman and son of a Philadelphia blacksmith, became its president. At that time Crown Cork lacked strong leadership and was dangerously close to bankruptcy. It suffered a first-quarter loss of over $600,000, and Bankers Trust was calling in a $2.5 million loan, with an additional $4.5 million due by the end of the year.

Connelly took dramatic measures. He halted can production altogether and filled the company's remaining orders with a large stockpile of unpurchased cans that had been allowed to accumulate. The customers did not object, and the money saved by selling old inventory instead of producing new cans brought Crown Cork close to solvency. In addition, unprofitable and unpromising product lines, such as ice cube trays, were immediately discontinued.

Connelly also reduced overhead costs, particularly those incurred by redundant labor. In one 20-month span the payroll was cut by 25 percent, with pink slips issued to managers and unskilled workers alike. The moves were drastic but necessary. By the end of 1957 the company was making both cans and profits. The following year Crown Cork moved its corporate headquarters to Philadelphia.

Once the initial bankruptcy crisis had passed, Connelly directed Crown Cork & Seal with renewed energy into two areas within which Crown had traditionally held an advantage: aerosol cans and foreign container markets. In the years immediately preceding Connelly's tenure, the company, while not neglecting these markets, had not pursued them with the vigor they warranted.

Crown Cork & Seal had pioneered the aerosol can in 1946 and Connelly was shrewd enough to recognize its potential. Hair spray, bathroom cleaning supplies, insecticides, and many other household products would come to be staples for the American consumer and would be marketed in aerosol dispensers.

In 1963, for example, Crown installed two aerosol can product lines in its Toronto factory, thinking that it would take the market five years to absorb the output. Within a year, however, another plant was required to handle the orders. A decade later, the same situation was repeated in Mexico. Only in the late 1970s and 1980s, when the negative environmental impact of aerosol cans became widely known (it was discovered that aerosol containers expel fluorocarbons which destroy the earth's fragile ozone layer), did Crown begin to reexamine this sector of its business. The company was among the first to develop an aerosol can that did not propel fluorocarbons into the atmosphere.

Connelly invested considerable capital to reclaim Crown's preeminence overseas in closures and cans. Between 1955 and 1960 the company received what were called "pioneer rights" from many foreign governments seeking to build up their industrial sectors. These "rights" gave Crown first chance at any new can or closure business being introduced into these developing nations. This kind of leverage permitted the company to make large profits while using industrial equipment that was, by U.S. standards, obsolete. Moreover, the pioneer rights allowed Crown to pay no taxes for up to ten years.

Crown's international operations were managed and staffed only by nationals of each country, with no Americans on Crown's payroll outside the United States. Connelly sent the foreign plants outdated but still-functioning equipment and let them begin. Crown profited from its disposal of antiquated machinery and created a far-ranging network of semiautonomous subsidiaries in the process.

1960s Through 1980s: Conservative Management

In the early 1960s, the can industry was losing more and more ground to the nonreturnable bottle. It appeared that cans would never be able to capture the lion's share of the beverage container market. For this reason American Can and Continental began experimenting with large-scale diversification into noncontainer fields. Crown Cork, however, did not follow the example; in fact, Connelly went against the prevailing wisdom and entrenched Crown Cork still further into the consumer product can business, spending $121 million on a capital improvement program initiated in 1962.

In 1963, just as the can making industry was experiencing its first recession in decades, the pulltab poptop was introduced. In the words of one can maker at the time, the new and seemingly simple innovation made opening a can "as easy as pulling the ring off a grenade, and a lot safer." The new pulltab opener revolutionized the industry while helping to dramatically increase canned beverage consumption. At the same time, Americans began drinking more beer and soft drinks than ever before, and the can industry experienced a seven-year period of unprecedented growth. Crown Cork, an early entrant in the pulltab can market, performed even better than American Can and Continental, and its year-to-year profits increased by double digit percentages.

In the early 1970s the beverage can market leveled out, with many of the major brewers and soft drink producers developing facilities to manufacture their own cans. A number of can companies, particularly American and Continental, did not adjust well to the diminishing growth in beverage can demand. They were overextended and operating at a greater capacity

Key Dates:

1892: William Painter invents the "crown cork," and soon starts the Crown Cork & Seal Company of Baltimore.
1927: Company is incorporated in New York City as Crown Cork & Seal Company, Inc. following its merger with New Process Cork Company Inc. and New York Improved Patents Corporation.
1936: Acme Can Company is purchased, marking entry into can making.
1957: John F. Connelly takes over presidency and turns the company around.
1958: Company moves its corporate headquarters to Philadelphia.
1962: Company spends $121 million on a capital improvement program.
1970: R. Hoe & Company, a metal decorating firm, is acquired.
1977: Net sales reach $1 billion.
1989: William J. Avery takes over company leadership.
1989–91: Continental Can's Canadian, U.S., and overseas plants are purchased in three deals, costing a total of $791 million.
1992: Company pays $519 million for CONSTAR International, Inc., a leading maker of plastic containers for beverages, food, household items, and chemicals.
1993: Cleveland-based Van Dorn Company, a maker of metal, plastic, and composite containers, is acquired.
1996: $5.2 billion acquisition of France's Carnaud-Metalbox S.A. is completed, vaulting Crown Cork into the top position in the global packaging market.

than necessary. Crown Cork, which did not rely as heavily on can customers like Schlitz and Pepsi, was not as severely affected when beverage companies began manufacturing their own cans. Furthermore, Crown's foreign enterprises, which were accounting for close to 40 percent of total sales, were expanding rapidly. They more than compensated for any domestic decrease in revenues. Crown also became involved in the printing aspect of the industry by acquiring the R. Hoe & Company metal decorating firm in 1970. With this addition to its operation, Crown had the equipment necessary for imprinting color lithography upon its cans and bottle caps. By 1974 Crown had a consolidated net profit of over $39 million—double that of its 1967 results. By 1977 net sales had reached $1 billion.

The first widespread production of two-piece aluminum cans began in the mid-1970s. Aluminum was relatively expensive, but simpler to manufacture, lighter for the consumer, and recyclable. Connelly, however, once again went against industry trends. Just as he had refused to participate in the diversification trend years before, he steered Crown Cork clear of the aluminum two-piece can. He decided instead to concentrate on the old-style three-piece steel can that had been the mainstay of the industry for years. Many industry analysts regarded this strategy as particularly risky since the Food and Drug Administration had indicated that it might outlaw the three-piece can because the lead used to solder the three seams of the can was considered a health hazard. To circumvent this problem Crown began welding rather than soldering its cans.

Connelly was against switching from steel to aluminum for two reasons. First, by relying on the steel can the company was relieved of the high research and development costs necessary for changing to aluminum can manufacturing. Second, Connelly realized that there were only a handful of corporations selling aluminum in bulk. This meant that the can makers would be paying a premium price for their raw materials. Crown, by using steel, could play the various steel producers off one another and drive the price of its materials down. The strategy worked, and Crown's company was making profits while his larger and more progressive competitors spent hundreds of millions of dollars on retooling for aluminum cans.

Connelly, it seemed, made very few mistakes. In all of his years as president, the company never suffered a quarterly loss and was virtually debt-free. During the 1980s, when competitors were spending and buying themselves into debt, Crown sat conservatively waiting. By the end of the 1980s the company was ready to position itself as a major player in the industry, taking advantage of weak economies and buying competitors' assets at low prices.

1990s: Acquiring Its Way to the Top

The man that lead Crown's amazing growth in the 1990s was not Connelly, but his protégé, William J. Avery. Avery joined Crown in 1959 as a management trainee and then worked in manufacturing and marketing. Connelly watched Avery's potential grow and groomed him to take over the company. One day, Connelly, who was described as an "ultraconservative, tight-lipped, and tightfisted boss," called Avery into his office and told him to stop being intimidated. Said Avery in a 1993 article in *Financial World,* "He told me, 'Bill, I am very disappointed in you. You have to set your sights higher. You have to think of taking my job.' " In 1989, after a period of diminishing health, Connelly died and Avery took over the company.

Avery remarked in *Financial World,* "When I became president in 1989, I had to light a fire and get the company going again. The company's growth had slowed down in the 1980s. John Connelly's health was not good, the company had no debt and we were very vulnerable to a takeover." Avery began acquiring companies at a rapid pace. In fact, in five years he purchased 20 businesses with combined sales in the billions. Under Avery, Crown's revenues doubled to $3.8 billion in 1993 and reached almost $4.5 billion in 1994.

Avery approached newer markets in developing countries cautiously through joint ventures. The acquisition of Continental Can's U.S., Canadian, and overseas plants where done in three deals from 1990 to 1991. It cost Crown $791 million, but gave it several foreign joint ventures and put the company in Korea, Saudi Arabia, Hong Kong, Venezuela, and China, where many of its U.S. competitors were not. This purchase brought in $2 billion in new sales, almost doubling Crown's size. Along with this purchase came Continental's technical center located outside of Chicago. Under Connelly, spending for research and development was almost nonexistent. But by the late 1980s, Crown's customers wanted more than just lower prices; they also wanted new products such as lighter weight, custom-designed cans and specific metal coatings. Continental's research center gave Crown the ability to develop new cans to meet their specific needs.

In October 1992, Crown paid $519 million for CONSTAR International, Inc., a leading maker of plastic containers for beverages, food, household items, and chemicals. In April 1993, Crown acquired the Cleveland-based Van Dorn Company, a $314 million maker of metal, plastic, and composite containers for a variety of industries. The total merger was valued at $175 million and enabled Crown to improve its economies of scale, as well as add to its technological and marketing expertise.

Other ventures during this time included an agreement in China with Shanghai Crown Maling Packaging Co. Ltd. to manufacture aluminum beverage cans and a joint venture with a Vietnamese company to produce two-piece aluminum beverage cans. In 1994 Crown Cork ranked as the world's second largest aluminum can maker with the expansion of its Aluplata facility near Buenos Aires, which included the addition of a second can line capable of producing 1,600 cans a minute, for a total of more than 800 million cans a year. In 1995 Crown announced that it was building a new $21.3 million corporate headquarters in Philadelphia; it moved into the new quarters in 1997.

In May 1995 Crown Cork announced that it would acquire France's CarnaudMetalbox S.A. One of the largest packaging companies in Europe and the number one maker of metal and plastic packaging on that continent, Carnaud was formed in 1989 from the merger of Groupe Carnaud S.A. of France and MB Group PLC of the United Kingdom. The deal, which was valued at $5.2 billion in stock and debt, was not completed until February 1996 thanks to an in-depth antitrust investigation launched by European Union authorities. The antitrust officials finally approved the takeover after the companies agreed to divest several aerosol can operations in Europe; the facilities were subsequently sold in September 1996 to U.S. Can Corporation for $52.8 million. Meantime, Crown sold its U.S.-based paint- and oblong-can operations to BWAY Corporation.

The completion of the Carnaud purchase vaulted Crown Cork into the top position in the global packaging market. The combined operations seemed to fit nearly perfectly, with Crown a major player in the United States, Carnaud a major player in Europe, and both companies with small but growing presences in Asia. The deal also provided Crown with a foothold in the specialty packaging area of cosmetics and perfume packaging, such as lipstick cases, mascara applicators, compacts, and fragrance pumps; this sector was a desirable one because of its higher profit margins. The acquisition also proved a boon for Crown Cork shareholders as the company resumed payment of a cash dividend in March 1996, the first such payment since August 1956; under Connelly, the company had adopted a policy of using cash to repurchase common shares instead of issuing cash dividends.

Crown Cork anticipated being able to wrest about $100 million in annual savings by eliminating jobs and closing plants in the aftermath of the Carnaud acquisition. In 1996 the company shuttered 40 plants and regional administrative offices, reorganized an additional 52 plants, and reduced the combined workforce by 6,500. Further restructurings followed during the next three years, including the closure of 13 additional factories and a further elimination of 2,900 jobs during 1998. Crown also sold its Crown-Simplimatic business, which was involved in manufacturing various packaging machinery, to a management-led group in 1997.

Even with these attempts to increase efficiency and divest noncore operations, Crown Cork saw its profits fall in the late 1990s, at the same time that revenues were flat. There were multiple reasons for the setback. Aluminum producers cut output and raised prices starting in 1994. The strength of the U.S. dollar reduced the value of overseas sales—which made up 60 percent of Crown's overall sales in the late 1990s—following conversion to the U.S. dollar. Crown also faced a formidable new rival starting in May 1997 when Pechiney S.A. and Schmalbach-Lubeca AG spun off their can making operations into a new venture called Impress Metal Packaging Holdings. Impress soon slashed can prices, forcing Crown to follow suit. The question Crown Cork & Seal faced as it entered the 21st century was whether or not its performance in the late 1990s represented only a temporary setback. The company appeared to be counting on another round of industry consolidation leading to fewer competitors and to a condition wherein Crown could raise prices and realize the profits it had anticipated when it had absorbed Carnaud.

Principal Subsidiaries

Crown Cork & Seal Company (PA) Inc.; Pennsylvania Crown Consultants, Inc.; Nationwide Recyclers; CONSTAR, Inc.; AH Packaging Co.; CONSTAR INTERNATIONAL INC; CarnaudMetalbox Enterprises, Inc.; CarnaudMetalbox Investments (USA), Inc.; CarnaudMetalbox Holdings (USA), Inc.; Risdon - AMS (USA), Inc.; Zeller Plastik, Inc.; Crown Cork & Seal Holdings, Inc.; Crown Cork & Seal Technologies Corporation; Crown Cork & Seal Company (USA), Inc.; Crown Financial Management, Inc.; Crown Overseas Investments Corporation; Crown Beverage Packaging, Inc.; Crown Cork de Puerto Rico, Inc.; Central States Can Company of Puerto Rico, Inc.; Aluplata S.A. (Argentina); Crown Cork de Argentina S.A.; Crown Cork & Seal (Barbados) Foreign Sales Corporation; Crown Cork Company (Belgium) N.V.; Crown Cork Holding Company (Belgium); Speciality Packaging Belgie NV (Belgium); Crown Brasil Holding Ltd. (Brazil); Crown Cork Embalagens S.A. (Brazil); Crown Cork do Nordeste Ltd. (Brazil); Crown Cork Tampas Plasticos, S.A. (Brazil); Crown Cork & Seal Canada Inc.; Risdon - AMS (Canada) Inc.; Crown Cork de Chile, S.A.I.; Beijing CarnaudMetalbox Co., Ltd.; Beijing Crown Can Co., Ltd. (China); CarnaudMetalbox Huapeng (Wuxi) Closures Co., Ltd. (China); Foshan Crown Can Company, Limited (China); Foshan Crown Easy-Opening Ends Co., Ltd. (China); Huizhou Crown Can Co., Ltd. (China); Shanghai Crown Packaging Co., Ltd. (China); Jiangmen Zeller Plastik, Ltd. (China); Crown Litometal S.A. (Colombia); Crown Colombiana, S.A. (Colombia); Crown Pakkaus OY (Finland); Astra Plastique (France); Risdon S.A. (France); CarnaudMetalbox S.A. (France); CarnaudMetalbox Group Services (France); CMB Plastique SNC (France); Crown Cork et Seal Finance S.A. (France); Crown Cork Company (France) S.A.; Crown Developpement SNC (France); Crown Financial Corporation France S.A.; Polyflex S.A. (France); Societe Bourguignonne D'Applications Plastiques (France); Societe de Participations Entrangers CarnaudMetalbox (France); Societe de Participations CarnaudMetalbox (France); Societe Francasie De Developpement De La Boite Boisson (France); Z.P. France; CarnaudMetalbox Deutschland GmbH (Germany); CarnaudMetalbox Nahrungsmitteldosen GmbH (Germany); CarnaudMetalbox Plastik Holding GmbH (Germany); Crown Bender (Germany) GmbH; Wehrstedt GmbH (Germany); Zeller Plastik GmbH (Germany); Zuchner Gruss Metallverpackungen GmbH (Germany); Zuchner Metallverpackugen GmbH (Germany); Zuchner Verpackugen GmbH & Co (Germany); Zuchner Verschlusse GmbH (Germany); Hellas Can Packaging Manufacturers (Greece); CarnaudMetalbox Magyarorszag (Hungary); CONSTAR International Plastics KFT (Hungary); CarnaudMetalbox Italia SRL (Italy); CMB Italcaps SRL (Italy); Crown Cork Company (Italy) S.P.A.; FABA Sud Spa (Italy); Risdon SRL (Italy); Superbox Aerosols SRL (Italy); Superbox Contenitori per Bevande SRL (Italy); Zeller Plastik Italia SPA (Italy); CarnaudMetalbox Kenya Limited; Societe Malgache D'Emgallages Metalliques (Madagascar); CarnaudMetalbox Bevcan SDN BHD (Malaysia); Crown Cork de Mexico, S.A.; Envases Generales Crown, S.A. DE C.V. (Mexico); Carnaud Maroc (Morocco); CMB Plastique Maroc (Morocco); CarnaudMetalbox NV (Netherlands); CMB Closures Benelux BV (Netherlands); CMB Promotional Packaging (Netherlands) BV; CONSTAR International Holland (Plastics) B.V. (Netherlands); Crown Cork Company (Holland) B.V. (Netherlands); Crown Cork Mijdrecht B.V. (Netherlands); Crown Cork Netherlands Holding B.V.; Speciality Packaging Nederland BV (Netherlands); CarnaudMetalbox Nigeria PLC; Zeller Plastik Philippines, Inc.; CarnaudMetalbox Gopak Sp. zo. o. (Poland); CarnaudMetalbox Tworzyna Sztuczne SP Z.O.D. (Poland); CarnaudMetalbox de Portugal; Crown Cork & Seal de Portugal Embalagens S.A.; CarnaudMetalbox (Asia-Pacific) Holdings PTE Ltd. (Singapore); CarnaudMetalbox Asia Limited (Singapore); CarnaudMetalbox Packaging PTE Limited (Singapore); CarnaudMetalbox Slovakia Spol. S.R.O.; Crown Cork Company, S.A. (Pty) Ltd. (South Africa); Crown Investment Holdings (Pty) Ltd. (South Africa); Crown Cork Company Iberica (Spain) SL; Envases CarnaudMetalbox S.A. (Spain); Envases Metalicos Manlleu S.A. (Spain); Envases Metalner S.A. (Spain); Envases Murcianos S.A. (Spain); Ormis Embalajes Espana S.A. (Spain); Risdon Productos de Metal LTDA (Spain); Crown Obrist AG (Switzerland); CarnaudMetalbox Tanzania Limited; CarnaudMetalbox (Thailand) PLC; CarnaudMetalbox Bevcan Limited (Thailand); Crown Cork & Seal (Thailand) Co., Ltd.; ZPJK (Thailand) Co., Ltd.; CarnaudMetalbox Ambalaj Sanayi (Turkey); CONSTAR Ambalaj Sanayi Ve Ticaret A.S. (Turkey); Emirates Can Company, Ltd. (Dubai, UAE) (United Arab Emirates); CarnaudMetalbox Bevcan PLC (U.K.); CarnaudMetalbox Closures PLC (U.K.); CarnaudMetalbox Engineering PLC (U.K.); CarnaudMetalbox Group UK Limited; CarnaudMetalbox Overseas Limited (U.K.); CarnaudMetalbox PLC (U.K.); CMB Bottles and Closures (U.K.); CONSTAR International U.K., Ltd.; Crown Cork & Seal Finance PLC (U.K.); Crown UK Holdings Ltd.; Speciality Packaging (UK) PLC; The Crown Cork Company Limited (U.K.); United Closures & Plastic PLC (U.K.); Zeller Plastik UK Limited; CarnaudMetalbox (Saigon) Limited (Vietnam); Vietnam Crown Vinalimex Packaging, Ltd.; CarnaudMetalbox (Zimbabwe) Ltd.; Crown Cork Company 1958 PVT Ltd. (Zimbabwe).

Principal Competitors

Alcoa Inc.; BWAY Corporation; Ball Corporation; Berlin Packaging; Century Aluminum Company; Continental Can Company, Inc.; Impress Metal Packaging Holdings; Kerr Group Inc.; Owens-Illinois, Inc.; Pechiney S.A.; Rexam PLC; Reynolds Metals Company; Schmalbach-Lubeca AG; Sealright Co., Inc.; Silgan Holdings Inc.; Tetra Laval International S.A.; Toyo Seikan Kaisha, Ltd.; U.S. Can Corporation; VIAG AG.

Further Reading

"Cross-Border Combinations Rife with Risk: Crown Cork & Seal Is Tripped Repeatedly in Carnaud Purchase," *Baltimore Sun,* August 10, 1998, p. 5C.

"Crown Cork & Seal," *Beverage World,* February 1992, p. 18.

"Crown Gets Its Company," *Beverage World,* January 1993, p. 22.

"Crown Launches Steel Can Unit," *American Metal Market,* August 16, 1994, p. 5.

Davis, Tim, "Crowning Achievement: Embarking on Its Second Century in Business This Year, Crown Cork & Seal Is Well Poised to Meet Its Mission of Becoming a World-Class Manufacturer," *Beverage World,* February 1992, pp. 66+.

Epstein, Joseph, "Crown Cork & Seal: A Boost from Brussels," *Financial World,* December 5, 1995, pp. 22, 24.

Halbfinger, David M., "Metals Companies All Made Critical '92 Acquisitions," *Philadelphia Business Journal,* May 31, 1993, p. B11.

Kahn, Sharon, "An In-House M&A Team Reshapes a Company," *Global Finance,* March 1997, pp. 39+.

Kamm, Thomas, and Douglas Lavin, "CarnaudMetalbox Calls Its Sale 'Perfect,' " *Wall Street Journal,* May 24, 1995, p. A10.

Khalaf, Roula, "New Era," *Forbes,* April 26, 1993, pp. 158+.

Lipin, Steven, and E.S. Browning, "Crown Cork & Seal to Buy France's CarnaudMetalbox," *Wall Street Journal,* May 23, 1995, p. A3.

Martin, Peter, "Making Money from a Mature Market," *Financial Post,* January 18, 1996, p. 58.

Millman, Joel, "Crown Cork to Pay Its First Dividend in Nearly 40 Years," *Wall Street Journal,* February 23, 1996, p. B4.

Morais, Richard C., "One World," *Forbes,* December 4, 1995, p. 156.

Murray, Shailagh, "Heavier Metal: Beverage-Can Firms in Europe Seek Edge on Costs, Recycling," *Wall Street Journal Europe,* April 7, 1997, p. 1.

Panchapakasen, Meena, "Indecent Expansion," *Financial World,* July 6, 1993, pp. 34+.

Pressley, James, "EU Seen As Likely to Approve Merger of Carnaud, Crown," *Wall Street Journal Europe,* November 8, 1995, p. 2.

Regan, Bob, "Crown Cork Bids $5.2B for French Aluminum Can Firm," *American Metal Market,* May 24, 1995, p. 2.

——, "Crown Cork in Third China Swing," *American Metal Market,* November 13, 1992, p. 2.

——, "Crown Cork Plans to Expand Argentine Can Production," *American Metal Market,* December 22, 1994, p. 12.

——, "Crown Plans $21M HQ," *American Metal Market,* May 31, 1995, p. 2.

——, "Vietnamese Venture," *Beverage World,* September 1994, p. 16.

Ridding, John, and Richard Waters, "Giants Wrap Up Package Deal," *Financial Post,* May 25, 1995, p. 61.

Somerville, Sean, "Crown Cork Seeks Global Gains," *Baltimore Sun,* June 12, 1996, p. 1C.

Welsh, Jonathan, "Crown Cork Warns on Earnings, Will Cut Staff," *Wall Street Journal,* September 23, 1998, p. A3.

—Beth Watson Highman
—updated by David E. Salamie

Czarnikow-Rionda Company, Inc.

One William Street
New York, New York 10004
U.S.A.
Telephone: (212) 806-0700
Fax: (212) 968-0825

Private Company
Incorporated: 1909 (dissolved 1999)
Employees: 48
Sales: $800 million (fiscal 1998 est.)
NAIC: 52314 Commodity Brokerage

Czarnikow-Rionda Company, Inc. was one of the largest sugar brokers in North America for almost a century, acting as a middleman between growers and refiners of sugarcane, with its principal focus on Cuba. Through affiliated companies, the firm also owned sugarcane farms and processing mills, cattle ranches, and alcoholic distilleries in Cuba and a Philadelphia sugar refinery. Czarnikow-Rionda lost all its Cuban property with the rise of Fidel Castro to power but remained one of the world's largest sugar brokers until 1999, when heavy losses on some contracts left it too deeply in debt to continue in business.

Cuban Sugar Powerhouse: 1903–20

Prussian-born Julius Caesar Czarnikow emigrated to England in 1854 and became a successful sugar broker, founding the firm of Czarnikow & Co. (later C. Czarnikow, Ltd.) in 1861. Czarnikow, MacDougall & Co., founded in 1891, was the New York-based North American branch of this brokerage house. Joining the firm as a commission agent in 1897 was Manuel Rionda, the younger brother of two Spanish-born brothers who had established a business empire based on Cuban sugar. By the end of 1898 both of Manuel's brothers were dead, and he was the head of the family's properties and business. Nevertheless, he continued working for Czarnikow, MacDougall which, by means of his energy and enterprise and the parent firm's capital, was the dominant power in the Cuban sugar trade by 1903.

Following the death of Czarnikow in 1909, Czarnikow-McDougall was reorganized as Czarnikow-Rionda, with Rionda as president and his nephew Manuel E. (Manolo) Rionda as secretary and treasurer. (MacDougall died in 1911.) Rionda was only one of five equal partners in the company, with the other four being partners in the parent firm. Relations between Rionda and the others were never good, since he believed they were too conservative to effectively compete for the U.S. sugar market and they were reluctant to invest in Cuba because of political instability on the island. In 1915 Rionda succeeded in reducing the parent firm's participation in the New York operation. All ties were severed at some undetermined later date.

In spite of its brokering activities, Czarnikow-Rionda's primary focus for its first 50 years was to import raw cane sugar and molasses from Cuban mills for delivery to refineries in the United States. Affiliates of the company did some of the planting, harvesting, transporting, and milling, but even many mills nominally independent were in fact tied to Czarnikow-Rionda by loans to finance the grinding of the cane. In turn, nominally independent planters were tied to the mills by the need to finance their activities. Czarnikow-Rionda also exported machinery, jute bags, and provisions to Cuba.

By 1913 Cuba was the world's leading sugar exporter. Czarnikow-Rionda was prominent in every part of the trade. In its heyday as a broker it handled over 60 percent of Cuban sugar sales in New York and some 60 percent in the United States. The Cuban Trading Co., established in 1907 as a subsidiary or affiliate, bought sugar, arranged loans to millers and farmers, sold jute bags for transporting the milled cane, handled insurance claims, and provided legal and notary services, even resolving local disputes and acting as liaison to the Cuban government.

Rionda family members were active in the business, especially Bernardo Braga Rionda, another nephew of Manuel Rionda. Several mills passed into the hands of Czarnikow, McDougall and Czarnikow-Rionda when their owners could not pay their debts. The Riondas then acquired these properties, including the sugar mills Central San Vicente, Central San Jose (reorganized as Washington Sugar Co.), Central Elia, and Central Cespedes. They also had earlier acquired Central Tuinucu. These were organized into affiliates of Czarnikow-Rionda.

Key Dates:

1909: Company is founded.
1916: Manuel Rionda is president of Cuba's biggest sugar enterprise.
1920: Collapse of sugar prices ends the firm's most lucrative period.
1943: Rionda dies at the age of 89.
1960–61: Fidel Castro nationalizes all the firm's Cuban holdings.
1969: Czarnikow-Rionda is purchased by C. Brewer and Co.
1999: The firm closes its doors after big trading losses.

Francisco Sugar Co., incorporated in 1899, purchased in 1921 the common stock of the company that owned Central Elia. Its holdings, then or later, included 117 miles of railroad, a port, a cattle ranch, and an alcohol distillery. Manati Sugar Co., incorporated in 1912, operated the Riondas' largest sugar mill, Central Manati, plus more than 200,000 acres of land. Other Cuban enterprises in which Czarnikow-Rionda was involved included another alcohol distillery, two more sugar mills, a paper mill that produced cellulose from cane bagasse, a wallboard factory, and a scheme to substitute Cuban-grown kenaf for imported Asian jute in producing bags for transporting sugar.

Manuel Rionda was an investor in, and first president of, the Cuba Cane Sugar Co., which in 1916 bought 17 mills, making it the largest sugar enterprise in Cuba. Backed by J.P Morgan & Co., this company controlled 16 percent of Cuba's sugar production. At its height Cuba Cane Sugar also held over 500,000 acres of purchased or leased land and 500 miles of railroad, complete with rolling stock for transporting sugarcane.

Czarnikow-Rionda's fortunes reached their zenith in this period. Sugar prices rose threefold during World War I, spurring a surge in production. The postwar lifting of U.S. price controls set off a speculative frenzy that increased the value of raw sugar at least three times more in 1919. The so-called Dance of the Millions bubble burst the following year, ruining hundreds of Cuban planters and merchants.

Less Dominant Role: 1920–60

Czarnikow-Rionda survived this crisis and even purchased a Philadelphia sugar refinery, W.J. McCahan Sugar Refining and Molasses Co., in 1920. However, overproduction and low prices were a problem for the Cuban sugar trade throughout the 1920s. For a brief period in the early 1920s, Walter E. Ogilvie, a businessman who helped Rionda break another firm's monopoly on coal distribution in Cuba, served as Czarnikow-Rionda's president and tried to reorganize its operations. This endeavor was not successful, and Rionda resumed the presidency.

Nearly 80 percent of all Cuban sugar was being sold to U.S. markets in 1929, but the industry had to compete against tariff-protected growers in the possessions of Hawaii, the Philippines, and Puerto Rico, as well as in the mainland United States. The situation worsened during the Great Depression, as demand fell. The Francisco, Manati, and Cespedes sugar companies, forced into receivership, were reorganized under the continued control of the Riondas. Washington Sugar and Central San Vicente were sold. Cuba Cane Sugar was dissolved in 1938.

Manuel Rionda died in 1943 at the age of 89 and was succeeded as president of Czarnikow-Rionda by Bernardo Braga Rionda. The sugar refinery was sold in 1944 to the American Sugar Co. The period after World War II saw the company's fortunes gradually revive. In 1960 and 1961, however, soon after Fidel Castro came to power, Czarnikow-Rionda lost all its property in Cuba, including six remaining sugar mills.

Post-Cuban Role: 1960–99

With all commercial links to Cuba also severed, Czarnikow-Rionda had to find new markets. Sugar from the Dominican Republic and the Philippines replaced much of the Cuban trade. In 1961 the company financed 15 percent of a cooperative venture to establish a mill in southern Florida, which became the nation's largest. Through a new subsidiary, Osceola Farms, Inc., Czarnikow-Rionda also dismantled a Louisiana mill and reassembled it on 4,000 acres of farmland newly drained by the U.S. Army Corps of Engineers near Canal Point, Florida. The Fanjul family, long associated with the Riondas (two Fanjuls had served as presidents of the Cuban Trading Co.), took a 20 percent stake in this enterprise and eventually came to own 160,000 acres of cultivated land in the area through its Flo-Sun Inc. company.

As a sugar broker, Czarnikow-Rionda was second in size only to Galban, Lobo & Co. This firm was unable to survive the Cuban crisis and was dissolved in 1965. Czarnikow-Rionda acquired its subsidiary, Olavarria & Co., which was selling Puerto Rican refined sugar to retail outlets in the mainland United States. Czarnikow-Rionda also established a subsidiary in Great Britain, where it competed with its former parent, C. Czarnikow, as a broker in the European beet-sugar market.

Czarnikow-Rionda had annual revenue of about $40 million when it was sold in December 1969 to C. Brewer and Co., Ltd., a majority-owned subsidiary of International Utilities Corp. (The molasses operation was not sold and continued as Braga Brothers, Inc.) Czarnikow-Rionda's eight subsidiaries at that time included the London brokerage, a Philippine firm, New York- and Panama-based shipping companies, and Closter Farms, Inc. of Florida, but in its annual report International Utilities merely described the firm as "a New York-based sugar merchant organization." Brewer sold the company to Czarnikow-Rionda's employees shortly after 1972.

The volatile sugar market continued to demonstrate in the 1970s why commodity trading is not a venture for the faint of heart. Large profits or losses ordinarily rest on fluctuations of only a fraction of a penny per pound, but in 1974 heated speculation, only partly based on rational expectations in the wake of a huge run-up in oil prices, drove the value of sugar from 16 to 66 cents. This was quickly followed by a reversion to the usual price level of less than 10 cents a pound. During this period Czarnikow-Rionda maintained close links with SuCrest

Corp., the third largest refiner in the United States. SuCrest was buying virtually all of its raw sugar in the Philippines.

Czarnikow-Rionda had estimated revenue of $100 million in 1990. By 1984 it had established Czarnikow-Rionda Trading Co. as a subsidiary. This became, in 1992, Czarnikow-Rionda Sugar Trading Inc., which had about $455 million in annual revenue two years later. Daniel Gutman, the firm's majority owner, became chief executive officer in 1993.

Czarnikow-Rionda was the world's third largest sugar-trading firm when it went under in 1999 as a result of sugar prices dropping to five cents a pound. The firm reportedly held many long-term contracts with China and Russia at prices well above that level. These customers were said to have defaulted on their contracts. Czarnikow-Rionda also suffered from extending sizable credits to sugar mills in Brazil, which was in the grip of a currency crisis in early 1999. A group of about 17 creditors was discussing restructuring debts totaling more than $70 million in April, but negotiations apparently failed to resolve the problem, for Czarnikow-Rionda closed its offices in July.

Principal Subsidiaries

Czarnikow-Rionda Sugar Trading Inc.

Further Reading

Editor's note: The chief easily accessible source is an abstract of the Braga Brothers Collection of the special collections of the University of Florida's George A. Smathers Libraries. This abstract is found at http://www.uflib.ufl.edu/spec/manuscript/Braga/Braga.htm. See also the following:

Albert, Bill, and Adrian Graves, eds., *The World Sugar Economy in War and Depression: 1914–40,* London and New York: Routledge, 1988.

''Bridge Update: Sugar,'' *Futures World News,* July 16, 1999.

''Czarnikow-Rionda Co. Settles SEC Complaint Tied to SuCrest Corp.,'' *Wall Street Journal,* June 29, 1977, p. 6.

Dye, Alan, *Cuban Sugar in the Age of Mass Production,* Stanford, Calif.: Stanford University Press, 1998.

Einhorn, Cheryl Strauss, ''Not So Sweet,'' *Barron's,* April 19, 1999, p. MW20.

''Florida Bets on a Boom in Sugar,'' *Business Week,* October 14, 1961, p. 59.

Janes, Hurford, and H.J. Sayers, *The Story of Czarnikow,* London: Harley, 1963.

Mayer, Jane, and Jose de Cordoba, ''First Family of Sugar Is Tough on Workers, Generous to Politicians,'' *Wall Street Journal,* July 29, 1991, pp. A1, A7.

''The Tempest in the Sugar Market,'' *Fortune,* February 1977, pp. 116, 118.

—Robert Halasz

Dairy Crest Group plc

Dairy Crest House
Portsmouth Road
Surbiton
Surrey KT6 5QL
United Kingdom
Telephone: +44 181 910-4000
Fax: +44 181 910-4111
Web site: http://www.dairycrest.co.uk

Public Company
Incorporated: 1987
Employees: 3,400
Sales: £773.8 million ($1.27 billion) (1999)
Stock Exchanges: London
NAIC: 311511 Fluid Milk Manufacturing; 311512 Creamery Butter Manufacturing; 311513 Cheese Manufacturing

Dairy Crest Group plc, the dairy products processing arm of the former British Milk Marketing Board milk monopoly, has developed into one of the United Kingdom's leading producers of consumer dairy products, dairy-based food services products, including doorstep milk delivery, and fresh milk products. The company has transformed itself considerably during the 1990s, from a milk processor dependent on fresh milk products for some 90 percent of its sales, to a diversified producer of a wide variety of dairy and dairy-based products, including cheeses, butters and other spreads, drinks, and—through its 49 percent participation in the joint venture Yoplait Dairy Crest—yogurt and ''fromage frais'' (fresh cheese) products under the Yoplait and other brand names. Dairy Crest is currently the U.K. brand leader in dairy spreads, through sales of its Clover brand. Moreover, the company's Cathedral City and Davidstow brands have enabled it to capture a strong share of the British cheddar cheese market, the largest cheese category in the United Kingdom. After acquiring Millway Foods in 1999, Dairy Crest has also strengthened its position as leader of another favorite British cheese category, that of Stilton cheese. Dairy Crest is among the United Kingdom's top five purchasers and processors of raw milk and supplies fresh milk products to leading retailers. While Consumer Foods forms the largest–and fastest-growing—part of the company, representing more than two-thirds of annual sales, the company also maintains a strong presence in the Food Services market. With foodservice sales of nearly £300 million in 1999, Dairy Crest is the United Kingdom's leading dairy ingredients supplier. The company also operates the leading doorstep delivery service in the East Anglia/London region. Dairy Crest has been led since 1990 by CEO W.J. Houliston.

Milk Monopoly Spinoff in the 1980s

While Dairy Crest itself was formed in the early 1980s, it nonetheless had its origin in Depression-era England. Britain's dairy farmers were under increasing pressure from the nationwide recession and resulting price instabilities. At the same time, the increasing use of automation in milking and milk preparation techniques made possible a vast increase in milk production, placing dairy farmers under even more pressure. Farmers began lobbying the government for some form of protection, which they received in 1934 with the establishment of the Milk Marketing Scheme. This scheme established a government-controlled milk buying and selling monopoly.

Dairy products manufacturers, having lost the ability to find competitive milk pricing, quickly began lobbying for a counterpart Milk Products Marketing Scheme to protect them from the Milk Marketing Scheme's monopoly pricing power. After some five years of negotiations, the government at last agreed to provide dairy products manufacturers with relief, creating the Milk Products Marketing Board in 1939. Britain's entry into World War II, however, quickly brought all of the United Kingdom's dairy industry under government control as rationing rules were placed in effect.

The dairy industry was then placed under the control of a single government department, the Milk Marketing Board. While rationing was eased after the war, the Milk Marketing Board continued to regulate the UK's dairy industry, not only fixing pricing levels, but also enacting production quotas. At this time, the dairy industry represented little more than traditional staple products, such as whole milks, butter, and cheese. Other products, such as yogurt and low-fat milk, were relatively unknown in the U.K. market of the time.

Company Perspectives:

We have established our operating base and achieved a position of financial strength from which to develop our future as a broadly based U.K. dairy food company. As one of the U.K.'s largest buyers of raw milk, Dairy Crest has always appreciated the vital role milk producers play in the success of the dairy business. The management's task is to continue to develop Dairy Crest's potential for the benefit of its shareholders.

The United Kingdom's entry into the European Community in 1973 not only forced a change in the functioning of the country's dairy industry, it also brought about changing consumer habits—and product demand—as well. An early effect of European Community membership was the institution of production caps on member states. Not only were member states placed under production quantity quotas, they were also required to export a fixed percentage of dairy production to other member states each year.

As foreign milk and dairy products began to appear on the U.K. supermarket shelves, the Milk Marketing Board responded with the creation of its own "brand" of milk and dairy products. In 1981, the Milk Marketing Board established Dairy Crest as its dairy products processing unit. Dairy Crest began introducing its own branded products to rival its new competitors, as the United Kingdom's consumers adopted new dairy consumption habits. The market share of low-fat milk, for example, rose from next to nothing to nine percent in the early 1980s; by the mid-1990s, that share had risen to 51 percent of the total milk market. Dairy Crest itself scored a success with the introduction of its Clover brand of imitation butter spread in 1984, as the U.K. consumer began seeking more healthful alternatives to butter. By the 1990s, Clover had taken the lead of the spreads market.

Dairy Crest was spun off as a company, still under the Milk Marketing Board's control, in 1987. As the European Market edged toward a single-market structure, the food industry had begun to experience dramatic changes. Increasing quotas encouraged greater exports to member countries; as a result, Dairy Crest had found itself facing stiffer competition on supermarket shelves, with a growing variety of dairy products fighting for consumer attention. Dairy Crest, while starting to diversify, still relied on liquid milk products for as much as 90 percent of its total business. In addition, the newly spun off company faced other pressures. First, it was forced to maintain a bloated production infrastructure of more than 32 dairies and creameries, as well as a workforce of some 32,000. The company also maintained an extensive doorstep delivery business, despite the fading popularity and increasing costs of this service in much of the country. Moreover, Dairy Crest was required by law to purchase all excess milk production in the United Kingdom, whether or not this was beyond the company's own needs.

Public Company in the 1990s

The British government came under increasing pressure to end the Milk Marketing Board's monopoly, especially as the countries' dairy producers and manufacturers were finding means of using the European Community trade rules to exploit loopholes in the Milk Marketing Board's control of the U.K. milk production market. Preparations to abandon the milk monopoly began in the early 1990s, including the division of the U.K.-wide Milk Marketing Board into separate, smaller boards for the regions of England, Wales, and Scotland. As part of the breakup of the Milk Marketing Board, a new voluntary cooperative body, dubbed Milk Marque, was created. Farmers were then allowed to sell their milk to Milk Marque or to one of its private competitors, including Northern Milk and Unigate. Nonetheless, Milk Marque managed to sign up more than 80 percent of U.K. dairy farmers.

The breakup of the Milk Marketing Board was originally intended to coincide with the listing of Dairy Crest on the London Stock Exchange. In preparation for the listing, Dairy Crest, under the leadership of W.J. Houliston since 1990, had undergone its own transformation. During the first half of the 1990s, Dairy Crest succeeded in slimming down its operations, eliminating nearly half of its production facilities to consolidate its processing operations into just 14 creameries, dairies, and other processing and packaging centers. The company also steadily trimmed its workforce, bringing its total employees below 4,000. Meanwhile, Dairy Crest chose to exit most of its doorstep delivery business, keeping only its East Anglia market, where it held a leading position. In 1995, Dairy Crest realized an important acquisition, buying Mendip Foods Ltd., which enabled it to gain a leading share of the cheddar cheese market, the largest-selling cheese category in the United Kingdom.

Dairy Crest's public listing was delayed because of government disagreement over the form of the milk industry's deregulation. It was not until August 1996 that the company finally went public. Under the offering, the country's 28,000 dairy farmers—considered the indirect owners of Dairy Crest after the breakup of the Milk Marketing Board—were given the option of taking shares in Dairy Crest or receiving a direct payment. More than 90 percent of the farmers opted for shares in Dairy Crest. This show of support also placed Dairy Crest under majority control of the farmers, which served to shield the company from any takeover attempt.

After its cost-cutting efforts and a strong investment program in revitalizing its industrial park, Dairy Crest turned to transforming its market focus. Seeking to reduce its exposure to the low-margin liquid milk business, Dairy Crest turned to higher-margin products such as yogurts and cheeses. By the late 1990s, the company had successfully reduced its liquid milk business to just 60 percent of its annual sales. Aiding this transformation was the joint venture company, Yoplait Dairy Crest, set up with France's Sondiaal to market the yogurt brand Yoplait in the United Kingdom. Dairy Crest's share of the partnership was 49 percent. The company's Petit Filous and other products proved quickly successful with the British consumer, and by mid-decade Yoplait Dairy Crest had taken the market lead in many of its product categories.

Dairy Crest was also finding success with its other brands, including the Clover spread, which had captured the country's lead in this category, and a line of fresh dairy drink products, called Frijj. Dairy Crest also began making a series of strategic acquisitions, including those of Anglia Dairies, for £4.6 million

Key Dates:

1939: The British Milk Marketing Board is created.
1973: United Kingdom enters into European Community (EC).
1981: Dairy Crest is formed as the processing arm of Milk Marketing Board.
1984: EC establishes milk quotas.
1987: Dairy Crest is spun off as a separate company.
1990: Yoplait Dairy Crest joint venture is created.
1994: Milk Marketing Board monopoly is broken up.
1996: Dairy Crest gains public listing on London Stock Exchange.

in 1997, and Raines Dairy Foods Operating Companies, bought for £66 million in 1998. The Raines purchase, made through the Yoplait Dairy Crest partnership, helped boost Dairy Crest's European position as well, adding plants in several countries, including five production plants in France, and plants in Spain, Poland, and the Czech Republic. Another acquisition, made in January 1999, of Longs Dairies, helped strengthen Dairy Crest's position in the East Anglia doorstep delivery market. At the same time, the company boosted its marketing of several of its key brands, including its Cathedral City cheese and other brands.

Dairy Crest's transformation into a value-added dairy products company helped ensure double-digit sales growth in the years following its public offering. The company showed no sign of slowing down at the turn of the century. The company took the leading position in the Stilton cheese market with the acquisition of Millway Foods, from France's Bongrain, in 1999.

Principal Subsidiaries

Philpot Dairy Products Ltd.; Millway Foods Ltd.; Yoplait Dairy Crest Ltd. (49%); The English Butter Marketing Company Ltd. (50%).

Principal Divisions

Consumer Foods; Food Services.

Principal Competitors

Groupe Danone; Express Dairies; Northern Foods plc; Unigate plc.

Further Reading

''Dairy Crest Joint Venture Trebles in Size with Pounds 66m Acquisition,'' *Independent*, February 6, 1998, p. 24.

Grimon, Magnus, ''Dairy Crest 'on Track for 10% Earnings Growth','' *Independent*, June 4, 1997, p. 26.

Mathieson, Clive, ''Dairy Crest Sees Growth in Sales of Key Brands,'' *Times* (London), November 12, 1999.

''Pastures New for Dairy Crest,'' *Daily Telegraph*, November 11, 1998, p. 39.

Reece, Damian, ''Fat Cats Get the Cream,'' *Sunday Telegraph*, August 15, 1999.

—M.L. Cohen

Daktronics, Inc.

331 32nd Avenue
Brookings, South Dakota 57006
U.S.A.
Telephone: (605) 697-4300
Fax: (605) 697-4700
Web site: http://www.daktronics.com

Public Company
Incorporated: 1968
Employees: 638
Sales: $95.9 million (1999)
Stock Exchanges: NASDAQ
Ticker Symbol: DAKT
NAIC: 339950 Scoreboards Manufacturing

Daktronics, Inc. is one of the world's largest suppliers of electronic scoreboards, computer programmable display systems, and large video displays for sport, business, and government applications. Its primary product groups are made up of Sports Products, Large Matrix Products, and Business Products. Product displays include standard scoreboards, timing and judging equipment, commercial information displays, custom scoreboards, voting systems, and traffic/transportation displays. Typically, Daktronics sells standard scoreboards to high schools as sports scoreboards and message centers. Timing and judging equipment is sold to high schools, colleges, swim clubs, YMCAs, and other health/sports organizations. The commercial information displays are sold to all types of businesses for indoor and outdoor advertising through sign companies. The custom scoreboards are sold to colleges, arenas, auditoriums, and pro sports facilities. The voting systems are used by state legislatures to record votes and display information to members. The traffic/transportation systems are sold to airports and highway departments. The company offers the most complete line of large display products of any single manufacturer, from smaller indoor scoreboards and displays to multimillion-dollar outdoor video display systems. Daktronics' displays communicate with millions of viewers in more than 60 countries worldwide. It is recognized globally as a technical leader with the capabilities to design, manufacture, install, and service complete systems displaying real-time data, graphics, animation, and video. Daktronics sells display systems ranging from small standard scoreboards priced under $1,000, to large complex displays priced in excess of $7 million.

1960s: Revolutionary Technical Advances Support Birth of New Company

Daktronics was founded in 1968 by Dr. Aelred Kurtenbach and Dr. Duane Sander, two professors of electrical engineering at South Dakota State University (SDSU) in Brookings. Kurtenbach received his B.S., M.S., and Ph.D. degrees in Electrical Engineering from South Dakota School of Mines and Technology, the University of Nebraska, and Purdue University, respectively. His experience spanned the fields of communication engineering and control system design, technical services, computer systems, electrical engineering education, and small business management. Cofounder Duane Sander began operating as a director and secretary of the company. He served as the Dean of Engineering at SDSU, where he taught electrical engineering courses and directed biomedical research projects since 1967. The founders utilized the talents of the school's graduates, in 1970 producing and selling their first product, a voting display system for the Utah legislature. The founders sold shares to the public, marketing their offering as an opportunity for people in the community to invest in a new start-up. People in the area recognized the talent coming out of SDSU and responded favorably. Following up on a tip from the university's wrestling coach, they built a small scoreboard for school meets, a project that ultimately catapulted the company into the limelight, when a Daktronics scoreboard was employed at wrestling competitions during the 1976 Olympics.

Daktronics began using the technology developed from voting display systems, expanding production to include large scoreboards and commercial displays. Typical users of commercial displays included banks, shopping centers, auto dealers, hotels, retail stores, advertising companies, and casinos. Attuned to technical innovations of the time, the company incorporated microprocessor-based computers to process information provided by an operator, and to formulate the information for presen-

Company Perspectives:

As a company, we continue our focus on providing the best possible service to our customers. We do this through concentrated attention to market needs, by improving the features of existing products and introducing new products that excite the marketplace, and by providing product and service quality and delivery in a manner that is expected from an industry leader. We continue to improve our after sale service offerings as well, in both the operation and maintenance of the display systems that we have in the field. It was [more than] ten years ago that we made a paradigm shift in our approach to the marketplace. At that time we changed from ''selling products'' to ''serving markets.'' We expect the payoff for that change to continue.

tation on a display. In the late 1970s the company began building computer-programmable information display systems utilizing standard modules or sections in a variety of systems. The use of modular sections allowed Daktronics to offer a broad range of standard as well as custom products. Daktronics' systems were comprised of two principal components, the display and the display controller. The display controller used computer hardware and software to process the information provided from the operator and formulated the information, graphics, or animation to be presented on the display. The display controller then controlled each of the picture elements or ''pixels'' on the display to present the message or image. Data was transferred between the display controller and the displays for both local and remote display sites. Local connections used twisted pair cables, fiber optic cables, infrared links, or radio frequency. Both standard and cellular telephone connections were used to connect remote display locations, connections which were generally purchased from third parties. Prior to the use of computer programmable signage—which either emits or reflects light depending on the specific display technology—the large video display business was dominated by the small cathode ray tube-based product, and the suppliers were generally the same companies that were in the television set business.

World-Class Events: 1970s–80s

Daktronics quickly became an established leader in the niche of computer programmable signs and by 1977 the company had surpassed $1 million in annual sales, forcing it to double the size of its facilities. Daktronics secured a contract to provide nine large scoreboards for the 1980 Winter Olympic Games in Lake Placid. During that period it also provided scoreboards for several large college installations. The company continued to enhance its controller and display technology, acquiring the Glow Cube reflective display technology along with Star Circuits, a manufacturer of printed circuit boards. In the mid-1980s the company installed its first major league scoreboard and provided systems to several other Olympic events as well as the PGA golf tour.

On New Year's Eve, 1984, Daktronics installed its first large Starburst technology display at Caesar's Palace in Las Vegas, and later converted the World famous ''Zipper'' display at Times Square in New York City to Daktronics LED (light emitting diode) technology. In an interview with Sharon Phillips of the *Wall St. Corporate Reporter*, Aelred Kurtenbach stated that ''We are building off the computer industry so there is definite expansion taking place. This is a growth-oriented business that addresses interesting applications.''

Entering the Global Market; Lighting Las Vegas: 1990s

During the 1990s Daktronics initiated a strategic business alliance with Omega Electronics, S.A. of Bienne, Switzerland, a leading timing systems manufacturer and a company of SMH. The two companies planned to utilize each other's complementary core business positions, with Omega distributing Daktronics scoreboards and matrix displays for use in sport applications around the world. In return, Daktronics added Omega Electronics sports timing and photofinish products to its product offering for sale in the United States and Canada. Daktronics was counting on Omega Electronics' established presence and reputation to open up areas of the world that were very difficult and expensive to penetrate. Within months of the alliance, projects for Daktronics scoreboard installations outside of North America included locations in Singapore, Egypt, France, Colombia, Switzerland, Portugal, India, and Scotland.

Another SMH company, Swiss Timing, the largest watchmaker in the world, contracted with Daktronics to provide more than 70 scoreboards for the 1996 Olympics to be held in Atlanta, Georgia. Everything from small, indoor reflective displays to large, outdoor incandescent displays using low-energy lamp/reflector/lens technologies were included in the installations, with the most sophisticated displays located in the Olympic Stadium, site of the opening and closing ceremonies and track and field events. After the Olympics, the stadium and scoreboards were reconfigured for baseball, where the Atlanta Braves began playing in the 1997 season. New service offices were opened in Atlanta, Columbus, and San Antonio, bringing the total number of Scoreboard Sales and Service offices to 11, as plans for further statewide openings were being considered.

Daktronics negotiated a multimillion-dollar contract with Artkraft-Strauss Sign Corporation to provide five large electronic displays and 24 digital clocks for installation in Times Square. Replacing the famous Zipper sign, the new 370-foot-long display used amber LEDs, controlled by the company's proprietary Venus 7000 software. The Venus control system was a Windows-based, large matrix control system that allowed customers to easily display text messages, colorful graphics and animation, statistics and data imported from other programs, out-of-town game scores, live video, and instant replays. Three of the displays were designed to scroll news headlines in 48-inch-high characters, for NASDAQ and NYSE market information. The other two showed additional financial information, still graphics, animation, and video-sourced graphics in 256 different shades of color.

Responding to the growth of the U.S. gaming industry—and due to the gaming industry's large use of programmable displays—the company developed special products for that market, a market of seemingly unlimited growth potential. In Las Vegas, new and bigger casinos continued to entice customers.

Key Dates:

1968: Daktronics incorporates.
1969: Company completes its first stock offering.
1976: Daktronics scoreboards are first used in Olympic competition (wrestling).
1984: The company is restructured from a product-driven to a market-driven organization.
1987: Daktronics acquires circuit board manufacturer Star Circuits.
1994: Daktronics stock is traded on the NASDAQ exchange.
1999: Daktronics sets record for annual orders with more than $100 million booked.

In response to that growth, the company consolidated its marketing efforts to casinos to take advantage of contacts and experience with electric sign companies. In addition to gaming growth in the Las Vegas area, Daktronics provided color displays to several riverboat and Native American casinos in other areas, and digital jackpot displays on billboards for the Oregon lottery. At dog and horse racetracks Daktronics' products were utilized to display odds, winners, track conditions, and other information.

Despite sales growth in 1996, profits dropped from those of fiscal 1995, attributed to a $900,000 projected cost overrun on a contract to supply variable message signs to the New Jersey Department of Transportation and competitive conditions in other market segments. Company executives countered the loss by initiating a strategy to focus on product improvement and to slow down the growth pace. They planned to continue expanding sales and profits from standard products and to limit the increase of selling, general, and administrative costs, and to concentrate on returning to a profitable position in its custom technical contracting business. The company introduced a number of new standard products and expanded its manufacturing space to accommodate the final assembly of standard products. Additional sales and service staff were added to support that manufacturing facility.

Daktronics' sport market niches continued to provide some 70 percent of sales in 1997. The company reorganized its Engineering Departments into three product groups: Sports Products (primarily scoreboards and timing equipment); Data Trac/InfoNet (primarily text based displays); and Large Matrix (graphics/animation/video displays). The reorganization was intended to allow the company's technical employees to interact more effectively with the marketplace and to bring more appropriate products to the market in less time. The groups focused on standardizing smaller products and subassemblies that were used in building larger display systems.

Company management remained committed to having the capability to offer a variety of different programmable display technologies for different customers. Many of Daktronics' competitors in the business markets produced only one type of display (lamp, LED, or reflective), limiting their offerings to customers, while Daktronics offered a solution for each unique situation. Management reasserted its desire to develop innovative products and updating existing ones with new features, reducing costs when possible to maintain a competitive edge. Their strategy paid off with improved profit margins—a net income increase in 1998 of 125 percent over the previous year. By May of that year company backlog exceeded $21 million and executives were confident that strong growth would continue. Following the introduction of the ProStar family of RGB (red/green/blue) LED displays, which were enhanced in both resolution and color depth, executives felt confident that the company could compete favorably with industry giants such as Sony, Mitsubishi, Panasonic, and other large screen video display companies.

Daktronics signed a multimillion-dollar contract with SMH to provide scoreboards, matrix displays, and technical support services at the 2000 Summer Olympics in Sydney, Australia. Daktronics had already installed equipment for certain venues at the site, including the International Aquatics Centre and the Sydney Showground. The equipment included more than 50 scoreboards and matrix displays to record scores, times, and other information at 34 different venues.

The company maintained its close relationship with South Dakota State University, attributing much of the company's technical expertise to the institution's policy of ongoing training and education. Some 300 of the university's students were employed at Daktronics in various capacities in 1998. The company reimbursed tuition costs for work-related courses and internal education. According to company sources, many of the company leaders were at one time working at Daktronics as students. Additionally, Daktronics offered a few internships with other regional universities.

James Morgan took over as president and COO of the company in 1999, at a time when the company ranked as one of "The 100 Best Stocks to Own for Under $20," in the book of the same name by Gene Walden. Morgan earned his bachelor's and master's degrees in electrical engineering from SDSU and joined Daktronics in 1970 as a graduate student. Morgan designed the first company scoreboard, the Matside wrestling scoreboard, in 1971. His other accomplishments included leading the design, manufacturing, and installation of the first Daktronics swim timing system, a control system for a municipal water treatment plant, various voting systems, and the first Daktronics outdoor electronic message center.

According to Jonah Keri of *Investor's Business Daily*, "A boom in new stadium construction, a greater focus on fan entertainment and corporations' heightened interest in sponsoring professional, college and high school sports has sent the scoreboard industry through the roof." Daktronics' main rival in the scoreboard market was Trans-Lux Corporation, and it, too, attracted high-profile sports clients, contracting projects such as the Rose Bowl and the San Francisco Giants' Pacific Bell Park, among others. Industry analysts predicted that superior product offerings by both Daktronics and Trans-Lux would enable them to be major contenders, with the other rival companies dropping off.

Principal Subsidiaries

Star Circuits, Inc.

Principal Operating Units

Sports Products; Large Matrix Products; Business Products.

Principal Competitors

Trans-Lux Corporation; Sony Corporation; Mitsubishi Corporation; Display Technologies Inc.

Further Reading

''Daktronics Adopts Rights Plan,'' *Wall Street Journal,* November 25, 1998, p. C12.

''Daktronics, Inc.,'' *First Coverage,* August 31, 1998, p. 3.

Keri, Jonah, ''On Display, Daktronics Scoring Big Profits with Its High-Tech Scoreboards,'' *Investor's Business Daily,* August 31, 1999.

Koenig, Bill, ''Indianapolis Motor Speedway Buys Television Screens,'' *Knight-Ridder/Tribune Business News,* December 16, 1998, p. p0KRB983500BD.

Oakley, Lawrence C., ''Special Situation,'' *Conservative Speculator,* August 1998.

Vrcan, Lori, ''Design a Pool, Keep It Running,'' *School Product News,* June 1983, p. 31.

—Terri Mozzone

D'Arcy Masius Benton & Bowles, Inc.

1675 Broadway
New York, New York 10019-5809
U.S.A.
Telephone: (212) 468-3622
Fax: (212) 468-4385
Web site: http://www.dmbb.com

Private Subsidiary
Incorporated: 1906 as D'Arcy Advertising; 1929 as Benton & Bowles
Employees: 6,000
Gross Billings: $5.8 billion (1998)
NAIC: 541810 Advertising Agencies

D'Arcy Masius Benton & Bowles (DMB&B), Inc., known informally as D'Arcy, was ranked the world's 15th largest advertising agency in 1998 with $5.8 billion in worldwide billings. The agency had 131 offices in 75 countries. It was formed in 1986 by the merger of two pioneering firms in the advertising industry: D'Arcy MacManus Masius, an agency based in the St. Louis area, and Benton & Bowles, a pillar of the New York advertising business. In November 1999 D'Arcy's parent holding company, The MacManus Group, announced it would merge with The Leo Group, parent of Leo Burnett Co., to form the world's fourth largest advertising holding company.

Prospering with Coca-Cola and Anheuser-Busch: 1906–20

The agency that would become DMB&B got its start on August 23, 1906, when William C. D'Arcy opened a six-person advertising firm in St. Louis. After graduating from a St. Louis public high school, D'Arcy took a job selling paint. Ten years later, he moved to the Western Advertising Company, a pioneering St. Louis firm, where he stayed for five years to learn the advertising business. D'Arcy struck out on his own when he saw an opportunity to prosper by promoting a fizzy brown beverage with a two-part name, Coca-Cola.

Coke's ad budget in D'Arcy's first year was only $3,000. D'Arcy had a small stable of other clients that year, including Plover Hams and Bacon, Cascade Whiskey, and Nature's Remedy, an elixir that claimed healing properties. The company earned $1,500 by the end of 1906.

The survival of D'Arcy's fledgling enterprise was guaranteed when Coke upped its ad budget to $25,000 in the firm's second year. Instantly, D'Arcy became an advertising agency with a national presence, placing ads for Coke in publications across the country. This track record helped D'Arcy win its next major account, St. Louis brewer Anheuser-Busch, Inc., in 1914. Anheuser-Busch put the agency to work promoting its products Bevo, a nonalcoholic soft drink, and Malt Nutrine, a premium bottled tonic.

The following year, D'Arcy landed Anheuser-Busch's Budweiser account. Technological innovations led to the use of refrigerated railroad cars and the development of a stabilized brewing formula—two factors that enabled Anheuser-Busch to sell Budweiser across the United States. The brewer therefore needed an advertising agency that could promote its products throughout the country. D'Arcy notched another major account in 1916, when the General Tire Company signed on. The following year, D'Arcy began its marketing research efforts, conducting its first interviews with consumers to determine their attitudes toward various products.

The advent of World War I slowed the U.S. economy, and clients reduced their advertising budgets. D'Arcy, however, survived the war without losing any accounts, despite the fact that wartime prohibition cut into the company's Anheuser-Busch business. By 1919 the ad agency had grown to 30 employees.

Prohibition and Radio: 1920s

In 1920, however, D'Arcy's key Anheuser-Busch account received another crushing blow when the 18th Amendment to the Constitution inaugurated Prohibition, a nationwide peacetime ban on the manufacture, transportation, and sale of alcoholic beverages. The brewer stepped up marketing of its nonalcoholic beverage, Bevo, and turned to sales of other related products, like yeast, to stay in business.

Company Perspectives:

At D'Arcy Masius Benton & Bowles we have a passion for creating brand leaders. It's what drives us and makes us unique. It's the richest part of our heritage and the touchstone for our future.

That same year, D'Arcy set up its research center, which began with the clipping and saving of advertisements from both current major publications and more than 30 years of backfiles. This resource allowed D'Arcy staff to trace the history of various advertising campaigns created for a given product over the course of decades, thereby aiding them in creating their own new advertising.

In 1923 D'Arcy opened its first office outside St. Louis. The Atlanta location served as a liaison with the flourishing Coca-Cola Company. Throughout the 1920s D'Arcy introduced several innovations in the production of print ads and began advertising on a new medium: radio. The first ads to be aired were for Anheuser-Busch on KMOX in St. Louis.

By 1929 D'Arcy's account with General Tire had grown large enough to merit the opening of a special office, and the company's operations expanded to Cleveland for this purpose. During this time, the company also conducted its first major effort at market research, surveying 733 airports to determine demand for Shell aviation fuel.

New Offices, and the End of Prohibition: 1930s

Two years later, D'Arcy began a decade of landmark work for Coca-Cola with a Christmas campaign that included an enduring depiction of Santa Claus. The artwork from this ad, showing Santa with twinkling eyes and a red fur-lined suit, would go on to shape the popular perception of this mythical figure. In addition to the Santa campaign, which ran every winter in an effort to get people to drink Coke even when it was cold out, D'Arcy introduced the Coke slogan, "The Pause That Refreshes," in the 1930s.

As Americans took to the highways, D'Arcy helped Coke develop filling station vending machines and also plastered the land with billboards. The agency would soon become the largest buyer of outdoor advertising space in the United States, pioneering the use of rotating cutouts to further attract attention to its ads.

With the repeal of Prohibition in 1933, D'Arcy's other major account came back to life, heralded by a print ad in every newspaper in the country that proclaimed, "Something More Than Beer Is Back," touting the economic and social advantages of legalized liquor.

Building on its successes with national accounts, D'Arcy undertook a geographical expansion in the 1930s. The company opened a New York office in 1934, a Toronto outpost in 1938, and a Los Angeles branch in 1939. Despite the general economic malaise of the Great Depression, William D'Arcy's enterprise prospered throughout the decade.

World War II, Television, and the Retirement of the Founder: 1940s–50s

The company underwent a much more severe test with the U.S. entry into World War II at the end of 1941. D'Arcy's staff was reduced as its employees joined the military, and almost all of its clients cut back on their advertising budgets as the economy shifted to war materiel production, which severely restricted the manufacture of consumer goods. With the resulting shortages of many products, ads urging people to buy became inappropriate. Instead, D'Arcy and its clients devoted themselves to the promotion of the war effort with ads urging Americans to buy war bonds.

Despite the privations of the war years, D'Arcy expanded further in 1942, opening a wholly owned subsidiary in Mexico City, Publicidad D'Arcy. At the conclusion of the conflict in 1945, the agency underwent another transition when its founder, William D'Arcy, announced his retirement. At the time he stepped down, billings at the company D'Arcy had built topped $21 million.

D'Arcy was replaced at the helm by his deputy and longtime employee, J.F. Oberwinder. During his tenure, D'Arcy began to employ the new medium of television to promote its clients' products. Anheuser-Busch became the sponsor of the "Ken Murray Show," aired over the CBS network on Saturday nights, and in 1955, Donald Woods became the on-air salesman for Budweiser, "The King of Beers."

Coca-Cola got on the television bandwagon when it signed up to sponsor "Kit Carson," a Saturday afternoon cowboy show for children. Four years after the agency's 1951 transfer of Coca-Cola dealings to its New York office, D'Arcy suffered the loss of this flagship account: Coca-Cola switched its business to McCann-Erickson, New York, a competing advertising firm with an international presence.

In the wake of this loss, D'Arcy won several other big clients, including Standard Oil of Indiana, Royal Crown Cola, and car manufacturer Studebaker-Packard. In the mid-1950s the company also opened an office in Chicago. Along with its branches in Detroit, Houston, Dallas, and Havana, Cuba, this gave D'Arcy 12 offices across North America.

An Innovative Ad Agency: 1960s

D'Arcy's use of outdoor billboard advertising expanded greatly during the 1960s, and the company introduced a number of technological innovations to the field. Among D'Arcy's most successful campaigns during this time was the launch of the red and blue Budweiser label as an advertising icon. The company first ran the label as a *Life* magazine ad in 1965. Soon, the demand for products bearing the label had taken off, and it was imprinted everywhere from beach towels to hot air balloons.

By 1966 D'Arcy was taking in $120 million a year, and the company acquired Johnson & Lewis, a San Francisco advertising agency. Revenues remained at that level for the following year but dropped to $110 million in 1968 and fell even further the next year to $102 million. One factor contributing to this slow-down was the account losses suffered by D'Arcy's New York office, which lost its $10 million Royal Crown Cola

Key Dates:

1906: William C. D'Arcy opens an advertising firm in St. Louis.
1914: D'Arcy wins the Anheuser-Busch advertising account.
1923: D'Arcy opens its first office outside St. Louis, in Atlanta, where client Coca-Cola is located.
1934: D'Arcy opens a New York office.
1970: D'Arcy merges with MacManus, John & Adams, Inc., a Detroit-based agency, and becomes D'Arcy-MacManus.
1972: Company merges with British agency Masius, Wynee-Williams and becomes D'Arcy-MacManus & Masius (DM&M).
1986: DM&M merges with New York ad agency Benton & Bowles and becomes D'Arcy Masius Benton & Bowles (DMB&B).
1996: DMB&B acquires N.W. Ayer and Partners and renames its holding company The MacManus Group.
1999: The MacManus Group announces a merger with The Leo Group, parent holding company of Leo Burnett Co.

account in 1969, as well as several other clients whose business totaled $6 million.

Cutbacks, Mergers, New Clients: 1970s

Difficulties continued in 1970, as the Chicago office lost its $7 million McDonald's Corporation fast food account, and the company shuffled members of its top management in an effort to stem the tide of client defections and set profits on the rise. D'Arcy had scaled back its full service offices to eight, and its billing was sliding toward the $100 million level.

In late 1970 D'Arcy merged with MacManus, John & Adams, Inc., an advertising agency headquartered in Detroit. Among the clients of this firm were General Motors and 3M. The plans to merge were disrupted initially by a suit brought by a disgruntled former D'Arcy executive, who charged that he had been fired improperly because he opposed the merger. After the suit was settled out of court, the two agencies combined their operations, consolidating offices in New York, Chicago, and Los Angeles and changing the agency name to D'Arcy-MacManus.

The agency went through a series of additional modifications during the 1970s, beginning with a name change in April 1972 to D'Arcy-MacManus International. Six months later, D'Arcy-MacManus underwent another transformation, merging with a British advertising agency, Masius, Wynne-Williams. This company had been founded in London by an American in the aftermath of World War II, and it had extensive operations in Europe, South Africa, Australia, and New Zealand. The firm then adopted the name D'Arcy-MacManus & Masius, or DM&M. In the following year, DM&M spun off its research arm as a subsidiary, called Media Information Research.

In the early 1970s DM&M began to systematize its marketing methods, developing theories to explain how consumers decided what products to buy. These methods would eventually become "Belief Dynamics," which would lead to the use of target audiences to increase the effectiveness of advertising campaigns.

During the mid-1970s D'Arcy worked for a variety of clients in diverse businesses, including the automobile and restaurant industries and the U.S. Armed Forces. The agency created successful campaigns to encourage enrollment in the U.S. Air Force and also handled advertising for the General Mills Restaurant Group's Red Lobster chain of seafood restaurants. In 1975 the company agreed to refrain from making deceptive claims of fuel economy in its ads for Cadillac's Eldorado model, after it was charged with doing so by the Federal Trade Commission a year earlier. Around the same time, DM&M began producing advertising to promote a new kind of beer, "light" beer, for calorie-conscious consumers.

International Expansion, Merger, and Reorganization: 1980s

DM&M began a push to expand global operations in the late 1970s. The company added offices in Australia, Hong Kong, Kenya, South Africa, Germany, Spain, and Zimbabwe and by 1984 had 46 offices around the world. At that time, it again altered its name slightly, to D'Arcy MacManus Masius, and instituted a new, more centralized corporate structure after it lost Colgate-Palmolive, a $35 million client. The company planned to compete more effectively for international accounts in its new incarnation and aimed to reach revenues of $2.1 billion by 1988.

D'Arcy MacManus Masius took a large step toward that goal in 1986, when it merged with Benton & Bowles, a venerable New York advertising agency. Benton & Bowles had been founded in July 1929 by Chester Bowles and William Benton, who started out with a staff of five. With a stable of General Foods products, including Hellman's mayonnaise, and Certo, a pectin extract for making jellies, the fledgling enterprise rode out the stock market crash of 1929 and the subsequent Depression to become a leading New York ad agency, retaining its affiliation with General Foods for more than five decades and adding such consumer giants as Procter & Gamble.

With the merger of the two privately held firms, then the largest in the advertising industry's history, D'Arcy Masius Benton & Bowles became the world's sixth largest advertising agency. Benton & Bowles brought to the union a portfolio of communications concerns that it had purchased over 15 years, including Medicus Intercon International, a medical communications company; Ted Colangelo & Associates, a corporate communications specialist; Manning, Selvage & Lee, a large public relations firm; and several others.

The merger was followed by staff cutbacks in October 1986, as DMB&B attempted to streamline its operations in response to a sluggish economy. The firm laid off 63 employees in New York and San Francisco, closed its Atlanta office, and began to shed its smaller regional bureaus, including those in Houston and Miami.

As DMB&B's overseas revenues grew, the company's U.S. operations remained static. The agency became known on Madison Avenue as the "bridesmaid agency" for its failure to succeed in competitions for a number of big new clients. Responding to an industry perception that DMB&B lacked creative sparkle, the company undertook a reorganization, putting creative directors in closer contact with account supervisors.

The reconfigured agency's push for new business finally bore fruit after three years, when in 1989 DMB&B snagged two big new clients: a $50 million Maxwell House coffee account from Kraft General Foods Group, and half of the $215 million Burger King fast food franchise job. It followed up these gains by augmenting its creative staff and paying record salaries to attract top executives in an effort to banish once and for all the idea that DMB&B was an unimaginative workplace. In November 1990, however, DMB&B lost the Maxwell House account and was forced to fire 70 employees at its New York office as a result of the drop in expected revenue.

More Expansion and Growth: 1990s

In that same year, the company purchased a 49 percent interest in Sosa, Bromley, Aguilar & Associates, an advertising agency specializing in appeals to the Hispanic population, and further expanded its communications holdings when it bought the Donald E. Whiting Yellow Pages business. In addition, DMB&B undertook significant international advances, buying part of an advertising agency in Malaysia and forming joint ventures in India and Pakistan to augment its network of Southeast Asian operations. Agreements with agencies in Brazil, Argentina, and Colombia added to the company's holdings in Latin America. It also acquired a British firm, Yellowhammer.

In a major move that signified a dramatically changing marketplace, DMB&B opened an office in 1991 in Guangzhou, China, to advertise products for Procter & Gamble, Sharp, and Philips. DMB&B's Asia-Pacific network included agencies in China, Japan, Hong Kong, Korea, Taiwan, the Philippines, Singapore, Australia (Sydney and Melbourne), and New Zealand.

Also in 1991 DMB&B opened agencies in Hungary and Czechoslovakia, building on the move it had made into the Eastern bloc in 1989, when it started DMB&B/Moscow, a joint venture with Promstroy Bank—the second largest bank in what was then the Soviet Union. In 1992, a Warsaw office was opened.

In addition, DMB&B augmented its holdings in the Hispanic and ethnic marketing field, purchasing 49 percent interest in two California firms: Noble & Asociados, a major packaged goods advertising agency, and Moya, Villanueva & Associates, a leading Hispanic public relations company. These new companies, coupled with Sosa, Bromley, Aguilar & Associates, gave DMB&B the strongest Hispanic-related communications capability in North America. The company also bought into a Puerto Rican advertising agency located in San Juan.

CEO Roy Bostock planned to bring the agency's far-flung advertising, public relations, and promotions operations closer together. Ranked 11th in worldwide billings, the agency was still perceived in the industry as "big and boring." Annual billings for 1992 were $4.7 billion, and the agency had 125 offices in 46 countries. Major clients included Budweiser, Cadillac, Burger King, Procter & Gamble's Scope and Pampers, and Kraft General Foods' Cool Whip. Recent new accounts included the GM gold card, Citizen watches in the United States, Hyatt International in the Pacific Rim, and Canon cameras in Germany.

In 1994 DMB&B lost the $100 million Budweiser account after 79 years, when Anheuser-Busch chairman August Busch III decided that the brewer's relationship with the agency had eroded over the years. The account went to DDB Needham Chicago. DDB Needham was already handling Bud Light advertising. In 1994 DMB&B added Blockbuster Entertainment as a client. By 1995 worldwide billings exceeded $6 billion.

From 1994 to 1996 DMB&B lost eight major accounts, including Magnavox, Anheuser-Busch, Kraft General Foods, Whirlpool, Denny's, and Amoco. In 1996 it lost the Blockbuster account. Following the loss of Denny's and Amoco, the agency closed its offices in Chicago and Greenville, South Carolina. The Los Angeles office was reorganized after a merger with Pacific Marketing Group and spun off as Highway One in 1995, but it re-opened in late 1996 with the DMB&B name following confusion on the part of clients over the new name.

Following a series of lost accounts, DMB&B began to set up a new tier of management to oversee the agency's North American operations. Leading the reorganization was the agency's North American CEO, Richard Hopple. U.S. and Canadian operations would be managed as a single unit. Previously the agency's regional offices had operated independently, with inconsistent standards.

Despite its problems in North America, the agency's global strategy continued to pay dividends. It was able to turn a relatively small assignment from Tyco Toys into a $75 million global account. The firm had also invested heavily in emerging markets such as Russia, China, and Latin America.

In 1996 DMB&B acquired N.W. Ayer and Partners, the oldest advertising agency in the United States. DMB&B subsequently changed the name of its holding company from D'Arcy Masius Benton & Bowles Communications Group to The MacManus Group in order to differentiate between the Ayer and DMB&B operations. Roy Bostock, DMB&B's CEO and chairman since 1990, held the titles of chairman and CEO at both The MacManus Group and DMB&B. The MacManus Group became the parent holding company over both Ayer and DMB&B. Ayer's principal offices were in New York, Chicago, and Los Angeles.

In 1997 Arthur Selkowitz, formerly president of DMB&B/North America, succeeded Roy Bostock and chairman and CEO of DMB&B on May 1, 1997. Bostock remained as chairman and CEO of DMB&B's parent holding company, The MacManus Group. John Farrell, formerly group chairman of DMB&B/United Kingdom, succeeded Selkowitz as president of DMB&B/North America.

DMB&B lost several accounts in 1997 due to organizational changes at its advertisers. These included the $70 million Tyco Toys account, after Tyco was acquired by Mattel Inc., the $25 million Baskin-Robbins business, and the $70 million Aleve account, following the brand's sale to Roche.

At the beginning of 1998 DMB&B picked up the advertising account for Ryder TRS, the number two consumer truck rental company, following a five-month agency review. The account was valued at $20 million in billings. Ryder advertising would be handled by DMB&B's Troy, Michigan, office, which also handled advertising for General Motors' Cadillac and Pontiac brands.

In 1998 DMB&B lost its account for SBC Communications, which it had handled through its St. Louis office for 30 years. SBC accounted for about $7.5 million of DMB&B's annual billings. However, the St. Louis office was subsequently awarded SBC's $70 million Pacific Bell business.

In 1998 the agency also lost the account for computer manufacturer Gateway 2000. The loss was attributed to Gateway's newly installed president and chief operating officer. DMB&B expected to handle $50–$70 million worth of business from Gateway. Following its dismissal, DMB&B initiated a rare lawsuit against Gateway to recover $9 million in costs associated with the former client.

Following extended negotiations, advertising giants Leo Burnett Co. and The MacManus Group called off a planned merger of their media operations at the end of 1998. The two holding companies shared some clients, including General Motors and Procter & Gamble, the two largest U.S. advertisers. It was rumored at the time that a full-fledged merger was also discussed.

In 1999 D'Arcy was selected by Molson Breweries of Canada for its $12–$15 million account for its flagship brand, Molson Canadian. The agency's St. Louis and Toronto offices would handle the account. It was D'Arcy's first beer advertising account since the departure of Anheuser-Busch in 1994.

The agency also picked up additional advertising from The Pillsbury Co., including its Progresso Soup, Totino's Pizza, and breakfast brands, accounting for some $60 million in billings. DMB&B's parent, The MacManus Group, also announced plans to shift all of its Procter & Gamble accounts—including Folgers coffee, Puffs tissue, and Hawaiian Punch beverages—from N.W. Ayer to D'Arcy in order to free Ayer to become a more creative agency. The change was part of an ongoing strategy to raise Ayer's creative profile.

With D'Arcy and MediaVest, The MacManus Group's media buying and planning subsidiary, handling Procter & Gamble's Sunny Delight, Coca-Cola decided to take its $50 million Minute Maid account away from D'Arcy and MediaVest and give it to Starcom Worldwide, Chicago.

D'Arcy picked up $65 million worth of billing when Avon Products decided to consolidate its advertising account and move it from Ayer to D'Arcy. An important factor in the move was D'Arcy's ability to support Avon's global vision with its 131 offices in 75 countries. Ayer, by contrast, only had four offices, two in the United States and two abroad. Ayer's entire Avon team moved with the account from Ayer's New York office to D'Arcy's New York office.

In mid-1999 DMB&B announced it would unofficially change its name from DMB&B to D'Arcy, preferring to be called D'Arcy rather than by its initials. At the time D'Arcy was the world's 15th largest advertising agency, with $5.8 billion in worldwide billings. As part of its reorganization, the agency added another layer of management for its newly created Trans-atlantic Region, which included North America, Europe, the Middle East, and Africa. In charge of the new regional group were current North American President John Farrell and Chief Branding Officer Susan Gianinno, who would share the title co-president. The new structure was intended to flatten the agency's hierarchy and encourage independent offices to work together.

New Parent Holding Company: 1999 and Beyond

During 1999 The MacManus Group explored a possible merger with the Interpublic Group of Companies. When nothing resulted, The MacManus Group and The Leo Group, parent of Leo Burnett Co., announced in November 1999 that they would merge to create the world's fourth largest advertising company. MacManus and Leo were the two largest privately held ad agency holding companies. The new company was tentatively titled BDM (for Burnett D'Arcy MacManus). Observers expected the new company would likely go public in 2000 with an estimated market value ranging from $3.6 billion to $5.4 billion. Also taking part in the deal was Tokyo-based Dentsu, which provided cash and took a 20 percent stake in the merged organization. BDM would have an estimated gross income of $1.8 billion based on 1998 figures. In the new organization, which would be headquartered in Chicago, Roy Bostock would become chairman, while Roger Haupt, CEO of The Leo Group, would become CEO.

With the change in ownership, D'Arcy, N.W. Ayer, Leo Burnett Co., and other agency brands were expected to continue. Some of the agencies falling under the DMB umbrella would have client conflicts, which could result in lost business. For example, Burnett handled advertising for Delta Air Lines, while Ayer had the Continental Airlines account and D'Arcy handled Trans World Airlines. It was up to the individual agencies within the DMB family of agencies to keep those accounts separate but equal.

Principal Competitors

Interpublic Group of Companies; True North Communications Inc.; BBDO Worldwide Inc.; Grey Advertising Inc.

Further Reading

"Ad Agencies Leo Burnett and the MacManus Group Said Last Week That They Have Abandoned Plans to Merge Their Worldwide Operations," *Broadcasting & Cable,* November 23, 1998, p. 72.

Between Us: D'Arcy-MacManus & Masius/St. Louis Newsletter, Seventy-Fifth Anniversary Edition, St. Louis: D'Arcy-MacManus & Masius, 1981.

Between Us: DMB&B Anheuser-Busch, Inc., Celebrating 75 Years of Partnership, St. Louis: D'Arcy Masius Benton & Bowles, October 1990.

"Chairman at D.M.B.&B.," *New York Times,* June 29, 1990, p. C5.

Chase, Dennis, and Howard Sharman, "DMM Mulls All Options for '88 Goal," *Advertising Age,* February 27, 1984.

''Coca-Cola Moves Minute Maid to Starcom,'' *Advertising Age,* June 7, 1999, p. 1.

Comiteau, Jennifer, ''AT&T Account and N.W. Ayer Find New Homes,'' *Adweek Eastern Edition,* June 24, 1996, p. 5.

——, ''DMB&B Offices Face Sharper Oversight,'' *Adweek Eastern Edition,* January 1, 1996, p. 2.

——, ''Mattel Axes DMB&B,'' *Adweek Eastern Edition,* July 21, 1997, p. 2.

''D'Arcy Advertising and MacManus-John Planning to Merge with Intermarco NV,'' *Wall Street Journal,* November 25, 1970.

''D'Arcy Masius Benton & Bowles Winning More Business a Priority,'' *Advertising Age,* March 30, 1998, p. S16.

Desloge, Rick, ''D'Arcy Brews Ad Campaign for Molson,'' *St. Louis Business Journal,* September 27, 1999, p. 5A.

——, ''Scaled-Down D'Arcy Changes Everything,'' *St. Louis Business Journal,* March 24, 1997, p. 32A.

——, ''SBC Hangs up on D'Arcy,'' *St. Louis Business Journal,* July 13, 1998, p. 1.

''DMB&B Out of Gas in Chicago,'' *Adweek Eastern Edition,* December 4, 1995, p. 38.

Elliott, Stuart, ''Are Emulation and Envy at Work As D.M.B.&B. Takes the Name of a Leader from Its Past?'' *New York Times,* July 17, 1996, p. C5.

Emmrich, Stuart, ''D'Arcy Revamps Agency Image,'' *Advertising Age,* January 16, 1984.

Farrell, Greg, and Jennifer Comiteau, ''Wake up Call,'' *Adweek Eastern Edition,* March 4, 1996, p. 9.

Gazdik, Tanya, ''Ryder Taps DMB&B,'' *Adweek Eastern Edition,* January 5, 1998, p. 6.

Grant, Don, ''D'Arcy Shifts Raidt, Reassigns Other Top Execs,'' *Advertising Age,* March 30, 1970.

Grover, Stephen, ''Benton & Bowles and D'Arcy Agree to Merge,'' *Wall Street Journal,* June 24, 1986.

''Interpublic, MacManus Rumored in Merger Talks,'' *Advertising Age,* March 29, 1999, p. 1.

Kirk, Jim, ''Busch Whacked! Why DMB&B Lost Budweiser,'' *Adweek Eastern Edition,* November 21, 1994, p. 2.

Konrad, Walecia, ''The 'Bridesmaid' Ad Agency Finally Catches the Bouquet,'' *Business Week,* June 12, 1989.

Lazarus, George, ''Chicago's Burnett, New York's MacManus to Create Advertising Superpower,'' *Knight-Ridder/Tribune Business News,* November 2, 1999.

——, ''Chicago Tribune Marketing Column,'' *Knight-Ridder/Tribune Business News,* November 3, 1999.

Lucas, Sloane, ''Gateway Fires DMB&B from $50–$70 Mil. Biz,'' *Adweek Eastern Edition,* March 23, 1998, p. 3.

Martin, Ellen Rooney, and Elefthenia Parpis, ''Ayer Chicago Not for Sale,'' *Adweek Eastern Edition,* July 29, 1996, p. 2.

McCarthy, Michael, ''MacManus Unravels Agency,'' *Adweek Eastern Edition,* November 4, 1996, p. 2.

——, ''World View,'' *Adweek Eastern Edition,* July 19, 1993, p. 21.

Morris, Lindsay, ''DMB&B Decides It's Happier Being D'Arcy,'' *Advertising Age,* June 14, 1999, p. 3.

Petrecca, Laura, ''DMB&B Sues Former Client Gateway for $9 Mil.,'' *Advertising Age,* June 8, 1998, p. 3.

——, ''MacManus' P&G Plan Would Free up Ayer,'' *Advertising Age,* February 15, 1999, p. 10.

Petrecca, Laura, and Hilary Chura, ''Big Players,'' *Advertising Age,* November 8, 1999, p. 3.

''Pillsbury Unveils Agency Changes,'' *Nation's Restaurant News,* March 8, 1999, p. 54.

Ross, Chuck, ''More Than Media Deal Died in Burnett, MacManus Flop,'' *Advertising Age,* November 23, 1998, p. 4.

Sampey, Kathleen, ''Ayer's Avon to D'Arcy,'' *Adweek Eastern Edition,* June 28, 1999, p. 4.

——, ''DMB&B Restructures Itself Along Global Lines,'' *Adweek Eastern Edition,* June 14, 1999, p. 7.

''Top Executive Changes at DMB&B,'' *Adweek Eastern Edition,* February 10, 1997, p. 68.

—Elizabeth Rourke
—updated by David P. Bianco

Datek Online Holdings Corp.

100 Wood Avenue South
Iselin, New Jersey 08830-2716
U.S.A.
Telephone: (732) 516-8000
Toll Free: (888) 463-2835
Fax: (732) 548-7668
Web site: http://www.datek.com

Private Company
Incorporated: 1978 as Datek Securities Corp.
Employees: 250
Sales: $75 million (1998 est.)
NAIC: 52312 Securities Brokerage; 52232 Financial Transactions Processing, Reserve, and Clearing House Activities; 541512 Computer Systems Design Services; 551112 Offices of Other Holding Companies

Datek Online Holdings Corp. is the holding company for Datek Online Brokerage Services Corp., one of the nation's busiest online brokers, which is known for low rates and speed of execution. Its other subsidiaries include a clearinghouse for trades and a developer and marketer of software for brokerage and trading firms, while an affiliate has created an electronic communications network for the same purpose. Throughout the 1990s the company was the subject of repeated regulatory and criminal investigations resulting from its trading practices. In an effort to shed its unsavory reputation and prepare the way for an expected initial public offering, in the late 1990s the firm sold its day trading unit and secured the resignation of its chairman and chief executive officer, Jeffrey A. Citron, who, however, remained its chief stockholder.

Brokerage House and Nascent Trading Operation: 1970–90

Datek Securities was founded in 1970 by Aaron Elbogen and George Weinberger, who opened a small office in Brooklyn to sell stocks and underwrite minor issues. By 1978, when the company incorporated, it had moved its quarters to Iselin, New Jersey. In 1975 and 1982 the company was censured and fined for technical rule violations by the National Association of Securities Dealers (NASD), a self-regulatory group established for trading stocks on the over-the-counter (OTC) market.

Datek established a trading operation in 1987 in New York City's financial district headed by Sheldon Maschler, an aggressive and abrasive broker who had been associated with Robert E. Brennan, a promoter of penny stocks who was eventually barred from the brokerage industry. (Brennan was later charged by the state of New Jersey with using Datek as an intermediary in the manipulation of the prices of four stocks that several brokerage firms controlled by Brennan were trading among themselves.) One of Maschler's first hires was Citron, the 17-year-old son of a friend, who started as a clerk. He was soon joined by Joshua Levine, a high-school dropout billed as a programming genius.

In 1989 Levine and Citron began to investigate faster, cheaper means of buying and selling stocks. Working in the basement of Maschler's Staten Island home, where Datek moved its four-man trading operation in 1990, Levine and Citron created Watcher, a software program that allowed day traders—so-called because most of their transactions were intended to be completed within a single day—to monitor more than one computer screen at a time and exploit the Small Order Execution System (SOES), an electronic system established by NASD to facilitate trading of OTC stocks by small investors. Watcher allowed Datek to take advantage of a weakness in the system—relatively slow updating of price quotes—in order to make money by taking a position on the margin.

Day-Trading Powerhouse: 1991–98

By 1991 Citron, by his own account, had earned $1 million. Datek earned about $2 million that year from its trading operation. The company was censured and fined by NASD in July 1988 and January 1991 for violations of fair-practice rules. Datek and Maschler were fined $10,000 and $50,000, respectively, in August 1991, and were suspended from using the SOES systems for ten and 35 days, respectively, for abusing the system. In August 1992 NASD suspended Datek and Maschler

Key Dates:

1970: Founded as Datek Securities Corp., a small Brooklyn broker.
1987: Datek opens a trading operation in lower Manhattan.
1995: Sophisticated software enables Datek to earn $75 million.
1996: Datek opens a unit for Internet retail trades.
1998: The company is reorganized and sells its day trading unit.
1999: Datek Online is the fourth largest Internet broker.

from the OTC market for three months for misuse of the system. The organization charged that Maschler had, in late 1991, executed large orders of a security by bundling them into smaller orders, thereby violating the regulation that the system was to be used only for the individual investment decisions of small investors.

In 1993 Maschler was censured by a NASD committee for "profane and indecorous language." A NASD executive conceded, in a May 24, 1993 *Wall Street Journal* article, that Wall Street traders "don't necessarily speak the queen's English" but added that Maschler's language "transcended anything that could be remotely considered proper even in those circles." The committee fined Datek and Maschler $5,000 each and suspended Maschler for one business day. Another NASD complaint against Maschler was overturned by the Securities and Exchange Commission (SEC), which ruled that the panel was biased against him.

Datek earned $3.8 million from its trading operation in 1992. Citron and Levine left the company that year in order to form an array of enterprises intended to serve Datek with new technologies. In 1993 Citron also purchased a brokerage firm that operated from Datek's offices and established another brokerage firm, also headquartered in Datek's offices, that he subsequently sold to Levine. Both also were partners with Maschler, who was supervising about 40 traders huddled in front of computer screens. By the end of 1996 Datek had 500 traders, many of them freshly out of Ivy League schools but already making as much as $750,000 a year. They were employing the SOES system for large trades, buying stocks and then selling them again within seconds.

Datek earned more than $75 million in 1995 and nearly $95 million on revenues of about $190 million in 1996—or about 50 cents on the dollar. While rivals continued to call Datek a "rogue trader" and "SOES bandit," they were imitating the firm's own practices by this time. They, as well as Datek, were using software programs, such as Watcher and Monster Key, developed by Citron and Levine. The two also developed Island ECN, which in 1997 became one of four electronic communications networks authorized by the SEC to handle quotes for the NASDAQ's more than 5,000 stocks (and which in July 1998 was accounting for about 15 percent of all NASDAQ trades).

In 1996 Citron and Levine (and Maschler, according to one account; Peter Stern, according to another) had formed Smith Wall Associates to develop and license trading software. Maschler, who left Datek in 1996, was fined $675,000 and suspended from trading for one year in December of that year. Citron was fined $20,000 and suspended for 20 days in 1996.

Still unresolved, in 1998, were other charges against Datek. The SEC had filed a civil suit charging that five persons, including Maschler as a Datek executive, had collaborated in 1993 to sell unregistered shares of stock to a fictitious foreign investor, with the proceeds placed in offshore accounts. The SEC was seeking the return of $6.5 million from this scheme. Datek itself was sued in 1997 by a petroleum company that contended the securities firm had collaborated with six foreign investors to manipulate its stock.

By 1997 Datek's profits from day trading were waning due to new NASD rules and also because so many other firms had either licensed or imitated the Citron-Levine software programs. The company was now placing its hopes for the future on Datek Online, the Internet retail brokerage operation it established in 1996. Datek Online became the first brokerage to take advantage of Island's ability to show quotes for all NASDAQ securities, thereby—it told its customers—increasing their chances of having their orders filled at the best price for all these stocks. It also undercut the competition by offering a bargain price of $9.99 per trade. By May 1998 Datek Online's roster of clients had grown eightfold in little more than a year, to 80,000, holding more than $1.5 billion in company accounts. It ranked fifth in volume of daily trades among brokerages engaged in Internet trading. Net income was about $1.5 million in 1998.

Datek Online Holdings: 1998–99

Datek Securities was restructured as Datek Online Holdings in February 1998. Datek Online Brokerage Services was the subsidiary for day trading and retail brokering. Other subsidiaries included Big Think, a software development and marketing support unit, and Datek Software Services. Island ECN remained autonomous, although 85 percent owned by Clearing, an operation to clear trades. Three other segments provided computer services: Datek Online Network Operations, Datek Online Management, and Datek's day trading unit, whose chief principals were Citron (the largest shareholder), Levine, Maschler, Elbogen, and Stern. In an apparent effort to distance the trading operation from the new company, this unit was sold a month later to Heartland Securities Corp., a money management firm headquartered in the same Iselin, New Jersey, building as Datek Online Holdings. Heartland's owners—or part-owners—were Elbogen and Erik Maschler, a son of Sheldon Maschler.

In spite of Datek Online Holdings' divestment of its controversial day trading unit, the new company was forced to postpone a planned initial public offering of its stock because of continued probes by the SEC of the divested unit's activities. Moreover, in July Vulcan Ventures Inc., a venture capital fund financed by Paul Allen, a cofounder of Microsoft Corp., canceled plans to invest as much as $100 million in Datek Online Holdings and Island ECN. The SEC, in 1999, found Datek guilty of violating federal securities law 12 times in the spring of 1998 but fined the firm only $50,000.

In May 1999 Vulcan Ventures joined with two other investors, Group Arnault , a French private holding company, and TA Associates Inc., a Boston private investment firm, to offer Datek $300 million in exchange for a minority stake in the company. The latter two put up $195 million in July, but Vulcan decided not to follow through, reportedly partly because of concerns about continuing criminal and regulatory investigations of Datek. TD Waterhouse later backed away from a proposal to take a one-eighth share in Island ECN.

By this time Datek was the fourth largest online broker in the United States, with 253,000 such accounts holding more than $6 billion in customer assets. Datek offered low-cost stock trading and promised to execute these trades in a minute or less but, unlike such full-service brokers as Charles Schwab Corporation, it did not offer research or such investment vehicles as bonds and options. Interviewed by the *Wall Street Journal* for a June 1999 supplement on investing, Citron said, ''At Datek we provide the same off-line services that Merrill Lynch would provide, except we don't do it in a physical location; you have to call us on the phone. But you can call us and get quite a bit of information and quite a bit of help—although we will not tell you or give you advice on what particular items to buy.''

Contrasting Schwab's clients, many of whom he characterized as ''people who really need help in investing,'' Citron went on to say, ''our customers are financially literate. . . . They understand the markets. They know exactly what they want to buy. . . . They require more real-time tools. They require real-time quotes. They require real-time account-balance information, real-time graphing.'' Citron described E*Trade Group, Inc., and Ameritrade Holding Corp. as Datek's chief competitors, rather than full-service firms such as Schwab, FMR Corp., and TD Waterhouse Group Inc.

Because of the continuing concerns about possible prosecution of Datek and its principals, Citron resigned as chairman and chief executive officer of the firm in October 1999. He continued to own about 30 percent of the firm's stock but agreed to surrender all voting and management rights to the company's board of trustees for two years. In a *New York Times* story, Edward J. Nicoll, Datek's former president and Citron's successor, conceded, ''There's no question we want to disassociate ourselves from the past. The company's value has been diminished as a result of the investigations.'' He was hoping to resolve these issues so that Datek could fulfill, perhaps as soon as mid-2000, its plans to convert itself to a public company. Datek also sought a clean bill of health from regulatory authorities because Island ECN was asking the SEC to allow it to form North America's first private for-profit stock exchange.

Principal Subsidiaries

Big Think Corp.; Datek Online Clearing Corp.; Datek Online Management Corp.; Datek Online Network Operations Corp.; Datek Online Software Services Corp.; Datek Online Brokerage Services Corp.

Principal Competitors

Ameritrade Holding Corp.; E*Trade Group, Inc.

Further Reading

Barboza, David, ''Datek's Online Chief Agrees to Step Down,'' *New York Times,* October 7, 1999, pp. C1, C8.

——, ''Golden Boy?'' *New York Times,* May 10, 1998, Sec. 3, pp. 1, 4–5.

——, ''Some Clouds Dim a Star of On-Line Trading,'' *New York Times,* July 8, 1998, pp. D1, D6.

——, ''Vulcan Ventures Withdraws from Planned Investment in Datek,'' *New York Times,* July 22, 1999, pp. C1, C10.

Birger, Jon, ''Bandits No More: Datek Makes Good on Net,'' *Crain's New York Business,* April 28, 1997, p. 16.

Brennan, Robert J., ''NASD Suspends Datek Securities and Top Trader,'' *Wall Street Journal,* August 13, 1992, p. B3.

Buckman, Rebecca, ''Datek's Nicoll Is Struggling to Overcome Firm's History,'' *Wall Street Journal,* October 19, 1999, pp. C1, C21.

Harlan, Christi, ''Wall Street Trader Censured by NASD for Profane Words,'' *Wall Street Journal,* May 24, 1993, p. A5E.

Knight, Jerry, ''Variety of Run-Ins Make Trader a NASDAQ Nemesis,'' *Washington Post,* September 13, 1995, p. H4.

Lohse, Deborah, ''Datek Online Says It Agreed to Sell Day-Trading Unit,'' *Wall Street Journal,* April 1, 1998, p. C22.

Morgenson, Gretchen, ''U.S. Is Said to Investigate Datek Trading,'' *New York Times,* July 23, 1998, pp. C1, C9.

Pettit, Dave, ''Making a Market,'' *Wall Street Journal,* June 14, 1999, pp. R18–R19.

''Suspension by N.A.S.D.,'' *Wall Street Journal,* August 13, 1992, p. D4.

Weisul, Kimberly, ''Datek Exposes Best Bids, Offers on All Stocks,'' *Investment Dealers' Digest,* August 11, 1997, pp. 10–11.

——, ''Datek Online Polishes up for Investors,'' *Investment Dealers' Digest,* November 24, 1997, pp. 60–61.

——, ''Upstart Datek Starts Looking Conventional,'' *Investment Dealers' Digest,* February 9, 1998, p. 13.

Willoughby, Jack, ''Datek's Deliverance?'' *Barron's,* June 7, 1999, p. 46.

—Robert Halasz

Degussa-Hüls

Degussa-Hüls AG

Weissfrauenstrasse 9
D-60311 Frankfurt am Main
Germany
Telephone: (49) 69-218-3165
Fax: (49) 69-218-3218
Web site: http://www.degussa-huels.de/dh/index.htm

Public Subsidiary of Veba A.G.
Incorporated: 1873 as Deutsche Gold-und Silber-Scheideanstalt vormals Roessler and 1953 as Chemische Werke Hüls AG
Employees: 44,892
Sales: $4.99 billion (1998)
Stock Exchanges: Frankfurt Düsseldorf
NAIC: 325211 Plastics Material and Resin Manufacturing; 32551 Paint and Coating Manufacturing; 325412 Pharmaceutical Preparation Manufacturing; 325212 Synthetic Rubber Manufacturing

Degussa-Hüls AG is a specialty chemicals company based in Germany. One of the largest chemical companies in Germany, the company was formed in late 1998 through the merger of Degussa AG and Hüls AG. Degussa-Hüls manufactures a number of chemical and metal products, including the plastic sheet brand Plexiglas. Its products are used to make tires, rubber and plastic goods, animal feed additives, pharmaceuticals, electronics, and paints. Other services offered by Degussa-Hüls include banking, venture capital, and analytical. Veba AG, a German energy company, owns 62.4 percent of Degussa-Hüls.

History of Degussa AG

Degussa's story begins in Frankfurt am Main in the first half of the 19th century. The Free City of Frankfurt, as it was known in those days, built its new mint in 1840 in the immediate vicinity of Degussa's present head office, following a commitment it had accepted in 1837 at the Mint Conference in Munich. Here, the South German states and the Free City of Frankfurt, which together made up the states forming the German Customs Union of the day, had agreed for the first time on a common monetary unit, the florin, and had undertaken to coin certain amounts of the new currency. The director of the mint, Friedrich Ernst Roessler, son of the mint counselor of the grand duchy of Hesse and living in the neighboring town of Darmstadt, at the same time established a precious-metals refinery within the mint at the behest of the city. He took a lease on the refinery and in January 1843 started operations at his own expense. Roessler thus laid the foundation for what was to become Degussa AG.

In addition, Friedrich Ernst Roessler established a chemical engineering laboratory not far from the Frankfurt Mint on the site now occupied by Degussa's head office. Byproducts of the sulfuric acid refinement process, in those days the standard method, were processed there, and silver nitrate for photography and cyanide compounds were produced.

As a consequence of the Austro-Prussian War of 1866, in which Frankfurt lost its political independence, Friedrich Ernst Roessler became a Prussian civil servant and had to discontinue his private refinery business. He was nevertheless able to acquire the now private refinery for his two eldest sons, Hector and Heinrich, both of whom had studied chemistry. They transferred refinery operations to the chemical engineering laboratory, located in a new factory built for the purpose, and continued to run both lines of business under the name Friedrich Roessler Söhne (Friedrich Roessler Sons) as a private company.

By developing an economical form of sulfuric acid refinement, a process which was still common—the electrolytic process was introduced in 1892 and 1895—Friedrich Roessler Söhne was technically well-equipped to take advantage of the creation of the new German Empire in 1871, when the coins of the former independent German states were replaced by the newly introduced mark currency, thus providing a favorable opportunity for extensive minting and refining activities. However, since the securities required by the empire on refinement orders could not be met, the precious-metals refinery Friedrich Roessler Söhne was converted into a joint-stock company, or *Aktiengesellschaft,* in January 1873 in order to enlarge its capital resources. Several banking institutions were behind the founding of the present Degussa, which from then on operated under the name of Deutsche Gold-und Silber-Scheideanstalt vormals Roes-

Company Perspectives:

Degussa-Hüls is a globally active chemicals company with value-oriented management. Our core business is specialist chemicals, which we will consistently expand upon. Besides that, we are today also active in select areas having synergies to chemicals. We are focusing on growing business with a low cyclicity, above average potential for appreciating value and leading competitive positions.

sler (German Gold and Silver Refinery, formally Roessler) for more than a century. Only in 1980 was the acronym and telegram address Degussa, in common use since the 1930s, entered into the trade register with the addition of the term *Aktiengesellschaft* identifying it as a share-issuing company.

Its initial capital amounted to 1.2 million gold marks. Of the 2,000 shares issued, 525 were held by the Roessler family, representing 26 percent of the stock capital. The company's identity as a family business was preserved nevertheless, owing to the appointment of the brothers Hector and Heinrich Roessler to Degussa's first board of directors.

Degussa's first great commercial success came about as a result of its newly developed method of producing bright gold for the fire-resistant embellishment of chinaware and glass, following the completion in 1879 of the large-scale minting contracts for the German Empire. Other ceramic colors were later added to the list of products. Shortly afterward in 1882, Degussa began to produce bright gold in the United States. This led to the foundation of the Roessler & Hasslacher Chemical Company of New York in 1889, with affiliated companies and a plant in Niagara Falls, New York, which gradually took on the entire Degussa production program. As a consequence of World War I, these companies were lost to Degussa after their confiscation as German property. They were acquired in 1930 by E.I. du Pont de Nemours & Company, with which they merged two years later.

After the end of the 19th century Degussa's trade business expanded particularly rapidly. The company acted as sales agent for individual products and product groups manufactured by other chemicals companies, and conventions regulating production and sales were set up in both Germany and Europe. In order to obtain access to new products, the company often participated, even in a minor role, in their production. This business policy enabled Degussa to make considerable profits, with a relatively restricted capital participation, over a considerable number of years.

In 1898, together with the Aluminium Company of London, Degussa founded the Electro-Chemische Fabrik Natrium GmbH in Frankfurt. At Rheinfelden, on the Upper Rhine not far from the Swiss border, the company established a plant to produce sodium using the Castner process. This substance was needed by Degussa for manufacturing cyanide salts. Over the years the Rheinfelden plant, owned exclusively by Degussa from 1918, was the site of many production developments, in particular of active oxygen compounds—peroxocompounds—and the fumed silica Aerosil. Later, catalytic converters for the purification of automobile exhaust emissions were made in Rheinfelden.

In 1905 the Degussa chemist, Otto Liebknecht, developed a process for the production of sodium perborate from a sodium peroxide base. Sodium perborate had already become a highly successful product in a matter of months, with the introduction onto the market of the Henkel company product Persil, the first active detergent, in 1907. Persil at that time consisted of 15 percent sodium perborate produced by Degussa and 85 percent bleaching soda manufactured by Henkel. Degussa's participation in the world's first electrolytic hydrogen peroxide factory at Weissenstein, Carinthia, in Austria, also dates back to this time.

As early as 1905 Degussa had already been involved in the establishment of the Chemische Fabrik Wesseling AG in Wesseling, near Cologne. It thus consolidated its position in cyanide chemistry, now one of its longest-established fields of activity. Expansion continued in the metals division as well. By taking a holding in the G. Siebert platinum smelting works in Hanau, Degussa became active in the production of semi-finished precious metal goods.

Because a policy of international expansion was no longer possible during and immediately after World War I, Degussa strove to acquire domestic production sites. As early as 1919, it accepted an offer from the precious metal refinery, Dr. Richter & Co., in Pforzheim, southwest Germany, to take over this company. Pforzheim would eventually become the main production plant for Degussa's dental products, which would form part of the pharmaceuticals division. Gold alloys for jewelry and dentistry, solders, silver amalgams, and dental equipment were produced here.

An important new field of activity, organic chemistry, was entered into by Degussa in 1930–31 following many years of negotiations concerning the acquisition of the two large German charcoal production companies, the Holzverkohlungs-Industrie AG in the town of Constance and the Verein für Chemische Industrie in Frankfurt, with its numerous plants. Degussa now had access to a wide variety of organic chemical products. The Holzverkohlungs-Industrie AG had already succeeded in modernizing its processes and changing over to new products such as adhesives—Atlas Ago—during the merger negotiations. The company expanded its product range on an even more intensive scale after the merger, moving from methanol to formaldehyde, and from formaldehyde to pentaerythritol and acrolein—which gained great significance in methionine synthesis after World War II, when the amino acid methionine was used to treat widespread malnutrition—and ultimately to the plastic polyoxymethylene, developed jointly with BASF AG.

The company also began acetone production, based on the low-cost raw material alcohol. British Industrial Solvents Ltd. was founded as a joint venture with a partner company, Distillers Co. Ltd., of Edinburgh, in 1928. Based on methods developed by the Holzverkohlungs-Industrie AG, a large-scale plant in Hull was built for the production of acetone, acetaldehyde, acetic acid, and butanol. A process for the manufacture of water-free alcohol, which met with considerable demand as an admixture for fuel, proved a commercial success. Soon many domestic and foreign licenses were using the method at a total of 68 plants, together

Key Dates:

1873: Founding of Deutsche Gold-und Silber-Scheideanstalt vormals Roessler (Degussa) in Frankfurt am Main.
1898: Degussa establishes a chemicals production plant in Rheinfelden.
1919: Degussa acquires Scheideanstalt Dr. Richter & Co. and enters the dental business.
1932: Purchase of carbon blacks plant makes Degussa the second largest producer of carbon blacks in the world.
1938: IG Farbenindustrie, along with partner Bergwerksgesellschaft Hibernia AG, form Chemische Werke Hüls GmbH to produce Buna.
1952: Degussa expands its chemicals operations in Wesseling, and IG Farbenindustrie is forced to disband by the Allies.
1953: Hüls is released from Allied control and allowed to incorporate as Chemische Werke Hüls AG; shareholders include Bayer AG, Kohleverwerungsgesellschaft, and Hibernia.
1970: Degussa builds a chemical plant in Belgium.
1973: Degussa founds a plant in the United States.
1979: Hüls becomes a wholly owned subsidiary of Veba AG.
1980: Degussa becomes known as Degussa AG.
1985: Hüls changes its name to Hüls Aktiengesellschaft, and Hüls America begins operations.
1998: Degussa AG and Hüls AG merge to form Degussa-Hüls AG.

producing over five million hectoliters of absolute alcohol per year. Acetone paved the way for the production of acetone cyanohydrin, and acetone cyanohydrin led to methylmethacrylate (MMA) and polymeric methylmethacrylate (PMMA).

In 1932 Degussa acquired a small flame soot factory in Kalscheuren, near Cologne, which had run into financial difficulties. Degussa's involvement with carbon black can be traced to this date. By 1934 it had already succeeded in producing active gas black CK3 at Kalscheuren. Gas black produced in the United States had been for many years an indispensable product in the tire industry, which used carbon black as a strengthening filler. In the late summer of 1933, the German Ministry for the Economy approached Degussa with the demand that Degussa produce active gas black, based on domestic raw materials, at Kalscheuren. In 1935 Degussa researchers succeeded in developing the so-called gas black production process. This breakthrough yielded a product which could finally compete in the market against so-called channel blacks, which had been dominated by U.S. manufacturers until then. Together with the German tire manufacturers, Degussa founded the Russwerke Dortmund GmbH in 1936 for the production of carbon black using the Degussa CK3 process. Furnace black was later used as a strengthening agent by the tire manufacturing industry.

In addition to metals and chemicals, Degussa had a pharmaceuticals division, which was established in 1933 when Degussa purchased the Chemisch-Pharmazeutische AG Bad Homburg in Frankfurt am Main from its Jewish owners. It was difficult for Jewish-owned companies to operate under Nazi economic restrictions, so the owners offered to sell to Degussa. Shortly before the outbreak of World War II Degussa had developed into a significant group of companies. During World War II, all of Degussa's links with Allied countries were severed. However, Degussa continued its traditional activities within the framework imposed on the German economy by the government's war policies. Its broad production base provided Degussa with a large number of starting points in the initial period of reconstruction after World War II, during which destruction was considerable. In addition to war damage, the dismantling of the hydrogen peroxide plant—virtually the only production site left intact—in Rheinfelden on the Swiss border, the loss of all foreign assets, and of all plants and holdings located in the Soviet-occupied sector of Germany, Degussa also lost a large part of its precious metal stocks. The progress of reconstruction before the 1948 German currency reform was further hindered by forced decartelization measures introduced against Degussa, the investigation of its technical and trade secrets by the Special Services of the occupying powers, and the forced sequestration of Degussa plants located in the French Zone of occupation, including the factories in Constance and Rheinfelden.

The June 1948 German currency reform created the foundation for a new economic beginning. In the same year, Degussa began to rebuild its head office on the original site in Frankfurt. An additional administrative building was erected in Frankfurt in 1953.

A new hydrogen peroxide plant in Rheinfelden, a replacement for the one dismantled, was one of the first construction projects realized in Germany in the early 1950s. Plants for production based on the anthraquinone method were built in the 1960s and 1980s. Production of the fumed silica Aerosil also commenced in Rheinfelden. It had first been produced successfully in 1942 in the course of efforts to manufacture a cheap substitute for carbon black from readily available raw materials such as sand or silicates.

In 1952 Degussa began to build its own hydrogen cyanide factory in the newly established plant at Wesseling, near Cologne, very close to the Chemische Fabrik Wesseling branch; both were referred to jointly as the Wesseling plant. Production was later switched to Degussa's own process based on methane and ammonia. New markets for hydrogen cyanide, produced in Wesseling, emerged along with the discovery of the amino acid methionine and cyanuric chloride. Methionine met with considerable demand as an animal feed additive, improving the quality of protein. Cyanuric chloride was a primary product for herbicides, optical brighteners in textiles and paper, and reactive dyes.

The first plans for an overseas production site after World War II dated back to the early 1950s. Degussa founded the company Bragussa in Brazil and built a plant for production of ceramic colors on a site not far from Sao Paulo. Production began in 1955. The company was later merged with other Brazilian subsidiaries to constitute Degussa S.A., operating in all three Degussa sectors: metals, chemicals, and pharmaceuticals.

As well as building up a worldwide sales network, Degussa focused its attention on research activities that had to be postponed immediately after the war in favor of reconstruction of production facilities. Prior to World War II Degussa's research center was housed at the head office in Frankfurt but had to be evacuated to various sites during the war years and could not be reestablished on its former site owing to insufficient space. Consequently, at the start of the 1960s, a chemicals research center with laboratories and workshops was built on the site of Degussa's subsidiary at Wolfgang, near Hanau. The chemicals research and applications technology facilities, which were also moved to Wolfgang, were constantly being expanded.

Metals research operations were also grouped together directly next to the chemicals research center, and the precious metals refining and metallurgy operations were moved away from the center of Frankfurt in 1972 to take up residence in a new metals plant in Wolfgang.

As Degussa's production capacities in the Federal Republic of Germany were no longer sufficient, a large-scale chemical plant was built in Antwerp, Belgium, around 1970. The first production plants for sodium perborate, Aerosil, hydrogen cyanide acid, and cyanuric chloride started operations in 1970. A few years later, in 1974, the company took the first steps towards the construction of another large-scale chemical plant, this time in the United States, more than 90 years after the establishment of Degussa's first U.S. production plant. The Degussa Corporation U.S. produced silicon tetrachloride, Aerosil, methionine, cyanuric chloride, the herbicide Bladex, hydrogen peroxide, formaldehyde, and hydrogen cyanide at its plant in Mobile, Alabama. Polyoxymethylene was produced jointly with the BASF Corporation.

The United States contained the largest proportion of Degussa's foreign investments. These belonged to the chemical division, which included such products as catalytic converters for automobile exhaust emissions and chemicals, precipitated silicas, the vitamin B nicotinamide and, since 1988, three large-scale carbon black plants. Degussa's activities in the United States also included metals.

Carbon black activities in the 1980s were not only restricted to the United States, where Degussa acquired the carbon black plants of Ashland Oil in Ashland, Kentucky, and grouped them together into a separate company, the Degussa Carbon Black Corporation, a fully owned subsidiary of the Degussa Corporation. Degussa also purchased the European carbon black plants of the Phillips Petroleum Company of Bartlesville, Oklahoma. The carbon black plants in Ambes, France; Botlek in the Netherlands; and Malmö in Sweden became Degussa's property entirely, while Degussa also acquired a 50 percent holding in a carbon black plant in Ravenna, Italy. The company also acquired a 50 percent stake in a carbon black plant in South Africa.

Degussa's pharmaceuticals division also underwent a major expansion in the 1970s and 1980s. A majority holding in the Bielefeld-based Asta Werke AG, which produced anticancer drugs, had been acquired by the end of the 1970s. In 1983, the company became a fully owned Degussa subsidiary. A few years later, in 1987, the entire domestic and foreign pharmaceuticals activities—the Chemiewerk Homburg Branch, Asta Werke AG, and various holdings in Brazil, Italy, Austria, Switzerland, and India—were amalgamated to form Asta Pharma AG, whose headquarters were in Frankfurt. A further important acquisition by the pharmaceuticals division in the same year was the French pharmaceuticals group Sarget S.A. in Mérignac, near Bordeaux, together with several European subsidiaries. The Sarget group's principal products were analgesics, cardiocirculatory compounds, antiseptics, vitamins, and amino acid preparations.

The increasing influence of Japan and the steadily growing economic impact of Southeast Asia prompted Degussa to establish, in addition to its organizational network, its own production sites, and technical application centers in the Pacific Basin region.

In the course of the company's worldwide expansion, Degussa's organization has been streamlined. In addition to disincorporating the pharmaceuticals division and converting it to the Asta Pharma AG, Degussa's oldest area of activities, the metals division, was the target of extensive restructuring measures, including the complete takeover of the high-tech company Leybold AG and the resumption of primary recovery activities after an interlude of almost 100 years.

Degussa continued to strengthen its operations in the 1990s, and revenues reflected the efforts. Sales increased steadily from 1993 to 1998, from DM 6.59 billion to DM 7.39 billion. Significant events during the early 1990s included the acquisition of pharmaceutical company Temmler Group in 1990 and the formation of Cerdec AG in 1993. Cerdec, a subsidiary, was in the ceramic colors segment, which involved such fields as glass, color solids, glazing systems, and mixed phase pigments. Also in 1993 Degussa acquired a 20.4 percent interest in Muro Pharmaceutical, Inc., of the United States. The company upped its stake in Muro three years later by acquiring the remaining shares. In 1994 Degussa formed Qingdao Degussa Chemical Company Ltd., a carbon blacks joint venture with China. A year later the company purchased an interest in Ducera Dental GmbH & Co. KG and consolidated its dental activities at the Hanau-Wolfgang site.

In March 1996 Degussa gained a new CEO: Uwe-Ernst Bufe. Bufe, who had worked at Degussa Corp. in the United States, was viewed by industry analysts as an innovator. Bufe quickly restructured company operations and focused on strengthening core businesses by grouping Degussa's 11 operating units into four core groups: chemicals, health and nutrition, precious metals, and banking. Bufe announced plans to boost revenues of underperforming businesses, such as precious metals, automotive catalysts, and acrylics, and spun off the acrylates business into Agomer GmbH, a separate entity, in April 1997. In 1997 Veba AG acquired a 36.4 percent interest in Degussa for US$1.7 billion, and talk of a merger of Veba-owned Hüls AG and Degussa began to circulate throughout the chemicals industry.

History of Hüls AG

While Hüls was founded in 1938, it owed much to the 1888 invention of tires. Without tires and the consequent demand for rubber, there would have been no synthetic rubber; without synthetic rubber, there would have been no Hüls. The first patent for synthesizing rubber was filed in 1909, but the process was too expensive for commercial exploitation. After the automobile increased the need for tires, experiments began in earnest again. Based on the work of the Nobel prize-winners Carl Bosch, Fritz Haber, and Friedrich Bergius, Buna was created. First made in 1926, Buna was an economical synthetic rubber, based on coal and using sodium as a catalyst.

In the fall of 1935, the first experimental plant for the production of Buna was built by I.G. Farbenindustrie. A year later, the German government issued its second Four Year Plan, in which the importance of Buna production to the country's strength was stressed. On May 9, 1938, Chemische Werke Hüls GmbH was founded specifically for the production of Buna, with a capital stock of 30 million marks. I.G. Farbenindustrie owned 74 percent and Bergwerksgesellschaft Hibernia AG owned 26 percent of the new company. The first managing directors were Otto Ambros and Friedrich Bruning, and on the board were Dr. Fritz ter Meer and Wilhelm Tengenmann. All four men were representatives of the shareholding companies.

Construction of new factories was difficult during wartime, yet labor was obtained because the Nazis urgently needed Buna. The factory was built very quickly and in August 1940 production began. The annual capacity for production was 18,000 tons of Buna. The capital stock was immediately increased to 80 million marks. The company also produced chlorine, antifreeze, and other chemicals. In 1941 the production of Buna was increased to 40,000 tons annually. From this time, the chemists at Hüls began to work on the production of solvents, softening agents, and resins. Production was increased to 50,000 tons in 1942 and capital was raised to 120 million.

It was not until 1943 that the war began to affect Hüls negatively. The company had great difficulty in obtaining raw materials and surviving bomb attacks. The worst was a heavy daylight air raid on June 11, 1943, when 1,560 bombs were dropped on Hüls factories. The works were devastated, 186 people were killed, and 752 were wounded. Production stopped for three months. In spite of heavier bombing of the hydrogenation plants to stop the supply of raw materials, by 1944 the Hüls works reached maximum production capacity again, though they were still a main target of the bomb attacks. On March 29, 1945 a special unit of the German Army appeared with orders to blow up all of Hüls. It was Hitler's command that "the enemy should find nothing." The unit was persuaded to disobey these orders by Dr. Paul Baumann. Two days later, American troops marched into the factories.

Paul Baumann was one of the chemists who had worked on the development of Buna. He fought in World War I, then studied in Heidelberg with the Nobel prize-winner Philipp Lenard. Baumann received his doctorate in 1923, and first worked for I.G. Farbenindustrie, spending time at their offices in Baton Rouge, Louisiana. At Hüls he was quickly promoted to production manager. In 1945, when the British troops replaced those of the Americans, Baumann was made manager of works, then chairman of the board.

In 1945 the British, who were paying high prices for natural rubber at home, allowed the resumption of the production of Buna. At their orders, the company's name changed to Chemische Werke Hüls. The Potsdam agreement then forbade the production of Buna in Germany, and in order to survive the company had to change its products immediately. Since the country was short of everything after the war, Hüls had no problem coming up with new products, but there were other problems, chiefly with the customers. Hüls sold a preparation that was meant to be used against scabies. When it was discovered that this was being used to make illegal liquor, the product had to be withdrawn. A lice-killer also had to be withdrawn when it was learned that people were using it as a substitute for petrol. The list of other products Hüls was permitted to make in 1945 included softening agents, artificial resins, detergents, gases, colorings, antifreeze, and pharmaceuticals. Its main product, after the erratically produced Buna, was acetic acid.

In November 1945 the entire company was taken over by the Allied authorities and put under a financial control office. The "de-Nazification" included the dismissal of Hans Gunther and Ulrich Hoffman. Other dismissals were planned but, as they would have meant the administrative collapse of the company, were not effected. The I.G. Farbenindustrie sales offices, Hüls's main outlets, were closed by the Allies. Hüls then cooperated with other companies on sales, but as this was regarded as joint operations, it too was stopped. All production of Buna was formally stopped by the British in 1948, partly as English, French, and Dutch colonies were experiencing a natural rubber boom, but also because the production of synthetic rubber was seen as potentially useful in the rebuilding of a German military effort. Hüls was faced with large numbers of employees and not enough work for them. The company began to produce vinyl chloride, propylene oxide, emulsifiers, and the polyvinyl chloride called Vestolit, but even so in 1949, many employees were made redundant, and plant works capable of producing 900 tons had to be dismantled.

In 1948 Hüls rather cleverly created "produkt 1973," a synthetic rubber made by the same process as that for Buna but with a few steps reversed. (It was also called "umgekehrt Buna," literally "Backward Buna.") This was to be used in linoleum. Both the forward and the backward Buna required butadien for production. In 1949 the Allied governments banned all butadien. Hüls protested, but, as it was one of the few companies to escape the total disbanding of its works by the allies, it restrained its protests. Generally, Hüls was better treated than other companies after the war, in part because of its ability to change its production to acceptable areas, and of the ability of Paul Baumann to get on so peaceably with the Allies. Additionally, Hüls was a major producer of fertilizers, which were considered vital to the agricultural economy.

In 1950, when the rest of the world dreaded that the Korean War might become World War III, Hüls was pleased to record that turnover increased by 50.4 percent. Colonial unrest cut off the supply of natural rubber to the Allies, and in 1951 the production of some 6,000 tons of Buna was permitted. This was on the condition that all coal export agreements were honored first. The mines of Germany could not produce enough coal, so Hüls was forced to import coal from the United States. Not enjoying this arrangement, Hüls built its own small, temporary mine until the German mines could increase production.

The I.G. Farbenindustrie was disbanded by the Allies in Frankfurt in 1952. On December 19, 1953 Hüls was released from Allied control and converted to a joint stock company with a capital stock of DM 120 million. The following year, the company invested DM 85 million to expand plant production capacity. New products included Vestolen, a high-density polyethylene, and Vestopal, a polyester resin.

For some time, the production of Buna had ceased to be profitable, and the company had been working on ways to improve and modernize the antiquated production procedures. A new plant was proposed and a new company, Bunawerke Hüls GmbH, was formed in 1955. The shareholders were Hüls, with 50 percent, and its old partners from I.G. Farbenindustrie, in the guise of the company's three successors. Dr. Baumann was the managing director. In a very short time, Bunawerke was the largest producer of synthetic rubber in Europe.

Hüls grew apace. It built Power Station II, the first coal power station to operate on supercritical steam. In 1956 Quimica Industrial Huels do Brasil Ltda. was formed in Brazil. Plants were either converted or constructed to produce reinforcing agents, phthalic anhydride, and more acetylene. In 1961 the capital stock was increased to DM 120 million and Faserwerke Hüls GmbH was founded, with a capital of DM 33.6 million, to produce synthetic fibers.

In 1959, a quarter of a century after Hüls had begun manufacturing heavy detergents, it was discovered that they were major polluters of the environment. A law was passed in 1961 requiring that all detergents be reducible by 80 percent by the existing sewage plants. Three years later Hüls produced Marlon, a biodegradable surfactant. The whole episode was a minor setback in the phenomenal growth of Hüls, which continued to form new companies, introduce new chemicals, and establish new partnerships until, in 1971, its capital reached DM 310 million.

Veba and Bayer had long been owners of equal amounts of Hüls stock. This led to squabbles. In 1978, Veba bought out Bayer, increasing its shareholding of Hüls to 87.6 percent, and thus acquiring control. A reorganization was arranged, transferring all of Veba-Chemie AG to Hüls. Throughout the early 1980s, Hüls built plants all over Germany for a variety of functions, from sludge burning to the production of n-but-l-ene and powdered rubber. Acquisitions were a focus for Hüls in the late 1970s and 1980s as well, and in 1985 Hüls acquired Nuodex Inc., a colorants manufacturer located in Piscataway, New Jersey. This purchase marked the foundation of Hüls America. Also that year the Chemische Werke Hüls changed its name to Hüls Aktiengesellschaft.

In 1988 Hüls grew larger when the chemical operations of Dynamit Nobel AG were acquired and merged into Hüls. Dynamit Nobel's operations included plants at Rheinfelden, Lülsdorf, and Witten. Dyanamit Nobel's U.S. facilities were combined with Nuodex under the Hüls America name. A year later the company acquired the silicon wafer business of Monsanto Company and joined it with analogous Dynamit Nobel operations under the company name of MEMC Electronic Materials. Hüls boosted its share of Röhm GmbH to a majority stake in 1989 as well. Continuing with its acquisition strategy, Hüls gained a majority interest in Chemische Fabric Stockhausen GmbH, a leading manufacturer of superabsorbents, in 1991. During the course of the acquisition-hungry decade, Hüls also purchased German methacrylates manufacturer Rhm. By 1991 Hüls's sales had doubled since 1978, reaching DM 10 billion.

In 1991 Bunawerke Hüls GmbH was dissolved, with Hüls gaining the Marl operations and Bayer assuming control of the plants in Dormagen and France. The following year Hüls adopted a restructuring strategy that included plans to divest itself of non-core operations. By 1994 the company had pulled out of a number of sectors, including industrial gases, plastics and polyolefins processing, and PVC compounding. Hüls had also sold the Kunstoffwerk Hohn and Faserwerk Bottrop subsidiaries, as well as the plastics operations of Hüls America. Though Hüls progressed with core operations, with several new facilities coming on stream, such as a polypropylene plant at Scholven, an isophorone derivates plant in the United States, and a hydrogen production facility at Marl, the company suffered a loss of DM 671 million in 1993.

In 1993 Hüls gained a new chairman, Erhard Meyer-Galow, who continued with the divestment strategy. Between 1994 and 1996, the company shed businesses with combined annual sales of DM 2.2 billion. It exited chloroparaffin, electrofused product, and rubber production and sold Faserwerk Bottrop GmbH and Deutsche Hefewerke GmbH, among other operations. By 1995 Hüls was again profitable.

As Hüls divested itself of non-core operations, it also attempted to strengthen its core operations. Hüls gained a majority stake in Phenolchemie, a leading phenol producer, in 1994 and established several joint ventures—the leather and fur operations were joined with Ciba Geigy AG's to create TFL Ledertechnik; the lubricant additives operations of Rhm were combined with Rohm and Haas's to form RohMax; and Bayer and Hüls combined their latex operations in order to maximize profitability and strengthen international operations. In 1996 Nalco Chemical Company announced it would sell its superabsorbent chemicals operations to Hüls's Stockhausen subsidiary. The sale included Nalco's plant in Louisiana.

Parent Veba planned to invest DM 9.6 billion in Hüls for the period from 1997 to 2001. The amount, a significant increase over previous investments, accounted for 30 percent of VEBA's total group investments. Veba hoped to expand Hüls's international operations, and Hüls said it would strive to shift its primarily European sales to a more balanced portfolio of 50 percent of sales in Europe, 30 percent in North America, and 20 percent in Asia by 2000. In order to become more international, Hüls began to search for possible acquisitions in the United States. When they were determined to be too expensive, Veba acquired a 36.4 percent interest in Degussa AG, which had strong operations in the United States. Hüls's Meyer-Galow offered a glimpse of the future when he told *Chemical Week* in late 1997 that it was not Veba's plan to keep two chemicals subsidiaries. ''It will be one activity in the future,'' indicated Meyer-Galow.

Late 1990s: Merger Between Degussa AG and Hüls AG

In early 1998 the announcement that Degussa AG and Hüls AG planned to merge was made. About 15 percent of company operations overlapped, which allowed for great growth potential, according to the companies. Both companies had neighboring facilities in Rheinfelden, Germany, Antwerp, Belgium. and Mobile, Alabama, which would be combined for greater production capacity. Proposed vice-CEO Klaus Albrecht announced in *Chemical Market Reporter* in November 1998,

"Degussa and Hüls share many strengths and complement each other perfectly. . . . The merger will lead to a strengthening of our market position in numerous products—in methacrylates, fine chemicals, coating raw materials, silanes and fillers, in particular." Expansion in North America and in Asia were noted as key objectives for Degussa-Hüls.

On December 18, 1998, a Degussa shareholders' meeting was held to vote on the planned merger. A majority 99.98 percent voted in favor of the merger, and on February 1, 1999, the new company was entered in German commercial registers. The merger was dated retroactively to October 1, 1998, which marked the beginning of the company's first fiscal year.

Despite high hopes for Degussa-Hüls, the new company's early performance was disappointing, primarily due to difficult economic conditions in Asia, Russia, and Brazil. For the first quarter ended January 1, 1999, the company reported a ten percent decline in sales. Degussa-Hüls eliminated more than 1,000 jobs between October 1998 and March 1999 to streamline operations, but profits continued to fall. For the first half of the fiscal year, the company's sales reached EUR 5.8 billion, an 11 percent decline from the same period a year earlier.

To boost operations, Degussa-Hüls announced it would spin off its precious metals division, automotive catalysts segment, and the Cerdec ceramic colors business into a new subsidiary, to be operational in January 2000. Degussa-Hüls acquired the remaining 30 percent interest in Cerdec AG Keramische Farben from Ciba Specialty Chemicals AG in March 1999 to become the sole shareholder. The new subsidiary, with plants in Europe, North and South America, Asia, and South Africa, would concentrate on performance ceramics, future-oriented electronics, automotive engineering, and metals chemistry. Degussa-Hüls also combined Röhm GmbH and Agomer GmbH, two methacrylate chemicals operations, in March with the intention of improving its market position in the methacrylate market.

Degussa-Hüls noticed improvement in some sectors in the third quarter of its first fiscal year, but earnings remained low compared to year-earlier figures. For the first nine months of Degussa-Hüls's first fiscal year, overall sales fell ten percent. Undaunted, the company continued to focus on improving performance. In June Degussa-Hüls's subsidiary Stockhausen GmbH & Co. KG formed a joint venture with Röhm and Haas Company of Philadelphia. The joint venture would produce acrylic acid at two sites: one in Marl, Germany, and the other in Deer Park, Texas. Another subsidiary, ASTA Medica AG, sold affiliate Temmler Pharma GmbH, which manufactured medicines that treated diseases of the central nervous system, pain, and gastrointestinal disorders.

In September 1999 the company announced plans to invest DM 500 million ($260 million) in its silanes operations. In addition to expanding organosilanes plants at Mobile, Alabama, and Antwerp, Belgium, Degussa-Hüls planned to build a second plant at Antwerp, to be operational in 2002. Also in September Degussa-Hüls indicated it would sell its stakes in the joint ventures Ultraform GmbH and Ultraform Company to BASF Aktiengesellschaft. Both companies made thermoplastic polyoxymethylene, which was used in automotive components and mechanical and electrical engineering.

As Degussa-Hüls approached the 21st century, the company was still in its infancy but confronted many challenges and changes. In October 1999 majority shareholder Veba A.G. announced plans to merge with competitor Viag AG, a Germany company with operations in telecommunications, energy, and manufacturing. The estimated $14.2 billion merger was motivated by consolidation in the energy industry in Europe. The resultant company, however, would focus on chemicals as a core operation. The deal would add Viag's subsidiary SKW Trostberg to the Degussa-Hüls group to create the largest German specialty chemicals corporation. Degussa-Hüls looked toward the proposed merger with anticipation; the company, with sagging profits, was under pressure to improve performance and bring profits up to expectation levels. Degussa-Hüls believed the merger would provide the company with market advantages and opportunities for growth.

Principal Subsidiaries

Degussa Bank GmbH; Infracor GmbH; CREAVIS GmbH; ASTA Medica AG; Stockhausen GmbH & Co. KG; Röhm GmbH; Vestolit GmbH; OXENO Olefinchemie GmbH; Phenolchemie GmbH & Co. KG; Cerdec AG.

Principal Divisions

Health and Nutrition; Specialty Products; Polymers and Intermediates; Performance Materials.

Principal Competitors

BASF Aktiengesellschaft; Bayer AG; Hoechst AG.

Further Reading

Alperowicz, Natasha, "Degussa's Turning Point: New CEO, Veba Stake Spell Change," *Chemical Week*, September 17, 1997, p. 26.

——, "Huls Takes on a New Shape; Seeking Integration with Degussa," *Chemical Week*, December 24, 1997, p. 12.

"Degussa and Hills Finalize Merger Forming a Specialties Powerhouse," *Chemical Market Reporter*, November 2, 1998, p. 8.

"Degussa-Huls Continues Integration; Focuses on Global Product Portfolio," *Chemical Market Reporter*, April 19, 1999, p. 16.

Deutsche Gold- und Silber Scheideanstalt vormals Roessler 1873–1923, Frankfurt am Main: Degussa, 1923.

Dittrich, Gunther, H. Offermanns, and H. Schlosser, "Von der Münzscheiderei zum L-Methionin," *Chet*, June 1977.

Hume, Claudia, "Veba-Viag Merger Creates a Specialties Giant," *Chemical Week*, October 6, 1999, p. 7.

Mayer-Wegelin, Heinz, *Aller Anfang ist schwer: Bilder zur hundertjährigen Geschichte der Degussa*, Frankfurt am Main: Degussa, 1973.

Pinnov, Hermann, *Degussa 1873–1948*, Frankfurt am Main: Degussa, 1948.

Wolf, Mechthild, *It All Began in Frankfurt: Landmarks in the History of Degussa AG*, Frankfurt am Main: Degussa, 1989.

——, "Porträt Heinrich Roessler 1845–1925," *Chemie in unserer Zeit*, June 3, 1986.

——, *Von Frankfurt in die Welt*, Frankfurt am Main: Degussa, 1988.

—Mechthild Wolf
—updated by Mariko Fujinaka

Dr Pepper/Seven Up, Inc.

5301 Legacy Drive
Plano, Texas 75024
U.S.A.
Telephone: (972) 673-7000
Fax: (972) 673-7867
Web sites: http://www.drpepper.com
http://www.7up.com

Wholly Owned Subsidiary of Cadbury Schweppes plc
Incorporated: 1988 as Dr Pepper/Seven Up Companies, Inc.
Employees: 1,200
Sales: $810.3 million (1999)
NAIC: 312111 Soft Drink Manufacturing

Dr Pepper/Seven Up, Inc. (DPSU) is the number three soft drink maker in the world, trailing only the two industry giants: Coca-Cola Company and PepsiCo, Inc. It is also the U.S. leader in noncola soft drinks, with its two flagship brands holding top ten positions among all soft drinks—Dr Pepper at number six and 7 Up at number nine. Wholly owned by U.K. confectionery and drink maker Cadbury Schweppes plc since 1995, DPSU also produces a number of other drink brands, including Welch's, IBC Root Beer and Cream Soda, Canada Dry, Schweppes, A&W, Crush, Sunkist, Squirt, Mott's, Hires, Sundrop, Vernors, and Country Time.

Early Development of Dr Pepper

Dr Pepper, the elder brand of the two flagship brands, was invented in Waco, Texas, at Morrison's Old Corner Drug Store. In 1885 a young pharmacist who worked for Morrison's, Charles C. Alderton, experimented on his own soft drink. He mixed phosphorescent water, fruit juice, sugar, and other ingredients to produce a new soft drink unlike any tasted before. With Morrison's approval, Alderton offered the drink to the store's customers. One of these jokingly called the concoction "Dr. Pepper's drink"—for Dr. Charles Pepper, the disapproving father of a woman Morrison had been courting, suggesting that Pepper might be flattered.

The name and the soft drink, with its tart, yet sweet flavor, became popular locally, and in 1887 Morrison offered beverage chemist Robert S. Lazenby the opportunity to participate in the marketing and development of this new product. After sampling "Dr Pepper's drink," Lazenby agreed to go into partnership with Morrison to produce the beverage at his Circle A Ginger Ale Company, also in Waco. Alderton, the drink's inventor, dissociated himself from Dr Pepper, opting instead to turn his talents to the pharmaceutical trade.

The new product, "Dr Pepper's Phos-Ferrates," was available only in soda fountains until 1891, when the manufacturers began bottling the beverage. With Lazenby handling the business end, Dr Pepper became a top seller in and around Texas. Expansion was inevitable, and Lazenby sought a marketing opportunity to introduce Dr Pepper to the world.

The ideal forum was the 1904 World's Fair, held in St. Louis. Lazenby and his son-in-law, J.B. O'Hara, demonstrated their product there, providing samples of Dr Pepper to some of the approximately 20 million World's Fair visitors. Incidentally, the 1904 exhibition also showcased other innovations, including the ice-cream cone and buns for hot dogs and hamburgers. Dr Pepper's success encouraged Lazenby and Morrison, who founded the Artesian Manufacturing and Bottling Company, which would eventually be renamed the Dr Pepper Company; by 1923, headquarters were moved from Waco to Dallas, Texas.

Early Development of 7 Up

Around 1920, while Dr Pepper was growing in favor, C.L. Grigg, an advertising veteran of 30 years, had formed the Howdy Company in St. Louis, Missouri. The company was named for the Howdy orange-flavored soft drink Grigg had developed, but the CEO had other ideas—specifically, to invent a new flavor of beverage. For two years, Grigg tested different combinations of lemon and other flavors. By the mid-1920s he had settled on a distinctive lemon-lime formula and in 1929 the Howdy Company introduced the soda to the general public.

Grigg and company were confident of their invention's appeal. As an early sales bulletin noted, consumers "are tired of

Company Perspectives:

Our CORE PURPOSE is: To maximize shareholder value by creating uniquely refreshing beverage experiences and a business environment that marries our talents and aspirations with our shareholders' objective to achieve superior returns and our customers' desires for high quality products and service.

the insipid flavors, and the aftertaste of the heavy synthetic flavors is more objectionable. . . . So in *our beverage* we have provided seven natural flavors so blended and in such proportions that, when bottled, it produces a big natural flavor with a real taste that makes people remember it.''

The only thing that might have stood in the way of the drink's early success was its name, ''Bib-Label Lithiated Lemon-Lime Soda.'' Griggs derived the new and much simpler name, 7 Up, from the beverage's ''seven natural flavors.'' The new name first appeared on the bottle later in 1929. The beverage sold well, and the new name made it easy for consumers to remember. In 1936, the Howdy Company became the Seven-Up Company, and by the 1940s its product became the world's third largest selling soft drink.

Marketing Developments: 1930s–80s

Although what distinguished both drinks from the rest of the market was unique flavor, neither beverage was marketed simply as a refreshment. Indeed, both Dr Pepper, whose name still retained the period at this time, and 7 Up were promoted as health drinks in their first decades. In the 1930s, Dr Pepper's famous slogan ''Drink a bite to eat at 10, 2 & 4'' capitalized on the idea that one typically experienced an energy slump during those hours; a serving of Dr. Pepper would presumably provide the energy boost needed to make it through the day. At the same time, 7 Up boasted in ads that it ''energizes . . . sets you up, dispels brain cobwebs and muscular fatigue.''

The fortunes of both companies grew during World War II, with Dr Pepper able to go public in 1946, while the postwar period saw the Baby Boom, which produced an unprecedented number of soft drink consumers. In their marketing efforts, both beverage companies sought to appeal to this lucrative market. Dr Pepper, for instance, became a regular sponsor of the hit teen show ''American Bandstand,'' while 7 Up became noted for its ''uncola'' campaign of the late 1960s, which capitalized on the individualistic tendencies of young people by distancing 7 Up from the cola market. In the 1970s Dr Pepper was marketed through the long-running ''Be a Pepper'' campaign.

Later advertising efforts avoided the so-called ''cola wars'' of the 1980s, focusing instead on what made Dr Pepper and 7 Up different. Dr Pepper ads declared the soft drink was ''just what the Dr ordered,'' while Diet Dr Pepper was ''the taste you've been looking for.'' 7 Up introduced an animated character, ''Spot,'' derived from the its long-used logo, a large 7 with a red spot in the middle, that revitalized the ''uncola'' theme that worked so well in the 1970s. Both companies also spent years testing and introducing new products while refining existing ones. Both Dr Pepper and 7 Up brought out ''diet'' versions by the early 1970s. In 1981 Dr Pepper purchased the rights to Welch's soft drinks.

1984–95: Ownership Changes, Then Dr Pepper/Seven Up

Dr Pepper was traded on the New York Stock Exchange until 1984, when it was taken private in a $615 million leveraged buyout by Forstmann Little & Co. Some of the company's assets were stripped to pay down debt, overhead was cut, and a new promotional campaign was launched. Meantime, Seven-Up was a privately owned family business that did not avail itself of public trading until 1967. In 1978 cigarette maker Philip Morris bought Seven-Up, which soon went into a profit slide. By 1986 Philip Morris was set to sell the struggling Seven-Up Company to PepsiCo while Coca-Cola was seeking to buy Dr Pepper. The Federal Trade Commission, however, blocked both proposed acquisitions for antitrust reasons, although Philip Morris was allowed to sell Seven-Up's international operations to PepsiCo. Dallas-based investment bank Hicks & Haas then entered the picture, purchasing Dr Pepper in another leveraged buyout for $406 million in August 1986. Participating in the buyout was Britain's Cadbury Schweppes, which gained a minority stake in Dr Pepper. Later in 1986, Hicks & Haas struck again, purchasing the U.S. operations of Seven-Up for $240 million. Two years later, Hicks & Haas merged Dr Pepper and Seven-Up, forming the Dr Pepper/Seven Up Companies, Inc. on May 19, 1988. The combined market strength of the two companies created a stronger contender in the soft drink market, against Coke and Pepsi. The new company began with a brand portfolio that included Dr Pepper and 7 Up (both in regular and diet versions), caffeine-free Dr Pepper and diet Dr Pepper, Cherry 7 Up (introduced in 1987), Welch's, and IBC Root Beer and Cream Soda.

In 1990 Dr Pepper/Seven Up entered the sport drink field with Nautilus Thirst Quencher. Like rival Gatorade, Nautilus was promoted as a high-electrolyte, energy-producing beverage to revive athletes. But Nautilus also stood out in its debut as the only major brand sport drink sweetened entirely by aspartame (the artificial sweetener marketed under the name NutraSweet).

In January 1993 Dr Pepper/Seven Up went public through an initial public offering. The $15 per share IPO raised $283.5 million, which was used to redeem the company's preferred stock and to retire debt. During the early 1990s DPSU enjoyed vigorous growth, with sales increasing from $658.7 million to $769 million from 1992 to 1994 alone. These gains came despite the continuing struggles of the 7 Up brand, which by this time had been surpassed by rival brand Sprite, owned by Coca-Cola. Dr Pepper's popularity, however, was on the increase; it was in fact the fastest-growing U.S. carbonated beverage, garnering a compound average growth of 8.5 percent a year from 1989 through 1993. Overall, DPSU's share of the domestic soft drink market increased from 9.8 percent in 1991 to 11.4 percent in 1994.

As of mid-1993 Cadbury Schweppes held a 5.7 percent stake in Dr Pepper/Seven Up, the holding stemming from its minority interest in Dr Pepper. Prudential Insurance Co. held a 22.2 percent stake in DPSU, which it sold to Cadbury in August 1993 for $231.8 million, raising Cadbury's stake in DPSU to 25.9

Key Dates:

1885: Pharmacist Charles C. Alderton invents Dr Pepper soft drink in Waco, Texas.
1891: Bottling of Dr Pepper begins.
1904: Dr Pepper is showcased at the World's Fair held in St. Louis.
1929: Adman Charles L. Grigg introduces Bib-Label Lithiated Lemon-Lime Soda, soon renamed 7 Up, to the general public.
1936: Grigg's company, the Howdy Company, changes its name to the Seven-Up Company.
1946: Dr Pepper Company goes public.
1967: Seven-Up Company goes public.
1978: Philip Morris buys Seven-Up.
1984: Forstmann Little purchases Dr Pepper through LBO.
1986: Hicks & Haas purchases Dr Pepper and Seven-Up in separate transactions.
1988: Hicks & Haas merges Dr Pepper and Seven-Up to form Dr Pepper/Seven Up Companies, Inc. (DPSU).
1993: Cadbury Schweppes increases stake in DPSU to 25.9 percent.
1995: Cadbury Schweppes completes full takeover of the company, with DPSU becoming a wholly owned subsidiary and being renamed Dr Pepper/Cadbury of North America, Inc.
1997: Company name is changed to Dr Pepper/Seven Up, Inc.
1998: 7 Up is reformulated for the first time ever.

percent. Under the leadership of John Albers, DPSU quickly adopted a poison pill measure which discouraged Cadbury from making any immediate moves to further raise its stake or initiate a complete takeover. Albers also refused to grant its suitor a seat on the board as it had requested. Meantime, Cadbury in October 1993 further increased its presence in the U.S. market through the acquisition of A&W Brands Inc., thereby gaining U.S. ownership or rights to the flagship A&W root beer brand, the citrus-flavored Squirt, Vernors ginger ale, and Country Time lemonades. Cadbury already controlled the Schweppes, Canada Dry, Crush, Mott's, and Sunkist brands.

Subsidiary of Cadbury Schweppes Starting in 1995

The addition of A&W Brands increased Cadbury's share of the U.S. soft drink market to 5.6 percent. But the U.K. company aimed to become the leading producer of noncola soft drinks in the world; the emphasis on the noncola sector made particular sense in the U.S. market, where noncola sales were increasing at a ten percent per year clip while cola sales were merely edging ahead at four percent a year. The quickest path to achieving this goal was the acquisition of DPSU, particularly since Cadbury believed the Dr Pepper brand had untapped potential outside the United States, as it held a mere one percent of the world market. In March 1995, then, Cadbury Schweppes acquired the 74 percent of Dr Pepper/Seven Up stock it did not already own for $33 per share, or $1.7 billion. Leading the newly named Dr Pepper/Cadbury of North America, Inc. was John F. Brock, a Cadbury veteran. Although it still lagged far behind industry behemoths Coca-Cola and Pepsi, Dr Pepper/Cadbury was a much stronger number three player in the United States, with a market share of 17 percent and a strong roster of brands, including: Dr Pepper, 7 Up, Welch's, IBC, Canada Dry, Schweppes, A&W, Crush, Sunkist, Squirt, Mott's, Hires, Sun-drop, Vernors, and Country Time. During 1997 the name of the company was changed to Dr Pepper/Seven Up, Inc. and Todd Stitzer, another Cadbury veteran, was named president and CEO of the new DPSU.

During the late 1990s DPSU made several moves to solidify the bottling and distribution of its brands in the United States. In May 1996 Coca-Cola Enterprises Inc., the nation's largest soft drink distributor, agreed to manufacture and distribute Dr Pepper brand products until at least year-end 2000 and several other DPSU brands–including Schweppes, Canada Dry, and Squirt—through the end of 1998. In January 1998 this licensing agreement was extended, with the above dates changed to year-end 2005 and year-end 2001, respectively. In December 1998 DPSU reached another multiyear agreement with the Pepsi Bottling Group, whereby the latter would continue bottling DPSU soft drink brands. Perhaps most importantly, Cadbury Schweppes and the Carlyle Group of Washington, D.C., in early 1998 formed a joint venture named the American Bottling Company, which was initially comprised of the merger of two leading independent bottling groups in the Midwest—Beverage American and Select Beverages. A year later American Bottling was combined with another independent bottler, Dr Pepper Bottling Company of Texas. The creation of American Bottling—whereby the company gained ownership of at least part of its bottling system—was designed to give Dr Pepper/Seven Up greater control over the distribution of its brands.

As it headed into a new century, Dr Pepper/Seven Up faced a number of challenges, perhaps most importantly the continuing need to revitalize the 7 Up brand. By the end of the 1990s, the brand had fallen to the number nine position in the U.S. soft drink market. A series of ad campaigns in the 1990s, a 1998 formula change—the first ever for the brand—and such packaging changes as the dropping of the ''Uncola'' slogan all failed to stem the brand's decline. Cadbury Schweppes had also attempted in 1999 to sell its soft drink brands—principally Schweppes, Dr Pepper, Canada Dry, and Crush—outside the United States, France, and South Africa to Coca-Cola for $1.85 billion. A number of nations raised antitrust concerns about the deal, however, and its fate was uncertain. Despite such question marks, Dr Pepper/Seven Up was the clear number three soft drink maker in the United States and appeared headed for a bright future based on the increasing popularity of the Dr Pepper brand and the company's emphasis on the hot noncola sector.

Principal Operating Units

Dr Pepper Company; Cadbury Beverages/Seven Up.

Principal Competitors

The Coca-Cola Company; PepsiCo, Inc.

Further Reading

Beck, Ernest, ''Cadbury's Dr Pepper Still Lags Far Behind Doctors Coke, Pepsi,'' *Wall Street Journal,* April 21, 1997, p. B5B.

Benezra, Karen, ''CadPepper: Brand Parity, Cultural Chasm,'' *Brandweek,* January 30, 1995, p. 5.

——, ''DP/7 Up Beats Marketing Drums, but Is Pepsi Alliance in Offing?,'' *Brandweek,* September 22, 1997, p. 9.

——, ''Fizz or Fizzle?,'' *Brandweek,* October 13, 1997, pp. 29–31.

Davis, Tim, ''Playing Like Champs,'' *Beverage World,* March 1, 1993, p. 47.

Deogun, Nikhil, ''Dr Pepper Unit of Cadbury to Slash Jobs,'' *Wall Street Journal,* November 4, 1997, p. B6.

——, ''It's an Upgrade Thing?: 7-Up Maker Plans New Formula to Challenge Sprite,'' *Wall Street Journal,* September 9, 1997, p. A3.

Doherty, Jacqueline, ''A Sparkling Strategy?: Cadbury Schweppes to Fiddle with Formula for 7-Up to Try for Market Effervescence,'' *Barron's,* September 15, 1997, p. 12.

''Dr Pepper/Seven Up,'' Standard NYSE Stock Reports, vol. 60, no. 62, sec. 6, entry no. 771U, Standard & Poors Corp., March 31, 1993.

Ellis, Harry E., *Dr Pepper: King of Beverages,* Dallas: Dr Pepper Co., 1979, 268 p.; centennial ed., Dallas: Dr Pepper Co., 1983, 96 p.

Ho, Rodney, ''Cadbury Extends Bottling Agreement with Coca-Cola Enterprises to 2005,'' *Wall Street Journal,* January 15, 1998, p. B10.

Howard, Theresa, ''Brand Builders: The Pepper Paradigm,'' *Brandweek,* November 2, 1998, pp. 24, 28.

Jackson, Susan, Stephanie Anderson Forest, and Lori Bongiorno, ''Can Cadbury Dodge Big Cola's Bullets?,'' *Business Week,* August 12, 1996, p. 70.

McKay, Betsy, ''7Up Drops 'Un' for a New Ad Campaign,'' *Wall Street Journal,* September 15, 1999, p. B8.

Palmer, Jay, ''Cadbury, You Cad: British Firm Grabs Dr Pepper/Seven-Up in Move That May Anger Pepsi and Coke,'' *Barron's,* January 30, 1995, p. 14.

——, ''Has Cadbury Gone Crazy?: Why the Company Is Pushing Boldly into the U.S. Soda Market,'' *Barron's,* November 8, 1993, p. 10.

Parker-Pope, Tara, ''Cadbury's Pitch Could Change Soft-Drink Landscape: Purchase of Dr Pepper Would Make British Concern No. 3 in U.S. Market,'' *Wall Street Journal,* January 24, 1995, p. B3.

Prince, Greg W., ''Cadbury Buys Pepper/Seven-Up and Everything Changes (Again),'' *Beverage World,* February 28, 1995, p. 1.

Rodengen, Jeffrey L., *The Legend of Dr Pepper/Seven-Up,* Ft. Lauderdale, Fla.: Write Stuff Syndicate, 1995, 144 p.

Rudnitsky, Howard, ''Lots of Fizz: John Albers Has Pulled Dr Pepper Out from Under a Load of Debt,'' *Forbes,* August 1, 1994, p. 44.

''Three's Charm,'' *Brandweek,* October 13, 1997, pp. 32–34, 36.

''Unimpressive Is the Word DPSU Executives Tag on 7 Up in '98,'' *Beverage World,* October 1998, pp. 18, 20.

Valente, Judith, ''Cadbury Hopes Dr Pepper Will Satisfy Its Sweet Tooth,'' *Wall Street Journal,* November 26, 1993, p. B4.

Warner, Bernhard, ''The Up Beat: With Music and Sound Effects, Brand Dialogue Puts Some Fizz into 7 Up's Gen-X Web Site,'' *Brandweek,* November 17, 1997, IQ sect., pp. 40–42.

—Susan Salter
—updated by David E. Salamie

Earl Scheib, Inc.

8737 Wilshire Boulevard
Beverly Hills, California 90211-2795
U.S.A.
Telephone: (310) 652-4880
Fax: (310) 659-4827
Web site: http://www.earlscheib.com

Public Company
Incorporated: 1962
Employees: 1,172
Sales: $55.01 million (1999)
Stock Exchanges: American
Ticker Symbol: ESH
NAIC: 811121 Automotive Body, Paint, and Interior Repair and Maintenance; 32551 Paint and Coating Manufacturing.

Earl Scheib, Inc. owns a national chain of automobile painting and body repair shops. Operating under the New Earl Scheib Paint & Body Shop name, the California-based chain consists of more than 175 stores in about 150 U.S. cities. Though the stores are primarily known for economically priced, production auto painting services, body and fender repair services are also offered. Earl Scheib manufactures its own paint at a company-owned facility in Missouri. The company established a fleet sales division in 1998. The Earl Scheib brand became well known largely through founder Earl Scheib, a pioneer of advertising.

Entrepreneurial Beginnings in the Late 1930s

Earl A. Scheib's association with automobiles began in the automobile mecca of southern California in the 1920s. After graduating from Los Angeles High School in the late 1920s, Scheib secured a job as a gas station attendant rather than pursuing college. Through numerous oil and tire changes completed for the General Petroleum Co., Scheib gained valuable experience. Soon Scheib branched off onto his own, purchasing his own service station in Los Angeles. Scheib fell into auto painting rather by accident. Customers frequently asked Scheib about auto painting shops, so Scheib decided to paint a few cars in the station's garage during the evening hours when the station was closed. What began as a small, after-hours endeavor soon blossomed, and Scheib could not keep up with demand. He thus sold his gas station and in 1937 opened Earl Scheib Paint and Body on a Los Angeles street corner near Beverly Hills.

Scheib was the first to introduce production painting of automobiles in the United States. Touting low prices of $29.95 for sedans and $24.95 for coupes, Scheib seriously undercut competitors' prices, which generally ran a few hundred dollars to paint an automobile. Because of the rock-bottom prices, customers rushed to Scheib's shop, reportedly causing traffic snarls that required assistance from the police. Open daily, Scheib and his ten employees painted between 150 and 210 cars per week during the early years.

Earl Scheib hit a snag in the 1940s with the advent of World War II. The war generated a great demand for paint, and paint supplies in the United States grew thin. Scheib was forced to lease a gas station to make ends meet, and he fought to keep his business open. In 1946, however, paint rationing ended, and the auto painting business experienced tremendous growth and popularity. Scheib opened additional stores in the San Fernando Valley, located just outside of Los Angeles, to accommodate the demand.

King of Advertising and National Expansion: 1950s–70s

Scheib began to expand nationally in the 1950s, and to raise awareness of his auto painting shops he turned to advertising. Earl Scheib marketed his shops through low-budget television commercials. Appearing on late-night television programs, Scheib soon became a national icon and celebrity, and his oft-heard sales pitch, "I'm Earl Scheib, and I'll paint any car, any color for $29.95. No ups, no extras," became an instantly recognizable phrase. Scheib, credited as being the first spokesperson for his own company, handled all advertising and developed and wrote his own television commercials. Scheib believed viewers would find his ads more convincing and genuine if he spoke directly to the viewers about the company's offerings.

Earl Scheib also handled media buys, placing his television and radio ads carefully. As son Donald explained in a company

Company Perspectives:

Earl Scheib Paint & Body is the world's largest company-owned and operated auto-painting and body repair service, painting more than 15,000 cars and trucks every year. Made famous in the early years by Earl's slogan, "I'll paint any car, any color for $29.95. No Ups! No Extras," the company has painted more than 10 million cars over its 62 years in business, and continues to adhere to Earl's original commitment of offering the best price in town on auto painting. A commitment they guarantee.

statement: "He'd personally call the station manager and tell him to interrupt a sponsored show at a pivotal moment and run his ad. . . . So you'd be watching a show, the villain's sneaking up behind the hero with a knife, and just when he's about to plunge the knife into the hero's back . . . Earl comes on the screen pitching his service." Scheib's commercials were seen and heard on television and radio stations in more than 100 cities, and he continued to film spots until his death in 1992. Despite his fame and television ad ubiquity, son Donald claimed that Scheib was less than fond of appearing in commercials. "In truth," Donald Scheib said in a company statement, "he hated doing those television spots. . . . He didn't like being in front of the camera, you'd have to drag him feet-first into that studio, screaming."

Expansion and Competition in the 1980s

Earl Scheib, Inc., which went public in 1963, was the largest non-franchised auto painting chain by the 1980s, thanks in large part to founder Earl Scheib's promotional efforts. Though the cost of a standard Earl Scheib paint job had grown to $99.95, the chain's prices were still among the lowest in the industry and appealed to budget-minded consumers. Car owners were choosing to keep their cars longer, and this trend was reflected in Scheib's sales; in the early 1980s the company's sales increased an average of 17.6 percent per year, and between 1982 and 1985 the firm's stock quadrupled. By 1985 there were 275 Earl Scheib stores, ranging from Hawaii to New York. The company opened its first store in Canada in 1984 and planned to open 25 new outlets in fiscal 1986. Overseas expansion was in the works as well, and an Earl Scheib store opened in London in 1985.

Despite sales growth in the 1980s, Earl Scheib faced increasing competition in the industry it had essentially created. Chains and franchises such as Maaco, which had 380 outlets in 1985, and One-Day Paint and Body were expanding more aggressively than Earl Scheib and taking away its market share. This competition, coupled with Scheib's commitment to low prices, presented challenges for the company. If the company continued to raise prices—the cost of an Earl Scheib paint job had increased 43 percent between 1982 and 1985—it risked losing its standing as the low-budget alternative to more expensive shops, some of which offered paint jobs starting at $129.95. In addition, Scheib paint jobs had earned a reputation as being rather shoddy, and the potential for customers to jump into a higher price range for better-quality work was something Earl Scheib was forced to face. Some industry analysts believed Scheib could grow through diversification and the offering of more expensive and upscale services, but the company was hesitant to change its tried-and-true formula.

Sales Slump in the Late 1980s and Early 1990s

After reaching record sales of $69 million in 1987, Earl Scheib entered a period of decline. At the end of 1987 Earl Scheib announced plans to close its European auto painting operations. Though the company had entered the European market only two years earlier, losses continued to build, and future prospects appeared gloomy. The domestic situation seemed no better. Under Earl Scheib's command, overall yearly sales sagged in the late 1980s, and though sales began to inch upward in the early 1990s, the company continued to rack up losses. For the third quarter ended January 31, 1991, Earl Scheib reported a net loss of $1.9 million on sales of $9.9 million.

On February 29, 1992, a day after turning 85, Earl Scheib passed away, leaving behind a legacy and a struggling business. A few days later, on Monday, March 3, the company's stock skyrocketed 47 percent as investors speculated about the future of the company. Many believed Scheib's 37 percent interest in the company would be sold in order to finance his estate taxes. Irwin Buchalter, an Earl Scheib board member and executor of Scheib's estate, indicated that the 37 percent stake would be divided between Scheib's three sons, all of whom were employed by the company. Buchalter acknowledged problems with Scheib's management and commented in the *Wall Street Journal* that Scheib "refused to take realization of the economy—of what was happening to the auto-painting business. . . . He always felt he had to have the lowest prices in the business by a wide stretch." Scheib's belief, Buchalter noted, prevented him from raising prices to compensate for slow sales. It was not until June 1991 that Scheib finally relented, raising the price of a basic paint job from $99.95 to $119.95. Buchalter believed the stock rise was indicative of stock buyers' optimism about the company's potential for growth.

A week after Earl Scheib's death, his son Donald was named president and CEO. Donald Scheib had previously served as vice-president. Irwin Buchalter was elected chairman. The company also announced that it had no plans to sell. The formidable task of turning around the ailing company was started. For fiscal 1993 the company reported sales of $53.64 million and a net loss of $110,000. The following fiscal year sales declined to $48.49 million, yet net loss grew to $1.82 million. In November 1994 Donald Scheib stepped down as president and CEO and was elected chairman, a position that had become vacant upon the death of Irwin Buchalter in August. Daniel Seigel was appointed president and CEO and handed the task of making the 250-store chain profitable once again.

The New Earl Scheib: 1995–2000

With a new CEO leading the company, Earl Scheib faced many changes in the second half of the decade. A major restructuring strategy was adopted in fiscal 1995, and as a result 84 unprofitable stores, most situated in the Midwest and East, were closed. The company took a pre-tax charge of $4.2 million for restructuring-related costs. The following fiscal year Earl Scheib reported its first profit in four years. The company earned

Key Dates:

1937: Earl A. Scheib opens the first Earl Scheib Paint and Body in Los Angeles.
1946: Scheib opens new branches just outside Los Angeles.
1962: Earl Scheib incorporates.
1963: Company goes public.
1985: Earl Scheib begins international overseas expansion with a new store in London.
1992: Founder Earl Scheib passes away; son Donald Scheib becomes president and CEO.
1997: Company establishes a fleet sales department and launches Euro-Paint, an exclusive, high-quality auto paint.

$895,000 on sales of $43.98 million, compared to a loss of $5.55 million on sales of $47.28 million in fiscal 1995. The company also spent about $4.6 million to renovate and convert 137 stores into the New Earl Scheib Paint and Body store format. The new stores boasted an updated look, including new paint and graphics, as well as new exterior signs. The shops also offered a customer information center and modern equipment, such as the Infrared Quartz Finish Drying System, used to facilitate the drying of car paint. Conversions of stores in California were completed in early fiscal 1996, and results were positive—during the first quarter comparable store sales grew by 24.2 percent compared to year-earlier figures. The upswing in sales spurred Earl Scheib to renovate the remainder of its shops.

Another challenge Daniel Seigel and Chief Operating Officer Christian Bement had to tackle was Earl Scheib's image. Many customers viewed the chain's auto painting work as being of poor quality, and new management needed to alter this perception if Earl Scheib was to once again reign the industry. Bement, reflecting upon the state of the company in 1995, admitted in the *Dallas Morning News* in 1998: "We mainly had the Earl Scheib name. That was the good news. That was also the bad news." The new shop format was designed to boost the chain's image, and to back up its new exterior, Earl Scheib started developing a new, top-quality paint. "We definitely had some of the worst paint in the industry," Bement recalled in the *Los Angeles Daily News.* "When I first got here I received letters from customers complaining about the paint jobs. The paint that was chipping off was actually in the envelopes," he added. The company-owned paint manufacturing plant in Missouri was called upon to create a high-quality auto paint, and the outcome was Euro-Paint, a 100 percent acrylic urethane paint. Introduced in 1997, the paint provided durability and a high-gloss finish and was rated as the best paint in production auto painting by Paint Research Association Laboratories Inc., a paint-testing firm. The paint, as well as other changes, effectively reduced the percentage of jobs that had to be redone because of poor quality. The company's "redo rate" dropped from 22 percent in 1995 to below six percent in the late 1990s.

Earl Scheib stepped up its expansion efforts beginning in 1997, concentrating on opening more stores in existing markets to diminish the need for increased advertising expenditures and to fully penetrate existing markets. The chain opened five new stores during fiscal 1997 and the following fiscal year opened 12 new shops. Sales continued to grow, reaching $48.34 million in fiscal 1997, up from $43.98 million the previous year. In late 1997 the company established a fleet sales department. The division, which initially had a staff of ten sales people, sought to establish multi-vehicle fleet sales accounts. It was hoped that fleet sales would help offset the regularly slow winter months. One of the first contracts secured by the fleet department was a three-year agreement with US Airways Inc. to paint about 3,500 ground vehicles and equipment. The fleet division also gained contracts with Orkin Exterminating, the Hertz Corporation, and several government agencies.

Hoping to grow to 200 shops and $100 million in sales, Earl Scheib opened 19 new stores during 1999. The company also closed six stores, bringing the year-end total to 174. Daniel Seigel resigned as president and CEO in January, and Donald Scheib retired from the board of directors in August. Seigel remained a member of the board, and Christian Bement was appointed president and CEO. Sales for fiscal 1999 increased 8.2 percent from the previous year to reach $55 million. Although comparable shop sales increased by 3.1 percent, earnings were essentially flat due to various non-recurring expenses. As increased sales returned, so did founder Earl Scheib's classic commercials, a result of a resurrection of old television programs and commercials. Not only did Earl Scheib's ads appear on Nickelodeon's "TV Land" cable network, which featured classic television shows and ads, but Earl Scheib merchandise, including T-shirts and hats, were offered for sale through specialty catalog merchants.

As Earl Scheib entered the year 2000, the company continued with its comeback strategy. The company hoped to increase sales in stores open for more than a year and to continue expansion. Earl Scheib also planned to seek strategic acquisitions to grow the company more quickly. As the year commenced, however, the outlook was restrained. Rising materials and administrative expenses, among other factors, affected first quarter sales, which reached $15.75 million, down from $15.90 million the previous year. Comparable store sales were hit harder, dropping 6.7 percent compared to the first quarter of fiscal 1999. As a result, first-quarter net income reached $345,000, down considerably from the year-earlier figure of $1 million. Earl Scheib remained focused and hopeful, however, and planned to continue painting cars—any car, any color—well into the 21st century.

Principal Subsidiaries

Earl Scheib Automotive Paint Finishes, Inc.

Principal Competitors

Ziebart International Corporation; Peach Auto Painting and Collision, Inc.

Further Reading

Box, Terry, "Earl Scheib Inc.'s Auto Painting Empire Returns to Profitability," *Dallas Morning News,* November 30, 1998.
Brommer, Stephanie, "Auto Paint King Scheib Dies at 85," *Los Angeles Daily News,* March 1, 1992, p. N1.

''Earl Scheib Inc. Seen Giving Posts to Donald Scheib,'' *Wall Street Journal,* March 3, 1992, p. B5.

Stevenson, Richard W., ''Making a Difference: 'Any Car Any Color','' *New York Times,* March 15, 1992, p. 10.

Ticer, Scott, ''Earl Scheib Is Still King of the No-Frills Paint Job,'' *Business Week,* May 27, 1985, p. 94.

White, George, ''Shares of Scheib Soar in Wake of Founder's Death,'' *Los Angeles Times,* March 3, 1992, p. D1.

Wilcox, Gregory J., ''From Red to Black; Earl Scheib Seeks Comeback with Quality Corporate Makeover,'' *Los Angeles Daily News,* March 21, 1999, p. B1.

—Mariko Fujinaka

eBay Inc.

2005 Hamilton Ave., Suite 204
San Jose, California 95125
U.S.A.
Telephone: (408) 558-7400
Fax: (408) 558-7401
Web site: http://www.ebay.com

Public Company
Incorporated: 1996
Employees: 138
Sales: $47.4 million (1998)
Stock Exchanges: NASDAQ
Ticker Symbol: EBAY
NAIC: 453998 Other Miscellaneous Store Retailers

Millions of buyers and sellers have made eBay Inc. the world's largest and most popular site on the Internet for individuals to exchange goods in person-to-person trading. Its second auction site, Great Collections, features fine art and antiques from galleries, dealers, and auction houses. As of the end of 1999, the company had more than 5.6 million registered users and listed over three million items for sale in more than 2,000 categories. The company also owns two traditional auction businesses, Butterfield & Butterfield and Kruse International, as well as online auction subsidiaries in Germany and Japan. Virtually all of its revenues come from fees and commissions from its online and traditional auction services.

Looking for Pez Dispensers: 1995–96

When Pierre Omidyar's fiancée complained that she could not find other people interested in collecting and trading Pez dispensers, Omidyar thought he might be able to help, so he opened a small online auction service on the Web. He formed a sole proprietorship in September 1995 and operated the auction service under the name of AuctionWeb.

At the time, Omidyar was working at General Magic Corp. as a software developer. His background included cofounding Ink Development Corp., which became eShop, one of the pioneers of online shopping before it was bought by Microsoft; developing consumer applications for Claris, a subsidiary of Apple Computer; and writing a software program for his high school library at the age of 14.

For five months, Omidyar offered his new service for free, building a base of buyers and sellers through word of mouth. In May 1996 he incorporated eBay, becoming CEO, and quit his day job. By the end of 1996 the company had six employees, including Jerry Skoll, eBay's original president.

The Concept

Prior to AuctionWeb, online auctions were either business-to-business or business-to-consumer. There was nothing comparable to Omidyar's concept either online or offline, with the most similar institutions being local flea markets and yard sales. Unlike traditional auctions, there was no auctioneer. At AuctionWeb, sellers posted information about their items, and buyers were able to browse the site and submit bids by e-mail. The actual auction for an item was held over three to four days, with bidders receiving e-mail notices when someone made a higher bid. They could counter that bid or drop out. The winning bidder made arrangements with the seller for payment and shipping.

eBay served the role of a broker. The company did not own any of the items being sold and was not responsible for distribution. Bidding was free, but it cost between 25 cents and two dollars to list an item for sale, plus a commission of between 2.5 and five percent of the sale price. The site was profitable almost from the beginning, unlike the vast majority of e-commerce sites. Much of the site's success appeared due to Omidyar's sense that while people wanted a central location to buy and sell items, they also wanted to be able to meet and talk with people with similar interests. From the beginning, eBay's auction service sought to create the sense of an old-fashioned market and encouraged communication between hobbyists and collectors.

During 1996, the site hosted more than 250,000 auctions in some 60 categories including Beanie Babies, stamps, coins, and computers. By the end of the year, it was overseeing about 15,000 simultaneous auctions daily, with 2,000 of them new

Company Perspectives:

We help people trade practically anything on earth. eBay was founded with the belief that people are honest and trustworthy. We believe that each of our customers, whether a buyer or seller, is an individual who deserves to be treated with respect. We will continue to enhance the online trading experiences of all our constituents—collectors, hobbyists, small dealers, unique item seekers, bargain hunters, opportunistic sellers, and browsers. The growth of the eBay community comes from meeting and exceeding the expectations of these special people.

each day. The site received over two million hits a week, and the amount of money exchanged for goods sold exceeded $6 million for the year.

Fighting Fraud: 1997

The site's popularity continued to increase. The first quarter of 1997 saw over 330,000 completed auctions, with the total transaction value of the goods sold worth more than $10.25 million. Among the items was an original 1959 "Suburban Shopper" Barbie doll, which sold for $7,999. In a May 1997 press release, eBay president Jerry Skoll stated that the growth "clearly demonstrates the receptivity and the eagerness of the general public to participate in online commerce. Our goal is to provide a fun, efficient, and reliable forum for both buyers and sellers."

Omidyar and Skoll decided the company needed venture capital and a more experienced management team. In mid-year, Benchmark Capital, a venture capital firm in Menlo Park, California, put $5 million into the company, acquiring a 22 percent stake. With their advice, the company began targeted advertising and, in September, the company renamed its auction service eBay and launched a second-generation service, with a redesigned site. By the end of 1997, the company had some 340,000 registered users and was hosting approximately 200,000 auctions at any one time. Furthermore, eBay had established a relationship with America Online Inc. (AOL), under which eBay was featured in AOL's Hobby and Classifieds channels. A year later, in 1998, eBay became the exclusive auctioneer in the Classifieds area, paying AOL a guaranteed $12 million over three years.

The problem of fraud on the Internet was a growing concern, as buyers paid for goods that were never delivered. In November 1997, the U.S. Senate's Permanent Subcommittee on Investigations conducted hearings. The National Consumers League found that fraud reports tripled after it created its Internet Fraud Watch project in March 1996. In addition to false promises for discounted services and charges for Internet services that were supposed to be free, more people were experiencing problems at auction sites. Between January and October 1997, Internet Fraud Watch received 141 complaints about auction sites. As Susan Grant of the National Consumers League told *Internet World,* "The problem basically is that auction sites really don't take responsibility for the sales if they go bad. They merely put the buyer together with the seller."

In that same article, eBay indicated that between May and August 1997, it had had only 27 disputes from its 1 million transactions. To keep such disputes to a minimum, eBay instituted a feedback system whereby buyers could post reviews of their transactions. eBay rated sellers based on their number of successful auctions: positive comments received one point, neutral responses a zero, and negative comments a minus one. Potential buyers were able to read the comments as well as view the rating. A rating of minus four resulted in a seller being denied use of the service.

Competition Appears: 1998

eBay continued its phenomenal growth, recording gross merchandise sales of $100 million and revenues of $6 million in the first quarter of 1998. The first quarter had become the company's best quarter, as eBay promoted auctioning off unwanted Christmas gifts.

Some competition was beginning to develop for the company. Late 1997 saw the business-to-business auction service OnSale Inc. add person-to-person auctions and the launch of Auction Universe Inc., a Web auction firm owned by *Los Angeles Times* parent Times Mirror Co. During 1998, that site began providing city-oriented auction sites through a group of affiliated newspapers, with each offering a local auction site run by Auction Universe. Such web sites, which were aimed primarily at the newspaper's local area, made it easier to auction large items, since it was expensive to ship a used car or a large piece of furniture across the country. It also offered newspapers a way to regain revenues lost when classified ads became too expensive for low-cost items.

The company bought Jump, Inc., the developer and operator of Up4Sale, an advertising-supported trading/auction site launched in 1997. Planning to use Up4Sale to introduce complementary future services, eBay operated the site as a separate service.

New CEO: 1998

In May 1998, Margaret C. (Meg) Whitman was appointed president and CEO of eBay, with Pierre Omidyar becoming chairman. Whitman came from Hasbro Inc.'s preschool division, where she had been general manager. Before that she headed up FTD Inc., overseeing the transition of that organization from a network of individual florists to a private company and launching its web site. Known for her experience in managing and marketing consumer brands, including Teletubbies and Playskool, Whitman concentrated on raising eBay's profile through increased advertising aimed at hobbyists and groups of collectors. At the time, eBay claimed more than 950,000 registered users and hosted more than two million auctions a month in 846 categories. Furthermore, more than 70 percent of the items put up for auction were sold.

The company had even started listing artwork for sale, although there was skepticism in the art world that this would become a significant category for eBay. As art dealer Andrew Terner told the Minneapolis *Star Tribune,* "It's important to know, to touch, to see, to do due diligence on the artwork, to know exactly what you're buying. For sophisticated collectors,

Key Dates:

1995: Pierre Omidyar launches AuctionWeb.
1996: Omidyar incorporates company as eBay Inc.
1998: eBay reincorporates in Delaware and goes public.
1999: Company acquires world's fourth largest auction house; launches ''Great Collections'' auction site for high ticket items.

buying art is in the details. I wonder whether an Internet auction can provide that information.''

Meanwhile, Sotheby's celebrated 254 years in the auction business with its first online auction, of books and manuscripts. The auction, which included some first editions of Poe and Hawthorne, generated $65,000. ''I don't want to be replaced by a computer quite yet, but I have to say I believe in them,'' Sotheby's executive vice-president and auctioneer David Redden told Allen Breed of the Associated Press.

Going Public

In September, Whitman and Omidyar reincorporated eBay in Delaware and took the company public, watching the price of their stock triple within a few days. Among those selling shares in the $63 million initial public offering was the eBay Foundation, established by eBay several months before the IPO with a grant of 100,000 shares. According to the Community Foundation Silicon Valley, which administered the foundation, this was the first time a company had launched a charitable fund with pre-IPO stock. ''It is fairly unusual, [and] it's a fairly effective way to do it because it doesn't cost them much,'' a Community Foundation official told the *Business Journal-San Jose*. At the IPO, the eBay Foundation sold just over 10,000 shares, generating cash with which to make grants.

At the end of 1998, eBay was hosting nearly 1.8 million auctions and reported a profit of $2.4 million on revenues of $47.4 million, making it one of the few Internet retailers to return solid profits. At the same time, its growth and popularity were putting the spotlight on the company and user expectations were becoming more sophisticated.

Acquisitions and Crashes: 1999

The first quarter was again record-setting, with gross merchandise sales of $541 million and net revenues of $34 million. During the quarter, eBay stopped the selling of guns and ammunition on its site. The company announced a second public offering and a four-year $75 million marketing alliance with AOL. It also saw a 3-for-1 stock split. The day before the secondary offering, Amazon.com, the Web's leading ''e-tailer,'' began hosting daily auctions.

In May, the company made three acquisitions. Both Butterfield & Butterfield, a 135-year-old San Francisco auction house, and Kruse International, an automobile auctioneer in Indiana known for collector cars, helped eBay move into a higher-priced market. The third purchase, Billpoint Inc., was a California company that made it easier to accept credit card payments over the Internet. Sellers on eBay could now use Billpoint to instantly accept credit cards and buyers would be able to receive reference reports listing all their transactions. The company issued $275 million in common stock to finance the purchases.

Moving overseas, eBay next entered a joint venture with Australia-based PBL Online. In addition, to provide its members with more news and information about their collectibles, eBay signed an agreement with the Collecting Channel to provide ''content'' on the site. The first offering was information about Star Wars memorabilia.

However, June was a rough month for eBay, as the company's web site experienced numerous crashes. The company was a few days away from completing installation of a backup system when outages began occurring, including one that lasted 22 hours. eBay refunded $3–$5 million in waived listing fees, conducted free auctions, and moved to hire more computer network experts and senior technology managers. As other big Internet companies such as AOL and E*Trade had found out, site reliability was a critical factor in retaining customer loyalty. Competitors such as Amazon.com and Auction Universe reported increased traffic at their sites as a result of eBay's problems.

Within days of the outages, however, eBay gave journalists something else to write about the company: its global expansion. It moved into Europe with the acquisition of Alando.de AG, Germany's largest online trading site, and added a Japanese-language corner to provide customer support for its 6,500 members in Japan and to attract additional Japanese users.

Competition moved to the high end of the auction market as 1999 drew to a close. Amazon.com, which had bought a minority stake in Sotheby's Holding Inc., paired up with its new partner to launch a joint auction site. Christie's International indicated that it would soon be adding an interactive section to its web site, and smaller companies handling decorative and fine art or antiques were also going online. Behind all the action was the tremendous potential for sales. Experts predicted the online auction field would grow to 17.5 million registered buyers and sales of $15.5 billion by 2001, up from 1.5 millions users and $1.5 billion in sales in 1998.

eBay had already recognized the opportunity to use online auctions for high-priced items, but noted that such offerings would have to be presented differently. After acquiring Butterfield and Butterfield, the world's fourth largest auction house, for $250 million, the company began structuring such a site. Great Collections was launched in October 1999, with partnering auction houses, galleries, and dealers having their own branded areas and offering the same authentication services they did in their brick-and-mortar locations. The branded areas, essentially storefronts, might be a forecast of things to come on the eBay site, where 20 percent of sellers accounted for 80 percent of the transactions.

The online auction business, which eBay pioneered by developing communities of collectors who wanted to buy and sell Beanie Babies, antique coins, and Elvis memorabilia, could obviously offer more than cyberspace flea markets. The issues of fraud and site reliability were still matters of concern, as they were for any e-commerce company. But eBay, with two sites for different segments of the market, 30 regional sites around the United States, German and Japanese subsidiaries, and a large and loyal community of 5.6 million users, was the company all the others had to beat.

Principal Subsidiaries

Butterfield & Butterfield; Kruse International; Alando.de AG.

Principal Competitors

Auction Universe; OnSale Inc.; First Auction; Amazon.com; Yahoo.com; Sothebys.amazon.com.

Further Reading

Alexander, Steve, ''Digital Auction,'' *Star Tribune* (Minneapolis), March 1, 1998, p. 1D.

Anders, George, ''Customers' Loyalty Tested As eBay Repairs System,'' *South Bend Tribune*, June 21, 1999, p. C7.

——, ''Nation's Latest Cybermogul Got the Bidding Started Online,'' *Orange County Register*, September 27, 1998, p. 22.

Avery, Simon, ''AOL, eBay in $75M Marketing Alliance,'' *National Post*, March 26, 1999, p. C8.

Bowers, Richard, ''Barbie Sold for $7,999 on Internet,'' *Newsbytes News Network*, February 14, 1997.

Buel, Stephen, ''Amazon.com to Challenge eBay for Online Auction Market,'' *San Jose Mercury News*, March 30, 1999.

——, ''Online Trader eBay Feeling Growing Pains,'' *San Jose Mercury News*, December 29, 1998.

''Business in Brief,'' *Atlanta Journal and Constitution*, November 24, 1999, p. 3D.

Carrell, Paul, ''eBay Buys German Online Trader,'' *National Post*, June 23, 1999, p. C11.

''Collecting Channel to Serve As Lead Content Partner for eBay,'' *PR Newswire*, June 4, 1999.

Delevett, Peter, ''eBay Uses New Wrinkle to Launch Charitable Fund,'' *Business Journal-San Jose*, August 3, 1998, p. 7.

''eBay Announces Acquisition of Jump Inc.,'' *Business Wire*, July 21, 1998.

''eBay's AuctionWeb Completes Record $10 Million in Auctions,'' *Business Wire*, May 1, 1997.

''eBay's AuctionWeb Tops One Million Bids,'' *Business Wire*, December 12, 1996.

Evangelista, Benny, ''New eBay Site Auctions High-Ticket Items,'' *San Francisco Chronicle*, October 20, 1999, p. C2.

''Foreign Companies in Japan,'' *Nikkei Weekly*, November 29, 1999, p. 8.

Gaw, Jonathan, ''Nearly Daylong Outage Plagues Online Auction House eBay,'' *Los Angeles Times*, June 12, 1999, p. C1.

Green, Heather, ''Online Merchants: Cyberspace Winners: How They Did It,'' *Business Week*, June 22, 1998, p. 154.

Hof, Robert D., ''eBay Vs. Amazon.com,'' *Business Week*, May 31, 1999, p. 128.

''Internet: eBay and AOL Extend Relationship,'' *Network Briefing*, September 3, 1998.

Kharif, Olga, ''Online Gun Sales,'' *Chicago Daily Herald*, May 24, 1999, p. Business 4.

''Meg Whitman: eBay,'' *Business Week*, May 31, 1999, p. 134.

Murphy, Kathleen, ''Fraud Follows Buyers onto Web,'' *Internet World*, October 20, 1997.

''Net Auctioneer eBay Names Hasbro GM As President and CEO,'' *Network Briefing*, May 8, 1998.

Smith, Rebecca, ''eBay, Butterfield Make a Bid for the Bourgeoisie,'' *San Francisco Chronicle*, June 28, 1999, p. E1.

''Time Will Tell If eBay's Able to Captivate the Art World,'' *Star Tribune* (Minneapolis), July 27, 1998, p. 9E.

Williams, Martyn, ''eBay Eyes Japan Market for Expansion,'' *Newsbytes*, June 22, 1999.

''U.S. Online Auctioneer Wooing Japanese Trade,'' *Nikkei Weekly*, June 28, 1999, p. 11.

Vierira, Paul, ''Going, Going . . . Online,'' *National Post*, November 27, 1999, p. C7.

—Ellen D. Wernick

Eckerd Corporation

8333 Bryan Dairy Road
Largo, Florida 33777
U.S.A.
Telephone: (727) 395-6000
Toll Free: (800) 325-3737
Fax: (727) 395-7934
Web site: http://www.eckerd.com

Wholly Owned Subsidiary of J.C. Penney Company, Inc.
Incorporated: 1961 as Eckerd Drugs of Florida
Employees: 55,000
Sales: $10.33 billion (1998)
NAIC: 446110 Pharmacies & Drug Stores

Eckerd Corporation operates a chain of about 2,900 drug stores located in 20 states in the Northeast, Southeast, and Sunbelt. With its acquisition by J.C. Penney Company, Inc. in February 1997, Eckerd grew substantially through its absorption of the existing drugstores operations of its new parent—vaulting the chain into the number four position among pharmacy chains, trailing only Walgreen Co., CVS Corporation, and Rite Aid Corporation. About 2,000 of the units in the chain are located in strip centers, but the company is shifting toward freestanding locations featuring drive-through pharmacy windows and larger layouts of about 11,000 square feet. Revenues at Eckerd units are derived in large part from the sale of prescriptions and over-the-counter medications; the stores also sell general merchandise, including health and beauty items, ready-to-eat food and beverages, and greeting cards. Photofinishing services are offered at most units, and 850 outlets operate minilabs with one-hour Express Photo centers. The company owns a pharmacy benefits management service, called Eckerd Health Services (EHS), which designs and manages comprehensive prescription benefit plans for employers and HMOs; EHS is also one of the largest retail mail-order pharmacies in the nation.

Cut-Rate Beginnings

Eckerd Corporation traces its history to the days when J. Milton Eckerd launched one of the country's first drugstore chains in Erie, Pennsylvania. Eckerd was born in Mechanicsburg, Pennsylvania, in 1871 and began working as an assistant to a drug wholesaler as a young man. This wholesaler was on the cutting edge of drugstore retailing, in that he was supplying drugstores with mass-produced prescription and over-the-counter drugs; previously, local pharmacies mixed their own medicines in batches. Eckerd's employer believed that a cut-rate drugstore could prove to be a profitable venture by buying supplies in bulk from wholesalers at discount rates and thereby offering lower prices than competing drugstores. He encouraged Eckerd to open such a store.

In September 1898 Eckerd became one of the pioneers of the discount drugstore industry. That month he opened a store in Erie using $600 in savings and a few thousand dollars in credit from his now former employer. The discount outlet soon found success offering over-the-counter medicines such as the newly invented Aspirin, personal hygiene items such as Listerine, and products usually found in grocery stores, including candy and tobacco. Although retailers at the turn of the century typically were barred from operating on weekends, Eckerd, because he acted as a pharmacist whose customers might be in need of his products at any time, was able to stay open seven days a week. This enabled him to increase profits at the expense of such retailers as grocers, who could operate only during the week. Within a few years, Eckerd had established his operation as one of the leaders of the region's drugstore sector.

In 1912 Eckerd decided to sell his Erie operation to his sons William and Ken and open a new discount drugstore in Wilmington, Delaware. His choice of location proved auspicious when Wilmington soon became the booming commercial center of the Delaware Valley. Among the innovations introduced by Eckerd at his new location in Delaware was the addition of a store manager to handle the overall operations of the store; this freed pharmacists to concentrate solely on prescription services, whereas before they had to manage the store as well. This practice was soon adopted by most competitors. During the 1920s beauty products became more respectable and upscale women were flocking to department stores to purchase makeup. Eckerd began selling discounted brand name cosmetics, thereby capturing sales from lower-income women. Eckerd also ex-

Company Perspectives:

The executives, store managers, sales associates, pharmacists, and many others who have made Eckerd Corporation a success are part of a proud tradition of American mercantile enterprise. Like their forebears, the merchants of Eckerd are proof that success is based upon innovation, adaptability, initiative, and teamwork. But most of all, Eckerd has thrived because its merchants and pharmacists have always put the customer first. They listen carefully to their customers, learn what they need, and provide them with the most up-to-date, cost-effective, high-quality merchandise and services.

panded his chain into North Carolina, opening units in Charlotte, Raleigh, and Asheville. By the 1930s Eckerd had become the leading drugstore chain in North Carolina. The North Carolina chain eventually became owned and operated by Ed O'Herron, Sr., while the Wilmington chain was likewise to be controlled by Mitchell Hill; O'Herron and Hill were sons-in-law of J. Milton Eckerd. (William and Ken Eckerd, meanwhile, continued to own the original Erie stores until selling them in the early 1960s.)

Jack Eckerd, youngest son of J. Milton, began working for his father's company during the Great Depression. He started off as the company pilot, flying his father on scouting missions aimed at identifying potential new locations on the East Coast. From that role Jack Eckerd moved on to a position as an Eckerd sales associate in Erie, working closely with his father and older brothers. In this way, he learned the business from the bottom up, despite his father's warning, ''You're going to work longer and harder than anyone else, and you're not going to make too much money.''

1940s and 1950s: Self-Service and the Move to Florida

In 1947 Eckerd encountered the new concept of self-service drugstores at a PayLess store during a trip to California. PayLess was a pioneer in this retailing innovation, which had enabled the regional chain to lower labor costs and offer significant discounts to its customers. Eckerd became convinced of the merits of the new system and returned to Erie in 1949 to open QuikChek, the first self-service drugstore on the East Coast. An instant success, QuikChek had a larger design than conventional drugstores, was systematically laid out to make finding items as easy as possible, and offered greater discounts than other Eckerd stores.

This success, however, also led to customer confusion between the two Eckerd-run drugstore brands in Erie. Jack Eckerd, therefore, decided to venture into an entirely new market. In 1952 he left his father's chain and purchased three struggling drugstores in Tampa and Clearwater, Florida, on the Gulf Coast. Using the self-service concept, he turned the three stores into financial successes. By 1955 Eckerd was running a five-store chain in Florida. The state had been well chosen; it was experiencing a postwar tourism boom and had an increasing population of senior citizen retirees, a prime demographic group for any drugstore chain.

According to friends and family, the Jack Eckerd chain also became successful because of Eckerd's honesty, hard work, dedication, and people-oriented philosophy of management. He told one interviewer, ''I made up my mind I would never do anything, if I could help it, that wasn't in the best interests of the customers, the employees, and the stockholders.'' His wife, Ruth, wrote that he could not drive by one of his stores without going in to talk to the employees. He himself said that understanding employees and making decisions based on fairness were essential to his success. He called his employees his company's greatest asset.

Eckerd tried to keep in touch with employees and listen to their suggestions because they were the ones who came in contact with the customers. To foster a sense of family, Eckerd sent personally signed birthday cards to all employees throughout the chain, stopping this practice only when the employee rolls grew to 8,000.

Eckerd drew attention when he successfully challenged Florida's ''fair trade law,'' which prohibited retailers from reducing prices below those charged by other retailers in the state. Eckerd successfully argued before the Florida Supreme Court that the law was unconstitutional and that he had the right to provide discounts to increase his share of the market.

Expansion and Diversification: 1959–85

In 1959 Publix markets, Florida's leading grocery chain, offered Eckerd the opportunity to build drugstores next to five of its supermarkets in strip shopping malls in Tampa, Clearwater, and St. Petersburg. Eckerd borrowed $1 million and committed to a 15-year lease on each of the stores. This partnership would eventually lead to the opening of 150 new Eckerd drugstores. Eckerd took his 15-store chain public in 1961 as Eckerd Drugs of Florida. Two years later an Orlando division was established, marking the beginning of a statewide expansion. Also during the early 1960s, the company built a state-of-the-art photofinishing plant in Clearwater to have full control of its photo processing services and thereby ensure consistent quality. In 1965 Eckerd stores introduced two-for-one prints of processed film to enormous success; this innovation was later widely adopted by the photofinishing industry. Another widely copied Eckerd innovation was very popular senior citizens' discounts.

In the late 1960s through the end of the 1970s, Eckerd bought a string of other Southeastern drugstores and participated in the drive to diversify that dominated U.S. business in that era. In 1966 Eckerd bought Old Dominion Candies (which he sold in 1972); in 1968 he purchased Jackson's/Byrons, a 12-unit junior department store chain based in Miami that was renamed J. Byron; and in 1969 he acquired the Gray Security Service, an installer of alarm and security systems, and the food service supplier Kurman Company. In 1970 Eckerd Drugs of Florida was renamed Jack Eckerd Corporation. The company's nondrugstore subsidiaries eventually were organized within a new corporate entity called Jack Eckerd Allied Company, which was headed by Stewart Turley, who was named CEO of Eckerd Drugs in 1974. Jack Eckerd Corporation expanded again

Key Dates:

1898: J. Milton Eckerd launches one of the country's first drugstore chains in Erie, Pennsylvania.
1912: Eckerd sells his Erie business to two of his sons and opens a new cut-rate drugstore in Wilmington, Delaware.
1949: In Erie, Jack Eckerd opens QuikChek, the first self-service drugstore on the East Coast.
1952: Eckerd purchases three struggling drugstores on Florida's Gulf Coast and turns them around.
1959: Eckerd begins partnership with Publix grocery chain.
1961: Company is taken public as Eckerd Drugs of Florida.
1970: Company is renamed Jack Eckerd Corporation; drugstore chains in Louisiana, Texas, and Florida are acquired.
1974: Stewart Turley is named CEO of the company.
1977: Eckerd North Carolina is acquired in largest merger in drugstore history; the Eckerd chain now includes 766 units and is the second largest in the country.
1985: Dart Group Corporation launches a hostile takeover of the company.
1986: Dart's takeover attempt is fended off through a management-led leveraged buyout that returns the company to private hands.
1990: Company acquires 220 Revco drugstores, primarily in Texas.
1992: Major restructuring cuts about 600 jobs and reduces the number of divisions from eight to six.
1993: Company returns to public ownership with the sale of 15 percent of its stock and changes its name to Eckerd Corporation.
1996: Frank Newman is named company CEO.
1997: Company is acquired by J.C. Penney Company, Inc.; Penney's Thrift Drug unit is merged into Eckerd, which becomes a wholly owned subsidiary of Penney.
1999: Genovese Drug Stores, a 141-unit chain based in New York, is acquired.

in 1973 with the opening of 12 Eckerd Optical Centers, which offered prescription eyeglass services. Within two years there were more than 50 of the centers, which were being supplied by two optical laboratories. Around this same time, Turley also moved to rein in the company's nondrugstore operations through the divestment of several subsidiaries, including Kurman Company and Gray Security, both sold in 1976.

On the drugstore side, Jack Eckerd Corporation in 1970 bought Louisiana-based Brown's Thrift City Wholesale Drugs, Houston-based Mading-Dugan Drugs, and Georgia-based Galaxy Drugs. The company also purchased Delaware-based Eckerd Drugs Eastern Inc. (from Milt Hill, J. Milton Eckerd's grandson) and Texas-based Ward Cut-Rate Drug in 1973. In 1977 Turley completed the consolidation of all Eckerd drugstores within Jack Eckerd Corporation through the acquisition of Eckerd North Carolina, the chain that had been founded in Charlotte by J. Milton Eckerd and then sold to Eckerd's son-in-law Ed O'Herron, Sr., in the 1930s. This merger was at the time the largest in drugstore history, increased the number of Eckerd stores to 766, and vaulted the company into the number two position among drugstore chains.

During the 1970s, Jack Eckerd made a number of unsuccessful bids for public office. He lost his first race when he ran in a primary election for governor of Florida in 1970. In 1974 he won the Republican nomination to run for the U.S. Senate but lost the election. Eckerd ran for governor again in 1979 but once again lost his bid for elected office. Eckerd held public office only when President Gerald Ford named him head of the General Services Administration (GSA) in 1975. During his tenure at the GSA, Eckerd turned over chairmanship of the company to Turley. Eckerd returned to the company as a member of its board in 1979.

In 1980 Jack Eckerd Corporation strengthened its presence in Texas by acquiring Sav-X drugstores of Abilene and 40 Sommers Drug Stores. The following year the company acquired 19 drugstores from the Thrift Drugs unit of J.C. Penney. Eckerd also entered the video market through the 1980 acquisition of American Home Video, which owned the Video Concepts stores. Eckerd sold both the video concern and the J. Byron stores in 1985 as the financial performance of the company's nondrugstore operations began to turn sour.

Jack Eckerd became a hero in the Christian press in the mid-1980s when he ordered *Playboy, Penthouse,* and *Hustler* magazines and other "questionable books" off the shelves of Eckerd Drugs stores, calling them "America's family drugstores." According to the *Christian Herald,* Eckerd also led a drive, through lobbying and public pressure, to convince other drugstore chains to "stop selling pornography."

Return to Private Ownership: 1986–93

The hostile takeover craze of the 1980s affected Jack Eckerd Corporation as well—the company being vulnerable because of its strong market position and weak stock price. The Dart Group Corporation launched a hostile takeover of Eckerd in 1985 but the attempt was fended off when Jack Eckerd sold his shares in the company to a management investment group in a leveraged buyout. Merrill Lynch Capital Partners negotiated the leveraged buyout (LBO) of the Eckerd Drugs company by its managers for $1.58 billion. The buyout left Merrill Lynch and affiliates with 58 percent share of the company, and Eckerd Drugs was once again a private company, retaining the name Jack Eckerd Corporation. Jack Eckerd's sale of his shares brought him $36 million.

The management buyout brought a new look to the drug chain, as the company spent $20 million a year to remodel more than 250 stores each year. The late 1980s also brought some massive closings and purchases in a continuing effort to reduce the more than $1 billion in debt the company had incurred in the LBO. Jack Eckerd Corporation shut down 45 of its least profitable stores and sold 11 of its Tulsa, Oklahoma stores. On the other side of the ledger, however, it bought 32 Shoppers Drug Mart Stores located in Florida in 1986 and opened 50 new stores. The company also expanded its optical and photofinishing services by adding 79 instore one-hour Express Photo minilabs and more than 20 Visionworks optical superstores. In 1989 Eckerd acquired Insta-Care Pharmacy Services, which provided prescription drugs and medical consulting services to long-term healthcare facilities in six states.

When Revco drugs declared bankruptcy in 1990, Eckerd immediately acquired 220 of its stores (primarily located in Texas) and engaged in protracted negotiations to acquire the remaining stores in the Ohio-based chain. Eckerd chairman Turley saw Revco and Eckerd as very compatible, given the similarity of size and the fact that geographically they complemented each other: half of Revco's stores were located in states in which Eckerd operated, but the other half were located in the Midwest, which would extend Eckerd's market. The merger of Revco and Eckerd would also have given Eckerd more clout in the prescription market. With competition tight for the third-party payment plans of government, unions, and company medical plans, volume was the key to prescription profits. If Eckerd became the largest drugstore chain, it could offer lower prices and become more attractive to third-party clients.

Eckerd's offer for Revco was worth almost $779 million, pushing challenger Rite Aid out of the running. Most creditors were now backing Eckerd's plan, which also called for turning Revco headquarters into a regional office and closing about 250 Revco stores. A last-minute reorganization plan by Revco, however, promised to save thousands of jobs and keep most Revco stores open, quashing Eckerd's bid in 1991. Revco agreed to pay Eckerd $7.5 million to cover the expenses generated by the bidding process.

In the early 1990s the managed care revolution continued and drugstores felt additional competitive pressures from discount retailers such as Wal-Mart Stores, Inc. and Kmart Corporation, which were carrying more health and beauty aids that were traditionally bought at drugstores. The drugstores had already lost business to supermarkets and were being forced to become more like corner convenience stores by carrying more foods and beverages. In 1992 Eckerd launched plans to increase its cosmetics and fragrance sales by adding new upscale product lines. Eckerd, as well as other chain drugstores, also began offering free home delivery for elderly customers and young parents.

Still burdened by debt, Eckerd was struggling to return to profitability, losing $300 million between 1987 and 1992; in four of those years operating profits did not even cover interest expenses. In 1992 the company consolidated its corporate structure in a major restructuring, reducing operating regions from eight to six, and cutting about 600 headquarters and field office jobs to reduce the number of bureaucratic layers between stores and top management. In the spring of 1993, Eckerd negotiated a refinancing deal with two banks, allowing it to simplify its debt structure and save considerably on interest and dividend costs. The company announced that the refinancing also would support expansion plans.

By 1993 Jack Eckerd Corporation was returning to financial health. To further reduce its debt and lay the groundwork for further expansion, the company returned to the New York Stock Exchange in August 1993 as a publicly traded company under a new name: Eckerd Corporation. Through an initial public offering (IPO) 15 percent of company stock was sold to the public, marking the beginning of the firm's second period of public ownership.

As of 1993 Eckerd owned 1,692 stores in 13 states. More than 540 Eckerd drugstores were located in Florida, 475 in Texas, almost 200 each in North Carolina and Georgia, more than 100 in Louisiana, and fewer than 100 in South Carolina. There were also Eckerd stores scattered throughout Tennessee, Mississippi, Oklahoma, New Jersey, Alabama, Delaware, and Maryland. Express Photo shops were located in 405 of these stores.

Mid-to-Late 1990s: From Acquirer to Acquiree

Eckerd returned to profitability in 1994, posting net income of $41.4 million on sales of $4.19 billion. That year the company sold its vision care operations, which at the time consisted of 47 Visionworks optical superstores and 29 Eckerd Optical Centers, to a management-led investment group. Eckerd also divested its Insta-Care unit, selling the institutional pharmacy business to Beverly Enterprises Inc. for about $112 million. These moves were designed to focus the company further on its core retail drugstore operations.

The pressures on drugstore companies to enlarge themselves through mergers continued throughout the 1990s. The industry's razor-thin profit margins encouraged firms to grow ever larger to buy pharmaceuticals and other products at greater quantities at lower prices and to pass the savings on to their customers—in the end increasing sales and earnings. Eckerd participated in this trend by buying North Carolina-based Crown Drugs and its 19 stores in 1994 and by purchasing the following year most of the assets of Rite Aid's Florida operations, including 37 drugstores and the prescription lists, inventory, and fixtures from another 72 Rite Aid stores slated for closure. In May 1995 the company formed a pharmacy benefits management service called Eckerd Health Services (EHS). In addition to designing and managing comprehensive prescription benefit plans for employers and HMOs, Clearwater-based EHS also launched a mail-order pharmacy operation in 1996. A mail-order facility was soon able to handle up to 2,500 prescriptions per day and within a few years EHS had gained a position as one of the largest retail mail-order pharmacies in the nation.

In 1996 Eckerd's president, Frank Newman, was named CEO as well, with Turley remaining as chairman. Before joining Eckerd as president in 1993, Newman had extensive experience at a number of retailers, including F.W. Woolworth & Co. and F&M Distributors Inc., a discount seller of health and beauty aids. A key development in the Newman-led era was the move away from locations in strip centers, which typically were anchored by supermarkets—most of which by now had pharmacies and were thus in direct competition with drugstores. Eckerd began opening new units and relocating existing units in freestanding locations. These larger outlets—of about 11,000 square feet—were able to offer an enhanced selection of convenience foods as well as adding drive-through pharmacy windows. Stores located from strip centers to freestanding locations typically saw their sales increase by 30 percent.

Eckerd continued to seek out acquisition targets; it had long coveted the Thrift Drug chain owned by J.C. Penney. The department store retailer rejected Eckerd's overtures and began building its drugstore unit through the acquisition of North Carolina-based Kerr Drug Stores in 1995 for $75 million and New York-based, 270-unit Fay's Drug in October 1996 for $285 million. Also in October 1996 Penney agreed to acquire 190 Rite Aid drugstores in North and South Carolina. The following month, however, Penney and Eckerd reached an agreement whereby the department store operator would acquire the drugstore specialist. To gain antitrust approval from the Federal Trade Commission, Penney was forced to sell 164 Rite Aid and Kerr stores in the Carolinas; in early 1997 it sold the units to a former member of Thrift management and others for $75 million. This paved the way for the consummation of the Eckerd acquisition, which occurred in February 1997 with Penney paying $2.5 billion in cash and assuming Eckerd's $760 million debt. Penney's Thrift unit was merged into Eckerd, which became a wholly owned subsidiary of Penney. Eckerd thereby added to its chain about 1,100 drugstores on the East Coast and in parts of the Midwest, with concentrations in New Jersey and Pennsylvania; all of the Penney drugstores were eventually rebranded under the Eckerd name. By the end of 1997 Eckerd was a chain of 2,778 stores with sales of $9.66 billion, making the company the number four drugstore operator in the nation, behind Walgreen, CVS, and Rite Aid. Growth that year was aided by the purchase of 114 Revco stores in Virginia.

In the late 1990s Eckerd continued to concentrate on the steady conversion of the chain from strip mall to freestanding locations. During 1998 Eckerd opened 220 stores, 175 of which were relocations. The company was expanding its photofinishing services by adding one-hour Express Photo centers to more of its drugstores; 850 units had the centers by the end of 1998, with about 320 opened in 1999 and 300 more slated for 2000. Synergies were also being sought between Eckerd and its parent. The drugstores began accepting the J.C. Penney credit card, and Penney catalog desks began to be added to Eckerd stores. The chain's sales increased to $10.33 billion in 1998, with comparable-store sales growing 9.2 percent.

In March 1999 Eckerd acquired Genovese Drug Stores, a 141-unit chain based in New York with annual sales of about $800 million. The purchase made Eckerd the number one drugstore operator in the state of New York. The Genovese stores soon were converted to the Eckerd banner. By late 1999 the Eckerd chain had nearly 3,000 stores and planned for an additional 575 new and relocated stores by 2001. Looking further down the road, Eckerd planned to convert as many as 2,000 strip center units to freestanding outlets by the end of the first decade of the 21st century. The company also was continuing its history of innovation with the testing of an automated prescription dispensing system. J.C. Penney, meanwhile, was preparing to take Eckerd public once again through the sale of about 20 percent of the company's stock through an early 2000 IPO.

Principal Competitors

Albertson's, Inc.; CVS Corporation; Drug Emporium, Inc.; Food Lion, Inc.; H.E. Butt Grocery Co.; Kmart Corporation; The Kroger Company; Phar-Mor, Inc.; Publix Super Markets, Inc.; Rite Aid Corporation; Safeway Inc.; Walgreen Co.; Wal-Mart Stores, Inc.; Winn-Dixie Stores, Inc.

Further Reading

Bradford, Stacey L., "Eckerd: Pennies from Hell?," *Financial World,* December 16, 1996, p. 24.

Clancy, Carole, "Wall Street Finds Itself Getting Hooked on Eckerd," *Tampa Bay Business Journal,* August 18, 1995, p. 1.

DeGeorge, Gail, "A Drugstore Cowboy Rides to Revco's Rescue," *Business Week,* January 27, 1992, p. 35.

DeGeorge, Gail, and Stephanie Anderson, "Partly Filled, Fully Billed," *Business Week,* February 23, 1998, p. 46.

DeTorok, Judy, "Jack Eckerd," *Tampa Bay Business,* January 10–16, 1988, p. S5.

"Eckerd/Genovese Merger Closes," *Drug Store News,* March 15, 1999, pp. 1, 3.

Fleming, Harris, Jr., "A Pharmacist's Pharmacy," *Drug Topics,* April 19, 1999, pp. 55–56, 58.

Hagy, James, "A Miracle Drug for Jack Eckerd," *Florida Trend,* February 1992, pp. 49–51.

Kimelman, John, "Eckerd: A Cheaper Prescription," *Financial World,* May 24, 1994, p. 18.

Lee, Louise, "Penney Aims for Growth in Drug Sales, Shopper Convenience in Eckerd Deal," *Wall Street Journal,* November 5, 1996, p. A3.

The Merchants and Medicines of Eckerd: Yesterday, Today, Tomorrow, Clearwater, Fla.: Eckerd Corporation, [n.d.].

Muirhead, Greg, "Monster Merger: J.C. Penney in $3.3 Billion Move to Buy Eckerd Chain," *Drug Topics,* November 18, 1996, pp. 14, 16.

Sigo, Shelly, "Proxies in the Mail, Eckerd IPO on Track for January," *Tampa Bay Business Journal,* October 18, 1999.

Smith, Katherine Snow, "Eckerd's Rx to Fight the Discount Habit," *Tampa Bay Business Journal,* April 29, 1994, p. 1.

——, "New Eckerd President Brings Reputation for Vision," *Tampa Bay Business Journal,* April 22, 1994, p. 14.

—Wendy J. Stein
—updated by David E. Salamie

Energizer Holdings, Inc.

800 Chouteau Avenue
St. Louis, Missouri 63164
U.S.A.
Telephone: (314) 982-2970
Toll Free: (800) 383-7323
Fax: (314) 982-2752
Web site: http://www.energizer.com

Public Company
Incorporated: 1986 as Eveready Battery Company, Inc.
Employees: 17,400
Sales: $2.07 billion (1998)
Stock Exchanges: New York
Ticker Symbol: (pending)
NAIC: 335912 Primary Battery Manufacturing

Energizer Holdings, Inc., formerly known as Eveready Battery Company, Inc., is one of the world's foremost manufacturers of dry cell batteries and flashlights. In the United States, it battles intensely for market share with the category leader, Duracell. Its share of the domestic market in the late 1990s was estimated at just over 30 percent, trailing Duracell's almost 40 percent. Energizer makes two mainstay brands, Energizer and Eveready. Its principal products are alkaline batteries, as well as other varieties including carbon zinc and lithium. The company also sells flashlights and other lighting products. Energizer makes and markets its products around the world, with over 40 production facilities overseas and distribution in over 160 countries.

Early History

Energizer Holdings was originally a battery and electric lighting firm known as American Ever Ready Company, with offices in New York and San Francisco. In the 1890s, this company was marketing a so-called electric hand torch—what we today call a flashlight. In 1913 this company was acquired by the National Carbon Company, Inc., a unit of Union Carbide & Carbon Corporation, later known simply as Union Carbide. National Carbon was already making batteries, advertising its Columbia brand dry cells with an eagle motif and the slogan "Columbia Batteries Circle the Globe." After the acquisition, National Carbon began using the Eveready name for its batteries. Later the battery business of National Carbon folded into the parent company, and Eveready batteries were made by the Battery Products Division of Union Carbide. Union Carbide was a leader in the United States battery market from early on, along with such other companies as General Electric, Electric Storage Battery, and Gulton Industries. Sales of its Eveready Layerbilt batteries grew rapidly in the 1920s, rising from 12.5 million batteries sold in 1922 to 303 million in 1926. The rise in sales was attributable to the new craze for the radio, which at first was battery operated. By the late 1920s, however, plug-in radios became the norm, and the market for batteries contracted.

During World War II the Germans developed a new battery made of sealed nickel cadmium plates, and Union Carbide brought this technology to the United States after the war, as did General Electric and Gulton. In 1947 Union Carbide came out with the first hearing aid batteries, and followed this with other advances in the next decade. The company developed watch cells in the late 1950s, as well as 9-volt transistor batteries. At this time Union Carbide's battery division also created the first alkaline batteries, the type which is so common in consumer products today. Although aware of its importance, Union Carbide did not press the alkaline battery as much as it might have, and continued to lead the market with its carbon zinc Eveready brand battery through the 1970s. It also made rechargeable batteries, which had military and space program uses, car batteries, and a variety of industrial batteries.

In the mid-1960s, Union Carbide's Eveready brand was estimated to have about half the market share in dry cell batteries, a total market said to be worth around $250 million annually. The industry as a whole was expanding rapidly in that era, as battery technology got better and more uses were found for battery power. In 1966, Union Carbide produced a battery made with hydrazine, a newly developed rocket fuel, and placed it in an electric motorcycle that could reach speeds of 25 miles per hour. This was a spectacularly useless development, as a slow, quiet motorcycle had very little consumer appeal. But it demonstrated the innovative strength of the battery industry at

Company Perspectives:

Energizer Holdings, Inc. is the largest manufacturer of dry cell batteries and flashlights and a global leader in the dynamic business of providing portable power. Energizer offers a full line of products in five major categories: alkaline, carbon zinc, miniature and rechargeable batteries; and lighting products. Our Energizer and Eveready brands are recognized around the world and are marketed and sold in more than 160 countries. Energizer's worldwide work force of approximately 17,400 produce more than 6 billion battery cells annually.

that time, where the possibilities for new applications seemed endless. Union Carbide worked with the Defense Department to develop its hydrazine battery, and in the same era industrial demand for batteries was growing enormously. Sales of industrial batteries grew by nearly 100 percent in the first half of the 1960s. This was the dawn of the era of portable, battery-operated toys and gadgets, too. A December 5, 1966 article in *Barron's* laid out a host of possible new uses for dry cell batteries, where Eveready was the leading brand. The article spoke wonderingly of the new fad for lighted beer steins and electric spaghetti forks. Gizmos like this prompted a rapid upswing in battery sales. Perhaps the most important battery-powered invention though was the portable transistor radio, which was being sold around the world. In 1959 Union Carbide formed a Consumer Products Division in order to capitalize on the trend toward portable radios and other battery-operated gadgets.

Entering the Alkaline Market in the 1980s

Perhaps because the battery business grew so easily, with rising consumer demand for battery-powered products naturally bringing in increasing sales, Union Carbide did not market its products aggressively. Although it had developed the first alkaline batteries in the 1950s, it continued to sell carbon zinc batteries, which did not last as long as alkaline. Meanwhile a competing brand, Duracell, owned by P.R. Mallory & Company, began attracting consumers. By the late 1970s, the percentage of the overall battery market made up of alkaline sales was growing swiftly, and Duracell had become a powerful competitor. The carbon zinc Eveready still had a strong following, but as alkaline batteries were demonstrably better, providing power longer, Union Carbide's brand was in danger of growing obsolete. However, it was not until 1980 that the company launched its first consumer-oriented alkaline battery. Named the Energizer, this battery quickly caught up with Duracell. Union Carbide lavished advertising on its new brand. Its spokesperson was the Olympic gymnast Mary Lou Retton, a powerful, energetic young woman. She continued with the brand until 1987.

Shortly after the Energizer's introduction, Union Carbide's brand claimed just over 40 percent of the alkaline battery market, while Duracell held just under 50 percent. The battery market continued to expand, driven by demand for things like the portable cassette player, which became ubiquitous in the mid-1980s. Overall, the battery industry grew at around seven percent a year in the early 1980s, and the alkaline segment of the market grew at close to double that. It was a highly profitable market, too, with margins as high as ten percent. Union Carbide's two brands and Duracell made up more than 90 percent of the total market, and battery sales in the United States surpassed $2 billion annually in the mid-1980s. Overseas, Union Carbide's brands held a 30 percent share of the market. It was a formidable business.

Eveready Sale to Ralston Purina in 1986

Union Carbide had great success with its Battery Products Division. Although it had reacted belatedly to competitive pressure to launch an alkaline battery, the company had come in powerfully at last with Energizer, and swept up an admirable chunk of the market. Sales rose worldwide as demand expanded, and the product was lucrative to manufacture. Yet in 1986 Union Carbide was forced to unload its productive battery unit. Union Carbide restructured in an effort to fend off a hostile takeover, and to make itself less attractive it decided to sell off what was considered perhaps the best part of its business. The buyer was Ralston Purina Company, the pet food giant. Ralston was also wary of a takeover. Because the company was rich in cash, it was a likely target for takeover artists. It paid $1.4 billion to get Union Carbide's battery division, thereby loading itself with unflattering debt. Both companies gained protection from takeover through the deal. Moreover, though Ralston was known for its Purina brand pet foods, it saw itself as a good marketer of consumer products in general, and so batteries were not such an odd fit with its core business. The former Battery Products Division became a wholly owned subsidiary, with the new name Eveready Battery Company.

By the late 1980s, the consumer battery market was still growing, thanks to the proliferation of portable electronics and walking, talking toys. Consumer battery sales overall stood at $2.5 billion annually in the late 1990s, and this figure was expected to grow to $3.5 billion over the next several years. Consequently, more companies entered the field, with Kodak introducing its battery brand in 1987, vying for the third place spot in the market held by Rayovac. The alkaline battery market was growing the fastest, and competition between brands was somewhat vicious. Each maker claimed its batteries lasted longer than the competitors, though *Consumer Reports* and people inside the industry agreed that there really was not much objective difference between Duracell, Energizer, and the others. Meanwhile under Ralston Purina, Eveready actually lost market share. Its two brands, Eveready and Energizer, had held 52 percent of the market in 1986, and by 1988 that figure had slipped slightly to 47 percent. In the alkaline market, Energizer fell from roughly 45 percent to 40 percent in the late 1980s.

Memorable Bunny Ads: A 1990s Sensation

As a unit of a food and pet food conglomerate, Eveready's marketing had not been that different from the way other grocery items were presented. Eveready came up with brand extensions, such as the Eveready Classic and the Eveready Super Heavy-Duty. New packaging to coordinate with wrapping paper came out as GiftMate Energizers around Christmas, and a brand aimed at audio equipment users came out, the

Key Dates:

1913: American Ever Ready is acquired by National Carbon.
1959: Union Carbide forms Consumer Products Division to market batteries.
1980: Union Carbide launches Energizer alkaline battery.
1986: Union Carbide sells its battery division to Ralston Purina.
2000: Ralston spins off Eveready subsidiary.

Conductor. This strategy was tried and true for many food items, but it was not working for batteries. In 1989 Eveready finally decided to try an advertising campaign that went head-to-head with its rival Duracell. Duracell had developed ads showing hordes of wind-up bunnies running on its batteries. Eveready's advertising agency, Chiat/Day, came up with a spoof on those bunnies, with a giant Energizer bunny breaking in on the Duracell gang, rudely banging a drum. The Energizer bunny campaign went on from there, with a unique series of fake advertisements that would be interrupted by the banging rabbit. The commercials began as what looked like straightforward ads for coffee or nasal spray, and suddenly the rabbit burst onto the screen, with the slogan "Still going. . . ." The campaign was extremely innovative, though it did not immediately affect Eveready's sales. It engendered its own spoofs, too. In 1991 the Adolph Coors Company aired an ad with a well-known comedic actor dressed in a bunny suit banging a drum with the words "Coors Light" on it. Eveready filed suit against Coors, claiming it had spent more than $55 million over two years developing its bunny ads, and it did not enjoy the parody. The Energizer ads continued to be popular throughout the 1990s, and the company attributed its seven percent rise in revenues in 1992 to the success of its bunny campaign.

Other Developments in the 1990s

Eveready increased its worldwide presence in the late 1980s and 1990s. In 1989 it acquired Cofinea, a French battery company, to bolster its position in Europe. Eveready also made acquisitions in the United Kingdom and Spain, and it beefed up its manufacturing and marketing in Turkey, China, and Czechoslovakia. The domestic battery market continued to grow, adding another billion dollars every five years or so. The proliferation of pagers and cellular phones spurred growth in the mid-1990s, and total battery sales were close to $4 billion by 1995. Alkaline batteries made up over 90 percent of the total consumer battery market. A small but growing segment, however, was rechargeable batteries. Rayovac's rechargeable brand held almost 60 percent of the category. Eveready made a strategic acquisition in 1993, buying rechargeable battery maker Gates Energy Products, Inc., in order to give itself a place in the rechargeable field. Eveready renamed the company Energizer Power Systems in 1994, and changed Gates's brand name from Millennium to Energizer. Another new product for Eveready in the mid-1990s was the lithium battery, which was both lightweight and long-lasting. Lithium batteries were used primarily in cameras. Eveready made three different styles of them and claimed to have very high sales volume by 1995.

In 1996 Eveready introduced batteries with testers on them. Consumers could press a test strip on the battery to see how much power it had. Duracell also introduced a virtually identical product. Both companies were said to have spent millions developing the testing systems, and they were still jockeying for market share. Figures for 1996 put Duracell in the number one spot, with 48 percent of the domestic battery market, and Eveready followed with 35 percent. Battery sales continued to increase, growing at six percent in 1996, a typical rate. An article in *Supermarket News* from February 10, 1997 noted that both leading brands were vying to add value to their products to gain a competitive edge. The testing strip was supposed to do just that. But the overall increase in sales seemed to have nothing to do with the manufacturers' efforts to provide better products. Analysts interviewed in *Supermarket News* noted that sales were going up for the same reason they always had—people had more gadgets to put batteries in.

Independent Company in 2000

Ultimately, the battery business seemed to have frustrated Eveready's parent, Ralston Purina. Despite innovative marketing, strategic acquisitions, and millions spent on developing new and better products, Eveready's brands could not catch up with market leader Duracell. Perhaps signifying the company's desperation, the Energizer bunny ads for 1999 showed the rabbit crushing, torching, and pummeling competitors' batteries. These ads were stopped by a judge's order. Eveready had sales of $2.07 billion in 1998, but it was adversely affected by the economic crisis in Asia that year, and its domestic marketing was not going well. Ralston decided that batteries were not a good fit with its core business, and in 1999 the parent company announced that it would spin off the subsidiary. Eveready Battery Company changed its name to Energizer Holdings Inc. and was to become a public company listed on the New York Stock Exchange in April 2000.

Principal Competitors

Rayovac Corporation; Duracell, Inc.

Further Reading

Ansberry, Clare, "Battery Makers See Surge in Competition," *Wall Street Journal,* November 30, 1987, p. 7.
Beam, Alex, "What's Recharging the Battery Business," *Business Week*, June 23, 1986, p. 124.
Dalton, Julie Carrick, "Spinning Off Problems," *CFO*, August 1999, p. 22.
Dreyfack, Kenneth, "What Purina Really Wanted from Carbide," *Business Week*, April 21, 1986, p. 33.
Foltz, Kim, "Amid TV's Ad Clutter, a Rabbit Runs Wild," *New York Times*, October 23, 1989, p. D11.
"Kill De Wabbit," *Business Week*, November 1, 1993, p. 6.
King, Thomas R., "Say, Doesn't That Big Pink Bunny Look Like the Guy in 'Airplane!'?," *Wall Street Journal*, April 26, 1991, p. B1.
Lipman, Joanne, "Too Many Think the Bunny Is Duracell's, Not Eveready's," *Wall Street Journal*, July 31, 1990, pp. B1, B7.
Loehwing, David A., "New Life in Batteries," *Barron's*, December 5, 1966, pp. 3, 17.
McMurray, Scott, and Matthew Winkler, "Eveready Has Lithium Battery for Consumers," *Wall Street Journal*, September 30, 1988, p. 4.

''New Ad Campaigns Enliven Battery Competition,'' *Discount Store News*, June 5, 1995, p. 42.

''Ralston Purina to Spin Off Battery Unit in April,'' *New York Times*, October 20, 1999, p. C4.

Simmons, Jacqueline, ''Rayovac Ads Power Rechargeable Battery,'' *Wall Street Journal*, December 23, 1993, p. B8.

Siskin, Jonathan, ''Testing the Charge,'' *Supermarket News*, February 10, 1997, p. 69.

Snyder, Beth, and Laura Petrecca, ''Eveready Keeps Going with New Products Review,'' *Advertising Age*, September 27, 1999, p. 2.

Stroud, Jerry, ''Judge Pulls Plug on Eveready's Energizer Bunny Ads,'' *Knight-Ridder/Tribune Business News*, May 14, 1999, p. OKRB99134I8E.

''Two Energetic Moves,'' *Sales & Marketing Management*, August 1986, p. 30.

—A. Woodward

EXXON CORPORATION

Exxon Corporation

5959 Las Colinas Boulevard
Irving, Texas 75039-2298
U.S.A.
Telephone: (972) 444-1000
Toll Free: (800) 252-1800
Fax: (972) 444-1348
Web site: http://www.exxon.com

Public Company
Incorporated: 1882 as Standard Oil Company of New Jersey
Employees: 79,000
Sales: $117.77 billion (1998)
Stock Exchanges: New York Boston Cincinnati Midwest Philadelphia Basel Dusseldorf Frankfurt Geneva Hamburg Paris Zurich
Ticker Symbol: XON
NAIC: 211111 Crude Petroleum & Natural Gas Extraction; 324110 Petroleum Refineries; 324191 Petroleum Lubricating Oil & Grease Manufacturing; 325110 Petrochemical Manufacturing; 447100 Gasoline Stations; 486110 Pipeline Transportation of Crude Oil; 486910 Pipeline Transportation of Refined Petroleum Products; 212110 Coal Mining; 212234 Copper Ore & Nickel Ore Mining; 212299 All Other Metal Ore Mining; 221112 Fossil Fuel Electric Power Generation

As the earliest example of the trend toward gigantic size and power, Exxon Corporation and its Standard Oil forebears have earned vast amounts of money in the petroleum business. The brainchild of John D. Rockefeller, Standard Oil enjoyed the blessings and handicaps of overwhelming power—on the one hand, an early control of the oil business so complete that even its creators could not deny its monopolistic status; on the other, an unending series of journalistic and legal attacks upon its business ethics, profits, and very existence. Exxon became the object of much resentment during the 1970s for the huge profits it made from the OPEC-induced oil shocks. The uproar over the *Exxon Valdez* oil tanker spill in 1989 put the corporation once more in the position of embattled giant, as the largest U.S. oil company struggled to justify its actions before the public. At the end of the 1990s Exxon stood as the second largest of the world's integrated petroleum powerhouses—trailing only the Royal Dutch/Shell Group. In addition to its oil and gas exploration, production, manufacturing, distribution, and marketing operations, Exxon was a leading producer and seller of petrochemicals and was involved in electric power generation and the mining of coal, copper, and other minerals. Exxon was also once again making history, through a proposed merger with Mobil Corporation, to create the largest petroleum firm in the world in one of the biggest mergers ever—and to reunite two of the offspring of the Standard Oil behemoth.

Prehistory of Standard Oil

The individual most responsible for the creation of Standard Oil, John D. Rockefeller, was born in 1839 to a family of modest means living in the Finger Lakes region of New York State. His father, William A. Rockefeller, was a sporadically successful merchant and part-time hawker of medicinal remedies. William Rockefeller moved his family to Cleveland, Ohio, when John D. Rockefeller was in his early teens, and it was there that the young man finished his schooling and began work as a bookkeeper in 1855. From a very young age John D. Rockefeller developed an interest in business. Before getting his first job with the merchant firm of Hewitt & Tuttle, Rockefeller had already demonstrated an innate affinity for business, later honed by a few months at business school.

Rockefeller worked at Hewitt & Tuttle for four years, studying large-scale trading in the United States. In 1859 the 19-year-old Rockefeller set himself up in a similar venture—Clark & Rockefeller, merchants handling the purchase and resale of grain, meat, farm implements, salt, and other basic commodities. Although still very young, Rockefeller had already impressed Maurice Clark and his other business associates as an unusually capable, cautious, and meticulous businessman. He was a reserved, undemonstrative individual, never allowing emotion to cloud his thinking. Bankers found that they could

Company Perspectives:

Ours is a long-term business, with today's accomplishments a reflection of well-executed plans set in motion years ago. Likewise, Exxon's success at building shareholder value in the future is dependent on plans we develop and implement today.

The following strategies have and will continue to guide Exxon as we strive to meet shareholder and customer expectations: identifying and implementing quality investment opportunities at a timely and appropriate pace, while maintaining a selective and disciplined approach; being the most efficient competitor in every aspect of our business; maintaining a high-quality portfolio of productive assets; developing and employing the best technology; ensuring safe, environmentally sound operations; continually improving an already high-quality work force; maintaining a strong financial position and ensuring that financial resources are employed wisely.

trust John D. Rockefeller, and his associates in the merchant business began looking to him for judgment and leadership.

Clark & Rockefeller's already healthy business was given a boost by the Civil War economy, and by 1863 the firm's two partners had put away a substantial amount of capital and were looking for new ventures. The most obvious and exciting candidate was oil. A few years before, the nation's first oil well had been drilled at Titusville, in western Pennsylvania, and by 1863 Cleveland had become the refining and shipping center for a trail of newly opened oil fields in the so-called Oil Region. Activity in the oil fields, however, was extremely chaotic, a scene of unpredictable wildcatting, and John D. Rockefeller was a man who prized above all else the maintenance of order. He and Clark, therefore, decided to avoid drilling and instead go into the refining of oil, and in 1863 they formed Andrews, Clark & Company with an oil specialist named Samuel Andrews. Rockefeller, never given to publicity, was the "Company."

With excellent railroad connections as well as the Great Lakes to draw upon for transportation, the city of Cleveland and the firm of Andrews, Clark & Company both did well. The discovery of oil wrought a revolution in U.S. methods of illumination. Kerosene soon replaced animal fat as the source of light across the country, and by 1865 Rockefeller was fully convinced that oil refining would be his life's work. Unhappy with his Clark-family partners, Rockefeller bought them out for $72,000 in 1865 and created the new firm of Rockefeller & Andrews, already Cleveland's largest oil refiners. It was a typically bold move by Rockefeller, who although innately conservative and methodical was never afraid to make difficult decisions. He thus found himself, at the age of 25, co-owner of one of the world's leading oil concerns.

Talent, capital, and good timing combined to bless Rockefeller & Andrews. Cleveland handled the lion's share of Pennsylvania crude and, as the demand for oil continued to explode, Rockefeller & Andrews soon dominated the Cleveland scene. By 1867, when a young man of exceptional talent named Henry Flagler became a third partner, the firm was already operating the world's number one oil refinery; there was as yet little oil produced outside the United States. The year before, John Rockefeller's brother, William Rockefeller, had opened a New York office to encourage the rapidly growing export of kerosene and oil byproducts, and it was not long before foreign sales became an important part of Rockefeller strength. In 1869 the young firm allocated $60,000 for plant improvements—an enormous sum of money for that day.

Creation of the Standard Oil Monopoly: 1870–92

The early years of the oil business were marked by tremendous swings in the production and price of both crude and refined oil. With a flood of newcomers entering the field every day, size and efficiency already had become critically important for survival. As the biggest refiner, Rockefeller was in a better position than anyone to weather the price storms. Rockefeller and Henry Flagler, with whom Rockefeller enjoyed a long and harmonious business relationship, decided to incorporate their firm to raise the capital needed to enlarge the company further. On January 10, 1870, the Standard Oil Company was formed, with the two Rockefellers, Flagler, and Andrews owning the great majority of stock, valued at $1 million. The new company was not only capable of refining approximately ten percent of the entire country's oil, it also owned a barrel-making plant, dock facilities, a fleet of railroad tank cars, New York warehouses, and forest land for the cutting of lumber used to produce barrel staves. At a time when the term was yet unknown, Standard Oil had become a vertically integrated company.

One of the single advantages of Standard Oil's size was the leverage it gave the company in railroad negotiations. Most of the oil refined at Standard made its way to New York and the Eastern Seaboard. Because of Standard's great volume—60 carloads a day by 1869—it was able to win lucrative rebates from the warring railroads. In 1871 the various railroads concocted a plan whereby the nation's oil refiners and railroads would agree to set and maintain prohibitively high freight rates while awarding large rebates and other special benefits to those refiners who were part of the scheme. The railroads would avoid disastrous price wars while the large refiners forced out of business those smaller companies who refused to join the cartel, known as the South Improvement Company.

The plan was denounced immediately by Oil Region producers and many independent refiners, with near-riots breaking out in the oil fields. After a bitter war of words and a flood of press coverage, the oil refiners and the railroads abandoned their plan and announced the adoption of public, inflexible transport rates. In the meantime, however, Rockefeller and Flagler were already far advanced on a plan to combat the problems of excess capacity and dropping prices in the oil industry. To Rockefeller the remedy was obvious, though unprecedented: the eventual unification of all oil refiners in the United States into a single company. Rockefeller approached the Cleveland refiners and a number of important firms in New York and elsewhere with an offer of Standard Oil stock or cash in exchange for their often-ailing plants. By the end of 1872, all 34 refiners in the area had agreed to sell—some freely and for profit, and some, competitors alleged, under coercion. Because of Standard's great size and the industry's overbuilt capacity, Rockefeller and Flagler

Key Dates:

1870: John D. Rockefeller and Henry Flagler incorporate the Standard Oil Company.
1878: Standard controls $33 million of the country's $35 million annual refining capacity.
1882: Rockefeller reorganizes Standard Oil into a trust, creating Standard Oil Company of New Jersey as one of many regional corporations controlled by the trust.
1888: Standard founds its first foreign affiliate, Anglo-American Oil Company, Limited.
1890: The Sherman Antitrust Act is passed, in large part, in response to Standard's oil monopoly.
1891: The trust has secured a quarter of the total oil field production in the United States.
1892: Lawsuit leads to dissolving of the trust; the renamed Standard Oil Company (New Jersey) becomes main vessel of the Standard holdings.
1899: Jersey becomes the sole holding company for all of the Standard interests.
1906: Federal government files suit against Jersey under the Sherman Antitrust Act, charging it with running a monopoly.
1911: U.S. Supreme Court upholds lower court conviction of the company and orders that it be separated into 34 unrelated companies, one of which continues to be called Standard Oil Company (New Jersey).
1926: The Esso brand is used for the first time on the company's refined products.
1946: A 30 percent interest in Arabian American Oil Company, and its vast Saudi Arabian oil concessions, is acquired.
1954: Company gains seven percent stake in Iranian oil production consortium.
1972: Standard Oil Company (New Jersey) changes its name to Exxon Corporation.
1973: OPEC cuts off oil supplies to the United States.
1980: Revenues exceed $100 billion because of the rapid increase in oil prices.
1989: The crash of the *Exxon Valdez* in Prince William Sound off the port of Valdez, Alaska, releases about 260,000 barrels of crude oil.
1990: Headquarters are moved from Rockefeller Center in New York City to Irving, Texas.
1994: A federal jury in an *Exxon Valdez* civil action finds the company guilty of ''recklessness'' and orders it to pay $286.8 million in compensatory damages and $5 billion in punitive damages.
1997: Company appeals the $5 billion punitive damage award; it reports profits of $8.46 billion on revenues of $120.28 billion for the year.
1998: Company agrees to buy Mobil in one of the largest mergers in U.S. history, which would create the largest oil company in the world, Exxon Mobil Corporation.

were in a position to make their competitors irresistible offers. All indications are that Standard regularly paid top dollar for viable companies.

By 1873 Standard Oil was refining more oil—10,000 barrels per day—than any other region of the country, employing 1,600 workers, and netting around $500,000 per year. With great confidence, Rockefeller proceeded to duplicate his Cleveland success throughout the rest of the country. By the end of 1874 he had absorbed the next three largest refiners in the nation, located in New York, Philadelphia, and Pittsburgh. Rockefeller also began moving into the field of distribution with the purchase of several of the new pipelines then being laid across the country. With each new acquisition it became more difficult for Rockefeller's next target to refuse his cash. Standard interests rapidly grew so large that the threat of monopoly was clear. The years 1875 to 1879 saw Rockefeller push through his plan to its logical conclusion. In 1878, a mere six years after beginning its annexation campaign, Standard Oil controlled $33 million of the country's $35 million annual refining capacity, as well as a significant proportion of the nation's pipelines and oil tankers. At the age of 39, Rockefeller was one of the five wealthiest men in the country.

Standard's involvement in the aborted South Improvement Company, however, had earned it lasting criticism. The company's subsequent absorption of the refining industry did not mend its image among the few remaining independents and the mass of oil producers who found in Standard a natural target for their wrath when the price of crude dropped precipitously in the late 1870s. Although the causes of producers' tailing fortunes are unclear, it is evident that given Standard's extraordinary position in the oil industry it was fated to become the target of dissatisfactions. In 1879 nine Standard Oil officials were indicted by a Pennsylvania grand jury for violating state antimonopoly laws. Although the case was not pursued, it indicated the depth of feeling against Standard Oil, and was only the first in a long line of legal battles waged to curb the company's power.

In 1882 Rockefeller and his associates reorganized their dominions, creating the first ''trust'' in U.S. business history. This move overcame state laws restricting the activity of a corporation to its home state. Henceforth the Standard Oil Trust, domiciled in New York City, held ''in trust'' all assets of the various Standard Oil companies. Of the Standard Oil Trust's nine trustees, John D. Rockefeller held the largest number of shares. Together the trust's 30 companies controlled 80 percent of the refineries and 90 percent of the oil pipelines in the United States, constituting the leading industrial organization in the world. The trust's first year's combined net earnings were $11.2 million, of which some $7 million was immediately plowed back into the companies for expansion. Almost lost in the flurry of big numbers was the 1882 creation of Standard Oil Company of New Jersey, one of the many regional corporations created to handle the trust's activities in surrounding states. Barely worth mentioning at the time, Standard Oil Company of New Jersey, or ''Jersey'' as it came to be called, would soon become the dominant Standard company and, much later, rename itself Exxon.

The 1880s were a period of exponential growth for Standard. The trust not only maintained its lock on refining and distribution but also seriously entered the field of production. By 1891 the trust had secured a quarter of the country's total output, most of it in the new regions of Indiana and Illinois. Standard's overseas business was also expanding rapidly, and in 1888 it founded its first foreign affiliate, London-based Anglo-American Oil Company, Limited (later known as Esso Petroleum

Company, Limited). The overseas trade in kerosene was especially important to Jersey, which derived as much as three-fourths of its sales from the export trade. Jersey's Bayonne, New Jersey refinery was soon the third largest in the Standard family, putting out 10,000 to 12,000 barrels per day by 1886. In addition to producing and refining capacity, Standard also was extending gradually its distribution system from pipelines and bulk wholesalers toward the retailer and eventual end user of kerosene, the private consumer.

Jersey at Head of Standard Oil Empire: 1892–1911

The 1890 Sherman Antitrust Act, passed in large part in response to Standard's oil monopoly, laid the groundwork for a second major legal assault against the company, an 1892 Ohio Supreme Court order forbidding the trust to operate Standard of Ohio. As a result, the trust was promptly dissolved, but taking advantage of newly liberalized state law in New Jersey, the Standard directors made Jersey the main vessel of their holdings. Standard Oil Company of New Jersey became Standard Oil Company (New Jersey) at this time. The new Standard Oil structure now consisted of only 20 much-enlarged companies, but effective control of the interests remained in the same few hands as before. Jersey added a number of important manufacturing plants to its already impressive refining capacity and was the leading Standard unit. It was not until 1899, however, that Jersey became the sole holding company for all of the Standard interests. At that time the entire organization's assets were valued at about $300 million and it employed 35,000 people. John D. Rockefeller continued as nominal president, but the most powerful active member of Jersey's board was probably John D. Archbold.

Rockefeller had retired from daily participation in Standard Oil in 1896 at the age of 56. Once Standard's consolidation was complete Rockefeller spent his time reversing the process of accumulation, seeing to it that his staggering fortune—estimated at $900 million in 1913—was redistributed as efficiently as it had been made.

The general public was only dimly aware of Rockefeller's philanthropy, however. More obvious were the frankly monopolistic policies of the company he had built. With its immense size and complete vertical integration, Standard Oil piled up huge profits ($830 million in the 12 years from 1899 to 1911). In relative terms, however, its domination of the U.S. industry was steadily decreasing. By 1911 its percentage of total refining was down to 66 percent from the 90 percent of a generation before, but in absolute terms Standard Oil had grown to monstrous proportions. Therefore, it was not surprising that in 1905 a U.S. congressman from Kansas launched an investigation of Standard Oil's role in the falling price of crude in his state. The commissioner of the Bureau of Corporations, James R. Garfield, decided to widen the investigation into a study of the national oil industry—in effect, Standard Oil.

Garfield's critical report prompted a barrage of state lawsuits against Standard Oil (New Jersey) and, in November 1906, a federal suit was filed charging the company, John D. Rockefeller, and others with running a monopoly. In 1911, after years of litigation, the U.S. Supreme Court upheld a lower court's conviction of Standard Oil for monopoly and restraint of trade under the Sherman Antitrust Act. The Court ordered the separation from Standard Oil Company (New Jersey) of 33 of the major Standard Oil subsidiaries, including those that subsequently kept the Standard name.

Independent Growth into a ''Major'': 1911–72

Standard Oil Company (New Jersey) retained an equal number of smaller companies spread around the United States and overseas, representing $285 million of the former Jersey's net value of $600 million. Notable among the remaining holdings were a group of large refineries, four medium-sized producing companies, and extensive foreign marketing affiliates. Absent were the pipelines needed to move oil from well to refinery, much of the former tanker fleet, and access to a number of important foreign markets, including Great Britain and the Far East.

John D. Archbold, a longtime intimate of the elder Rockefeller and whose Standard service had begun in 1879, remained president of Standard Oil (New Jersey). Archbold's first problem was to secure sufficient supplies of crude oil for Jersey's extensive refining and marketing capacity. Jersey's former subsidiaries were more than happy to continue selling crude to Jersey; the dissolution decree had little immediate effect on the coordinated workings of the former Standard Oil group, but Jersey set about finding its own sources of crude. The company's first halting steps toward foreign production met with little success; ventures in Romania, Peru, Mexico, and Canada suffered political or geological setbacks and were of no help. In 1919, however, Jersey made a domestic purchase that would prove to be of great long-term value. For $17 million Jersey acquired 50 percent of the Humble Oil & Refining Company of Houston, Texas, a young but rapidly growing network of Texas producers that immediately assumed first place among Jersey's domestic suppliers. Although only the fifth leading producer in Texas at the time of its purchase, Humble would soon become the dominant drilling company in the United States and eventually was wholly purchased by Jersey. Humble, later known as Exxon Company U.S.A., remained one of the leading U.S. producers of crude oil and natural gas through the end of the century.

Despite initial disappointments in overseas production, Jersey remained a company oriented to foreign markets and supply sources. On the supply side, Jersey secured a number of valuable Latin American producing companies in the 1920s, especially several Venezuelan interests consolidated in 1943 into Creole Petroleum Corporation. By that time Creole was the largest and most profitable crude producer in the Jersey group. In 1946 Creole produced an average of 451,000 barrels per day, far more than the 309,000 by Humble and almost equal to all other Jersey drilling companies combined. Four years later, Creole generated $157 million of the Jersey group's total net income of $408 million and did so on sales of only $517 million. Also in 1950, Jersey's British affiliates showed sales of $283 million but a bottom line of about $2 million. In contrast to the industry's early days, oil profits now lay in the production of crude, and the bulk of Jersey's crude came from Latin America. The company's growing Middle Eastern affiliates did not become significant resources until the early 1950s. Jersey's Far East holdings, from 1933 to 1961 owned jointly with Socony-Vacuum Oil Company—formerly Standard Oil Company of

New York and now Mobil Corporation—never provided sizable amounts of crude oil.

In marketing, Jersey's income showed a similar preponderance of foreign sales. Jersey's domestic market had been limited by the dissolution decree to a handful of mid-Atlantic states, whereas the company's overseas affiliates were well entrenched and highly profitable. Jersey's Canadian affiliate, Imperial Oil Ltd., had a monopolistic hold on that country's market, while in Latin America and the Caribbean the West India Oil Company performed superbly during the second and third decades of the 20th century. Jersey had also incorporated eight major marketing companies in Europe by 1927, and these, too, sold a significant amount of refined products—most of them under the Esso brand name introduced the previous year (the name was derived from the initials for Standard Oil). Esso became Jersey's best known and most widely used retail name both at home and abroad.

Jersey's mix of refined products changed considerably over the years. As the use of kerosene for illumination gave way to electricity and the automobile continued to grow in popularity, Jersey's sales reflected a shift away from kerosene and toward gasoline. Even as late as 1950, however, gasoline had not yet become the leading seller among Jersey products. That honor went to the group of residual fuel oils used as a substitute for coal to power ships and industrial plants. Distillates used for home heating and diesel engines were also strong performers. Even in 1991, when Exxon distributed its gasoline through a network of 12,000 U.S. and 26,000 international service stations, the earnings of all marketing and refining activities were barely one-third of those derived from the production of crude. In 1950 that proportion was about the same, indicating that regardless of the end products into which oil was refined, it was the production of crude that yielded the big profits.

Indeed, by mid-century the international oil business had become, in large part, a question of controlling crude oil at its source. With Standard Oil Company (New Jersey) and its multinational competitors having built fully vertically integrated organizations, the only leverage remained control of the oil as it came out of the ground. Although it was not yet widely known in the United States, production of crude was shifting rapidly from the United States and Latin America to the Middle East. As early as 1908 oil had been verified in present-day Iran, but it was not until 1928 that Jersey and Socony-Vacuum, prodded by chronic shortages of crude, joined three European companies in forming Iraq Petroleum Company. Also in 1928, Jersey, Shell, and Anglo-Persian secretly agreed to limit each company's share of world production to their present relative amounts, attempting, by means of this "As Is" agreement, to limit competition and keep prices at comfortably high levels. As with Rockefeller's similar tactics 50 years before, it was not clear in 1928 that the agreement was illegal, because its participants were located in a number of different countries each with its own set of trade laws. Already in 1928, Jersey and the other oil giants were stretching the very concept of nationality beyond any simple application.

Following World War II, Jersey was again in need of crude to supply the resurgent economies of Europe. Already the world's largest producer, the company became interested in the vast oil concessions in Saudi Arabia recently won by Texaco and Socal. The latter companies, in need of both capital for expansion and world markets for exploitation, sold 30 percent of the newly formed Arabian American Oil Company (Aramco) to Jersey and ten percent to Socony-Vacuum in 1946. Eight years later, after Iran's nationalization of Anglo-Persian's holdings was squelched by a combination of CIA assistance and an effective worldwide boycott of Iranian oil by competitors, Jersey was able to take seven percent of the consortium formed to drill in that oil-rich country. With a number of significant tax advantages attached to foreign crude production, Jersey drew an increasing percentage of its oil from its holdings in all three of the major Middle Eastern fields—Iraq, Iran, and Saudi Arabia—and helped propel the 20-year postwar economic boom in the West. With oil prices exceptionally low, the United States and Europe busily shifted their economies to complete dependence on the automobile and on oil as the primary industrial fuel.

Exxon, Oil Shocks, and Diversification: 1972–89

Despite the growing strength of newcomers to the international market, such as Getty and Conoco, the big companies continued to exercise decisive control over the world oil supply and thus over the destinies of the Middle East producing countries. Growing nationalism and an increased awareness of the extraordinary power of the large oil companies led to the 1960 formation of the Organization of Petroleum Exporting Countries (OPEC). Later, a series of increasingly bitter confrontations erupted between countries and companies concerned about control over the oil upon which the world had come to depend. The growing power of OPEC and the concomitant nationalization of oil assets by various producing countries prompted Jersey to seek alternative sources of crude. Exploration resulted in discoveries in Alaska's Prudhoe Bay and the North Sea in the late 1960s. The Middle Eastern sources remained paramount, however, and when OPEC cut off oil supplies to the United States in 1973—in response to U.S. sponsorship of Israel—the resulting 400 percent price increase induced a prolonged recession and permanently changed the industrial world's attitude to oil. Control of oil was, in large part, taken out of the hands of the oil companies, who began exploring new sources of energy and business opportunities in other fields.

For Standard Oil Company (New Jersey), which had changed its name to Exxon in 1972, the oil embargo had several major effects. Most obviously it increased corporate sales; the expensive oil allowed Exxon to double its 1972 revenue of $20 billion in only two years and then pushed that figure over the $100 billion mark by 1980. After a year of windfall profits made possible by the sale of inventoried oil bought at much lower prices, Exxon was able to make use of its extensive North Sea and Alaskan holdings to keep profits at a steady level. The company had suffered a strong blow to its confidence, however, and soon was investigating a number of diversification measures that eventually included office equipment, a purchase of Reliance Electric Company (the fifth largest holdings of coal in the United States), and an early 1980s venture into shale oil. With the partial exception of coal, all of these were expensive failures, costing Exxon approximately $6 billion to $7 billion.

By the early 1980s the world oil picture had eased considerably and Exxon felt less urgency about diversification. With the price of oil peaking around 1981 and then tumbling for most of the decade, Exxon's sales dropped sharply. The company's confidence rose, however, as OPEC's grip on the marketplace proved to be weaker than advertised. Having abandoned its forays into other areas, Exxon refocused on the oil and gas business, cutting its assets and workforce substantially to accommodate the drop in revenue without losing profitability. In 1986 the company consolidated its oil and gas operations outside North America, which had been handled by several separate subsidiaries, into a new division called Exxon Company, International, with headquarters in New Jersey. Exxon Company, U.S.A. and Imperial Oil Ltd. continued to handle the company's oil and gas operations in the United States and Canada, respectively.

Exxon also bought back a sizable number of its own shares to bolster per-share earnings, which reached excellent levels and won the approval of Wall Street. The stock buyback was partially in response to Exxon's embarrassing failure to invest its excess billions profitably—the company was somewhat at a loss as to what to do with its money. It could not expand further into the oil business without running into antitrust difficulties at home, and investments outside of oil would have had to be mammoth to warrant the time and energy required.

The Exxon Valdez*: 1989–98*

In 1989 Exxon was no longer the world's largest company, and soon it would not even be the largest oil group (Royal Dutch/Shell would take over that position in 1990), but with the help of the March 24, 1989, *Exxon Valdez* disaster the company heightened its notoriety. The crash of the *Exxon Valdez* in Prince William Sound off the port of Valdez, Alaska, released about 260,000 barrels, or 11.2 million gallons, of crude oil. The disaster cost Exxon $1.7 billion in 1989 alone, and the company and its subsidiaries were faced with more than 170 civil and criminal lawsuits brought by state and federal governments and individuals.

By late 1991 Exxon had paid $2.2 billion to clean up Prince William Sound and had reached a tentative settlement of civil and criminal charges that levied a $125 million criminal fine against the oil conglomerate. Fully $100 million of the fine was forgiven and the remaining amount was split between the North American Wetlands Conservation Fund (which received $12 million) and the U.S. Treasury (which received $13 million). Exxon and a subsidiary, Exxon Shipping Co., also were required to pay an additional $1 billion to restore the spill area.

Although the *Valdez* disaster was a costly public relations nightmare—a nightmare made worse by the company's slow response to the disaster and by CEO Lawrence G. Rawl's failure to visit the site in person—Exxon's financial performance actually improved in the opening years of the last decade in the 20th century. The company enjoyed record profits in 1991, netting $5.6 billion and earning a special place in the *Fortune* 500. Of the annual list's top ten companies, Exxon was the only one to post a profit increase over 1990. *Business Week*'s ranking of companies according to market value also found Exxon at the top of the list.

The company's performance was especially dramatic when compared with the rest of the fuel industry: as a group the 44 fuel companies covered by *Business Week*'s survey lost $35 billion in value, or 11 percent, in 1991. That year, Exxon also scrambled to the top of the profits heap, according to *Forbes* magazine. With a profit increase of 12 percent over 1990, Exxon's $5.6 billion in net income enabled the company to unseat IBM as the United States' most profitable company. At 16.5 percent, Exxon's return on equity was also higher than any other oil company. The company also significantly boosted the value of its stock through its long-term and massive stock buyback program, through which it spent about $15.5 billion to repurchase 518 million shares—or 30 percent of its outstanding shares—between 1983 and 1991.

Like many of its competitors, Exxon was forced to trim expenses to maintain such outstanding profitability. One of the favorite methods was to cut jobs. Citing the globally depressed economy and the need to streamline operations, Exxon eliminated 5,000 employees from its payrolls between 1990 and 1992. With oil prices in a decade-long slide, Exxon also cut spending on exploration from $1.7 billion in 1985 to $900 million in 1992. The company's exploration budget constituted less than one percent of revenues and played a large part in Exxon's good financial performance. Meantime, Exxon in 1990 abandoned its fancy headquarters at Rockefeller Center in New York City to reestablish its base in the heart of oil territory, in the Dallas suburb of Irving, Texas. In 1991 the company established a new Houston-based division, Exxon Exploration Company, to handle the company's exploration operations everywhere in the world except for Canada.

At the end of 1993 Lee R. Raymond took over as CEO from the retiring Rawl. Raymond continued Exxon's focus on cost-cutting, with the workforce falling to 79,000 employees by 1996, the lowest level since the breakup of Standard Oil in 1911. Other savings were wrung out by reengineering production, transportation, and marketing processes. Over a five-year period ending in 1996, Exxon had managed to reduce its operating costs by $1.3 billion annually. The result was increasing levels of profits. In 1996 the company reported net income of $7.51 billion, more than any other company on the *Fortune* 500. The following year it made $8.46 billion on revenues of $120.28 billion, a seven percent profit margin. The huge profits enabled Exxon in the middle to late 1990s to take some gambles, and it risked tens of billion of dollars on massive new oil and gas fields in Russia, Indonesia, and Africa. In addition, Exxon and Royal Dutch/Shell joined forces in a worldwide petroleum additives joint venture in 1996.

Exxon was unable—some said unwilling—to shake itself free of its *Exxon Valdez* legacy. Having already spent some $1.1 billion to settle state and federal criminal charges related to the spill, Exxon faced a civil trial in which the plaintiffs sought compensatory and punitive damages amounting to $16.5 billion. The 14,000 plaintiffs in the civil suit included fishermen, Alaskan natives, and others claiming harm from the spill. In June 1994 a federal jury found that the huge oil spill had been caused by "recklessness" on the part of Exxon. Two months later the same jury ruled that the company should pay $286.8 million in compensatory damages; then in August the panel ordered Exxon to pay $5 billion in punitive damages. Although Wall Street reacted positively to what could have been much larger damage amounts and Exxon's huge profits placed it in a position to reach a final settlement and perhaps put the *Exxon Valdez* nightmare in its past, the company chose to continue to take a hard line. It vowed to exhaust all its legal avenues to having the verdict overturned—including seeking a mistrial and a new trial and filing appeals. In June 1997, in fact, Exxon formally appealed the $5 billion verdict. Exxon seemed to make another PR gaffe in the late 1990s when it attempted to reverse a federal ban on the return to Alaskan waters of the *Exxon Valdez,* which had by then been renamed the *Sea-River Mediterranean.* Environmentalists continued to berate the company for its refusal to operate double-hulled tankers, a ship design that may have prevented the oil spill in the first place. In addition, in an unrelated but equally embarrassing development, Exxon in 1997 reached a settlement with the Federal Trade Commission in which it agreed to run advertisements that refuted earlier ads claiming that its high-octane gasoline reduced automobile maintenance costs.

Nearing the Turn of the Century: Exxon Mobil

In December 1998 Exxon agreed to buy Mobil for about $75 billion in what promised to be one of the largest takeovers ever. The megamerger was one of a spate of petroleum industry deals brought about by an oil glut that forced down the price of a barrel of crude by late 1998 to about $11—the cheapest price in history with inflation factored in. Just one year earlier, the price had been about $23. The oil glut was caused by a number of factors, principally the Asian economic crisis and the sharp decline in oil consumption engendered by it, and the virtual collapse of OPEC, which was unable to curb production by its own members. In such an environment, pressure to cut costs was again exerted, and Exxon and Mobil cited projected savings of $2.8 billion per year as a prime factor behind the merger.

Based on 1998 results, the proposed Exxon Mobil Corporation would have combined revenues of $168.8 billion, making it the largest oil company in the world, and $8.1 billion in profits. Raymond would serve as chairman, CEO, and president of the Irving, Texas-based goliath, with the head of Mobil, Lucio A. Noto, acting as vice-chairman. Shareholders of both Exxon and Mobil approved the merger in May 1999. In September of that year the European Commission granted antitrust approval to the deal with the only major stipulation being that Mobil divest its share of a joint venture with BP Amoco p.l.c. in European refining and marketing. Approval from the Federal Trade Commission proved more difficult to come by, as the agency was concerned about major overlap between the two companies' operations in the Northeast and Mid-Atlantic region. The FTC was likely to force the companies to sell more than 1,000 gas stations in those regions as well as accede to other changes to gain U.S. antitrust approval.

Principal Subsidiaries

Ancon Insurance Company, Inc.; Esso Australia Resources Ltd.; Esso Eastern Inc.; Esso Hong Kong Limited; Esso Malaysia Berhad (65%); Esso Production Malaysia Inc.; Esso Sekiyu Kabushiki Kaisha (Japan); Esso Singapore Private Limited; Esso (Thailand) Public Company Limited (87.5%); Exxon Energy Limited (Hong Kong); Exxon Yemen Inc.; General Sekiyu K.K. (Japan; 50.1%); Esso Exploration and Production Chad Inc.; Esso Italiana S.p.A. (Italy); Esso Standard (Inter-America) Inc.; Esso Standard Oil S.A. Limited (Bahamas); Exxon Asset Management Company (75.5%); Exxon Capital Holdings Corporation; Exxon Chemical Asset Management Partnership; Exxon Chemical Eastern Inc.; Exxon Chemical HDPE Inc.; Exxon Chemical Interamerica Inc.; Exxon Credit Corporation; Exxon Holding Latin America Limited (Bahamas); Exxon International Holdings, Inc.; Esso Aktiengesellschaft (Germany); Esso Austria Aktiengesellschaft; Esso Exploration and Production Norway AS; Esso Holding Company Holland Inc.; Exxon Chemical Antwerp Ethylene N.V. (Belgium); Esso Nederland B.V. (Netherlands); Exxon Chemical Holland Inc.; Exxon Funding B.V. (Netherlands); Esso Holding Company U.K. Inc.; Esso UK plc; Esso Exploration and Production UK Limited; Esso Petroleum Company, Limited (U.K.); Exxon Chemical Limited (U.K.); Exxon Chemical Olefins Inc.; Esso Norge AS (Norway); Esso Sociedad Anonima Petrolera Argentina; Esso Societe Anonyme Francaise (France; 81.54%); Esso (Switzerland); Exxon Minerals International Inc.; Compania Minera Disputada de Las Condes Limitada (Chile); Exxon Overseas Corporation; Exxon Chemical Arabia Inc.; Exxon Equity Holding Company; Exxon Overseas Investment Corporation; Exxon Financial Services Company Limited (Bahamas); Exxon Ventures Inc.; Exxon Azerbaijan Limited (Bahamas); Mediterranean Standard Oil Co.; Esso Trading Company of Abu Dhabi; Exxon Pipeline Holdings, Inc.; Exxon Pipeline Company; Exxon Rio Holding Inc.; Esso Brasileira de Petroleo Limitada (Brazil); Exxon Sao Paulo Holding Inc.; Exxon Worldwide Trading Company; Imperial Oil Limited (Canada; 69.6%); International Colombia Resources Corporation; SeaRiver Maritime Financial Holdings, Inc.; SeaRiver Maritime, Inc.; Societe Francaise EXXON CHEMICAL (France; 99.35%); Exxon Chemical France; Exxon Chemical Polymeres SNC (France).

Principal Divisions

Exxon Company, U.S.A.; Exxon Company, International; Exxon Coal and Minerals Company; Exxon Chemical Company; Exxon Exploration Company.

Principal Competitors

7-Eleven, Inc.; Amerada Hess Corporation; Ashland Inc.; Atlantic Richfield Co.; BP Amoco p.l.c.; Caltex Corporation; Chevron Corporation; Conoco Inc.; Elf Aquitaine; ENI S.p.A.; Mobil Corporation; Norsk Hydro ASA; Occidental Petroleum Corporation; Pennzoil Company; Petroleo Brasileiro S.A.; Petroleos de Venezuela S.A.; Petroleos Mexicanos; Phillips Petroleum Company; RaceTrac Petroleum, Inc.; Repsol-YPF, S.A.; Royal Dutch/Shell Group; Saudi Arabian Oil Company; Sunoco, Inc.; Texaco Inc.; Tosco Corporation; TOTAL FINA S.A.; Ultramar Diamond Shamrock Corporation; Unocal Corporation; USX-Marathon Group; YPF Sociedad Anonima.

Further Reading

Akin, Edward N., *Flagler: Rockefeller Partner and Florida Baron,* Kent, Ohio: Kent State University Press, 1988.

Beatty, Sally, "Exxon-Mobil Is Marketing Dilemma," *Wall Street Journal,* December 3, 1998, p. B11.

Byrne, Harlan S., "Well-Oiled: Exxon Has Shaped Itself into a Nimble—and Even More Formidable—Giant," *Barron's,* May 20, 1996, pp. 17–18.

Caragata, Warren, ''Union of Giants: Exxon and Mobil Create a Colossus,'' *Maclean's,* December 14, 1998, pp. 44–46.

Chernow, Ron, *Titan: The Life of John D. Rockefeller Sr.,* New York: Random House, 1998.

Cooper, Christopher, ''Fears Linger on 10th Anniversary of *Exxon Valdez* Spill,'' *Wall Street Journal,* March 23, 1999, p. B4.

Cooper, Christopher, and Steve Liesman, ''Exxon Agrees to Buy Mobil for $75.3 Billion,'' *Wall Street Journal,* December 2, 1998, p. A3.

Cropper, Carol M., et al., ''The *Forbes* 500's Annual Directory,'' *Forbes,* April 27, 1992.

''Exxon-Mobil, Total-Petrofina Mergers Slated,'' *Oil & Gas Journal,* December 7, 1998, pp. 37–38, 40–41.

Finch, Peter, ''The *Business Week* 1000,'' *Business Week,* special issue, 1992.

Gibb, George Sweet, and Evelyn H. Knowlton, *History of Standard Oil Company (New Jersey): The Resurgent Years, 1911–1927,* New York: Harper & Brothers, 1956.

Grabarek, Brooke H., ''Exxon: Forget the *Valdez,*'' *Financial World,* September 27, 1994, p. 14.

Hedges, Stephen J., ''The Cost of Cleaning Up,'' *U.S. News & World Report,* August 30/September 6, 1993, pp. 26–28, 30.

Hidy, Ralph W., and Murrel E. Hidy, *History of Standard Oil Company (New Jersey): Pioneering in Big Business, 1882–1911,* New York: Harper & Brothers, 1955.

''Inside the Empire of Exxon the Unloved,'' *Economist,* March 5, 1994, p. 69.

Larson, Henrietta M., Evelyn H. Knowlton, and Charles S. Popple, *History of Standard Oil Company (New Jersey): New Horizons, 1927–1950,* New York: Harper & Row, 1971.

Liesman, Steve, ''Exxon Suspends Exploration in Russia,'' *Wall Street Journal,* August 19, 1999, p. A2.

Liesman, Steve, and John R. Wilke, ''Exxon and Mobil Get Antitrust Approval in Europe for Their Planned Merger,'' *Wall Street Journal,* September 30, 1999, p. A4.

Longman, Phillip J., and Jack Egan, ''Why Big Oil Is Getting a Lot Bigger,'' *U.S. News & World Report,* December 14, 1998, pp. 26–28.

Mack, Toni, ''The Tiger Is on the Prowl,'' *Forbes,* April 21, 1997, p. 42.

McCoy, Charles, ''Exxon's Secret *Valdez* Deals Anger Judge,'' *Wall Street Journal,* June 13, 1996, p. A3.

Nevins, Allan, *Study in Power: John D. Rockefeller—Industrialist and Philanthropist,* 2 vols., New York: Charles Scribner's Sons, 1953.

Norman, James R., ''A Tale of Two Strategies,'' *Forbes,* August 17, 1992, p. 48.

''Oil Majors Make Tough Decisions on Jobs, Assets,'' *Chemical Marketing Reporter,* July 13, 1992.

Raeburn, Paul, ''It's Time to Put the *Valdez* Behind Us,'' *Business Week,* March 29, 1999, p. 90.

Richards, Bill, ''Exxon Is Battling a Ban on an Infamous Tanker,'' *Wall Street Journal,* July 29, 1998, p. B1.

Rogers, Alison, ''The *Fortune* 500: It Was the Worst of Years,'' *Fortune,* April 20, 1992.

Sampson, Anthony, *The Seven Sisters: The Great Oil Companies and the World They Made,* New York: Viking, 1975; New York: Bantam, 1991.

Solomon, Caleb, ''Exxon Is Told to Pay $5 Billion for *Valdez* Spill,'' *Wall Street Journal,* September 19, 1994, p. A3.

——, ''Exxon Verdict Comes Amid Problems of Old Oil Fields, Few New Prospects,'' *Wall Street Journal,* September 19, 1994, p. A3.

——, ''Jury Decides Exxon Must Pay $286.8 Million,'' *Wall Street Journal,* August 12, 1994, p. A3.

——, ''Jury Finds Exxon Reckless in Oil Spill,'' *Wall Street Journal,* June 14, 1994, p. A3.

Sullivan, Allanna, ''Exxon and Mobil Are Already Devising Their New Brand,'' *Wall Street Journal,* April 6, 1999, p. B4.

Tarbell, Ida M., *The History of the Standard Oil Company,* New York: Harper & Row, 1966.

Teitelbaum, Richard, ''Exxon: Pumping Up Profits,'' *Fortune,* April 28, 1997, pp. 134–36, 140–42.

Wall, Bennett H., *Growth in a Changing Environment: A History of Standard Oil Company (New Jersey),* New York: McGraw-Hill, 1988.

Wilke, John R., and Steve Liesman, ''Exxon, Mobil May Be Forced into Divestitures,'' *Wall Street Journal,* January 20, 1999, p. A3.

—Jonathan Martin and April Dougal
—updated by David E. Salamie

Facom S.A.

6, rue Gustave Eiffel
91423 Morangis (Essonne)
France
Telephone: (33) 1.64.54.45.45
Fax: (33) 1.69.09.60.93
Web site: http://www.facom.fr

Public Subsidiary of Fimalac S.A.
Incorporated: 1918 as Franco-Américaine de Construction d'Outillage Mécanique
Employees: 4,300
Sales: FFr 5.2 billion (US$860 million) (1998)
Stock Exchanges: Paris
NAIC: 332212 Hand and Edge Tool Manufacturing; 336399 All Other Motor Vehicle Parts Manufacturing

Facom S.A. is one of the world's leading manufacturers of hand tools, equipment, and parts for the garage market and automotive aftermarket. Based near Paris, Facom boasts one of the most extensive ranges of hand tools in the world, with more than 8,000 catalog references covering specialized tools for the automotive, aerospace, electrical engineering, electronics, offshore, and heavy duty industry markets, as well as tools for the maintenance, general applications, and consumer markets. Facom operates 13 production facilities in Europe and the United States, while sales and support services are provided through 15 centers located in Europe, the United States, and Asia, which provide distribution to more than 100 countries through a network of 5,500 distributors. The company also operates a fleet of some 100 demonstration trucks, which allow in-field technical and product demonstrations for more than 3,500 Facom products. Each year Facom's field demonstrators log more than 100,000 visits. In the late 1990s, Facom was building its garage equipment activity, principally through its German Beissbarth subsidiary. The company also branched out into the automotive aftermarket business, with the cash purchase of Autodistribution S.A. in May 1999. Formerly known as Strafor-Facom, the company shed its furniture operations (including its joint ownership position of the Steelcase Strafor furniture group), as well as its traditional steel foundry operations. In May 1999, Facom was acquired by the French holding company Fimalac, which bought out more than 96 percent of Facom's stock. Under new CEO Alain Gomez, appointed in June of that same year, Facom announced its intention to become one of the world's top three hand tool manufacturers, ahead of Snap On, Stanley Works, Danaher, and SPX Corp.

Foundry Founding in 1918

World War I had devastated much of northern France, but had also pointed the way to a new emphasis on machinery and precision engineering. Rebuilding the country's industrial and manufacturing infrastructure gave rise to new opportunities. Among those seeking his fortune was young engineering graduate Louis Mosès. With funding from his family, Mosès opened a small forge and workshop near Paris's Gare de Lyon in 1918. Calling his company ''Franco-Américaine de Construction d'Outillage Mécanique,'' from which the acronym FACOM was later drawn, Mosès and a staff of ten workers began crafting precision tools for the booming mechanical and manufacturing markets. The ''Américaine'' in the company's name was a shrewd marketing ploy, conjuring up the technical sophistication and diversity of the U.S. military equipment brought over during the war.

Facom's original products were based on Mosès' own designs; Mosès also acted as the company's salesman. Initial production centered on a single product, which remained the company's only product during its first year of business. Later known as ''Madame 101,'' this product was an adjustable wrench, one of the first of its kind, with a distinctive round head and curved cast-iron handle. The product, which remained in the company's catolog into the 1960s, was quickly adopted by the French railroad industry, which was rebuilding after the war.

The strength of Facom's sales and a growing range of wrench designs led the company to expand its facilities. Building on Mosès family land in Gentilly, a suburb of Paris, Facom opened a 16,000-square-foot workshop containing machining, hardening, grinding, honing, and fitting setups, as well as its own power source. Facom also began adding sales staff. The first of Facom's sales force was one Gustave Schoettlé, who went on to found Etablissments Schoettlé, a prominent Alsace

Company Perspectives:

The Facom Group is focusing development on several major growth avenues: Proximity to end-users and close cooperation with distributors; greater innovation in all fields, particularly for the improvement of product ranges and service offered to end-users; constant improvement in products and processes in the Group's Centres of Competence; strengthening of Group brands; continued development of Garage Equipment in cooperation with hand-tool brands for the automotive aftermarket; internationalisation.

region distributor of automotive parts and industrial tools and supplies, and lead the way toward the building of Facom's worldwide distribution network.

During the 1920s, Facom's market focus expanded from the national railroad industry to the booming automotive market. The company began designing tools for France's automakers, starting with a monkey wrench for Renault and soon followed by a wood-handled screw wrench for Peugeot. By 1924, Facom was ready to publish its first sales pamphlet, which started with just a few pages for only some 60 product references, but later grew to nearly 600 pages, referencing more than 8,000 products, with over 800,000 copies distributed worldwide. Among the products featured in the 1924 catalog was the "Autobloc" self-adjusting wrench.

This was followed by another strong success. In the mid-1920s, Facom introduced the Stillson-type pipe wrench to the French market. The success of this and the company's other products led to rapid growth. By the end of the decade the company employed more than 100 workers, and its sales staff had grown to six people.

The 1930s offered the company a new market for growth. The rising strength of the airplane industry—which had grown from a craftsman-based cottage industry to full-scale industrial production—brought Facom a new range of customers. Quickly adapting its production to the aircraft industry, Facom became a principal supplier of hand tools and equipment to the new national airline, Air France, which was inaugurated in 1933. The company's involvement in the growth of the aircraft industry encouraged Facom to adopt a new symbol, that of a winged bolt, which remained a company hallmark throughout the century.

By then, Facom's catalog had grown to some 500 products, including a variety of wrench designs—such as the Bulldog, a cycling favorite—adapted to the specialized needs of the various industries. Facom was also building a reputation for high quality, as well as innovative designs. In the late 1930s, the company also began positioning itself as a leader in the high-end tool market, offering products such as interchangeable sockets for its socket wrenches and chromed—as opposed to the standard burnished—steel tools.

Meanwhile, the company diversified beyond tools per se, turning its forge and machining shops to such products as meat mincers and other kitchen tools. Despite a decade of social unrest, as French industry was rocked by a long series of strikes, Facom remained relatively stable, enjoying good employee relations. The company also managed to get through World War II in good shape, maintaining control of its assets and even protecting most of its workforce from labor draft by the German occupiers. Facom, then, was poised for new growth as the war drew to an end.

Postwar Boom

Leadership of Facom was given to Louis Mosès son André in 1945. A graduate of the prestigious engineering school Ecole Centrale, André Mosès remained at Facom's head until 1974, along the way elevating the company as one of France's largest manufacturers, while also turning its focus to the international market. With an extensive catalog of tool designs and a commitment to technological advancements, the company was well placed to take advantage of the economic boom in postwar Europe. The rebuilding effort—and Facom's commitment to making the capital investment needed to increase production capacity and expand its product range—brought a new era of company prosperity. Over the next 30 years, Facom registered an average annual sales increase of some 13 percent. With production quickly quadrupled, Facom also began innovating with its sales activities.

The company's sales literature was formalized into the Facom Catalog, which, published every four years, quickly became a reference for the French and international tool markets. Facom was also shifting its sales force from direct sales to a distributorship model, eventually building a network of more than 5,500 distributors. At the same time, Facom borrowed a technique from its U.S. rivals, taking to the road with a fleet of demonstration vehicles. The trucks, fitted with much of Facom's growing range of tools, paid visits to the company's distributors and customers, offering demonstrations of new products, as well as noting customer reactions and suggestions, which were then incorporated into the company's future products.

By the beginning of the 1950s, Facom's production levels had grown to some 50,000 products per month. The company launched a large number of new products, including pullers, ratchet wrenches, and torque wrenches, while expanding its automotive range with products including wheel balancers. Facom continued to bring U.S.-inspired marketing techniques to the European marketplace, including a lifetime guarantee on all of its products, which was introduced in 1952. By the end of the decade, the company's sales had expanded across the European continent, and Facom had made strong inroads into the South American, African, and Asian markets as well.

With the start of the 1960s, Facom had taken its position as the European leader in hand tools sales. The company also began diversifying at this time, adding to its core foundry and hand tools operations product lines such as office furniture and baking machinery. The company's office furniture line eventually took on a substantial position in the company, leading to a name change of Strafor Facom. In the early 1970s, Facom placed its Strafor subsidiary operations into a joint venture with Steelcase, of the United States, to form the Steelcase Strafor office furniture manufacturer. Facom continued to build its furniture activities, adding the office partition maker Clestra, and moving into the high-end furniture market with the Italian Cassina.

Key Dates:

1918: Company is founded by Louis Mosès.
1945: Andrés Mosès is named president of company.
1970: Facom is listed on the Paris stock exchange.
1980s–90s: Company pursues a number of acquisitions, including Bost, Garnache, Virax, Dela, Britool, SK Hand Tools, Sykes Pickavant, and Beissbarth.
1995: Company begins major restructuring.
1998: Facom sells its baking machinery and office furniture subsidiaries.
1999: Company purchases Autodistribution S.A.

Facom was also building its capital infrastructure. After opening a new forge at Villeneuve-le-Roi in the mid-1950s, the company began opening other industrial facilities, including production sites at Ezy-sur-Eure in 1967 and Nevers in 1974. The company's headquarters moved to Morangis in 1970. That year the company went public, placing its stock on the Paris exchange.

The new capital generated by its stock listing enabled Facom to make stronger moves on the international front. The company began opening full-fledged subsidiary operations in many of its international markets, including Belgium and Germany in 1970, followed by Italy in 1971. By the time of André Mosès's death in 1974, Facom had built up a catalog of some 4,000 product references, with print runs of more than 300,000 copies and translations into multiple languages.

If André Mosès had been responsible for turning Facom into one of France's major manufacturers, his successors, Roger Desvignes, from 1974 to 1988, and Henri Lachman, who guided the company into the late 1990s, were credited with building Facom into a truly international company. By the beginning of the 1980s, the company had extended its subsidiary operations to the Netherlands, the United Kingdom, the United States, and Switzerland. The company added a Spanish subsidiary in 1988. Facom also continued to build up its peripheral activities, including garage equipment and service industry equipment.

By the end of the decade, Facom had grown to take not only the leadership of the European hand tools market, with some nine percent market share, but had also become one of the world's top three hand tools manufacturers. International sales had grown to such an extent that more than one-third of Facom's sales were made outside of France. Facom began boosting its market position with a series of strategic acquisitions, adding new product lines and markets, including Piolé, a sheet metal manufacturer; pliers from Bost; screwdrivers with Garnache; pipeworking tools from Virax; the measuring tools maker Dela; the automotive tool maker Britool, based in the United Kingdom; Italy's largest hand tools producer, USAG; and U.S. hand tools manufacturer SK Hand Tool Corporation. These acquisitions not only helped consolidate Facom's market status, they also strengthened its international foothold, adding a string of production facilities in the United States, the United Kingdom, and Italy.

Retooling for the 21st Century

While the company continued its international expansion, adding locations in new markets including Poland, Singapore, Russia, and Denmark, an extended economic crisis forced Facom to reevaluate its diversified status. By the late 1990s, Facom made the decision to regroup around its core business of hand tools, while boosting its garage equipment activities and entering the automotive aftermarket—two relatively unconsolidated markets offering strong growth prospects. By late 1998 and early 1999, Facom had begun to pare down its operations, selling off its foundry and baking machinery operations, while exiting the Steelcase Strafor joint-venture partnership. After purchasing the automotive aftermarket specialist Autodistribution for some FFr 3.4 billion in May 1999, the company exited the furniture market completely, simplifying its name once again to Facom.

By then, the company had come under new ownership as well. In March 1999, the holding company Fimalac, led by Marc Ladreit de Lachamière, launched a hostile takeover of Facom. After an attempt to resist the takeover, Facom finally agreed to the purchase in May 1999, giving Fimalac more than 96 percent control of Facom's stock. The change in ownership put an end to the short-lived leadership of CEO Paul-Marie Chavanne, who had replaced Henri Lachmann in 1998. In his place, Alain Gomez was named CEO. In late 1999, Facom moved to boost its garage equipment operations with the acquisitions of three companies: Fog, in France; Zippo, in Germany; and Tecalemit, in the United Kingdom.

Principal Subsidiaries

Facom (Singapore); Facom (Netherlands); Facom (Germany); Facom (Switzerland); Facom (Spain); Facom (Belgium); Facom (Denmark); Facom (U.K.); Britool (U.K.); Sykes Pickavant (U.K.); Auto Tools (U.K.); Vitrex (U.K.); USAG (Italy); Pastorino (Italy); Coficom; Vidmar; BGI; Dela; Virax; Facom Tools (U.S.A.); Facom USA; SK Hand Tool (U.S.A.); Facom Automotive Group GmbH (Germany); Facom Automotive Group Italia; Beissbarth (Germany); Sicam (Italy).

Principal Competitors

The Stanley Works; Snap On, Incorporated; SMED International.

Further Reading

Debontride, Xavier, "Facom acquiert trois sociétés européenes spécialisés dans l'éqipment de garage," *Les Echos*, October 14, 1999, p. 12.

Deep in the Heart of the 20th Century Industrial Evolution, Morangis: Facom S.A., 1993.

Laforce, Margueritte, "Facom vise le podium mondial," *Les Echos*, June 30, 1999, p. 13.

"Strafor Facom se separe de son pole ameublement," *Le Figaro*, February 4, 1999.

"Strafor Takeover Battle Heats Up," *Financial Times*, April 12, 1999.

—M. L. Cohen

Feld Entertainment, Inc.

8607 Westwood Center Drive
Vienna, Virginia 22182
U.S.A.
Telephone: (703) 448-4000
Fax: (703) 448-4100
Web site: http://www.feldentertainment.com

Private Company
Incorporated: 1932 as Ringling Bros. and Barnum & Bailey Combined Shows, Inc.
Employees: 2,500
Sales: $500 million (1999 est.)
NAIC: 71131 Promoters of Performing Arts, Sports, and Similar Events Without Facilities

Feld Entertainment, Inc., formerly Irvin Feld & Kenneth Feld Productions, Inc., is one of the foremost live entertainment firms in the United States. Approximately 25 million people attend its live shows each year, drawing more customers than any other live entertainment venue except the Disney theme parks. The core of Feld Entertainment is the Ringling Brothers Circus, the legendary U.S. circus with roots in the 19th century. Feld operates two Ringling Brothers shows, a Red show and Blue show, so that audiences can see entirely different acts each time the circus comes to town. These circuses perform in indoor arenas in North America. An international unit travels to Mexico and South America. In addition, the company operates a circus called Barnum's Kaleidoscape, which uses a traditional canvas tent. Kaleidoscape is smaller than the other units, and more upscale. Feld also operates nine touring ice shows including the popular Disney on Ice, and the top-grossing Las Vegas act Siegfried & Roy. Feld has also promoted and invested in Broadway shows, and run other entertainments such as a life-size model of the space shuttle and a touring show based on George Lucas's *Star Wars* movies. The company's revenues come not only from its ticket sales, but from concessions, which it runs through a subsidiary called Sells-Floto.

Ringling Brothers and Barnum & Bailey

P.T. Barnum was a legendary U.S. showman who exhibited midgets and Eskimos, beautiful babies and bearded ladies. Most of his life he ran stationary or traveling exhibitions, and it was not until he was 60 years old, in 1870, that he established a genuine circus. Barnum's circus had one major rival, that run by James A. Bailey. In 1879 the competitors merged, to form Barnum & Bailey's Circus—The Greatest Show on Earth. This was a huge hit in the United States, and in 1887 it departed for a five-year tour of Europe. During Barnum & Bailey's European sojourn, another U.S. circus came into prominence. This was Ringling Brothers. The Ringlings–Albert, Otto, Alfred, Charles, and John—grew up in Baraboo, Wisconsin, where they began performing musical concerts, skits, and clown acts. By 1884, Ringling Brothers was touring out of Baraboo with an animal show and a band. Early acts featured a ''Hideous Hyena Striata Gigantum'' and the brothers singing, spinning plates, and dancing in big wooden shoes. They bought an elephant in 1888, and two years later, they had become a formidable competitor to the absent Barnum & Bailey, touring coast to coast. P.T. Barnum died in 1891, and Barnum & Bailey's and Ringling Brothers eventually worked out non-conflicting tours. Then when James Bailey died in 1907, the Ringlings bought his circus for something less than half a million dollars. The two circuses operated separately until 1919, when they combined into the Ringling Brothers and Barnum & Bailey Combined Show, Inc. By 1930 this was the world's biggest circus, with 5,000 employees and a main tent seating capacity of 10,000 people. It moved by railroad, requiring 249 cars at its peak. John Ringling, the youngest of the Ringling Brothers, died in 1936, and leadership of the circus passed to a nephew, John Ringling North. The circus continued to tour, but began losing its audience to other forms of entertainment. The circus clung to its traditional marketing, putting up posters in alleys and on barnsides, though radio and then television would have been advertising options. It needed open space to set up its tents, and its shows were pushed increasingly to the edges of towns. By 1956 the circus was a decrepit organization, antiquated, outmoded, and $1.8 million in debt. John North announced that the great canvas ''big top'' would fold for the last time in Pittsburgh that year.

Company Perspectives:

Feld Entertainment Inc. is the largest producer of live family entertainment in the world today. Under the dynamic leadership of Chairman and Chief Executive Officer Kenneth Feld, this organization is poised to become an even larger force in the entertainment industry and an innovator in family entertainment internationally.

The Feld Takeover: 1957–67

The tent folded, yet the circus reopened the next season, transformed into an indoor show. The agent of this change was a rock-and-roll promoter, Irvin Feld. Feld was born in Hagerstown, Maryland, where his father ran a clothing store. The family was always short of money, and in 1931, when Irvin was 13, he and his brother Israel joined a traveling carnival and sold the proverbial snake oil. Peddling bottles of dubious medicine netted the brothers $8,000 over the summer, and they returned to the carnival in subsequent summers. After Feld graduated from high school, he and his brother opened a novelty shop in a poor neighborhood of Washington, D.C. In 1939 the NAACP offered to pay the Felds to operate a pharmacy in the store, if they would also open a soda fountain that would serve black customers. The Felds went along with the idea, and their store became the Super-Cut-Rate Drugstore. Irvin was interested in music, and the store also sold records. Irvin soon prepared to open a chain of record stores, and he scouted for talent for his Super Disc record label. In 1945 Feld's label produced a million-record hit, Arthur Smith's ''Guitar Boogie.'' In the 1950s Irvin Feld went on to become a hit-maker for his own and other record labels, and then he began packaging rock-and-roll tours. Artists he handled included many of the top acts of the era, including Chubby Checker, Fats Domino, Paul Anka, Fabian, Bill Haley, Frankie Avalon, and the Everly Brothers. Feld toured his ''Biggest Show of Stars'' in 80 cities nationwide. Indoor arenas were being built across the country at that time, and Feld saw that these heated venues could create opportunities for other entertainment as well. Inspired by his youth on the carnival circuit, Feld wanted to run a circus, and when the Ringling Brothers circus announced it would shut down, Feld immediately called on its owner, John North. North offered to sell him the circus if he would also absorb all the organization's debts, but Feld had a different idea. The circus remained in North's hands, with Feld managing it as an indoor enterprise.

The change of venue made an immediate impact. The tent show had been restricted to summer months or warm-weather climates. Now it could go year-round. In addition, without the tent to put up, the circus saved vastly on its labor costs. Savings were said to be $50,000 the very first week the indoor show opened. Feld took over marketing, advertising, renting the arenas, and planning the tour, for a percentage of the revenue. This arrangement lasted until 1967. According to Feld, the problem was that the circus had become stale. The performers were old, their acts did not change, and it remained an antiquated form of entertainment. Feld wanted to do more with the circus. In partnership with his brother Israel and Judge Roy Hofheinz, builder of the Houston Astrodome, Irvin raised $8 million to buy out North. In true showman style, Feld had the consummation of the deal photographed. He handed over the check to North in the Coliseum in Rome, in the company of a rented lion cub.

Expansion in the 1970s and 1980s

Feld and his partners bought themselves an organization full of problems. Even after a decade of the cost-saving switch to indoor arenas, the circus was still $1 million in debt. Its clowns ranged in age from 50 to 75, some of its showgirls too were past their prime, and the performers' costumes, music, and lighting were outdated. Feld began investing in new equipment and seeking out new talent. He founded a Clown College in order to train new performers, and very soon the average age of Ringlings' entertainers dropped from 46 to 23. Feld also decided that he would double the circus, producing two shows, the Red and the Blue. Then if each show revamped its acts entirely every other year, he could manage tours in which no city saw the same show twice. It made the circus fresh. Eventually the two circuses between them covered 90 cities across the United States, for a total of 550 shows a year. Feld wanted the core of his new show to be a great animal act, and he decided on the most famous European animal trainer, Gunther Gebel-Williams. But Gebel-Williams was under contract to a German circus that did not want to let him go. Ultimately, Feld bought Circus Williams for $2 million, in order to get its star.

Feld and his partners paid for the new acts and equipment in several ways. They cut labor costs by putting the performers on salary, so that they were paid the same no matter how many shows they did. And they did a lot of shows, now working six days a week. Feld also extended the season for more weeks a year. With relentless promotion of the new, improved circus, Feld upped attendance. The circus brought in more money, though tickets remained modestly priced. In 1969, the company went public. Feld carried his showmanship even into the company's annual report and stock certificates, printing them in bright colors and writing a special year-end report just for children. The public offering raised a lot of cash for the company, but it also made the corporation open to takeover. Two years after going public, Mattel, Inc., the giant toy company and maker of Barbie dolls, bought the circus for close to $50 million. The Ringling Brothers Circus was folded into Mattel's entertainment division, though Irvin Feld continued to run it as chief executive officer. Israel Feld died in 1972, and Irvin's son Kenneth entered the business. They continued as hands-on managers, personally auditioning every new act as well as handling all the financial and logistical decisions. According to an interview with Irvin Feld in the February 1983 *Inc.*, Mattel did not interfere directly with the managing of the circus. Yet it did have financial expectations that the Felds found unrealistic, such as looking for an automatic 15 percent increase in revenues annually. Mattel also suggested raising ticket prices, something that was anathema to Irvin Feld. He wanted the circus to remain affordable for everyone. Although in the *Inc.* article the Felds declared that the circus had been consistently profitable through the Mattel years, the Mattel entertainment division nevertheless suffered a loss of $1.1 million in 1982. Even if, as Feld insisted, the loss was attributable to other Mattel divisions, the company nevertheless agreed to sell off the circus in 1983. Irvin and Kenneth Feld raised $22.8 million—less than half what they

Key Dates:

1879: Barnum & Bailey's Circus–The Greatest Show on Earth is formed.
1907: Ringling Brothers and Barnum & Bailey form combined circus.
1956: Big top folds.
1957: Under Irvin Feld's management, circus moves to indoor arenas.
1967: Feld and investors buy Ringling Brothers.
1969: Company goes public.
1971: Toymaker Mattel, Inc. buys the circus.
1983: Mattel sells circus back to Felds; holding company of Irvin Feld & Kenneth Feld Productions, Inc. is formed.
1988: Circus tours Japan.
1996: Company changes name to Feld Entertainment, Inc.
1999: Barnum's Kaleidoscape opens.

had been paid for it in 1971—and bought the circus back. Their holding company for the circus and other units was named Irvin Feld & Kenneth Feld Productions, Inc.

Diversification in the Late 1980s and 1990s

A year after reacquiring the circus, Irvin Feld died. His son Kenneth took over as chief executive of Feld Productions, and the circus continued to grow and change. By 1987, Ringling Brothers was the only circus in the United States that still traveled by railroad, though there were some two dozen smaller circuses in the country that traveled by truck. The combined shows employed 280 performers who toured close to 90 cities to an audience total of 11 million people. Ticket prices remained moderate, costing from $6 to $11.50 in 1987, but the shows raked in money through concessions. Kenneth Feld extended the concessions offerings after his father's death, adding circus videos and other products. The circus was unusual among entertainments playing at indoor arenas, because most other shows were required to split their concessions take with the arena owners. But Ringling Brothers kept 100 percent of its concessions, which accounted for a large chunk of its profits. Total revenues for the circus doubled between 1983 and 1987, to reach $250 million.

Feld Productions also branched out into other live performances. While still owned by Mattel, the company had invested in two skating shows, the Ice Follies and Holiday on Ice. These shows soon proved to be uneconomical, because they depended on big-name star skaters who commanded a hefty percentage of the revenues. Kenneth Feld managed this difficulty by firing the stars, and instead licensed characters from Walt Disney. Walt Disney on Ice used professional skaters in bulky costumes. Within a few years, this popular show was traveling the world. By the late 1980s, Feld Productions operated three ice shows and the Las Vegas magic act Siegfried & Roy. In 1988, the circus toured Japan for the first time as a 100-animal and 160-performer act. Japanese investors paid a flat fee of approximately $11.4 million for the seven-month tour.

By the mid-1990s, the company had branched out to include a variety of entertainment projects. It owned a life-size replica of the U.S. space shuttle which toured the world; invested in Broadway shows; owned a circus equipment manufacturer and the company that managed its concessions; and had put together an extravagant live-action entertainment based on George Lucas's *Star Wars* films. The circuses had evolved into much more modern shows, with hip music and glitzy choreography. The company developed a third circus unit in 1994 in order to take the show abroad. Logistics had made this difficult in the past, so the company hired new managers with experience in other industries to oversee the intricate travel and equipment arrangements. Feld Productions had seven ice shows by that time, which toured Australia, Japan, and Europe regularly.

The company had grown so much domestically that international expansion seemed a logical next step. In 1996 Kenneth Feld hired a president and chief operating officer from outside the industry to help oversee the firm's future growth. The new COO was Stuart Snyder, who came to Feld from Turner Home Entertainment. He was to oversee much of the nuts and bolts of the corporation, as well as help plan for future expansion. The company hoped to become more of an integrated family entertainment company, branching out perhaps even into television. In addition, the firm saw plenty of room to grow abroad. Target areas included Central America and the Asia/Pacific region. The company changed its name that year, from Irvin Feld & Kenneth Feld Productions to the simpler Feld Entertainment, Inc.

Feld Entertainment made a large investment in the late 1990s to develop an entirely new circus. The company spent approximately $10 million to come up with a new style circus that could capture an upscale audience. Called Barnum's Kaliedoscape, the show took place in a tent, recalling the traditional circus of Ringling Brothers and Barnum & Bailey. But this was a plush, comfortable tent on an intimate scale, seating only 1,800 people. Amenities included flower-decked restrooms and concessions sales of Wolfgang Puck pizza, a brand created by the famous California chef. Kaleidoscape was launched to rave reviews and took the 1999 Golden Clown Award at the International Circus Festival in Monte Carlo.

At the approach of the new millennium, Feld was a growing and dynamic company, ready for many more possibilities beyond circuses and ice skating. CEO Kenneth Feld mused in a November 8, 1999, *Fortune* feature about expanding the Feld brand into restaurants, television, and the Internet. ''We'd like to be there every day,'' he said, rather than as a once-a-year event. Whether this dream was possible or not, the company had certainly made much out of the once-moribund circus industry. Skilled management and promotion had brought the circus back from near extinction, and it seemed likely that brand extension or a new business direction were not out of reach for the firm's capable managers.

Principal Subsidiaries

Hagenbeck-Wallace, Inc.; Sells-Floto.

Principal Competitors

Walt Disney Company; Cirque du Soleil Inc.

Further Reading

Deckard, Linda, ''Fall '95 Debut for Ringling's First International Unit,'' *Amusement Business,* August 1, 1994, p. 14.

Fitzgerald, Kate, ''On the Circus Circuit,'' *Advertising Age,* July 12, 1999, pp. 30–31.

Gilpin, Kenneth, ''The Circus Is Just One of His Acts,'' *New York Times,* March 24, 1993, p. D1.

Gunther, Mark, ''The Greatest Business on Earth,'' *Fortune,* November 8, 1999, pp. 228–38.

Hirsch, James, ''Big Business Under the Big Top,'' *New York Times,* October 4, 1987, pp. F1, F29.

''John Ringling North,'' *Variety,* June 12, 1985, p. 94.

Kobell, Rona, ''Feld Entertainment CEO Touts Evolution of Circus As Art Form,'' *Knight-Ridder/Tribune Business News,* October 28, 1999.

La Franco, Robert, ''The Tightest Man in Show Business?'' *Forbes,* November 8, 1993, pp. 67–75.

Langdon, Dolly, '''Lord of the Rings' Irvin Feld Has Made a Fading Circus the Greatest Show on Earth Again,'' *People,* May 12, 1980, pp. 49–57.

Melvin, Mary Kay, ''Feld 'Outsider' Prez/Coo Snyder to Help Company Broaden Its Scope,'' *Amusement Business,* December 16, 1996, p. 25.

''The Show Goes On,'' *Sales & Marketing Management,* March 1997, p. 16.

Solomon, Abby, ''Lords of the Rings,'' *Inc.,* February 1983, pp. 101–08.

—A. Woodward

Fisher-Price Inc.

636 Girard Ave.
East Aurora, New York 14052
U.S.A.
Telephone: (716) 687-3000
Toll Free: (800) 432-5437
Fax: (716) 687-3476
Web site: http://www.fisher-price.com

Wholly Owned Subsidiary of Mattel Inc.
Incorporated: 1930
Employees: 5,600
Sales: $693.9 million (1998 est.)
NAIC: 339932 Games, Toy, and Children's Vehicle Manufacturing; 339931 Doll and Stuffed Toy Manufacturing

Fisher-Price Inc. is the world's largest preschool products company. Fisher-Price has dominated the infant and preschool toy market for over 60 years and has become known for the high quality and durability of its products. Wholly owned by Mattel Inc. since 1993, Fisher-Price consolidated with other divisions of its parent to make up a single, massive marketer of toys principally for children under the age of five. Some of its best-known products include Little People playsets and Power Wheels ride-on toys. It markets several licensed toy lines, such as Sesame Street products and Disney, Winnie the Pooh, Blue's Clues, and Bear in the Big Blue House toys and games. The company makes toys for both boys and girls, with strong sellers in each category. It is also a leading manufacturer of infant furniture and car seats. Fisher-Price has outstanding brand name recognition and customer loyalty. The company operates as an umbrella over several Mattel units: Fisher-Price, based in East Aurora, New York; Tyco Preschool, based in Manhattan; and Mattel's Preschool unit, based in El Segundo, California.

Early Years

Fisher-Price was founded in East Aurora, New York, in 1930, by Herman G. Fisher, Irving L. Price, and Helen M. Schelle. While Price and Schelle had worked in retail businesses that featured toys among their inventory, Fisher brought to the group his experience in the advertising and sale of games. All three proved adept at knowing what children liked and were committed to the idea that the public would appreciate high quality toys. Though the founders knew little about the actual manufacture of toys, they reasoned that popular products would have, according to the company's first catalog, "intrinsic play value, ingenuity, strong construction, good value for the money and action." Specifically, they observed, "children love best the gay, cheerful, friendly toys with amusing action, toys that do something new and surprising and funny!"

Such beliefs proved correct. From a frame and concrete-block house turned manufacturing headquarters in East Aurora, Fisher-Price manufactured 16 different toys during its first year of operation. This line included Granny Doodle and Doctor Doodle, brightly colored wooden ducks that, when pulled, opened their beaks and quacked. During this time, Fisher-Price made its toys out of Ponderosa pine, a splinter-resistant wood. The wooden pieces were then joined by heavy steel parts and decorated with non-toxic lithographs and finishes, resulting in a uniquely durable and appealing product.

Withstanding the effects of the Great Depression, Fisher-Price reported losses during its first four years of business and eventually developed a healthy reputation and customer base. In the early 1950s, Fisher-Price augmented its line of wooden toys by fashioning new products from a popular new material, plastic.

Production After World War II

During the period of increased consumerism following World War II, the toy industry grew and changed dramatically. Herman Fisher retired from his post as president of Fisher-Price in 1966 and was succeeded by Henry Coords, who had been recruited from AT&T's affiliate company Western Electric. Shortly thereafter, the Quaker Oats Company expressed interest in acquiring Fisher-Price, and in 1969, Quaker Oats purchased Herman Fisher's 67.4 percent voting stock and 14.1 percent nonvoting stock, along with Fisher-Price's additional outstanding shares, for

Company Perspectives:

Our mission is to support today's families with young children, through a breadth of products, including toys and children's products that make early childhood more fun and enriching.

$122 per share, the same amount paid Mr. Fisher. At the time of the purchase, Fisher-Price had sales above $30 million.

Also during this time, other cereal companies, including General Mills, General Foods Corp., and Nabisco, acquired toy companies. While some industry analysts speculated that cereal companies were purchasing toy manufacturers that would produce ''premiums''—the small, inexpensive toys offered free inside cereal boxes—one toy company executive told *Advertising Age* that ''the toy business is not really geared to premium offers. The merchandise is too expensive to be a successful premium item. It can't build business.'' Rather, some suggested, cereal and toy companies were merged, in part, to ''piggy-back'' toy and cereal commercials. ''It's a natural thing to form marriages of convenience with toys and cereals. They're aimed at the same market,'' one adman told *Advertising Age*.

The ad agency of Waring and LaRosa handled advertising for both Quaker Oats and Fisher-Price, and under Quaker Oats ownership, Fisher-Price's spending on advertising increased. In 1970, in what was then the largest advertising campaign in the company's history, Waring and LaRosa created a campaign emphasizing the quality and sturdiness of Fisher-Price toys. The estimated $1.25 million ad campaign declared Fisher-Price made toys to last a ''whole childhood, and another childhood, and a childhood after that.'' Aimed at parents, the print ads ran in *Family Circle*, *Good Housekeeping*, *Ladies' Home Journal*, *Parents*, and *Women's Day*.

By 1976, Fisher-Price had diversified into three different businesses. While the majority of its business still lay in preschool products for children 18 months through 4 years, the company also marketed a line of toys for children aged four to nine years and another line for infants. The newest additions to the company's toy lines were the 1974 introduction of dolls, the 1975 introduction of the Adventure Series, which included Adventure People for early grade school children, and the 1976 introduction of the Play Family Hospital for preschoolers.

As Fisher-Price entered new markets, it also expanded the scope of its advertising, offering commercial spots during children's television programming for the first time in 1976. Responding to criticism from such special interest groups as Action for Children's Television (ACT), concerned about advertising's potential for exploiting children, Fisher-Price president Henry Coords maintained that the ads would not exert high pressure and would be moderate in number. Fisher-Price continued advertising its toys on prime and daytime network television, as well as in women's service magazines, but also focused on reminding retailers in trade journals that Fisher-Price now serviced three distinct age groups. Though Fisher-Price consistently increased its ad budget, spending almost $2.15 million on network advertising in 1975, the company spent considerably less than did its top rivals. General Mills Fun Group, for example, spent $8.8 million on network advertising in 1975; Mattel and Hasbro spent $6 million and $4 million, respectively.

Competition in the 1980s

While Fisher-Price had turned its attention to its new markets in the 1970s, significant increases in the birth rate revived the stagnant preschool market, Fisher-Price's mainstay, in the mid-1980s. As toy giants such as Hasbro, Kenner Products, and Mattel expanded their presence in the preschool market, and other companies, including Matchbox Toys Ltd., Panosh Place, and Schaper Mfg. Co., entered the market with new lines ranging from baby exercise tapes to washable vinyl plush toys, Fisher-Price found its leading position in the preschool market threatened.

''In the face of major competition, Fisher-Price has become very aggressive in ad support for all its products,'' Fisher-Price's director of advertising Robert Moody told *Advertising Age*, reaffirming the company's commitment to ''advertising of over 75 of the new and existing toys in its line on a year-round basis.'' To support its new plan, Fisher-Price increased its ad budget by 90 percent to $50 million in 1986. The company also afforded significant portions of its account to the advertising firms of J. Walter Thompson USA in Chicago and Backer & Spielvogel in New York. Funding for its new marketing expenditures came through reductions in overhead and controlling manufacturing costs.

With the help of ad support, Fisher-Price's new toy lines made 1986 a profitable year. An integral part of the company's product line during this time was represented by its Gummi Bear merchandise, toys based on a very popular Walt Disney Productions cartoon series featuring magical, medieval bears. Gaining the license to use the trademarked Gummi Bear characters, Fisher-Price produced poseable figures, puzzles, stuffed animals, and other toys based on the cartoon. The Gummi Bear license, according to *Advertising Age*, was Fisher-Price's most profitable television license since that of the Sesame Street characters, which the company had obtained in the 1970s. Also during this time, Fisher-Price introduced a Toddler Kitchen, a Magic Vac (a toy vacuum cleaner that blew bubbles), and Puffalumps, ultra soft, silky stuffed animals. Puffalumps became the most successful new product in Fisher-Price's history, achieving sales of approximately $25 million in its first year.

As Fisher-Price revived its preschool line in 1986, it also pushed its fastest growing segment, an audiovisual toy division, created in 1982, which produced durable audiovisual products, simple in design, specifically for children. Among the division's most popular products were a phonograph, a tape recorder, and an AM-FM radio with a sing-along microphone. The company planned to increase its advertising support of the division by 40 percent in 1986, in response to an expected increase in the number of older children to whom the products would appeal.

In 1987, the company introduced the first video camcorder for children. Priced at around $200, the PXL 2000 Deluxe Camcorder System was well received at the American International Toy Fair in New York City, the annual showing of new products in the industry, and had sold out at retailers for the

Key Dates:

1930: Founded by Fisher, Price, and Schelle.
1969: Quaker Oats acquires company.
1976: Company begins promoting its products through television ads.
1982: Creates audiovisual toy division.
1991: Fisher-Price trades on New York Stock Exchange as independent company.
1993: Company acquired by Matttel.

calendar year by late spring. Public response to the camcorder was bolstered by an aggressive $3 million ad campaign that featured 30-second television ads on network television and the Nickelodeon cable channel, as well as print ads in *Life*, *Newsweek*, *People*, *Sports Illustrated*, and *Time*. Unlike most toy ads, the camcorder print ads targeted men; J. Walter Thompson executive Matt Kurtz explained to *Advertising Age* that ''most electronics purchases are made by fathers,'' and the magazines had been chosen because of their large male readership. The ad headline challenged readers to ''Picture what your kid can do with the new PXL 2000,'' offering the camcorder as ''a great way to turn on your kid's imagination.''

While the camcorder met with initial success, Moody asserted in *Advertising Age* that ''the camcorder shouldn't disguise what Fisher-Price is all about,'' which was toys for preschoolers. Nevertheless, Fisher-Price's offerings had expanded to include much more than preschool toys between 1984 and 1989, and the company now encompassed four main operating groups: the Infants Products Group, which included crib and playpen products as well as juvenile furnishings, accounting for 30 percent of the company's U.S. business; the Traditional Products Group, which included preschool toys, accounting for 60 percent of U.S. business; the Promotional Products Group, which included highly publicized toys like the Puffalumps and the PXL 2000 Deluxe Camcorder System, accounting for ten percent of sales; and International Business, which included sales in Canada and Europe, accounting for 25 percent of Fisher-Price's sales in 1987. As the company increased its efforts at expansion, management observed demographic trends indicating that the level of new births would remain static into the early 1990s and the number of older children would increase. Therefore, Fisher-Price's preparations for expansion into non-traditional products and products for older children were on target for future profits.

The company's expansion did not go as planned, however. According to some critics, as Fisher-Price entered the promotional products toy market in 1987, it shortchanged its preschool line, which had helped it grow steadily from 1930 to 1986. Though the first promotional products met with success and brought additional revenues to the company, by 1988 resources had to be shifted from the company's preschool, infant, and juvenile lines to support the failing promotional line, according to *Children's Business*. In the late 1980s, Fisher-Price began losing money, due largely to the failure of its promotional products (including a battery-powered sports car and a children's video camera), order cancellations because of some late merchandise deliveries, and intensified competition from Hasbro, Rubbermaid, and Mattel in the preschool market.

To combat these difficulties, Fisher-Price discontinued its line for older children and refocused its attention on its preschool line. In addition, newly appointed president Ronald Jackson and his management team began trying to turn the company around by cutting expenses. Toward that end, four of the company's 13 manufacturing plants and two distribution centers were closed, and the workforce was reduced by more than 3,000. Production of some lines were moved overseas, while advertising and selling costs were reduced by $17 million, according to the *Business First-Buffalo*. The restructuring efforts had returned Fisher-Price to profitability by 1991.

Still, the company continued to struggle with the effects of its unsuccessful bid to market toys and furnishings for older children. Despite Fisher-Price's leading position in the market for preschool toys, industry analyst John G. Taylor suggested in the *Buffalo News* that ''Fisher-Price is somewhat of an underdog in this competition. Fisher-Price doesn't have the financial resources that the other companies (Little Tikes and Playskool) have—they're owned by people with deep pockets.''

New Ownership in the 1990s

In 1991, Quaker Oats decided to spin off Fisher-Price as an independent company, and, in the summer of that year, Fisher-Price began trading on the New York Stock Exchange. During this time, Mattel expressed an interest in acquiring the steadily improving Fisher-Price, but Quaker Oats had rejected the idea. In December 1993, however, Fisher-Price became a wholly owned subsidiary of Mattel, making Mattel the leading toy company in the United States. Analysts referred to the deal as the most significant acquisition in the toy industry since Hasbro bought Tonka Corp. in 1991, as it allowed Mattel to challenge Hasbro's top position in the $17 billion toy industry.

Mattel and Fisher-Price fit together well. Mattel consolidated Fisher-Price's Mexican production, European sales offices, and media planning and buying with its own to make a ''stronger, more focused entity,'' according to the *Buffalo News*. Journalist Frank Reysen told the paper that Mattel and Fisher-Price succeeded together because ''neither is a hot-item type of company. They look to developing (toy) lines over the long term.'' Fisher-Price's infant and preschool lines became Mattel's second largest product category, after Barbie, making up an estimated one-fourth of Mattel's 1994 sales.

After several years of restructuring, Fisher-Price began to expand in 1994 with a new line of outdoor toys. According to the *Buffalo News*, Fisher-Price saw ''outdoor play yard toys as a means of increasing its sales without the risks associated with diversification outside the infant and preschool toy category.'' To support the new line, the company opened two new factories (the first such openings in 20 years), purchased additional equipment, added 300 production plant jobs and 50 white collar jobs, and began considering building a research and development center near its headquarters in East Aurora, New York. ''We are going after market share, and we intend to grow,'' Fisher-Price president James A. Eskridge (who succeeded Ronald Jackson after the takeover) told the *Buffalo News*.

Though the outdoor playthings market was dominated by Rubbermaid subsidiary Little Tikes, Fisher-Price represented a challenge to competitors through lower manufacturing costs and sound merchant relations. Responding to the move, Little Tikes executive Kevin G. Curran remarked, "I wish them success, but Little Tikes invented this category 20 years ago, and we are going to defend it aggressively."

Fisher-Price's efficient operations and quality products garnered awards in the industry, including the title of 1993 Vendor of the Year, awarded by *Discount Store News*. Fisher-Price was the first toy manufacturer to ever win the vendor category award, the top award given manufacturers by the discount retailing chains. In addition, Fisher-Price ranked fifth in Total Research Corp.'s 1993 Equitrend survey of brand quality. Indeed, according to one stock analyst quoted in the *Buffalo News*, "the goodwill the toy maker has developed with consumers . . . was instrumental in the firm's rapid recovery after it suffered record losses in 1990 and early 1991."

Fisher-Price remained the leader in the $1 billion infant and preschool plaything market and was achieving sales records into the mid-1990s. The company's Little People playsets, Corn Popper, Bubble Mower, and other toys proved invaluable to parent Mattel, and the outdoor play toys also met with initial success. In addition, Fisher-Price was taking advantage of Mattel's global distribution and marketing network to bolster sales in Mexico, Italy, Germany, and Spain.

To increase exposure on retail shelves, Fisher-Price entered three new markets in 1994: games, dolls, and electronic learning toys. Unlike its expansion under Quaker Oats, Fisher-Price remained committed to marketing toward the age range with which it had its greatest success. "We aren't getting outside of what we do best: toys for children zero to five years of age," Fisher-Price president James A. Eskridge told the *Buffalo News*.

Yet the company continued to open creative new outlets for itself. In January 1996 Fisher-Price announced it was embarking on an expensive joint venture with Compaq Computer Corporation to develop home computers for young children. The companies planned to spend as much as $15 million to make educational and fun computer toys and software. Products included large-sized computer keyboards designed for young hands, software that came with a steering wheel attachment that let children "drive" through a game landscape on the computer screen, and other game and adventure software programs. Fisher-Price's entry into this segment came as other companies too were pouring resources into educational and entertainment software. Sales of electronic learning toys of all types grew at over 25 percent in the mid-1990s. Yet competition in the toy industry was intense, and sales slumped at Fisher-Price, dropping almost 20 percent from 1996 through 1997.

Despite difficult conditions, which affected the entire toy industry, Fisher-Price had some strong sellers. One was its line of Power Wheels ride-on toys. These were sturdy motorized cars and motorcycles that children could ride in or out of the house. They moved at about five miles per hour, and retailed for around $70 to several hundred dollars for the top of the line models. By 1998, the company had sold approximately ten million of the battery-powered cars, which were popular among both boys and girls and ran to nearly 100 different models. But gradual recognition of complaints from consumers that the vehicles had ignited and caused fires led to a huge recall of Power Wheels in 1998. The U.S. Consumer Products Safety Commission began receiving reports from fire departments in late 1996 that the vehicles had caught fire, and in November 1998, the agency spurred Fisher-Price to issue a massive recall. Its recall of the estimated ten million vehicles made this one of the largest toy recalls in the history of the industry. Though Fisher-Price maintained that the fires were in virtually every case caused by consumers tinkering with the engines, the company nevertheless spent approximately $30 million (through parent Mattel) to recall and repair all its Power Wheels.

The recall contributed to a slight decrease in sales at Fisher-Price for 1998. In the fall of that year, the company took the first step in a major reorganization. At that time, the company began to put its "F-P" trademark on some of the preschool toys made by other Mattel-owned companies. Then in the spring of 1999, the company announced that Fisher-Price Inc. would encompass both Mattel's preschool line and the Tyco Preschool brand. Tyco was based in New York City and was best known for its licensed products. These included Blue's Clues, a late 1990s hit, and Sesame Street character toys, longstanding veterans that continued to sell well. Mattel's preschool unit, based at Mattel's home base in El Segundo, California, also featured a host of licensed products, including Disney characters and Winnie the Pooh. Licensing was proving to be the hottest area in toy sales, and Fisher-Price had lacked any licensed products. By putting its well-known brand name on the other divisions' licensed toys, the company hoped to get in on the licensing magic. The company was operated within Mattel as Fisher-Price Brands, with Fisher-Price Inc.'s president, Neil Friedman, traveling continuously between East Aurora, Manhattan, and El Segundo. The company had no plans to consolidate physically, but marketing and management for the three companies now operated together. This consolidation made Fisher-Price the number one preschool toy company in the world.

Principal Subsidiaries

Fisher-Price House (U.K.); Fisher-Price Spielwaren GmbH (Germany).

Principal Operating Units

Tyco Toys; Mattel Preschool.

Principal Competitors

Hasbro, Inc.

Further Reading

Baker, M. Sharon, "Quick, Decisive Moves Gave Fisher-Price a New Playground," *Business First-Buffalo*, May 11, 1992, p. 19.

Begley, Sharon, "Little Cars, Big Issues," *Newsweek*, November 2, 1998, p. 50.

Biltekoff, Judith A., "Fisher-Price Stuffs Ad Budget," *Advertising Age*, February 24, 1986, p. 62.

Chadwick, John, "El Segundo, Calif.-Based Fisher-Price Recalls Riding Toy," *Knight-Ridder/Tribune Business News*, October 22, 1998, p. OKRB929506E.

Colman, Gregory J., ''Fisher-Price Leaves Home,'' *Children's Business*, August 1991, p. 8.

''Fisher-Price: Fighting to Recapture the Playpen,'' *Business Week Industrial Edition*, December 1990, p. 70.

Fitzgerald, Kate, ''Fisher-Price Leads Pack: Back-to-Basics Is Key for Toy Fair,'' *Advertising Age*, February 8, 1988, p. 72.

Forkan, James P., ''TV Use Is Key to Fisher-Price Profitability Plan,'' *Advertising Age*, March 15, 1976.

Jaffe, Thomas, ''Fisher-Price Overpriced?,'' *Forbes*, August 19, 1991, p. 148.

Lefton, Terry, ''How the Big Brands Rank,'' *Brandweek*, March 29, 1993, pp. 26–30.

Linstedt, Sharon, ''Mattel Raises Preschool Profile of Western New York-Based Fisher-Price,'' *Knight-Ridder/Tribune Business News,* May 17, 1999, p.OKRB99137020.

—— ''Mattel Reports Mixed Results for 1998,'' *Knight-Ridder/Tribune Business News*, February 3, 1999, p. OKRB99034023.

Madore, James T., ''Competitors Crowd Fisher-Price's Market,'' *Buffalo News*, February 20, 1994.

——, ''Fisher-Price Poised for Major Expansion,'' *Buffalo News*, July 24, 1994, p. B13.

——, ''They're Pulling Hair in the Playpen,'' *Buffalo News*, February 9, 1992.

McWilliams, Gary, ''Babes in Cyberland,'' *Business Week*, January 15, 1996, p. 38.

O'Connor, John J., ''Cereal Men Aren't Playing When They Enter Toy Marketing,'' *Advertising Age*, December 14, 1970, pp. 1, 74.

Pollack, Andrew, ''No. 2 Official Out at Mattel in Shake-Up,'' *New York Times*, March 4, 1999, pp. C1, C21.

Stern, Sara E., ''Youth Movement: Fisher-Price Turns on Kid Video,'' *Advertising Age*, October 5, 1987, p. 90.

—Sara Pendergast
—updated by A. Woodward

FMR Corp.

82 Devonshire St.
Boston, Massachusetts 02109
U.S.A.
Telephone: (617) 563-7000
Fax: (617) 476-6153
Web site: http://www.fidelity.com

Private Company
Incorporated: 1946 as Fidelity Management and Research Company
Employees: 28,000
Total Assets: $765.2 billion (1998)
NAIC: 52392 Portfolio Management (pt); 52393 Investment Advice; 52312 Securities Brokerage; 52311 Investment Banking and Securities Dealing; 523991 Trust, Fiduciary, and Custody Activities (pt); 523999 Miscellaneous Financial Investment Activities (pt)

Boston-based FMR Corp. is a diversified financial services company with operations in banking, mutual funds, life insurance, and retirement services. FMR is the parent company of Fidelity Investments, the largest mutual fund group in the world with more than $765 billion under management. The company's Fidelity Brokerage Services Inc. subsidiary is the second largest discount brokerage house in the United States. FMR has direct investments covering a wide range of industries, including telecommunications, real estate, publishing, and transportation. The privately held financial giant's extraordinary growth is closely tied to the powerful influence of one family, that of Edward ''Ned'' Johnson III.

The Early Decades: 1930s–60s

FMR traces its history to 1930, when the Boston money management firm of Anderson & Cromwell—later Cromwell & Cabot—organized Fidelity Shares. Designed to serve smaller investment accounts, the firm's steady $3 million in assets were invested in Treasury notes rather than stocks. Efforts to boost the shareholder base using various distribution arrangements proved unsuccessful, although the firm did become a pioneer in shareholder communications by regularly updating shareholders through letters and reports on portfolio holdings. In 1938 Fidelity Fund opened its own offices, and Cromwell & Cabot began receiving a fee for its investment advice. Later that year, as the fund evolved and became more of an independent entity, Fidelity's president and treasurer began to draw salaries from the fund itself. Two years later a regulatory statute, the Investment Company Act of 1940, went into effect and enabled the accelerated growth of such mutual fund houses as Fidelity.

When Fidelity Fund's president resigned in 1943, the fund's directors recruited Edward C. Johnson II to take over, while he retained his position as treasurer and counsel to the large Boston investment trust Incorporated Investors. Johnson, a graduate of Harvard Law School, came from a wealthy Boston family—his father was last in the line of Johnson family partners in Boston's premier retail dry goods store, C.F. Hovey & Company. Serving his father as trustee on family trust funds, Johnson's position with Fidelity Fund provided him with an opportunity to consolidate his family's investments and give free rein to his fascination with picking stocks.

Johnson had found his calling, and his uncanny gift for choosing moneymaking stocks provided the fuel for the company's remarkable expansion—by 1945 the fund's assets had risen to $10 million, and Johnson gave up his position with Incorporated Investors to devote his time to Fidelity. The following year Fidelity's contract with Cromwell & Cabot expired, and rather than renew it, Johnson chose to manage the fund himself and create a new firm, Fidelity Management & Research Company, to act as advisor. Also in 1946 Johnson began developing a group of Fidelity funds, beginning with the launch of the Puritan Fund. In the ensuing decade a variety of different investment groups were started, all under the umbrella of the Fidelity Group of Funds. Johnson continued to supervise Fidelity's portfolio until the mid-1950s, when the company's rapid growth necessitated shifting his attention to executive and administrative tasks. In the decade from 1947 to 1957, under his guidance, assets under management at Fidelity soared from $16 million to $262 million.

A well-established leader of the Boston financial community and a Wall Street legend, Johnson was a strong-willed chief

Company Perspectives:

With our success, we have grown to an organization of more than 28,000 people, with businesses throughout the United States and across the globe. We must balance our growth by retaining the entrepreneurial spirit of a small company, where each individual knows how much his or her efforts count. Fidelity's culture is to build on our existing strengths as we explore future opportunities, to balance tradition with new thinking. Working together, we can provide valuable products and services for our customers.

executive who took an almost paternalistic interest in the company and in nurturing talent at the fund. Throughout his life, he never wavered in his fascination with the vagaries of the stock market, keeping a daily stock market diary for over 50 years, in order to sharpen his understanding of market fluctuations.

One of the talented young men who came under Johnson's tutelage was his son, Edward C. ''Ned'' Johnson III, who joined Fidelity in 1957 after working at State Street Bank. In that year two ''growth'' funds were added to the Fidelity Group. Ned was put in charge of the Trend Fund, while Gerry Tsai, another protégé of the senior Johnson, became manager of the Capital Fund. Tsai was a young, inexperienced immigrant from Shanghai when Johnson hired him as a stock analyst in the early 1950s. Tsai bought such speculative stocks as Polaroid and Xerox when he took control of the Capital Fund. His performance gained him fame and customers, and in less than ten years he was managing more than $1 billion. Tsai, considered the prodigy of the investment world, eventually left Fidelity in 1965 after recognizing that it was Ned who was destined to succeed the elder Johnson as CEO.

The 1960s were a golden period for Fidelity, with the Trend and Capital Funds the high-performance heroes of that decade. From 1960 to 1965 assets under management swelled from $518 million to $2.3 billion. In 1962 the company established the Magellan Fund, which eventually became the largest mutual fund in the world. The firm also launched FMR Investment Management Service Inc., in 1964, for corporate pension plans; the Fidelity Keogh Plan, a retirement plan for self-employed individuals, in 1967; and, to attract foreign investments, established Fidelity International the following year in Bermuda. In addition, it formed Fidelity Service Company in 1969 to service customer accounts in-house, one of the first fund groups to do so.

Diversification and Expansion: 1970s–Early 1990s

By 1972, when Ned Johnson took over executive control from his father, the seemingly boundless growth of the 1960s had dissipated, and Fidelity was experiencing an uncharacteristic downturn in business—during the two years from 1972 to 1974, assets had shrunk 30 percent. Under Ned's control, the company began an ambitious expansion program, diversifying from its mutual fund base into a broad range of financial services. The new strategy seemed to work and by the late 1970s, Fidelity regained the momentum it had lost. Among the new services made available by the company was the Fidelity Daily Income Trust (FDIT), the first money market fund to offer check writing, which was launched in 1974. Bypassing traditional brokerage distribution channels, Fidelity offered the new fund directly to the public, using print advertising and direct mail. Two years later, Fidelity launched the first open-end, no-load municipal bond fund, and in 1979 Fidelity became the first major financial institution to offer discount brokerage services. That year Fidelity also organized an arm of the company to serve institutional investors.

During the late 1970s and much of the 1980s, Fidelity became the envy of the investment industry with the remarkable success of its Magellan equity fund. Under the management of investment wizard Peter Lynch, Magellan became the best-performing mutual fund in the nation. Beginning in 1977, when Lynch became manager, the mutual fund seemed to take off through a run of inspired stockpicking. Leading the ten-year fund performance rankings for most of the 1980s, Magellan consistently posted higher percentage gains than the Standard & Poor (S&P) 500 stock index. Typical of its performance, the fund scored an average annual gain of 21.1 percent in the five-year period ending March 31, 1989, which compared favorably to the 17.4 percent annual gain posted by the S&P 500.

Magellan had more than 1,000 companies in its portfolio—many more than the 200 or so that most big equity funds held. Industry observers traced Magellan's success to the combination of Lynch's remarkable knowledge, his gift for picking stocks, a willingness to take risks, and the heavy promotion undertaken for the fund by Fidelity. During the 13 years that Lynch was in charge, Magellan grew at a breakneck pace—from $20 million in 1977 to $12 billion by 1990.

Because Lynch did not invest heavily in conservative stocks and kept very little liquid capital, the Magellan Fund was hit hard by the crash that shook Wall Street on October 19, 1987. Caught off-guard, Fidelity was forced to sell shares heavily in a plummeting market to meet redemptions. On that day alone, nearly $1 billion worth of stock was sold. By the end of the week, Fidelity's assets had dropped from $85 billion to $77 billion. Still, almost all of the firm's equity funds beat the market on Black Monday. In 1988, the year following the crash, Fidelity's revenues were down a quarter and profits were 70 percent lower. Determined never to suffer another Black Monday, Johnson cut personnel by almost a third (from a pre-crash high of 8,100), began sharpening the company's international presence, and prepared to enter the lucrative insurance field. In 1989, with more than $80 billion in assets under management, the firm had captured about nine percent of the entire mutual fund industry; a year later these figures leapt to nearly $119 billion in assets with over 35 million mutual fund transactions in 1990, the year Peter Lynch surprised the industry by resigning from the Magellan Fund to spend more time with his family and write (he rejoined the company as a part-time adviser in 1992).

By the early 1990s Magellan had lost its star status, although it still ranked among the top ten best-performing funds in the industry. In the meantime another Fidelity fund, Fidelity Select Health, a biotech fund, had taken over the number one spot, as Magellan moved to number three. The top five was rounded out by yet another one of Fidelity's funds, Fidelity Destiny 1. Most of Fidelity's top performers at that time came from its 36 ''select'' funds based on narrow industry segments.

Key Dates:

1930: Fidelity Fund is formed by Anderson & Cromwell.
1943: Edward C. Johnson II becomes president of the Fidelity Fund.
1946: Johnson establishes Fidelity Management and Research.
1962: Magellan Fund is established.
1969: Company begins serving international investors through Fidelity International.
1972: FMR Corp. is formed. Edward ''Ned'' C. Johnson III takes over control of the company.
1977: Peter Lynch becomes manager of the Magellan Fund.
1979: FMR offers discount brokerage services.
1984: Company offers computerized trading services.
1990: Peter Lynch retires from Magellan Fund.
1993: Assets under management surpass $200 billion mark.
1996: Fidelity introduces its redesigned web site.

Magellan was not the only fund to reap the rewards of Fidelity's advertising campaign. Beginning with Ned Johnson's leadership, the company began to more aggressively promote its services, keeping a high profile in the industry and before the general public through its big-budget marketing efforts. By the early 1990s the company's advertising budget was $28 million per year, making it the biggest advertiser in the mutual fund industry. Meanwhile, Fidelity was also reaching the public through a nationwide network of branch offices, launched in 1980.

Like his father, Ned Johnson was also fascinated by Japanese culture, inspiring him to adopt Japanese-style management. The company was vertically integrated in order to make it more self-sufficient. One of the functions brought inhouse was the account processing that banks usually handled for mutual funds. Fidelity was then able to capitalize on these operations by selling its services to other investment firms. Johnson was also prompted to create a closer relationship with employees and management. Ideas for improving business were solicited, while promoting an atmosphere of team loyalty.

In the late 1960s Fidelity began—before many other banking and investment firms—to invest a large share of its budget in technology, with an eye toward becoming technologically self-reliant. As a result Fidelity was able to stay on top of the data processing and telecommunications revolution that was beginning to transform the financial industry. This strategy continued, and as the company entered the 1990s Fidelity was spending more than $150 million a year in the technology realm. The company was at the forefront of the group of financial firms making the transition from traditional roles to one of technology-based customer service, offering a kind of one-stop financial services shop.

An example of these advances was the interactive, automated telephone system that Fidelity was among the first to install in 1983. The following year the firm began offering computerized trading through Fidelity Investors Express. This service allowed customers to perform their own stock trades through home personal computers—what had become known as desktop investing. Fidelity also had custom-designed software to help representatives tap more information, including margin calculations and options analysis, while responding swiftly to customer requests. By the early 1990s Fidelity had upgraded its phone answering system to the point where it could handle 672 calls simultaneously on its automated toll-free lines, while a master console in Boston routed calls to the first available operator around the country. Fidelity also had its own electronic stock trading system, called the Investor Liquidity Network, that matched buy and sell orders from its brokerage and fund operators with those of outside institutional investors.

With the advent of the 1990s Fidelity had embarked on a new strategy to maintain its competitive advantage. Increasingly, it was aiming to be a low-cost personal financial advisor, moving in on territory traditionally associated with banks and brokers. Fidelity first crossed the line into banking's territory in 1983, by offering its USA checking service to customers with a minimum balance of $25,000. At the same time, Fidelity's enormous research and technology capabilities were being mobilized to provide customers with guidance in a wide range of areas, from retirement savings to planning for a college education.

Previously, Fidelity's custom services had been targeted at its richest clients, but by the early 1990s the firm was offering a wide range of services to all of its six million customers. After a slow start, the discount brokerage operation, which lost money in its first nine years, was expanded in the late 1980s with the addition of three new offices. This service eventually became the second largest in the country. In 1987 Fidelity also moved into the insurance and annuity business by offering its customers in certain states such products as single premium policies, deferred annuities, and variable life policies. In 1989 Fidelity offered the new Spartan Fund, which featured a low expense charge for larger, less active investors. Throughout the 1980s the company's institutional business grew, and by the end of the decade, Fidelity had become the largest manager of 401(k)s. From 1984 to the end of the decade, institutional assets under Fidelity management grew from $9.9 billion to $40 billion.

By the end of the first 20 years of Ned Johnson's reign, assets under Fidelity Investment's management had grown 21 percent annually, and with the close of 1991 FMR Corp. had posted record revenues of $1.5 billion, and record profits as well. During those two decades FMR became a highly diversified corporation with some 41 companies under its umbrella—among the financial companies were such firms as an art gallery, a limousine service, an employment agency, and a publishing concern. In addition, in April 1992 Fidelity Investments purchased 7.5 percent of banking giant Citicorp's common stock. Worth $480 million, this stake made Fidelity the largest single shareholder of common stock in the nation's largest banking company.

Over the course of the company's history, Fidelity proved itself time and again by taking risks and seizing opportunities, and despite a skittish investor market and a sluggish economy in the late 1980s and early 1990s, the company maintained its competitive edge. The Johnson family owned 47 percent of the stock—worth approximately a billion dollars—and most of the voting shares. The other 53 percent of the stock was owned by employees, principally senior managers, who were obligated to sell their shares back to the company when they left.

Continuing Growth and Challenging Times in the 1990s

The year 1993 was a banner one for FMR, and the company's total assets under management increased 36 percent, from $190 billion to $258 billion. Performing especially well in 1993 was Fidelity's growth fund group, which included Magellan. Nearly all of Fidelity's stock funds bettered the S&P 500, and Magellan alone grew from $22 billion in 1992 to $31 billion in 1993. Much of Magellan's success was attributed to manager Jeffrey Vinik, who assumed control of the fund in mid-1992. Vinik invested heavily in technology, cyclical, foreign, and natural gas stocks. Fidelity's market share in the mutual fund industry, which had hovered around the ten percent mark for four years, rose to 11.5 percent in 1993. In order to provide clients with a wide array of mutual fund choices, FMR in July launched Fidelity FundsNetwork, which offered non-Fidelity funds with no transaction fee. More than 250,000 new retail brokerage accounts and 1.5 million new retail mutual fund accounts, the highest number since 1987, were opened in 1993. John Rekenthaler, editor of the publication *Morningstar Mutual Funds,* which followed the activity of mutual funds, commented on Fidelity's performance in *Business Week*, "Any way you cut the numbers, Fidelity is doing spectacularly."

Also in 1993 FMR made headway in its capital group. Its Community Newspaper Company completed the acquisition of Beacon Communications from Chronicle Publishing Company of San Francisco. The purchase, which included 15 weekly newspapers and one daily, made Community Newspaper the largest operation of weekly newspapers in New England. FMR also founded a new company, City of London Telecommunications (COLT), and started Fidelity Personal Trust Services in three New England states.

The unsurpassed growth and success were not to continue so easily, however, and FMR faced increasing challenges in the mid-1990s. Though FMR enjoyed increased revenues, 1994 also brought rising interest rates and a volatile market. Small stocks suffered, and because many Fidelity funds invested heavily in smaller companies, FMR suffered as well. The U.S. bond market was, according to FMR, one of the worst since 1927, and the firm's fixed-income funds outperformed only 23 percent of their competitors. The company restructured its fixed income group management in order to increase efficiency. Gross retail sales for 1994 declined 35 percent.

In addition to Fidelity's losses in 1994, the company struggled to maintain consumer confidence after several incidents had sullied its reputation. The first occurred with the 1992 conviction of former portfolio manager Patricia Ostrander for accepting bribes from Drexel Burnham Lambert's Michael Milken in the late 1980s. Then came three revelations in 1994: the deliberate transmission of day-old prices for about 150 mutual funds; a company reversal after stating that the Magellan Fund would pay a year-end distribution, when in fact it would not; then another gaffe when incorrect 1099-DIV forms were mailed to shareholders of two international funds. Yet despite these problems and negative economic factors, Fidelity still managed to beat over 83 percent of its fund competition, posted increases for most of its business units, and raised assets under management to $297 billion, a climb of nearly 15 percent for 1994.

In 1995 the S&P 500 had a return of 37.58 percent, its top performance since 1958. Still, because a large percentage of the rise resulted from a small number of large company stocks, FMR struggled to maintain its pace. Though some of FMR's stock funds, such as the growth group, performed well in 1995, others did not. The growth and income group, with heavy investments in retail and energy industries, did poorly, as did the asset allocation group and the international group. FMR's high-income funds outperformed more than 75 percent of its peers, but the Capital & Income fund's poor performance impacted the group. A considerable Capital & Income investment in Harrah's Jazz went sour when the company declared bankruptcy.

In 1996 revenues and assets under management increased, but net income dropped from $4.31 billion in 1995 to $4.23 billion. The U.S. economy was strong, inflation low, and the stock market active, but just as in 1995, the best-performing stocks were a small number of large companies. As a result, only about 26 percent of Fidelity's stock funds outperformed the S&P 500. Magellan was one of the funds that performed poorly; its holdings in cash and bonds hurt results, and it was not as invested in well-performing industries, such as healthcare and technology. FMR restructured its equity group, reassigning a number of managers and dividing the group into eight business units. The restructuring of the fixed income group in 1994 had led to increased performance—in 1996 its funds outperformed 74 percent of the competition—and FMR hoped the same would happen with the equity division.

Despite some challenging years, FMR continued to expand and diversify. In 1994 the company announced plans to open a fifth regional operations center, in Marlborough, Massachusetts, and Fidelity Capital Markets opened a new trading floor at the World Trade Center in Boston. Fidelity's market share in the mutual fund market grew to 12.8 percent, up from 11.5 percent, and almost 1.5 million new customer accounts were opened. Also in 1994 Ned Johnson gave daughter Abigail Johnson a 24 percent interest in FMR, leading many to speculate that she was being groomed to take over the company upon Ned Johnson's retirement.

FMR opened its fifth regional operations center, in Merrimack, New Hampshire, in 1996. The company entered the commercial software business with the establishment of Fidelity Technologies, a company geared toward developing and marketing software to other businesses. FMR advanced on the technology front in another aspect with the redesign and relaunch of a new web site. By year-end, the Fidelity web site was being visited about 476,000 times a day, up from 43,000 during the fourth quarter of 1995. FMR's telecommunications company, COLT, went public in late 1996.

FMR and Fidelity faced many changes in 1997 and 1998 as the financial services climate grew increasingly competitive. In November Fidelity Investments announced a company reorganization effort designed to streamline operations and help boost mutual fund sales, which were sluggish during the first half of the year. James Curvey, who became FMR's chief operating officer that year, explained to *USA Today,* ''The key reason why we made the change: We need to simplify our organization. . . . Absolutely, we will become more efficient.'' Though the firm's fund performance began to improve toward the end of 1997, it was still not doing as well as the company hoped. According to Financial Research Corp., a firm that tracked mutual fund purchases, sales of Fidelity's mutual funds fell for the fourth year in a row in 1997. Also during this transition year FMR sold some non-strategic operations, such as its credit card business and its stake in Wentworth Gallery Ltd. FMR also closed its retail brokerage operations in the United Kingdom due to poor performance. The company was able to open some new operations in 1997 as well, including client service offices in Latin America. Energized by COLT's promising performance, Fidelity formed MetroRed, a telecommunications start-up business in South America.

In 1998, just months after closing its discount brokerage operations in the U.K., Fidelity opened a similar operation in Tokyo, Japan. Japan represented an untapped market, with the majority of personal finances stored in low-interest savings accounts. Also in 1998 Fidelity opened a sixth regional operations center, in Rhode Island. The company divested its Capital Publishing unit, publisher of *Worth, Civilization,* and *The American Benefactor,* presumably to focus on building its mutual fund operations. To reinforce its brand, Fidelity launched a national advertising and marketing campaign in 1998. Television and print ads featured Peter Lynch and the tag line, ''Know What You Own, and Know Why You Own It.''

Management changes in the late 1990s included the appointment of Bob Pozen as president of FMR in 1997, the same year James Curvey became chief operating officer. J. Gary Burkhead was promoted to vice-chairman of FMR from director, and Abigail Johnson took on a management role, leading the specialized growth group. In 1998 James Curvey took on the additional role of president of FMR. Pozen remained president of Fidelity Management & Research Company.

The stock market continued to perform strongly into the late 1990s, and the S&P 500 increased more than 28 percent in 1998, achieving more than 20 percent rises for the fourth straight year. Fidelity's mutual fund assets under management rose 25 percent over 1997, reaching $694.4 billion. In addition, the firm's funds beat 73 percent of their competitors, the best performance since 1993, and Fidelity funds made up 42 percent of the U.S. mutual funds that outperformed the S&P 500 in 1998. Despite such positive performances and a sales increase of 15 percent over 1997, net income fell from $535.6 million to $445.7 million. The company attributed the decline to drops in brokerage commissions, increasing expenses, and performance penalty fees.

As FMR neared 2000, the outlook appeared positive. For the first quarter of 1999, revenue shot up 27 percent to reach $2 billion, thanks to increases in brokerage commissions and mutual fund management fees. Net income increased more than fourfold to reach $294.1 million. In June FMR announced plans to raise $750 million, its most significant effort to raise money in company history. The firm indicated the money was needed to finance expansion of facilities and fund investment opportunities. FMR also planned to launch a savings and loan, called Fidelity Personal Trust Company.

With a long and rich history, FMR was by the late 1990s a global financial giant. The diverse conglomerate was not only the largest mutual fund company in the world but also the top provider of individual retirement plans in the United States, as well as the second largest discount brokerage firm. FMR had more than 15 million customers, more than $765.2 billion in assets under management, and more than 280 funds under its administration. With the U.S. economy showing no signs of a slowdown, and FMR demonstrating a willingness to advance and adapt with the times, it seemed likely FMR and the Fidelity name would continue to succeed and dominate the financial services sector.

Principal Subsidiaries

Fidelity Institutional Retirement Services Company; Fidelity Investments Actuarial Consulting Services; Fidelity Investments Public Sector Services Company; Fidelity Employer Services Company; Fidelity Investments Tax-Exempt Services Company; Fidelity Group Pensions International; Fidelity Group Pensions Japan; Fidelity Management Trust Company; Fidelity Brokerage Services Inc.; Fidelity Customer Marketing and Development Group; Fidelity Distributors Corporation; Fidelity Retail Distribution and Services; Fidelity Retail Operations and Technology; Fidelity Service Company, Inc.; National Financial Services Company; Fidelity Investments Canada Limited; Fidelity Money Management, Inc.; Strategic Advisers, Inc.; BostonCoach; Fidelity Interactive Company; J. Robert Scott; Community Newspaper Co.; Fidelity Investments Life Insurance Company; The Seaport Hotel; Devonshire Custom Publishing; Fidelity Investments Personal Trust Company; Tempworks/Tempsource; World Trade Center Boston.

Principal Operating Units

Fidelity Investments Institutional Retirement Group; Fidelity Personal Investments & Brokerage Group; Fidelity Investments Institutional Services Company, Inc.; Fidelity Brokerage Services Japan, LLC; Fidelity Management & Research Company; Fidelity Corporate Systems and Services; Fidelity Capital; Fidelity Ventures.

Principal Competitors

The Charles Schwab Corporation; T. Rowe Price Associates, Inc.; The Vanguard Group, Inc.

Further Reading

Browning, Lynnley, ''Fidelity's Unassuming Heir,'' *Boston Globe,* August 8, 1999, p. A1.

Churbuck, David, ''Watch Out, Citicorp,'' *Forbes,* September 16, 1991.

Eaton, Leslie, ''Junk Ethics: Michael Milken's Powers of Persuasion Included Bribery,'' *Barron's,* August 3, 1992, pp. 8–9, 20–26.

''Fidelity Fights Back,'' *Economist,* August 8, 1992, pp. 67–68.

Fierman, Jaclyn, ''Fidelity's Secret: Faithful Service,'' *Fortune,* May 7, 1990, pp. 86–92.

Helm, Leslie, et al, ''Fidelity Fights Back: Can CEO Johnson Revive the Behemoth of the Mutual Fund Industry?,'' *Business Week,* April 17, 1989, pp. 68–73.

Hechinger, John, ''Fidelity Investments Unveils Plan for Raising $750 Million in Debt,'' *Wall Street Journal,* June 16, 1999, p. A4.

Henderson, Barry, ''Magellan Steams Ahead: Fund Beats S&P, Putting Fidelity on Course for Big Revenues,'' *Barron's,* December 13, 1999, p. F3.

Hirsch, James S., ''Fidelity Sells Publishing Unit, Posts Gains,'' *Wall Street Journal,* April 6, 1998, p. B21.

McCartney, Robert J., ''Mutual Fund Firm Fidelity Buys Big Stake in Citicorp,'' *Washington Post,* April 28, 1992, pp. D1, D4.

Schwartzman, Sharon, ''Fidelity's Formula: Technology Keeps Customers Happy,'' *Wall Street Computer Review,* July, 1991, pp. 27–32.

Smith, Geoffrey, ''Fidelity Jumps Feet First into the Fray,'' *Business Week,* May 25, 1992, pp. 104–06.

——, ''What's Behind Fidelity's Riveting Results,'' *Business Week,* November 22, 1993, p. 114.

Stern, Richard L., ''Henry Ford Meet Ned Johnson,'' *Forbes,* September 3, 1990, pg. 42.

Waggoner, John, ''Fidelity Investments Retools Fund-Selling Structure,'' *USA Today,* November 4, 1997, p. B6.

—Timothy Bay and Kim M. Magon
—updated by Taryn Benbow-Pfalzgraf
and Mariko Fujinaka

Foster Poultry Farms

1000 Davis Street
Livingston, California 95334
U.S.A.
Telephone: (209) 394-7901
Toll Free: (800) 344-3116
Fax: (209) 394-6342
Web site: http://www.fosterfarms.com

Private Company
Incorporated: 1939
Employees: 7,000
Sales: $990 million (1998 est.)
NAIC: 311615 Poultry Processing

Long the leading poultry producer in California, Foster Poultry Farms has expanded its operations into Washington and Oregon to become the largest producer of chicken and turkey on the West Coast. The privately held company is a vertically integrated business which controls most aspects of its poultry production process. Foster Farms hatches, raises, slaughters, and processes chickens and turkeys. In addition, it manufactures its own feed, runs its own refrigerated trucks to bring its birds to market, and operates processing plants in Livingston and Fresno, California; Creswell, Oregon; and Kelso, Washington. Foster Farms also produces grain at a Colorado facility, and has other operations located in Alabama and Illinois. The company sells over 750 products to retail supermarkets and foodservice wholesalers under its own label, as well as under the Fircrest Farms, Lynden Farms, and Pederson Farms brands.

Launching of a Family Business

Foster Farms was founded in 1939 when Max and Verda Foster borrowed $1,000 against their life insurance policy to buy a repossessed 80-acre farm near Modesto, California. While Max continued to work as a reporter and the city editor at the *Modesto Bee,* Verda concentrated on raising turkeys. By 1942 the couple's venture had succeeded to the point that Max was able to quit his job at the paper and commit himself to the family business full time.

Although Foster Farms concentrated solely on turkeys during its early years, the company had expanded into chickens and dairy cattle by the late 1940s. After buying a second farm, the company acquired a feed mill in 1950. With the addition of this feed mill, Foster Farms would no longer depend on an outside supplier to feed its chickens. At the time, the Fosters were not the only poultry producer striving for vertical integration of the different aspects of their business. In fact, the entire poultry industry was in the midst of a massive reorganization. Fueled by monumental changes both in the technology of food production and in how Americans obtained their food, poultry producers increasingly came to see themselves less as family farms and more as automated factories.

A Changing Industry

Like other agricultural sectors, poultry production was revolutionized by the rise of large supermarkets. While consumers had once bought their meat from local butchers (as well as their produce from local growers and their bread from local bakeries), beginning in the 1950s, large supermarket chains—which sold all of these items and more under one roof—began to alter the country's patterns of food shopping and supply. As these chains encompassed ever larger geographical areas, they turned to major regional suppliers for their poultry, vegetables, and other perishable goods. The new interstate highway system made it cheaper and easier to move products over land, and the development of refrigeration technology meant that perishable items could be trucked for some distance without spoiling. The result of these changes for poultry producers was that larger operations that provided processed chicken at high volume were favored by supermarket chains. ''The poultry industry, once a collection of thousands of backyard operations'' evolved into ''a highly integrated and automated business,'' explained the *Chicago Tribune.*

Expansion in California: 1959–87

Foster Farms embraced this trend in 1959 when it bought a processing plant in Livingston, California. Live birds were trucked to the facility, slaughtered, processed, and packaged. Staffed by workers who repeatedly performed one part of the

Company Perspectives:

Excellence, honesty, quality and service. These are the Foster Family's principles that have shaped and continue to guide this solid, growing and fully integrated company.

Excellence: It is accomplished by hands-on management and strict attention to detail at every level, by people who make excellence a personal goal, as well as a corporate one. Given the best resources and encouragement in aggressive investment and thoughtful risk-taking, we maintain our leadership position.

Honesty: It starts with a fair and open sharing of expectations between each and every employee. It guides us throughout the business day, with our suppliers, our customers, and within the communities we call home. The result is a hard-earned reputation for honesty and credibility in all that we do.

Quality: More than any other single value, quality at Foster Farms cannot be compromised. We ensure this by a shared recognition that our future is determined by our ability to select and retain a team of quality people, and that the superiority of our product is a measure of these individuals.

Service: Honest dealings with customers and consumers, coupled with outstanding people and products, add up to the high level of customer service expected of Foster Farms. In short, we will be our customer's most valued supplier.

Committed to and living by these values, we at Foster Farms believe that success is assured, yet never assumed. We also believe that a feeling of accomplishment for a job well done, a clear sense of individual direction and worth, and an open, enjoyable atmosphere on the job contribute to a company continually on the forward move.

whole operation—much like auto workers on an assembly line—the Livingston plant also incorporated new technology that sped up the tasks. (Although a fire destroyed the original Livingston processing plant in the early 1960s, Foster Farms quickly rebuilt it on a nearby site.) In the 1960s, the company moved its corporate headquarters from the original family farm to Livingston.

Although Max and Verda Foster remained at Foster Farms' helm, their eldest son, Paul, was the dominant force in the company's rapid expansion. While Max concentrated on the fledgling dairy operations, Paul oversaw the burgeoning poultry production arm. In 1969, Paul officially took the company's reigns, and was named president. Under his guidance, Foster Farms acquired a distribution and sales center in El Monte, California, in 1973. This new facility allowed the company to act as a major distributor of poultry products in southern California. Paul died suddenly of a heart attack in 1977, and was succeeded by his brother, Thomas.

Following in his brother's footsteps, Tom Foster led the family business into new territory. In 1982, the company purchased the assets of The Grange Company and its subsidiary, Valchris Poultry. This deal provided two particular benefits to Foster Farms: it enabled the company to re-enter the turkey processing business after a long hiatus, and it also let the company enter a new segment of the poultry industry. Grange produced packaged deli products, especially luncheon meats, and after the acquisition it continued to do so, but now under the Foster Farms name. By the mid-1980s, Foster Farms offered a number of new products, including poultry franks, bologna, and luncheon meats.

The company's pace of growth was brisk—sales tripled between 1975 and 1988, according to the September 29, 1988 edition of the *San Francisco Chronicle.* By 1987, Foster Farms was the largest chicken producer in California, churning out some 140 million chickens per year. The company's success was due in part to its total vertical integration. "Our production pipeline goes from egg to package," a company spokesperson told the *Chronicle.* Foster Farms' operations were a model of industrial efficiency. Chickens were conceived on one of 12 breeder farms within 35 miles of the processing plant in Livingston. After the hens laid their eggs (a total of approximately 2.2 million a week), the eggs were trucked to hatcheries, where they were kept in controlled conditions in an incubator for 18 days. When the newborn chicks hatched, they were taken to one of several ranches, where they remained for about 52 days. During that time, the chickens had constant access to the company's own corn and soybean meal feed. "They are pampered," a Foster Farms spokesperson explained to the *San Francisco Chronicle* on June 2, 1987. "Good chicken is good business."

After their time at the ranches, the birds were trucked to the Livingston processing plant. Workers hung the chickens by the ankles upside down on a metal conveyor line. The chickens were then shocked with an electric current to stun them before their throats were cut by an automated blade. Still on the conveyor line, the bodies were scalded with hot water, had their feathers removed by plucking machines, and were eviscerated by yet other machines. Next, some 500 workers cut and packaged the birds: some bagged whole chickens; others removed breasts and boxed them; others cleaved off legs and packaged the parts. At the end of the assembly lines, the packages were mechanically sealed with cellophane, and promptly shipped to supermarkets and food-service vendors via Foster Farms' own fleet of refrigerated trucks. The entire process illustrated the observation of *Southern California Business* that "the conversion of poultry raising from a handicraft into a mass production basis" had occurred.

Foster Farms' sales had risen so rapidly in the mid-1980s that the company announced plans substantially to increase its poultry producing capacity in 1988. That year, Foster Farms constructed a new fryer ranch with one million square feet of poultry housing in Merced County, California, and upgraded its feedmill in Ceres, California. It also built in Livingston a new 85,000-square-foot distribution facility, and a sales office for northern California. In addition, the company erected a plant to process chicken byproducts. Most importantly, Foster Farms acquired a turkey processing plant in Fresno, California, from Roxford Foods in November 1989. Foster Farms immediately converted the facility to a chicken processing plant, by adding new equipment and making structural additions. The Fresno plant was slated to process an additional 80 million chickens each year.

Foster Farms' booming sales were driven by a number of factors, foremost of which was the growing popularity of

Key Dates:

1939: Max and Verda Foster found Foster Farms.
1959: Foster Farms purchases a poultry processing plant in Livingston, California.
1982: Foster Farms acquires the assets of The Grange Company and its subsidiary, Valchris Poultry.
1987: Foster Farms acquires Fircrest Farms.
1990: Company purchases an additional chicken processing plant in Fresno, California.
1994: Foster Farms acquires Lynden Farms.
1997: Foster Farms acquires Pederson's Fryer Farms.
1998: Company opens new processing plant in Kelso, Washington.

chicken in the United States. With the discovery that saturated fat intake was linked to heart disease, Americans began to consume less red meat, which was often fattier than poultry and contained more cholesterol. In place of meats such as steak, roast beef, and pork, Americans increasingly opted for chicken, which typically contained less saturated fat. According to the March 5, 1996, *USA Today,* poultry's share of the meat market rose from 24 percent in 1976 to 41 percent in 1996, and per capita poultry consumption rose from 40.6 pounds in 1970 to about 72 pounds in 1996. In 1987, per capita poultry consumption surpassed beef for the first time in history.

Chicken's more prominent role in the American diet was not only attributable to its lower fat content. Innovations made by the poultry industry itself also spurred demand for the fowl. For most of their history, poultry processors had offered whole chickens and little else. But a new trend hit the market in the early 1980s. As the September 17, 1987, *Wall Street Journal* explained, the fast-food chain McDonald's had greatly influenced the poultry industry. In 1982, McDonald's introduced a new product—nuggets of boneless, deep-fried chicken that came with a dipping sauce. These McNuggets sold briskly at McDonald's, and also inspired a bevy of knockoffs. According to the *Wall Street Journal,* the lesson that McNuggets imparted to poultry processors was the ''value of moving beyond standard chicken.'' A huge and untapped market was discovered for prepackaged and jazzed-up chicken products. To capitalize, leading poultry producers—including Foster Farms—quickly released a variety of so-called ''value-added'' products, such as boneless-skinless chicken breasts, chicken tenders, and marinated chicken strips.

Poultry's meteoric rise up the American food chain was slowed in 1987 by a report broadcast on the television news magazine show ''60 Minutes'' which claimed that a high percentage of chicken was infected with salmonella. This bacteria, a naturally occurring organism that tainted meats and vegetables, could cause illness ranging from flu-like symptoms to death. Because the bacteria could be spread between birds in fecal matter and blood, the close proximity of so many birds—both on the ranches and in the processing plants—made it more prevalent as the poultry industry became more automated. Poultry prices dropped precipitously in the wake of these revelations as consumer demand slackened.

Foster Farms emerged from the salmonella crisis unscathed, however. The company, notorious for its aversion to publicity, took the uncharacteristic step of inviting members of the media into its processing operations to witness its state-of-the-art anti-contamination measures. The positive coverage generated by this effort boosted public confidence in the company's products. Moreover, Foster Farms was able to rely on its strong brand image to assuage consumers' concerns. In fact, a company spokesperson told the *San Francisco Chronicle* on September 29, 1988, that ''the salmonella scare indirectly boosted Foster sales, because consumers became pickier about the chickens they bought.''

In the aftermath of the salmonella scare, other poultry producers realized the importance of branding as well. According to the *Atlanta Journal-Constitution,* brand name birds could command an extra ten cents a pound over their generic counterparts in the supermarket. One of Foster Farms' major competitors, Perdue Farms Incorporated, had been advertising since 1967, but stepped up its branding efforts in the late 1980s. Perdue aired a series of commercials featuring the company's eponymous chairman, Frank Perdue, proclaiming that ''it takes a tough man to make a tender chicken.'' Recognizing the need to defend its position, Foster Farms also increased its television marketing presence in 1988. One spot, portraying a mother-in-law showing her daughter how to prepare chicken, received a prestigious Clio Award that year. Foster Farms subsequently launched a sales promotion aimed at Latinos in 1990.

Expansion into Oregon and Washington: 1987–98

Along with its ongoing branding efforts, the late 1980s saw Foster Farms decide to expand its geographical presence. Already the undisputed market leader in California, the company eyed the rest of the West Coast as possible territory for expansion. Foster Farms had first ventured into the Northwest in 1987, when it acquired Fircrest Farms. Located in Creswell, Oregon, Fircrest was one of the leading poultry producers in Oregon, and had a firmly-ensconced regional brand. In 1994, Foster Farms made a more aggressive move into the markets of the Northwest when it purchased Lynden Farms for an estimated $8.2 million. Foster Farms shipped the chickens from both Fircrest and Lynden to its Livingston and Fresno plants to be processed.

Although the Foster family continued to play an active role in managing the company, brothers George and Tom had relinquished the role of president and chief executive to Robert Fox (a non-family member) in 1992, while the brothers continued to serve on Foster Farms' board. But the company's growth continued throughout the early- and mid-1990s. Though the privately held operation was tightlipped about its sales figures, Foster Farms did announce that its 1996 sales had topped $900 million. By then, the company had become the largest poultry producer on the entire West Coast, and the eighth largest in the nation, ranking 231st among all *Fortune* 500 companies. Moreover, the Livingston plant was the largest slaughterhouse in the world, processing 480,000 chickens each day.

The company wanted to keep growing, though. In 1997, Foster Farms spent roughly $7 million to buy the leading poultry producer in the state of Washington—Pederson's Fryer

Farms. Pederson's offered Foster Farms a unique opportunity to gain control of most Western markets. As Bob Fox told the *Daily News* on September 2, 1997, ''Washington . . . is the second-most populated state in the Western United States. We believe it's an extension of our California-area business.''

Even with the purchase of Pederson's, however, Foster Farms continued to truck its Pacific Northwest-grown birds back to California for processing. This arrangement was both inconvenient and expensive. To remedy the situation, Foster Farms constructed a $45 million processing facility in South Kelso, Washington. ''It's a very major step for us,'' Fox noted to the *Daily News* on May 15, 1997. ''It's the biggest single from-the-ground investment we've made.'' After opening in 1998, the Kelso facility added over 500 workers to the Foster Farms fold. The company closed Pederson's processing operations in Tacoma, Washington (although it kept the brand name), and shifted processing over to the Kelso site. By the close of 1998, Foster Farms processed about 130 million pounds of poultry at its Northwest facilities.

1998 and Beyond

As it continued to expand its poultry empire, Foster Farms did not lose sight of the strategies that had helped establish the company. Marketing the Foster Farms brand remained an important aspect of business. During the 1998 Super Bowl, for example, the company launched a major advertising campaign that brought Foster Farms the accolades of both media critics and consumers. The spots, which featured straggly, junk-food eating chickens who tried to masquerade as Foster Farms chickens, boosted the company's brand image as a producer of high-quality, carefully vetted chicken. The campaign continued through 1999.

The company continued to grow through acquisition, as well. In 1999, Foster Farms acquired Butterball Turkey Co.'s turkey processing plant and feed mill in Turlock, California, along with a hatchery in Fresno, California. That same year, Foster Farms also purchased Griffith Foods—an Alabama-based producer of corn dogs. The company's future prospects were bright. Although Tom Foster died in 1999, brother George remained active in the company, as did CEO Bob Fox. Foster Farms produced more than 750 million pounds of fresh poultry in 1999, and was the second largest corn dog producer in the United States. As the *Modesto Bee* noted on October 28, 1999, in what seemed a perfect understatement, ''Foster Farms' presence in the industry and the West has been increasing in recent years.''

Principal Competitors

Perdue Farms Incorporated; Tyson Foods, Inc.; Zacky Farms, Inc.; ConAgra, Inc.; Hormel Foods Corporation.

Further Reading

Beckett, Jamie, ''Foster Feathering Nest,'' *San Francisco Chronicle,* September 29, 1988.

Bizjak, Tony, ''Where 22,000 Chickens Watch B-52s and Think Big,'' *San Francisco Chronicle,* June 2, 1987.

Britton, Charles, ''Zacky Farms . . . Is No Turkey,'' *Southern California Business,* November 1, 1987.

Estrada, Richard, ''Livingston, California-Based Poultry Farm Goes Online,'' *Modesto Bee,* October 28, 1999.

Hallman, Tom, ''The Chicken Name Becomes an All-Out War,'' *Atlanta Journal-Constitution,* April 25, 1988.

LaBeck, Paula, ''550 Jobs Coming Home to Roost in Kelso,'' *Daily News,* May 15, 1997.

Lindblom, Mike, ''Small Town Likes Its Huge Chicken Plant,'' *Daily News,* September 2, 1996.

Smith, Timothy, ''Changing Tastes: By End of This Year Poultry Will Surpass Beef in the U.S. Diet,'' *Wall Street Journal,* September 17, 1987.

Tyson, Rae, ''Beef Industry Hits Hard Times,'' *USA Today,* March 5, 1996.

—Rebecca Stanfel

Frito-Lay Company

7701 Legacy Drive
Plano, Texas 75024-4099
U.S.A.
Telephone: (972) 334-7000
Fax: (972) 334-2019
Web site: http://www.fritolay.com

Division of PepsiCo, Inc.
Incorporated: 1961 as Frito-Lay, Inc.
Employees: 92,000
Sales: $10.98 billion (1998)
NAIC: 311919 Other Snack Food Manufacturing; 311821 Cookie and Cracker Manufacturing

Frito-Lay Company is the world leader in the salty snack category, controlling more than 35 percent of the world market in snack chips and 60 percent in the United States. Among the company's well-known brands are five that generate annual sales of $1 billion each: Lay's, Ruffles, Doritos, Tostitos, and Chee-tos. In addition to its dominance of the potato chip, tortilla chip, and corn chip sectors (the last of these led by the Fritos brand), Frito-Lay has major brands in other categories, such as Rold Gold pretzels, Cracker Jack candy-coated popcorn, and Grandma's cookies. About $4 billion of the company's overall net sales are generated outside the United States, with sales in 42 countries. Lay's, Ruffles, and Chee-tos are among Frito-Lay's major international brands, along with such local favorites as Walker's in the United Kingdom and Sabritas in Mexico. Frito-Lay Company is the snack food division of PepsiCo, Inc., generating about half of the parent company's revenues and two-thirds of its profits.

Early Years of the Frito Company

Frito-Lay traces its origins to the early 1930s. In the midst of the Great Depression, the lack of job prospects spurred a number of young people to turn to entrepreneurship in order to get ahead. Among these were the founders of the two companies that would merge in 1961 to form Frito-Lay. Elmer Doolin's entrance into the snack food industry was one of happenstance. In 1932 the Texas native was running an ice cream business which was struggling because of a price war. Doolin began seeking a new venture and happened to buy a five-cent, plain package of corn chips while eating at a San Antonio café. At the time, corn chips or "fritos" (the word *frito* means fried in Spanish) were a common fried corn meal snack in the Southwest. Typically, cooks would cut flattened corn dough into ribbons, then season and fry them.

Impressed with his five-cent snack, Doolin discovered that the manufacturer wished to return to Mexico and would sell his business for $100. Doolin borrowed the money from his mother, purchasing the recipe, 19 retail accounts, and production equipment consisting of an old, handheld potato ricer. Initially setting up production in his mother's kitchen, Doolin spent his nights cooking Frito brand corn chips and sold them during the day from his Model T Ford. Early production capacity was ten pounds per day, with profits of about $2 per day on sales ranging from $8 to $10 per day.

Doolin soon expanded to the family garage, and increased production by developing a press that operated more efficiently than the potato ricer. Within a year of his purchase of the business, Doolin moved the headquarters for the Frito Company from San Antonio to Dallas, the latter having distribution advantages. Sales began expanding geographically after Doolin hired a sales force to make regular deliveries to stores. The Frito Company also began selling the products of potato chip manufacturers through license agreements. The company soon had plants operating in Houston, Tulsa, and Dallas.

In early 1941 Doolin expanded to the West Coast by opening a small manufacturing facility in Los Angeles. Only the onset of World War II and rationing slowed Frito's growth. But sales quickly picked up again following the war's end, and by 1947 revenues exceeded $27 million. Doolin moved his company toward national status through licensing agreements. The first came in 1945, when Frito granted H.W. Lay & Company an exclusive franchise to manufacture and distribute Fritos in the Southeast. This marked the beginning of a close relationship between the two companies, and would eventually lead to their 1961 merger. In 1946 another franchise was launched in Bethesda, Maryland, followed by a Hawaii-based franchise in 1947. The following year, Frito introduced Chee-tos brand Cheese Flavored Snacks, which gained immediate popularity.

Company Perspectives:

Our Mission Statement: To be the world's favorite snack and always within arm's reach.

Meantime, the Fritos brand went national in 1949 when Doolin purchased color advertisements in several magazines, including *Ladies' Home Journal, Better Homes and Gardens,* and *Life.*

By 1954 the Frito Company business included 11 plants and 12 franchise operations. In 1953 the Frito Kid made his debut as a company spokesman; the character continued to be used in Fritos advertising until 1967. In 1956 the Frito Kid made an appearance on the "Today" show with host Dave Garroway, marking the Frito Company's first use of television advertising. Fritos gained a new advertising theme in 1958 with the debut of "Munch a Bunch of Fritos." That year, the Frito Company acquired the rights to Ruffles brand potato chips. The following year, Doolin died, having led his company to its status as a major snack food maker, with revenues exceeding $51 million. The Frito Company continued to operate 11 plants, but its franchise operations had been reduced to six after the company bought out several franchisees. John D. Williamson took over as president of the company. Within two years of Doolin's death, the Frito Company would merge with H.W. Lay.

Early Years of H.W. Lay & Company

H.W. Lay & Company, Inc. was founded by another entrepreneur, Herman W. Lay. Born in humble circumstances in 1909 in Charlotte, North Carolina, Lay had worked a variety of jobs and run a few small businesses from the age of ten, including an ice cream stand, before taking a position as a route salesman at the Barrett Food Products Company, an Atlanta-based potato chip manufacturer, in 1932. Later that year, Lay borrowed $100 to take over Barrett's small warehouse in Nashville on a distributorship basis. This was coincidentally the same year that Doolin had established the Frito Company.

Lay started out selling Barrett's Gardner brand products from his 1928 Model A Ford, initially pocketing about $23 a month. Growth came rapidly, however. In 1933 Lay hired his first salesman, and by the following year his company had six sales routes. By 1936 Lay employed a workforce of 25 and had moved his company from its original warehouse to another Nashville building. From this location, Lay began manufacturing products himself, including peanut butter cracker sandwiches and french fried popcorn. In 1938 the latter became the first item marketed under the Lay's name, specifically Lay's Tennessee Valley Popcorn. By that year Lay was distributing snack foods throughout central Tennessee and southern Kentucky, and had opened a new warehouse in Chattanooga. The most significant development of 1938, however, came as a result of financial difficulties encountered by Barrett Food Products. After securing $60,000 in financing through business associates and friends, Lay bought Barrett, its plants in Memphis and Atlanta, and the Gardner's brand name. He changed the name of the company to H.W. Lay & Company, Inc., with headquarters in Atlanta.

During the early 1940s H.W. Lay added manufacturing plants in Jacksonville, Florida; Jackson, Mississippi; Louisville, Kentucky; and Greensboro, North Carolina. Lay also built a new plant in Atlanta featuring a continuous potato chip production line, one of the first in the world. In 1944 the company began marketing potato chips under the Lay's name, with the Gardner's brand becoming a historical footnote. That same year, H.W. Lay became one of the first snack food concerns to advertise on television, with a campaign featuring the debut of Oscar, the Happy Potato, the company's first spokesperson. The following year, H.W. Lay gained from the Frito Company an exclusive franchise to manufacture and distribute Fritos corn chips in the Southeast.

After establishing a research laboratory to develop new products in 1949, H.W. Lay expanded its product line during the 1950s to include barbecued potato chips, corn cheese snacks, fried pork skins, and a variety of nuts. The company also expanded outside the Southeast and acquired a number of weaker competitors. In 1956 H.W. Lay went public as a company with a workforce exceeding 1,000, manufacturing facilities in eight cities, and branches or warehouses in 13 cities. Revenues in 1957 stood at $16 million, making Herman Lay's company the largest maker of potato chips and snack foods in the United States. H.W. Lay had also gained fame for carefully developing and utilizing its sales routes. Company salespeople were among the first to go beyond simply delivering their merchandise to store owners, as they also stocked the merchandise for the owners, set up point-of-purchase displays, and helped to assure product quality by pulling stale bags off the shelves and displays before they could be sold. This "store-door" delivery system helped to increase revenues as the salespeople were able to "work" a particular sales territory more intensely. By the spring of 1961, H.W. Lay had operations in 30 states, following the purchase of Rold Gold Foods, makers of Rold Gold Pretzels, from American Cone and Pretzel.

Frito-Lay, Inc.: 1961–65

In September 1961 H.W. Lay and the Frito Company merged to form Frito-Lay, Inc., a snack food giant headquartered in Dallas with revenues exceeding $127 million. The new company began with four main brands—Fritos, Lay's, Ruffles, and Chee-tos—and a national distribution system. Williamson served as the first chairman and CEO of Frito-Lay, with Lay taking the position of president. In 1962 Lay took over as CEO, with Fladger F. Tannery becoming president; two years later, Lay added the chairmanship to his duties.

In 1963 Frito-Lay began using the slogan "Betcha Can't Eat Just One" in its advertising for Lay's potato chips. Two years later comedian Bert Lahr began appearing in ads in which he attempted—always unsuccessfully—to eat just one Lay's chip. Annual revenues for Frito-Lay exceeded $180 million by 1965, when the company had more than 8,000 employees and 46 manufacturing plants.

June 1965: Frito-Lay + Pepsi-Cola = PepsiCo

In June 1965 Frito-Lay merged with Pepsi-Cola Company to form PepsiCo, Inc., with Frito-Lay becoming an independently operated division of the new company. Pepsi's CEO and president became CEO and president of PepsiCo, while Herman Lay

Key Dates:

1932: Elmer Doolin founds the Frito Company in San Antonio, Texas, and begins making Fritos corn chips.
1938: Herman W. Lay buys Atlanta potato chip maker, changes name to H.W. Lay & Company, Inc., the following year.
1944: H.W. Lay begins marketing potato chips under the Lay's name.
1948: Frito Company introduces Chee-tos snacks.
1958: Frito Company acquires the rights to Ruffles brand potato chips.
1961: The Frito Company and H.W. Lay & Company are merged to form Frito-Lay, Inc.
1965: Frito-Lay, Inc. and the Pepsi-Cola Company merge to form PepsiCo, Inc., with Frito-Lay becoming a division of the new company.
1967: Doritos tortilla chips make their national debut.
1970: Frito Bandito advertising campaign is abandoned following complaints from Mexican American organizations.
1981: Company introduces Tostitos tortilla chips.
1991: Sunchips multigrain snacks are introduced.
1997: Company acquires the Cracker Jack brand.
1998: Wow! line of low-fat/no-fat chips debuts.

was named chairman, a position he held until 1971. Lay then served as chairman of the executive committee until 1980, when he retired. He died in December 1982.

There were a number of forces that drove the two companies together. The 1960s was an era of consolidation, with a number of food and beverage firms being gobbled up by larger entities. Pepsi-Cola was considered a takeover target not only because it ran a distant second in the soft drink sector to industry giant Coca-Cola Company, but also because little of the company's stock was in the hands of management. Following the creation of PepsiCo, however, the new company's directors held a much larger proportion of shares, with Lay holding a 2.5 percent stake himself. A second force behind the merger was Frito-Lay's desire to more aggressively pursue overseas markets. The company's sales had largely been restricted to the United States and Canada, but it could now take advantage of Pepsi's strong international operations, through which Pepsi products were sold in 108 countries.

A third force was the perceived synergy between salty snacks and soft drinks. As Kendall succinctly related to *Forbes* in 1968, ''Potato chips make you thirsty; Pepsi satisfies thirst.'' The plan was to jointly market PepsiCo's snacks and soft drinks, thereby giving Pepsi a potential advantage in its ongoing battle with Coke. Unfortunately, these plans were eventually scuttled by the resolution of a Federal Trade Commission antitrust suit brought against Frito-Lay in 1963. The FTC ruled in late 1968 that PepsiCo could not create tie-ins between Frito-Lay and Pepsi-Cola products in most of its advertising. PepsiCo was also barred from acquiring any snack or soft drink maker for a period of ten years.

New Products, the Frito Bandito, and Increased Competition: 1965–79

Frito-Lay began its PepsiCo era with the same lineup of brands it had when Frito-Lay was created in 1961: Fritos, Lay's, Ruffles, Chee-tos, and Rold Gold. Shortly after the creation of PepsiCo, Lay's became the first potato chip brand to be sold nationally. Of even greater importance was increased new product development activity. In 1966 Frito-Lay began test-marketing a new triangular tortilla chip under the brand name Doritos. Compared to regular tortilla chips, Doritos were more flavorful and crunchier. Launched nationally in 1967, Doritos proved successful, but additional market research revealed that many consumers outside the Southwest and West considered the chip to be too bland—not spicy enough for what was perceived as a Mexican snack. Frito-Lay therefore developed taco-flavored Doritos, which were introduced nationally in 1968 and were a tremendous success. Four years later, national distribution began of nacho cheese-flavored Doritos, which were also a hit. Ironically, with increasing popularity, Doritos became less and less identified as a ''Mexican snack,'' a development that echoed the earlier brand history of Fritos. During the 1970s Doritos became Frito-Lay's number two brand in terms of sales, trailing only Lay's. This spectacular growth was fueled by heavy advertising expenditures—as much as half of the company's overall $23 million ad budget in the mid-1970s. The ''Crunch'' campaign began in the early 1970s, and gained added impetus in 1976 when Avery Schrieber began crunching Doritos on national television. Frito-Lay also found lesser success in this period with other new products, including Funyuns onion-flavored rings, which debuted in 1969, and the Munchos potato crisps that were launched in 1971.

In 1968 Frito-Lay began a new Fritos advertising campaign featuring the Frito Bandito, a Mexican bandit complete with a long mustache, sombrero, and six-gun who spoke in a heavy accent. Ads showed the cartoon character robbing and scheming to get his beloved Fritos corn chips. The campaign quickly drew heavy criticism from Mexican American groups who alleged that it showed a prejudice against Mexican Americans and perpetuated a stereotype. Responding to the protests, radio and television stations in California began pulling Frito Bandito spots off the air. Frito-Lay finally ended the campaign in 1970.

During the 1970s Frito-Lay began feeling the effects of increased competition. The Lay's brand was challenged not only by more aggressive regional brands but also by such newfangled chips as Pringles and Chipos. These chips were made from mashed or dehydrated potatoes molded into a uniform shape, which enabled them to be stacked into a can or packaged in a box. In either case, they had several advantages over regular potato chips: they were less fragile, their packaging was less bulky, and they had a longer shelf life. Most importantly, they could be made in one location and shipped nationally, rather than having to be made in a nationwide system of regional plants. Pringles and Chipos were also backed by the national advertising prowess of two consumer product giants—Procter & Gamble Company and General Mills, Inc., respectively. Additional competition in the 1970s came from Nabisco Inc., maker of Mister Salty pretzels and such extruded snacks as Flings and Corkers, and Standard Brands Inc., which was expanding its Planters brand beyond nuts into corn and potato chips, cheese curls, and pretzels. Despite its formidable foes, Frito-Lay remained the clear leader in the U.S. snack industry, with sales by the late 1970s exceeding the $1 billion mark, more than double that of the nearest competitor, Standard Brands. Moreover, Frito-Lay was far from resting on its laurels. It increased its overall production capacity by one-third by 1979 through the opening of a new plant in Charlotte, North Carolina, and the culmination of expansion programs at ten existing plants. Keeping Frito-Lay ahead of the competition during this period was D. Wayne Calloway, who became president and chief operating officer in early 1976.

New Product Ups and Downs in the 1980s

The 1980s started out promisingly, with Frito-Lay acquiring the Grandma's regional brand of cookies in 1980 for $25 million, in a venture outside of its salty snack stronghold. In 1983 the company made a national launch of the Grandma's brand, and soon was selling five varieties. Among these was a homemade-style cookie that was soft on the inside but crispy on the outside. In 1984 Procter & Gamble sued Frito-Lay and two other cookie makers for infringing on its patent for Duncan Hines crispy-chewy cookies. The parties reached a settlement in 1989, whereby Frito-Lay agreed to pay about $19 million to Procter & Gamble, while the bulk of the $125 million settlement was shared equally by the two other defendants, Nabisco and Keebler Co.

In addition to the acquisition of Grandma's, the early 1980s also saw Frito-Lay introduce Tostitos tortilla chips. Debuting in 1981, Tostitos was the most successful new product introduction yet in Frito-Lay history, garnering sales of $140 million in the first year of national distribution. The development of Tostitos came out of market research on Doritos indicating that some consumers felt the latter chips were too heavy, too thick, and too crunchy; at this time, there was a general trend toward consumer preference for ''lighter-tasting'' foods, as well as an increased interest in Mexican food. Frito-Lay thus created the thinner, crispier Tostitos, which could be eaten alone, made into nachos, or dipped into increasingly popular salsas. By 1985 Tostitos was Frito-Lay's number five brand, with sales of about $200 million, trailing only Doritos ($500 million), Lay's ($400 million), Fritos ($325 million), and Ruffles ($250 million). Also in 1985 Frito-Lay expanded its tortilla chip line with the introduction of Santitas white and yellow corn round chips.

In 1983 Calloway shifted to the PepsiCo headquarters in Purchase, New York, to become the parent company's CFO (and eventually its chairman and CEO). Taking over as president of Frito-Lay was Michael Jordan, who held the position for two years before also heading to Purchase and eventually becoming PepsiCo president. Willard Korn served as president of Frito-Lay during the mid-1980s, a period coinciding with the company's relocation of its headquarters from Dallas to Plano, Texas, but more importantly with a spate of failed product introductions. In 1986 Frito-Lay rolled out a slew of new products, several in the nonsalty snack sector, including Toppels cheese-topped crackers, Rumbles crispy nuggets, and Stuffers dip-filled shells. The company also attempted to penetrate the growing market for kettle-cooked chips, a variety harder and crunchier than regular potato chips, with a brand called Kincaid. The barrage of new products was too much for Frito-Lay's 10,000-strong sales force to handle; products were lost on store shelves and all of the new brands were quickly killed. Korn resigned from his post in November 1986, with Jordan returning to Texas to head Frito-Lay once again.

Under Jordan's leadership in the late 1980s, Frito-Lay focused on revitalizing its existing brands rather than developing new brands. Among the successful line extensions introduced in this period were Cool Ranch flavor Doritos and a low-fat version of Ruffles. In 1989 Frito-Lay acquired the Smartfood brand of cheddar-cheese popcorn, a regional brand it hoped to roll out nationwide. The company was also finding success in the international market, where profits were increasing 20 percent per year, revenues exceeded $500 million by the end of the decade, and Frito-Lay products were being sold in 20 countries. Overall sales stood at about $3.5 billion.

Rising Fortunes in the 1990s

Entering the 1990s, Frito-Lay faced continuing challenges from both regional and national players, including the upstart Eagle Snacks brand, owned by beer powerhouse Anheuser-Busch Cos. Eagle Snacks gained market share in the 1980s with premium products that sold for low prices, some of which were 20 percent lower than those of Frito-Lay. In addition to the increased competition, Frito-Lay also suffered in the late 1980s through 1990 from self-inflicted wounds, such as increasing prices faster than inflation, letting the corporate payroll become bloated, and allowing product quality to decline. As a result, profits were on the decline in the early 1990s.

In early 1991, Roger A. Enrico was named to the top spot at Frito-Lay, after most recently serving as president of PepsiCo Worldwide Beverages. Enrico, a former Frito-Lay marketing vice-president, immediately set out to turn around the stumbling but still formidable snack giant. During 1991 the company eliminated 1,800—or about 60 percent—of its administrative and managerial jobs, creating a much more streamlined structure. Four of the company's 40 plants were closed or sold off, and more than 100 package sizes and brand varieties were dropped from what had become an unwieldy product portfolio. These moves resulted in annual savings of approximately $100 million. On the selling side, Frito-Lay created 22 sales/marketing offices to bring decision-making closer to retailers and consumers. The company also slashed its prices. In its first big new product success since Tostitos, Frito-Lay launched SunChips in 1991, garnering $115 million in sales during the first year; the multigrain, low-sodium, no-cholesterol chip/cracker found a ready market among adults seeking a more healthful snack. In moves designed to revitalize its longstanding brands, Frito-Lay redesigned the packaging for several products, including Fritos and Rold Gold pretzels, and reformulated both Lay's and Ruffles potato chips—the first time the Lay's formula had ever been changed. To enhance the flavor of both chips, the company developed a new frying process and switched from soybean oil to cottonseed oil. With consumers preferring less salty snacks, the sodium content of the chips was also reduced. The new Lay's chips were introduced in 1992 through an ad campaign featuring the tag line, ''Too Good to Eat Just One!,'' a variation on the old ''Betcha Can't Eat Just One'' slogan. In 1993 Rold Gold pretzels were the subject of the product's first network television campaign, with ads featuring

''Seinfeld'' star Jason Alexander as ''Pretzel Boy.'' The following year the formula for Doritos was reformulated to make the chips 20 percent larger, 15 percent thinner, and stronger tasting—changes that were based on careful market research. Frito-Lay also continued to roll out new products, including Wavy Lay's potato chips and Baked Tostitos (1993), Cooler Ranch flavor Doritos (1994), and Baked Lay's (1996).

By the mid-1990s, as the snack food sector entered a slower growth period marked by heavy price competition, it became increasingly clear that Frito-Lay would remain the industry front-runner by a wide margin. The company increased its share of the salty snack market in the United States from 38 percent in the late 1980s to 55 percent by 1996. Competitive pressure from Frito-Lay led two of its fiercest rivals to wave the white flag. Borden sold most of its snack businesses in the mid-1990s as part of a massive restructuring. In early 1996 Anheuser-Busch shut down its Eagle Snack unit after failing to find a buyer for the unit; it sold four of Eagle's plants to Frito-Lay, which converted them to production of its main brands.

In 1996 PepsiCo merged its domestic and international snack food operations into a single entity called Frito-Lay Company, consisting of two main operating units, Frito-Lay North America and Frito-Lay International. The following year Frito-Lay bought the Cracker Jack brand from Borden, marking the company's reentrance into the nonsalty snack food sector. Also in 1997 Frito-Lay reentered the sandwich cracker market with the national introduction of seven varieties. Frito-Lay expanded internationally in 1998 through the acquisition of several salty snack assets in Europe and Smith's Snackfood Company in Australia from United Biscuit Holdings plc for US$440 million. In late 1998 Frito-Lay announced that it had formed a broad Latin American joint venture with Savoy Brands International, part of a Venezuelan conglomerate, Empresas Polar SA. Covering Venezuela, Chile, Colombia, Ecuador, Guatemala, Honduras, Panama, Peru, and El Salvador, the joint venture was designed to enable Frito-Lay to better penetrate the $3 billion salty snack sector in Latin America. Also in 1998 Frito-Lay began selling its Wow! line of low-fat and no-fat versions of Doritos, Ruffles, Lay's, and Tostitos. Made with a fake fat called olestra developed by Procter & Gamble (ironically the maker of rival chip Pringles), the Wow! products were controversial because of reports and studies that indicated that the chips could cause gastric distress. All olestra products carried warning labels stating that they ''may cause abdominal cramping and loose stools.'' Despite waves of negative publicity, the Wow! line was the best-selling new consumer product of 1998, garnering a whopping $350 million in sales.

By the end of the 1990s, Frito-Lay's aggressive new product development, advertising, and marketing efforts had further increased the company's share of the U.S. salty snack market to 60 percent. With the domestic market so firmly in its control, Frito-Lay was sure to look increasingly overseas for growth opportunities, particularly because there was no other global competitor in the industry. In the early 21st century, the company was likely to continue its expansion of its main brands—especially Lay's, Ruffles, Chee-tos, and Doritos—into new markets and to seek additional acquisitions and joint ventures in order to add more brands to its non-U.S. portfolio, which featured Walker's in the United Kingdom and Sabritas in Mexico.

Principal Divisions

Frito-Lay North America; Frito-Lay International.

Principal Competitors

Borden, Inc.; Campbell Soup Company; ConAgra, Inc.; General Mills, Inc.; Golden Enterprises, Inc.; International Home Foods, Inc.; Keebler Foods Company; Lance, Inc.; Nabisco Holdings Corp.; Poore Brothers, Inc.; The Procter & Gamble Company.

Further Reading

Adler, Jerry, ''The Soul of a New Snack,'' *Newsweek,* April 16, 1984, pp. 13, 16.

Bayer, Tom, and B.G. Yovovich, ''Snacking on Success: New Product Prowess? That's Frito-Lay's Bag,'' *Advertising Age,* March 15, 1982, p. M10.

Benezra, Karen, ''Frito-Lay Dominates, While Others Pick up Loose Chips,'' *Brandweek,* February 7, 1994, pp. 31ff.

——, ''Frito-Lay's Last Challenge,'' *Brandweek,* March 18, 1996, pp. 33ff.

Block, Maurine, ''Doritos Feel the Crunch—of Success,'' *Advertising Age,* October 2, 1972, p. 26.

''Boards of Pepsi-Cola and Frito-Lay Approve Merging As PepsiCo,'' *Wall Street Journal,* February 26, 1965, p. 8.

Bork, Robert H., Jr., ''Of Potato Chips and Microchips,'' *Forbes,* January 30, 1984, pp. 118–19.

Calloway, D. Wayne, ''Case History of Frito Lay,'' *Planning Review,* May 1985, p. 13.

Chakravarty, Subrata N., ''The King of Snacks,'' *Forbes,* October 20, 1997, p. 213.

Collins, Glenn, ''Pepsico Pushes a Star Performer,'' *New York Times,* November 3, 1994, pp. D1, 8.

Deogun, Nikhil, ''PepsiCo Forms Big Venture in Latin America,'' *Wall Street Journal,* November 25, 1998, pp. A12, 13.

——, ''PepsiCo's Frito-Lay Unit to Buy Some Assets of United Biscuits,'' *Wall Street Journal,* November 18, 1997, p. B4.

——, ''Sailor Jack and Bingo Join Frito-Lay Team in Cracker Jack Deal: Can Famed Sweet Snack Offer a Prized Change of Pace for Firm's Salty Lineup?,'' *Wall Street Journal,* October 9, 1997, p. B6.

——, ''U.S. Probe into Practices by Frito-Lay Ends Without Charges Being Brought,'' *Wall Street Journal,* December 22, 1998, p. A4.

Dunkin, Amy, ''Frito-Lay's Cooking Again, and Profits Are Starting to Pop,'' *Business Week,* May 22, 1989, pp. 66, 70.

Feder, Barnaby J., ''Frito-Lay's Speedy Data Network,'' *New York Times,* November 8, 1990, pp. D1, 7.

Feld, Charles S., ''Directed Decentralization: The Frito Lay Story,'' *Financial Executive,* November/December 1990, pp. 22ff.

Fisher, Anne B., ''Peering Past Pepsico's Bad News,'' *Fortune,* November 14, 1983, pp. 124ff.

Forest, Stephanie Anderson, and Julia Flynn Siler, ''Chipping Away at Frito-Lay,'' *Business Week,* July 22, 1991, p. 26.

Frank, Robert, ''Frito-Lay Devours Snack-Food Business,'' *Wall Street Journal,* October 27, 1995, p. B1.

——, ''Frito-Lay Puts up More Than Chips in Deal for Olestra,'' *Wall Street Journal,* May 31, 1996, pp. A3, 4.

''Frito-Lay May Find Itself in a Competition Crunch,'' *Business Week,* July 19, 1982, p. 186.

Gibson, Richard, ''Frito-Lay Has Eagle Snacks out on a Limb,'' *Wall Street Journal,* March 1, 1994, p. B7.

Greenwald, John, ''Frito-Lay Under Snack Attack,'' *Time,* June 10, 1996, pp. 62ff.

Grossman, Laurie M., ''Frito-Lay Chief Aims to Cut Unit's Fat and Give Snack Food a Spicier Image,'' *Wall Street Journal,* July 11, 1991, p. B1.

——, "Price Wars Bring Flavor to Once-Quiet Snack Market," *Wall Street Journal,* May 23, 1991, p. B1.

"Gulp, Munch & Merge," *Forbes,* July 15, 1968, pp. 20–21.

Hall, Trish, "President Quits at PepsiCo's Largest Unit—Korn Leaves Frito-Lay Job," *Wall Street Journal,* November 25, 1986, p. 2.

"Herman W. Lay of PepsiCo," *Nation's Business,* September 1969, pp. 88–89, 92–95.

"Holders of Pepsi-Cola and Frito-Lay Approve Proposal for Merger," *Wall Street Journal,* June 9, 1965, p. 8.

"Innovators in the Salted-Snacks Market: New Products and New Packaging Challenge Industry Leader Frito-Lay," *Business Week,* October 30, 1978, pp. 73–74.

Johnson, Robert, "In the Chips: At Frito Lay, the Consumer Is an Obsession," *Wall Street Journal,* March 22, 1991, pp. B1ff.

Kaplan, Elisa, "Frito-Lay: Still King of the Snack Food Hill," *Advertising Age,* April 30, 1979, pp. S2, 48–49.

Lawrence, Jennifer, "Frito-Play: New 'Basics' Strategy Takes on Regional Rivals," *Advertising Age,* March 30, 1987, pp. 1, 70, 71.

——, "Taco Bell Calls on Supermarkets: Frito-Lay to Test Mexican Food Line Under Sister PepsiCo Unit's Name," *Advertising Age,* February 8, 1993, pp. 3, 47.

Levine, Art, "Food Fight in Indianapolis: A Test Market for Fat-Free, Olestra-Based Snacks Gets Messy," *U.S. News & World Report,* May 5, 1997, pp. 53ff.

Lisser, Eleena de, "Tortilla Chips Tempt Snackers with Changes," *Wall Street Journal,* May 6, 1993, p. B1.

McCarthy, Michael J., "Added Fizz: Pepsi Is Going Better with Its Fast Foods and Frito-Lay Snacks," *Wall Street Journal,* June 13, 1991, pp. A1ff.

——, "Frito-Lay Bets Big with Multigrain Chips," *Wall Street Journal,* February 28, 1991, p. B1.

——, "PepsiCo, in a Surprise Reshuffle, Names Roger A. Enrico to Lead Frito-Lay Unit," *Wall Street Journal,* December 12, 1990, p. B6.

McGraw, Dan, "Salting Away the Competition: Frito-Lay Launches a Powerful Snack Attack and Crunches the Competition," *U.S. News & World Report,* September 16, 1996, pp. 71ff.

McKay, Betsy, "Russians Go Nuts for Snacks As Planters, Frito Duke It Out," *Advertising Age,* December 13, 1993, pp. I3, 14.

Morrison, Ann M., "Cookies Are Frito-Lay's New Bag," *Fortune,* August 9, 1982, pp. 64–67.

"Our First Fifty Years: The Frito-Lay Story, 1932–1982," special issue of *Bandwagon,* Dallas: Frito-Lay, 1982.

Parker-Pope, Tara, and Nikhil Deogun, "Frito-Lay to Begin Selling Wow! Chips Made with Olestra Later This Month," *Wall Street Journal,* February 10, 1998, p. B2.

"Party Gets Rough for Potato Chippers," *Business Week,* November 8, 1969, p. 36.

"PepsiCo—More Than Just 'Pepsi,' " *Financial World,* November 4, 1970, pp. 5, 26.

Pollack, Judann, "Frito-Lay Revamps Strategy for Struggling Wow!," *Advertising Age,* September 14, 1998, p. 1.

——, "New-Product Feast Readied by Frito-Lay," *Advertising Age,* February 12, 1996, pp. 1, 37.

Prokesch, Steven E., "Frito-Lay's Go-It-Alone Policy," *New York Times,* December 2, 1985, pp. D1, 4.

Sellers, Patricia, "If It Ain't Broke, Fix It Anyway," *Fortune,* December 28, 1992, pp. 49ff.

"Steady Gains for PepsiCo," *Financial World,* March 1, 1972, pp. 7, 19.

Thomas, Robert McG., Jr., "Herman W. Lay, 73, Is Dead: Success Tied to Potato Chips," *New York Times,* December 7, 1982, p. D30.

Warner, Fara, "Empowered by Enrico," *Adweek's Marketing Week,* May 4, 1992, pp. 16ff.

Whalen, Jeanne, "Tostitos Tastes New Life," *Advertising Age,* December 11, 1995, p. 42.

"Who Acquired Who?," *Forbes,* April 1, 1967, p. 69.

Willman, John, "Salty Snack Attack on Europe," *Financial Times,* February 2, 1998, p. 13.

Yung, Katherine, "Concerns About Sales Leave Only a Few Making Fat-Free Chips," *Dallas Morning News,* January 25, 1999.

Zellner, Wendy, "Frito-Lay Is Munching on the Competition," *Business Week,* August 24, 1992, pp. 52–53.

—David E. Salamie

Genentech, Inc.
Genentech, Inc.
Genentech, Inc.
Genentech, Inc.
Genentech, Inc.

Genentech, Inc.

One DNA Way
South San Francisco, California 94080-4990
U.S.A.
Telephone: (650) 225-1000
Fax: (650) 225-6000
Web site: http://www.gene.com

Public Company/66 Percent Owned Subsidiary of Roche Holding Ltd.
Incorporated: 1976
Employees: 3,389
Sales: $1.15 billion (1998)
Stock Exchanges: New York Pacific
Ticker Symbol: DNA
NAIC: 325412 Pharmaceutical Preparation Manufacturing; 325414 Biological Product (Except Diagnostic) Manufacturing; 541710 Research & Development in the Physical, Engineering, & Life Sciences

Genentech, Inc. became a pioneer of biotechnology when it was founded in the late 1970s. A publicly traded company, Genentech is controlled by Roche Holding Ltd. (parent of Swiss pharmaceutical giant Hoffmann-La Roche) through that company's 66 percent stake, but is allowed to operate independently. Genentech discovers, develops, manufactures, and markets human pharmaceuticals for significant medical needs. The company fabricates organisms from gene cells, organisms that are not ordinarily produced by the cells. Conceivably, this process, referred to as gene splicing or recombinant DNA, may lead to cures for cancer or AIDS. The potential success of this young science causes it to flourish, attracting entrepreneurs and investors. After being swept up in a wave of takeovers and mergers that shook the industry in the late 1980s, Genentech emerged in the 1990s as one of the most solid biotechnology companies in the world. At the turn of the century the company marketed seven products in the United States: Protropin, Nutropin, and Nutropin AQ, all for the treatment of growth deficiency or failure; Activase, used to dissolve blood clots in heart attack and stroke patients; Pulmozyme, a therapy in the treatment of cystic fibrosis; Rituxan, used to treat non-Hodgkin's lymphoma, a cancer of the immune system; and Herceptin, for the treatment of breast cancer.

Early Years

Founded in 1976, Genentech was financed by Kleinman, Perkins, Caufield and Byers, a San Francisco high-tech venture capital firm, and by its cofounders, Robert Swanson and Herbert Boyer. Swanson, a graduate of the Sloan School of Management at the Massachusetts Institute of Technology, was employed by Kleinman, Perkins, where he learned of the achievements of Cetus, a biotechnology firm founded in 1971; he decided to investigate the prospect of marketing DNA products. Initially, the concept was met with little enthusiasm, but in Herbert Boyer, a distinguished academic scientist, Swanson found someone who enthusiastically supported his plan. One of the first scientists to synthesize life (he had created gene cells with Stanley Cohen), Boyer wanted to take his research further and to create new cells.

Boyer and Swanson decided to leave their respective jobs and to found Genentech (genetic engineering technology). Thomas J. Perkins, a partner with Kleinman, Perkins, who became Genentech's chairman, suggested that the new company contract out its early research. Swanson followed Perkins's advice and contracted the City of Hope National Medical Center to conduct the company's initial research project.

Boyer and Swanson wanted to exhibit their grasp of the relevant technology before they attempted to market products—to achieve credibility for Genentech. To accomplish this goal, Boyer intentionally selected an easily replicated cell with a simple composition, Somatostatin. The first experiment with Somatostatin required seven months of research. Scientists on the project placed the hormone inside E. coli bacteria, found in the human intestine. The anticipated result was that the bacteria would produce useful proteins that duplicated Somatostatin, but that did not happen. Then a scientist working on the project hypothesized that proteins in the bacteria were attacking the hormone. Somatostatin was protected, and the cell was success-

Company Perspectives:

Our mission is to be the leading biotechnology company, using human genetic information to develop, manufacture and market pharmaceuticals that address significant unmet medical needs. We commit ourselves to high standards of integrity in contributing to the best interests of patients, the medical profession, and our employees, and to seeking significant returns to our stockholders based on the continued pursuit of excellent science.

fully produced. Although it established credibility for the company, the experiment brought no real financial returns. Boyer and Swanson intended to produce human insulin as Genentech's first product.

Early in the summer of 1978 Genentech experienced its first breakthrough in recreating the insulin gene. This development required an expenditure of approximately $100 million and 1,000 human years of labor. By 1982 the company had won approval from the Food and Drug Administration (FDA). Eli Lilly and Company, the world's largest and oldest manufacturer of synthetic insulin, commanded 75 percent of the U.S. insulin market, and Swanson knew that Genentech stood little chance of competing with them. He informed Lilly's directors of Genentech's accomplishments, hoping to attract their attention: he believed that the mere threat of a potentially better product would entice Lilly to purchase licensing rights to the product, and he was correct. Lilly bought the rights and marketed the product as Humulin. This maneuver provided ample capital for Genentech to continue its work. By 1987 the company was earning $5 million in licensing fees from Lilly.

Swanson pursued a similar strategy with the company's next product, Alpha Interferon. Hoffmann-La Roche purchased the rights to Interferon—which it marketed as Roferon-A—and paid approximately $5 million in royalties to Genentech in 1987. Revenues from these agreements helped to underwrite the costs of new product development, which ran from $25 million to $50 million per product prior to FDA approval. Meanwhile, Genentech went public in 1980, raising $35 million through an initial public offering.

Entering the Marketing Arena in the Middle to Late 1980s

The first product independently marketed by Genentech, human growth hormone (HGH) or Protropin, generated $43.6 million in sales in 1986. Demand for HGH increased as the medical profession learned more about the drug's capabilities and diagnosed hormone inadequacy more frequently. Protropin enjoyed record-setting sales over the next six years, topping $155 million by 1991. Approved by the FDA in 1985, Protropin helped prevent dwarfism in children. Genentech's entry into the market was facilitated by an FDA decision to ban the drug's predecessor because it was contaminated with a virus. By the end of the 1980s a ''new and improved'' version of HGH patented by Eli Lilly also had received approval from the FDA. Lilly's drug, unlike Genentech's version, actually replicated the growth hormone found in the human body. To counter this potential threat to their market, Genentech sued the FDA to force the agency to determine which company held exclusive rights to the product. At the end of 1991, Genentech's Protropin maintained an impressive 75 percent share of the HGH market.

Such legal disputes were not unusual for biotechnology firms still in their infancy. Because the products of the industry duplicated substances found in nature, they challenged long-established patent laws. Traditionally, products and discoveries determined as not evident in nature receive patent awards. Biotechnology firms contested these standards in the courtroom, attempting to force alterations in the law, to make it conform to the needs of the industry. Companies applied for broad patents to secure against technological innovations that could undermine their niche in the marketplace. For start-up firms such as Genentech, patent battles consumed large sums of money in both domestic and foreign disputes.

Genentech introduced tissue plasmogen activator (t-PA) in 1987 as Activase, a fast-acting drug that helped to break down fibris, a clotting agent in the blood. At $2,200 per dose, t-PA was marketed as a revolutionary drug for the prevention and treatment of heart attacks. When Genentech failed to provide the FDA with evidence that Activase prolonged the lives of heart attack victims, the federal agency delayed approval until 1988. The drug brought in almost half of the company's $400 million in 1989 revenues.

But Activase was soon battered with legal and clinical setbacks. Genentech's claim to exclusive ownership of natural t-PA and all synthetic variations on it was struck down in Britain when the British firm Wellcome Foundation Ltd. challenged Genentech's patent in the British courts, claiming it was overly broad. In 1993, however, Genentech won a court victory against Wellcome, preventing the U.K. firm from marketing t-PA in the United States until 2005, when Genentech's patent was due to expire. Clinical data showed that the drug caused serious side effects, including severe internal bleeding. A European study indicated that the drug was faster, but no more effective, than some competitors costing just $200 per dose. The troubles continued when a controversial study comparing Activase, SmithKline Beecham plc's Eminase, and another firm's streptokinase was released in March 1991. The International Study of Infarct Survival (ISIS-3) found all three drugs to be equally effective at keeping people alive, which again reflected badly on Activase's high cost. Genentech discounted several of the research methods used, then commissioned its own 41,000-patient comparative trial (at a cost of $55 million), which was completed in 1993 and vouched for the superiority of Activase over streptokinase. By the mid-1990s, however, Genentech was selling just $300 million worth of Activase per year, a far cry from the $1 billion annual sales it had projected for the product in the late 1980s.

Early to Mid-1990s: From Roche Merger to CEO Controversy

The regulatory, legal, and clinical roadblocks that stymied Genentech's introduction of Activase, combined with competition from large pharmaceutical and chemical companies that

Key Dates:

1976: Robert Swanson and Herbert Boyer found Genentech, Inc.
1978: Company scientists recreate the insulin gene—Genentech's first marketable product.
1980: Company raises $35 million through an IPO.
1982: Human insulin clone wins FDA approval and is marketed as Humulin under license by Eli Lilly.
1985: Protropin, the first product independently marketed by Genentech, receives FDA approval for the treatment of dwarfism.
1987: Company begins marketing Activase as a way to dissolve blood clots in heart attack victims.
1990: Switzerland's Roche Holding Ltd. purchases a 60 percent stake in the company for $2.1 billion.
1993: Pulmozyme receives FDA approval for the treatment of cystic fibrosis.
1994: Company begins marketing a second human growth hormone (HGH), Nutropin.
1995: Roche agrees to extend its option to buy remainder of Genentech for four more years; Genentech board forces CEO G. Kirk Raab to resign after allegations of ethical improprieties arise; Dr. Arthur Levinson is named as successor.
1996: Nutropin AQ, the first liquid HGH and Genentech's third HGH product, receives FDA approval.
1997: Company begins marketing Rituxan for the treatment of non-Hodgkin's lymphoma; revenues surpass $1 billion for the first time.
1998: FDA approves Herceptin in the treatment of breast cancer.
1999: Company pays $50 million to settle charges that it had illegally marketed Protropin for unapproved uses; Roche exercises option to buy remainder of the company, then sells about 34 percent of its stock back to the public through two public offerings; Genentech agrees to pay the University of California at San Francisco $200 million to settle a patent dispute involving Protropin.

bought into biotechnology in the late 1980s, culminated in Genentech's 60 percent acquisition by Switzerland's Roche Holding Ltd. The merger was one of many in 1989 and 1990, which resulted in such pharmaceutical giants as SmithKline Beecham plc and Bristol-Myers Squibb Company. Genentech used the $2.1 billion influx of capital to fund research, finance patent disputes, and invest in cooperative ventures to develop synthetic drugs using biotechnological discoveries. Also in 1990, G. Kirk Raab, whom the *Wall Street Journal* described as a ''master marketer,'' was named CEO of Genentech. That year, the company launched the first commercial life sciences experiment in space when it sponsored research aboard the space shuttle *Discovery,* and it received FDA approval to expand the marketing of Activase to include the treatment of acute massive pulmonary embolism (blood clots in the lungs).

Activase had faced stiff competition when it first entered the market in the late 1980s. Delays in approval gave competitors such as Biogen and Integrated Genetics the opportunity to catch up with the industry leader. A dozen or so companies filed patents for similar drugs. Genentech could not expect to easily secure foreign markets for its new drug, either. Competition was stiff; this relatively new industry had little time to carve out established markets, and there were important competitors, particularly in Western Europe. In 1991, however, Genentech won an exclusive patent for recombinant t-PA in Japan. Genentech also had several new products in FDA trials in 1991. An insulin-like growth factor for the treatment of full-blown AIDS patients and relaxin, an obstetric drug, were in development that year. Genentech's DNase (pronounced dee-en-ayse), for use in the management of cystic fibrosis and chronic bronchitis, entered Phase III FDA trials. The firm's HER2 antibody entered clinical trials in 1991 as well. This treatment for breast and ovarian cancer was first developed from mouse cells. Genentech also was able to begin marketing of interferon gamma, or Actimmune, in 1991. The product's relatively meager sales of $1.7 million were connected to the small number of patients suffering from chronic granulomatous disease, an inherited immunodeficiency.

In 1993 Genentech received regulatory approval to market Pulmozyme, its brand name for DNase, in the United States, Canada, Sweden, Austria, and New Zealand, for the treatment of cystic fibrosis. The company's relationship with Roche led to the establishment of a European subsidiary of Genentech to develop, register, and market DNase in 17 primary European countries. Genentech also allotted Roche an exclusive license to sell DNase anywhere but Europe, the United States, Canada, and Japan. DNase was considered the first major advance in the treatment of cystic fibrosis in 30 years. Sales of Pulmozyme—which had gone from conception to market in just five years, half the industry average—reached $76 million by 1996.

Genentech continued to expand its product line as the 1990s continued. In March 1994 the FDA approved a new Genentech human growth hormone, Nutropin, for the treatment of growth failure in children. Other uses for Nutropin soon followed, including the treatment of adults suffering from growth hormone deficiency and of short stature associated with Turner syndrome. A third Genentech HGH, Nutropin AQ—the first liquid HGH—received its first FDA approval in 1996. That year the company's line of growth hormone products generated $218.2 million in revenues.

By mid-1995 Roche's holding in Genentech had increased to about 65 percent. As part of its original stake purchased in 1990, Roche had received the option of purchasing the remainder of the company at $60 per share, an option that expired June 30, 1995. In May 1995, however, Genentech and Roche reached an agreement whereby the option would be extended to June 30, 1999. The option was set to begin at $61.25 per share, then increase each quarter by $1.25 until expiring at $82.50. As part of the agreement, Roche took over Genentech's Canadian and European operations, with Genentech agreeing to receive royalties on sales of Pulmozyme in Europe and on sales of all of the company's products in Canada.

In the midst of the negotiations on this deal, Raab approached Roche to seek a $2 million guarantee of a personal loan. When Genentech's board found out about this improper move, it conducted a broad review of his leadership. Finding other problems, including ongoing federal regulatory investigations into charges that Genentech was promoting the use of its products in unapproved ways, the board forced Raab to resign in July 1995. Named to replace him as president and CEO was Dr. Arthur Levinson, a molecular biologist who had headed the company's research operations. One outcome of the federal probes came in April 1999, when Genentech finalized an agreement to pay $50 million to settle charges that it had illegally marketed Protropin for unapproved uses, such as a kidney disorder and severe burns, from 1985 to 1994. The company also pleaded guilty to a criminal violation, "introducing misbranded drugs in interstate commerce."

Revitalizing the Product Pipeline in the Late 1990s

Although many questioned the wisdom of appointing as CEO a scientist who had never before run a company, Levinson helped restore the company's reputation by shifting its focus away from the marketing arena and back to the laboratory. Genentech reached new heights in the late 1990s, with revenues surpassing the $1 billion mark for the first time in 1997 before reaching $1.15 billion the year after. The reemphasis on research revitalized the company's product pipeline, leading to a substantial increase in the sales of products Genentech marketed itself. In 1998 such sales reached $717.8 million, an increase of nearly 23 percent from the previous year. The growth was attributable to the sales of two new products. In November 1997 Genentech began selling a monoclonal antibody called Rituxan, the first such entity approved to treat a cancer, specifically a form of non-Hodgkin's lymphoma (a cancer of the immune system). Sales of Rituxan, which was codeveloped with La Jolla, California-based IDEC Pharmaceuticals Corporation, were $162.6 million in 1998, the first full year of sales. Monoclonal antibodies are designed to zero in on cancer cells and kill a tumor without harming healthy tissue. A second Genentech-developed monoclonal antibody, Herceptin, was approved by the FDA in September 1998 to treat breast cancer. In clinical trials at this time was a third cancer treatment, called Anti-VEGF, which was being studied as a treatment for several types of solid-tumor cancers.

In June 1999 Roche exercised its option to acquire the 33 percent of Genentech it did not already own for $82.50 per share, or about $3.7 billion. Just one month later, however, Roche sold about 16 percent of Genentech stock back to the public in an IPO that raised about $2.13 billion at the offering price of $97 per share. Genentech thereby resumed trading on the New York Stock Exchange but under a new symbol, DNA. In October 1999 Roche made a secondary offering of 20 million Genentech shares at $143.50, raising $2.87 billion in the largest secondary offering in U.S. history. Following the offerings, Roche held a 66 percent stake in Genentech, which retained the operational autonomy through which it had thrived.

In November 1999 Genentech agreed to pay $200 million to the University of California at San Francisco to settle a nine-year dispute over a patent underlying Protropin. The university had charged that Genentech scientists had stolen a DNA sample from a lab in 1978 and used the specimen to develop Protropin, which by the end of the 1990s had generated $2 billion in sales over its lifetime. The university had sought $400 million in lost royalties and other damages. Despite this latest embarrassment, Genentech entered the 21st century as the most highly respected biotechnology company. With more than a dozen promising products in various stages of clinical development and plenty of cash on hand to fund its aggressive research efforts, Genentech seemed certain to maintain this position well into the new century.

Principal Competitors

Abbott Laboratories; American Home Products Corporation; Amgen Inc.; Bayer AG; Biogen, Inc.; Bristol-Myers Squibb Company; Chiron Corporation; E.I. du Pont de Nemours and Company; Eli Lilly and Company; Genzyme Corporation; Glaxo Wellcome plc; Hoechst AG; Immunex Corporation; Johnson & Johnson; Merck & Co., Inc.; Novartis AG; Novo Nordisk A/S; Pfizer Inc.; Pharmacia & Upjohn, Inc.; Rhone-Poulenc Rorer Inc.; Schering-Plough Corporation; SmithKline Beecham plc.

Further Reading

Arnst, Catherine, "After 27 Years, a Big Payoff," *Business Week,* June 1, 1998, p. 147.

Baum, Rudy, "Knotty Biotech Issues Receive Attention," *Chemical & Engineering News,* April 27, 1992, pp. 30–31.

Blumenstyk, Goldie, "U. of California Patent Suit Puts Biotech Powerhouse Under Microscope," *Chronicle of Higher Education,* August 6, 1999, pp. A45–A46.

Bylinsky, Gene, "Got a Winner? Back It Big," *Fortune,* March 21, 1994, pp. 69–70.

Chase, Marilyn, "Hedged Bet: As Genentech Awaits New Test of Old Drug, Its Pipeline Fills Up," *Wall Street Journal,* April 30, 1993, p. A1.

Fisher, Lawrence M., "Rehabilitation of a Biotech Pioneer," *New York Times,* May 8, 1994, Sec. 3, p. 6.

Grabarek, Brooke H., "Genentech: Still Nowhere But Up?," *Financial World,* June 21, 1994, pp. 16, 18.

Hamilton, Joan, "How Long Can Biotech Stay in the Stratosphere?," *Business Week,* November 25, 1991, p. 224.

——, "It Ain't Over Till It's Over at Genentech," *Business Week,* July 24, 1995, p. 41.

——, "A Miracle Drug's Second Coming," *Business Week,* June 3, 1996, p. 118.

——, "A Star Drug Is Born," *Business Week,* August 23, 1993, p. B6.

"Heart Attack Drugs: Trials and Tribulations," *Economist,* March 19, 1991, pp. 86–87.

King, Ralph T., Jr., " 'Assembly Line' Revs Up Genentech," *Wall Street Journal,* March 12, 1998, p. B1.

——, "Genentech Inc. Names Its CEO As Chairman," *Wall Street Journal,* September 23, 1999, p. B18.

——, "Genentech to Pay $200 Million to End Suit Over Patent," *Wall Street Journal,* November 17, 1999, p. B7.

——, "Profit Prescription: In Marketing of Drugs, Genentech Tests Limits of What Is Acceptable," *Wall Street Journal,* January 10, 1995, p. A1.

——, "Roche to Unload As Much As 17% of Genentech," *Wall Street Journal,* October 11, 1999, p. B2.

Levine, Daniel S., "Genentech Finds a Swiss Cure for Its Wall Street Ills," *San Francisco Business Times,* June 16, 1995, p. 6.

McCoy, Charles, "Genentech's New CEO Seeks Clean Slate," *Wall Street Journal,* July 12, 1995, p. B6.

"Mergers and Acquisitions: Strategic Is the Word," *Institutional Investor,* January 1991, pp. 74–81.

Moukheiber, Zina, "The Great White Hunter," *Forbes,* July 26, 1999, pp. 133–36.

''A Natural Selection,'' *Chief Executive,* May 1992, pp. 34–39.

Rigdon, Joan E., ''Fatal Blunder: Genentech CEO, a Man Used to Pushing Limit, Exceeds It and Is Out,'' *Wall Street Journal,* July 11, 1995, p. A1.

Slutsker, Gary, ''Patenting Mother Nature,'' *Forbes,* January 7, 1991, p. 290.

Thayer, Ann, ''Biotech Firms' Revenues Up But Earnings Win First Half,'' *Chemical & Engineering News,* August 31, 1992, pp. 15–16.

Westphal, Christoph, and Sherry Glied, ''AZT and t-PA: The Disparate Fates of Two Biotechnological Innovations and Their Producers,'' *Columbia Journal of World Business,* Spring/Summer 1990, pp. 83–100.

—April S. Dougal
—updated by David E. Salamie

Global Crossing Ltd.

150 El Camino Drive, Suite 204
Beverly Hills, California 90212
U.S.A.
Telephone: (310) 385-5200
Toll Free: (800) 314-3749
Fax: (301) 281-4942
Wessex House
45 Reid Street
Hamilton HM12
Bermuda
Telephone: (441) 296-8600
Fax: (441) 296-8607
Web site: http://www.globalcrossing.com

Public Company
Incorporated: 1997
Employees: 148
Sales: $424 million (1998)
Stock Exchanges: NASDAQ Bermuda
Ticker Symbol: GBLX
NAIC: 234920 Telecommunications Line Construction

Bermuda-based Global Crossing Ltd., the first independent owner and operator of undersea fiber optic cables, is building a system and offering telecommunication and Internet product services to link telecommunications carriers, multinational businesses, and small businesses anywhere in the world. Its completed transatlantic cable provides high capacity for transmitting telephone, fax, e-mail, and web pages between the United States and Europe, and its terrestrial Pan European network connects major commercial centers. The company is also building submarine cables linking the United States with Japan, the Caribbean, and Central and South America, which were expected to become operational in 2000. At the same time, the company was acquiring land-based networks, including Frontier Communications, and developing joint ventures with owners of fiber optic networks in Asia and Europe. When complete, its global fiber optic network would stretch over 90,000 miles and serve five continents, 24 countries, and more than 170 major cities. In addition to providing bandwidth to carriers and Internet service providers, the company owns the world's largest fleet of cable laying and maintenance vessels, and its Global Centers provide a variety of telecommunication and Internet services, including Web-hosting facilities and cache management, as well as hosting more than 300 of the top Internet brands.

An Independently Owned Subsea Cable: 1997

The story of Global Crossing Ltd. combines fiber optic technology, undersea construction, the tremendous global demand for voice and data transmissions, and one man's belief that he could beat "the big guys." When venture capitalist and financier Gary Winnick established Global Telesystems in March 1997, all the fiber optic cables that crisscrossed the ocean floors were built and owned by consortia of large telecommunications firms. These companies, such as AT&T, Deutsche Telecom, and Nippon Telegram and Telephone, would put up large amounts of money to design a cable and lay it beneath an ocean. Once it was completed, the consortia member were guaranteed a portion of the cable's capacity to send long distance telephone calls, faxes, e-mail, and Web pages. The capacity they were not using they would sell to smaller companies, often at a very significant markup.

Winnick believed it was possible for an independent company to build and own a cable running beneath the Atlantic Ocean, connecting the United States and Europe. A former furniture salesman, Winnick spent nearly a decade at Drexel Burnham Lambert with Michael Milken, the junk-bond guru. He left there in 1985 and formed the Pacific Capital Group, an investment firm, buying and selling companies. For his Atlantic Crossing (AC-1) cable venture, he formed Global Telesystems Ltd. and brought Lodwrick Cook, the former chairman and CEO of Atlantic Richfield Co., out of retirement. In March, they signed a deal with AT&T Submarine Systems, a cable-laying subsidiary of AT&T, and began raising funds to lay a 14,000 kilometer, state-of-the-art cable that would provide high capacity transmissions between the United States, the United Kingdom, Germany, and the Netherlands. Global Telesystems Ltd., the owner of the cable, was capitalized by Pacific Capital group and several other institutional investors.

Company Perspectives:

Global Crossing's mission is to develop, own and operate the world's first independent integrated global network to help satisfy the explosive demand for reliable, high quality undersea transmission capacity. Global Crossing is rapidly developing major fiber optic undersea cable systems and terrestrial facilities to reliably and cost-effectively connect the leading cities in the world.

The cable network itself, according to *EDGE,* was the most advanced undersea telecommunications system ever constructed. It was a high-capacity four fiber self-healing Synchronous Digital Hierarchy ring network, capable of providing 40 gigabits per second of initial service, double the capacity of existing systems. The company later increased capacity to 80 gigabits. In mid-1997, AT&T sold its submarine systems business to Tyco International, which formed Tyco Submarine Systems Ltd. (TSSL).

Going Global

In November 1997, Winnick announced the formation of a holding company, Global Crossing Ltd. This reflected his interest in building a global network of submarine cables to link major cities around the world. Before the end of the year, Global Crossing had announced plans for three new operations to accomplish this. The Mid-Atlantic Crossing (MAC-1) was a joint venture with cable system owner TeleBermuda International Ltd. to build and own an undersea cable connecting New York, Bermuda, the Caribbean, and Florida. The new cable would connect with AC-1 in New York.

The Pan American Crossing (PAC-1) undersea cable would link California, Mexico, Panama, Venezuela, and the Caribbean. The Pacific Crossing (PC-1) cable, a joint venture with Japanese trading firm Marubeni, would link California and Washington and Japan. Ultimately, Global Crossing planned to build and own a 31,000 mile cable network running beneath the Atlantic, Caribbean, and Pacific Oceans.

Internet service providers in particular were demanding high bandwidth single channels, and Global Crossing was not the only company looking to the Pacific Rim. China-U.S. Cable Network, a consortium of carriers (AT&T, MCI WorldCom, Sprint, Teleglobe of Canada, and China Telecom) planned to build a $950 million, 30,000-kilometer cable between China and the United States, and Neptune Communications Corp., a private company, announced it would build the Pacific Express Cable Network between Hawaii, Japan, the Republic of Korea, and Canada.

Creating the Network: 1998

Global Crossing would have to make money by selling capacity on its cables. Unlike the telecommunications consortia that owned existing submarine cables, Global Crossing opened its cable to anyone who wanted to use it. Traditionally, a company wanting to buy capacity on a cable, whether it was land based or submarine, had to sign a long-term contract for a fixed amount of capacity from point A to point B. Since different parties owned different cables, a customer had to have separate agreements with each owner of a land or oceanic cable along the route it wanted to use, say from Houston to Rome. Global Crossing offered customers the flexibility to use capacity anywhere along its network as they needed it. In addition to AC-1 and the other subsea lines it was building, Global Crossing was also constructing or hooking up with terrestrial cable owners, so that its customers were not left to fend for themselves on the shore of a foreign country.

As AC-1 was being constructed, carriers began buying capacity, including New Jersey-based IDT, Unisource (PTT Telecom of the Netherlands, Telia of Sweden, and Swisscom), PSINet, and Deutsche Telekom. The deal with Deutsche Telekom included "backhaul services" whereby all AC-1 customers would have access to that company's land network. Global Crossing also signed an agreement with Qwest Communications International to swap capacity, so that Qwest would use AC-1 to transmit to Europe and Global Crossing would use Qwest's Macro Capacity Fiber Network, which, when completed in 1999, would serve more than 125 cities in the United States.

Going Public

In April 1998, John M. Scanlon left Motorola Inc.'s cellular division to become CEO of Global Crossing, while Lodwrick Cook and Winnick became co-chairmen. On May 26, ten months after construction began, the first phase of AC-1 initiated commercial service, allowing data and voice transmissions between the United States and the United Kingdom. The start-up coincided with the tenth anniversary of the first submarine fiber-optic cables. According to John Burgess of the *Washington Post*, the cable could "handle more than 480,000 simultaneous two-way transatlantic conversations, each duplicated for protection." Tyco Submarine Systems Ltd., which was the hardware developer and primary contractor during the construction of the system, was now responsible for operating and maintaining AC-1.

In June 1998, Global Crossing finished raising the $800 million needed to build PC-1 through a private note offering to major institutions and mutual funds. The company had $3 billion of projects underway, and while profits remained well out of sight, as of April 1998, it had more than $400 million in binding agreements with customers for AC-1 and more than $175 million in non-binding agreements.

Winnick took the company public in August, raising $399 million in net proceeds. The stock, traded on the NASDAQ, opened at $19 per share and closed at $25.50. The proceeds were used primarily to complete the AC-1 financing.

In October, the company announced it was building a $700 million fiber optic network (Pan Europe Crossing, PEC) to link 18 cities in Europe to AC-1 and the rest of its cable system. In November, one of the company's indirect subsidiaries, GC Pacific Landing Corp., merged with Neptune Communications, LLC, which was controlled by The Carlyle Group, an international investment firm.

The company was having an impact. At the end of the year, CEO Scanlon told *Investor's Business Daily* that prices for leased

Key Dates:

1997: Global Telesystems Ltd. begins building Atlantic Crossing subsea fiber optic cable; holding company Global Crossing Ltd. is created.
1998: Atlantic Crossing begins commercial service; Global Crossing goes public.
1999: Company acquires Frontier Communications.

lines beneath the Atlantic had dropped by half since AC-1 began operating in May. In December, Global Crossing announced its second terrestrial network, to connect major cities in Japan. The company owned 49 percent of the new network, called Global Access Limited (GAL), and Marubeni Corporation, its partner in PC-1, owned the rest. The company was heavily in debt. At the end of the year, it had $1.3 billion in total liabilities.

Fighting a Consortium and Selling Capacity: 1999

Global Crossing began 1999 by asking the Federal Communications Commission (FCC) to defer approval of a landing license in Japan for the telecommunications consortium building the Japan-U.S. Cable System. The company contended that such approval might be anti-competitive because the three Japanese companies in the 30-member consortium (which also included AT&T, Sprint, MCI WorldCom, and British Telecommunications) would control transmission prices within Japan. After several months, as Global Crossing's lobbyists haunted Capitol Hill, the FCC granted the license free of any conditions.

The attempt to break up the consortium did not stop AT&T from leasing capacity on Global Crossing's transatlantic cable. With the tremendous demand by carriers for more bandwidth, AC-1 was proving even more popular than anticipated. The company reported it had generated $1 billion in contract sales during 1998, although most of that ($634 million) would be realized over the next three years. In the fourth quarter alone, the company had revenues of $205 million and a net income of $56 million. It also announced it would begin developing a second transatlantic cable (AC-2) as well as a system (South American Crossing, SAC) to link the U.S. Virgin Islands, Brazil, Argentina, Chile, Peru, Columbia, and Panama.

Work continued on the other legs of the company's network. For the terrestrial Pan European cable, the company announced a $150 million deal with Lucent Technologies to supply technology and systems that provided high bandwidth connections and allowed carriers to integrate voice and data on fiber backbones. Lucent's experience with both subsea and land systems helped win the contract.

A New CEO Moves Quickly

Also in January, Global Crossing got a new CEO. Robert Annunziata, the head of AT&T's business services, replaced Jack Scanlon, who became vice-chairman. Annunziata was hired to take Global Crossing from its position as a wholesale carrier to a full-fledged telecommunications competitor by adding local networks and customers. The plan was to make its network truly global, with underwater cables connected to countrywide networks linked to local networks serving major cities. The Pan European Crossing would begin to serve that purpose in Europe. What Global Crossing needed was a network, or backbone, in the United States, with existing customers.

Three weeks after coming onboard, Annunziata began merger talks with Rochester, New York-based Frontier Communications, the fifth largest long-distance carrier in the United States. In addition to Frontier's nationwide fiber optic network, the deal would bring Global Crossing two million customers using Frontier's local and long-distance telephone, Internet, data, cellular, and paging services as well as 34 local telephone companies in 13 states, and it appeared to be closed in March. The company then bought Cable & Wireless's undersea cable operations for $885 million, and in May announced a $35.5 billion agreement to take over Denver-based U S West, Inc., the smallest of the Baby Bells but a $12.4 billion corporation.

Global Crossing's bid to buy U S West was stymied when Qwest Communications International went after Frontier. Qwest, like Global Crossing, was primarily a network builder and operator looking for end use customers. After a takeover battle lasting five weeks, Global Crossing ended up buying Frontier for $10.9 billion, and U S West merged with Qwest.

Selling Services As Well As Capacity

With its acquisition of Frontier, Global Crossing moved from simply providing ultra-high long-distance capacity to carriers, a wholesale operation, to also operating local networks and providing telecommunication and Internet services on a retail basis to customers—carriers, corporations, small businesses, and consumers.

Over the next several months, it introduced new telecommunications and Internet product services, including WebSaver, with discounted long distance telephone rates; audioconferencing; uCommand, an account and network management tool; ISP Advantage for Internet service providers; web hosting and managed caching services to distribute web content more quickly. For its wholesale carrier customers, it launched Asynchronous Transfer Mode (ATM), which made it possible to support several applications (data, Internet, voice, and video) over a single platform by increasing bandwidth incrementally. To bring its products to international markets, the company announced it was building ten new Global Centers worldwide.

Still, Annunziata was not ignoring the network. Global Crossing began expanding its city-to-city concept as it announced a joint venture with Microsoft and Softbank. The new venture, called Asia Global Crossing, was to build a $1.3 billion broadband network (East Asia Crossing) to link Japan, China, Singapore, Hong Kong, Taiwan, South Korea, Malaysia, and the Philippines with Global Crossing's network. Shortly thereafter, Global Crossing acquired Racal Telecom, which owned a 4,500-mile fiber optic network in England, giving Global Crossing another land network to link with the Pan European Crossing and more customers for its services.

As all this was occurring, Winnick assumed the position of chairman of the board. In November, the company announced a joint venture with Hutchison Whampoa Ltd., named Hutchison Global Crossing, to sell telecommunications and Internet services over Hutchison's network in Hong Kong. The new venture was worth an estimated $1.2 billion.

With its national networks and international pipelines, Global Crossing was an attractive takeover target in the fast-moving, quickly consolidating telecommunications field. In November 1999, Deutsche Telekom reportedly offered $60 a share, which the company allegedly rejected. Winnick had anticipated the phenomenal demand for bandwidth and the need to provide carriers with a simple, single connection across borders and shorelines. He recognized the potential growth of Internet traffic, which was soon outdistancing that within the U.S. market, and concentrated on submarine cables. Whether it continued as an independent company or not, Global Crossing had already changed the telecommunications industry.

Principal Subsidiaries

Global Crossing Network Center, Ltd.; Global Marine Systems Ltd.; Global Crossing International, Ltd.; Atlantic Crossing Holdings, Ltd.; Pacific Crossing Holdings Ltd.; Mid-Atlantic Crossing Holdings Ltd.; Pan American Crossing Holdings Ltd.; Global Crossing Landing Holdings Ltd.

Principal Competitors

AT&T Corp.; MCI WorldCom, Inc.; Bell Atlantic Corporation; BellSouth Corporation; GTE Corporation; FirstCom; Qwest Communications International; Sprint Communications Company; Global Telesystems Groups Inc.

Further Reading

''AT&T to Build World's Most Powerful Undersea Network,'' *Business Wire*, March 24, 1997.

Bloomberg News, ''Global to Build New Fiber Optic Network,'' *New York Times*, October 2, 1998.

Booth, Jason, ''Financier Raises Vast Sums for Fiber-Optic Operations,'' *Los Angeles Business Journal*, July 27, 1998, p. 7.

Dickinson, Mike, ''Global Crossing Faces New Battles,'' *Rochester Business Journal*, October 1, 1999, p. 1.

''FCC Ponders Validity of Undersea Cable Consortiums,'' *Communications Today*, January 22, 1999.

Gilder, George, ''Undersea Treasure,'' *Forbes*, December 28, 1998.

''Global Crossing Loses Regulatory Battle,'' *Fiber Optics News*, July 26, 1999.

''Global Crossing, Lucent Strike $150 Million Deal,'' *Communications Today*, February 1, 1999.

''Global Crossing Picks Up $399 Million in IPO,'' *Communications Today*, August 24, 1998.

''Global Crossing's New WebSaver Plan Leverages Power of Internet to Fuel E-Business,'' *Cambridge Telecom Report*, November 1, 1999.

''Global Crossing, Softbank and Microsoft Establish Joint Venture to Build Telecom Network Providing Advanced Services Throughout Asia,'' *EDGE: Work-Group Computing Report*, September 13, 1999.

''Global Crossing Swims in Cable Deals,'' *Fiber Optics News*, January 12, 1998.

Grover, Ronald, ''High Times for a Former Milken Man,'' *Business Week*, October 12, 1998, p. 56.

Grover, Ronald, and Peter Elstron, ''An Undersea Creature with a Big Appetite,'' *Business Week*, May 31, 1999, p. 42.

Holman, Kelly, ''Global Crossing Charts Public Waters,'' *Private Equity Week*, August 24, 1998.

Krause, Reinhardt, ''Phone Maverick Surfaces Among Telecom's Sharks,'' *Investor's Business Daily*, December 1, 1998, p. A8.

Lynch, Karen, ''Local Boy Goes Global,'' *tele.com*, September 20, 1999.

Madigan, Nick, ''Connecting Americas,'' *Daily Variety*, December 29, 1997, p. 2.

Meyers, Jason, ''Pioneers of the World Network,'' *Telephony*, February 15, 1999.

Molony, David, ''Internet the Catalyst for New Wave of Subsea Pipes,'' *CommunicationsWeek International*, March 2, 1998, p. 2.

——, ''U.S. Carriers Move in on European Targets, *CommunicationsWeek International*, October 25, 1999, p. 47.

Moore, W. John, ''The Water Boys,'' *National Journal*, May 8, 1999, p. 1,276.

''Qwest, Global Crossing Divvy Up Their Quarry,'' *Chicago Times*, July 20, 1999, Bus. Sec. p. 4.

Schiesel, Seth, ''Neat Package Hides Issues in Phone Deal,'' *New York Times*, July 20, 1999, p. C1.

Sloan, Allan, ''Financial Haute Couture,'' *Newsweek*, May 31, 1999, p. 52.

Strauss, Jennifer C., ''Trio Links Up Pacific Crossing,'' *Bank Loan Report*, July 6, 1998.

''Tyco's Submarine Systems Purchase Final,'' *Record* (Bergen, N.J.), July 3, 1997, p. B2.

''US-Japan Undersea Fiber-Optic Network Financing Completed,'' *ASIA PULSE*, May 12, 1998.

Vrana, Debra, ''California Dealin': Underwater Cable Company to Float $300 Million IPO,'' *Los Angeles Times*, July 27, 1998, p. D5.

Wirbel, Loring, ''Single Company Tackles Transoceanic Cable Jobs,'' *Electronic Engineering Times*, January 5, 1998.

Young, Anne, ''Profile: Jack Scanlon,'' *CommunicationsWeek International*, April 20, 1998, p. 39.

—Ellen D. Wernick

Golden State Foods Corporation

18301 Von Karman Avenue
Suite 1100
Irvine, California 92612
U.S.A.
Telephone: (949) 252-2000
Fax: (949) 252-2080

Private Company
Incorporated: 1969
Employees: 1,800
Sales: $1.6 billion (1998)
NAIC: 42241 General Line Grocery Wholesalers

Golden State Foods Corporation is a food processor and distributor, supplying more than 130 products to McDonald's Corporation, its only customer. The company's main products are hamburger patties, buns, ketchup, mayonnaise, and other sauces. Golden State is one of McDonald's largest suppliers, providing product to approximately 2,000 of the company's 25,000 restaurants. Headquartered in Irvine, California, Golden State maintains 12 production plants and distribution centers in the United States, Egypt, and Australia.

1947–70: One-Stop Shopping for the Food Service Industry

Golden State Foods was formed in 1947 by William Moore. Originally named Golden State Meat, the small business started as a meat supplier to restaurants, hotels, and institutional food services in the Los Angeles area. In the late 1950s, Moore acquired as a client a franchisee of a new restaurant chain called McDonald's. McDonald's, a fast-food hamburger stand, had been founded in 1948 in San Bernardino, California, by brothers Dick and Mac McDonald. In 1954, an enterprising salesman from Illinois named Ray Kroc had approached the brothers to inquire about the possibility of turning the successful hamburger stand into a chain. When the McDonald brothers agreed, Kroc quickly began opening a series of McDonald's restaurants in Illinois, Indiana, and California.

In 1961, Kroc bought out the McDonald brothers and became the owner of the rapidly growing McDonald's chain. A year later, he moved to California to oversee a major expansion initiative in that state, and befriended Moore, who was serving as a supplier to the chain. In 1965, Moore and a partner purchased their own McDonald's franchise, and over the next two years acquired four more. When Moore's partner died, however, he sold the restaurants back to McDonald's in exchange for stock.

Meanwhile, McDonald's was experiencing explosive growth. In 1965, the company went public and three years later celebrated the opening of its 1,000th restaurant. As Kroc's restaurant chain grew, so did Golden State's business. Toward the end of the 1960s, the company built a new meat-processing plant and warehouse in City of Industry, California, just outside Los Angeles. It also changed its name, incorporating as Golden State Foods. Shortly after building its new facilities, Moore introduced an innovation that was to alter both the course of his company and the nature of the fast-food industry supply business. He decided to begin supplying his McDonald's customers with virtually everything they needed to run their businesses.

This "one stop shopping" notion was a dramatic departure from the norm. At the time, the average McDonald's unit had a whole series of suppliers, each of which provided a different category of product. With deliveries from the meat supplier, dairy supplier, bakery supplier, frozen foods supplier, and various other distributors, it was not uncommon for a franchisee to receive up to 15 deliveries per day. While inefficient and time-consuming, this multiple-supplier method was the only option available to restaurant owners.

Golden State's ability to offer a full range of food products—including hamburger patties, buns, sauces, and soft drink syrups—made it stand out among other suppliers. Once it had established its food lines, however, it went a step further and began providing cleaning supplies and paper goods, such as cups, napkins, and containers. The company's ability to deliver everything in a single trip enabled McDonald's franchisees to receive all their supplies in just three to four deliveries each week.

Key Dates:

1947: William Moore forms Golden State Meats to supply meat products to Los Angeles area restaurants and hotels.
1950s: Golden State begins supplying several McDonald's franchises.
1969: Company incorporates as Golden State Foods.
1972: Golden State goes public; deciding to focus solely on McDonald's, it drops all its other customers.
1978: Founder William Moore dies; vice-president of sales James Williams becomes president and CEO.
1980: Moore leads a group of Golden State executives in taking the company private.
1992: Company moves headquarters from Pasadena to Irvine, California
1998: The Yucaipa Cos. and Wetterau Associates purchase Golden State.

1970–90: A One-Customer Company

During the 1970s, the McDonald's chain was growing at breakneck speed, adding approximately 500 new restaurants each year. As such, the fast-food chain was supplying Golden State with as much business as it could handle. In 1972, the company decided to shed all of its other clients, in order to focus exclusively on McDonald's needs. Although a gamble, it was a calculated one. Moore was a firm believer in Kroc's philosophy of providing good, hot food inexpensively and felt certain that the chain would continue to thrive. That same year, Golden State went public, with year-end sales of $65 million.

In 1978, the company's founder and CEO, William Moore, died. He was replaced by James Williams, the company's vice-president of sales. Williams had a long history with Golden State. He had started his employment there in 1961, just a few years after the company had begun supplying McDonald's. At that time, Golden State had 15 employees, a single delivery truck, and annual sales of around $500,000. In 1972, Williams had been promoted to vice-president of sales and given responsibility for more than 100 McDonald's units in southern California. When he became CEO of Golden State, 17 years after joining the operation, he found himself heading up a company with $272 million in sales.

Soon after becoming Golden State's leader, Williams began investigating the possibility of taking the company private. In 1980, he headed a group of company executives in a $29 million buyout, purchasing 1.05 million outstanding shares of common stock, many of which were held by Moore's family. According to Williams, the move to privatize was partially due to Moore's death and partially due to his dislike of securities analysts rating the company's shares in accordance with the fast-food industry's performance as a whole.

Golden State continued to add new McDonald's franchises to its customer base and to expand its operations. By 1987, the company had estimated annual sales of $800 million and 1,300 employees. It had distribution facilities in eight states—California, Washington, Arizona, Georgia, Hawaii, New York, North Carolina, and Virginia—but its operations were primarily concentrated in the western and southeastern United States. Through its distribution network, Golden State supplied some 425 different items to approximately one-fifth of the McDonald's franchisees in the United States. The company's total product mix consisted of frozen foods, produce, dairy, groceries, disposable products, glassware, and cleaning supplies.

As Golden State approached the end of the 1980s, its annual sales approached the $1 billion mark. With the company showing strong and steady gains, its owners—Williams and 14 other company insiders—began considering an exit scenario. In the fall of 1989, the company announced that it had hired a financial advisor to begin exploring the possibility of a merger. ''We believe now may be an opportune time to investigate a merger of the company in light of current market conditions and the growth in the company's business,'' Williams said in an October 13, 1989 press release. By early 1990, Golden State was officially for sale, and one of its top bidders was the Quaker Oats Company. Williams and the other investors were unable to reach a satisfactory agreement with a buyer, however, and they eventually took the company off the market.

1990s and Beyond: Continued Growth, New Owners

In 1992, Golden State moved its corporate headquarters from Pasadena to a 20,000-square-foot penthouse office in Irvine, California. By the time the company relocated, its annual sales had climbed to approximately $1.2 billion, and it was ranked number 139 on the *Forbes* 400 list of the largest privately owned companies. It was McDonald's third largest supplier—behind Keystone Foods Corp. and the Martin-Brower Corp.—providing items to 1,800 of the chain's restaurants.

In addition to its Irvine headquarters and its eight distribution facilities, Golden State operated two food processing factories: a 106,000-square-foot plant in City of Industry, California, and a 250,000-square-foot plant in Conyers, Georgia. The City of Industry plant produced goods for McDonald's in the western United States and also for units in the countries of Hong Kong, Singapore, Taiwan, Australia, and Japan. Golden State's Georgia plant supplied McDonald's in the southeastern United States, Latin America, and the Caribbean.

Despite the fact that McDonald's was Golden State's sole customer, the company did not hold a long-term supply contract with the fast-food giant. It was McDonald's practice to offer its franchisees an approved supplier list, from which individual franchisees could choose. Therefore, virtually all of Golden State's business was conducted with individual franchisees who could switch suppliers at will. This arrangement meant that the company had to maintain high product and service quality and offer competitive pricing in order to sustain its sales levels. ''We make a good product, or McDonald's is not going to buy from us; it's that simple,'' Williams said in a January 1993 interview with the *Orange County Business Journal.* ''We have to be a value to a system, or we're not going to be in business. It doesn't matter to them if you've been doing business for two years or 30 years. The quality is never negotiable,'' he added.

In 1994, Williams recruited a new face for Golden State's management team. Richard Gochnauer joined the company as president, while Williams himself kept the title of CEO. Gochnauer had previously served as an executive vice-president of Dial Corp. and as president of a division of Universal Foods.

The following year, Golden State was again listed in the *Forbes* 400 list of largest private companies, with a ranking of 120th. It was thus the largest privately held business in Orange County. In 1996, the company opened another distribution center in Portland, Oregon. It also expanded internationally, establishing distribution centers in Egypt and Australia. Golden State's growth was not surprising, given the increasing demands of its customer. During the middle of the 1990s, McDonald's was expanding at a frenzied pace, adding as many as 1,100 new domestic units in a year. The burger giant was also making tremendous strides in foreign markets; by the end of the decade, there were more international stores than domestic ones, and foreign business made up 56 percent of the company's operating profits.

In 1997, with annual sales approaching $1.5 billion, Williams and Golden State's other owners once again began thinking of cashing out. Hiring the New York investment firm Lazard Freres & Co. to analyze its options, the owners offered the company up for sale in late 1997. This time, they found the right buyers and the right deal. The purchase price was an estimated $400 million, more than 13 times what Williams' investors had paid to take the company private in 1980.

The buyers were The Yucaipa Cos., which acquired 70 percent of the company, and Wetterau Associates LLC, which bought the remaining 30 percent. Yucaipa was a Los Angeles-based private investment company headed by Ron Burkle. Golden State represented the company's first investment in foodservice distribution. Its other holdings were primarily in the supermarket industry; Yucaipa had a stake in companies operating 850 supermarkets throughout the country. Wetterau Associates was a St. Louis-based management company run by Mark and Conrad Wetterau, brothers and former executives of a multibillion-dollar Midwestern food distributorship. Having sold their distributorship to SuperValu Inc. in the early part of the 1990s, the Wetteraus had been looking for likely acquisitions when Golden State went on the market. Recruiting Yucaipa as a financial partner, the brothers finalized the deal in April 1998. Under the terms of the agreement, Wetterau Associates assumed responsibility for running the daily operations of Golden State. Williams agreed to remain with the company for at least one year, but a number of other executives and former shareholders used their gains to retire.

Williams stayed with Golden State no longer than he had agreed to. In May 1999, he announced his retirement, ending 38 years of employment with the company. Mark Wetterau became the company's new CEO, while Richard Gochnauer stayed on as its president.

No major changes had taken place since Yucaipa's and Wetterau's acquisition of Golden State. The company remained headquartered in California, and continued to cater exclusively to McDonald's. Although the company's new owners had been quiet about their plans for the future, no alterations in its course were foreseen.

Principal Divisions

Golden State Foods-City of Industry; Golden State Foods-Georgia Division; Golden State Foods-Hawaii Division; Golden State Foods-North Carolina Division; Golden State Foods-Northwest Division; Golden State Foods-Oak Brook Division; Golden State Foods-Phoenix Division; Golden State Foods-Rochester Division; Golden State Foods-South Carolina Division; Golden State Foods Suffolk.

Principal Competitors

J.R. Simplot Company; Keystone Foods Corp.; The Martin-Brower Company.

Further Reading

Britton, Charles, ''Golden State Foods . . . Under the Arches,'' *Southern California Business*, July 1, 1987, p. 8.

Desloge, Rick, ''Wetterau Says McDonald's,'' *St. Louis Business Journal*, March 2, 1998, p. 1A.

Hernandez, Greg, ''Golden State's Chief Executive Retires,'' *Los Angeles Times, Orange County Edition*, May 28, 1999, p. C6.

Segal, Robert, ''McDonald's Primary Distributors Are Sold,'' *The Voice of Foodservice Distribution*, July 1998, p. 33.

Stanton, Russ, ''Duo Purchases Golden State Foods,'' *Los Angeles Times, Orange County Edition*, February 24, 1998, p. D21.

—Shawna Brynildssen

The Green Bay Packers, Inc.

1265 Lombardi Avenue
Green Bay, Wisconsin 54304
U.S.A.
Telephone: (920) 496-5700
Fax: (920) 496-5738
Web site: http://www.packers.com

Nonprofit Company
Incorporated: 1923 as Green Bay Football Corporation
Employees: 95
Sales: $102.7 million (1999)
NAIC: 711211 Sports Teams and Clubs

The Green Bay Packers, Inc. is a nonprofit corporation held by the citizens of Green Bay to run its football team. The Packers are the only publicly owned team in the National Football League (NFL), and the team is the only surviving franchise in the NFL still playing in its original small town. Green Bay Packers, Inc. has roughly 100,000 shareholders, but the shares produce no dividends, and all profits the team makes go to the American Legion. The team's wins, therefore, produce no financial gain for stockholders. Yet this arrangement virtually precludes the Packers from moving to another city. Green Bay remains the only town of its size to have a major league football team. The Packers' unusual corporate status attests to the huge loyalty Wisconsonites have for the team. The Green Bay team has a celebrated history. It was one of the most successful teams in the sport in its earliest years, and had a golden period in the early 1960s, when it was graced with many top players. The team returned to the top ranks in the 1990s, led by such star players as Brett Favre and Reggie White.

Early Years Under Lambeau

The Green Bay Packers team was founded and led by a remarkable player and coach, Earl L. "Curly" Lambeau. Lambeau was born in Green Bay in 1898, and grew up to be the star of his high school football team. He attended Notre Dame University in 1918, and as a freshman played on the varsity team under the legendary coach Knute Rockne. An illness kept Lambeau home from college the next year, and he began working at the Indian Packing Company, a meat-packing plant in his home town. Lambeau missed playing football, so in the summer of 1919 he helped organize a local team. Lambeau convinced his employer to put up money for uniforms and equipment. The team was known briefly as the Indians, but soon became the Green Bay Packers, after the meat-packing company. For its first two seasons, the team played games against other teams from small towns in Wisconsin and Michigan. The players' only pay was what could be collected in a hat passed among spectators at halftime. The proceeds per player for the whole 1919 season were $16.75. The Packers played in a vacant field in a downtown park, and the members of the team of necessity had regular day jobs.

But Lambeau was ambitious. He was an extraordinary player himself, and pioneered the passing style of play. Earlier players did not rely on throwing the ball to the extent Lambeau did, and opponents were often infuriated by Lambeau's winning technique. In 1921 Lambeau again appealed to the Indian Packing Company to put up $50 to buy the Packers a franchise in the newly formed American Professional Football Association (later renamed the National Football League). The team did well, playing against clubs from Ohio, Indiana, and Illinois. When the Packers joined the professional league, the competition got better, and Lambeau began to recruit players from outside of Green Bay. In order to lure players, he needed to guarantee them some financial gain beyond loose change in a hat. Thus in 1923, a group of five area businessmen got together and launched the Green Bay Football Corporation, a nonprofit entity to provide financial backing for the team. Shares of stock sold for $5 each and paid no dividends. Purchasers were obligated to buy at least six season tickets. The corporation had a five-member executive committee and 15 elected directors. As a nonprofit, the corporation was tax-exempt, and all profits were to go to the American Legion. Lambeau signed some impressive players, among them Verne Lewellen, Lavvie Dilweg, and Johnny Blood. In the 1920s and early 1930s Lambeau's team was a powerhouse, winning three national championships from 1929 to 1931. Lambeau had his last season as a player in 1930, but he continued to coach the team.

Despite the team's success on the field, it had financial difficulties during the Depression years. Because of a bleacher

Company Perspectives:

Since the team's inception in 1919, the Green Bay Packers have had a special bond with its fans and neighbors. Its unique ownership structure—the only community owned team in professional sports—as well as the team's small market origins only reinforce the Packers' link to their fans and their community.

accident in which a fan was injured, the team was required to settle a $5,000 lawsuit, and when its insurer went bankrupt, the team accrued even more debt. In 1935, Green Bay Football Corporation was put into receivership. Professional football changed for the better in the mid-1930s, when a fair college draft system was instituted. Previously, the four best teams in the NFL dominated year after year, because the good college players would only sign on with the leading teams. Competition within the league evened out after a draft was initiated in 1934, and football became more popular. The Packers had a championship team in 1936, and by 1937 they were out of receivership. The corporation reorganized as the Green Bay Packers, Inc.

Transitional Years After World War II

Curly Lambeau continued to coach the Packers through the 1940s. But after 1945, many of the team's great heroes had retired, and the Packers began to lose. An All-American Football Conference was organized in 1946, splitting the sport between the old NFL and the new league. This drastically increased the number of professional teams on the American scene. As a result, good players were in high demand, and they began to command large salaries. Because of this, running the Packers became more expensive. Lambeau muddied the Packers' financial picture too by using the corporation's assets to buy an expensive lodge north of Green Bay to house the team. The players then had to be bused into town to practice. The team's record slid. In 1948 they won 3 games out of 12, and the next year won only two. In order to bring money to the team, the board of directors decided to sell more stock. Lambeau led a behind-the-scenes move to sell the stock to four backers who would put in $200,000 if the corporation could be changed to a for-profit one. He was outvoted on this move, and a stock sale went ahead in 1950. Single shares went for $25 each, and the sale raised $125,000. Shortly after this Lambeau left the Packers to become head coach of the Chicago Cardinals.

The conflict between the two major football leagues ended in 1949 when the All-American Football Conference came to an arrangement with the NFL, and the country was divided into a National Conference and an American Conference. The Packers secured a new coach, Gene Ronzani, in 1950. But the team continued to lose. Verne Lewellen, one of the early great Packers players and later a lawyer and Standard Oil executive, became the team's business manager in 1954. Lewellen began looking for a new coach. In 1954 Lisle Blackbourn became coach, but he fared no better than Ronzani. He lasted until 1957, when he was replaced by Ray McLean. The team won only one game in 1958.

The Packers did make some positive changes during this disastrous decade. The stadium by the high school where the team had started was hopelessly outdated. Its wooden structure had deteriorated, it had no bathrooms, and it was too small. In 1956 the Green Bay Packers, Inc. broke ground for a new stadium on the southwestern edge of town. The total cost was just under $1 million, and the financing was split between the corporation and the city. Its original seating was for 32,150, thought to be frighteningly large. The team won its first game there, in September 1957, with Vice-President Richard Nixon on hand for the dedication. Originally called City Stadium, its name was changed to Lambeau Field in 1965, after the death of Curly Lambeau. The Packers also gained increasing financial benefit from radio and television broadcasting during the 1950s. The corporation was able to sell radio rights to its games for $20,000 in 1952. The first televised Packers game was in 1953, and the team was paid $5,000 for each of three broadcast games. By 1956, television rights were going for a lot more. CBS paid the team $75,000 that year to televise all its games. Because the Green Bay area was such a small television market, the Packers' contract was worth far less than what teams in such cities as Los Angeles and New York were getting. In the early 1960s, this disparity among league teams was worked out. The NFL negotiated as a whole, and television proceeds were split evenly between teams. This was much to the advantage of Green Bay.

Lombardi Brings Back the Pack in the 1960s

Despite building a new stadium and gaining lucrative television coverage, the team still had precarious finances and, worst of all, a losing record. The Packers' executive committee let Ray McLean go, and in 1959 brought in a relatively unknown man to be head coach, Vincent Lombardi. Lombardi had been a high school coach, a lawyer, an assistant coach for West Point, and then an assistant coach for the New York Giants before he came to Green Bay. He immediately instituted changes, trading players and redefining strategy. The sorry Packers were transformed. In Lombardi's first season, they had seven wins, and the next year the team won the Western Division title. The 1960s were the glory years for the Packers. The team was filled with such legendary players as Bart Starr, Paul Hornung, and Jerry Kramer. Under Lombardi, the Packers never finished below second place, and they won championships in 1965, 1966, and 1967. The corporation's finances improved markedly when broadcast revenues increased. In 1967 the team received more than $1 million in television fees. The rising popularity of the team meant the stadium in Green Bay needed more seats. By 1965, Lambeau Field seated over 50,000 fans, and every single home game was sold out.

At Sea in the 1970s and 1980s

Exhausted after the climactic 1967 season, Lombardi became General Manager and gave his coaching job to his assistant, Phil Bengston. Lombardi died just two years later. With Bart Starr injured, other players aging, and the costs of hiring top players becoming more than the small Green Bay franchise could afford, the team went downhill. A series of coaches succeeded Bengston, who coached from 1968 to 1970. Dan Devine had the job for the next three seasons. The Packers' percentage of wins under him was .474, that is, they won less than half their games. Under former quarterback Bart Starr's coaching, the team did even worse. Starr coached from 1975 through 1983, with a career record of .410. The numbers went down even more sadly under

Key Dates:

1919: Curly Lambeau organizes first team.
1923: Packers' nonprofit structure is initiated.
1929–31: Team wins three consecutive championships.
1950: Lambeau leaves the team.
1959: Vince Lombardi has first season coaching.
1966: First of two back-to-back Superbowl wins.
1991: Mike Holmgren begins building a winning team.
1996: Packers take the Superbowl.
2000: Coach Ray Rhodes is fired after the Packers close out a losing season; Mike Sherman is named as the new head coach.

the next coach, Forrest Gregg, to .405 over his three seasons. When Gregg left, Lindy Infante took the position, and between 1988 and 1991, the Packers won 24 games and lost 40. Green Bay's fans were intensely loyal, and every home game was sold out from 1960 on. Nevertheless, the team was clearly lacking in direction and not fun to watch. This changed beginning in 1991, with new coach Mike Holmgren.

New Success in the 1990s

Financially, Green Bay Packers, Inc. fared better than the team it stood for. By 1990, the net worth of the franchise was estimated at over $125 million. Revenue from television rights had continued to climb, so that in 1990 the team pulled in $25 million from broadcast rights, and reported a profit of $2 million, which was of course reinvested. The corporation added more seating to Lambeau Field, including 36 boxes and 1,920 theater-style club seats in 1990. The corporation's president since 1989, Robert Harlan, significantly boosted the team's income by aggressively marketing the Packers logo and opening a Packer Pro Shop to sell Packers gear and paraphernalia. But the corporation's board was not satisfied with financial solvency when the team was no good. President Harlan decided in 1991 to replace the head of operations, Tom Braatz, with Ron Wolf. Wolf was given sole responsibility for the team. He even had the authority to fire the coach. So he did. Coach Infante had a salary guarantee of $1.65 million on a three-year contract. Wolf decided the team could afford to swallow the loss in order to get rid of Infante, and he soon hired Mike Holmgren, an assistant coach of the San Francisco 49ers. Over the next four years, Holmgren and Wolf revamped the Packers lineup, so that at the end of that time only three players were left from the Infante era. Wolf was responsible for picking up Brett Favre, a lowly draft choice who became the team's star quarterback. Then, in 1993, the team signed Reggie White, the best defensive end in the NFL. Signing White shocked the football community. Green Bay was the smallest town in the NFL, not considered likely to hold much attraction for a player of White's renown. Moreover, the team had to pay $17 million (over four years) to get him, at the time the third highest salary in the history of the NFL. White was a leading light of the league, and the most sought-after player of that year. Other teams had wined and dined him, treating him and his wife to extravagant tours of their cities. White was African American and a minister as well as a football player, and evidently he saw an opportunity in Green Bay that other cities lacked. He wanted to set up counseling and education programs for inner city youth, and he was able to do that in nearby Milwaukee. At the same time Brett Favre, once an odd choice for the team, had become an impressive player by the mid-1990s. In 1994 he signed a five-year, $19 million contract. The Packers were winning again.

In spite of the expense of hiring and keeping star players like Favre and White, the Packers still had money to spend. The corporation improved Lambeau Field throughout the 1990s, adding more seating in 1995 and upgrading the sound system, adding a new scoreboard, and installing a new ground drainage and heating system in other years. In 1994 the corporation spent $4.7 million replacing the team's indoor practice center with a new facility. The team was losing roughly $2.5 million a year by playing home games in nearby Milwaukee and Madison, whose stadiums did not have lucrative luxury seats. Beginning in 1995, the Packers played all their regular season home games at Lambeau Field in Green Bay.

The mid-1990s were a great time for the Green Bay Packers. They won the Superbowl in 1996, and came close in 1997. The year 1998 became the sixth in a row the Packers had advanced to the playoffs, and their seventh consecutive winning season. Still needing to upgrade their stadium, the Packers made a new stock offering in 1997, offering 400,000 shares of common stock to raise $80 million for the building fund. Though stockholders received no dividends, the enormous popularity of the team meant many fans did not hesitate to plunk down $200 for a share. By 1999, coach Holmgren had moved on, leaving Ray Rhodes in his place. Reggie White retired, and several other key players were injured. Perhaps the team was coming down from its peak in the mid-1990s. Financially, president Harlan announced that the corporation had a negative cash flow in 1998 and expected the same in 1999. Noting that every other team in the league would have either new or improved stadiums by 2003, which would include year-round revenue sources such as restaurants and shops, Harlan petitioned Wisconsin state legislators for help in "saving the franchise." According to a December 10, 1999 article in the *Wisconsin State Journal*, Harlan claimed that without stadium improvements, the Packers would be "dead last in this league in revenue," in four years, and he looked to the state to save the team. Legislators came up with several tentative plans, including sales tax surcharges and selling special Packers license plates to back state bonds. Clearly, despite the team's new power in the 1990s, it was still struggling with financial issues. The plans for helping the team in 1999 were notable in that several were statewide, in effect extending the franchise beyond the city of Green Bay to include the entire state of Wisconsin.

Principal Competitors

Chicago Bears; Minnesota Vikings; Tampa Bay Buccaneers; Detroit Lions.

Further Reading

Deckard, Linda, "Figures in for Green Bay Packers," *Amusement Business*, July 1, 1989, p. 13.
Doherty, Jim, "In Chilly Green Bay, Curly's Old Team Is Still Packing Them In," *Smithsonian*, August 1991, pp. 80–90.
Hajewski, Doris, "Green Bay Packers Victory a Boon to Wisconsin Retailers," *Knight-Ridder/Tribune Business News*, February 7, 1997, p. 207B1222.

Helyar, John, "Green Bay Packers Are Threatened by Football's Changing Economics," *Wall Street Journal*, December 14, 1984, p. 29.

Isaacson, Kevin, *Return to Glory: The Inside Story of the Green Bay Packers' Return to Prominence*, Iola, Wis.: Krause Publications, 1996.

King, Peter, "The Green Bay Packers," *Sports Illustrated*, August 30, 1999, p. 185.

Mayers, Jess, and Scott Milfred, "Packers Lobby for 2003," *Wisconsin State Journal*, December 10, 1999, pp. 1A, 3A.

"A Perspective on Dollars and Sense," *Sporting News*, January 31, 1983, p. 47.

"A Piece of the Pack," *Sports Illustrated*, November 24, 1997, p. 24.

Silverstein, Tom, "Axing the Picks," *Sporting News*, August 9, 1999, p. 44.

Smith, Timothy W., "Packers Aim to Revive a Winning Tradition," *New York Times*, July 21, 1993, p. B15.

Torinus, John B., *The Packer Legend: An Inside Look*, Neshkoro, Wis.: Laranmark Press, 1982.

Vecsey, George, "Socialism Keeps Pack in Green Bay," *New York Times*, October 14, 1994, p. B11.

—A. Woodward

Greyhound Lines, Inc.

15110 North Dallas Parkway
Dallas, Texas 75248
U.S.A.
Telephone: (972) 789-7000
Toll Free: (800) 231-2222
Fax: (972) 789-7234
Web site: http://www.greyhound.com

Wholly Owned Subsidiary of Laidlaw Inc.
Incorporated: 1926 as Motor Transit Corporation
Employees: 13,400
Sales: $846 million (1998)
NAIC: 485210 Interurban and Rural Bus Transportation; 485510 Charter Bus Industry; 492110 Couriers; 551112 Offices of Other Holding Companies; 722211 Limited-Service Restaurants

Greyhound Lines, Inc. is the sole national provider of intercity bus service in the United States. Its fleet of 2,400 buses carries more than 22.5 million passengers each year over a route system that extends for more than 75,000 miles. Greyhound travels to more than 2,600 destinations, with 18,000 daily departures. In addition to its scheduled passenger services, the company offers charter bus service, express package service through Greyhound Package Express, and food service at some of its terminals. Greyhound is also involved in cross-border bus service through joint ventures with Mexican transportation companies. In March 1999 the company became a wholly owned subsidiary of Laidlaw Inc., a Canadian firm involved in bus transportation through its ownership of Greyhound Canada Transportation Corp., which was subsequently merged into Greyhound Lines.

Early History: From Hibbing to Coast-to-Coast

The bus company that became Greyhound was founded in 1913 by Carl Earl Wickman. Wickman was an immigrant who settled in Hibbing, Minnesota, because the weather there reminded him of his native Sweden. Wickman's first ambition was to be a car salesman, but when he could not sell a single seven-passenger ''Hupmobile'' he founded the first U.S. bus company.

The company started by transporting miners from Hibbing to Alice, Minnesota, along the Mesaba Iron Range. The first roundtrip fares cost 25 cents. The secret to Wickman's early success was maximizing ridership, which took the form of stuffing 18 miners into a seven-passenger Hupmobile. Wickman's revenues began to increase, and he took on partners who helped him invest in larger vehicles. Since there were no buses in 1914, Wickman had large touring cars, mostly Studebakers and Packards, sawed in half and elongated. In 1916 the company, then known as ''Hibbing Transportation,'' had its own bus station which was located in a firehouse.

Wickman and his partners were not the only motor coach entrepreneurs in Hibbing. By 1915 a motorcycle racer named Ralph Bogan began transporting miners from Hibbing to Alice for 50 cents. Hibbing Transport responded by reducing its fares to 40 cents. Thus began the first known price war among bus companies. Wickman eventually offered Bogan a share in Hibbing Transport, establishing a pattern of merging with competitors that would eventually result in the formation of the largest bus company in the world.

By the mid-1920s Wickman's company, renamed Mesaba Transportation Company, was worth several million dollars and had numerous partners. In 1925 the man who had started it all left the company and purchased a fledgling firm known as the White Bus Line. The following year Wickman and his partner, Orville Caesar, merged this company with others to form the Motor Transit Corporation, nicknamed ''Greyhound'' because the buses it used, which were built by Safety Coach of Muskegon, Michigan, were sleekly designed and sported gray paint.

Greyhound came along at a time when the idea of the ''vacation'' became firmly entrenched in the American psyche. The motorcoach, whose operating costs were a small fraction compared to trains, soon became the transportation of choice for vacationers, salesmen, and even jazz bands.

Despite the popularity of this new form of transportation, Greyhound nearly failed after the stock market crash of 1929. In 1929 Greyhound's net income was $1.3 million, but this dropped to $38,000 in 1930, the year the company changed its name to Greyhound Corporation. By 1932 Greyhound was $140,000 in debt. It was the 1933 World's Fair in Chicago that

Company Perspectives:

The Company's mission is to provide the opportunity for anyone to travel between cities in North America with safety, dignity and convenience.

saved Greyhound by dramatically increasing ridership. Historian Carlton Jackson, in his *Hounds of the Road,* a history of Greyhound, claimed that ridership also increased after a 1934 movie entitled *It Happened One Night* was released, in which movie stars Claudette Colbert and Clark Gable take a cross-country bus trip.

During the following years Greyhound revenues climbed steadily, reaching $6 million before the end of the decade. In 1939 management of Greyhound anticipated the coming war, and began to stockpile parts. Greyhound suspected both that its buses would have a part in the U.S. war effort and that its supplier, General Motors, would be busy manufacturing jeeps. Both intuitions were correct.

One of Greyhound's principal duties during the war was to transport workers to shipyards and munitions factories. Military personnel were often transported via Greyhound to their bases. Wartime responsibilities and gas shortages made it difficult for Greyhound to serve all its civilian customers, and the company actually used advertisements to discourage ridership. ''Serve America Now So You Can See America Later'' and ''Don't Travel Unless Your Trip Is Essential'' were two Greyhound advertisements during World War II.

A 35 m.p.h. speed limit, imposed to save rubber, and a continual shortage of parts vexed Greyhound management throughout the war. America's most well-known motorcoach company found consolation in its balance sheets, however, as profits climbed to $10 million by the mid-1940s. At that time, Greyhound served more than 6,000 towns and carried one-fourth of all U.S. bus passengers—more than any other company. Its bus routes stretched like a net across the continental United States and Canada.

Increased Competition in the Postwar Era

In 1946 Carl Wickman retired as president of Greyhound and returned to Sweden. There he was knighted by King Gustav V ''for serving the unserved.'' Upon Wickman's retirement, Orville Caesar became president of Greyhound. Caesar lobbied intensely for wider highways to accommodate his buses and fought to change the laws restricting the length of a bus to 35 feet. His new ''Scenicruisers'' were 40 feet long and illegal in certain states.

The growth of Greyhound slowed to two percent a year in the late 1940s. Postwar prosperity brought with it thousands of new passenger cars, and the increase in cars meant fewer bus patrons. In addition, severe labor problems did not help the company. A series of walkouts in 1950 was prompted by a well-publicized incident in which 19 drivers suspected of skimming fares were lured to a hotel and held there against their will for 36 hours. Labor difficulties were nothing new for Greyhound. During World War II the Navy commandeered shipyard buses when the Greyhound drivers decided to strike.

In 1956 the company's president, Arthur Genet, decided to move Greyhound into the car rental business. There were several reasons for this move. One reason was that the car rental offices could operate out of Greyhound's urban terminals. The rental business would allow Greyhound to capitalize on something that had been a problem, namely, the popularity of the automobile. There was an unforeseen problem with the car rental strategy, however, and this was that the typical Greyhound bus passenger, to whom the rental business was geared, was not likely to rent a car. Within two years the car rental division was depressing revenues and had to be abandoned.

Not all of Greyhound's early attempts at diversification were as unsuccessful as the car rental business. Beginning in the 1940s Greyhound established a chain of restaurants, called ''Post Houses,'' in its larger terminals. These were successful, as was the express package business, the implementation of which cost almost nothing at all.

Until the mid-1960s, Greyhound was primarily a bus company, and company management did everything it could to prevent passengers from defecting to trains or planes. Studies at the time showed that a large proportion of Greyhound's passengers were African American, and by the early 1960s Greyhound's marketing strategy was oriented toward this demographic. In fact, Greyhound was the transportation of choice for the freedom riders of the civil rights movement, and Greyhound buses were sometimes attacked by the Ku Klux Klan. While the company's promotion of black ridership was motivated by its quest for profits, Greyhound was also one of the first companies to implement something resembling an affirmative action program.

Beyond Transportation in the 1960s and 1970s

Greyhound began to diversify in earnest during the 1960s. Previously, diversification had been limited to the operation of restaurants in terminals, a van line, the express package service, and the manufacture of buses and bus accessories. All of Greyhound's original expansions were connected to its main business, namely, interurban transportation. Even the unsuccessful car rental business was meant to appeal to bus passengers, who were expected to rent a Greyhound car during their stay in the city. After 1962, however, Greyhound began to diversify into businesses not related to transportation.

In 1962 Greyhound purchased Booth Leasing and soon became the largest industrial leasing company in the world. Among the items offered for leasing were computers, locomotives, and jet airplanes. (In 1966 a separate computer leasing company was formed.) In addition, a money order firm, Traveller's Express, and an insurance company, General Fire and Casualty, had been added to Greyhound's list of purchases by 1965. Greyhound's food services were expanded in 1964 with the acquisition of a roadside restaurant chain, Horne's, and Prophet Foods, a large industrial and institutional caterer. In 1967 Greyhound continued to make acquisitions in the service industry. One of these purchases, Aircraft Services International, provided ground handling and janitorial services. Greyhound also began to provide food for the airlines.

Key Dates:

1913: Carl Earl Wickman founds America's first bus company in Hibbing, Minnesota.
1926: Wickman merges several bus lines together to form the Motor Transit Corporation, nicknamed "Greyhound."
1930: Company changes its name to Greyhound Corporation.
1933: The World's Fair in Chicago saves Greyhound by dramatically increasing ridership during the Great Depression.
1946: Wickman retires as president of the company.
1962: Diversification beyond transportation-related businesses starts with the purchase of Booth Leasing.
1970: Armour Foods is acquired for $400 million.
1978: CEO Gerald Trautman takes charge of the company's bus operations and upgrades its facilities, resulting in increased profits.
1983: A violent 47-day bus driver's strike results in $25 million in lost revenues and ends with drivers accepting a 15 percent wage reduction.
1986: Ridership has declined 55 percent since 1980.
1987: The bus operations of Greyhound Corporation are purchased by a Dallas-based investment group through a leveraged buyout (LBO), and are renamed Greyhound Lines, Inc.; archrival Trailways Lines, Inc. is acquired.
1990: A bitter and sometimes violent driver's strike leads to huge first quarter loss and a bankruptcy filing.
1991: CEO Currey is pressured out by the company's creditors; Frank J. Schmieder takes over the company leadership; Greyhound emerges from bankruptcy in October.
1993: A nationwide rollout out of a computerized reservation system turns disastrous.
1994: Schmieder is forced to resign; Craig Lentzsch takes over and begins turning the company around; company reports net loss of $65.5 million.
1998: Company records its first full-year profit since 1993 and its most profitable year since the 1987 LBO.
1999: Company is acquired by Laidlaw Inc.

The companies purchased by Greyhound during its 1960s acquisition program were all small, and the majority of Greyhound profits still came from the operation of buses. Even after its expansion, food services only accounted for five percent of profits, and financial and leasing activities for 20 percent.

The diversification of Greyhound into nonbus activity was necessary because the motorcoach industry was steadily shrinking, partly in response to an increase in inexpensive airfares. Even with some lucrative acquisitions, Greyhound lost money because profits from the bus line were down. Bus line profits hit a low point in 1967, when riots after the death of Martin Luther King depressed ridership.

Company management thought that a major acquisition would help Greyhound considerably. As a result, in 1970 Greyhound acquired Armour Foods for $400 million. To reduce its investment Greyhound immediately sold $225 million of Armour assets, leaving only the meatpacking and consumer products operations. Armour's pharmaceutical division was sold to Revlon in 1977. Despite some problems with the low-margin meatpacking business, the two remaining divisions generated a net income of $25 million on an investment that had been reduced to $100 million. Armour's contribution to Greyhound was superseded, however, by the financial services division with 1978 profits of $25.8 million.

Greyhound's success with its expansion into financial services and its initial success with Armour continued to be overshadowed by difficulties with bus operations throughout the 1970s. Though some decline in ridership was inevitable as people chose the convenience of air travel, many of Greyhound's problems resulted from poor management. One major problem was that Greyhound scheduling and routing favored long distance ridership, while over 80 percent of the company's customers used Greyhound for distances of 200 miles or less. This inappropriate routing and scheduling discouraged some short-haul passengers, as did the bus stations themselves, whose interiors were often regarded as uncomfortable and unpleasant; in fact, the washrooms were a major passenger complaint. To aggravate matters, rather than making an investment in upgrading facilities, the bus division engaged in a costly price and advertising war with Trailways motorcoach company.

In 1978 Greyhound's chief executive officer, Gerald Trautman, concluded that the company's health still depended on its bus operations. Since he wanted to leave the company in good financial condition when he retired, Trautman postponed his retirement, demoted his protégé James Kerrigan, and placed himself in charge of the bus operations that Kerrigan had supervised. After Trautman took charge of the bus line, more attention was paid to details such as clean washrooms and bus maintenance. Measures such as these, coupled with the gas shortage (which made car travel less desirable), helped increase bus profits 83 percent between 1978 and 1979.

Deregulatory Difficulties in the 1980s

In 1982 Trautman decided to retire. His successor, John Teets, while not unappreciative of Trautman's final efforts, had a different approach to the management of Greyhound. Upon becoming CEO, Teets immediately began to sell subsidiaries that were not performing well. The meatpacking division, which was earning $10 million on sales of $2 billion, was among the first to be sold. Teets blamed higher than average employee wages for Armour's difficulties; when the unions refused to accept a reduction in pay Teets closed all 29 meatpacking plants in one day.

Teets' handling of the violent 47-day bus driver's strike in 1983 was no different. With the deregulation of the U.S. transportation system leading to cheaper airfares and significant decreases in bus ridership, this strike was precipitated by management's demand that the drivers accept a 17 percent cut in wages and benefits. After a bitter series of negotiation meetings, the drivers were forced to accept a 15 percent wage reduction. Greyhound had won a major concession, but the price was costly—$25 million in lost revenues.

Overall, from 1980 to 1986, Greyhound suffered a decline in ridership of 55 percent. Part of the drop was engendered by Greyhound itself, which took advantage of the deregulated environment by closing unprofitable bus routes. The other factor was, of course, cheaper airfares which were drawing people away from bus lines. Greyhound's package delivery business was also feeling the effects of competition, as Federal Express and United Parcel Service were taking business away by offering faster service.

Late 1980s and Early 1990s: Bankruptcy

In March 1987 a Dallas-based investment group led by Fred G. Currey purchased the struggling bus line from Greyhound Corporation through a $350 million leveraged buyout (LBO). The bus operations were renamed Greyhound Lines, Inc., the headquarters of which were relocated to Dallas. Currey served as chairman and CEO of the now privately held company. (Greyhound Corporation continued as a separate firm involved in consumer products and services. It changed its name to the Dial Corporation in 1991, then divided into two companies in 1996, with the services operations becoming Viad Corp. and the consumer products businesses continuing as Dial.)

Currey's first major move was to acquire archrival Trailways Lines, Inc. and merge it into Greyhound. Upon the completion of the acquisition in July 1987, Greyhound Lines became the only national provider of intercity bus service in the United States, although it continued to face competition from regional lines. Currey moved quickly to revamp Greyhound, spending $30 million to renovate dilapidated terminals and to open new ones; increasing the company's advertising budget 50 percent to $27 million; and installing a computerized reservations and ticketing system to increase ridership and decrease the amount of time customers had to wait in lines. Ridership did in fact increase in both 1988 and 1989, and the company was able to post a small profit in the latter year on sales of nearly $1 billion. The turnaround proved short-lived.

When Greyhound headed into contract talks with its unionized employees (members of the Amalgamated Transit Union) in early 1990, Currey decided to take a hard line, telling the union that the company would hire permanent replacement workers if the union went out on strike. Underscoring his approach, he began hiring replacement workers even before the union decided to strike. The strike quickly turned violent, with drivers angered by some of Currey's proposals, most notably a route consolidation that would lead to the elimination of 2,000 jobs. Currey anticipated being able to maintain 80 percent of the bus line's routes by the end of March, but because of difficulty finding replacement workers and because very few of the unionized drivers elected to cross the picket lines, Greyhound was operating at only 36 percent of its normal capacity by that time. In early May the company, which was saddled with $340 million in debt from the LBO and the acquisition of Trailways, announced that it was near bankruptcy after suffering losses of $55.8 million during the first quarter of 1990. Having missed a $9.8 million interest payment due on June 1, Greyhound filed for Chapter 11 bankruptcy protection a few days later.

While the company attempted to reorganize, its creditors engineered the ouster of Currey. Frank J. Schmieder took over leadership of the company in July 1991. Three months later Greyhound emerged from bankruptcy as a publicly traded company with a restructuring plan that centered on cutting costs, including workers, routes, and the bus fleet itself, which was reduced from 3,700 to 2,400. In emulation of the airline industry, Schmieder adopted a hub-and-spoke system, which eliminated numerous long-haul—and direct—routes, forcing many travelers to take longer trips to reach their destinations. In July 1993 Greyhound launched a nationwide rollout of a computerized reservation system called "Trips," which executives viewed as the key to the company's future. Trips turned out to be a disaster: 80 percent of the reservations were for passengers who did not show up, the system's computers were quickly overloaded from the sheer complexity of the bus line's routes, the company's toll-free customer service center was understaffed and overwhelmed, and numerous passengers missed connections and lost luggage because of ticketing delays in the terminals. Customers were further alienated by a two-tier fare system charging passengers more for walk-up tickets than those made in advance. From a passenger standpoint, the new reservation system made little sense, given that most bus travelers make last-minute decisions to travel.

Greyhound's difficulties continued into 1994, when it posted a net loss of $65.5 million and carried only 14.9 million passengers, a steep decline from the 16.2 million figure of two years earlier. The company was near bankruptcy again when Schmieder resigned under pressure from shareholders in August 1994. Thomas G. Plaskett took over on an interim basis, before Craig R. Lentzsch was named president and CEO in November of that year. Lentzsch was a former executive of bus manufacturer Motor Coach Industries International and was part of the investor group that purchased Greyhound Lines from Greyhound Corporation in 1987, working at Greyhound Lines as vice-chairman and executive vice-president from 1987 to 1989. In early 1995 Plaskett was named chairman of Greyhound.

Mid-1990s and Beyond: Beginning a Turnaround

The new management team quickly secured an out-of-court refinancing with the company's creditors, thereby avoiding another bankruptcy filing. They also scaled back the reservation system, eliminated the hub system, fixed the phone system, reduced walk-up fares for long trips, brought back many of the long-haul routes that had been eliminated, increased departures, purchased more buses, and hired more drivers. The result was steadily increasing revenues, from $616.3 million in 1994 to $846 million in 1998. In addition, ridership increased to 22.5 million passengers by 1998. That year, the company posted net income of $35.2 million—its first full-year profit since 1993 and its most profitable year since the 1987 LBO.

Meantime, Greyhound entered the growing market for U.S.-Mexico cross-border bus service through joint ventures it set up with Mexican transportation companies. The Mexican market was an attractive one because many Mexicans working in the United States rode buses home to visit their families and because 98 percent of long distance trips in Mexico occurred via buses, compared to less than two percent in the United States. Greyhound also beefed up its U.S. network through the 1997 and 1998 acquisitions of Valley Transit, Carolina Trailways, and Golden State, the last of these a southern California line providing service to cities on the Mexican border. Additionally, Greyhound began seeking out alternative ways to grow its passenger volume and started delivering passengers to special destinations, such as casinos, airports, and Amtrak stations. The growth of the gambling market made casino service particularly lucrative and Greyhound carried more than 1.2 million passengers to casinos in 1998, garnering $30 million in revenue in the process.

It was thus a revitalized Greyhound that reached an agreement in October 1998 to be acquired by Laidlaw Inc., a Canadian firm based in Burlington, Ontario. Completed in March 1999 at a cash plus debt price of about $650 million, the transaction turned Greyhound into a wholly owned subsidiary of Laidlaw. At the time of the acquisition, Laidlaw owned Greyhound Canada Transportation Corp., an intercity bus operation serving five Canadian provinces from Ontario to British Columbia and the Yukon Territory. Greyhound Canada, which Laidlaw had acquired in October 1997, was subsequently merged into Greyhound Lines, creating the largest intercity bus line in North America. Laidlaw announced in September 1999 that it planned to focus on its bus passenger operations, which included school and municipal bus operations in addition to Greyhound. The company would divest its other interests, which included emergency and nonemergency ambulance services, a physician practice management service, and a minority interest in an environmental services firm. As part of Laidlaw, Greyhound would have access to increased capital to make further expansionary moves and to maintain its vastly improved level of customer service.

Principal Subsidiaries

Amarillo Trailways Bus Center, Inc.; Atlantic Greyhound Lines of Virginia, Inc.; Continental Panhandle Lines, Inc.; Gateway Ticketing Systems, Inc.; Greyhound de Mexico, S.A. de C.V.; Peoria Rockford Bus Lines, L.L.C.; Transportation Realty Income Partners L.P.; Union Bus Station of Oklahoma City, Oklahoma; Wilmington Union Bus Station Corporation; GLI Holding Company; ASI Associates, Inc.; Carolina Associates, Inc.; Carolina Coach Company; Red Bus Systems, Inc.; Seashore Transportation Company; LSX Delivery, L.L.C.; On Time Delivery Service, Inc.; Peoria Rockford Bus Lines, L.L.C.; Texas, New Mexico, & Oklahoma Coaches, Inc.; T.N.M. & O. Tours, Inc.; Valley Garage Company; Valley Transit Co., Inc.; Vermont Transit Co., Inc.; Sistema Internacional de Transporte de Autobuses, Inc.; American Bus Sales Associates, Inc.; Americanos U.S.A., L.L.C.; Autobus Leasing Co., L.L.C.; Autobuses Americanos, S.A. de C.V.; Autobuses Amigos, L.L.C.; Autobuses Amigos, S.A. de C.V.; Autobuses Crucero, S.A. de C.V.; Gonzalez, Inc. (dba Golden State Transportation); Los Buenos Leasing Co., Inc.; Los Rapidos, Inc.; Omnibus Americanos, S.A. de C.V.

Principal Competitors

America West Holdings Corporation; AMR Corporation; National Railroad Passenger Corporation; Coach USA, Inc.; Continental Airlines, Inc.; Delta Air Lines, Inc.; FDX Corporation; The Hertz Corporation; Northwest Airlines Corporation; Roadway Express, Inc.; Southwest Airlines Co.; Trans World Airlines, Inc.; United States Postal Service; UAL Corporation; United Parcel Service, Inc.; US Airways Group, Inc.; Yellow Corporation.

Further Reading

Allen, Margaret, ''Bus Company Gets Back on Profit Road,'' *Dallas Business Journal,* April 25, 1997, pp. 1+.

——, ''Greyhound: Teaching the Old Dog Some New Tricks,'' *Dallas Business Journal,* May 15, 1998, pp. 1+.

Bernstein, Aaron, and Jim Bartimo, ''Wrong Time for Scare Tactics?,'' *Business Week,* April 16, 1990, p. 27.

David, Gregory E., ''Greyhound Lines: Goodbye, Dog Days?,'' *Financial World,* July 5, 1994, p. 16.

De Santis, Solange, and Robert Tomsho, ''Laidlaw Agrees to Acquisition of Greyhound,'' *Wall Street Journal,* October 20, 1998, p. A4.

Geer, John F., Jr., ''Why Greyhound Is No Longer a Dog,'' *Financial World,* January 30, 1996, pp. 64–66.

''Greyhound Lines: Bused Again?,'' *Economist,* November 12, 1994, p. 81.

Hamilton, Martha M., ''Regaining Stride at Greyhound Lines,'' *Washington Post,* June 16, 1992, p. C1.

Henderson, Barry, ''Go Greyhound: Long-Beleaguered Bus Line Is Finding the Route Back to Profitability,'' *Barron's,* May 11, 1998, pp. 24, 26–27.

Jackson, Carlton, *Hounds of the Road: A History of the Greyhound Bus Company,* Bowling Green, Ohio: Popular Press, 1984, 214 p.

Kelly, Erin, ''Greyhound Ignores Wall Street and Thrives,'' *Fortune,* April 26, 1999, pp. 48+.

Kelly, Kevin, ''Greyhound Is Bringing Travelers Down to Earth Again,'' *Business Week,* June 19, 1989, p. 52.

——, ''Greyhound May Be Coming to the End of the Line,'' *Business Week,* May 21, 1990, p. 45.

Lee, Louise, ''Greyhound CEO, Schmieder, Quits Under Pressure,'' *Wall Street Journal,* August 10, 1994, p. B8.

Maxon, Terry, ''On Eve of Sale, Greyhound Turns First Profit Since 1993,'' *Dallas Morning News,* February 17, 1999.

Schisgall, Oscar, *The Greyhound Story: From Hibbing to Everywhere,* Chicago: J.G. Ferguson, 1985, 309 p.

Sherer, Paul M., ''Greyhound and Laidlaw's Pact to Alter Deal Is a Lesson for Issuers of Convertible Shares,'' *Wall Street Journal,* November 6, 1998, p. C2.

Tomsho, Robert, ''Craig Lentzsch Returns As Chief of Greyhound,'' *Wall Street Journal,* October 21, 1994, p. B5.

——, ''Greyhound Drives Down New Road in Quest for Success,'' *Wall Street Journal,* February 25, 1998, p. B4.

——, ''Greyhound Files for Chapter 11 to Guard Assets,'' *Wall Street Journal,* June 5, 1990, p. A3.

——, ''Greyhound Lines Files Revamp, Giving Unsecured Creditors Notes, 95% Stake,'' *Wall Street Journal,* November 20, 1990, p. A11.

——, ''Real Dog: How Greyhound Lines Re-Engineered Itself Right into a Deep Hole,'' *Wall Street Journal,* October 20, 1994, p. A1.

Zellner, Wendy, ''Another Dogfight at Greyhound?,'' *Business Week,* September 2, 1991, p. 43.

——, ''Greyhound Is Limping Badly,'' *Business Week,* August 22, 1994, p. 32.

——, ''Leave the Driving to Lentzsch,'' *Business Week,* March 18, 1996, p. 66.

—updated by David E. Salamie

DANONE

Groupe Danone

7, rue de Téhéran
75381 Paris Cedex 08
France
Telephone: (01) 44-35-20-20
Fax: (01) 42-25-67-16
Web site: http://www.danonegroup.com

Public Company
Incorporated: 1966 as Boussois Souchon Neuvesel
Employees: 78,945
Sales: FFr 84.85 billion (US$15.11 billion) (1998)
Stock Exchanges: Paris London Switzerland Brussels New York
Ticker Symbol: DA
NAIC: 311421 Fruit and Vegetable Canning; 311422 Specialty Canning; 311511 Fluid Milk Manufacturing; 311513 Cheese Manufacturing; 311514 Dry, Condensed, and Evaporated Dairy Product Manufacturing; 311520 Ice Cream and Frozen Dessert Manufacturing; 311812 Commercial Bakeries; 311821 Cookie and Cracker Manufacturing; 311941 Mayonnaise, Dressing, and Other Prepared Sauce Manufacturing; 312111 Soft Drink Manufacturing; 312112 Bottled Water Manufacturing; 312120 Breweries; 327213 Glass Container Manufacturing

Known until 1994 as BSN Groupe S.A., Groupe Danone is one of the largest food companies in the world. It is the leading food company in France, Italy, and Spain and is ranked third in Europe and seventh worldwide. The company's operations revolve around three core businesses: dairy products, which includes yogurts, cheeses, desserts, baby foods, and other products; beverages, which is mainly comprised of mineral water and beer; and biscuits, which includes cookies, crackers, cakes, and other baked items. Groupe Danone holds the number one position worldwide in dairy products, with Danone (Dannon in the United States) the world's top dairy product brand; the number two position worldwide in bottled waters, with Evian the leading mineral water brand in the world; and the number one position worldwide in sweet biscuits (cookies). Five of the company's brands generate more than half of overall revenues: Danone, Evian, Lu (a major European biscuit brand), Galbani (a leading Italian-style cheese brand), and Kronenbourg (the leading beer brand in France). Other key brands include Blédina, a leading French baby food brand, San Miguel and Mahou beer in Spain, the water brands Volvic and Ferrarelle, and in the biscuits sector: Jacob's in the United Kingdom and Ireland, Papadopolous in Greece, Saïwa in Italy, De Beukelaer in Germany, Bolshevik in Russia, Opavia in the Czech Republic, Britannia in India, Bagley in Argentina, and Campineira and Aymoré in Brazil. Outside of its three core areas, Danone (which is pronounced dah-KNOWN) owns sauce brands in the United Kingdom (HP) and the United States (Lea & Perrins) and owns a minority stake in the number two maker of glass containers in Europe, BSN Emballage. Groupe Danone products are sold in more than 150 countries; 37 percent of revenues are generated in France, about 39 percent in the remainder of the European Union, 7.5 percent from Latin America, seven percent from Asia, 6.5 percent from North America, two percent from Central Europe, and the remaining one percent from elsewhere.

Bottlemaking Beginnings

In 1958, 39-year-old Antoine Riboud inherited the glassmaking company founded by his great uncle nearly a century before in Lyons. Riboud had begun his career working in its factory during World War II. Souchon-Neuvesel produced hollow glass, bottles, jars, flasks, and glass tableware. A small company, it recorded only about US$10 million in sales that year.

Riboud concentrated on hollow glassmaking until 1966, when La Verrerie Souchon-Neuvesel merged with Glaces de Boussois, a maker of flat glass for automobiles and housing. The new company was named Boussois Souchon-Neuvesel, and Riboud was named president.

In 1967 the company boasted FFr 1.1 billion in sales and was renamed BSN. It had become a major European maker of glass

Company Perspectives:

As a leader in our businesses, we must use our specialized expertise to understand, anticipate and stimulate demand with each type of consumer. Which means that we must continue to stand for what Danone has always represented—enthusiasm, openness and recognition of human worth.

containers, but was still dwarfed by its competitor and France's largest glassmaker, Compagnie de Saint-Gobain, founded in 1665 by Louis XIV. The next year Riboud made one of the largest French takeover bids ever for this company, with more than ten times as many employees as BSN, using tactics considered radical in France at the time: he proposed to swap BSN convertible bonds for Saint-Gobain stock. Saint-Gobain's board members fended off the offer by claiming that it violated French laws and European Economic Community rules on monopolies. Saint-Gobain also launched a major publicity campaign to rally support from stockholders against BSN's "cheap" bid. The *Wall Street Journal* called it "the David-vs.-Goliath campaign," and Riboud's tactics brought him the admiration of younger businessmen ready for fresh air in the French business establishment. Sadly, in the midst of such publicity, Riboud's apartment in Paris was bombed by a terrorist gang. In the end, shareholders came to Saint-Gobain's rescue, acquiring a 40 percent holding to BSN's ten percent, and BSN dropped the bid.

1970–85: Diversification into Filling the Bottles

BSN's defeat led Riboud to diversify into the food industry. "I saw it would be better to fill the bottles rather than just make them," he explained to *Forbes* in 1980. In 1970 BSN acquired Société des Eaux d'Evian, Société Européenne de Brasseries, and Brasseries Kronenbourg, becoming a leader in natural spring water and baby food, as well as the largest brewer in France. The next year, in an effort to tap the consumer taste for premium beers, BSN introduced its Kanterbraü beer.

In the meantime, BSN established its first flat-glass manufacturing subsidiary, Flachglass A.G., in West Germany in 1970, and two years later it acquired a controlling interest in Glaverbel, a Belgian flat-glass producer. Together with earlier expansion programs in West Germany, Austria, and the Benelux countries, these acquisitions gave BSN almost half the European market for flat glass.

The establishment of the Common Market at the end of the 1950s forced French companies to be more competitive, and between the early 1960s and 1973 France became the fastest-growing industrialized country after Japan. BSN also experienced rapid growth, culminating in 1973 with a merger between BSN and Gervais Danone, France's largest food company and the leader in yogurt, natural cheese, deserts, and pasta. That year sales for the new BSN-Gervais Danone topped FFr 9 billion.

By 1973, however, BSN began to suffer from the impact of the energy crisis, which had severe consequences for the two main markets for flat glass, the construction and automotive industries. For the next five years the profits of many major French companies declined sharply, mainly because of higher costs for energy and raw materials. After a period of growth, the French foreign trade balance fell into deficit. Fortunately BSN had made most of its acquisitions with stock rather than cash, so the company's finances were able to weather the crisis. Riboud tried to help the flat-glass sector recover by building three new glass units in northern France and adding more efficient float glass equipment to BSN plants all over Europe. Nonetheless, beginning in 1974, the company shut down 22 furnaces and reduced its workforce by 30 percent. In five years of restructuring the company spent FFr 2.5 billion. The crisis was a turning point for the company; from now on glass would be primarily a complement to its food and beverage businesses.

BSN acquired a minority interest in Ebamsa (later known as Font Vella S.A.), the leading Spanish bottler of natural spring water in 1973, and between 1974 and 1977 introduced several new products, including Lacmil and Gervillage. In an effort to dominate the European beer market, in 1978 BSN acquired a minority interest in Alken, a large Belgian brewery. A year later it acquired one-third interests in the breweries Mahou in Spain and Wührer in Italy, and a majority interest in Anglo-Belge in Belgium. BSN next bought four French food manufacturing firms through an exchange of stock interests with Générale Occidentale, a move encouraged by the French government, which was eager to invigorate the food industry and actually drew up a special incentive agreement for investments in food processing and food exports. In 1980 the company entered Japan's dairy market through a joint venture with Japan's Ajinomoto. BSN also bought two French producers of frozen foods and ice cream and two breweries in Nigeria. As it moved into these new fields, BSN nearly doubled its annual sales in grocery products.

At the same time, BSN was finally leaving the flat-glass industry, prompted in part by the fear that another oil crisis was imminent. In 1980 BSN sold its West German flat-glass ventures to the British company Pilkington Brothers, and by 1981, BSN had sold its flat-glass subsidiaries in Germany, Austria, Belgium, and the Netherlands. The following year, it sold the French Boussois subsidiary, the last of its flat-glass operations, leaving it with only nine glass container factories. Also in 1981 BSN acquired Dannon, the largest U.S. yogurt-maker, from Beatrice for US$84.3 million.

In 1983 BSN-Gervais Danone changed its name back to BSN. In an effort to increase efficiency, Riboud installed computerized production lines, which meant that the company had to lay off 1,000 of its 40,000 employees, a move opposed by the unions but encouraged by French President François Mitterand, who praised BSN for its contribution towards modernizing French industry. By 1984, BSN had acquired all shares of the champagne makers Pommery et Greno and Lanson Pere et Fils, and had introduced a number of new yogurt products, as well as the Plastishield plastic-coated bottle. Since 1981, the company's sales had risen sharply, and that year it made a record capital investment totaling FFr 2.4 billion. But in July, the European Economic Community imposed fines of about US$3.2 million on BSN and Saint-Gobain for price-fixing in the Benelux glass market.

Key Dates:

1958: Antoine Riboud inherits a glassmaking company called La Verrerie Souchon-Neuvesel.
1966: La Verrerie Souchon-Neuvesel merges with Glaces de Boussois, to form Boussois Souchon-Neuvesel.
1967: Company is renamed BSN.
1970: Company diversifies, acquiring Société des Eaux d'Evian, Société Européenne de Brasseries, and Brasseries Kronenbourg.
1973: BSN merges with Gervais Danone, France's largest food company, to form BSN-Gervais Danone.
1981: Dannon, the largest American yogurt-maker, is acquired.
1982: Company sells the last of its flat glass operations.
1983: Company name is changed back to BSN.
1986: Genérale Biscuit S.A., the top producer of biscuits and toasted bread in Continental Europe, is acquired.
1989: The European operations of RJR Nabisco are purchased.
1992: Acquisition of Volvic brand vaults company into the top spot worldwide in mineral water.
1994: BSN becomes Groupe Danone, incorporating its top international brand into its name.
1996: Franck Riboud succeeds his father as chairman and CEO.
1997: Company adopts new strategy focusing on dairy products, beverages, and biscuits.

BSN continued to grow in the latter half of the 1980s. In 1985 BSN sold its glass-jar and glass-tableware operations to Verreries Champenoises and acquired a minority interest in that company. BSN also bought the pharmaceuticals-maker Bottu, which specialized in pain relievers and artificial sweeteners.

1986–89: Snapping Up the Cookie Market

In 1986, the company's 20th anniversary year, sales were 35 times higher than the FFr 1.1 billion of its first year. That year, BSN acquired Générale Biscuit S.A., the top producer of biscuits and toasted bread in Continental Europe. BSN also merged its Kronenbourg and Société de Brasseries breweries under the Kronenbourg name. The company acquired Sonnen Basserman in West Germany, and became the world's largest bottler of natural spring water. It also bought a majority interest in Angelo Ghigi, an Italian pasta maker.

In August 1988 BSN acquired the Belgian Maes Group Breweries, the British H.P. Foods, and the American Lea & Perrins as part of Riboud's strategy to gain a more substantial market in Britain and the United States for BSN products (64 percent of BSN's total sales still came from France). Concentrating on growth, Riboud also built several new yogurt plants and bottling facilities in strategic locations, and he spent more than US$100 million on European television advertisements for BSN brands.

In 1989 BSN bought the European operations of RJR Nabisco for US$2.5 billion, making it the world's second largest producer of biscuits. Also in 1989 BSN made several Italian acquisitions and became the leader in food production in that country.

1990–96: Global Expansion

The early 1990s were marked by BSN's aggressive expansion into the newly opened markets of Eastern Europe, as well as into Asia, Latin America, and South Africa. In Eastern Europe, BSN began by extending the marketing and manufacturing of its existing brands into the region. It later started acquiring or taking controlling stakes in companies, such as cookie makers Cokoladovny of the Czech Republic and Bolshevik of Russia. In Asia, BSN entered into a joint venture, called Britannia Brands, with an Indian partner in 1990 to acquire RJR Nabisco's Asia-Pacific businesses, which included the leading biscuit maker in India and units in New Zealand, Singapore, Malaysia, and Hong Kong manufacturing and marketing biscuits, snacks, nuts, and other products. Three years later, BSN bought out its Asian partner, taking full control of the Britannia companies. China was another target of BSN growth; by the mid-1990s the company had established several joint ventures there producing biscuits, dairy products, Asian-style sauces, and other products. In Latin America, the company in 1994 took a 49 percent stake in Campineira de Alimentos, the number two producer of biscuits in Brazil.

Back in Western Europe, BSN was active consolidating its position by taking control of several companies, including cookie makers Papadopoulos of Greece and W&R Jacob of Ireland, French mineral water manufacturer Mont Dore, and Spanish dairy product producer Danone SA. The company also made selective divestments in areas in which it was unable to gain the number one or two position; an example of this was the champagne sector, which saw BSN sell its Lanson and Pommery brands to LVMH Moet Hennessy Louis Vuitton for about FFr 3.1 billion (US$613.7 million) in 1990.

BSN also received much press in 1992 for its intervention in a takeover battle between the Agnelli family of Italy and Nestlé S.A. for control of the French mineral water company Source Perrier. BSN made a bid itself for the company that controlled Perrier, but only to signal that it sided with Nestlé, from which it hoped to buy Perrier's Volvic mineral water brand. In the end, Nestlé prevailed and agreed to sell Volvic to BSN for about US$500 million. The addition of Volvic vaulted BSN into the top spot worldwide in noncarbonated mineral water.

In mid-1994 the company jettisoned its BSN name, which, according to the company ''seemed to reflect the company's past rather than looking ahead to the future.'' In fact, glass containers, the founding business, were by this time responsible for less than ten percent of overall revenues. In addition, the BSN name was not well known outside of France. The company settled on the name Groupe Danone, because the Danone brand was its number one international brand, accounting for about a quarter of revenues, and Danone products were produced in 30 countries and sold internationally. At the same time, the company adopted a new logo picturing a young boy looking up at a star. Soon thereafter, the company began expanding its use of the Danone brand beyond dairy products into biscuits, mineral water, and baby foods.

By 1995 Danone's sales had reached US$16.18 billion, nearly double the 1989 figure of US$8.43 billion. This growth was largely the result of Antoine Riboud's aggressive global expansion program in the 1990s, which included US$5 billion spent on acquisitions. Riboud chose this juncture of Danone's history to retire, and named his 40-year-old son, Franck Riboud, to succeed him as chairman and CEO in mid-1996. A few months later, Danone entered into a joint venture with the Coca-Cola Company through which the companies agreed to sell refrigerated juice in Europe and Latin America under the joint Minute Maid and Danone brand names.

Late 1990s: Focusing on Three Core Areas

In May 1997 Franck Riboud announced the adoption of a new company strategy focusing on three core business areas—dairy products, biscuits, and beverages (specifically water and beer)—in which the company had global leadership. These areas also represented 85 percent of group sales. In the second half of 1997 and in 1998, Danone sold more than half of its grocery product holdings and its entire confectionery business. These disposals included the Panzani, La Familia, Maille, Amora, William Saurin, Agnesi, Liebig, Carambar, and La Pie qui Chante brands. During 1999 Danone sold off additional grocery businesses, including Spanish frozen food maker Pycasa (sold to Nestlé), frozen and chilled ready-to-serve meal units Marie Surgelés and Générale Traiteur (sold to Unigate plc), and its 50 percent stake in Star S.p.A., an Italian maker of a wide range of food products. As a result of these divestments, in late 1999 Danone retained in its grocery sector only HP Foods Ltd., a U.K.-based maker of brown sauces and Asian specialties under the HP, Lea & Perrins, and other brands.

Danone also substantially reduced its holdings in the glass container sector, moving closer to its complete exit from the founding business. The company's container activities were first merged with the food and beverage glass packaging operations in Germany owned by Gerresheimer AG. This enlarged glass container operation adopted the BSN Emballage name, with a U.K. management buyout firm called CVC Capital Partners purchasing a 56 percent stake in the entity and Danone retaining a 44 percent interest. Having established a much finer focus on its three main sectors, Groupe Danone was likely in the early 21st century to seek additional opportunities for global growth in these areas.

Principal Subsidiaries

DAIRY PRODUCTS: Bledina SA; Danone GmbH (Germany; 99.9%); Danone SA (Argentina; 99.5%); NV Danone SA (Belgium); Danone SA (Brazil); Danone Inc. (Canada); Danone SA (Spain; 55.7%); Danone Kft (Hungary); Danone SpA (Italy; 99.7%); Danone de Mexico SA de CV; Danone Sp zoo (Poland); Danone Portugal SA (52.8%); Danone A/S (Czech Republic; 95.1%); Danone Clover SA (South Africa; 66.8%); The Dannon Company (U.S.A.; 89%); Galbani (Italy; 90%). Beverages: Aguas de Lanjarón (Spain; 78.5%); Aguas Minerales (Argentina; 50%); Alken-Maes (Belgium; 99.6%); Birra Peroni Industriale (Italy; 24.4%); Evian; Font Vella SA (Spain; 77.8%); Italaquae SpA (Italy; 91%); Kronenbourg; Mahou SA (Spain; 33.3%); San Miguel (Spain; 80.5%); Volvic. Biscuits: Bagley SA (Argentina; 91%); Bolshevik (Russia; 72.8%); Danone Cokoládovny A/S (Czech Republic; 49.1%); Danone SA (Brazil); Griesson-De Beukelaer GmbH & Co.KG (Germany; 40%); Heudebert; Irish Biscuits (Ireland); The Jacob's Bakery Ltd (U.K.); LU; LU Benelux (Belgique) (Belgium; 99.6%); LU Benelux (Pays-Bas) (Netherlands; 99.6%); LU España (Spain); Papadopoulos (Greece; 60%); Saiwa SpA (Italy). OTHER: HP Foods Ltd (U.K.); BSN Emballage (44%); Amoy Food Ltd (Hong Kong; 90.3%); PT Aqua Golden Mississippi (Indonesia; 36.1%); Britannia Brands (Malaysia) SDN BHD (90.3%); Britannia Industries Ltd (India; 18.4%); Calpis Ajinomoto Danone Co Ltd (Japan; 25%); Continental Biscuits Ltd (Pakistan; 44.7%); Griffin's Foods Ltd (New Zealand; 90.3%); Hangzhou Wahaha Co. Ltd (China; 41%); Shanghai Danone Biscuits Foods Co. Ltd (China; 54.2%); Shenzhen Danone Health Drinks Co. Ltd (China; 54.2%); Tangshan United European & Haomen Brewery Co. Ltd (China; 63.2%); Wuhan Euro Dongxihu Brewery Co. Ltd (China; 54.2%); Danone International Brands Paris; Great Brands of Europe.

Principal Competitors

Anheuser-Busch Companies, Inc.; Bass PLC; Biscuits Gardeil; The Coca-Cola Company; ConAgra, Inc.; Dairy Farmers of America; Diageo plc; General Mills, Inc.; Heineken N.V.; H.J. Heinz Company; Kirin Brewery Company, Limited; Kraft Foods, Inc.; McKesson HBOC, Inc.; Nabisco Holdings Corp.; Nestlé S.A.; PepsiCo, Inc.; Suntory Ltd.; Unilever plc; Vivendi.

Further Reading

Browning, E.S., "BSN Agrees to Sell Two Champagnes to Moet Vuitton," *Wall Street Journal,* December 10, 1990, p. A8.

——, "BSN Finds Eastern Europe Expansion Hard to Swallow," *Wall Street Journal,* January 5, 1993, p. B4.

"BSWho?," *Economist,* May 14, 1994, p. 70.

La construction du Groupe: 30 ans de passion, Paris: Groupe Danone, 1996, 55 p.

"Danone Group: Feeding the Pacific Century Consumer," *Institutional Investor,* November 1995, p. C5.

Dawkins, William, "BSN in Takeover of Asian Nabisco," *Financial Times,* March 9, 1990, p. 28.

De Jonquieres, Guy, "Dynastic Hopes Fall Flat in France," *Financial Times,* March 25, 1992, p. 18.

Edmondson, Gail, et al., "Danone Hits Its Stride: Franck Riboud Is Turning the French Food Titan into a World-Beater," *Business Week,* February 1, 1999, p. 52+.

"Friend or Foe?," *Economist,* February 29, 1992, p. 77.

Gleason, Mark, "Dannon Water Springs into U.S.," *Advertising Age,* January 15, 1996, p. 6.

Goad, G. Pierre, "Groupe BSN's Buyout of Joint Venture Simplifies Food Maker's Recipe in Asia," *Wall Street Journal,* August 9, 1993, p. B5A.

Housego, David, "BSN Finds Its Gateway to the East," *Financial Times,* February 22, 1990, p. 38.

Jack, Andrew, "Danone to Book FFr 1bn Gain on Disposals," *Financial Times,* October 10, 1997, p. 28.

Koselka, Rita, "A Tight Ship," *Forbes,* July 20, 1992, p. 141.

Lubove, Seth, "Perched Between Perrier and Tap," *Forbes,* May 14, 1990, p. 120.

Owen, David, "Son to Succeed Chairman at Danone," *Financial Times,* May 3, 1996, p. 22.

Rawsthorn, Alice, "Gloves Come Off in Fight for Exor," *Financial Times,* February 24, 1992, p. 17.

Ridding, John, "BSN Puts New Name on the Table: Danone Wants to Expand Across the Globe," *Financial Times,* May 11, 1994, p. 31.

Rosenbaum, Andrew, "BSN Challenging Nestlé, Unilever," *Advertising Age,* June 25, 1990, p. 37.

Tagliabue, John, "A Corporate Son Remakes Danone: By Focusing on Best-Selling Brands, French Food Maker Grows Globally," *New York Times,* April 1, 1998, p. D1.

Toy, Stewart, "The Son Also Rises at Danone: As Chairman, Franck Riboud Will Keep Up the Push Overseas," *Business Week,* May 20, 1996, p. 21.

Willman, John, and Samer Iskander, "Ahead of the Crowd: Profile of Franck Riboud, Chairman and Chief Executive of Danone," *Financial Times,* January 4, 1999, p. 14.

—updated by David E. Salamie

Guthy-Renker Corporation

41-550 Eclectic Street
Suite 200
Palm Desert, California 92260
U.S.A.
Telephone: (760) 773-9022
Fax: (760) 773-9016
Web site: http://www.guthy-renker.com

Private Company
Incorporated: 1988
Employees: 200
Sales: $350 million (1998 est.)
NAIC: 51312 Television Broadcasting

Guthy-Renker Corporation is one of the world's largest direct-response television marketing companies, selling products worldwide through strategic alliances with various television and cable networks. Its primary focus is the production of infomercials, half-hour television programs that market various products. The company also markets products through short-form direct response television spots, telemarketing, direct mail, and a large Internet mall.

1981–88: The Beginnings of a Partnership

Guthy-Renker arose from a chance meeting of two young men with a zest for entrepreneurship. Bill Guthy and Greg Renker met in 1981 at a resort near Palm Springs, California. Guthy, in his mid-20s, was already the owner of a successful audiotape duplication company, which he had started while still in college. Renker worked in the marketing department of the Indian Wells Racquet Club, which his family owned. When Guthy purchased a home in the Renker family's resort, the two men struck up a friendship based on common interests.

Guthy and Renker shared an entrepreneurial spirit that dated back to their high school days. They also shared a passion for motivational books, especially *Think and Grow Rich* by Napoleon Hill. The two men stayed in touch for several years, trading books and ideas for moneymaking ventures. Renker continued to work for his family's business, while Guthy focused on running Cassette Productions Unlimited, his audiotape duplication business.

In 1984, an unusually large order for cassette tapes caught Guthy's attention. The customer was Paul Simon, an Arizona real estate tycoon, and he wanted 120,000 audiotapes. Curious about the size of the order, Guthy began investigating what Simon was doing. He discovered that Simon had videotaped one of his own real estate seminars, and was airing it on cable stations in the form of a two-hour infomercial. Guthy immediately recognized the synergistic potential of combining the cassette duplication and infomercial businesses. "I figured if I could start my own infomercial company, I could be my own best customer," he said in an October 1994 interview with *Entrepreneur.*

In 1986, Guthy approached Renker about the possibility of creating an infomercial, and Renker began researching infomercials. At that time, there was very little information available about the nascent industry, which had started with the 1984 FCC deregulation of advertising limits. Reading books on direct marketing and calling companies that were already using infomercials, however, the partners managed to piece together the information they needed. Determining the product they wanted to pitch was much easier; the pair readily agreed upon Napoleon Hill's *Think and Grow Rich.*

With $100,000 in capital, Guthy and Renker obtained the rights to *Think and Grow Rich* and set about finding a celebrity spokesperson for their production. Selecting football star Fran Tarkenton for the job, they shot an infomercial that pitched both the book and audiocassettes of Napoleon Hill giving lectures. The program was aired on six small-market cable stations. The partners' *Think and Grow Rich* piece proved successful, running for almost two years and grossing nearly $10 million.

It also provided an important connection, one that led Guthy and Renker to the production of their next infomercial. Both partners were devotees of the motivational book *Unlimited Power*, written by Tony Robbins. Aware that Robbins was also a fan of *Think and Grow Rich*, they asked him if he would be willing to do an unpaid testimonial for their product. Robbins

Company Perspectives:

Ten Commandments of Management: 1. Thou shalt not be afraid to take risks. 2. Thou shalt make thy competitor thy friend. 3. Thou shalt pick great partners. 4. Thou shalt build thy rolodex and use it. 5. Thou shalt test, test, and test again. 6. Thou shalt cultivate the mini-media universe. 7. Thou shalt join and lead thy association and trade group. 8. Thou shalt cultivate the press and build thy company's brand name at all times. 9. Thou shalt not limit thy upside. 10. Thou shalt be prepared to eliminate all these commandments and start over.

agreed. When Guthy and Renker watched the author and speaker's testimonial, they were immediately struck by his on-camera presence. Convinced that he should have his own infomercial, the two men acquired rights to all of Robbins's products and set about producing *Personal Power.* During production of *Personal Power* in 1988, Guthy and Renker officially formed their company—the eponymously named Guthy-Renker Corp.

1989–93: Pioneers in a New Industry

From its inception, Guthy-Renker took a slightly different approach than most other infomercial producers. In an era when most such programs had a somewhat shoddy, home-video quality, Guthy and Renker strove for a professional look. They also avoided the practice used in many infomercials of making exaggerated claims about their products. Their integrity won them the notice of the federal government. In 1990, when the government began investigating consumer protection and infomercial advertising, Renker was called to testify before a Congressional subcommittee. The government investigation led Renker and other infomercial producers to form the National Infomercial Marketing Association to set industry standards.

Another thing that set Guthy-Renker apart from its competitors was its practice of identifying itself at the beginning of every infomercial. Starting each program with a notice that "the following is a paid production of Guthy-Renker," or a similarly worded caption, not only made the company appear more reputable, but it was also good advertising. Soon, people started calling Guthy and Renker to pitch ideas for new programs.

The company fared well in 1990, posting earnings of $36 million. The year 1991, however, got off to a difficult start. With the onset of the Persian Gulf War and the accompanying media coverage, interest in infomercials waned. The company lost more than $1 million in the first days of the war. Only by paring operations down did Guthy-Renker manage to stay afloat.

The company's situation began to brighten again in the second half of the year, when it put together an infomercial for a line of skin care products by actress Victoria Principal. Rather than using their standard method of test marketing the program—airing it in several different cities and monitoring response—they decided to take a different approach. They tested consumer response to the product by having Principal do a live segment on a home shopping channel. By watching real-time viewer response in the form of phone-in orders, Guthy and Renker were able to determine exactly what parts of Principal's pitch produced the best results. Using that information, they reshot the infomercial, introducing it in July 1991. It quickly became one of the company's top producing programs, grossing $75 million in three years.

Other products and other celebrities followed. Among them were a teeth whitening system pitched by Vanna White and an acne treatment solution touted by Judith Light. Within a few years, Guthy-Renker was one of the five largest infomercial producers in the United States, with annual sales approaching $90 million.

In November 1993, Guthy-Renker got a cash boost in the form of a $25 million investment by Ronald Perelman. A player in the media game, Perelman owned a Los Angeles television production and distribution company, a television syndicator, and a chain of major market network affiliates. He also owned cosmetics giant Revlon Group and Marvel Entertainment Group, which produced Marvel Comics and various toys. The alliance with Perelman, which gave him a minority interest in the business, provided Guthy-Renker with preferential access to air time on his TV stations. It also gave the company access to new infomercial products and spokespersons by association with Revlon and Marvel.

1995–97: Diversification and Vertical Integration

In 1995, Guthy-Renker took its direct-response expertise and applied it to a new medium: the Internet. Forming a subsidiary called Guthy-Renker Internet, the company launched a cybermall called America's Choice Mall. Part of Guthy-Renker's Internet business was simply selling mall "space" to online merchants. A second aspect of the company, however, was educating people about e-commerce. This was accomplished by offering $69-per-person seminars on the topic. In true infomercial form, the company's seminars contained a sales pitch that often convinced attendees to purchase a site in America's Choice Mall.

Also in 1995, a second Guthy-Renker subsidiary was formed, specifically to market exercise products. Fitness products were a very popular item for infomercial marketers at the time; between 1994 and 1995, the number of exercise items promoted on television increased by 50 percent. To capitalize on this growing segment of the market, Guthy and Renker recruited a fitness marketing professional, and put him in charge of product procurement. The subsidiary's first fitness product was the Power Trainer, with an infomercial hosted by Bruce and Kris Jenner. More products quickly followed, including the Power Rider, Perfect Abs, Turbo Glider, and Fitness Flyer. Guthy-Renker's fitness products quickly became major producers, generating almost 40 percent of the company's total revenues in 1996.

Guthy-Renker launched yet another subsidiary in January 1996: Guthy-Renker Television Network. GRTV was a 24-hour single-channel TV network devoted to direct-response programming. By developing the network Guthy-Renker was able to become its own programmer and distributor, thereby partially

Key Dates:

1981: Bill Guthy and Greg Renker meet and become friends.
1987: Guthy and Renker produce their first infomercial.
1988: Guthy-Renker Corporation is officially formed.
1993: Media mogul Ronald Perelman buys a minority interest in Guthy-Renker.
1995: Guthy-Renker's Internet subsidiary launches America's Choice Mall, an online retail mall.
1996: Guthy-Renker forms its own television network, GRTV. Rupert Murdoch's New's Corp. acquires Ronald Perelman's stake in Guthy-Renker.
1997: Guthy-Renker Select Network is formed to focus on short-form direct response marketing.
1999: GRTV is sold to TVN Entertainment Corporation.

protecting itself from the rising cost of broadcast and cable airtime.

While building its domestic sales by adding new products, Guthy-Renker was also working to expand its international presence. In October 1996, the company finalized agreements with several Japanese television networks, allowing its infomercials to reach 23 million Japanese homes. Just two months later, Guthy-Renker launched its programs in China, broadcasting on five of the nation's eight main television stations. Consumer response in China was particularly promising; within 20 minutes of debuting the Power Rider program on Shanghai Television, the company sold an entire month's worth of its inventory.

In the fall of 1996, Ronald Perelman's holding company—which owned a 37.5 percent stake in Guthy-Renker—was sold to Rupert Murdoch's News Corp. The sale allied Guthy-Renker with one of the largest media companies in the world, whose vast holdings included the Fox Network and numerous satellite cable companies, both in the United States and overseas. ''We were looking for distribution platforms for our programs,'' Renker said in an October 1996 interview with *Forbes,* adding ''Murdoch has the biggest and best. It's an out-of-the-park home run.''

1997–99: Strategic Alliances and Further Growth

Guthy-Renker developed more subsidiaries in the first half of 1997. One of the most significant was Guthy-Renker Direct, a company formed to specialize in short-form direct response TV marketing. Short-form programs were, as the name implied, shorter than the 30-minute long-form infomercials and fit more easily into blocks of regular programming. The development of short-form marketing capacity was particularly important in the light of Guthy-Renker's new relationship with the Fox Network. Fox and its stations and affiliates were primarily interested in short-form, rather than long-form, direct response.

Guthy's and Renker's approach to forming and growing their various subsidiaries was one of empowerment. In most cases, the partners recruited an experienced leader in the specific industry they wanted to focus on, then gave him both the latitude and the support necessary to build a subsidiary. ''They're limited on the legal side, and they should use our operations and accounting—the stuff we must watch at corporate every day,'' Renker said in an August 1997 interview with *Response TV.* ''Beyond that,'' he noted, ''they're free to build the company as they see fit.'' Guthy and Renker viewed their company's growth strategy as a sort of hub-and-spokes model, with each subsidiary a spoke feeding business into the hub.

In 1998, Guthy-Renker entered into an agreement with Nissho Iwai Corporation, a $79 billion Japanese trading company. The agreement, under which Nissho Iwai purchased a minority interest in Guthy-Renker's Asian subsidiary, provided Guthy-Renker with access to Nissho Iwai's extensive worldwide manufacturing and distribution networks. This allowed it to outsource production of its products at more competitive prices.

While Guthy-Renker built its television business through the second half of the 1990s, consumers were falling in love with a new way to shop. E-commerce was rapidly gaining acceptance, as advances in encryption technology made online shopping more secure. Guthy-Renker had been an early proponent of e-commerce, working to educate the public about the potential of the Internet since 1995. Since that time, the company's web site, Choicemall.com, had grown to include more than 1,400 retailers and services in 16 different categories. Guthy-Renker had also formed alliances with various other Internet companies that served to drive traffic to the Choicemall site. The company cross-promoted its Internet business by mentioning the Choicemall site in every infomercial, as well as advertising the site in materials sent with each product shipped.

As Internet technology developed and the number of Internet viewers grew, Guthy-Renker continued to look for new ways to leverage the web's marketing potential. In the spring of 1999, Guthy-Renker Internet teamed up with GoOn-line.com, a subsidiary of Jones Naughton Entertainment, to take advantage of a technology called streaming video. The streaming technology allowed viewers to watch a video, complete with sound, on a web site. The GoOn-line site, which was unveiled in July 1999, featured streaming video and audio of approximately 100 products from various vendors.

Another significant Internet partnership occurred during this time as well, when Guthy-Renker partnered with Looksmart, one of the web's largest directories of reviewed and categorized sites. Under the terms of the agreement, Guthy-Renker acquired an equity position in Looksmart, and agreed to promote the Looksmart site during its infomercials.

In June 1999, Guthy-Renker agreed to sell its television network—GRTV—to TVN Entertainment Corporation, a supplier of programming for the cable and satellite TV industries. The network, which reached more than 40 million cable and satellite viewers, was slated to continue focusing on infomercials and direct response sales. TVN planned to operate under the GRTV name at first, and to continue offering Guthy-Renker's products. The company looked at the sale as an opportunity to broaden its broadcast reach. ''TVN is perfectly positioned to maximize the distribution potential of GRTV,'' Renker said in a June 14, 1999 press release. ''We look forward to maintaining a long and mutually profitable relationship with TVN as a valuable distributor of our direct response programming,'' he wrote.

2000 and Beyond

As Guthy-Renker prepared to move into a new millennium, it seemed almost certain to maintain a strong focus on direct response marketing. As it had done in the past, the company was likely to continue using a ''hub-and-spokes'' approach, building its original infomercial business ''hub,'' while continuing to seek new and related income ''spokes.'' Web-related initiatives were especially likely, as developing technologies continued to offer increasingly powerful ways to market online. Further strategic alliances with Internet and media companies also seemed probable.

Principal Competitors

Access Television Network, Inc.; Cybex International, Inc.; e4L, Inc.; GoodTimes Entertainment; QVC, Inc.; Shop at Home, Inc.; USA Networks, Inc.; ValueVision International, Inc.

Further Reading

Gladwell, Gina, ''Guthy-Renker: 10 Years of Trailblazing in Direct Response Marketing,'' *Response TV*, August 1, 1997, p. GR2.

Ingram, Leah, ''Birth to Billions: Guthy-Renker Screen Gems,'' *Entrepreneur*, August 1994, p. 118.

Leavitt, Neal, ''Highly Motivated,'' *Response TV*, March 1994.

Richman, Louis, ''Entrepreneurs: Pioneers of a New Way to Sell,'' *Fortune*, October 31, 1994, p. 248.

''Superselling: How Infomercials Became a $4.5 Billion Industry,'' *Success*, September, 1993, p. 12.

Whitelaw, Kevin, ''Not Just Slicing and Dicing,'' *U.S. News & World Report*, September 9, 1996, p. 43.

—Shawna Brynildssen

Hard Rock Cafe International, Inc.

6100 Old Park Lane
Orlando, Florida 32835
U.S.A.
Telephone: (407) 445-7625
Fax: (407) 445-9709
Web site: http://www.hardrock.com

Wholly Owned Subsidiary of Rank Group PLC
Incorporated: 1977 as Hard Rock International PLC
Employees: 5,900
Sales: $396.7 million (1998)
NAIC: 722110 Restaurants, Full Service; 72111 Hotels (Except Casino Hotels) and Motels; 53110 Brand Name Licensing

Without rival for years, themed restaurant phenomenon Hard Rock Cafe International, Inc. has enjoyed a stellar success that has brought forth several like-minded competitors, including Planet Hollywood, Rainforest Café, and the House of Blues. The Rank Group PLC subsidiary was founded in London in 1971 by Isaac Tigrett and Peter Morton. Separated by a bitter dispute, the founders later sold their interests and left Rank to put the pieces together. With more than 104 restaurants in 36 countries, as well as three hotel complexes, and the successful "Hard Rock Live!" television concerts series, the Hard Rock name nearly 30 years later represented a powerful and enduring brand, and a business that was still a dominant force in its industry.

An Incredible Concept: 1971–79

The popularity of the Hard Rock Cafes grew exponentially from the inception of the first cafe on June 14, 1971, in London. Two young Americans, Isaac Tigrett and Peter Morton—who were the quintessential odd couple—borrowed money from their parents to open a quirky restaurant. They were only 22 years old at the time, and they selected Park Lane in London's fashionable Mayfair district as the site of their "Hard Rock Cafe." The decor and menu contrasted sharply with the lavish hotels lining posh Park Lane, where strictly enforced dress codes were the norm, and hamburgers, milk shakes, and the music of the Rolling Stones most certainly were not.

Tigrett, son of a wealthy Tennessee financier named John Burton Tigrett, had moved to England with his family at age 15, attended private school in Lugano, Switzerland, and then later spent his days in London selling used Rolls Royces to Americans. Morton came from a wealthy and venerable Chicago restaurant family, a heritage he tapped into when he opened The Great American Disaster, an American-style restaurant located in Chelsea, London. As a restaurateur, Morton was immediately successful, but his first venture was all but forgotten after he hooked up with Tigrett.

The excitement generated by the first cafe, an opening that quickly drew queues of patrons eager to take part in the Hard Rock Cafe's carnival-like atmosphere, was duplicated with each additional opening of restaurants in other cities and other countries, becoming, if anything, more intense, as the restaurants themselves became grander and earned the reputation as popular gathering spots for celebrities.

The story of Hard Rock's growth took on a contentious flavor early. Outside of youth and family wealth, Tigrett and Morton had little in common. Morton was later described as aloof, reserved, and a "business-first businessman," personality traits that initially complemented and then later butted against Tigrett's impulsiveness. A self-described "raving Marxist," Tigrett became legendary for his flamboyance and recklessness, renowned for being an eccentric figure who played the principle role in many of the titillating stories composing Hard Rock Cafe lore. One such story put Tigrett behind Hard Rock's public address microphone after London had been devastated by an Irish Republican Army bombing, announcing to the cafe's patrons that anyone holding an Irish passport could eat and drink for free. Another described Tigrett stamping across the Hard Rock's tables shouting at patrons, "This is my restaurant! What are you doing here! Get out! This is my restaurant!"

Such incidents, as well as the storied sightings of celebrities, added to the mystique and unpredictability of a visit to Tigrett and Morton's establishments, creating invaluable marketing material

Company Perspectives:

Throughout its history, Hard Rock Cafe has been governed by a guiding service philosophy—''Love All-Serve All.'' HRC is a place where all have always been welcome, regardless of age, sex, or class. This unconditional welcoming hand, first extended by Messrs. Tigrett and Morton, continues today as integral to Hard Rock's present and future as it was to its beginnings.

for an organization that invested little time or money on traditional advertising. In fact, reports of celebrities seen imbibing or eating at a Hard Rock Cafe, coupled with Tigrett's fabled antics, began working to the two restaurateurs' advantage soon after they opened the initial Hard Rock Cafe. It was a time when the rock-n-roll genre from which the business took its name was just emerging. The eatery needed the luminaries from rock's list of idiosyncratic entertainers to make its definitive leap from a popular London restaurant to the internationally recognized nexus of celebrities, celebrity-watchers, and celebrants the Hard Rock later became, but initially it prospered as a welcome alternative to the otherwise reserved atmosphere pervading Park Lane. Its menu diverged from typical Park Lane fare as well, offering customers a simple, decidedly American selection of food and drink that included hamburgers, barbecued ribs, milk shakes, sundaes, corn-on-the-cob, and apple pie, in addition to a wide variety of beer, hard liquor, and suffusive rock-n-roll.

Before long celebrities began patronizing the cafe; the rock group Led Zeppelin reportedly sent whiskey bottles crashing against the walls one evening, and Carole King wrote a musical tribute to the rock-n-roll haven. Eric Clapton's guitar found its way onto a hook on the cafe's wall, and then Pete Townshend of The Who donated his guitar in riposte, along with a note that read, ''Mine's as good as his.'' The two guitars became part of the cafe's growing rock memorabilia collection, while the magnetic power of the Hard Rock to attract celebrities also pulled in notable personages from outside the world of music: the Duke of Westminster stopped by, director Steven Spielberg ate lunch there every day during the filming of *Raiders of the Lost Ark,* and numerous other celebrities made widely reported visits to the raucous anomaly on Park Lane.

The publicized reports of who did what at the Hard Rock benefited Morton and Tigrett commensurately. Soon, the London restaurant was the destination for tourists and local denizens, a site to pay homage to the famous and the peculiar. Although the Hard Rock was a marketing boon, the swell of excitement it generated created one obstacle for Tigrett and Morton to hurdle: customers lingered, dawdled, and gawked, remaining for hours to take part in the paparazzi-filled days and nights, but they purchased little, engendering a debilitatively slow customer turnover rate stunting profits. The solution Tigrett and Morton reached, however, was relatively simple; they turned up the volume of their music, increasing the decibel level in the cafe and, as a result, increasing the patron turnover rate. Louder music meant people talked less, ate and drank faster, and loitered less, a change that quintupled the cafe's turnover rate and lifted its profit performance to match its popularity. Tigrett and Morton also moved into merchandising during this time, offering shirts, hats, watches, and coffee mugs with the Hard Rock logo, which contributed significantly to Hard Rock's bottom line.

As the restaurant became increasingly popular and successful, however, the relationship between Tigrett and Morton was becoming increasingly strained. In 1974 Tigrett made an about-face in his personal life, when the former ''raving Marxist'' became a Hindu convert and devoted follower of spiritual leader Sai Baba. Espousing a ''Love All, Serve All'' tenet, Tigrett moved in with Ringo Starr's ex-wife, Maureen Starkey, in 1976. He later married her, referring to her, with typical Tigrett bravado, as his greatest piece of rock memorabilia. By the end of the 1970s, however, Tigrett's all-inclusive doctrine of love excluded Morton, and the two partners went their separate ways, beginning with Morton's return to the United States in 1979.

The End of an Era: 1980–89

A protracted separation ensued between Tigrett and Morton, during which the two former partners fought a battle over the legal rights to the Hard Rock name. Three years later, in 1982, the situation was resolved when Morton gained the rights to the Hard Rock name for all the world west of the Mississippi River, and all the world east of the Mississippi River was granted to Tigrett. There were exceptions to this demarcation line (Morton was given the rights to Chicago, and Tigrett was awarded Dallas), but from 1982 forward there would be two companies controlling the Hard Rock name and operating Hard Rock Cafes—Morton's Hard Rock America, Inc. and Tigrett's Hard Rock Cafe International, Inc. What followed was a more truculent era in Hard Rock's history.

Morton's Hard Rock America beat Tigrett's Hard Rock Cafe International to the punch when it opened the first Hard Rock in the United States in 1982. Located in Los Angeles, Morton's Hard Rock was backed financially by Hard Rock devotee Steven Spielberg, Hollywood film studio magnate Barry Diller, actor Henry Winkler, and singers Willie Nelson and John Denver, who helped Morton transport the Hard Rock concept across international borders for the first time. But, although Morton first brought the concept to the United States, Tigrett was the first to realize immediate success with the concept, opening a Hard Rock in New York City with the financial assistance of comedian Dan Aykroyd and actor Yul Brynner. Critics hailed Tigrett's New York restaurant as the first successful effort to incorporate the disparate elements that made the London Hard Rock the success that it was, and crowds flocked to the new venue. Inside the New York Hard Rock, Tigrett assembled the first guitar-shaped bar, the largest collection of rock-n-roll memorabilia, and his ''God Wall,'' a tribute to the inspirational forces guiding people's lives, featuring, among other things, a photograph of Sai Baba, a giant Krugerrand, and an enormous Quaalude.

After the opening of the New York Hard Rock, the two former partners continued to compete. Morton opened a café in San Francisco in an old automobile showroom; Tigrett opened one in Stockholm in 1985 and then opened the largest Hard Rock up to that time in Dallas in 1986. While Tigrett and Morton built their respective empires, others joined the fray by

Key Dates:

1971: First Hard Rock opens in London.
1977: Company is incorporated as Hard Rock Cafe International PLC.
1982: Founders Isaac Tigrett and Peter Morton split up the company and go their separate ways.
1984: Hard Rock goes public.
1986: Tenth Hard Rock opens in Dallas.
1988: Tigrett sells his interest in Hard Rock International to Robert Earl.
1990: 25th Hard Rock opens in Montreal.
1995: 50th Hard Rock opens in Calgary.
1996: Rank Group PLC buys Morton's Hard Rock America and Nick Bitove's Hard Rock Canada.
1997: Hard Rock Live! debuts on VH1.
1998: First Hard Rock Hotel opens in Bali.
1999: 100th Hard Rock opens in Amsterdam.

appropriating the Hard Rock name and independently opening ersatz Hard Rock Cafes in Amsterdam, Bombay, Bangkok, and Manila. By the late 1980s, after nearly 20 years in existence, the Hard Rock concept had engendered a confusing mess. Of all the proprietors operating Hard Rock Cafes, both legitimate and illegitimate, those who knew each other did not like each other, and those who did not know each other had every incentive to remain incognito. The restaurants themselves were flourishing, but behind the scenes a tempest was gathering force.

Then Robert Earl approached Tigrett with an offer of acquisition. The son of a British pop singer, Earl was several years younger than Tigrett and Morton. He had attended the University of Surrey, where he took courses in operating food and drink establishments. Thereafter he was involved in several food industry successes and had quickly amassed a restaurant empire totaling 70 restaurants by the time he merged his company President Entertainments with Pleasurama PLC, a London-based leisure group, in 1987. The transaction yielded Earl \$63 million.

One of the first deals Earl completed for Pleasurama was the acquisition of Tigrett's half of the Hard Rock business. Tigrett had since taken his Hard Rock Cafe International public, selling a small portion of the company to London investors in 1984. Three years later, Drexel Burnham Lambert sold another parcel of the company to American investors, an ill-timed \$40 million offering made prior to the stock market plunge in October 1987, which sent Tigrett's stock cascading downward. Less than a year later, in August 1988, Tigrett sold his Hard Rock holdings to Earl and Pleasurama for \$100 million, ending his 17-year tenure as a Hard Rock showman.

Hard Rock's notoriety earned it several pages in Milton Moskowitz's 1988 book *The Global Marketplace.* The author cited Hard Rock as a winning formula, one that worked irrespective of geographic boundaries and divergent cultures, with a Hard Rock Cafe performing as well in Australia as one in Iceland. This universal popularity of the Hard Rock concept represented a rare achievement in the global restaurant industry; traditional, full-service restaurants like Hard Rock seldom managed to move across international borders with any success. In addition, Hard Rock Cafes achieved their success without benefit of any prodigious marketing effort; to a large degree they generated business merely by their existence—and this was an unprecedented feat.

Meanwhile, Tigrett went on to superintend the development of a pyramid-shaped sports arena in Memphis and the construction of a hospital for the poor in India, while Earl took the four Hard Rocks located in Tigrett's eastern sector and quickly sought to increase their number. Earl's corporate affiliation with Pleasurama, meanwhile, came to an end in 1989, when the leisure company was acquired by Mecca Leisure PLC.

A Renaissance for Hard Rock: 1990–95

After Mecca Leisure PLC acquired Pleasurama, it in turn was swallowed by the Rank Organisation PLC, a British-based conglomerate, in 1990. By the time the dust had settled, there were 25 Hard Rocks dotting the globe, counting both Morton's and Earl's, the newest, largest, and most successful being the Orlando, Florida Hard Rock, which opened in 1990 and almost immediately began serving 5,000 customers a day.

The Orlando Hard Rock belonged to Earl, as did nine more Hard Rocks slated for construction in the coming years. Surprisingly, during this time, Tigrett and Morton found themselves agreeing on one issue: neither could abide Earl. Tigrett condemned Earl for treating the Hard Rock concept like a cash cow to be duplicated again and again until its novelty was exhausted, and Morton and Earl had become adversaries during the course of their business relationship. Earl and Morton jointly owned Hard Rock Licensing Corporation, the company controlling the exclusive rights to Hard Rock's lucrative trademarks. The licensing entity also served as a proving ground for both Hard Rock owners' divergent views as to which direction the name should be taken. A running feud between the two had begun almost as soon as Earl bought Tigrett's half of the Hard Rock empire, and as time progressed the animosity had intensified.

Earl irrevocably aggravated tensions in 1991 when he opened Planet Hollywood in New York, one block away from the Hard Rock Cafe, with his own band of celebrity investors, including film producer Keith Barish, director John Hughes, and actors Arnold Schwarzenegger and Bruce Willis. Designed by Anton Furst (who created the sets for the first *Batman* film), Planet Hollywood was to the film world what Hard Rock was to rock-n-roll, a restaurant that housed memorabilia from the film industry and provided customers with an opportunity to enjoy the glamour of Hollywood. Earl's new establishment angered Morton, who charged that Earl had illegally copied the Hard Rock concept. Earl flatly denied Morton's charge, stating to *New York* magazine, "Planet Hollywood was carefully designed so there would be no accusation whatsoever of duplication. You'll find zero similarity."

By the summer of 1992, however, less than a year after the New York Planet Hollywood had opened, Morton had found enough similarities between Planet Hollywood and Hard Rock Cafes to bring three lawsuits against the Rank Organisation and Robert Earl. Earl responded later in the year by announcing his intentions to leave Rank and pursue his Planet Hollywood-related business interests, which opened the door for a new leader of Tigrett's former Hard Rock holdings.

Stepping into the breach was Art Levitt, formerly of the Walt Disney Company, who was selected as the president and CEO of Hard Rock Cafe International in early 1993. Assuming his new post, Levitt inherited 22 Hard Rock Cafes in 13 countries, almost all of which were vestiges of Earl's prolific years at Rank. With these highly successful properties—the New York Hard Rock, for instance, ranked as the city's third largest tourist attraction (trailing only the Empire State Building and the Statue of Liberty)—Levitt had his hands full in steering the Hard Rock franchise and keeping an eye on its former wunderkinds. In 1992 another musically themed restaurant threatened Hard Rock's reign—the House of Blues, from another former insider, Isaac Tigrett. His new brainchild centered on the blues rather than rock-n-roll and offered live performances and late dining with the ambience of a nightclub.

In 1993 new Hard Rocks opened in a host of exotic locations, including San Juan, Miami, Mexico City, Bali, and Taipei. The following year, another four international restaurants opened (in Beijing, Cozumel, Kowloon, and Madrid), while Hard Rock set out to conquer the country music capital of the world, Nashville. Although many had criticized Robert Earl's rapid expansion, Hard Rock had brought 20 more restaurants into its fold in under three years. Competition had something to do with it, as Earl's Planet Hollywood continued to branch out and another themed restaurant chain, Rainforest Café, debuted in 1994. By the next year, as Hard Rock sprouted 14 new locations, Rainforest Café went public, as did Planet Hollywood. Both were initially successes, and Hard Rock quaked just a bit.

Themed Restaurants Hit Their Zenith: 1996–2000

With competitors popping up around the globe, often within spitting distance, Hard Rock continued its aggressive expansion with 13 new restaurants in 1996. Yet the biggest news of the year was the Rank Organization, which had changed its name to Rank Group PLC, scoring a coup by acquiring Peter Morton's Hard Rock America as well as the ownership to Hard Rock Canada, owned by Nick Bitove. The Hard Rock name and brand, a formidable and lucrative force around the world, was now owned by one entity in total control of the increasingly popular trademark. Meanwhile, Tigrett's House of Blues chain opened a heavily touted restaurant/club in Chicago and Earl's Planet Hollywood aggressively expanded as well. Yet all was not well in the flashy industry, as the market seemed to overload on garishly themed restaurants.

By early 1997, Hard Rock underwent a major change; its reputation came to mean much more than a chain of phenomenally successful restaurants with rock-n-roll history on its walls. Soon Hard Rock actually came to mean music, as the company teamed up with VH1 for ''Hard Rock Live!,'' a weekly television series. Each show featured performances by top names from the music industry, from the hottest new groups to legends from the annals of rock history. Aired on MTV's younger and increasingly popular sibling VH1, ''Hard Rock Live!'' was a hit and soon spawned a concert series and record deal with Rhino Records. Stages were added to the Hard Rock restaurants in Orlando and Mexico City, creating complexes for food, fun, and live rock-n-roll performances.

Fresh from its flourishing television series, Hard Rock Cafe International leapt in three disparate directions in 1998: the first was inking a deal with the NBA (National Basketball Association) in February to open ten basketball-themed restaurants; the second was a jump into the hospitality industry when the first Hard Rock Hotel opened in Bali in May; and the third was the debut of the company's official web site, www.hardrock.com. The Bali beach complex was a tropical paradise with Hard Rock's signature restaurant and 418 luxurious, musical era-themed rooms; the web site touted a wide range of activities (news, webcasts, promotions, sweepstakes, online shopping) and company information.

In 1999 Peter J. Beaudrault was named president of Hard Rock Cafe International, a year that marked the fall of Robert Earl's Planet Hollywood chain into Chapter 11. Among the downtrodden were the sports-themed All Star Cafes, part of Earl's crumbling empire. An undisclosed number of Planet Hollywoods and All Star Cafes were either closed or soon would be, while Hard Rock opened new eateries in Indiana, Florida, Tennessee, and Japan, bringing the total tally to 104 Hard Rock Cafes in 36 countries, with no sign of slowing down. One new restaurant, in particular, was bittersweet, as the chain went back to its birthplace, England, to open a café in Manchester. Although neither Tigrett nor Morton was involved, in a sense, Hard Rock had come full circle. The chain's memorabilia collection, originally begun as a whim, now traveled from one restaurant to another, made up of more than 60,000 one-of-a-kind items that Sotheby's valued at more than $30 million.

Although it was probably true that Tigrett and Morton had high hopes for their unique restaurant concept, neither had imagined just how successful the Hard Rock Cafes would be. With a story as colorful as its decor, the 29-year-old chain showed no signs of slowing down as it approached the new millennium. Like the 50-something Mick Jagger and Eric Clapton, Hard Rock Cafe International proved its rock-n-roll empire aged quite nicely.

Principal Operating Units

Hard Rock Cafes; Hard Rock Hotels; Hard Rock Records; Hard Rock Live!; Hard Rock Concerts.

Principal Competitors

Planet Hollywood International, Inc.; Rainforest Café, Inc.; HOB Entertainment Inc.

Further Reading

Ball, Aimee Lee, ''Mr. Universe,'' *New York,* July 15, 1991, p. 38.

''CEO Is Named,'' *Travel Weekly,* February 18, 1993, p. F1.

Efrat, Zilla, ''Hard Rock International Hits the Cape,'' *Business Times,* http://www.btimes.co.za, November 1996.

Finkelstein, Alex, ''Hard Rock Cafe Sues Hard Hats Cafe,'' *Orlando Business Journal,* February 7, 1992, p. 3.

Giles, Jeff, ''No Fear of Frying,'' *Rolling Stone,* November 14, 1991, pp. 15, 18, 21.

''Hard Rock Cafe Cranks Up the Volume By Launching Its Music-Oriented Internet Site,'' press release, Nov. 18, 1998, www.hardrock.com.
''Hard Rock Cafe Plans to Open a Hotel/Casino in Las Vegas,'' *Travel Weekly,* June 13, 1991, p. 1.
''The Hard Rock Café Story: A Brief History of a Global Phenomenon,'' Dec. 28, 1999, www.hardrock.com.
''Hard Rock Hotel to Headline in Vegas,'' *Restaurant/Hotel Design International,* October 1991, p. 14.
Hayes, Jack, ''Earl to Rank Leisure: Hasta la Vista Baby!,'' *Nation's Restaurant News,* December 14, 1992, p. 1.
''HRC's Morton Files New Suit to Block Chicago 'Knock-Off,' '' *Nation's Restaurant News,* June 29, 1992, p. 2.
Jackson, Jerry, ''Planet Hollywood Files for Bankruptcy and Closes in Miami, Lauderdale,'' *Orlando Sentinel,* http://www.sun-sentinel.com, October 11, 1999.
Martin, Richard, ''Hard Rock Hits Planet Hollywood with Copycat Suit,'' *Nation's Restaurant News,* March 16, 1992, p. 3.
Middleton, Christopher, ''The Hard Rock with a Soft Sell,'' *Marketing,* April 25, 1991, p. 23.
Moskowitz, Milton, *The Global Marketplace,* New York: Macmillan Publishing, 1987, pp. 248–51.
O'Conner, Amy, ''The Man Who Puts the Rock in the Hard Rock Cafe,'' *Restaurants & Institutions,* February 15, 1994, p. 14.
''Planet Hollywood International,'' *Daily Double,* http://www.fool.com, August 1, 1997.
''This Hard Rock Is Rolling,'' *Florida Trend,* January 1992, p. 18.
Zacharias, Beth, ''Art Levitt Rolls into Hard Rock,'' *Orlando Business Journal,* January 11, 1993, p. 3.

—Jeffrey L. Covell
—updated by Nelson Rhodes

hartmarx

Hartmarx Corporation

101 North Wacker Drive
Chicago, Illinois 60606
U.S.A.
Telephone: (312) 372-6300
Fax: (312) 444-2695
Web site: http://www.hartmarx.com

Public Company
Incorporated: 1911 as Hart Schaffner & Marx
Employees: 9,200
Sales: $725.0 million (1998)
Stock Exchanges: New York Chicago
Ticker Symbol: HMX
NAIC: 315222 Men's and Boys' Cut and Sew Suit, Coat, and Overcoat Manufacturing; Men's and Boys' Cut and Sew Shirt (Except Work Shirt) Manufacturing; Men's and Boys' Cut and Sew Trouser, Slack, and Jean Manufacturing; 315228 Men's and Boys' Cut and Sew Other Outerwear Manufacturing; 315232 Women's and Girls' Cut and Sew Blouse and Shirt Manufacturing; 315233 Women's and Girls' Cut and Sew Dress Manufacturing; 315234 Women's and Girls' Cut and Sew Suit, Coat, Tailored Jacket, and Skirt Manufacturing; 454110 Electronic Shopping and Mail-Order Houses; 551112 Offices of Other Holding Companies

Hartmarx Corporation is a holding company for a number of clothing companies, including its flagship brands of men's tailored clothing (suits, sportcoats, and slacks): Hart Schaffner & Marx and Hickey-Freeman. From its tailored beginnings, Hartmarx expanded into men's and women's sportswear—including golfwear, shirts and ties, and women's career apparel. A maker and marketer but no longer a retailer of apparel, Hartmarx owns other brands such as Sansabelt and Racquet Club and offers products under such licensed brands as Jack Nicklaus, Bobby Jones, Tommy Hilfiger, Burberry, Perry Ellis, Evan-Picone, and Pierre Cardin. The history of Hartmarx was, in large part, noneventful until the 1960s, when wise merchandising decisions brought the venerable Hart Schaffner & Marx name to a broader market. This was followed by strong internal growth in the 1970s and an initially successful acquisition campaign in the 1980s. But by 1990 the once profitable company was deeply in debt and losing money, primarily because of its massive network of clothing shops located mostly in shopping malls. In response, Hartmarx's management began a massive restructuring of the business, including the divestment of all of its retail operations by 1995.

Early Decades

Hartmarx traces its history to 1872 when, immediately after the great Chicago Fire, brothers Harry and Max Hart pooled their life savings of $2,700 and opened a small men's clothing store on Chicago's State Street. ''Harry Hart and Brother'' opened a second store a few blocks south in 1875. Max Hart became fascinated with labeling after working as a delivery boy for his father's butcher shop. His job, applying labels to delivery packages, taught him the importance of branded products. At the clothing store, he pursued this interest by asking tailors to affix Hart brand labels to the clothes they sold. A short time later, a downstate Illinois merchant expressed an interest in the label and asked to sell Hart suits.

In 1879 the Harts' brothers-in-law, Levi Abt and Marcus Marx, joined the partnership, which was renamed Hart, Abt and Marx. The small shop continued to prosper on sales to businessmen in Chicago's Loop financial district.

At the same time, however, the wholesale business began to grow, overtaking the retail operations. On the strength of wholesale production, Hart, Abt and Marx won contracts to produce clothing for the U.S. military. This introduced the partners to prefabricated off-the-rack clothing and marked their entry into the ready-made suit trade.

Marx and Abt left the business in 1887. A cousin named Joseph Schaffner took their place, however, whereupon the company was renamed Hart Schaffner & Marx. Schaffner was an excellent businessman who oversaw much of the early growth of the small firm.

Company Perspectives:

Hartmarx is a manufacturer and marketer of apparel products created to meet the dress and casual needs of consumers. The Company is focused on providing competitive values through cost effective sourcing. Providing a wide variety of apparel products, Hartmarx markets its brands through an extensive range of retail channels.

The industrial revolution added newer, more efficient tailoring methods that reduced the time to make a suit. With such favorable economics, many suit manufacturers entered the catalog business, introducing their own brands. Hart Schaffner & Marx responded in 1897 by running national advertisements for its products and began selling off-the-rack suits through a variety of distributors. Hart Schaffner & Marx commissioned well-known illustrators to paint pictures for style books and retail posters. These ads portrayed the company's latest fashions in rich surroundings, establishing Hart Schaffner & Marx as a premium brand.

By 1906 the company had branched into sizes for men who were unusually tall, short, or overweight. Hart Schaffner & Marx thus became a mass-market brand, enabling virtually any man to have a fine quality suit at a lower price than a custom tailored suit. On May 10, 1911, after years of steady growth, the partnership was incorporated.

In 1917 the company introduced the first tropical worsted suits. Hart Schaffner & Marx's production facilities also were pressed into service during World War I making uniforms.

Although it operated a number of small retail outlets of its own in 1926, the company expanded its retail presence considerably with the acquisition of Wallach's, a large clothing chain. Hart Schaffner & Marx continued its expansion over the next 30 years by taking over the operations of numerous other smaller retailers, opening new stores, and placing a strong emphasis on advertising.

Postwar Acquisition Spree Followed by Internal, Brand-Focused Growth

After producing a large quantity of uniforms for the government again during World War II, Hart Schaffner & Marx began making bolder acquisitions. In 1954 the company took over Society Brand, a major manufacturing house. Ten years later Hart Schaffner & Marx added Hickey-Freeman, a premium brand. The company acquired Jaymar-Ruby in 1967 and, in 1969, added M. Wile. In fact, Hart Schaffner & Marx made so many acquisitions between 1966 and 1969 that the U.S. Justice Department became involved. The government filed suit against the company on antitrust grounds, complaining that Hart Schaffner & Marx had established an anticompetitive domination of the clothing market. The company settled with Justice Department lawyers by signing a consent decree in which Hart Schaffner & Marx was obliged to sell off several recent acquisitions and promised to purchase no more companies, without court approval, for a period of ten years. This agreement took effect in June 1970.

The consent decree was not a serious setback for Hart Schaffner & Marx. Instead of external growth, the company merely changed its emphasis to internal growth. This was actually a better strategy because the company had launched several successful lines during the 1960s that required attention.

One night in 1966, television host Johnny Carson walked on stage to deliver his nightly "Tonight Show" monologue wearing a turtleneck sweater and a collarless Nehru jacket. Within a week the nation's stores had been depleted of both items, and Carson had unwittingly established himself as a fashion trendsetter. Celebrity endorsements were not new, but the episode demonstrated to many the value of using stars to introduce new styles. The idea was not lost upon Hart Schaffner & Marx, which got an agreement to market a new casual line of suits under the Johnny Carson name and, later, under Jack Nicklaus's name.

Hart Schaffner & Marx introduced the Austin Reed brand name during the 1960s. In 1974 the company rolled out a line of tailored clothing under the Christian Dior name, followed by Nino Cerruti, Allyn St. George, and Playboy. These new lines were created under contract to their designer namesakes and proved highly successful as fashion leaders.

Also in 1974, as part of its divestiture, Hart Schaffner & Marx sold 20 stores to Hughes & Hatcher, a rival chain of shopping mall clothing stores. In September 1979, nearly a year before the expiration of the consent decree, Hart Schaffner & Marx acquired Intercontinental Apparel under special agreement for $2.9 million. Intercontinental was the U.S. licensee of the Pierre Cardin line and brand name. With strong brand names and a wide variety of styles available, Hart Schaffner & Marx had built a very solid position in the market.

Acquisitive 1980s

When the terms of the consent decree expired in June 1980, Hart Schaffner & Marx, with 275 retail outlets, immediately embarked on an acquisition binge. The company took over Bishop's men's shops in September 1980 and branched into women's clothing by taking over the Country Miss chain for $12.5 million in January 1981.

While Hart Schaffner & Marx had registered strong gains of six percent annually, the market was growing at twice that rate. Despite the strength of its Hickey-Freeman and Christian Dior lines, the company was being ravaged by discount brands, which had become especially popular during the recessions of the 1970s. The company's own Playboy line flopped because "men didn't want bunnies on their buttons" and may have regarded the logo as tired and pretentious.

Thus, on December 1, 1982, after losing out significantly to discount brands, Hart Schaffner & Marx acquired the Kuppenheimer Manufacturing Company for $25.8 million. Kuppenheimer, a major factory retail operation with 41 outlets, dominated the market of inexpensive suits, defined as those costing $200 or less, and had been a strong competitor of Hart Schaffner & Marx. The acquisition gave Hart Schaffner & Marx a greater piece of the $4 billion suit market, 80 percent of which was controlled by discount brands such as Kuppenheimer. It also enabled the company to avoid diluting its premium brands with the lower-scale Kuppenheimer line.

Key Dates:

1872: Brothers Harry and Max Hart open small men's clothing store on Chicago's State Street, called Harry Hart and Brother.
1879: The Harts' brothers-in-law, Levi Abt and Marcus Marx, join the partnership, which is renamed Hart, Abt and Marx.
1887: Marx and Abt leave the business and are replaced by a cousin, Joseph Schaffner; the firm is renamed Hart Schaffner & Marx.
1911: The partnership is incorporated.
1926: Wallach's, a large New York-based clothing chain, is acquired.
1927: Chicago retail clothier Baskin is acquired.
1954: Company takes over Society Brand, a major manufacturing house.
1964: Hickey-Freeman, a premier men's clothing brand and retailer, is acquired.
1967: Jaymar-Ruby is acquired.
1970: Antitrust suit against company leads to consent degree barring any further acquisitions, without court approval, for ten years.
1979: Firm acquires Intercontinental Apparel, U.S. licensee of the Pierre Cardin brand.
1981: Country Miss chain is purchased, extending the company into women's clothing.
1982: Kuppenheimer Manufacturing Company, retailer of inexpensive suits, is acquired for $25.8 million.
1983: Company changes its name to Hartmarx Corporation, with the new parent acting as a holding company for various subsidiaries.
1992: Continued losses leads to the divestment of all retail outlets, except the Kuppenheimer chain.
1996: Plaid Clothing Group, Inc., is acquired, adding such brands as Burberry, Claiborne, Evan-Picone, Palm Beach, and Brannoch.

The company acquired Briar Neckwear in July 1985 and in December 1986 acquired the casual suit jacket manufacturer H. Ortisky. The following year Hart Schaffner & Marx took over the nine-store Detroit retail chain Anton's, and in 1988 purchased Boyd's, a small retail chain in St. Louis, and the Washington, D.C.-based upscale retailer Raleigh's. In February 1989 the company also added the Biltwell Company, a clothing manufacturer.

Along with the strong external expansion carried out during the 1980s, Hart Schaffner & Marx carried out a large modernization campaign aimed at updating equipment and processes. The company also underwent a profound restructuring. The business of Hart Schaffner & Marx had grown so large that the flagship company in the organization was unable to run it efficiently. In effect, Hart Schaffner & Marx had become an enterprise consisting of more than a dozen separate little companies, each with its own administrative structure. To better coordinate the activities of these independent little operations, the company decided to create a new parent organization.

In keeping with voguish corporate names such as Navistar, Unisys, Ameritech, and Primerica, a team of senior executives led by John R. Meinert settled upon the truncated name Hartmarx Corporation, which allowed the company to preserve the exclusivity of its Hart Schaffner & Marx name. When the name change was made official on April 13, 1983, the new holding company took possession of Hart Schaffner & Marx and its numerous subsidiary companies. Along with the creation of Hartmarx came a reorganization plan aimed at eliminating 23 redundant administrative functions within the company (roughly 800 jobs) and a campaign to redecorate the Kuppenheimer outlets. These efforts, which ate up more than $41 million in earnings by 1987, went $10 million over budget and yielded far less than the projected $12 million annual savings.

Amidst this crisis, on October 27, 1986, Chairman and CEO Richard P. Hamilton resigned suddenly and without official explanation. The company was stunned by Hamilton's immediate departure and analysts speculated that Hamilton's disagreements over the company's strategy compelled him to leave.

He was replaced by a troika consisting of Meinert, Harvey Weinberg, a former head of the retailing group, and Elbert Hand, who headed the company's manufacturing group. The new leadership team pressed ahead with the consolidation effort, centralizing purchasing, payroll, credit, and distribution at offices in Chicago, Dallas, and Columbus, Ohio. Having increased operating efficiency, the company now had only to increase its sales volume.

Meanwhile, Hartmarx struggled to expand Kuppenheimer and began advertising promotions with a fictional "Mr. Kuppenheimer" character. The timing could not have been worse. As the nation emerged from the 1982–85 recession, consumers' tastes went back to more expensive name brands. Despite Kuppenheimer's facelift, men avoided the stores.

Generally, however, sales from all 440 of the company's retail outlets were up, in large part because of the success of the conservatively tailored Hickey-Freeman and Hart Schaffner & Marx lines, as well as new brands such as Racquet Club and Henry Grethel, which Hartmarx purchased from Manhattan Industries. This enabled the company to obtain and service financing necessary to acquire the companies it had. But, while the balance sheet remained strong, debt remained high. When sales began to lag, profits fell quickly. By 1990 impatient investors had begun to abandon Hartmarx, beating its share price to 18, about half of what it had been only three years earlier.

Major 1990s Restructuring

Weinberg attempted to stem losses by bringing on John Eyler, a former CEO of Kohl's Main Street chain. Eyler recommended price decreases on several high-end suit lines and pressed for greater utilization of the computer network. In 1991 Hartmarx borrowed the superstore ploy from The Limited, opening as many as three retail stores in a single, larger space. This brought down rent fees and allowed the company to run a single back office. Still, Hartmarx proved unable to take advantage of the economies it had set up. The manufacturing and licensing operations remained strong, but the retail business incurred heavy losses. In January 1992 the company suspended dividends for the first time in 53 years.

Faced with a fifth consecutive year of lowered returns, Hartmarx finally took action on September 18, 1992. On that day, the company announced that it had sold its HSSI retail stores subsidiary for $43 million, basically exiting the retail store business. The Kuppenheimer operation, however, with its 120 retail operations, remained intact. Then, on September 21, the company announced the issue of $30 million in new shares to raise cash, and on October 10 it announced the closure of its Old Mill/Country Miss outlet stores. Hartmarx also began negotiations with its creditors to gain more favorable terms on its outstanding obligations.

The $30 million capital infusion came from a single company called Traco International N.V., controlled by Saudi businessman Abdullah Taha Bakhsh. Traco (the name is a conglomeration of ''trading and construction'') thus emerged with a 22 percent stake in Hartmarx. Little was known about Bakhsh or his company, and Hartmarx directors voiced concern over his motives but were content that he had helped the company avoid bankruptcy. An additional 21.4 percent of Hartmarx shares were controlled by Taiba Corporation, owned by Abdel Mohsen Y Abu Shukhaiden, another Middle Eastern businessman about whom little was known. Taiba authorized Traco to vote its shares, giving that company nearly 44 percent voting rights.

The decision to exit the retail business was necessary and long overdue. As long as Hartmarx was in the retail business, it could not sell its products to hundreds of other retailers. In effect, it was in competition with potential customers. Now just a marketing and manufacturing company, Hartmarx counted on high cash flow from these profitable businesses to offset investor concern with its high debt. Under the direction of Hand, as chairman and CEO, and Homi Patel, president and chief operating officer, Hartmarx also strategically refocused its business on apparel other than suits and boldly expanded its promising sportswear lines, particularly golfwear. Hartmarx's Bobby Jones upscale golfwear line, which made its national debut in 1991, had proved almost immediately successful. The company soon added a second golfwear line under the Jack Nicklaus label, with these items selling at more affordable prices than those carrying the Bobby Jones label. Both lines were sold mostly through pro shops. By the mid-1990s Hartmarx was selling $50 million of golfwear per year.

Meanwhile, several more operations were sold off, including the company's 14 Sansabelt outlets and its 37.5 percent interest in Robert's, a retail chain in Mexico City. Hartmarx completed its exit from the retail sector in 1995 when it sold its 91-store Kuppenheimer unit and two tailored clothing factories to a private investment group headed by Gene Kosack, former president and chief executive of NBO Stores Inc. The company also made major changes in its sourcing system, closing ten domestic factories and shifting production to the Far East, Mexico, and Costa Rica. By this time, Hartmarx had returned to profitability, reduced its debt by 40 percent, and increased shareholder equity by 82 percent. Although the company's turnaround was far from complete, its move to expand its sportswear lines was a case of nearly perfect timing, as the 1990s were marked by increasingly casual dress, especially in the workplace. Hartmarx found particular success with its Tommy Hilfiger line of casual businesswear. Despite the attention placed on the sportswear area, tailored clothing was not being ignored. Two new lines, Perry Ellis and Daniel Hechter, were introduced; the latter was positioned within the popular-priced segment and the former resided within the moderate sector. Still, by the mid-1990s, approximately one-quarter of sales came from outside the tailored clothing lines.

Over the course of its three-year restructuring, Hartmarx's revenues were cut by more than half, dropping from $1.22 billion in 1991 to $595.3 million in 1995. Growth returned to the company agenda, and in late 1996 Hartmarx paid about $27 million to acquire the bankrupt Plaid Clothing Group, Inc., a maker and marketer of men's tailored suits, sportcoats, and slacks under the licensed brands Burberry, Claiborne, and Evan-Picone, as well as under such brands as Palm Beach and Brannoch, which it owned. In November 1998 Hartmarx acquired the wholesale apparel business of Pusser's Ltd., including the Pusser's of the West Indies line of nautical and tropical sportswear and outerwear. Through a December 1998 purchase, Hartmarx gained Coppley, Noyes and Randall Limited, a leading Canadian maker of men's tailored clothing. In August of the following year, the company acquired Royal Shirt Company, a Canadian maker of women's and men's dress and sports shirts.

Hartmarx also made a return of sorts to retailing in late 1998. The company earlier that year reached an agreement with licensee David Johnson, president of Rancho Santa Fe, California-based Golf Specialty Retail Stores Inc., whereby Johnson would launch a chain of Bobby Jones upscale golfwear boutiques. Johnson was the owner and operator of the chain, which debuted in November 1998 with the first Bobby Jones store in Beverly Hills, California. Hartmarx hoped to gain brand recognition and increased sales volume out of the endeavor and had plans for a similarly structured Jack Nicklaus chain. In addition, the company successfully launched a third golfwear brand in the late 1990s: Desert Classic, a popular-priced private label available exclusively at Sears, Roebuck & Co. stores.

With the men's suit industry likely to remain stagnant into the early 21st century, Hartmarx was maintaining its strategy of beefing up its casual clothing offerings. Toward a goal of increasing sales of sportswear to one-third of overall sales, Hartmarx was even considering adding jeans to its ever more diverse product portfolio. During 1999 the company announced that it would cut back its presence in the moderate-priced $200 to $300 suit sector, while emphasizing its upper-end tailored clothing, which was more profitable. The bottom line was clearly a major concern of Hand and Patel, as evidenced by their setting a goal of recording earnings-per-share increases of 20 percent per year starting in 2000. Summarizing Hartmarx's future direction, Hand told shareholders at the 1999 annual meeting: ''This company has to be known as an apparel enterprise, not as a suit company.''

Principal Subsidiaries

Coppley Apparel Group Limited (Canada); Direct Route Marketing Corporation; Hart Schaffner & Marx; American Apparel Brands, Inc.; National Clothing Company, Inc.; Winchester Clothing Company; Hickey-Freeman Co., Inc.; International

Women's Apparel, Inc.; Jaymar-Ruby, Inc. (dba Trans-Apparel Group); Anniston Sportswear Corporation; E-Town Sportswear Corporation; Rector Sportswear Corporation; Biltwell Company, Inc.; Men's Quality Brands, Inc.; M. Wile & Company, Inc. (dba Intercontinental Branded Apparel); Intercontinental Apparel, Inc.; Novapparel, Inc.; Plaid Clothing Company, Inc.; Pusser's of the West Indies Apparel Company; Royal Shirt Company (Canada); Universal Design Group, Ltd.

Principal Operating Units

Men's Apparel Group; Women's Apparel Group.

Principal Competitors

Ashworth, Inc.; Brooks Brothers; The Gap, Inc.; Haggar Corp.; Lands' End, Inc.; Levi Strauss & Co.; Nautica Enterprises, Inc.; Oxford Industries, Inc.; Perry Ellis International, Inc.; Phillips-Van Heusen Corporation; The Pietrafesa Corporation; Polo Ralph Lauren Corporation; Tropical Sportswear Int'l. Corporation.

Further Reading

Brumback, Nancy, "Hartmarx Deemphasizing $200 to $300 Suits, Revving Up Sportswear," *Daily News Record,* April 16, 1999.

Fox, Bruce, "For Hartmarx, Hard Times Fuel Ingenuity," *Chain Store Age Executive,* September 1993, p. 59.

Gellers, Stan, "Hartmarx Spotlights Four Top Designer Labels in New Bottoms Unit," *Daily News Record,* September 21, 1998, p. 7.

——, "Reinventing Hartmarx: Sportswear to Fuel the Future," *Daily News Record,* January 30, 1995, p. 12.

George, Melissa, "Hartmarx Teeing Up for New Retail Push: Apparel Maker Links with Licensee to Open Bobby Jones Golf Chain," *Crain's Chicago Business,* May 4, 1998, p. 3.

"Hartmarx: Cashing in on Discount Suits Without Losing Its Upscale Image," *Business Week,* May 14, 1984, p. 200.

"Hartmarx Corp.," *Moody's Industrial Manual,* 1992.

"Hartmarx Is Suddenly Looking Threadbare," *Business Week,* January 29, 1990, p. 40.

"Hartmarx: Restoring the Specialty Group," *Daily News Record,* February 11, 1991, pp. 10–11.

"Hartmarx Unveils Its Game Plan," *Daily News Record,* October 15, 1992, pp. 1–5.

"Hart, Schaffner & Marx: Expanding Boldly from Class to Mass Markets," *Business Week,* October 20, 1980, pp. 74–75.

"Hart, Schaffner & Marx: Suiting up for the Eighties," *Duns' Business Review,* September 1, 1980, pp. 20–21.

"Has Anyone Seen This Man?," *Chicago Tribune,* April 16, 1993, Sec. 3, p. 3.

"How Hartmarx Plans to Recapture Its Youth," *Adweek's Marketing Week,* May 1, 1989, pp. 34–38.

"A New Cut for the Gray Flannel," *Forbes,* December 28, 1987, pp. 61–64.

Palmieri, Jean E., "Gene Kosack Group Buying Kuppenheimer from Hartmarx," *Daily News Record,* May 10, 1995, p. 1.

Patterson, Gregory A., "Hartmarx, Having Restyled Itself, Sees Robust Profits," *Wall Street Journal,* May 31, 1995, p. B4.

Pauly, Heather, "Hartmarx Tailors Plan: Apparel Firm Aims to Reverse Its Fortunes in the Stock Market," *Chicago Sun-Times,* September 2, 1999, p. 48.

Podmolik, Mary Ellen, "Hartmarx Executives Find Jean Idea Riveting," *Chicago Sun-Times,* April 15, 1999, p. 56.

"A Retailored Hartmarx Still Needs Some Altering," *Business Week,* March 9, 1987, p. 109.

Rose, Barbara, "Elusive Saudi Investor Ups Local Stakes," *Crain's Chicago Business,* January 11, 1993, p. 1.

Sharoff, Robert, "Hartmarx Sees Its Growth in Sportswear, CEO Bert Hand Tells Stockholders," *Daily News Record,* April 17, 1995, p. 2.

Stern, William, "Brave Beginnings," *Financial World,* April 25, 1995, pp. 46–47.

"Tailored Growth," *Barron's,* December 4, 1984, pp. 55–56.

Veverka, Mark, "Hartmarx Hitting Sportswear Links," *Crain's Chicago Business,* April 19, 1993, p. 3.

——, "Restructuring, Focus on Casual Dress Up Hartmarx Bottom Line," *Crain's Chicago Business,* May 29, 1995, p. 60.

"Whole Cloth," *Barron's,* April 4, 1983, p. 59.

—John Simley
—updated by David E. Salamie

Hazlewood Foods plc

Rowditch
Derby DE1 1NB
United Kingdom
Telephone: (+44) 1332 295295
Fax: (+44) 1332 292300
Web site: http://www.hazlewoodfoods.com

Public Company
Incorporated: 1900 as Hazlewood (Products) Ltd.
Employees: 11,000
Sales: £788.9 million (US$1.27 billion) (1999)
Stock Exchanges: London
Ticker Symbol: HZLE.L
NAIC: 311412 Frozen Specialty Food Manufacturing; 3119999 All Other Miscellaneous Food Manufacturing; 42241 General Line Grocery Wholesalers; 111419 Herb Farming; 422490 Sandwiches Wholesaling

Hazlewood Foods plc is one of Europe's leading producers of convenience foods, including frozen foods and other ready-to-eat food products. With 51 production facilities in the United Kingdom and Europe, many in the Netherlands, Hazlewood has captured a leading share in most of its product categories. Hazlewood leads the U.K. market as producer of chilled and frozen prepared foods and is the world's leading producer of sandwiches to the third-party market. In addition, Hazlewood's greenhouse horticulture production facilities place it as the world leader in hothouse tomatoes and fresh herbs. The company has achieved strong growth and profits by concentrating on product categories that provide the strongest growth potential, including sandwiches; ready meals and other convenience meals such as pizza and quiche; snack foods; recipe sauces; specialized fresh produce, including cherry and vine tomatoes; and celebration cakes. Hazlewood does not manufacture any products under its own brand names. Instead, the company acts as a major private label supplier to third-party retailers, including the top five U.K. supermarket retailers, as well as retailers in continental Europe. The United Kingdom and Ireland generate 86 percent of the company's sales, while the Netherlands generates seven percent. Hazlewood Foods is led by Chairman Peter Barr and co-CEOs John Simon (in the United Kingdom) and Tom van Gurp (in continental Europe).

Saucy Start at the Turn of the 20th Century

Hazlewood Foods originated at the turn of the century as a manufacturer of sauces. Founded by brothers Arthur and William Hazlewood, with backing from their families, the company's first facility was located in Belper, in Derbyshire. The company's sauces found a ready market in the British kitchen. One Hazlewood brand in particular, Beetop Sauce, remained a company staple until well into the 1980s, when it was discontinued.

By the 1930s the company had grown sufficiently to take a listing on the London Stock Exchange under the name Hazlewood (Products) Ltd. The company's catalog had grown to include pickles and vinegar production. Hazlewood moved to expanded facilities in Rowditch, Derby, where it maintained its headquarters through the end of the century. During the 1930s, Hazlewood placed an increasing emphasis on self-sufficiency. In 1937 the company added its own glassworks, as well as a printing and labeling machine, enabling the company to control the entire production and packaging process with the single exception of the caps for the bottles. This early vertical integration not only helped the company weather the lean Depression years, but also face up to the years of World War II, when rationing and supply shortages forced many of its competitors out of business.

By the end of the 1960s, however, Hazlewood's best years seemed to be behind it. While its products continued to find distribution in the Midlands, Lancashire, and Yorkshire regions, the company was not growing beyond these boundaries, and by the early 1970s, failure threatened.

In 1973, Peter Barr, then 31 years old, was hired as the company's managing director. Barr had previously been a director of a supermarket chain, Fine Fare, which later changed its name to Somerfield and grew to become one of the top five supermarket chains in the United Kingdom, as well as a top

Company Perspectives:

Hazlewood Foods is, or has a clear objective to be, market leader in a selected range of key convenience food categories. These categories, which Hazlewood Foods calls its "drive" categories, are rapidly growing markets and ones in which the Group can significantly increase its market share and for which it often acts as category manager. Hazlewood Foods' "drive" categories, which now account for 78 percent of turnover, are: ready meals; sandwiches; chilled pizza; quiche; recipe sauces; snacks; cakes & desserts; delicatessen; glasshouse horticulture.

Hazlewood customer. Barr was given a simple mission: turn Hazlewood's fortunes around in just ten weeks, or else the company would be closed down altogether. Barr not only met this challenge, but transformed Hazlewood into a leading U.K. food products supplier.

Cooking up Success in the 1980s

Barr dramatically restructured the company's manufacturing processes and introduced a wide variety of new products, working to modernize Hazlewood in the face of a radically changing supermarket landscape. The rise of the large, self-service supermarket had begun to change the way people shopped; at the same time, people began to rely increasingly on ready-made convenience foods, opening new markets to producers such as Hazlewood.

Barr was ready to take the company to the next level. In the mid-1970s, he set up a so-called "reverse takeover," in which Hazlewood was acquired by two food producers in the north of England: The Beetroot Company, which had been a major supplier to the Tesco supermarket giant, and Humber Pickle, based in Hull. The new company continued to operate under the Hazlewood name and retained its public status. Meanwhile, the founders of both The Beetroot Company and Humber Pickle remained with the company and were named to the executive board. In its next phase of growth, Hazlewood made a practice of retaining the management of companies it acquired.

Hazlewood quickly began an aggressive growth-by-acquisition drive that lasted into the late 1980s and placed the company among the United Kingdom's top three publicly listed growth companies for much of the period. For most of the decade, Hazlewood's growth rate for both revenues and profits exceeded 30 percent per year. In 1979 the company acquired Manor Vinegar Company, which brought future CEO John Simons to Hazlewood's management team. In 1984 Hazlewood purchased its first company in the Netherlands, which brought in future CEO Tom van Gurp and initiated a focus on the Dutch market. Other acquisitions added such product categories as meats, fish, horticulture, confectionery, and chilled and frozen foods. Most of these acquisitions were funded through exchanges of Hazlewood stock, providing a low-cost entry into these new markets. The company's insistence on retaining the existing management at its new acquisitions enabled production to remain steady.

As Hazlewood phased out its own-brand production, its emphasis turned more and more to supplying the rapidly consolidating supermarket field. The shakeout of the food retailing industry eventually concentrated much of the retail food markets into the hands of just five retailers–Tesco, ASDA, Safeway, Somerfield, and J. Sainsbury. As part of this movement, the supermarket industry's leaders increasingly began to challenge the name brand foods market with their own private label brands. Hazlewood had by then positioned itself as a primary supplier of private label foods and other products, just as the major retailers began seeking to expand their own private label sales. Launched initially as lower-priced "generic" alternatives to the major brands, private label brands became increasingly sophisticated during the 1980s and 1990s, rivaling the name brands in quality while remaining competitive in price. This trend enabled Hazlewood to achieve sustained growth throughout the decade.

During the late 1980s, Hazlewood also began to step up its acquisitions on the European continent, focusing its growth especially on the Netherlands. In 1989 the company acquired two Dutch companies, Advang Groep and Diepvries Monnickendam. Other European acquisitions included those of Evers Specials, Gebr. Hansen, Gebr. Sterk, Vishandel Gebr. Van der Veen, and Wafel Janssen, in the Netherlands; Feldhues Fleischwarenbetriebe in Germany; and Hectare Agro Industria in Portugal. By 1990, the company's European expansion had become significant enough to create a chief executive position for its Continental Europe activities, a position that was given to Tom van Gurp. Acquisitions of FH Lee Limited and Maharry Holdings brought the company into the paper goods and feminine hygiene products markets.

Regrouping in the 1990s

Hazlewood's rapid expansion gave it the critical mass to weather the deep recession of the late 1980s that crippled the British economy. Nonetheless, the company was forced to slow its growth, cutting back on acquisitions before embarking on a restructuring in the mid-1990s. As part of its regrouping, Hazlewood moved to exit a number of markets where it would otherwise be forced to make heavy investments in order to achieve a leadership position or where the high cost of commodities cut too heavily into profit margins. Hazlewood sought to concentrate on its core markets, particularly those with the highest profitability.

This regrouping led Hazlewood to exit such markets as fruit juices, shellfish, confectionery, and other markets. At the same time, Hazlewood turned its focus to increasing its share of the convenience foods sector, one of the fastest-growing markets in the retail food industry. These food categories included a number of Hazlewood mainstays, such as sauces, sandwiches, pizza, and frozen meals. As part of its new focus, Hazlewood engaged in a massive investment drive, increasing plant capacity while strengthening its operations with new strategic acquisitions. John Simon, who was named CEO for the company's U.K. operations, took on the task of redirecting the company's growth.

By the late 1990s, Hazlewood had firmly established itself as market leader in a number of key categories, including ready-

Key Dates:

1900: Hazlewood is founded.
1937: Company brings all aspects of the production process inhouse.
1960s: Hazlewood enters a slump.
1973: Peter Barr joins company as managing director, beginning turnaround and initiating a period of dramatic growth.
1980s: Company is positioned as a leading supplier of private label brands.
1990s: CEO John Simon directs focus toward most profitable product lines and drops others.

made sandwiches—the company had become the world's largest sandwich maker—and greenhouse horticulture products, especially potted herbs. The company's greenhouse operations expanded to become the largest in the world. The company opened its own greenfield mineral water production site in Campsie, Scotland, and became one of the largest bottled water producers in the United Kingdom. The company also built two new state-of-the-art ready-meal production plants in Warrington and Wrexham. By the late 1990s, the company had built a manufacturing network of more than 51 plants across Europe, with a total workforce of more than 11,000.

In the late 1990s, the company began to consolidate its leadership positions, especially its position in the sandwich market, with a new string of acquisitions. These included the 1997 acquisitions of The Sandwich Man in Germany and the 1998 acquisition of U.K. sandwich maker Breadwinner Foods. Hazlewood also boosted its frozen foods capacity, acquiring the R&B Group in 1997, while rolling out a line of frozen entrees, Rhodes to Home, featuring recipes created by famed chef Gary Rhodes. Meanwhile, Hazlewood continued to work closely with its major supermarket clients, designing new and more sophisticated prepared meals, with an increasing target on the upscale foods market. In 1999 the company unveiled a new generation of convenience foods for the J. Sainsbury supermarket chain, featuring all the ingredients a customer needed to prepare a given recipe. As it approached its 100th anniversary, Hazlewood's keen attention to the food market and its willingness to adapt itself to the retailing industry's major trends made it a likely industry leader in the 21st century.

Principal Subsidiaries

Advang Groep BV (Netherlands); Breadwinner Foods Ltd.; Diepvries Monnickendam BV (Netherlands); Evers Specials BV (Netherlands); Feldhues Fleischwarenbetriebe GmbH (Germany); FH Lee Ltd.; Gebr. Hansen Beheer BV (Netherlands); Gebr. Sterk Beheer BV (Netherlands); Hazlewood Convenience Group I Ltd.; Hazlewood Convenience Food Group Ltd.; Hazlewood Europe BV (Netherlands); Hazlewood Frozen Products Ltd.; Hazlewood Grocery Ltd.; Hazlewood Holdings GmbH (Germany); Hazlewood International Ltd.; Hazlewood Delicatessen and Meat Group (U.K.) Ltd.; Hazlewood Product Ltd.; Hectare Agro Industria SA (Portugal); Henri van de Bilt Beheer BV (Netherlands); Maharry Holdings (Ireland); R&B Group Ltd.; The Sandwich Man GmbH (Germany); Vishandel Gebr. van der Veen BV (Netherlands); Wafel Janssen BV (Netherlands).

Principal Competitors

Albert Fisher Group; Nestlé; Groupe Danone; Northern Foods; Geest; Unigate; Hibernia Foods; Unilever SA; Hillsdown Holdings; United Biscuits.

Further Reading

Anderson, Simon, "Hazlewood to Face Pounds 3m Costs on New Brands," *Daily Telegraph*, December 2, 1998.
Cope, Nigel, "Hazlewood Plays Down Talk of Bid," *Independent*, December 2, 1998, p. 21.
Grimond, Magnus, "Hazlewood to Focus on Own-Brand Foods," *Independent*, June 18, 1997, p. 26.
"Hazlewood Looks for Convenient Growth," *Reuters*, June 15, 1999.
Potter, Ben, "Tasty Fare at Hazlewood," *Daily Telegraph*, June 17, 1998.

—M.L. Cohen

H.B. Fuller Company

1200 Willow Lake Boulevard
St. Paul, Minnesota 55110-5101
U.S.A.
Telephone: (651) 236-5900
Fax: (651) 236-5898
Web site: http://www.hbfuller.com

Public Company
Incorporated: 1887 as Fuller Manufacturing Company
Employees: 6,000
Sales: $1.35 billion (1998)
Stock Exchanges: NASDAQ
Ticker Symbol: FULL
NAIC: 325510 Paint & Coating Manufacturing; 325520 Adhesive Manufacturing; 325998 All Other Miscellaneous Chemical Product & Preparation Manufacturing

A top performer among specialty chemicals firms, H.B. Fuller Company markets adhesives, sealants, coatings, paints, and several other specialty chemical products in 42 countries. Fuller's international markets, which have been aggressively pursued since the 1970s, account for more than 40 percent of the company's overall revenue. The company originated during the late 19th century as the first paste and glue manufacturer in Minnesota. Despite a long list of successes, Fuller ranked as the second smallest adhesive firm in the country up until World War II, at which time majority ownership and management of the company was passed from one of the founder's sons, H.B. Fuller, Jr., to Elmer Andersen, a highly successful sales manager. Andersen inaugurated a ''double it in five'' strategy, a systematic campaign for decentralized growth that would ensure 14 percent annual sales increases, or the doubling of sales every five years. By 1950, the company had become the fourth largest adhesives manufacturer in the country. When Andersen's son, Tony, assumed leadership of the company in 1971, further rapidly paced growth came through overseas expansion. Since the early 1980s, Fuller's growth has generally slowed; in addition, net earnings have decreased in five of the last ten years. But a major restructuring was initiated in 1998 by new company President and CEO Albert Stroucken, who aims for a quick turnaround.

Early Years

The company was launched in 1887 when Harvey Benjamin Fuller, Sr., traveled from Chicago to St. Paul, Minnesota, with the sole intention of inventing and selling glue. In Chicago Fuller had experimented with glue mixing, while successfully buying, repackaging, and marketing an existing adhesive that was guaranteed to ''cement everything.'' His marketing took the form of various promotional rhymes, including clever Mother Goose spoofs: ''Maid was in the garden, hanging out her clothes/Along came a blackbird, and nipped off her nose/When she found her nose was off, what was she to do/But go and stick it on again with FULLER'S 'PREMIUM GLUE.' '' Fuller regarded St. Paul, together with its ''twin city'' Minneapolis, as the ideal urban center to establish his business, for general industry was thriving there and competition was scarce. In addition, flour, then a key ingredient in gluemaking, was in abundant supply because of a strong agricultural base and such rising concerns as Pillsbury and General Mills's precursor, Washburn-Crosby Company.

Fuller's business plan was simple. ''What the world needed,'' according to *A Fuller Life* and H.B. Fuller, Sr., ''was a convenient, economical, strong adhesive—an adhesive so versatile that homemakers and manufacturers could both use it.'' His equipment was also simple: an iron kettle and the family's wood-burning stove. Soon Fuller concocted a wet, flour-based paste with which he was satisfied. He then began selling the mixture in small batches to local paperhangers, who were generally glad not to have to make their own glue. As the Fuller brand name gained recognition, Fuller realized his business required outside capital to sustain growth. The company was incorporated when three Minneapolis lawyers agreed to invest a total of $600. Thereafter, Fuller Manufacturing Company marketed its glue to a wide variety of customers, including flour mills, shoe companies, box manufacturers, bookbinders, printers, and households. The company also made and sold laundry blueing and did a brisk business in ink for the city schools. By 1888, the company, which was

Company Perspectives:

The H.B. Fuller's Corporate Mission is to serve its customers as a leading worldwide formulator, manufacturer and marketer of technology-driven specialty chemicals and other products related to its area of expertise. H.B. Fuller is committed to the balanced interests of its customers, employees, shareholders and communities; and, accordingly, H.B. Fuller will conduct business ethically and profitably, support the activities of its employees in their communities, and exercise leadership as a responsible corporate citizen.

really just Fuller serving as jack-of-all-trades, added its first employee, Fuller's oldest son, Albert. Two years later the company moved into its own manufacturing facility, where Albert assumed primary responsibility for filling orders and discovering new formulas while Harvey generated more revenues by expanding his sales areas.

In 1892 the company acquired a Minneapolis competitor, The Minnesota Paste Company, for $200. Although several decades later such acquisitions would become regular occurrences, Fuller meanwhile was destined to grow by internal development, particularly through a succession of inventions by the founder that greatly expanded both its product line and its manufacturing capabilities. In late 1893 Harvey successfully produced Fuller's Cold Water Dry Wall Cleaner, intended for use on wallpaper (at that time it was customary to clean walls twice yearly, but existing cleaners tended to decompose under warm conditions), and applied for a patent. The item was in wide production by the following spring and became enormously popular. The elder Fuller's next invention was Fuller's Cold Water Dry Paste, which became even more successful than Fuller's Cleaner. Because it was packaged dry, without the added weight of water, the product could be shipped at lower cost, saving both the manufacturer and the customer money. In addition, Fuller's Paste was remarkably easy to work with, and advertisements boasted that "a child can mix and use it." By 1898, Fuller Manufacturing was posting annual sales of $10,000. By 1905, the company was not only shipping its paste and cleaner to both coasts, it also had entered markets in England, Germany, and Australia.

One setback for the firm, however, was the lack of an obvious successor to the post of president, for Albert and Roger, Fuller's middle son, both left the business. Furthermore, Fuller's youngest son, Harvey, Jr., was more inclined to a career in art than manufacturing. Nevertheless, upon his graduation from the University of Chicago in 1909, Harvey, Jr., joined the company full time and made an immediate impact by bolstering advertising and creating the first comprehensive catalog of Fuller products.

Increasing its workforce to include an experienced bookkeeper, a stenographer, and a sales manager, Fuller Manufacturing entered the 1910s prepared for heightened growth. In 1915 the firm reincorporated as H.B. Fuller Company and issued stock valued at $75,000. World War I, already underway, was to be the primary impetus for Fuller's short-term growth. With the engagement of American troops came the need for shipping mass quantities of food overseas. U.S. canneries were ready to comply but had a need for a quality adhesive that would speed the labeling process. Fuller filled that need and prospered. After the war, however, Fuller's sales dropped off and Harvey, Sr., fell ill, dying late in 1921.

Struggles in the 1920s and 1930s

During this difficult period, when the company faced the possibility of bankruptcy, Harvey, Jr., made what was undoubtedly his greatest decision: that of hiring a full-time chemist named Ray Burgess. By the time Harvey inherited the presidency from his father, the company had regained its momentum, due in large part to Burgess's self-taught genius and his ability to develop customized adhesives and formulas for the industrial market. The list of Fuller products expanded to several dozen by the mid-1920s and record-setting sales of $157,000 capped the end of the decade.

In 1930, following the stock market crash, Fuller acquired The Selvasize Company of St. Paul, the maker of a combination plaster and wallpaper adhesive, for $2,000. Fuller, with steady customers in 38 states and a near monopoly on glue production in the Twin Cities, remained relatively healthy throughout the Great Depression. A number of events highlighted the 1930s. The company hired its first degreed chemist, who became responsible for several new patents, such as Ice Proof, a glue resistant to cold water. In addition, a research team was formed, Fuller began a full-scale entry into international markets, and Elmer Andersen, a business administration graduate and budding salesman, joined the company, which celebrated its 50th anniversary in 1937.

Also during this time, Burgess developed an important new product known as Nu-Type Hot Pick-Up. Until Burgess's invention, the company, like its competitors, had marketed several hot pick-up glues for use in automated labeling; all such glues, however, were notoriously difficult to work with, either too hard or too sticky in bulk form, and always cumbersome to apply in measured amounts. Nu-Type Hot Pick-Up was the first glue that solved each of these problems. Consequently, Fuller cornered the hot glue market nationwide.

Not all the corporate news was as favorable, however. The company, with just half of one percent of industry sales, was still conspicuously overshadowed by such giants as National Adhesives Corporation, which controlled approximately 65 percent of the market. Every new sale, therefore, mattered greatly, which made all the more devastating the revelation in late 1937 that three of Fuller's regional salesmen had been undercutting the company's orders through the creation of a bogus firm, which they now claimed to represent. Sales, depressed already by the still struggling economy, dropped from $212,000 that year to $165,000 the following year. Even more devastating to the company's long-term prospects was the debilitating stroke Harvey Fuller suffered in 1939.

In March 1941 a large Chicago competitor named Paisley Products approached the ailing St. Paul firm with an acquisition offer. Both Fuller, then in his mid-50s, and Andersen, 32, attended a meeting with Paisley's representatives, who formally

Key Dates:

1887: Fuller Manufacturing Company is founded by Harvey Benjamin Fuller, Sr.
1915: Firm is reincorporated as H.B. Fuller Company.
1921: Harvey B. Fuller, Jr., takes over presidency upon the death of his father.
1941: Elmer Andersen takes majority position in and leadership of the company.
1958: H.B. Fuller Company (Canada) Ltd., based in Winnipeg, is launched.
1968: Company goes public.
1971: Tony Andersen, son of Elmer, becomes company president.
1980: Sales reach $296 million.
1992: Walter Kissling is named president of Fuller.
1994: Sales surpass $1 billion.
1998: Albert Stroucken is named president and CEO, becoming the first outsider so named; major restructuring is launched.

proposed to purchase H.B. Fuller Company for $50,000. Fuller was prepared to retire but was also discouraged by the low offer he had received. Andersen provided an alternative solution. His plan involved assuming leadership of and a majority position in the company himself, while still allowing Fuller to retain at least a 25 percent stake. The deal was completed in July after Andersen borrowed heavily to finance a $10,000 down payment on the stock he was required to purchase. Mere months later, Pearl Harbor was attacked.

World War II and Postwar Growth

Far more so than the previous war, World War II afforded the company a chance to develop a broad line of adhesives that the government demanded for an equally broad array of uses. Fuller became one of the nation's first companies to specialize, among other areas, in waterproof adhesives. It thus earned a place on the government's recommended suppliers list which, in turn, brought it enhanced recognition nationally. The company scored another victory when it was able, during the midst of rationing, to supply Nabisco with raw glucose from its inventory, which had been dramatically enlarged by Andersen as a cost-saving measure. Nabisco subsequently became a major user of Fuller's adhesives for its boxed foods and other products. Both during and following the war, the company focused on decentralizing operations—bringing the product closer to the customer—by establishing a number of branch plants, beginning with Kansas City in 1943. At the close of the decade, Fuller ranked fourth among U.S. adhesives companies, behind National Starch (later owned by Unilever, then Imperial Chemical Industries PLC), Paisley Products (acquired by Fuller in 1975), and Swift.

In 1949, Andersen was elected to the state senate and became a part-time company president. Al Vigard assumed control of day-to-day operations in Andersen's absence; he later became president when Andersen extended his political career by receiving the governorship of Minnesota in 1960. A steady introduction of new products, a systematic development of a strong nationwide sales force, and a greater attention to international expansion typified this transitional era. In 1958, the company launched H.B. Fuller Company (Canada) Ltd. in Winnipeg. Shortly thereafter, Fuller Adhesives International of Panama was established. Numerous other international subsidiaries followed, each of which conformed to the Fuller blueprint for growth. A three-stage process, this blueprint called for: (1) building export volume to a high level; (2) forming or acquiring a subsidiary, or sometimes establishing a co-venture with a noncompetitor, in a clearly defined market; and (3) sustaining the business by hiring and training a local workforce to produce customized products.

One of Fuller's most significant ventures outside the United States was Kativo Chemical Industries Ltd. A promising but nearly bankrupt paint, inks, plastics, and chemicals business based in Costa Rica, Kativo was begun by a Kansas inventor named Dr. Frank Jirik. During the early 1960s, Fuller acquired a minority interest in the company, but by early 1967 Jirik approached Elmer Andersen with a proposal that Fuller assume a majority interest to fuel the company's plans for expansion. In *A Fuller Life,* Andersen recounted the visit that clinched his decision: "It was Kativo's people who made all the difference to us. . . . We trusted them. We had confidence in them and we cut them loose. We decided to send no U.S. Fuller employees to work in the Kativo operation." In addition, Andersen awarded the 13 Kativo executives the right to own stock in the company they had helped build. Soon Kativo became the heart of Fuller's Latin American operations, from Mexico to Argentina. Surviving plant and monetary losses from both the June 1979 revolution in Nicaragua and General Noriega's rampages during the U.S. invasion of Panama ten years later, Kativo and its related businesses ranked among the fastest-growing in the Fuller fold into the 1990s. One of Kativo's original executives, Costa Rican native Walter Kissling, eventually served as president and chief operating officer of Fuller.

Late 20th Century: International Growth and Restructuring

In 1971, three years after Fuller went public, Tony Andersen became company president. International sales accounted for around 15 percent of total revenues, and Andersen was given the primary responsibility of boosting this figure, while increasing overall volume. Consequently, he became a president routinely in transit, flying from one country to the next. Not until 1980 did he return to head U.S. operations full-time. During the interim, he oversaw some two dozen acquisitions—half in foreign countries—and, significantly, the first of these provided important new market entries into Japan and Europe. From 1971 to 1980, sales grew from $60 million to $296 million. Andersen's greatest contribution to the company, however, came shortly after his return to the St. Paul headquarters. In what was then an unpopular maneuver, he decided to revamp the company's entire infrastructure, which because of rapid geographic-oriented expansion had become both inefficient and inconsistent. A market-driven organization stressing product and price uniformity was Andersen's answer. Due to an economic downturn, the payoff was slow to come. By 1985, however, earnings had improved dramatically, and three years later,

Andersen was named executive of the year by *Corporate Report Minnesota.*

Fuller inaugurated the 1990s by broadening its Asia/Pacific operations with a hot-melt production plant in Guangzhou, China. Plant expansions around the globe, as well as continuing investment in research and development, typified the company through 1992. In April of that year, Elmer Andersen officially stepped down as company chairperson. In a speech to shareholders, he optimistically stated, "The past is prologue: you ain't seen nothing yet." During this time, however, Andersen's statement was somewhat eclipsed by publicity surrounding Fuller's Resistol glue and its use as an inhalant by children in Latin America. Widely respected for its sponsorship of charitable and educational causes, Fuller pulled the product from markets in Honduras and Guatemala in the fall of 1992 and continued to fund social programs that helped minimize such abuse. Despite these moves, the Resistol issue simply would not go away. More negative publicity came in 1996 when the company was sued for negligence by the family of a 16-year-old Guatemalan boy. The suit, brought in U.S. District Court in St. Paul, claimed that the boy died as a result of years of inhaling Resistol. The judge in the case dismissed the suit, having concluded that it lacked jurisdiction.

When Elmer Andersen retired in 1992, Tony Andersen took over as chairman and Kissling became president. Kissling added the CEO position as well in 1995. Under Kissling's leadership, Fuller in the mid-1990s worked to reduce its operating expenses through the closure and consolidation of plants, particularly in Europe and Latin America. The company was aided in these efforts by the liberalization of tariffs in these regions. Whereas previously the company was forced to locate a plant in nearly every country in which it hoped to sell its products, it could now consolidate its factories on a regional basis. In concert with these moves came a reorganizing of the European and Latin American operations into strategic business units that were based on product lines rather than on geography. Company sales, meantime, surpassed the $1 billion mark for the first time in 1994 and then grew to $1.28 billion by 1996.

In 1997 Fuller joined its automotive adhesives, sealants, and coatings operations (with annual sales of $100 million to $115 million) with the automotive adhesives business of Zurich-based EMS-Chemie Holding AG to form EFTEC. The Detroit-based joint venture had revenues of about $250 million, making it the second largest automotive supplier, after Dow's Essex, and enabling it to operate on a global basis.

The following year Kissling retired from the company. His successor as president and CEO was Albert Stroucken, the first outsider in the company's 111-year history to take over the top positions. A native of The Netherlands, Stroucken was a 29-year veteran with Bayer A.G. Stroucken's first major task as head of Fuller was to improve the company's net earnings, which had for years stood at around three percent. The investment community had long complained that Fuller's corporate culture, which helped earn the company a consistent place on lists of the best places to work, did not place enough emphasis on the bottom line. The company had a longstanding pledge that "its responsibilities, in order of priority [are] to its customers, employees, stockholders and communities."

It became immediately clear that this outsider would bring startling changes to Fuller and propel it into a new era. Most strikingly, in 1998 the Stroucken-led Fuller changed its mission statement, which now read in part, "H.B. Fuller is committed to the balanced interests of its customers, employees, shareholders and communities." In August 1998, a mere four months after his arrival, Stroucken announced a major restructuring aimed at reducing costs by $30 million per year and improving net margins to five percent through the closure of about a dozen plants, the divestment of underperforming units, and the elimination of about 600 jobs worldwide—all over an 18-month period. Stroucken also took a more aggressive stance toward acquisitions, aiming to displace Imperial Chemical Industries' National Starch subsidiary from the number one position in the global adhesives market. During 1998 Fuller spent $92.4 million on acquisitions, purchasing the Australian and New Zealand adhesives business of Croda International PLC and Peterson Chemicals Adhesives from Ecolab Inc. Stroucken told analysts in mid-1999 that he was identifying acquisition targets with sales of at least $100 million, a huge jump from the $5 million to $10 million companies that Fuller typically purchased. With its newfound focus on cost containment and improved profitability and a more aggressive attitude toward acquisitions, H.B. Fuller was certain to be a much more formidable competitor in 2000 and beyond.

Principal Subsidiaries

H.B. Fuller Company Puerto Rico, Inc.; H.B. Fuller International Inc.; F.A.I. Trading Company; Fiber-Resin Corporation; H.B. Fuller Automotive Company; EFTEC North America, LLC (70%); EFTEC Latin America (88.5%); EFTEC Europe Holding AG (Switzerland; 30%); EFTEC Asia Pte. Ltd. (Singapore; 80%); Foster Products Corporation; TEC Specialty Products, Inc.; Linear Products, Inc.; H.B. Fuller Licensing & Financing Inc.; Kativo Chemical Industries, S.A. (Panama; 99.7%); Pinturas Ecuatorianas, S.A. (Ecuador); Glidden Avenida Nacional, S.A. (Panama); Fabrica Pinturas Glidden, S.A. (Panama); H.B. Fuller Holding Panama Co.; H.B. Fuller Austria Gesellschaft m.b.H.; H.B. Fuller Belgium N.V./S.A.; H.B. Fuller GmbH (Germany; 99.9%); H.B. Fuller Italia s.r.l. (Italy); H.B. Fuller Nederland B.V. (Netherlands); Prakoll, S.A. (Spain); H.B. Fuller Sverige AB (Sweden); H.B. Fuller Holdings Limited (U.K.); H.B. Fuller Canada, Inc.; H.B. Fuller Mexico, S.A.; H.B. Fuller Company Australia Pty. Ltd.; H.B. Fuller (China) Adhesives Ltd. (97%); H.B. Fuller Japan Company, Ltd.; H.B. Fuller Korea Co., Ltd.; H.B. Fuller (Malaysia) Sdn. Bhd.; H.B. Fuller Company (N.Z.) Ltd. (New Zealand; 99.9%); H.B. Fuller (Philippines), Inc. (80%); HBF Realty Corporation (Philippines; 40%); H.B. Fuller Taiwan Co., Ltd.; H.B. Fuller (Thailand) Co., Ltd. (99.9%); Nippon Tilement Company, Ltd. (Japan; 9.1%).

Principal Competitors

Akzo Nobel N.V.; American Biltrite Inc.; Borden Chemicals and Plastics Limited Partnership; Cytec Industries Inc.; Dexter Corporation; Elf Atochem; Henkel KGaA; Hercules Incorporated; Imperial Chemical Industries PLC; Loctite Corporation; Minnesota Mining and Manufacturing Company; NS Group, Inc.; Pacer Technology; Rohm and Haas Company; RPM, Inc.;

Sekisui Chemical Co., Ltd.; TOTAL FINA S.A.; The Valspar Corporation; W.R. Grace & Co.

Further Reading

Carlson, Scott, ''U.S. Judge Dismisses Suit Against St. Paul-Based H.B. Fuller,'' *St. Paul Pioneer Press,* September 25, 1996.

Croghan, Lore, ''Family Values: Why Paternalistic H.B. Fuller Gives Wall Street Fits,'' *Financial World,* November 7, 1995, pp. 46–47, 50.

Davis, Riccardo A., ''New President Targets Net Profit Margin at Minnesota's H.B. Fuller,'' *St. Paul Pioneer Press,* July 2, 1998.

Feyder, Susan, ''Fuller Plans Cost-Cutting Effort,'' *Minneapolis Star Tribune,* December 22, 1995, p. 1D.

A Fuller Life: The Story of H.B. Fuller Company, 1887–1987, St. Paul: H.B. Fuller Company, 1986.

''Fuller's Brush with Fame,'' *Corporate Report Minnesota,* June 1984, p. 23.

Fuller World, January/February 1992 (full issue).

Gelbach, Deborah L., ''H.B. Fuller Company,'' in *From This Land: A History of Minnesota's Empires, Enterprises, and Entrepreneurs,* Northridge, Calif.: Windsor Publications, 1988, pp. 358–61.

''Glue Issue Dominates Fuller Meeting,'' *Minneapolis Star Tribune,* April 16, 1993, p. 3D.

''H.B. Fuller Co.,'' *City Business,* March 26, 1993, p. 18.

''H.B. Fuller Jockeys for Position to Become No. 1 Adhesives Player,'' *Chemical Marketing Reporter,* June 14, 1999, p. 7.

''H.B. Fuller Net Falls 51% in Quarter; Nonrecurring Sales Adjustment Cited,'' *Minneapolis Star Tribune,* March 23, 1993, p. 5D.

''H.B. Fuller Reports Lower Second-Quarter Earnings,'' *Minneapolis Star Tribune,* June 23, 1993, p. 5D.

Henriques, Diana B., ''Suit Against Fuller Over Death of Guatemalan Youth Dismissed,'' *New York Times,* September 25, 1996, p. D5.

Kelly, Marjorie, ''Though H.B. Fuller May Wish It, Resistol Issue Won't Go Away,'' *Minneapolis Star Tribune,* December 4, 1995, p. 3D.

Kunz, Virginia Brainard, *A Modern Renaissance St. Paul,* Northridge, Calif.: Windsor Publications, Inc., 1986, pp. 142–45.

Levering, Robert, Michael Katz, and Milton Moskowitz, *The 100 Best Companies to Work for in America,* Reading, Mass.: Addison-Wesley, 1984, pp. 112–14; new edition, New York: Doubleday, 1993, pp. 136–40.

Malamud, Steven, ''H.B. Fuller: A Different Record Home and Abroad,'' *Business and Society Review,* January 1, 1996.

McEnroe, Paul, and Susan E. Peterson, ''H.B. Fuller Sued in Teen's Death,'' *Minneapolis Star Tribune,* January 4, 1996, p. 1D.

Mundale, Charles I., ''H.B. Fuller's Caribbean Initiative,'' *Corporate Report Minnesota,* July 1983, pp. 55–60.

Papa, Mary Bader, ''Executive of the Year (Anthony L. Andersen): Building for the Future by Sticking to the Basic Values of the Past,'' *Corporate Report Minnesota,* January 1988, pp. 31–39.

Peterson, Susan E., ''Fuller Names Bayer Exec to Replace Kissling As CEO,'' *Minneapolis Star Tribune,* March 28, 1998, p. 1D.

——, ''H.B. Fuller Honors Outgoing Chairman Andersen, Celebrates Company's Continuing Good Health,'' *Minneapolis Star Tribune,* April 17, 1992, p. 1D.

——, ''H.B. Fuller President Kissling to Retire from Post in 1998,'' *Minneapolis Star Tribune,* July 19, 1997, p. 1D.

——, ''H.B. Fuller Will Cut 600 Jobs,'' *Minneapolis Star Tribune,* August 12, 1998, p. 1D.

——, ''Judge to Decide Venue of Fuller Case,'' *Minneapolis Star Tribune,* May 30, 1996, p. 1D.

——, ''This Al's No 'Chainsaw,' '' *Minneapolis Star Tribune,* July 6, 1998, p. 1D.

Pitzer, Mary J., ''Fuller's Worldwide Strategy: Think Local,'' *Business Week,* November 16, 1987, p. 169.

Schafer, Lee, ''H.B. Fuller and the Indignities of War,'' *Corporate Report Minnesota,* March 1990, p. 14.

Scheraga, Dan, ''Fuller Acquires Coating Technologies from NiTech,'' *Chemical Marketing Reporter,* October 19, 1998, p. 16.

——, ''Fuller Poised to Reap Rewards from Restructuring,'' *Chemical Marketing Reporter,* February 22, 1999, p. 20.

——, ''Fuller's Success Based on European and Latin Support,'' *Chemical Marketing Reporter,* April 12, 1999, pp. 4, 26.

——, ''H.B. Fuller Streamlines to Counteract Effects of Economic Slowdown,'' *Chemical Marketing Reporter,* August 17, 1998, pp. 3, 18.

Teresko, John, ''Too Fast a Pace? Andersen Has a Strategy for the Next Leg of the Race,'' *Industry Week,* September 15, 1986, pp. 59–60.

Walsh, Kerri A., ''A Fresh Start for H.B. Fuller,'' *Chemical Week,* February 3, 1999, pp. 39, 41.

——, ''Fuller, EMS-Chemie Stick Auto Adhesives Together,'' *Chemical Week,* May 28, 1997, p. 14.

Zemke, Ron, and Dick Schaaf, ''H.B. Fuller,'' *The Service Edge: 101 Companies That Profit from Customer Care,* New York: Penguin Books, 1989, pp. 458–61.

—Jay P. Pederson
—updated by David E. Salamie

H.E. Butt Grocery Company

646 South Main Avenue
San Antonio, Texas 78204
U.S.A.
Telephone: (210) 938-8000
Fax: (210) 938-8169
Web site: http://www.heb.com

Private Company
Founded: 1905 as C.C. Butt Grocery Store
Employees: 45,000
Sales: $7 billion (1998 est.)
NAIC: 445110 Supermarkets and Other Grocery (Except Convenience) Stores; 447110 Other Gasoline Stations; 311511 Fluid Milk Manufacturing; 311421 Fruit and Vegetable Canning; 311520 Ice Cream and Frozen Dessert Manufacturing; 311610 Animal Slaughtering and Processing; 311812 Commercial Bakeries; 311830 Tortilla Manufacturing; 326160 Plastics Bottle Manufacturing; 812920 Photofinishing

H.E. Butt Grocery Company (H-E-B) is the nation's 15th largest grocery chain in revenue terms and is one of the leading chains in Texas, with number one positions in Austin, Corpus Christi, and San Antonio. The largest private company in Texas, H-E-B has been owned and operated by the H.E. Butt family since its early 20th-century founding. Of the company's 269 units, most are large-format, combination food and pharmacy stores. About 90 of them are H-E-B Pantry Stores, which are smaller-sized, feature extra low prices, and are designed to be particularly convenient; these are mainly located in rural areas between southeast Texas and southwest Louisiana. Approximately 60 of the company's stores feature self-service Gas N Go gasoline islands. In addition to its units in Texas and Louisiana, H-E-B runs six stores in Mexico in states that border the United States. Among the products that the company makes or processes itself for sale in its own stores are milk, yogurt, sour cream, cottage cheese, ice cream, baked goods, tortillas, meat, orange juice, and fruit drinks. The company also makes its own plastic bottles and operates a photofinishing laboratory.

Early Decades: From Kerrville to San Antonio

H-E-B started out as a single store in Kerrville, a small town in the Texas Hill Country. Charles C. and Florence Butt moved to Kerrville from Memphis, Tennessee. Charles was suffering from tuberculosis, and they hoped that the drier climate would improve his condition. Once the family was settled in Kerrville, Florence was faced with supporting the family herself. She decided to open a grocery store. The family purchased a two-story house, planning to live upstairs and operate the store downstairs. With investment capital of $60, the family opened the C.C. Butt Grocery Store on November 26, 1905. They began selling food in bulk as a charge and delivery operation. Florence's young sons delivered the food via baby carriage until they could afford to buy a little red wagon.

By 1908 the Butt store had established itself within the local community as ''dealers in staples, fancy groceries and fresh meats.'' The boys had even been able to buy a horse and wagon to make deliveries. Also, Florence was building a profitable fresh-baked bread business as a sideline. She arranged for bread to be delivered by train from San Antonio and then immediately delivered to residences by her sons. The market for fresh bread was relatively new at the time because many women were hesitant to buy bread for fear of being considered too lazy to bake their own. Nevertheless, bread deliveries increased, initiating what would become a legacy of innovation at Butt Grocery.

All three of the Butt brothers—Charles, Eugene, and Howard E.—worked in the family business while they were growing up. However, it was Howard who took an early liking to the business, and was even described in company annals as a ''grocery man'' from the beginning. At the age of 22, in 1917, Howard was still working in the grocery store. Shortly after the United States entered World War I, however, Howard joined the Navy. After a two-year tour he returned to Kerrville to take over the store. He had a lot of ideas and was eager to implement them. His first move was to relocate the store to a busier corner in the burgeoning downtown area. In the new location, Butt installed the first in-store meat market and delicatessen. He also began a policy of constantly offering new and different items to patrons.

Company Perspectives:

We remain committed to providing our customers with three things: consistently superior Customer Service, the best quality and freshness in all of our products, and low prices with great value. Attaining these goals each day makes H-E-B the best it can be in each community we serve.

Importantly, Butt also tried a risky new experiment. Traditionally, customers had delivered or phoned in their orders, and the grocer had gathered and delivered the groceries along with a bill due at the end of the month. By the early 1920s, though, a growing number of people had their own cars and were able to more easily transport their own groceries. Butt believed that those customers, and maybe many others, would be willing to wait on themselves, pay cash, and transport their own groceries if they could save money. The savings would come from reduced labor and equipment costs at the store, and from the elimination of unpaid grocery bills. In December 1921 Butt sent out handwritten penny postcards to his customers, explaining the change. On New Year's Day the store opened under the new name of C.C. Butt Cash and Carry.

The cash-and-carry experiment was an instant hit. In fact, Butt decided in 1924 that it was time to expand. He opened a new store about 60 miles from Kerrville in a town called Junction. Although other stores were already established there, Butt's innovative cash-and-carry system and superior inventory allowed his store to thrive. Meanwhile, Butt continued to tweak his formula by experimenting with new services and products. Most importantly, he began to question why a housewife should not be able to get common household items other than food and staples from a grocery store. Throughout the 1920s he slowly began adding to his inventory: everything from pots and pans to tools and textiles.

In 1926 Butt discovered a new avenue to growth. Piggly-Wiggly, a grocery store chain that had become well-known in the region by utilizing many of the same tactics that Butt was using, began selling franchises. Butt purchased some of the franchise rights, reasoning that he could successfully combine his views about customer service, as well as his experience with cash-and-carry, with the recognized Piggly-Wiggly name. Butt opened his first Piggly-Wiggly in Del Rio in 1926. The success of that venture led him to open two more stores in 1927 in Brady and Gonzales, purchase three additional Piggly-Wiggly's in 1928, and build two more new outlets in San Benito and Harlingen. After roaring through most of the 1920s, Butt moved the company's headquarters to Harlingen in 1928 to get closer to his Piggly-Wiggly stores. By that time, Butt's first Piggly-Wiggly store in Del Rio was serving 5,000 customers each day.

The stock market crashed in 1929, spawning the Great Depression. Fortunately, Butt was relatively well positioned for the downturn in comparison to many other businesses at the time. His stores were geared for value, and grocery items were among the last goods that people stopped buying during the Depression. In fact, rather than slowing down, Butt continued to grow during the late 1920s and early 1930s, opening stores throughout the Rio Grande Valley and remodeling existing stores. By 1931 Butt Grocery was operating a total of 24 stores, and plans were being made for new outlets.

Butt suffered a major setback in 1933, when a hurricane swept from the coast into the Rio Grande Valley and damaged many of Butt's stores and warehouses. Interestingly, Butt's Piggly-Wiggly in Harlingen was the only grocery store in its area to open immediately after the hurricane. Despite the bad luck, Butt quickly restored his businesses and even managed to pursue a charitable venture. In 1934, when he was still in his 30s, Butt formed the H.E. Butt Foundation, a charitable organization created to aid the community. That effort was the first of many charitable acts that would earn Butt a reputation as a dedicated philanthropist. In 1935 Butt changed the name of his company to H.E. Butt Grocery Company.

H.E. Butt began to integrate vertically when it opened its own bakery and purchased a canning company in 1936. By that year, Butt was generating about $2 million worth of business annually from 31 stores. A new outlet built in Kerrville sported a parking lot with 100 spaces—quite a step up from the horse hitching post stationed in front of the original Kerrville store. In 1938, moreover, Butt expanded into the 75,000-person Austin market, the largest metropolitan area that it had entered. The company was also doing business in San Antonio by 1942 and was increasing its presence in its established markets. Meantime, headquarters were moved again in 1938, this time to Corpus Christi.

Postwar Era: Expansion of Scope and Facilities

Butt Grocery contributed to the World War II effort during the 1940s by supplying canned vegetables and fruits from its canning facility to troops overseas. In addition, many company employees served in the armed forces. At the same time, the company continued to progress. It opened the first air-conditioned grocery store and also began offering frozen foods, which were considered a novelty at the time. Shortages of many food items continued after the war, but by the late 1940s Butt's business was back to normal. Encouraged by the success of the air-conditioned store, Butt opened one of the first truly large grocery stores in Texas in 1949. The Corpus Christi store had 22,500 square feet of space and was the first to have a separate drug department, cosmetic area, and lunch counter.

The large grocery store was a hit, and H.E. Butt focused on the concept from that point forward. In 1950 the company opened a large store in Waco—the company's 53rd outlet—that featured an unheard of 12 checkout stands, two parking lots, and a self-service meat counter. Within two years several similar stores had been built and H.E. Butt's chain had swelled to 58. The company continued to push for more growth. To increase sales at existing stores, it began operating the Texas Gold Stamp Company as a subsidiary in 1955; the promotion gave customers stamps for each purchase, which they could then exchange for household items. Butt continued to add new stores during the late 1950s and early 1960s. One store even featured spectacular "magic carpets" (automatic doors), parking for 300 cars, and 12 separate departments.

By the end of the 1960s, H-E-B, as it had become known, was ready for a change. The dynamic and innovative Howard Butt

Key Dates:

1905: Florence Butt opens the C.C. Butt Grocery Store in Kerrville, Texas.
1921: Howard E. Butt, son of Florence, begins experimenting with a cash-and-carry format.
1935: H.E. Butt Grocery Company name is adopted.
1936: Vertical integration begins via new bakery and canning facility; company generates sales of $2 million.
1949: The chain's first truly large grocery store, with 22,500 square feet, opens in Corpus Christi.
1971: Charles Butt, son of Howard, assumes the helm as president; sales reach $250 million.
1981: First superstore, with 56,000 square feet, is opened in Austin.
1985: Headquarters shift to San Antonio.
1991: 93,000-square-foot H-E-B Marketplace, including restaurants and a coffee shop, opens in San Antonio; company reaches $3 billion in sales.
1996: First expansion outside of Texas occurs with the opening of a Pantry store in Louisiana; James F. Clingman becomes the first non-family member named president.
1998: Sales reach $7 billion.

officially passed the torch to his sons, Howard E., Jr., and the younger Charles. After Howard, Jr., took over management of the H.E. Butt Foundation, Charles Butt, a Wharton graduate, assumed the helm as president in 1971, a year in which sales of $250 million were recorded. He restructured the company's management and recruited several experienced grocery executives to help him make H-E-B a force in the 1970s and 1980s. To that end, H-E-B opened its own ice cream plant, a new bread bakery, a large pastry bakery, and new offices and warehouses during the early and mid-1970s. The new president in 1976 abandoned the firm's long-outdated policies that barred the sale of alcohol and kept the chain's stores closed on Sunday. In addition, H-E-B gained dominant shares of its major markets by drastically lowering its prices, forcing a number of competitors out of business. Butt also began designing the company's first ''Futuremarket,'' which would incorporate a gourmet deli, flower market, and in-store bakery among other features. Meanwhile, Howard E. Butt, Sr., fulfilled a longtime dream when, in 1974, he opened the H.E. Butt Camp, an 1,800-acre camp in the Texas Hill Country where nonprofit and Christian groups could retreat.

1980s–90s: New Store Concepts

H-E-B opened its first superstore, or Futuremarket, in Austin in 1981. The then massive store had 56,000 square feet and was considered a one-stop shopping center. Also in the early 1980s, H-E-B began selling generic goods and added a photo-processing plant to support in-store photo departments. Going into the mid-1980s, H-E-B was operating nearly 150 stores throughout central and south Texas and serving more than one million families. It continued to expand its store offerings with an array of new departments ranging from seafood shops and salad bars to nutrition centers and fast-food, take-home departments. Furthermore, Charles Butt was branching into new markets outside of the grocery store industry. Most notably, H-E-B opened its first H-E-B Video Central/H-E-B Video Superstore outlet in 1987 to capitalize on the booming home video industry; within a few years, H-E-B would tag more than 20 additional video stores onto that division. Another headquarters shift occurred in 1985, when the company moved into San Antonio's Arsenal Complex, the renovated U.S. Army Arsenal; H-E-B had purchased the arsenal from the U.S. government in 1981 and maintained its historical landmarks as part of the renovation.

A secondary benefit of H-E-B's foray into the video store business was that it gave the company an inroad into the massive Houston and surrounding East Texas markets, which it still had not entered by the late 1980s. Indeed, in 1988 H-E-B entered the East Texas market with a new store concept called H-E-B Pantry Foods. These stores were smaller than the superstores and featured only four departments: grocery, meat, produce, and health and beauty. They also focused on value, attempting to minimize operating costs by eliminating nonessential, low-profit departments. H-E-B quickly added to the chain and by 1991 was working to build 22 more Pantry stores in Houston within a year. Debuting in San Antonio in 1991—a year in which the company reached $3 billion in sales—was a much larger format, the H-E-B Marketplace, which spanned 93,000 square feet and included restaurants and a coffee shop/ice creamery. Also in 1991, H.E. Butt, Sr., died. Among his legacies was the successful Howard E. Butt Foundation that he had established in 1934. By the time he died, the foundation had built libraries, swimming pools, charitable food centers, and other amenities in the communities in which Butt stores operated. It had also reached out to the needy in other parts of Texas and even Mexico, among other initiatives. In 1993 H-E-B sold its 33-unit video store chain to Hollywood Entertainment.

At the same time that H-E-B was expanding with smaller stores, it was also engaged in the development of a new venture that would lead to the chain's biggest ever store. In the late 1980s, the innovative Charles Butt dispatched a team to study the great food merchandisers of the world in London, New York, Atlanta, and other places. He used the ideas they brought back to create the unique Central Market, a superstore that threw out the concept of one-stop shopping and emphasized perishable goods. The company opened the first Central Market in Austin in 1994. The store boasted 60,800 square feet and a large, tree-shaded parking lot. In contrast to conventional superstores, the Central Market offered a plethora of fresh foods and flowers, including many exotic goods, while it shunned common items such as detergent, packaged baked goods, and ordinary sodas and cereals. Although the store still emphasized value, it was geared more toward upscale buyers with a greater amount of disposable income.

Mid-1990s and Beyond

By the mid-1990s, the H-E-B chain included 230 stores—65 of the Pantry format. Sales surpassed $5 billion in 1995, when the company celebrated its 90th anniversary. Growth remained on the agenda, and H-E-B took its first step outside of Texas in 1996 with the opening of a Pantry store in Lake Charles, Louisiana. That same year, Charles Butt retired as president of the company, remaining chairman and CEO; James F. Clingman then became the first non-family member to assume the title of president.

The following year H-E-B ventured south, entering Mexico with the opening of a store in Monterrey. By the end of 1999 the company was operating six stores in Mexico—five in Monterrey, a prosperous city with a population of 3.5 million, and one in Saltillo, a town located about 60 miles southwest of Monterrey; one of the stores operated under the name EconoMax, and was similar to the H-E-B Pantry stores. The retail food industry in the United States was becoming increasingly competitive, with H-E-B feeling pressure from retail giant Wal-Mart's move into the grocery trade and from the entrance of the country's number four grocery chain, Safeway, into the Texas market through its 1999 acquisition of Houston-based Randall's Food Markets, Inc. There thus appeared to be more opportunities for growth in Mexico than in the United States. H-E-B succeeded in its first foreign foray by catering to the local consumer—offering only Mexican-made products, which had the additional benefits of lowering transportation costs and eliminating any duties. Meanwhile, back home, H-E-B opened a second Central Market in Austin in 1999.

By the end of the 1990s H-E-B held commanding shares in two of its major markets: 61 percent of the $2.1 billion market in San Antonio and 56 percent of the $1.7 billion market in Austin. In Houston, the company was the number four chain, with 10.1 percent of a $5.4 billion market. Thus, the company began looking both north and south for expansion and began laying the groundwork for a move into the $4.8 billion Dallas/Fort Worth market, with tentative plans to open its first stores there in 2000. In Mexico, where H-E-B was finding the competition less severe and the profit margins higher than at home, the company was planning aggressive growth. H-E-B envisioned a total of 40 stores by 2004 or 2005, with additional stores slated to land in Monterrey; in the border towns of Nuevo Laredo, Reynosa, and Matamoros; and further afield in the south central Mexican towns of Aguascalientes and San Luis Potosí.

Principal Competitors

Albertson's, Inc.; Brookshire Brothers, Ltd.; Brookshire Grocery Company; Carrefour S.A.; Controladora Comercial Mexicana, S.A. de C.V.; Costco Companies, Inc.; Drug Emporium, Inc.; Eckerd Corporation; Fiesta Mart Inc.; Food Lion, Inc.; Grupo Gigante, S.A. de C.V.; IGA, Inc.; Kmart Corporation; The Kroger Co.; Organizacion Soriana, S.A. de C.V.; Randall's Food Markets, Inc.; Rice Food Markets Inc.; Safeway Inc.; 7-Eleven, Inc.; Tosco Corporation; Wal-Mart Stores, Inc.; Walgreen Co.; Whole Foods Market, Inc.

Further Reading

''Charles Butt Fulfills Dream,'' *San Antonio Express-News,* February 21, 1997.

Douglas, Michael, ''H-E-B Bites into Houston Market with Discount Grocery Stores,'' *Houston Business Journal,* November 4, 1991, p. 12.

Dunlap, Lisa, ''HEB Cracks Houston Market with Videos Instead of Groceries,'' *San Antonio Business Journal,* January 9, 1989, p. 3.

Garry, Michael, ''HEB: The Tech Leader?,'' *Progressive Grocer,* May 1996, pp. 63–64, 66, 68.

Halkias, Maria, ''H-E-B Coming to Area: Grocery Chain Strong in Other Texas Cities,'' *Dallas Morning News,* January 14, 1999, p. 1C.

Harper, Roseanne, ''H-E-B Store Connects to Cuisine, and Sales Cook,'' *Supermarket News,* July 21, 1997, pp. 23–27.

Hicks, Leslie, ''H-E-B Growth to Include Louisiana, Maybe Dallas,'' *San Antonio Express-News,* April 15, 1996.

The History of H.E. Butt Grocery Company, San Antonio: H.E. Butt Grocery Company, 1994.

''In an Unfamiliar Limelight: Shy H-E-B Boss to Be Honored for 36-Year Career,'' *San Antonio Express-News,* January 12, 1996.

Kamerick, Megan, ''H-E-B Has Big Plans for Mexican Market,'' *San Antonio Business Journal,* April 2, 1999, p. 1.

Nannery, Matt, ''Minding the Store,'' *Chain Store Age,* April 1998, pp. 61–63.

Pletz, John, ''H-E-B, Then and Now,'' *Austin American-Statesman,* September 12, 1999, p. J1.

Sharpe, Patricia, ''Central Marketing: H.E.B.'s Research Said Austinites Would Rush to a Huge Gourmet Grocery. It Was Right,'' *Texas Monthly,* May 1994, p. 98.

Stuever, Hank, ''A Gourmet World in a Paradigm Shift,'' *Austin American-Statesman,* February 21, 1999, p. L1.

Sultenfuss, Diana, ''H-E-B Processes 130,000 Gallons of AMPI Milk Daily,'' *San Antonio Light,* March 28, 1992.

''Trying to Bag Business: Supermarkets Like H-E-B Hope to Fend Off Wal-Mart in a Soft Economy,'' *U.S. News & World Report,* February 26, 1996.

Vaughan, Vicki, ''H-E-B to Go Further South,'' *San Antonio Express-News,* September 10, 1999.

—Dave Mote
—updated by David E. Salamie

Henry Modell & Company Inc.

498 Seventh Avenue
New York, New York 10018
U.S.A.
Telephone: (212) 822-1000
Toll Free: (800) 275-6633
Fax: (212) 822-1051
Web site: http://www.modells.com

Private Company
Founded: 1889
Employees: 3,200
Sales: $360 million (1998 est.)
NAIC: 45111 Sporting Goods Stores

Henry Modell & Company Inc. is the owner and operator of Modell's Sporting Goods, a retail chain consisting of 84 stores in Delaware, Maryland, New Jersey, New York, Pennsylvania, Virginia, and Washington, D.C. Founded in 1889 by Morris Modell in New York City, the company has grown by offering exceptional value to its customers, based on tough bargaining with suppliers and low overhead. Its expansion has, since the 1960s, been largely due to the purchase of store locations from bankrupt rivals. The firm remains a family-run concern, with the fourth generation of Modells serving as co-presidents. The eighth largest sporting goods retailer in the United States, Modell's Sporting Goods sells athletic apparel, accessories, and footwear as well as sports equipment.

Early History: Thriving on Army Surplus Goods

Morris A. Modell was a Hungarian immigrant who arrived in New York City in the early 1880s, finding work selling clothes to sailors on shore leave. He established his store on a lower Manhattan site (later cleared for the World Trade Center) and founded a company in 1889. Modell supplied outfits for Theodore Roosevelt's Rough Riders during the Spanish-American War and bought surplus army clothing after the war. All of his seven sons worked in the store, but it was Henry who inherited the business after World War I service. He became the company's president in 1920 and chairman in 1937; during this time the business became known as Henry Modell Company, Inc. (and later as Henry Modell & Company Inc.). Modell's, which had stocked up on army surplus merchandise again after World War I, enjoyed record growth during the Great Depression because of its cut-rate prices.

Modell's business also boomed during World War II, when the firm again outfitted soldiers. Its chairman, who was commander of an American Legion post, announced shortly after the end of the war that he would sell the company's entire stock of menswear—which was then in short supply—to war veterans exclusively. In March 1946 the firm opened the Modell Veteran Training Center on lower Broadway. Stocked with surplus war merchandise, this outlet also offered six months of on-the-job paid training to veterans.

When Henry Modell opened the largest of his five stores eight months later in Brooklyn, 15 company-trained veterans constituted the sales staff.

Modell's was creatively combating the peacetime shortage of civilian goods by recycling shell cases into lamp bases, protective covering against attacks into low-priced emergency raincoats, helmets into toys, surplus khaki blankets into children's snow suits, and Air Force trousers into slippers. In 1947 Modell urged merchants to reduce their prices. ''Our stores sold 1,000 dozen of white shirts at $1.95 which cost us $18 per dozen,'' he was quoted as saying in a *New York Times* story, ''and in normal times such merchandising policies are considered unsound. The fact remains that these are not normal times. Merchants owe it to themselves to offer goods at a lower figure, particularly in view of the fact that they themselves are being offered better buys which should be passed on to the public.'' By this time Modell's had sold more than one million pairs of cotton socks at 17 cents each.

When Jackie Robinson made history in 1947 by joining the Brooklyn Dodgers major league baseball team, after a long ban on hiring African American players, Modell's placed Robinson's likeness in the company's advertisements. ''As Jews, we knew what it meant to be outsiders,'' Henry's son, William, later told Ylonda Gault of *Crain's New York Business.* ''Noth-

Corporate Perspectives:

Modell's Sporting Goods strives for quality and excellence by listening, respecting and responding to the needs of our valued associates and customers. We pledge to continue to find innovative ways to deliver exceptional value and quality service.

ing is more important than a sense of community and harmony. My Dad taught me that,'' he added.

Growing in Good and Bad Times: 1963–86

By 1963 Henry Modell Company, Inc. consisted of six stores, including two Modell's Shoppers World outlets in East Meadow, Long Island, and Paramus, New Jersey, which functioned as discount department stores. In that year the company purchased the bankrupt eight-store Davega Stores Corp. sporting goods chain for $311,100. Modell's closed two Davega locations and restaffed the retained stores with young veterans. In 1975 the Modell's chain, now chiefly run by William Modell, consisted of ten stores in New York City and Long Island with sales, in 1974, of $10.5 million and record profits, despite a national recession that struck the metropolitan area particularly hard.

''We are a depression-proof business,'' William Modell told Michael Stern of the *New York Times* at this time. He continued: ''In times like these, we don't have to look hard for [bargain] goods. They are offered to us by the big chains and the manufacturers who want to lighten their inventories for ready cash, and we pass the savings on to our customers.'' The company's forte was high-volume sales of a relatively narrow range of staple items, such as jeans, casual shoes, and work clothing, as well as sporting goods. Stores were plain but often strategically placed in high-traffic locations, such as midtown Manhattan's 42nd Street and downtown Brooklyn's Fulton Street.

By 1986 Henry Modell & Co. was operating 20 stores in the metropolitan area, including one in New Jersey. Sales of its sporting goods and apparel, menswear, athletic footwear, and luggage exceeded $50 million in 1985. By this time William Modell's sons, Michael and Mitchell, were vice-presidents in the firm. Interviewed by Carol R. Riggs for *D&B Reports,* Michael Modell described the company's traditions as the key to its success. ''We're very paternal,'' he said, adding ''The people who work with Modell's are part of the so-called Modell family. Our relationship with our customers is based on two things: Never lose sight of who our customer is and always give him good value. And our relationship with our suppliers is based on loyalty. Our vendors know that although we may negotiate hard on the price, once we agree to pay, that's as good as gold.''

Quadrupling Its Outlets: 1987–99

Although the company sold three Modell's Shoppers World stores to Home Depot Inc. in 1988—turning the business into a real-estate company serving as a landlord to the other stores—it had purchased bankrupt Philadelphia-based Polly Brothers the previous year, and it converted other Shoppers World outlets to sporting goods stores. The company began a major renovation of its no-frills stores and an expansion of its merchandise selection in 1991. By 1995 the chain, now known as Modell's Sporting Goods, had 48 outlets, of which 32 were in the New York metropolitan area and 16 in and around Philadelphia. Annual sales were estimated at about $140 million.

Based in Long Island City, a neighborhood in New York City's borough of Queens, Modell's Sporting Goods Inc., a subsidiary, was being run by Michael Modell. Speaking to a workshop in 1994, he revealed that the chain was fending off mass marketers such as Wal-Mart Stores and The Sports Authority by guaranteeing not only to meet a competitor's price but to rebate 25 percent of the difference between the two prices. Modell's kept its prices low by such means as purchasing six-month-old sneaker styles for sale to customers willing to forgo the latest Air Jordan.

In 1996 Modell's Sporting Goods expanded from 52 to 67 stores by purchasing, for about $2.5 million, 15 outlets in New Jersey and the Baltimore and Washington, D.C. metropolitan areas from bankrupt Herman's World of Sporting Goods, which had been one of Modell's larger competitors. A retail consultant told Gault the reason for the bargain price was that ''They're tough negotiators. They hammer away until the economics work for them. And if the numbers don't add up, they just walk away.'' Prior to the acquisition, Modell's was the 26th largest sporting goods retailer in the United States, with $229 million in annual sales. Modell's Sporting Goods was also planning to open at least five to ten new stores each year for the next five years. The now refurbished chain consisted of larger stores, averaging 15,000 to 20,000 square feet in size, and carried more merchandise, including 400 footwear styles and 200 popular brands and licensed apparel, including Nike and Reebok. Gault wrote that William Modell and his sons were ''as tightfisted when it comes to store design as they are in their lease deals.'' According to the consultant she interviewed, after they took over a Port Chester, New York, linen chain, ''They were in there in three days. A public company would have done surveys, design drawings, construction and months of planning.''

While not turning its back on suburban mall and shopping center outlets, Modell's Sporting Goods was also making inner-city locations profitable by stocking a streetwise eclectic merchandise mix that included trendy clothing and accessories as well as sporting goods and featuring a catchy ''Gotta Go to Mo's'' jingle in radio and television commercials. Many of its stores paid tribute to appropriate sports heroes; the Brooklyn shopping center location bore Dodgers memorabilia and the East Meadow store celebrated hockey's Long Island-based New York Islanders. ''Concept stores,'' such as three Manhattan outlets, carried what was described as in-store miniature boutiques. By this time the chain had found room for women's apparel.

Modell's Sporting Goods opened five Washington, D.C.-area stores in 1996 in former Herman's locations and opened four additional area outlets in 1997, including a Modell Team Stores in the MCI Center, a new downtown arena housing professional basketball's Wizards and hockey's Capitals. But William Modell told Gault that New York City represented the company's ''past, present and future.'' Its warehouse remained in the city's borough of The Bronx, despite what he called

Key Dates:

1889: Morris Modell founds a New York City clothing store.
1946: Modell's opens its fifth store in Brooklyn.
1963: The company purchases bankrupt Davega Stores Corp.
1987: Modell's enters the Philadelphia area through acquisition.
1988: Sale of discount department stores makes Modell's primarily a sporting goods chain.
1996: Modell's buys 15 stores from the bankrupt Herman's chain.

cheaper sites elsewhere, because, he said, ''There's more to life than saving a buck. We have a connection to New York. It's the reason we are successful.''

In 1997 Modell's paid New York's Metropolitan Transportation Authority more than $100,000 to place its logo on Metrocards—good for fares on the city's subway and buses—given out free to baseball fans attending the first regular season game between the Yankees and the Mets. The chain also offered a one-month 15 percent discount to customers carrying the card. Modell's enhanced its ties to New York professional sports teams in 1998, when it opened a mini-store at the training camp of professional football's New York Jets in Hempstead, New York.

By the late 1990s Modell's was spending $20 million annually on advertising its wares on radio and television, in newspapers, and at ball parks such as Yankee Stadium, where its stadium and arena signs could be seen by television viewers as well as ticket holders. William Modell was chairman of the parent company, while sons Michael and Mitchell were co-presidents. To lessen any potential conflicts, Michael was in charge of real estate and finance, while Mitchell was responsible for merchandise and marketing. Each had children but maintained that no pressure would be put on the next generation to join the business. ''You really have to love what you do and enjoy what you do,'' Michael Modell told a CNN interviewer, adding ''So that's a choice only they could make.''

Principal Subsidiaries

Modell's Sporting Goods Inc.

Principal Competitors

The Sports Authority, Inc.; Venator Group Inc.

Further Reading

''Calls on Stores to Cut Mark-Ups,'' *New York Times,* April 10, 1947, p. 42.

''Competing with Category Killers,'' *Chain Store Age Executive,* May 1994, p. S31.

Gault, Ylonda, ''Good Sports,'' *Crain's New York Business,* July 22, 1996, pp. 1, 29.

——, ''Sporting Retailer's Dealmaking Keeps the Ball High in the Air,'' *Crain's New York Business,* April 14, 1997, p. 20.

Geller, Adam, ''Modell's Taking over 16 Herman's Leases,'' *Bergen Record,* July 23, 1996, p. B1.

''Gotta Go to Mo's?: Retail Legend Modell's Keeps Scoring According to 109-Year-Old Game Plan,'' http://cnnfn.com/hotstories/busunu/9807/17/modells_pkg/, July 17, 1998.

Halbfinger, David M., ''M.T.A. Turns Deal Maker in Promoting Metrocards,'' *New York Times,* June 5, 1997, p. B9.

Lisanti, Tony, ''First, Think Out of the Box, Then Get Out of the Box,'' *Discount Store News,* August 10, 1998, p. 17.

Lundegaard, Karen M., ''Modell's Expands in D.C. Area,'' *Washington Business Journal,* May 9, 1997, p. 5.

''Mayor Opens Store Staffed by Veterans,'' *New York Times,* March 23, 1946, p. 28.

Murray, Caryn Eve, ''Modell's Pumped for Growth,'' *Newsday,* September 11, 1996, p. F11.

''New Modell Chain Opening Tomorrow,'' *New York Times,* July 9, 1963, p. 39.

''Preview of Store Staged by Modell,'' *New York Times,* November 13, 1946, p. 45.

Reyes, Sonia, ''Modell's Is on the Move,'' *New York Daily News,* July 22, 1996, p. 18.

Riggs, Carol R., ''Modell's: Family Owned Since 1889,'' *D&B Reports,* July/August 1986, pp. 26–27.

Stern, Michael, ''Business Here Taking Steps Against Recession,'' *New York Times,* February 2, 1975, pp. 1, 42.

Toch, Mark, ''The Modell's Method,'' *WWD—Women's Wear Daily,* January 26, 1995, p. S18.

Waggoner, Walter H., ''Henry Modell, 91; Headed Sporting-Goods Chain,'' *New York Times,* February 16, 1984, p. D27.

—Robert Halasz

Hydro-Quebec

75 Boulevard Rene Levesque West
Montreal, Quebec H2Z 1A4
Canada
Telephone: (514) 289-2211
Fax: (514) 289-3658
Web site: http://www.hydroquebec.com

Joint-Stock Company Owned by the Government of the Province of Quebec
Incorporated: 1944
Employees: 19,500
Sales: $8.8 billion (1998)
NAIC: 221111 Electric Power Generation, Hydroelectric

Hydro-Quebec is one of the world's largest generators of "green" energy. With its subsidiaries, the company constitutes the third largest electric utility in North America. In 1998 Hydro-Quebec provided electricity to more than 3.5 million customers in the Canadian province of Quebec and also supplied electricity to nine municipal systems, one regional cooperative, and 15 electric utilities in the northeastern United States, Ontario, and New Brunswick. As a power marketer, Hydro-Quebec made direct sales to U.S. power wholesalers; through its high-voltage, high-power research center, IREQ, the company was involved in energy-related research and testing. Sales outside Quebec accounted for nearly 11.5 percent of the company's total in 1998.

Montreal Light, Heat & Power Company: 1901–18

The province of Quebec emerged as one of the world's major producers of hydroelectricity in the late 19th century. Construction of the province's first large dam began in 1898, just three years after completion of the world's first hydroelectric plant at Niagara. Hydroelectricity was a powerful force behind the development of Quebec's economy, since many other industries, including aluminum and carbide production, relied on the cheap, abundant power produced on Quebec's raging rivers.

Montreal Light, Heat & Power Company (MLH&P) was formed in 1901 under the leadership of two powerful Montreal financiers, Louis-Joseph Forget and Herbert S. Holt, from three electric companies (Royal Electric Company, Montreal & St. Lawrence Light & Power Company, and Imperial Electric Light Company) and one gas company (Montreal Gas Company). The new organization soon dominated power distribution in and around the city of Montreal.

In 1916 the Civic Investment & Industrial Company, a holding company, was created to acquire the capital stock of MLH&P and the Cedars Rapids Manufacturing & Power Company. The company name was changed to Montreal Light, Heat & Power Consolidated in 1918 to reflect the incorporation of practically all the gas, electric light, and power business in Montreal as one enterprise.

Consolidation and the Great Depression: 1920–41

During the 1920s many energy companies were absorbed by MLH&P, and by 1930 the company owned or controlled six of its former competitors, an electric railway, and a coal and coke plant. The monopoly allowed MLH&P to set prices and reap big profits. From 1910 to 1930, domestic electric rates dropped from nine to three cents per kilowatt hour, and costs fell even faster. Holt held Quebecers' domestic rates at twice those offered in Ontario. Opposition to the "electricity trust" focused on these big profits and came primarily from local businessmen. Others were outraged at the perpetual land leases granted to the MLH&P along with rights to use the streets in suburbs within 100 miles of Montreal.

The Great Depression undermined the finances of many hydroelectric companies around Montreal during the 1930s. MLH&P gained control of Beauharnois Power Company, a large producer of energy on the St. Lawrence River, in 1933. It also took advantage of the economic opportunity to acquire municipal utility companies in Pointe Claire, Baie d'Urfe, and St. Anne de Bellevue. By 1941, MLH&P owned three hydroelectric plants and operated a fourth in cooperation with Shawinigan Water and Power.

Company Perspectives:

Hydro-Quebec's mission is to supply power and to pursue endeavors in energy-related research and promotion, energy conversion and conservation, and any field connected with or related to power and energy.

Provincial Control: 1940s

The Lapointe Commission, formed in 1934, recommended the creation of an Electrical Commission in 1935. The Electrical Commission (later named the Provincial Electricity Board), regulated electric distribution, focusing on rates and services. In 1937 the provincial government adopted a bill that favored municipal control of electrical service.

The Quebec Hydro-Electric Commission, better known as Hydro-Quebec, was created on April 14, 1944, and took over the assets of Montreal Light, Heat & Power Consolidated the next day. The new commission compensated MLH&P shareholders in 1947 but did not settle contracts with minority shareholders in MLH&P subsidiaries Beauharnois Light, Heat & Power and Montreal Island Power until 1953. By 1948 the government had gone a long way toward achieving its goals of reducing rates and standardizing service: residential rates were cut by 20 percent and commercial power prices went down 26 percent.

Building to Meet Demand: 1950s

Demand for cheap power was driven by the defense industry. Aluminum, copper, and nickel refining were in high demand during World War II and on into the military build-up during the Cold War. As a result, many major hydro projects were undertaken in the 1950s.

Hydro-Quebec's first bond offering to U.S. markets was used to finance a project on the Bersimis River. In 1953 Hydro-Quebec undertook a project to widen the Beauharnois canal, which diverted water from the St. Lawrence River to drive hydroelectric plants. The project kept Quebec in the forefront of hydroelectric development in Canada. The next year, the company installed the world's largest submarine power cable, connecting the Bersimis generating facility with the Gaspe Peninsula. The discovery of rich copper mines in this previously undeveloped region raised demand for inexpensive power. The area had been electrified by diesel generators, which cost two to three times as much as hydropower. The cables provided for the complete electrification of the area, 20 percent of which had been without power up to that time.

In 1957 the company sold its gas system to concentrate on water power. After that year, virtually all of Hydro-Quebec's generating capacity came from hydroelectric generators. By the end of the decade, the province of Quebec produced 48.9 percent of Canada's hydroelectricity and was the greatest producer of power per capita in the country. Hydro kept costs low, too: the price per kilowatt hour in Quebec was 33 percent less than that of the United States.

Government Nationalization of Electricity: 1960s

The 1960s were characterized by the purchase by Hydro-Quebec of the private electrical distribution companies. The Shawinigan Water & Power Company, Quebec's largest non-government hydroelectric company, was bought out in 1963 in an effort to standardize rates and services throughout the province. Between 1963 and 1965, 45 rural electrical cooperatives and 19 municipal systems came under government control. They had constituted about one-third of Quebec's power sources. The 1960s also brought technological strides for Hydro-Quebec. In 1963 the company co-sponsored extra-high voltage experiments with Pittsfield Massachusetts's General Electric Company. The 700-kilovolt tests surpassed U.S. voltage limits by 200 kilovolts.

During the 1950s an unfavorable balance of trade with the United States led the Canadian Exporters Association to discourage electric exports because of U.S. quotas and tariffs on many Canadian products. But in 1963, the federal government began to encourage the export of hydroelectricity to U.S. markets. In 1966, after two years of talks, Hydro-Quebec entered into agreements with British Newfoundland Corporation (Brinco) to begin a massive project at Churchill Falls of Newfoundland. The falls at Churchill were a tremendous untapped resource: at 245 feet (50 percent higher than Niagara Falls), Churchill was considered the western world's largest single source of power. Work began at the site in 1967 and was completed in 1970. Hydro-Quebec co-sponsored the project, which diverted the river above the falls into a tunnel to an underground powerhouse. When finished, the project produced more power than all the U.S. and Canadian plants at Niagara Falls.

The James Bay Project and Great Whale: 1971–84

In 1971 the James Bay Development Corporation was created by an act of the Quebec National Assembly to develop natural resources. Increased demand for electricity inspired a plan known as the James Bay project to develop generating stations. The venture was controversial from its inception and throughout its development, with plans calling for the construction of over 200 structures that would alter the courses of 19 waterways in northwest Quebec.

The James Bay project consisted of three different complexes hundreds of miles apart. The La Grande Complex, commonly referred to as James Bay 1, consisted of a series of dams and dikes stretching a total of 41 miles, guiding regional rivers through three generating stations. Despite efforts to stop the project the undertaking was completed in 1985. James Bay 2, commonly known as the "Great Whale" project, began in 1987. The $13.5 billion plan called for the construction of a hydroelectric plant on the Great Whale River and the construction of facilities on the Nottaway, Broadback, and Rupert Rivers.

The project drew opposition from Cree and Inuit Indians, and from international environmentalists, who cited the possibility of higher mercury levels in fish, destruction of caribou habitat, and the unpredictable geological impact of massive artificial reservoirs on the earth's crust as reasons to stop the project.

Key Dates:

1898: Construction begins on Quebec's first large dam.
1901: Montreal Light, Heat & Power Company is formed.
1930: MLH&P has a monopoly on gas and electric light.
1944: Quebec Hydro-Electric Commission (Hydro-Quebec) is created, taking over the assets of MLH&P.
1962: Government nationalizes the electricity industry under Hydro-Quebec.
1967: Construction begins on the Churchill Falls project.
1971: James Bay Development Corporation is created to develop natural resources.
1994: Great Whale project is canceled.
1997: Hydro-Quebec wins approval to sell power in the United States at market rates.

Utility and government officials, on the other hand, pointed out that hydro power does not produce air pollution or wastes, and that if the equivalent of the annual production of the Great Whale complex was produced by thermal power stations, it would be necessary to burn at least 26 million barrels of oil per year. Furthermore, the James Bay Project created thousands of jobs and opened up more than 1,000 miles of roads in previously inaccessible areas. Hydro-Quebec's increased generating capabilities would also enable the company to sell surplus electricity to neighboring provinces and to the United States.

Hydro-Quebec took a number of steps to resolve the concerns that impeded the conclusion of the James Bay projects. In cooperation with the provincial government and native groups, the company participated in environmental impact studies and drafted agreements to hire Native Americans and to award contracts to their firms. Although Hydro-Quebec's own $400 million study suggested that the demand for electricity would justify the $13 billion project, it was canceled by Premier Jacques Parizeau in November 1994.

Reorganization: Early 1990s

Despite the negative publicity it received from Great Whale, Hydro-Quebec instituted several successful programs during the early 1990s that improved both customer and employee relations. In 1993 the company reorganized the administrative structure of its major activities in hopes of improving efficiency and lowering operating expenses—two of the primary goals behind its growing *Defi performance* or ''performance challenge'' program. This long-range project, with its 400 improvement teams involving more than 3,000 employees, played a large part in boosting customer approval ratings to 95 percent in 1994. A broad range of Energy Efficiency Projects helped customers save money without a reduction in comfort.

Hydro-Quebec also earned high marks during the 1990s for its commitment to research and technology. Devoting almost two percent of its revenues and more than 800 employees to developing new computer software, electronics equipment, and various other high-tech projects, the company was generally acknowledged to be one of the Canadian leaders in R & D. In May 1995 the company was named a finalist for the Edison Award in recognition for its many technological breakthroughs during the previous year, which ranged from the Language Expert System, a sophisticated diagnostic software program, to the Organic Electrosynthesis Program, a more efficient method of producing a wide array of chemicals and pharmaceuticals. Once new technologies such as these were developed at its two research sites in Quebec, they were marketed by one of the company's subsidiaries, Nouveler, which negotiated licensing agreements representing some $14 million in revenue during 1994. Nouveler also launched several new companies, such as Scompitech, a firm engaged in the manufacture of a Hydro-Quebec's own newly developed robotic solder system.

Beginnings of Deregulation: 1995–97

By 1995, Quebec had more power than it knew what to do with. Hydro-Quebec's surplus inventory reached 4.2 million kilowatts and the company indicated the province would not need to add any new sources of electricity to its power grid until 2000. Hydro continued its research work on batteries: with its partners, 3M and Argonne National Laboratories, the company was developing prototypes of lithium-polymer storage batteries for electric vehicles, and in Japan, it announced construction of a plant to manufacture small, non-rechargeable batteries for radio frequency identification cards.

The privatization of Hydro remained an issue. In 1996, after a year of province-wide public discussion, industry and political leaders favored the move, but a report by a panel appointed by the government unanimously rejected the idea, pointing out that Quebec's utility rates were 30 to 40 percent cheaper than those of Ontario. The panel acknowledged that the Quebec government could privatize a portion of the company ''for financial reasons.'' These included a debt of $40 billion, the annual awarding of untendered contracts worth $380 million, and a top-heavy, well-paid management structure. The government agreed to create an energy board to regulate Hydro-Quebec, as recommended by the panel.

Meanwhile, deregulation of, and increased competition in, U.S. electricity markets was causing Canada's provincial utilities to make changes. In response to requirements of the U.S. Federal Energy Regulatory Commission (FERC), Hydro-Quebec had already restructured, separating its transmission, generation, and distribution services. In May 1997, the company created a new division, TransEnergy, to operate its transmission network completely separate from its energy services. With that step, along with opening its grid to all suppliers and allowing Quebec municipalities to choose their wholesale power suppliers, Hydro received permission from FERC to sell electricity in the United States at market-based rates, instead of just trading it.

The company's exports to the United States were already triple the amount sent south in 1990. In addition, Hydro was also aggressively diversifying into natural gas, as part of a strategy to provide both types of energy in Canada and the United States.

Moving into New Areas: 1998

Increased exports, international investments, venture capital—1998 was a year of new undertakings for Hydro-Quebec. It created H.Q. Energy Marketing, a holding company charged with conducting energy transactions in Canada and H.Q. Energy Services (U.S.), based in Pittsburgh, to market energy generated outside Quebec. The company indicated it planned to spend some $8 billion over the next ten years to increase its generation capacity by 25 percent, in order to increase its power exports. In line with those plans, it announced an agreement for a new 440 megawatt plant and river diversion plan. Hydro also opened a wind power test facility, exploring renewable energies.

Through its subsidiary, Hydro-Quebec International (HQI), the company developed new international markets for Hydro. These included building a gas turbine in Senegal, purchasing a third of that country's privatized electric company and taking responsibility for providing power to many of its towns, and heading a consortium to build and operate a connection between Peru's northern and southern power grids.

1999 to the Present

Hydro-Quebec was in a good position to take advantage of the changes occurring in the North American and global energy markets. While the province's demand for electricity was predicted to increase moderately, there was little expectation that the retail market would be opened for competition because of Hydro's competitive electricity rates. Not having to worry about retail competition at home, the company was able to concentrate on the deregulated wholesale market in the U.S. Furthermore, through its stake in the holding company Noverco, Hydro was involved in the transportation and distribution of gas. Finally, the company continued to make investments in international energy-related opportunities. With this three-pronged approach, Hydro hoped to become a major energy hub, as called for in the Quebec government's 1996 Energy Policy.

Principal Subsidiaries

Hydro-Quebec International; CapiTech; Societe d'energie de la Baie James; H.Q. Energy Marketing Inc.; H.Q. Energy Services (US) Inc.; H.Q. TransEnergy Inc.; Churchill Falls Corporation (34.2%); Noverco Inc. (41%).

Further Reading

Armstrong, Christopher, and H.V. Nelles, *Monopoly's Moment: The Organization and Regulation of Canadian Utilities, 1830–1930*, Philadelphia: Temple University Press, 1986.

Authier, Philip, ''Why Was Hydro-Quebec Buying Power?'' *Gazette* (Montreal), June 5, 1995, p. A1.

Bolduc, Andre, Clarence Hogue, and Daniel Larouche, *Hydro-Quebec After 100 Years of Electricity,* translated by Sheila Fischman, Libre Expression, 1989.

Coffee, Hoyt E., ''James Bay Power Project Hits a Dam,'' *Site Selection,* February 1992.

''Debate Intensifies over Hydro-Quebec Privatization,'' *Electricity Daily,* April 12, 1996.

Gagnon, Lysiane, ''Great Whale Was Headed for the Beach Long Before Coon Come's Speech,'' *Globe and Mail,* November 26, 1994, p. D3.

Gibbon, Ann, ''Druin Quitting Hydro-Quebec Early,'' *Globe and Mail,* May 4, 1995, p. B10.

——, ''Hydro-Quebec Loses Court Fight,'' *Globe and Mail,* February 25, 1994, p. A1.

Gottschalk, Arthur, ''Hydro-Quebec Gets Nod to Sell Power in the U.S.,'' *Journal of Commerce,* November 17, 1997, p. 3A.

''Hydro-Quebec and 3M Receive $US27.4 Million Contract Through December 1997,'' *Canada NewsWire,* February 20, 1996.

''Hydro-Quebec and Yuasa to Set up Japan's First ACEP Battery Plant,'' *Canada NewsWire,* March 25, 1996.

''Hydro-Quebec Forms New Transmission Unit to Provide Services to Deregulated U.S. Markets,'' *Foster Electric Report,* May 7, 1997, p. 15.

Linteau, Paul-Andre, et al, *Quebec: A History, 1867–1929,* Toronto: James Lorimer & Co., 1983.

McCabe, Aileen, ''Chretien, Hydro-Quebec Light up Senegal,'' *Gazette* (Montreal), November 9, 1999, p. A14.

McKenna, Barrie, ''Study Backs Great Whale Plan,'' *Globe and Mail,* September 1, 1993, p. B1.

McNish, Jacquie, ''Hydro-Quebec Facing Loss of Second Contract,'' *Globe and Mail,* March 30, 1994, p. A1.

''People,'' *Electrical World,* February 1992.

Picard, Andre, ''Is Hydro-Quebec the Wal-Mart of Energy?,'' *Globe and Mail,* May 19, 1994, p. A29.

Ravensbergen, Jan, ''Hydro Digs Deeper into Gas,'' *Gazette* (Montreal), July 9, 1997, p. D1.

Riga, Andy, ''Hydro Exports Booming,'' *Gazette* (Montreal), July 15, 1999, p. F1.

Selby, Beth, ''Hydro-Quebec's Big Power Play,'' *Institutional Investor,* February 1992.

Strategic Plan 2000–2004, Montreal: Hydro-Quebec, 1999.

—April S. Dougal and Jason Gallman
—updated by Ellen Wernick

IMCO Recycling, Incorporated

5215 North O'Connor Boulevard, Suite 94
Irving, Texas 75039
U.S.A.
Telephone: (972) 401-7200
Fax: (972) 401-7342
Web site: http://www.imcorecycling.com

Public Company
Incorporated: 1985 as Frontier Texas Corporation
Employees: 1,867
Sales: $568.5 Million (1998)
Stock Exchanges: New York
Ticker Symbol: IMR
NAIC: 42193 Recyclable Material Wholesalers; 331314 Aluminum Recovering from Scrap; 339999 All Other Miscellaneous Manufacturing

IMCO Recycling, Incorporated is the world's largest recycler of both aluminum and zinc. The company also processes magnesium. IMCO has 23 production facilities in the United States, and owns an aluminum recycling plant in Swansea, Wales, as well as 50 percent of a joint venture that operates two recycling and foundry alloy plants in Germany. IMCO's primary business entails the processing of aluminum, which includes used beverage cans (UBCs), scrap, and dross (a byproduct of aluminum production). In its zinc operations, the company uses furnaces to convert zinc scrap and dross into various value-added zinc products including zinc oxides, dust, and metal. Most of IMCO's processing capacity is utilized to recycle customer-owned materials, for which the company charges a fee—a service called "tolling." Approximately 68 percent of IMCO's total pounds of metal melted involves tolling. The balance of the company's business involves the purchase of scrap and dross for processing, recycling, and reselling. Principal customers of aluminum operations include major aluminum companies as well as manufacturers of automobiles and their suppliers. They, in turn, produce products for transportation, packaging, and construction. A 1991 *Forbes* magazine listing of the 200 best small U.S. companies ranked IMCO 33rd out of the 4,400 publicly traded companies considered for the listing.

Organized as Frontier Texas Corporation in 1985, the company entered the metals arena in September 1986 by purchasing International Metal Company, a recycler of aluminum and magnesium, and renaming itself IMCO. Ralph L. Cheek, formerly the vice-president of the sheet and rod divisions of Kaiser Aluminum and Chemical Corporation, led the company as CEO. By 1987, IMCO was operating two recycling production facilities and reporting revenues of about $40 million. IMCO began developing its network of tolling arrangements with primary producers, as well as expanding its production facilities. To the company's advantage was its capacity to deliver metal in molten form, enabling customers to avoid the cost of remelting.

In response to the increasing demand for its services, the company spent $3.7 million to upgrade and expand its Rockwood, Tennessee aluminum recycling facility in 1992, increasing the plant's capacity by 20 percent. The increased demand for IMCO's services resulted in part from stepped-up production of aluminum can stock by the company's customers, and customer satisfaction with the quality of IMCO's recovery product. In addition to building a new furnace at the Rockwood facility, new shredding and de-lacquering equipment was installed, increasing the plant's ability to recover metal from used beverage cans while improving the quality of metal generated from them.

1992: Support of National Deposit Law

Following the company's facility upgrade at Rockwood, IMCO was prepared for an increased recycling rate. Ten states had already legislated recycling laws, increasing recycling rates to an average of 90 percent. In the other states, recycling rates averaged only 40 to 50 percent, prompting president-elect Bill Clinton, who advocated environmental protection efforts, to speak in favor of mandatory national deposit legislation. Speaking for the recycling industry, Cheek told the New York Society of Security Analysts that "The president-elect is on record favoring national deposit legislation," adding, "Passage of the law could result in a 44 percent increase in the recycling rate to

Company Perspectives:

In its relatively short history, IMCO has achieved an impressive record of meeting our customers' needs and steadily increasing our capacity, diversification and earnings capability. Most important, we have the people, the facilities and the strategy to build on those past achievements and to create further success. The company strategy includes: A commitment to more profitable operations through the Operational Excellence Program, which improves efficiencies at all phases of the business; The company's continued emphasis on supplying the auto industry; And growing through expansion and acquisition activities that have greatly increased IMCO's leadership role within the metals recycling industry.

the 90 percent level over the next two to three years,'' according to Edward Worden of *American Metal Market*. A spokesperson for the Aluminum Company of America stated that a national deposit law would increase beverage prices, inconvenience consumers, and reduce consumer recycling choices. Opposition to mandatory deposits was formidable, especially from lobbyists representing the supermarket industry and the soft drink companies. IMCO, calling itself the ''world's largest independent'' recycler of UBCs, processed 56.8 billion cans in 1991, although it rarely took ownership of the cans and was not a direct player in the can scrap market. Ralph Cheek explained, ''We don't compete with our customers for used beverage cans. We don't buy them. So we have to assume that if we have national deposit legislation, our customers would require additional capacity, and we'd like to offer it.''

IMCO's management evaluated various methods of increasing growth, including the construction of more dedicated capacity operations near customers' plants, expanding facilities, and making acquisitions outside the aluminum recycling area. Operating at near-capacity, the company implemented a secondary stock offering, yielding $5.3 million to finance growth opportunities. In preparation for increased demand, IMCO added 50 percent to its recycling capacity when it opened a $12 million plant in Uhrichsville, Ohio. The new plant added 265 million pounds of annual processing capacity, producing molten aluminum from scrap tolled for the nearby Barmet Aluminum Company. IMCO entered into a contract agreement with Barmet, which gave IMCO the exclusive right to recycle Barmet's scrap over a ten-year period. Scrap delivered by truck to the plant was run through machines that broke the bales, shredded the scrap, removed ferrous materials, and stripped off any coatings before being charged into IMCO's rotary furnaces. The molten metal was then transported in specially designed crucibles to Barmet's holding furnaces, where it remained until cast and rolled into sheet and coil products.

Although the company's zinc recycling segment was operating at only 55 percent of capacity, IMCO's management predicted higher levels of production by hot-dip galvanizers, suppliers of the feedstock, for 1993. The company then acquired Interamerican Zinc, Inc. of Adrian, Michigan, for $5 million cash.

IMCO was honored when it became the 1993 recipient of the Kentucky Governor's Environmental Excellence Award for Industrial Environmental Leadership. *American Metal Market* reported that ''in making the award, the state called the company's Morgantown, Kentucky plant 'an environmental success story,' and praised IMCO Recycling as a company dedicated to environmental protection.'' Accepting the award, Executive Vice-President Richard Kerr said that the facility had a landfill built to hazardous waste standards to store saltcake, a nonhazardous byproduct of aluminum recycling. He commented, ''It protects our customers from third-party mixed landfill clean-up problems and it eliminates the possibility of saltcake leaching into groundwater supplies.'' The company committed further resources into developing a ''closed loop'' production system in which virtually all materials used in the aluminum recycling process would be reclaimed or consumed, greatly reducing the need for landfilling, as well as reducing disposal costs. Byproducts generated in zinc manufacturing, oxides and zinc fines, are either sold to third parties or melted in another process in the zinc manufacturing cycle.

Wall Street analysts were generally optimistic about the outlook for IMCO, describing the company as solid with conservative management practices. When it became apparent that it was time to follow opportunities in the international marketplace, IMCO undertook an executive management reorganization. Ralph Cheek stepped down from his domestic leadership position in order to pursue international opportunities for the company. Replacing him as interim CEO was Don V. Ingram, formerly a chairman of International Metal Company, IMCO board member, and a major shareholder of IMCO stock, with ownership interest of about 11 percent. In 1994, Frank H. Romanelli, former executive vice-president, commercial, for Occidental Chemical Corporation in Dallas, was named president and CEO of IMCO. Romanelli had also served as executive vice-president, petrochemicals, and managed Occidental Chemical's international division, which operated 15 plants in seven countries. Romanelli said he would continue to stress profitable expansion of recycling capacity and cost containment while emphasizing quality service to aluminum industry customers. Richard L. Kerr was named president of the metals division and chief operating officer. Formerly, Kerr had worked for a period of 15 years with Aluminum Company of America, followed by executive management positions with IMCO.

1995: Supplying the Transportation Industry

The U.S. aluminum industry continued to grow rapidly, largely through the use and recycling of beverage cans. The company expected the recycling rate for UBCs to continue to grow, especially compared to other materials such as glass or plastic. IMCO anticipated increased possibilities in other countries as well. In 1995 primary aluminum accounted for 35 percent of the metal used to make aluminum cans, down from 73 percent in the prior decade. During that period recycling and imports supplied the metal for growth. One of the hurdles the industry faced was the intense competition from makers of polyethylene terephthalate bottles. Responding to competition from plastic container producers, aluminum recyclers began looking to the transportation industry as a growth market through the wider use of aluminum parts in automobiles and

Key Dates:

1985: Company is founded and headquartered in Irving, Texas.
1987: IMCO purchases International Metal Company.
1992: IMCO completes $3.7 million upgrade of its Rockwood Tennessee aluminum recycling facility.
1995: IMCO reaches record-high revenues, with processing volume passing one billion pounds.
1998: IMCO buys U.S. Zinc Corporation for $72 million.
1999: General Motors agrees to buy more than $1 billion worth of recycled aluminum, which will be processed by IMCO.

trucks. The aluminum castings market was expected to rise significantly because of the transportation industry's interest in producing lighter-weight vehicles.

IMCO began focusing on the aluminum scrap-based manufacture of specification aluminum ingot for die casters as part of its latest strategy. At the close of 1995, IMCO formed a 50 percent joint venture with VAW Aluminum AG, the largest aluminum company in Germany. VAW owned and operated two recycling and foundry alloy facilities, and principally served the European automotive markets. The company also acquired five aluminum recycling plants. The five facilities had a combined annual capacity of 390 million pounds. Four were obtained through the purchase of privately held Alumar Associates, Inc., of Chicago Heights, Illinois, owner of Metals Mark, Inc., which operated aluminum recycling plants in Chicago Heights, Illinois; Pittsburg, Kansas; Sikeston, Missouri; and had a 50 percent-owned facility in East Chicago, Indiana. IMCO also acquired Phoenix Smelting Corporation, an aluminum recycling plant in Loudon, Tennessee. IMCO announced that its ''recently purchased'' aluminum recycling plant in Pittsburgh, Kansas, was ''outdated and inefficient,'' and would be closed down—and the scrap processed at that facility was shifted to the company's other facilities. The company then began making financial arrangements for the purchase of three western U.S. aluminum recycling plants and other assets from EnviroSource Inc. for $58 million. The companies were among the few in North America capable of treating nonhazardous byproducts of primary and secondary aluminum smelting, such as cake and drosses, which otherwise were shipped to landfills.

1996: Restructuring into Four Business Segments

IMCO established four company segments: commercial (which encompassed sales, marketing, customer relations, business development, emerging technologies, international activities, metal procurement, and trading, headed by Richard Kerr); manufacturing; purchasing, chasing and engineering; and finance. After about two years in office, Frank Romanelli resigned from his position as IMCO president, CEO, and board member. A press release stated that he ''left to pursue other business interests.'' U.S. exports of aluminum remelt secondary ingot (RSI) became flat during that period, largely due to China's withdrawal from the market. Japan had been a driving force in the RSI export market until 1996 when demand dried up because of Japan's excess smelter furnace capacity being put to use in providing UBC/RSI to can sheet rolling mills. Following the loss of the Asian business IMCO shut down its RSI plant in Corona, California. The company began construction of an aluminum recycling facility in Coldwater, Michigan, for a joint venture with Alchem and reached full operating capacity by the end of 1997. Through its IMCO Recycling Ltd. subsidiary in the United Kingdom, IMCO constructed an aluminum recycling facility in Swansea, Wales, adjacent to a plant owned by a subsidiary of Alcoa, the Swansea facility's principal customer under a long-term tolling agreement.

In late 1997 the company sold more than 2.6 million shares of common stock in a public offering and modified agreements with lenders to make as much as $200 million available for acquisitions. In the following year, IMCO purchased Houston, Texas-based U.S. Zinc Corporation and its subsidiaries, for $72 million, giving the company a second business segment, and adding five production facilities in Illinois, Texas, and Tennessee. IMCO also acquired all the assets of a zinc oxide production facility from North American Oxide in Clarksville, Tennessee. Two aluminum recycling businesses, IMSAMET and Rock Creek Aluminum Inc., were acquired. IMSAMET owned or had a majority interest in three plants located in Idaho, Arizona, and Utah. The company had a 50 percent interest in SALTS, a Utah facility that used a proprietary process to reclaim materials from salt cake. Rock Creek operated two facilities in Ohio that utilized milling, shredding, blending, testing, and packaging equipment to process various types of raw materials, including aluminum dross and scrap, into aluminum products used as metallurgical additions in the steelmaking process for steel producers. Through IMCO's purchase of Alchem, the company increased its participation in the automotive industry, broadening its customer base and expanding its product range to include specification alloys.

1999: Two Major Contracts Signed

Production of recycled aluminum creates energy savings of 95 percent when compared with production of primary aluminum from ore. About 65 percent of the aluminum used in vehicles is recycled metal, and it can be recycled again and again without loss of its original properties. In order to meet production requirements for supplying the auto industry, IMCO's subsidiary Alchem Aluminum announced plans to build a large smelting plant on a Saginaw, Michigan site, but was stymied by protests from the community. Public concern centered on the potential dangers presented by the large number of trucks carrying molten metal that would be in the area. The smelting facility was scheduled to have opened by the first quarter of 2000, but was delayed until a more suitable site could be found. IMCO needed a plant capable of producing secondary aluminum specification alloys for General Motors, including cylinder blocks and heads for the automaker's ''Atlas'' I-6 overhead-cam engines for light-duty trucks. General Motors signed a 13-year contract with IMCO, representing $1 billion worth of recycled aluminum. The company responded to potential production delays by temporarily shifting the GM order to its other alloy-producing facilities in Michigan and Tennessee. By 1999, the transportation sector represented about 30 percent of the company's annual scrap processing volume, compared to less than five percent in 1994.

In addition to broadening its customer base via the automotive industry, IMCO stepped up production of aluminum products needed in the building and construction industry. A major plant expansion and upgrade was implemented in IMCO's Uhrichsville, Ohio facility to better serve that market. The company signed a ten-year contract with Alcan Aluminum Ltd. to buy primary aluminum—from wheels to body panels—at predictable prices for ten years. IMCO would then supply more than three billion pounds of recycled aluminum to a rolling mill owned by Commonwealth Industries.

Volume at facilities that served the auto and truck component market were quite strong in 1999, but production levels at some of the company's plants that served the can market were negatively affected by the narrow spread between the aluminum scrap price and the primary metal price which reduced customer demand for recycled metal. IMCO adjusted by changing operating and employment levels. In an effort to meet the long-term agreement with GM, IMCO finalized plans to build a $22 million plant in Zilwaukee, Michigan. The company expected aluminum content in GM vehicles to rise seven percent or more a year for the foreseeable future. GM and Alcan agreed to share technology on new alloys that could lead to more aluminum being used in cars and trucks, and to work together in recycling that aluminum. A company report quoted John Stiles, GM executive director of worldwide purchasing–metallic, "Our engineers will be able to take advantage of the newest technology as they plan future cars and trucks because we will have a steady supply of aluminum," adding that "The increased use of aluminum is helping to significantly reduce the weight of our cars and trucks." The amount of IMCO's capacity dedicated to recycled aluminum alloys for the transportation industry continued to grow—and was expected to triple over the next several years.

Principal Subsidiaries

Alchem Aluminum Incorporated; Alchem Aluminum Shelbyville, Incorporated; Imsamet Incorporated; Interamerican Zinc, Incorporated; Mark Metal Incorporated; U.S. Zinc Corporation; Pittsburgh Aluminum, Incorporated; Rock Creek Aluminum, Incorporated; IMCO Energy Corporation; IMCO Investment Company; IMCO Management Partnership L.P.; IMCO Recycling of California, Incorporated; IMCO Recycling of Ohio, Incorporated.

Principal Competitors

Kaiser Aluminum Corporation; Alcoa Aluminum Corporation.

Further Reading

"IMCO Appoints Executives As Firm Restructures," *American Metal Market,* November 11, 1994, p. 9.

"IMCO Wins Environmental Award," *American Metal Market,* October 25, 1993, p. 20.

Marley, Michael, "Kerr Cites Can for Aluminum Rise," *American Metal Market,* November 15, 1995, p. 6.

Palmeri, Christopher, "Obscure Is Beautiful," *Forbes,* April 24, 2995, p. 406.

Selland, Kerri J., "IMCO Unveils New Uhrichsville Plant," *American Metal Market,* June 14, 1993, p. 8.

Tanner, Lisa, "Recycler Expects Boost from New White House," *Dallas Business Journal,* November 13, 1992, p. 39.

Worden, Edward, "Aluminum RSI Export Market Flat," *American Metal Market,* October 2, 1997, p. 7.

Worden Ralph, "IMCO Chief Backs Bottle Bill," *American Metal Market,* November 12, 1992, p. 2.

——, "IMCO Looks to Hike Zinc Recycling Rate; Used Just 55 Percent of Capacity in 1992," *American Metal Market,* April 16, 1993, p. 9.

——, "IMCO Recycling Sets up Four Business Segments," *American Metal Market,* February 23, 1996, p. 7.

——, "U.S. Zinc Buy Makes IMCO Top Zinc Recycler," *American Metal Market,* July 27, 1998, p. 7.

—Terri Mozzone

Imperial Sugar Company

One Imperial Square
Post Office Box 9
Sugar Land, Texas 77487-0009
U.S.A.
Telephone: (281) 491-9181
Toll Free: (800) 727-8427
Fax: (281) 491-9895
Web site: http://www.imperialholly.com

Public Company
Incorporated: 1924
Employees: 3,800
Sales: $1.78 billion (1998)
Stock Exchanges: American
Ticker Symbol: IHK
NAIC: 311312 Cane Sugar Refining; 311313 Beet Sugar Manufacturing; 311999 All Other Miscellaneous Food Manufacturing

Imperial Sugar Company holds the number one position in refined sugar in the United States, with a market share of about 33 percent. The company refines raw cane sugar at four facilities in Texas, Georgia, Florida, and Louisiana, and processes beet sugar at 11 processing plants in California, Wyoming, Montana, and Michigan. Its line of sugar products includes several well-known regional brands: Imperial Sugar (Southwest), Dixie Crystals (Southeast), Pioneer Sugar (Great Lakes region), Holly Sugar (intermountain West), and Spreckels Sugar (California). The company also sells sugar under private labels and markets the Wholesome Foods brand, the national leader in organic sweeteners. In addition to its sugar operations, Imperial Sugar derives about one-quarter of its revenues from its foodservice business, which sells a variety of nonsugar products—from drink mixes to plastic cutlery—to restaurants, healthcare institutions, schools, and other entities. Imperial Sugar traces its history back to 1843, when a sugar refinery was erected on a small sugar plantation in Sugar Land, Texas. The fledgling sugar enterprise grew as the nation grew, adopted the name Imperial Sugar Company during the early 20th century, then merged in 1988 with Holly Sugar Company—a beet sugar producer with roots stretching back to 1905—to form Imperial Holly Corporation. Following the acquisitions of Spreckels Sugar Company in 1996, Savannah Foods & Industries, Inc. in 1997, and Wholesome Foods L.L.C. and Diamond Crystal Specialty Foods, Inc. in 1998, the company changed its name back to Imperial Sugar Company in 1999.

19th-Century Origins

In 1820 a rush of Anglo-American settlers began colonizing the vast region that 25 years later would become the state of Texas. Through the recruiting efforts of Moses and Stephen Austin, who promised to carry out their father's plan to populate the territory, Texas' population swelled enormously in the years following 1820, jumping from 7,000 in 1821 to 50,000 by 1836—by far exceeding Stephen Austin's promise to bring at least 300 families into the area. Texas became an independent republic in 1835, and its citizens voted the following year in favor of annexation by the United States. Statehood would be another nine years away, however, delayed as lawmakers debated whether or not to extend slavery into the new region. Another 60 years would pass before oil, the chief engine that would drive the state's economy, first erupted from a well near Beaumont, Texas. During the six decades that separated Texas' admittance to the Union and the discovery of oil, other agricultural and manufacturing industries fueled the region's growth, including the cultivation and processing of sugarcane.

Although the first sugar refinery in the United States began operations in 1689, sugar production did not become a major U.S. industry until the 1830s. Early settlers into Texas took up the trade upon their arrival. One such colonist was Samuel May Williams, who owned a sugar crop on Oakland Plantation in southeast Texas in a community that later would be aptly named Sugar Land. Initially, the sugarcane was used to produce syrupy sweeteners, but by 1843—two years before Texas became a U.S. state—Williams and other neighboring farmers were harvesting sufficient sugarcane to warrant the construction of a commercial raw sugar mill. Completed that same year, the mill enabled the cooperative of sugar farmers to make granulated sugar. Imperial Sugar Company was spawned from this first

Company Perspectives:

In 1999, we changed our name from Imperial Holly Corporation to Imperial Sugar Company. A name recognized and trusted in the food industry for over 150 years. Although our name says ''sugar'' we are much more. Imperial Sugar Company maintains a portfolio of successful consumer sugar brands, has expanded its distribution and production facilities from coast to coast, and reaches further into the specialty products, foodservice and healthcare industries. Now with over 500 years of combined experience, Imperial Sugar is equipped and prepared to continue the reputation of dedication to quality.

mill, with the site Williams chose for Sugar Land's first sugar refinery serving as the site of Imperial Sugar/Holly's sugar production over the next 150 years.

Before long, Williams's Oakland Plantation and the mill were sold to W.J. Kyle and B.F. Terry, under whose stewardship the property became known as Sugar Land Plantation, one of several sugarcane farms in a region referred to as the ''sugar bowl.'' Kyle and Terry profited from their investment, as Sugar Land Plantation flourished in the years leading up to the Civil War, but the outbreak of the war signaled more prosaic growth for many of the sugar bowl's farmers. Once the war ended, sugar production in the region declined considerably and the number of sugar mills dropped to slightly more than a handful.

After the deaths of Kyle and Terry, Sugar Land Plantation and a majority of the other plantations in the area that had withstood the effects of the depressed agricultural climate were purchased by Edward H. Cunningham. Cunningham spent a considerable amount of money modernizing Sugar Land Plantation, investing more than a million dollars in machinery and construction projects by 1890. Slightly more than a decade later, however, Cunningham's holdings devolved into receivership and were stripped away from him by disgruntled and unpaid creditors. Sugar Land Plantation, along with the other properties formerly belonging to Cunningham, was acquired in 1905 by I.H. Kempner, his mother, and siblings, as well as W.T. Eldridge.

Early 20th Century: Development of Imperial Sugar

In the nearly 60 years since the first sugar mill was erected in Sugar Land, the property had passed through three sets of hands, and now, with the arrival of the new century, Kempner and Eldridge had become its fourth owners. There it would stay, remaining in the Kempner family for the next 80 years. I.H. Kempner and his descendants steered the company through its development from a small collection of sugar production properties to one of the largest sugar producers in the United States.

Kempner and Eldridge, like Cunningham, poured capital into their newly acquired properties, renovating the sugar production facilities and the community of Sugar Land itself. Toward the end of the 19th century Sugar Land was ignominiously branded ''Hell Hole of the Brazos''—a swampy area populated by ex-convicts, drifters, professional gamblers, and deserters from ships sailing to and from the port of Galveston. Kempner and Eldridge sought to ameliorate this disreputable image of their town by draining the land and paving new gravel streets. In the process, Sugar Land became a company town, managed by the company, with company-owned stores—such as the Imperial Mercantile Company general store—catering to the residents. Later, churches, hospitals, and schools were constructed, additions that attracted more respectable Sugar Land denizens and gave Kempner and Eldridge a community upon which to build their sugar empire.

The sugar properties owned by Kempner and Eldridge were known as Sugarland Industries until 1924. At that time, Imperial Sugar Company was incorporated to take over the properties owned by Sugarland Industries, including Sugar Land Feed Company and Imperial Mercantile Company. The name ''Imperial'' came from New York City's Hotel Imperial, one of the lavish hotels that graced the city's Herald Square in the 1890s. As a college student, Kempner had visited the hotel, been impressed by it, and decided to borrow its name as the name of his sugar company, co-opting the crown symbol from the hotel's stationery as well.

Imperial's sugar refinery by this point could produce 1.5 million pounds of sugar per day, a production capacity that required the importation of raw sugar from Cuba and the West Indies to keep the facility in operation throughout the year. Raw sugar was shipped to Galveston, unloaded in 300-pound burlap bags, then sent by rail to the refinery at Sugar Land, where granulated sugar was packaged in 25-, 50-, and 100-pound cloth bags bearing the Imperial brand name. By 1927, the company was producing slightly more than 300 million pounds of sugar per year and annual revenues had climbed to nearly $19 million. These results were encouraging, but the company would not eclipse these figures until the eve of World War II.

1930s Through Early 1980s: Fluctuating Fortunes

When the Great Depression descended on the country, stifling economic growth and forcing many businesses into bankruptcy, Imperial Sugar was not immune to its effects. The company's yearly sugar production and revenue totals both dropped substantially during the decade-long economic downturn. Revenues plunged from $18.8 million in 1927 to $6.3 million in 1932, and annual sugar production during the period fell from 219 million pounds to 165 million pounds—exceeding the magnitude of the recessive conditions following the Civil War. Moreover, the decline recorded between 1929 and 1932 did not represent the end of Imperial Sugar's financial woes. As the Depression dragged on into the mid-1930s, the company went into the red and was forced to cut its workforce from 500 to 373. Imperial Sugar lost money every year between 1932 and 1937, recording its greatest loss in 1932, when the company showed nearly $300,000 in negative net income, down from the $750,000 gain it had posted in 1928.

Despite the losses, Imperial Sugar—through a wholly owned subsidiary named Fort Bend Utilities Company—spent $300,000 on a power plant, which supplied the sugar producer's energy needs. When the power plant was completed in 1937, the company was beginning to emerge from the effects of the Depression, generating $15.9 million in revenues that year and

Key Dates:

1843: A commercial raw sugar mill is constructed in a southeast Texas community later named Sugar Land.
1905: The Sugar Land Plantation and sugar mill are acquired by I.H. Kempner and partner and are operated as Sugarland Industries; the first Holly Sugar factory is built in Holly, Colorado.
1924: Sugarland Industries is incorporated as Imperial Sugar Company.
1927: Company is producing more than 300 million pounds of sugar per year; annual revenues reach nearly $19 million.
1932: At height of Great Depression, company posts a $300,000 net loss.
1938: Production increases to nearly 400 million pounds of sugar.
1988: Imperial Sugar merges with Holly Sugar Company, a sugarbeet processor, to form Imperial Holly Corporation, a publicly traded firm.
1996: Imperial Holly acquires California-based Spreckels Sugar Company, Inc.; Dublin-based Greencore Group PLC acquires a 27 percent stake in Imperial Holly.
1997: Company acquires Savannah Foods & Industries, Inc. for $567 million.
1998: The acquisitions of Diamond Crystal Specialty Foods and Wholesome Foods, L.L.C. are completed.
1999: Imperial Holly changes its name back to Imperial Sugar Company.

$19.7 million the following year, at last eclipsing the total recorded in 1927. Annual sugar production increased as well, climbing to nearly 400 million pounds in 1938, offering persuasive proof that the hard times were over.

After the war, the Eldridges sold their stake in Imperial Sugar and the Kempners became majority owners of the company, which by the end of the 1940s was recording nearly $1 million a year in net income. The production capacity of the refinery at Sugar Land by this time had been increased to two million pounds per day, and by a decade later reached 2.25 million pounds per day, as the company expanded to meet rising demand during the postwar economic boom period. During the 1950s, Imperial Sugar's financial performance fluctuated wildly, in part due to President Eisenhower's embargo against Cuba, then the company's principal source of raw sugar. The company's annual net income wavered between $395,000 and $1.2 million during the decade, foreshadowing more difficult years to come.

Since the beginning of the century, the sugar industry had been subjected to federal regulation that, as time wore on, threatened to price sugar out of the U.S. market. During the 1960s and 1970s, as regulatory measures continued to inflate the price of domestic raw sugar, Imperial Sugar avoided much of the damage incurred by sugar producers located elsewhere. The migration of candy factories and bottlers into the Sun Belt during the period buoyed the company's business. By the end of the 1970s, however, the sugar industry had changed significantly and Imperial Sugar's position began to appear tenuous.

Sugar use experienced a precipitous decline during the 1970s, falling even as total sweetener consumption remained steady. From 1973 to 1983, Americans consumed 124 pounds of sweetener per person annually, yet sugar's share dropped from 107 pounds of the annual total to 71 pounds during the ten-year period. Corn sweeteners moved into the breach, increasing in usage by 130 percent. Exacerbating matters for sugarcane processors was the burgeoning popularity of artificial sweeteners such as saccharin and aspartame, as well as the rising price of domestic raw sugar. By the early 1980s, domestic raw sugar sold for 22 cents a pound, double the world market price. Imperial Sugar's management, now led by I.H. Kempner III, searched for a solution to the difficulties that lay ahead.

Late 1980s and Early 1990s: Merger with Holly Sugar

Imperial Sugar by this time was generating roughly $230 million a year in revenue, recording nearly $13 million a year in net income, and producing nearly a billion pounds of sugar annually. The totals were prodigious for a producer in the U.S. sugar industry, but they also reflected the uncertainties of a business derived exclusively from the refining of sugarcane. What the company lacked was a stake in those segments of the sugar market that were expanding, including companies that produced sugar from stock feed other than sugarcane. The realization of this need brought Imperial Sugar's management in contact with Holly Sugar Company, a producer that used sugarbeets instead of sugarcane to make sugar. The resulting association between the two companies would alter Imperial Sugar's future dramatically.

In 1905, the same year Kempner and Eldridge acquired Sugar Land Plantation, the first Holly Sugar factory was constructed in Holly, Colorado, just in time for the sugarbeet harvest that year. From the harvest the fledgling company produced 60,000 100-pound bags of sugar, enough to justify and help pay for the addition of a second factory in Swink, Colorado. Several years later, in 1911, expansion continued, this time across state borders into California, where Holly Sugar constructed a beet sugar factory in Huntington Beach. After the company's expansion into Wyoming in 1915, a wealthy Colorado businessman named A.E. Carlton acquired the company and spearheaded its subsequent vigorous growth. Either through acquisition or plant construction, Holly Sugar added ten factories to its growing list of facilities between 1916 and 1931. As the company expanded its sugarbeet operations, it also diversified into other business arenas, including livestock feeding operations and oil production and refining. By the mid-1980s, however, as Imperial Sugar was weighing its future moves in an increasingly volatile sugar market, Holly Sugar had been forced to close 12 beet sugar factories and divest its other business interests.

Imperial Sugar's management began actively courting Holly Sugar in 1987, convinced that the two companies would be more capable of competing in the sugar industry together than they would be apart. In October 1987, Imperial offered to pay

Holly Sugar's stockholders $68 for each of Holly Sugar's 1.1 million outstanding shares, in addition to giving them one share in the combined company, which would cede a 23 percent stake in the merger to Holly Sugar's stockholders. Imperial Sugar's offer, however, was not the only one Holly Sugar's management had to consider.

Just prior to Imperial Sugar's attempt at effecting a merger between the two companies, a Melville, New York-based investment group named Plum Associates, led by Illinois businessman Peter R. Harvey, offered Holly Sugar a $94.3 million, two-stage takeover plan. Holly Sugar initially rebuffed Imperial Sugar's proposal, favoring instead Plum Associates' offer, but before two months had passed, Plum Associates cut its tender offer to $85 million. As a result, negotiations with Imperial Sugar resumed, leading to a definitive agreement between the two in December 1987 that stipulated Imperial Sugar would acquire Holly Sugar for $78.5 million plus cede a 25 percent stake in the merged company. The following April, Holly Sugar's shareholders approved the merger, joining together Holly Sugar's eight beet sugar processing facilities—four in California, two in Wyoming, and one each in Montana and Texas—and Imperial Sugar's Sugar Land refinery, which created a new $660 million sugar concern named Imperial Holly Corporation. Also as a result of the merger, Imperial Holly became a publicly traded firm for the first time, although the Kempner family retained a stake of about 38 percent. Initially traded on the NASDAQ, the stock moved to the American Stock Exchange in 1990.

After the merger, Imperial Holly's annual revenues initially rose to $717 million in 1990, but then the company recorded consecutive declines in 1991, 1992, and 1993. Entering the mid-1990s, Imperial Holly continued to suffer from external market forces that prevented the company from realizing the true benefits of the 1988 merger. The most damaging of these developments continued to be the depressed prices for refined sugar, which fell 11 percent between 1989 and 1994. More unexpected were losses resulting from adverse weather and disease in 1994, which froze beets in the Midwest and infected them in California, contributing to the $7.9 million loss the company recorded in 1994. Meanwhile, on the management front, James C. Kempner was named company president and CEO in 1993, with I.H. Kempner III, brother of James, continuing as chairman.

Late 1990s: Acquisitions Spree and the Return of Imperial Sugar

In the wake of the 1996 Farm Bill, which eliminated certain government controls on sugar allotments, the sugar industry entered a period of consolidation, with Imperial Holly being one of the most active consolidators. In April 1996 the company acquired California-based Spreckels Sugar Company, Inc. for about $28 million in cash. Spreckels was a beet sugar processor and marketed a leading West Coast sugar brand, Spreckels. Imperial Holly, which held approximately 16 percent of the national sugar market at this time, managed to post its first profit since 1990 for the 1996 fiscal year. In August 1996 Dublin-based Greencore Group PLC, the only processor of sugar in Ireland, spent about $50 million to take a 27 percent stake in Imperial Holly and gain two seats on the company board. Imperial Holly used the injection to pay down debt and accelerate its capital improvement program.

In December 1997 Imperial Holly completed a $567 million acquisition of Savannah Foods & Industries, Inc., which had fiscal 1996 revenues of about $1.2 billion. Based in Savannah, Georgia, Savannah Foods was best known for its Dixie Crystals sugar brand, which was marketing throughout the Southeast. Savannah Foods operated three cane sugar refineries in Georgia, Louisiana, and Florida, and four sugarbeet processing plants in Michigan, with the latter stemming from its 1984 acquisition of Michigan Sugar Company and 1985 purchase of Great Lakes Sugar Company. The combination of Imperial Holly and Savannah Foods created the leading sugar refiner and processor in the United States, with a market share of 33 percent. Imperial Holly now owned five leading regional consumer sugar brands: Imperial Sugar, Dixie Crystals, Pioneer, Holly, and Spreckels (the Pioneer brand came to the company through Savannah Foods' Michigan operations). Imperial Holly also became a national supplier of sugar and sweetener products to industrial food manufacturers. The acquisition also helped increase the company's revenues to $1.78 billion for the 1998 fiscal year, more than double the year-earlier figure of $766.1 million.

In the late 1990s Imperial Holly remained vulnerable to the fluctuations engendered by government intervention in the sugar industry and by the industry's cyclical nature. As it looked to the 21st century, the company sought to ameliorate these influences by diversifying its operations into higher margin, higher growth, noncommodity sectors of the food industry. It already had a start on this through Dixie Crystals Brands, Inc., which was acquired with Savannah Foods and was a leading supplier of packaged sugar, sugar substitutes, and related products to the foodservice industry. In November 1998 Imperial Holly acquired Wilmington, Massachusetts-based Diamond Crystal Specialty Foods, Inc. for $143 million in cash, stock, and assumed debt. Diamond Crystal produced nutritional dry mixes, sauces, seasonings, drink mixes, and desserts for distribution to the foodservice industry, including hotels, restaurants, hospitals, and schools. Imperial Crystal combined Dixie Crystal and Diamond Crystal into a new foodservice operation called Diamond Crystal Brands, Inc. In less than a year, foodservice revenue had grown to represent one-quarter of overall revenues. In another move that increased Imperial Crystal's involvement in higher margin sectors, the company spent $5.1 million to acquire Daytona Beach, Florida-based Wholesome Foods, L.L.C., the leading marketer of organic sweeteners in the nation as well as the marketer of Sucanat, the number one organic sweetener in the United States. In the aftermath of all of these acquisitions, Imperial Holly's leaders concluded that the company's name was no longer appropriate for a firm with a national presence and a number of brands. In early 1999, then, the company returned to its roots and readopted the name Imperial Sugar Company.

Principal Subsidiaries

Holly Sugar Corporation; Savannah Foods & Industries, Inc.; Savannah Foods Industrial, Inc.; Dixie Crystals Brands, Inc.; Michigan Sugar Company; Imperial Sugar LP; Savannah Sugar

LP; Imperial Distributing, Inc.; Diamond Crystal Specialty Foods, Inc.

Principal Competitors

Alliant Foodservice Inc.; American Crystal Sugar Company; CSM nv; Corn Products International, Inc.; SYSCO Corporation; Tate & Lyle PLC; U.S. Foodservice.

Further Reading

Antosh, Nelson, ''For Growers of Sugar Beets and Cane, Business Is . . . Sweet and Sour,'' *Houston Chronicle,* 2 Star Sec., p. 1.

——, ''Holly Gets Sweeter by the Day: Sugar Maker Buys Food Service Firm,'' *Houston Chronicle,* September 9, 1998, 3 Star Sec., p. 1.

——, ''Imperial Buys Niche Sugar Firm,'' *Houston Chronicle,* 3 Star Sec., p. 1.

——, ''Imperial Holly, Irish Firm Cut Deal: Greencore Acquires 27% of Stock,'' *Houston Chronicle,* July 27, 1996, 2 Star Sec., p. 1.

——, ''Investors Cane Imperial Sugar,'' *Houston Chronicle,* 3 Star Sec., p. 1.

Armstrong, R.M., *Sugar Land, Texas, and the Imperial Sugar Company,* Sugar Land, Tex.: R.M. Armstrong, 1991.

Baldwin, William, ''Bitter Taste,'' *Forbes,* November 7, 1983, p. 128.

Bodipo-Memba, Alejandro, ''Savannah Foods to Be Acquired by Imperial Holly for $525 Million,'' *Wall Street Journal,* September 9, 1997, p. B10.

Bodipo-Memba, Alejandro, and Jennifer Lee, ''Imperial Holly Seeks To Acquire Savannah Foods,'' *Wall Street Journal,* August 27, 1997, p. A4.

''Imperial Holly Annual Sales Pegged at $2 Billion Following Merger,'' *Milling & Baking News,* December 9, 1997, p. 11.

''Imperial Sugar Agrees to Buy Holly for Cash and a Portion of Stock,'' *Wall Street Journal,* December 28, 1987, p. 24.

''Ireland's Greencore to Acquire 27% of Imperial Holly Corp.'' *Milling & Baking News,* August 6, 1996, p. 9.

''Merger of Sugar Companies to Create 'National Scope,' '' *Milling & Baking News,* September 30, 1997, p. 9.

Moreno, Jenalia, ''Imperial Holly Aims to Be No. 1 in Sugar with Deal,'' *Houston Chronicle,* August 28, 1997, 3 Star Sec., p. 1.

——, ''Imperial's Realm Grows with Victory,'' *Houston Chronicle,* September 13, 1997, 3 Star Sec., p. 1.

''Shareholders Approve Merger with Texas Sugar Concern,'' *Wall Street Journal,* April 27, 1988, p. 7.

''Sugar Processor Cuts Payout by Two-Thirds, Sets Layoffs,'' *Wall Street Journal,* October 29, 1993, p. B9A.

Totty, Michael, ''Holly Sugar Receives Bid by Texas Firm,'' *Wall Street Journal,* October 13, 1987, p. 4.

—Jeffrey L. Covell
—updated by David E. Salamie

INTERMET

Intermet Corporation

5445 Corporate Drive, Suite 200
Troy, Michigan 48098
U.S.A.
Telephone: (248) 952-2500
Fax: (248) 952-2501
Web site: http://www.intermet.com

Public Company
Incorporated: 1984
Employees: 6,890
Sales: $841.6 million (1998)
Stock Exchanges: NASDAQ
Ticker Symbol: INMT
NAIC: 331511 Iron Foundries; 331312 Primary Aluminum Production; 331524 Aluminum Foundries (Except Die-Casting); 33633 Motor Vehicle Steering and Suspension Components (Except Spring) Manufacturing; 33634 Motor Vehicle Brake System Manufacturing

Intermet Corporation is one of the largest independent foundry companies in the world, involved in producing ferrous and non-ferrous casting products for the automotive and industrial equipment industries. Intermet manufactures ductile iron, gray iron, and aluminum castings at 19 locations in North America and Europe, deriving approximately 85 percent of its revenue from sales to the automotive market. The company's products include castings for steering components, camshafts, crankshafts, chassis, and brake parts used in passenger vehicles, industrial vehicles, and in marine applications. During the 1990s, the company entered the aluminum business, quickly developing a strong market presence through acquisitions that built on its mainstay involvement in ductile iron castings.

19th-Century Origins

Intermet's lineage winds its way through a tangle of subsidiaries and predecessor companies to one of the oldest chartered companies in the United States, Columbus Iron Works, established in 1846. As a founding predecessor, Columbus Iron Works lent Intermet the type of prestige only history can impart: Aside from manufacturing armor plate for military applications, the 19th-century metal-worker was involved in the development of the first breech-loading cannon, and later, manufactured the cast iron pipe used in Manhattan Island's turn-of-the-century water system.

Intermet's modern-day origins begin in 1971, when Columbus Foundries Inc. was founded, incorporating the link to the past, the 19th-century Columbus Iron Works. During its first decade of operation, Columbus Foundries' internal growth was augmented by a methodical acquisition campaign. A machinery facility was acquired in 1976, followed by the purchase in 1980 of a foundry located in Germany, and the acquisition of the Lynchburg Foundry Company in 1983, which owned three Virginia-based foundries. Intermet, founded by George Mathews, Jr., was formed a year after Columbus Foundries acquired the three Virginia foundries. The new company, which was based in Columbus, Georgia, assumed control over Columbus Foundries.

More than a century after Columbus Iron Works' pioneering military work, Intermet geared itself for an entirely different sort of existence. The company manufactured cast iron pieces for the automobile industry, operating as an automotive parts supplier to original equipment manufacturers (OEMs) such as Ford, General Motors, and Chrysler. In 1985, a year after its formation, Intermet's stock began trading on the public market, touching off an energetic acquisition spree. In 1986, the company purchased Northern Casting Company, based in Hibbing, Minnesota, and New River Castings Company, based in Radford, Virginia. Two years later, Intermet acquired the Ironton Iron foundry in Ironton, Ohio, completing an initial surge of welcome additions to the company's fold. However, with the good came the bad. In an effort to extend its geographic reach and strengthen its capabilities and capacity, Intermet became involved in deals its management would later regret. Although the company eventually would rank as the largest concern of its kind in the world, its path to future dominance would not prove an easy road.

International Mistakes of the Late 1980s

As Intermet pursued an aggressive expansion campaign during its first decade of business, its zeal resulted in two acquisitions that represented notable failures. Intermet purchased a

Company Perspectives:

At Intermet we believe that the most valuable resource we have is our people. Advanced technology means little without the skilled technicians to manage it. We are as confident in the quality of our workforce as we are in the quality of our products. Some of our employees have been with us for nearly half a century, developing the kind of priceless experience that only comes from years on the job. The strong and stable relationship we enjoy with our workforce is Intermet's true strength. Intermet is also strengthened by our relationships with personnel at other companies—relationships that broaden our capabilities and allow us to offer more options to customers. We have very successful working relationships with a number of well-regarded technical services firms that specialize in advanced design and engineering. Our well-trained and technically proficient employees complement our advanced technology . . . making the company an unbeatable resource for the design, manufacture and assembly of world-class products.

foundry in Sweden, intent on bolstering its international presence, but slackening demand by European automobile manufacturers delivered a fatal blow to the new acquisition. The foundry failed to attract sufficient business to remain profitable and, consequently, the entire facility was shuttered, save a machinery division.

Intermet's progress was hobbled by another misguided overseas adventure, a joint venture named INTAT Precision. The company was formed through a partnership agreement between Intermet and a Japanese concern named Aisin Takaoda. Together, Intermet and Aisin Takaoda invested $25 million in an automotive parts facility located in Indiana, with Intermet controlling 60 percent of the joint venture and Aisin Takaoda controlling the remainder. Through INTAT Precision, automotive parts were to be manufactured first for Toyota, then for Honda, Mitsubishi, and Nissan, and finally for Japanese brake manufacturers. Under the terms of the agreement, Aisin Takaoda assumed control over the marketing and sales of the products manufactured by INTAT Precision, convincing Intermet officials that Aisin Takaoda's management possessed a greater understanding of the Japanese market and business customs governing trade in Japan. Ceding control to Aisin Takaoda proved to be a costly mistake, as Mathews later acknowledged in a March 1992 interview with *Business Atlanta,* saying, "We were asleep at the switch when we made the rudiments of that transaction." Projected sales of the new joint venture failed to materialize, but Intermet's partners preached patience, promising that sales would recover. Mathews and his staff waited, but eventually the losses became too significant to endure, forcing Intermet to withdraw from the joint venture with only financial losses to show for its efforts. "It drained our money from the company and drained theirs, too," Mathews explained in his interview with *Business Atlanta.* "Only thing, it was draining 40 percent of theirs and 60 percent of ours," he added.

Despite the costly miscues, Intermet's stature within the industry was impressive. By the early 1990s, the company was generating in excess of $320 million a year in sales through its worldwide operations. Intermet employed 3,600 workers spread among 12 foundries and two machining operations, primarily involving itself in ductile iron casting, which was stronger and lighter than traditional gray iron. Although the company manufactured housings, hubs, gear boxes, and other parts for farm and construction equipment, as well as parts for industrial manufacturers, the overwhelming majority of its sales were derived from OEM car and truck manufacturers. The company's major customers included Ford, Chrysler, General Motors, Toyota, Honda, Caterpillar, and Bendix. For these and other customers, Intermet manufactured casting products such as brake parts, steering and transmission components, camshafts, and crankshafts, earning distinction not so much for the particular products it produced but more for the manufacturing processes it employed. The company was capable of producing a broad range of casting products, from small castings to castings weighing up to 400 pounds, which enabled Intermet to pursue a commensurately broad range of contracts.

The opportunities available to Intermet promised to increase significantly as the company's management surveyed the industry during the early 1990s. Domestically, the automotive market was mired in a decisive slump during the early years of the decade. In 1991, the industry sold 12.3 million cars and light trucks, 11 percent less than it had sold the previous year. Further, the one-year drop in sales appeared to be part of an unwelcome trend: unit sales had peaked at 16.3 million in 1987, then began a five-year decline that intensified during the economically recessive early 1990s. At first blush, the anemic performance of Intermet's mainstay market pointed toward a commensurate decline in Intermet's business; a likely scenario considering OEM suppliers would suffer along with the manufacturers they supplied products to. For Intermet, however, the recessive conditions worked to the company's benefit. Because of the economic decline, major automobile manufacturers were forced to implement sweeping measures to improve efficiency and reduce costs. As they scaled down their operations, the automobile manufacturers increasingly turned to outside suppliers for the components they had traditionally produced on their own, using outsourcing as a means to reduce costs. For Intermet, the trend toward outsourcing not only led to an increase in business, but also reduced the strength of some of the company's largest competitors. In addition to competing against other independent foundry companies, Intermet battled for market share with companies such as General Motors' Central Foundries, which dramatically reduced the scope of its operations in the midst of the recessive early 1990s. Accordingly, while the automotive market suffered, Intermet increased its market share, exuding a vitality that was exemplified by the announcement in 1992 of a three-year, $100 million capital-expenditure program.

Diversification into Aluminum: Early 1990s

From an early 1990s vantage point, there were other positive developments that pointed toward promising growth for Intermet in the years ahead. The company was searching to add to its already formidable market position in iron casting by diversifying into aluminum, which was expected to be a high-growth segment of the automotive market in the future. During the early 1990s, a typical car manufactured in the United States

Key Dates:

1846: Intermet's earliest predecessor company, Columbus Iron Works, is founded.
1984: Intermet is formed.
1995: Bodine-Robinson Aluminum Foundry is acquired, ushering Intermet into the aluminum castings business.
1996: Sudbury, Inc. is acquired, substantially increasing production capacity of iron castings and lifting sales by $300 million.
1999: Company's aluminum business is bolstered with the acquisition of Ganton Technologies and Diversified Diemakers.

contained 175 pounds of aluminum, a proportion that was expected to double to 350 pounds per vehicle by 2000 as automobile manufacturers sought to reduce the weight of their various models. Intermet was intent on tapping into the burgeoning aluminum castings market and took its first steps into the business during the early 1990s. In 1992, the company formed a new division, Intermet Aluminum Inc., to produce cast aluminum chassis parts and signed a joint venture agreement with Australia-based Comalco Ltd. The joint venture, named ICA Castings, comprised a pilot plant and a smelting and rolling facility in Kentucky, which were to be used to make cast aluminum cylinder heads and engine blocks for U.S. automobile manufacturers. The agreement was terminated two years later, however, primarily because manufacturers were reluctant to place orders until further competition in the industry ensured competitive prices. Although its initial foray into aluminum suffered a setback, Intermet was determined to push ahead. In 1995, the company achieved its goal.

Midway through the decade, Intermet's iron castings business was growing robustly, enabling it to reach the half-billion-dollar mark in sales, which ranked the company as one of the largest independent foundry concerns in the world. In late 1995, Intermet added to its massive iron castings business by acquiring the Bodine-Robinson Aluminum Foundry, marking the company's formal entry into aluminum castings production. Based in Alexander City, Alabama, the foundry, which was renamed Alexander City Casting Co., was equipped to make automotive intake manifolds, transmission clutch parts, marine engine components, and castings for lawn and garden engines, possessing an annual capacity of more than 12 million pounds of light-alloy castings. For Intermet, the Bodine-Robinson acquisition represented an important first step into aluminum, touching off further aluminum acquisitions to follow, but the company's acquisitive activities were not restricted to building a presence in the fast-growing light-alloy market. The 1990s were heady years for Intermet, highlighted by an aggressive expansion campaign that cemented the company's standing as a global giant, particularly after a significant transaction in 1996 was completed.

Roughly a year after the Bodine-Robinson acquisition, Intermet struck again, purchasing Ohio-based Sudbury, Inc. for a reported $195 million. The acquisition lifted Intermet past all rivals, pushing its annual sales to $845 million and making it the largest independent ferrous castings foundry in the United States. Sudbury, a manufacturer of castings and machined parts and a provider of powder coating services primarily to the automotive industry, comprised five operating companies employing 2,300 workers, the largest of which, Wagner Castings Co., made the same kind of ductile iron castings as Intermet. Aside from adding substantially to Intermet's casting capacity, the Sudbury acquisition also expanded Intermet's product lines and capabilities to include zinc and aluminum die-casting, cantilevered cranes, and specialty service truck bodies.

Late 1990s Expansion

During the late 1990s, Intermet continued with its prevailing theme of the decade: expansion through acquisition. In May 1998, the company entered a joint venture for PortCast, a foundry company located in Portugal. In December 1998, the company completed another strengthening move overseas when it purchased an iron foundry in eastern Germany, but the biggest development of the month was Intermet's announcement that it was acquiring the Minnesota-based Tool Products division belonging to Quadion Corp. The purchase represented another important step toward the expansion of Intermet's aluminum business, giving the company the capacity to produce an additional 17–18 million pounds of aluminum castings annually. Tool Products, with plants in New Hope, Minnesota, and Jackson, Tennessee, manufactured precision die-castings for automotive and industrial electronic products, as well as small castings for anti-skid braking systems, fuel pumps, and steering wheel cores, deriving 60 percent of its annual revenue from the automotive market.

Intermet ended its most prolific decade of growth with yet another aluminum acquisition, leading some industry observers to speculate that the company would eventually abandon ferrous castings. The acquisition, announced in November 1999, included two companies, Ganton Technologies, Inc. and Diversified Diemakers, Inc., which, combined, were expected to generate $235 million in sales in 1999. Ganton Technologies, one of North America's largest aluminum die casters, operated three manufacturing facilities, two located in Wisconsin and another in Tennessee, and an engineering center in Wisconsin. Diversified Diemakers specialized in magnesium die-cast products such as brake pedal brackets, instrument panel frames, and housings used by automotive, commercial, and electronics industries, operating three production facilities in Michigan. With the addition of the two companies, Intermet's annual revenues were expected to reach $1.3 billion by the end of 2000, four times the total generated eight years earlier. The growth, however, was not being achieved at the expense of the company's longstanding involvement in the iron castings business, according to Intermet officials. Although the company announced the closure of its Ironton Iron foundry in December 1999 because of declining business, Intermet management scotched rumors that it was pursing a long-term strategy that excluded the company's involvement in ferrous castings. Instead, the company declared it was pursuing a growth strategy that would shape Intermet into a full-service metal caster. As the company pursued its comprehensive growth strategy, the likelihood of further acquisitions was strong, setting the stage for the company's progress in the 21st century.

Principal Subsidiaries

Cast-Matic Corp.; Frisby PMC, Inc.; Iowa Mold Tooling; Intermet Wagner Castings Co.

Principal Competitors

Worthington Industries, Inc.; Citation Corporation; Precision Castparts Corp.

Further Reading

''Alvin W. Singleton, Intermet President, Dies,'' *Foundry Management & Technology,* February 1991, p. 9.

''Ductile Iron As Good As Steel,'' *Ward's Auto World,* May 1999, p. 3.

''Intermet Acquires Leading Automotive Suppliers; Major Boost to Aluminum Manufacturing Capability,'' *PR Newswire,* November 17, 1999.

''Just-in-Time Manufacturing Is Working Overtime,'' *Business Week,* November 8, 1999, p. 36.

Kingman, Nancy, ''Drive for Lighter Cars Sets Intermet on Expansion Path,'' *American Metal Market,* April 26, 1993, p. 14.

Smith, Faye McDonald, ''Self-Inflicted Wounds All Healed,'' *Business Atlanta,* March 1992, p. 72.

Vanac, Mary, ''Ohio-Based Automobile, Industrial Parts Manufacturer to Be Bought Out,'' *Knight-Ridder/Tribune Business News,* November 20, 1996.

Wrigley, Al, ''Aluminum Castings Deal Canceled,'' *American Metal Market,* December 29, 1994, p. 5.

——, ''Intermet Gets Deeper into Aluminum,'' *American Metal Market,* December 29, 1998, p. 7.

——, ''Intermet Moves to Aluminum,'' *American Metal Market,* October 4, 1995, p. 2.

—Jeffrey L. Covell

ITOCHU Corporation

5-1-2 Kita-Aoyama
Minato-ku
Tokyo 107-8077
Japan
Telephone: (03) 3497-7295
Fax: (03) 3497-7296
Web site: http://www.itochu.co.jp

Public Company
Incorporated: 1914 as C. Itoh & Company
Employees: 5,775
Sales: ¥13.90 trillion (US$115.31 billion) (1999)
Stock Exchanges: Tokyo Osaka Nagoya Kyoto Hiroshima Fukuoka Niigata Sapporo
NAIC: 551112 Offices of Other Holding Companies

ITOCHU Corporation is the third largest of Japan's general trading companies—which are known as *sogo shosha*–trailing only Mitsui & Co., Ltd. and Mitsubishi Corporation. These companies are general in nature both in that they handle a wide range of products and services in nearly every industry, and in that they can handle a broad range of functions. General trading companies specialize in bringing together—on a global level—buyers and sellers of a variety of products and services and handling finance and transport of the resulting transaction; the companies derive most of their revenues from commissions earned through these short-term transactions. In the late 20th century, however, many of the *sogo shosha,* including ITOCHU, were increasingly turning to longer term equity investments in joint ventures and affiliates. Known as C. Itoh & Company, Ltd. from 1949 through 1992, ITOCHU was also in the process of shifting to a holding company structure as it approached the 21st century. At the same time, ITOCHU was focusing more of its resources on key strategic business areas: information and multimedia industries, with involvement in broadcasting, content, network businesses, and mobile multimedia; consumer and retail, with activities in convenience stores, food, and textiles; financial services, including foreign exchange trading, securities investments, business financing, insurance, and online securities brokerage services; and natural resource development, which includes investments in petroleum, liquefied natural gas, and other fuels. ITOCHU has a global network of more than 1,000 subsidiaries and affiliated companies in more than 80 countries.

Early History

ITOCHU's founder, Chubei Itoh, was born in 1842, the son of a dry goods merchant. In 1853, the year Admiral Perry from the United States ''opened'' Japan to international trade, Itoh began to accompany his older brother on sales trips to Osaka and Kyoto. By 1858 the younger Itoh was making his own sales trips, selling cloth to merchants in Okayama and Hiroshima. Two years later, at the age of 18, he established his own wholesale business and worked diligently to expand his small operation.

The 1860s were a time of upheaval and change in Japan. The 264-year-old government of the Tokugawa Shogun was overthrown in 1868 by loyalists of the Meiji Emperor. Itoh's business continued to prosper in spite of the civil war. In 1872 he opened a small shop in Osaka and within five years was one of the largest textile wholesaler-retailers in the city. A branch was opened in Kyoto in 1883, and the Osaka shop was designated the Itoh *Honten,* or ''head office.''

Chubei Itoh and his nephew Tetsujiro Sotoumi opened a third shop in Kobe in 1885. The Itoh-Sotoumi Company was primarily involved in the exportation of textile goods through *shokan,* or foreign trading agents. The export trade was very profitable, in spite of the *shokan,* who collected large commissions. Profits from export sales were reinvested in the company's domestic operations. Itoh opened a foreign office in Shanghai in an effort to bypass the *shokan* and their commissions. It was a difficult market to enter, however, and the company's representatives lacked the proper skills needed to deal effectively with Chinese merchants. As a result, the Shanghai office consistently lost money. In 1893 Itoh established Itoh Itomise (Thread and Yarn Store), from which C. Itoh & Company and ITOCHU were directly descended.

Itoh died in 1903 and his second son, also named Chubei, inherited the business. The younger Itoh was well trained and proved to be every bit as adept in business affairs as his father.

Key Dates:

1858: Chubei Itoh, company founder, begins linen trading operations.
1872: Itoh opens a shop in Osaka.
1903: Itoh dies and his second son, also named Chubei, inherits the business.
1914: Itoh Itomise is reorganized under the name C. Itoh & Company.
1918: C. Itoh becomes a public stock company and changes its name to C. Itoh & Company, Ltd.
1921: Serious recession leads C. Itoh deeply into debt; it is forced to restructure and is renamed the Marubeni Company; Daido Trading is created from a division of C. Itoh Trading.
1941: Itoh merges with Marubeni and Kishimoto & Company to form Sanko K.K.
1944: Japanese government orders Sanko, Daido Trading, and a subsidiary of Itoh called Kureha Textiles to merge and form a new company, Daiken Manufacturing.
1949: SCAP, the military occupation authority, orders Daiken divided into several separate companies, including C. Itoh & Company, Ltd.
1977: The Japanese government arranges for the acquisition of Ataka & Co., Ltd. by Itoh.
1985: Company takes 40 percent stake in new joint venture, Japan Communications Satellite Co.
1992: Company changes its name to ITOCHU Corporation.
1994: Company writes off US$662 million in nonperforming assets in aftermath of the bursting of the Japanese bubble economy.
1997: Restructuring continues with the disposal or writing off of US$1.8 billion in bad loans and nonperforming assets.
1999: Global-2000 strategic plan is launched, aiming to shift ITOCHU to a holding company structure by March 2001; US$2.38 billion in additional nonperforming assets are written off.

A few years before, Japan asserted its political dominance in northeast Asia when it defeated Russia in a war for influence in the region. In particular, Chosen (Korea) became a neocolonial possession of Japan. In 1898 a new *shokan* called Chosenya was established to handle trade between Japan and the Korean peninsula. It was a lucrative and developing market in which Chosenya had a monopoly. In 1905, however, the younger Itoh once again attempted to bypass the middlemen. He posted two company representatives in Korea, and later opened a full branch office in Seoul.

Itoh's business ventures on the Asian mainland deteriorated during 1907. In Chosen there was increasing dissatisfaction with the ''low quality of Japanese products.'' On the other hand, representatives in Shanghai found it increasingly difficult to manage exchange rate fluctuations between the gold-based yen and the silver-based Chinese currency. Mismanagement at the Shanghai office became so acute that by 1908 it was sold to its employees and severed from the Itoh company.

The company recovered quickly, due mainly to a rapid increase in domestic trading activity. In March 1910 Chubei Itoh, aged 23, went to London reportedly to study business administration. It is more likely, however, that he spent his time negotiating arrangements with English merchants. He discovered that the *shokan,* who presented themselves as powerful international figures in Japan, were actually small agencies with relatively little influence overseas. Itoh purchased large quantities of high-grade wool and other products directly from wholesalers in London and sent them to his company in Japan. Itoh also discovered that bank loans in London were commonly set at around two to three percent, substantially less than the 11 to 13 percent charged by the Yokohama Specie Bank in Japan. Taking advantage of these two factors enhanced Itoh's ability to undersell competitors in Japan and reinvest a larger portion of the company's profits. In 1914, meantime, Itoh reorganized Itoh Itomise under the name C. Itoh & Company. Four years later the company became a public stock company and changed its name to C. Itoh & Company, Ltd.

World War I to World War II

Japan was a victorious nation in World War I and, as a result, was awarded substantial commercial and military rights in the Pacific. It was a period of tremendous growth for large Japanese companies, particularly the large conglomerates which had become known as *zaibatsu,* or ''money cliques.'' C. Itoh & Company was not considered a *zaibatsu* like Mitsui, Mitsubishi, or Sumitomo. It was, however, a substantial company, engaged in commercial trading at a time when trade had become extremely important to the continued growth of the Japanese economy.

The strong economy and rising demand for textile products transformed the import trading division of C. Itoh virtually overnight. Demand for Itoh's products continued to grow faster than supply, causing prices (and therefore, profit margins) to rise with them. By 1919 the trading division had grown to twice the size of its parent company, and foreign offices had been established in New York, Calcutta, Manila, and four cities in China. As Itoh's volume of trade grew, so did its variety of products. In addition to textile and agricultural products, the company handled machinery, iron and steel products, and automobiles.

Like most economies that experience strong economic reversals during periods of rapid expansion, Japan entered a serious recession in 1920 which adversely affected consumer demand. Due to the fact that C. Itoh was still a relatively small company without the full backing of a *zaibatsu* bank, it was forced to borrow heavily in order to cover its obligations and went deeply into debt. The following year the company reorganized. C. Itoh & Company was restructured and named the Marubeni Company. Another new company called Daido Trading was created from a division of C. Itoh Trading. It had previously been responsible for trade with southeast Asia and the United States, but was ruined when demand for imports disappeared.

All three Itoh companies were forced to lay off hundreds of workers and suspend stock dividends for several years. Their recovery was slow, but gained momentum later in the 1920s. Ironically, these companies experienced their strongest post-recession growth during the worldwide depression of the 1930s.

The Calcutta branch, which was closed in 1921, reopened in 1931. In the following years new offices were opened in Australia, Thailand, and Indonesia. It was during this period that the benevolent one-man-rule of Chubei Itoh II was replaced by a more consensus-oriented presidential form of management.

The decade of the 1930s was a difficult period for Japanese business and politics. Right-wing militarists had terrorized their way to power and threatened not only to nationalize the nation's industries, but to dominate all of East Asia and the western Pacific. In the short term, the *zaibatsu* and other large companies stood to benefit greatly because they were the primary suppliers of machinery, weapons, and provisions to the growing Japanese military. In the long term, however, these same militarists had pledged to nationalize the *zaibatsu* and other companies. The Itoh companies were only three of hundreds that were placed in the difficult position of collaborating with the military government.

The militarists led Japan into a war against China in 1937, and later against Britain in 1940, and the United States in 1941. That year Itoh merged with Marubeni & Company and Kishimoto & Company to form a new company called Sanko K.K. The concentration of resources was intended to facilitate greater efficiency and conserve limited resources.

Despite the position of Japanese industry and the military, neither had the ability to mobilize or develop new technologies quickly enough to prevent the Allies from turning the war in their favor. Matters became particularly desperate when the Japanese mainland (and its factories) came within range of American bombers. In 1944, as part of an effort to rationalize Japanese industry, the government ordered Sanko, Daido Trading, and a subsidiary of Itoh called Kureha Textiles to merge. The new company, called Daiken Manufacturing, existed for about a year before Japan surrendered.

Postwar Reorganization

After the war, the military occupation authority, "SCAP" (for Supreme Commander of Allied Powers), implemented a complete reorganization of Japanese industry. Many American-style commercial laws were enacted, including an antimonopoly law which outlawed the *zaibatsu.* Although Daiken (Itoh) was not as large as the *zaibatsu,* SCAP ordered it divided into several companies.

When the reorganization was completed in 1949 C. Itoh & Company, Ltd.; Kureha Cotton Spinning Co., Ltd.; Marubeni Co., Ltd.; and a small manufacturer of nails called Amagasaki Nail Works, Ltd. were made independent companies under separate management groups. Both Itoh and Marubeni were given the authority to conduct both domestic and international business. Itoh exported Japanese textile products on a barter basis in return for foreign grain. The trade was stable and profitable, and enabled the company to establish itself quickly. In 1950 Itoh trade representatives were dispatched to India, Pakistan, and the United States. The United Nations war effort in Korea necessitated a change in commercial policies in Japan. On short notice Japanese companies, including Itoh, were contracted to supply food, clothing, and other provisions to United Nations forces in Korea. Itoh, which had already established an international network of suppliers, was quickly prepared to meet the sudden increase in business. The company product line, long dominated by textile products, was diversified to include petroleum, machinery, aircraft, and automobiles.

When the Korean War ended in 1952 many of Itoh's military contracts were canceled. The demobilization in Korea caused a serious recession during 1953 and 1954. Hundreds of smaller trading companies were forced into bankruptcy. C. Itoh, however, was larger and better able to endure the poor economic conditions. It later took over the business of the smaller bankrupt companies and continued to expand its product line.

Unlike the former *zaibatsu* groups, the postwar Itoh companies (C. Itoh, Marubeni, and Kureha) did not merge back together. During this period *zaibatsu* groups circumvented many antimonopoly laws by coordinating their individual company strategies through banking groups (called *keiretsu*). C. Itoh was neither a prewar *zaibatsu* nor a member of a postwar *keiretsu* group. During the later 1950s, however, the company accumulated enough capital to begin large-scale lending operations.

Evolving from Sogo Shosha *to Holding Company: 1960s–90s*

C. Itoh & Company and *keiretsu* group leaders such as Mitsui Bussan, Mitsubishi, and Sumitomo were engaged primarily in trading. They became know as *sogo shosha,* or "general trading companies." C. Itoh experienced strong growth during the 1960s, particularly on the strength of its trading activities. An international information network was created which made the company more responsive to business opportunities around the world.

In the late 1960s Itoh identified an opportunity to develop a nickel and cobalt mine at Greenvale in northeastern Australia. Itoh, in partnership with Australian interests, Mitsubishi, and Nissho Iwai, started the project in 1971. Raw materials from the mine were to be sold to Kawasaki Steel and Nisshin Steel, among others, and used to produce stainless steel.

When OPEC countries forced a dramatic increase in the price of oil in 1973, oil-dependent countries such as Japan found themselves seriously vulnerable to inflation and interruptions of supply. C. Itoh recognized this as an area of great opportunity. In coordination with C. Itoh Fuel Company, Itoh invested heavily in the development of new technologies for petroleum production.

In the mid-1970s the Japanese government became concerned about another trading company called Ataka & Co., Ltd., which was nearly bankrupt. Ataka had gained a reputation for mismanagement and inefficiency. It was repeatedly warned by banks and the government to practice greater discipline. When it appeared that Ataka's demise was inevitable, the Japanese government stepped in. In order to prevent the failure of such a large company (Ataka was Japan's tenth largest trading firm), the government hastily arranged for a major portion of it to be absorbed by Itoh. When the merger was affected on October 1, 1977, C. Itoh & Company moved from being the fourth to the third largest Japanese trading firm. The merger greatly increased Itoh's interests in steel and chemicals, and further reduced textiles to about 20 percent of total sales volume.

In addition to its trading activities, C. Itoh was involved in a number of large industrial projects in the 1980s, acting as a coordinator and providing financial support. Itoh's largest foreign projects were the Hassi-R'Mel natural gas plant in Algeria, a cashmere factory in Mongolia, the Baoshan steel complex near Shanghai (led by Nippon Steel), and the Kaduna oil refinery in Nigeria (with Chiyoda Chemical). Early in 1987, however, Itoh backed out of the Greenvale Mine project when it appeared that demand for nonferrous metals would not recover. The company was also involved in the development of natural resources, including petroleum products and uranium, and metals (despite ending its involvement with Greenvale).

The late 20th century was marked by the steady decline of the traditional *sogo shosha* activities–providing marketing, financial, and distribution services to other companies. Their customers grew more powerful thanks to the help of the trading companies, but as their customers grew in size they increasingly decided to bring in-house the services they had once paid the *sogo shosha* to perform. As noted in a 1988 *Financial World* article, the trading companies were putting themselves out of business.

Under the leadership of president Isao Yonekura, Itoh responded to this fundamental shift by adding to its trading activities longer term equity investments in joint ventures and affiliates actually producing products and services—thereby shifting from a pure trader to more of an investment holding company. Two of the main areas for the company's investments were the related fields of telecommunications and multimedia. In 1985 Japan Communications Satellite Co. (JCSAT) was formed as a joint venture of C. Itoh (40 percent), Hughes Communications (30 percent), and Mitsui (30 percent). Four years later JCSAT became the first company in Japan to launch and operate a private communications satellite. In 1991 Itoh and Toshiba Corporation each contributed US$500 million to gain a combined 12.5 percent stake in Time Warner Inc.'s movie, television, and cable TV businesses. The partners also formed a joint venture, Time Warner Entertainment Japan Corp., to operate Time Warner's operations in Japan, including home video, movie, and TV program distribution. Itoh and Toshiba each held 25 percent of this venture, with the U.S. firm holding the remaining half. In 1992 C. Itoh & Co. changed its name to ITOCHU Corporation, adopting a transliteration of its Japanese name. At the time of the name change, ITOCHU had held the position as the largest of the *sogo shosha* for several years; consolidated sales for the year ending in March 1992 stood at ¥20.6 trillion (US$154 billion).

The bursting of the late 1980s Japanese economic bubble led to prolonged difficulties for most of the *sogo shosha.* As a byproduct of the stagnation of their core trading activities, nearly all of the *sogo shosha* had diversified aggressively into financial investments during the speculative bubble, which reached its peak in 1988–89. The trading companies built up large stock portfolios and became hooked on the revenues they could gain through arbitrage (or *zaiteku,* as it is known in Japan). Once the bubble burst, the *sogo shosha* were left with huge portfolios whose worth had plummeted; the companies were forced to eventually liquidate much of their stock holdings. ITOCHU's troubles were even greater because the company had made large investments in the hot Japanese real estate market during the bubble. In fiscal 1994 ITOCHU recorded about US$662 million in extraordinary losses to write off insolvent financial and real estate subsidiaries and other nonperforming assets. This led the company to post a net loss of ¥14.13 billion (US$137.5 million) for the year.

The entire decade of the 1990s was a challenging one for the *sogo shosha* not only because of the lingering effects of their overzealous 1980s investments but also due to the stagnant Japanese economy of the early and mid-1990s, the Asian economic crisis that began in 1997, and the Japanese recession that followed the latter. ITOCHU was heavily involved in such troubled nations as Thailand and Indonesia. In late 1997, then, ITOCHU continued to restructure with the disposal or writing off of ¥230 billion (US$1.8 billion) in bad loans and nonperforming assets. This led to an even larger loss of ¥91.93 billion (US$713.9 million) for fiscal 1998. Still reeling from its financial difficulties, the company raised additional cash—US$1.17 billion—through the sale of its Time Warner stake in three separate transactions in 1998 and 1999. Losses for fiscal 1999 were reduced to ¥34.09 billion (US$283 million), but the company did not pay a dividend for the first time in 50 years. By this time, ITOCHU had fallen to the number three position among *sogo shosha,* having been surpassed by Mitsui and Mitsubishi.

Under the leadership of President and CEO Uichiro Niwa, ITOCHU in April 1999 initiated a two-year strategic plan called Global-2000. A key aspect of the plan was the shifting of the company to a holding company structure, with ITOCHU's seven division companies gaining greater management autonomy. Headquarters staff would be slashed from 280 to about 100 and would be responsible only for corporate planning and auditing. In another streamlining move, the company's board of directors would be reduced from 45 members to between 10 and 15. In addition, consolidated subsidiaries would be reduced by about one-third by March 2001, with a goal of increasing the portion of profitable subsidiaries from about 60 percent to 80 percent. The increased emphasis on profitability was a major shift for a trading company as the *sogo shosha* had traditionally valued market share and sales growth ahead of returns on investments. The newfound pursuit of profits was also evident in the industries ITOCHU targeted for future growth, which included such potentially lucrative fields as information, multimedia, and financial services. It was difficult to predict whether the Global-2000 program would position ITOCHU to profitably succeed in the more highly competitive, deregulated environment of the early 21st century. But the October 1999 announcement of yet another huge nonperforming asset writeoff—this one concentrating on real estate projects and totaling ¥253 billion (US$2.38 billion)—was certain to lead the company to its largest net loss yet for the fiscal 2000 year.

Principal Subsidiaries

ITOCHU has 1,027 subsidiaries and associated companies in more than 80 countries. Its overseas trading subsidiaries are: ITOCHU International Inc. (U.S.A.); ITOCHU Latin America S.A. (Panama); ITOCHU Brasil S.A. (Brazil); ITOCHU Europe PLC (U.K.); ITOCHU Deutschland GmbH (Germany); ITOCHU France S.A.; ITOCHU Italiana S.p.A. (Italy); ITOCHU Middle East E.C. (Bahrain); ITOCHU Australia Ltd.; ITOCHU Asia Pte., Ltd. (Singapore); ITOCHU Hong Kong

Ltd.; ITOCHU (China) Holding Co., Ltd.; ITOCHU Taiwan Corporation.

Principal Divisions

Textile Company; Plant, Automobile & Industrial Machinery Company; Aerospace, Electronics & Multimedia Company; Metals & Minerals Company; Energy & Chemical Company; Food, Forest Products & General Merchandise Company; Finance, Realty, Insurance & Logistics Services Company.

Principal Competitors

Archer-Daniels-Midland Company; Daewoo Group; Hutchison Whampoa Limited; Hyundai Group; Inchcape plc; Jardine Matheson Holdings Limited; Kanematsu Corporation; LG Group; Marubeni Corporation; Mitsubishi Corporation; Mitsui & Co., Ltd.; Nichimen Corporation; Nissho Iwai Corporation; Samsung Group; Sumitomo Corporation; Swire Pacific Limited; TOMEN Corporation.

Further Reading

Fairlamb, David, ''The Sogo Shosha Flex Their Muscles,'' *Dun's Business Month,* July 1986, pp. 44+.

Hulme, David, ''Giant Fights Off Extinction,'' *Asian Business,* June 1994, pp. 12–13.

''Itochu and Mitsubishi: Unclear Interests,'' *Business China,* October 27, 1997, pp. 6–7.

''Itochu to Market Gasoline Brand,'' *Asian Wall Street Journal,* April 1, 1997, p. 24.

Iwao, Ichiishi, ''Sogo Shosha: Meeting New Challenges,'' *Journal of Japanese Trade & Industry,* January/February 1995, pp. 16–18.

''Japanese Trading Companies: The Giants That Refused to Die,'' *Economist,* June 1, 1991, pp. 72+.

''Japanese Trading Companies: The Web Rips,'' *Economist,* August 8, 1992, p. 68.

''Japan's Trading Houses: March of the Middlemen,'' *Economist,* September 24, 1988, pp. 93–94.

Meyer, Richard, and Dexter Hutchins, ''Battling Behemoth,'' *Financial World,* November 1, 1988, pp. 30–31, 34, 36–37.

Momose, Toshiaki, ''The General Trading Companies of Japan,'' *Tokyo Business Today,* February 1989, pp. 50+.

Nakamoto, Michiyo, ''Itochu Sells 40% of Its Time Warner Holding,'' *Financial Times,* September 23, 1998, p. 28.

——, ''Itochu Unveils Plan for ¥230bn Restructuring,'' *Financial Times,* November 18, 1997, p. 32.

——, ''Itochu Warns of Loss and Steps Up Revamp,'' *Financial Times,* April 14, 1999, p. 28.

——, ''Trading Groups Reveal Heavy Indonesian Exposure,'' *Financial Times,* May 28, 1998, p. 27.

Ono, Yumiko, and Audrey McAvoy, ''Japan's Itochu Is Latest Trading Firm to Plan Revamp and a Related Loss,'' *Wall Street Journal,* October 14, 1999, p. A23.

Ono, Yumiko, and Jacob M. Schlesinger, ''C. Itoh, Toshiba Forge Time Warner Link,'' *Asian Wall Street Journal,* October 30, 1991, p. 1.

Rosario, Louise do, ''Lose and Learn: Japan's Firms Pay Price of Financial Speculation,'' *Far Eastern Economic Review,* June 17, 1993, pp. 60–61.

Sapsford, Jathon, ''Itochu Cuts Earnings Forecast, Sets Goal of 10% for Investment Yields,'' *Asian Wall Street Journal,* April 14, 1999, p. 3.

Schlesinger, Jacob M., and Yumiko Ono, ''Toshiba, C. Itoh Aim to Close Product Gaps,'' *Asian Wall Street Journal,* October 31, 1991, p. 1.

Sender, Henny, ''Let Me Introduce You: The Shosha Are Making It Easier to Set Up in China,'' *Far Eastern Economic Review,* February 1, 1996, p. 51.

——, ''The Sun Never Sets,'' *Far Eastern Economic Review,* February 1, 1996, pp. 46–48, 50.

Shao, Alan T., and Paul Herbig, ''The Future of Sogo Shosha in a Global Economy,'' *International Marketing Review,* vol. 10, no. 5 (1993), pp. 37+.

Spindle, Bill, ''Itochu Sells U.S. Assets to Acquire Capital to Allay Domestic Woes,'' *Asian Wall Street Journal,* March 23, 1998, p. 3.

''The Titans of Trade: At Home and Abroad, Japan's Trading Companies Are Helping Businesses Do Business,'' *Focus Japan,* December 1993, pp. 6, 8.

Udagawa, Hideo, ''Dawning of a New Age for the *Sogo Shosha* Traders,'' *Tokyo Business Today,* January 1992, pp. 54–57.

Yonekawa, Shin'ichi, ed., *General Trading Companies: A Comparative and Historical Study,* Tokyo: United Nations University Press, 1990, 229 p.

Yonekawa, Shin'ichi, and Hideki Yoshi Hara, ed., *Business History of General Trading Companies,* Tokyo: University of Tokyo Press, 1987.

Yoshihara, Kunio, *Sogo Shosha: The Vanguard of the Japanese Economy,* Tokyo: Oxford University Press, 1982, 358 p.

Young, Alexander, *The Sogo Shosha: Japan's Multinational Trading Companies,* Boulder, Colo.: Westview Press, 1979, 247 p.

—updated by David E. Salamie

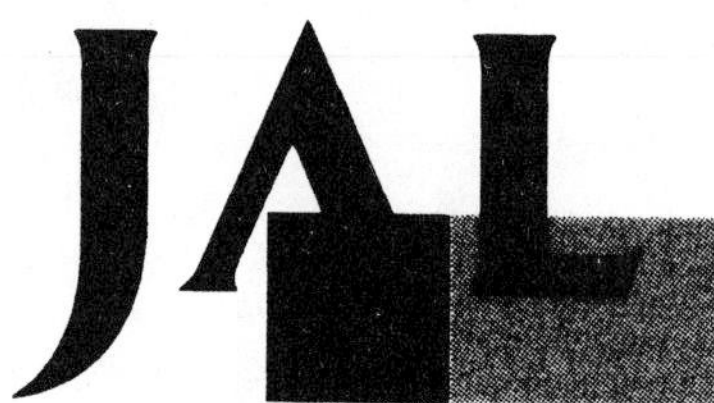

Japan Airlines Company, Ltd.

4-11, Higashi-shinagawa 2-chome
Shinagawa-ku
Tokyo 140-8637
Japan
Telephone: (03) 5460-3191
Fax: (03) 5460-5929
Web site: http://www.jal.co.jp

Public Company
Incorporated: 1953 as Japan Air Lines Company, Ltd.
Employees: 20,367
Sales: ¥1.57 trillion (US$13.05 billion) (1999)
Stock Exchanges: Tokyo Osaka Nagoya NASDAQ
Ticker Symbol: JAPNY
NAIC: 481111 Scheduled Passenger Air Transportation; 481112 Scheduled Freight Air Transportation; 481211 Nonscheduled Chartered Passenger Air Transportation; 485999 All Other Transit and Ground Passenger Transportation; 488190 Other Support Activities for Air Transportation; 561520 Tour Operators; 561590 Other Travel Arrangement and Reservation Services; 721110 Hotels (Except Casino Hotels) and Motels; 722310 Food Service Contractors

Japan Airlines Company, Ltd. is the largest airline in both Japan and Asia. Japan Airlines (JAL) operates a worldwide system serving 75 cities in 29 countries. Its fleet of jets numbers 135, with the vast majority being Boeing models, including 79 747s and 21 767s. JAL carries approximately 35 million passengers each year, with about two-thirds using the company's domestic routes within Japan. In addition to its domestic and international passenger operations, JAL has a number of other wholly or partly owned operations, including: cargo transportation via air, aircraft maintenance and ground support services, in-flight catering services, computer reservation systems, travel services such as packaged tours, and the management of nearly 400 hotels worldwide. The company also holds a 25 percent stake in DHL International, a leading worldwide courier service.

Early History

In 1952 the governments of Japan and the United States signed a bilateral agreement which established normal air services between the two countries. During the postwar American occupation Northwest and Pan Am were the two principal air carriers serving Japan. The formation of a Japanese airline was not permitted until the occupation ended in 1951. At that time Japanese Air Lines was established and placed in charge of domestic flight services between a number of major Japanese cities. By 1952, however, it was in need of capital. The following year, the Japanese government purchased an entire stock issue which doubled the company's capital, but also gave the government a 50 percent interest in the airline, which was renamed Japan Air Lines Company, Ltd.

The airline suffered from a shortage of experienced pilots. Nearly all Japanese aviators were drafted into the air service during the war and very few survived. As a result, American, British, and other Commonwealth aviators were required to operate the company's fleet of aircraft (which consisted of Martin 202s leased from Northwest and, later, a number of DC-4s) until Japanese pilots could be trained and assimilated into the flight crews.

Japan Air Lines grew quickly under the leadership of Seijiro Yanagida. In early February 1954, JAL inaugurated its first international route, a semiweekly service which connected Tokyo, Honolulu, and San Francisco. Plans were made to extend JAL services to Hong Kong and Sao Paulo, Brazil, the center of a large Japanese community in South America. Also that year, JAL opened offices in Los Angeles, San Francisco, and Chicago. A route connecting Tokyo and London was established when the airline purchased several de Havilland Mark II Comet jetliners.

In its first year of operation JAL secured a significant share of the trans-Pacific market. The company lost money, however, despite a $3 million government subsidy. In its rush to acquire the latest aircraft, JAL purchased production orders for DC-6Bs from other airlines. This plan for securing early delivery of the airplanes obliged JAL to pay a compensatory premium. Another costly factor was the training program which placed an unusually high number of employees on the payroll. In addition,

Company Perspectives:

JAL is determined to operate in a transparent fashion, treat customers and partners fairly, make decisions rapidly, show strategic foresight and take a global perspective in all its activities. Together, these qualities define how JAL is tackling the issues that face all group members.

JAL's maintenance and repair work was being performed by United Airlines until Japanese personnel could be trained.

Japan Air Lines offered its first issue of public stock in May 1956. ¥500 million (US$1.38 million) was raised to finance the purchase of several new DC-8 passenger jets from the Douglas Aircraft Company. The company made a number of subsequent public offerings and had increased its share capital to ¥5.3 billion (US$14.7 million) in 1960. That figure was increased to ¥11.7 billion (US$32.5 million) in 1962 and ¥18.2 billion (US$50.5 million) in 1965. The increased capital at JAL's disposal enabled it to implement a rapid expansion program.

In 1958 JAL extended its Bangkok service to Singapore, marking a significant return to southeast Asia for Japanese interests. The Japanese occupation of Malaya (peninsular Malaysia) and the East Indies during World War II has remained a politically sensitive issue for southeast Asian governments. The return of the Japanese flag to Singapore on commercial terms began a normalization process between Japan and southeast Asia.

Japan Air Lines created a subsidiary in 1957 called the Airport Ground Service Co., Ltd., which provided a variety of maintenance services to JAL and other airlines serving Japan. The company's personnel training programs were completed that same year, and for the first time JAL was operating regular flights with all-Japanese crews. Two years later a JAL crew training center was opened at Tokyo's Haneda Airport.

1960s and 1970s: Growth and Diversification

The company began a Tokyo to Paris service in conjunction with Air France in 1960. This route was unique because it was one of the first regular services to fly over the North Pole. Air France provided the Boeing 707 jetliners which were required for the long stretch over the Arctic.

Later that year JAL entered the jet age when it received its first DC-8 commercial jetliner. Less than a month later the jet was put into service on the Tokyo to San Francisco route. By the end of the year JAL DC-8s were flying to Los Angeles, Seattle, and Hong Kong. The company ended its arrangement with Air France and inaugurated its own DC-8 service from Tokyo to London and Paris via Anchorage on June 6, 1961.

The next jetliner to enter service with JAL was the Convair 880 which was used primarily on domestic and southeast Asian routes. After appropriate arrangements were concluded with various governments, JAL established a "Silk Road" service between Europe and Japan via Hong Kong, Bangkok, Calcutta, Karachi, Kuwait, Cairo, Rome, and Frankfurt. The route was inaugurated in October 1963 with the new Convair jets.

The Boeing Company sold its first airliner, a 727, to JAL in 1965. This purchase marked the beginning of a close relationship between the airline and Boeing. Over the years JAL would become Boeing's best foreign customer. In addition, that same year JAL adopted the *tsuru* (which means crane) as its official symbol. The crane is a symbol of good luck in Japan and is regarded as an appropriate motif for the Japanese airline.

Shortly after setting up a new computerized reservations system called JALCOM early in 1967, Japan Air Lines completed a route network that stretched around the world. The trans-Pacific service to San Francisco was linked to New York and London, where it connected with the "Silk Road" back to Japan. It was an honor for an airline to boast around-the-world service. Few were able to maintain them for more than just a few months. JAL's worldwide service, however, lasted for six years.

A dispute over the Soviet occupation of several Japanese islands prevented a full normalization of relations between those two countries following World War II. Once again, Japan Air Lines helped to promote a normalization of relations between Japan and a foreign country. In 1967 JAL inaugurated a service in conjunction with the Soviet airline Aeroflot which linked Moscow and Tokyo. The Soviets provided the aircraft (a Tupelov 114) and flight crew, but the cabin attendants were a combination of JAL and Aeroflot personnel.

JAL created a subsidiary called Southwest Airlines on June 22, 1967. The new airline operated domestic services between Japanese cities and vacation spots in the Ryukyu Islands in southern Japan (it was later renamed Japan Trans Ocean Air Co., Ltd.). JAL's tourist business continued to grow as the country became more affluent. In 1969 the company founded another subsidiary called JAL Creative Tours, whose purpose was to market travel packages and excursions. Around this same time, JAL began developing its chain of Nikko International Hotels.

On July 22, 1970, Boeing delivered the first of several 747s to JAL. Three months later the aircraft was introduced on the Tokyo-Los Angeles route. In addition to jumbo jets, JAL had three Concorde and five Boeing supersonic transports (SSTs) on order. These jetliners were later canceled when the price of a Concorde increased and the Boeing project was abandoned.

Shizuma Matsuo, who succeeded Seijiro Yanagida as president of the airline in 1961, was promoted to the position of chairman in 1971. Another company officer, Shizuo Asada, took Matsuo's place. During this period of time questions were raised about JAL's management. A series of major accidents throughout 1972 culminated with the crash of a JAL DC-8 after takeoff from Moscow's Sheremetyevo Airport. These accidents were blamed on the pilots' lack of experience. Commercial pilots in western nations usually come from the military where they gained thousands of hours of flight experience. Japan, however, had only a small "self-defense force" whose pilots were forbidden from taking higher-paying jobs in civilian aviation. As a result, less experienced JAL pilots (it was reported) tended to lack certain instinctual skills during crisis situations. The airline investigated this problem, but in the meantime the loss of its DC-8 created an equipment shortage which forced JAL to cancel the London-U.S. portion of its around-the-world

Key Dates:

1951: Japanese Air Lines is established.
1952: In need of capital, airline sells 50 percent interest to the Japanese government, and is renamed Japan Air Lines Company, Ltd.
1954: Company inaugurates its first international route, which connects Tokyo, Honolulu, and San Francisco.
1956: Company offers its first issue of public stock.
1960: Airline enters the jet age upon receiving its first jetliner, a DC-8.
1965: JAL buys its first jet from the Boeing Company, a 727, marking the beginning of a close relationship between the two firms.
1967: A domestic airline subsidiary is established, Southwest Airlines, which is later renamed Japan Trans Ocean Air.
1970: Airline takes delivery of its first Boeing 747.
1974: Air service to Taiwan is suspended and service is inaugurated between Japan and the People's Republic of China.
1975: Air service to Taiwan is resumed through a new subsidiary, Japan Asia Airways.
1985: Japanese government grants company the authority to fly more domestic routes; JAL flight 123 crashes into a mountainside, killing all but four of the 524 passengers in the worst single-airplane accident in history, and leading to the resignation of the company president.
1987: JAL is fully privatized.
1989: Company changes its name to Japan Airlines Company, Ltd.
1992: Japan Air Charter, a lower-cost international charter subsidiary, is formed; company posts a net loss of US$100.2 million, the first of seven straight years in the red.
1998: Continuing difficulties, including a ¥154.6 billion (US$1.2 billion) writeoff, lead to the resignations of the company chairman and president; JAL Express—a new low-cost domestic airline subsidiary—begins scheduled service.
1999: Japan Air Charter is transformed into a scheduled carrier and renamed JALways; company establishes code-sharing agreements with American Airlines, British Airways, and Qantas.

service. Consequently, the company took a number of steps to ensure that accidents of this kind would not occur in the future.

On April 21, 1974, as part of a wider government campaign to normalize relations with the People's Republic of China, Japan Air Lines suspended its service to Taipei, Taiwan. Six months later JAL opened air service between Osaka and Shanghai in the People's Republic of China. The following year JAL created a separate subsidiary called Japan Asia Airways Co., Ltd., which resumed the air service to Taiwan.

Japan Air Lines continued to add Boeing 747s to its growing airliner fleet. In 1977, however, a number of Japanese politicians were implicated in a scandal which involved illegal payments from the sale of Boeing airplanes. An investigation by the Japanese government led to the resignations of several Japanese officials before any formal charges of wrongdoing could be initiated. Boeing's chief competitor, McDonnell Douglas, had not sold a new airplane to JAL in over ten years. That company's latest entry in the commercial jetliner market was the wide body DC-10. The DC-10 was smaller than Boeing's 747, but it was also more suitable for a number of JAL's routes. Soon thereafter, the airline purchased a number of DC-10s and introduced them on routes previously served by DC-8s, which were converted for freight service.

Boeing, however, was still JAL's number one aircraft supplier. JAL had a special need for aircraft capable of carrying very large numbers of passengers and only Boeing manufactured an airliner as large as the 747. In 1980 JAL accepted delivery of its first 747SR, a special 747 capable of carrying 550 passengers. It was used mainly for domestic flights between Tokyo and Okinawa.

Japan Air Lines was recognized for its numerous successes when it was chosen "1980 Airline of the Year" by the editors of *Air Transport World.* While JAL had made its mark in the air, it was also very active on the ground. Tokyo's Narita Airport was built to accommodate Tokyo's growing air traffic and relieve the pressure of air traffic at the older Haneda Airport. The problem with Narita, however, was that it was located 66 kilometers from downtown Tokyo. JAL officials had long expressed an interest in developing a high-speed train that would cover the distance in 20 minutes. After many years of experimentation, JAL introduced the HSST (high speed surface transport), built in conjunction with Sumitomo Electric Industries and Tokyo Car Manufacturing Company. The HSST (also known as a "maglev" vehicle because of the way it works) does not touch the rails it rides over. The train is magnetically suspended approximately one centimeter above the rails. Since it never touches the rails, there is no friction and, as a result, the train can travel at greater speeds. On February 14, 1978, the HSST achieved its intended operating speed of 300 kilometers per hour. It was demonstrated on a special 400 meter track at the Tsukuba Exposition in 1985 with the hope that it might attract buyers searching for a high-speed public transportation system.

1980s: Deregulation and Privatization

Shisuo Asada announced his retirement as president of JAL in 1981. He was succeeded by Yasumoto Tagaki. Under Tagaki, Japan Air Lines entered a new phase in the world airline market. Deregulation in the United States inspired increased airline competition in foreign markets. By 1983 a committee recommended that JAL should be operated more like a commercial operation, and perhaps even privatized.

In 1985 the Japanese government authorized JAL's domestic rival, All Nippon Airways, to fly international routes and operate cargo services in competition with JAL. In return, JAL was given the authority to fly more domestic routes in competition with All Nippon, which had a monopoly on many Japanese routes. It was also suggested that Toa Domestic Airways (later known as Japan Air System Co. Ltd.) and a number of other foreign airlines be given greater freedom to operate in Japan.

During this period JAL suffered from a number of brief but highly publicized strikes. Perhaps the biggest blow to the company's credibility came in February 1982, when the pilot of a JAL jet (who was later diagnosed as a schizophrenic) crashed his airplane into Tokyo Bay, killing 24 passengers. Many air travelers subsequently avoided JAL, severely depressing the company's earnings.

On August 12, 1985, JAL flight 123 from Tokyo to Osaka took off with 524 passengers. Shortly after takeoff, while the cabin was pressurizing, the rear bulkhead ruptured and severely damaged the 747's tail fin. The airplane had no maneuverability but stayed aloft for 30 minutes before crashing into a mountainside, killing all but four passengers. This was the most serious single-airplane accident in aviation history, and it kept thousands of customers away from JAL. Yasumoto Tagaki assumed full responsibility for the tragedy and offered his resignation to Prime Minister Yasuhiro Nakasone, who publicly berated Tagaki for lax discipline. Japan Air Lines held memorial services and offered to pay all educational costs of any children who lost parents in the crash. Later, Tagaki personally went to visit the surviving members of the crash victims, offering one last apology before his resignation took effect.

Susumu Yamaji was appointed JAL's president in December 1985 and Junji Itoh was named the airline's chairman in June 1986. Itoh became the first chairman of JAL with a background in marketing. Under Itoh's leadership JAL was restructured and organized under three main operating divisions: international passenger service, domestic passenger service, and cargo (including mail) service. Itoh also made progress with the company's strained state of labor relations.

The most obvious feature of chairman Itoh's leadership was the company's emphasis on marketing. Under the previous management the loyalty of Japanese customers was largely taken for granted. In a more deregulated market, however, JAL was forced to fight for its share of the market. The American airline companies were expected to compete intensely in Japan. JAL prepared for their arrival by securing agreements with Delta Air Lines and Western Airlines which linked JAL to an extensive American flight network.

By 1987 the Japanese government's ownership of Japan Air Lines had been reduced to 34.5 percent. In late 1987 the government sold its stake to the public, completing JAL's privatization and giving it more decision-making freedom. In 1989 the company shortened its name to Japan Airlines Company, Ltd. and adopted a new craneless logo.

1990s: Hitting Turbulence

JAL—headed by chairman Susumu Yamaji starting in June 1991—began to founder not long after it was fully privatized. The company was expanding its fleet tremendously in the early 1990s, at the same time that the Gulf War, economic recessions in the United States and the United Kingdom, and the beginning of a prolonged downturn in the Japanese economy were all making for difficult operating conditions. Perhaps most importantly, the Japanese economic troubles led many of the country's companies to cut back dramatically on highly profitable business and first class fares. For the fiscal 1992 year, JAL company posted its first loss since 1985, a loss of US$100.2 million; the company stayed in the red through fiscal 1998. Compounding the company's troubles was its inability to expand its domestic operation because the major airports in Japan were all operating at capacity. The Japanese airport crisis was relieved only in 1994, when the Kansai International airport opened in Osaka. While the new airport—as well as expansions at others in Japan—provided JAL with new opportunities, the new capacity also brought increased competition from foreign airlines offering lower-cost fares.

One of the company's responses to its crisis was to launch a lower-cost international charter subsidiary called Japan Air Charter in 1992. Among the cost-saving measures employed at the charter was the employment of Thai stewardesses who were paid less than a quarter of the salary paid to Japanese. Another cost-cutting move came in 1993 when JAL and All Nippon Airways reached a cooperation agreement in the area of aircraft maintenance. JAL was also attempting to reduce its bloated staff through attrition. For fiscal 1993, JAL posted a net loss of ¥54.9 billion (US$416.8 million) on revenues of ¥1.28 trillion (US$11.18 billion); the company stopped paying dividends that year.

Alliances emerged as a key strategy for airlines struggling to survive in the hypercompetitive environment of the 1990s, and Japan Airlines joined in, entering into a marketing alliance with American Airlines in 1995. Overall, JAL continued to struggle in the mid-to-late 1990s, despite its cost-cutting measures which included a 4,000-person reduction in the workforce from 1993 to 1998. In March 1998 the company announced that it would use shareholder equity to write off ¥154.6 billion (US$1.2 billion), ¥57.6 billion (US$447 million) of which was used to dispose of accumulated debt and the remaining ¥97 billion (US$753 million) to restructure its hotel and resort operations. JAL had spent heavily in the late 1980s buying property and building hotels in Hawaii and elsewhere but had been hurt by slumping property values and hotel business in the 1990s. For the year ending in March 1998 JAL posted a record loss of ¥94.2 billion (US$476.7 million). The company's dismal state of affairs led Yamaji and company president Akira Kondo to resign their posts; taking over as president was 40-year veteran Isao Kaneko, but no chairman was immediately named.

One challenge immediately faced by the new president was the signing in early 1998 of a new bilateral U.S.-Japan aviation treaty, which appeared certain to bring still more competition to JAL from several American carriers. Kaneko continued his predecessors' drive to cut costs, reducing the payroll by an additional 1,500 employees during fiscal 1999. He also led a restructuring of subsidiary and affiliate operations. In July 1998 JAL Express Co., Ltd., a new low-cost domestic airline subsidiary, began scheduled service. The following year, Japan Air Charter was transformed into a scheduled carrier and renamed JALways Co., Ltd. JALways took over JAL routes to and from tourist destinations in southeast Asia, Oceania, and other locations in the Pacific. JAL also began reorganizing its cargo operation as an internal ''virtual company'' with greater autonomy. The company was actively seeking out alliances and established code-sharing agreements with several airlines—including American Airlines, British Airways, and Qantas Airways—in 1999. JAL also sold off some of its largest hotels, as part of an effort to eliminate unprofitable businesses. In March

1999 the company announced that it would eliminate an additional 1,300 jobs and reduce its board from 28 to 11 members in order to speed decision-making.

Despite returning to profitability in fiscal 1999, Japan Airlines faced an uncertain future. Even though it had cut costs substantially during the 1990s, JAL was still confronted with the high cost of using Japan's largest airports and downward pressure on fares from increasing competition. As it looked toward the 21st century, JAL was planning to spin off to the public several subsidiaries within the catering, distribution, and information systems divisions—moves that would further its focus on its core airline activities. It was also likely to sell off more of its hotel and resort operations. In addition, JAL was considering joining one of the large global airline alliances, most likely the Oneworld grouping led by American Airlines and British Airways.

Principal Subsidiaries

Airport Ground Service Co., Ltd. (95.5%); Airport Transport Service Co., Ltd.; DHL International (25%); AXESS International Network Inc. (75%); J Air Co., Ltd.; JAL Express Co., Ltd.; JAL Finance Corporation; JAL Hotels Co., Ltd. (89.3%); JALPAK Co., Ltd. (76.8%); JAL PLAZA Co., Ltd.; JAL Royal Catering Co., Ltd. (51%); JALSTORY Co., Ltd. (70.9%); JAL Trading Inc. (69.5%); JALways Co., Ltd. (82.4%); Japan Airlines Development Co., Ltd.; Japan Airport Ground Power Co., Ltd. (63.3%); Japan Asia Airways Co., Ltd. (90.5%); Japan Creative Tours Co., Ltd.; Japan Trans Ocean Air Co., Ltd. (51.1%).

Principal Competitors

Air Canada; All Nippon Airways Co., Ltd.; AMR Corporation; British Airways Plc; Cathay Pacific Airways Ltd.; Central Japan Railway Company; China Airlines; China Eastern Airlines Corporation Limited; Compagnie Nationale Air France; Continental Airlines, Inc.; Delta Air Lines, Inc.; Deutsche Lufthansa AG; East Japan Railway Company; Evergreen Marine Corporation (Taiwan) Ltd.; PT Garuda Indonesia; Japan Air System Co. Ltd.; Kinki Nippon Railway Co., Ltd.; KLM Royal Dutch Airlines; Korean Air Lines; Northwest Airlines Corporation; Singapore Airlines Limited; Skymark Airlines Co.; Thai Airways International Public Co. Ltd.; Trans World Airlines, Inc.; UAL Corporation; Virgin Atlantic Airways; West Japan Railway Company.

Further Reading

Abrahams, Paul, "Heroic Effort in Flight for Survival," *Financial Times,* October 29, 1999, p. 28.

Amaha, Eriko, "High Flyer," *Far Eastern Economic Review,* February 26, 1998, p. 66.

Burton, John, "JAL Records First Loss Since 1985," *Financial Times,* May 29, 1992, p. 26.

Carey, Susan, "DHL International Stake to Be Bought by Three Concerns," *Wall Street Journal,* May 30, 1990, p. A4.

Greiff, Peter R., "Lufthansa, JAL and a Trading Firm Acquire Majority Stake in Courier DHL," *Wall Street Journal,* August 24, 1992, p. A5A.

Harney, Alexandra, "JAL Admits to Racketeer Link," *Financial Times,* August 18, 1998, p. 20.

——, "JAL Counts Costs of Swimming with the Sharks," *Financial Times,* March 6, 1999, p. 17.

——, "JAL to Cut 1,300 Jobs and Slash Board Size," *Financial Times,* March 17, 1999, p. 20.

Hutton, Bethan, "JAL Uses Shareholder Equity for Write-Offs," *Financial Times,* March 18, 1998, p. 46.

Jones, Dominic, "From One Crisis to Another," *Airfinance Journal,* September 1998, pp. 48–50.

——, "Sun Rises in the East," *Airfinance Journal,* Business Yearbook 1999, pp. 7-9.

Labich, Kenneth, "Air Wars over Asia," *Fortune,* April 4, 1994, pp. 93+.

Landers, Peter, "Flying into Trouble: A Weakened Japan Airlines Faces New Competition," *Far Eastern Economic Review,* June 25, 1998, pp. 61–62.

Mecham, Michael, "JAL Realigns Itself for a Discount World," *Aviation Week & Space Technology,* July 19, 1999, p. 46.

Moorman, Robert W., "Changing Course: Japan Airlines Gets Inventive," *Air Transport World,* June 1994, pp. 185–86.

Nakamoto, Michiyo, "JAL Maps Out a Route to Recovery: Japan's Flag Carrier Is Fighting for Survival," *Financial Times,* March 23, 1993, p. 29.

——, "JAL to Spin Off Some Domestic Operations," *Financial Times,* October 21, 1996, p. 23.

——, "Japan Air Lines Pins Its Hopes on Cutting Costs," *Financial Times,* February 3, 1994, p. 21.

Nelms, Douglas W., "JAL Above and Beyond," *Air Transport World,* March 1992, pp. 92–94.

O'Connor, Anthony, "No Lack of Interest," *Airfinance Journal,* March 1996, p. 28.

Paul, David, "Climbing Above the Clouds," *Asian Business,* December 1989, p. 12.

Rapoport, Carla, "JAL Gets Ready for Privatisation," *Financial Times,* November 19, 1987, p. 33.

——, "JAL Share Sale Goes Off Smoothly," *Financial Times,* December 22, 1987, p. 24.

Sampson, Anthony, *Empires of the Sky: The Politics, Contests, and Cartels of World Airlines,* New York: Random House, 1984, 254 p.

Schlesinger, Jacob M., "Japan Airlines Leads Investment Group to Bail Out 'Maglev' Train Developer," *Wall Street Journal,* December 27, 1991, p. B4.

Shirouzu, Norihiko, "Japan Air to Write Off $1.2 Billion in Losses," *Wall Street Journal,* March 18, 1998, p. A17.

Small, Stacy H., "Rising to the Challenge," *Travel Agent,* February 16, 1998.

Smith, Charles, "Brace Yourselves: Japan Airlines Struggles to Pull Out of a Nosedive," *Far Eastern Economic Review,* December 23, 1993, pp. 43–44.

Woolsey, James P., "Building for the 'New Era,' " *Air Transport World,* June 1992, pp. 22–26.

—updated by David E. Salamie

JB Oxford Holdings, Inc.

9665 Wilshire Boulevard, Suite 300
Beverly Hills, California 90212
U.S.A.
Telephone: (310) 777-8888
Toll Free: (800) 799-8870
Fax: (310) 777-8820
Web site: http://www.jboxford.com

Public Company
Incorporated: 1987 as OTRA Securities Group, Inc.
Employees: 255
Sales: $67.3 million (1998)
Stock Exchanges: NASDAQ
Ticker Symbol: JBOH
NAIC: 52312 Securities Brokerage

JB Oxford Holdings, Inc. offers brokerage and financial services primarily through subsidiary JB Oxford and Company (JBOC). The company provides full-service discount and online brokerage services, including mutual funds, securities, security options, annuities, and fixed-income products. JB Oxford also offers clearing services to more than 30 independent broker-dealers as well as market maker services in stocks for about 500 corporations. The firm has three offices in the United States. JB Oxford's growing online services allow customers to access account information; place orders for equities, options, and mutual funds; and obtain news and stock information, as well as stock quotes.

Early Years As a Clearing Agent

The history of JB Oxford may be traced to OTRA Securities Group. Established in 1986 in Glendale, California, OTRA Securities Group began as a holding company that provided clearing services to securities broker-dealers, or correspondents, through primary subsidiary OTRA Clearing, Inc. OTRA processed stock trades (issuing stock to buyers and transferring the cash to sellers), confirmed securities trades, and provided financing services for about two dozen small stock brokerage firms. OTRA was incorporated on March 31, 1987, and completed its initial public offering in September. At that time OTRA was authorized to conduct business in the District of Columbia and 43 states.

OTRA's beginnings were auspicious, with revenues increasing steadily. For the nine months ended September 29, 1987, OTRA reported revenues of $3.02 million, compared to the previous year's revenues of $845,375. Cofounder, chairman, and largest stockholder William R. Stratton attributed the more than threefold revenue increase to expansion and the rise in the number of correspondents OTRA served; the company's broker-dealer list grew from 24 to 39 firms by November 1987.

To maintain its sales growth in the late 1980s, OTRA continued to expand and seek strategic acquisitions. By 1989 OTRA had 85 employees and served about 60 corporate customers. In January the company announced it would acquire Certificate Transfer Co., a seven-year-old California company that maintained stockholder lists and recorded stock transactions for about 200 companies. The transfer business was considered a logical addition to OTRA's existing services and was in line with the company's diversification strategy. By early 1991 OTRA had operations in three areas of the financial services industry: subsidiary OTRA Clearing continued to provide securities clearing services; subsidiary Oxford Transfer & Registrar, Inc. provided transfer services; and subsidiary Houlihan Valuation Advisors offered evaluation and corporate business plan development services.

For the fiscal year ended December 31, 1989, OTRA reported revenues of $10.03 million. A year later sales jumped significantly, reaching $12.59 million. OTRA's clearing services had undeniably proved profitable, but chairman Stratton believed further diversification was necessary to gather momentum in the financial services sector. Because OTRA's clearing services were dependent on its network of independent broker-dealers, which numbered 26 in mid-1991, the company could not reliably predict the amount of business headed its way. "One of the things that's always bothered me about being a wholesale clearing firm is you don't have any control over your revenue base," Stratton explained in the *Los Angeles Times*. "When we come to work, we don't know if we're going to clear

Company Perspectives:

Our company is now stronger and more competitive than ever before. Our customers are growing like never before. And this management is more focused than ever before on generating revenue growth and building the value of JB Oxford for shareholders. We intend to do that by continuing to provide high-quality service and cutting-edge investment resources to clients while building brand awareness and attracting a wider customer base.

3,000 trades that day or 1,000. We have to be prepared to do 3,000, but we also have to be profitable at 1,000.'' OTRA, which cleared a daily average of 1,700 trades in 1991, hoped to remedy the problem by opening its own retail brokerage firm, thus ensuring ample demand for its clearing services.

Expansion and Diversification in the Early 1990s

As promised, OTRA opened a retail brokerage division in late 1991. A division of OTRA Clearing, Reynolds Kendrick Stratton was based in San Francisco and offered full-service investor services. Continuing with its expansion strategy, OTRA also gained a 90 percent stake in Prolyx Data Systems, Inc., with Wm. Michael Reyn & Associates, a business valuation company. Prolyx was a provider of wide-area network and terminal emulation products and services.

To mark its entry in the brokerage industry and signal its expanded repertoire, OTRA changed its name to RKS Financial Group, Inc., on May 22, 1992, the initials RKS representing the name of the Reynolds Kendrick Stratton subsidiary. Stratton remarked in a prepared statement: ''This change is a reflection of the company's shift from focusing only on the securities industry to the broader, financial services area that the company now encompasses.'' The newly christened company made another major change in 1992; RKS Financial moved its headquarters from Glendale to Beverly Hills. The Beverly Hills location provided 20 to 30 percent more space than the Glendale offices. RKS Financial planned to open a second Reynolds Kendrick Stratton office in the Beverly Hills office and increase its staff by about a dozen brokers. RKS also renamed OTRA Clearing in September 1992, changing the name to Reynolds Kendrick Stratton, Inc. In a company statement, William Stratton commented on the name change, ''I don't believe a generic name is suitable for a company that has as much personality as we do. . . . With our new name, I believe our firm will be more readily recognized as a full service brokerage by those in the securities industry.''

Despite continually rising revenues—sales increased nearly 32 percent during the first half of 1992—RKS Financial was not without problems. In July 1991 a lawsuit was filed against OTRA. The lawsuit, which gained class-action status in 1993, alleged that OTRA defrauded more than 100,000 investors by charging illegal annual maintenance fees. OTRA did begin applying a fee, generally not exceeding $25, in 1990 for maintenance of dormant stock accounts. Investors who did not provide payment for such fees discovered that OTRA sold their stock to collect the outstanding amount. OTRA gained about $1.6 million in 1990 from such fees. The lawsuit claimed that investors were not given the opportunity to close or transfer accounts to avoid the fees; investors who chose to close accounts were charged processing fees. OTRA denied any wrongdoing and indicated that only a handful of investors voiced complaints regarding the new maintenance fee. The suit requested out-of-pocket damages of a maximum of $50 for each plaintiff, as well as millions in punitive damages. The case was settled with little fanfare in 1996.

Major Changes and Scandal in the Mid-1990s

More controversy hit RKS Financial in the mid-1990s. In the spring of 1993 a 51 percent share in RKS Financial was acquired by a group of investors that included Walter Senior, an executive for 20th Century Fox; Christopher Sues, a New York attorney; and Rafi Khan, a stockbroker with Reynolds Kendrick Stratton. The three investors gained seats on RKS Financial's board. Problems arose quickly, however, and in October of that same year, a mere six months after joining Reynolds Kendrick Stratton, Rafi Khan quit his job and resigned his seat on the board, offering little explanation. Khan was in the midst of attempting to gain control of ICN Pharmaceuticals Inc., a company in which Khan and his family had acquired a significant number of shares.

Though Khan's activities brought unwanted attention to RKS Financial, it was the company's relationship with Irving J. Kott that became increasingly troublesome and damaging. Kott became affiliated with the company when he assisted the group of investors that included Rafi Khan with the development of a turnaround strategy. Kott had a long and controversial history in the securities industry. He had been convicted of stock fraud in his native Canada in 1976 and was involved with questionable securities activities in Amsterdam in the mid-1980s. In the Amsterdam case, Kott was accused of running a boiler-room operation, a firm that employed aggressive sales tactics to promote small, highly speculative stocks, known as First Commerce. One of the stocks the company promoted was DeVoe-Holbein International, a company claiming to have developed a process for the extraction of valuable minerals from water. It was estimated that investors lost between $100 million and $400 million as a result of First Commerce's operations. Reynolds Kendrick Stratton claimed that Kott served only as a consultant, but many insiders stated otherwise. Also, it was shortly after Kott joined the company that brokers began to promote shares of Harison Corp., a company eerily similar and with strong ties to DeVoe-Holbein. Reynolds Kendrick Stratton became known as a boiler-room operation itself, and its activities sparked lawsuits and investigation by the National Association of Securities Dealers (NASD).

In 1994 RKS Financial changed its name to JB Oxford Holdings, Inc., and entered the discount brokerage industry. William Stratton left the company, and Stephen Rubenstein became CEO. Felix Oeri, a Swiss banker and a major shareholder, assumed the role of director. The company also discontinued the operations of Reynolds Kendrick Stratton in order to focus on the securities clearing and discount brokerage segments rather than the full-service brokerage business, and per-

Key Dates:

1986: OTRA Securities Group, Inc. forms.
1991: OTRA begins offering brokerage services through subsidiary OTRA Clearing, Inc.'s Reynolds Kendrick Stratton division.
1992: OTRA changes company name to RKS Financial Group, Inc.
1994: Company changes name to JB Oxford Holdings, Inc., and enters the discount brokerage trade. Reynolds Kendrick Stratton discontinues operations.
1998: New management takes over operations at JB Oxford Holdings.

haps also to move beyond its scandalous recent past. Reynolds Kendrick Stratton was replaced by JB Oxford & Company.

JB Oxford was very active in the mid-1990s, and many changes were implemented. The company entered the Swiss market by establishing a representative office in Basel, Switzerland, headed by Felix Oeri, in 1994. A year later the office was reorganized into a full-service branch. JB Oxford sold its Houlihan Valuation subsidiary and closed the operations of Prolyx Data Systems to focus more fully on developing JBOC. The company opened a JBOC office in New York in 1995 and later opened additional offices in Boston, Dallas, and Miami. JB Oxford also worked to gain name recognition and exposure through advertising campaigns and began to target Asian populations, such as the Los Angeles Chinese community. Asian investors were considered a key target market for discount investing services, and the company hired Chinese-speaking brokers and advertised in Chinese newspapers and on television to attract and accommodate customers.

In the hope of gaining new customers and to serve a wide range of clientele, JB Oxford adopted a restructuring strategy in late 1994. The firm planned to offer a greater array of products, including mutual funds, fixed-income products, insurance services, and variable and fixed-rate annuities. JB Oxford greatly increased its market-making stocks, from 20 in 1994 to more than 100 in 1995, and opened a capital markets division. JB Oxford also offered customers with personal computers the opportunity to place orders electronically and increased its online trading services by introducing a Windows-based product in 1996. With the rising popularity of the Internet—orders placed through JBOC's electronic trading services more than doubled during the third quarter of 1996—JB Oxford planned to continue upgrading its online products.

The changes paid off, and JB Oxford's revenues began to pick up. The company broke even in the first quarter of 1995 after six consecutive quarters of losses. Net income reached $5.02 million in fiscal 1995, compared to a loss of $7.58 million in 1994, and 1996 revenues were $57.59 million, up 45 percent from 1995 sales. Still, one thing the company seemed unable to shake was Irving Kott, who continued to resurface at JB Oxford as a marketing consultant. Though JB Oxford maintained that Kott's services were used only on occasion, *Time* reported that Kott spent more than half of his time at JB Oxford headquarters, in an office larger than Rubenstein's. The magazine also indicated that a number of JB Oxford's major shareholders possessed close ties to Kott or with Kott-related stocks and that Kott was instrumental in helping the company begin its discount brokerage business. Kott was also behind JB Oxford's advertising and marketing endeavors.

JB Oxford finally severed ties with Kott in September 1997, a month after agents from the Federal Bureau of Investigation raided its Beverly Hills office and seized boxes of files as part of an investigation into alleged stock manipulation and other abuses. Swiss authorities simultaneously raided the Basel, Switzerland, offices. Ian Kott, Kott's son, continued on as chief operating officer of JB Oxford, despite reservations concerning Irving Kott's influence.

A Clean Slate in the Late 1990s

In May 1998 a group of investors led by Christopher L. Jarratt acquired a controlling interest in JB Oxford. Jarratt, a principal of merchant banking firm Third Capital, LLC, replaced Felix Oeri as chairman and Stephen Rubenstein as CEO. James G. Lewis, also a principal of Third Capital, was appointed chief operating officer and interim president of JB Oxford. Jarratt shared his enthusiasm for JB Oxford's potential in a prepared statement and noted: ''We believe JB Oxford is a good Company with good employees and a healthy customer base from which to develop and expand existing business lines. It suffered some unfortunate setbacks recently and our immediate goal is to put these problems behind us.''

New management quickly began to implement a restructuring strategy that included streamlining operations for maximum efficiency and increased profitability. Ian Kott was dismissed from his position in June and a national search for a chief operating officer was launched. Though Rubenstein remained president of JBOC after management changes, he left the company in the fall. JB Oxford began consolidating its offices, closing branches in Dallas, Boston, and Basel, Switzerland, in 1998 and 1999. The company also consolidated its Stocks-4-Less subsidiary into JB Oxford and hired a new advertising agency, Tracey/Ryan & Partners, to develop an aggressive marketing campaign that spotlighted JB Oxford's discount and online trading services.

Internet trading reached a fever pitch in the late 1990s, and JB Oxford took full advantage. The firm unveiled a newly redesigned web site in July 1998 that enhanced online trading capabilities. In early 1999 the stocks of small brokerage firms offering online trading surged, JB Oxford's among them; in one day in February, according to Automatic Data Processing, more than 33 million shares of JB Oxford were traded. In the first quarter of 1999, reported Bill Burnham of CS First Boston, online trading volumes increased 30 to 35 percent over fourth quarter figures, reaching about 450,000 trades daily.

The popularity of online trading helped JB Oxford attain profitability sooner than anticipated, during the fourth quarter of 1998. Revenues reached $19.4 million, a rise of 21 percent over fourth quarter revenues in 1997. JB Oxford reported record revenues of $23.7 million for the first quarter of 1999, up 22 percent from the previous quarter. To maintain its meteoric rise in sales, JB Oxford announced plans to purchase a small brokerage to increase its accounts, which numbered 115,000 at the end of 1998. The company changed advertising agencies in May 1999, hiring Think New Ideas Inc., and nearly doubled its advertising budget for the second half of 1999 to $10 million. A national, multimedia advertising campaign was launched in September.

That same month JB Oxford launched its redesigned web site, which not only allowed customers to place online trades and access a wealth of financial information but also provided the ability to communicate in real time with a JB Oxford representative. JB Oxford also introduced the *npower* account, which provided free, unlimited Internet access to customers who maintained a $2,000 cash balance. The account included electronic banking services, such as online bill payment, after-hours trading, and access to up-to-date financial information.

As the company headed toward the new millennium, JB Oxford planned to continue growing its business, particularly its online division. According to Forrester Research, a market research firm, the number of online brokerage accounts was projected to grow to 14 million between 1999 and 2002. By continually upgrading its services, providing cutting-edge technology, and expanding through acquisitions and increased product offerings, JB Oxford hoped to tap into its unrealized potential and attract new customers.

Principal Subsidiaries

JB Oxford & Company; JB Oxford Insurance Services, Inc.

Principal Competitors

Charles Schwab & Co., Inc.; Fidelity Brokerage Services, Inc.; Waterhouse Securities, Inc.; Ameritrade, Inc.; E*TRADE Group, Inc.

Further Reading

Emshwiller, John R., ''Convicted Swindler Is Securities-Firm Consultant,'' *Wall Street Journal,* May 3, 1995, p. C1.

Gollner, Philipp, ''2 Investors Sue Glendale-Based OTRA Securities Over Annual Fees,'' *Los Angeles Times,* July 23, 1991, p. A9.

Gurwin, Larry, ''The Secret Life of JB Oxford—Why the Power Behind a Discount Broker Wants to Stay out of Sight,'' *Time,* December 9, 1996, p. 52F.

Lucchetti, Aaron, and Larry Bauman, ''Small Brokerage Firms Surge on Internet Fever,'' *Wall Street Journal,* February 5, 1999, p. C7.

Peltz, James F., ''Glendale Securities Firm Seeks to Increase Its Presence Trading: OTRA Wants to Supplement Its Clearinghouse Function by Also Becoming a Retail Brokerage,'' *Los Angeles Times,* June 18, 1991, p. 10.

Reerink, Jack, ''Stock Trades Via Internet up 30%, Set Record,'' *San Diego Union-Tribune,* April 6, 1999, p. C3.

Rundle, Rhonda L., ''Khan Pursues Effort for ICN Pharmaceuticals,'' *Wall Street Journal,* October 11, 1993, p. A4.

Weber, Jonathan, ''Beverly Hills Firm's Stock Offer Is Similar to Major Fraud Case Investments: Reynolds Kendrick & Stratton Has Allied Itself with Controversial Stock Promoter Irving J. Kott,'' *Los Angeles Times,* December 18, 1993, p. 1.

Zeidler, Sue, ''Brokerage Targeted in Stock-Manipulation Case,'' *San Diego Union-Tribune,* August 21, 1997, p. C2.

—Mariko Fujinaka

J.D. Power and Associates

30401 Agoura Road, Suite 200
Agoura Hills, California 91301
U.S.A.
Telephone: (818) 889-6330
Fax: (818) 889-3719
Web site: http://www.jdpower.com

Private Company
Incorporated: 1968
Employees: 475
Sales: $71.6 million (1998)
NAIC: 541910 Marketing Research and Public Opinion Polling

By the early 1990s, the name J.D. Power and Associates had become synonymous with automotive quality in the minds of consumers. Power's surveys defined quality in terms of how consumers judged it, rather than from the manufacturers' point of view. Power's surveys influenced not only consumers, but also manufacturers. Power has been recognized as playing a major role in propelling the U.S. auto industry toward improving quality in the late 1980s and 1990s.

Power bears the cost of conducting the surveys, which could run as much as $300,000 or more. The firm then generates revenue by selling the results of its surveys to interested companies for $50,000 to $100,000. In addition, advertisers must also buy the rights to use the Power name for an additional sum. Agency founder Dave Power himself admits that the surveys are used as a marketing tool by the auto manufacturers as well as a measure of manufacturing quality and customer satisfaction.

Collecting Data and Conducting Surveys: 1968–80

J.D. Power and Associates was founded in 1968 as a market research firm in Agoura Hills, a suburb of Los Angeles, by James David (Dave) Power III. He grew up in Worcester, Massachusetts, and went to local college Holy Cross (class of 1953). After a stint in the U.S. Coast Guard, he went to the Wharton School of Business at the University of Pennsylvania and received his MBA in 1959. He was recruited by Ford Motor Company and became a financial analyst at the company's headquarters in Dearborn, Michigan. He spent two years with Ford, then joined Marplan/Detroit, a subsidiary of Interpublic and the research arm of advertising agency McCann-Erickson. There he did market research studies for Buick for three-and-a-half years.

After a few more job changes, Power established a market research agency in April 1968 called J.D. Power and Associates. The firm's first clients included chainsaw manufacturer McCulloch Corporation, for whom Power had done market research, U.S. Borax, United California Bank, and MSI Data Systems. The firm's first big break came when Toyota, which had just opened a sales office in Torrance, California, hired Power to do market research.

Power then began preparing independent surveys that were sold to automakers on a subscription basis in the early 1970s. The first was a national ownership survey of the Mazda rotary engine. The survey revealed that owners were having major problems with the unique engine. Although Mazda initially denied the problems, the company later acknowledged them. The survey gave Power great credibility and showed that the agency was not just a spokesperson for the auto industry.

In the mid-1970s Power surveyed American car owners about front-wheel-drive vehicles. At the time U.S. automakers were not offering that option; only Honda and Subaru were. Power's front-wheel-drive survey showed that American consumers were interested in front-wheel-drive if it performed well and was reliable. The survey clinched Power's position as an auto industry prophet. Still, the Power agency was one of several statistics-gathering organizations in the 1970s and did not really stand out among automakers.

Customer Satisfaction Surveys Becoming Well-Known: 1980s

Power's annual Consumer Satisfaction Index, first published in 1981, measured satisfaction among customers who had owned their cars for one year. Consumers were asked to rate their vehicles as well as dealer service during the first year of

Company Perspectives:

Established in 1968, the firm's primary objective is to assist companies in achieving their operating goals by providing relevant information and business solutions based on the expectations of their customers. J.D. Power and Associates has gained practical experience developing customer service models across industries by becoming intimately familiar with consumer decision-making, habits and perceptions. As a result, the firm can quickly assist companies in better understanding their customer base by analyzing consumer experiences with products and services and translating that information into actionable improvement initiatives.

ownership by checking off a list of defects and service problems. The 1983 survey indicated the overall index was up 9.5 percent, which could be taken as an indication that automobile manufacturers were becoming more concerned with quality. While imports dominated the list, Ford was able to pull ahead of a number of imports in the survey.

It was not until the mid-1980s that Power was able to sell his research findings to the big three automakers in Detroit. By then approximately half of Power's revenues were from various studies on the automotive business. To improve the firm's credibility and stop complaints about its methodology, Power opened its studies to three statisticians from graduate business schools for auditing.

Power's revenues were $7.5 million in 1987, the year in which the agency introduced its Initial Quality Study (IQS), which covered automobile owner experiences during the first 90 days of ownership. The study was released every May. In the first IQS the Toyota Cressida was ranked first with a score of 69 problems per hundred cars.

Power became involved in a dispute with Ford Motor in the late 1980s. Ford's own in-house studies ranked it above its domestic competitors in terms of initial customer satisfaction and quality. Power's IQS ranked Ford below its domestic competitors. The two sides discussed their different methods of data collection and interpretation and appeared to resolve the dispute. By 1992 Ford outranked both General Motors and Chrysler in the IQS.

By 1989 the Power agency was sending out four million questionnaires annually to car owners and taking in $12 million. About 35 percent of the mailed surveys were answered, a higher than average response rate. At the end of the 1980s quality was the biggest issue among carmakers. They were spending millions of dollars promoting the findings of the Power organization, which had grown in status during the 1980s due to three main factors: increased professionalism of the Power staff; increased attention given to domestic automakers; and a substantial increase in the number of winners who purchased advertising to promote the Power findings and the organization.

Automakers cited Power's improved technical support. They were completely confident in the Power organization's ability to conduct interviews and code results properly, without bias. At the end of the 1980s Power was publishing four major automotive reports annually, plus numerous minor ones. Its best-known surveys were the Customer Satisfaction Index and the Initial Quality Study. Customers were not allowed to publish or release the contents of an entire survey, but they could report and publicize favorable findings as long as Power approved it for accuracy.

Branching out into Other Industry Surveys: 1990s

By 1990 Power was growing at an annual rate of 25 percent, with 100 full-time employees and 150 part-time employees. In addition to its Agoura Hills headquarters, the firm had a Detroit office that also handled its Canadian operations. It had recently entered into a 50–50 market research venture in Japan called R&D/J.D. Power. It also conducted its first annual automotive advertising strategy conference, which became a sold-out event among advertising and marketing professionals.

In addition to its automotive CSI and IQS, Power was also producing a Sales Satisfaction Index, whose key elements were the salesperson, initial product quality, and actual delivery of the car to the customer; the Vehicle Performance Index, which covered the first two to three years of ownership; and the Vehicle Dependability Index, which looked at owner satisfaction and the incidence and type of problems during the first four to five years of ownership.

More carmakers than ever were citing the results of Power surveys in their 1990 model introduction ads. As a result, the firm tightened its guidelines for the next year. Under then current guidelines, advertisers were not allowed to extract just one factor from the Customer Satisfaction Index (or any other Power index) to support overall claims. For example, an automaker could not say it provided the best road service if its overall customer satisfaction rating was not even in the top 20.

When Buick's LeSabre was ranked number one in Power's Initial Quality Survey, Buick launched an advertising campaign touting the LeSabre as "the most trouble-free car built in America." Sales subsequently jumped by 32.5 percent in June, 91 percent in July, and 98 percent in August, enabling Buick to report a sales gain of one percent over 1989 instead of a decline. Power's guidelines allowed Buick to promote its 1990 models based on 1989 survey results. The Power survey was "one of the key factors in the tremendous resurgence that Buick has had in the last few years," according to David Cole, director of The Center for Study of Automotive Research, quoted in *California Business.*

"Quality" was *the* buzzword of the 1990s as automakers touted their cars as "best built," "most trouble-free," and "highest quality." According to *Automotive Industries* magazine, J.D. Power's Initial Quality Survey and *Consumer Reports'* Frequency of Repair Records were the two most respected independent measures of car quality.

In 1991 Power released its first Computer Industry Satisfaction Program study, which measured customer satisfaction with personal computers, in time for the annual spring Comdex show. Sixteen manufacturers were included in the study, based on Power's judgment of who the leading companies were. Results of the survey were available for around $50,000; only

Key Dates:

1968: John David Power III founds market research agency J.D. Power and Associates in southern California.
1973: Power publishes results of national ownership survey that reveals problems with the Mazda rotary engine.
1981: Power publishes the first annual Consumer Satisfaction Index.
1987: Power introduces the Initial Quality Study.
1991: Power releases its first annual Computer Industry Satisfaction Program study.
1993: Power begins developing the Power Information Network to capture daily sales data of automobile dealers.
1997: Power introduces its first annual study of the used-vehicle market.
1999: Power completes its first survey of the RV market.

companies involved in the survey were likely to purchase the report. Dell and Apple were ranked one and two. The study was based on phone calls to companies with fewer than 500 employees. Two additional studies were planned, one on PCs in large corporations and one on PCs at home. Following release of the survey results, Dell ran a full-page ad in the *Wall Street Journal.*

Revenues for 1991 reached $18 million. To maintain and guard its credibility, Power tightened the rules regarding advertising. When Infiniti and Lexus tied for first place in the IQS, both were barred from naming the study in their ads without mentioning the tie. The variety of surveys and proliferation of categories, if not policed by the Power organization, tended to result in some confusion and a potential erosion of the firm's credibility.

In addition, Power decided in 1991 that its name could only be associated in advertising with the top car in four categories: best American, Asian, and European brands, and best overall. Since Lexus occupied three of the four top spots, advertising references to J.D. Power and Associates were not as numerous.

By tightening the rules and guarding its credibility, Power was responding in part to an advertising campaign involving Chevrolet's Lumina. Chevrolet had advertised its Lumina as the ''most trouble-free two-door car in the midsize segment'' and referred to Power by name. When it came to light that all of the models in that segment performed below average, Chevrolet pulled the ads.

By 1992 Power was producing 12 studies that measured the performance of automakers and their dealers. It launched its first Canadian CSI in 1991. The first Japanese CSI on luxury cars was due the fall of 1992, the result of Power's joint venture with a Japanese research firm. Negotiations were underway to set up similar ventures in Europe and Australia. Power's 1992 revenues were expected to reach $22.5 million. It was estimated that industry surveys, such as the CSI, accounted for about one-third of Power's revenues. Another third came from proprietary research for individual clients. Such research supported a growing management consulting business as well as extensive training for manufacturers and dealers. No single company accounted for more than five percent of the firm's business.

For the first time since its founding, Power began recruiting MBAs from college campuses in the spring of 1992. Power traveled a lot on behalf of his business, visiting Detroit once a month, Japan every two months, and Europe three times a year. He was on the road an estimated 80 percent of the time. The agency announced it would release its first consumer satisfaction survey for the airline industry in December 1992. The company asked 40,000 frequent travelers to file reports on business trips.

In 1995 Power introduced a new survey on credit cards. The agency surveyed 7,200 cardholders and reported on 21 card issuers that accounted for about 75 percent of the market. The survey found that customer service and billing were key factors in determining customer satisfaction with cards they held. Industry experts, though, still considered fees, rewards, and rates as the main factors in determining what credit cards consumer chose. Power also began conducting a similar survey in Canada.

J. David Power unveiled a new daily sales reporting network for automobile dealers at a University of Michigan conference in August 1996. Power claimed the network could cut distribution costs by $4 billion a year by reducing dealer inventories to a 30-day supply. Power had invested $6 million in the network, which was started in 1993 and already included 1,000 of California's 3,600 automobile dealers. By 1997 the Power Information Network was gathering daily sales transaction data from 1,250 California dealerships. Power took that data, analyzed it, and provided the dealers with information useful for distribution, price, and marketing strategies. In 1998 Power added dealers in several major markets, resulting in 3,000 dealers providing daily sales information to the network. Power projected that the network would cover areas representing at least two-thirds of automotive sales in the United States by the end of 1999.

In 1996 revenues reached $46 million. Power continued to run into resistance in Europe, where automakers did not believe his surveys could help them sell more cars. Also hindering international expansion was the lack of a vehicle registration system comparable to that of the United States.

In 1996 Power introduced the Residential Local Telephone Service Study to measure customer satisfaction with local telephone service. From 1996 to 1999 the top ranked provider was BellSouth.

During the 1990s the automotive industry became more responsive to customer needs and desires. Power's surveys, always conducted from the customer's perspective, contributed to the auto industry becoming more customer-driven. According to *Automotive Industries,* J.D. Power and Associates was ''a name that's become ubiquitous in the automotive world, virtually synonymous with automotive quality and reliability.'' In 30 years the firm grew from an obscure southern California market research firm ''to become the nation's arbiter of customer satisfaction.'' Power's surveys created an awareness of customer satisfaction and defined ways in which customer expectations could be both measured and met.

Some auto manufacturers turned to outside consultants to help improve their ratings in the Power surveys. In 1994 and 1995 Chrysler hired a consultant to improve its internal audit process. Chrysler discovered its own audit procedures did not catch certain things that Power respondents would complain about, such as the lack of a center armrest on certain models. As a result, Chrysler learned not only how to emulate Power internally, but also how to use the methodology to fix problems.

Power's 1997 Initial Quality Study found that overall vehicle quality continued to improve. The study found an average of 86 problems per hundred vehicles, compared to 110 problems per hundred vehicles in 1996. The 22 percent improvement was the best since the study began in 1987.

The 1997 survey was based on questionnaires sent to 110,000 randomly selected new car owners. Results showed Ford with 81 defects per hundred cars, a 40 percent improvement; General Motors with 97 defects per hundred cars; and Chrysler, with a 20 percent improvement to 103 defects per 100 cars. The clear winners, though, were Japanese automakers such as Honda (62 defects per hundred vehicles), Toyota (64 defects per hundred vehicles), and Nissan (79 defects per hundred vehicles). The winner in the passenger car category was the Lexus LS 400, with only 38 defects per hundred cars.

In 1997 Power introduced its first annual study of the used vehicle market. The survey noted that used vehicle sales in the United States were growing, while sales of traditional entry level vehicles continued to fall. By 1998 the survey showed an increase in the percentage of people concerned that new vehicles depreciated too much. It also noted that used vehicles were becoming important to luxury brands, with consumers increasingly purchasing used luxury vehicles instead of comparably priced new vehicles. The 1999 survey revealed that more than one-fourth of used vehicle buyers used the Internet for assistance and information to help with their purchase decision.

In the 1997 survey the gap between the top and bottom had narrowed considerable since the first survey in 1987, when 340 points separated the top and bottom models. In 1998 Power modified its IQS by giving consumers more defects they could choose—135 versus 90 in previous versions of the survey. Survey results for 1998 would thus show more defects per hundred vehicles. Added to the list of possible defects were many technological gadgets that had been added to cars since the first IQS in 1987. Some defects that did not occur very often, such as engine dieseling and body rust, were dropped from the survey. The changes were made in response to criticism that the difference between model quality was becoming difficult to judge, with many models having less than one defect per car in the 1997 survey. Power also introduced the APEAL (Automotive Performance Execution and Layout) study, which focused on what went right with a vehicle rather than what went wrong.

In 1998 Power expanded into the recreational vehicle (RV) market. It received approval from the Go RVing Coalition's Committee on Excellence for a proposed research project. The Committee earmarked $298,000 to contribute to the study, which would determine the important factors in customer satisfaction with RVs. The Power survey would be tailored to the RV industry and would not include individual model rankings. Survey results would be used to support an overall industry advertising campaign to promote the use of RVs.

Power completed its RV survey in 1999. Results were based on 12,000 owners of 1997 model year RVs. Product issues accounted for about two-thirds of RV customer satisfaction, according to the survey, with the sale and delivery experience being the next most important factor. Disclosure of the survey results was to be determined by the major RV industry associations, with proprietary reports sent to individual participating manufacturers.

In the summer of 1998 Power released the results of its first new home buyers survey. Power surveyed home buyers in southern California, Phoenix, and Denver, targeting customers of builders who accounted for the top 70 percent of the market. The survey results were based on 3,200 responses in southern California, 8,800 responses in Phoenix, and 4,300 responses in Denver. For 1999 the company planned to survey Dallas-Fort Worth, Atlanta, and Chicago.

As of 1999 Power continued to expand into new industries. It was evaluating the marine market for possible surveys. It also conducted an annual Cable/Satellite TV Customer Satisfaction Study, and in 1999 the agency introduced a new study of automobile insurance.

Principal Competitors

Consumer Reports (Consumers Union); AutoPacific Group; Strategic Vision Inc.; IDC; InfoCorp; Dataquest Inc.

Further Reading

Alpert, Mark, "Power Surge," *Fortune,* September 11, 1989, p. 209.

Brooke, Lindsay, "The Quest for Quality," *Automotive Industries,* January 1990, p. 36.

Callahan, Joe, "Power's a Winner Now," *Automotive Industries,* November 1989, p. 21.

"Canada Trust Card Wins Customer Satisfaction Survey," *American Banker,* October 20, 1998.

Colman, Price, "Charter Disputes Survey," *Broadcasting & Cable,* September 13, 1999, p. 32.

Craig, Charlotte W., "J.D. Power Expands Quality Survey on New Cars," *Knight-Ridder/Tribune Business News,* May 26, 1998.

"Digest," *Automotive News,* October 4, 1999, p. 18.

Eisenstein, Paul A., "Behind the Power: How Does J.D. Power Decide Which Companies and Vehicles Have the Best Quality?" *Automotive Industries,* May 1997, p. 51.

Farrell, Michael, "J.D. Power Ponders Rating Marine Market," *Boating Industry,* May 1998, p. 6.

Files, Jennifer, "Southwest Bell, GTE Rank Below Average in Customer Survey," *Knight-Ridder/Tribune Business News,* August 4, 1999.

Goldenberg, Sherman, "Go RVing Committee on Excellence Approves J.D. Power Research," *RV Business,* July 1998, p. 7.

Hinsberg, Pat, "J.D. Power Keeps Raising the Chinning Bar," *Adweek Eastern Edition,* September 9, 1991, p. 17.

"J.D. Power Releases RV-Satisfaction Study," *RV Business,* September 1999, p. 10.

Kerry, Lee, "Powering up a Market Research Firm," *Adweek Western Advertising News,* November 5, 1990, p. 8.

Kiley, David, "Ad Overkill Threatens J.D. Power's Impact," *Adweek's Marketing Week,* November 27, 1989, p. 5.

Lurz, William H., "J.D. Power Surveys Seem Sure to Influence Buyers," *Professional Builder,* December 1998, p. 42.

Martin, Dave, "J.D. Power & Associates' Ongoing Success Can Be Traced to Its Doing Research That Consistently Reflects Consumers' Needs and Desires," *Mediaweek,* May 3, 1993, p. 9.

Mateja, Jim, "Jim Mateja Column," *Knight-Ridder/Tribune Business News,* October 14, 1999.

McElroy, John, "Quality: The New Yardstick," *Automotive Industries,* December 1983, p. 47.

Meece, Mickey, "Auto Rating Firm Rolls out New Survey—on Credit Cards," *American Banker,* November 9, 1995, p. 1.

Miller, Joe, "Study: Market Craves More Used Vehicles," *Automotive News,* December 21, 1998, p. 30.

"Net a Prime Resource for Lemon Alerts," *Content Factory,* August 3, 1999.

O'Keefe, Susan, "BellSouth on Top Again," *Telecommunications,* October 1, 1998, p. 24.

Rechtin, Mark, "As Quality Graph Narrows, Power Rethinks the IQS," *Automotive News,* May 12, 1997, p. 3.

Sawyers, Arlena, "Power Expands Daily Sales Data Network," *Automotive News,* November 9, 1998, p. 25.

Sedam, Scott, "The Surveys Are Coming! The Surveys Are Coming!," *Builder,* September 1998, p. 160.

Smith, David C., "Northern Disclosure," *Ward's Auto World,* September 1996, p. 95.

Svetich, Kim, "More Power to You," *California Business,* September 1991, p. 46.

Taylor, Alex, III, "A Peek Inside the Auto Industry's Most Respected Survey," *Fortune,* October 26, 1998, p. 46.

"Thanks for Your Concern, But What Are Your Rates?," *Adweek Eastern Edition,* October 4, 1999, p. 52.

Underwood, Elaine, "J.D. Power Will Rate, Rank Airlines," *Brandweek,* October 5, 1992, p. 10.

Venditto, Gus, "J.D. Power Tackles the Big Job of Ranking PC Customer's Satisfaction," *PC Magazine,* August 1991, p. 29.

Warshaw, Michael, "Know Your Customer," *Success,* February 1997, p. 36.

White, Todd, "Attitude Surveyor Drives into Computers, Airlines; Automotive Survey Firm J.D. Power Plans to Expand," *Los Angeles Business Journal,* December 7, 1992, p. 39.

—David P. Bianco

JJB Sports plc

Martland Park
Challenge Way
Wigan
Lancashire WN5 0LD
United Kingdom
Telephone: +44 1942 221400
Fax: +44 1942 629809
Web site: http://www.jjb.co.uk

Public Company
Incorporated: 1971
Employees: 5,000
Sales: £372.97 million (US$636.60 million) (1999)
Stock Exchanges: London
Ticker Symbol: JJB
NAIC: 45111 Sporting Goods Stores

JJB Sports plc is in the big leagues of U.K. sports retailing. The leading sports equipment and sports apparel retailer operates 450 stores under the JJB Sports and Sports Division names throughout the United Kingdom. More than 180 of these stores feature a superstore format of more than 10,000 square feet. The company is phasing out its smaller stores in favor of converting most of its shops to the superstore concept. JJB Sports is also phasing out the Sports Division name, replacing the storefronts gained from its acquisition of its main U.K. rival with its own name. While absorbing the larger Sports Division has been difficult for the company, JJB Sports continues an aggressive expansion, opening 25 sites—including 21 superstores—during 1999. Unlike such competitors as Intersport and JD Sports, JJB Sports focuses on sporting goods, rather than the fading leisure and sportswear trends of the late 1990s. Nonetheless, clothing represented 43 percent (49 percent at Sports Division) of the company's sales in 1999, with footwear adding 30 percent (33 percent at Sports Division). The company also generated 14 percent of sales with so-called replica football (soccer) and rugby kits, featuring the colors of U.K. clubs. All of JJB Sports' sales are made in the United Kingdom. The company continues to be led by founder David Whelan, as well as his son-in-law (and heir apparent) Duncan Sharpe.

Coal Mines to Goal Lines in the 1960s

David Whelan came from a mining background. All of the male members of the Whelan family had worked the Wigan, Lancashire, mines. However, Whelan's father was determined to spare his sons from the same life of hardship; he forbade them from following the family mining tradition, insisting instead that Whelan become an engineer's apprentice. At the age of 15, however, Whelan left school in order to pursue a career in professional football (soccer). At the age of 17, Whelan had been signed to play for the Blackburn Rovers, earning £5 per week. By the age of 23, however, Whelan's football career was over. Having helped his team reach the FA Cup final round, at Wembley Stadium, Whelan, playing fullback, broke his leg in three places.

Whelan made a go at returning to the field, after two years of recovery, only to break his leg a second time. With no education and no more than the £400 bonus paid to him by Blackburn for helping the team reach the finals, Whelan was forced to find a new career. Whelan used the bonus money to buy out a stall in Blackburn's outdoor market, where he began selling toiletry items and groceries. Whelan's talents as a salesman and entrepreneur quickly came to light. Soon after, Whelan opened a second stall, at Wigan's market. By the end of the 1960s, Whelan had moved to an actual shop, on the edge of Wigan, before opening a second shop in the center of town. Whelan incorporated his stores under the name Whelan's Discount Stores, expanding to a full supermarket concept and building up a chain of ten stores by the end of the 1970s. In 1978, Whelan agreed to sell his chain to the northern-based Wm. Morrison chain of supermarkets, which paid Whelan £1.5 million.

Rather than retire, at age 60, Whelan turned to a new retailing direction. In 1971, Whelan had purchased and incorporated a small bait-and-tackle and sports shop on the outskirts of Wigan. The store had been in existence since 1903, when it was opened by rugby player J.J. Broughton. After Broughton, the store came under the ownership of another former athlete,

> **Company Perspectives:**
>
> *Company strategy is to strengthen and expand the business by a controlled increase in the number of stores and, in particular, to develop a chain of larger out-of-town stores. The company's ambition was to build a network of over 500 outlets; this has now been achieved.*

J.J. Bradburn, with fishing equipment and model railroads providing the bulk of sales. Whelan took the shared initials of the store's former owners, naming the store JJB Sports. After the sale of Whelan's Discount Stores, Whelan decided to spend his "retirement" building JJB into the United Kingdom's largest sports retailer—and making himself one of the U.K.'s wealthiest businessmen.

JJB Sports' first year of business under Whelan produced a modest £22,000 in sales, the largest portion of which represented sales of bait, namely maggots. When the store's refrigerator broke down, Whelan decided to redirect his shop's focus to a less perishable product. As such he began stocking his shelves with sports equipment and related items, eliminating model railroads, and reducing emphasis on fishing supplies. By 1979, JJB Sports had become solely dedicated to sports equipment and to strong growth. By the end of 1979, Whelan's retail experience had enabled him to build a chain of seven stores.

JJB Sports arrived just in time to ride a boom in the sporting goods market. Beginning in the late 1970s and taking off into the early 1980s, the United Kingdom, like the United States, saw a huge increase in consumer interest in sporting activities, and in the products that accompanied the various sports. Inspired in part by a building awareness of the importance of personal health and fitness, consumers began looking to fill their leisure time with participation in sports. While consumers continued to play traditional sports, new sports categories and their supporting products had appeared, thanks to booms in jogging, aerobics, and general fitness. JJB Sports quickly became a regional center for the new wave of amateur athletes.

U.K. Leader in the 1990s

Whelan was joined by son-in-law Duncan Sharpe in 1983. Already a professional golfer for some seven years, Sharp, then 23, started out as an area manager with JJB Sports, before rising to become the company's managing director—and chosen heir to Whelan's leadership. Whelan and Sharpe continued to build JJB Sports and to refine their sporting goods concept through the 1980s. While stores tended to be small, city-center based shops, the company began introducing the superstore concept adapted from the United States. The company also launched a side chain of Alpine Sports shops, concentrated on items for the climbing, hiking, and ski markets. However, in 1988 JJB Sports acquired the 11-store chain of Howards Sports, from rival Blacks' Leisure, in exchange for the Alpine Sports concept. Whelan continued to pursue other entrepreneurial side projects. In 1992, for example, he purchased a Wigan pie shop and renamed the shop's pie specialty as "Wigan's Pie," which he then began marketing throughout northwestern England. In the same year, JJB Sports opened its 100th store.

JJB Sports continued its growth into the 1990s, eschewing further acquisitions to focus on organic growth. With the sporting goods boom in full-swing, driven by a growing trend that adopted sportswear—and sporting brand names—as fashion apparel, JJB engaged in an aggressive store opening schedule that brought the chain to 119 stores by 1994. In order to fuel further growth, the company went public in that year, taking a listing on the London stock exchange. Whelan and his family, however, retained majority control of the company he had founded.

Whelan attempted a brief international excursion, opening three JJB stores in Spain in the mid-1990s. The move proved unsuccessful, however, and the three Spanish stores were closed in 1997. Back home, however, JJB continued to ride the growth of the sporting goods market, adding a new warehouse and distribution center in 1996 in order to accommodate the chain's growth. In that year, JJB opened more than 35 stores. By 1997, the company, with 170 stores, announced its intention to open some 50 stores per year for ten years—with a growing percentage of new store openings represented by the larger superstore format—as well as its intention to build the chain to a nationwide concern of 500 "high street" stores and 200 suburban stores. The company also began testing a new store format, aimed at the burgeoning children's sports apparel market, dubbed Future Stars.

JJB Sports took a huge leap toward meeting its goal in 1998 when it surprised the sporting goods industry by acquiring larger rival Sports Division. Slumping retail sales in general, and fears that the sporting goods and sports apparel trends had peaked, as well as growing competition as the United Kingdom's fragmented sporting goods market began to consolidate, had combined to force the private Sports Division to abandon its plans for going public that year. Founded in 1984 by Tom Hunter, who started the company selling sports shoes from his garage, Sports Division had acquired former Sears subsidiary Olympus Sports in the late 1980s to become the United Kingdom's largest sporting goods retailer. Upon the collapse of Sports Division's proposed public flotation, Hunter agreed to allow JJB Sports to acquire his company, for £290 million, in July 1998. While this price was considered high by many industry analysts, the acquisitions more than doubled the size of JJB Sports, enabling it to top the 500-store mark, and making it far and away the leading sporting goods retailer in the United Kingdom. Hunter, age 37, initially took a position as vice-chairman of the company, which remained under the JJB Sports name. After Whelan's insistence, however, that son-in-law Sharpe remained in line to take over the leadership of JJB Sports, Hunter left the company.

Although skeptical about the purchase prices, analysts greeted the merger with approval. The complementary nature of the two retail chains—with JJB Sports concentrated in the north and Sports Division focused on the south—created a truly national entity, with enough purchasing clout to reinforce its bargaining strength with sporting goods and sportswear manufacturers. Merging the operations proved more difficult than expected, however. The company ran into embarrassing difficulties when attempting to transfer Sports Division's stock to

Key Dates:

1979: David Whelan acquires JJ Bradburns and renames it JJB Sports.
1983: Son-in-law Duncan Sharpe joins firm.
1988: Company acquires 11-store Howards Sports chain from Blacks' Leisure.
1992: Company opens 100th JJB Sports store.
1994: JJB Sports goes public on London Stock Exchange.
1999: Company opens Soccer Dome in Wigan.

JJB Sports' warehouse and distribution facilities. The result was a two-week break in deliveries to the company's stores, forcing JJB Sports to pull its advertising. At the same time, Sports Division's cashier system turned out to be not Y2K compliant; stores were forced to close for half-days in order to update their cash registers.

Nonetheless, the company seemed to have solved most of its merger difficulties by mid-1999. The company also announced its decision to phase out the Sports Division name and to place those stores under the JJB Sports signage. This transformation was expected to take several years to complete—however, by the end of 1999 the company reported that the rebranding process was ten months ahead of schedule, and that all of the high street Sports Divisions had already been renamed JJB Sports. Meanwhile, JJB continued to announce aggressive organic expansion, calling for the opening of 26 stores—now primarily in the superstore format—by the start of 2000. At the same time, JJB opened the first of what it hoped would be a new winning format. In June 1999, the company prepared to open the Soccer Dome, in Wigan, featuring 11 indoor soccer fields, as well as a JJB Sports superstore and other amenities.

Principal Competitors

Blacks' Leisure; JD Sports; Intersport; Decathlon.

Further Reading

Blackhurst, Chris, "Coal Miners' Sons Who Struck a Rich Seam," *Independent on Sunday*, November 3, 1996, p. 8.

Cope, Nigel, "JJB Runs into Trouble After Acquiring Rival," *Independent*, January 13, 1999, p. 19.

——, "Sports Shops Set for Merger Wave," *Independent*, July 24, 1998, p. 17.

Herbert, Ian, "It's a Sporting Life, David," *Independent*, September 8, 1999, p. 3.

Szretzer, Adam, "Wigan's Answer to Jack Walker Will Always Be a Blackburn Fan at Heart," *Daily Telegraph*, December 30, 1997.

—M.L. Cohen

Just Born, Inc.

1300 Stefko Boulevard
Bethlehem, Pennsylvania 18016
U.S.A.
Telephone: (610) 867-7568
Toll Free: (800) 445-5787
Fax: (610) 867-3983
Web site: http://www.marshmallowpeeps.com

Private Company
Incorporated: 1923
Employees: 240
Sales: $24 million (1998 est.)
NAIC: 31134 Non-Chocolate Confectionary Manufacturing

Just Born, Inc. is the number one manufacturer of marshmallow candies in the United States. It makes both Marshmallow Peeps and Marshmallow Bunnies, which are the nation's leading non-chocolate Easter candy. In addition to marshmallow confections, the company also produces several well-known candy brands, including Mike and Ike and Hot Tamales. Both the company's corporate headquarters and manufacturing facilities are located in Bethlehem, Pennsylvania.

Early History

Just Born sounds like it refers to the new chicks hatching out of marshmallow in its Marshmallow Peeps, but the name actually originated with the company's founder, Samuel Born. Born was a native Russian who emigrated to the United States in 1910. Apparently he had already been a candymaker in his homeland, and he brought the trade with him. His first fame in the United States was the invention in 1916 of the Born Sucker Machine, a mechanism for automatically inserting sticks into lollipops. For this marvel, San Francisco awarded Born the keys to the city.

In 1923, Born opened a small candy shop in Brooklyn, New York. Here he made his own candy and sold it retail. Because he made fresh candy every day, he hit on the idea of displaying some of the day's batch in the window with a sign reading "Just Born." This gave the name to his company, and also its early logo, which was a baby in a candy scale. Soon after he opened his store, Born invited two family members, his brothers-in-law Jack and Irv Shaffer, to become his business partners. Born was above all an inventor and entrepreneur, and he wanted his partners to handle the more mundane aspects of the new company. As sales grew and the small factory increased its output, Born turned to inventing chocolate novelties, and came up with two which are still common today. He is responsible for chocolate jimmies, the small chocolate sprinkles that go on ice cream cones, and for the kind of chocolate that is used as an ice cream coating. Another new Just Born product that persists today was Mike and Ike, which made its first appearance in 1928. These were small, soft-shelled fruit flavored candies somewhat like a skinny jellybean. The names Mike and Ike were apparently a popular 1920s pairing, and Born chose this for his new product. Also in 1928 Just Born debuted Hot Tamales. These were cinnamon flavored red hot candies. Both new items came in distinctive boxes.

Relocation and Expansion Through the 1950s

The 1920s were a time of general prosperity in the United States, and Just Born grew and expanded in its first decade. Even when the Great Depression hit with the stock market crash of 1929, Just Born continued to do well. But eventually it outgrew its New York headquarters. The company began to look around for a place to relocate to, and finally settled on Bethlehem, Pennsylvania. Bethlehem's advantages were that it had good rail connections, so it was easy to receive raw materials and ship products, the price on the land was acceptably low, the labor force was considered good, and the trolley to New York City stopped right in front of Just Born's new facility.

Three years after moving to Bethlehem, Just Born expanded again, through an acquisition. In 1935 the company bought Maillard Corporation, an esteemed maker of both chocolate and non-chocolate confections. Maillard made mints, jellies, crystallized fruits, and what was touted as "the best bridge mix in the country," as well as unique chocolates decorated by hand. Maillard had a reputation for elegant, upscale candy, and its products were marketed to fine department stores such as Macy's and Neiman-Marcus.

Company Perspectives:

Today, Just Born is the premier provider of marshmallow confections in the U.S., with Marshmallow Peeps and Bunnies hailing as the top-selling non-chocolate Easter candy. Both Mike and Ike and Hot Tamales enjoy year-round popularity across all age groups.

In 1946, Samuel Born's son Bob joined the company, getting the second generation of Borns into the family business. Shortly after, in 1953, the company made what was perhaps its most decisive acquisition. Just Born's principal candies, including Mike and Ike and Hot Tamales, were what are known as soft panned confections, made by a slow process that allowed multiple sugar layers to build up while remaining soft and flexible. Perhaps the best-known soft panned candy in the United States is the jelly bean, a fruit-flavored oblong most often seen around Easter. Consequently, when Just Born learned in 1953 that the Rodda Candy Company, a jelly bean maker in nearby Lancaster, Pennsylvania, was for sale, it seemed a natural fit of product lines, and Just Born made the acquisition. Though Rodda was best known for its jelly beans, the company also had a small sideline making another popular Easter candy, solid marshmallow chicks. At the time of the acquisition, Rodda made these so-called Marshmallow Peeps through a laborious process that involved squeezing the softened marshmallow by hand through pastry tubes to form the desired shape. The marshmallow chicks took 27 hours to make, and the eyes had to be painted on individually by hand. Bob Born showed he had inherited his father's knack for inventions when he was determined to mechanize the Marshmallow Peep manufacturing process. Convinced it could be done, he worked with his plant manager to come up with a viable automatic method that would reduce the costly and time-consuming hand work. Born was successful, and the company went on to become the leader in the Easter marshmallow market.

Changes in the 1980s

After making these acquisitions, Just Born operated several divisions under its corporate umbrella. The Maillard division continued to market its upscale candies; the Rodda division was responsible for the Easter candies jelly beans and Marshmallow Peeps, and under the name Just Born the company marketed its soft panned Mike and Ikes, Hot Tamales, and several new ones. Just Born came up with another fruit-flavored candy in 1960, a grape treat similar to Mike and Ike. This was called Jolly Joes. Two years later, in 1962, the company put out a spearmint candy named Cool Kids. Around this time, the company halted production of chocolate candies to focus entirely on non-chocolate and marshmallow confections. The company was still in family hands, run by descendants of the original founders Samuel Born and Jack Shaffer. Though it had not grown to be a nationally prominent company in the ranks of Hershey or Mars, it had a settled niche, and its brands were sold across the country. But the company did little advertising, and had not made much of an effort to market itself more vividly.

By 1983, the third generation of Borns and Shaffers had taken leadership positions in the company. David Shaffer and Ross Born entered the company, sharing executive responsibility with their fathers. The company was in the minority in the candy industry as a private, family-run institution, but Just Born was not interested in selling out to a bigger company or finding outside management. Yet the company did change decisively under the younger generation's guidance. Beginning in 1985, Just Born changed its focus and became more concerned with its marketing. Ross Born described the company's old philosophy in a July 1989 interview with *U.S. Distribution Journal* as "If we can make it, we can sell it." He went on to explain that the company knew how to make candy, but it had no idea how to take advantage of marketing opportunities. Ross Born and David Shaffer hired a consultant to help the company market its products better. They also initiated consumer focus groups, so that they could gather feedback directly from consumers. Through information from the consultant and the focus groups, Just Born arrived at a four-year plan to increase its presence and reach out to potential customers. Soon the formerly quiet company was coming up with creative promotions, expanding its product lines, and changing its packaging and logo. It also sought talent from outside the company to head its sales and marketing operations, hiring a man with 25 years of such experience at General Foods. A new national sales manager had previously worked for Hershey and Willy Wonka.

Just Born used its consumer focus groups to help guide its packaging. In 1988 the firm came out with new, brighter boxes for Mike and Ikes, Jolly Joes, and Hot Tamales. Just Born also began offering different sized packages of these old standards, including very small boxes that could be given away as Halloween treats. By 1989, the new packaging alone was estimated by the company's sales manager to have boosted total volume by around 30 percent. Mike and Ikes also received major exposure when the company for the first time promoted them by putting sample packs in cereal boxes. Sample boxes of the fruit candies went to four million consumers in 1988, inside General Mills' sweet Cocoa Puffs cereal. The Cocoa Puffs boxes also featured Mike and Ikes advertising on the back.

The company deemed fruit candies a growing segment of the U.S. candy market, and worked to come up with new fruit flavors for Mike and Ike. Just Born also tried to free itself from its dependence on Easter as its major sales maker by producing marshmallow candies for Christmas and Halloween. These included marshmallow ghosts, pumpkins, and spooky cats, and for Christmas, trees and snowmen. The company estimated it could double its production, and in the late 1980s it made plans to install new machinery, at the cost of $5 million.

Acceleration in the 1990s

By the late 1980s, Just Born was producing approximately 250 million marshmallow chicks and bunnies and six million jelly beans every year. Its marshmallow division, Rodda, was the largest maker of marshmallow candies in the world. Just Born made not only standard Easter jelly beans, but was selling gourmet beans called Teenee Beanees through its Maillard division. These caught the marketing updraft created by Ronald Reagan's passion for jelly beans. Teenee Beanees were sold through upscale marketers, including the candy counters at Macy's and Neiman-Marcus. About 60 percent of Just Born's sales came through candy and tobacco distributors. With the

Key Dates:

1923: Samuel Born opens first store in Brooklyn.
1928: Debut of Mike and Ike.
1932: Business relocates to Bethlehem, Pennsylvania.
1935: Just Born acquires Maillard.
1953: Just Born acquires Rodda.
1992: Grandsons of founder and founding partner become co-presidents.

changes instituted by Ross Born and David Shaffer in the mid-1980s, the company was once again on the upswing. These two became officially co-presidents of the company in 1992. Changes abounded. The design for the old favorite Marshmallow Peep was altered in 1991, with a new wingless shape. Peeps had been available in only three colors for ages: yellow, pink, and white. In 1995 Just Born brought out its first lavender Peeps. The new color apparently contributed to the product's growing sales, and in 1998 the company added another color, blue. This decision was not made lightly. Just Born used its consumer focus groups in order to determine if a new hue would sell. Blue was the prevailing choice of those polled. The company had worked diligently to build marketing momentum, and in the late 1990s its Marshmallow Peeps were the number one non-chocolate Easter candy year after year. Then in 1999 Just Born released television advertising for Peeps for the very first time. The ad featured a 15-second Broadway rendition of the song ''Rockin' Robin,'' with a cast of computer-animated Peeps swing dancing on a glittering stage. By that time, sales of Peeps had swollen to over 600 million units a year, up from 250 million a decade earlier. The company also hoped its television campaign would strengthen brand awareness for Just Born's new marshmallow products, which included Valentine's Day specialties, Peeps Jellybeans, and Peeps Eggs.

Meanwhile, the fruit candy side of the company also continued to expand through marketing. In 1996 Just Born brought out new flavors for Mike and Ike, including tropical fruit. The next year saw the addition of Bodacious Berry. With the new flavors, Mike and Ike finally passed up Hot Tamales as the company's best seller. Just Born ventured into television again in 1999, through a cross-promotion with Atlantic Records. In this arrangement, Mike and Ikes and Hot Tamales packages featured several Atlantic Records performing artists on the back. A sweepstakes offered instant cash prizes as well as a chance to win a compact disc compilation of the Atlantic artists. The CD, called ''The Absolute Hits,'' came with a coupon for a free box or bag of either Mike and Ikes or Hot Tamales. The sweepstakes and ''The Absolute Hits'' were advertised on television in the spring of 1999. According to industry analysts cited in *Brandweek* for January 18, 1999, sales of Mike and Ikes grew tremendously in the late 1990s, surging over 18 percent in the last several years of the decade. Hot Tamales too grew by over eight percent in the same period, with total sales of $11 million in 1998. This new, more aggressive and creative marketing of Just Born's products transformed the small, family-run company into a modern and growing enterprise. As the decade came to a close, Just Born was certain that the markets for its products were still opening. The company planned to continue its course of expanded product lines.

Principal Divisions

Rodda; Maillard.

Principal Competitors

Ferrara Pan Candy Company; Herman Goelitz, Inc.; Ben Myerson Candy Co.

Further Reading

Beirne, Mike, ''Just Born Candies Get Big Bang with Atlantic Records Cross-Promo,'' *Brandweek*, January 18, 1998, p. 4.
''Blue Is Red-Hot, Even for Easter,'' *U.S. Distribution Journal*, January-February, 1998, p. 50.
Broekel, Ray, *The Great American Candy Bar Book*, Boston: Houghton Mifflin, 1982, p. 126.
''Just Born Proves It's No Marshmallow,'' *U.S. Distribution Journal*, July 1989, p. 54.
Lehrer, Jeremy, ''Peeps Make Some Noise,'' *Shoot*, April 2, 1999, p. 5.

—A. Woodward

KOHLER®

Kohler Company

44 Highland Drive
Kohler, Wisconsin 53044
U.S.A.
Telephone: (414) 457-4441
Fax: (414) 457-1271
Web site: http://www.kohlerco.com

Private Company
Incorporated: 1873 as Kohler & Silberzahn
Employees: 19,000
Sales: $2.4 billion (1998 est.)
NAIC: 326191 Plastics Plumbing Fixture Manufacturing; 327111 Vitreous China Plumbing Fixture and China and Earthenware Bathroom Accessories Manufacturing; 327122 Ceramic Wall and Floor Tile Manufacturing; 331511 Iron Foundries; 332913 Plumbing Fixture Fitting and Trim Manufacturing; 332998 Enameled Iron and Metal Sanitary Ware Manufacturing; 335312 Motor and Generator Manufacturing; 335313 Switchgear and Switchboard Apparatus Manufacturing; 337110 Wood Kitchen Cabinet and Countertop Manufacturing; 337121 Upholstered Household Furniture Manufacturing; 337122 Nonupholstered Household Furniture Manufacturing; 337211 Wood Office Furniture Manufacturing; 713910 Golf Courses and Country Clubs; 721110 Hotels (Except Casino Hotels) and Motels

Kohler Company is one of the largest privately operated firms in the United States. Unlike others that were once public companies but were taken private through debt-ridden leveraged buyouts, Kohler has always been owned and run by a circle of family members who descended from the founder. One of Wisconsin's largest employers, Kohler is best known for its line of baths, sinks, toilets, and other bathroom fixtures. The company is also a leading producer of electric generators and small engines, owns two distinguished furniture manufacturers, and operates successful hospitality and real estate businesses in Kohler, Wisconsin, where it has its corporate headquarters and largest manufacturing facilities.

Late 19th-Century Roots

The Kohler Company was established in 1873, at the beginning of a debilitating five-year economic depression. That year the company's founders, John Michael Kohler and Charles Silberzahn, purchased an iron foundry from Kohler's employer and father-in-law, Jacob Vollrath, for $5,000. Kohler, a 29-year-old Austrian immigrant, was the senior partner in the business, which was located in Sheboygan, Wisconsin.

In their first year, Kohler & Silberzahn were hit hard by the depression. But, as manufacturers of agricultural implements, such as watering troughs and scalding vats (to remove hair from animal carcasses), they had a good market: people had to eat, and farmers had to feed them.

In November 1878, at the end of the depression, Silberzahn sold his interest in the business to Herman Hayssen and John H. Stehn, who were employees of the enterprise. In 1880, with improved business prospects, the company established a newer, larger machine shop; however, this plant was destroyed by fire only months after opening, forcing the operation to move to a new location.

Rebounding from this costly setback, the small company introduced a line of unique enameled plumbing fixtures in 1883. While its significance was not yet fully realized, this line would propel Kohler into a period of strong growth. The company sold thousands of enameled sinks, cuspidors (spittoons), stove reservoirs, kettles, and pans, as well as the first Kohler bathtubs, fashioned from one of the company's watering troughs. By 1887, the year the company was formally incorporated, these products accounted for 70 percent of Kohler's revenues.

The Kohler Company encountered its first labor difficulties in March 1897, when 21 members of the AFL Iron Molder's Union struck over new pay rates. After some of the molders returned to work and others were replaced, the strike ended without any formal settlement.

Company Perspectives:

From potteries in Mexico and China, to showrooms in Japan and France, KOHLER ideas, craftsmanship and technology are at work today leading the way to more gracious living in plumbing products, exquisite furniture, engines and generators, hospitality and real estate.

Early 20th Century: Rocky Road to Industry Leadership

By 1900 Kohler employed more than 250 people, with 98 percent of its revenues coming from enameled iron products such as tubs, sinks, and water fountains. The factory in Sheboygan had become too small to meet growing production needs. Because it was not practical to expand the plant, which was now surrounded by homes, John Michael Kohler began building a new factory four miles west of Sheboygan in the small community of Riverside. The company entered a period of extraordinarily bad luck when John Michael Kohler died in November 1900 at the age of 56. Less than three months later, before a new chairman could be selected, the company's new iron foundry and machine and enamel shops burned down. Herman Hayssen and John Stehn's widow sold their interests in the company to the Kohler family, and in February 1902 the company was reorganized as the J.M. Kohler Sons Company under the leadership of Robert, Walter, and Carl Kohler, the oldest sons of John Michael Kohler. Two years later Carl died at the age of 24, and in 1905 Robert died at the age of 35, leaving the entire company to Walter Kohler.

Walter Kohler was a strong believer in corporate responsibility. As most of his employees were newly arrived immigrants, Kohler built the American Club, a stately boarding hotel where employees could live until they had enough money to purchase housing and send for their families. He established a benefit organization to provide employees with sickness and death benefits, and even provided lessons in civics, English, and American history so they could pass citizenship exams.

Kohler also laid plans to establish an entirely new community built around the company. He commissioned architects, city planners, and landscape architects, including the Olmsted Brothers (who designed New York's Central Park), to develop a city plan.

In 1911, after some years of stability, the workforce had grown to 950 and the company had ten sales offices, including one in London. That year the company introduced a revolutionary one-piece enamelware built-in bathtub with integral apron that was more sanitary than conventional two-piece tubs. The village of Kohler, meanwhile, had grown to 40 houses, and was incorporated in 1912 with a population of 254. In 1917 the Kohler Improvement Company began building houses in the planned community, selling them to Kohler Co. employees at cost. A second development was started in 1923, and others followed.

By the mid-1920s Kohler had become the third largest plumbing products company in the United States, adding such sales boosters as vitreous china toilets and wash basins and brass faucets, shower heads, and other fittings. The company also introduced a revolutionary new product called the "electric sink." Essentially a dishwasher, but 20 years ahead of its time, the device did not catch on. Shortly afterward, Kohler introduced a slightly more successful novelty, the electric clothes washer.

In 1929 the company's products were chosen on the basis of their excellent design for inclusion in an exhibition at New York's Museum of Modern Art celebrating "the artistic qualities of the bath." The following year Kohler began manufacturing cast iron boilers and radiators for increasingly popular hot water and steam heat systems.

As one of the leaders in Wisconsin industry, Walter Kohler held substantial political power. In 1929 he ran successfully as a Republican for governor of Wisconsin. Distinguished for his administrative acumen rather than his political instincts, he was termed a "poor politician." He vigorously supported the unpopular President Herbert Hoover in 1932, a move that undoubtedly caused him to lose reelection to a second term.

Inspired by the growth of electrical appliances but faced with poor electrical distribution, Kohler began developing small electrical generators. The first unit, introduced in 1920 as the "automatic power and light," provided 1,500 watts of 110-volt DC power from a generator driven by a four-cylinder gasoline engine. The small generator marked a significant improvement over existing generators, which merely charged batteries at 32 volts and were not as portable.

While the generators were intended for farm electrification, they were pressed into service by maritime and railroad companies, European castle owners, and others in need of portable power sources. Admiral Richard Byrd later took five Kohler generators with him on his first expedition to the South Pole in 1926, and took seven Kohler generators with him on his return in 1933. Revisiting his original base station on the frozen continent, his team found the generators from the first expedition in perfect working order. Byrd named an Antarctic mountain range for Kohler and later became a close friend of the family.

Great Depression and World War II: Adjusting to New Circumstances

By 1932, however, residential building rates had fallen to just 11 percent of their 1928 levels, and Kohler was facing the prospect of massive employee layoffs. Because the company was not in debt and retained favorable terms for raw materials, Kohler resolved to keep the company in operation, and to stockpile whatever products could not be sold. This full employment policy had the effect of saving the local economy from ruin.

The company was revisited by labor unrest in July 1934 when a portion of the workforce struck Kohler for the right to be represented by the Federal Union. The strike was canceled later that year when the union lost an employee vote to represent all of Kohler's production and maintenance employees. In arbitration, however, the National Labor Relations Board instructed the company to recognize a smaller, independent union, the Kohler Workers' Association.

In 1940 Walter Kohler died, and a battle for control of the firm broke out between Walter's children and their father's younger

Key Dates:

1873: Kohler & Silberzahn is established.
1883: Line of enameled plumbing fixtures makes its debut.
1887: Company is incorporated as Kohler Company.
1905: Cofounder's son, Walter Kohler, takes over company leadership.
1912: Village of Kohler is incorporated.
1920: Production of small electrical generators begins.
1940: Walter's younger brother, Herbert Kohler, takes control of company.
1954: Six-year-long strike against the company begins.
1968: Nonfamily members lead the company for the first time.
1972: Herbert Kohler, Jr., is named chairman of Kohler Company.
1984: Sterling Faucet Company of Schaumburg, Illinois, is acquired.
1985: The Kohler Design Center opens.
1986: Company enters furniture manufacturing through acquisition of Grand Rapids, Michigan-based Baker, Knapp & Tubbs.
1989: San Francisco-based McGuire Furniture is acquired.
1993: Company expands into cabinetmaking with acquisition of Sanijura, S.A. of France.
1998: Ownership reorganization plan meets with resistance from dissident shareholders.

brother, Herbert Kohler, who was running the company. While the children argued for strict hereditary succession, the situation was further complicated by the fact that Herbert's mother and Walter's mother were sisters. In the end, Herbert prevailed.

When the United States became involved in World War II, much of Kohler's commercial operations ground to a halt. Iron, brass, and chrome supplies were diverted for war use by the government, which asked Kohler to resume production of military wares (during World War I Kohler had made mine anchors, projectiles, and shells). The company's first military products were precision valves and fittings for use in aircraft, such as the DC-3 and B-29. Kohler also built a variety of electric generators for the armed forces.

Based on Kohler's experience in precision crafted metallurgy, the government asked the company to produce 105mm and three-inch artillery shells, as well as forgings for rockets and other shells, fuses, torpedo tubes, piston rings, shell rotating bands, and engine bearings. After the war, Kohler discontinued much of its military production, but resumed building 105mm shells during the Korean War. The company did, however, continue to manufacture precision products and generators, albeit for different markets.

Postwar Developments

Given the occasional unreliability of utility-supplied power, many hospitals, banks, and other offices had to have their own emergency standby power, but required larger capacities than the ten megawatt models Kohler manufactured. Eager to supply this market, Kohler began development of 100 kilowatt diesel-powered systems. As the market continued to grow, Kohler introduced a 230 kilowatt model and, some years later, a massive 500 kilowatt system.

Kohler also manufactured small gasoline engines, which were first built to power the company's electric generators. During the 1950s, the small engines found an explosive market in Thailand and Vietnam, where they were used to power boats, pump water on rice paddies, and drive air compressors. Virtually all the air-cooled engines in Southeast Asia at this time were made by Kohler and sold through a distributor in Hong Kong.

In 1951 Walter Kohler, Jr., a former officer and director of the company, followed in his father's footsteps to become the governor of Wisconsin. He was reelected twice, serving until 1957. At the company, labor trouble arose again in April 1954 when the UAW-CIO local called a walkout to protest changes in union shop rules, seniority, and pay increases without regard to merit. Seeing these demands as unfair and potentially crippling to the profitable operation of the corporation, the company resisted. The strike continued until September 1960, when bargaining resumed, and a new contract was concluded two years later. The strike earned a place in the *Guinness Book of World Records* as the longest strike in American history.

Entering the 1960s, the company's engine division, still strong in Asia, gained momentum in the United States, where Kohler motors were used to power lawnmowers, garden tractors, construction equipment, and even snowmobiles. International Harvester, John Deere, Wheel-Horse, Jacobsen, and Bombardier (inventor of the snowmobile) incorporated Kohler engines in their products. By 1963 Kohler was one of the leading small engine suppliers in the industry.

In order to keep pace with this growing demand, Kohler established two new production facilities, in Mexico City and Toronto. The company ran into strong competition, however, from Japanese and German manufacturers who had extensive experience with two- and four-stroke engines. Kohler suffered market share loss, but won back a significant share of the market by introducing higher technology two-cycle engines in 1968. It later won a suit against market leader Briggs & Stratton, which had tried to coerce its distributors to stop handling Kohler engines.

The company experienced another leadership crisis in 1968 when Kohler's president, J.L. Kuplic, died unexpectedly. Only six days later, Herbert Kohler, Sr., chairman and CEO of the company for 28 years, also died. Herbert Kohler, Jr., heir to the company, was at the time a self-described "hippie," pursuing a career outside the company. He later told *Supply House Times,* "By preplanning my life, my father removed my right to fail. As a result, for a portion of my life I experienced nothing but failure. That led me to become a substantial rebel."

Company directors elected to pass over the younger Kohler, and named an interim chairman. In an unusual departure from company traditions, the directors named nonfamily members Lyman Conger and Walter Cleveland as chairman and president, respectively. When Conger retired in 1972, Herb Kohler was appointed chairman, and two years later he succeeded Cleveland as company president. In 1978, concerned about the company slipping from family control, Kohler engineered a 1-for-20 reverse stock split, which reduced the number of shareholders in the private company from more than 400 to about 250 and the number of outstanding shares from 161,105 to about 8,000. The maneuver also forced a number of nonfamily shareholders to sell out at $412.50 per share, leaving the Kohler family with 96 percent of the voting shares.

Late 20th Century: Growth Through Acquisition

Under Herb Kohler's leadership, Kohler Company more than tripled in size to an estimated $1.34 billion in annual sales by the late 1980s. After 110 years of strictly internal growth, much of the expansion came from the company's new venture into acquisitions. In 1984 the company acquired the Schaumburg, Illinois-based Sterling Faucet Company. Two years later, Kohler purchased Baker, Knapp & Tubbs, a high-end furniture manufacturer headquartered in Grand Rapids, Michigan, and Jacob Delafon, a plumbing products manufacturer headquartered in Paris. The company also established a Japanese subsidiary. In 1989 Kohler purchased the McGuire Furniture Company, a San Francisco-based manufacturer, Oakland-based Kallista, Inc., Portland-based Ann Sacks Tile and Stone, and Dupont Sanitaire-Chauffage, in Paris.

By this time, Kohler had also expanded into the leisure industry, turning the company's one-time workers' hotel, the American Club, into a successful full-scale convention and recreation resort hotel. Having poured about $50 million into the resort from 1978 through the mid-1990s, Kohler created the only resort in the Midwest to receive AAA's top five-diamond rating. The resort's centerpiece was Blackwolf Run, which offered two world championship golf courses created by a top course designer, Pete Dye. Blackwolf Run hosted the 1998 U.S. Women's Open Championship. The bathrooms in the American Club's fancy guest rooms also served as showcases for Kohler Company products. Serving a similar function was the Kohler Design Center, which opened in Sheboygan in 1985 as a 36,000-square-foot showcase of Kohler plumbing fixtures, faucets, engines, and generators; Baker and McGuire furniture; Ann Sacks tile and stone; and other company products.

Kohler continued to expand in the 1990s through acquisition, increasingly venturing overseas to do so. In 1993 the company acquired Sanijura, S.A., a French maker of bathroom cabinets. The following year, Kohler purchased Osio, a maker of enamel baths based in Italy. The company ventured further into the cabinet sector through the 1995 acquisition of Pennsylvania-based Robern, Inc., which specialized in mirrored cabinets, lighting fixtures, and accessories; and the 1996 addition of Canac Kitchens, Ltd., a maker of wood kitchen cabinets based in Ontario, Canada. Another France-based firm, Holdiam, S.A., was added in 1995, bringing to Kohler the leading French maker of acrylic baths, whirlpools, synthetic kitchen sinks, and artistic faucets. In the late 1990s the company established Kohler China Ltd., which had locations in Shanghai, Beijing, and Guangzhou province, from which it manufactured and distributed throughout the People's Republic a full line of plumbing products.

In 1993 Kohler Company sales reached a record $1.53 billion; earnings stood at $15.5 million, a figure substantially reduced by a $33 million charge resulting from a change in accounting for retiree health benefits. By 1997 earnings had increased to $88 million on sales of $2.2 billion. Concerned again about the loss of family control as well as anticipating the need to hold down estate taxes, Herb Kohler proposed another restructuring of the company's stock in early 1998. At the time, there were 7,445 shares outstanding, with 75 percent of them controlled by Herb and his sister, Ruth DeYoung Kohler. Over the years, about four percent of the stock had fallen into the hands of nonfamily members through the sale of the thinly traded stock by family members. In April 1998 Kohler shareholders approved a plan whereby all the nonfamily shareholders would be bought out at $52,700 per share. The plan also offered other family members the option of cashing in their stock or taking a mix of voting and nonvoting shares, with the added stipulation that if they chose the latter they could only sell their shares at a later date back to the company. At the end of 1997 Kohler stock had a book value of about $100,000 per share and shares had been selling in early 1998 for as high as $135,000 per share. The plan therefore angered the outside shareholders, some of whom felt the stock was worth as much as $400,000 per share, as well as dissident members of the Kohler family, who bristled both at the buyback offer and at the plan's restrictions on selling to outsiders. Under Wisconsin law, shareholders had the ability to take a disputed stock valuation to court and ask a judge to increase the per share offer. A trial was therefore set for April 2000 in Sheboygan County Circuit Court to determine the value of Kohler Company stock, with owners of 811 shares asking for redress. Meanwhile, dissident shareholders also filed suit in U.S. District Court in Milwaukee to stop the entire reorganization plan, with a trial set for late 1999. The outcome of these lawsuits seemed certain to play a key role in determining Kohler's direction well into the 21st century, both in terms of ownership control and financial health—the latter because a substantial valuation increase could prove quite costly to the company.

Principal Subsidiaries

Baker Knapp & Tubbs, Inc.; McGuire Furniture Company; Crosswinds Furniture Company; Dapha, Ltd.; Sterling Plumbing; Ann Sacks Tile & Stone, Inc.; Robern, Inc.; Canac Kitchens, Ltd. (Canada); Kallista, Inc.; Jacob Delafon, S.A. (France); Jacob Delafon, Espana, S.A. (Spain); Jacob Delafon, Maroc, S.A. (Morocco); Jacob Delafon, Italia, S.r.l. (Italy); Holdiam, S.A. (France); Sanijura, S.A. (France); KOHLER China, Ltd.; KOHLER de Mexico, S.A. de C.V.; Helvex, S.A. de C.V.; P.T. Artcraft (Indonesia); P.T. Port Rush (Indonesia); KOHLER Europe (France); Foshan Kohler, Ltd. (China); Beijing Kohler, Ltd. (China); Shanghai Kohler, Ltd. (China); KOHLER Power Systems Asia Pacific (Singapore).

Principal Competitors

American Standard Companies Inc.; Armstrong World Industries, Inc.; Bassett Furniture Industries, Incorporated; The Black & Decker Corporation; Briggs & Stratton Corporation; Chicago Faucet Company; Cooper Industries, Inc.; Crane Co.; Dal-Tile International Inc.; The Dyson-Kissner-Moran Corporation; Elkay Manufacturing Company; Falcon Building Products,

Inc.; Fortune Brands, Inc.; Gerber Plumbing Fixtures Corporation; Honda Motor Co., Ltd.; Klaussner Furniture Industries Inc.; LADD Furniture, Inc.; Leggett & Platt, Incorporated; Masco Corporation; Mueller Industries, Inc.; Newell Rubbermaid Inc.; NIBCO Inc.; Premark International, Inc.; Tecumseh Products Company; TOTO Ltd.; Triangle Pacific Corp.; U.S. Industries, Inc.; Waxman Industries, Inc.; Yamaha Motor Co. Ltd.

Further Reading

The American Club: A Heritage and History Remembered, Kohler, Wis.: Kohler Company, 1993.

Bold Craftsmen, Kohler, Wis.: Kohler Company, 1973.

Kilman, Scott, "Family Squabble Brews at Kohler over Control," *Wall Street Journal,* March 23, 1998, p. A4.

——, "Head of Kohler Family Unveils Plan to Buy Out Holders of Fixtures Firm," *Wall Street Journal,* April 7, 1998, p. B16.

"Kohler Company," *Forbes,* December 11, 1989.

Lank, Avrum D., "Wisconsin-Based Kohler Seeks to Stay Private in Stock Buy-Back Plan," *Milwaukee Journal Sentinel,* April 7, 1998.

Lank, Avrum D., and Kathleen Gallagher, "Kohler Family, Outside Shareholder Dispute Stock Value," *Milwaukee Journal Sentinel,* April 10, 1998.

McCune, Heather, "Kohler Co. Establishes Global Faucet Operations," *Supply House Times,* March 1998, p. 16.

McNamee, Tom, "Plumbing Kohler's Pleasures," *North Shore,* July 1999, pp. 52–62.

Melcher, Richard A., "Can Kohler Keep It All in the Family?," *Business Week,* May 4, 1998, p. 98.

Samuels, Gary, "Generational Investor," *Forbes,* October 16, 1995, p. 70.

"This Is Herb Kohler, Like Him or Not," *Supply House Times,* November 1986.

—John Simley
—updated by David E. Salamie

L.A. Gear, Inc.

5900 Rodeo Road
Los Angeles, California 90016-4313
U.S.A.
Telephone: (310) 822-1995
Fax: (310) 581-7709
Web site: http://www.lagear.com

Private Company
Incorporated: 1979 as Good Times, Inc.
Employees: 10
Sales: $50 million (1998 est.)
NAIC: 533110 Lessors of Nonfinancial Intangible Assets (Except Copyrighted Works)

Near the end of a tumultuous decade, L.A. Gear, Inc. emerged from bankruptcy in late 1998 as a pure licensor—and former manufacturer—of the L.A. Gear brand for footwear, apparel, and accessories. The company's most significant partner is ACI International, with which L.A. Gear has a licensing agreement to produce women's, children's, and men's footwear (the owners of ACI also hold a stake of about 50 percent in L.A. Gear itself through a Los Angeles-based investment company, PCH Investments). L.A. Gear has other licensing agreements covering women's and girl's active/lifestyle clothing, children's swimwear and activewear, eyewear and sunglasses, hosiery, and watches. The company revolutionized the world athletic shoe market in 1985 by developing shoes that incorporated the comfort of sneakers with the frills of fashion shoes. Company founder Robert Greenberg's ability to design shoes that appealed to young women fueled L.A. Gear's rapid rise to third place in athletic shoe sales behind Nike and Reebok by 1990. The success of the shoe sales led to L.A. Gear's diversification into the men's and children's shoe markets and the casual apparel market. L.A. Gear's product appeal was not universal, however. As L.A. Gear tried to expand into the men's market, its shoes were not well received, sales plummeted, and a string of loss-making years ensued. Several turnaround attempts, management shuffles, and staff reductions later, the company filed for bankruptcy protection in early 1998, emerging after several months as a privately held licensing company.

1985–90: The Phenomenal Rise

L.A. Gear evolved out of the longtime entrepreneurial adventures of Robert Greenberg. Greenberg attributed his entrepreneurial bent to his father, who sold fresh produce in Boston, and to his father's subscription to *Forbes* magazine. "I always wanted to be the president of a company on the New York Stock Exchange," Greenberg told *Los Angeles Magazine,* adding that had his father subscribed to *Sports Illustrated* he would probably have been a baseball player. As an entrepreneur, Greenberg had a legacy of picking and riding trends. The one-time hairdresser incorporated a roller skating rental shop in 1979 under the name Good Times, Inc., and that company eventually grew into a skate-manufacturing business called United Skates of America. But when skate sales waned, he spotted the profitability of novelty shoelaces and sold $3 million worth in three months. In 1982 Greenberg opened a Los Angeles women's apparel store on Melrose Avenue which sold major brand name clothes, shoes, and accessories. In this store Greenberg launched the L.A. Gear clothing label.

The L.A. Gear brand name actually came from a T-shirt saleswoman's comment in the company warehouse. After the saleswoman declared her shirts were "real L.A. gear," a clerk jotted down the name and submitted it for the contest Greenberg had introduced to find the right name for the retail store. "Of course, I looked at the piece of paper and threw it away," Greenberg told *Los Angeles Magazine.* "But at four in the morning, I woke up and thought, 'My God, L.A. Gear!' " Initially, the L.A. Gear label signified casual clothes, shoes, and sandals. By 1984, however, Greenberg decided to concentrate the company's efforts on wholesale shoe sales, and closed the unprofitable retail store. Business partner Ernest Williams, however, "felt there was no room for another athletic-footwear company," Greenberg told *Los Angeles Magazine,* and Williams broke their partnership.

It did not take Greenberg long to establish a presence in the athletic shoe market. Greenberg tapped his lengthy experience with companies in the Far East to find independent companies who would produce and distribute his shoes. L.A. Gear entered the athletic shoe market with the Canvas Workout shoe in 1985, and the company soon met with great success. Greenberg's shoe designs were targeted at fashion-conscious females between the

Company Perspectives:

"L.A. Gear is structured for the future. Our customer has grown more complex, and inherently more interesting. To that end, we will continue to redefine who we are and what we are to offer the best product available."

—David Gatto, CEO

ages of 12 and 35 who wanted stylish, comfortable shoes, according to *Forbes*. The overwhelming reception in the marketplace pushed sales from $200,000 at the beginning of the year to $1.8 million at the end of 1985.

In 1986 L.A. Gear became a public company, and the money raised from the stock offering allowed the company to diversify. L.A. Gear's main business was footwear, but in the late 1980s it began producing sport and casual wear for men, women, and children. The apparel division featured knit tops and sweat clothes with bold L.A. Gear graphics and basic five pocket jeans decorated with frills. The company also continued to develop its shoe lines. Building on the enormous success of the Canvas Workout shoe for women, L.A. Gear began to spruce up its line of basic women's shoes with gold lamé, fringe, pastel colors, and spangles. For men, the company produced bold, jazzy hightops for basketball. L.A. Gear's children's shoes stimulated young eyes with black and white checkerboard and cow spot designs. The company also marketed street shoes called Street Hikers that combined an urban appearance with the comfort of sneakers. Even though L.A. Gear continued to market its original styles into the early 1990s, it unveiled new styles every year.

Business Week contributor Kathleen Kerwin attributed L.A. Gear's almost instant success in footwear sales to their ability to appeal to the 80 percent of customers who "rarely set foot on a tennis or basketball court." L.A. Gear's growth in sales and product recognition surpassed that of the entire footwear market. Sales increased 200 percent in 1986 and doubled the next year. In 1988 and 1989, *Business Week* selected L.A. Gear as one of the best small American companies. *Business Week,* the *Wall Street Journal,* the *Los Angeles Times,* and *Fortune* highlighted L.A. Gear's stock as the best performer on the New York Stock Exchange in 1989. In 1990 company sales peaked at $818.8 million, as did its share of the U.S. athletic shoe market; its 11.8 percent share placed it third behind Nike and Reebok.

Despite L.A. Gear's phenomenal performance, skeptics questioned the endurance of the brand. In 1990 L.A. Gear was thought to be a "flash in the pan," Montgomery Securities' apparel analyst Alice Ruth told *Institutional Investor.* Skeptics based their fad theory on L.A. Gear's relatively weak sales in sporting goods stores, the conventional athletic shoe outlets. But Ruth touted the staying power of L.A. Gear because it was inundating department stores and mass merchandisers. Noting the narrow focus and clientele of sporting goods stores, *Los Angeles Magazine* contributor David Jefferson called Greenberg's decision to capture a larger clientele in department stores such as Nordstrom, May Co., and Bullock's a "brilliant marketing strategy."

By 1990 Greenberg felt the company was secure in its niche. "We've taken the number three position now. Our brand is growing and consumer confidence is gaining every day," he told the *Wall Street Transcript,* adding that he expected the company "should only fuel itself now." The majority of L.A. Gear's success, however, laid in the hands of the two men responsible for the L.A. Gear image: Greenberg and Sandy Saemann. Greenberg designed the shoes. His friend and former colleague in the skate business, Sandy Saemann, masterminded the marketing. Greenberg's and Saemann's appeal to fashion-conscious females was unique. "L.A. Gear has really hit on a formula no one else has," John Horan, publisher of *Sports Management News,* told *Advertising Age* in 1989. "They take a shoe that's not a real technical shoe, so not expensive to produce, put some spangles and some colored trim on it," and "put their money into marketing and advertising." Saemann designed ads that were not as "slick" as ads for Reebok or Nike but were "effective," according to Marcy Magiera in *Advertising Age.* "They sold sex and sizzle," noted *Business Week.*

L.A. Gear's ads focused on the sunny glamour of the Los Angeles lifestyle, featuring beautiful young blondes wearing little else besides their L.A. Gear shoes. In 1990 Horan told *Advertising Age* that "of all the ads out there, [L.A. Gear's] seem to turn the sales on and off."

Encouraged by its success in the women's market, L.A. Gear decided to expand its sales in the men's market in 1989. L.A. Gear employed the same fashionable design and glamorous marketing techniques that had proved successful in the women's market to enter the men's market. Relying on jazzy designs and what industry analysts considered unusual endorsers, L.A. Gear marketed shoes in what they called the "fashionable" basketball market, featuring boldly designed hightops called Street Slammers, Hot Shots, and Brats. The men's market, however, was highly competitive; men's athletic shoes accounted for 70 percent of L.A. Gear's competitors' total sales but only 20 percent of L.A. Gear's total sales. Yet L.A. Gear's strategy of emphasizing fashion in the men's market seemed an odd strategy for growth because "men typically pay less attention to style," wrote Kerwin in *Business Week.* Avia marketing chief Bruce W. MacGregor added in *Business Week* that "technology has been the fashion" in the men's market.

Rather than hiring a young sports superstar such as Bo Jackson, Nike's endorser at the time, L.A. Gear hired retiring Los Angeles Laker Kareem Abdul-Jabbar to endorse a line of basketball shoes called Jabbars. One analyst predicted in *Business Week* that this move would appeal to the "geriatric crowd," rather than foster the category growth the company wanted. The company's main endorser was an even more unlikely athletic shoe sponsor. Pop singer Michael Jackson was paid close to $10 million to be the company spokesperson and to design a line of shoes and T-shirts. The company's use of Michael Jackson was "more than a growth opportunity, they're trying to maintain their fashion image," Paine Webber analyst Frank Podbelsek told *Advertising Age.* Under the umbrella theme "Unstoppable," L.A. Gear prepared to tap Michael Jackson's worldwide popularity by coordinating the Jackson line rollout with the release of a collection of his greatest hits called *A Decade.* Michael Jackson's album was never released and his black, heavily buckled shoes did not sell well. His endorsement and the line were both quickly discontinued. This series of events cost the company several million dollars.

Key Dates:

1979: Robert Greenberg incorporates a roller skating rental shop as Good Times, Inc., the forerunner of L.A. Gear, Inc.
1982: Greenberg opens women's apparel store in Los Angeles and launches the L.A. Gear label.
1984: Greenberg closes retail store to concentrate on wholesale shoe sales.
1985: L.A. Gear enters the athletic shoe market with the Canvas Workout women's shoe.
1986: The company goes public, using the IPO proceeds to diversify beyond women's footwear.
1990: L.A. Gear catapults into third place in athletic shoe sales, behind only Nike and Reebok; company sales peak at $818.8 million.
1991: Company posts $66.2 million loss, the first of several straight years in the red; Trefoil Capital Investors, L.P., an investment fund, injects $100 million into L.A. Gear and gains a 34 percent stake in the company.
1992: Sales decline to $430.2 million, market share to five percent; Greenberg resigns from the company.
1994: Company abandons its foray into men's performance shoes.
1997: Trefoil sells its interest in the company to PCH Investments for $228,000.
1998: L.A. Gear files for Chapter 11 bankruptcy protection, emerging late in the year as a pure licensing company.
1999: L.A. Gear-branded products manufactured under license make their first appearances.

1991–97: The Spiral Downward

L.A. Gear paid the price for these misadventures in increased inventories and diminished profits. Inventory stockpiling due to unrealistically high sales projections caused the company to discount almost all their shoe styles to liquidate the inventories. Yet selling the shoes at discounts angered retailers because it made their prices seem exorbitantly high and degraded the L.A. Gear brand image, according to the *Los Angeles Times.* Bad marketing decisions, coupled with rebellious retailers who began to refuse L.A. Gear shelf space contributed to a net loss of $66.2 million for the company in 1991. The company's market share continued to expand in 1991, but at the expense of profits.

Aware that fashionable men's athletic shoes would not generate profits, the company decided to branch into the men's technical shoe market with the introduction of the Catapult basketball shoe in 1991. The $100 Catapult, which featured a fiberglass and graphite heel supporting an air cushion, was marketed without the L.A. Gear brand name to ''distance Catapult from L.A. Gear's young, low-price image,'' creative director Michael Albright told *Advertising Age.* As part of its new strategy, the company chose a more typical endorser: Karl Malone, a Utah Jazz basketball star. Unfortunately, problems with product quality interfered with initial sales. After the company outfitted a Marquette University basketball team in Catapult shoes, one player tripped on his shoe sole as it peeled off during a televised game. The company reported that it was working to improve the shoes' quality and the university team continued wearing the shoes.

L.A. Gear's entrance into the technological shoe market was not without other problems. Initially, L.A. Gear failed to differentiate its technology enough to please competitors. Nike filed a suit against L.A. Gear in 1991 alleging the Catapult infringed on Nike's patented ''spring moderator'' technology. In a similar case, L.A. Gear paid Reebok $1 million and licensing fees in an out-of-court settlement in 1992. L.A. Gear's Regulator series infringed on the patented technology of the Reebok Pump. Under the licensing agreement, L.A. Gear continued to develop its line of inflatable shoes under the Regulator and the Gauge brand names. Moreover, it built on Catapult technology with the Twist-a-pult shoe, which allowed the wearer to adjust the amount of cushion offered by the Catapult mechanism. Meanwhile, also in 1991, the company introduced the L.A. Lights series of lighted athletic shoes for children, which fared better than the men's line.

L.A. Gear's efforts to establish a significant presence in the men's market left it facing financial troubles. In 1991 the company went into technical default on its bank loan, and to free itself from the confines of the bank's regulations, it looked for an investor to support the company through its slump. Trefoil Capital Investors, L.P.—an investment fund managed by Shamrock Advisors, Inc. and led by Roy E. Disney, nephew of Walt Disney and vice-chairman of the Walt Disney Co.—invested $100 million in L.A. Gear, giving Trefoil a 34 percent stake in the company. In accordance with its investment agreement, Trefoil assumed control of the board after L.A. Gear was unable to pay Trefoil dividends for three consecutive quarters, and they began to make a number of changes. Mark Goldston, a one-time Reebok marketing executive, was given responsibility for L.A. Gear's business dealings as president and chief operating officer; several new managers were hired to bring the company back to profitability; and Greenberg was encouraged to concentrate on what he did best—designing shoes and picking trends. Greenberg announced he would work without pay until the company made money. By the end of the year, however, *Advertising Age* reported that L.A. Gear's market share had dropped to eight percent from its high of 11.8 percent in 1990.

As Trefoil increased its control of the company's operations and added new senior managers, Greenberg decided to resign in early 1992. He told the *Los Angeles Times* that ''after eight years of constant involvement with L.A. Gear, I can now devote more time to my family.'' As a one-time L.A. Gear employee told the *Los Angeles Magazine,* ''People who build a billion-dollar company aren't always the people who can run a billion-dollar company.'' Upon Greenberg's resignation, Stanley Gold, a man known for his ability to return companies to profitability, was positioned as chairman and CEO by Trefoil. The Trefoil-picked management had a record of success in the footwear industry, as well as a reputation for saving floundering companies.

The new management began to pare down the business as the company's drop in market share moved it from third to fourth place among footwear companies. Scattered corporate offices were consolidated in a new Santa Monica, California, headquarters, which reduced costs and brought all senior management together. To further reduce costs, the company closed its apparel production and marketing facilities, opting to license its name to a few garment-making companies instead. Goldston stressed in *PR Newswire* that the licensing agreements increased "the range and quality of non-footwear products that will be offered both domestically and internationally under the L.A. Gear brand name." In 1992 the cost-cutting measures included a 45 percent staff reduction.

To lend consistency to the company's image, Goldston announced in a 1992 article in *Advertising Age* that the company would separate the fashion and fitness products into distinct lifestyle and athletic shoe divisions that "will run as standalone companies in the marketplace." The divisions would be distinguishable by the diamond-shaped L.A. Gear logo for the lifestyle shoes and the square L.A. Tech logo for the high-tech athletic line. The children's shoes would also be marketed separately using the Bendables logo that featured a drawing of a baby. Such demarcations would allow the divisions to market their products to suit the needs of very different markets. Shoe quality and distribution were also enhanced after the company reevaluated the independent manufacturers and distributors with whom it was doing business. In 1992 L.A. Gear signed a sourcing agreement with LASCO, an affiliate of Pentland Group plc, the world's largest sourcing agent, respected throughout the footwear industry. LASCO would be responsible for inspecting the quality of the finished products as well as supervision of production, scheduling, and all foreign shipping. The company's shoes continued to be manufactured mainly in the People's Republic of China, Indonesia, South Korea, and Taiwan. On the distribution side, L.A. Gear moved away from selling its shoes at discount outlets, convenience stores, and supermarkets (a semi-desperate strategy to sell off unwanted inventory anyplace possible, which included flea markets) and placed emphasis on department stores and shoe stores, hoping to further enhance its image through this full-priced strategy.

Trefoil also updated the "dated blondes-at-the-beach" advertising strategy, noted *Advertising Age* contributor Marcy Magiera. The company decided to break with the industry marketing trend of using a media buyer and search for a full-service outside advertising agency that would handle both creative work and media planning. Ogilvy and Mather was chosen to create ads and buy media space in late 1991. "Get in Gear," the new umbrella theme, was unveiled at the 1991 Sporting Goods Manufacturer's Association Super Show in Atlanta, Georgia. Goldston, concerned about contemporizing L.A. Gear's image, said of the new theme that "our strategy is athletic lifestyle and the theme line is one that can be used for years and years," according to *Advertising Age.*

Along with the new advertising theme came a new advertising strategy. The company would no longer spend mammoth amounts on superstar sponsors; a three-year endorsement budget was set at $8 million, according to the *Los Angeles Magazine.* The long list of celebrity endorsers was pared to three: Hakeem Olajuwon, Joe Montana, and Karl Malone, who would continue to represent the men's line of technical sport shoes.

As losses continued despite the numerous turnaround moves, L.A. Gear announced in June 1994 that Goldston had resigned and was being replaced by William L. Benford, who had been executive vice-president and CFO. At the same time, the company announced an agreement with Wal-Mart Stores, Inc., whereby the discount retail giant would buy at least $80 million of L.A. Gear shoes per year over a three-year period starting in 1995. Wal-Mart outlets began selling specially designed, lower-end L.A. Gear footwear that year. This move seemed to contradict L.A. Gear's upscale marketing strategy adopted only recently but the company apparently felt it could not pass by such a lucrative opportunity. L.A. Gear made another strategy shift in the summer of 1994, electing to abandon its foray into men's performance shoes altogether. The new emphasis would be on women's and children's shoes. L.A. Gear also intended to pursue a multibrand strategy through the acquisition and licensing of key brands; its first step to this end, however, the acquisition of Ryka, Inc., a troubled maker of high-performance women's athletic shoes, was abandoned in mid-1995 because of the further deterioration in Ryka's financial performance. In September 1995 L.A. Gear announced that it would close its eight retail outlets and reduce its workforce by an additional 30 percent. Results for the fiscal year ending in November 1995 were abysmal: a $51.4 million loss on sales of just $296.6 million. L.A. Gear had also fallen to sixth place in the U.S. athletic shoe market, with a market share of only three percent.

In April 1996 the company was unable to pay the $50 million in dividends it owed to Trefoil, so the investment firm accepted a preferred stock swap that increased its ownership interest in L.A. Gear to 42 percent. In November of that year, hurt by a decline of its sales to Wal-Mart and a drop in demand for its lighted children's shoes, L.A. Gear announced the elimination of another 55 percent of its workforce (from 310 to 140) and a one-time charge of more than $28 million. Benford resigned as president and COO, with Bruce MacGregor, senior vice-president of marketing, replacing him on an interim basis. The company's downward spiral continued in 1997, however, when sales fell still further, to $125 million. In October 1997 Trefoil sold its 42 percent stake in L.A. Gear at a self-described "substantial" loss, accepting just $228,000 from PCH Investments, a Los Angeles-based investment partnership headed by Steven Jackson and Richard Hollander. Gold and six of the eight other directors of L.A. Gear's board immediately resigned. Of Trefoil's turnaround attempts, Gold told the *Wall Street Journal,* "We tried three different management teams. We clearly didn't have the key to unlocking the profits." David F. Gatto was named the new chairman and CEO of L.A. Gear, having previously worked at software company Syncronys Softcorp before joining L.A. Gear in June 1997 as chief administrative officer.

1998 and Beyond: The Manufacturer-Turned-Licensor

In January 1998 L.A. Gear filed for Chapter 11 bankruptcy protection in order to implement a reorganization plan with its bondholders. By the time the company emerged from bankruptcy in late 1998 its new managers had settled on a radical plan to transform the company from manufacturer to licensor of the L.A. Gear brand. Gatto told *Apparel Industry Magazine,* "With an emphasis on growing L.A. Gear's valuable trademarks and trade names, licensing efforts will focus on key apparel and accessory categories [as well as] existing lines of footwear.'' Having voided its existing stock, it also emerged as a private company, controlled and owned by PCH and the bondholders. The new L.A. Gear had a workforce of just ten.

The company's largest initial licensee was ACI International, a Los Angeles-based footwear manufacturer, which was itself run by Steven Jackson. In the spring of 1999 ACI rolled out a new line of L.A. Gear footwear, including women's and men's casual athletic shoes and children's L.A. Lights shoes. In this and other licensing deals, L.A. Gear received a percentage of the resulting sales for the use of its brand and also worked closely with its licensees on the marketing and distribution sides. Gatto told *Sporting Goods Business,* ''We have pretty strict contractual controls built in. We'll set the direction for the brand within each category. We'll review samples and get involved in distribution if it becomes an issue.'' Gatto also said the company planned to stay away from discount channels, such as Wal-Mart and Target. Among L.A. Gear's other early licensees were New York-based Kidfusion, for a children's swimwear and windsuit collection; Los Angeles-based Jerry Leigh, for a line of women's and girls' active apparel; South Hackensack, New Jersey-based Farash & Robins, for a line of digital and analog watches for men, women, and children; and Fyffe, Alaska-based Kilgore Hosiery, for athletic and fashion socks in sizes from infants to adults. This move toward licensing—as well as another diversification beyond footwear—was clearly the boldest attempt yet to revitalize a brand that had once known glory, if ever so briefly.

Principal Competitors

adidas-Salomon AG; Converse Inc.; Fila Holding S.p.A.; K-Swiss Inc.; New Balance Athletic Shoe, Inc.; NIKE, Inc.; Reebok International Ltd.; Russell Corporation.

Further Reading

Adamson, Deborah, ''L.A. Gear Changes Strategy to Regain Its Market Share,'' *Los Angeles Daily News,* April 24, 1995, p. B6.

Burchfield, Stephanie, ''L.A. Gear Announces Licensing Agreements Signed with Sweatshirt Apparel, U.S.A.; Steinwurtzel Acquisition and Coordinated Apparel,'' *PR Newswire,* August 25, 1992.

Cole, Benjamin Mark, ''Stanley Gold's Blunder: The L.A. Gear Deal,'' *Los Angeles Business Journal,* September 30, 1996, p. 1.

Cullinane, Kevin, ''L.A. Gear's 3rd Quarter Shows $11-Million Loss,'' *Los Angeles Times,* October 5, 1991, p. D3.

Darlin, Damon, ''Getting Beyond a Market Niche,'' *Forbes,* November 22, 1993, p. 106.

Ellis, Kristi, ''Building the Brands Through Licensing,'' *Women's Wear Daily,* May 26, 1999.

Gellene, Denise, ''Out of Step: L.A. Gear, in Athletic Shoe Race, Seeks to Regain Foothold,'' *Los Angeles Times,* September 20, 1996, p. D1.

Grish, Kristina, ''L.A. Gear Swims into Kids Pool of Active Market,'' *Sporting Goods Business,* November 6, 1998, p. 26.

Hollreiser, Eric, ''L.A. Gear Recasts for Women, Kids,'' *Brandweek,* January 30, 1995, p. 13.

Jefferson, David J., ''Don't Walk a Mile in His Shoes: Can Disney Magic—and Money—Put Former L.A. Gear Shoe King Robert Greenberg Back on the Fast Track?,'' *Los Angeles Magazine,* December 18, 1991, p. 114.

Kerwin, Kathleen, ''L.A. Gear Is Going Where the Boys Are,'' *Business Week,* June 19, 1989, p. 54.

Kranhold, Kathryn, ''Group Including Disney Family Sells Its 42% Interest in L.A. Gear at a Loss,'' *Wall Street Journal,* October 14, 1997, p. B8.

''L.A. Gear Bouncing Back: Largest Licensee ACI Acts As Main Spring,'' *Footwear News,* July 13, 1998, p. 5.

''L.A. Gear Coming Out of the Fog,'' *Sporting Goods Business,* July 24, 1998, p. 23.

''L.A. Gear Emerges As Licensor,'' *Apparel Industry Magazine,* November 1, 1998, p. 14.

''L.A. Gear Inc., Bordan Shoe Suit Settled,'' *Footwear News,* January 11, 1999, p. 2.

''L.A. Gear, Inc. (L.A.),'' *Wall Street Transcript,* August 6,1990, pp. 98, 110.

''L.A. Gear + 184.6% (No. 2),'' *Institutional Investor,* March 1990, pp. 52–53.

''L.A. Gear's Chapter 11 Puts 'Our House in Order,' '' *Footwear News,* January 19, 1998, p. 2.

''L.A. Gear Vs. Bordan: It's Truth or Consequences,'' *Footwear News,* July 27, 1998, p. 2.

Lazzareschi, Carla, ''L.A. Gear CEO Greenberg Says He'll Step Down,'' *Los Angeles Times,* January 27, 1992, p. D1.

Lippman, John, ''L.A. Gear Makes Chapter 11 Filing, Sets Creditor Pact,'' *Wall Street Journal,* January 14, 1998, p. B13.

Lubman, Sarah, ''Goldston Quits at L.A. Gear,'' *Wall Street Journal,* June 16, 1994, p. B13.

Magiera, Marcy, ''L.A. Gear's Comeback Plan: Fashion, Fitness Shoes to Get Separate Identities,'' *Advertising Age,* June 29, 1992, p. 12.

——, ''L.A. Gear Creative Review Ahead?,'' *Advertising Age,* June 17, 1991, p. 48.

——, ''L.A. Gear Looks for New Image,'' *Advertising Age,* November 4, 1991, p. 2.

——, ''L.A. Gear Shifts Ahead,'' *Advertising Age,* December 23, 1991, p. 26.

——, ''L.A. Gear Toughens Up,'' *Advertising Age,* January 30, 1989, p. 76.

——, ''Rebound Team: L.A. Gear Relies on Montana, Jackson,'' *Advertising Age,* July 2, 1990, pp. 3, 30.

——, ''Small Rivals Leap As L.A. Gear Stumbles: But No. 3 Shoe Marketer Is Planning Comeback,'' *Advertising Age,* June 8, 1992, p. 12.

McAllister, Robert, ''L.A. Gear Still Reaching for Brass Ring,'' *Footwear News,* February 17, 1997, p. 26.

Paris, Ellen, ''Rhinestone Hightops, Anyone?,'' *Forbes,* March 7, 1988, pp. 78, 80, 84.

Peltz, James F., ''L.A. Gear Runs Hard, but Isn't Gaining,'' *Los Angeles Times,* February 2, 1993.

Rose, Frederick, ''L.A. Gear, More Losses in Sight, to Cut Staff 55%, Take a Charge,'' *Wall Street Journal,* November 29, 1996, p. B4.

Savona, Dave, ''Can Foreigners Save L.A. Gear?,'' *International Business,* December 1994, p. 18.

Tedeschi, Mark, ''L.A. Gear Coming Out of the Fog,'' *Sporting Goods Business,* July 24, 1998, p. 23.

Zoltak, James, ''L.A. Gear Looks for Resurgence with DGWB,'' *Adweek,* August 23, 1999, p. 4.

—Sara Pendergast
—updated by David E. Salamie

MacDermid Incorporated

245 Freight Street
Waterbury, Connecticut 06702-0671
U.S.A.
Telephone: (203) 575-5700
Fax: (203) 575-5630
Web site: http://www.macdermid.com

Public Company
Incorporated: 1922
Employees: 1,900
Sales: $382.6 million (1999)
Stock Exchanges: New York
Ticker Symbol: MRD
NAIC: 32551 Paint and Coating Manufacturing; 325612 Polish and Other Sanitation Good Manufacturing; 32591 Printing Ink Manufacturing; 42183 Industrial Machinery and Equipment Wholesaling; 42261 Chemicals and Allied Products, Not Elsewhere Classified

MacDermid Incorporated develops, acquires, manufactures, markets, and services specialty chemicals and systems for the chemical treatment, surface preparation, and finishing of metals, plastics, and other materials. Its principal products are more than 5,000 chemical compounds manufactured by the company and used in finishing metals and non-metallic surfaces, printing, and offshore-drilling lubricants. MacDermid also produces equipment in support of the chemical business and markets supplies and equipment related to the use of these chemicals but produced by other companies. It maintains manufacturing facilities in six countries and sells its products in more than 25 countries. A flurry of acquisitions in the late 1990s was expected to almost double MacDermid's annual sales, to $750 million, in fiscal 2000.

MacDermid Through the 1970s

MacDermid was founded by Archibald J. MacDermid, a Scot who had worked on the construction of the Panama Canal. He left a sales position with a chemical distributor to found the company in 1922 and, with a grubstake of $4,000, began producing and marketing an electrolytic brass cleaner, in Waterbury, Connecticut, a major center of the brass industry in the United States. Sales reached an annual $391,000 by 1929, only to fall by more than half in the depths of the Great Depression, but were back on track by 1935.

Harold Leever—coincidentally also of Scottish extraction—joined the firm in 1938 as a research chemist, developed another lucrative product, and succeeded to the presidency in 1954. Archibald MacDermid sold his firm to 57 employees in 1959. Net sales rose rapidly in the 1960s, increasing from $4.8 million in fiscal 1962 to $16.8 million in fiscal 1966. MacDermid became a public company in that calendar year, selling less than 20 percent of its outstanding common stock at $17.50 per share. In addition to its Waterbury headquarters, laboratories, and manufacturing and warehouse facilities, the firm operated a smaller plant in Ferndale, Michigan, and leased sales offices and warehouse facilities in Dallas, Denver, Kansas City, Los Angeles, and St. Louis. It also held a majority interest in production companies in Spain and Australia.

By the 1970s MacDermid believed it was providing the most complete line of proprietary chemical compounds and supporting services in the fields of industrial metal and plastics finishing and plating on plastics. It was producing and marketing more than 250 proprietary chemical products used for these purposes and selling them to more than 6,000 companies. Additional plants had been established in Dallas and St. Louis. Typical end products finished by MacDermid chemical processes included office equipment, automobiles, cameras, refrigerators, and plumbing hardware, as well as engineering applications in aerospace and printed circuitry. Related chemicals, supplies, and equipment were being sold in New England and the Southwest. A subsidiary was manufacturing and selling tanks and other equipment to withstand chemical corrosion and other forms of attack, such as radiation.

In fiscal 1973 MacDermid purchased Occidental Petroleum Co.'s share in a joint venture that was manufacturing and selling the company's products abroad. This acquisition gave MacDermid full control of the Australian company and 90 percent

Company Perspectives:

We will create an industry image that automatically causes people in the industries we serve to think first of MacDermid.

We will justify their action by first thinking of the customers' needs—what's right for them makes it right for MacDermid—by supplying a total system including processes, know-how, and services that assist in meeting all their needs.

control of the Spanish one, plus full ownership of subsidiaries in Switzerland and Hong Kong. A German subsidiary was established as well, and manufacturing plants in Spain and England came into operation. MacDermid also took a majority interest in Plastron Systems Inc., a developer of a new technology for printed circuit boards, and increased its interest in the firm to 94 percent in fiscal 1974. This subsidiary became Etched Plastics Inc. the following year. MacDermid's sales continued to grow throughout the 1970s, and its net earnings declined only during the recessionary period of fiscal 1975 and 1976.

Stagnant Earnings in the 1980s

MacDermid reported record net sales of $56.8 million and earnings of $5.3 million in fiscal 1980. By this time it had acquired two more companies, Specialty Polymers Inc., located in Leominster, Massachusetts, and Vapocure International Pty. Ltd. (which it sold in 1983), and had established a Canadian subsidiary. MacDermid opened a larger English manufacturing plant in fiscal 1981 and a research and development center in Waterbury in 1982. In fiscal 1983 it acquired 3M's Plating Systems department, which included a factory in Vernon, Connecticut. A research laboratory also was established in Israel.

In 1981 MacDermid started marketing the chemical products it had begun developing four years earlier for a niche market in the microelectronics industry called submicron technology, geared to customers' particular needs as printed circuits shrank in size. MacDermid claimed to be the only company manufacturing all three essential chemical processes for making printed circuit boards: plating solutions, etchants, and resists.

MacDermid continued to expand in the latter part of the decade. It opened a copper recovery plant in West Germany in fiscal 1985 and a factory and laboratory in Taiwan in fiscal 1986.

A technical center was opened in Japan in 1986 to develop special chemicals for electronics. Another technical center opened in Hong Kong in fiscal 1987. MacDermid also opened a Nashville factory and laboratory in fiscal 1989. During 1989 the company acquired Circuit Services-W.R. Hatch Corp., a maker of chemicals for the electronics market; Henkel Corp.'s electroplating chemical-supply business; and ELNIC Corp., a producer of electroless nickel chemicals. In 1990 MacDermid swapped its semiconductor proprietary chemical sector in exchange for Dynachem Electronic Materials' electroless copper and screen resist businesses.

MacDermid's net sales almost tripled during the 1980s, but its net earnings peaked at $7.6 million in fiscal 1984. Fiscal 1986 saw a drop in revenues of 15 percent and in earnings of over 40 percent, which the company attributed in its annual report to the "most difficult electronics business climate in recent memory." Nevertheless, MacDermid, in contrast to many other suppliers to the electronics industry, did not lay off workers; indeed, it invested $11 million in new plant and equipment. During this decade of mergers, leveraged buyouts, and hostile takeovers, stagnant or falling profits might have resulted in wrenching changes. However, with a majority of its stock in the hands of company officers, directors, and present or retired workers—both individually and through an employee profit-sharing plan—MacDermid stuck to old-fashioned values. Each year, for example, company officers presided over an awards ceremony in which, clad in kilts, they presented service pins to employees honored for special contributions.

One investment manager told Kathleen S. Failla of *Chemical Week* in 1987, "The company thinks the way Japanese do. They run the business with a view to the long-term success of the company, and most companies are prone to short-term pressures." Failla quoted Chairman Leever in these words: "My goals are still very simple. Take care of the people and the people will take care of the stockholders." Arthur J. LoVetere, who had replaced Leever as chief executive officer in 1982, told her: "There is more to life than the almighty dollar." The two men were said to know each of the 650 employees by first name.

Aggressive Growth in the 1990s

This era of paternalism ended in 1990, when LoVetere accepted a demotion to devote more time to Roman Catholic lay activities. In Harold Leever's son Daniel, who succeeded him, MacDermid got a chief with his eye firmly fixed on the bottom line. Leever closed six facilities, including the Leominster, Nashville, and Vernon plants, in fiscal 1992, and cut the U.S. workforce by 30 percent. He made company executives share rooms in Best Western hotels and even eliminated the office water coolers. "If I see waste of even five dollars, it makes my guts churn," he told Silvia Sansoni of *Forbes* in 1998. Leever raised MacDermid's profits in spite of a sales drop during the recessionary fiscal year 1992 and reduced corporate debt from $26.2 million in fiscal 1990 to $8.5 million in fiscal 1994. A new earnings record of $7.7 million was set in fiscal 1993.

By this time MacDermid was producing more than 1,200 chemical compounds, with manufacturers of printed circuit boards accounting for two-thirds of its business. These chemicals were being used for cleaning, plating, and otherwise preserving the metal surfaces of these boards. More than half of all sales were coming from other countries, at least partly because MacDermid's main customers were moving manufacturing operations to East Asia. By mid-1993 the company had 22 foreign subsidiaries.

In 1992 Olin Corp. sold its European- and Singapore-based printed wireboard chemical operations to MacDermid and its worldwide exclusive rights to Olin's "black hole" technology for metal plating the holes in the boards, a carbon-based chemical system that could possibly replace electroless copper plating in circuit board manufacturing. Replacement of the conductive

Key Dates:

1922: Company is founded by Archibald J. MacDermid.
1966: MacDermid becomes a publicly owned company.
1981: MacDermid introduces chemicals for submicron technology.
1991: Numerous plants are closed and employees dismissed.
1993–94: New annual earnings record of $7.7 million is set.
1998: MacDermid is now world leader in metal-treatment chemicals.
1999: Acquisition makes MacDermid the leader in the North American flexographic printing market.

copper plating usually used would result in fewer toxic byproducts in the manufacturing process and protect MacDermid against lawsuits for violations of hazardous-substance laws.

MacDermid was also entering the field of photolithography, a $500-million-a-year chemical photoimaging process being used to define the image of a circuit on a printed board. Much of the necessary technology was being developed at the research and development facility in Israel. The company enhanced its capabilities in 1995, when it purchased, for $130 million, a unit of Hercules Inc. making photoresists, used to imprint electrical patterns on circuit boards, and a photopolymer printing-plate system, including solvent inks, to reproduce graphics for package printing.

The company was not neglecting its metal-cleaning market among traditional manufacturers in the United States and Europe. This market consisted of chemicals used to coat metal and plastic surfaces for the application of chrome or corrosion-protective coatings. ''Just about everything under the hood of a car is protected against corrosion by the chemicals we make,'' Leever told Daniel J. McConville of *Chemical Week* in 1994. He was placing hopes for the future on Viatek electroless nickel, a plating technique that he said offered a cheaper, better coating than the electrolytic process, but that did not debut until 1999. Also in 1994, MacDermid established an Industrial Cleaners Group. Among its products were cleaners provided by Allied-Kelite Co., a metal-finishing business recently purchased from Witco Corp.

By the end of fiscal 1999 MacDermid could point to outstanding gains. Net sales had more than doubled in the five-year period starting in fiscal 1995, and net income had more than tripled, with a new record set in each year. Company stock rose roughly tenfold over this period. Debt increased from $22.6 million to $258.7 million, but the money was used for acquisitions in order to increase market share. After purchasing Canning, a British firm, for about $150 million in 1998, MacDermid became the world leader in metal-treatment chemicals, according to both companies. MacDermid was prepared to sell some of Canning's other operations but intended to keep its unit for synthetic offshore-drilling lubricants. MacDermid had just finished acquiring Ytema, a Swedish firm, and earlier in the year had taken a 30 percent share in Galvanevet, Italy's largest producer of metal-finishing chemicals.

MacDermid enhanced the graphic arts sector of its business by purchasing Polyfibron Technologies International, a producer of photopolymers with annual sales of about $245 million a year, in early 1999. By adding photopolymers to MacDermid's production of water-based inks, the company would nearly double the sales of its graphic arts segment, increasing this sector to 38 percent of its total, compared to 31 percent each for electronics and industrial products. It also would make MacDermid the leader in the flexographic printing market in North America and second in the world. MacDermid issued seven million shares of stock and assumed $155 million of Polyfibron's debt to finance the purchase, which was valued at about $392 million. But as of November 1999 the transaction still had not closed because of an antitrust review by the Federal Trade Commission.

In fiscal 1999 MacDermid's revenue came 84 percent from proprietary chemicals, nine percent from equipment in support of the chemical business, and seven percent from the resale of chemicals and supplies manufactured by others. About 20 percent of its sales of proprietary chemicals derived from products covered by patents owned by the company or produced under patent licensing agreements. Members of the Leever family held about 20 percent of the company's stock in 1999, while an employee stock-ownership plan held about 15 percent.

In the United States, MacDermid was maintaining manufacturing plants in Waterbury; Ferndale; Middletown, Delaware; and Waukegan, Illinois. It maintained laboratories in Waterbury, Middletown, Waukegan, and New Hudson, Michigan. Factories abroad were in Panyu, China; Birmingham, Telford, and Wigan, England; Eure and Villemeux, France; Dusseldorf and Zulpich, Germany; Barcelona, Spain; and Hsin Chu, Taiwan. Laboratories were in Barcelona, Birmingham, Eure, and Telford, and also in Sheffield, England, and Hong Kong.

Principal Subsidiaries

MacDermid Asia, Ltd. (Hong Kong); MacDermid Benelux BV (Holland); MacDermid Chemicals, Inc. (Canada); MacDermid Equipment, Inc.; MacDermid Equipment Asia, Ltd. (Taiwan); MacDermid Equipment GmbH (Germany); MacDermid Espanola, S.A. (Spain); MacDermid Europe, Incorporated; MacDermid France, S.A. (France); MacDermid G.B., Ltd. (U.K.); MacDermid GmbH (Germany); MacDermid Hong Kong, Ltd. (Hong Kong); MacDermid Imaging Technology Asia (Hong Kong); MacDermid Imaging Technology Belgium NV (Belgium); MacDermid Imaging Technology Europe BV (Holland); MacDermid Italiana SRL (Italy); MacDermid New Zealand, Ltd. (New Zealand); MacDermid Overseas, Asia, Incorporated; MacDermid Scandinavia (Sweden); MacDermid S.A. (Pty.) Ltd. (South Africa); MacDermid Singapore, Pte. Ltd. (Singapore); MacDermid Suisse, S.A. (Switzerland); MacDermid Taiwan, Ltd. (Taiwan); Nippon MacDermid Co., Inc. (Japan); W Canning, MacDermid UK Ltd. (U.K.).

Principal Competitors

Atotech USA Inc.; Ethone-OMI Inc.; E.I. duPont de Nemours & Company; Minnesota Mining & Manufacturing Company; Röhm and Haas Company.

Further Reading

Failla, Kathleen S., ''MacDermid Is 'Following the Road Less Traveled,' '' *Chemical Week,* August 26, 1987, pp. 53, 56–57.

Galle, William, ''Chemical Products Natural Profits Catalyst at MacDermid,'' *Investment Dealers' Digest,* March 2, 1971, pp. 17–18.

''Hercules Inc. Agrees to Sell a Unit to MacDermid,'' *New York Times,* September 29, 1995, p. D3.

''Industry Activities,'' *Metal Finishing,* July 1994, p. 89.

''International All-Stars,'' *International Business,* June 1993, pp. 55–56.

McConville, Daniel J., ''MacDermid Charts Expansion to Hike Profits,'' *Chemical Week,* June 1, 1994, pp. 37, 40.

Moore, Samuel K., ''MacDermid Boosts European Profile with Canning Purchase,'' *Chemical Week,* November 4, 1998, p. 18.

——, ''MacDermid Clan's Balancing Act,'' *Chemical Week,* September 22, 1999, pp. 68–69.

——, ''MacDermid Sharpens Its Graphic Arts Focus,'' *Chemical Week,* March 3, 1999, p. 18.

Sansoni, Silvia, '' 'Waste Makes My Guts Churn,' '' *Forbes,* November 2, 1998, p. 228.

Walsh, Kerri, ''MacDermid Modifies Polyfibron Deal,'' *Chemical Week,* November 10, 1999, p. 15.

Wyatt, Edward A., ''Battling the Giants,'' *Barron's,* April 26, 1993, p. 14.

—Robert Halasz

Mandalay Resort Group

3950 Las Vegas Boulevard South
Las Vegas, Nevada 89119
U.S.A.
Telephone: (702) 632-6700
Fax: (702) 632-6714
Web site: http://www.mandalayresortgroup.com

Public Company
Incorporated: 1974 as Circus Circus Enterprises, Inc.
Employees: 33,966
Sales: $1.48 billion (1999)
Stock Exchanges: New York
Ticker Symbol: MBG
NAIC: 551112 Offices of Other Holding Companies; 721120 Casino Hotels; 713210 Casinos (Except Casino Hotels); 721110 Hotels (Except Casino Hotels) and Motels

Mandalay Resort Group is one of the leading hotel-casino companies in the United States, and is the largest such company in the Las Vegas market in terms of square footage of casino space and number of hotel rooms. Known as Circus Circus Enterprises, Inc. until June 1999, Mandalay Resort operates ten hotel-casinos in Nevada, including four elaborate properties on the Las Vegas Strip: Mandalay Bay, Luxor, Excalibur, and Circus Circus. It is also a partner with Mirage Resorts, Incorporated in a joint venture that owns and operates the Monte Carlo, another Strip denizen. Outside of Nevada, the company owns a dockside casino in Tunica County, Mississippi (near Memphis, Tennessee); has a joint venture interest in the Grand Victoria, a riverboat casino located in Elgin, Illinois; and is developing casinos in Detroit, Michigan, and on the Mississippi Gulf Coast. With the exception of the upscale Mandalay Bay, the company's properties are mainly aimed at middle-class vacationers; to appeal to this market segment, the company offers reasonably priced rooms and food, and has pioneered the concept of the casino as an entertainment theme park for the entire family.

Early Years: From a Baby Elephant to Topless Dancers

Circus Circus, the first casino of what would later become Mandalay Resort Group, began as the brainchild of Jay Sarno, a Las Vegas businessman with reputed ties to organized crime. Sarno had made his name as the operator of a chain of motels and had also developed Caesars' Palace, a casino and hotel with a Greco-Roman theme. In 1968 Sarno opened a casino with a circus theme on Las Vegas Boulevard, more commonly known as the Las Vegas Strip. Never one to think small, the promoter installed a circus arena, a carnival midway, a casino, restaurants, and shops under an enormous pink and white-striped tentlike roof. A baby elephant roamed the premises pulling the handles of slot machines and aerialists whirled through the air, their nets hovering just above the gaming tables. On the midway customers threw baseballs at targets and were rewarded for a bull's-eye by a topless woman springing out of a bed to dance for them. Stunned by the excess of the display, rivals on the Las Vegas Strip declared Circus Circus a combination of Sodom and Disneyland.

Sarno had hoped that the extravagant displays of Circus Circus would attract high rollers to his baccarat tables, but the circus theme—with clowns and animals and the children they attracted—was at war with the ambiance of a posh gambling hall. Trapeze artists whizzing overhead were a constant distraction to gamblers and the casino was not the big money-maker that Sarno had envisioned.

Although a 400-room, 15-story hotel tower was completed in 1972, Circus Circus continued losing money; within two years Sarno was broke. In February 1974, the casino and hotel operation were formally incorporated as Circus Circus Enterprises, Inc.; three months later, in May, the setup was purchased for $50,000 by two new investors, William N. Pennington and William G. Bennett, a former furniture store executive who became chairman and CEO of the company.

1974–79: Making Circus Circus a Success

Bennett and Pennington set out to revamp Circus Circus. After briefly attempting to cater to big spenders with perks and free services, the new managers soon became convinced that a

Key Dates:

1968: Jay Sarno opens Circus Circus casino on the Las Vegas Strip.
1972: A 400-room, 15-story hotel tower is added to Circus Circus.
1974: The hotel-casino is incorporated as Circus Circus Enterprises, Inc.; company is acquired by William N. Pennington and William G. Bennett.
1975: A second 15-story tower, with 395 more rooms, is added to the casino.
1978: A second Circus Circus casino is opened in Reno, Nevada.
1979: Company purchases Slots-A-Fun, a Las Vegas casino located next to Circus Circus.
1981: Silver City Casino, located in Las Vegas, is acquired.
1983: Company goes public with a listing on the NYSE; the Edgewater Hotel and Casino in Laughlin, Nevada, is acquired.
1986: The addition of Circus Skyrise and West Casino to the Circus Circus-Las Vegas complex gives the company the largest gaming capacity in the industry.
1987: Company opens its first casino developed from the ground up, the Colorado Belle, located in Laughlin.
1990: The company opens what is then the world's largest resort, Excalibur, a casino with a castle theme located on the Strip.
1991: Company adds a high-rise hotel tower with almost 1,000 rooms to the Edgewater casino.
1993: The $390 million Luxor opens on the Strip next to the Excalibur.
1995: Gold Strike Resorts is acquired for about $500 million.
1999: The $950 million upscale Mandalay Bay resort opens on the Strip; company changes its name to Mandalay Resort Group.

circus theme would never attract high rollers. ''Circus acts and kids and high rollers—it doesn't mix,'' Bennett later theorized in *Fortune* magazine. Bucking the industry trend, Bennett and Pennington decided to try to make their greatest weakness a strength by seeking out family business. In place of the traditionally coveted high-stakes customer, they would try to attract the masses, going after the middle-class tourist.

Implementing a shift in marketing emphasis and strict financial controls, the new owners remade their casino. The circus was moved to the second floor to cut down on interference with the gambling, the slot-playing elephant was retired, and the company banished the topless dancers. Bennett removed the high-stakes baccarat tables, ended complimentary services for big spenders, and stopped issuing credit to gamblers. Instead Circus Circus installed nickel slot machines, blackjack games, and $1 tables on the gaming floor. In addition to the circus acts, the company provided video games for kids and additional children's games on the mezzanine-level carnival midway; adult gaming activities were, therefore, separated from children's activities in compliance with state gaming regulations.

Most importantly, Circus Circus began to provide low-cost rooms and food to attract vacationers looking for a bargain. The company offered $28 rooms and inexpensive all-you-can-eat buffet meals. The buffet's purpose was to pull people in, not to make money on the food; indeed, the company lost about 50 cents on each meal served. Circus Circus also lost money on the hotel operations, but was subsidized by the casino. Patronized by hordes of people attracted to inexpensive food and lodging, the Circus Circus casino became one of the busiest and most profitable gaming arenas on the Strip. Bennett and his cohorts had refined their vision of what Circus Circus ought to be, becoming the first of a new generation of casino operators who saw their business not as an offshoot of a slightly shady underworld practice, but as an entertainment franchise designed to attract people of all income levels and all ages.

By June 1974 Circus Circus was turning a large profit. In the following year, the opening of a second 15-story hotel tower provided an additional 395 rooms.

Four years later, the company duplicated the Las Vegas operations in Reno, Nevada, opening a second Circus Circus casino in a space that had formerly been a department store. The new casino was accompanied by a 104-room hotel. In addition, the company opened a five-story garage in Las Vegas to serve the original casino.

This facility was expanded in the next year with the opening of the Circusland RV Park, part of the company's strategy to attract vacationers looking for a bargain. The park had slots for 421 recreational vehicles, complete with electric hookups to power utilities, a 24-hour convenience store, a laundromat, a children's playground, a pet-walking area, a community room, pools, saunas, a Jacuzzi, and a game arcade. Vacationers paid just $10 a night to use the park's facilities.

Circus Circus's steady construction of parking facilities resulted from heavy reliance on patrons who drove from areas around the Southwest, primarily southern California, to Las Vegas. This dependence left the company vulnerable to fluctuations in the oil industry. A gasoline shortage, resulting in long lines at service stations, lessened Circus Circus's profits for several months in 1979.

1979–87: Steady Expansion Beyond Circus Circus

Slot machines remained a staple of Circus Circus's strategy to keep costs down and returns high. Unlike table games, the machines did not need casino attendants and were extremely inexpensive to operate. Furthermore, visitors found them unintimidating, so the machines typically had a high rate of use despite the fact that the house paid out a smaller percentage of winnings on slot machines than on other games. In 1979 Circus Circus purchased Slots-A-Fun, located next door to the first casino on the Las Vegas Strip, and a dramatic renovation of this once-ailing facility soon followed.

Circus Circus added more hotel rooms in 1980. Circus Manor consisted of five three-story buildings; this project included 810 hotel rooms and a mini-casino. To link the different areas of the company's extensive Las Vegas operation, Circus Circus constructed a $5 million amusement-park-like elevated car system named the Circus Sky Shuttle. Pink and white air-conditioned cars glided along a monorail 18 feet above Circus Circus Drive carrying casino patrons between the big top and their hotels starting in 1981.

Circus Circus's rapid expansion continued in 1981 with the purchase of the Silver City Casino, a failing casino located one-quarter mile south of the company's headquarters on the Las Vegas Strip. The new owners revamped the property's exterior and expanded and updated the interior. In Reno, Circus Circus had an additional 725 hotel rooms in a new 22-story building.

In an effort to keep the flagship property fresh, the company spent $7 million in 1982 remodeling Circus Circus-Las Vegas. The casino, restaurant, and parking facilities were enlarged and a new front entrance marquee was built. By 1983, 20,000 people utilized the facilities each day and Circus Circus reported $240 million in revenues, making the venture the most profitable public gaming company.

In order to finance more expansion, Circus Circus went public in October 1983, offering four million shares on the New York Stock Exchange. The stock was introduced at $15 a share and quickly rose to $16.25 in trading, the start of a process that would lead to rich rewards for the shareholders, notably chairman William G. Bennett and president William N. Pennington. ''We changed this business when we went public,'' Bennett later acknowledged in the *New York Times.* ''People knew we were doing well, but until then nobody knew how well. Once they found out, everyone went after the so-called family business.''

With the influx of funds that resulted from the stock offering, Circus Circus extended the operations to a third city in Nevada, purchasing the Edgewater Hotel and Casino on the Colorado River in Laughlin, Nevada, in 1983. Shortly thereafter the company announced plans for a $12 million expansion and renovation of the property, which had fallen on hard financial times. This expansion, based on a Southwestern theme, included the construction of an additional 450 hotel rooms, quadrupling the Edgewater's existing 150 rooms to 600, and the enlargement and total overhaul of the casino. Other facilities appealing to middle-class vacationers, such as a Keno lounge, a sports betting center, a swimming pool, and a bowling alley, were also added.

As part of these plans Circus Circus purchased the Colorado Belle Casino—located next to the Edgewater—in 1984, for $4 million. The company wanted to move the original Colorado Belle building out of the way of the Edgewater's view of the Colorado River to make space for the expansion of adjacent property. The following year the company announced that the Colorado Belle would be reincarnated as a new resort in the shape of a $70 million replica of a three-deck Mississippi paddlewheel riverboat.

Circus Circus expanded the Reno facilities in 1985 as well: a 27-story hotel, the Skyway Tower, boasted more than 1,625 rooms and suites. The company's revenues in Reno, however, failed to match capacity. Harsh winter weather, in particular, resulted in an extremely poor showing for the Reno properties during 1986.

Construction in Laughlin and Reno did not stop the pace of expansion in Las Vegas, though, as Circus Circus added a new casino, which provided 17,000 more square feet to the gaming area, and also opened a large garage. Since occupancy rates for the existing hotels remained high, the company began constructing a 29-story hotel tower in 1985, called Circus Skyrise. The new accommodation provided an additional 1,188 hotel rooms. When inaugurated early the following year, Circus Skyrise and West Casino gave the company the largest gaming capacity in the industry. The property was not immediately profitable, however, and revenues remained sluggish for the next six months.

On July 1, 1987, Circus Circus opened its first casino developed from the ground up, the Colorado Belle, in the booming Laughlin, Nevada, market. Designed to attract a slightly more affluent customer than the company's staple blue-collar gamblers, the Belle was decked out in authentic riverboat decor. With a 210-foot ''smokestack,'' elaborate lighting to give the effect of a turning paddle wheel, and a length three times that of the actual river boats, the casino site dominated the banks of the Colorado River and was accompanied by a hotel building with more than 1,200 rooms. The Colorado Belle and the Edgewater quickly became the top two money-makers in the Laughlin market and Circus Circus ended 1987 with earnings of nearly $56 million.

1988–98: The Megaresort Era Begins

Despite persistent rumors that Circus Circus would follow other Las Vegas casino companies to New Jersey's Atlantic City, chairperson Bennett insisted that the cost of doing business in the East Coast city, where land prices were far higher than in Nevada, made such a decision unlikely. Instead Circus Circus looked to develop another massive resort in Las Vegas. In April 1988 the company purchased a large parcel of land once owned by Howard Hughes on the Las Vegas Strip and designated a sizeable chunk as the site for a new megaresort bearing a castle theme. The castle was intended to be the first thing motorists saw as they left the highway. The project—a large casino, a shopping arcade, a ''dungeon'' with miniature golf and other amusements, and more than 4,000 hotel rooms—was slated to cost $290 million. After a contest the castle was dubbed ''Excalibur'' and groundbreaking ceremonies were held in October 1988.

In February 1989 Circus Circus relinquished its only nongaming unit, Circus Hobbies, Inc., a money-losing enterprise that marketed radio-controlled toy planes. The company sold the unit to chairperson Bennett, who put up approximately $11.5 million in stock for the purchase.

When Circus Circus opened Excalibur in June 1990, the enterprise became the world's largest resort. With multicolored towers and crenelated battlements, the castle established new standards of flashiness for Las Vegas properties. In keeping with Bennett's belief that ''the non-casino areas have to be winners for the casino to succeed,'' as reported in the *Wall Street Transcript,* the hotel featured jousting tournaments in the main dining hall, strolling minstrels, fire-eaters in medieval garb, and periodic sword fights between knights in armor in the hallways. In an appeal to the prearranged tour market, the company promised fairs, festivals, rides, and shows. The hotel was almost always full.

Circus Circus continued growing steadily. Early the next year, the company unveiled a new high-rise hotel tower with nearly 1,000 rooms, attached to the Edgewater Casino in Laughlin. Only the Reno property remained largely unchanged. By the end of the first nine months of 1991, the company had earned $84.3 million on sales of nearly $620 million, despite a general recession in the gaming industry.

Circus Circus announced plans for the other half of its parcel of the Las Vegas Strip in November 1991, unveiling ''Project X,'' a $300 million development shaped like a pyramid with a glass facade. Slated to have 2,500 rooms and 30 stories, the pyramidal casino would be located next to the Excalibur. President William Bennett, who was nearing retirement age, announced that he would change his plans and stay on at the helm of the company in order to supervise the new project.

Four months later Circus Circus made a serious stab at opening a casino outside of Nevada. The company joined with two competitors—Hilton Hotels Corp. and Caesars World Inc.—to propose a $2 billion joint gambling and entertainment project to be built in the Chicago metropolitan area. Although Illinois had legalized gambling on Mississippi riverboats, land-based casinos were still forbidden; the realization of the plan depended on a large number of significant factors. This plan represented the company's first serious bid to expand beyond Nevada, but it was soon abandoned following the emergence of local political squabbling.

The Circus Circus-Las Vegas complex gained another entertainment venue in August 1993 with the opening of Grand Slam Canyon, a $90 million domed amusement park. Gland Slam failed to become the drawing card envisioned, however, with officials admitting it was ''underattractioned'' and needed to be expanded. Two months later came the long anticipated opening of the Egyptian-themed Luxor, which ended up costing $390 million to build because of construction problems. Boasting 120,000 square feet of gambling space, the Luxor had a debut that was marred by numerous glitches; it was eventually able to overcome these problems and become a successful property. The executive who oversaw the opening, William J. Paulos, became the latest high-profile departure, when he resigned in January 1994 to become a top executive at an Australian casino company. The following month, Bennett unexpectedly stepped aside as CEO of Circus Circus, remaining chairman, with Turner assuming the roles of CEO and president. According to *Forbes,* the management turmoil proved a distraction for the company, whose growth slowed at a boom time for the industry; for the fiscal year ending in January 1994, Circus Circus posted revenue growth of 13 percent (to $954.9 million), nearly all of which was attributable to Luxor's opening, while net income fell one percent, to $116.2 million.

Mounting pressure from institutional shareholders, other investors, and the company's board itself finally forced Bennett out in July 1994. Bennett resigned as chairman, and soon thereafter gave up his board seat and sold most of his 7.8 percent stake—although not before tussling with the board one more time over the Hacienda hotel-casino, which Bennett attempted to purchase before Circus Circus snatched it away from him in an acrimonious dispute. Following Bennett's resignation, Turner took over as chairman. Soon thereafter, Circus Circus had to fend off a takeover attempt by Chicago-based casino rival Bally Entertainment Corp. Around this same time, the company finally made its first foray outside of Nevada with the opening of a new Circus Circus in Tunica County, Mississippi. The dockside casino was located on the Mississippi River about 20 miles south of Memphis, Tennessee. Also debuting at this time was the Silver Legacy, a joint venture hotel-casino in Reno in which Circus Circus was a 50 percent participant. Attempts to expand into Atlantic City and Louisiana failed during this period.

A key development in 1995 was the acquisition of privately held Gold Strike Resorts Inc. for about $500 million. An operator of small casinos, Gold Strike was coveted more for its management ranks than for its properties. About 100 of the company's managers had once worked at Circus Cirçus, including Schaeffer and another one-time Bennett heir-apparent, Michael S. Ensign, a principal partner in Gold Strike. Ensign became vice-chairman and chief operating officer of Circus Circus, while Schaeffer became president and CFO. In addition to shoring up the Circus Circus management team, Gold Strike brought to the company two small casinos in Jean, Nevada—the Gold Strike and Nevada Landing; a 50 percent interest in a joint venture with Hyatt Development Corporation, which owned and operated the Grand Victoria riverboat casino in Elgin, Illinois; and a 50 percent interest in a joint venture with Mirage Resorts that was building the Monte Carlo casino. Located on the Strip on part of the property where the Dunes Hotel used to stand, the Monte Carlo was a 3,000-room resort catering to middle-class clientele through an atmosphere of ''casual elegance.'' It opened in June 1996 and cost $350 million to develop. The acquisition of Gold Strike also led to Circus Circus Mississippi being rechristened Gold Strike-Tunica. By early 1998 a 1,066-room, 31-story hotel tower had been constructed and opened adjacent to this casino.

In January 1998 Turner resigned from the company and Ensign became chairman, CEO, and COO. Around this time the company was in merger discussions with several real-estate investment trusts. These discussions led nowhere, as did talks with Hilton Hotels Corp. in early 1998 regarding a merger to create the largest U.S. gambling concern. Circus Circus's earnings were suffering from increased competition in the casino industry and its stock price was depressed.

1999 and Beyond: Going Upscale As Mandalay

In the midst of a Las Vegas Strip building boom that promised to add thousands of new hotel rooms to the gambling mecca, Circus Circus was betting its future on its biggest resort yet, Mandalay Bay. Construction of the hotel-casino began in 1997 on the site of the Hacienda, which was imploded on New Year's Eve 1996. Opened in March 1999, Mandalay Bay marked Circus Circus's move upscale. Costing $950 million to build, the South Seas-themed megaresort included 3,700 hotel rooms and 100,000 square feet of casino space; 15 restaurants, a 12,000-seat sports and entertainment complex, a Broadway-style theater, and a House of Blues nightclub; and an 11-acre pool ''environment'' featuring a beach, a shark tank, and a wave machine through which world-class surfing competitions were able to be held. Adjacent to the new casino, Circus Circus also built a high-class, 424-room Four Seasons Hilton, which did not offer gambling but became the first hotel in Las Vegas to receive the coveted five-diamond rating from the American Automobile Association.

The initial results at Mandalay Bay were positive, and the increased traffic within Circus Circus's ''Masterplan Mile'' helped to improve results at the struggling Luxor. Circus Circus moved its headquarters to Mandalay Bay following its opening and further signaled its future direction by changing the company name to Mandalay Resort Group in June 1999. As it looked toward the early 21st century, Mandalay Resort had no immediate plans to develop another megaresort on the Strip, although it had land set aside for that purpose. It did have in the works smaller additions to the Mandalay Bay area, including a time-share condominium development. Also in the development stages were a casino in Detroit, Michigan, being developed through a joint venture 45 percent owned by the company; and a hotel-casino resort on the Mississippi Gulf Coast, the third largest U.S. gambling market after Las Vegas and Atlantic City.

Principal Subsidiaries

Circus Circus Casinos, Inc. (dba Circus Circus Hotel & Casino-Las Vegas, Circus Circus Hotel & Casino-Reno, and Silver City Casino); Slots-A-Fun, Inc. (dba Slots-A-Fun Casino); Edgewater Hotel Corporation (dba Edgewater Hotel & Casino); Colorado Belle Corp. (dba Colorado Belle Hotel & Casino); New Castle Corp. (dba Excalibur Hotel & Casino); Ramparts, Inc. (dba Luxor Hotel & Casino); Circus Circus Mississippi, Inc. (dba Gold Strike Casino Resort); Pinkless, Inc.; Mandalay Corp. (dba Mandalay Bay Resort & Casino); Circus Circus Development Corp.; Ramparts International; Galleon, Inc.; M.S.E. Investments, Incorporated; Last Chance Investments, Incorporated; Goldstrike Investments, Incorporated; Diamond Gold, Inc.; Oasis Development Company, Inc.; Goldstrike Finance Company, Inc.; Railroad Pass Investment Group (dba Railroad Pass Hotel & Casino); Jean Development Company (dba Gold Strike Hotel and Gambling Hall; Jean Development West (dba Nevada Landing Hotel & Casino); Nevada Landing Partnership; Gold Strike L.V.; Jean Development North; Lakeview Gaming Partnerships Joint Venture; Goldstrike Resorts, Inc.; Gold Strike Fuel Company; Jean Fuel Company West; Goldstrike Aviation, Incorporated; Circus Circus Louisiana, Inc.; Circus Circus Michigan, Inc.; Circus Australia Casino, Inc.; Circus Circus New Jersey, Inc.; Pine Hills Development II; Scentsational, Inc.; Darling Casino Limited (Australia; 50%); Circus and Eldorado Joint Venture (50%); Detroit Entertainment, L.L.C. (45%); Victoria Partners (50%); Elgin Riverboat Resort (50%); Pine Hills Development (90%); Circus Circus Leasing, Inc. (78.7%); New Dirt, Inc.; Ramparts International PTE Ltd. (Singapore); Time Share Operating Co.

Principal Competitors

Aztar Corporation; Boomtown, Inc.; Boyd Gaming Corporation; Harrah's Entertainment, Inc.; Hollywood Casino Corporation; MGM Grand, Inc.; Mirage Resorts, Incorporated; Park Place Entertainment Corporation; Santa Fe Gaming Corporation; Starwood Hotels & Resorts Worldwide, Inc.; Station Casinos, Inc.; Trump Hotels & Casino Resorts, Inc.

Further Reading

——, ''Circus No More,'' *Las Vegas Review-Journal,* June 18, 1999, p. 1D.

——, ''Controversial Lenin Head Disappears from Mandalay,'' *Las Vegas Review-Journal,* May 18, 1999, p. 1D.

Binkley, Christina, ''Circus Circus CEO to Resign: Ensign Will Assume Titles,'' *Wall Street Journal,* January 20, 1998, p. B17.

——, ''Gamble on Las Vegas Hotel-Casinos May Not Pay Off,'' *Wall Street Journal,* April 1, 1998, p. B4.

Einhorn, Cheryl Strauss, ''Hot Hand: But Will Circus Circus Keep Turning Up Aces After 1999?,'' *Barron's,* May 24, 1999, pp. 24, 26.

Grover, Ronald, ''At Circus Circus, It's Build Build,'' *Business Week,* September 25, 1995, p. 84.

——, ''Circus Circus Rakes in the Bread Bread,'' *Business Week,* February 27, 1989.

——, ''Circus Circus' Ringmaster–the One and Only—Casino Legend Bill Bennett Keeps Forcing Out His Heirs Apparent,'' *Business Week,* May 10, 1993, p. 84.

Gumbel, Peter, ''Las Vegas Hotel Boom Begins Paying Off,'' *Wall Street Journal,* April 20, 1999, p. B1.

Harris, Roy J., Jr., ''Circus Circus Succeeds in Pitching Las Vegas to People on Budgets,'' *Wall Street Journal,* July 31, 1984.

Koselka, Rita, ''The Last Pharaoh,'' *Forbes,* April 11, 1994, p. 118.

McKee, Jamie, ''Chairman Says Circus Circus President Resigned After Takeover Attempt,'' *Las Vegas Business Press,* April 5, 1993, p. 1.

——, ''Circus Circus Has Rollercoaster Year,'' *Las Vegas Business Press,* December 20, 1993, p. 3.

Seligman, Daniel, ''Turmoil Time in the Casino Business,'' *Fortune,* March 2, 1987.

Stevenson, Richard W., ''Cloning Casinos with Appeal for the Masses,'' *New York Times,* December 8, 1991.

Yoshihashi, Pauline, ''Casino Companies Say Chicago Is Their Kind of Town,'' *Wall Street Journal,* March 25, 1992.

——, ''Circus Circus, After a Spate of Bad Luck, Is on a Roll,'' *Wall Street Journal,* March 27, 1995, p. B4.

——, ''Circus Circus Agrees to Buy Hacienda for $80 Million and Drop Bennett Suit,'' *Wall Street Journal,* March 7, 1995, p. B11.

——, ''Circus Circus Chief Leaves Post, Remains Chairman,'' *Wall Street Journal,* February 25, 1994, p. B2.

——, ''Circus's Chairman William Bennett Resigns Under Pressure to Boost Stock,'' *Wall Street Journal,* July 11, 1994, p. A2.

—Elizabeth Rourke
—updated by David E. Salamie

McLeodUSA Incorporated

6400 C Street SW, P.O. Box 3177
Cedar Rapids, Iowa 52406-3177
U.S.A.
Telephone: (319) 790-7800
Toll Free: (800) 896-8330
Fax: (319) 790-7767
Web site: http://www.mcleodusa.com

Public Company
Incorporated: 1991 as McLeod Telecommunications, Incorporated
Employees: 7,800
Sales: $604.14 million (1998)
Stock Exchanges: NASDAQ
Ticker Symbol: MCLD
NAIC: 51331 Wired Telecommunications Carriers; 513310 Telecommunications Networks, Wired; 511140 Telephone Directory Publishers

McLeodUSA Incorporated is a major provider of integrated telecommunications services to businesses and residential customers in 12 Midwestern and Rocky Mountain states. It is one of the nations's fastest-growing telecommunications companies. The core business of McLeodUSA is to provide "one-stop," integrated communications services including local, long distance, voice mail, paging, and Internet access services, all from a single company on a single bill, tailored to the customer's needs. The company derives its revenues from the sale of telecommunications services, the sale of advertising space in telephone directories, and telemarketing sales. McLeodUSA Publishing prints and distributes nearly 24 million telephone directories in 22 states.

Anticipating Industry Deregulation: 1990

McLeodUSA was founded in 1991 by Clark McLeod. In the year prior to his formation of the company, Clark McLeod sold Telecom USA, which he and several partners had built into the nation's fourth largest long distance company, to MCI Communications Corporation for $1.2 billion. In the early 1980s the telecommunications industry had been monopolistic and services were inadequate. Typically designed to accommodate only one service, the infrastructure could not handle the high-speed computing traffic that consumers required, and pricing was prohibitive. Increased competition in the long distance market was the first step toward improving the situation—and McLeod's Telecom USA had reaped the benefits of deregulation in that market. McLeod became interested in trying the local phone market, planning to create a "super-regional" phone company offering local, long distance, paging, and Internet access on one bill. He was aware of consumer demand for a broader scope of high-capacity telecommunications at a lower cost. Legislators, regulators, and consumers were demanding that the industry be opened up to more competition, and McLeod anticipated sizeable opportunities for the future.

In 1992 the company began providing fiber optic maintenance services for the Iowa Communications network. In the following year, McLeod Telecommunications, Inc. was reincorporated as McLeod, Inc. The company began offering local and long distance services to Iowa and Illinois businesses in 1994. McLeod planned to concentrate on second- and third-tier cities in Midwestern and Rocky Mountain areas because no one else was focusing there. The company identified a 12-state area from the Great Lakes to the Rockies for expansion. With the help of managers who had contributed to Telecom's success, McLeod began his assault on two entrenched regional Bells: U S West and Ameritech.

Following regulatory approval, revenues soared 417 percent, from $1.6 million in 1993 to $8 million in 1994, reflecting in particular an increase of $1.9 million in revenue from the Iowa Communications Network Maintenance Contract and its commencement of local and long distance services. Positioning itself for rapid growth, McLeod launched its PrimeLine service, its first bundled telephony product for residential customers, and completed its initial public offering in 1996, adding $258 million in equity capital, followed by a second offering which added $138 million. Clark McLeod commented: "This is probably the largest sum ever raised in the shortest amount of time by an Iowa-based company," according to *Knight-Ridder/Tri-*

Company Perspectives:

Our mission is to become the number one provider and most admired company in the communities we serve. The principal elements of the Company's business strategy include: Providing integrated telecommunications service; Building market share through branding and customer service; Expanding our fiber optic network; And, migrating existing customers to our own network.

bune Business News. The funds allowed for the accelerated hiring of personnel, construction of its own fiber optic communications network, the construction of a technology park at its corporate headquarters in Cedar Rapids, Iowa, and for service expansion into new areas.

The federal Telecommunications Act of 1996 was enacted during this period. It pushed for deregulation and increased competition among local providers. McLeod worked to assemble an executive management team with decades of experience in telecommunications, while establishing a network to support the enhanced services it wished to provide. While building its network the company had long-term contracts with two regional Bell operating companies, allowing it to lease lines and switches. Once a customer chose McLeod, the Bell company would assign a line and telephone number. From there, McLeod controlled local line features, long distance service, voice mail, and Internet access for that customer. McLeod entered the local service market by doing an end-run around U S West, reselling the incumbent's own product, Centrex, according to the *Denver Business Journal,* which was a vehicle to provide local connections. Centrex avoided "many of the issues plaguing new competitors trying to enter the local market, especially the complex problem of interfaces." Centrex was basically an electronic PBX (private branch phone exchange), connecting callers via a switch at the phone company's central office rather than through an operator at a switchboard. It was capable of being loaded with features such as call waiting, voice mail, and caller ID. When U S West understood what McLeod was doing, it began a state-by-state regulatory offensive to withdraw Centrex from service. McLeod argued that U S West's regulatory actions created an unlawful barrier to competition, an argument which prevailed in every state petitioned through 1997. Following the construction of its own network, McLeod served customers without leasing capacity from U S West Communications and other carriers, selling its own network capacity to other telecommunications providers.

1996: Creating Brand Awareness

McLeod purchased one of the largest non-Bell publishers of white and yellow page directories in 1996, forming a subsidiary, McLeodUSA Publishing. The directories were a means of creating brand awareness by showcasing the company's name, logo, and telephone services. McLeod also acquired a telemarketing company, Ruffalo, Cody & Associates, a company which sold long distance services for a major telephone company and was ranked as the 26th fastest-growing private company in the United States, according to *Inc.* magazine. McLeod converted the experienced sales team into a long distance sales team to sell PrimeLine service. By this time, the company was serving residential and business customers in Iowa, Illinois, Minnesota, and Wisconsin.

McLeodUSA and AT&T signed an agreement to provide dedicated access service within 30 Midwestern cities. The agreement provided an alternative connection to the local telephone company for AT&T to serve business customers. According to *Knight-Ridder/Tribune Business News*, "This agreement allows McLeodUSA to provide dedicated access service to AT&T in key second-and-third-tier cities," adding: "Currently, AT&T is using the networks provided by the local incumbent telephone company to serve its customers." The McLeod network was constructed to meet AT&T specifications, enabling both companies to utilize current technologies within a high quality network. AT&T had announced various agreements with seven alternative access providers allowing businesses in 130 cities to connect with its network as an alternative to access provided by incumbent local phone companies. At McLeod's annual shareholder meeting in 1997, shareholders approved changing the company's name to McLeodUSA Incorporated.

Analysts estimated that the telecommunications revenue potential in McLeod's 14-state area should approximate $23 billion by the year 2007. Bolstered by projections, the company emphasized market penetration rather than geographic expansion. Its employee base had grown from 400 to over 4,500 within two years, with about 25 percent of that force devoted to sales and marketing services. McLeod completed a merger with Consolidated Communications Incorporated (CCI) of Mattoon, Illinois, creating the first Super Regional CLEC (Competitive Local Exchange Carrier). As a result of the merger, the company took ownership of all former CCI subsidiaries, including ICTC, an independent local exchange carrier serving east central Illinois; CCTS, a local exchange carrier offering integrated local, long distance and other services to customers in central and southern Illinois and in Indiana; CCD, a telephone directory company; an operator service company; an inmate pay-phone company; a full service telemarketing agency; a majority interest in a cable television company; and a minority interest in a cellular telephone partnership. The acquisition positioned McLeod for expansion in the targeted markets. As of late 1998, the company served almost 367,000 local lines in 267 cities and towns. Other opportunities were also seized, including mergers with Dakota Telecommunications Group (DTG) of Irene, South Dakota, and Ovation Communications of Minneapolis, Minnesota.

Westward Expansion: 1999

Encroaching deeper into U S West's territory, McLeod purchased two Salt Lake City, Utah, telecommunications businesses, Access Communications, Inc. and S.J. Investments Inc. Access provided voice and data long distance services to 30,000 customers in nine states. A major selling point for the company was Access's special 800 service for local and national accounts. The technology allowed the programming of incoming toll-free calls to "behave" differently depending on where the call originated, the time of day, and other variables. Steve Gray, McLeod president and COO, stated in *Knight-Ridder/Tribune Business News* that "We believe this is just the beginning for

Key Dates:

1992: Company begins providing fiber optic maintenance services for the Iowa Communications Network.
1993: McLeod reincorporates as McLeod, Incorporated.
1996: McLeod completes its initial public offering.
1997: Company merges with Consolidated Communications, Incorporated.
1998: Company acquires Access Communications, Inc.
1999: McLeod negotiates a long-term partnership with Forstmann Little & Co.

this new technology,'' adding ''From a futuristic perspective, the same logic built into the enhanced 800 routing platform can be adapted to direct e-commerce applications.'' Under terms of the deal, the owners of Access Long Distance received about 1.9 million shares of unregistered McLeodUSA stock and about $50 million in cash. McLeod also assumed about $97 million in Access debt. Following the acquisition, the company began planning expansion into Arizona, New Mexico, Oregon, and Washington, increasing its market area to 16 states—and increasing McLeod's market by 23 percent.

Anne Bingaman, former assistant U.S. attorney general in charge of the antitrust division, was elected to the board of McLeodUSA, becoming the first woman to serve on the company's board of directors. While working for the Department of Justice, Bingaman had focused on telecommunications, international antitrust, and intellectual property. She left the government in 1997 for the private sector to serve as senior corporate vice-president and founding president of the local services division of LCI International Telecom, Inc., in McLean, Virginia. While at LCI, Bingaman was responsible for regulatory affairs, filing numerous petitions with the Federal Communications Commission and testified before the Senate Commerce Committee to promote local service competition under the Telecommunications Act of 1996. She left LCI when the company was acquired by Qwest.

Bingaman's expertise was, indeed, needed. One of McLeod's major competitors, Ameritech, sought legal sanction allowing it the freedom to set its own rates for local telephone service, claiming that it faced ample competition to justify its claim. The Citizens Utility Board, along with ''at least one of Ameritech's competitors'' argued that there isn't enough competition in those markets to warrant rate deregulation, according to *Knight-Ridder/Tribune Business News*. The Citizens Utility Board argued that Ameritech's move to free itself from price regulation in 19 communities was improper because many consumers had no choice other than Ameritech for local phone service. In the Champaign-Urbana, Illinois-area, the principal alternative to Ameritech was McLeodUSA. Ameritech had begun reclassifying residential phone service in the 19 communities as ''competitive.'' That meant that the company could raise rates in those regions when it wanted to. An Ameritech spokesperson argued that the company was regulated by the Illinois Commerce Commission under a 1994 ''alternative regulatory plan,'' allowing the company to declare its services ''competitive'' when there was an alternative in the marketplace—and argued that the prices for Ameritech's phone services had actually decreased since 1994. McLeod argued that there still was not enough competition, and that Ameritech still held the upper hand. At press time the matter was still pending.

Former White House Chief of Staff Erskine Bowles joined the board of directors of McLeod, following a $1 billion investment in the company by Forstmann Little & Company, giving the firm a 12 percent stake in McLeod. Bowles was a general partner in Forstmann Little, along with fellow director, Theodore Forstmann, senior partner of the New York private investment firm. As general partner, Bowles focused on the firm's portfolio companies and on the development of new investments. He was involved in the firm's decision to invest in McLeod and to fund its business plan. Bowles told *Knight-Ridder/Tribune Business News* that ''One of the most compelling reasons for selecting McLeodUSA for this substantial investment was the quality of their leadership team and their track record of outstanding execution.'' The investment was one of the largest individual investments made by Forstmann Little. McLeod planned to use the capital to develop its fiber optic network and to penetrate new markets to add new customers.

In the autumn of 1999, McLeod dedicated an 80,000-square-foot facility in the Missouri Research Park in Weldon Spring, Missouri, consolidating three St. Louis-area offices. The company invested approximately $30 million in development in the region, having captured 32 percent of the business lines. Mcleod contracted with Network Management to provide engineering services and lay 75 miles of fiber optic network in the St. Louis area, an area which company managers considered an emerging center for technology in the United States.

At it entered 2000 McLeod had consistently met or surpassed its goals since the company's founding, succeeding in developing customer bases in targeted secondary markets. Speaking for the company, Clark McLeod has boldly stated that ''We want to be the number one provider in every market that we're in,'' adding ''Our strategy has been to enter a marketplace, gain share in the marketplace and then build fiber networks to get closer and closer to our customers.'' So far, favorable legislation and the company's grass-roots approach has positioned McLeod for continued growth.

Principal Subsidiaries

Consolidated Communications Directories Inc.; Consolidated Communications Telecom Services, Inc.; Illinois Consolidated Telephone Co.; McLeodUSA Diversified, Inc.; McLeodUSA Media Group, Inc.; McLeodUSA Network Service, Inc.; McLeodUSA Publishing Company; McLeodUSA Telecommunications Service, Inc.

Principal Competitors

U S West, Inc.; Ameritech Corporation.

Further Reading

Bates, Mary W., ''Business Calling Plans: What Some of the Major Telecommunications Companies Are Offering,'' *Indiana Business Magazine*, June 1999, p. 37.

Burnette, Lacey, ''Telecommunications Firm Opens New Building in Research Park, *St Louis Post-Dispatch,* October 12, 1999, p. 3.

''Cedar Rapids, Iowa, Telecommunications Firm, McLeodUSA, Moves Quickly,'' *Knight-Ridder/Tribune Business News,* August 31, 1997, p. 831B0934.

Ford, George C., ''Cedar Rapids, Iowa-Based Telecommunications Firm Adds Woman to Board,'' *Knight-Ridder/Tribune Business News,* July 18, 1999, p. OKRB991991DF.

——, ''Former White House Official Joins Board of Iowa Telecom Firm McLeodUSA,'' *Knight-Ridder/Tribune Business News,* September 20, 1999, p. OKRB9926303E.

——, ''McLeodUSA to Acquire Utah Telecommunications Firm,'' *Knight-Ridder/Tribune Business News,* June 3, 1999, p. 0KRB99154040.

——, ''Telecommunications Company McLeodUSA Finances Large Expansion in Iowa,'' *Knight-Ridder/ Tribune Business News,* March 10, 1997, p. 330B1014.

Green Leslie, ''Forstmann Little Funds Telecom Company,'' *Private Equity Week,* September 20, 1999, p.11.

''Illinois Regulators Debate Ameritech's Freedom in Setting Local Rates,'' *Knight-Ridder/Tribune Business News,* August 17, 1999, p. OKRB99229050.

''Iowa-Based McLeodUSA, AT&T Sign Agreement,'' *Knight-Ridder/ Tribune Business News,* November 3, 1997, p. 1103B0944.

Kronemyer, Bob, ''Dial Tones: Choice of Local Phone Service Providers Is Finally Here,'' *Indiana Business Magazine,* December 1998, p. 19.

Zeiger, Dinah, ''Newcomer Rattles Telephone Business,'' *Denver Business Journal,* August 1, 1997, p. 1.

—Terri Mozzone

The Mentholatum Company Inc.

707 Sterling Drive
Orchard Park, New York 14127
U.S.A.
Telephone: (716) 882-7660
Toll Free: (800) 688-7660
Fax: (716) 882-6563
Web site: http://www.mentholatum.com

Wholly Owned Subsidiary of Rohto Pharmaceutical Co. Ltd.
Founded: 1889 as The Yucca Company
Employees: 200
Sales: $200 million (1999 est.)
NAIC: 325411 Medicinal and Botanical Manufacturing; 325412 Pharmaceutical Preparation Manufacturing; 32562 Toilet Preparation Manufacturing

The Mentholatum Company Inc. is a world leader in the manufacture and marketing of nonprescription drugs and healthcare products. Since 1889, The Mentholatum Company has grown and prospered from a small purveyor of soaps and toiletries into an international company, marketing quality proprietary medicines around the world. Worldwide sales in 1999 reached approximately $200 million and primarily involved the following product categories: external analgesics, oral care, skin care, lip care, and laxatives. The three major brands which account for over 75 percent of the company's sales worldwide are: Mentholatum Ointment, Mentholatum Deep Heating Rub, and Mentholatum Lip Care, the number one selling lip care line in China, Hong Kong, Japan, and Taiwan, and the fastest-growing in the United States. Manufacturing is carried out in 26 locations around the globe and marketing and distribution in over 150 countries.

The company, privately held for 99 years, was acquired by Rohto Pharmaceutical Co. Ltd. of Osaka, Japan, in 1988. Rohto is a major player in the Japanese pharmaceutical market, with top-selling products in the eye care, topical, and stomach relief categories.

Pioneer Days: The Hyde Family and The Yucca Company: 1889–1935

The Mentholatum Company's roots date back to the late 1800s in Wichita, Kansas, but the story starts earlier than that. Albert Alexander Hyde was born in Lee, Massachusetts, in 1848, and moved to Leavenworth, Kansas, in 1865 with his brother, where he was employed as a bank clerk at Clark & Company Bank until 1872. In 1872, Hyde's company sent him to Wichita to open a new bank, where he remained until 1887. Hyde left the company at that time and entered the booming real estate market. Following the collapse of that market in 1889, and despite being $100,000 in debt during a severe economic depression, Hyde began a new partnership called The Yucca Company, which began manufacturing and marketing laundry and toilet soap and shaving cream. In 1889, Hyde bought out his partners and became the sole proprietor.

In addition to soap and shaving cream, one of Yucca's earliest products was a cough syrup called Vest Pocket Cough Specific, which contained a blend of camphor and menthol and had a soothing effect against burns and inflammation. Hyde became intrigued by menthol and sought to develop a new product which would take advantage of its ability to soothe and relieve pain. His idea was to make an ointment that would relieve a head or chest cold, headache, or sore throat.

In 1894, after four years of research, experimentation, and consultation with pharmacists and physicians, the company introduced "Mentholatum Ointment" that December. The product was named by combining "menthol" and "petrolatum," and enjoyed highly favorable sales. Hyde, suddenly flush with cash, decided his money would better be used to the benefit of the local community, and donated most of his earnings to churches and Christian missions. With the expansion of business, the head office and factory moved to Buffalo, New York, in 1903. In 1906, the firm adopted the name The Mentholatum Company, after its flagship product.

During the 1920s, Hyde's son, Albert Todd Hyde, who is often overlooked as a co-creator of Mentholatum, moved to Dos Palos (now known as Mitchell Ranch), California, where he bought land. He planted mint, which he harvested and shipped

Company Perspectives:

It is our goal to become a company that aims to continuously improve quality and profits. The company will strive to achieve category leadership through innovation. Mentholatum will constantly develop unique new products with recognizable points of difference. We will commit to introduce at least two or three new products every 12 months for the next 5 years. In accomplishing these goals, we will increase our shareholder value and advance the growth of the company and development of our people.

to his father for use in their famous ointment, which utilized the juice of pressed mint leaves. Mint Road in rural Dos Palos was named after Albert Todd Hyde's mint farm. Albert Alexander Hyde passed away in 1935 and, in 1998, was posthumously inducted into the Leavenworth, Kansas, Business Hall of Fame.

The Vories Connection and Expansion into Japan: 1913–75

The company expanded into Japan due to the work of an American missionary. William Merrell Vories was born in Leavenworth, Kansas, on October 28, 1880, not far from where Hyde was working in Wichita. He moved to Omi Hachiman, Japan, to become a missionary when he was 24 as part of the YMCA Missionary Program, teaching high school English and marrying a local woman. He founded The Vories Architectural Company in 1907 and went on to design over 1,600 buildings throughout Japan, Korea, and China, including hospitals, churches, schools, and houses during his lifetime. He also founded The Omi Brotherhood Co. in 1920 to support his Christian missionary work. Vories also created The Omi Hachiman YMCA; The Omi Sanitarium and Hospital, originally designed for the treatment of tuberculosis; and The Omi Christian School System, all of which still exist today.

Vories's connection to Mentholatum began in 1913, when he acquired the rights to sell Mentholatum products in Japan under his Omi Brotherhood Pharmaceutical Company. Vories began importing and selling the product there in 1920 under the name ''Menturm,'' which was marketed through yet another company he founded that year, called The Omi Sales Company. Sales in Japan continued to grow over the years and Vories became a revered member of the business community in Japan.

Vories was instrumental in negotiations between Emperor Hirohito and General Douglas MacArthur following World War II, and is credited with Hirohito remaining emperor after the occupation of U.S. forces. Vories died in Japan in 1964, but, in 1997 (mostly due to his successful career and charity work, and partly due to his association with Mentholatum), Omi Hachiman became a sister city with Leavenworth.

East Meets West: Mentholatum and Rohto: 1975

The Rohto Pharmaceutical Co. Ltd., an Osaka, Japan-based pharmaceutical giant, had its own roots about the same time as The Mentholatum Company. Rohto was founded on February 22, 1899 as Shintendo Yamada Anmin Pharmacy, located in Osaka. In April 1909, the company released Rohto Eye Drops; when it received a newly designed container in 1931, it became a best-selling product. Yamada Pharmaceutical, as it became known in the 50 years it was in business, was renamed Rohto Pharmaceutical Company Ltd. in September 1949, and was incorporated on the 15th of that month and capitalized at ¥10 million.

A few years later, in December 1952, Rohto Peni-my Eye Drops were released and supported by radio advertisements. The following year, in September 1953, Siron, a gastrointestinal medicine, was released, and Rohto captured 47.5 percent of the market share for such products. In September 1959, growing rapidly, the company completed construction of an integrated main office, manufacturing, research and development, and distribution facility in Osaka. By October 1961, the company was listed on the second board of the Osaka Stock Exchange, and then moved to the second board of the Tokyo Stock Exchange the following year. By August 1964, the company was listed on the first boards of both the Tokyo Stock Exchange and the Osaka Securities Exchange, with an increased capitalization of ¥1.378 billion.

New products followed over the years, including Pansiron, a new and improved version of Siron, in December 1962; V Rohto, an ophthalmic medicine, in February 1964; and Namida Rohto, artificial tears, in October 1973. In January 1985, Rohto entered the home care test kits market with the introduction of Checker, a pregnancy test kit. Two years later, the company followed with Rohto Alguard, an ophthalmic medicine for allergy-related diseases, such as pollenosis.

Acquisitions began in 1974, when the company acquired the management rights to Josephine Cosmetics, a cosmetics manufacturing and sales company, and, in August 1975, The Rohto Pharmaceutical Co. Ltd. of Japan and The Mentholatum Company Inc. of the United States crossed paths for the first time, as the Japanese company acquired the trademark rights to Mentholatum and began manufacturing and selling Mentholatum Ointment and Mentholatum Medicated Lip Stick. Sales continued to grow, and the company was worth ¥2.64 billion by April 1981.

In June 1988, the management rights to The Mentholatum Company Inc. were acquired by The Rohto Pharmaceutical Co. Ltd., and the nearly 100-year-old company was delivered into the hands of the nearly 90-year-old Japanese firm.

Expansion, 1988 and Beyond

In October 1991, Mentholatum Zhongshan Pharmaceuticals, a joint venture company, was founded in Zhongshan, Guandang Province, China, as headquarters for the development of business in the Chinese marketplace for both Rohto and Mentholatum products, and P.T. Rohto Laboratories, Indonesia, was created in September 1996 to further the business expansion of both companies in that market. Rohto's Tokyo Branch Office was established in December 1996, and a new manufacturing plant was built in Ueno City, Mie Prefecture, Japan, in mid-1997.

New products continued to emerge, including Rohto's Dotest home pregnancy test kit in February 1993; a joint venture in early 1997 with Sebapharma (Germany) for the launch of Sebamed; and a joint venture in late 1997 with Whitehall, U.S.A. to enter the cold remedy market with a

Key Dates:

1889: The Yucca Company is founded.
1894: Mentholatum Ointment is introduced.
1906: Business adopts the name The Mentholatum Company.
1949: Rohto Pharmaceutical is incorporated.
1975: Rohto acquires trademark rights to Mentholatum name.
1988: Mentholatum Company is acquired by Rohto.
1999: Mentholatum celebrates its 110th year in business.

preparation that dissolved in hot water. Mentholatum's Deep Heating Rub, Fletcher's Castoria, and other products, representing a $1 million account, were turned over from inhouse advertising to New York-based advertising giant Campbell-Mithun-Esty for marketing.

When Rohto C3 came out in November 1995, it marked the company's entry into the contact lens supplies market. Pursuing that market with vigor, Mentholatum's eye drops began local production and sales in China in May 1996, followed in September of that year by the production and sales of intraocular lens and OTC eye drops. January 1997 brought the company exclusive rights to sell contact lenses from Cooper Vision, U.S.A.

In 1995, the company began looking for a new location for a research and development facility. Erie County, New York, where the company had retained its home since at least 1903, making it one of the oldest companies in the area, launched a bid to keep the company in its demesnes. Teamed with everyone from local CEOs and the University of Buffalo to Roswell Park Cancer Institute to the governor of New York, the county won its battle, as Mentholatum moved its headquarters into a 102,000-square-foot building on Sterling Drive in Orchard Park in 1998, which had been erected by Moog Controls Inc.

In mid-1999, the company released a new eye product called Zi. Containing natural camphor, the pH-balanced purified water solution was designed to cool and refresh the eyes. Targeted at style-conscious, 16- to 30-year-old women with ''active lifestyles,'' the product was supported by a $3 million advertising campaign for television and women's magazines in its bid to capture the top spot in an industry estimated at $27 million. Zi for Eyes would go on to win Best New Eyecare Product in the 1999 Superdrug Health & Beauty Awards after only six months on the market. Another new product, Migraine Ice, chill pads for migraine sufferers, was rolled out in June of that year, to compete head-on with such products as Glaxo Wellcome's Imitrex, the sales leader in the $1.2 billion migraine drug market; AstraZeneca's Zomig; Merck & Co.'s Maxalt; Glaxo's Amerge; and Bristol Myers-Squibb's Excedrin Migraine. According to a June 1999 article in *Knight-Ridder/Tribune Business News*, some industry analysts estimated that ''some 33 million Americans, or approximately 15 percent of the population, primarily women, suffer from the debilitating headaches at least once a year. The annual price tag of the painful affliction includes the purchase of close to $4 billion in pain relievers. . . .''

By 1999, Mentholatum alone had annual sales of more than $150 million in approximately 150 countries around the world, with such best-selling products as Migraine Ice, Softlips lip protectant, Deep Heating Rub, Natural Ice Medicated Lipbalm, Pain Patch, Fisherman's Friend cough drops, Fletcher's Castoria, Red Cross Toothache Remedy, and Red Cross Canker Sore Medication all bolstering its first and flagship product, Mentholatum Ointment. As the company entered the 21st century, Joni Sahhar, Mentholatum's director of new products, summed up the company's position. ''We're a 110-year-old company,'' she said, ''but we're not done growing.'' Rohto, meanwhile, enjoyed sales of ¥41.66 billion in 1999, with branch offices in Osaka, Tokyo, Nagoya, Sapporo, and Fukuoka, Japan.

Principal Subsidiaries

Mentholatum (Asia Pacific) Ltd. (Hong Kong); Mentholatum Australasia Pty. Ltd. (Australia); Mentholatum de Mexico, S.A. de C.V.; Mentholatum Pharmaceuticals P.V.E. Limited (India); Mentholatum South Africa (Pty.) Ltd.; Mentholatum Taiwan Ltd. (Taiwan) Korea; The Mentholatum Company Inc.; The Mentholatum Company Ltd. (U.K.); The Mentholatum Company of Canada, Limited (Canada); The Mentholatum (Zhongshan) Pharmaceuticals Co., Ltd. (P.R. China); P.T. Rohto - Mentholatum (Vietnam); Rohto - Mentholatum (Malaysia) SDN BHD; Rohto - Mentholatum Research Laboratories, Inc.; Rohto - Mentholatum Thailand Ltd.; Rohto U.S.A., Inc.

Principal Competitors

Glaxo Wellcome PLC; Merck & Co., Inc.; Bristol-Myers Squibb Company; Johnson & Johnson.

Further Reading

Angrist, Stanley W., ''Rubbing It In,'' *Forbes*, December 20, 1982, p. 147.
''CME Gets Dose of Mentholatum,'' *ADWEEK Eastern Edition*, August 24, 1992, p. 50.
''A Cooling Revival for the Eyes,'' *Chemist & Druggist*, April 3, 1999, p. 10.
''An Eye-Opening Campaign for Zi,'' *Chemist & Druggist*, May 1, 1999, p. 12.
Fink, James, ''Mentholatum Co. Evaluating Expansion Alternatives,'' *Business First of Buffalo*, October 16, 1995, p. 3.
——, ''Mentholatum Likely Buyer of Moog Plant,'' *Business First of Buffalo*, November 11, 1996, p. 1.
——, ''Niagara Compact Gets 'Save' in Bid to Keep Mentholatum,'' *Business First of Buffalo*, November 18, 1996, p. 16.
——, ''Tax Breaks, Grants Aimed at Keeping Mentholatum,'' *Business First of Buffalo*, February 26, 1996, p. 1.
''It's Zi Winner,'' *Chemist & Druggist*, October 9, 1999, p. 19.
Lauro, Patricia Winters, ''Cold Comfort for Migraines,'' *New York Times*, July 18, 1999, p. BU4.
Linstedt, Sharon, ''Orchard Park, N.Y.-Based Firm to Launch New Migraine Cooling Pads,'' *Knight-Ridder/Tribune Business News*, June 3, 1999, p. OKRB99154020.
''Mentholatum Co.,'' *Advertising Age*, August 31, 1992, p. 39.
Petrecca, Laura, and David Goetzl, ''Glaxo Shifts $40 Million Imitrex Account to Grey,'' *Advertising Age*, October 11, 1999, p. 1.
''Two Inducted into Hall of Fame,'' *Topeka Capital-Journal*, February 11, 1998, p. NA.

—Daryl F. Mallett

Mesa Air Group, Inc.

410 North 44th Street, Suite 700
Phoenix, Arizona 85008
U.S.A.
Telephone: (602) 685-4000
Toll Free: (800) MESA-AIR; (800) 637-2247
Fax: (602) 685-4350
Web site: http://www.mesa-air.com

Public Company
Incorporated: 1983 as Mesa Air Shuttle, Inc.
Employees: 2,500
Sales: $423.54 million (1998)
Stock Exchanges: NASDAQ
Ticker Symbol: MESA
NAIC: 481111 Scheduled Passenger Air Transportation; 481112 Scheduled Freight Air Transportation; 481212 Nonscheduled Chartered Freight Air Transportation; 481211 Nonscheduled Chartered Passenger Air Transportation

Five million passengers a year fly Mesa Air Group, Inc., although they may not know it by name: the company operates regional feeder flights under the brands America West Express and US Airways Express. It flies under its own brand in New Mexico. The group's young fleet visits 130 cities in the United States and also flies to Canadian and Mexican destinations. More than 90 percent of revenues come from America West Express and US Airways Express.

Beginnings

By his own admission, Larry L. Risley barely graduated from high school, having judged anything above a ''C'' grade ''a wasted effort.'' He then enlisted in the U.S. Army and eventually obtained an aviation mechanic's license, aspiring to nothing more than emulating his two older brothers, who were employed as union mechanics for two major airlines. However, following the career path chosen by his brothers proved difficult for Risley, who became a somewhat itinerant worker, securing employment at general aviation fields then quickly losing his job or quitting in anger, as he disliked working under anyone's supervision. In between his stints as an aviation mechanic, Risley found employment where he could get it, including selling burglar alarms and working as a janitor in a baby clothes factory. Later recalling this period of his life, Risley noted, ''I was really out of my element.''

Risley's prospects brightened in 1970 when he found his first opportunity to work alone, unfettered by a supervisor, opening an aircraft engine shop in Waxahachie, Texas. This comfortable niche, however, soon deteriorated. Several of his customers reneged on payments, debts mounted, and Risley's engine shop dissolved. It would be roughly another decade before an opportunity for success arrived, but when it did, Risley took hold and entrenched himself in the industry that had for so long eluded him.

In 1979, through the efforts of his brother-in-law, Risley was hired by Four Corners Drilling Co., an oil company based in Farmington, New Mexico, to manage its charter airline service. Oil was a plentiful and lucrative commodity in the region during this period, and Risley was kept busy maintaining a fleet of 14 small planes that shuttled oil drillers to and from the desert. The oil boom era in the region was short-lived, however, shuddering to a stop in 1980. The downward spiral of oil prices forced Four Corners Drilling to sharply reduce its drilling activities. The company's fleet of planes was sold as a consequence, but Risley convinced the company to keep one plane, a five-seat Piper, so he could try to establish a shuttle airline service between Farmington and Albuquerque.

With this one small plane, Risley established the foundation from which Mesa Airlines evolved. He advertised on local radio, placed signs along the roads surrounding Four Corners Regional Airport, and, perhaps most importantly, charged half the ticket price of his rival, Frontier Airlines Inc. After two years, during which both Risley and his wife worked seven days a week maintaining and operating the shuttle service, the couple decided to purchase the plane, offering their pickup truck and house as collateral against a $125,000 loan. The following year, 1983, their fledgling enterprise was incorporated as Mesa Air Shuttle, Inc.

Key Dates:

1982: Mesa Shuttle begins flying between Farmington and Albuquerque, New Mexico.
1985: Company begins a five-year growth spurt that will quadruple its size.
1987: Company goes public as Mesa Airlines, Inc.
1988: *Inc.* magazine names Mesa one of the fastest-growing small companies in the United States.
1992: Acquisition of WestAir doubles Mesa's size.
1997: United Airlines dumps Mesa, instantly cutting revenues 40 percent.
1998: Founder Larry Risley retires; Jonathan Ornstein takes over.

From the beginning Risley's operating philosophy was to fly only small planes between cities and towns in need of additional airline service and to pay close attention to the company's operating costs. Those costs largely resulted from aircraft maintenance, a task for which Risley was particularly well suited. Keeping costs low also carried over into other areas, such as having the pilots of the shuttle service assist in loading passengers' baggage, reducing the number of gate crew at arrival and destination points, and keeping the number of reservation agents to a minimum. Risley's strategy was to have a comparatively small workforce operating small planes that flew their routes with greater frequency—initially five times a day between Farmington and Albuquerque—than the company's competitors. If all reservation agents were busy booking flights, the incoming calls were directed to other Mesa employees, and if the entire staff was busy handling reservations, as they often were during Mesa's first decade of operation, Risley himself would answer the phone and book a passenger's flight.

Acquisitions: 1980s

Very early then, the characteristics that would set Risley's company apart from other regional/commuter airline companies were established, and the shuttle service prospered. From the single, five-seat Piper, the company's fleet gradually grew, with each new plane and each new service route enabling the company to generate greater revenues. With the exception of a small loss in 1984, Mesa recorded a profit throughout the 1980s and reached a financial level that enabled it to begin acquiring other companies, thus broadening its presence in the southwestern United States.

A majority of Mesa's acquisitions in its first decade were not outright purchases of other airline companies, but instead were code-sharing agreements reached with major airline companies, a necessary arrangement for a small airline company following the deregulation of the airline industry in 1978. A code-sharing agreement is a franchise that enables smaller airlines to benefit from the air traffic attracted by larger carriers without incurring their enormous marketing expenses.

In the mid- and late 1980s, Mesa signed two such agreements, first with Midwest Express, then with United Airlines, and additional agreements followed. Generating nearly $5 million in sales in 1985, Mesa embarked on a five-year period of prodigious growth, elevating itself to the top ranks of regional/commuter airlines in the United States. In 1986 it forced a much larger airline company, Air Midwest, out of the New Mexico region. The following year the company changed its name to Mesa Airlines, Inc., went public, and increased its sales volume to $14.3 million, a nearly 200 percent increase from two years earlier.

That year, 1987, proved to be a busy one for Risley's company and not without its disappointments. Mesa acquired the assets and the Denver, Colorado-based route system of Centennial Airlines, a purchase that resulted in a $250,000 loss for Mesa. The decision to acquire Centennial's service routes emanating from Denver and thereby compete against much larger, more entrenched air carriers represented a step away from Risley's initial corporate strategy to only enter markets suffering from a dearth of established air carriers. Operating as an independent in a market occupied by airline companies possessing much larger financial resources, Mesa found that its approach of offering low air fares and more frequent service was not enough to unseat the larger air carriers.

Despite this setback, Mesa continued to expand. By 1989, the airline's annual sales had reached more than $22.5 million, more than four times the revenues recorded four years earlier, and the mainstream press began to take notice. A year earlier *Inc.* magazine had named Mesa as one of the country's fastest-growing small public companies. In 1989 Mesa formed Skyway Airlines as a wholly owned subsidiary to fly in conjunction with Midwest Express Airlines out of Milwaukee, Wisconsin, extending Mesa's reach northward. In the same year, the company became the only commuter airline in the world authorized by Pratt & Whitney, an aircraft engine manufacturer, to perform complete overhauls of the PT6, the primary type of engine used by Mesa's planes. Mesa's construction of a $1 million engine shop illustrated Risley's focus on reducing aircraft maintenance costs. Within a year, the costs incurred from building the engine shop were recouped, positioning Mesa as one of the few vertically integrated commuter airlines in the world.

Mesa Airlines quadrupled in size between 1985 and 1990, and doubled in size in roughly the five months preceding the company's tenth anniversary in October 1990 by acquiring Aspen Airways' United Express franchise at United's Denver hub. Risley could look back on a decade of enormous success. By letting each market dictate the size of the plane serving that market, Mesa had perennially recorded one of the lowest seat-per-mile costs in the industry and could efficiently operate its 33 planes. Mesa planes by this time serviced a considerable portion of the United States: its Skyway planes serviced Iowa, Wisconsin, Illinois, Indiana, Michigan, and New York; its United Express code-sharing agreement took Mesa planes throughout Colorado, Wyoming, Nebraska, and South Dakota; and its original route system, evolving from the company's Farmington-to-Albuquerque flight, now covered New Mexico, Arizona, Texas, and Colorado. All this was enough to make Mesa one of the ten largest commuter/regional airlines in the nation. The airline's greatest growth, however, was still to come at the hands of Jonathan Ornstein, an airline financier who joined the company during its tenth year of operation. Ornstein had originally approached Risley to inquire about purchasing Mesa, an offer

Risley declined, but the meeting eventually led to Ornstein's employment by Mesa. Once Ornstein arrived, he began prodding Risley to pursue purchases of additional airline-related assets and to increase Mesa's influence in the commuter/regional airline industry, aggressively following a course Risley had previously pursued with moderation.

One year after Ornstein's arrival, Mesa acquired Air Midwest, Inc., an airline that operated under a code-sharing agreement with USAir Inc. The purchase extended Mesa's presence into Missouri by virtue of USAir's base operations in Kansas City and signaled the beginning of an era in which Ornstein and his desire to increase Mesa's magnitude would figure prominently. Later that year, in 1991, Mesa formed a new subsidiary, FloridaGulf Airlines, spreading the company's influence into the southeastern United States. By the conclusion of 1991, a disastrous year for many air carriers, particularly for Eastern, Pan-Am, and Midway Airlines, each of which ceased operation, Mesa continued to exhibit robust performance. The company posted a 39 percent increase in earnings from 1990, a 69 percent increase in revenues to $78 million, and a 50 percent increase in passengers from the previous year.

These positive results were dwarfed by what was to follow. In May 1992, Mesa announced the completion of a merger combining Mesa Acquisition Corp., a wholly owned subsidiary of Mesa, with WestAir Holding Inc., California's largest regional airline. For Mesa the acquisition was enormous, doubling its size and vaulting the airline from the tenth largest in the country to the largest regional/commuter airline in the United States. WestAir Holding was organized as a wholly owned subsidiary after the merger and continued to operate under its code-sharing agreement with United Airlines as United Express, based in Fresno, California.

New Challenges in the 1990s

As Mesa entered the mid-1990s, it continued to look for additional acquisitions, guided by both Risley and Ornstein. In 1994, a year in which the company expected to post $354 million in sales, Risley was contemplating the purchase of CCAir Inc., a commuter airline based in Charlotte, North Carolina, for $32 million, as well as other, smaller, acquisitions, such as a $3 million acquisition of SunAir, an airline serving the Virgin Islands and Puerto Rico, and a 24 percent share in a small commuter carrier based in Britain. As the company continued to expand, succeeding where other airlines had failed, it gained the attention of investors and competitors alike, becoming, for some, the prototype of a regional/commuter airline for the future. *Air Transport World* named it Regional/Commuter Airline of the Year in 1993.

Mesa's corporate holdings were renamed Mesa Air Group in December 1994. However big and powerful it was becoming, Mesa was also developing a reputation for delayed flights and overbooking, particularly at Denver International Airport. The FAA investigated this and allegations of poor maintenance, ultimately fining the carrier and recommending that several of the carrier's operations be merged. In essence, the FAA felt the carrier's operations had not kept pace with its furious growth.

As sales approached the half-billion dollar mark in 1996, Mesa's growth propelled the airline to order 16 Canadair Regional Jets worth $20 million apiece. It sent ten of them to Fort Worth's Meacham International Airport, which had no scheduled passenger service at the time, although American Airlines operated a huge hub at nearby Dallas-Fort Worth International. However, regulations limited Mesa to flights within Texas, traffic did not meet projections, and this operation folded within a year.

An even more devastating setback came when United Airlines replaced Mesa with SkyWest for its West Coast regional feeder services. The loss was severe, as Mesa had garnered 47 percent of its sales from United. Mesa lost $45 million on sales of $423 million in 1998, down from $510 million in 1997, and employment was cut nearly in half.

Risley announced his retirement against this dismal backdrop in early 1998. Ornstein, who had left the company to become CEO of Virgin Express, had led a group of investors that acquired 6.6 percent of Mesa shares and won two board seats. He became CEO of Mesa Air Group himself in May 1998 and set out to reverse the carrier's decline, cutting unprofitable routes, refining Mesa's pricing formula, and disposing of excess aircraft. He also fired 17 of his executives, retaining just one.

Mesa's next largest partner after United was US Airways, which was scrambling to keep up with competitors offering jet service on feeder routes. Although other carriers, Chautauqua and CCAir, also partnered with US Airways on the East Coast, Mesa was the only one operating regional jets at the time. Ornstein planned to expand the US Airways Express operations still further. Mesa Air Group bought CCAir Inc., another US Airways Express partner headquartered in Charlotte, North Carolina, for about $53 million worth of stock. By 1999, Ornstein had succeeded in directing the carrier back toward profitability as he had previously done during a brief tenure at Continental Express. It did not hurt that Bombardier paid Mesa $9 million to settle claims related to aircraft financing and trade-in options. Mesa operated 30 Canadair Regional Jets and 22 de Havilland Dash 8 turboprops at the time, making it one of Bombardier's largest customers.

The company relocated its headquarters to Phoenix from Farmington, New Mexico, in late 1998, and soon afterward, a new corporate logo was unveiled that featured a red sun, which represented a new sun rising for Mesa. As *Forbes* reported, Ornstein's first career as a stockbroker ended with him being fined and suspended for lying to clients. In his career as an airline executive, however, restored profits and on-time performance of better than 90 percent gave him credibility among Mesa's passengers, shareholders, and employees.

Principal Subsidiaries

Mesa Airlines, Inc.; Air Midwest, Inc.; WestAir Holdings, Inc.

Principal Divisions

America West Express; Air Midwest; US Airways Express; Mesa Airlines; Desert Turbine Services; Regional Aircraft Services; Mesa Pilot Development.

Principal Competitors

Continental Express; United Express; SkyWest, Inc.; Southwest Airlines Co.

Further Reading

Barrett, William P., ''Second Act,'' *Forbes,* August 9, 1999, pp. 113–14.

''Commuter Airline of the Year,'' *Air Transport World,* February 1993, p. 35.

''Flight Leader,'' *Success,* January 1993, p. 30.

Frink, S., and Jack Hartsfield, ''On the Wings of Eagles: The Air Industry,'' *New Mexico Business Journal,* February 1992, p. 26.

McCartney, Scott, ''Mesa Air Consents to an FAA Fine and Improvements,'' *Wall Street Journal,* September 26, 1996, p. B2.

''Mesa Airlines Embraces Code Sharing,'' *Air Transport World,* September 1990, p. 178.

Moorman, Robert, ''Playing Catch-Up,'' *Air Transport World,* September 1998, pp. 131–35.

——, ''Riches to Rags,'' *Air Transport World,* April 1998, pp. 66–69.

Phillips, Edward H., ''Mesa Seeks to Boost Houston Traffic,'' *Aviation Week and Space Technology,* August 11, 1997, p. 88.

Reagor, Catherine, ''Mesa Airlines Makes Offer to WestAir,'' *Business Journal,* November 18, 1991, p. 1.

Shine, Eric, ''Is Mesa Airlines Flying Too High?,'' *Business Week,* May 9, 1994, p. 82.

Teitelbaum, Richard S., ''Mesa Airlines,'' *Fortune,* May 4, 1992, p. 88.

''Temporary Downdraft,'' *Forbes,* June 22, 1992, p. 244.

''Woes of Big Airlines Mean Boom Times for Mesa, StatesWest,'' *Business Journal,* October 21, 1991, p. 11.

Zellner, Wendy, ''A Small-Jet Dogfight over Texas,'' *Business Week,* March 24, 1997, p. 36.

—Jeffrey L. Covell
—updated by Frederick C. Ingram

Murphy Oil Corporation

200 Peach Street
Post Office Box 7000
El Dorado, Arizona 71731-7000
U.S.A.
Telephone: (870) 862-6411
Fax: (870) 864-6373
Web site: http://www.murphyoilcorp.com

Public Company
Incorporated: 1950 as Murphy Corporation
Employees: 1,566
Sales: $1.69 billion (1998)
Stock Exchanges: New York Toronto
Ticker Symbol: MUR
NAIC: 211111 Crude Petroleum and Natural Gas Extraction; 324110 Petroleum Refineries; 422710 Petroleum Bulk Stations and Terminals; 447110 Other Gasoline Stations; 486110 Pipeline Transportation of Crude Oil; 486910 Pipeline Transportation of Refined Petroleum Products

Murphy Oil Corporation is one of the smallest of the U.S.-based integrated oil companies. Murphy conducts onshore and offshore exploration activities mainly in the United States (particularly the Gulf of Mexico), western Canada, the United Kingdom's North Sea, and Ecuador. The company owns two U.S. oil refineries located in Meraux, Louisiana, and Superior, Wisconsin, and holds a 30 percent stake in a U.K. refinery in Milford Haven, Wales. On the marketing side, Murphy sells refined products through more than 560 SPUR and Murphy USA gasoline stations in 17 states in the Southeast and Upper Midwest of the United States and in the Thunder Bay area of Ontario, Canada. About 45 of the stations are located in the parking lots of discount retail giant Wal-Mart Stores, Inc. In the United Kingdom, Murphy sells refined products via nearly 400 MURCO and EP gasoline stations. The company also holds stakes in four crude oil pipelines in western Canada, and in several crude oil and refined petroleum product pipelines in the United States.

Early Years: From Timber to Oil Exploration

The Murphy story began in the early 1900s in El Dorado, Arkansas, where Charles H. Murphy, Sr., started a lumber company with thousands of acres of timberland along the Arkansas-Louisiana border. Although he drilled his first oil well in the Caddo Pool of northern Louisiana in 1907, his primary efforts in oil exploration did not actually commence until 1936–37, when he and his associates discovered two large oil fields in southern Texas and Arkansas. At this time Murphy realized his land holdings were worth more for oil than for timber.

Murphy's business interest gradually expanded into a loose collection of partnerships, corporations, and individual holdings. In 1944, after he and his associates discovered their largest deposit near Delhi, Louisiana, they brought their diverse entities together as C.H. Murphy & Company.

Charles H. Murphy suffered a stroke late in the decade, and his son, 21-year-old Charles H. Murphy, Jr., was put in charge during his subsequent illness. With his new role in the company the younger Murphy was not able to attend college but eventually educated himself by reading the classics and learning foreign languages, and his ambitions grew with the goals of the company. He saw that corporate status would be necessary to achieve company objectives, so, in 1950, he reincorporated C.H. Murphy & Company as Murphy Corporation, the direct predecessor of Murphy Oil Corporation.

During the early 1950s, Murphy continued to explore for oil on the more than 100,000 acres of company-owned land, which also contained timber and farming operations. In 1956, two years after Charles H. Murphy, Sr., died, his son brought the company public, offering shares on the New York Stock Exchange.

Late 1950s Through Early 1970s: Creating an Integrated Oil Company

Toward the end of the decade Murphy began an expansion program that eventually led to the company's status as an integrated oil company. He helped found the 51 percent owned Ocean Drilling and Exploration Company (ODECO), an outfit one reviewer called "one of the true pioneers and innovators in the off-shore drilling industry." In 1958 he exchanged 71,958 shares for Murphy's first refinery: Lake Superior Refining Company's Superior, Wisconsin, installation.

In 1960, Murphy continued to grow, acquiring Amurex Oil Co., River States Oil Co., and National Petroleum Corp. Most importantly, that year a merger took place with Spur Oil Co., an

Key Dates:

1944: Charles H. Murphy, Sr., and associates form C.H. Murphy & Company.
1950: Incorporation of the company as Murphy Corporation.
1956: Company is taken public on the New York Stock Exchange.
1958: First refinery, located in Superior, Wisconsin, is purchased.
1960: First service stations are acquired through acquisition of Spur Oil Co.
1964: Company is reorganized as Murphy Oil Corporation; farm and timber interests are placed into a wholly owned subsidiary, Deltic Farm & Timber Co., Inc.
1973: OPEC oil embargo leads to increased revenues and profits for the company.
1980: Revenues surpass $2 billion for the first time.
1983: Murphy Oil is reorganized as a holding company; Murphy Oil USA, Inc. is created to oversee domestic oil interests and Canadian marketing division is sold.
1986: Low crude prices lead to the layoff of 30 percent of the Murphy workforce and an annual loss of $194.7 million.
1996: Company launches alliance with Wal-Mart Stores, Inc., under which Murphy gas stations are added to the retailer's store properties; Deltic Farm & Timber is spun off to company shareholders.

outfit whose extensive service station network would become Murphy's own.

After acquiring a second refinery in 1961—Ingram Oil and Refining Company's Meraux, Louisiana, installation—Murphy began expanding the company's drilling network. In 1962 he obtained the Western Natural Gas Company's Venezuelan properties and production. In the following years the company would begin exploring the Persian Gulf, Libya, the North Sea, the Louisiana shore, and other lands in the continental United States. It would also take large land positions in British Columbia, off the shore of Nova Scotia, in New Zealand's Tasman Sea, and off the coast of New South Wales in Australia.

As a result of this overwhelming concentration on fossil fuels, Murphy reorganized the company as Murphy Oil Corporation on January 1, 1964, placing the company's farm and timber interests—which now included 200,000 owned acres and 100,000 acres managed for others—into a wholly owned subsidiary, Deltic Farm & Timber Co., Inc.

In the mid-1960s, the company scored large successes in Iran's Sassan Field and in Libya. Between 1964 and 1969 the company's production of crude oil and liquids increased from 16,000 barrels per day to 37,000 barrels per day, while refinery intake rose from 43,000 barrels per day to 90,000 barrels per day. Much of the gasoline refined by the company went to owned or independently operated gas stations using the SPUR name. By 1969 there were 942 leased and owned SPUR stations and 1,332 SPUR stations operated by others. Of these, 548 were in the United Kingdom, 315 in eastern Canada, and 127 in Sweden.

ODECO also grew during the late 1960s. Between 1964 and 1969, its revenues more than doubled from $12.4 million to $28.5 million. Of all drilling contractors ODECO was in a unique position to help its corporate parent. The company contracted work for itself in addition to farming some jobs out, and therefore received portions of successful leases on their proceeds, adding to Murphy's total reserves. By 1968 ODECO was operating 12 drilling barges and according to the *Wall Street Transcript* was considered "one of the best growth stocks in the oil industry."

About the only Murphy product which did not grow during the 1960s was natural gas production, which fell from a record 65.6 million cubic feet per day in 1962 to 60.3 cubic feet per day in 1969. However, rising production did not always translate into rising profits. Steep transportation costs, high exploration costs, weak refined products prices, and losses in Europe led to declining profits from 1967 through 1969, when net income fell from $8.2 million to $6.2 million.

Despite these losses, Murphy—who still controlled 51 percent of the stock—continued to expand the company. In 1969, he created Murphy Eastern Oil Company in London, to monitor diversified overseas operations. The same year he signed off on ODECO's formation of Sub Sea International, Inc. to operate various undersea systems such as diving bells and underwater welding chambers.

In 1970, a year in which profits rose to $9.3 million, reflecting higher prices and lower ocean freight costs, Murphy Oil began drilling in the British North Sea through an eight percent participation with Burmah Oil and Williams Bros. To finance this project as well as drilling barges for ODECO and additional acreage in the Gulf of Mexico, the company sold $34 million in convertible debentures in 1969 and 800,000 shares of common stock in June 1971.

By 1971, the company as a whole was reporting revenues of $300 million. While two-thirds of its crude reserves were in Iran, Libya, and Venezuela, it had also created Murphy Oil Company, Ltd., which oversaw exploration, production, and marketing operations in Canada and was headquartered in Calgary, Alberta.

The 1970s–80s: Profiting from High Oil Prices

The OPEC oil embargo of 1973 was a boon for Murphy Oil. Sales shot up from $377.6 million in 1972 to $499 million and $862 million in 1973 and 1974, respectively. At the same time profits ballooned from $14.3 million to $48.5 million and $60.9 million. In 1977 the company surpassed $1 billion in sales for the first time, selling $1.11 billion worth of fossil fuel products and services.

Prices remained high at the end of the decade. In 1979, after North Sea drilling paid off in the huge Ninian Field (the United Kingdom's third largest), the company racked up three consecutive years of record sales and income. Revenues surpassed $2 billion for the first time in 1980 while in 1981 profits reached $163 million despite a total $119 million increase in American, Canadian, and British crude oil excise taxes.

Throughout the industry, high prices made higher cost and higher risk exploration activities economically viable. Murphy invested heavily in prospects in Alaska and off the coast of Spain, and although he balanced these more risky plays with leases near established properties in the Gulf of Mexico, the company's activities reflected those of an industry that was taking more chances and using more drilling rigs. This was good news at ODECO, where executives ordered several new platforms to satisfy demand.

On February 15, 1982, the company experienced a tragedy inherent in the ocean drilling business. During a severe storm off the coast of Newfoundland, ODECO's semisubmersible Ocean Ranger sank. Eighty-four people were on board and all were lost.

Although margins, particularly for refined products narrowed in the early 1980s, Murphy remained highly profitable. In 1983, the company began pumping oil from the Gaviota field off the north coast of Spain. The same year, it reorganized as a holding company, creating Murphy Oil USA, Inc. to oversee domestic oil interests and selling its Canadian marketing division, consisting of 100 owned or leased SPUR stations, a dealer network, and three product terminals.

Ups and Downs Through Early 1990s

In 1984 Charles H. Murphy, Jr., while retaining his role as the company's chairperson, turned the positions of CEO and president over to Robert J. Sweeney, an engineering physicist with a long career at Murphy. Sweeney faced an industry in which overcapacity and conservation had begun to pressure crude prices, and, consequently, refining and drilling margins. For example, as crude prices fell from $34 a barrel to $27 a barrel, there were periods in which the cost of products refined at company facilities were $2 higher than the same products on the spot cargo market.

In the fourth quarter of 1985, crude prices fell into the $15 to $20 range. Given reasonable returns for much of the year, Sweeney was able to salvage profits of $79.7 million, but in 1986 continued low prices forced him to take drastic economic measures. He slashed exploration budgets, terminated scientist positions, reduced support personnel by 15 percent, and let hundreds go at ODECO. Overall, he laid off over 1,600 employees—almost 30 percent of the company's total. Despite these efforts, the company lost $194.7 million, in what Sweeney in his annual report called "a terrible year."

Prices began to rise again in 1987, and all of the company's sectors rebounded except for ODECO, which suffered in a generally poor drilling climate. Since ODECO's capital costs were very high, underutilization of rigs meant heavy losses. In 1987 ODECO lost $61 million and at one point during the year was using only 29 percent of capacity. Excluding ODECO's figures, Murphy made $18 million that year; taking ODECO's losses into account, the company lost $44 million.

During these low years, management retained its credibility with stockholders by maintaining a $1 per share dividend. Moreover, Sweeney did make some moves toward growth. He used company land holdings to enter the real estate business in Little Rock, Arkansas, where the company was building homes and a PGA quality golf course. In 1986, he bought ten drilling rigs, reasoning that a shakeup was underway and that ODECO might profit from being one of the few surviving firms. In 1987, he bought out the 23 percent minority interest in Murphy Oil Company Ltd., Murphy's London-based subsidiary. That year the company also replaced its oil and gas reserves on an energy equivalent basis.

In 1988, Jack W. McNutt succeeded Sweeney as CEO. Like Sweeney, McNutt presided over a basically profitable company whose drilling subsidiary was what the *Arkansas Gazette* called the "monkey" on its back. ODECO was one of the nation's top three drilling companies, but like the industry as a whole, it had overbuilt and was carrying too many underutilized rigs.

During his first year, McNutt tried to gain more leverage in ODECO by buying out its minority owners. Though unsuccessful in this endeavor, Murphy reported a net income of $39 million in 1988—the first profit in three years. By 1990 the company had made a major rebound. Because of higher prices induced by Iraq's invasion of Kuwait, sale of the Sub Sea International (ODECO's diving segment), and divestment of a share of its interest in Ninian Field, Murphy reported net income of $114 million, the best overall result since 1983.

The year 1990 was also marked by an industrywide trend toward increased production of natural gas, a fuel whose environmental benefits many believed would prove valuable to utility and automotive companies in the future. At Murphy this trend was evidenced by record production and by the fact that for the first time natural gas production exceeded liquid hydrocarbon production on an energy equivalent basis.

In 1991, McNutt finally disposed of Murphy's ODECO problem. After several unsuccessful attempts, he acquired the minority interest in ODECO through a tax free exchange of shares and then sold ODECO for $372 million to Diamond M Corp., a contract drilling subsidiary of Loews Corp. Though the deal was not actually consummated until January 30, 1992, it was reported in 1991 as an $83.9 million charge against earnings and resulted in a loss for the year of $11.2 million. The company gained a much stronger balance sheet as a result, however. Part of the proceeds were used to pay debt down to just $24 million by the end of 1992, leaving it in a cash-rich position, with a little more than $300 million on hand.

Mid-1990s and Beyond

In the mid-1990s Murphy Oil chose to invest this money in its exploration and production operations (the upstream side of the oil industry) rather than in refining and marketing (the downstream side). The company's upstream strategy was to purchase interests—largely nonoperated—in high-risk, high-potential, very large global exploration ventures, balancing this with investment in lower risk prospects in the Gulf of Mexico and western Canada. In 1993, then, Murphy expanded its interests in North Sea production operations through the purchase of an 11.3 percent stake in the "T-Block"—a venture between Italy's AGIN, the field's operator, British Gas PLC, PetroFina S.A. of Belgium, and others—for about $145 million. Murphy also bought a 6.5 percent stake in the Hibernia field, which was located off Newfoundland and was a potential 615 million barrel find. Also in 1993, the company purchased from the province of Alberta a five percent interest—equivalent to 100 million barrels—in Syncrude, an oil shale project in the northern reaches of the province. Moreover, in late 1994 it acquired a

10.7 percent stake in the Terra Nova field, which had the potential of producing 400 million barrels and was located 20 miles southeast of Hibernia. Murphy Oil was also targeting several other areas for exploration, including fields in Peru, Ecuador, and China. By the end of 1994 the company had increased its proven reserves to 327.6 million barrels, a significant jump from the year-end 1992 figure of 187 million barrels.

Other key developments in 1994 involved the company's management. In October of that year, R. Madison Murphy, who had been serving as CFO, was named to the largely ceremonial post of chairman, replacing his father. That same month, McNutt was replaced as president and CEO by Claiborne P. Deming, a cousin of Madison who had been chief operating officer. Almost immediately, Murphy Oil became more visible to the press and the investment community, reflecting the influence of Deming; under Charles Murphy, Jr.'s leadership, the company had kept a very low profile for a public company.

Deming proceeded with several major restructuring moves. In 1995 the company reported a net loss of $118.6 million that was entirely attributed to writedowns of previously overvalued assets. In August 1996 Deming sold 48 U.S. onshore oil and gas fields to a group of institutional investors for more than $47 million. At year-end 1996, in a move aimed at refocusing the company on its core petroleum operations, Murphy Oil spun off to its shareholders Deltic Farm & Timber, its farm, timber, and real estate subsidiary, which was reincorporated as Deltic Timber Corporation.

Deming also attempted to revive the company's long struggling downstream activities. In November 1996 Murphy Oil entered into an agreement to merge its U.K. refining and marketing interests with those of Chevron Corporation and France's Elf Aquitaine S.A. However, it withdrew from the merger in early 1997, choosing to go it alone in the difficult U.K. retailing environment. Murphy subsequently entered into an alliance with U.K. convenience chain Costcutter, whereby Costcutter stores were added to existing Murphy gas stations. The ensuing increase in volume helped turn the U.K. downstream operations from loss-making to profitable. Murphy Oil followed a similar strategy in the United States, where it joined with Wal-Mart Stores, Inc. to test the addition of gasoline stations to the retail giant's stores. The test proved so successful that Murphy had 145 stations operating on Wal-Mart parking lots by the end of 1999, with plans laid to more than double the amount by the end of 2000. The Wal-Mart program began in the Southeast, using gasoline from Murphy's Meraux, Louisiana, refinery, then expanded to the Upper Midwest, where the stations were serviced from the refinery in Superior, Wisconsin. Murphy Oil's commitment to its partnership with Wal-Mart was underscored by the announcement in August 1999 of the sale of 60 company-owned SPUR gas stations.

Meanwhile, an oil glut forced down the price of a barrel of crude by late 1998 to about $11, the cheapest price in history with inflation factored in; just one year earlier, the price had been about $23. The oil glut was caused by a number of factors, principally the Asian economic crisis and the sharp decline in oil consumption engendered by it, and the virtual collapse of OPEC which was unable to curb production by its own members. The low prices were the principal factor in a 20 percent decline in revenues for Murphy Oil in 1998, from the $2.13 billion figure of 1997 to $1.69 billion. The company also took a $57.6 million after-tax charge to write down the value of some of its properties, leading to a net loss for the year of $14.4 million. With oil prices bouncing back up in 1999, this appeared to be only a temporary setback. In late 1999 the company announced capital expenditures totaling $457 million for 2000, an 18 percent increase over 1999, with the bulk of the funds going toward exploration in the Gulf of Mexico, development of the Terra Nova field, which was expected to start production in early 2001, and expansion of the Wal-Mart retailing program.

Principal Subsidiaries

Murphy Eastern Oil Company (U.K.); Murphy Exploration & Production Company; Murphy Oil Company, Ltd. (Canada); Murphy Oil USA, Inc.

Principal Competitors

Alberta Energy Company Ltd.; Apache Corporation; BP Amoco plc; Canadian Occidental Petroleum Ltd.; Chevron Corporation; The Coastal Corporation; Enterprise Oil plc; Exxon Mobil Corporation; Kerr-McGee Corporation; Marathon Ashland Petroleum LLC; Noble Affiliates, Inc.; Petro-Canada; RaceTrac Petroleum, Inc.; Ranger Oil Limited; Royal Dutch/Shell Group; 7-Eleven, Inc.; Southern Mineral Corporation; Suncor Energy Inc.; Texaco Inc.; Texoil, Inc.; Union Pacific Resources Group Inc.; Unocal Corporation.

Further Reading

"Chevron Corp., Elf, Murphy Oil to Merge Operations in U.K.," *Wall Street Journal,* November 6, 1996.

"Chevron, Elf, and Murphy's British Downstream Merger Is Not Surprising," *Petroleum Finance Week,* November 11, 1996.

Fan, Aliza, "Deming's New Management Style Lifts Murphy Oil's Traditional Veil of Secrecy," *Oil Daily,* September 27, 1995, p. 1.

Ford, Kelly, "Murphys Plan Transition: Madison Murphy to Direct El Dorado Oil Firm," *Arkansas Business,* June 6, 1994, p. 30.

Garner, W. Lynn, "Cash-Rich Murphy Oil Continues Search for Big Strike with Big Exploration Budget," *Oil Daily,* October 18, 1993, p. 1.

Gullage, Peter, "Hibernia Partners Are Mired in Lawsuits," *Platt's Oilgram News,* February 4, 1997, p. 2.

Johnston, David, "Murphy, Wal-Mart Face Ruling in Below-Cost Fuel Pricing Case," *Platt's Oilgram News,* May 3, 1999, p. 2.

Mack, Toni, "Roots: The Third Generation in His Family to Run Murphy Oil, Claiborne Deming Is Bringing It Back to the Business That Made the Murphys Rich," *Forbes,* October 7, 1996, p. 60.

"Murphy Oil Corp.," *Oil and Gas Investor,* October 1, 1999, p. 16.

"Murphy Oil Finds Refining and Marketing Up-Side in Wal-Mart Parking Lots," *Petroleum Finance Week,* September 27, 1999.

"Murphy Oil Focus Remains U.S. Gulf," *Platt's Oilgram News,* March 31, 1993, p. 5.

Ozanian, Michael K., "Murphy Oil: A Great Way to Play Oil Prices," *Financial World,* July 19, 1994, p. 22.

Toal, Brian A., "In Search of Greener Grass," *Oil and Gas Investor,* November 1995, pp. 33–35.

"Two Midcontinent Majors Reconfigure to Improve Their Wall Street Profiles," *Petroleum Finance Week,* September 16, 1996.

Washer, James, "Murphy Surviving As Niche Player in UK Retail Market," *Platt's Oilgram News,* March 19, 1998, p. 1.

Zipf, Peter, and Jim Washer, "Murphy Out of Milford Haven Deal," *Platt's Oilgram News,* March 14, 1997, p. 1.

—Jordan Wankoff
—updated by David E. Salamie

National Association for Stock Car Auto Racing

1801 W. International Speedway Boulevard
Daytona Beach, Florida 32115
U.S.A.
Telephone: (904) 253-0611
Fax: (904) 252-8804
Web site: http://www.nascar.com

Private Company
Incorporated: 1948
Sales: $2 billion (1999 est.)
NAIC: 71132 Promoters of Performing Arts, Sports, and Similar Events Without Facilities

The National Association for Stock Car Auto Racing, known as NASCAR, is the official sanctioning body for the sport of stock car racing. Stock car racing is a competition between cars that use standard auto bodies instead of specially designed exteriors. Stock car racing had a tremendous rise in popularity in the 1990s, and it is now the second most popular televised spectator sport in the United States, second only to major league football. Branching out from its base in the South, NASCAR runs races at tracks across the nation. Its Winston Cup series draws over six million fans annually, and 17 of the top 20 best-attended sporting events in 1998 were NASCAR races. The company brings in revenues through racing fees, licensing of its name, corporate sponsorships, and television rights. The company is privately held by descendants of its founder, Bill France.

Early Years

Stock car racing as a sport developed out of the need for fast and efficient delivery of illegal alcohol. The earliest racers were actually drivers for bootleg whiskey made in the Appalachian mountains of the American South. Homemade whiskey was a profitable sideline for poor farmers in Appalachia, who were able to sell their goods in urban centers when Prohibition made alcohol production illegal in the United States. Prohibition lasted from 1919 to 1933. Yet even after 1933, so-called moonshine remained in high demand, as it was inexpensive. Homemade alcohol was called moonshine because it was made at night, in order to avoid detection by federal revenue agents. The government levied high taxes on legal alcohol production, and the moonshiners sought to avoid paying. By the 1930s, a running battle between federal agents and moonshiners was underway, carried on up and down steep mountain roads between midnight and dawn. The distillers worked hard on their cars to give them speed and power, and built in features that helped them handle the cruel curves of the Appalachian roads. The cars themselves became the subject of folk legends, bearing names like the Black Ghost, the Grey Ghost, and the Midnight Traveler. The moonshine drivers were exceptionally skilled, and eventually they wanted to compete with each other in the daylight. The first such race was held in 1937 in Stockbridge, Georgia, and soon the sport was drawing thousands of spectators. Races were held on dirt tracks, which were usually officially horse racing ovals, although sometimes races were held in a plowed field. The most famous racers of the 1930s were all bootleg whiskey drivers, including Fonty Flock, Buddy Shuman, and Junior Johnson. The sport was rough, dirty, and apparently exhilarating. But it was not organized in any way until the intervention of Big Bill France.

Big Bill was born William Henry Getty France, the son of a banker from Washington, D.C. In the 1920s, Big Bill dropped out of high school in order to build and race cars in suburban Maryland; he also became a skilled mechanic. By 1934 France had a wife and a young son, and he decided to move the family to Florida for the warm weather. Originally headed for Miami, the family stopped off in Daytona Beach, and settled there instead. Daytona Beach was a haven for racers, who used its hard-packed beach as a speedway. Drivers from all over the world descended on Daytona to race. In 1935 Sir Malcolm Campbell, the most famous English racer, attempted to set a land speed record of 300 miles per hour at Daytona Beach. His attempt was foiled by strong ocean winds, and the next year, he and the world's other leading drivers moved from Daytona's speedway to the open desert of the Bonneville Salt Flats in Utah. Speedweek, as the Daytona event was called, was a huge financial boon for Daytona Beach, bringing in thousands of tourists. The city organized races in 1936 and 1937, but without the big stars, both of these lost money, and the sport seemed doomed. Bill France at that time was not only a stock car driver

Key Dates:

1947: ''Big Bill'' France organizes National Championship Stock Car Circuit.
1948: Company incorporates as NASCAR.
1958: Bill France builds new Daytona track.
1972: Big Bill retires; leadership passes to Bill France, Jr.
1979: First national broadcast of live NASCAR event takes place.
1991: Brian France takes over NASCAR marketing.

but also owned a gas station and mechanic's shop favored by other racers. The Daytona Beach Chamber of Commerce approached France about organizing a 1938 race, and France gladly stepped in. He booked a date, signed up drivers, and solicited local businesses for prizes, which included such items as a case of beer and a box of cigars. Tickets went for 50 cents each, and the race drew 4,500 spectators. The first race was a success, and France began planning for the next one. By 1939, he had organized a set of basic rules and found more local sponsors. With ticket sales raised to $1, he was able to pay his costs as well as rake in several thousand dollars profit.

Big Bill's adventure in race promoting came to a halt when the United States entered World War II and he was commissioned to work in a shipyard. After the war, France returned to Daytona and tried to pick up where he had left off. He lacked the financial backing to put a race together in Daytona, but he decided to sponsor a 100-mile national championship stock car race at a track in Charlotte, North Carolina. However, journalists France approached were uninterested in writing about a supposed ''national championship'' when there were no national rules governing the sport. Other problems plagued stock car racing as well. Each track made its own rules, so drivers frequently had to re-fit their cars to meet differing standards, and owners were often unscrupulous, absconding with prize money before the race was over. France added legitimacy to his sport by forming his own national sanctioning body, named the National Championship Stock Car Circuit (NCSCC), and set up a point system for drivers and a prize money fund. He ran the 1947 season under the NCSCC auspices. The next year, France wanted to expand the NCSCC's powers, giving it governing authority over all the major Southern tracks. He gathered 35 major racing figures in a Daytona hotel room to hammer out the specifics of the organization in December 1947. The following year the group incorporated as the National Association for Stock Car Auto Racing, with four stockholders, including Big Bill, who was elected president.

NASCAR in the 1950s and 1960s

Stock car racing grew into a tremendously popular sport in the South in the 1950s and 1960s. France was a visionary promoter, and he was aided by track owners who wanted NASCAR's sanctioning to make their races official. A new raceway was built in Darlington, North Carolina, by a local entrepreneur, and NASCAR sanctioned the track's first Southern 500 race in 1950. The track was built to hold 9,000 spectators, but its first event drew a crowd of 25,000. Five years later, the Southern 500 had become the biggest sporting event in the entire South, drawing a crowd of at least 50,000. Attracted by Darlington's success, other track owners upgraded their raceways or built new ones. The sport remained rough and dangerous. To control unruly crowds in the infield, local sheriffs would set up a temporary jail inside the oval. This was easier than dragging offenders across the track. France wanted to move the sport away from small dirt tracks and run races at more modern, paved raceways like Darlington. The speedway at Daytona Beach had been deteriorating for years, and after several seasons of running a ''last'' race at the beach, France convinced the city to let him build a paved, 2.5 mile speedway, breaking ground in 1957. Big Bill went deeply into debt, but his gamble paid off when the track opened in 1959 to a crowd of 42,000, rivaling Darlington's draw.

In the 1960s, many new speedways were built. There were perhaps a hundred different dirt tracks across the South by the early 1960s, and NASCAR sanctioned more than 50 races during the season. In 1960 builders in Atlanta opened the Atlanta International Raceway, and Charlotte, North Carolina, saw the inauguration of the Charlotte Motor Speedway. A year later Bristol Speedway debuted in Bristol, Tennessee, and in 1965 promoters built the North Carolina Motor Speedway in the Sandhills area of that state. France busily promoted races and certified cars and drivers. In 1969 major tracks opened in Michigan and Delaware, expanding the geographical reach of the sport. As stock car racing became bigger business, NASCAR reached out to corporate sponsors to provide purse money in exchange for advertising. In the early 1950s France had signed up the big Detroit automakers as sponsors, and other loyal backers of the sport included tire companies and other automotive-related businesses. NASCAR's business was quite lucrative, as it received sponsorship money from corporations, while track owners were responsible for the expenses of running the track. NASCAR organized and promoted the races and handled logistics. Its responsibilities included qualifying drivers, keeping records of the point system, and declaring winners.

Second Generation Takes over in the 1970s

As stock car racing grew, Big Bill France found himself hard put to keep up. Besides his track at Daytona, France had invested in another at Talladega, Alabama, which meant that he had less time to run NASCAR. He ceded the business to his son Bill, Jr., in 1972. Big Bill was 62; his son, 28. Bill Jr. made immediate changes. Most importantly, he found a new corporate sponsor for the races in the R.J. Reynolds tobacco company, which had been banned from advertising on television. In 1971 R.J. Reynolds agreed to sponsor a 500-mile race at Talladega called the Winston 500, after its leading cigarette brand. In 1972 Reynolds asked for a bigger role in NASCAR. It wanted the company to reduce the total number of races in the season from around 50 to just 31 so that the season would be shorter and more fans would concentrate at each race. In exchange, Reynolds offered major prize money, including a $100,000 bonus to be split among the season's top racers. It also took over the job of promoting the Winston Cup series races.

NASCAR continued to expand. It penetrated into the Northeast with tracks in Pennsylvania and New York. The sport grew in popularity, fueled in part by the explosive personalities of the star drivers. Leading racers such as Carl Yarborough, Richard Petty, and Bobby Allison grew in fame beyond the confines of the South as racing fans were drawn from a larger cross-section of the United States. With the rise of new, paved tracks in the 1960s, the infield brawling of the sport's early years mostly passed. Women fans became increasingly prominent, and the Winston Cup saw its first female driver in 1976 in the person of Janet Guthrie, a former University of Michigan physics major. In 1979 NASCAR reached a major milestone when it convinced the CBS television network to broadcast a championship race. The Daytona 500, the first televised NASCAR race, drew approximately 16 million viewers, or twice the audience the network had expected. NASCAR took ten percent of television revenues, so this was an extremely important revenue stream. The cable sports network ESPN began broadcasting Winston Cup races in 1981, and by the 1990s all three major networks ran NASCAR races.

Marketing in the 1990s

Though explosive growth seemed to have characterized the sport all through its existence, in the 1990s stock car racing was a juggernaut, becoming not only the fastest-growing sport in the country but finding itself second only to major league football as a spectator sport. Attendance at the championship series Winston Cup races grew more than 65 percent between 1990 and 1996, with average attendance in the late 1990s ranging from 100,000 to 150,000. In the early 1990s, NASCAR was still run very much as it had been when the company started. The bulk of its revenues came from sanctioning fees, which each track paid in order to have an official NASCAR race. The number of races had grown tremendously, with nearly 150 U.S. racetracks holding NASCAR events and additional tracks in Japan, for a total of more than 2,000 events. NASCAR's marketing staff in 1991 comprised only three people, as most of its promotion was handled by R.J. Reynolds.

When the third generation of the France family entered the business in the early 1990s, the company began to find more ways of bringing in money. Brian France, Bill, Jr.'s son, became head of marketing in 1991. In 1990, fans spent approximately $80 million on licensed NASCAR merchandise, and NASCAR itself made roughly $1 million off licensing fees. Brian France worked to increase NASCAR's licensing revenues by putting the NASCAR name on more items. Not only T-shirts, but also car batteries and Barbie dolls soon could be found emblazoned with the NASCAR name and logo. The company opened a licensing division in Huntersville, North Carolina, in 1995. The original staff of six had grown to more than 20 a few years later. In 1996 NASCAR sold rights to Gaylord Entertainment, a Tennessee entertainment and media firm, to operate and manage a chain of stores selling NASCAR goods. The chain, NASCAR Thunder, opened in Atlanta and in Winston-Salem, North Carolina, and soon expanded to other locations. By the end of the 1990s, NASCAR's revenue from licensing fees had grown to approximately $35 million annually. Sales of licensed goods had grown to $1.1 billion. Brian France also endeavored to bring more corporate sponsorship money directly to NASCAR. Previously, most sponsorship money went to racers, whose cars then advertised the company backing them. Brian France convinced major corporations such as Coca-Cola, Visa, and Anheuser-Busch to become sponsors, with approximately $45 million in 1999 going directly to NASCAR. Big Bill's grandson also worked to negotiate better television rights for NASCAR. At the time, NASCAR races were shown on all three major networks as well as cable stations, and each track worked out its own deal with whichever station it wanted. This meant that races were shown on many different channels, and NASCAR had little bargaining leverage. France wanted to consolidate television rights so that races would be broadcast by fewer stations. This move was expected to increase the amount NASCAR brought in from broadcast rights, from $10 million to possibly four times that much.

As NASCAR prepared to enter the 21st century, its phenomenal growth did not seem to be slowing. It was reaching more fans than ever through television and at more and more live events as tracks continued to be built across the country. It had changed from a lowly, dirt-track sport to a polished form of mass entertainment that appealed to entire families. Seventy *Fortune* 500 companies were NASCAR sponsors to some degree. The sale of licensed goods continued to rise, bringing in revenue not only to NASCAR but also to other companies such as Action Performance, Inc., which made NASCAR collectibles. Stock car drivers continued to be as charismatic as the colorful figures of the 1940s and 1950s, and leading racers from the 1990s such as Dale Earnhardt, Jeff Gordon, and Rusty Wallace were heroes to young fans. Profit margins for NASCAR were estimated to be as high as 35 to 40 percent in the late 1990s, and it seemed evident the company would continue to prosper as stock car racing captivated an ever wider audience.

Further Reading

Bernstein, Andy, "In the Driver's Seat," *Sporting Goods Business,* May 12, 1997, p. 60.

Fleischman, Bill, and Al Pearce, *The Unauthorized NASCAR Fan Guide '99,* Detroit: Visible Ink Press, 1999.

Friedman, Wayne, "NASCAR Opens Drive for More Profitable Sponsorship Deals," *Advertising Age,* March 22, 1999, p. 22.

Hagstrom, Robert G., *The NASCAR Way,* New York: John Wiley & Sons, 1998.

"NASCAR Thunder Revs Up," *Chain Store Age Executive,* October 1996, p. 78.

"Numbers Reflect NASCAR's Growth," *Knight-Ridder/Tribune Business News,* April 6, 1998.

Spiegel, Peter, "Southern-Fried Dynasty," *Forbes,* October 11, 1999.

—A. Woodward

National Envelope Corporation

29-10 Hunters Point Avenue
Long Island City, New York 11101
U.S.A.
Telephone: (718) 786-0300
Toll Free: (800) 808-8455
Fax: (718) 706-7663
Web site: http://www.nationalenvelope.com

Private Company
Incorporated: 1952
Employees: 2,800
Sales: $360 million (1998 est.)
NAIC: 322232 Envelope Manufacturing; 42212 Stationery & Office Supplies Wholesalers

National Envelope Corporation is the largest privately held envelope manufacturing company in the United States, turning out up to 100 million envelopes every day in some 2,500 varieties. Its assortment includes commercial and official regulars, custom-designed booklet envelopes for special direct-mail uses, and everything in between. The company has grown in part by acquisition of other firms. Its founder, after 47 years, was still chief executive officer in 1999.

William Ungar, a Holocaust survivor of two Polish concentration camps, came to New York City in 1946 on the first ship transporting displaced persons to America after World War II. Arriving with $15 in his pocket, he found work with F.L. Smith, a manufacturer of envelope-making machines. Ungar founded National Envelope in a tiny space on Manhattan's Lower East Side in 1952. The firm originally was staffed with five employees and turned out 200 envelopes per day.

National Envelope—North: 1971–96

By 1971 National Envelope was big enough to move into New England, building a plant in Worcester, Massachusetts, and stocking it with the equipment and employees of the United States Envelope Co.'s Worcester facility, which had recently closed its doors. This operation became National Envelope—North, manufacturing envelopes for such firms as BayBanks Inc., Raytheon Co., and the publisher of the *Boston Globe.* In 1996 the 133,000-square-foot facility was turning out millions of envelopes a day, operating around the clock five days a week.

Reporting on the factory's silver anniversary in 1996, *Globe* staffer Jennifer Lee wrote that National Envelope's milestone ''stands as a testament to the enduring vitality of niche manufacturing in Massachusetts and to the ability of such manufacturing to continue to provide blue-collar workers with secure wages and jobs.'' Some of the employees attending a birthday party at the factory spoke of good pay and benefits, progressive hiring policies, and room for advancement. Layoffs had been unknown except for a two-week period in the 1980s involving only a handful of workers. The 200 employees had an in-house union, wages said by the company to be competitive with other New England manufacturers, company-paid pensions, full medical and dental insurance, life insurance, sick leave, and earned vacation time. ''It's the kind of thing that attracts good-quality employees and retains them,'' said the factory's general manager. ''It allows us to compete by producing quality.''

Old Colony Envelope in 1994

National Envelope picked up 440 employees in 1994, when it acquired Old Colony Envelope Co. of Westfield, Massachusetts, a firm dating from 1920. A national leader in the paper-conversion industry and an official converter for several leading mills, Old Colony was supplying prominent fine-paper merchants with envelopes in a variety of paper grades, colors, and textures. Its envelopes had been used for President Bush's White House parties, President Clinton's first inaugural celebrations, and stationery addressed by Jacqueline Kennedy and Barbara Bush. The Envelope Manufacturing Association recently had honored Old Colony for the most improved safety record in the industry. In the year before, the company was recognized for the best safety record for U.S. envelope manufacturers employing 250 or more workers.

Company Perspectives:

At National we have one focus, supplying envelopes to the trade! If it's considered an envelope, we make it. Our assortment includes envelopes from commercial and official regulars to custom designed booklets for special direct mail uses, and everything in between. By specializing in one thing, envelopes, National is able to offer the best quality and service and millions of envelopes in stock daily!

Key Dates:

1952: National Envelope is founded by William Ungar.
1971: Company launches National Envelope—North in Worcester, Massachusetts, as it expands throughout New England.
1994: Company acquires Old Colony Envelope Co. and plans major expansion.
1998: National Envelope moves into the Southwest with the purchase of Texas-based envelope manufacturer Colortree.

National Envelope purchased Old Colony from its parent, International Paper Co., after a difficult period in which it was on the block for about two years. ''We did a great deal of soul-searching during the recession,'' Old Colony's general manager told Suzanne May of *BusinessWest,* a regional Massachusetts publication. ''We had gotten into all kinds of things that were not germane to who we are, and we were trying to be all things to all people. Once we regained our focus, however, and got back to doing what we do very well—which is manufacturing fine quality envelopes—we started to see improvement.''

In announcing the acquisition, Ungar said the existing Old Colony site in Westfield's Turnpike Industrial Park would be doubled to 240,000 square feet with the construction of a new adjacent building to replace another Westfield plant used by Old Colony but retained by International Paper. Ungar said that management and workers would be kept as part of an independent and autonomous operation and that the purchase would combine National Envelope's strength in the commodity envelope field with Old Colony's leadership in mill-branded envelopes.

National Envelope in the 1990s

With the Old Colony acquisition, National Envelope now had ten fully integrated manufacturing facilities in California, Georgia, Kansas, Massachusetts, Missouri, New Jersey, and New York. In late 1996 the parent company was threatening to leave New York City by moving its headquarters and plant in Long Island City—a community in the borough of Queens—to Union, New Jersey, where it already had a plant. The firm said it had outgrown its two-building complex in Long Island City and could save more than 20 percent in costs by moving to New Jersey. National Envelope was the only remaining one of the five or so envelope manufacturers operating in the city when Ungar founded the firm. Earlier in the year, his company had closed its Brooklyn plant and moved much of the work to Union to save money. National Envelope subsequently decided not to move after city and state officials offered the firm a multimillion-dollar package of tax concessions and other incentives.

National Envelope acquired a presence in the Southwest in 1998 by purchasing the Texas envelope manufacturer Colortree. This firm, renamed National Envelope of Texas, then ceased to serve envelope users directly and instead became a wholesaler to National Envelope and other paper customers. Based in Grand Prairie, Texas, Colortree had counted among its customers Dallas envelope distributors Clampitt and Olmstead Kirk as well as Dallas County firms Unisource and XPEDX, the latter a subsidiary of International Paper. National Envelope said it would transfer its own Dallas distribution operation to Grand Prairie. The envelope market, after a period of consolidation by manufacturers and paper merchants because of increased use of the Internet and fax machines, was said to be improving because of the growth of direct mail and small and home offices.

National Envelope's New York Envelope Co. was the parent firm's biggest unit in 1996, with about $160 million of National Envelope's estimated $300 million in sales. Old Colony accounted for about $60 million, and National Envelope—Central, based in Earth City, Missouri, for about $35 million. Other company units, in 1999, aside from the aforementioned and the Westfield and Worcester units, were Aristocrat Envelope Corp., based in Long Island City; National Envelope—East (Union); National Envelope—Midwest (Lenexa, Kansas); National Envelope—Northwest (Tukwila, Washington); National Envelope—South (Austell, Georgia); and National Envelope—West (Chino, California). The Chicago Area Distribution Center was in Warrenville, Illinois. National Envelope's sales office was also in Warrenville. Corporate marketing was in Union. The sample department was in Westfield.

National Envelope's array of envelopes in 1999 included commercial and official ones, both made of regular and recycled papers; window envelopes; booklet-style envelopes; and translucent ones, in 24 colors. There were also open-end specialty envelopes; open-side specialty ones, including blank forms, proxy, collect-to-mailers, filing jackets, and remittance envelopes; and open-end catalogs/coins envelopes, including policy, glove, and scarf ones. Fine-paper envelopes were available from more than 30 different mills and ranged from standard kraft to specialty woven. Also available were clasped envelopes and retail/soho/super size ones. Presentation portfolio envelopes were offered in micro linen or micro strife and available in 15 colors, with an interior holding two four-inch-deep pockets for insertions, including business cards and floppy discs. National Envelope also was presenting a full-line color catalog that it said presented the most complete line of products in the envelope industry.

Principal Operating Units

Aristocrat Envelope Corporation; Chicago Area Distribution Center; National Envelope Corporation—Central; National Envelope Corporation—East; National Envelope Corporation—Midwest; National Envelope Corporation—North; National Envelope Corporation—Northwest; National Envelope Corporation—South; National Envelope Corporation—West; National Envelope of Texas; New York Envelope Company; Old Colony Envelope Company.

Principal Competitors

American Business Products Inc.; American Mail-Well Envelope; Gilman Paper Co.

Further Reading

Bay, Suzanne, ''Old Colony, New Beginning: Envelope Manufacturer Has New Owner and Big Expansion Plans,'' *BusinessWest,* December 1994, p. 31.

Grant, Peter, ''Envelope Skirmish: A Queens Firm with 500 Jobs Eyes NJ Move,'' *New York Daily News,* December 24, 1996, p. 44.

Lee, Jennifer, ''The Science of Letters: In Era of E-Mail, Worcester Firm Continues to Thrive,'' *Boston Globe,* June 18, 1996, p. 39.

Powell, Barbara, ''National Envelope Buys Colortree in Grand Prairie,'' *Fort Worth Star-Telegram,* July 31, 1998, p. 4.

—Robert Halasz

National R.V. Holdings, Inc.

3411 North Perris Boulevard
Perris, California 92571
U.S.A.
Telephone: (909) 943-6007
Fax: (909) 943-5204
Web site: http://www.nrvh.com

Public Company
Incorporated: 1964 as Dolphin Trailer Company
Employees: 1,903
Sales: $360.3 million (1998)
Stock Exchanges: New York
Ticker Symbol: NVH
NAIC: 336213 Motor Home Manufacturing; 336214 Travel Trailer and Camper Manufacturing

National R.V. Holdings, Inc. is a leading manufacturer of recreational vehicles (RVs). Together with its wholly owned subsidiary Country Coach, National R.V. makes a line of 13 motor homes, travel trailers, and conversion vans under brands such as Dolphin, Sea Breeze, Sea View, Affinity, Allure, and Concept. Named as one of *Fortune* magazine's fastest-growing companies in 1999, National R.V. is benefiting from the aging of the massive baby boom generation. As they approach retirement, these consumers enter their prime R.V.-buying years. National R.V. sells its vehicles at 190 dealers in 38 states, Canada, and Europe.

The Roots of the Recreational Vehicle Industry

The American recreational vehicle industry dates back to the early 20th century. Some of the first RV devotees were Henry Ford and Thomas Edison, who teamed up in 1916 with naturalist John Burroughs and tire manufacturer Harvey Firestone to travel and camp across the United States in converted motor cars. These ''Four Vagabonds''—as they liked to call themselves—brought some of the comforts of home with them on the road. Like current RVs, these early models provided electric lighting and a cook stove.

RVs did not gain a wide following until after World War II, when mass production of the vehicles began. Like the broader automobile industry, RV production boomed in the postwar era of prosperity and optimism. The construction of an interstate highway system made it feasible for the first time for people to drive easily across the country, and the rise of RVs were another example of Americans taking to roads to see their nation. Moreover, camping became an increasingly popular way to vacation, and RVs enabled families to experience the outdoors without giving up comfortable amenities. As the U.S. rapidly became a ''car culture''—with suburbs and shopping malls springing up outside urban areas—RVs became the perfect symbol for the new American way to vacation.

Despite its early momentum, the RV industry remained a small one during the 1960s. As Dave Humphries, president of the Recreational Vehicle Industry Association, explained to the *Los Angeles Times* on November 7, 1987, ''it took us 20 years after the war to get all the elements in place: manufacturers, suppliers, dealers, campgrounds, and so forth.''

Dolphin Trailer Company: 1964–72

Wayne Mertes entered this nascent industry in 1964, when he launched Dolphin Trailer Company with his father. The younger Mertes had moved to California from North Dakota when he was only 15, and had immediately found a job with a mobile home manufacturer. For the next few years, Mertes had worked in every facet of the RV business—from electrical work to plumbing systems to final finishing. Armed with his experience in the field, Mertes ventured out on his own. The father-son pair mortgaged their homes to raise the $6,500 they needed for seed money.

The first eight years of Dolphin Trailer Company's business coincided with a growth spurt in the overall RV market. However, the young company did not challenge industry leaders such as Fleetwood Enterprises, Inc., which produced Class A motor homes—the largest and most luxurious type of motorized RVs. Instead Dolphin concentrated on the manufacture of camper shells, as well as ''Micro-mini motor homes.'' These ''Micro-mini'' RVs consisted of a small motor home shell built on a pickup truck chassis. (Class A motor homes are much

Company Perspectives:

Over the decades, National R.V. has established a solid reputation in the marketplace for high quality, innovative products that deliver superior value. By building upon and leveraging this strong track record, the company is able to enhance its position among the nation's leading RV manufacturers. This focused strategy has been responsible for a four-fold increase in the company's share of the Class A market over the last five years. A parallel development is the aging of the Baby Boomer population into their peak RV buying years. The combination of National R.V.'s powerful market position and the positive demographic trends driving the RV industry should provide future growth.

larger and utilize a specially designed chassis). In 1970, Mertes rechristened his business National R.V., Inc., although the company continued to focus on its line of Dolphin products.

Like most other firms in the industry, National R.V. was a diminutive company during this period. As *Barron's* explained, most RV companies were ''tiny operations concentrating on small geographic areas [and] niche products.'' In 1972, the RV industry achieved its best year to that date, when a total of 582,900 vehicles were shipped. Although hundreds of small and medium-sized RV manufacturers had sprouted up during the 1960s, record sales supported the entire industry.

Crisis in the Recreational Vehicle Industry: 1973–92

The sector's good fortunes came to an abrupt halt in 1973 with the onset of the Arab oil embargo. Even ''Micro-mini'' RVs were gas guzzlers, and concerned Americans worried about future gas prices and eschewed the hulking vehicles in favor of more fuel efficient alternatives. RV sales took another steep drop in 1979 during the next fuel crisis. Gas rationing and long lines at service stations made it not only expensive but also impractical to drive RVs. Informed by the general tenor of the times—that unnecessary consumption of oil resources was frivolous and wasteful—RV purchases declined. With President Jimmy Carter admonishing Americans to ''wear a sweater'' and lower the temperature of their houses, RVing seemed almost immoral.

RV production fell by about 70 percent in the 1970s, and nearly half of all manufacturers closed, according to the January 9, 1991, *Los Angeles Times*. In 1980, only 181,400 recreational vehicles were produced, as consumer confidence plummeted and interest rates (which impacted both RV and home sales) rose. But National R.V. weathered this storm, as well as the subsequent recession of the early 1980s.

In 1985 Mertes took steps to shield National R.V. from subsequent downturns. After moving the company's production facilities from Sylmar to Perris, California, National R.V. entered the Class A motor home segment of the market in 1985 with the introduction of the Sea Breeze model line. By expanding its product lines and boosting sales, National R.V. sought to make its position in the industry more stable. After some successes, the company was acquired by the New York investment firm Siegler, Collery & Co. in 1989, and shortly thereafter was rechristened National R.V. Holdings, Inc. (Gary N. Siegler would serve as the company's chairman through 1999).

The entire motor home market tightened once again in the early 1990s, though, as the country fell into a recession. On November 11, 1992, the Recreational Vehicle Industry Association told the *Riverside Press-Enterprise* that as a result of this economic downturn, ''consumer confidence remain[ed] depressed and RV dealer inventories [were] at near record lows.'' Consequently, the RV industry went through another period of mass consolidation. Despite these difficulties, National R.V. survived, although its share of the Class A motor home market remained below one percent and the company was only the 16th largest motor home manufacturer in the country.

Significant Growth in the 1990s

National R.V.'s place in the Class A motor home market changed dramatically in 1992, when the company introduced a bus-style version of its Sea Breeze motor home. Instead of conforming to the typical boxy RV design, National R.V. pioneered the sleeker bus-styling that soon became the industry standard. In addition to giving the huge vehicles a more stylish and contemporary look, the bus-style RVs–with their vertical front windshields—afforded the often inexperienced RV drivers who purchased the new model greater visibility. Moreover, the new design ''gave people the feeling they were getting more for their money,'' Kenneth Ashley, the company's chief financial officer, told *RV Business* on September 1, 1998. Consumers noticed the difference. According to the May 23, 1994, *Riverside Press-Enterprise*, the new design also ''helped National R.V. increase its market share even during the depth of the recession.'' Indeed, the company's share of the Class A market grew from 1.4 percent in 1992 when National R.V. debuted the Sea Breeze to 3.4 percent in 1993. Moreover, the company reported a net income in 1992 after several years of losses, generating about $1 million of profit on sales of over $45 million.

But the company realized that it remained subject to the vicissitudes of the motorized segment of the RV market. Although the success of the new Sea Breeze model was a boon, the overall market for motorized RVs remained weak. Towable RV sales, on the other hand, had proved to be more resilient in the face of recession. While motor home sales increased 4.8 percent from 1992 to 1993, towable RV sales grew 15.8 percent during the same period. The towable segment of the RV industry included inexpensive folding tent trailers, as well as travel trailers (which ranged from 12 to 35 feet long and were intended to be pulled by a car, van, or pickup truck) and fifth-wheel travel trailers (which reached 40 feet in length, could be two stories, and required a special hitch to tow).

With the approximately $2.7 million it raised from an initial public offering of stock in late 1993, National R.V. decided to pursue the towable segment of the RV market as well. ''We are totally dependent on the motorized market,'' the company's chief financial officer told *Press-Enterprise* on August 21, 1993. ''We would like to grow the company to a bigger size than it is, and to do that we need to diversify into trailers.''

National R.V.'s initial entry in the towable segment was a 30-foot fifth-wheel travel trailer, which was marketed under the

Key Dates:

1964: Wayne Mertes founds Dolphin Trailer Company.
1970: Company is renamed National R.V., Inc.
1985: National R.V. introduces its Sea Breeze motor home.
1989: National R.V. is acquired by Siegler, Collery & Co., and is renamed National R.V. Holdings, Inc.
1993: National R.V. makes its first public stock offering.
1996: National R.V. acquires Country Coach.

company's Dolphin line. At the close of 1993, National R.V. reported a net income of $3.1 million in total sales of $71.8 million. (The year also marked the end of the company's production of its original Micro-mini units, a shift triggered by Toyota's decision to stop making the special chassis that the product required.)

Further expansion was on National R.V.'s horizon. In 1994, the company introduced its first diesel pusher model—a motor home with a diesel engine mounted on the rear of the vehicle—as well as an updated bus-style model of its Dolphin motor home. At the same time, National R.V. extended its sales operations into Canada, a market which was expected to generate an additional $5 million in revenue for the company. At the same time, the company launched its Dolphin Camper Club—an association open to all member of National R.V.'s motor homes—in an effort to foster a sense of community among RV owners.

The company's efforts to cater to its customers in ways overlooked by its competitors were logical. After weathering several difficult periods in the previous three decades, the RV industry as a whole could look forward to bright prospects—based almost entirely on demographics. The baby boomers (the largest generation in American history) were entering into their prime RV-buying years. As Wayne Mertes explained to *Investor's Business Daily* in 1994, ''the number one trend is that the baby boomers are maturing into our buyers who are mostly between 50 and 65 years old.'' A *Wall Street Journal* analyst estimated that the population of RV-buying Americans would grow by 14 million people beginning in the mid-1990s. Moreover, baby boomers on the whole were wealthier than previous generations, having reaped the benefits of an unprecedented economic expansion. This development was particularly welcomed by National R.V. as, by 1994, the company's products ranged in price from $52,000 to over $100,000.

In 1995, National R.V. once more made industry history with the introduction of a widebody motor home. While motor homes were typically 96 inches wide, National R.V. was one of the first companies to develop the ''slideout'' room which increased the width of its motor homes to 102 inches. After the company debuted a widebody Dolphin motor home in 1995, demand quickly outstripped National R.V.'s limited supply, and backlog orders tripled in three months. Not only did the company's share of the Class A motor home market grow in 1995, but the once-tiny manufacturer had earned the respect of industry analysts. ''They're one of the up-and-comers who are creating excitement in this industry,'' one such analyst told the *Ontario Business Press* in 1996. Fueled by the initial success of the ''slideout''-equipped Dolphin, National R.V. redesigned its Tropi-Cal motor home to incorporate a widebody feature in 1996. By 1997, the company offered 11 different ''slide-out'' models across its product lines.

Buoyed by its design innovations, National R.V. had a record-breaking year in 1996, attaining a six percent share of the Class A market, and reporting $6.6 million of profit on sales of over $137 million. The industry as a whole fared well, too, and in 1996 National R.V. teamed up with other RV manufacturers and dealers to help ensure overall future growth. Armed with the knowledge that baby boomers were turning 50—and that the industry could more than double in shipments if it convinced boomers to purchase RVs–the Recreational Vehicle Industry Association launched a $15 million print and television advertising campaign targeting aging baby boomers. Themed ''Recreation Vehicles: Wherever You Go, You're Always At Home,'' the campaign relied on nostalgic images of families enjoying the RV lifestyle.

National R.V. concluded 1996 with a bold move. Well established in what the *Eugene Register-Guard* termed the ''moderately-priced motor home'' market (its RVs ranging from $50,000 to $110,000), National R.V. sought to expand into new segments of the market. As part of this effort, the company acquired Country Coach Inc.—an Oregon-based manufacturer of luxury motor homes (with RV prices ranging from $170,000 to $700,000) whose 1995 sales topped $70 million. As the *Register-Guard* explained, the two companies, ''which compete[d] in drastically different price brackets, . . . join[ed] forces in hopes of securing a wider share of the overall RV market.'' Although Country Coach became a wholly owned subsidiary of National R.V., the companies' manufacturing facilities and management remained separate. Soon after announcing its acquisition, National R.V. began a massive expansion of its own manufacturing facilities that would ultimately raise the company's production capacity by a third.

Financial and industry analysts took note of National R.V.'s successes. Between 1992 and 1996, the company's share of the Class A market had increased threefold. In 1997, that share grew to 6.6. percent, while its sales reached $286 million. *Forbes* named National R.V. one of the 200 best small companies in 1997. To ensure its continued vigor, the company continued to introduce new models. Tradewinds—a $140,000 motor home priced to bridge the gap between National R.V.'s own offerings and those of Country Coach—was rolled out in 1997. The following year, the company debuted the Sea View motor home, a mid-range motor home costing about $79,000. The Surf Side, a 31-foot motor home priced at $65,000, was introduced in 1999, and the Islander and Caribbean motor homes were slated to appear for model-year 2000.

The roaring economy of the late 1990s fueled growth in the RV industry as a whole, and National R.V.'s sales continued to flourish. In 1998—a year when the motor home market experienced double digit growth and RV sales reached a 20-year high—National R.V.'s sales topped $360 million, while the company became the fifth largest producer of motor homes. Future prospects looked even rosier. Company officials predicted that National R.V.'s target market would grow nearly 40 percent between 1998 and 2008. Moreover, the company's two primary segments—Class A motor homes and fifth-wheel travel trailers—were two of the fastest-growing sectors of the overall RV market, accounting for nearly two-thirds of the industry's overall dollar volume. By 1999, National R.V. had become the fourth largest manufacturer of Class A motor homes, and announced further plans to expand its production facilities. Included in both *Fortune* magazine's list of "100 Fastest-Growing Companies," as well as *Business Week's* "100 Hot Growth Companies," National R.V. maintained a strong appeal with investors.

Principal Subsidiaries

Country Coach Inc.

Principal Competitors

Blue Bird Corporation; Coachmen Industries, Inc.; Fleetwood Enterprises, Inc.; KIT Manufacturing Company; Monaco Coach Corporation; Rexhall Industries, Inc.; Skyline Corporation; SMC Corporation; Thor Industries, Inc.; Winnebago Industries, Inc.

Further Reading

Burnham, Rick, "National RV to Go Public, Add Workers," *Riverside Press-Enterprise,* August 18, 1993.

Frey, Peter, "Californians Ride Away for Their Weekends in Recreational Vehicles of All Shapes and Sizes," *Los Angeles Times,* November 7, 1987.

Howard, Bob, "Company Profile: National R.V. Holdings," *Ontario Business Press,* July 29, 1996.

Huggler, Tom, "Home on the Road," *Outdoor Life,* April 1, 1994.

"Industry Rebounds," *San Diego Union-Tribune,* July 2, 1984.

James, Joni, "California Firm to Buy Country Coach," *Eugene Register-Guard,* October 24, 1996.

Kisiel, Ralph, "RV Industry Plans Blitz for Boomers," *Automotive News,* December 11, 1995.

Lau, Gloria, "National R.V. Holdings, Inc.," *Investor's Business Daily,* July 22, 1994.

Leung, Shirley, "Demographic Boom Could Bring Investors on Board National R.V.," *Wall Street Journal,* May 5, 1999.

McAuliffe, Don, "RV Industry Cautious As Shipments Rise," *Riverside Press-Enterprise,* November 11, 1992.

"National R.V.: Designing for Growth," *RV Business,* September 1, 1998.

Rescigno, Richard, "Recreational-Vehicle Makers Seem Ready to Roll Again," *Barron's,* June 17, 1991.

Roberts, Rich, "Riding the Wild Turf in Comfort Travel: Recreational Vehicles Offer Many of the Amenities of Home for Outdoor Enthusiasts," *Los Angeles Times,* January 9, 1991.

Sanchez, Jesus, "Rougher Road for RVs," *Los Angeles Times,* May 29, 1989.

Smith, Rosalind, "Stepping Out of the Big Guy's Shadow," *Riverside Press-Enterprise,* May 23, 1994.

Wadley, Jared, "RV Builders' Shipments up in 2nd Quarter," *Riverside Press-Enterprise,* September 15, 1999.

Wiedrich, Bob, "Age Means Vigor for RV Business," *Chicago Tribune,* March 19, 1989.

—Rebecca Stanfel

Neff Corp.

3750 N.W. 87th Avenue, Suite 400
Miami, Florida 33178
U.S.A.
Telephone: (305) 513-3350
Fax: (305) 513-4155
Web site: http://www.neffcorp.com

Public Company
Incorporated: 1995
Employees: 1,600
Sales: $324.09 million (1998)
Stock Exchanges: New York
Ticker Symbol: NFF
NAIC: 532412 Construction Machinery and Equipment Rental or Leasing Without Operator

Neff Corp., a leading U.S. construction and industrial equipment rental company with 89 locations in the United States and South America, has witnessed substantial, steady growth during the past three years. It prides itself as being a top of the line company for earth moving equipment, compressors, generators, and lifts. It also acts as a new equipment dealer, sells used equipment and parts, and provides repair and maintenance services. Earth moving equipment comprises 40 percent of its fleet. Until it signed an agreement to sell Neff Machinery, Inc. on November 12, 1999, and sold S.A. Argentina on November 24, 1999, Neff Corp. had three segments: Neff Rental, Inc., Neff Machinery, Inc., and S.A. Argentina. The divestments were part of a new, and apparently necessary, strategy to increase shareholder value and refocus the company on its core rental business. However, the strategy perhaps also signaled that what remained of Neff would, very shortly, be up for sale. GE Capital owns 24 percent of the company and members of the Mas family, who are also principal shareholders for telecommunications network builder MasTec, own about 40 percent.

Early 1990s: The Beginning of an Equipment Rental Company

Neff Corp. began in 1988 with only one store located in Miami, Florida. Little information is available regarding the company's early years. Big changes arrived for the company, however, in 1995, when it incorporated in Delaware and welcomed GE Capital as a major shareholder. GE Capital's role involved providing strategic counsel, acquisition support, and five series of financings to facilitate Neff's growth. GE Capital increased its ownership in Neff in 1996.

During 1995, Neff also began an aggressive new business plan to foster financial growth. The company established a goal of becoming a nationwide rental company with the best people and highest quality fleet by making additional acquisitions of equipment rental companies, increasing fleet at its existing rental locations in both existing and new product lines, continuing to open new equipment rental locations, and expanding its dealership operations. At the time the plan was administered, the company had six Florida locations.

Late 1990s: Rapid Growth

Since that time, Neff opened 26 start-up rental equipment locations. As it did so, the company noticed a trend toward the start-up locations generating significant revenue but marginal profits during the first three years of operations; generally, the stores became profitable in the third year. The delayed profitability was attributed to the gradual addition of more equipment and the maturity of the rental location.

From 1996 to 1997, revenues increased by nearly 50 percent. The company was still operating in the red, however, as it awaited future profits. In August 1997, the company purchased Industrial Equipment Rentals, Inc., the parent company of Buckner Rental Service, Inc., for approximately $63.6 million. Industrial Equipment Rentals had similar operations as Neff in Alabama, Louisiana, Mississippi, and Texas. In 1997 the company suffered a loss of $6.4 million on sales of $142.22 million.

In January 1998, Neff acquired Richbourg's Sales and Rentals, Inc. for approximately $100 million. Richbourg boasted

Company Perspectives:

Neff Corp. is one of the fastest growing equipment rental companies, with operations throughout the United States and in South America. The company rents construction and industrial equipment through 89 locations. Neff's fleet is comprised of the latest equipment from leading manufacturers, and includes earthmoving equipment, compressors, generators, and aerial lifts.

Customers benefit from Neff's commitment to providing quality fleet, 24-hour on-call technical support, and a local store presence. In addition, Neff rental stores utilize an advanced management information system to monitor operations at all company sites. This system maximizes fleet utilization and determines which equipment is in demand on a regional basis, thus speeding customer delivery.

The corporate mission is to build shareholder value through strong internal growth and strategic acquisitions. By leveraging corporate strengths, Neff is striving to be recognized as the leading equipment rental company, with the best people and finest quality fleet.

15 locations in three states. During April, Neff announced its purchase of Road Machinery, Inc. and Iliff Rent Center, Inc., equipment rental companies with a total of four locations in Denver, Oregon, and Washington. That year the company rebounded somewaht, generating net income before extraordinary charges of $1.2 million on sales of $324.09 million.

Despite its short and tenuous track record, the company also went public in 1998. Using the approximately $94 million in proceeds from the public offering, Neff purchased eight companies, strengthened management's infrastructure by hiring key people, broadened its store base, and completed two bond offerings. Notable among Neff's purchases was that of a 65 percent stake in S.A. Argentina, for approximately $36.1 million, and earn-out payments equal to 82.8 percent of S.A. Argentina's net income for 1998 and 1999. S.A. Argentina rented and sold industrial and construction equipment throughout South America.

The following year, in a strategic about-face, Neff turned to the investment firm of Donaldson, Lufkin & Jenrette Inc. (DLJ) for financial assistance. Neff Corp. announced its partnership with the firm in March as an effort to explore various ways of enhancing shareholder value. At the time of the announcement, Kevin P. Fitzgerald, president and CEO of Neff, said that "the Company will work with DLJ to explore strategic alternatives, including a sale of all or a part of the Company, a recapitalization, or a spin-off. The Company's board of directors has decided that in the current business environment, it should actively consider strategic alternatives that would increase shareholder value in the near future."

Looking Toward the New Millennium: The Trend of Selling

On October 6, 1999, Neff announced that it had signed a definitive agreement to sell its equity interest in Sullair Argentina, S.A. (S.A. Argentina) to Alejandro Oxenford, S.A. Argentina's president. S.A. Argentina had 1998 revenues of approximately $54 million. The sale closed on November 24, 1999, netting Neff $42.5 million. Some $30 million was paid at closing and the remaining amount was to be paid to Neff in February 2000. Fitzgerald, president and CEO of Neff, stated, "The sale of our interest in S.A. Argentina is an important first step in our previously stated objective of increasing shareholder value through the strategic evaluation process we initiated earlier this year."

Neff also announced on November 12, 1999 that it had signed a definitive agreement to sell Neff Machinery Inc., its wholly owned construction dealership business, to NORTRAX. Total 1998 revenues for Neff Machinery were approximately $103 million. John Deere Construction owned a minority interest in NORTRAX. The sale would bring approximately $91 million to Neff. Illuminating Neff's cloudy future, Fitzgerald commented, "Neff Corp. will now be a pure rental company. In this regard, we are continuing to evaluate other strategic alternatives including a sale or merger."

Key Dates:

1988: Company opens first store in Miami, Florida.
1995: Business incorporates in Delaware; GE Capital becomes a major shareholder.
1997: Neff acquires Industrial Equipment Rentals, Inc.
1998: Company goes public, raising $94 million in its first stock offering.
1999: Neff announces a restructuring of its Gulf Coast stores in an effort to mitigate any oil industry impact; company also announces a partnership with the investment firm of Donaldson, Lufkin & Jenrette Inc. (DLJ) to consider strategic alternatives to enhance shareholder value.

Final Analysis

Due to the fact that earnings were less than anticipated in 1999, Neff made some significant decisions to sell two-thirds of its company. The company claimed that earnings were negatively impacted by rental rate pressures, the Gulf Region stores performance, short-term closures in the Southeast due to several hurricanes, a tremendous equipment sale in the Gulf Region stores, and expenses related to the company's change in business strategy. Based on trends during 1999, selling could be expected to continue in 2000 as Neff relied on its partnership with Donaldson, Lufkin & Jenrette Inc. Whether the company would survive under its own name for any length of time remained to be seen.

Principal Competitors

The Hertz Corporation; Rental Service Corporation; United Rentals Inc.

Further Reading

Fitzgerald, Kevin P., "Interview," *Wall Street Reporter*, New York.

—Kimbally A. Medeiros

Newsquest plc

Newspaper House
34-44 London Road
Morden
Surrey SM4 5BR
United Kingdom
Telephone: +44 181 640-8989
Fax: +44 181 646-3997
Web site: http://www.newsquest.co.uk/corporate

Wholly Owned Subsidiary of Gannett Co., Inc.
Incorporated: 1995
Employees: 5,700
Sales: £305.8 million (US$507.6 million) (1998)
NAIC: 51111 Newspaper Publishers

In less than five years, Newsquest plc has risen to become England's largest regional newspaper publisher and the third largest in the United Kingdom. Since the company's takeover by Gannett in June 1999, Newsquest is also part of one of the world's leading media companies. Yet Newsquest's focus remains the local and regional news front, where the company owns some 180 titles, including the world's oldest newspaper in continuous circulation, *Berrow's Worcester Journal*, first published in 1690. Some 51 of Newsquest's titles list are paid weeklies; another 11 titles are paid dailies. The bulk of the company's titles are free regional, local, and specialty advertising newspapers. The company's publishing portfolio ranges from the *Northern Echo*'s 200,000-strong circulation to local papers with circulation of less than 15,000. More than 80 percent of the company's revenues are generated through advertising, especially through classified advertising. The company has also been an early entry into the Internet news market, with its trademarked collection of ''This Is . . .'' Internet sites. Newsquest also provides direct marketing and third-party printing services using the company's leftover printing capacity.

Origins in a 1995 Management Buyout

The United Kingdom's regional newspaper market of the 1990s was highly fragmented and technology poor in the mid-1990s. More than two decades of strict government-led merger controls—meant to prevent the appearance of monopolies in the country's highly popular local and regional newspaper circuit, which numbered more than 1,200 titles—had left many newspaper concerns cash-strapped, without the critical mass required for much needed capital investments. The government began to relax its rules in the 1980s, starting with the country's ''Fleet Street'' of national news titles. The resulting consolidation of the national newspaper market enabled a massive investment program, bringing new printing and input technologies and machinery to the industry. These improvements not only helped the newspapers—and their owners—but the consumer also saw a better-printed, more easy to read product.

The regional market, however, remained highly fragmented among many smaller companies. Unable to make the needed investments and unable to grow through acquisition, many local and regional companies had no choice but to slash costs by reducing staff and sacrificing production quality in order to remain afloat. Meanwhile, a share of the market was held by several of the country's media giants, including Pearson, Reed-Elsevier, and Emap. Unable to expand their shares of the regional market, and seeking instead to capture more of the higher-end, higher-margin publishing markets, these companies began looking to shed their regional holdings in the mid-1990s.

By 1995, the government's willingness to allow greater consolidation in the regional market had resulted in a flurry of acquisitions. Consolidation took on greater steam as the major media groups began selling off their regional and local newspaper holdings. Reed-Elsevier, the Dutch-British media power, decided to shed its Reed Regional Newspapers subsidiary as part of its mid-1990s restructuring. While profitable, Reed Regional's 125-title holdings of regional and local newspapers no longer fit its parent company's focus. Upon learning of this decision, Reed Regional's CEO, Jim Brown, together with finance director John Pfail, asked to be allowed to perform a management buyout of the division.

Scottish-born Brown started his newspaper career as a junior reporter for Scotland's *Ayreshire Post.* Brown went on to build a well-respected career as a journalist, moving to the Glasgow arena, then joining Thomson Newspapers, where he was pro-

Company Perspectives:

Newsquest's objective is to hold market leading local information franchises which deliver valuable, trusted products satisfying the needs of their audience. The business is market led and technology driven, focused on generating sustained superior profit growth.

moted into management. At the beginning of the 1980s, Brown was hired away by Reed-Elsevier, where he was placed in charge of the Reed Regional division. By the mid-1960s, Brown, at 60 years old, was facing retirement. However, Reed-Elsevier accepted his proposal to organize a management buy-out bid to compete with other suitors of Reed-Regional.

For this, Brown and Pfail turned to buyout specialist Kohlberg Kravis Roberts (KKR), which had recently made headlines with the acquisition of Nabisco. KKR agreed to support the buyout, helping to raise a winning bid of £210 million. Brown, Pfail, and other management received a 12 percent share of the new company, while KKR held the remaining share. As Reed-Elsevier insisted on a name change, the new company took on the name ''Newsquest,'' suggested by Brown's secretary during a brainstorming session.

Building a Name in the 1990s

Newsquest Media Group immediately set out to establish itself as a major player in the United Kingdom's regional newspaper market. The company's first expansion moves were made in April 1996, when Newsquest agreed with rival Johnston Press to exchange a number of titles. As part of that transaction, Johnston Press paid £15 million for Newsquest's Yorkshire-based newspapers, while Newsquest purchased the Johnston Press Bury, Lancashire, titles for £75 million. Newsquest sold another piece of its holdings in July of that same year, receiving £12.3 million from Midland Independent Newspapers for Newsquest's midlands region titles. These transactions set the stage for the company's next move, which catapulted Newsquest into the lead of the country's regional newspaper market. Meanwhile, Newsquest also invested in upgrading its machinery and technology, consolidating its printing and other activities. The company was also among the first newspaper companies in the United Kingdom to offer its news services on the Internet.

In December 1996, Pearson announced its intention to sell off its 65-title strong regional newspaper division, Westminster Press. Newsquest's bid, backed by KKR and CINven, a U.K. media investment fund, was finally accepted at £305 million. The purchase doubled Newsquest's size and made it a key player among the country's other new regional giants, Johnston Press, Trinity International, and Midland. Throughout the following year, Newsquest worked to absorb its new acquisition, which, although profitable at some £25 million per year, had been struggling. Many of the Westminster titles had suffered strong circulation declines, with resulting declines in advertising revenues.

Newsquest began trimming its titles in some places, including the sale of its Wessex group of titles to Bristol United Press for £35 million in October 1997, while launching new titles elsewhere. Among the papers launched in 1997 were the *Harrow Times*, a free paper; the *Gravesham News Shopper*, as part of the company's ten-title News Shopper series; and the *Chessington and Hook Surrey Comet*, launched in June 1997. By October of that year, Newsquest was ready to prepare a public offering. Pricing for the company's stock was expected to range from 250 pence to 290 pence per share. Although the company entered the London Stock Exchange at the low end of this range, the listing still valued Newsquest at some £500 million.

Public ownership allowed Newsquest to begin a new investment drive in expanding the company. After spending some £15 million on capital improvements, the company began an aggressive campaign of new title launches and acquisitions of existing titles. Among the company's acquisitions in 1998 were Contact-a-Car, based in Sussex; the London Property Weekly group of real estate newspapers, with their circulation of 230,000 households; Kinsman Reeds Ltd., with two northwest England titles; and the Review Group, with three newspapers in Hertfordshire. In 1998 alone the company spent more than £9 million on acquisitions of new titles. Newsquest's new launches included the *Walton and Weybridge Guardian*; the *Sutton Comet*, a paid-for weekly, the eighth in the company's Comet series; and the *Staines Property Weekly*, extending the company's newly acquired Property Weekly series. Beyond targeting the local market, Newsquest also expanded its niche titles, adding *Auto Weekly,* a car magazine published in conjunction with the Northcliffe Newspapers.

Early 1999 saw the launch of the company's ''This Is . . .'' Internet series. Offering portals to the company's regionally focused online titles, the ''This Is . . .'' series—already profitable, with revenues of more than £5 million—was seen as one of the company's most potent assets for the future. Newsquest was also finding success elsewhere on the net, with its AuctionHunter web site and with a deal to provide ''thin content'' (headlines that linked to the ''This Is . . .'' sites) to major Internet providers. In March 1999, the company's Internet activities took on a further importance as the company joined with rivals Trinity and Associated Newspapers to extend the ''This Is . . .'' regional series to a ''This Is Britain'' national site, with links to content provided from the three publishing groups' online and print titles. Operating such a strategic portal was seen as a means to ensure a strong early position in the expected dominance of the Internet in the early 21st century.

Acquisition by Gannett in 1999

Seeking to expand still further in the U.K. market—including placing a bid to buy the Portland and Sunderland newspaper group—Newsquest began shopping itself as an acquisition target. In June 1999, Gannett Co., Inc., the U.S. media giant and publisher of *USA Today,* announced its intention to acquire Newsquest for US$1.43 billion (£904 million). The purchase offer quickly won agreement from the company's largest shareholders, including KKR, which still held 36 percent of Newsquest.

Key Dates:

1995: Management buys out Reed Regional Newspapers and forms Newsquest Media Group plc.
1996: Company acquires Westminster Press from Pearson plc.
1997: Public offering occurs on London Stock Exchange.
1998: Newsquest launches "This Is Britain" partnership with Trinity and Associated Newspapers.
1999: Company is acquired by Gannett Co., Inc.

While Gannett denied that it meant for the Newsquest acquisition, its first in Europe since the early 1970s, to be a spearhead for a new European entry drive, Newsquest, now with the backing of Gannett's deep pockets (with nearly US$3 billion available in 1999), continued to seek to expand its own position. In November 1999, the company completed the purchase of the Hampshire Chronicle group of newspapers, including the *Hampshire Chronicle* itself, another of the United Kingdom's oldest continuing newspaper titles.

Principal Divisions

Blackburn Citizen (Lancashire); *Blackpool Citizen* (Lancashire); *Bolton Evening News* (Lancashire); *Bolton Journal* (Lancashire); *Bradford Star* (Bradford); *Brighton & Hove Leader* (Sussex); *Enfield Independent* (London); *Evening Argus—Brighton* (Sussex); *The Evening Press* (York); *The Hereford Times* (Midlands South); *Lancashire Evening Telegraph* (Lancashire); *The Northern Echo* (North East); *Oxford Mail* (Oxfordshire); *Oxford Star* (Oxfordshire); *The Oxford Times* (Oxfordshire); *Sale & Altrincham Messenger* (Cheshire/Merseyside); *Swindon Evening Advertiser* (Wiltshire); *St. Helens Star* (Lancashire); *Sutton Guardian Series* (London); *Telegraph & Argus* (Bradford); *Times Advertiser Series* (North East); *Warrington Guardian* (Cheshire/Merseyside); *Warrington Midweek Guardian* (Cheshire/Merseyside); *Westmorland Gazette* (Kendal); *Wirral Globe* (Cheshire/Merseyside); *Worcester Evening News* (Midlands South); *York Star Series* (York).

Principal Competitors

Daily Mail and General Trust plc; Hollinger International Inc.; Independent News; Johnston Press; Scottish Media Group plc; Trinity Mirror.

Further Reading

Horsman, Mathew, "Pressing On with Building a Regional Newspaper Empire," *Independent*, August 12, 1996, p. 17.
Intindola, Brendan, "Gannett Seeks to Buy Newsquest, British Chain," *Reuters*, June 24, 1999.
Larsen, Peter Thal, "Newsquest Links with Rivals to Give Local News on the Net," *Independent*, March 23, 1999, p. 19.
Shu Shin Luh, "Gannett to Buy U.K. Publishing Company," *Washington Post*, June 25, 1999, p. E3.
Thackray, Rachelle, "Me and My Partner: John Pfeil and Jim Brown," *Independent*, May 12, 1999, p. 12.
Young, Andrew, "Gannett Bids for Britain's Newsquest," *Reuters Business Report*, June 24, 1999.

—M.L. Cohen

DAILY NEWS

The Most New York You Can Get.

New York Daily News

450 West 33rd Street, 3rd Floor
New York, New York 10001
U.S.A.
Telephone: (212) 210-2100
Fax: (212) 643-7831
Web site: http://www.nydailynews.com

Private Company
Incorporated: 1919
Employees: 1,500
Sales: $377 million (1997)
NAIC: 511110 Newspaper Publishers

Called "too tough to die," the *New York Daily News* was the largest circulation metropolitan daily newspaper in the United States for much of the 20th century. The pioneering tabloid, and its eponymous holding company, fell on hard times in the 1980s, though, and a five-month strike in 1990 forced its parent company, the Tribune Company, to put it up for sale. British publisher Robert Maxwell took over the paper in 1991, but died later that year under mysterious circumstances. The paper found new ownership in Mortimer Zuckerman and Fred Drasner at the beginning of 1993. It soon returned to profitability and has become New York's leading tabloid.

From Pioneering Tabloid to Largest Daily Newspaper: 1919–80

The first issue of the *New York Daily News* was published on June 26, 1919. It was a pioneer of the tabloid format. In his introductory editorial, Joseph Patterson wrote, "The policy of the *Daily News* will be your policy. It will be aggressively for America and for the people of New York." The newspaper was owned by the Tribune Company, which was based in Chicago and published the *Chicago Tribune*.

In 1926 circulation reached nearly one million, making the *New York Daily News* the largest newspaper in the United States. Following World War II, American newspapers were in their heyday, and "the brassy, pictorial *New York Daily News* led all the rest," according to a *Time* magazine tribute. Its 1947 circulation was 2.4 million daily and 4.7 million on Sunday. The paper's leadership continued into the 1950s, when the *Daily News* was the largest newspaper in the United States with a daily circulation of more than two million and a Sunday circulation of four million.

Hard Times—Losses and Strikes: 1980–90

In the 1980s the paper was hit by hard economic times. During the years when the newspaper was profitable, its management had yielded to union demands for more jobs, overtime, and restrictive work rules. By the 1980s the newspaper was averaging losses of $1 million a month in spite of annual revenues of nearly $425 million. Its parent, the Tribune Company, explored the possibility of closing the newspaper, but it would cost more than $100 million, mainly for severance pay and pensions.

When union contracts expired in March 1990, the Tribune Company confronted the unions and demanded huge concessions to make the paper profitable again. It claimed that the newspaper had lost $115 million in the past ten years on revenues of $4 billion, with labor costs eating up 44 percent of the revenue. The company wanted to cut 700 to 1,000 jobs and complained about union overstaffing of drivers and pressmen. The Tribune Company had a reputation as a union-buster, following a 1985 strike at the *Chicago Tribune* that resulted in the hiring of non-union workers as permanent replacements.

The newspaper's ten unions, joined together under the umbrella organization Allied Printing Trades Council, responded by going on strike in October 1990. During the strike the *Daily News* continued to publish, using non-union replacement workers and non-striking union staff. For 1990 the *Daily News* reported a pre-tax operating loss of $114.5 million, including a $69.3 million fourth quarter loss attributed to the strike.

Newspaper in Turmoil: 1991–93

British media mogul Robert Maxwell acquired the newspaper from the Tribune Company in March 1991, ending the strike. Other bidders included Mortimer Zuckerman, owner of

Company Perspectives:

As the first hometown owners of the Daily News, *Zuckerman and Drasner have demonstrated a strong and continuous commitment to the newspaper as well as the city and its people. A year into their ownership, the* Daily News *was operating in the black. And today, it is the largest-selling newspaper in the New York metropolitan area.*

U.S. News and World Report and the *Atlantic Monthly.* Actually, the Tribune Company paid Maxwell $60 million to take the paper off its hands, most of which went for severance pay and buyouts. Maxwell negotiated $72 million in union concessions and reduced the paper's workforce from 2,600 jobs to 1,800, of which 1,500 were unionized. The allied unions agreed to a one-year wage freeze and to changes in work rules, but retained the right to have staff levels determined by contract rather than by management. Following the strike the paper's circulation was down to fewer than 800,000 copies daily and less than one million on Sunday.

Robert Maxwell drowned on November 5, 1991, and the newspaper filed for bankruptcy in December. Following Maxwell's death it was revealed that over $1 billion was missing from his British pension funds, and his media empire was riddled with debt. His British companies sued the *Daily News* to recover the missing funds amid rumors that Maxwell had used the funds to cover losses at the *Daily News.*

During subsequent negotiations in 1992 Mortimer Zuckerman outbid Canadian Conrad Black, owner of newspaper holding company Hollinger, Inc., for the *Daily News.* He negotiated contracts with nine of the paper's ten unions, failing to reach an agreement with its largest union, the New York Newspaper Guild, which represented about 450 workers. In one agreement with the New York Typographical Union, Zuckerman was allowed to disregard lifetime job guarantees for 167 printers whose jobs had become obsolete and were costing the paper $10 million a year. By October 1992 the unions' support of Zuckerman forced the newspaper's management to drop its support for rival bidder Conrad Black, who had offered $75 million for the paper—considerably more than Zuckerman's offer.

Becoming a "Serious Tabloid" Under New Owners: 1993–99

In January 1993 Mortimer B. Zuckerman and Fred Drasner acquired the newspaper for $36 million after prolonged negotiations. They had previously acquired and turned around *U.S. News and World Report* and the *Atlantic Monthly.*

Nine of the newspaper's ten unions, negotiating under the umbrella organization Allied Printing Trades Council, had reached agreements with Zuckerman prior to the acquisition. For the most part the agreements called for staff cuts and changes in work rules that Zuckerman deemed inefficient. Only the New York Newspaper Guild, which broke away from the umbrella organization, failed to reach an agreement with Zuckerman.

Following his acquisition of the newspaper, Zuckerman fired about 185 employees, mostly reporters, including about one-third of the Guild's members. The Guild threatened to boycott the paper and cut its circulation by 100,000. The Allied Printing Trade Council criticized the Guild's actions, noting the Zuckerman's acquisition of the *Daily News* had preserved 1,535 union jobs.

It was expected that Zuckerman would remake the *Daily News* into a "serious tabloid," something closer in tone and substance to *New York Newsday* than to the *New York Post.* He would need to replace the paper's editor-in-chief, James Willse, who announced he would be leaving the paper. In July 1993 Martin Dunn, originally from Great Britain and former editor-in-chief of the *Boston Herald,* was named editor-in-chief.

In September 1993 Zuckerman committed $60 million for the purchase of color presses, which would be installed at the company's new printing facility being built in Jersey City, New Jersey. At the time *New York Newsday* was the city's only color tabloid. The Goss four-color presses would enable the *Daily News* to publish color of the quality found in *USA Today.* Getting new presses was a top priority, as the *Daily News* was being printed on outmoded letterpress equipment that was 30 to 40 years old.

The *Daily News* began operating in the black. Reduced labor costs, lower rent, and a $10.8 million gain in advertising revenue helped the *Daily News* show an operating profit in its first year under Zuckerman's ownership. Zuckerman planned to raise the cover price in an effort to achieve a better balance between circulation revenues and advertising revenues. Toward the end of 1993 he expressed concern over the future of the newspaper's advertising revenues.

In 1995 the *Daily News* moved from its traditional location on 42nd Street and Second Avenue to a single floor of an office building at 33rd Street and Tenth Avenue. In 1996 the paper began publishing a national insert called *BET Weekend,* in association with Black Entertainment Television Inc., for African Americans. It began as a quarterly and became monthly in 1997 with a distribution of 1.1 million copies. In 1997 it appeared in 15 markets around the country.

In June 1996 the New York Newspaper Guild, the only union that Zuckerman failed to settle with when he acquired the *Daily News,* rejected the newspaper's latest contract proposal. Guild members in circulation, advertising, and news had been working without a contract since Zuckerman acquired the paper in 1993.

In October 1996 the *Daily News* began publishing parts of the paper on the World Wide Web. During the year the price of the Sunday edition was increased from $1.25 to $1.50. In 1997 the newsstand price went down to one dollar.

In January 1997 Pete Hamill, 61, became the editor-in-chief of the *Daily News.* Hamill was a veteran reporter and editor who began his career with the *New York Post* in 1960. Now his assignment was to battle the *Post* for readers. Hamill replaced former editor-in-chief Martin Dunn, who left in October to return home to England. Under Dunn, the *Daily News* staff had become split into factions made up of old-timers who had been

Key Dates:

1919: First issue is published on June 26.
1926: Circulation reaches nearly one million, making the *New York Daily News* the largest newspaper in the United States.
1947: *Daily News* reaches peak circulation of 2.4 million daily and 4.7 million on Sunday.
1990: The newspaper's ten unions go on strike in October.
1991: Robert Maxwell acquires the newspaper from the Tribune Company in March, then drowns in November; the *Daily News* files for bankruptcy in December.
1993: Mortimer B. Zuckerman and Fred Drasner acquire the *Daily News*.

around since the Tribune Company owned the newspaper and newcomers recruited by Zuckerman. With the arrival of Hamill, it appeared that the various factions would begin to work together and set aside their differences.

In March 1997 the *Daily News* launched an insert publication called *Caribbean Monthly,* which was aimed at Caribbean nationals and Caribbean Americans in New York. Approximately 400,000 copies were inserted into zoned editions of the *Daily News,* with some copies being distributed at newsstands in Caribbean neighborhoods and at selected commuter points.

Estimated revenues for 1997 were $177 million from circulation and $200 million from advertising. The paper was expected to show a profit of about $10 million. During 1997 production was moved to a new $150 million printing plant in Jersey City, New Jersey, which gave the newspaper four-color capacity. The *Daily News* began publishing weekday editions in color in September 1997 but discontinued the use of color in March 1998. Shortly afterward the national edition, which had been using color before the daily editions, reverted to black and white. By June 1998 the Sunday editions also had lost their color.

The paper was having problems with the new Goss Newsliner presses it had acquired from Rockwell Graphic Systems. It was one of the first newspapers to buy the presses and the only one to use Rockwell's original keyless inking system. When Goss acquired Rockwell's press business, the *Daily News* sued both Goss and Rockwell, claiming technical shortcomings and breach of contract, but the lawsuit was dismissed and two appeals failed to revive the lawsuit.

In October 1997 Debby Krenek was promoted to the position of editor-in-chief, replacing Hamill. She was the first woman to hold the senior newsroom management spot in the newspaper's history. Editorial improvements included the restoration and expansion of sections covering borough politics, parenting, and immigration news. An investigative reporting group was established and built. The paper also featured award-winning sports coverage. It introduced a New York-focused entertainment and lifestyle section, the "Sunday Extra," to attract more women and young readers as well as new immigrants.

With Zuckerman as publisher and Krenek as chief editor, the *Daily News* developed a reputation, through litigation, for protecting First Amendment rights. For example, it forced the courts to unseal documents relating to the state's eight pending death penalty cases. It made public information about the city's Board of Education and strengthened public access to family court records. Zuckerman received one of the New York Press Club's highest honors, the John Peter Zenger Freedom of the Press Award. He also received the New York Society of Professional Journalists' First Amendment Award.

Other awards included two Pulitzer Prizes for Distinguished Commentary, one in 1996 to columnist E.R. Shipp and one in 1998 to columnist Mike McAlary for his reports on police brutality. In addition the editorial board won a Pulitzer Prize in 1999 for its investigation of alleged mismanagement at Harlem's famous Apollo theater. The series aimed to save the legendary venue.

In March 1999 the *Daily News* unveiled a revamped Sunday edition with more entertainment, lifestyle, and opinion pages. The paper had been losing a significant portion of its Sunday readership. Sunday circulation had dropped from 978,000 readers in 1995 to 807,000 in 1997, before rising to 810,000 in 1998. During the same period the *Daily News's* two main competitors, the *New York Post* and *Newsday,* both saw Sunday circulation increase. Changes in the *Daily News's* Sunday edition included the addition of new columnists, a new editor in Ed Kosner (*Newsweek, New York,* and *Esquire),* and two new sections titled "Showtime" and "Lifeline." One of the new columnists was Mike Barnicle, who had left the *Boston Globe* the previous year following accusations of plagiarism.

As of March 1999 the *Daily News* had a daily weekday circulation of 729,449, ahead of competing tabloids *Newsday* (573,542) and the *New York Post* (433,774). It was the fifth largest metropolitan daily newspaper in the United States. It claimed to be the only major metropolitan daily newspaper to be completely electronically published, which enabled it to include late-breaking news reports. Its new slogan, "The most New York you can get," reflected its commitment to the people of New York.

Principal Competitors

New York Post; Newsday.

Further Reading

Bessie, Simon M., *Jazz Journalism: The Story of the Tabloid Newspapers,* New York: Russell & Russell, 1969.
"Big Apple Bites Back," *Economist (U.S.),* January 26, 1991, p. 61.
"Daily News: 'Serious Tabloid' with Local NY Strength," *PR Week,* August 2, 1999.
Davies, Nicholas, *Death of a Tycoon: An Insider's Account of the Rise and Fall of Robert Maxwell,* New York: St. Martin's Press, 1993.
Demery, Paul, "Slim Hope for Survival of News," *L.I. Business News,* January 21, 1991, p. 21.
Farnham, Alan, "Zuckerman Vs. the Odds, Again," *Fortune,* November 30, 1992, p. 126.
Garneau, George, "Evaluate Offers to Buy New York Daily News," *Editor & Publisher,* April 18, 1992, p. 16.

——, ''Home Stretch; Zuckerman Set to Close Deal to Acquire New York Daily News Despite Lack of Contact with the Newspaper Guild,'' *Editor & Publisher,* January 9, 1993, p. 13.

——, ''Just a Matter of Time: Unions Confident That Zuckerman Will Acquire New York Daily News,'' *Editor & Publisher,* October 3, 1992, p. 15.

——, ''New Life: British Publisher Robert Maxwell Agrees on Staff Cuts with Nine Striking New York Daily News Unions,'' *Editor & Publisher,* March 16, 1991, p. 14.

——, ''Talks Go Round the Clock to Sell N.Y. Daily News,'' *Editor & Publisher,* August 15, 1992, p. 8.

——, ''Zuckerman Takes the Helm,'' *Editor & Publisher,* January 16, 1993, p. 12.

Gatewood, Worth, editor, *Fifty Years: The New York Daily News in Pictures,* New York: Doubleday, 1979.

Giobbe, Dorothy, ''N.Y. Labor Talks Falter,'' *Editor & Publisher,* June 22, 1996, p. 11.

Guy, Pat, '' 'Daily News' in the Black,'' *USA Today,* January 21, 1994.

Harris, John, ''This Guy Eats Nails,'' *Forbes,* January 21, 1991, p. 109.

Henry, William A., III, ''Captain Bob's Amazing Eleventh-Hour Rescue,'' *Time,* March 25, 1991, p. 52.

Jennings, Kenneth M., *Labor Relations at the New York Daily News: Peripheral Bargaining and the 1990 Strike,* Westport, Conn.: Greenwood Publishing Group, 1993.

Lesly, Elizabeth, ''The Monster Tab,'' *New York Magazine,* September 22, 1997, p. 26.

Liebman, Hanna, ''Daily News to Hike Cover Price,'' *Mediaweek,* November 15, 1993, p. 5.

——, ''Daily News to Spend $60M to Purchase Color Presses,'' *Mediaweek,* September 13, 1993, p. 3.

——, ''Zuckerman Takes over at Troubled Daily News,'' *Mediaweek,* January 11, 1993, p. 2.

Martin, Douglas, ''Moving Day at the News,'' *New York Times,* May 4, 1995.

''Media Notes,'' *Mediaweek,* July 19, 1993, p. 28.

''More Losses for the Daily News,'' *L.I. Business News,* February 11, 1991, p. 24.

Reina, Laura, ''N.Y. Daily News Debuts Niche Product,'' *Editor & Publisher,* March 15, 1997, p. 18.

Rosenberg, Jim, ''Color Again for the Daily News?'' *Editor & Publisher,* April 17, 1999, p. 55.

Ruffini, Gene, ''News to Unions: Drop Dead,'' *The Nation,* May 7, 1990, p. 620.

Sacharow, Anya, ''N.Y. Tab Vet Takes Charge,'' *Mediaweek,* January 13, 1997, p. 9.

Strupp, Joe, ''Revamped Sundays at New York Daily News,'' *Editor & Publisher,* March 27, 1999, p. 16.

—David P. Bianco

New York Restaurant Group, Inc.

1114 First Avenue
New York, New York 10021
U.S.A.
Telephone: (212) 838-2061
Fax: (212) 758-6027

Private Company
Founded: 1977 as Smith & Wollensky
Employees: 879
Sales: $52.8 million (1998)
NAIC: 72211 Full-Service Restaurants

The New York Restaurant Group, Inc. (NYRG) owns and operates high-priced restaurants in New York City and several other cities. Founded by Alan Stillman, who originated the T.G.I. Friday's restaurant chain, NYRG is best known for its Smith & Wollensky steakhouse in Manhattan. Of NYRG's 12 restaurants in 1999, eight were owned and four were operated by the firm; six were located in Manhattan. The company was planning to make an initial public offering of stock, probably in 2000. It was then expected to change its name to that of its flagship Manhattan restaurant, Smith & Wollensky, which was said to be the most successful single à la carte restaurant in the nation.

Smith & Wollensky and Others: 1977–89

Alan Stillman was a salesman living on Manhattan's Upper East Side in the mid-1960s. Perceiving that the many affluent unattached young people in the neighborhood needed more places to meet and mix, he took a lease on a rundown bar on First Avenue and 63rd Street with $5,000 borrowed from his mother and opened one of the first singles bars, which he called T.G.I. Friday's. Stillman opened, with partners, about a dozen other Friday's in other cities as well as several Manhattan restaurants with names such as Tuesday's, Wednesday's, and Thursday's. In the mid-1970s he sold his share of the Friday's chain (an act he later described as his biggest mistake), reportedly for $1 million, to Carlson Companies, except for the original, which he kept until 1987 and then sold for a reported $3.8 million.

By this time Stillman had turned to serving a more mature—and more affluent—clientele. Backed by Ben Benson and other investors, in 1977 he purchased Manny Wolf's, a restaurant in a landmark 1897 building on Third Avenue at 49th Street, and converted it into a steakhouse named, for reasons still obscure, Smith & Wollensky. The restaurant was not an instant success, and in spite of gimmicks such as slices of roast beef offered to passersby, few people entered at first. ''We came very, very close to selling,'' Stillman recalled to Pamela Kruger of the *New York Times* in 1993.

Instead, Stillman went back to the investors for money, added a 100-seat lower-priced grill next door, and launched an effective advertising campaign. Gael Greene, the restaurant critic for *New York* who rated Smith & Wollensky last among the ten steakhouses she reviewed in late 1978, conceded, ''The house is often crowded. The faces are young and seem happy.'' By 1984 the restaurant, several times refurbished and enlarged since its opening, was worthy of inclusion in *Gourmet,* where Jay Jacobs noted, ''Typically, the place is about as serene as an ordinary day in a boiler factory.'' He called the meats and fish ''top-quality stuff . . . served in massive portions, and with very few exceptions . . . prepared precisely as they should be.''

By 1990 Smith & Wollensky was a smashing success, perhaps ''not the best steakhouse in town,'' wrote restaurant reviewer Bryan Miller of the *New York Times,* ''but it is probably the busiest. ... Smith & Wollensky is an efficient feeding machine . . . that churns out more than 700 meals daily.'' By this time the 380-seat restaurant was more than a steakhouse. Although steak and prime rib continued to be best-selling individual entrees, seafood now made up 40 percent of the menu. Sales volume, including the adjoining grill, came to $17 million in 1989, with the average check for the main room at $38 for lunch and $50 for dinner.

Stillman opened two more midtown Manhattan restaurants in the early 1980s. The Post House, launched in 1980, was a steak and chop house with an American theme. Restaurant reviewer Moira Hodgson of the *New York Times* wrote, ''This unpretentious yet elegant restaurant offers high quality, straightforward food in a thoroughly pleasant, relaxed atmosphere. . . . This is not the fare of Puritan austerity. The propor-

Company Perspectives:

We strive to provide a consistent, high-quality dining experience in order to foster customer satisfaction and brand loyalty. To achieve this goal, we focus on providing our customers with attentive and professional service by training and encouraging our employees to exceed guests' expectations.

tions are enormous. . . . The choices are the same at lunch and dinner, with prices identical, at expense-account level.'' The Manhattan Ocean Club, opened in 1984, was a high-end seafood restaurant. Reviewing it some months later for the *Times,* Marian Burros wrote that the eatery ''is playing to large crowds, despite high prices and some inconsistencies.''

By 1984 these three restaurants formed the New York Restaurant Group, which in 1993 encompassed a complex series of partnerships, with Stillman as general partner and owner of 25–85 percent of each restaurant. (NYRG, for example, was the operator, not owner, of Smith & Wollensky. Its owner, in 1999, was St. James Associates, in which Smith & Wollensky Operating Corp., controlled by Stillman, was a general partner.) Each of the group's nine managers had been with the company for more than a decade in 1989, and 25 of the 450 employees had shares in the enterprise. Michael Byrne, who began as a bartender, had been director of operations since 1980 and had been supervising Smith & Wollensky on a daily basis for more than ten years.

Stillman, not a hands-on manager, spent at least two months of each year on combined business and pleasure travel abroad. A lover of fine wines and artwork as well as haute cuisine, he owned a vineyard near his Long Island oceanfront estate and had been featured on Robin Leach's television program ''Lifestyles of the Rich and Famous.'' The luxurious restaurants of the New York Restaurant Group reflected his epicurean tastes. Smith & Wollensky carried at least 45,000 bottles of wine. The Post House was decorated with American folk art, and the Manhattan Ocean Club displayed Stillman's collection of Pablo Picasso's pottery.

Expansion in the 1990s

La Cité, described by New York Restaurant Group as a Parisian cafe-style restaurant, opened in midtown Manhattan near the end of 1989. It was still struggling to make money in 1993, although Stillman had revised the menu, lowered prices, added a 70-seat grill, and shortened the name to simply Cité. Reviewing it late that year, Gael Greene approved the changes, noted a greater emphasis on meat and a longer wine list, and added, ''I find it the handsomest steakhouse in town.''

Park Avenue Cafe, characterized by the company as offering ''cutting-edge new American cuisine in a cafe atmosphere,'' opened on the Upper East Side, but only a few blocks north of midtown, in 1992. It was under the direction of chef David Burke, who had been lured from River Cafe, his previous home, where he made a name for concoctions whimsical and even bizarre. Greene declared, ''Burke's tornado of creativity is delivering mostly remarkable food,'' including a ''swordfish chop'' carved from the seldom-used collarbone and neck, house-smoked salmon atop corn blini, scallops on braised oxtail, and duck-and-chicken pie rich with wild mushrooms, asparagus, and potato in a biscuit-like crust. New York Restaurant Group sold The Post House that year but continued to operate it under contract.

By 1993 Stillman was estimating that he was feeding one million people a year, with the dinner check at New York Restaurant Group's five operations averaging at least $47.50 and perhaps as much as $60. Described by Kruger as ''Using marketing savvy-street smarts and a Donald Trump-sized ego,'' Stillman had built an organization that claimed to have annual sales of $42 million, including $19 million for Smith & Wollensky. More than $1 million a year was being spent on promotion, including full-page ads in the *Times, Forbes,* and *Fortune* and commercials on cable television. Stillman had employed at least four advertising agencies in the last five years and was fond of such publicity stunts as roasting an entire steer outside The Post House.

During twice-a-year Wine Week, beginning in 1986, his customers were offered a choice of free wines for sampling during lunch; at Cité unlimited free wine was offered beginning at 8 p.m. to fill a room typically vacated by diners moving on to nearby theaters.

Park Avenue Cafe introduced a Chicago locale in 1994, closely duplicating the original, on the second floor of the Guest Quarters Suites hotel (later the Doubletree Guest Suites hotel). New York Restaurant Group already had opened a more casual Mrs. Park's Tavern on the ground floor of the hotel. Both were later sold to Doubletree, but NYRG continued to operate them.

New York Restaurant Group, L.L.C. was formed in 1995 as a holding company for a series of partnerships and limited liability companies anchored by Stillman but involving as many as 40 investors. In early 1996 Stillman sold 23 percent of the company to the Thomas H. Lee Co., a Boston-based investment house, for as much as $15 million. This sale wiped out the company's debt, according to Stillman, reduced the number of NYRG's investors to about ten, and provided the means for financing Stillman's plans to expand the group's operations to other cities.

In 1996 New York Restaurant Group launched Maloney & Porcelli. Located close to Smith & Wollensky and named for two lawyers Stillman had hired to negotiate a liquor license, the new restaurant was essentially a steakhouse, although its *piece de resistance* was a 2½-pound hunk of ''crackling'' pork shank that Corby Kummer of *New York* wrote ''looks like a deflated soccer ball.'' The influence of Burke, now corporate chef for all of the group's eateries, could be found in what Kummer called ''lots of little tricks that make dinner seem like a long McDonald's birthday party for grown-ups,'' including ''a mile-high slab of chocolate cake . . . topped by a dark-chocolate crossbar supporting a big white-chocolate cow.'' This restaurant was operated, but not owned, by NYRG.

After what Stillman described as 16 or 17 years of trying, his Smith & Wollensky partners agreed to license the name to NYRG and allow expansion. The group then spent almost $8.5 million to convert a former seafood restaurant in Miami Beach

Key Dates:

1977: Alan Stillman opens Smith & Wollensky.
1984: NYRG now includes The Post House and Manhattan Ocean Club.
1993: NYRG is feeding an estimated one million people per year.
1996: Stillman sells a 23 percent stake in NYRG to Thomas H. Lee.
1998: Four Smith & Wollenskys opened in other cities.
1999: NYRG postpones a plan to offer stock to the public.

into a replica of the original Smith & Wollensky. When it opened in late 1997, this branch had the largest seating capacity—670—of any NYRG restaurant at the time. Other versions of Smith & Wollensky opened in 1998 in Chicago (overlooking the Chicago River), Las Vegas (on the Strip, with 675 seats), and New Orleans (on the site of a registered national landmark) and in 1999 in Washington, D.C. All were owned by NYRG and were on leased property except for the New Orleans site. Appointed president of New York Restaurant Group in 1998, James Dunn was in charge of opening the new restaurants. Byrne remained director of New York operations and was a limited partner in St. James Associates.

New York Restaurant Group in 1999

New York Restaurant Group, Inc. was formed in 1997 by a merger with New York Restaurant Group, L.L.C. The cost of opening new restaurants threw this enterprise into the red, with a combined loss of almost $5.5 million during the years 1996–98, despite the rise in revenues (for group-owned restaurants) to $52.8 million in the latter year. The long term debt was $17.6 million. Counting restaurants operated but not owned by NYRG, sales came to $89 million. Sales of $24.7 million for the year ended June 28, 1999 made Smith & Wollensky's Manhattan site one of the highest grossing single restaurant locations in the country.

Second place in revenues for this period—$10.3 million—belonged to Maloney & Porcelli. In third place—and first among NYRG-owned restaurants—was the Chicago Smith & Wollensky, followed by Cité, Manhattan Ocean Club, and Park Avenue Cafe. The Las Vegas Smith & Wollensky, although open for only the last seven months of this period, had sales of $7.9 million, the same amount as the Miami Beach Smith & Wollensky, which was open for the entire period. The average check per person in this period ranged from $73.60 at The Post House to $24.30 at Chicago's Park Avenue Cafe (including Mrs. Park's Tavern). NYRG was stocking 92,000 bottles of wine. Stillman held 30 percent of the company's shares and Lee held 23 percent in mid-1999.

Stillman planned to make an initial public offering for the New York Restaurant Group—which he planned to rename Smith & Wollensky Restaurant Group—in the fall of 1999. The company issued a prospectus that, at 972 pages in length, reflected the complexity of its organization but postponed the offering because of lukewarm investor interest. While awaiting a new offering date, NYRG announced a joint venture with New York City's Plaza Hotel to create and run a new restaurant concept in the space previously taken by the Edwardian Room. It also was planning to open Smith & Wollensky units in Atlanta, Boston, and Philadelphia. A Maloney & Porcelli was scheduled to open in January 2000 in Washington, D.C.

Principal Competitors

Morton's Restaurant Group, Inc.; Ruth's Chris Steak House.

Further Reading

Agovino, Theresa, "Traveling Epicure Embarks on Bistro," *Crain's New York Business,* April 24, 1989, pp. 3, 49.
Battaglia, Andy, "David Burke," *Nation's Restaurant News,* January 1999, pp. 42, 44.
Burros, Marian, "Down to the Sea on West 58th Street," *New York Times,* September 21, 1984, p. C20.
Frumkin, Paul, "Stillman's NYRG Heeds Soft Market, Delays IPO," *Nation's Restaurant News,* October 11, 1999, pp. 1, 6.
Gault, Yalonda, "N.Y. Steak Man Wants More to Chew On," *Crain's New York Business,* March 29, 1993, pp. 3, 41.
Greene, Gael, "Little Chop Around the Corner," *New York,* February 4, 1992, p. 127.
——, "Prime Time: The Best Steaks in Town," *New York,* December 18, 1978, pp. 72, 76–77.
——, "Sizzling Steak Wars," *New York,* January 3, 1994, p. 29.
Hodgson, Moira, "Elegant, High-Quality New Steak House," *New York Times,* October 24, 1980, p. C20.
Jacobs, Jay, "Specialties de la Maison," *Gourmet,* September 1984, pp. 24, 26.
Kamen, Robin, "Insatiable Appetite," *Crain's New York Business,* February 12, 1996, pp. 1, 21.
Kruger, Pamela, "Selling New York on the $60 Dinner," *New York Times,* May 23, 1993, Sec. 3, p. 10.
Kummer, Corby, "Slab-Happy," *New York,* September 23, 1996, p. 103.
Miller, Bryan, "Smith & Wollensky," *New York Times,* March 30, 1990, p. C20.
Papiernik, Richard L., "NYRG Divulges Losses Linked to Expansion As IPO Awaits," *Nation's Restaurant News,* August 9, 1999, pp. 6, 111.
Prewitt, Milford, "Investment Firm Buys 25% of NY Restaurant Group," *Nation's Restaurant News,* January 8, 1996, pp. 1, 4.
Prial, Frank J., "Restaurants That Pour Freely," *New York Times,* March 8, 1995, p. C9.
Sanders, Lisa, "New Eateries, Full Plate," *Crain's New York Business,* August 31, 1998, p. 15.
"Smith & Wollensky," *Nation's Restaurant News,* May 7, 1990, p. S25.
Strauss, Karya, "Smith & Wollensky Hits Big, NYRG Plans More Portfolio Expansions," *Nation's Restaurant News,* April 12, 1999, pp. 4, 90.
Walkup, Carolyn, "NY Restaurant Group Opens 1 Concept, Plans 2nd in Chi," *Nation's Restaurant News,* November 28, 1994, p. 7.

—Robert Halasz

Nikken Global Inc.

15363 Barranca Parkway
Irvine, California 92618
U.S.A.
Telephone: (949) 789-2000
Fax: (949) 789-2085
Web site: http://www.nikken.com/global

Wholly Owned Subsidiary of Nihon Kenko Zoushin Kenkyukai
Founded: 1975 as Nihon Kenko Zoushin Kenkyukai
Employees: 250
Sales: $1.5 billion (1998 est.)
NAIC: 42145 Medical, Dental, and Hospital Equipment and Supplies Wholesalers; 325412 Vitamin Preparations Manufacturing

Nikken Global Inc. is one of the world's largest multilevel marketing (MLM) and health products firms, based on its annual sales of over $1.5 billion. Its roots are in Japan, the world leader in the multilevel or network marketing industry, where one in eight homes have a Nikken wellness product. Operating in about 20 nations in Asia, North America, and Europe, hundreds of thousands of independent distributors make Nikken the world leader in selling magnetic health products. Although magnets have a long history in healing, Nikken incorporates its magnets in several kinds of products, such as shoe inserts, flexible support wraps, clothing, water purification devices, sleep masks, mattresses, and other sleep products. It also sells nutritional supplements, massage products, pet care items, jewelry, skin care products, and clothing and other items made with ceramic-reflective fibers to maintain an ideal body temperature. Although Nikken is a large international firm expanding rapidly in the United States and elsewhere, little is available in American publications about this debt-free and well-managed company.

Historical Background of Magnetic Therapy

Some say that historic figures such as Aristotle, Cleopatra, and Galen, a famous physician of ancient history, used lodestones (magnetic rocks) for healing. The Chinese as far back as 2000 B.C. used magnetic stones, along with heat and acupuncture, to help the body correct unhealthy imbalances. Ancient Hindu scriptures, the Vedas, mentioned using stone instruments, probably lodestones, for treating disease. Medieval European doctors reported using magnets to cure gout, arthritis, baldness, depression, and some kinds of poisonings. Paracelsus, the famous physician born in 1493 in Switzerland, used magnets to treat many forms of illness, including epilepsy, diarrhea, and hemorrhage. In 1775 Franz Anton Mesmer wrote *On the Medicinal Uses of the Magnet* and became well-known for his concepts of animal magnetism and mesmerism, or hypnosis. In the 1800s, with the discoveries of the connections between electricity and magnetism, even more people used electrical or magnetic devices to treat the sick. Many people, however, considered such methods a hoax or quackery, so it was not surprising that most doctors opposed magnetic healing in the 20th century.

Origins of Nikken in Japan

In 1973 Isamu Masuda, a desk clerk for a Japanese bus company, blamed his own poor health when his baby was born without ears. Masuda began using magnetic shoe inserts and in 1975 launched his firm Nihon Kenko Zoushin Kenkyukai in Fukuoka, Japan. He promoted his company on what he called the "five pillars of health," namely healthy body, mind, family, finances, and society. In its first four years, Nihon broke all previous records for a Japanese start-up firm, a record still in place in the late 1990s, according to a promotional video produced by independent Nikken distributors Kurt and Kathy Wilkins of Star, Wyoming.

In the 1980s other firms began marketing magnetic products. For example, Fred Rinker in England started in 1981 making magnetic products to wrap around horses' legs, but three years later his firm called, Magna-Pak Inc., began selling magnets for humans, which soon outsold the equine items.

Nikken had operated in at least six nations, including Japan, Hong Kong, and Taiwan, and had accumulated a total of at least $5.5 billion in retail sales before deciding in April 1989 to start operations in the United States. Nikken U.S.A. Inc. began in a

Key Dates:

1975: Isamu Masuda founds the parent company in Fukuoka, Japan.
1985: Hong Kong operations are started.
1988: Firm expands into Taiwan.
1989: Company begins operating in the United States and Portugal.
1996: North American operations move to Irvine, California, which becomes the world headquarters for Nikken; company operations begin in Sweden, Holland, Germany, and the United Kingdom.
1997: Company starts operating in Italy and the Philippines.
1998: Firm expands into France.
1999: Nikken and Amway file lawsuits against each other; Nikken begins operating in Finland.

high-rise building in Westwood, California. Concentrating on the Asian markets of Los Angeles and New York City, the subsidiary did $3 million in U.S. sales in 1989, but rapid expansion was forthcoming.

The 1990s

Nikken's American sales reached $41 million in 1992, $54 million in 1994, and $135 million in 1995. However, it remained primarily a Japanese and Asian firm. The parent company, Nihon Kenko Zoushin Kenkyukai, traded on the Tokyo Stock Exchange and sold a more diverse line of products, such as portable saunas and cookware. In 1996 Nikken distributor Jeff VanBlaircum of Oregon said that the firm in Japan garnered $700 million in annual sales, but 99 of 100 Americans knew nothing about Nikken, thus presenting new opportunities.

Although Nikken had considerable success with its magnetic products, called Kenko Technology in company literature, in the early 1990s the firm had no way to apply magnetism to elbows, knees, and other often-bent body parts. So in 1993 the company began a major research project. ''Their mission was to create an advanced version of Kenko Technology—a comfortable support wrap that would be stretchable, flexible and durable. Finding nothing suitable already available, Nikken invented a rubber-based product with magnets inside. The result was the firm's trademarked Elastomag Support Wraps, highlighted in company literature as ''an evolution in wellness technology.'' Elastomag products in 1999 included wraps for the elbow, hand, knee, thigh, ankle, shoulder, back, and wrist. Nikken also sold its black, zippered Elastomag Vest in both men's and women's sizes.

Nikken by the early 1990s also had developed a line of new products based on what it called in its product literature ''Far-Infrared Technology—The Newest Innovation in Warmth.'' Far-Infrared used ceramic-reflective fibers that ''act like millions of tiny heat sponges that then reflect the warmth . . . as deep heat. Excess heat is released into the atmosphere, so you'll experience exceptionally comfortable warmth that is continuously activated by your natural body temperature.'' One distributor who wished to remain anonymous said Far-Infrared was derived from or inspired by the use of ceramic fibers in American space suits used to keep astronauts from overheating from the sun's direct rays or becoming cold in the chill of outer space.

Far-Infrared Products in 1999 included Nikken's trademarked KenkoTherm Summer and Winter Comforters, both made with 50 percent ceramic fibers and 50 percent wool, and dress and sports sox for men and women made with copper fibers to prevent static cling. Others were ThermoWear Long Johns made of 51.6 percent ceramic-reflective fibers, 36.5 percent cotton, and 11.9 percent nylon, and ThermoWear Vests in black or khaki.

Nikken also sold nutritional supplements and drink mixes that included herbs such as ginseng, valerian root, and camomile, and various vitamins and minerals. Its sleep products included pillows, mattresses, and pads with built-in magnets. Nikken skin care products included cleansers, toners, and lotions, some with herbal extracts. Nikken also provided magnets it claimed prevented mineral buildup inside pipes and decreased any mineral deposits on human skin. In addition, its noncarbon chlorine filter removed chlorine from shower water and also helped decrease any lead, hydrogen sulfide, iron oxide, and sediments. Specially designed handheld metal balls and other self-massage items were sold to help users relieve their stress. Nikken sold blankets with magnets for both household pets and horses. Both ceramic fibers and magnets were used in its Kenko PetPads for pets to rest on. The company also sold nutritional supplements designed just for pets.

Nikken's trademarked SoliTENS unit was the firm's only federally approved medical device and thus required a prescription from a healthcare professional. According to a 1999 company product brochure, ''TENS units have gained increased acceptance by the American medical community over the years and are now acknowledged as effective therapy devices for the relief of aches and discomforts all over the body. TENS stands for Transcutaneous Electrical Nerve Stimulator. Structured like a flattened writing pen, this lightweight instrument emits an electronic pulse that can be directed very specifically at an area that requires treatment, using a set of controls that adjusts for intensity and duration.''

In 1996 Nikken moved into its North American headquarters in Irvine, California, and later expanded to make Irvine the center of its global activities. Nikken in 1999 remained under the leadership of Chairman Isamu Masuda. Another key leader was Toshizo (Tom) Watanabe, who had earned a B.S. degree from Brandeis University, an MBA from Pepperdine University, and studied at Massachusetts Institute of Technology and Tokyo's Keio University. He joined Nikken in 1984 as its director of training, directed the formation of the U.S. subsidiary in 1989, in 1992 became president of Nikken, USA, oversaw the expansion of the firm into several other nations, and in January 1999 became president/CEO of Nikken's worldwide operations.

Nikken hired Advent Communications, headed by Clifton Jolley, PhD, to take care of its public relations. A former writer for Salt Lake City's *Deseret News*, Jolley advocated the merits of multilevel marketing, speaking at other MLM firms such as Tele-Sales, Inc.

Like other network marketing firms, Nikken relied on its independent distributors to sell their products. John Kalench in 1998 started his Nikken business after promoting multilevel marketing as an author and speaker. In 1991 he had published *Being the Best You Can Be in MLM*, followed by *The Greatest Opportunity in the History of the World* in 1992 and *17 Secrets of the Master Prospectors* in 1994. Formed in 1987, Kalench's firm, Millionaires in Motion, was described by writer Ana McClellan as "one of the world's premiere training and educational companies for the network marketing industry."

Kalench's turning point came in 1994 when his son was born. He realized that his speaking engagements and other business activities left insufficient time for his wife and child. However, it was not until he recovered from a serious illness that he made the decision to join Nikken. In May 1998 he became a distributor and in just seven months reached the Diamond level, the fastest in Nikken's history, according to McClellan.

Kalench's use of modern technology illustrated how network marketers and other business leaders succeeded in the Information Age. "Technology has become an instrumental force in building a successful network in the new millennium," said Kalench in the McClellan article. "We still use large events to bring the family, the unity, the camaraderie, for people to catch the big vision. However, it's technology that allows us to leverage the personal contacts that really make a difference in building an effective team. The Internet, teleconferencing, conference calls, three-way calls have transformed business in the 90s. In building my Nikken network, I've used video-conferencing extensively. . . . I have a video-teleconferencing unit right in my home office that allows me to be in different cities. . . . When I'm finished . . . I walk out of the room, and there are my two boys. I can pick them up, hug them, and finish breakfast. This is freedom." Other prominent Nikken distributors included Marty Jeffery, the owner of two large Canadian newspapers, and Dave Johnson, a former Amway distributor who reportedly made $260,000 a month with Nikken.

Of course, few Nikken distributors reached such levels of success. Most network marketing distributors, whether in Nikken, Amway, or other firms, made modest incomes from their efforts. To encourage its distributors, Nikken offered many bonuses, including an auto incentive program in which the corporation paid monthly car payments for qualified distributors.

Nikken's training entity, called Team Diamond, organized large meetings for the firm's growing number of distributors. For example, in 1999 some 7,000 Nikken distributors attended a quarterly conference in the Buffalo, New York Convention Center, the largest gathering in the center's 21-year history. Such sales rallies were common among MLM firms.

In the 1990s several athletes and even some sports teams used magnetic devices, including those from Nikken. For example, the Denver Broncos football team purchased Nikken mattresses. Nikken spokesmen included former Miami Dolphins Bob Kuechenberg, Jim Kiick, Nat Moore, and Don Nottingham, and also former St. Louis Cardinals outfielder John Morris and tennis champion Peter Fleming. Dolphins quarterback Dan Marino and professional golfers Bob Murphy, Jim Colbert, and Donna Andrews endorsed Tectonic products made by Nikken rival Magnet Therapy, Inc. of West Palm Beach, Florida

Amway Challenge: 1999

Amway, the world's largest multilevel marketing firm, in May 1999 began selling its own magnetic products, and then the Ada, Michigan firm filed a patent infringement lawsuit against Nikken. Nikken in turn in June sued Amway in the U.S. District Court for the Central District of California. On October 15, 1999 the U.S. District Court, Middle District of Tennessee, Nashville Division, dismissed the Amway suit, while the Nikken suit was still pending at the end of 1999.

According to a Nikken press release, Amway's literature compared its magnets to those made by Nikken. Kendall Cho, Nikken executive vice president, said in the press release that, "It's obvious to us that Amway sees Nikken as its major competitor in this market." Dr. Clifton Jolley added that the firm from the beginning had considered the Amway suit "bizarre," because Nikken had been selling magnets for many years before Amway even entered that particular market.

In 1999 Nikken signed a multiyear manufacturing contract with Natural Alternatives International, Inc., a public corporation (NASDAQ: NAII) that provided nutritional product design and clinical testing.

Preparing for a Bright Future, Despite the Skeptics

As the 20th century ended and after a long history of magnetism used for health purposes, users and scholars remained divided on the effectiveness of such products. Baylor College of Medicine conducted a double-blind study most often cited by advocates of magnetic healing. Baylor found that magnets provided some relief to 50 individuals with post-polio pain. In the *Washington Post* of April 19, 1999, Carlos Vallbona, M.D., said, "Based on our study, there is no question on the efficacy of magnets for the control of pain in the population we studied," but he cautioned that the study should be repeated before making any general conclusions. Dr. Vallbona and his coauthors also reported in their medical journal article that the "safety of application of these electromagnetic fields is attested by the World Health Organization. . . ."

J.T. Ryaby of Tempe, Arizona's OrthoLogic published a review article about the clinical uses of electromagnetism to heal fractures that began in the 1970s. A National Library of Medicine abstract stated that since the 1970s, "several technologies have been developed and shown to promote healing in difficult to heal fractures."

These medical studies did not test Nikken products, but still they added credibility to the whole field of magnetic therapy. With more research underway, the use of magnets for health was discussed at professional meetings, including the First World Congress on Magnetotherapy held in 1996 in London and the Bioelectromagnetic Society in Bologna, Italy, in 1997.

Yet others remained skeptical. James D. Livingston, author and professor at Massachusetts Institute of Technology, agreed magnets were safe, but he also thought they might be a waste of money since more research was needed. "It remains to be proven," said Livingston in the *Washington Post.* "The overwhelming majority of the claims of magnetic therapy have been either pure hokum or just some form of the power of suggestion, or secondary things, like local warming, and not related to the magnetic field itself."

Nikken wisely avoided legal difficulties, with the FDA for example, by not claiming its magnets reduced pain and generally being quite careful in its product descriptions. When Nikken Vice-President Larry M. Proffit was interviewed for a 1996 article in the *Los Angeles Times*, he said, "we have to be careful," and thus the company usually shunned publicity. Since Nikken and its public relations firm declined to provide any information for this profile, that company policy to avoid media attention seemed to continue in 2000.

In spite of skepticism among some people, Nikken's future looked bright, as consumer demand seemed to be increasing for not only its magnets but also its other products. More competitors entered the field, and the whole area of alternative healing gained respectability. In addition, the economic opportunities from network marketing offered people new options as thousands lost their jobs from corporate layoffs.

Principal Subsidiaries

Nikken U.S.A. Inc.; Nikken U.K., Ltd.; Nihon Kenko Zoushin Kenkyukai Canada, Ltd.; Nikken de Mexico; Nikken Puerto Rico; Nikken Dominican Republic; Nikken Sweden; Nikken Finland; Nikken Holland; Nikken France; Nikken Germany; Nikken Spain; Nikken Portugal; Nikken Italy; China Nikken (Taiwan); Nikken Hong Kong; Nikken Philippines, Inc.; Nikken Sales Thailand Company, Ltd.

Principal Competitors

BIOflex; Amway Corporation; Magna-Pak Inc.; Magnetic Health Therapy; Homedics Inc.; Magnetherapy; Biomagnetics.

Further Reading

Blum, Justin, "Polarized Opinions; Magnets' Curing Power Debated," *Washington Post*, April 19, 1999, p. B1.

Clark, Christopher, "Magna-Pak Inc. Attracts Attention," *London Free Press*, March 29, 1999, p. 3.

Czarnik, Stanley A., "Electricity and Medicine in the 19th Century," *Popular Electronics*, September 1992, pp. 58–62, 92.

Dorr, Dave, "Do Magnets, Wristbands Ease Pain?" *St. Louis Post-Dispatch*, October 28, 1998, p. E1.

Hudson, Berkley, "A Growing Attraction to a New Field," *Los Angeles Times*, July 8, 1996, p. E1.

Lawrence, Ron, Paul J. Rosch, and Judith Plowden, *Magnet Therapy: The Pain Cure Alternative,* Rocklin, Calif.: Prima Publishing, 1998.

Livingston, James D., *Driving Force: The Natural Magic of Magnets,* Cambridge, Mass.: Harvard University Press, 1996.

McClellan, Ana, "The Journey of John Kalench," *Network Marketing Lifestyles*, December 1999, pp. 70–75.

Meyer, Brian, "Economic Impact of Convention Bookings Down 46 Percent in Buffalo, N.Y.," *Buffalo News*, September 21, 1999.

"Natural Alternatives International Announces New Contracts, Increased Backlog and Redesigned Website," *PR Newswire*, September 23, 1999.

Nodell, Bobbi, "Magnetic Pitch Attracts Scrutiny," *Los Angeles Business Journal*, June 21, 1993, p. S1.

Ryaby, J.T., "Clinical Effects of Electromagnetic and Electric Fields on Fracture Healing," *Clinical Orthopedics*, October 1998, pp. S205–15.

"United States District Court Dismisses Amway Suit," *PR Newswire*, October 21, 1999.

Vallbona, Carlos, et al., "Response of Pain to Static Magnetic Fields in Postpolio Patients: A Double-Blind Study," *Archives of Physical Medicine and Rehabilitation*, November 1997, pp. 1200–203.

—David M. Walden

Ontario Hydro Services Company

250 Yonge Street, 6th Floor
Toronto, Ontario M5B 2L7
Canada
Telephone: (416) 592-5111
Fax: (416) 592-2178
Web site: http://www.ohsc.com

State-Owned Company
Incorporated: 1974
Employees: 6,000
Sales: C$8.98 billion (US$6.24 billion) (1998)
NAIC: 221121 Electric Bulk Power Transmission and Control; 221122 Electric Power Distribution

Ontario Hydro Services Company (OHSC) is a government-owned energy services provider based in Ontario, Canada. Spun off from utilities giant Ontario Hydro in April 1999 in preparation for privatization of the electric utility industry in 2000, OHSC handles distribution of electricity and retail operations. The firm provides electricity to three types of customers: industrial; retail, including residential customers, farms, and small businesses; and municipalities. The more than 250 municipalities served by OHSC in turn supply electricity to more than 2.7 million consumers. Serving nearly a million customers, OHSC has more than $9 billion in assets and operates one of the most extensive transmission and distribution systems in North America.

Early History: 1895–1950

The powerful Niagara Falls is located in Ontario, in an area that was populated by the majority of the province's citizens in the late 19th century. In 1895 the first major generating station was built, harnessing the power of the Niagara Falls, which was for many years the province's most vital source of electricity. Still, only local areas were able to take advantage of the power provided by a number of private companies given waterpower leases on the falls.

At the turn of the century, a group of prominent Ontario citizens began to advocate public ownership of the hydroelectric industry. Foremost among the proponents was Adam Beck, the mayor of London, Ontario. A vociferous, energetic supporter of public ownership of electric power, he threw the entire weight of his office and his powerful connections behind lobbying the Ontario legislature in favor of the idea, arguing that the thinly populated province would benefit from having a one-company monopoly rather than rival private competitors. Before approval could be given, however, legal battles had to be fought with the United States to regain control of parcels of the Canadian Niagara Falls that had been purchased by U.S. companies. In addition, the public had to be won over to the idea of a government monopoly of electric power.

Finally in 1906 the Ontario legislature passed a statute creating the Hydro Electric Power Commission of Ontario, headed by Sir Adam Beck, as he later became. The commission was given a mandate to provide all citizens with electricity at the lowest possible cost. This ''socialist'' measure, although viewed with alarm in the United States and Great Britain, achieved its desired results.

Initially Hydro purchased electric power from private entrepreneurs for distribution to those municipalities that had contracts with the commission. However, the utility gradually began to purchase and, much later, to build its own hydroelectric generators, in addition to transmission systems.

World War I enormously expanded the need for electricity. The demand for electric power in Ontario tripled during the war and continued at the higher rate even after the war's end. In 1914 Hydro purchased its first generating station, and later the same year construction was completed on the first generating station to be built by the commission. Thus began an aggressive purchasing and building campaign, necessary to meet the increased demand, due in part to the soaring popularity of such electric appliances as irons, vacuum cleaners, and washing machines.

By 1922 Hydro was the largest, most powerful utility in the world, with a demand for electricity of 496,000 kilowatts, up from 4,000 kilowatts just 12 years before. To help meet the growing demand, in 1922 Hydro completed construction of its first major power station, Queenston-Chippawa, later renamed

Company Perspectives:

The Ontario Hydro Services Company is a services-based growth company maximizing shareholder value through excellence in energy transmission and distribution businesses. Building off our strong platform of asset ownership, operational excellence and customer approval, we diversify into related, financially attractive businesses. The Values of Ontario Hydro Services Company: Operational Excellence (Capital Efficiency, Productivity and Customer Responsiveness); Competitiveness; Fiscal Responsibility; Environmental Stewardship; Public Safety; Leadership.

the Sir Adam Beck-Niagara Generating Station No. 1. It had taken 2,000 men to build and was the largest power generator in the world.

In the 1930s the commission took over administration of a series of small northern systems—later to be known as the Northern Ontario Properties—that primarily provided service to the paper and mining industries in that region. Three systems, serving the southern, more populated, area of Ontario, were consolidated into the Southern Ontario System in 1944. These two systems were eventually combined into one in 1962, although two others, divided at Sault Ste. Marie into the East System and West System, remained separate. In 1970 all of them were finally merged into one province-wide integrated system, with enough capacity to supply electricity to the United States at a handsome profit.

Diversification and Expansion: 1950s–Early 1990s

The years after World War II saw a huge expansion of utility companies, including the Hydro Electric Power Commission of Ontario. Immediately after the war, Hydro began construction of eight additional hydroelectric stations. In the late 1950s—with demand for electricity still unsatisfied—the commission decided to harness the St. Lawrence River, Ontario's last major undeveloped hydraulic site. The St. Lawrence project was undertaken jointly with the State of New York, and, when completed, added an extra one million kilowatts to the Hydro system, which, at the time, included 65 hydro stations and two fossil-fueled plants.

With the completion of the St. Lawrence project in 1958, Ontario had only minor waterways available for hydroelectric development. While thermal-electric plants were efficient generators during peak usage periods, these did not provide a viable alternative to meeting the spiraling demand for electricity, due to the expense of importing the fossil fuels necessary to run the plants. Nuclear power seemed to be the answer, and Ontario was richly endowed with the uranium that was used in the nuclear reactors. As early as 1951 Hydro had begun to experiment with nuclear power for commercial use, completing its first experimental nuclear power plant in 1962, followed in 1967 by a much larger one. While nuclear power was clean and efficient, it was also costly. Hydro engineers began experimenting successfully with increasing the size of nuclear power generators, developing the CANDU, or Canadian-type reactor, later used by all nuclear power stations in Canada. CANDU reactors were successfully installed in the Pickering A generating station, Canada's first major nuclear power facility, completed in 1971.

Diminishing natural resources, soaring costs, growing environmental consciousness, and the rise of aboriginal movements in Canada signaled that it was time for the Hydro Electric Power Commission to evaluate its direction for the future. An Ontario legislative task force was established in 1971 to examine these changes and to determine how Hydro could best meet them. The result was a major reorganization that enabled the company to better respond to the social and economic complexities of the late 20th century. Hydro ceased being a commission and became incorporated as a crown corporation in 1974, adopting the name Ontario Hydro. While still a government monopoly, the company became financially independent and was expected to turn a profit. The new Hydro was managed by a 17-member board of directors, 16 of which, including the chair, were appointed by the provincial lieutenant governor, while the president was appointed by the board itself. Although the newly reorganized company began to focus on social and environmental issues in addition to producing electricity, Ontario Hydro's mandate remained as it was in 1906, although expanded: not only electricity, but also electrical services including inspection and repair of electrical wiring and equipment, would be provided to Ontario citizens.

Throughout the 1970s and 1980s Ontario Hydro faced the public's growing concern about the world's shortage of fossil fuels and mounting damage to the environment. In an effort to deal with these problems, as well as keep costs down and moderate demand, conservation became an important company initiative. By late 1991 Ontario Hydro had invested nearly $179 million in energy conservation, which produced a reduction in demand, in that year, of 250 megawatts and resulted in a savings to customers of $28 million. Other measures undertaken to aid the environment included companywide recycling and the installation of scrubbers in many of the hydroelectric plants.

Although Ontario Hydro continued to show a modest profit, it found it necessary to reduce its workforce and restructure its operations in response to the recession of the early 1990s. Throughout the early 1990s Ontario Hydro executives worked to streamline the organization. The company was praised, however, for its humane downsizing, in which employees whose jobs were targeted for elimination were given the option of assessing their abilities and determining how and where they could best fit into other areas of the company. Those employees who left the company received generous severance packages. Salary freezes were approved for senior management for the foreseeable future. To further offset increased costs and the effects of the recession, the Ontario Energy Board gave its approval for a sizable rate hike of 11.8 percent.

Ontario Hydro continued to generate profits and increase its exports during the early 1990s. It signed 76 new contracts to provide its services abroad in 1991, for example, and managed to boost revenues ten percent to about $7.14 billion. Sales grew similarly in 1992 and net income increased to a healthy $312 million. Throughout the period, Ontario Hydro managers worked to cut costs and improve efficiency. In 1993 Ontario Hydro appointed Allan Kupcis CEO.

Key Dates:

1895: First major hydroelectric station is built in Niagara Falls, New York.
1906: Ontario Hydro-Electric Power Commission is formed by Sir Adam Beck.
1914: The Commission purchases its first generating station.
1922: Construction of the Commission's first major power station is completed.
1944: The Southern Ontario System is created through the combination of three divisions.
1962: First experimental nuclear power plant is completed.
1974: Hydro becomes incorporated and adopts the name Ontario Hydro.
1998: Ontario's electricity industry is deregulated through the Energy Competition Act.
1999: Ontario Hydro is restructured, resulting in the creation of Ontario Hydro Services Company.

Under Kupcis's direction Ontario Hydro continued to cut costs, reduce the size of its workforce, and reposition itself for future gains. Restructuring efforts showed up on the bottom line in 1994 when the company recorded net income of $855 million. Although its debt was still more than $34 billion going into 1995, the company's liabilities had been significantly reduced since the late 1980s. Furthermore, Ontario Hydro had reduced its workforce to less than 21,000 from more than 32,000 just a few years earlier. Although Ontario Hydro's competitive stance was improved over the early 1990s, its long-term success was contingent on some factors outside its control—including the possibility of deregulation, or ''open access,'' in the Ontario electricity supply market.

Moving Toward a Free Market in the Late 1990s

In 1995, following in the footsteps of electric industry trends in the United States, Ontario began a process to restructure its electricity industry. The deregulation of Ontario Hydro was a major campaign issue in the June provincial election in Ontario, and the winner, Mike Harris of the Ontario Progressive Conservative Party, had spoken in favor of privatization of Ontario Hydro's non-nuclear assets. Harris had stated that privatization earnings would be used to reduce the monopoly's significant debt. Ontario Hydro, too, welcomed deregulation. Maurice Strong, Ontario Hydro's chairman since 1992, had been lobbying for privatization since he joined the firm, only to face opposition from the government. With a new premier in office, however, Ontario Hydro once again began to vocalize its opinions. CEO Strong stated in a speech to the Canadian Electrical Association in mid-1995: ''In the election campaign . . . Premier Harris indicated that his government would consider major changes in Ontario Hydro, including at least some degree of privatization. We welcome—and we need—his leadership in effecting changes. Ontario Hydro is ready.'' Harris appointed William Farlinger, former chairman and CEO of accounting firm Ernst & Young, as chairman of Ontario Hydro, and Farlinger also agreed that the firm needed to be privatized quickly. With Ontario Hydro's debt mounting and retail prices rising, fear that consumers would switch to alternative power sources, such as the new gas turbine technology, was warranted.

The road to privatization was not a smooth one, however, and the call for timely deregulation was left unanswered for several years as the government pondered how best to restructure the electricity industry. By late 1998 Ontario Hydro had C$23.3 billion in stranded debts—money borrowed for projects not expected to be financially viable after the privatization process. A significant portion of the stranded debts was a result of the billions Ontario Hydro had invested in building a nuclear power generating network, a network deemed to be nearly worthless on the retail market. The firm reported a net loss of C$6.3 billion for fiscal 1997, the largest net loss ever recorded in Canadian corporate history. The unusually high loss was due to C$6.7 billion worth of write-offs and charges.

The Electricity Act of 1998 succeeded in pushing forward the breakup of Ontario Hydro. The Act called for Ontario Hydro to be split into five entities, the two most prominent being Ontario Hydro Services Company, which would handle electricity transmission, distribution, and retail operations; and Ontario Power Generation, to operate hydroelectric, nuclear, and fossil fuel generating stations. The three remaining groups were Electrical Safety Authority, to perform electric installation inspection operations; Independent Electricity Market Operator, to oversee the system and make sure electricity is distributed to all customers; and Ontario Electricity Financial Corp., to manage Ontario Hydro's debt that would not be taken over by the new companies. The debt, estimated to be around $20.9 billion, was to be pared down through a surcharge billed to electricity customers. The restructuring into five groups was the first stage toward an open market for electricity in 2000.

Ontario Hydro Services Company was born on April 1, 1999, when Ontario Hydro was officially broken up. OHSC was to function as it had prior to restructuring until sometime in 2000, when access to the market opened to outside entities. The new CEO and president of OHSC was Eleanor Clitheroe, and William Farlinger remained chairman. OHSC's worth was estimated by the province to be C$8.6 billion.

The new entity wasted no time getting started on its mission to expand its energy network and to prepare for the impending free market. OHSC acquired the electricity distribution assets of Artemesia Township for C$600,000, its first purchase under Bill 35, also known as the Energy Competition Act. Bill 35, which passed in November 1998, was designed to stimulate competition and lower utility prices. Several months after the Artemesia deal, in July, OHSC acquired six municipal utilities in southwestern Ontario for about C$11.5 million. The municipalities served nearly 9,000 customers. Because OHSC already served more than 12,000 customers in the same county, the acquisition was considered to be ideal. The company unveiled its new diesel generating station in Armstrong, located in northwestern Ontario, in August. Because of Armstrong's remote location, customers in those communities were unable to be serviced through OHSC's existing power grid; rather, local generation was required. The estimated C$3.5 million project used new technologies intended to reduce environmental hazards and increase safety.

OHSC, though a young company, exuded confidence and made preparations as it grew closer to an open utilities market. The prospects of new competitors and customers being able to freely select their utilities providers were viewed as opportunities rather than hindrances. OHSC looked forward to being able to expand and seek new customers in Ontario and beyond, and also to offering a wide array of new products and services. The company planned to leverage its existing fiber-optics system, used to transmit information regarding its power grid, to expand into the communications sector. OHSC also planned to enter such service arenas as gas and water distribution. CEO Clitheroe commented on the future in a speech made at the Canadian Transmission Restructuring Conference in June 1999: ''We feel a deep connection with those pioneers, led by Sir Adam Beck, who at the beginning of this century took up the challenge of bringing abundant, affordable energy to every corner of this vast province. We've not only inherited their success . . . we've also held on to the values behind that success, which are timeless. These are the lighthouses, so to speak, that will guide us through the uncertain waters of the first few years of an open marketplace in which we—and everyone else in the industry today—are the new generation of pioneers.''

Principal Competitors

Consolidated Edison, Inc.; Hydro-Quebec; Power Authority of the State of New York.

Further Reading

''Canadians Replace Layoffs with Voluntary Rightsizing,'' *Personnel,* May 1991.

Corcoran, Terence, ''Time for New Ideas at Ontario Hydro,'' *Globe and Mail,* July 5, 1995, p. B2.

Crone, Greg, ''Ontario Hydro Heads into New Territory,'' *National Post,* December 31, 1998, p. D4.

''Marc Eliesen: Ontario Hydro's New Chairman Says the Public's Interests Are Best Served by Ensuring That It Remains a Crown Corporation,'' *Financial Times of Canada,* October 14, 1991.

Mittelstaedt, Martin, ''Electricity Users Face Bill in Billions,'' *Globe and Mail,* April 2, 1999, p. A2.

——, ''Ontario Hydro Carrying Massive Debt,'' *Globe and Mail,* October 27, 1998, p. B1.

——, ''Ontario Hydro to Cut Debt 11%; Plans $3.6-billion Reduction by 1997,'' *Globe and Mail,* June 15, 1995, p. B7.

Nelles, H.V., *The Politics of Development: Forests, Mines and Hydroelectric Power in Ontario, 1849–1941,* Toronto: Macmillan Publishing Co., 1974.

''Ontario Hydro Privatization Urged,'' *Petroleum Economist,* May 1991.

''Ontario Hydro Profit $587 Million for 1994,'' *Toronto Star*, March 14, 1995, p. D7.

''Ontario Hydro Says Savings Will Allow It to Defer New Plants,'' *Wall Street Journal,* January 17, 1992.

''Privatization of Hydro-Quebec Likely As Ontario Election Draws to a Close,'' *Northeast Power Report,* June 9, 1995, p. 7.

Ruimy, Joel, ''Five Firms Rise from Hydro's Ashes—Giant Utility's End the First Step to Privatization,'' *Toronto Star,* April 1, 1999, p. 1.

Toughill, Kelly, ''Parts of Hydro Could Be Sold McLeod Says,'' *Toronto Star,* May 23, 1995, p. A8.

''Utility Chooses Nuclear Power, *Christian Science Monitor,* January 16, 1990.

Van Alphen, Tony, ''Hydro's Failed Overhaul,'' *Toronto Star,* October 24, 1994, p. B1.

Weber, Terry, ''Ontario Hydro Confirms New CEO,'' *Financial Post,* January 28, 1995, p. 11.

——, ''Ontario Hydro Trims 1,025 Jobs in Buyout Program,'' *Financial Post,* March 23, 1995, p. 12.

Wells, Jennifer, ''Power Play: Why Did Mike Harris Take a Pass on His Biggest Privatization Candidate—Ontario Hydro, the Country's Largest Electrical Utility?'', *Globe and Mail,* May 28, 1999, p. 36.

—Sina Dubovoj and Dave Mote
—updated by Mariko Fujinaka

Protection One, Inc.

600 Corporate Pointe, 12th Floor
Culver City, California 90230
U.S.A.
Telephone: (310) 342-6300
Toll Free: (800) 738-4255
Fax: (310) 649-1385
Web site: http://www.protectionone.com

Public Subsidiary of Western Resources, Inc.
Incorporated: 1991
Employees: 4,577
Sales: $421.1 million (1998)
Stock Exchanges: New York
Ticker Symbol: POI
NAIC: 561621 Security Systems Services (Except Locksmiths) (pt); 561612 Security Guards and Patrol Services; 23531 Electrical Contractors

Protection One, Inc. provides security monitoring services to more than 1.5 million customers in the United States, Canada, the United Kingdom, and Western Europe. As one of the leading home security companies in the United States, Protection One installs security systems, monitors the systems, and also provides such services as paging, smoke detectors, and patrol and alarm response. The company has grown significantly in the late 1990s as a result of an aggressive acquisition and growth strategy. The majority of the firm's subscribers are residential customers, and the bulk of its revenue comes from the monitoring of security systems. Western Resources, Inc., a consumer services company with major interests in energy and monitored services, owns approximately 84 percent of Protection One.

Formative Years in the Late 1980s and Early 1990s

Protection One was born in 1988 when electric utility company PacifiCorp, Inc. decided to form a security company. As the utility industry faced flat growth in the late 1980s, many utility companies turned to diversification, something the Portland, Oregon-based PacifiCorp was familiar with—in the 1950s the company expanded its operations to include telecommunications and mining, which by the late 1980s contributed more than half of PacifiCorp's total earnings. Because of stagnant sales in electric utilities and telecommunications, PacifiCorp decided to invest in the security alarm business, an as yet untapped market.

The newly formed Protection One Alarm Services opened a branch in Burbank, California, in August 1988 to better serve the rapidly growing California market. In the course of a year Protection One built a subscriber base in southern California counties ranging from Ventura to San Diego. In September 1989 the company opened a Home Builder Services Division in southern California. The division developed contacts with real estate developers and offered programs to put security systems in homes being built.

In 1991 PacifiCorp spun off the security unit in the wake of regulatory conflicts. Protection One was acquired by an investor group of alarm industry executives, including James M. Mackenzie, Jr., John E. Mack, III, John W. Hesse, and Thomas K. Rankin, and incorporated on June 21, 1991. James Mackenzie took on the roles of president and CEO, and the company headquarters was established in Culver City, California.

Exponential Growth Through Acquisitions in the Mid-1990s

Protection One failed to turn a profit during the early 1990s, but the security industry showed immense promise, and Protection One enjoyed increasing revenues—sales grew from $17.6 million in 1992 to $21.9 million the following year. The company had grown through small acquisitions and the purchase of customer accounts. According to William C. Cunningham, president of a security consulting firm, the private security industry in the United States generated sales of about $64.4 billion in 1993. ''The security industry as a whole is experiencing fairly robust growth,'' Cunningham told the *Portland Oregonian.* ''It is one of the fastest-growing segments of the service sector.''

By mid-May 1994 Protection One had more than 71,700 subscribers spread throughout Washington, Oregon, California, Arizona, and Nevada. More than 80 percent of the company's

Company Perspectives:

Our vision is to be the most trusted provider of peace of mind through extraordinary monitored security systems and services, protecting people and the things they care about, wherever and whenever needed.

subscribers were residential customers. Protection One's IPO took place in September 1994. The company traded on the NASDAQ under the symbol ALRM.

The U.S. security market was highly fragmented and filled with independent, regional operators, but Protection One sought to consolidate, hoping to become one of the nation's top providers of security systems. To meet its ambitious goal, Protection One began a flurry of acquisition activities, focusing initially on increasing its presence in familiar markets. In November 1994 the company acquired the alarm monitoring accounts of Knight Protective Industries Inc., gaining about 9,200 residential accounts, 85 percent of which were in California. The Knight purchase marked Protection One's largest account acquisition to date. A week later, the company bought the security alarm monitoring accounts of AAA Alarm Systems, bringing Protection One's subscriber count to more than 95,000. By the end of 1994 the company had more than 98,000 subscribers, an increase of 73 percent over the previous year.

Protection One continued to grow through acquisitions in 1995, beginning the year with the purchase of Custom House Security Inc. Protection One gained about 6,500 subscriber accounts and became the largest residential alarm monitoring company in the Seattle, Washington area. The company also boosted its account base in Portland, Oregon, through the acquisition. Protection One's total number of subscribers rose to more than 103,000, generating monthly recurring revenue of $3.3 million. In May the firm gained about 22,700 additional subscribers through the $18.5 million purchase of Alert Centre Inc.'s accounts in Oregon, Washington, Arizona, California, and Nevada. Alert, one of the largest alarm monitoring companies in the United States, continued its operations in the Southeast and Southwest. In December Protection One grew larger once again through the acquisition of the subscriber base of San Francisco Bay Area-based Bolt Security. The move expanded Protection One's presence in the San Francisco Bay Area region—the second most attractive residential security alarm market on the West Coast, according to Protection One. The company also acquired the residential subscriber base of Wells Fargo Alarm Services Inc. Most of the subscribers were located in southern California and Arizona. In combination, the two acquisitions added about 6,000 subscribers to Protection One's account base, bringing the total to more than 129,000, a 52 percent rise over the previous year.

For the fiscal year ended September 30, 1995, Protection One reported revenues of $55.9 million, up 62 percent from fiscal 1994 sales of $34.5 million. Net losses increased as well, however, reaching $18.5 million, compared with $9.2 million in fiscal 1994. Protection One noted that about $8.9 million was due to an extraordinary charge and remained confident that earnings would increase. CEO Mackenzie indicated satisfaction with fiscal 1995 results in a company statement and stated, ''We believe fiscal 1995 results affirm the soundness of the Protection One strategy—the pursuit of subscriber growth in the residential security alarm market, clustered around the company's branch areas.''

Protection One continued to pursue its growth strategy in 1996. In March the company acquired about 18,000 additional alarm monitoring subscribers from Intercap Funds Joint Venture dba (doing business as) Security Data Group and Eagle Sentry Inc. The $18 million purchase consisted primarily of residential subscribers situated in southern California and Las Vegas. The acquisition significantly increased Protection One's presence in the Las Vegas area; Jim Mackenzie noted in a prepared statement, ''With the acquisition of the subscribers and assets of Eagle Sentry, we estimate Protection One today has in excess of 30% market share in the residential security alarm market in Las Vegas, and the next largest competitor has no more than 5% market share.'' In May Protection One paid about $15 million for Metrol Security Services, Inc., an alarm company with about 19,000 alarm monitoring subscribers in Arizona and New Mexico, a new region for Protection One. Metrol also had about 5,500 customers using its alarm response services. The acquisition gave Protection One a leadership position in the Arizona market. At the end of 1996 Protection One added to its subscriber base in Portland, Oregon, through the acquisition of Phillips Electronics Inc. for $14.5 million. Phillips had about 12,000 subscribers, 70 percent of whom were residential customers, and the acquisition made Protection One four times larger than its closest rival in the Portland region.

Innovative marketing was another means for Protection One to expand its subscriber base. The company did not have its own sales force but sold security systems through an authorized dealer network. Protection One also pursued marketing deals with other businesses, such as electric utility companies. In October 1996 Protection One announced a marketing venture with former parent PacifiCorp in which Protection One offered home security systems to residential and small business customers served by PacifiCorp's Pacific Power and Utah Power operations. The agreement gave Protection One access to new territory, namely Utah. Matt De Voll, Protection One's vice-president of marketing, explained the company's expansion strategy in *Enterprise:* ''Our strategy has been to expand continuously . . . and the Utah market, obviously being a high growth market—very family oriented with a lot of homeowners—is a very appealing market for us.''

National and International Expansion in the Late 1990s

Protection One, which had built up its business to become the largest provider of security alarm systems on the West Coast, went nationwide in November 1997 when it acquired the home security businesses of WestSec, Inc., Westar Security, Inc., and Centennial Security Holdings, Inc., subsidiaries of Kansas-based electric and gas utility company Western Resources, Inc. The deal made Protection One one of the largest security companies in the United States, boosting its subscriber base to about 670,000 customers in 48 states, and gave Western Resources an 82.4 percent stake in Protection One. Western

Key Dates:

1988: PacifiCorp, Inc., establishes Protection One Alarm Services.
1991: PacifiCorp spins off security alarm division as Protection One.
1994: Protection One goes public and is traded on the NASDAQ.
1997: Acquires the security alarm operations of Western Resources, Inc.; Western Resources becomes a majority owner of Protection One.
1998: Protection One expands into Europe and moves to the New York Stock Exchange.

Resources had entered the security industry only a few years earlier and had quickly grown to become the third largest security company in the United States. In 1996 Western Resources purchased Westinghouse Security Systems from Westinghouse Electric Corporation, substantially increasing its number of subscriber accounts. The agreement with Protection One, then the seventh largest U.S. provider of home security services, was part of Western Resources' diversification strategy.

According to Morgan Stanley Dean Witter & Co., the U.S. security alarm industry grew five percent in 1997 to become a $14 billion market. The industry also showed tremendous growth potential, as only about 11 percent of U.S. households subscribed to security alarm services. Analysts believed the industry could grow to about 50 percent of households. Protection One and its new majority shareholder, Western Resources, hoped to take full advantage of the industry possibilities and continued to pursue acquisitions aggressively. At the beginning of 1998 Protection One purchased Network Multifamily Security Corporation for about $180 million. The alarm company had a subscriber base of about 200,000 customers and provided alarm monitoring services to apartment complexes and other multifamily residences. Protection One then acquired the tenth largest monitored alarm company in the United States, Multimedia Security Services, Inc., from Gannett Co., Inc., for about $220 million in March. Multimedia served about 140,000 subscribers in such states as California, Florida, Kansas, Oklahoma, and Texas. Also in March, Protection One acquired Comsec Narragansett Security, Inc. and its 30,000 customers for $65 million.

In May Protection One made its first overseas investment when it acquired Hambro Countrywide Security, one of the largest security companies in the United Kingdom, for about $18 million. The company also moved into Canada when it purchased Rogers CanGuard, Inc., a subsidiary of Rogers Cablesystems Limited, in June. Rogers was the fifth largest security services provider in Canada and served about 38,000 subscribers. Protection One made another move in Europe through the acquisition of a 65.6 percent stake in Compagnie Européenne de Télésecurité (CET), a French security alarm business. CET had offices in Germany, Switzerland, Belgium, and The Netherlands in addition to offices in France. CET's subscriber base of about 60,000 customers securely pushed Protection One's subscriber numbers to more than 1.4 million.

Protection One made a move from the NASDAQ to the New York Stock Exchange in November 1998. The company experienced its first profitable quarter since incorporating during the third quarter that ended September 30, 1998, earning $2.8 million on sales of $103.3 million. For the same quarter of 1997 the company reported a loss of $6.8 million on revenue of $32.8 million. For the fiscal year ended December 31, 1998, Protection One reported sales of $421.1 million and $10.4 million of net income, up from $144.77 million and a loss of $49.3 million in 1997.

Protection One's financial situation may have appeared more stable and promising, but 1999 was not to be a good year. In October 1998 the company announced plans to purchase Lifeline Systems, Inc. for $174 million. Lifeline provided emergency response and personal security monitoring services in the United States, and the acquisition would have expanded Protection One's roster of services. The deal was put on hold, however, as the Securities and Exchange Commission (SEC) began to question Protection One's accounting and amortization methods. Protection One agreed to restate its financial results for 1997 and the first three quarters of 1998. As a result, Protection One's previously reported $10.4 million of net income in 1998 was revised to a loss of $2.46 million, and the previous year's net loss of $49.3 million was revised to $42.73 million. The SEC investigation sparked several lawsuits against Protection One, and many industry analysts began to question whether the company's aggressive acquisition and expansion strategy had not created a burden of debt too immense to overcome. In mid-August the company's stock plummeted to a 52-week low of $3.38.

In addition to financial problems, Protection One faced challenges on its service front. Customer attrition began to rise as service glitches frustrated subscribers. By November 1999 Protection One's annualized attrition rate had shot up to 16 percent. The company explained that the service problems, which included long response times and false alarms, were due to upgrading and consolidation efforts in the company's call centers. To improve service, Protection One hired 150 customer service representatives in the second quarter of 1999 and focused efforts on improving training.

Despite struggles and challenges, Protection One fought to survive. CEO Mackenzie resigned in March and was replaced by John Mack. Western Resources, concerned over Protection One's poor performance, placed some of its officers in Protection One's management in hopes of a turnaround. Annette M. Beck, a senior officer with Western Resources, was appointed president and chief operating officer of Protection One in July, and Tony Somma, a Western Resources executive director of finance, became Protection One's chief financial officer.

In August Protection One sold its Mobile Services Group to ATX Technologies, Inc. for about $28 million. Protection One continued to provide security tracking systems for ATX through a reseller arrangement. ATX and Protection One provided mobile services and systems to such automobile companies as Mercedes-Benz North America, Ford Motor Company, and Nissan Motor Company. In September Protection One signed an agreement with Paradigm Direct LLC, a direct marketing company, to acquire new security accounts. Protection One hoped to gain 50,000 new accounts in the first year. Western Resources owned a 40 percent share of Paradigm Direct.

Western Resources and Protection One announced in October 1999 that financial alternatives for Protection One were being explored. These alternatives included the possibility that Protection One would be sold. Western Resources indicated in a prepared statement, ''Western Resources believes it's important to address ways to eliminate the negative effect of Protection One's losses on Western Resources' income statement.'' For the nine months ended September 30, 1999, reported revenues were about $175.4 million, a 63.3 percent increase over the comparable period of 1998. Net income of $2.34 million, however, became a net loss of $53.45 million.

Although Protection One's future seemed uncertain, the company planned to carry on, focusing on improving customer service and reducing attrition rather than growing its subscriber accounts. By late 1999 Protection One was the second largest home security company in the United States, serving more than 1.5 million subscribers through its network of 57 North American service branches, 11 satellite offices, and 51 European service branches. With rapidly expanding European operations and a U.S. security alarm market growing up to 15 percent annually, demand for services offered by Protection One was one thing that appeared definite.

Principal Subsidiaries

Protection One Alarm Monitoring, Inc.; Network Multifamily Security, Inc.; Protection One Continental Europe; Protection One United Kingdom.

Principal Competitors

Pittston Brink's Group; SBC Communications Inc.; Honeywell International Inc.; Tyco International Ltd.

Further Reading

Cohn, Lisa, ''All Things to All People,'' *Oregon Business,* April 1, 1988, p. 19.

Holden, Benjamin A., ''Western Resources, Protection One Plan Merger Deal,'' *Wall Street Journal,* July 31, 1997, p. B15.

''Investors Feel Secure with Protection One,'' *Going Public,* July 25, 1994.

Jones, Lara, ''PacifiCorp Inks Marketing Pact with Alarm Systems Firm,'' *Enterprise,* October 14, 1996, p. 1.

Kranhold, Kathryn, ''Western Resources to Restate Earnings for 1998 Due to Unit Accounting Glitch,'' *Wall Street Journal,* April 2, 1999, p. A4.

Leeds, Jeff, ''Protection One Is Hit by Fear Over Debt, SEC Probe Markets: Its Shares Touch 52-Week Low,'' *Los Angeles Times,* August 19, 1999, p. C1.

Mayes, Steve, ''Portland Security Company Bought Up,'' *Portland Oregonian,* December 19, 1996, p. D1.

''Spending on Private Security Climbs Steadily,'' *Portland Oregonian,* January 9, 1994, p. 4.

Vrana, Debora, ''California Dealin' Protection One Is No. 2 Through Acquisitions,'' *Los Angeles Times,* January 11, 1999, p. C1.

''Western Resources and Protection One to Form Second Biggest Security Firm,'' *Electric Utility Week,* August 4, 1997, p. 1.

—Mariko Fujinaka

Purina Mills, Inc.

1401 S. Hanley Road
St. Louis, Missouri 63144
U.S.A.
Telephone: (314) 768-4100
Fax: (314) 768-4636
Web site: http://www.purina-mills.com

Wholly Owned Subsidiary of Koch Industries, Inc.
Incorporated: 1894 as Robinson-Danforth Commission Company
Employees: 2,700
Sales: $998.7 million (1998)
NAIC: 311119 Other Animal Food Manufacturing; 444220 Feed Stores (Except Pet)

Purina Mills, Inc. is the largest manufacturer of animal feed products in the United States, producing more than five million tons of feed each year. Through its 50 feed mills, the company produces thousands of feed formulations specially designed for various types of animals, including beef and dairy cattle, goats, horses, sheep, pigs, poultry, pets, and lab and zoo animals. Purina also operates more than 35 retail outlets, which sell animal feed, lawn and garden supplies, hardware, and related items.

1890s–1910s: William Danforth and the Checkerboard Empire

Purina Mills' forerunner, the Robinson-Danforth Commission Company, was formed in 1894 by George Robinson, Will Andrews, and William Danforth. The three founders were looking for a business that could thrive despite the depressed economy when, after some debate, they decided upon the manufacture of horse and mule feed. Their reasoning was that animals had to eat, come good times or bad. With $12,000 in borrowed capital, they started their new business in a storefront near the St. Louis riverfront. Their feed product—a combination of corn, oats, and molasses—was mixed by shovels and poured into 175-pound sacks, which were then sewn shut by hand.

Just two years after Robinson-Danforth Commission got underway, it suffered a major setback. In May 1896, a tornado destroyed the company's milling facility. William Danforth saved the struggling business by borrowing $10,000 to build a new mill. Until that time, Danforth's position in the business had been that of bookkeeper and salesperson. Upon building the new mill, however, he effectively became the company's leader. Soon, he would carve a niche in history for himself and his company as one of the United States' most colorful business successes.

Danforth was a man of strong personal convictions. Believing that the ''ingredients'' of life were body, mind, personality, and character, he strove to balance all four in his own life and to help his employees do the same. A zealot about healthy living, he boasted that he had never missed a day of work due to illness. It was, in part, Danforth's interest in health that helped him succeed in diversifying from animal feed into consumer goods.

In 1898, while traveling in Kansas, Danforth met a miller who had developed a way to prevent rancidity in whole wheat. Packaging the miller's wheat, Danforth named it ''Purina Whole Wheat Cereal,'' and began selling it to St. Louis grocers. The name Purina was derived from Robinson-Danforth's company slogan: ''Where purity is paramount.'' To promote his new cereal, Danforth approached one of the most famous health spokespersons of the day, a Dr. Ralston. Ralston, whose precepts were followed by thousands, agreed to endorse the cereal only if it were named after him. Danforth quickly renamed the product ''Ralston Wheat Cereal,'' and the campaign began. By 1902, there was a whole line of Ralston cereals boasting various health benefits. The names Purina and Ralston had, by that time, become so well known that Danforth changed the company's name to Ralston Purina Company.

Also in 1902, Danforth created a marketing gimmick that was to serve the company well for its many years of business. Looking for a way to set Purina products apart from competitors' and make them easy to spot, Danforth remembered a family he had known from his childhood in Charleston, Missouri. The family, who visited Danforth's father's general store each Saturday, always wore clothing made from a red-and-white checkerboard-patterned cloth. Danforth decided to try

Company Perspectives:

The corporate philosophy of Purina Mills is to continue our tradition of providing both the necessary nutritional products and the value-added services that producers, processors and retailers need to satisfy the demands of a growing end-consumer market. We remain committed to expanding our research and development to enable American agricultural entrepreneurs to capitalize on the opportunities ahead.

using the distinctive checkerboard pattern on his product packaging. The ploy was highly successful—and the checkerboard eventually came to play a very important role in Purina's corporate culture. Danforth took to wearing checkerboard ties, shirts, and coats. He established a "Checker Gallery," containing pictures of his employees wearing checkered clothing, and designated an annual Checker Day. The company's headquarters even became known as Checkerboard Square.

Another of Danforth's marketing techniques emerged from his stint as YMCA secretary for the Third Army Division during World War I. While serving in France, the savvy Danforth noticed that solders' rations were often called "chow." He also noticed that soldiers responded positively to the term, seeming to warm more to the idea of "chow" than to "food." When he returned from the war, Danforth substituted the word "chow" for "feed" on all of Purina's animal products. He also created the company's Chow Division, which was later to become subsidiary Purina Mills.

Soon after the war, Purina introduced another innovation to the animal feed business when it began compressing its feed products into small pellets. Soon, the entire U.S. feed industry followed suit, and began producing pellet-style feed products.

Second Generation of Danforth Leadership: 1920s–60s

In the early 1920s, Danforth's son Donald joined Purina and began convincing his father that the company needed to build a research facility. Eventually, the elder Danforth conceded, and the company established a research center near Gray Summit, Missouri. Also in the 20s, Purina began making a commercial pet food, which was primarily used for hunting dogs and working farm dogs.

With the advent of the Depression in the early 1930s, Ralston Purina saw its sales drop from $60 million to $19 million in two years' time. The company posted losses of $500,000 and $168,800 in 1931 and 1932, respectively. In 1932, William Danforth retired, turning the business over to Donald. The younger Danforth successfully navigated the company through the difficulties, adding six new mills to establish a decentralized production and distribution network.

Under Donald Danforth's leadership, Ralston Purina also developed and began producing a new commercial pet food to be distributed through grocery outlets. The product, Purina Dog Chow, went into national distribution in 1957 and immediately proved a huge success. Dog Chow captured 14.8 percent of the dog food market by the end of 1957, and became the market leader in August 1958. Purina's highly successful launch of its Dog Chow—and later of its Cat Chow—served to strengthen the company's foothold in the grocery products industry.

Donald Danforth retired in 1963, after piloting Purina for slightly more than 30 years. He was replaced as chairman of the board and CEO by Raymond E. Rowland. Rowland had been with Purina since 1926, when he started his career there as a sales trainee. Rowland was nearing 60 when he became Purina's leader, however, and as such, his tenure was comparatively short. He retired in December 1967, and was replaced by R. Hal Dean, a Purina veteran of almost 30 years.

New Direction for Ralston Purina, New Ownership for Purina Mills: 1970s–80s

Ralston Purina took a markedly different direction after Dean assumed control, with diversification being the predominant theme. Having already purchased the Van Camp seafood line while Rowland was still in charge, Purina in 1968 hastily began acquiring new businesses in what often seemed to be a random manner. Among the company's acquisitions were a business that prepared and supplied food for a chain of fast-food restaurants; a ski resort; mushroom farms; a business that raised rats for laboratory experiments; and the St. Louis Blues National Hockey League franchise, along with its arena.

By 1981, when Dean retired, Ralston Purina was a hodgepodge of unrelated companies, with some doing well and some doing very poorly. It fell to Dean's successor, William Stiritz, to clean up the company and tighten its focus. He did so by selling off several subsidiaries, including the restaurant operations company, the hockey franchise, and the Van Camp seafood line. With these subsidiaries out of the way, the company could better focus on what was to be its core business: consumer packaged goods.

Another branch of Ralston Purina that Stiritz decided to prune was Purina Mills—the animal feed business, which had been the basis of the company's inception. In 1986, Purina Mills was sold to London-based conglomerate British Petroleum PLC for $545 million. The sale did not include the pet food lines, which were kept by Ralston Purina. Both Ralston and Purina Mills continued to use the checkerboard trademark in the United States, but Purina Mills was prohibited from using the Purina brand and trademark in foreign markets.

Purina Mills joined British Petroleum's animal nutrition subsidiary, which was comprised of 120 companies operating in 30 nations. It immediately became the top moneymaker for BP Nutrition, generating about one-third of the subsidiary's sales and approximately 45 percent of its profits. British Petroleum stepped up investment in Purina's research, manufacturing, and quality, and began to export its feeds to Canada, Mexico, Asia, and the Caribbean under the trade name PMI Feeds.

Changing Hands Again . . . and Again: 1990s

In 1992, British Petroleum began a period of restructuring, during which it decided to exit its nutrition business and refocus its energies on its core petroleum business. In March 1993, the

Key Dates:

1894: The Robinson-Danforth Commission Company is founded.
1902: Company name is changed to Ralston Purina Company. Company adopts the red-and-white checkerboard logo.
1986: Ralston Purina sells its Purina Mills subsidiary to British Petroleum.
1993: British Petroleum sells Purina Mills to a management group led by the Sterling Group, of Houston, Texas.
1997: Purina Mills rolls out America's Country Store retail chain, begins buying and reselling hogs in an effort to bolster swine feed sales.
1998: Koch Industries acquires Purina Mills.
1999: Purina Mills files for Chapter 11 bankruptcy reorganization.

company put its entire BP Nutrition subsidiary on the block, including Purina Mills. After exploring several options—including selling Purina to another feed company and spinning off the business in a public offering—BP agreed to sell the business to a group that included an outside investment firm, Purina managers, and an employee stock ownership plan. The $425 million buyout, led by The Sterling Group, a Houston-based private investment firm, was highly leveraged and left Purina with $358.5 million in debt. But when the deal was finalized in September 1993, Purina Mills was, for the first time in its history, a stand-alone company with no large parent corporation.

In the mid-1990s, Purina was faced with major changes in the feed industry. Both the feed and livestock industries were beginning to consolidate, with smaller operations being absorbed or driven out of business by larger, more powerful ones. Consolidation was especially noticeable in the pork industry, where the trend toward mammoth farming operations was steadily driving smaller farms out of business. More significant for Purina Mills, however, was the fact that many of the large pork producers had begun to build vertically integrated operations, through which they controlled every phase of the farm-to-market cycle—from feed production to processing—with minimal reliance on outside parties. These trends toward integration and consolidation had the potential to seriously damage Purina Mills' business.

In response to the industry's "bigger-is-better" movement, Purina pursued some consolidation of its own. In January 1995, the company acquired one of its rival feed producers, Golden Sun Feeds Inc., of Estherville, Iowa. Golden Sun, which had six mills, produced approximately 335,000 tons of feed annually. A few months later, Purina made another acquisition: the Test Diet business of U.S. Biochemical Inc. The newly acquired business produced animal feeds that were developed to the specifications of scientists, to be used in research. By integrating the Test Diet business with its existing Specialty Products business, Purina was able to position itself as a bigger player in the research and test diet segment of the feed industry.

In 1997, the company branched out in an entirely new direction, introducing its own chain of retail stores. The stores, called America's Country Stores, offered "country lifestyle" merchandise, including lawn and garden products, animal feed, hardware, and, in some cases, housewares. The concept was designed to appeal to hobby farmers and "ruralpolitan" homeowners—individuals living in previously rural areas that had since become outer suburbs. The Country Stores were owned and operated by independent retailers, with Purina providing products, site selection, market research, and store design. By the end of 1998, the company had opened almost 20 of the stores in various locations through the West and Midwest, and in the Carolinas. It planned to open as many as 600 by the year 2000.

Another of Purina Mills' 1997 initiatives was designed to prop up its sales of swine feed, which had declined dramatically. Deciding to become more directly involved in the pork industry and thereby establish a captive market, the company began contracting to buy baby pigs from breeders. It then resold the pigs to independent hog producers who, in turn, agreed to buy Purina feed.

The end of 1997 brought yet another change in ownership for Purina Mills. In December, the company agreed to be purchased by Koch Industries Inc. Koch, the United States' second largest private company, was an energy and agricultural firm with some $30 billion in annual revenues. Koch believed that Purina would be a good fit for its farm-related businesses, which included cattle feedlots and an experimental drying technology that could convert food waste into an inexpensive feed ingredient. Koch finalized the Purina acquisition in March 1998, for a price of $660 million. Approximately $110 million of the purchase price was financed with equity, $200 million came from bank loans, and $350 million came from public bonds that refinanced the debt from the Sterling buyout.

Bankruptcy: 1999

Purina's 1997 decision to enter the hog business was to prove disastrous in late 1998 and 1999. The hog market, which had been excellent in the mid-1990s, reversed dramatically a few years later when a surfeit of hogs tipped the supply-and-demand balance. Prices dropped to their lowest level in 26 years, and farmers lost money on every hog they sent to market.

Purina was hurt by the market reversal on several fronts. As hog farming ceased to be profitable, many farmers either quit or were forced out of the business. This led to a decrease in swine feed sales—which accounted for 20 percent of Purina's total sales. Far more significant, however, was the loss Purina took on its own hog operation. Not only did the company lose money on the hogs it already owned, but it was under contract to buy 9.8 million more pigs over an eight-year period. It had contracts to sell only 3.4 million. The financial exposure on the contracts amounted to approximately $236 million.

In September 1999, Purina was unable to make a $16 million interest payment on its public debt. Koch, which had not guaranteed the debt, failed to come to the rescue, and in October, Purina filed for Chapter 11 bankruptcy. In early November, the company announced that it had filed a preliminary draft of its plan for reorganization and anticipated emerging from bankruptcy in the early part of 2000. After reorganization, the company was again to be a stand-alone entity, independent of Koch.

Principal Subsidiaries

Carolina Agri-Products Inc.; Coastal Ag-Development Inc.; Cole Grain Co. Inc.; Dairy Management Services LLP; Golden Sun Feeds, Inc.; PM Holding Corp.; PM Nutrition Co. Inc.; PMI Agriculture L.L.C.; PMI Nutrition Inc.; Purina Nutrition International Inc.; Purina Livestock Management Services Inc.

Principal Competitors

Archer Daniels Midland Company; Ag Processing Inc.; Agway Inc.; Bartlett & Company; Cargill, Incorporated; Colgate-Palmolive Company; ConAgra, Inc.; ContiGroup Companies, Inc.; Hartz Group Inc.; The Iams Company; Mars, Inc.

Further Reading

''A Checkered Past,'' *St. Louis Post-Dispatch*, September 25, 1994.

Copple, Brandon, ''Checkered Future,'' *Forbes*, November 1, 1999.

Danforth, William, *I Dare You!*, St. Louis: American Youth Foundation, 1969.

Faust, Fred, ''Purina Mills Its Own Boss Now,'' *St. Louis Post-Dispatch*, September 28, 1993.

Holyoke, Larry, and Desloge, Rick, ''Purina Mills Defaults,'' *St. Louis Business Journal*, Week of November 1, 1999.

Nicklaus, David, ''Debt, Low Hog Prices Pull Purina Down,'' *St. Louis Post-Dispatch*, November 7, 1999.

——, ''Feedmaker Purina Mills Files for Bankruptcy,'' *St. Louis Post-Dispatch,* October 29, 1999.

Stroud, Jerri, ''CEO, Workers Relieved by Purina Mills Buyout,'' *St. Louis Post-Dispatch*, June 27, 1993.

——, ''Purina Mills Goes on Sale Block,'' *St. Louis Post-Dispatch*, March 5, 1993.

——, ''Purina Says Buyout Is Strategic,'' *St. Louis Post-Dispatch*, December 7, 1997.

—Shawna Brynildssen

REXAM

Rexam PLC

114 Knightsbridge
London SWIX 7NN
United Kingdom
Telephone: (0171) 584-7070
Fax: (0171) 581-1149
Web site: http://www.rexam.co.uk

Public Company
Incorporated: 1910 as W.V. Bowater & Sons, Limited
Employees: 22,700
Sales: £1.90 billion (US$3.15 billion) (1998)
Stock Exchanges: London Toronto Montreal NASDAQ
Ticker Symbol: REXMY
NAIC: 322212 Folding Paperboard Box Manufacturing; 322215 Nonfolding Sanitary Food Container Manufacturing; 322221 Coated and Laminated Packaging Paper and Plastics Film Manufacturing; 322222 Coated and Laminated Paper Manufacturing; 322223 Plastics, Foil, and Coated Paper Bag Manufacturing; 325992 Photographic Film, Paper, Plate, and Chemical Manufacturing; 326160 Plastics Bottle Manufacturing; 326199 All Other Plastics Product Manufacturing; 327213 Glass Container Manufacturing; 332431 Metal Can Manufacturing; 333298 All Other Industrial Machinery Manufacturing; 333513 Machine Tool (Metal Forming Types) Manufacturing

Rexam PLC is one of the world's ten largest consumer packaging companies. Its wide-ranging packaging operations are divided into four sectors: healthcare, with such products as sterilized medical packaging, pharmaceutical cartons, including child-resistant and tamper-evident containers, and blister packaging; beauty, with fragrance sprays, skin-care pumps, lipstick cases, cosmetics compacts, and samplers; specialty foods, with thin-wall plastic containers and trays, flexible packaging solutions, and carton systems for such liquids as milk and juice; and beverages, with metal cans and plastic bottles for beverages and glass bottles and containers for beverages, food, and healthcare products. Approximately 70 percent of company revenues are generated from consumer packaging operations. Another 20 percent of revenues stem from Rexam's coated films and papers sector, which offers coating and laminating services and products, including paint film for plastic automobile body parts; ink jet and electrographic material for imaging systems; release liners used for a wide range of tape, label, and medical applications; and latex saturated paper, which is coated, embossed, and sometimes printed for such applications as book and photo album covers, decorative packaging for jewelry and other consumer products, and security printing (e.g., passports, bank books). The remaining ten percent of revenue derives from the company's building and engineering sector, which is composed of two autonomous businesses, both of which hold the number one global position in their business area: MiTek Inc., supplier of metal connector plates and engineering software for the building industry; and TBS Engineering Limited, maker of specialized machines for assembling lead acid batteries.

Paper Beginnings

William Vansittart Bowater was the firm's founder. As a young man he joined James Wrigley & Sons, a Manchester papermaking firm, where he became a manager. He is reputed to have been ill-tempered, tyrannical, and hard-drinking, traits that eventually led to his dismissal by Wrigley. By 1881, at the age of 43, he was in business on his own in the City of London, the heart of the U.K. newspaper publishing and printing industries, operating as a paper wholesaler and as an agent for the purchase of newsprint on behalf of newspaper publishers. The final decades of the 19th century saw the birth of the popular press in Britain and soaring demand for newsprint. Bowater secured contracts with two of the most dynamic newspaper and magazine tycoons, Alfred Harmsworth, publisher of the *Daily Mail* and the *Daily Mirror,* and Edward Lloyd, publisher of the *Daily Chronicle.* Three of William Bowater's five sons joined him in partnership, and the firm—now renamed W.V. Bowater & Sons—gradually prospered and expanded, although in 1905 the personnel comprised only the four partners, six clerks, two typists, and an office boy.

Key Dates:

1881: William Vansittart Bowater opens business as a paper wholesaler and newsprint purchasing agent.
1910: Company is incorporated as W.V. Bowater & Sons, Limited.
1926: Expansion into paper manufacturing begins with the start-up of the company's first paper mill.
1927: Eric Bowater, grandson of founder, becomes chairman and managing director; firm becomes a public company.
1936: Purchase of two more paper mills gives the company 60 percent of the U.K. newsprint market and makes it the number one newsprint company in Europe.
1938: Company expands into pulp with the purchase of pulp mills in Sweden, Norway, and Canada.
1944: Diversification into paper packaging begins with purchase of Acme Corrugated Cases.
1947: Company is made into a holding company with the new name Bowater Paper Corporation.
1954: Production begins at first U.S. paper mill in Calhoun, Tennessee.
1984: North American newsprint and pulp operations are demerged from the rest of the firm, as Bowater Inc.; U.K. rump changes name to Bowater Industries plc.
1987: North Carolina-based Rexham Corporation, maker of coated and laminated products, is acquired for US$240 million.
1990: Norton Opax PLC, a specialized print and packaging group, is acquired for £382 million; company changes its name to Bowater PLC.
1993: Specialty Coatings International Inc., a U.S. maker of coated products, is bought for £297.7 million.
1995: Company changes its name to Rexam PLC.
1996: Major restructuring is launched.
1999: Swedish beverage packaging firm PLM is acquired for £588 million.

The years immediately before World War I saw important developments in the management of the firm and in the pattern of its activities. The death of the founder in 1907 was followed three years later by Bowater's adoption of limited liability as a private company (named W.V. Bowater & Sons, Limited). This status made it easier to bring the next generation into the business. In 1913 the head of the firm, Sir Thomas Vansittart Bowater, the founder's eldest son, who was knighted in 1906, became lord mayor of London, leaving the running of the family business to his younger brothers. Besides wholesaling and agency activities, during the Edwardian era the company moved into large-scale dealing in wastepaper, including the export of surplus newspapers to the Far East, where they were used for the protection of young tea plants. These years also saw the commencement of the export of newsprint to Australia, leading to the establishment of a U.S. marketing subsidiary, Hudson Packaging & Paper Company, in 1914 and an office in Sydney, Australia, in 1919. These were the first steps in Bowater's development into a multinational corporation.

World War I boosted newspaper sales and demand remained buoyant in the postwar years. Yet Bowater's role as a middleman was increasingly uncomfortable in an industry in which there was more and more integration between newspaper publishers and newsprint manufacturers.

Interwar Period: Europe's Largest Newsprint Manufacturer

Bowater's first step towards becoming a paper manufacturer was the purchase of a site at Northfleet on the south side of the Thames estuary near Gravesend in May 1914. World War I interrupted the firm's plans and it was not until 1923 that the construction of a paper mill could be considered. The contractor was Armstrong, Whitworth & Co. Limited, a major armaments manufacturer which turned to other activities after the end of the war and had recently built a paper mill at Corner Brook in Newfoundland. Bowater too had an interest in the Corner Brook development, since its U.S. marketing subsidiary was sole agent for the sale of Corner Brook's output. There were serious flaws in Armstrong's design of the Northfleet mill, and modifications had to be made during construction. These changes led to large cost overruns and delayed the commencement of full production from July 1925 until almost a year later.

The resolution of the serious problems at Northfleet was the work of Eric Bowater and this achievement was his stepping stone to the leadership of the firm. A grandson of the founder, he entered the firm in 1921. In 1927, at the age of 32, he became chairman and managing director of W.V. Bowater & Sons and was the leading figure in the firm for the following three and a half decades. He dominated Bowater's affairs by sheer force of personality. There was no doubt of his utter dedication to his company's success, yet his austerity and aloofness inspired admiration rather than affection. He behaved as if he owned the firm, although it became a public company in 1927, and relied heavily upon a small circle of close advisers.

Eric Bowater was determined to establish Bowater as a major force in U.K. papermaking as fast as possible. To this end he negotiated the sale of a controlling interest in the firm to the newspaper magnate Lord Rothermere, which reduced the family's shareholding to 40 percent. Rothermere's backing allowed Bowater to raise the finance to double the output of the Northfleet mill in 1928. He looked immediately for further opportunities to expand and a new project was initiated to build a large paper mill on the Mersey, near Liverpool, which was financed jointly by Bowater, Rothermere, and Beaverbrook newspapers. The latter entered a long-term contract to receive supplies of newsprint from the new undertaking. By the end of 1930 the output of Bowater's mills was 175,000 tons of newsprint per year, 22 percent of the U.K.'s total output. In order to achieve this result, it had been necessary to cede control of the business to a pair of press barons. Rothermere's business, however, was badly affected by the slump at the beginning of the 1930s and in 1932, to raise cash, he sold his Bowater shareholding back to Bowater. Beaverbrook followed suit. Eric Bowater thus found himself in absolute control of the firm again, now the U.K.'s largest newsprint producer.

Newspaper circulations rose again in the 1930s and Eric Bowater's response was to double the capacity of the Mersey mills. Even more audacious was his purchase in 1936 of paper mills at Sittingbourne and Kemsley from Edward Lloyd Ltd., which doubled the firm's output of newsprint to around 500,000 tons per annum. In little more than a decade since the start of manufacturing, Bowater was producing 60 percent of British newsprint and had become the largest newsprint undertaking in Europe.

The expansion of Bowater's activities enabled the firm to take advantage of economies of scale, and it was a highly efficient and competitive producer. Nevertheless, it occupied a strategically vulnerable position between the producers of pulp, its raw material, and the consumers of paper, its finished product. In 1937 profits were squeezed hard by a large and unforeseen rise in pulp prices engineered by a cartel of Scandinavian producers. This was a chastening experience for Eric Bowater, who resolved to prevent its repetition by securing the firm's own pulp supplies. Bowater immediately acquired interests in Swedish and Norwegian pulp mills and in 1938 it purchased the massive mill at Corner Brook, Newfoundland's most important industrial undertaking with newsprint capacity of 200,000 tons per year and resources of 7,000 square miles of timberland. These moves were described by Eric Bowater as a ''raw material insurance policy.'' Thus by the eve of World War II Bowater was a multinational manufacturer producing 800,000 tons of newsprint annually and a host of other products for an international clientele.

1939–62: Expanding on Both Sides of the Atlantic

Wartime controls to divert resources to the war effort had a devastating impact on Bowater's U.K. newsprint production, which fell to a fifth of the prewar level. The Northfleet mill closed down completely, ''a heart-breaking sight,'' as the chairman commented. Bowater himself was diverted from the firm's affairs from 1940 to 1945 by work for the Ministry of Aircraft Production, for which he was knighted in 1944. Since a rapid revival of demand for newsprint appeared unlikely, Sir Eric Bowater adopted a policy of diversification into paper packaging. This diversification began with the purchase of Acme Corrugated Cases in 1944, and in 1947, these interests were organized into a wholly owned subsidiary, Associated Bowater Industries. The war had much less impact upon Bowater's North American operations, since U.S. demand for newsprint experienced only a brief downturn before resuming a vigorous advance. From 1944 to 1950 U.S. consumption almost doubled. During the downturn, Bowater adopted a policy of accepting losses on contracts with U.S. newspapers in order to maintain its client base. The firm was soon rewarded, and in 1946 it was necessary to add a further 75,000 tons capacity at Corner Brook to meet the order-book. The end of the war was a fitting time for a major reorganization of the firm that had developed piecemeal during the previous two decades. In 1947 a streamlined structure was instituted, in which a number of wholly owned operating companies reported to a holding company which was given a new name, the Bowater Paper Corporation.

For Sir Eric Bowater the formation of the Bowater Paper Corporation marked a new point of departure. Over the ensuing decade and a half he worked tirelessly to build up the business on both sides of the Atlantic. In the United Kingdom, the strategy of diversification away from newsprint continued through the late 1940s and early 1950s with further acquisitions of paper products firms. In North America, by contrast, the relentless rise in U.S. demand for newsprint led to the construction of a paper mill at Calhoun, Tennessee, marking the firm's debut as a producer in the United States. The choice of location was determined not only by the availability of timber but also by its proximity to a group of Southern newspapers with which the firm had strong and longstanding connections. Financing the simultaneous expansions in the United Kingdom and the United States almost proved too much, but once again Bowater's personality saved the day: ''The crowning glory of my business life,'' remarked Bowater when production began at Calhoun in October 1954. Six months later, it was producing 145,000 tons of newsprint yearly.

By the mid-1950s Bowater was the largest producer of newsprint in the world, a position Bowater had no intention of relinquishing. Eric Bowater's strategy to ensure Bowater's continued preeminence was further expansion. A plan made in 1956 envisaged a 60 percent increase in the company's North American newsprint production to 840,000 tons per annum and a 40 percent expansion in the United Kingdom to 860,000 tons. To accomplish this increase, Bowater acquired the Mersey Paper Co. of Liverpool, Nova Scotia, which added a further 140,000 tons of newsprint output and doubled capacity at Calhoun. In the United Kingdom, the end of government paper control in 1956 inspired a resurgence of optimism regarding demand for newsprint, and further capacity was added at Kemsley and on Merseyside. As in the 1930s, self-sufficiency in raw materials was considered to be essential, leading to the opening of a new pulp mill at Catawba, South Carolina, in 1959. Self-sufficiency had previously been taken a step further by the formation of the firm's own shipping fleet in 1954. Diversification continued to be an objective in the United Kingdom, leading to expansion of the building products and packaging activities and most importantly to entry into the rapidly growing tissue market through the acquisition of the St. Andrews tissue mill in 1955 and the formation in 1956 of the Bowater-Scott Corporation, a company jointly owned with the market leader in tissue technology, the Scott Paper Company of Philadelphia. Continental Europe was believed to offer tremendous growth potential and the late 1950s saw the establishment of a Bowater presence in Belgium, Switzerland, and Italy. The firm also became the largest newsprint maker in France, with the acquisition of the Les Papeteries de la Chapelle works with a capacity of 180,000 tons. The latter merged with Les Papeteries Darblay in 1968 to become Les Papeteries de la Chapelle-Darblay. In 1959 Bowater entered a joint venture to produce pulp and newsprint in New Zealand to supply the Australian market. This extensive expansion program required substantial funding and Bowater's borrowings increased greatly.

By the beginning of the 1960s it was plain that Bowater's strategy was flawed. Other competitors had made substantial investments in newsprint capacity and from 1957 the market was oversupplied, causing prices to weaken and profits to disappear, a very serious matter for the world's largest producer of newsprint. In U.K. packaging the story was much the same. Although the expansion program was curtailed, the firm was already heavily burdened with debt and the advance into Europe continued to absorb capital. Matters were made worse by production problems at the new Catawba pulp mill and by the move to prestigious new headquarters in London's Knightsbridge in 1958, which doubled per capita office costs. The death of Sir Eric Bowater in August 1962 in the midst of the financial crisis marked the end of an era in the history of Bowater.

1962–84: Retrenchment and Diversification

Retrenchment was a hallmark of Bowater's strategy in the decade 1962–72. Between 1962 and 1969 the firm was led by Sir Christopher Chancellor, who made his reputation with Reuters and had previously been chairman of Odhams Press, and starting in 1969 by Martin Ritchie, who had joined the firm in 1956 when his family packaging business was acquired by Bowater. Overcapacity in U.K. newsprint was tackled by the conversion of machines to other types of papermaking, and eventually by closures, including Northfleet in 1973. Calhoun continued to be profitable in the 1960s. The problems at Catawba were solved. Corner Brook operations became unprofitable and capacity was cut. Overall, the reduction in capacity in the United Kingdom and North America by 1972 totaled 300,000 tons. In Europe, where the business had never lived up to Bowater's expectations, there was wholesale retreat, culminating in the sale of the loss-making French company—Les Papeteries de la Chapelle-Darblay–in 1971. Diversification away from newsprint was the other side of the strategy, with successful expansion in areas of activity such as building products in the United Kingdom, and tissue production in both the United Kingdom and Australia.

Diversification on a dramatic scale was achieved in 1972 with the purchase of Ralli International, a commodity trading company whose sales were roughly equal to those of Bowater. Although the acquisition of Ralli fitted Bowater's longstanding strategy of diversification, it was not a move initiated by the firm. It was proposed by the investment bank Slater Walker, which had close connections with Ralli, and Bowater's assent was an opportunistic move to frustrate a hostile bid for the firm launched by Trafalgar House. Lord Eroll, a former Conservative minister, became chairman of the enlarged group in 1972. During the 1970s Bowater made further moves away from newsprint production in the United Kingdom, culminating in the closure of the last machine dedicated wholly to newsprint manufacture in 1982. The same year saw an output reduction of 130,000 tons in North America. The expansion of packaging, tissue products, and building products operations continued and there were some notable acquisitions in Germany. The firm also operated as a commodity trader on a large scale, in 1978 acquiring Gibbs Nathaniel, an importer of dried fruit, edible nuts, and other foodstuffs. There was little synergy between the two sides of the business and in 1981 the diversification of 1972 was reversed by the sale of Ralli.

1984–95: Focusing on Core Areas

The strategy of the mid-1980s to the mid-1990s—under a succession of three chairman: Aylmer Lenton, 1984–87, Norman Ireland, 1987–93, and Michael Woodhouse, 1993–96—was to focus upon activities in which the firm enjoyed managerial expertise and excellence. The strategy was taken to its logical conclusion in 1984 when the North American newsprint and pulp operations were demerged from the rest of the firm, as Bowater Inc. Bowater Industries plc, as the U.K.-based firm was known after the demerger, became a business with five functionally organized operating groups: packaging and industrial products, builders' merchants group, building products group, freight services group, and Australian group. In the United Kingdom, the manufacture of packaging was the leading activity, as it became in the United States following the 1987 acquisition of the Rexham Corporation of North Carolina, specializing in coated and laminated products, for US$240 million (£136 million). This acquisition provided a new base for the development of the firm's North American activities. The building products activities were mostly in the United Kingdom and Europe, though again a U.S. presence in this sector was secured in 1987 through the acquisition of an interest in St. Louis, Missouri-based MiTek, supplier of metal connector plates and engineering software for the building industry. Tissue manufacturing was the firm's foremost activity in Australia following the acquisition of Scott's 50 percent interest in Bowater-Scott of Australia in 1986, in return for the sale of Bowater's interest in Bowater-Scott's U.K. firm to Scott. Further consideration of Bowater's strategic direction led in 1989 to the disposal of the freight group and in 1990 to the £382 million takeover of Norton Opax PLC, whose strengths lay in the complementary fields of printing and publishing. The creation of the combined entity was marked by a new name—Bowater PLC.

Bowater positioned itself in the early 1990s as a maker of products either fiber-based or resin-based. It organized its operations into four main clusters: packaging for medical and pharmaceutical products, packaging for toiletries and cosmetics markets, packaging for food and beverage markets, and coated products mainly for industrial markets. The company also maintained additional businesses in industrial packaging, security and special printing, building products, tissue, and engineering. This more tightly organized structure resulted from a number of significant acquisitions as well as additional divestments. In 1992 Bowater acquired DRG Packaging, a maker of food and healthcare packaging, for £216 million; and Cope Allman Packaging, a supplier of cosmetics and pharmaceutical packaging, for £235 million. During 1993 a total of £403 million was spent on acquisitions, the most noteworthy of which were: Specialty Coatings International Inc., a U.S. maker of coated products bought for £297.7 million; Tower Packaging, a U.S. maker of medical packaging bought from Baxter Healthcare Corporation for US$105 million; and the remaining stake in MiTek not already owned by Bowater. In late 1994 Bowater strengthened its cosmetics packaging operations through the £66 million acquisition of France-based SOFAB SA, a maker of pumps and valves used to dispense fragrances and cosmetics, as well as pharmaceuticals. Then in early 1995 the company completed its gradual exit from the paper industry through the sale of its Australian tissue operations to Carter Holt Harvey of New Zealand for A$342 million (£158 million).

Through its numerous acquisitions and disposals during this period, Bowater not only refocused its operations on a more manageable number of core areas but also improved its overall financial performance. The company's operating margin stood at 4.7 percent in 1986 but increased to 10.1 percent by 1994. During the same span, group revenues increased from £1.37 billion to £2.21 billion. Also by 1994 the acquisition of

Rexham, among other developments, had once again gained the company a significant presence in North America, with that continent accounting for 41 percent of group profits. Bowater, however, had given up the right to use its corporate name in North and South America as part of the 1984 demerger of Bowater Inc. This led to increasing confusion, and to the company's decision to change its name. In May 1995, then, Bowater PLC became Rexam PLC, a moniker concocted, according to the *Financial Times,* ''when chief executive Mr. David Lyon removed the 'h' from Rexham while doodling on a note pad.'' (Unbeknownst to Lyon, the Rexham name itself had a similar origin, having been created by the removal of the ''w'' from Wrexham, a town in Wales where one of that firm's factories had been located.)

Late 1990s: Major Restructuring

In mid-1996 Woodhouse and Lyon both retired from their positions. Stepping in as chairman was Jeremy Lancaster, who had been the longtime chairman of the Wolseley building products group, while Rolf Börjesson was named chief executive, having previously served for eight years as chief executive of PLM AB, a beverage packaging company based in Sweden. The new management team took over a company reeling from the effects of market forces, most notably volatility in raw material prices in the second half of 1995 and the resultant customer demand during 1996 for less costly packaging designs. Sales in 1996 were subsequently flat and the company's profit margin fell to 7.9 percent. Lancaster and Börjesson responded by reorganizing the company into seven market-focused sectors: food and beverage packaging (renamed specialty food packaging in 1997), industrial packaging, healthcare packaging, beauty packaging, printing, coated films and papers, and building and engineering. In December 1996 a separate subsidiary called Octagon was created that combined about 20 businesses identified as noncore and earmarked for disposal. With these actions, Rexam took a goodwill writeoff of £254 million during 1996, resulting in a net loss for the year of £238 million.

During 1997 Rexam divested 17 of the Octagon businesses as well as an additional three non-Octagon units. The jettisoned operations represented more than ten percent, or about £260 million, of group sales. The pruning continued in 1998 and 1999, with the completion of the Octagon disposal program and the selling off of several other businesses. In February 1999 Rexam sold its corrugated packaging division—an operation that comprised the bulk of the company's industrial packaging sector—to SCA Packaging International BV for £195 million. Rexam began selling off its printing division in 1999 and in October sold its last windows manufacturing operation, Bowater Windows Limited, to a management-led buyout team for £122.5 million. The last of these sales left Rexam's building and engineering sector with just two operations: MiTek and TBS Engineering.

In the midst of this major effort to ''clear the decks,'' in the words of Börjesson, Rexam began shopping for acquisitions to bolster its core packaging operations. The company's largest purchase of the late 1990s came in late 1998 and early 1999 when it purchased PLM—Börjesson's former employer—in two stages for a total of £588 million. PLM was the number four European maker of beverage packaging—including cans, plastic containers, and glass bottles—and its acquisition propelled Rexam into the number ten position among the world's consumer packaging companies. It also provided Rexam with a much enlarged presence within Continental Europe, from which only about 12 percent of revenues were derived in 1998. PLM formed the core of a newly created beverage packaging sector. With the eventual completion of the disposal of Rexam's printing sector, the company would enter the 21st century with six main sectors, four of which were in consumer packaging—healthcare, beauty, specialty food, and beverage—with the others being coated films and papers and a much reduced building and engineering unit. With its days as a conglomerate almost in the history books, Rexam appeared positioned for a new period of profitable growth and had about £1 billion available for additional acquisitions.

Principal Subsidiaries

MiTek Inc. (U.S.A.); Rexam France SA; Rexam Holdings Pty Limited (Australia); Rexam Inc. (U.S.A.); Rexam Overseas Holdings Limited; Rexam Packaging Limited; Rexam Printing Limited; Rexam UK Holdings Limited; TBS Engineering Limited.

Principal Operating Units

Coated Films and Papers Sector; Beauty Packaging Sector; Healthcare Packaging Sector; Beverage Packaging Sector; Specialty Food Packaging Sector; Building and Engineering Sector.

Principal Competitors

Alcoa Inc.; AptarGroup, Inc.; AssiDomän AB; Autobar Group Ltd.; Ball Corporation; Bemis Company, Inc.; Coster Technologie Speciali S.p.A.; Crown Cork & Seal Company, Inc.; Danisco A/S; E.I. du Pont de Nemours and Company; Elopak; Groupe Danone; Groupe Qualipac; Hitachi, Ltd.; Huhtamaki Van Leer Oyj; International Paper Company; Klöckner & Co. AG; Minnesota Mining and Manufacturing Company; Oce N.V.; Owens-Illinois, Inc.; Pactiv Corporation; Pechiney S.A.; Risdon-AMS Corp.; RPC Group PLC; Compagnie de Saint-Gobain; Schmalbach-Lubeca AG; Sihl GmbH; Techpack International; Tetra Laval International S.A.; Tetra Pak; Toyo Seikan Kaisha, Ltd.; VIAG AG; Yoshino.

Further Reading

Buckley, Neil, ''Bowater's Supermodel Image: The Bottom Line,'' *Financial Times,* September 10, 1994.

Burt, Tim, ''Rexam to Accelerate Disposal Programme,'' *Financial Times,* December 4, 1998, p. 24.

Harverson, Patrick, ''Bowater Renamed Rexam to End Confusion in U.S.,'' *Financial Times,* April 25, 1995, p. 22.

——, ''Pragmatist Booked to Reshape Rexam,'' *Financial Times,* January 13, 1996, p. 8.

——, ''Wanted: New Management Team,'' *Financial Times,* January 4, 1996, p. 16.

History and Activities of the Ralli Trading Group, London: Ralli Brothers (Trading) Ltd, 1979.

Hollinger, Peggy, and Terry Hall, ''Bowater to Depart Paper Business with £158m Sale,'' *Financial Times,* November 5, 1994, p. 8.

Marsh, Virginia, "Determined, Restless Swede Driven, Not by Money Alone, but a Yen for Achievement," *Financial Times,* March 28, 1998, p. 20.

——, "Rexam Could Spend £1bn on Purchase," *Financial Times,* September 10, 1999, p. 24.

——, "Rexam Focuses on Packaging As It Exits Windows," *Financial Times,* October 15, 1999, p. 27.

——, "Rexam Has Its Decks Cleared for Action but the Market Has a Bout of Jitters," *Financial Times,* January 7, 1999, p. 28.

——, "Rexam Seeks to Spend Up to £1bn on Acquisitions," *Financial Times,* October 8, 1998, p. 25.

——, "Rexam to Sell Printing and Window Businesses," *Financial Times,* March 12, 1999, p. 24.

Martin, Roscoe C., *From Forest to Front Page,* Birmingham: University of Alabama Press, 1956.

McIvor, Greg, and Jonathan Ford, "Rexam Sells Corrugated Board Unit for £195m," *Financial Times,* December 22, 1998, p. 21.

Muir, Augustus, *The British Paper and Board Makers' Association 1872–1972: A Centenary History,* London, privately printed, 1972.

Reader, W.J., *Bowater: A History,* Cambridge: Cambridge University Press, 1981.

Thornhill, John, "A Timely Move by Sober Management," *Financial Times,* March 3, 1992, p. 25.

—Richard Roberts
—updated by David E. Salamie

Saab Automobile AB

SE-461 80 Trollhätten
Sweden
Telephone: (0520) 850 00
Fax: (0520) 815 38
Web site: http://www.saab.com

50–50 Joint Venture of General Motors Corporation and Investor AB
Incorporated: 1990
Employees: 9,974
Sales: SKr 22.59 billion (US$3.51 billion) (1998)
NAIC: 336111 Automobile Manufacturing; 421110 Automobile and Other Motor Vehicle Wholesalers; 421120 Motor Vehicle Supplies and New Part Wholesalers; 522291 Consumer Lending; 532112 Passenger Cars Leasing

Saab Automobile AB is a Swedish maker of passenger automobiles in the premium sector of the market. The company makes two lines of cars: the 9-3, which comes in two-door, five-door hatchback, and convertible models; and the 9-5, which includes luxury sedan and station wagon models. Considered a small automaker in the globalized auto industry of the late 20th century, Saab produces about 125,000 cars each year, with most built at its factory in Trollhätten, Sweden, where the company is also headquartered. The largest markets for Saab automobiles are the United States, Western Europe, Australia, Japan, Canada, and Taiwan. Saab began as an aircraft manufacturer, then launched automotive production in 1949. Its automobile operations became a division of Saab-Scania AB following the 1969 merger of Saab AB and Scania-Vabis AB, a maker of trucks, buses, and diesel engines. Saab Automobile AB was officially formed in 1990 when General Motors Corporation purchased 50 percent of Saab-Scania's passenger car business. The following year Investor AB gained the other 50 percent interest following Investor's leveraged buyout of Saab-Scania.

From Airplanes to Automobiles: 1937–68

With the threat of another war in Europe building in the 1930s, it became imperative for Sweden to improve its defenses. Not least important was the need for a domestic aircraft industry large enough to supply the Swedish forces with military aircraft. This led to the formation in April 1937 of the Svenska Aeroplan Aktiebolaget, abbreviated SAAB. Two years later, SAAB, with headquarters in Trollhättan, took over the aircraft division of the Aktiebolaget Svenska Jarnvagsverkstaderna, or Swedish Railroad Works, located in Linköping. SAAB subsequently transferred its corporate headquarters and construction and design departments to Linköping.

Construction was accelerated at both the Linköping and Trollhättan plants, which were building aircraft designed by Bristol, Junkers, and Northrop. During this period work proceeded on the first SAAB aircraft, the Svenska B-17 dive bomber, which made its first flight in 1940. When war came to Europe, however, Sweden declared itself neutral. As a result the country was spared from occupation by Nazi troops which had already taken control of its Scandinavian neighbors Norway and Denmark.

Plans for car production at the SAAB plant at Trollhättan started evolving as World War II neared an end, and management sought to widen the production program to meet an expected decline in military aircraft requirements. The success of small European cars in the Swedish market just prior to the war provided management with confidence that cars of the same type would also prove popular in the future, and that demand would be steady enough to ensure the success of a SAAB automobile.

A talented aircraft engineer named Gunnar Ljungström was placed in charge of the development of the SAAB auto, the first prototype of which, the 92.001, was ready by the summer of 1946. The body design, however, was neither practical nor aesthetically pleasing. A new prototype was developed with an improved external design and was designated the 92.002. First unveiled in 1947, actual production began two years later. The design of this model—which was known as the SAAB 92 and was initially available only in moss green—was to characterize SAAB automobiles for the next 30 years. Streamlining helped to reduce fuel consumption and engine wear, and enabled the car to reach speeds of 60 miles per hour. Despite a number of minor shortcomings, the car's road performance was excellent, and its appearance was stylish and popular.

Company Perspectives:

Saab Automobile is an international automobile company with its traditions firmly established in Sweden. Our background as an aircraft manufacturer has given us the broad-based foundation of technical expertise and innovative concepts which characterise the company just as much now as they did when it was originally established more than 50 years ago. This is precisely what typifies us in our role as car manufacturers—we never follow traditions simply for the sake of it but always search for methods and approaches in which we can believe. New approaches to develop our cars and our organisation, by leaving plenty of scope for our employees' creative ability. The results speak for themselves. Saab Automobile has always been at the leading edge when it comes to design, performance and safety. Our history is full of technical innovations which are now standard in the majority of cars—and we are planning to continue along the same lines.

Saab Automobile is a dynamic company which always makes human beings the focus of attention. This applies to everything from the way we design our cars to how we take care of our staff and deal with our customers. It is one of the reasons why the Saab will always be far more than an exclusive car. A Saab will also be synonymous with a powerful personality.

Improved versions of Ljungström's original design appeared throughout the 1950s—with the SAAB 93 replacing the 92 in 1955—and by 1955 SAAB automobiles had become the most popular in Sweden; one car left the assembly line every 27 minutes. In order to meet anticipated demand, more plant space was required, and a new factory was established at Göteborg to manufacture engines and gearboxes. New models were also developed, with the 92 model replaced in 1955 by the SAAB 93, followed by the SAAB 95 station wagon in 1959 and one year later by the SAAB 96, which went on to be the mainstay of the company's sales throughout most of the 1960s.

SAAB continued to develop a variety of aircraft, particularly military fighter jets. The first of these was introduced in 1949, and production in various forms was maintained throughout the 1950s. The SAAB aircraft division also held licenses to manufacture foreign-designed aircraft and produce aircraft components for foreign manufacturers.

As early as 1953 SAAB management started exploring the possibility of selling cars in the United States, but hesitated to enter that market until 1956, when a more promising atmosphere had developed. Using New York City as a base of operations, a U.S. subsidiary called SAAB Motors Inc. was created to import SAAB automobiles, and a depot was established near Boston to receive cars and store spare parts. It was a modest beginning for a small foreign company in the world's largest automobile market, and growth was difficult and slow.

During the 1960s the scope of SAAB's operations expanded from automobiles and aircraft into satellites, missiles, and energy systems. On May 19, 1965, as its business continued to grow, the company changed its name to Saab Aktiebolag (the acronym had become so popular as to warrant the elimination of the old name). Over the next four years, officials of Saab and Scania-Vabis began to investigate the viability of operating as a single corporation. In the meantime, Saab introduced its first completely new model since the 92 when it began production of the larger Saab 99 in the fall of 1968.

Saab-Scania Era: 1969–89

Saab and Scania-Vabis merged their operations during 1969, and absorbed two other military contractors, Malmo Flygindustri and Nordarmatur. All automotive operations of the new Saab-Scania AB were centered at the facility in Södertälje, with production continuing in Trollhätten, while the aircraft division headquarters, which produced the JAS-35 Draken and JAS-37 Viggen fighter jets, remained at Linköping. Also in 1969, Saab-Scania, in cooperation with the Finnish company Valmet Oy, established an automobile factory at Uusikaupunki, Finland. In 1972 Saab-Scania's automotive division was divided into the Saab Car Division, which concentrated on passenger cars, and the Scania Division, focused on trucks. That year the Saab 99 was named Car of the Year in Sweden. By this time the 99 offered several innovative features, including headlight wipers and washers, electrically heated driver's seat, self-repairing five-m.p.h. bumpers, and side-impact door beams.

Saab decided to focus its efforts on competing for a significantly larger share of the U.S. automobile market, the main goal being to define its cars as a better choice than those offered by BMW, Mercedes-Benz, and Volvo. These cars had been highly successful with more affluent American consumers. The expanded marketing campaign produced few results over the first half of the decade, but by 1978 began to pay off handsomely. The company's sales increased by 19 percent in the United States and by 17 percent in Scandinavia. That year saw the launch of the upscale Saab 900, which was based on the 99 platform but featured a longer wheelbase, a longer body, a new front, and an all-new interior. Offered initially in three- and five-door hatchback models, a four-door sedan version was introduced in 1980. Innovations with the 900 series included a cabin ventilation air filter (1978), asbestos-free brakes (1982), and the first turbocharged engine featuring 16 valves—four per cylinder (1984). Production of the Saab 96 ended in January 1980, concluding the 30-year history of the 92-93-95-96 family—with overall production of more than 730,000 cars. The Saab 99 remained in production until 1984, at which point nearly 590,000 of the model had been built.

The Saab 9000, built on a new large-car platform, was introduced in 1984 and was only the third all-new model in Saab history. The car had a luxury four-door sedan profile but offered the practicality of a hatchback. The 9000 proved to be popular but problems related to retooling production plants thwarted a planned expansion of production capacity by ten percent during 1985. Arriving on the scene in 1986 was the Saab 900 convertible. Driver's side airbags were introduced in 1988.

In the late 1980s, Georg Karnsund, Saab-Scania's president, placed greater emphasis on marketing programs in Europe, particularly in France and Italy, as well as in Australia and Japan. Karnsund believed that Saab's ability to develop advanced technology would give its cars a distinct advantage in increasingly competitive international markets.

Key Dates:

1937: Svenska Aeroplan Aktiebolaget (SAAB) is formed to build military aircraft.
1939: Company acquires aircraft division of the Swedish Railroad Works, located in Linköping, where the company's headquarters are relocated.
1949: Production begins on the company's first car model, the SAAB 92.
1956: SAAB Motors Inc. is formed as a U.S. sales subsidiary.
1965: Company changes its name to Saab Aktiebolag.
1968: Production of the Saab 99 begins.
1969: Saab merges with Scania-Vabis to form Saab-Scania AB.
1978: Production of the Saab 900 begins.
1984: Production of the larger format Saab 9000 starts.
1990: General Motors purchases 50 percent interest in Saab car division, which is reorganized as Saab Automobile AB, a 50–50 joint venture of GM and Saab-Scania.
1991: Investor AB completes leveraged buyout of Saab-Scania, thereby becoming a joint owner of Saab Automobile.
1993: All-new Saab 900 is launched.
1996: Robert W. Hendry, a top GM executive, is named president and CEO of Saab.
1997: The Saab 9-5 series is launched with a sedan model.
1998: The Saab 9-3 series debuts with two-door, five-door, and convertible models; the Saab 9-5 station wagon makes its debut.

1990s: The Joint Venture Decade

The 1990s began with the conclusion of a pivotal deal whereby Saab-Scania ceded half of its Saab automobile division to General Motors Corporation. Prior to the consummation of the 50–50 joint venture with Saab-Scania, General Motors (GM) had sought to acquire Jaguar Cars Ltd., a British manufacturer of luxury cars, but in November 1989 the U.S. car maker was beaten to the prize by rival Ford Motor Company. Still in the mood to acquire, and seeking to increase its presence in the European luxury car market, GM announced its joint venture with Saab-Scania the following month. The deal was completed in early 1990, with GM paying US$600 million to gain 50 percent interest in the prestigious yet troubled car maker, which was reorganized as Saab Automobile AB.

By the late 1980s, the Saab division had become a perennial financial loser, crippled by declining sales in the United States, the company's largest single market for car sales. The affiliation with General Motors was expected to ameliorate Saab's position overseas, but at home, larger, more formidable obstacles faced the company and its enormously powerful part-owner, Peter Wallenberg. In addition to holding a controlling interest in Saab-Scania, Wallenberg maintained sizable investments in many other large Swedish companies, including appliance maker Electrolux Corporation and L.M. Ericsson, Sweden's largest communications company. Wallenberg's empire accounted for a third of Sweden's US$165 billion economy—a much-coveted portfolio when the country's economy was robust, but a financial nightmare when economic conditions soured as they did entering the 1990s. To make Wallenberg's position more precarious, by 1990 Sweden was prepared to join the European Community, which would force the country to drop its protective economic barriers. These barriers had insulated Wallenberg against foreign corporate raiders and thus enabled him to control companies that represented US$55 billion in market value with only US$5 billion in equity.

Fearing a hostile takeover, Wallenberg increased his ownership of Saab-Scania in 1990 from 36 percent to 58 percent, then initiated the largest leveraged buyout in Swedish history the following year—purchasing, through his holding company Investor AB, all of Saab-Scania for US$2.3 billion—after learning that outside investors were planning to acquire ten percent of the company's stock. Saab Automobile thereby became 50–50 owned by Investor and GM. Against the backdrop of Wallenberg's strategic maneuvers, Saab Automobile continued to lose money, recording a loss of US$848 million in 1990, which translated into an alarming US$9,200 loss for each car sold. Meantime, Saab's history of innovation continued, when it became the first automaker to offer CFC-free air conditioning systems in 1991.

By 1992, it appeared that Saab Automobile was destined for a more profitable future, thanks in large part to the assistance of General Motors' management, who greatly improved the segment's manufacturing efficiency. When GM management arrived at Saab in 1990, it took 100 hours to produce a single car, but by 1992 the hours required per car had been whittled down to 50 or 60 hours, cutting in half the production quota required to generate a profit. Although Investor and General Motors needed to effect further improvements to spark a complete resurgence of Saab automobiles, progress was being made. The introduction of an all-new Saab 900 in mid-1993 fueled hopes for a recovery of Saab's U.S. sales, a necessary ingredient in Saab's revitalization. Available first in a five-door sedan, then in three-door coupe and convertible models, the 900 helped Saab Automobile post in 1994 its first profit of its joint venture era. Production of the 900 nearly doubled between 1993 and 1996, with units built increasing from about 33,600 to more than 62,400. Sales of the 900 suffered, however, because of early quality problems and negative press coverage.

Saab began backsliding into the red in 1995 and 1996 buffeted by high marketing and product development costs as well as downward pressure on prices. In August 1996 GM sent one of its top executives, Robert W. Hendry, to Sweden to take on the position of president and CEO of Saab. Two months earlier GM and Investor agreed to pump another SKr 3.48 billion (US$524 million) into the troubled automaker to help it through a five-year recovery period. During this time, Saab planned to replace the 9000 and 900 models with two new lines. It also needed to sell a higher volume of the new models—overall sales of 150,000 cars per year—to return to profitability, and to do so it needed to move its image more into the mainstream. Saab was almost invariably referred to as a ''quirky'' carmaker and it had long aimed its advertising at ''driving enthusiasts.'' With its new models, Saab aimed to emphasize the uniqueness and quality of its products rather than the eccentricity of its customers.

The Saab 9-5, the larger of the two new lines and a replacement for the 9000, debuted in 1997 with a luxury sedan model. A 9-5 station wagon followed the next year. Also in 1998 came the debut of the Saab 9-3 series, which replaced the 900 series and included two-door, five-door hatchback, and convertible models. The new models were slowly increasing Saab's overall sales, with 98,036 cars sold in 1996, 100,275 the following year, and 118,581 in 1998, but losses deepened to SKr 1.91 billion (US$240.8 million) in 1997 before improving to SKr 620 million (US$76.5 million) in 1998.

The year 1999 had the makings of a turnaround year for Saab Automobile as the company was projecting a return to profitability, a further increase in worldwide sales to between 130,000 and 140,000 units, and expected sales in the United States (the company's largest market) of about 40,000, a substantial increase over the 28,253 of 1996. Further ownership changes were also a looming possibility in late 1999 or early 2000. General Motors had an option to acquire Investor's stake in Saab and make the Swedish carmaker a wholly owned GM subsidiary. Should GM not exercise this option, Investor had the right to force GM to buy half of its 50 percent stake in the spring of 2000. It seemed likely that General Motors would in fact acquire Saab outright. Saab retained a solid brand reputation, and as a member of the GM family would be positioned to take full advantage of the auto giant's strategy of shared global platforms and its worldwide purchasing network. GM would also be able to help Saab develop the wider product line it needed to further boost sales; plans were already being laid for the replacement of the 9-3 series in 2002 or 2003 and a Saab sport-utility vehicle was also under consideration.

Principal Subsidiaries

Saab Opel Sverige AB; Saab Cars Holdings Corp. (U.S.A.); Saab Great Britain Ltd.; Saab Deutschland GmbH (Germany); Saab Norge A/S (Norway); Saab Automobile Australia Pty Ltd; Saab France S.A.; Saab-Ana Finans AB; Saab Denmark A/S; Saab Japan Inc; Saab Canada Inc.; Saab Automobile Investering AB; Saab Automobile Schweiz AG (Switzerland); Saab Korea.

Principal Competitors

Bayerische Motoren Werke AG; DaimlerChrysler AG; Fiat S.p.A.; Ford Motor Company; Honda Motor Co., Ltd.; Hyundai Motor Company; Mazda Motor Corporation; Mitsubishi Motors Corporation; Nissan Motor Co., Ltd.; PSA Peugeot Citroen S.A.; Renault S.A.; Toyota Motor Corporation; Volkswagen AB.

Further Reading

Birch, Stuart, ''. . . And in the Beginning,'' *Automotive Engineering,* September 1, 1997, p. 14.

Burt, Tim, ''Hope for GM's Saab Saga: Board Says Swedish Car Maker Will Report Profit in 1999 After Years of Painful Restructuring,'' *Financial Times,* September 14, 1998, p. 26.

——, ''Saab Eyes Common Platform,'' *Financial Times,* December 21, 1998, p. 21.

——, ''Saab Set for Further SKr1bn Investment,'' *Financial Times,* May 22, 1998, p. 27.

Carnegy, Hugh, ''Battles for Survival Continue: Volvo and Saab See Sales Dip As Development Costs Continue to Rise,'' *Financial Times,* March 6, 1997.

Dawley, Heidi, ''Saab: Why GM Sent in Its Ace Mechanic,'' *Business Week,* September 2, 1996, p. 55.

Dymock, Eric, *Saab: Half a Century of Achievement, 1947–1997,* Newbury Park, Calif.: Haynes North America, 1997, 192 p.

Feast, Richard, ''Jaguar and Saab: Bullish on America; Ford and GM Patiently Groom Their Latest European Acquisitions for the Long Haul,'' *Automotive Industries,* May 1991, p. 14.

Flint, Jerry, ''Europe to the Rescue,'' *Forbes,* February 3, 1992, p. 19.

Gardner, Greg, ''Will GM 'Saternize' Saab?,'' *Ward's Auto World,* August 1996, p. 37.

Henry, Jim, ''Saab Scrambling to Meet Lofty Sales Goals,'' *Automotive News,* November 11, 1996, p. 6.

Hökerberg, Jan, *Spelet om Saab: en biltillverkares uppgång, fall och väg tillbaka,* [Stockholm]: Bonnier Alba, 1992, 353 p.

Johnson, Richard, ''Europeans Pinched, but Most Are Profitable in Market Dip,'' *Automotive News,* May 27, 1991, p. 2.

Kapstein, Jonathan, ''Fortress Wallenberg Is Showing Some Cracks,'' *Business Week,* December 10, 1990, p. 45.

——, ''Wallenburg's New Walls,'' *Business Week,* March 11, 1991, p. 46.

Kurylko, Diana T., ''GM Global Platform Is Key to Saab's Future Products,'' *Automotive News,* November 8, 1999, p. 24L.

——, ''New Saab Boss Focuses on Europe,'' *Automotive News,* November 8, 1999, p. 24L.

——, ''Profit in Sweden on the Horizon,'' *Automotive News,* May 16, 1994.

Miller, Scott, ''Saab Has Plans to Widen Its Model Line and Double Output Within Five Years,'' *Wall Street Journal,* November 18, 1999, p. A21.

''Saab Rallied Round a Mountain to Earn Attention in U.S.,'' *Automotive News,* April 24, 1996, p. 70.

''Saab Taking a Gamble with 9-5 Saloon,'' *Financial Times,* August 7, 1997, p. 26.

Sandell, Kaj, and Bo Streiffert, *Scania 100 år, 1891–1991: ett sekel industri- och fordonshistoria,* Södertälje: Saab-Scania, Scaniadivisionen, 1990, 264 p.

Templeman, John, ''Saab: Halfway Through a U-Turn,'' *Business Week,* April 27, 1992, p. 121.

Washington, Frank S., ''Saab Counts on Image Make-Over to Attract Older, Luxury Buyers,'' *Automotive News,* March 10, 1997, p. 23.

Wielgat, Andrea, ''Future Still Uncertain but Looking Up for Saab,'' *Ward's Auto World,* October 1999, p. 45.

Wright, Chris, ''Saab Looks for Boost from 9-5 Station Wagon,'' *Automotive News Europe,* December 7, 1998, p. 18.

—Jeffrey L. Covell
—updated by David E. Salamie

The Salvation Army USA

615 Slaters Lane
Alexandria, Virginia 22314
U.S.A
Telephone: (703) 684-5500
Toll Free: (800) 725-2769
Fax: (703) 684-3478
Web site: http://www.salvationarmyusa.org

Nonprofit Company
Incorporated: 1899
Employees: 39,883
Sales: $1.6 billion (fiscal 1998)
NAIC: 624210 Food Banks; 81311 Religious Organizations; 813311 Human Rights Organizations

From baking donuts during World War I to the ubiquitous bell ringers and red kettles of the last years of the 20th century, The Salvation Army is one of the most visible charitable organizations in the world. With world headquarters based in London, and U.S. operations based in Virginia, The Salvation Army is active in over 103 countries and its officers and personnel speak 160 languages. Stateside, the Army served over 32 million people in 1998, spreading its message of hope, love, and redemption through nearly 1.6 million volunteers who committed themselves to providing disaster relief and fighting hunger, illness, homelessness, and other social ills.

Man with a Message: 1829–78

William Booth was born in 1829 in Nottingham, England, and privately educated. He was ordained as a Methodist minister in 1852 at the age of 23, and took his calling to God as a crusade. He traveled the country as an emissary of the New Connexion Church, and began noticing, in increasing numbers, the forgotten souls of his surrounding communities. These forgotten or forsaken, living on the fringes of England's polite society, were not attending church. They could not or would not, and even if they had the desire, they were turned away as vagrants, drunkards, pimps, or prostitutes. Booth believed these people had the same if not more need for worship, to hear and learn of the Gospel, to be given the hope of redemption.

In 1860s Great Britain, Queen Victoria ruled and Edward, the Prince of Wales, married Princess Alexandra of Denmark. Although much of the country was caught up in the nuptials, Booth was more concerned with rampant poverty of London. Moreover, while the powers-that-be of British Methodism preferred worship and religious practice in a traditional manner, i.e. in a church with the proper pulpit, music, hymnals, and setting—Booth had become disenchanted and officially left the Methodist church in 1861. Since scores of the most desperate needed spiritual guidance and simply were not getting it, Booth resolved to take the church to them. He and his wife, Catherine, began traveling throughout the country, delivering the teachings of Jesus Christ to all who would listen.

During a tent revival in an abandoned Quaker cemetery in Whitechaple, word spread of Booth's charismatic message, and a multitude of the needy showed up. Booth soon settled his evangelical fervor on the destitute East Enders, who lacked spiritual guidance as well as food and shelter. Booth and Catherine came to believe that moral, physical, and spiritual well being were interdependent and aimed to provide a balance of all three. By July 1865 the Booths and several charitably minded colleagues began calling themselves the Christian Mission, and earnestly offered their message to the "unchurched" of the East End. Within two years, General Superintendent Booth had a staff of ten full-time local missionaries (including Catherine, a skillful preacher, dubbed the "Army Mother") and an increasing number of converts.

Throughout the 1870s the Booths and their growing band of believers continued to minister to the lost souls of London. Yet the squalor and helplessness of many of Britain's 26 million people was beginning to be noticed: Octavia Hill's tenement reforms had taken hold, debtors' prisons had been abolished, British Parliament legalized labor unions, electric street lighting was introduced, and the Booths brought many salvation through the Gospel. As their reputations grew among the poverty-stricken of London and beyond, many came to the Mission for salvation. The converts, known as the "Hallelujah Army," taught the Mission's message by singing or preaching on the streets, and the group's congregation multiplied. By 1874, the Mission had some 1,000 converted volunteers and 42 full-time evangelists. Ironically, these religious messengers still were not

Company Perspectives:

The Salvation Army, an international movement, is an evangelical part of the universal Christian Church. Its message is based on the Bible. Its ministry is motivated by the love of God. Its mission is to preach the gospel of Jesus Christ and to meet human needs in His name without discrimination.

allowed into traditional churches, because many had once been prostitutes, gamblers, thieves, or drunks.

In 1878 the Booths and the Christian Mission regrouped under a new name, The Salvation Army. The move was precipitated by the wording of an annual report; Booth had been proofing the printed document and read a statement about the Christian Mission's ''Volunteer Army,'' which he changed to ''Salvation Army.'' From this revision came the organization's new name and the institution of a militaristic structure, to organize and fight for Jesus and to bring friendship and love to those who had neither. General Superintendent Booth became simply ''the General,'' and the rank of ''officer'' was given to all ministers within the new organization. The Salvation Army continued in the same manner as the Christian Mission, accepting anyone into its fold without discrimination, and its ranks swelled. Wearing military-type uniforms and called salvationists, they were often the victims of ridicule and/or violence. In this vein, Catherine Booth designed a sturdy bonnet for women salvationists, which protected their faces and eyes from flying objects. Yet William Booth's message was firm: ''Go for souls, and go for the worst.''

Coming to America: 1879–99

The message of the salvationists was carried to the United States by Lt. Eliza Shirley after she followed her parents overseas. Shirley held her first meeting in 1879 in Philadelphia. Upon hearing of Lt. Shirley's popularity and success, a group of salvationists was sent to the United States the following year to spread the word. In March 1880 the group, thankful for their safe arrival, held their first public meeting in Battery Park, New York. Though generally well-received, the U.S. salvationists often suffered the same occasional attacks and persecution as their English counterparts. The latter had converted 250,000 people from 1881 to 1885; the former, though gaining recognition, paid higher prices—some salvationists were jailed in the United States and others were killed. Yet neither prejudice nor punishment daunted the salvationists, further strengthening their resolve and in turn their message.

By 1886 the U.S. salvationists had received a ringing endorsement from President Grover Cleveland, and had moved from Philadelphia to the West Coast (California), the East Coast (Connecticut, Massachusetts, and New Jersey), the Midwest (Indiana, Michigan, Missouri, Ohio, and Pennsylvania), and the South (Kentucky). After expansion in the United States and Canada, the salvationists took their message worldwide, traveling to Australia, France, Germany, Iceland, India, South Africa, and Switzerland. General Booth began writing an organization newsletter, *The War Cry*, as well as several books.

General Booth and Catherine, who had had eight children, were the first to bring a second generation into their organization. Among their children were sons Bramwell and Ballington, and daughter Eva, all of whom had been active in their parents' evangelical work. Yet due to a dispute with his father, Ballington left The Salvation Army and founded his own charitable organization, Volunteers of America, in 1896. Some of the Army's officers and volunteers followed Ballington, much to the dismay of the other Booths, though everyone carried on with their missions.

A New Century: 1900s–50s

The Salvation Army's religious goodwill had continued to gain momentum with the turn of the century. A devastating blow came in 1912 with the death of General Booth; yet The Salvation Army remained stalwart and committed. Within a year of his death, General William Booth was immortalized by American poet Vachel Lindsey, who wrote a poem entitled ''General Booth Enters into Heaven,'' and published a book bearing the same name. The poem eloquently told Booth's story and was a lasting memoir of the General's devotion to God and his fellow human beings.

Next came the advent of World War I in 1914, and The Salvation Army gained recognition in its many services for Allied soldiers. Lt. Colonel Helen Purviance, sent to France, began a new tradition by baking homemade donuts for the ''doughboys'' in France, using rations, a wine bottle, and open-fire stove. Rolling the dough with the wine bottle and cooking the donuts over the fire, Purviance and her fellow Salvationists saw demand soar to 9,000 a day. Bramwell Booth, who had taken over leadership of the organization upon his father's death, saw the group through World War I and to 1929, when Edward J. Higgins was voted in as the first elected general. Eva, who had served throughout Great Britain and Canada, migrated to the United States and became that country's commander in 1904, changing her name to Evangeline. She served as commander until 1934 when she took over the generalship from Higgins, becoming the Army's first female general. Five years into her leadership, Britain and France declared war on Germany and World War II was underway. Though Evangeline retired during this year at age 70, she had contacted President Woodrow Wilson and offered The Salvation Army's help in any manner needed. Many war-related activities ensued for Allied soldiers, from mobile canteens with food, beverages, books, and writing gear to camps where the enlisted could dance, sing, and attend religious services. The War Work Council, which in turn created the War Service League, made clothing to be distributed by the Red Cross; the American Expeditionary Forces overseas were tended to by salvationists who went to the frontlines, bringing home-baked treats, including the world-famous donuts, as well as pies, cakes, and cookies.

After World War II ended, The Salvation Army helped veterans and their families, and initiated a wide range of programs for men, women, and children. There were teen programs to prevent juvenile delinquency, building services, aid for the handicapped, and, as always, preaching of the Gospel. In 1950, the Army lost another of its most ardent leaders when Evangeline Booth died at age 85.

The Modern Salvation Army: 1960s–70s

Like a military hierarchy, The Salvation Army's structure grew to consist of interlocking units answering to divisional

Key Dates:

1865: Organization founded by William Booth, an ordained minister, in London.
1878: The Christian Mission is renamed the ''Salvation Army'' and adopts a military structure.
1879: First salvationist journeys to the United States.
1885: Volunteer salvationists have converted 250,000.
1896: Booth's son Ballington breaks away and founds Volunteers of America.
1912: William Booth dies.
1934: Evangeline Booth, daughter of the founder, becomes General.
1950: Evangeline Booth dies.

chiefs. The General oversaw all operations from the organization's world headquarters in London, while a national commander directed activities in the United States, at national headquarters in Alexandria, Virginia. In the United States, there were four tax exempt territories (Central, South, East, and West), each with a territorial commander who oversaw smaller units called divisions. There were in turn 40 divisions, each with its own divisional commander, and each division consisting of numerous social and religious outlets within its area.

Other members of the group included rankings from lieutenant to major, as well as soldiers, cadets, ''adherents,'' and laypersons. Soldiers were required to profess their faith and sign a declaration called the ''Articles of War,'' guaranteeing The Salvation Army two years of volunteer service (raised from the original nine months of service). Once a soldier was in the program for six months, he/she was eligible for Officers' Training at one of the Army's four U.S. colleges in Illinois, New York, Georgia, and California. After successfully completing a two-year residence program, each cadet was awarded the rank of ordained minister (lieutenant), then given an assignment and living quarters. Nonmilitary personnel, on the other hand, consisted of ''adherents'' and laypersons, the former as people who designated Salvation Army churches as their place of worship and the latter from many walks of life, such as civic or business leaders, who wished to further the organization's reach.

The Army was a national, regional, and local organization, though funds were raised only through regional and local units with no national campaign (though most divisions participated in such fundraisers as the famed bell ringing during the Christmas shopping season). Like the military, The Salvation Army had instituted a strict code of conduct; uniformity and consistency were key to the organization's longevity.

Responding to New World Crises: 1980s–90s

In 1986 The Salvation Army elected its second woman general, Eva Burrows. It was a time of change for the Army, as the world around it was discovering the devastation of AIDS. Though the Army's religious mantra never became dated, the need for more modern assistance was necessary. With the advent of HIV and AIDS, greater awareness of spousal and child abuse, widespread drug abuse, and global devastation in the forms of hurricanes, floods, earthquakes, and civil warfare, the Army sought to become more proactive. The organization continued to reach farther into the lives and general welfare of the world's inhabitants, not just in times of extreme need or emergencies, but in order to support career counseling, vocational training, senior citizen services, and outreach programs for recently released convicts. In Florida, the Army began seeking custody of newly paroled prisoners, first-timers who had served their sentences and needed assistance to get back on their feet. Rather than see many of these convicts become habitual criminals, the Army created rehab programs to assimilate them back into society with great success.

Luckily, awareness of the needy had increased across the board in the 1980s and 1990s in the United States and the world, as nonprofit organizations multiplied. With more competition for charity dollars, the Army began using direct-mail brochures to bring awareness to its causes. By 1993 the international Salvation Army rivaled the armed forces with operations in 99 countries, a membership of over three million people, and 25,000 officers of diverse backgrounds.

According to *Forbes* magazine, by 1996 there were over 600,000 organizations vying for U.S. dollars; yet Americans gave varied charities upwards of $120 billion during the year. The Salvation Army USA, for its part, received close to $2 billion of these dollars in 1996 and spent $1.56 billion on helping men, women, and children around the globe. The organization spent 86 cents of every dollar furthering its causes, with the remainder going to administrative costs. This ratio of 86 percent ranked The Salvation Army at the top of the U.S. charities list, and as *Forbes* pointed out in April 1998, similar organizations spent significantly less on those in need and more on expenses. Additionally, the Army received less from the government (around 15 percent) than other organizations, many of which had received from 25 to 60 percent of their funding. These numbers were in part why legendary management consultant Peter F. Drucker told *Forbes* The Salvation Army was ''by far the most effective organization'' in the United States. In the interview, Drucker heaped further praise on the organization: ''No one even comes close to [The Salvation Army] in respect to clarity of mission, ability to innovate, measurable results, dedication and putting money to maximum use.''

Global expansion was another key issue in 1996, with new recruits taking Korea, Tanzania, Kenya, and Uganda by storm. The Salvation Army, better known than many of its competitors—be they hospitals, museums, symphonies, colleges and universities, or research facilities—funded its programs through tenacity and the sheer willpower of its volunteers. In 1997, the Army had 9,633 centers of operations (shelters, camps, churches, thrift stores, day care centers, clinics, etc.); helped 2,177 people find lost relatives; conducted 3.7 million Sunday ''holiness'' meetings; operated 669,061 group homes; and served holiday meals to 6.9 million people nationwide. Salvation Army thrift stores, which numbered 1,576, were another of the organization's successful venues, popping up all over the nation, offering clothing, toys, and household goods at a fraction of their retail prices. The stores were responsible for contributing over 15 percent of the Army's annual revenues.

In 1998, the Army was again the focus of a *Forbes* profile, this time telling the story of Commissioners Robert and Alice Watson, lifelong salvationists who ran the organization's U.S. operations. The Watsons oversaw more than 500,000 volunteers, with outposts in every state, and controlled operating funds of over $1.5 billion for 1997 and $1.6 billion in 1998. The Army's worldwide growth was up by ten percent from 1994 to 1998, and the *New York Times* reported that 1998 donors in the United States gave more than ever before (up by 16 percent) and the number one recipient was The Salvation Army with $1.2 billion in cash and goods. While the Army did not consider itself a true competitor, its chief international rival was Goodwill Industries, the Maryland-based charity founded in 1910. This service organization, whose motto was ''a hand up, not a handout,'' had a worldwide workforce of 60,000 (significantly higher than the Army's nearly 40,000), and brought in revenues of $1.5 billion for 1998.

In 1999, the Army was able to continue its deeds, as 42 percent of all Americans gave to charity, according to the *Chronicle of Philanthropy.* That September the Watsons were replaced by new National Commanders John and Elsie Busby. The Busbys were previously commanders of the Southern territory, based in Atlanta. Approaching the new millennium, The Salvation Army operated much as it had at the previous turn of the century. Though it reached billions instead of hundreds of thousands, the message and mission were the same, brought by third and fourth generation salvationists. While Ballington Booth's defection from the family cause had pained his parents, they should nonetheless have been proud—the entire family succeeded in bringing help to those in need. Ballington's Volunteers of America, based in New Orleans, was nowhere near as large as his father's creation, but both had survived in the tradition of their founders.

Principal Divisions

Central Territory; Eastern Territory; Southern Territory; Western Territory.

Principal Competitors

Goodwill Industries International, Inc.

Further Reading

''Gifts to Charities up 16 Percent,'' *New York Times,* November 1, 1999, p. 14.

Kilgannon, Cory, ''Wary of an Invasion of Cars, Street Shuns New Neighbor,'' *New York Times,*October 31, 1999, p.13.

Lee, Susan, and Ashlea Ebeling, ''Can You Top This for Cost-Efficient Management?,'' *Forbes,* April 20, 1998.

Lenzer, Robert, and Ashlea Ebeling, ''Peter Drucker's Picks,'' *Forbes,* August 11, 1997.

''Raising the Roof: The Philanthropy 400,'' *Chronicle for Philanthropy,* http://www.philanthropy.com, November 4, 1999.

—Nelson Rhodes

Sandvik AB

SE-811 81 Sandviken
Sweden
Telephone: (26) 26 00 00
Fax: (26) 26 10 22
Web site: http://www.sandvik.com

Public Company
Incorporated: 1868 as Sandvikens Jernwerks Aktiebolag
Employees: 37,520
Sales: SKr 42.40 billion (US$5.23 billion) (1998)
Stock Exchanges: Stockholm London
NAIC: 331210 Iron and Steel Pipe and Tube Manufacturing from Purchased Steel; 331221 Rolled Steel Shape Manufacturing; 331222 Steel Wire Drawing; 331421 Copper Rolling, Drawing, and Extruding; 331491 Nonferrous Metal (Except Copper and Aluminum) Rolling, Drawing, and Extruding; 331513 Steel Foundries (Except Investment); 332212 Hand and Edge Tool Manufacturing; 332999 All Other Miscellaneous Fabricated Metal Product Manufacturing; 333120 Construction Machinery Manufacturing; 333131 Mining Machinery and Equipment Manufacturing; 333512 Machine Tool (Metal Cutting Types) Manufacturing; 333515 Cutting Tool and Machine Tool Accessory Manufacturing

Sandvik AB is an industrial engineering group based in Sandviken, Sweden, and trading through an international network of 300 companies in 130 countries. About 94 percent of Sandvik's sales are from outside Sweden, with 39 percent stemming from European Union countries (other than Sweden), 25 percent from North America (including Mexico), and 15 percent from the Australasian region. Originating from a steelworks using the Bessemer method in the 1860s, the company has developed into a group with three main business units, each of which holds world-leading positions in several niches. Sandvik Tooling specializes in tools and tooling systems for metalworking applications, with Sandvik Coromant holding the global lead in the manufacture of cemented-carbide tools and CTT Tools also leading the world in the manufacture of high-speed steel tools. Sandvik Mining and Construction is a leading global supplier of rock-working equipment, tools, and services for mining and civil engineering. Sandvik Specialty Steels is principally comprised of Sandvik Steel, a world leader in the manufacture of products made of stainless steel and of titanium, nickel, and zirconium alloys; and Kanthal, a world leader in the production of metallic and ceramic resistance materials in the form of wire, strip, and electric heating elements.

Steelworks Beginnings

The origins of Sandvik can be traced back to the formation of the Högbo Stål & Jernwerks AB in 1862. The company was set up to build a new steelworks at Sandviken—150 miles north of Stockholm, the capital of Sweden—by Göran Fredrik Göransson. Sandvik claims that Göransson, who obtained a license to use the Bessemer process, was the first to get the new process to work on an industrial scale. The Bessemer method, unlike earlier methods, allowed the production of heavy castings and forgings in one piece from one melt. In the process, air is blown through molten pig-iron and a vigorous combustion results from the reaction of the blast and the hot iron in the converter. Sandviken is located in the southeastern corner of the region of Sweden where iron products had been produced for hundreds of years prior to the formation of the new company. The original iron industry was based on local deposits of iron and the ready availability of wood to make charcoal.

Johan Holm, the main financial backer of Göransson's company, however, got into financial difficulties that resulted in his and the company's downfall. The company was declared bankrupt in 1866; after financial restructuring, Sandvikens Jernwerks (Steelworks) Aktiebolag was founded in May 1868. Anders Henrik Göransson, the son of the founder, became the manager of the new company and set Sandvik on the course that would lead to its future success. By international standards, Sweden offered a small home market for the new company. From the start Sandvik exported products which, because of the company's location far from the main industrial markets, had to be highly upgraded steel products. The high quality of Swedish

Company Perspectives:

Sandvik shall contribute actively to improving the productivity and profitability of its customers. Products and services offered by the Group shall provide customers with maximum value in terms of performance, quality, speed, safety, flexibility and total economy. Sandvik shall be the obvious first choice for customers.

Operations shall be concentrated primarily in niche sectors where Sandvik is–or has the potential to become—a world leader.

iron ore and the Bessemer process urged the company in the same direction. Even during the first years of the new company, Anders Göransson traveled widely in Europe, taking orders for products and establishing agencies.

By the 1890s the company was making some manufactured products, such as saws, from the steel it produced. In the latter part of the 19th century, the company's specialties included boiler tubes for installation in steamships and railway engines, rock drilling steels, and wire for umbrellas. By the outbreak of World War I, exports accounted for up to 80 percent of Sandvik's output.

By 1914 employment at Sandviken exceeded 2,200. During World War I the export share shrank, but was offset by the booming domestic market for steel. During the interwar period the company was hit hard by recession, in the early 1920s and again in the early 1930s. The workforce declined, but by 1937 had risen again to 5,380. During this period, the production of steel by the open-hearth process and electro process replaced the Bessemer process that had been instrumental in the foundation of the company. Sweden's cheap hydroelectric power provided an advantage for steelmakers using the electro process.

Between 1918 and 1939 exports as a proportion of sales varied between 60 and 70 percent. Throughout this period, steel was the dominant product group; manufactured products such as saws, conveyor belts, complete conveyors, and razor blades accounted for only six percent of sales. Within the area of steel products, tube products were increasingly important; these included seamless stainless tubes for the food, pulp and paper, and chemical industries.

From 1920 until 1958 the dominant figure in the company was Karl Fredrik Göransson, grandson of the company's founder. When he returned to Sweden in 1901 after studying in the United States, he brought with him the company's, and probably Sweden's, first microscope for metallurgical studies. He was managing director from 1920 until 1948 and chairman from 1929 until 1959.

By the beginning of World War II, Sandvik's production amounted to 90,000 tons of steel ingots a year and 65,000 tons of finished products. In terms of ingots, the company accounted for about ten percent of Sweden's output, but because the final products were highly upgraded this understates the company's relative importance in terms of the value of output. During World War II, exports collapsed again and output was diverted to the home market. During this period, however, an event of immense importance for the development of the company occurred.

Increasing Importance of Cemented-Carbide Products: 1940s–60s

In 1941 the company decided to enter the cemented-carbide trade. Cemented-carbide is a powder-metallurgical product of which tungsten carbide is the main constituent. It may also contain carbides of other metals such as titanium, tantalum, and niobium. Powders prepared from the various metal carbides are mixed with fine-grained powdered metal, most commonly cobalt. The mix is pressed to the desired shape and is treated at a high temperature; the cobalt melts and functions as a binding agent for the carbide grains which are sintered in. The sintered product has multiple advantages: hardness, ductility, and resistance to wear. A sintered blank can be ground to high edge sharpness, affixed to a holder, and used as a tool for metal cutting.

Fried. Krupp AG, the German steel and engineering company (which was later subsumed into Thyssen Krupp AG), had invented cemented-carbide tools in the 1920s and was the leading supplier before World War II. The war separated Krupp from many of its markets and provided opportunities for new entrants to the trade.

Sandvik used the name Coromant for its new venture, which was initiated by production manager Carl Sebart. Previously, cemented-carbide had been sold in the form of blanks to be fashioned and sharpened into tools by the users. Sandvik's new approach, to supply ready-made tools, was first applied to rock-drills, which were developed and marketed in collaboration with Atlas Copco AB, another Swedish company, and were an immediate success. The cooperative arrangement with Atlas Copco continued until 1988. Michael Porter, author of *The Competitive Sources of Power,* suggested that one reason for Sweden's success in producing internationally competitive rock drilling equipment is that its rock is among the hardest in the world. Cemented-carbide metalworking tools were slower to achieve popularity, but development after 1956 was rapid. Sandvik Coromant expanded by building new factories in Sweden and other countries and by acquiring existing producers. Wilhelm Haglund, who had managed the development of Sandvik's cemented-carbide operation from the start in 1941, was appointed managing director of Sandvik in 1957 by K.F. Göransson, and held the position until 1967.

The Göransson family was the company's major shareholder and controlled Sandvik until 1957, when additional capital was raised by an issue of shares, and the investment company Kinnevik acquired a stake in the company. In 1967 Hugo Stenbeck, chairman of Kinnevik, became chairman of Sandvik, and Arne Westerberg–a former manager of a subsidiary of Kinnevik–took over as managing director.

An important change of corporate strategy occurred in 1967 at about the time of the changeover in management from Wilhelm Haglund as managing director and Gustaf Söderlund as chairman to Hugo Stenbeck and Arne Westerberg, respectively. Hitherto, the company's policy had been to market products made by the parent company or by its subsidiaries starting from products made by the parent company. Between 1962 and

Key Dates:

1862: Göran Fredrik Göransson forms Högbo Stål & Jernwerks AB to build a new steelworks at Sandviken, Sweden.
1866: Company is declared bankrupt.
1868: Sandvikens Jernwerks Aktiebolag is founded in May 1868, with Anders Henrik Göransson, son of the founder, as general manager.
1920: Karl Fredrik Göransson, grandson of the founder, becomes managing director.
1941: Company enters the cemented-carbide trade.
1957: Company goes public through an issue of shares; investment company Kinnevik acquires stake in the company.
1967: Hugo Stenbeck, chairman of Kinnevik, becomes company chairman; Arne Westerberg, formerly of Kinnevik, becomes managing director.
1971: Sales of cemented-carbide products exceed those of steel products for the first time.
1972: Company changes its name to Sandvik AB; the U.S. rock drilling manufacturing operation of Fagersta is purchased.
1983: Skanska AB acquires Kinnevik's holding and builds up a 37 percent stake in the company; Percy Barnevik, chief executive of ASEA AB, is appointed chairman.
1984: Company's operations are restructured into six core business areas: Sandvik Tooling, Sandvik Rock Tools, Sandvik Hard Materials, Sandvik Steel, Sandvik Saws and Tools, and Sandvik Process Systems.
1987: The Carboloy Division of General Electric Company is acquired.
1989: Per-Olof Eriksson is named president and CEO; Skanska's holding stands at 26 percent.
1991: Bahco Tools Group is acquired and added to Sandvik Saws and Tools.
1993: Company completes acquisition of CTT Tools from AB SKF.
1994: Clas Åke Hedström takes over as president and CEO.
1997: Sandvik takes full control of Tamrock, Kanthal, and Precision Twist Drill; Skanska sells the bulk of its stake in Sandvik, with large portion sold to AB Industrivärden.
1999: Company's operations are concentrated around three core business areas: Sandvik Tooling, Sandvik Mining and Construction, and Sandvik Specialty Steels; Sandvik Saws and Tools unit is sold to Snap-On Incorporated.

1966, parent company sales represented 78 percent of group sales. From 1967 more products, particularly cemented-carbide products, were manufactured by the company's overseas subsidiaries.

In 1971 sales of cemented-carbide products exceeded those of steel products for the first time. In 1972 this was acknowledged by a change in the company's name from Sandvikens Jernwerks Aktiebolag to Sandvik AB.

Expansion Through Acquisition: 1970s–80s

Sandvik's other divisions were also making progress in developing products and markets while the carbide-tool business took off; they certainly could not afford to be idle in the intensely competitive environment of the steel and engineering industries during the 1970s and 1980s. While other steel companies faced repeated if not terminal crises, Sandvik succeeded as a result of its policies of investment in the latest technology and by developing specialty products to be sold in world markets. In world terms, Sandvik was a small-scale producer of steel; it survived in spite of the existence of large economies of scale for steel production by concentrating on the production of types of specialty steel and making high quality special products, such as surgical needles, scalpels, and probes that require special strength and resistance to corrosion, bone pins, artificial hip-joints, cladding in nuclear reactors, and springs.

The pace of expansion through acquisitions in Sweden and abroad was stepped up after 1967. In 1968 a joint venture, the Saeger Carbide Corporation, was set up in the United States with the Greenleaf Corporation. Between 1970 and 1973, manufacturers of rock drilling equipment in France and Spain were acquired. In 1972 the U.S. rock drilling manufacturing operation of another Swedish steel company, Fagersta, was purchased. In 1973 the U.K.-based Wickman-Wimet group was acquired, and during 1978 and 1979 tool manufacturers in Germany and France were bought. Between 1971 and 1974 the steel division made acquisitions in Spain, West Germany, and the United Kingdom; saw, hand-tool, and conveyor manufacturers were also taken into the group.

Although it was better placed than many other Swedish steel producers, Sandvik took part in the successive rationalizations of the Swedish special steels industry during the early 1980s. The result of the rationalizations was that there were only two principal special steel manufacturers in Sweden—Sandvik and Avesta—with Sandvik specializing in strip, wire, and tube products.

Following the second oil crisis in 1980, Sandvik suffered from the effects of the recession in many of its major markets. In 1983 the company's profits were reduced by Skr 219 million (US$30 million) owing to an exchange rate loss brought about by unauthorized foreign-exchange speculation by an employee. In the aftermath of this disaster, Skanska AB, a construction company with diversified interests, acquired Kinnevik's holding and built up a 37 percent stake in Sandvik. In October 1983 Percy Barnevik, the chief executive officer of the Swedish electrical giant ASEA AB, was appointed chairman of Sandvik in succession to Arne Westerberg. In 1984 Per-Olof Eriksson was appointed president. In 1989 Percy Barnevik remained chairman while Per-Olof Eriksson became president and CEO of Sandvik, and Skanska AB controlled 26 percent of shareholders' votes. Meantime, in 1984 the company restructured its operations into six core business areas: Sandvik Coromant, Sandvik Rock Tools, Sandvik Hard Materials, Sandvik Steel, Sandvik Saws and Tools, and Sandvik Process Systems.

Acquisitions continued to be made during the 1980s. An important one was the Carboloy Division of the General Electric Company, of the United States, in 1987. In 1989 Metinox Steel Ltd., a small U.K. company making medical products out of stainless steel, was acquired.

During the years 1987 to 1989, Sandvik's operating profit—after charging depreciation—represented more than 15 percent of sales. Expenditure on research and development was more than four percent of sales while capital expenditure averaged more than five percent of sales.

Strengthening and Focusing on Three Core Areas: 1990s

The early 1990s were difficult years for Sandvik as recession gripped much of the world from 1990 through 1993. Despite declining sales, the company remained profitable thanks to management's heeding signs of the downturn as early as mid-1989. Eriksson began cutting staff around the world, reducing the workforce by 20 percent by the end of 1992. He also held off on making any significant acquisitions in 1989 or 1990, returning the company to its more acquisitive nature starting in 1991—but at a slower pace than in the past. During 1991 Sandvik spent SKr 358 million to acquire ten enterprises in whole or in part. The largest of these was the December purchase of the Bahco Tools Group, which had annual revenue of SKr 700 million and about 1,700 employees. The addition of Bahco bolstered Sandvik Saws and Tools. In late 1992 and early 1993 Sandvik acquired CTT Tools from AB SKF in a two-step transaction. CTT Tools–which was formed in 1990 through the merger of SKF Tools and the German firm Günther & Co.—was the world leader in the manufacture of high-speed steel tools for metalworking, such as drills, thread-cutting tools, milling cutters, and reamers. CTT Tools and Sandvik Coromant were grouped into a new Sandvik Tooling business area.

In 1993 Sandvik formed a subsidiary in China, Sandvik China Ltd., which began construction of a cemented-carbide tools factory in Langfang City. The following year Eriksson turned over the reigns to a new president and CEO, Clas Åke Hedström. In February 1994 Sandvik reached an agreement to acquire the cemented-carbide operations of Krupp Widia GmbH (the original producer of cemented-carbide products) from Fried. Krupp AG Hoechst-Krupp. German antitrust authorities, however, concluded that Sandvik would gain too dominant a position in particular product segments of the German market and squelched the deal.

From 1993 through 1995 Sandvik recorded steadily rising revenues and profits as the business climate was generally favorable worldwide. With the late 1990s difficulties experienced in Japan, other parts of Asia, Russia, and Latin America, net profits declined from SKr 3.73 billion in 1995 to SKr 2.10 billion in 1998. Revenues, however, moved in the opposite direction, increasing from SKr 29.7 billion to SKr 42.4 billion during the same period, aided by several major acquisitions. During 1997 alone, Sandvik took full control of Tamrock, Kanthal, and Precision Twist Drill. Finland-based Tamrock, which Sandvik acquired in two phases in 1996 and 1997, was a world-leading maker of rock-drilling equipment. The three main operations of Tamrock were combined with Sandvik Rock Tools to form a new Sandvik Mining and Construction business area. This area included four separate business sectors: the newly named Sandvik Tamrock, producer of drilling rigs, loaders, trucks, hydraulic hammers, and cemented-carbide products; Voest-Alpine Eimco, maker of equipment and tools for the mining of coal and other soft minerals; Driltech Mission, maker of drilling rigs and cemented-carbide tools for rotary and down-the-hole drilling; and Roxon, provider of equipment for conveyors and systems for handling of bulk materials.

Also acquired in two steps in 1996 and 1997 was Kanthal AB, a leading maker of high-temperature metallic and ceramic materials in the form of wire, strip, and electric heating elements. Kanthal had strong ties to Sandvik Steel and the two units were grouped within a new business area called Sandvik Specialty Steel. In September 1997 Sandvik acquired Crystal Lake, Illinois-based Precision Twist Drill Co. for SKr 1.06 billion. With annual sales of more than US$110 million, Precision was one of the leading manufacturers of high-speed steel twist drills in the world. It became part of CTT Tools.

In mid-1997 Skanska sold the bulk of its significant holding in Sandvik. Skanska sold part of its stake to AB Industrivärden, a Swedish investment company that held an 11.7 percent voting stake at the end of 1998. In April 1999 Sandvik announced that it would sell Sandvik Saws and Tools to Kenosha, Wisconsin-based Snap-On Incorporated. The SKr 3.3 billion (US$400 million) deal was completed in September of that year, with Sandvik recording a capital gain of about SKr 1.6 billion. Sandvik Saws and Tools was renamed Bahco Group AB and continued to be based in Sandviken, Sweden. With this divestment pending, Sandvik in May 1999 announced that it would restructure its operations into three main areas. The first was Sandvik Tooling, which continued to include Sandvik Coromant and CTT Tools and also gained Sandvik Hard Materials, producer of cemented-carbide blanks, components, and rolls. The second was Sandvik Mining and Construction. And the third was Sandvik Specialty Steels, which comprised Sandvik Steel and Kanthal as well as the newly added Sandvik Process Systems, maker of steel belts and steel-belt-based process plants. Sandvik was now well-positioned for the 21st century, as Sandvik held leading global positions in specific niches within each of these areas.

Principal Subsidiaries

Dormer Tools AB; Dropler High Tech AB; Ecocat AB; Edmetson AB; Fragoso AB; Guldsmedshytte Bruks AB; Gusab Holding AB; Gusab Stainless AB; AB Sandvik Belts; AB Sandvik Calamo; AB Sandvik Coromant; Sandvik Coromant Norden AB; AB Sandvik Falken; Sandvik Far East Ltd. AB; AB Sandvik Hard Materials; Sandvik Hard Materials Norden AB; AB Sandvik Information Systems; AB Sandvik International; Sandvik Invest AB; AB Sandvik Powders; AB Sandvik Process Systems; AB Sandvik Rock Tools; Sandvik Rock Tools Svenska Försäljnings AB; AB Sandvik Service; AB Sandvik Steel; Sandvik Stål Försäljnings AB; AB Sandvik Teknik; AB Sandvik Tranan; AB Sandvik Västberga Service; Sandvik rebro AB; AB Sandvik rnen; ZP Sandvik (Belarus); Dormer Tools S.A. (Brazil); Sandvik do Brasil SA. (Brazil); Sandvik China Ltd.; Sandvik International Trading (Shanghai) Co. Ltd. (China); Sandvik Colombia S.A.; Sandvik CZ s.r.o. (Czech Republic); Sandvik

GmbH (Germany); Sandvik Holding GmbH (Germany); Sandvik A.E. Tools and Materials (Greece); Sandvik KFT (Hungary); Sandvik Asia Ltd. (India; 73%); Sandvik Choksi Ltd. (India; 51%); CML Handling Technology S.p.A. (Italy); Sandvik K.K. (Japan); Sandvik Kenya Ltd. (96%); Sandvik Korea Ltd.; Sandvik Méxicana S.A. de C.V. (Mexico); Sandvik Maroc S.A. (Morocco; 94%); CTT Cutting Tool Technology B.V. (Netherlands); Sandvik Benelux B.V. (Netherlands); Sandvik Finance B.V. (Netherlands); Sandvik del Perú S.A.; Sandvik Baildonit S.A. (Poland); Sandvik Polska Sp.z. o.o. (Poland); Sandvik Portuguesa Lda (Portugal); Sandvik Slovakia s.r.o.; Minas y Metalurgia Espanola SA (Spain); Sandvik Endüstriyel Mamüller Sanayi ve Ticaret A.S. (Turkey); Sandvik (Zambia) Ltd.; Sandvik (Private) Ltd. (Zimbabwe).

Principal Operating Units

Sandvik Tooling (including Sandvik Coromant, Sandvik CTT, and Sandvik Hard Materials); Sandvik Mining and Construction (including Sandvik Tamrock, Voest-Alpine Eimco, Driltech Mission, and Roxon); Sandvik Specialty Steels (including Sandvik Steel, Kanthal, and Sandvik Process Systems).

Principal Competitors

Atlas Copco AB; Boart Longyear Group; Bridgeport Machines, Inc.; Carpenter Technology Corporation; Flow International Corporation; Furukawa Co., Ltd.; Greenfield Industries, Inc.; Harnischfeger Industries, Inc.; Ingersoll-Rand Company; Joy Mining Machinery; Kennametal Inc.; Long-Airdox Company; Mannesmann AG; Milacron Inc.; Mitsubishi Steel Mfg. Co., Ltd.; Nippon Steel Corporation; The Stanley Works; Sumitomo Metal Industries, Ltd.; Thyssen Krupp AG; Toshiba Corporation.

Further Reading

Aronson, Robert B., "Journey to Sweden," *Manufacturing Engineering,* July 1998, pp. 134–38.

Burt, Tim, "Snap-On Buys Sandvik Unit," *Financial Times,* April 23, 1999, p. 31.

Garnett, Nick, "Carbide Tool Groups Sharpen Up Their Image," *Financial Times,* April 6, 1988.

Hedin, Göran, *Ett Svenskt Jernwerk, Sandviken, 1862–1937,* Uppsala: [n.p.], 1937.

McIvor, Greg, "Skanska to Sell Its Holding in Sandvik," *Financial Times,* April 15, 1997, p. 27.

Reier, Sharon, "Against the Tide," *Financial World,* May 10, 1994, pp. 48–49.

"Sandvik, Inc. to Acquire Precision Twist Drill," *Industrial Distribution,* August 1997, pp. 16, 23.

Shutte, Lesley, "Sandvik Shows Its Metal," *Director,* December 1996, pp. 54–58.

Transformation: Sandvik, 1862–1987, Sandviken: Sandvik AB, 1987.

Wright, Chris, "Sandvik Ready for the Increase in Competition," *Corporate Finance,* January 1999, p. 29.

—Cliff Pratten
—updated by David E. Salamie

SBC Communications Inc.

175 East Houston Street
San Antonio, Texas 78205
U.S.A.
Telephone: (210) 821-4105
Fax: (210) 351-2274
Web site: http://www.sbc.com

Public Company
Incorporated: 1920 as Southwestern Bell Telephone Company
Employees: 203,000
Sales: $46 billion (1998)
Stock Exchanges: New York
Ticker Symbol: SBC
NAIC: 513310 Wired Telecommunications Carriers; 513322 Cellular and Other Wireless Telecommunications; 511140 Telephone Directory Publishers

Originally one of the seven regional holding companies formed after the breakup of American Telephone & Telegraph Corporation's (AT&T) Bell System in 1983, SBC Communications Inc. has emerged in the 1990s as a national provider of local telephone services. It acquired other regional bell operating companies (RBOCs)—Pacific Telesis, Southern New England, and Ameritech—in the 1990s following passage of the Telecommunications Act of 1996. Second in size only to the proposed Bell Atlantic-GTE combination, SBC was poised to offer a full range of local, long-distance (not yet permitted, but expected in 2000), and wireless services throughout the United States and internationally.

Early History to 1920

Southwestern Bell Telephone Company was created in 1920 from about 20 predecessor companies. The four largest of these were American District Telegraph Company, formed in St. Louis, Missouri, in 1878; the Kansas City Telephone Exchange, formed in Kansas City, Missouri, in 1879; Southwestern Telegraph & Telephone Company, which began serving Texas and Arkansas in 1881; and Pioneer Telephone & Telegraph Company, which provided telephone service beginning in 1904 in Oklahoma—not then a state, but known as Indian Territory—and in parts of Kansas. During their early years these four companies became affiliated with the Bell System, acquired other companies, and went through a number of name changes. In 1912 they consolidated various operating functions and became the Southwestern Bell Telephone System.

In 1917 the four companies began moving toward a more formal merger, with the Missouri & Kansas Telephone Company—the new name of the Kansas City Telephone Exchange—acquiring Bell Telephone Company of Missouri, successor to American District Telegraph. The resulting company was named Southwestern Bell Telephone Company (Missouri). In 1920 this company bought Southwestern Telephone & Telegraph and Southwestern Bell Telephone Company (Oklahoma), the successor to Pioneer Telephone & Telegraph, establishing the new Southwestern Bell Telephone Company, which was a subsidiary of AT&T. The new company had headquarters in Kansas City, Missouri, but moved to St. Louis the following year. Its president was Eugene D. Nims, a veteran executive at several other companies.

Growth and Consolidation: 1920s

During the 1920s Southwestern Bell absorbed several other companies. In 1923 it bought the Kinloch Telephone System, which had been a competitor in St. Louis. Southwestern Bell and Kinloch had been two of the last telephone companies to compete in a major U.S. city. In 1925 Southwestern Bell bought back from the Dallas Telephone Company the Dallas-based telephone business that Southwestern Telephone & Telegraph had sold in 1918. In 1927 Southwestern Bell Telephone made another reacquisition, this time of the Kansas City phone business, which the Southwestern system had sold to a non-Bell company in 1919. Southwestern Bell did divest itself of a few operations, selling 23 Missouri telephone exchanges to Southeastern Missouri Telephone Company in 1929.

In 1926, the year Southwestern Bell installed its one millionth telephone, the company completed its new operations

Company Perspectives:

SBC Communications Inc. is a global telecommunications company offering a wide range of innovative services and solutions to meet customers' needs. Through leading brands, the SBC Telecom strategy (an initiative to expand nationally into 30 top markets outside of our traditional service region), and investments in telecommunications businesses in 22 countries outside the U.S., SBC stands ready to serve customers, wherever they may be.

center in St. Louis. At 31 stories, the building was the tallest in Missouri at that time. New or renovated administrative offices followed in Dallas, Kansas City, and Oklahoma City in 1929.

Weathering the Great Depression: 1930s

During the Great Depression that followed the 1929 stock market crash, Southwestern Bell bought up numerous small telephone companies in its region. Often these companies were on the brink of insolvency. The largest Depression-era purchase was United Telephone Company of Kansas, bought in 1938. In the Depression years, Southwestern Bell took on some employees from its parent company, AT&T, which did not want to lay them off; the Bell System operating companies were not hit as hard by the Depression as AT&T's Western Electric manufacturing arm. Southwestern Bell felt the effects of the Depression sufficiently, however, to give employees incentives to bring in new customers or to persuade existing customers not to have their phone service shut off. During the Depression, unionization of Southwestern Bell's workforce was heightened. Several of U.S. President Franklin D. Roosevelt's New Deal programs, such as the Wagner Act of 1935, encouraged the formation of labor unions and protected workers from being penalized for joining unions. Southwestern Bell and its unionized employees had relatively cordial relations during this period.

Expanding Following World War II: 1940s

More than 3,000 Southwestern Bell workers served in the armed forces in World War II. The company took steps to conserve materials, such as copper and rubber, that were in short supply during the war. Telephone sets also were scarce, but Southwestern Bell's territory held a position of priority in their allocation, because the five-state area contained many defense plants and military training facilities. Other Bell operating companies transferred parts of their inventory to Southwestern Bell. The number and length of telephone calls, particularly long-distance calls, increased greatly during the war, often resulting in long delays for callers. Southwestern Bell launched an advertising campaign encouraging customers to hold their calls to five minutes each, and operators interrupted conversations that went past this limit.

After the war ended, Southwestern Bell expanded its engineering operations to meet pent-up demand for phone service; at one point in 1945 the company had a waiting list of 205,000. The number of phones the company operated had reached two million in 1944 and soared to three million by 1948. Southwestern Bell also stepped up the marketing of enhanced telephone equipment and services, such as extensions; this effort had begun in the late 1930s but was pushed aside by more pressing matters during the war.

The late 1940s brought a break in the company's peaceful labor relations. The National Federation of Telephone Workers, the union that later became the Communications Workers of America, organized the first nationwide strike against telephone companies in 1947. The strike lasted more than 40 days. In 1953 Missouri governor Phil Donnelly signed the King-Thompson Act that outlawed utility strikes in the state, but unions and their supporters subsequently won a repeal of the act.

Responding to Social Changes: 1950s–60s

In 1951 Southwestern Bell acquired Southeastern Missouri Telephone Company, the company that had bought some of Southwestern Bell's exchanges in 1929. In 1952 it added Southwest Telephone Company of Kansas. The number of phones operated by Southwestern Bell reached four million in 1952, five million in 1956, and six million in 1960. The figure was ten million by 1969.

The 1950s and 1960s brought a wave of new products and services from Western Electric and Bell Laboratories, two other AT&T companies. These innovations included phones in various colors and styles, the ability to interrupt or forward calls, and push-button service. To sell all these products, Southwestern Bell Telephone created its first marketing department in 1967.

The 1950s and 1960s also were a time of social change. During the 1950s Southwestern Bell shut down a St. Louis customer service office that had been staffed entirely by blacks since the 1940s. The company had set up this office so that black customers dealt with only black employees; the growing civil rights movement, however, led the company to integrate its workforce. In 1966 Southwestern Bell named its first woman manager of a business unit.

Promotion of minorities and women in Bell System companies was not moving fast enough to please the U.S. Equal Employment Opportunity Commission (EEOC), however. In 1970 the EEOC accused AT&T and its Bell System of discrimination on the basis of race and sex. The companies responded that they were moving minorities and women gradually into parity with white males. In 1973 and 1974, AT&T and the Bell companies agreed to provide millions of dollars in back pay and salary increases to thousands of minority and women employees, although the companies did not admit to having discriminated in the past.

Government and Labor, New Challenges: 1968–1980

In the late 1960s the first challenges to the Bell System's monopoly appeared. In 1968 came the Federal Communications Commission's (FCC) Carterfone decision, which struck down prohibitions on connections of other companies' equipment or systems with the Bell telephone system. Then, in 1969, the FCC decided to allow Microwave Communications, Inc. (MCI) to build a long-distance line between St. Louis and

Key Dates:

1920: Southwestern Bell Telephone Company is consolidated from about 20 predecessor companies.
1926: Southwestern Bell installs its one millionth telephone and completes its operations center in St. Louis, Missouri.
1978: Southwestern Bell installs its 15 millionth telephone, making it the largest company in the Bell System.
1984: Southwestern Bell Corporation, a holding company, officially takes ownership of Southwestern Bell Telephone Company following the breakup of AT&T.
1990: Edward Whitacre becomes CEO of Southwestern Bell.
1995: Southwestern Bell changes its name to SBC Communications Inc.
1996: SBC acquires Pacific Telesis Group for $16.5 billion.
1998: SBC acquires Southern New England Telecommunications Corp. for $4.4 billion and Ameritech for $62 billion.

Chicago. In 1974 the U.S. Department of Justice filed an antitrust suit against AT&T—the suit that broke up the Bell System a decade later.

In the meantime, many of the Bell companies were having labor problems. A 1968 strike lasted 18 days at Southwestern Bell, although it stretched to five months in some other parts of the system. Another strike followed in 1971; workers at Southwestern Bell and most other system companies settled within six days.

A crisis of 1974 involved management-level employees. T.O. Gravitt, who ran Southwestern Bell's Texas operations, committed suicide that year, leaving behind papers that alleged bribery of regulators and other offenses by the company. In civil litigation, Gravitt's widow won substantial compensation from Southwestern Bell, but the court's decisions were reversed on appeal. The allegations prompted an audit by AT&T of all Bell operating companies; the audit found questionable practices only in Texas and North Carolina. The situation also prompted the state of Texas, which heretofore had left telephone regulation to its cities, to establish the Public Utility Commission of Texas in 1976. It had been the last state in the union without such a commission. In one of its first actions, the commission granted Southwestern Bell less than 20 percent of a $298 million rate increase the company had requested.

In 1978 Southwestern Bell installed its 15 millionth telephone; it was the first company in the Bell System to reach this level. By 1982, 70 percent of Southwestern Bell's customers were served by electronic switching systems, a percentage that also was the highest among Bell companies. In 1982 the company made another acquisition, of the El Paso, Texas, telephone business that had been operated by Mountain States Telephone Company.

Competing with Other Bell Companies: 1980s

In 1982 AT&T and the Justice Department approved the consent decree that broke up the Bell System. AT&T agreed to divest itself of the Bell operating companies, and the department agreed to drop its antitrust suit. In 1983 Southwestern Bell Corporation was formed as the regional holding company for Southwestern Bell Telephone Company.

Before the breakup was effected, there was another nationwide telephone strike, which lasted for 21 days in 1983. Workers won improved benefits as well as provisions for additional severance pay or retraining if they lost their jobs—a particular concern at the time of the divestiture.

Ownership of Southwestern Bell Telephone Company was officially transferred to Southwestern Bell Corporation on January 1, 1984. SBC had three other subsidiaries: Southwestern Bell Publications, Inc., a directory publisher; Southwestern Bell Mobile Systems, Inc., in the business of mobile telephone service; and Southwestern Bell Telecommunications, Inc., focusing on marketing phone equipment to business customers. The new holding company's president, chairman, and CEO was Zane Edison Barnes, who had been president of the telephone company since 1973. SBC moved its headquarters into a new 44-story building in St. Louis.

Unlike some other regional Bell holding companies, which diversified into such fields as real estate and computer sales, SBC stuck with businesses closely related to telephone service. Through several acquisitions, it solidified its position as the largest directory publisher in the United States. It purchased Mast Advertising & Publishing, Inc., from Continental Telecom for $120 million in 1985. Mast was the 12th largest U.S. directory publisher and brought SBC a national sales force and an entrance into the publication of directories for independent telephone companies. SBC took its publishing ventures to the international market when its publications subsidiary in 1984 won a contract to be the Yellow Pages sales and collection agent for Telecom Australia.

SBC's customers were hurt by the recession in the oil business in the mid-1980s, and this in turn affected SBC. By 1986 the company's sales growth was the slowest of any regional telephone holding company, and its earnings growth was next to last. The situation began to turn around, however, after SBC bought Metromedia Inc.'s cellular and paging business in 1987. This purchase made SBC the third largest cellular-communications company in the United States, behind McCaw Cellular and Pacific Telesis. In 1989 SBC's cellular business began to be profitable, while its larger competitors were still showing losses. In overall profitability, SBC ranked second only to Pacific Telesis among regional telephone holding companies in 1989.

Aggressive Acquisitions Strategy Under Whitacre: 1990s

In January 1990 Edward Whitacre succeeded Barnes. Whitacre had been with SBC and Southwestern Bell Telephone for 27 years. During 1990 SBC increased its international focus. Its subsidiary, Southwestern Bell International Holdings Corporation (SBIHC), joined a consortium that bought 20.4 percent of the total equity and 51 percent of the shares with full voting rights in Télefonos de México, S.A. de C.V., Mexico's national telephone company. SBIHC's partners in the consortium were France Cables et Radio, S.A.—a subsidiary of France Telecom—and Mexican company Grupo Carso. The total purchase price was $1.76 billion; SBIHC's share of this was $486 million. Participation gave SBC a chance to sell services, such as long-distance telephone communications, that it was prohibited from offering in the United States. Mexico had an antiquated telephone system, but potential for significant growth; only one in 17 households had a telephone. Another international move in 1990 was SBC's agreement to purchase West Midlands Cable Communications in the United Kingdom; this system included the largest cable television franchise in that country. In 1991 SBC increased its ownership to 98 percent of the United Kingdom's Oyston Cable.

In the early 1990s, SBC, like other regional holding companies, was seeking changes in the regulations that arose from the AT&T breakup. These regulations restricted the businesses that regional holding companies could enter; among those prohibited were video programming production and various other communications products. As it awaited the outcome of its fight to lift these constraints, SBC continued to focus on its core businesses, as it had done ever since the divestiture.

In February 1993 SBC moved its headquarters from St. Louis to San Antonio, Texas. It joined a local group of businesses to acquire the San Antonio Spurs basketball team for $75 million. It also became the first regional Bell telephone company to acquire a cable television company outside of its service area when it paid $650 million to Hauser Communications for two cable systems in Maryland and Virginia.

In 1994 SBC called off a proposed $1.6 billion acquisition of a 40 percent interest in Cox Cable of San Diego Inc. SBC's management felt that the FCC's rulings regarding cable television would negatively impact the company's cash flow. Over the next several years SBC would divest its remaining interests in cable television companies.

Emerging As a National Local Service Provider: 1996–2000

Following a 1995 name-change to SBC Communications, the company combined its Southwestern Bell Telecom division, which provided telephone equipment, with Southwestern Bell Telephone Co. as a cost-saving measure. Under new federal rules customers were allowed to purchase local phone connections and phone equipment or systems from the same source. Under the 1984 breakup of AT&T, regional Bell companies had been required to operate their phone service and phone equipment businesses as separate divisions or subsidiaries.

In April 1996 SBC announced it would acquire Pacific Telesis Group (PacTel), an RBOC serving California and Nevada, for $16.5 billion. The two companies' service regions were not contiguous, but both had interests in phone service in and to Mexico. For the previous year SBC had $12.7 billion in revenues and 14.1 million local access lines, while PacTel had $9.0 billion in revenues and 15.8 million local access lines. The merger received the necessary approvals from SBC shareholders, the FCC, and the California Public Utilities Commission in 1997. SBC planned to build a cellular service in California as well as an Internet service. California accounted for an estimated 25 percent of all U.S. Internet users.

For 1996 SBC posted its fifth consecutive year of double-digit increases in earnings. The company reported earnings of $2.1 billion for 1996, a 12 percent increase from $1.9 billion in 1995. Its wireless business added 739,000 subscribers, and overall the company added 1.5 million customer lines during the year. Internationally the company's customer base increased to one million access lines, 307,000 wireless customers, and 350,000 video subscribers. SBC retained a ten percent interest in Télefonos de Mexico (Telmex), but was facing increased competition there due to Mexican deregulation. Under the Telecommunications Act of 1996, SBC was looking forward to entering the long-distance market. With competition now permitted in local telephone service, SBC signed 56 interconnection agreements in 1996 with 32 companies that planned to enter local markets.

In 1997 rumors of a proposed merger between AT&T, the United States' largest long-distance carrier, and SBC, the largest local service provider, came to an end when the FCC voiced its disapproval. Later in the year SBC completed its exit from cable television when it sold the two systems in Maryland and Virginia it had acquired from Hauser Communications in 1993. The company was also in the process of completing negotiations to leave the Americast joint venture it had formed in 1995 with Ameritech, BellSouth, and the Walt Disney Co. In December 1997 SBC sold Pacific Bell Video Services, the digital wireless cable operation it had acquired as part of PacTel. For 1997 SBC had more than $23 billion in revenues.

Hoping to enter the long-distance field, SBC announced in January 1998 it would acquire Southern New England Telecommunications Corp. (SNET) for $4.4 billion in stock. SNET was based in New Haven, Connecticut. SBC had recently won a court judgment that would make it easier for RBOCs to enter the long-distance market, but the decision was still being challenged by AT&T and the FCC. The FCC approved SBC's acquisition of SNET in October 1998, giving SBC a total of 36.9 million local access lines.

In May 1998 SBC and Ameritech, two of the remaining five RBOCs, announced a planned $62 billion merger, with SBC taking over Ameritech. The acquisition added Ameritech's 21 million local telephone lines in five Midwest states to the SBC system. The FCC approved the merger in October 1999 and attached a list of 30 conditions that SBC must meet. SBC planned to move Ameritech's corporate functions to San Antonio, and Ameritech's top executives were given a multimillion-dollar severance package. For the time being, the merger made SBC the largest RBOC, at least until the FCC approved a merger between Bell Atlantic and GTE.

Also in 1998 SBC strengthened its position in the rapidly growing data service market by paying $22 million for a four percent interest in Concentric Network Corp. of Cupertino, California. The two companies planned to develop a collection of business products that would include virtual private networks, web hosting, shared software, and electronic commerce. Combined 1998 revenues were $46 billion, including Ameritech, placing SBC among the top 15 companies in the *Fortune 500.*

In January 1999 SBC announced it would purchase Comcast Cellular, the wireless subsidiary of Comcast Corporation, for $1.7 billion, including the assumption of $1.3 billion of debt. Under the agreement SBC's wireless service regions (Washington-Baltimore, Connecticut, Rhode Island, Massachusetts, and upstate New York), would join with Comcast Cellular's wireless systems in Philadelphia, New Jersey, and Delaware. SBC would also acquire wireless systems in Illinois and personal communications system licenses in Pennsylvania. SBC would add about 800,000 customers to its wireless customer base of more than 6.5 million people.

Continuing to prepare for the day when it would be allowed to compete for long-distance service, SBC announced in February 1999 it would acquire up to ten percent of Williams Companies' telecommunications division for about $500 million. Williams was about two-thirds of the way to completing a nationwide fiber-optic network and would carry SBC's long-distance traffic.

In the first quarter of 1999 SBC reported net income of $1.1 billion on revenue of $7.3 billion. As 1999 drew to a close, the company was not yet permitted to offer long-distance services, but it fully anticipated that approval would be granted in 2000. SBC operated more than 59 million access lines and had more than ten million domestic wireless customers. It served eight of the United States' ten largest metropolitan areas, and it had strategic investments in 23 countries worth an estimated $22 billion.

Principal Subsidiaries

Southwestern Bell Telephone Company; Pacific Bell; Ameritech Corporation; Cellular One; Nevada Bell.

Principal Competitors

BellSouth Corporation; Bell Atlantic Corporation; MCI WorldCom, Inc.; AT&T Corp.

Further Reading

''Acquisition: SBC Communications Expands Wireless Reach,'' *InfoWorld,* January 25, 1999, p. 20.
''A.M. Report: And Then There Were Four: FCC Oks SBC/Ameritech Merger,'' *Telephony,* October 11, 1999.
Avalos, George, ''SBC, Pacific Telesis Merger Wins Federal Approval,'' *Knight-Ridder/Tribune Business News,* February 2, 1997.
''A Bid Too Far?'' *Economist (U.S.),* May 16, 1998, p. 63.
Brown, Rich, ''Southwestern Bell Makes First RBOC Cable Entry for $650 Million,'' *Broadcasting,* February 15, 1993, p. 3.
Carter, Wayne, and Beth Snyder, ''Always a Bridesmaid . . . SBC, AT&T End Brief Courtship,'' *Telephony,* July 7, 1997, p. 6.
Colman, Price, ''SBC Selling LA Wireless Cable,'' *Broadcasting & Cable,* December 8, 1997, p. 90.
Dwyer, Joe, III, ''Bell Telephone, Telecom Merging,'' *St. Louis Business Journal,* January 22, 1996, p. 1A.
Essick, Kristi, ''SBC Plans Huge Telecom Takeover,'' *InfoWorld,* May 18, 1998, p. 55.
Ferranti, Marc, ''SBS, Pacific Telesis Group Combine, Address Global Issues,'' *InfoWorld,* April 14, 1997, p. 58.
Files, Jennifer, ''Phone Companies' Earnings Grow,'' *Knight-Ridder/Tribune Business News,* April 21, 1999.
Hayes, David, ''Telecommunications Act Continues to Reshape the Industry,'' *Knight-Ridder/Tribune Business News,* October 4, 1999.
Higgins, John M., ''Unhappy Returns for Comcast,'' *Broadcasting & Cable,* February 1, 1999, p. 42.
Kupfer, Andrew, ''A Whirlwind Romance Leads to Wedding Bells,'' *Fortune,* April 29, 1996, p. 42.
Park, David G., Jr., *Good Connections: A Century of Service by the Men & Women of Southwestern Bell,* St. Louis, Mo.: Southwestern Bell Telephone Company, 1984.
Poole, Claire, ''Home Court Advantage,'' *Forbes,* March 29, 1993, p. 16.
Rose, Barbara,''SBC Ready to Ring up Big Changes: After Merger, Ameritech to Adopt Whitacre's Code,'' *Crain's Chicago Business,* August 30, 1999, p. 3.
Rudnitsky, Howard, ''Value in Cable,'' *Forbes,* April 12, 1993, p. 144.
''SBC Leaves Cable,'' *Television Digest,* October 6, 1997, p. 6.
''SBC Makes a Long-Distance Deal,'' *Business Week,* February 22, 1999, p. 45.
''SBC Makes Long-Distance Acquisition,'' *Computerworld,* January 12, 1998, p. 48.
''SBC/SNET Merger Complete,'' *Telephony,* November 2, 1998.
Sheron, Don, ''Earnings up 12 Percent at SBC Communications,'' *Knight-Ridder/Tribune Business News,* January 22, 1997.
——, ''SBC Shareholders Approve Pacific Telesis Merger,'' *Knight-Ridder/Tribune Business News,* August 1, 1996.
''Southwestern Bell,'' *Television Digest,* August 19, 1991, p. 6.
Stroud, Jerri, ''SBC to Acquire Stake in Cupertino, Calif.-Based Telecommunications Firm,'' *Knight-Ridder/Tribune Business News,* October 20, 1998.
''SWB-Cox Deal Dies,'' *Television Digest,* April 11, 1994, p. 4.
Taub, Daniel, ''Mixed Results After PacBell, SBC Merger,'' *Los Angeles Business Journal,* August 3, 1998, p. 3.
Vittore, Vince, ''SBC Completes Video Pullout,'' *Telephony,* October 6, 1997, p. 13.
Vogelstein, Fred, ''By the Power Vested in Me: No,'' *U.S. News & World Report,* July 14, 1997, p. 47.

—Jim Bowman and Trudy Ring
—updated by David P. Bianco

scottish media group

Scottish Media Group plc

Cowcadden
Glasgow G2 3PR
United Kingdom
Telephone: (+44) 141 300-3300
Fax: (+44) 141 300-3033
Web site: http://www.scottishmedia.com

Public Company
Incorporated: 1957 as Scottish Television plc
Employees: 1,524
Sales: £207.4 million (US$344.3 million)(1998)
Stock Exchanges: London
Ticker Symbol: SSM
NAIC: 51312 Television Broadcasting; 51111 Newspaper Publishers; 51112 Periodical Publishers

Scottish Media Group plc is one of the largest cross-platform media companies serving Scotland. The company, formerly known as Scottish Television, has held the STV license, serving central Scotland and more than 3.4 million television viewers since 1957, and the license for Grampian Television, Scotland's second largest television broadcaster, serving 1.1 million viewers across northern Scotland, since 1997. Together, these two members of the United Kingdom's ITV (Independent Television) network produce more than 1,400 hours of programming each year. With the legislation passed in 1996 allowing cross-media ownership in the United Kingdom, Scottish Media Group has expanded beyond television broadcasting to include such market leaders in newspaper publishing as the *Herald*, the *Evening Times*, and the *Sunday Herald*; magazine publishing, through subsidiary Caledonian Magazines; and electronic publishing, through subsidiary Delphic Interactive. Scottish Media Group has also branched into outdoor advertising with the acquisition of Primesight in March 1999. Consistently rumored as a takeover target for the consolidating U.K. television and publishing markets, Scottish Media Group has affirmed its intention to retain its independence and its base in Scotland. Nonetheless, the company has been 20 percent owned by English independent television heavyweight Granada Group since June 1999.

Independent Pioneer in the 1950s

Until the mid-1950s, television in the United Kingdom remained under the strict control of the British Government, which served its television viewing audience through its world famous BBC stations. The introduction of an independently owned broadcast network in the 1950s, however, opened the way for a new range of television companies. The country was divided into a number of broadcast regions, with each region representing a single license. In 1957, Roy Thomson, from Canada, was awarded the license for the central Scotland region. Thomson named James Coltart as the company's first managing director.

Scottish Television began its first transmissions on the new ITV network that year with the popular "This Is Scotland" broadcast, featuring such local talent as Deborah Kerr, David Niven, and Moira Shearer. The company's initial audience was limited to only 187,000 television sets. Nonetheless, its first transmissions attracted some 750,000 viewers. By the end of its first year, more than 430,000 households in the central Scotland region had television sets. The first broadcasts of the "One O'Clock Gang," a weekday show, gave STV its first hit program and one of the longest-running of its early shows, with more than 1,760 programs lasting until 1966. That show's success, however, paled beside the success of "Scotsport," which debuted in September 1957 and continued to boast strong audience shares through the end of the century, making it the longest-running program in the entire U.K. television market.

After going public in 1965, STV won an increase in its programming requirements, adding some three-and-a-half hours per week. This increase prompted the company to open new studios, in Edinburgh, in 1969. The new studios, called Gateway Studios, opened just in time; that same year, a fire destroyed the company's main studios at Cowcadden. Work on rebuilding the Cowcadden Studios began in 1972; the reopening of the new Cowcadden Studios came in 1974. STV's studio complexes were further expanded in 1977, in order to accom-

> **Company Perspectives:**
>
> *We deliver a mix of information and entertainment across a range of different media. In doing so we fulfil the needs and demands of our advertisers, viewers and readers.*

modate an increase in programming. STV had meanwhile scored a coup when it handled the broadcast of the European Cup soccer finals from Hampden Park, the largest outdoor sporting event yet broadcast by a member of the ITV network.

STV remained one of the smaller of the United Kingdom's broadcasters, focusing on its own central Scotland region. A number of the company's programs, however, went on to reach worldwide audiences. Such was the case with the series ''Taggart.'' Featuring a detective in Glasgow, ''Taggart'' was first broadcast in 1983 as a three-part miniseries. Popular acclaim led to the creation of a series, starring Mark McManus in the title role. As audiences topped 18 million viewers for some episodes, ''Taggart'' became one of the United Kingdom's longest running series, with new shows being produced for the beginning of the new century. The series even proved capable of surviving McManus's death in 1994. Another popular and long-running series, ''High Road,'' debuted in the first half of the 1980s, giving STV a new programming success. In 1984, STV scored another programming triumph with the broadcast of the 24-part history of Scotland, ''Scotland's Story.''

Scottish Media Giant in the 1990s

Led by William Brown, who had joined STV in 1958 and had served as the company's managing director since 1966, STV began to seek new blood and a new look in the 1980s. In 1985, the company hired Gus Macdonald, former journalist, and later producer with rival Granada Television, as the company's director of programs. Macdonald was named managing director in 1990, as Brown became company chairman. One of the first moves Macdonald made was to lead a change of identity, adopting the name Scottish Television and a new logo featuring a thistle design. The new name and logo were meant to underscore the company's commitment to its home base and to set off its identity as a Scottish broadcaster against the dominant English nature of the United Kingdom's broadcast community.

By the 1990s, Scottish Television recognized that it would need to grow in order to maintain its independence in a media landscape promising radical changes over the coming decade. The emergence of new competitors—in the form of cable television and satellite television operators—produced new threats to the company's position and advertising revenues. While the United Kingdom had been relatively late in adding cable and satellite television systems, these new competitors, including the BSkyB satellite network, finally began to launch in the late 1980s. At the same time, repeated calls for new legislation governing media ownership were expected to open the media market to cross-ownership possibilities in the 1990s. The new legislation promised not only the consolidation of the U.K. television market, but also the emergence of a new breed of U.K. multimedia giant.

In reaction to this trend, Scottish Television began to seek means of diversifying its own interest. An early effort, with the acquisition of Alternative International, a temporary employment agent with operations throughout the United Kingdom and in Italy, Luxembourg, Germany, and Belgium, brought the company a bit too far from its core operations, and was sold off again in 1994. Instead, Scottish Television turned to the television market itself, with its expanding number of broadcasters, for its diversification. In 1993, the company launched a new subsidiary, Scottish Television Enterprises (STE), devoted to creating programming not only for Scottish Television, but also for the entire ITV network. STE quickly found customers among the worldwide television market as well. The company also sought to enter the cable television field, buying a 20 percent interest in Good Morning Television Ltd. (GMTV); that investment, however, remained passive, and, after years of write-offs, was finally sold in 1999. Meanwhile, Scottish Television itself became attractive to other buyers: in 1994, the publishing company Mirror Group purchased a 20 percent position in Scottish Television; the following year, the cable programming company Flextech bought up another 20 percent of Scottish Television.

Scottish Television turned to satellite television, launching Sky Scottish, a joint-venture operation with BSkyB, in 1996. Meant to broadcast Scottish programming to a U.K.-wide audience, Sky Scottish's transmissions were available to both cable and satellite television audiences. Yet the venture met with only limited success and was ended in 1998.

After Gus Macdonald had been appointed chairman in 1995, his position as managing director was filled by Andrew Flanagan, who was later named company CEO in 1997. Macdonald and Flanagan found better success with the company's other diversification efforts. The new legislation passed in 1996 allowing cross-media ownership had opened the way to a consolidation of the U.K.'s media markets. Scottish Television took advantage of the changing media landscape by transforming itself. After starting up its Voice electronic publishing subsidiary in 1995, the company acquired Caledonian Publishing. More than a newspaper and magazine publisher, Caledonian held two key properties: the *Scottish Herald* and the *Evening Star*, two of Scotland's most prominent and widely read newspapers. The move not only promised opportunities for cross-media advertising sales, it also enabled Scottish Television to reinforce its image as one of Scotland's only Scotland-based and Scotland-owned media groups.

Indeed, in order to reinforce its new multifaceted organization, Scottish Television changed its name to Scottish Media Group (SMG) in 1997. The company quickly followed this change with the acquisition of Grampian Television, the ITV broadcaster holding the license for Scotland's northern region. Adding 1.2 million viewers to SMG's audience, Grampian also boasted the largest geographical base of all ITV broadcasters. At the same time, the company suggested that it was not opposed to a future acquisition of Border Television, the third ITV licensee in Scotland.

SMG's reaffirmation of its Scottish roots came at the same time as support for the breakup of the United Kingdom into independent regional countries was growing. Demands for

Key Dates:

1957: Roy Thomson is awarded ITV license for central Scotland, and Scottish Television programming begins.
1966: Company gains listing on London Stock Exchange.
1969: Gateway Studios opens in Edinburgh.
1974: Cowcadden Studios is inaugurated.
1983: "Taggart" television series debuts.
1993: Scottish Television Enterprises is formed.
1996: Sky Scottish joint venture with BskyB is launched; company acquires Caledonian Publishing.
1997: Name is changed to Scottish Media Group; company purchases Grampian Television, ITV broadcaster for northern Scotland.

Scottish independence, with the creation of Scotland's own parliament, led to a referendum vote in 1997. With the referendum passed, SMG found itself in a strong position to attract an audience flush with a new national pride. At the same time, other media groups, including the London-based giants, were eyeing the Scottish market, adapting their newspapers and magazines to include new region-specific editions.

Nonetheless, SMG comforted itself with its early lead and strong Scotland focus. The company also increased its interests in the burgeoning electronic media market. After forming the Delphic Interactive joint-venture between its Voice subsidiary and Delphic Media & Communications, a multimedia developer, SMG went on to acquire all of Delphic Interactive in 1999. In that same year, SMG, having strengthened its media offerings, moved to fortify its crucial advertising potential by buying up Pearl & Dean, an agency that catered to the movie theater industry, and Primesight and Baillie Advertising, both involved in outdoor advertising. At the beginning of 1999, SMG also made a move to enter one of Scotland's most important newspaper markets, with the creation of the *Sunday Herald*. Judged something of a risk by analysts, as the new *Herald* edition proposed to go head-to-head with the dominant *Scotland on Sunday* and its circulation of some 125,000, the *Sunday Herald* underscored SMG's commitment to becoming the dominant Scot-centric media force for the 21st century. Meanwhile, the company continued to proclaim its intention to remain an independent company, despite a change in its major shareholders. In late 1999, the Mirror Group sold its 20 percent stake to ITV competitor Granada Television, which itself had begun seeking to expand as one of the United Kingdom's major media groups for the new century.

Principal Subsidiaries

Caledonian Magazines; Caledonian Publishing; Delphic Interactive; Grampian Television Ltd; Pearl & Dean Cinemas; Primesight plc; Scottish Media Newspapers Ltd; Scottish Television Ltd; Scottish Television Enterprises Ltd; Scottish Media Publishing Limited.

Principal Competitors

British Broadcasting Corporation Ltd. (BBC); Johnston Press; BSkyB; Newsquest plc; Carlton Communications plc; Trinity Mirror; Hollinger International Inc.; United News & Media plc; Independent News.

Further Reading

Brown, Rob, "And Finally . . . the Dirks Are Out for an English McDonald," *Independent*, June 9, 1997, p. 6.

Daeschner, Jeff, "Scottish Media Guards Its Independence," *Reuters*, March 8, 1999.

"Granada 'Eyeing Scottish Media Group'," *Daily Telegraph*, November 30, 1999.

Horsman, Mathew, Scottish TV Pays Pounds 120m for Publisher, *Independent,* July 26, 1996, pp 21.

——, "STV Ponders Its Own Scottish Empire," *Independent*, March 06, 1996, p. 16.

Jaspan, Andrew, "No Sassenachs Please, We're Scottish," *Independent*, July 16, 1996, p. 18.

Larsen, Peter Thal, "Mirror to Sell Scottish Media Stake," *Independent*, March 05, 1999, p 18.

Weir, Keith, "Granada Buys 18 Pct of Scottish Media," *Reuters*, March 23, 1999.

Williams, Rhys, "Scots Paper in Crowded Market," *Independent*, February 08, 1999, p 4.

—M. L. Cohen

Seaman Furniture Company, Inc.

300 Crossways Park Drive
Woodbury, New York 11797
U.S.A.
Telephone: (516) 496-9560
Toll Free: (800) 332-5340
Fax: (516) 682-1610
Web site: http://www.seamans.com

Private Company
Incorporated: 1933
Employees: 1,130
Sales: $270 million (1998 est.)
NAIC: 44211 Furniture Stores

Seaman Furniture Company, Inc., a high-volume retailer targeted to appeal to the price-conscious middle-income consumer, believes itself to be the largest specialty furniture retailer in the northeast United States. Its more than 40 stores are located in the New York, Philadelphia, and Cleveland/Akron metropolitan areas. Seaman stocks a variety of living room, dining room, bedroom, and other home furniture and accessories. By offering few alternatives to items shown on the retail floor, the company is able to purchase in large quantities and pass on the savings to the consumer.

Rise to Riches: 1954–87

Julius Seaman left his Brooklyn school in the seventh grade to help his family make ends meet, eventually opening a furniture store in 1933. This enterprise gradually increased to an annual $150,000 in sales and allowed Seaman to send his two sons to the University of Pennsylvania's elite Wharton School of Business. ''His big goal in life,'' Morton Seaman later told Burr Leonard of *Forbes,* ''was that his boys would follow him and build up his business.''

Julius Seaman was only 48 when he died of a heart attack, leaving Morton—the elder son and a recent Wharton graduate—to help his mother save the business, while Carl, still in school, did what he could to pitch in on weekends and vacations. One lesson the sons had learned at Wharton was that it paid to advertise, and so in 1955 they spent $1,000 for the store's first ad, a full-page spread in a local tabloid. When sales tripled that week, Morton remembered another piece of Wharton advice—achieve economy of scale—and decided to open a second store to reduce advertising costs per unit. By 1971 there were seven Seaman outlets.

The next big move—and one that established Morton Seaman as a merchandising genius in the furniture retailing field—came in 1980, when the brothers gave up the traditional practice of ordering piece by piece from manufacturers and wholesalers and began buying in bulk instead at discount prices. They took a risk by anticipating demand but were able to offer shoppers bargain packages of coordinated furniture, with immediate delivery. Heavy use of television commercials successfully promoted the business with the jingle, ''See Seaman's First.'' Sales soared from $44.1 million in fiscal 1981 (the year ended April 30, 1981) to $101.6 million in fiscal 1984, when there were 22 stores, all in the metropolitan New York area. Nearly all of Seaman's furniture came from domestic sources until 1983, but by mid-1985, 19 percent of its merchandise was being imported from the Far East, Europe, and Canada.

Seaman entered the Philadelphia area in 1986 and rose to seventh place among U.S. furniture retailers with sales volume of $186.7 million in the fiscal year. The company had gone public in 1985, raising $47 million from sale of stock and about the same amount in 1986 from a secondary offering. The Seaman family, which retained about 43 percent of the shares, pocketed most of this money and used the rest for the expansion into Philadelphia, new corporate offices in Uniondale, Long Island, and the opening of a furniture factory in Conover, North Carolina. In 1987 Seaman opened its first Connecticut store and a new warehouse in Central Islip, Long Island. Morton Seaman was planning to open more suburban stores, stock them with higher-end furniture, and step up advertising to as much as $24 million a year.

The Seaman formula for success seemed unstoppable. Sales rocketed to $224.8 million in fiscal 1987, when net income reached $15.2 million. The firm's sales per square foot was

Company Perspectives:

Seaman's pledges to remain among the best full-line retailers in the United States.

Seaman's pledges to offer to our customers a pleasant and exciting shopping environment, with a wide selection of quality and value-priced furniture and accessories. We also pledge to enhance the shopping experience with quick, courteous delivery and, when needed, professional follow-up service.

We pledge to provide our employees with a friendly but challenging workplace where each individual's ideas and skills will be fostered and developed.

We pledge to continue to deal with our valued suppliers with openness and integrity.

second among furniture retailers and about three times the industry average.

In September 1987 the cumulative value of Seaman stock was more than $400 million, nearly twice the company's annual sales level. Before the end of the year the leveraged buyout firm Kohlberg Kravis Roberts & Co. (KKR) had agreed to purchase 77 percent of Seaman for $26 a share, or $354 million. The Seaman family collected about $150 million in cash and bonds and still remained in managerial control, retaining some 17 percent of the stock. KKR, in keeping with standard leveraged buyout practices of the era, took out huge bank loans and also issued high-yielding but speculative-grade ''junk'' bonds to finance the purchase, putting up only $40 million in cash.

Road to Ruin: 1989–92

During fiscal 1989 Seaman was the nation's second largest furniture retailer, with 31 stores and annual revenue of about $275 million. Nevertheless, its sales gains were falling far short of the average annual rise of about 20 percent that it had achieved for a decade—and short of even the five to ten percent gain that KKR more realistically anticipated. Consequently, its fiscal year operating profit of $23 million was not enough to pay the $39 million or so due in interest on the heavy debt that had been incurred to take the company private.

When Seaman was unable to meet an interest payment due in August 1989, restructuring negotiations began, with a settlement reached three months later. The 29 participating banks agreed to reduce the debt from about $275 million to $125 million in return for 46 percent of the company's shares. Most junk bond holders accepted an exchange of their securities for lesser-valued ones at a lower interest rate and an aggregate stake of seven to eight percent in the firm. KKR, its buyout fund, and the Seamans contributed a $42 million cash reserve to tide the company over.

With the national economy falling into recession and Long Island especially hurt by military cutbacks in the wake of the end of the cold war, however, Seaman's sales fell to about $259 million in fiscal 1990, and its operating income dropped to $11 million. Morton Seaman resigned as chief executive officer in February 1990 and soon was running a Florida-based furniture company called Rooms To Go. He was succeeded by Matthew D. Serra, president of a department store chain. Serra brought in many of his own people, reduced the number of employees, hired a contractor for the company's inhouse finance program, and dropped the firm's delivery company, opening a warehouse in Woodbridge, New Jersey. But the news remained bad in fiscal 1991, with revenue dropping to $255.8 million, despite the opening of eight new stores, bringing the total to 38. Operating income fell to $2 million, and the company incurred a net loss of $12.8 million.

Seaman filed for Chapter 11 bankruptcy protection from its creditors in January 1992, announcing that it planned to close the 15 of its 37 stores that were collectively accounting for only 20 percent of current sales. Nine months later, the company emerged from bankruptcy with its long-term debt cut from $370 million to $14 million. In return for accepting stock in place of debt, three Wall Street investment firms now owned 51 percent of the company. The bank lenders received 24 percent of the stock, with the remainder allocated to bondholders, trade creditors, and KKR partners. A total of 21 stores remained after those in Connecticut, the Philadelphia area, and some in New York were shed.

Recovery: 1993–98

A new management team, now based in Woodbury, Long Island, and headed by former Seaman executive Alan Rosenberg, vowed to get the company back to basics. The chain had been relying less on room sales and more on big sales days and events, but Rosenberg said he would return it to its former focus and, indeed, to an emphasis on even bigger assemblages of furniture. Futures sales, he said, would give the customer a reason to return by offering only certain items, rather than just about everything in the store. The company went public again, and its shares had tripled in value by the summer of 1993, trading at about book value.

Seaman opened three New York stores in 1993 and reentered the Philadelphia market the following year with three more outlets. It also opened a Connecticut store. By the end of 1994, 13 stores had been renovated, featuring a new, brighter, and more colorful lifestyle-oriented interior design. A no-money-down revolving line of credit replaced installment loans. Updated new options included a special price on five-piece living room packages with an additional two lamps, $100 off the boxspring and mattress and a free frame when buying the bedroom package, and $100 off the wall unit for the living room.

Seaman started spending a larger proportion of its advertising budget on television than in the past. A new soft-sell advertising campaign aimed to improve the company's image while continuing to draw in value-conscious customers. Rosenberg appeared in some television spots emphasizing a one-year ''peace of mind'' full warranty on everything Seaman sold and up to five years' limited warranty against structural defects. ''This should be a campaign that doesn't end,'' he told Clint Engel of *Furniture Today.* He said the spots were getting people to thinking about furniture ''without the sickening message of sale, sale, sale.''

Seaman entered the Midwest for the first time in 1995, when it opened stores in four Cleveland suburbs. The company added

Key Dates:

1933: Julius Seaman opens a furniture store in Brooklyn.
1971: The number of Seaman stores reaches seven.
1980: Seaman begins featuring sales of furniture by the room.
1985: Seaman becomes a public company.
1988: The firm goes private again in a leveraged buyout.
1992: Seaman files for Chapter 11 bankruptcy.
1993: The company emerges from bankruptcy and goes public again.
1997: Seaman once more becomes a private company.

a Cleveland warehouse to its existing ones in Central Islip and Woodbridge. Fiscal 1997 sales reached $251.2 million, with net income of $4.1 million. Continuing expansion had raised the number of stores—all leased—to 41, with 27 in the metropolitan New York area, eight in the Philadelphia area, and six in the Cleveland/Akron area. The company, profitable in every quarter since emerging from bankruptcy, ranked 15th or 16th among U.S. furniture retailers. The Ohio and Pennsylvania stores had yet to turn a profit, however.

Despite Seaman's successful resurrection, the three investment firms that now owned 80 percent of its stock—M.D. Sass Associates, T. Rowe Price Recovery Fund, and Carl Marks Management—were disappointed at the failure of the publicly held shares to rise above the 1993 level. In the summer of 1997 they took the company private again, paying $25 a share, or about $22 million, for the remainder of the stock. The speculation was that another public offering would be made in about three years, when higher profits had raised the value of the company. In 1998 the chain opened two Seaman's Kids stores on Long Island to sell furniture and accessories for minors ranging in age from post-crib toddlers to teenage youths. These stores also carried lines of extra-bedroom furniture. Each showroom displayed more than 20 sets of affordable, midrange merchandise.

In 1999 Seaman was offering a two-year peace-of-mind warranty and a five-year fabric and leather protection warranty. It was requiring a one-third deposit at the time of purchase by cash, credit, or personal check. The company also offered a credit plan with minimum purchase of $300. Delivery was promised within seven to ten days of purchase on most items, based on routing schedule. Of Seaman's 43 stores, 19 were in New York, ten in New Jersey, six in Ohio, five in Pennsylvania, and three in Connecticut.

Principal Competitors

Heilig-Meyers Co.; IKEA Holdings Inc.; Levitz Furniture Inc.; Wickes Furniture Co. Inc.

Further Reading

Anders, George, "Seaman Furniture Files for Chapter 11, Cites Long Slump in New York Market," *Wall Street Journal,* November 6, 1992, p. A4.

Engel, Cliff, "Revitalized Seaman's Ready for Growth," *Furniture Today,* September 12, 1994, pp. 1, 28–29.

——, "Room-Package Pioneer Seaman Polishes Merchandising Strategy," *Furniture Today,* February 9, 1993, pp. 1, 22.

——, "Seaman's to Enter Cleveland," *Furniture Today,* June 28, 1995, pp. 1, 50.

——, "Seaman to Add Five Philadelphia Stores," *Furniture Today,* April 25, 1994, p. 2.

Flack, Stuart, "See You in Bankruptcy Court," *Forbes,* October 16, 1989, pp. 77, 80.

Green, John H., "Seaman Plans Major Growth," *HFD,* June 24, 1985, pp. 15–16.

Howard, Henry, "Seaman Emerges from Chill," *Furniture Today,* October 26, 1992, pp. 1, 51.

Leonard, Burr, "Heir Raising," *Forbes,* September 7, 1987, pp. 74, 78, 80.

Rigg, Cynthia, "Clock's Ticking for Seaman's," *Crain's New York Business,* August 19, 1991, pp. 1, 21.

——, "Seaman's Debt May Overload New CEO," *Crain's New York Business,* February 12, 1990, p. 2.

Scully, Tara A., "Furniture Fit for Children," *Newsday,* August 17, 1998, p. C7.

"Seaman Furniture Board Accepts Bid of Kohlberg Kravis," *Wall Street Journal,* December 1, 1987, p. 34.

"Seaman Furniture Completes Its Move for a Restructuring," *Wall Street Journal,* November 21, 1989, p. A12.

"Seaman Moves Up with New Mix," *HFD,* June 9, 1986, p. S10.

Temes, Judy, "Seaman Goes Private to Polish Its Finances," *Crain's New York Business,* July 21, 1997, pp. 3, 55.

—Robert Halasz

Semtech Corporation

652 Mitchell Road
Newbury Park, California 91320
U.S.A.
Telephone: (805) 498-2111
Fax: (805) 498-3804
Web site: http://www.semtech.com

Public Company
Incorporated: 1960
Employees: 572
Sales: $114.51 million (1999)
Stock Exchanges: NASDAQ
Ticker Symbol: SMTC
NAIC: 334413 Semiconductor and Related Device Manufacturing; 33422 Radio and Television Broadcasting and Wireless Communications Equipment Manufacturing; 335999 All Other Miscellaneous Electrical Equipment and Component Manufacturing; 42161 Electrical Apparatus and Equipment, Wiring Supplies, and Construction Material Wholesalers

Semtech Corporation, headquartered in Newbury Park, California, develops and manufactures analog and mixed-signal semiconductor products for such industries as communications, computer, video, automated test equipment, automotive, aerospace, and military. The company's circuits are used in communications, advanced power management, protection, and interface products to protect equipment from damaging power surges and to regulate power distribution. Semtech has a number of manufacturing facilities, located in the United States, Mexico, and Scotland.

1960–80: Serving the Military and Aerospace Industries

Semtech Corporation was founded in 1960 by Gustav H.D. Franzen and Harvey Stump, Jr., who together had established semiconductor company Diodes Inc. in 1959. When investors assumed control of Diodes after only a year, Franzen and Stump formed Semtech to provide components for companies with military contracts, as well as aerospace companies. Semtech was quickly successful, and in 1967 the company went public and was listed on the American Stock Exchange. The firm specialized in the manufacture of power rectifiers, which were used in such end products as jet airplanes and X-ray machines.

By the late 1970s Semtech's annual sales hovered around the $15 million mark, and the company's net income was about $1 million. Smooth sailing was not to endure, however, and trouble began to brew in 1979 and 1980. Semtech had since its beginnings used pure silver in its components, specifically in rectifier wires, or leads. The price of silver increased dramatically in 1979 and 1980, soaring from $5 per ounce to about $50. Semtech's manufacturing costs rose radically as a result, and the panic-stricken company began to use copper, a less costly alternative to silver. The company had unfortunately not anticipated or researched the consequences of replacing silver with copper, and problems arose. Copper was unable to withstand high temperatures, and Semtech's semiconductors were rendered useless. Semtech suffered through nearly a year when very little product was shipped.

Losses Mount in the Early 1980s

Semtech had a difficult time recovering from the silver crisis and struggled from 1980 to 1985. As sales fell, losses grew; for the fiscal year ended January 31, 1982, Semtech reported losses of $36,000 on sales of $13.81 million. A year later the company had losses of $113,000 on sales of $11.69 million, and fiscal 1984 losses grew to $668,000 on sales of $11.41 million. For the year ended February 2, 1985, losses mounted dangerously, reaching $3.97 million on sales of $10.94 million. The company attributed the declines to reduced demand and a severe slump in the semiconductor industry.

As Semtech fought to remain in business, changes in management threatened the company's future. Cofounder Stump was elected Semtech chairman in February 1984 only to resign six months later, citing personal reasons. J. Spencer Letts, a director and an attorney for a Los Angeles firm, was elected to take

Company Perspectives:

Semtech's mission is to be a leading manufacturer of high quality analog and mixed-signal products, dedicated to providing our customers with cost effective, innovative solutions for power management, protection, communications and interface issues.

Stump's place. A year later, in May, president and CEO Sidney A. Wales stepped down. Wales, only the second president in the company's history, had headed the company for just over a year, taking the place of Stump when Stump became chairman. Semtech announced that the CEO and president positions would be filled temporarily by cofounder and Executive Vice-President Gustav Franzen, Vice-President Allen Gateka, and Chairman J. Spencer Letts. In September, unbeknownst to Franzen, who was on vacation in Europe, John "Jack" Poe was hired to take the helm. Franzen remained executive vice-president. Finally, in November, Letts resigned as chairman.

Slow Recovery and Restructuring: 1985–90

Jack Poe faced enormous challenges in his first position as a CEO of a company. Poe was familiar with the semiconductor market, having worked at Fairchild Camera & Instrument and acted as vice-president of operations at Silicon General prior to joining Semtech, but those experiences did not prepare him for his first day at the crumbling Semtech. Poe shared his experiences with writer Jennifer L. Baljko of *Electronic Buyers' News*, noting that on that first day his secretary was absent because she was having surgery, two company attorneys handed him masses of paperwork and told him the Securities and Exchange Commission had questions about the company's failure to post a profit in four years, and a manager informed him that the company did not have enough funds to make the week's payroll. To add insult to injury, Poe gave a speech to Semtech's factory employees in the afternoon, only to discover afterwards that he had left his pants unzipped.

Poe implemented a restructuring strategy and set about turning Semtech around. To cut costs, Semtech cut its workforce 14 percent, from 264 to 227 workers, and sold a warehouse located in Nevada. Poe also kept a close watch on the company's expenditures. He explained to the *Los Angeles Times* how he managed to save money: "The way you do that is you sign every purchase requisition." Poe added that "absolutely anything that is not essential to keep the company going, you don't spend it. We were living on checks that we got in that day to pay bills we had to send out that afternoon." Slowly, losses were reduced. For the third quarter ended November 2, 1985, losses declined 11 percent from the comparable period in 1984, reaching $195,000. Then, for the first half of fiscal 1987, Semtech reported sales of $5.92 million. Sales were lower than the $6.10 million reached during the first half of fiscal 1986 because of a soft semiconductor market, but Semtech managed to pare down losses further, from $692,000 to $36,000. Fiscal 1987, which ended January 31, 1987, marked a turning point for Semtech. The company reported an annual profit of $179,000, the first time Semtech had reported an annual profit since fiscal 1981.

Another aspect of Semtech's restructuring was to focus more heavily on research and development. New technical and engineering divisions were established, including one to investigate new technology in microelectronic design and another to enhance existing semiconductor products. Semtech also beefed up its manufacturing processes, adding manufacturing equipment and upping plant capacities. These enhancements enabled Semtech to cut its lead times from 24 weeks to 12 weeks for a product line of military diodes. The family of diodes was among Semtech's most popular, and the diodes were used in a number of U.S. defense programs. Also in 1988 the company launched a line of power rectifiers. The fast rectifiers possessed higher voltage handling capabilities and were used in military and industrial applications. To keep up with the increased demand for its semiconductor products, Semtech acquired Polycore Electronics Inc. in September 1988. Polycore, which primarily served military customers, operated a silicon foundry and custom-die design business.

Though Semtech appeared to have evaded extinction, challenges still existed. The end of the 1980s brought the end of the Cold War, which led to a decrease in military contracts. A decline in the semiconductor industry hit Semtech as well, and Semtech saw its sales drop once again. In fiscal 1989 the company earned $1.7 million on sales of $19 million, but during the fourth quarter of that fiscal year profit declined 40 percent from the corresponding year-earlier period. Sluggish demand for semiconductors was blamed, and the company braced itself for an industrywide slump, a regular occurrence in the highly cyclical semiconductor business.

Transition to Commercial Markets in the Early 1990s

Semtech was by the early 1990s a survivor, and Poe was determined to lead the company to success. In response to falling defense contracts, Semtech diversified, turning toward commercial markets. The company dedicated resources to find new markets for its analog semiconductors and began to develop products geared specifically toward those markets. To quicken its foray into commercial markets, Semtech acquired Lambda Semiconductors, the semiconductor division of Lambda Electronics Inc., a power supply manufacturer, in 1990. Lambda Semiconductors specialized in the voltage regulator business and manufactured power transistors and bipolar integrated circuits. The acquisition provided Semtech with a more commercial sales mix, lessening its dependence on military and aerospace contracts from about 90 percent of total sales to approximately 50 percent. Also that year Semtech sold Polycore Electronics.

In 1991, to streamline operations and in response to slow activity, Semtech reduced its workforce by 28 percent. The company also sold its microelectronics business, which it had founded in 1987, to Natel Engineering Co. Inc. To further establish its presence in the power regulator business, Semtech purchased the assets of Modupower Inc. in 1992. Modupower, which was formed in 1990, manufactured DC/DC converters, power-supply modules, and voltage regulators. Semtech also hired Modupower founder Art Fury, appointing him vice-president of sales and marketing. In 1993 the company launched its first commercial line of transient voltage suppressor (TVS) diodes. The diodes were targeted for applications in telecommu-

Key Dates:

1960: Semtech Corporation forms.
1967: Company goes public.
1985: John "Jack" Poe is elected CEO and president of Semtech.
1990: Semtech enters commercial markets.
1995: Semtech switches from the American Stock Exchange to the NASDAQ.
1998: Company sales exceed $100 million.

nications, data processing, office automation, and consumer electronics.

As Semtech adjusted to its new role serving commercial markets, so did its finances, which fluctuated wildly during the first half of the decade. Net income dropped from $840,000 in fiscal 1990 to $452,000 in 1991, despite higher sales. By 1993 sales to military and aerospace interests had dropped significantly. Net income sagged once again in fiscal 1994, reaching $95,000 on sales of $21.29 million, compared with net income of $431,000 on sales of $20.16 million in fiscal 1993. Semtech was not discouraged, however, noting that fiscal 1994 marked the first time the company received more orders in commercial and industrial markets than in military and aerospace businesses. In addition, the company remarked that it had invested heavily in new product development and promotional efforts to help with the transition to new markets.

Intensifying Growth: 1995–2000

Semtech gained momentum as it headed toward the 21st century. Sales began to improve, reaching $25.81 million in fiscal 1995, up 21 percent from fiscal 1994. After two years of flat sales and sagging profits, Semtech posted a net income of almost $1.2 million. The company focused on businesses involved in telecommunications and personal computer manufacturing, introducing more than a dozen new products geared toward notebook and desktop computers during the fourth quarter of fiscal 1995 alone. Semtech also launched a number of new products designed to provide solutions for low voltage power conversion applications in such battery-powered products as cellular phones, pagers, and notebook computers. One innovation Semtech made was in the development of a low voltage regulator that converted the industry standard five volts to 3.3 volts. Low voltage regulators had a growing market in computer and telecommunications businesses, which relied on lower voltages to enhance battery life and boost performance.

To increase exposure and liquidity for Semtech common stock, Semtech made a move from the American Stock Exchange to the NASDAQ National Market System in March 1995. The transition occurred at an opportune time, as the semiconductor industry staged a strong recovery. As a result, shares of Semtech jumped from about $2 a share to more than $19 a share during the first six months of 1995.

Focused on growth, Semtech acquired Gamma Inc.'s ECI Semiconductor, an analog semiconductor manufacturing firm. The purchase advanced Semtech's ability to produce linear voltage regulators and TVS products. In June 1996 Semtech announced plans to establish a design center in Santa Clara, California. The company hired two analog integrated circuit designers to head the center, which would focus on developing products for the portable electronic and networking markets, including cellular phones and notebook computers. CEO Poe commented on the importance of the design center in a company press release, stating "While we have been tremendously successful in transitioning from a military customer base to a predominantly commercial and industrial customer base, Semtech knows it cannot rest on the laurels of its success. New products are the lifeblood of a company, and Semtech will be very aggressive in pursuing business opportunities within our areas of expertise and in the emerging markets that hold promise."

According to plan, military and aerospace accounts dropped to about 30 percent of the company's sales in the mid-1990s as Semtech broadened its visibility in commercial sectors. Net income for fiscal 1996 surged 401 percent, hitting $7.53 million. Revenues increased 78 percent over fiscal 1995 sales to reach $61.68 million. In October 1996, Semtech was ranked number 51 in *Fortune* magazine's list of the 100 fastest-growing companies in the United States; the following year, the company climbed to number 30 on the list.

In anticipation of expansion in the automated test equipment market, Semtech acquired Edge Semiconductor in October 1997 through a stock swap estimated at about $50 million. Edge, based in San Diego, California, made analog and mixed-signal products used in automated test equipment. In April 1998 Semtech purchased Acapella Ltd., a United Kingdom-based designer of mixed-signal integrated circuits for fiber-optic communications. Acapella also acted as a design consultant for various electronics companies. This acquisition greatly enhanced Semtech's presence in the high-growth fiber-optic communications market. Then, in September 1999, Semtech purchased Practical Sciences, Inc., which specialized in the design of high-speed communications components and analog integrated circuits. This acquisition complemented the Acapella purchase and further boosted Semtech's presence in the fiber optic market.

Semtech also continued to develop technology for creating analog semiconductors, which were enjoying increased demand because they were instrumental in regulating the power to digital semiconductors. Expanding the company's design efforts, Semtech established a design center in Glasgow, Scotland, in fiscal 1998. In May 1998 a third design center was created. Located at Research Triangle Park, North Carolina, the center employed designers focused on data acquisition, power management, and video and interface solutions. In November 1999 Semtech completed expansion of the North Carolina facility, which grew from 4,700 square feet to 7,700. The company planned to hire 15 new engineers to add to its existing staff of 19 employees.

Despite sagging sales caused in large part by the economic crises in Asia, Semtech continued to grow and rack up impressive annual sales. In fiscal 1998, Semtech's sales surpassed the $100 million mark for the first time in the company's history. The following fiscal year, sales climbed 11 percent over the previous year. Semtech hired 52 new engineers that year, 36 of whom were dedicated solely to research and design, and launched 43 new product families, a 48 percent increase over the previous year. The third quarter of fiscal 2000 continued Semtech's upward trend, with sales reaching $47.1 million, a jump of 65 percent over the comparable period of 1999.

As Semtech faced the future, it planned to focus on high-growth areas to ensure its continued success and expansion. Developing solutions for the growing number of portable devices and enhancing technology for fiber-optic communications were among the areas on which Semtech planned to concentrate. The company also planned to investigate acquisition opportunities and to diversify its product portfolio in order to gain a leadership position in the constantly changing and growing communications industry.

Principal Subsidiaries

Semtech Limited (Scotland); Semtech Corpus Christi; Semtech Santa Clara; Semtech Corpus Christi S.A. de C.V. (Mexico); Edge Semiconductor; Acapella Limited (U.K.).

Principal Competitors

Analog Devices, Inc.; National Semiconductor Corporation; STMicroelectronics N.V.; Unitrode Corporation; Micrel Inc.

Further Reading

Baljko, Jennifer L., "John D. Poe—Led a Dramatic Financial Reversal and a Shift in Business Strategy," *Electronic Buyers' News,* December 22, 1997, p. 74.

Gold, Martin, "Semtech to Purchase Lambda Semi Division," *Electronic Engineering Times,* August 27, 1990, p. 95.

Peltz, James F., "Leader Revives Ailing Semtech Corp.," *Los Angeles Times,* May 23, 1989, p. 9A.

Ryan, Margaret, "Commercial Transition a Matter of Survival," *Electronic Engineering Times,* October 14, 1996, p. 50.

Smith, Leo, "Semtech Finds Shift From Defense Paying Off," *Los Angeles Times,* August 26, 1997.

Sullivan, Ben, "Local Firms Pegged for Fast Growth," *Los Angeles Daily News,* June 4, 1998, p. B1.

Thryft, Ann R., "Modupower Bought: Semtech Acquires Key Assets, Product Lines," *Electronic Buyers' News,* September 21, 1992, p. 3.

——, "Semtech Enters Commercial Market," *Electronic Buyers' News,* February 1, 1993, p. 57B.

Wilcox, Gregory J., "Buy, Buy to Slumping Local Economy," *Los Angeles Daily News,* September 23, 1997, p. N1.

Yoshitake, Dawn, "Tiny Semtech Becomes Big Market Attraction," *Los Angeles Daily News,* June 19, 1995, p. B1.

—Mariko Fujinaka

7-Eleven, Inc.

2711 North Haskell Avenue
Dallas, Texas 75204-2906
U.S.A.
Telephone: (214) 828-7011
Toll Free: (800) 255-0711
Fax: (214) 828-7848
Web site: http://www.7-eleven.com

Public Subsidiary of IYG Holding Company
Incorporated: 1961 as The Southland Corporation
Employees: 32,368
Sales: $7.26 billion (1998)
Stock Exchanges: NASDAQ
Ticker Symbol: SVEV
NAIC: 445120 Convenience Stores; 447110 Gasoline Stations with Convenience Stores

7-Eleven, Inc.—known as The Southland Corporation until April 1999—is the world's largest operator, franchisor, and licensor of convenience stores, with more than 18,200 stores in 18 countries, the vast majority of which carry the 7-Eleven banner. About 2,200 of the outlets offer self-service gasoline, almost all of which is sold under the Citgo brand through a long-term product purchase agreement with Citgo Petroleum Corporation. The company's operations include 5,560 7-Eleven convenience stores in 30 U.S. states and five Canadian provinces. 7-Eleven's largest area licensee is Seven-Eleven Japan Co., Ltd., which operates 7,605 7-Eleven stores in Japan and 48 in Hawaii. Other major foreign territories include Taiwan with 1,908 units, Thailand with 1,105, China with 398, Australia with 177, South Korea with 171, Malaysia with 151, and the Philippines with 149. The debt load from a 1987 leveraged buyout led the company into bankruptcy by 1990, which in turn led to a Japanese corporation securing a majority stake in it during 1991. 7-Eleven, Inc. is 65 percent owned by IYG Holding Company, which is in turn jointly owned by Ito-Yokado Co., Ltd. and Seven Eleven Japan. The latter is itself a 50.3 percent owned subsidiary of Ito-Yokado, which is a leading Japanese retailer.

Creation of the Convenience Store: 1927–45

The company began as a brainstorm of John Jefferson Green. In 1927 Green approached Joe C. ''Jodie'' Thompson, one of five founding directors of the Dallas Southland Ice Company, with a new idea. He wanted to sell milk, eggs, and bread through his retail ice dock. ''You furnish the items,'' he suggested, ''and I'll pay the power bills.'' Thompson agreed, and together they established the first known convenience store.

The newly formed Southland Ice Company was composed of four separate ice companies and operated eight ice plants and 21 retail ice stations. An early attempt at advertising occurred after one Southland manager visited Alaska in 1928. Upon his return to Texas, he planted a souvenir totem pole in front of his store. The pole attracted so much attention that the employees suggested placing one at every Southland-owned retail ice dock and naming the stores ''Tote'm Stores,'' since the consumers toted away their purchases.

Southland decided to go with the new name; it unified the company's diversified stores and provided a distinct identity, a key ingredient in the successful operation of numerous retail outlets. Joseph Thompson, secretary-treasurer of Southland Ice, unified the stores further by training staff with daily sales talks. He also chose a company uniform for ice station service men. Thompson recognized early on that consumers should receive the same quality and service at every store. During this time Southland also began to experiment with constructing and leasing gasoline stations at ten of its Dallas-area stores.

The Great Depression plunged Southland into bankruptcy in 1931. During a period of receivership and reorganization, Joseph Thompson was named president, a move that ensured continuity during the rocky period. The management team chosen during this time was especially strong and led Southland for a number of years. W.W. Overton, Jr., a Dallas banker, helped disentangle the young company's finances by organizing the purchase of all Southland bonds for seven cents on the dollar, which eventually put ownership of the company under the control of the board of directors. Despite the financial confusion, profits from the Tote'm Stores continued to climb, and with the repeal of Prohibition in 1933, ice and beer sales surged.

Company Perspectives:

For 62 years, the Southland name united many diverse businesses while preserving our heritage. However, ten years ago Southland began divesting its other operations to focus on convenience retailing and has consequently decided to rename the company "7-Eleven, Inc.", better reflecting our business focus. The name is appropriate now because 7-Eleven's strategic initiatives have brought about such dramatic changes in performance and culture that the company truly is not the same.

7-Eleven is again raising customer expectations as new information systems enable store managers and franchisees to anticipate customers' needs and serve them better. Each day, a network of commissaries, bakeries and distribution centers provides 7-Eleven stores with an unmatched selection of the freshest products, yielding true differentiation. This unique, proprietary infrastructure creates a strategic advantage over competitors and will enable 7-Eleven to produce sustainable and profitable growth over the long term. 7-Eleven will enter the new millennium a transformed company with new business tools and a name that reflects its identity and focus.

Once it was on more stable footing, Southland began vertical integration with construction of Oak Farms Dairies in 1936, using public relations to market its new dairy products by offering a free movie for six of its milk bottle caps. A crowd of 1,600 attended the Dallas theater sponsoring the event. By 1939 Southland operated 60 Tote'm Stores in the Dallas-Fort Worth area, triple the number operating when the company was founded 12 years earlier.

With the onset of World War II, demands for ice peaked; Southland became the chief supplier of ice for the construction and operation of Camp Hood, the U.S. Army's largest training camp. The dramatic increase in business prompted reorganization of the company. Southland bought City Ice Delivery, Ltd.; the acquisition included two modern ice plants, 20 retail stations, and property on Haskell Avenue, where the new company headquarters was situated. Southland became the largest ice operator in Dallas.

Rapid Postwar Expansion: 1945–69

By 1945 Southland owned stores scattered over north-central Texas, operating from 7 in the morning to 11 at night, seven days a week. In 1946 the firm Tracey-Locke, commissioned to create a new name, chose "7-Eleven" to emphasize the firm's commitment to long operating hours to serve customers better. At this time Southland remodeled all 7-Eleven stores, doubling the amount of floor space at each retail outlet.

After the war, the United States' pent-up consumer appetite surged. Refrigerators, however, were not yet readily available to the public. To meet demands for block ice, Southland bought Texas Public Utilities, which owned 20 ice plants, in 1947, making Southland the largest ice operator in Texas. In 1948 Joseph Thompson's oldest son, John P. Thompson, was named to the board of directors.

At a management meeting in Washington, D.C., in 1956, a blizzard blanketed the city. John Thompson noticed that in densely populated areas, people could walk to the stores even when the weather made driving impossible, and that 7-Eleven's long operating hours and unusual stock could provide exactly what customers might need, from canned soup to tissues to aspirin. Southland began to focus on the traffic patterns around potential store sites, choosing high-volume corners whenever possible.

At the end of the 1950s, John Thompson, now vice-president, began to introduce 7-Eleven stores outside of Texas, in Virginia, Maryland, and eastern Pennsylvania. In reaction to mass migration to the suburbs, Southland opened more suburban stores. Southland also refined its marketing by studying customer traffic in its stores and eliminating products that moved slowly.

In 1961 Joseph Thompson named his son John as the second president of Southland. His son Jere W. Thompson was elected vice-president of sales. Upon the elder Thompson's death that year, the *Dallas Morning News* credited Thompson with transforming "the ordinary corner ice house from an ice dispensary to a multimillion-dollar drive-in grocery enterprise." John Thompson's first goal as president was to propel Southland from $100 million in annual sales to $1 billion within ten years.

Southland, incorporated in 1961, moved quickly to national prominence. The unprecedented expansion began with dairy acquisitions, notably Midwest Dairy Products in 1962, with production plants and branches in Illinois, Arkansas, Louisiana, and Alabama. Purchasing continued through the 1960s and 1970s, as Southland bought existing convenience market chains in Arizona, New Jersey, Colorado, Illinois, Georgia, and Tennessee. In addition, Southland experimented with its first 24-hour store, in Las Vegas, and expanded to the East Coast and into Canada in 1969.

With the acquisition of 100 SpeeDee Marts in California in 1963, Southland was introduced to the concept of franchising, a system already in operation at the very successful SpeeDee Mart stores. The company developed two-week training sessions for prospective franchisees, which allowed greater decentralization of stores. By 1965, Southland had climbed to 49th in *Fortune* magazine's top 50 merchandising firms. In January 1965, 1,519 7-Eleven stores were operating; by December 1969 the number had increased to 3,537. Meanwhile, the Slurpee slush drink made its debut in 7-Eleven stores in 1965.

Acquisitions and Foreign Expansion: 1970–86

Through a new computer inventory system, 7-Eleven was able to pinpoint its strengths and discover that single purchase items were its best sellers. But with such growth, problems began to surface: due in part to the operation of 24-hour stores, high employee turnover and insufficient security systems drew management attention. The company committed itself to the 24-hour store nonetheless, and the number of 24-hour 7-Eleven stores rose from 817 in 1972 to 3,703 by the end of 1975.

Key Dates:

1927: John Jefferson Green and Joe C. Thompson establish Southland Ice Company and the first known convenience store.
1928: Southland stores begin operating as ''Tote'm Stores.''
1931: Great Depression plunges Southland into bankruptcy.
1933: Following the repeal of Prohibition, ice and beer sales surge.
1936: Vertical integration begins with construction of Oak Farms Dairies.
1939: Company is operating 60 Tote'm Stores in the Dallas-Fort Worth area.
1946: The stores are rebranded ''7-Eleven'' to emphasize their long operations hours—7 a.m. to 11 p.m.
1947: Purchase of Texas Public Utilities makes the company the largest ice operator in Texas.
1961: The Southland Corporation is incorporated; Joseph Thompson names son John as the company's second president; son Jere is elected vice-president of sales.
1963: Company begins franchising after being introduced to the concept through its acquisition of 100 Spee-Dee Marts in California this same year.
1965: The Slurpee makes its debut in 7-Eleven stores, which now number 1,159.
1969: Company expands to the East Coast and into Canada; store count reaches 3,537.
1971: Sales reach $1 billion.
1973: Area license for Japan is granted to Ito-Yokado Co., Ltd.
1974: The 5,000th 7-Eleven opens at site of the company's original ice dock.
1983: Citgo Petroleum Corporation is acquired for $780 million.
1986: Company sells 50 percent interest in Citgo to the Venezuelan state-owned oil company.
1987: The Thompson brothers complete an LBO of Southland.
1988: Company completes series of divestitures to streamline operations and reduce debt.
1990: After defaulting on $1.8 billion in publicly traded debt, Southland files for bankruptcy.
1991: Company emerges from bankruptcy with debt restructured and with IYG Holding Company of Japan owning 70 percent of its common stock.
1992: To focus on core 7-Eleven business, company exits from the distribution and food processing businesses.
1996: Most extensive store remodeling program in company history is completed.
1999: Company changes its name to 7-Eleven, Inc.

Southland reached $1 billion in sales by 1971 and became a member of the New York Stock Exchange the following year. The first regional distribution center was opened in Florida in 1971; by 1977 several such centers were fully functioning and serving more than 3,000 7-Eleven stores. Jere Thompson, named president of Southland in 1973, continued Southland's U.S. retail store expansion.

Southland began to use microwaves for fast-food sales and introduced self-service gasoline through its newly acquired Pak-a-Sak stores. In 1974, the 5,000th 7-Eleven store opened in Dallas at the site of John Jefferson's original ice dock.

Penetration of the European market occurred with Southland's purchase of a 50 percent interest in Cavenham Ltd., a manufacturing corporation controlling 840 retail outlets in Great Britain. By early 1974, Southland's international operations included 50 percent interest in 1,096 United Kingdom outlets, 75 7-Eleven stores in Canada, and four Super-7 Stores in Mexico.

Negotiations for the introduction of 7-Eleven to Japan were completed in December 1973, when Southland granted Ito-Yokado Co., Ltd., one of Japan's largest retailers, an area license. Like the franchise concept in the United States, area licensing worked well in Japan because of its emphasis on the individual businessperson operating a store but able to take advantage of 7-Eleven's name and established systems of management and accounting. By late 1978, 188 7-Eleven stores were open for business in Japan.

Also in 1978, Southland bought Chief Auto Parts, a California chain of 119 retail automobile parts stores. By 1986 Chief Auto Parts was the largest convenience retailer of automobile parts in the nation, operating 465 stores. Another Southland acquisition was Tidel Systems, a manufacturer of cash-dispensing systems and underground gasoline-tank-monitoring systems.

But Southland's most significant acquisition by far was the Citgo Petroleum Corporation, purchased in August 1983. Southland hoped that the $780 million acquisition would provide a smooth supply of gasoline for its convenience stores. But because of a decrease in demand and a glut in capacity throughout the oil refining industry, the Citgo purchase resulted in a pretax loss of $50 million for Southland. Profits in 1985 exceeded the previous year's loss by $20 million, but nevertheless, Southland cut Citgo's petroleum production in half, expecting Citgo's Lake Charles, Louisiana refinery to be unprofitable. In September 1986 Southland decided to sell a 50 percent interest in Citgo to a subsidiary of Petroleos de Venezuela, S.A., the Venezuelan state-owned oil company; Southland also signed a 20-year product purchase agreement with Citgo through which Southland agreed to purchase a certain minimum amount of gasoline from Citgo at market prices.

From LBO to Bankruptcy: 1987–91

In mid-1987 the Thompson brothers, spurred in part by the threat of a hostile takeover bid by Canadian raider Samuel Belzburg, initiated a leveraged buyout. The buyout, which involved the formation of a temporary holding company called JT Acquisitions, was completed on July 6, 1987.

By the end of 1988 Southland had completed a series of divestitures to streamline operations. Southland sold Chief Auto Parts, the snack foods division, the dairies group, Reddy Ice, Chemical/Food Labs, Tidel Systems, 1,000 convenience stores, and related real estate properties. Proceeds from the divestitures, as well as the transfer of royalties from licensees in Japan, went to repay a portion of the $4 billion debt Southland had incurred through the leveraged buyout.

Southland may well have rebounded by the early 1990s were it not for competition from convenience stores operated by the major oil companies. Although these stores emphasized gasoline retailing rather than other merchandise, they did sell the primary products of convenience stores—soft drinks, cigarettes, and beer. Their sheer number and financial strength changed the nature of the convenience retailing industry. Their effort was exacerbated by the decline in the U.S. economy that began in the late 1980s. Southland, along with a number of other convenience store chains, had limited capital to invest in its store base due to heavy debt loads.

Under President and CEO Clark J. Matthews II, the company began to work on a plan to restructure its balance sheet. During 1990 Southland sold its remaining 50 percent stake in Citgo to Petroleos de Venezuela. In October 1990, after defaulting on $1.8 billion in publicly traded debt, Southland filed a bankruptcy plan of reorganization after securing preliminary approval from its bondholders. The company emerged from bankruptcy less than five months later. As part of the reorganization, Southland exchanged its old leveraged buyout bonds for approximately half of the principal amount of new bonds—which had substantially lower interest rates. In addition Southland sold 70 percent of its common stock to IYG Holding Company of Japan for $430 million. Ito-Yokado Co., Ltd., the most profitable retailer in Japan, owned 51 percent of IYG, and Seven-Eleven Japan Co., Ltd., the longtime 7-Eleven licensee in Japan, owned 49 percent.

Focusing on 7-Eleven: 1992 and Beyond

In 1992 Southland completed additional financing for a $400 million commercial paper facility backed by Ito-Yokado. Also in 1992, Southland decided to leave the distribution and food processing business to focus on its core business, 7-Eleven. The company sold certain distribution centers and food processing facilities to McLane Co., Inc., a subsidiary of Arkansas-based Wal-Mart stores. Southland also signed a service agreement with McLane, the country's largest convenience store distributor, to provide coast-to-coast distribution service to the company's 5,700 stores in the United States.

Matthews capitalized on the company's nationally recognized 7-Eleven name and enhanced the quality, appearance, and service of the famous convenience store. In late 1991, Southland remodeled and remerchandised its 50 stores in Austin, Texas, to test its new physical standards, commissary foodservice program, and new merchandising process.

The new process, which deleted slow-moving items and introduced new products, had been refined and introduced to 7-Eleven stores across the country by the end of 1992. Because of the initial capital infusion by its majority owners in 1991 as well as their backing of the commercial paper facility established in 1992, Southland was able to make long-term capital investment plans for the first time in many years.

Southland's remodeling program continued throughout the mid-1990s. By 1996 the company had completed the most extensive store remodeling program in its history. The new 7-Eleven look included improved exterior and interior lighting, a store layout with wider aisles and better organization, improved signage, and upgraded gasoline pumps that included pay-at-the-pump systems. 7-Eleven stores also changed their pricing policies, most notably doing away with what Southland itself called "insult pricing"—the huge markups that customers were forced to pay for convenience. The chain thereby lowered prices on much of its inventory, adopting an "everyday fair pricing" policy. In addition, Southland closed additional underperforming stores in the mid-to-late 1990s, shuttering 202 units from 1996 through 1998.

As the next step in its slow recovery, Southland put growth back on the agenda in late 1996; beginning in 1997 store openings began outpacing closings. The following year, Southland decided to step up the pace of its U.S. expansion, aiming to open 300 to 400 units per year. During 1998 the company added 299 stores through acquisitions and new construction—the biggest jump since 1986. The acquisitions included two that closed in May 1998: the purchase of Massachusetts-based Christy's Markets, Inc., an operator of 135 convenience stores in New England; and that of 20 red D mart convenience stores in South Bend, Indiana, which were purchased from MDK Corporation of Goshen, Indiana.

Another key strategy that Southland adopted to revitalize the chain was to improve the quality and value of the convenience items and services offered by the stores. This included moving toward daily deliveries of fresh perishables and the introduction of new ready-to-eat fresh foods, such as sandwiches and pastries, and eventually dinner entrees. 7-Eleven stores also began an aggressive expansion of the financial services it offered. Having already gained the position as the U.S. retailer with the most ATM machines, Southland began offering prepaid phone cards in 1995 and quickly became a leading seller of money orders. In 1998 the company began selling pagers and pager services in all U.S. 7-Elevens. That year it also began testing "financial service centers"—automated computer terminals that, in addition to standard ATM transactions, allowed customers to cash checks, wire money, pay bills electronically, and buy prepaid phone cards and postage stamps. After a successful trial at 36 Austin, Texas stores, Southland began planning for the expansion of the centers into more than 200 7-Elevens in the Dallas-Fort Worth area.

Perhaps the most important element of the 7-Eleven overhaul in the United States was the implementation of a chainwide proprietary retail information system, the development of which began in 1994. Such a system had already been installed by the highly successful Seven-Eleven Japan operation, which through its nearly 8,000-unit chain was one of the most profitable retailers in Japan. Installed in phases in the United States through the end of the 1990s, the system was designed to enable each store to improve its inventory management, reduce the incidence of out-of-stock items, and tailor its product mix to better match the needs of its customers.

In April 1999 the Southland Corporation changed its name to 7-Eleven, Inc. in a move reflecting the fact that the corporation was involved in only one business. It also seemed an appropriate time for such a change as the company was well on its way to a full recovery with revenues and sales on the increase and the once-heavy debt burden significantly reduced. By mid-1999 7-Eleven had recorded eight straight quarters of U.S. same-store sales growth, the longest such stretch in the 1990s. As it looked ahead, 7-Eleven was counting on the full implementation of its retail information system to be the engine driving its growth well into the 21st century.

Principal Subsidiaries

Bawco Corporation; Bev of Vermont, Inc.; Brazos Comercial E Empreendimentos Ltda. (Brazil); Christy's Market, Inc.; Cityplace Center East Corporation; Melin Enterprises, Inc.; Philippine Seven Properties Corporation (Philippines); Puerto Rico - 7, Inc. (59.07%); 7-Eleven Beverage Company, Inc.; 7-Eleven Comercial Ltda. (Brazil); 7-Eleven of Idaho, Inc.; 7-Eleven of Massachusetts, Inc.; 7-Eleven of Nevada, Inc.; 7-Eleven of Virginia, Inc.; 7-Eleven Sales Corporation; Southland Canada, Inc.; Southland International, Inc.; Southland International Investment Corporation N.V. (Netherlands Antilles); Southland Investment Canada Limited; Southland Sales Corporation; TSC Lending Group, Inc.; The Southland Corporation; Valso, S.A. (Mexico; 49%); 7-Eleven Mexico, S.A. de C.V. (99.96%).

Principal Competitors

Casey's General Stores, Inc.; Chevron Corporation; Cumberland Farms, Inc.; Dairy Mart Convenience Stores, Inc.; Exxon Corporation; FINA, Inc.; Holiday Companies; The Kroger Company; Mobil Corporation; The Pantry, Inc.; QuikTrip Corporation; RaceTrac Petroleum, Inc.; Sheetz, Inc.; Royal Dutch/Shell Group; Texaco Inc.; Tosco Corporation; Ultramar Diamond Shamrock Corporation; Uni-Marts, Inc.; Wawa Inc.; White Hen Pantry Inc.

Further Reading

''Bondholders Withdraw All Objections to Southland Plan (Bankruptcy Organization Plan),'' *Los Angeles Times,* January 24, 1991.

''Exciting Times at Southland,'' *Convenience Store News,* March 22, 1999, p. 25.

Fairclough, Gordon, and Udorn Thani, ''Shopping on the Fly: Thais Catch On to the Benefits of Convenience Stores,'' *Far Eastern Economic Review,* December 9, 1993, p. 70.

Francella, Barbara Grondin, ''Southland and New Jersey Franchisees Face Off in a Range of Disputes,'' *Convenience Store News,* September 8, 1997, p. 16.

Gubernick, Lisa, ''Thank Heaven for 7-Eleven,'' *Forbes,* March 23, 1987, p. 52.

Hackney, Holt, ''Southland: The Junk Also Rises,'' *Financial World,* January 3, 1995, p. 24.

Klinkerman, Steve, ''Why Southland Won't Unload Its Albatross,'' *Business Week,* July 1, 1985, p. 71.

Kotabe, Masaaki, ''The Return of 7-Eleven . . . from Japan: The Vanguard Program,'' *Journal of World Business,* Winter 1996, pp. 70+.

Landers, Peter, ''In Japan, the Hub of E-commerce Is a 7-Eleven,'' *Wall Street Journal,* November 1, 1999, pp. B1, B4.

——, ''Softbank, 7-Eleven Japan Go Online to Sell Books As E-commerce Expands,'' *Wall Street Journal,* June 4, 1999, p. A12.

Lee, Louise, ''Southland Plans to Accelerate Store Openings,'' *Wall Street Journal,* April 6, 1998, p. A4.

Liles, Allen, *Oh Thank Heaven! The Story of the Southland Corporation,* Dallas: The Southland Corporation, December 1977.

McCarthy, Michael, ''Shake Up at 7-Eleven,'' *Brandweek,* July 11, 1994, pp. 20–22, 24–27.

Miller, Karen Lowry, ''A New Roll of the Dice at 7-Eleven,'' *Business Week,* October 26, 1992.

Nelson, Emily, ''Product Development Is Always Difficult; Consider the Frito Pie,'' *Wall Street Journal,* October 25, 1999, pp. A1, A22.

Opdyke, Jeff D., ''7-Eleven Tests Check-Cashing in Texas Stores,'' *Wall Street Journal,* April 29, 1998, p. T1.

Rudnitsky, Howard, ''Billion-Dollar Fire Sale,'' *Forbes,* November 17, 1986, p. 44.

Shirouzu, Norihiko, and Jon Bigness, ''7-Eleven Operators Resist System to Monitor Managers,'' *Wall Street Journal,* June 16, 1997, p. B1.

''Southland Chief Fires Top Aides to Cut Costs,'' *Wall Street Journal,* June 25, 1992.

Tannenbaum, Jeffrey A., ''Franchisee Lawsuit Seeks $1 Billion from Southland,'' *Wall Street Journal,* April 8, 1994, p. B2.

Taylor, John H., ''The Texas Chain Store Massacre,'' *Forbes,* February 6, 1989, p. 54.

Weber, Joseph, ''7-Eleven Wants Out of the Glare,'' *Business Week,* July 20, 1987, p. 78.

Weil, Jonathan, ''Taking Big Gulp, Southland Moves to Revamp Stale 7-Eleven Chain,'' *Wall Street Journal,* September 9, 1998, p. T2.

Zellner, Wendy, and Emily Thornton, ''How Classy Can 7-Eleven Get?,'' *Business Week,* September 1, 1997, pp. 74–75.

—Sina Dubovoj
—updated by David E. Salamie

Shearman & Sterling

599 Lexington Avenue
New York, New York 10022-6060
U.S.A.
Telephone: (212) 848-4000
Fax: (212) 848-7179
Web site: http://www.shearman.com

Partnership
Founded: 1873
Employees: 1,800
Sales: $425.5 million (1998)
NAIC: 54111 Offices of Lawyers

Shearman & Sterling is one of the largest law firms in the United States, if not the world. It is famous for representing Citigroup, and its predecessors Citibank and the National City Bank of New York, a client relationship stretching back to 1891. It represents not only large banks but other financial institutions such as Merrill Lynch and Goldman Sachs, and numerous other corporate clients in many industries, from energy and utility clients to the high-tech field. Shearman & Sterling's expertise centers on corporate concerns, from financing, tax, and bankruptcy to mergers, acquisitions, and antitrust. The firm's international practice is most prominent in Germany, where it is nicknamed ''German & Sterling,'' but it has clients in many nations in Europe, Asia, Latin America, and the Middle East. Its overseas offices are located in London, Paris, Frankfurt, Dusseldorf, Hong Kong, Tokyo, Beijing, Singapore, Toronto, and Abu Dhabi, United Arab Emirates. Its representation of international clients brings in about 40 percent of its annual revenues. With a long history of participation in industrialization, globalization, privatization, and other historic events and trends, Shearman & Sterling sets a great example of openly telling its story, unlike some law firms that seem ultrasecretive by comparison.

Origins in the Gilded Age

Thomas Shearman, the senior partner who founded Shearman & Sterling, was born in 1834 in Birmingham, England, and came to the United States in 1843 with his family. In the 1850s he worked as a law reporter for the *New York Times* and studied the law on his own before being admitted to the New York Bar in 1859. Meanwhile, John Sterling, the other founder, was born in Stratford, Connecticut, in 1844 and in1867 graduated from Columbia Law School before joining the New York Bar.

In the 1860s both Shearman and Sterling worked for the Field law firm headed by a prominent Republican named David Dudley Field. Probably the largest New York City law firm at the time, the Field firm represented railroad men James Fisk and Jay Gould in the 1860s. However, in May 1873 Field dissolved his firm, so in November 1873 Shearman and Sterling organized their own partnership with five lawyers and two other employees.

Shearman, an outgoing individual heavily involved in community affairs, excelled in the courtroom drama of litigation, the traditional style of law practice. In contrast, introverted Sterling became one of the first lawyers to serve as a corporate counsel, working as an insider ''tactician'' and ''boardroom gun'' helping companies grow, according to a phone interview with Bruce Weindruch, CEO of The History Factory, a history consulting firm hired by Shearman & Sterling in 1997. Gerald W. Gawalt's 1984 book *The New High Priests* described how big city law firms, such as Shearman & Sterling, grew after the Civil War to meet the needs of the country's expanding corporations.

The new partnership took six former Field law firm clients who helped the new law firm get off the ground. Those clients led Shearman & Sterling to represent Jay Gould from day one. Gould had plenty of work for the new partnership, for in 1873 he faced 63 cases and a year later he had 97 cases pending. Shearman & Sterling, for example, helped Gould hand Cornelius Vanderbilt a rare setback when the latter tried to take over the Erie Railroad, and later the law firm helped Gould gain control of the Union Pacific and Western Union Telegraph.

At about the same time, in 1875 the trial of the prominent Reverend Henry Ward Beecher began, with Thomas Shearman, a member of his church, as his defense attorney. Accused of adultery with one of his church members, Beecher was acquitted by the jury and was able to return to his ministry after one of the era's most sensational cases.

Key Dates:

1873: Shearman & Sterling is founded.
1891: Firm is retained by National City Bank of New York, a predecessor of Citigroup.
1919: Firm merges with Cary & Carroll, a major expansion that adds ten new partners.
1963: First overseas office is opened in Paris.
1972: London office is started.
1979: Firm begins its first West Coast office in San Francisco.
1985: Los Angeles office opens.
1987: Firm starts offices in Tokyo and Washington, D.C.; after 114 years on Wall Street, New York headquarters is moved to the Citicorp Center.
1994: Hong Kong office opens.
1995: The Singapore office is established.
1998: Firm opens its Menlo Park, California office and celebrates its 125th anniversary.

In 1884 six utilities serving Manhattan merged to create Consolidated Gas Company, a consolidation that was typical of utilities around the turn of the century. Later Shearman & Sterling gained Consolidated Gas as a major client.

During the depression that started in 1893, Shearman & Sterling helped the National City Bank of New York triple its assets and become the nation's largest bank by purchasing the Third National Bank of New York in 1897. From that point, ''Citibank,'' which was National City Bank's wire code address, helped numerous businesses consolidate, and it also became Shearman & Sterling's major long-term client.

The Partnership from 1900 to 1945

Following the passage of the 1890 Sherman Antitrust Act, especially in the early 1900s, Shearman & Sterling represented many corporations, including American Sugar Refining Company, and company leaders accused of illegal monopolies. For example, the firm successfully defended Edward Harriman during Senate hearings about his control of the Union Pacific and the Chicago & Alton railroads, Mutual of New York in a 1905 investigation, and Standard Oil's William Rockefeller and Henry Rogers during a House of Representatives investigation.

After the turn of the century, Shearman & Sterling gained as a major client the Consolidated Gas Company that had been formed in 1884 when six firms serving Manhattan had merged. The law firm counseled the merged utility on policy, financing, and litigation issues. It also helped the Saratoga Gas Company win in 1908 a major court battle involving gas rates set by the New York State Commission for Gas and Electricity.

Shearman & Sterling's work for National City Bank of New York led to its participation in major national and international events of the 20th century. When the Bolsheviks (Communists) took over the Russian government in 1917, they also confiscated money held by branches of foreign banks. Shearman & Sterling in the 1920s helped National City Bank depositors recover their funds in the bank's branch in Petrograd.

In 1918 the law firm had just two partners, plus 11 associates and 18 clerks. Its client National City Bank felt that its outside law firm needed more help, so in 1919 Shearman & Sterling completed its first merger. It merged with Cary & Carroll and added ten new partners, which allowed the merged law firm to retain National City Bank as its major client, similar to the New York law firm of Milbank, Tweed representing the predecessor of the Chase Manhattan Bank.

In the 1920s Shearman & Sterling gained the following new clients: Chemical National Bank, Home Insurance Company, Combustion Engineering Company, Consolidated Coal Company, Cuba Railroad Company, Herring Hall Marvin Safe Company, Montana Consolidated Copper Company, and Old Ben Coal Company.

In the Great Depression of the 1930s, Shearman & Sterling successfully defended National City Bank directors as others tried to blame them for money lost in the stock market crash and depression. It also represented the bondholders of New York City's private Interborough Rapid Transit Company as the failing company restructured and combined with the Brooklyn Manhattan Transit Corporation to create the municipally owned ''largest mass transportation system in the United States.'' The law firm history *Enterprise* also stated the merged system featured ''308 miles of underground and elevated track with more subway cars than the London, Moscow and Tokyo systems combined.''

Post-World War II Practice

After World War II, Boykin Wright and several other lawyers left what became Cahill Gordon to join Shearman & Sterling. They brought new clients and generally helped the firm grow, and for a few years the firm was called Shearman & Sterling & Wright.

Shearman & Sterling by 1953 had helped 42 German corporations and 14 German municipalities arrange to pay their debts. The firm also helped some German companies survive breakup attempts by occupation officials and aided recovered firms like BASF and Siemens to restart business operations in the United States. Thus the New York law firm played a key role in assisting West Germany become a friend of the United States and an economic powerhouse during the Cold War.

The Ford family and Ford Foundation turned to Shearman & Sterling when it decided the Ford Motor Company should become a public corporation while maintaining family control. Thus in 1956 the law firm helped in the ''largest equity offering to date—involving more than 700 underwriters—and the last of the great private industrial family enterprises'' became a public corporation, according to *Enterprise*.

When Malcolm McLean invented shipping containers in the early 1950s, Shearman & Sterling helped him gain the private financing needed to start Sea-Land. McClean's containers revolutionized both land and maritime shipping.

The firm also represented Greek businessman Aristotle Onassis when he started to transform ocean shipping by building larger vessels, using Liberian registration, and other means. Shearman & Sterling continued to represent Onassis after he married the widowed Jacqueline Kennedy, helping him, for example, start and finance his Olympic Airways and defending his controlling interest in the famous Monte Carlo Casino. Finally, the law firm represented his daughter Christina in estate negotiations with his widow after he died in 1975.

In 1959 Shearman & Sterling aided Merrill Lynch when it became "the first major brokerage firm to incorporate," according to *Enterprise*. Other brokerages, again assisted by the law firm, later followed Merrill Lynch's example as a way to gain investments and limit liability. Not surprisingly, Merrill Lynch remained a Shearman & Sterling client into the 1990s.

In the 1950s Shearman & Sterling, with 35 partners and 90 associates, was the largest law firm in the United States. Only three other Wall Street firms had more than 100 lawyers. By the early 1960s just 21 New York City law firms and 17 firms in other cities had 50 lawyers or more, but rapid growth in the legal profession was forthcoming.

The law firm in the 1960s concentrated on corporate, banking, and trust law, while its litigation practice was "comparatively insignificant," according to a company timeline. Highlights of its practice in the 1960s included the incorporations of American Express and Studebaker-Worthington Corporation. It also began representing SONATRACH, the Algerian government-owned gas and oil company, when it negotiated with multinational oil companies. SONATRACH remained a client at the end of the century.

Shearman & Sterling in 1967 made banking history when it helped its long-term client National City Bank of New York create the nation's first one-bank holding company, later called Citicorp, that was able to offer a variety of new financial products and services. Other banks, including Bank of America, Chase Manhattan, and Manufacturers Hanover, followed this example within six months, and eventually most major banks did likewise.

In 1976 Lockheed retained Shearman & Sterling to investigate its business practices after its reputation was hurt by revelations it had spent $30 million in questionable overseas payments. In this post-Watergate era, many were hostile to the widespread bribery of foreign officials by corporations. The law firm's report, along with the resignation of top Lockheed executives, helped Lockheed survive this crisis.

During the Carter presidency, Muslim fundamentalists led by the Ayatollah Khomeini took over the nation of Iran, and then Iranians captured 52 U.S. hostages in 1979. Carter diplomacy and military efforts failed to rescue the hostages. Since Carter froze Iranian assets in U.S. banks and many individuals as well as U.S. corporations had invested in the Iranian oil-rich economy, lawyers for major U.S. banks negotiated with lawyers representing the Iranian interests. Negotiations occurred in the New York offices of Shearman & Sterling that represented Citibank. Told in detail in a chapter in *The Partners*, this story illustrated how lawyers worked behind the scenes to resolve a major international crisis.

Like many other large law firms, Shearman & Sterling grew rapidly in the 1980s. From 284 lawyers in 1978, the firm expanded to 387 lawyers in 1983 and 440 lawyers in 1990. New offices were opened and gross revenues rose from $137 million in 1986 to $281 million in 1989, with profits per partner increasing at the same time from $480,000 to $800,000.

The 1990s

In the wake of the 1991 Persian Gulf War, Iraq deliberately started about 500 oil well fires in Kuwait, provoking doomsday predictions from some environmentalists who felt the massive air pollution would damage the world's climate. The fires were put out in about a year, and Kuwait retained Shearman & Sterling and other international law firms to help it seek reparations from Iraq for its environmental damages.

Meanwhile, the Mexican government hired Shearman & Sterling to assist in negotiating the 1992 North American Free Trade Agreement (NAFTA) with the United States and Canada. Later the firm played a key role in gaining U.S. Senate ratification during the Clinton administration.

From 1989 to 1991 the Cold War ended as the Berlin Wall was destroyed, Germany was reunited, communism failed throughout Eastern Europe, and the Soviet Union was broken up into Russia and several other smaller governments. In 1992 the newly formed Republic of Kazakhstan hired Sherman & Sterling to help create a national oil company, develop its major oil and gas reserves, resolve border disputes, and write legislation involving foreign investment and other matters.

In 1997 Shearman & Sterling represented Morgan Stanley when it merged with Dean Witter, "creating the largest U.S. securities firm ranked by equity capital," according to *Enterprise*. The law firm in 1997 also represented Robertson Stephens and Alex, Brown when the two securities firms were acquired by BankAmerica and Bankers Trust, respectively.

In 1998 the law firm represented Citicorp when it merged with Travelers Group to form Citigroup, a transaction worth $140 billion that consolidated insurance and banking entities. Its lawyers in Frankfurt and Dusseldorf advised Germany's Daimler-Benz when it merged with Chrysler.

The *American Lawyer* in its July/August 1998 issue ranked Shearman & Sterling as the ninth largest U.S. law firm, based on 1997 gross revenues of $356 million. In the July 1999 issue, the magazine ranked Shearman & Sterling as the seventh largest U.S. firm, due to its 1998 gross revenues of $425 million, and also listed it as number 13 in terms of revenue per lawyer ($625,000).

In 1998 Shearman & Sterling went to great lengths to celebrate its 125th anniversary. With the help of The History Factory and Thomas Heinrich, a Baruch College business history professor, the law firm established a company archive, created a historical exhibit, and published *Enterprise* to highlight the firm's major deals and clients since 1873. The firm's exhibit and publications "illustrate an important, if seldom-acknowledged, relationship between business and the law," said senior partner Stephen Volk in the April 22, 1999 *New York Law Journal*. The firm's web site included most of the material from *Enterprise*, in contrast to some law firm web sites that seldom mention any firm clients or history. Bruce Weinruch,

CEO of The History Factory, gave speeches on Sherman & Sterling's heritage to the firm's lawyers.

"The underlying purpose is to help define what Shearman & Sterling really is as a professional institution: its culture, if you will," said Larry Smith in a 1999 article. "Yet Shearman didn't go to all this trouble just to name-drop dead clients. The practical reason for partners to celebrate history, or to even care about culture, is that the bond thus forged is crucial once they sit down together to actually practice law."

Shearman & Sterling faced numerous challenges as the year 2000 began, including 11 of the 15 European Union nations adopting the "euro" as their common currency, new laws concerning banking and insurance, the booming electronic economy, and growing resistance to globalization, as seen in the 1999 "Battle in Seattle" protesting meetings of the World Trade Organization. With stiff competition from much larger consolidated law firms and also the big accounting firms that employed thousands of lawyers, Shearman & Sterling seemed well prepared by balancing its sense of heritage with new technology and innovative legal thinking.

Principal Competitors

Baker & McKenzie; Jones, Day; Skadden, Arps, Slate, Meagher & Flom.

Further Reading

Cherovsky, Erwin, "Shearman & Sterling," *The Guide to New York Law Firms,* New York: St. Martin's Press, 1991, pp. 179–82.

Earle, Walter, *Mr. Shearman and Mr. Sterling and How They Grew: Being Annals of Their Law Firms,* New Haven: Yale University Press, 1963.

Earle, Walter, and Charles Perlin, *Shearman & Sterling 1873–1973,* New York, 2nd edition, 1973.

Enterprise, New York: Shearman & Sterling, 1998.

Galanter, Marc, and Thomas Palay, *Tournament of Lawyers: The Transformation of the Big Law Firm,* Chicago: University of Chicago Press, 1991.

Gawalt, Gerald W., *The New High Priests: Lawyers in Post-Civil War America,* Westport, Conn.: Greenwood Press, 1984.

Lavelle, Marianne, "Mexico's NAFTA Hand; He Doesn't Lobby; Instead, This Lawyer Shaped the Debate," *National Law Journal,* November 15, 1993, p. 1.

Smith, Larry, "How One Megafirm Uses the Past to Buttress the Future," *Of Counsel,* March 15, 1999.

Snider, Anna, "Shearman & Sterling Marks Its Place in History," *New York Law Journal,* April 22, 1999.

Stewart, James B., "Iran: Shearman & Sterling; Davis Polk & Wardwell," in *The Partners: Inside America's Most Powerful Law Firms,* New York: Simon and Schuster, 1983, pp. 19–52.

—David M. Walden

Siebert Financial Corp.

885 Third Avenue
New York, New York 10022
U.S.A.
Telephone: (212) 644-2400
Toll Free: (800) 872-0711
Fax: (212) 486-2784
Web site: http://www.siebertnet.com

Public Company
Incorporated: 1969 as Muriel Siebert & Co., Inc.
Employees: 100
Sales: $25.7 million (1998)
Stock Exchanges: NASDAQ
Ticker Symbol: SIEB
NAIC: 52231 Mortgage & Other Loan Brokers; 52311 Investment Banking & Securities Dealing; 52312 Securities Brokerage; 52392 Portfolio Management

Siebert Financial Corp. is the holding company for Muriel Siebert & Co., Inc., one of the largest discount brokerage firms in the United States. The firm, which has been in business and a member of the New York Stock Exchange longer than any other discount broker, also offers, uniquely among discount brokers, a wide variety of underwriting and investment banking services. The company believes that it is the largest woman-owned capital markets business enterprise in the United States. Muriel Siebert, the first female member of the New York Stock Exchange, held about 92 percent of the company's common stock in 1998. When the price of the stock suddenly surged in early 1999, she became—briefly—Wall Street's first woman billionaire.

Muriel Siebert & Co.: 1969–96

Cleveland-born Muriel (''Mickie'') Siebert dropped out of college after her father died and drove to New York City in a used Studebaker, where, claiming to have earned a degree, she secured a position as a research analyst trainee. Shuttling from one Wall Street firm to another during the next decade, she sought to advance her career and sidestep sex discrimination by such means as circulating her resumé under the name ''M.F. Siebert.''

Siebert had been a partner in three firms by 1967, when she decided to purchase a seat on the New York Stock Exchange because her male colleagues were being paid 50 to 100 percent more money than she. Nine men turned her down before one agreed to sponsor her, and the exchange refused to sell her a seat until she fulfilled the unprecedented condition of obtaining a bank letter promising to loan her $300,000 of the $445,000 price. Then she had to overcome the reluctance of banks to make such a loan without a corresponding commitment from the exchange. Of the more than 1,000 members, she remained the only woman for another ten years.

Siebert scored another ''first'' in 1969, when she formed the firm bearing her name, thus becoming the first woman to own and operate a brokerage firm that was a member of the New York Stock Exchange. Sex discrimination continued to hamper her career, however. Interviewed by Ed Leefeldt for *Bloomberg Personal Magazine* in 1994, she recalled that ''We did a private placement for Ryder System in 1969, but when the company did a public underwriting in 1970, I wasn't good enough for Salomon Brothers, the lead underwriter. Every underwriter was listed in alphabetical order on the ad except Siebert. We were at the bottom . . . even though I brought them the deal. . . . I'm proud to say that most of the firms that wouldn't put their names under mine are no longer in business.''

Following legislation that put an end to mandatory fixed broker's commissions, Siebert again rankled the establishment by offering discounted rates at the opening bell of trading on May 1, 1975, the day the law went into effect. In retaliation, the clearing house handling her company's trades dropped the firm, forcing her to scramble to find another house or be expelled by the Securities and Exchange Commission. In 1977 Siebert placed her company in a blind trust so that she could take the post of superintendent of banking for the state of New York. She held this position until 1982, when she ran unsuccessfully for the Republican Party nomination for the U.S. Senate.

Siebert's long vacation from active management of her firm cost her between $15 million to $20 million, she later calcu-

Company Perspectives:

It's simple. We know what independent investors want and we've been exceeding their expectations for more than 30 years.

lated, because of bad decisions made in her absence. She hired new managers and, in 1985, purchased the discount brokerage operations of two bankrupt firms, raising her own company's level of net commissions to $3 million a year. Muriel Siebert & Co., which now had about 50,000 accounts, began operating as a municipal bond underwriter in 1989. By 1992 the firm had entered the mortgage-backed-securities business with the help of the federal government's Resolution Trust Corp., which had been mandated by law to include minority- and women-owned firms in its underwriting groups.

Muriel Siebert & Co. returned this favor by donating half of its underwriting commissions from new issues of municipal and corporate securities to charity. As a way to drum up new business, the firm made the same offer to the buyers of these securities, who could choose the beneficiaries. In the program's first full year, 1991, Muriel Siebert & Co. gave $310,000 to more than 40 charities, and by 1997 the figure had reached almost $5 million. Its founder also established a philanthropic foundation for her own favorite charities.

By mid-1992 some 20 or so money management firms were taking part in the Siebert Entrepreneurial Philanthropic Plan. This high-minded initiative understandably did not win unanimous cheers from the financial community. One executive told Fred R. Bleakley of the *Wall Street Journal,* "We have enough pressures on profit margins from competition and risk-taking without our customers saying, 'If Mickey Siebert's firm can give half to charity, why can't you?' " Siebert had no sympathy for this viewpoint, replying, "The money [in profits] downtown is vast, almost lewd."

By early 1994 Muriel Siebert & Co. had a branch in Los Angeles as well as its base in New York City. That year the company opened a third office, in Boca Raton, Florida. It was, however, facing price competition from a new breed of superdiscounting brokers. In television ads, Muriel Siebert declared that its prices were "70% below Schwab's" and "consistently less" than Fidelity Brokerage Services Inc. and Quick & Reilly, but at the same time warned the public to beware of "untested Johnny-come-latelies, with lowball rates, unexpected charges, and restrictions."

Public Company: 1996–99

Muriel Siebert & Co. had about 80,000 active customers and a fourth branch, in Naples, Florida, by early 1996, when it went public by merging with publicly traded J. Michaels, Inc., a struggling furniture retailer with five stores. After the merger, J. Michaels liquidated its assets but took a small share in the newly formed Siebert Financial Corp. That year the company also entered municipal bond underwriting by acquiring the remnants of a dissolved minority-owned investment bank, Grigsby Brandford & Co., which became the Siebert, Brandford, Shank division of Siebert's investment banking group. In 1998 this division became Siebert, Brandford, Shank & Co., L.L.C., a partnership 49 percent owned by Siebert.

Siebert Financial was still viewed as a minor player among discount brokers at this time, because it had no market-making operations, did not clear its own trades, and did not go online until late 1996. By early 1999, however, when the firm raised $7.2 million to expand its web site, Siebert was very much a major factor among the 130 or so online brokerage firms. By June 1999 the company was conducting 37 percent of its business through SiebertNet, compared to 16.5 percent during the first quarter of 1998.

After opening the year at $9 a share, Siebert Financial became a hot stock itself, rising as high as $70 a share on February 16, 1999. Since only two million shares were available to the public and 10.4 million shares were traded on a single day, this meant the average share changed hands five times during the day. Siebert was herself disturbed by the rollercoaster ride of her company's stock, which on April 14th again briefly soared to $58 after being recommended on an online site, only to fall back to its previous level of $19. Interviewed by Gretchen Morgenson of the *New York Times* in August, she said, "There's a lack of accountability in these chat rooms, and it's necessary for the regulators to do something if these people move individual stocks."

At a fee of only $14.95 per trade, Siebert Financial could only hope to make significant profits from online brokerage operations if it achieved economies of scale. Accordingly, Siebert and her new vice-chairman, Daniel Jacobson, were planning to acquire smaller discount brokerages. In 1997 the company purchased Stock Mart, the retail brokerage business of William O'Neil & Co. By mid-1999 the firm also had acquired the discount brokerage business of California's Cowles & Sabol & Co. and had reached a tentative agreement to purchase Andrew Peck & Associates of Jersey City.

Siebert Financial Corp. in 1998

In 1998 Siebert Financial was providing discount brokerage and related services to more than 70,000 retail investor accounts, including online trading on the Internet site SiebertNet. This site offered free real-time quotes, a listing of current bond offerings, news, research, and investment-planning tools. Mobilebroker, an interactive palmtop service, enabled clients to make equity trades, receive confirmation, get real-time quotes and alerts, access account data, and send and receive e-mail, by two-way pager instead of a telephone or computer. Marketphone allowed customers to trade by means of touchtone phones and to check balances and executions and receive real-time quotes, with automatic transfer to a live broker, if desired, or the use of a fax-on-demand feature to select a research report available 24 hours a day.

Siebert's products and services also included no-fee, no-minimum check writing, a program for automatically reinvesting cash dividends and capital gains distributions, and retirement accounts (at no fee if in excess of $10,000) in more than 12,000 publicly traded securities and mutual funds. The company offered access to about 7,000 no-load mutual funds, of

Key Dates:

1969: Company is founded as Muriel Siebert & Co., Inc.
1975: Siebert executes its first discounted-commission trade.
1989: Siebert adds underwriting to its list of activities.
1990: The company begins donating to charity half of its commissions from some underwriting activities.
1996: The company goes public as Siebert Financial Corp.
1999: Online traders make Siebert a hot stock and the company's founder a billionaire on paper.

which about 1,000 came without transaction fees. Selectnet and Instinet gave customers access to extended trading hours. Performancefax allowed them to receive a comprehensive profit-and-loss analysis of their portfolios faxed each morning before the market opened. A Siebert Visa debit card was available, as was a VIP statement offering a more sophisticated view of account information, including an asset-allocation pie chart and a detailed income-summary section. Customer financing was available for margin accounts.

Siebert Financial's Capital Markets division was principally engaged in investment banking and institutional equity-execution services. The company was offering the former to corporate and municipal clients, participating as an underwriter for taxable and tax-exempt debt. Since it began underwriting in 1989, the firm had co-managed more than $100 billion in municipal debt and had participated either as an underwriter and/or selling-group member in over 210 offerings, including corporate debt issuances totaling more than $137 billion.

Siebert Financial also was executing equity orders for about 400 institutional accounts through a network of up to 15 independent floor brokers strategically located on major exchanges. These clients included some of the largest pension funds, investment managers, and banks in the United States. The Siebert Real-Time List Execution system, designed and developed by inhouse professionals, enabled the company's Capital Markets division to simultaneously manage an array of baskets for multiple clients while providing real-time analysis. This division was also participating in the secondary markets for municipal and U.S. Treasury securities and trading listed closed-end bond funds and certain other securities for its own account.

Siebert Financial maintained its corporate headquarters in midtown Manhattan. It had retail offices in Beverly Hills, California; Morristown, New Jersey; and Boca Raton, Naples, Palm Beach, and Surfside, Florida. Investment banking offices, including operations of Siebert, Brandford, Shank & Co., were in Chicago, Dallas, Detroit, Houston, Los Angeles, San Francisco, and Seattle. All these facilities were being leased. Of the company's revenues of $25.7 million in 1998, commissions and fees accounted for 75 percent; investment banking for 13 percent; trading profits for five percent; income from equity investees for five percent; and interest and dividends for two percent. Net income came to $4.3 million.

Principal Subsidiaries

Muriel Siebert & Co., Inc.; Siebert, Brandford, Shank & Co., L.L.C.

Principal Competitors

Ameritrade Holding Corp.; Charles Schwab & Co. Inc.; E*Trade Group, Inc.; FMR Corp.; National Discount Brokers Group; Quick & Reilly Group Inc.; TD Waterhouse Group.

Further Reading

Birger, Jon, ''Broker Siebert Struggles to Bond with Munis,'' *Crain's New York Business,* October 13, 1997, p. 12.

——, ''Going Brokerage Shopping,'' *Crain's New York Business,* June 14, 1999, p. 35.

Bleakley, Fred R., ''Broker's Generosity Generates Business, Worries Wall Street,'' *Wall Street Journal,* July 7, 1992, pp. C1, 25.

Gilbertson, Dawn, ''Broker Still Kicking in Doors After Years on Wall Street,'' *Arizona Republic,* January 13, 1996, pp. E1–2.

Hansell, Saul, ''Vast Riches and Rude Vagaries of Internet Trading,'' *New York Times,* February 7, 1999, pp. C1, 7.

Henriques, Diana B., ''Ms. Siebert, Still on the Barricades,'' *New York Times,* July 5, 1992, Sec. 3, p. 15.

Horowitz, Jed, ''Broker Uses CRA As a Lure,'' *American Banker,* January 6, 1992, p. 8.

Huntley, Helen, ''Muriel Siebert's Innovative Marketing Sets Her Apart at New York Exchange,'' *St. Petersburg Times,* January 9, 1996.

Kamen, Robin, ''Still Controversial After All These Years,'' *Crain's New York Business,* March 25, 1996, p. W29.

Morgenson, Gretchen, ''Wild Rides on Stock Market Begin in Internet Chat Rooms,'' *New York Times,* August 21, 1999, pp. A1, C14.

Plitch, Phyllis, ''Wall Street Pioneer Muriel Siebert Is Still Making a Mark with New Deals,'' *Wall Street Journal,* May 27, 1997, p. A13B.

Rowland, Mary, ''Rebel of Wall Street,'' *Working Woman,* April 1986, pp. 64, 68, 70.

Schultz, Abby, ''Resolution Trust Corp. Boosts Minority Firms,'' *Investment Dealers' Digest,* May 18, 1992, pp. 12–13.

Tran, Mark, ''Siebert Chief Is First Wall St Billionairess,'' *Guardian,* February 5, 1999, Sec. 1, p. 25.

Wooley, Suzanne, ''Are Superdeep Discounters As Cheap As They Seem?'', *Business Week,* August 29, 1994, pp. 68–69.

Wyatt, Edward, ''Wall St.'s Top Woman Slips in the Back Door,'' *New York Times,* February 11, 1996, Sec. 3, pp. 1, 6.

—Robert Halasz

Sleepy's Inc.

175 Central Avenue South
Bethpage, New York 11714
U.S.A.
Telephone: (516) 844-8800
Toll Free: (800) SLEEPYS; (800) 753-3797
Fax: (516) 844-8896
Web site: http://www.sleepys.com

Private Company
Incorporated: 1957 as Bedding Discount Center
Employees: 700
Sales: $110 million (1997 est.)
NAIC: 44211 Furniture Stores

Sleepy's Inc. is a mattress and bedding chain with more than 150 stores, mostly in the tri-state New York City metropolitan area. It carries ten major mattress brands in offering what the company calls the largest selection in the United States, all in stock for immediate delivery. In addition to mattresses and box springs, which make up almost 85 percent of company sales, Sleepy's offers a selection of brass and iron beds, platform beds, day beds, futons, headboards, and related bedroom items. Harry Acker, Sleepy's founder, also owns a share of the Kleinsleep bedding chain and serves as its chairman.

Sleepy's Before 1990

Harry Acker learned the bedding trade by hand-tying box spring mattresses in his father's Brooklyn store, Midwood Mattress. In 1957, two years after his father's death, Acker opened Bedding Discount Center, a 1,100-square-foot Brooklyn store. It was acquired in the early 1960s by another business, but Acker had seven stores in the mid-1970s. These stores had taken the Sleepy's name in 1972.

Sleepy's came close to foundering during this decade. A sour national economy, coupled with New York City's own fiscal woes and competition from department and furniture stores almost drove the enterprise into Chapter 11 bankruptcy. Instead, Acker told Michael D. McNamara of *HFD* in 1991, he "went to every vendor and said I want to borrow the money I owe you. I'll pay you back in two years, and all I ask is that you don't stop shipping me. From then on, we started to take off." By 1979 the chain had expanded to 12 stores and was doing more than $1 million in annual sales for the first time. A year earlier, Sleepy's had moved its headquarters from Brooklyn to a 20,000-square-foot facility in New Hyde Park, Long Island.

Sleepy's ranked 43rd in the United States among furniture and bedding retailers in 1985, with 32 stores and $38.1 million in sales. Its main rival was Klein Sleep Products Inc., with 19 stores and $39 million in sales that year. Founded in 1952 by Herbert and Gloria Klein with their life savings of $600 and $1,000 from relatives, Kleinsleep, known for its "Have more fun in bed" jingle, was growing faster than Sleepy's. The company was also selling brass and white iron beds.

Surviving the Early 1990s

The economic downturn that began at the end of the 1980s took its toll on a number of New York-area bedding chains. In June 1991 Klein Sleep Products, which had filed for Chapter 11 bankruptcy in 1976, did so again. This time the company was unable to emerge from receivership under its existing owners, and in January 1993 K.S. Acquisitions Inc., whose principals included Acker, purchased the Kleinsleep name, trademark, and three of its remaining four stores, for $1.4 million. "We hope to build a 20 to 30 store chain in the metro area to bring Kleinsleep back to where it was in the early '70s, which was the dominant sleep shop in New York," Acker told Pam Schancupp of *HFD.* "It will carry more upscale bedding and merchandise that you won't find in a normal sleep shop or furniture store."

Acker had claimed, in 1991, that Sleepy's was riding out the recession in comfortable fashion, with sales having increased appreciably because of 11 new store openings. But the chain was not without its problems. Like other sleep shops, Sleepy's risked losing credibility because of questionable advertising cited by New York City's Department of Consumer Affairs. In 1990 the agency filed suit against Sleepy's in state court, charging that the firm advertised "sales" that continued for

Key Dates:

1957: Harry Acker opens his first store in Brooklyn.
1972: Acker adopts the Sleepy's name.
1979: The Sleepy's chain consists of 12 stores.
1990: Acker is a principal in the purchase of the Kleinsleep chain.
1994: Sleepy's moves its headquarters to Bethpage, New York.
1998: Sleepy's opens a store chain for children.

months—meaning, in effect, according to the agency, that the sale price was the same as the regular price.

While defending his company against charges of deceptive advertising, Acker told McNamara that he was worried that some of his competitors were ruining the credibility of the industry by bait-and-switch tactics, phony model names, and outrageous product warranties. ''What happens when those less than honest practices occur in sleep shops,'' he said, ''is that 70 percent of the people walk out of the store because they know they have been taken. What does that do to that store? It kills its credibility. What does it do to the sleep shop industry? It kills it.''

Another problem for Sleepy's and other traditional bedding shops was competition from Dial-A-Mattress Inc., a city-based telemarketing operation that combined low prices and quick delivery. Speaking to McNamara, Acker was scornful of the idea. ''Would you buy your car, or your home, or even pick your wife over the phone?'' he asked rhetorically. ''If not, why should you choose your bed, something you spend eight hours a night on, over the phone?'' Acker told Cynthia Rigg of *Crain's New York Business,* ''I think manufacturers are stupid to sell to any telemarketing people. They don't see that their better mattresses won't be sold anymore because shoppers won't be able to see the differences in their product.''

Acker voiced this warning about buying a mattress unseen not only to reporters but by means of radio commercials. ''We have to tell the story why sleep shops are important,'' he conceded to McNamara, ''and why the consumer should come to a sleep shop. We avoided television and radio advertising because we were successful without it. 50 percent of our business comes from referrals, but we have found we have to get across to consumers what we are all about, and that means advertising.'' The company was publicizing its wares in the major city newspapers and was considering television commercials for the first time.

Sleepy's had 53 stores in 1991 and was looking to New Jersey for further expansion. Showrooms, chosen by the company on the basis, Acker said, of ''location, location, location,'' on major roads, were averaging about 3,000 square feet. The stores were carrying the Eclipse, Englander, Kingsdown, Sealy, Serta, Simmons, and Spring Air brands, with each brand selling equally, according to Acker. Queen-sized mattresses averaged a little more than $600 in price. A telephone intercom system was allowing Sleepy's store managers not only to talk to their counterparts and to headquarters but also to obtain information on inventory levels and advertisements, to receive product and sales tips, and even to obtain industrywide news. A rigorous three-week sales training program—four weeks by 1998—was in place for new hires.

Sleepy's had moved its headquarters from New Hyde Park to Port Washington by 1994, when it announced it would move again, to a newly purchased facility in Bethpage, another Long Island community. The 135,000-square-foot building on 13 acres, acquired from General Motors Corporation, was three times the capacity of its previous space and included 100,000 square feet for warehousing. Sleepy's was planning to add a 15,000-square-foot training and telemarketing center to the facility. In early 1998, the company completed an 80,000-square-foot addition to the warehouse, thereby adding storage space for more than 15,000 items. Nineteen shipping bays and ten receiving docks were constructed, bringing the total to 37 and 18, respectively.

To better compete with Dial-A-Mattress, which Acker tried but failed to purchase, Sleepy's added an 800 number in 1995 and, mimicking this competitor, offered two-hour delivery in the New York metropolitan area for Sealy, Serta, and Simmons bedding. To fight the ever-growing rival, Sleepy's offered, in 1999, a ''price challenge'' of 25 percent off Dial-A-Mattress's best price or the mattress free.

Major Expansion in 1998–99

In 1998 the company opened a Sleepy's Kids chain for five-year-olds and up as an outgrowth of its earlier store-within-a-store for children's mattresses, furniture, and accessories. The selection of products included comforter sets and bean bag chairs. The display was in room vignettes showing everything from bunk beds to sleep, study, and storage centers. A Sleepy's executive told Nina Farrell of *HFN/Home Furnishing News,* ''What we do differently than some of the other traditional youth furniture stores, as far as presentation and motif, is that our colors are incredibly bright. We're using a lot of Crayola colors, so it's bright and cheery when customers come in. This makes a huge difference in overall store presentation and the impact it has on customers.''

Sleepy's had more than 150 locations in 1999. There were more than 100 in the New York metropolitan area alone, including about 30 on Long Island and others in New Jersey and Connecticut, besides those in New York City and suburban parts of the state other than Long Island. Sleepy's also had entered the Philadelphia area, with as many as 30 stores opened there in 1998. There was also a Sleepy's in Springfield, Massachusetts. Aside from its giant Bethpage distribution center, Sleepy's continued to operate a 20,000-square-foot warehouse in New Hyde Park and it opened another one in central New Jersey.

On its web site, Sleepy's was offering the following models as exclusives in late 1999: Simmons Beautyrest with Lumbar Support; Sealy Posturepedics with Mid-Zone Support; Sera Perfect Sleeper with Comfort Tech 250; Kingsdown Sleeping Beauty Coil with up to 1,320 coils; and Spring Air Spine Saver with up to 2,000 coils.

In late 1999 Sleepy's was offering prospective customers a free mattress and $500 in cash if they could find the same mattress for less at any furniture, department store, or telemarketer. (The offer, however, was not good on all models.) A 60-day trial also was offered, with an exchange if not completely satisfied. Sleepy's carried ten major brands, all in stock for immediate delivery morning, afternoon, or night. The stores were open seven days a week.

Kleinsleep had the same corporate headquarters and central warehouse as Sleepy's. Acker was chief executive officer of both companies and his son David was second in command of both. The chain's 21 stores in 1999 were located mainly on Long Island but also included five in New York City, three in New Jersey, and one in Connecticut. Aireloom, Kingsdown, Sealy, and Serta were the brands displayed. The company served all of New York City and Long Island and, within a 75-mile radius of midtown Manhattan, offered to deliver any in-stock set of bedding on the same day in the evening if ordered before 3:00 p.m. Kleinsleep guaranteed to beat any department store's best sales price on Sealy Posturepedics, Simmons Beautyrests, or Kingsdown Sleeping Beauties or the mattress would be free. Kleinsleep also was selling hi-risers and brass, iron, electric, and day beds. Its revenue was about one-fifth that of Sleepy's in the late 1990s.

Principal Competitors

Dial-A-Mattress Inc.; Seaman Furniture Co., Inc.

Further Reading

Farrell, Nina, "Sleepy's Makes the Grade," *HFN/Home Furnishings News,* March 1, 1999, p. 16.

Gilgoff, Henry, "Going to the Mattress: NYC Sues Over Bed Ads," *New York Newsday,* April 6, 1990, p. 49.

"Kleinsleep Joins the Upper Half," *HFD,* June 9, 1986, p. S12.

"Kleinsleep Masters the New York Market," *HFD,* August 11, 1986, p. S12.

Madore, James T., "Bethpage Sleepy's Expansion Ends," *Newsday,* March 10, 1998, p. A38.

"Mattresses Are Bedrock of Acker's Success," *LI Business News,* April 6, 1998, p. 20.

McNamara, Michael D., "Acker: 'Honesty Best Bedfellow,' " *HFD,* June 10, 1991, pp. 17–18.

Rigg, Cynthia, "Bedding Stores Endure Sleepless Nights," *Crain's New York Business,* September 30, 1991, p. 8.

Schancupp, Pam, "K.S. Acquisition Buys Kleinsleep," *HFD,* February 22, 1993, p. 21.

"Sleepy's Chain to Relocate Offices to Bethpage, N.Y.," *Furniture Today,* August 8, 1994, p. 34.

Thomas, Larry, "Sleepy's Adds 800 Number in NYC," *Furniture Today,* April 17, 1995, pp. 4, 28.

—Robert Halasz

SB
SmithKline Beecham

SmithKline Beecham plc

New Horizons Court
Brentford, Middlesex TW8 9EP
United Kingdom
Telephone: (0181) 975-2000
Fax: (0181) 975-2090
Web site: http://www.sb.com

Public Company
Incorporated: 1989
Employees: 58,300
Sales: £8.08 billion (US$13.42 billion) (1998)
Stock Exchanges: London New York
Ticker Symbol: SBH
NAIC: 325412 Pharmaceutical Preparation Manufacturing; 325611 Soap and Other Detergent Manufacturing; 325620 Toilet Preparation Manufacturing; 312111 Soft Drink Manufacturing; 541710 Research and Development in the Physical, Engineering, and Life Sciences

SmithKline Beecham plc, which was formed in 1989 from the merger of the Beecham Group of the United Kingdom and the U.S. company SmithKline Beckman, is one of the world's largest pharmaceutical companies, and one of the top two in Britain (the other being Glaxo Wellcome plc). SmithKline discovers, develops, manufactures, and markets prescription drugs, vaccines, over-the-counter (OTC) medicines, and health-related consumer products. Among the company's more than 400 branded products are Augmentin, a leading antibiotic; Relifex/Relafen, an anti-inflammatory used to treat arthritis; Seroxat/Paxil, a leading antidepressant; Havrix/Engerix-B/Twinrix hepatitis vaccines; LYMErix, the first vaccine for the prevention of Lyme disease; Panadol, an OTC analgesic; several consumer products to deal with stomach and digestive ailments, including Tums, Tagamet HB, and Phillips Milk of Magnesia; Horlicks, Lucozade, and Ribena nutritional drinks; Aquafresh toothpaste and toothbrushes; OTC cold and flu medications, including Beechams, Contac, and Sucrets; and smoking cessation aids, including Nicorette and NicoDerm CQ.

Beecham's Modest Beginnings

One of the first British companies to undertake intensive advertising, Beecham grew from a small regional pill-peddling operation to a multinational patent medicine company at a time when very few companies branched beyond their own communities. In 1847 Thomas Beecham began hawking his own brand of pills throughout the town of Wigan and the surrounding countryside. He soon set up shop as an herbalist and grocer in Wigan. Beecham, born the son of a farm worker in 1820, had spent his youth as a shepherd boy, and in that job he had learned a good deal about herbal remedies. Beecham was said to have had a special knack for healing sick animals and, on occasion, even humans. For several years Beecham sold his laxatives at local markets with a sales pitch that included showing off a jar of intestinal worms.

In 1859, after mixed results in Wigan, Beecham moved his operation to nearby St. Helens, where he focused on two products: a cough tablet and the famous laxative Beecham's Pills, advertised in the local newspaper as "worth a guinea a box." Both products were available through mail order and Beecham increased spending on advertising to take advantage of a rapidly growing demand for health products.

In 1881, when Thomas Beecham's son Joseph took effective control of the company, Beecham's sales were at £34,000, demonstrating average annual growth of about 18 percent, a rate it had sustained since 1865. The elder Beecham remained active in the operations of the company until his official retirement in 1895.

Joseph Beecham increased the company's advertising expenditures considerably. By 1891 annual advertising expenditures had increased to £120,000, from £22,000 in 1884, and Beecham introduced more creative ads. Advertising gimmicks included free distribution of sails printed with Beecham slogans to boat owners and inexpensive general information booklets bearing Beecham's messages.

During the 1880s Joseph Beecham spearheaded the company's expansion overseas. First, Beecham's Pills were exported to countries throughout the British Empire. In 1888 they

Company Perspectives:

At SmithKline Beecham, healthcare—prevention, diagnosis, treatment and cure—is our purpose. Through scientific excellence and commercial expertise we provide products and services throughout the world that promote health and well-being.

The source of our competitive advantage is the energy and ideas of our people. Our strength lies in what we value: customers, innovation, integrity, people and performance.

At SmithKline Beecham, we are people with purpose, working together to make the lives of people everywhere healthier, striving in everything we do to become The "Simply Better" Healthcare Company as judged by all those we serve: customers, shareholders, employees and the global community.

were distributed in the United States and Canada, and two years later a manufacturing facility was set up in New York.

Extensive advertising had made Beecham's Pills practically a household word on several continents by the end of the 19th century. This success was not at first duplicated after the turn of the century, however. Although Beecham remained profitable, its rate of growth slowed considerably. Joseph Beecham spent more of his time on projects unrelated to the business, including numerous philanthropic endeavors and patronage of his music-minded son, Thomas, later to become a renowned conductor. In 1913 sales remained static at £290,000, although the firm's profitability had improved.

In 1916 Joseph Beecham died, leaving a complicated estate. Beecham had never incorporated the pill business and it remained entwined with his other affairs. Henry Beecham, Joseph's younger son, ran the business with three other executors until 1921, but had no active role after that time. Three years later the pill business was acquired by financier Philip Hill. Hill incorporated the company as Beecham's Pills in 1928 and launched a new period of growth.

Expanding and Diversifying into Pharmaceuticals: 1930s–70s

For the next ten years Hill made acquisitions broadening the product line of the company. He purchased patent medicines such as Yeast Vite, Iron Jelloids, Phosferine, and Phyllosan. In the later 1930s the company entered the toiletries business with the acquisition of Prichard and Constance, a shampoo manufacturer that distributed the brand name Amami. In 1938 Beecham acquired Macleans Ltd., well-known for toothpaste; County Perfumery, manufacturers of Brylcreem; and Eno Proprietaries, makers of a popular antacid. In 1938 Beecham acquired Lucozade, a popular glucose drink, from its inventor W.W. Hunter, to enter the health-drink field. The company changed its name to Beecham Group Ltd. in 1945 to reflect its diversified nature.

When Beecham acquired Maclean's in 1938 it unknowingly changed its direction. With the purchase came company secretary and director H.G. Leslie Lazell. Lazell became corporate secretary of Beecham's Pills, and during the war took over as managing director of the Maclean's unit. Leslie Lazell had always been a firm believer in research, and he developed a research department at the company, which soon entered the medicines field.

Formed in 1943, Beecham Research Laboratories Ltd. employed 115 people, 34 of them graduate-level scientists. In 1947 a 27-acre facility was opened at Surrey, with Alexander Fleming, the discoverer of penicillin, presiding over the opening ceremonies. Beecham Research Laboratories started out researching both pharmaceuticals and food products but before long concentrated solely on pharmaceutical research. In 1949 Beecham's acquisition of the C.L. Bencard company, a manufacturer of allergy vaccines, paved the way for entry into the prescription drug field.

During the 1950s Beecham expanded its consumer products line and pumped the profits into drug research. It purchased new health drinks, including Ribena blackcurrant juice, Shloer apple and grape drinks, and Horlicks beverages were acquired in 1969. The toiletries division also expanded, adding Vosene shampoo among others. A real breakthrough came in 1957 when company researchers isolated the penicillin nucleus 6-aminopenicillanic acid (6-APA). This discovery opened the door to the manufacture of a multitude of new antibiotics.

In 1959 Beecham marketed Broxil (phenethicillin), followed shortly by Celbenin (methicillin). The introduction of these products represented a medical breakthrough, as many bacterial strains had built up a resistance to the original penicillins–Penicillin G and Penicillin V. In 1961 Penbritin (ampicillin) hit the market, and soon Beecham's facilities were inadequate for the worldwide demand. A 35-acre complex at Worthing came on line in the early 1960s to produce 6-APA, the base for semisynthetic penicillins. Beecham's lead in antibiotics brought tremendous growth in the 1960s and 1970s.

Lazell's emphasis on marketing was also key to Beecham's growth. By 1960 the company was the second largest advertiser in the United Kingdom. Beecham was one of the first British firms to put the CEO directly in charge of the marketing team, long a standard practice in the United States.

In the mid-1960s, Beecham products penetrated the European continent. Within 20 years, this region comprised Beecham's largest single market. In the later 1960s Beecham Pharmaceutical marketers turned their attention to the United States, where an expanding business had been built on foundations provided by Brylcreem hair dressing. In 1967 the company opened an antibiotics factory in Piscataway, New Jersey. In 1971 Beecham bought the U.S. feminine hygiene company S.E. Massengill.

In 1972 the company planned to increase the size of its prescription drug business by merging with one of its chief British competitors, the Glaxo Group. The British government blocked the merger, citing the possibility of reduced spending on research and development within the industry. Glaxo was particularly attractive because it had a large network overseas.

Also in 1972 Beecham launched Amoxil, which went on to become one of the most widely prescribed antibiotics, often

Key Dates:

1830: John K. Smith opens his first drugstore in Philadelphia through a company called John K. Smith & Company.
1847: Thomas Beecham begins hawking his own brand of pills in and around the town of Wigan.
1875: Smith's company is renamed Smith, Kline & Company, ten years after Mahlon Kline joined the company, first serving as bookkeeper then moving into management.
1881: Joseph Beecham takes effective control of his father's company.
1891: Smith, Kline acquires French, Richards & Company and changes its name to Smith, Kline & French (SK&F).
1916: Joseph Beecham dies.
1924: Financier Philip Hill acquires the Beecham business.
1928: Hill incorporates Beecham's Pills and launches a new period of growth.
1945: Beecham's Pills changes its name to Beecham Group Ltd. to reflect its diversification.
1952: SK&F launches Dexedrine, the first time-released capsule.
1957: Beecham researchers isolate the penicillin nucleus 6-APA, a discovery that opens the door to the manufacture of a multitude of new antibiotics.
1960: SK&F begins marketing Contac, the first all-day cold remedy.
1972: Beecham launches Amoxil, which becomes one of the most widely prescribed antibiotics.
1976: SmithKline Corporation (new name for SK&F) revolutionizes peptic ulcer treatment through the introduction of Tagamet.
1981: Beecham introduces Augmentin, an antibiotic used to treat an array of bacterial infections.
1982: SmithKline acquires Allergan, a maker of eye and skin care products, and Beckman Instruments, a leading manufacturer of diagnostic and measurement instruments and supplies; it also changes its name to SmithKline Beckman Corporation.
1985: Norcliff Thayer, a U.S. maker of OTC drugs including Tums, is acquired by Beecham; SmithKline Clinical Labs merges with American BioScience Laboratories to form SmithKline BioScience Laboratories.
1986: Robert P. Bauman becomes chairman of Beecham and disposes of £400 million of noncore, consumer product businesses.
1988: SmithKline BioScience Labs becomes the industry leader with the purchase of one of its biggest competitors, International Clinical Laboratories, Inc.
1989: Tagamet becomes the world's first drug to have annual sales in excess of US$1 billion; SmithKline's James Black is awarded the Nobel prize in medicine for his Tagamet research; Beecham and SmithKline merge to form SmithKline Beecham plc.
1993: Company spends US$125 million to enter into a genetic research collaboration agreement with Human Genome Sciences Inc.
1994: Company acquires Diversified Pharmaceutical Services, Inc., a leading U.S. pharmaceutical benefit manager; it also acquires Sterling Health, a specialist in OTC medicines, from Eastman Kodak, then sells Sterling's North American operations to Bayer AG; the company sells its animal health business to Pfizer Inc.
1998: Company enters advanced mergers talks with Glaxo Wellcome, but the deal falls through.
1999: Diversified Pharmaceutical Services and the company's clinical laboratory unit are divested.

used to treat bacterial infections, including those involving the ear and throat. Amoxil was the brand name for amoxycillin, which had been discovered by Beecham scientists. The company's growing antibiotic line also included Floxapen (flucloxacillin) and Ticar (ticarcillin). In the mid-1970s new non-antibiotic drugs were introduced, such as the allergy vaccine Pollinex and the antidepressant Norval.

Late 1970s to Late 1980s: Acquisitions Followed by Divestments

Acquisitions of U.S. drug and consumer products companies accelerated toward the end of the decade and into the 1980s. In 1977 Beecham bought Sucrets throat lozenges for US$76 million and acquired the floundering Calgon bath products line. Beecham turned the businesses around, revamping old products and packaging, and using aggressive marketing strategies. In 1979 Beecham purchased Jovan, the U.S. perfume manufacturer, for US$85 million. Other fragrance lines were later acquired, including Diane Von Furstenberg in 1983 and the cosmetics and fragrances of BAT Industries plc in 1985. Other big acquisitions in the early 1980s included the J.B. Williams company, makers of Geritol, Sominex, Aqua Velva, and Lectric Shave among others for US$100 million in 1982; DAP, Inc., manufacturer of caulk and other home improvement products for US$68 million in 1983; and Norcliff Thayer, a major manufacturer of OTC drugs including the well-known antacid Tums, in the United States for US$369 million in 1985. Beecham also acquired a number of European pharmaceutical companies in France, West Germany, and Italy. On the drug development front, Beecham in 1981 introduced Augmentin, an antibiotic used to treat an array of bacterial infections.

In 1984, Beecham's profits began to level off, due in part to decreased popularity of ampicillin, caused by increased antibiotic competition, and pressure from the British government to cap profits on drugs. Following Lazell's formula, Beecham's new chairman, Sir Ronald Halstead, hoped to pay for rising research and development costs through profits on consumer goods. A number of acquisitions of consumer products companies in 1984 and 1985 seemed to the company's directors too costly and out of line with Beecham's overall thrust. Halstead was let go in 1985. In 1986 Robert P. Bauman became chairman of Beecham. The company's first U.S. chairman, Bauman knew the North American market well, having worked at General Foods, Avco, and Textron. Bauman sold off some of Beecham's consumer products lines, primarily soft drinks lines, although he retained the successful Ribena, Horlicks, and Lucozade brands, and implemented cost-cutting measures worldwide. Between 1986 and mid-1989, Bauman disposed of £400 million of noncore businesses.

By the mid-1980s Beecham had made significant headway into the U.S. marketplace and continued to hold its place as the largest OTC drug producer in its home market. Beecham's pharmaceutical research focused on three general areas: cardiovascular therapy, diseases affecting the central nervous system, and anti-infectives. Demand for healthcare products increased substantially as the wealthy U.S. market grew older. Relifex, a nonsteroidal anti-inflammatory used by arthritis patients, began limited marketing in 1985 and by the late 1980s showed promise for the company. An anticlotting agent, Eminase, introduced in Europe in 1987, also appeared to be a significant breakthrough for cardiac patients. Two new antibiotics, Augmentin and Timentin, earned the Queen's Award for technological achievement in 1986. Both drugs received widespread acceptance throughout the medical community.

Brief History of SmithKline Beckman

In July 1989 Beecham merged with an equally well established business, Philadelphia-based SmithKline Beckman Corporation. SmithKline Beckman's roots extended back to 1830, when John K. Smith opened his first drugstore in Philadelphia through a company called John K. Smith & Company. The firm soon became a leader in drug wholesaling. It was renamed Smith, Kline & Company in 1875, ten years after Mahlon Kline joined the company, first serving as bookkeeper, then moving into sales and management. In 1891 Smith, Kline acquired French, Richards & Company and changed its name to Smith, Kline & French (SK&F). At this time, SK&F produced and sold fine perfumes, liniments, tonics, hair oil, cough medicine, and various home remedies.

In 1910 SK&F expanded its product offerings through the addition of the "Blue Line," which included such standard drugs as poison ivy lotion, iron tablets, and lozenges. Around the same time as the establishment of Beecham Research Laboratories, SK&F established its own research arm called Smith Kline & French Laboratories. In the 1950s SK&F scientists developed the antipsychotic Thorazine, which started a revolution in the treatment of mental illness. In 1952 came the launch of Dexedrine, the first time-released capsule. This was followed in 1960 by another time-release product, Contac, the first all-day cold remedy.

During the 1970s SK&F shortened its name to SmithKline Corporation. The revolutionary peptic ulcer medication Tagamet was introduced in the United Kingdom in November 1976 and in the United States in August 1977. Tagamet went on to become, in 1989, the first drug in the world to have annual sales in excess of US$1 billion. Also in 1989 SmithKline's James Black was awarded the Nobel prize in medicine for his research involving Tagamet and other beta-blockers and H_2 blockers. In 1982 SmithKline acquired Allergan, a maker of eye and skin care products, and Beckman Instruments, a leading manufacturer of diagnostic and measurement instruments and supplies. On completion of the latter purchase, the company changed its name to SmithKline Beckman Corporation. By this time, SmithKline had also diversified into the clinical laboratories business. It entered that sector in the 1960s through the acquisition of seven labs in the United States and one in Canada. SmithKline Clinical Labs then merged with American BioScience Laboratories in 1985 to form SmithKline BioScience Laboratories, which became the industry leader in 1988 with the purchase of one of its biggest competitors, International Clinical Laboratories, Inc.

Merger of Beecham and SmithKline in 1989

The merger of Beecham and SmithKline Beckman formed what was at the time one of the top five pharmaceutical companies in the world. The new SmithKline Beecham plc, based in London, tallied US$6.9 billion in sales annually. Beecham was widely considered the healthier half of the new company. With Eminase and Relifex about to hit the U.S. market, Beecham looked solid enough to shore up its ailing U.S. partner for at least a short time. SmithKline had failed to come up with a blockbuster product since it introduced the ulcer remedy Tagamet in the mid-1970s, despite substantial research and development expenditures. New competition from Glaxo's Zantac had eroded some of Tagamet's expected market share, and SmithKline was accused by stock analysts of lacking direction. A headline in the *Wall Street Journal,* July 7, 1989, called the merger "just what the doctor ordered" for SmithKline.

SmithKline's chairman Henry Wendt became chairman of the merged company while Robert Bauman, who became the new company CEO, faced combining two distinct corporate cultures and had little time to spare: just one week after the Beecham SmithKline merger was finalized, two U.S. giants, Squibb and Bristol-Myers, announced their own merger plans (forming Bristol-Myers Squibb Company). Beecham, with its new prescription drugs and strong presence in the over-the-counter drug market, looked like a good partner for SmithKline, with its strong U.S. sales staff. The SmithKline Beecham merger permitted both companies to compete on a global level neither could manage alone. In addition, the companies' R&D programs were complementary. Beecham had several new products ready for market while SmithKline was at the opposite end of the R&D cycle, promising results down the road. Geographically, Beecham's strength in Europe fit well with SmithKline's coverage in the United States and Japan. Bauman expressed his intentions to cut costs by eliminating administrative and production personnel, rather than by paring sales or research staffs.

1990s and Beyond

In the early 1990s SmithKline Beecham concentrated on reducing the debt it had taken on to complete the merger. The company made a number of disposals, mainly in the consumer products area, including its cosmetics businesses, its adhesives unit, Brylcreem and other hair care brands, and other non-healthcare products. In early 1994 its consumer side was reorganized as the consumer healthcare division, focusing solely on OTC drugs, toothpaste and toothbrushes, and nutritional drinks. The company's OTC drug offerings were later expanded through the introduction of nonprescription versions of prescription drugs, including the launch of Tagamet HB. On the pharmaceutical side, SmithKline announced in late 1992 that it would withdraw from long-term research into gastrointestinal drugs to concentrate its R&D efforts on five areas: the central nervous system, the heart and lungs, anti-infectives, inflammation and tissue repair, and vaccines. Among the pharmaceuticals introduced by SmithKline in the early and mid-1990s were Relafen, an anti-inflammatory drug for the treatment of arthritis; Engerix B, a hepatitis B vaccine; Havrix, a hepatitis A vaccine; Kytril, an antinausea product used in treating cancer patients; and Seroxat/Paxil, an antidepressant. These introductions helped counter the plummeting sales of the prescription version of Tagamet, which went off patent in 1994.

In 1993 SmithKline spent US$125 million to enter into a research collaboration agreement with and take a seven percent stake in Human Genome Sciences Inc., a newly formed enterprise actively identifying and describing the functions of human genes. The agreement gave SmithKline rights to develop drugs based on the gene sequencing information discovered by Human Genome Sciences. This collaboration was slow to pay off in terms of new medicines.

Jan Leschly, a native of Denmark who as a young man was a professional tennis player ranked as high as number ten in the world, was named CEO of SmithKline in 1994. In May of that year, the company acquired Diversified Pharmaceutical Services, Inc.—a leading U.S. pharmaceutical benefit manager (PBM)—for US$2.3 billion (£1.6 billion). PBMs, which acted as drug wholesalers for managed care organizations, were growing rapidly in the United States, in tandem with the growth of health maintenance organizations and other managed care enterprises. SmithKline continued its acquisitive ways in 1994 with the August purchase of Sterling Health, a specialist in branded OTC medicines, for US$2.9 billion. A few weeks later SmithKline sold Sterling's North American operations to Bayer AG for US$1 billion. The net result of these moves was that SmithKline expanded its OTC presence in Western Europe significantly and even more dramatically in Eastern Europe and Asia; the company became the third largest seller of OTC products in the world, and the largest in Europe. It gained several key brands, including the analgesic Panadol and the gastrointestinal remedy Phillips Milk of Magnesia. Rounding out a year filled with large transactions, SmithKline in late 1994 sold its animal health business to Pfizer Inc. for US$1.45 billion (£920 million), a move enabling SmithKline to focus further on the human healthcare market.

During the mid-to-late 1990s SmithKline Beecham began marketing a number of new products. On the OTC side, the company moved into the smoking cessation sector with the launch of Nicorette gum. In 1996 the FDA approved NicoDerm CQ, a smoking cessation patch. These products held 90 percent of the OTC smoking cessation market in the United States through the late 1990s. Also in 1996 came the launch of the pharmaceutical Hycamtin, which was designed to treat ovarian cancer and small cell lung cancer. In the vaccine arena, SmithKline introduced Twinrix, the first combined hepatitis A and B vaccine; the Infanrix line of combination vaccines, which included protection against diphtheria, tetanus, and pertussis (or whooping cough) in its basic formulation, with additional protection against other diseases provided through other formulations; and LYMErix, which was introduced in 1998 as the first vaccine in the world for the prevention of Lyme disease.

SmithKline's collaboration with Human Genome Sciences had yet to pay off in terms of new medicines, but was uncovering numerous leads for potential development. SmithKline simply did not have the resources, however, to follow up on every lead. Therefore, in 1996 the company began licensing the Human Genome Sciences data to other pharmaceutical companies, including Schering-Plough Corporation, Takeda Chemical Industries Ltd., and Merck. The following year, SmithKline joined with Incyte Pharmaceuticals to create another biotechnology venture called diaDexus. This venture was focused on developing new diagnostic tests based on gene discoveries. One of its first undertakings was the development and commercializing of a new cervical cancer screening technology which had been originally conceived by Cancer Research Campaign Technology Limited.

The need for greater resources to investigate the many opportunities being uncovered by the biotechnology revolution led SmithKline to enter merger discussions, first with American Home Products Corporation, which began in 1997 and ended in early 1998, and then with U.K. rival Glaxo Wellcome. In late January 1998 Glaxo and SmithKline announced that they were on the verge of announcing a merger valued at between US$65 billion and US$70 billion. This would have been the largest corporate merger ever, but the deal fell apart in late February following disagreements between the two companies' CEOs over leadership of the combined company.

In the aftermath of this botched union, SmithKline refocused its operations on two core areas: pharmaceuticals and consumer healthcare. To this end, in April 1999 it sold Diversified Pharmaceutical Services to Express Scripts Inc. for £422 million (US$700 million) in cash, resulting in an after-tax loss of £446 million (US$740 million), which was recorded in 1998. Around this same time, the company announced a four-year restructuring plan in which it would close down excess manufacturing plants and lay off about 3,000 people, resulting in annual savings of £200 million (US$332 million) by 2002. SmithKline planned to take pretax charges of up to £750 million (US$1.25 billion) over the four-year period. In August SmithKline completed the sale of its clinical laboratory unit—SmithKline Beecham Clinical Laboratories—to Quest Diagnostics, Incorporated for £618 million (US$1.03 billion) and a 29.2 percent equity interest in Quest.

In mid-1999 SmithKline received FDA regulatory approval of Avandia, a diabetes drug which it began comarketing with Bristol-Myers Squibb; and for a new use for Paxil, that of treating people suffering from severe "social phobia"—extreme bouts of shyness that could be severely debilitating and traumatic. In December 1999 Leschly announced that he would retire as chief executive in April 2000 and be replaced by COO Jean-Pierre Garnier. Rumors instantly began to surface suggesting that the leadership change would lead to renewed merger talks with Glaxo, but there was no immediate suggestion that SmithKline Beecham was certain to change direction with Leschly's departure. The company appeared capable of continuing on a path of organic growth, with several pharmaceuticals in advanced stages of development, including: Ariflo, for chronic obstructive pulmonary disease and for asthma; Idoxifene, for osteoporosis and breast cancer; Factive, an antibiotic for the treatment of respiratory tract and urinary tract infections; Bexxar, for non-Hodgkin's lymphoma, a cancer of the immune system; and Locilex, a topical antibiotic for the treatment of infected diabetic foot ulcers.

Principal Subsidiaries

Beecham Group p.l.c.; SB Pharmco Puerto Rico Inc. (U.S.A.); SmithKline Beecham Corporation (U.S.A.); SmithKline Beecham (Australia) Pty Ltd; SmithKline Beecham Biologicals S.A. (Belgium); SmithKline Beecham Biologicals Biotech S.A. (Belgium); SmithKline Beecham Biologicals Manufacturing S.A. (Belgium); SmithKline Beecham Brasil Ltda (Brazil); Sino-American Tianjin Smith Kline & French Laboratories Ltd (China; 55%); SmithKline Beecham Laboratoires Pharmaceutiques S.A. (France); SmithKline Beecham Consumer Healthcare G.m.b.H. (Germany); SmithKline Beecham Pharma G.m.b.H. (Germany); SmithKline Beecham (Cork) Ltd (Ireland); SmithKline Beecham Dungarvan Ltd (Ireland); SmithKline Beecham S.p.A. (Italy); SmithKline Beecham Seiyaku K.K. (Japan); SmithKline Beecham Mexico S.A. de C.V.; SmithKline Beecham S.A. (Spain).

Principal Competitors

Abbott Laboratories; American Home Products Corporation; AstraZeneca PLC; Bayer AG; Bristol-Myers Squibb Company; Colgate-Palmolive Company; Corning Incorporated; Eli Lilly and Company; Glaxo Wellcome plc; Hoechst AG; Johnson & Johnson; Laboratory Corporation of America Holdings; Merck & Co., Inc.; Mylan Laboratories Inc.; Novartis AG; Pfizer Inc.; Pharmacia & Upjohn, Inc.; The Procter & Gamble Company; Rhone-Poulenc Rorer Inc.; Roche Holding Ltd.; Schering-Plough Corporation; Unilever; Warner-Lambert Company.

Further Reading

Abrahams, Paul, ''Honeymoon Over at SmithKline: The Merged Group Must Now Increase Sales,'' *Financial Times,* October 21, 1992, p. 22.

Bauman, Robert P., Peter Jackson, and Joanne T. Lawrence, *From Promise to Performance: A Journey of Transformation at SmithKline Beecham,* Boston: Harvard Business School Press, 1997, 302 p.

''Beecham Group PLC: A Brief History,'' Beecham corporate typescript, 1989.

Corley, T.A.B., ''Sir Joseph Beecham'' and ''Thomas Beecham,'' in *Dictionary of Business Biography: A Biographical Dictionary of Business Leaders Active in Britain in the Period, 1860–1980,* vol. I, edited by David Jeremy, London: Butterworth, 1985.

de Jonquieres, Guy, ''Buying the Bactroban with the Bath Oil: Why SmithKline Beecham Has Reshaped Its Consumer Brands Side,'' *Financial Times,* January 10, 1994, p. 18.

Flynn, Julia, et al., ''Is SmithKline's Future in Its Genes?,'' *Business Week,* March 4, 1996, pp. 80–81.

Francis, Anne, *A Guinea a Box: A Biography,* London: Hale, 1968, 191 p.

Green, Daniel, ''Merger of Equals Sinks into Drug-Induced Hallucination,'' *Financial Times,* February 25, 1998, p. 19.

——, ''SmithKline Awaits Results of Expansion Trial,'' *Financial Times,* December 2, 1994, p. 22.

——, ''SmithKline's Well-Sugared Pill,'' *Financial Times,* February 22, 1997, p. 5.

——, ''Team Player Leschly Likes to Prove a Point: A Competitive Streak Makes the Head of SmithKline Beecham a Tough Opponent,'' *Financial Times,* July 29, 1996, p. 7.

Guyon, Janet, ''A Mangled Merger,'' *Fortune,* March 30, 1998, p. 32.

Hindley, Diana, and Geoffrey Hindley, *Advertising in Victorian England, 1837–1901,* London: Wayland, 1972, 208 p.

Holland, Kenneth, ''Pharmaceutical Industry Profiles: Beecham Group PLC,'' *The Pharmaceutical Journal,* vol. 238, 1987.

Jackson, Tony, and Daniel Green, ''SmithKline Pays 2bn for US Group,'' *Financial Times,* May 4, 1994, p. 1.

Langreth, Robert, ''Depression Pill May Help Treat the Acutely Shy,'' *Wall Street Journal,* May 3, 1999, p. B1.

Langreth, Robert, and Steven Lipin, ''Glaxo, SmithKline Reel in Battle of Egos,'' *Wall Street Journal,* February 25, 1998, p. A3.

Lazell, H.G., *From Pills to Penicillin: The Beecham Story, a Personal Account,* London: Heinemann, 1975, 208 p.

Maremont, Mark, and Joseph Weber, ''The First Acid Test of the Drug Megamergers,'' *Business Week,* February 19, 1990, pp. 62–63.

Marion, John Francis, *The Fine Old House,* Philadelphia: SmithKline Corp., 1980, 251 p.

Moore, Stephen D., and Michael Waldholz, ''SmithKline's Science-Tech Chief, Poste, to Quit,'' *Wall Street Journal,* October 29, 1999, p. B8.

''The Mother of All Mergers,'' *Economist,* February 7, 1998, pp. 63–64.

Stephens, Harrison, *Golden Past, Golden Future: The First Fifty Years of Beckman Instruments, Inc.,* Claremont, Calif.: Claremont University Center, 1985, 144 p.[ke.

Syedain, Hashi, ''SmithKline Beecham's Early Trials,'' *Management Today,* November 1989, pp. 98+.

Tanouye, Elyse, and Robert Langreth, ''Genetic Giant: Cost of Drug Research Is Driving Merger Talks of Glaxo, SmithKline,'' *Wall Street Journal,* February 2, 1998, p. A1.

Tanouye, Elyse, and Stephen D. Moore, ''Chief Prescribes Research for SmithKline: Expected Sales of Units Set, with Big Charge, Layoffs,'' *Wall Street Journal,* February 10, 1999, p. B6.

Waldholz, Michael, ''SmithKline Head to Retire After 10-Year Reign,'' *Wall Street Journal,* December 3, 1999, p. B6.

Waldholz, Michael, Elyse Tanouye, and Gardiner Harris, ''With Executives Aging and Patents Expiring, Industry Is Ripe for Megamergers,'' *Wall Street Journal,* November 4, 1999, pp. B1, B4.

Weber, Joseph, Julia Flynn, and Karen Lowry Miller, ''SmithKline's New World Order,'' *Business Week,* September 12, 1994, p. 35.

—Thomas M. Tucker
—updated by David E. Salamie

Spar Aerospace Limited

121 King Street West, Suite 2100
Toronto, Ontario
Canada M5H 4C2
Telephone: (416) 682-7600
Fax: (416) 682-7601
Web site: http://www.spar.ca

Public Company
Incorporated: 1968 as Spar Aerospace Products Ltd.
Employees: 600
Sales: C$251.18 million (US$163.5 million) 1998)
Stock Exchanges: Toronto Montreal
Ticker Symbol: SPZ
NAIC: 336413 Other Aircraft Parts and Auxiliary Equipment Manufacturing; 54171 Research and Development in the Physical, Engineering, and Life Sciences

Spar Aerospace Limited is perhaps better known for what it once was than what it is. Once Canada's largest space contractor, it produced the robotic Canadarm, a centerpiece of that nation's technological achievement, and was a market leader in space robotics. Divestitures have pared Spar down to its Aviation Services division. It maintains the only North American service center for the ubiquitous Lockheed Martin C-130 Hercules transport (there are 1,800 of these planes worldwide). It also services and upgrades Sea King military helicopters and Boeing 737 commercial airliners.

Origins

In the 1950s and 1960s, the Special Products and Applied Research division of de Havilland Aircraft of Canada Limited developed missile components and other advanced aerospace products. Its STEM (Storable Tubular Extendible Member) products dominated the satellite antenna market and its BI-STEM tripod was just being tested.

Management bought the company in 1967 and took it public the next year. Spar soon added X-ray equipment, battery chargers, and urethane structures to its product line. Its first full year in operation as an independent company brought sales of C$5.1 million. Aircraft equipment repair and overhaul was the company's largest product segment, accounting for C$2 million of its sales. Spar had 300 employees at the time.

The year 1969, which saw the first human step onto the surface of the moon, ironically brought Spar serious setbacks. The Nixon administration cut back sharply on military aerospace programs, and Spar's takeover of Levy Industries Limited's York Gears Division produced complications in the form of difficult-to-collect receivables and unprofitable, unfulfilled contracts. Spar lost C$556,000 on sales of C$7.2 million for the year.

Although sales reached C$9.8 million in 1970, the company still posted a loss, of C$371,000. In these years that were so difficult for the industry in general, Spar did find some success in supplying satellite components for the Hughes Aircraft Co. and, through its York Gears subsidiary, gears for the Bell Helicopter Company.

Spar developed the Canadarm robotic control arm in the late 1970s. Spar gave the first one to NASA in 1981. Emblazoned with a maple leaf, the Canadarm caught the world's attention when it began operations on the second flight of the space shuttle *Columbia.* The program fostered more than national pride: by the 1990s it was bringing in C$20 million a year for maintenance support.

In the mid-1980s, Spar built communications satellites for Hughes Aircraft and Telesat Canada (the Anik-E). The company manufactured Olympus-1 (or L-Sat) satellites in collaboration with Fokker. Its Communications Systems Division also developed equipment for satellite communications for the energy industry.

Some contractors resented Spar's prime contractor status and felt that the company reserved the choicest high technology assignments for itself. Com Dev, Inc., a C$60 million microwave component specialist, unsuccessfully bid against Spar to build the MSat, a Canadian mobile communications satellite. Spar, however, was precariously dependent on these ''golden chains'': its government contracts amounted to C$275 million

Company Perspectives:

Spar had grown over the years into a complex company with a number of lines of business operating in a variety of markets. One of the management team's guiding principles over the past couple of years has been to reduce that complexity—to streamline Spar—so we can focus on fewer, large, core businesses. The result will be a company that is more manageable and better able to grow profitably, while being easier for the investment community to analyse.

That being said, our strategic direction for Spar is two-fold: Number One: Spar will be a profitable, North American provider of Services both to the Aviation and Robotics sectors. Number Two: Spar will provide components and systems that enable bandwidth anywhere, anytime in emerging space and terrestrial communications markets.

in 1991. At one point, the Canadian space budget was projected to be only C$100 million by 2000, one-fifth of its 1995 level.

Com Dev, MacDonald Dettwiler and Associates (MDA), and Spar did cooperate in the Radarsat International joint venture, formed to market data from the world's most advanced radar satellite. The first one was launched in November 1995. MDA, a Canadian subsidiary of U.S.-based Orbital Science Corporation, beat out Spar for the contract to build Radarstat-2, targeted for launch in 2001. Spar owned an 11 percent interest in MDA and planned to buy the remainder for about C$50 million; however, these negotiations broke off abruptly in July 1992.

Branching Out in the 1990s

Although dependent upon the ups and downs of government procurement, at least Spar was not devoted exclusively to military programs at the end of the Cold War. Half of its revenues came from space communications hardware. Space-related work accounted for 82 percent of the company's revenues; aviation and defense, 13 percent.

Spar wanted to diversify even more. In late 1992, it bought ComStream Corp., a US$30 million San Diego digital communications company, for US$58 million. ComStream was known for its data compression technology and lucrative modem manufacturing business. It had also teamed with the giant Canadian telephone company Satellite Telecommunications Laboratory in a research venture.

In 1992 NASA gave Spar a C$67 million contract for follow-up support for the Canadarm. Follow-up work had brought in C$200 million already. An October launch of the space shuttle *Columbia*, manned by Canadian astronaut Steve MacLean, also displayed the new Space Vision System, a joint project of Spar and the National Research Council. It was the Canadarm that was used to perform repairs on the Hubble space telescope in 1993.

As impressive as the Canadarm was, the next generation of robot arms in development eclipsed it handily. The vision, sensory, and "expert" systems of the new "smart arms" allowed them to perform many complex and delicate tasks virtually unaided by manual input. The Space Station Remote Manipulator System's Special Purpose Dexterous Manipulator was designed to replace space-walking astronauts for many tasks. They were controlled by two Robotic Workstations inside the Space Station. Spar made the systems on the new arms modular so that components could be replaced as technology advanced over their expected 30-year service life.

Another advanced research project involved American Mobile Satellite Corp., Hughes Aircraft Corp., Spar Aerospace, and Telecast Mobile, another Canadian firm, which worked to produce two MSats, or mobile satellites. The system used satellites instead of towers to relay signals. Spar supplied the antennae and transponder. In addition, its Sun Microsystem computer network linked the four firms throughout design, testing, and manufacturing. The MSat program began in the mid-1980s and cost US$500 million. The first, MSat-1, was launched on April 20, 1996. It opened most of Canada's wide-ranging, underdeveloped geography to the possibility of mobile communications.

Spar worked on bringing its robot arm expertise to land-based applications. The company also produced flight data recorders and communications equipment for military clients, for whom it continued to provide maintenance. Not surprisingly, it sought to attract more civilian clients to this division. Communications and space programs accounted for slightly more than 40 percent each of Spar's revenues in 1995, while the Aviation and Defense unit added another 13 percent. ComStream posted a profit of C$10.5 million on revenues of C$250.7 million in 1995.

In 1996 Spar won a C$30 million contract to supply the International Space Station with two robotic workstations for the Mobile Servicing System (MSS). The Canadian Commercial Corp., a government agency, made the award. A launch date of January 1998 was anticipated for the first pieces of the space station, with the MSS to follow in 1999. SED Systems, MDA, IMP, CAE Electronics, and CAL Corp., all Canadian firms, were on board as subcontractors. Japanese and Italian firms also tapped Spar for its robotic expertise in preparing their countries' respective ISS components.

Scaling Back in the Late 1990s

Spar had a horrendous first quarter in 1996. Its share price fell 25 percent and its dividend was eliminated. The results were attributed to poor performance of the new ComStream subsidiary, and critics opined that Spar, so accustomed to government work, was not cut out for the highly competitive communications field. They complained that the management team led by John MacNaughton was too hesitant in making critical decisions. For example, ComStream went for months without a CEO in 1995 and 1996.

Colin D. Watson became president and CEO of Spar in 1996. Watson had previously led the cable television operations of Rogers Communications Inc. He arrived just in time to announce the surprise loss in the first quarter that caused Spar's share price to fall another 50 percent. When Watson took over at Spar, many of ComStream's technical staff were demoralized that the company had not followed through with a promised initial public offering for the unit. It had lost its primary customer, Thomson Consumer Electronics, a maker of satellite

Key Dates:

1967: Management buys out De Havilland's Special Products and Applied Research Division.
1969: Nixon cuts military aerospace programs.
1981: Spar delivers the first Canadarm robotic control arm to NASA.
1992: Spar tries hand at telecommunications with purchase of ComStream Corp.
1995: Spar-built Radarsat-1 is launched by NASA.
1996: Losses mount as ComStream flounders.
1998: Spar divests ComStream.
1999: New board pays out millions in dividends and sells off all areas of business except Aviation Services.

television components, when Thomson began making its own chips. After attempts to sell or revive the company through new CEOs and workforce reductions, Spar arranged to sell the unit to Radyne Corp. for US$17 million in cash and promissory notes in August 1998.

Government support for the ''Canada Hand''—$170 million worth—gave Spar some much-needed good news in the spring of 1997. It also won contracts to maintain Sea King helicopters for the armed forces of the United States, Brazil, Malaysia, and others. However, in July, 14 insurance companies sued Spar for US$135 million, alleging that the company's satellite communications system caused a Lockheed Martin satellite launched in 1995 to fail. Spar felt the ground operator deserved some of the blame. Spar settled this case in July 1999 for US$15 million.

After losing C$34 million in 1997, Spar posted a C$31 million profit on sales of C$251 million in 1998. One of 1998's highlights came when the Canadarm completed its 50th mission in space aboard the space shuttle *Columbia.* The program by that time represented C$500 million in exports. The arm's maintenance and support requirements brought in C$20 million a year.

Such milestones were bittersweet. Watson had sought to make Spar a C$1 billion company by 2000, but the problem of profits prevented that. The Asian financial crisis extinguished enthusiasm in one of Spar's hottest markets. In the face of competition from much larger manufacturers, Spar refocused its production from complete satellites to components such as antennae. It sold off its applied systems business. In the spring of 1999, it also agreed to sell its robotics division, which would leave it with aviation services.

An investment group led by New York-based Crescendo Partners LP, IMP Group Ltd. of Nova Scotia, and Toronto's C.A. Delaney Capital Management Ltd. gained control of the Spar board through its 58 percent share ownership. It soon had most of the company's C$150 million cash paid out in dividends, forsaking any acquisition plans. Watson became vice-chairman to board chairman Eric Rosenfeld.

Many of Spar's high-profile businesses were sold after the ownership shift. MacDonald, Dettwiler and Associates, Ltd. (MDA) bought Spar's robotics business for C$63 million. Spar sold Astro Aerospace Corporation to TRW Inc. for C$30.6 million in December 1998. Aviation Services accounted for C$14.4 million of profits and C$123.1 million of sales in 1998. Space Robotics had profits of C$16.9 million on sales of C$128 million. The Satellite Products Unit was then sold to Electromagnetic Sciences Inc. for C$29.5 million.

In December 1999, Spar announced that it had not been able to sell its aviation services division at an acceptable price. The company retained the unit and planned to pay out more cash to shareholders. The board also continued to entertain offers to buy the remainder of the company.

Principal Competitors

NAPCO International, Inc.; Raytheon Aircraft; Rockwell Collins, Inc.; Honeywell Defense Avionics Systems.

Further Reading

Beckert, Beverly A., ''Satellite Design Soars to New Heights,'' *Computer-Aided Engineering,* October 1993, p. 24.
Berman, David, ''When Bad Companies Happen to Good People,'' *Canadian Business,* March 27, 1998, pp. 78–81.
Calamai, Peter, ''Canada Mulls Shifting Space Contract to Europeans: U.S. Ban on Flow of Information, Technology Blamed,'' *Toronto Star,* May 29, 1999.
Covault, Craig, ''Ariane Launches Canadian MSat-1,'' *Aviation Week and Space Technology,* April 29, 1996, p. 29.
De Santis, Solange, ''In Reaching to Diversify, Spar Aerospace Loses Its Grip—New Chief at Maker of Canadarm Has Hands Full with Leftover Problems,'' *Wall Street Journal,* June 26, 1996, p. B4.
Hubbard, Craig, ''Shuttle's Canadarm Earns Its 50-Mission Cap,'' *Computing Canada,* August 10, 1998, p. 4.
Knapp, Bill, ''Masters of the Universe,'' *Canadian Business,* November 1992, pp. 119–24.
Litvak, Isaiah A., ''Instant International: Strategic Reality for Small High-Technology Firms in Canada,'' *Multinational Business,* Summer 1990, pp. 1–12.
Morgan, Walter L., ''The Olympus Family,'' *Satellite Communications,* June 1985, p. 35ff.
Savona, Dave, and Stephen W. Quickel, ''Steel's New Gleam; Sparring Partner,'' *International Business,* March 1993, p. 126.
Southerst, John, ''An Arm with a Mind of Its Own,'' *Canadian Business,* March 1992, pp. 60–64.
''Spar Aerospace Launches New Data Collection System,'' *Plant Engineering & Maintenance,* March/April 1993, pp. 15–18.
''The Year of Living Differently,'' *Canadian Business,* June 1997, p. 16.

—Frederick C. Ingram

Speedway Motorsports, Inc.

Post Office Box 600
U.S. Highway 29 North
Concord, North Carolina 28026
U.S.A.
Telephone: (704) 455-3239
Fax: (704) 455-2547
Web site: http://www.speedwaymotorsports.com

Public Company
Incorporated: 1994
Employees: 970
Sales: $229.8 million (1998)
Stock Exchanges: New York
Ticker Symbol: TRK
NAIC: 711212 Racetracks; 339932 Game, Toy, and Children's Vehicle Manufacturing

Speedway Motorsports, Inc. is a leading promoter, marketer, and sponsor of motorsports entertainment in the United States, operating six racetracks that host dozens of National Association for Stock Car Auto Racing-sanctioned events. Speedway Motorsports also sanctions its own racing series called the Legends Car Racing Circuit, which features ⅝-scale vehicles that the company manufactures and sells to amateur racing enthusiasts. The company is the product of O. Bruton Smith's aggressive attempt to develop the largest racetrack operation in the country. Starting with Charlotte Motor Speedway, Smith added Atlanta Motor Speedway in 1990, Bristol Motor Speedway and Sears Point Raceway in 1996, Texas Motor Speedway in 1997, and Las Vegas Motor Speedway in 1999. Smith owns 67 percent of Speedway Motorsports, presiding as chairman and chief executive officer of the company.

Late 1950s Origins

Although Speedway Motorsports did not exist until 1994, the legacy of the organization stretches back 35 years earlier, back to the early career of the company's founder, O. Bruton Smith. Smith made an attempt at establishing himself as a professional driver, but failed, settling instead on being near the sport that would prove to be his lifelong passion. Smith began promoting races at small dirt tracks in his native North Carolina during the 1950s, work that kept him employed in the racing world while he hatched plans for his dream project. Smith wanted to build a premier racetrack, a facility that would stand as a monument of the automobile racing world. In 1959, he formed Charlotte Motor Speedway (CMS) to build a $600,000 facility. Smith was able to raise $450,000 through financing arrangements, and broke ground on the ambitious project—the first example of the lofty vision that would later characterize his business approach to the sport of stock car racing. As construction was underway, however, Smith found it difficult to raise the remaining $150,000 he needed to complete CMS. His attempt to create a regional epicenter of stock car racing failed. By 1961, CMS was exhausted of funds and had entered reorganization proceedings dictated by the U.S. bankruptcy code. Smith left town, relocating in Illinois where he embarked on another career as a car dealer. However, Smith would later achieve his success in the racing industry by demonstrating the same ambitiousness that had forced his retreat in 1961.

While in Illinois, Smith proved he was a shrewd businessman, perhaps overly shrewd considering that in the 1960s a federal judge ruled Smith had defrauded some business partners, as reported in the March 30, 1997 issue of the *St. Louis Post-Dispatch.* His car dealership, Town & Country Ford, Inc., developed into a lucrative business, eventually ranking as the sixth largest car dealership chain in the United States. Smith would need the steady and heavy stream of cash provided by his car dealership because by the early 1970s he was attracted again to the prospect of CMS. The court-appointed directors of the speedway were at an impasse. The directors began to squabble, and Smith stepped in, using the substantial cash he was accumulating with Town & Country Ford to buy back shares in CMS. By 1975, he owned nearly all of the racetrack he had left nearly 15 years earlier, exerting his newfound influence from his office as CMS's new chief executive officer. The same year Smith gained executive control over the racetrack, H.A. ''Humpy'' Wheeler joined CMS. A year later, in 1976, Wheeler was named general manager of CMS; together, Smith and Wheeler

Company Perspectives:

The operating subsidiaries of Speedway Motorsports have a 38-year history in which we have dedicated our talents to growing the entire motorsports entertainment industry.

would develop the North Carolina speedway company into stock car racing's largest racetrack operator.

Smith's reemergence into the arena of stock car racing occurred at a pivotal point in the sport's history. Since its inception, stock car racing had been a local and regional pursuit populated by drivers who generally owned their own teams and by tracks that were individually owned. It was a product of the Southeast that stayed tied to its roots, attracting little national following. The dynamics of the sport would radically change, however, transforming stock car racing into a multibillion-dollar business. In the new lucrative era of stock car racing, track owners operated multiple speedways, facilities that were located in markets large and small, from coast to coast. The growth of the sport from its rural Southeastern beginnings to its modern dimensions as a national phenomenon was aided by the formation of the sport's sanctioning body, the National Association for Stock Car Auto Racing (NASCAR) in 1947, and by several developments that coincided with Smith's return to CMS. During the mid-1970s, tobacco giant R.J. Reynolds began funneling vast sums of sponsorship money into the sport for the first time in its history, providing a financial foundation for stock car racing's future growth. In 1979, network television broadcasters began airing NASCAR races live, providing many throughout the country with their first glimpse of the sport.

Stock car racing was beginning to grow beyond its historical proportions, but of equal importance to the growth of the sport was the presence of Smith in the industry. As he had with CMS, Smith demonstrated no wariness in staking everything he had on grandiose projects, believing that massive, luxuriant facilities were central to stock car racing's, and his own, success. Smith's reputation as a risk taker was cemented during the 1990s, stock car racing's decade of prolific growth. Not coincidentally, the popularity of NASCAR-controlled events and the growth of stock car racing itself mirrored the rapid development of CMS into a multi-speedway track operator named Speedway Motorsports.

Acquisitions and Growth in the 1990s

Smith first began developing a portfolio of speedway properties in 1990. Smith positioned himself on the vanguard of the industry's growth with the acquisition of Atlanta Motor Speedway (AMS), his second racetrack and his first step toward accumulating speedways and other related properties. As he had done with CMS during the 1980s, Smith constructed additional grandstand seating at AMS, adding luxury suites, improving concession facilities, and, in an example of his far-reaching vision of stock car racing's potential, developing condominiums that overlooked the speedways. At the heart of Smith's strategy was controlling a number of speedways near large, metropolitan markets, each capable of seating legions of spectators and each offering a breadth of conveniences and luxury services. By controlling massive, state-of-the-art racing complexes, Smith hoped his speedways would be awarded popular NASCAR-sanctioned events, none more coveted than the NASCAR Winston Cup series. As the popularity of stock car racing grew during the 1990s, so too did the revenue-generating potential of hosting a Winston Cup race, which, if included on a speedway's annual schedule of events, nearly guaranteed profitability for the racetrack. Smith, as he made his first advance on the acquisition front, endeavored to create racing facilities that, in consideration of their size and proximity to large markets, could not be denied the opportunity to host Winston Cup events. Toward this end, Smith aggressively pursued the expansion of his stock car racing holdings, convinced that massive investment in the sport would be substantiated by its widespread appeal.

In 1992, Smith's maverick ways and his faith in stock car racing's potential were evinced by two decisions he made. The year marked the debut of nighttime racing at CMS, the first speedway in the country to offer nighttime races. Also in 1992, the company developed the Legends Car Racing Circuit, giving aficionados of stock car racing the chance to compete in ⅝-scale versions of the cars driven by early NASCAR drivers. Smith's company manufactured and sold the cars, developing a racing schedule that was sanctioned through a subsidiary named 600 Racing. While the foray into amateur racing proved a prudent move, creating a meaningful tributary of revenue ($5.7 million by 1994, and $10.9 million by 1998), Smith's primary focus was on adding more speedways to his name, an objective that gained momentum by the mid-1990s.

In December 1994, Smith formed Speedway Motorsports. If outside observers and competitors did not perceive the formation of Speedway as the beginning of Smith's aggressive assault on stock car racing, then his next, unprecedented move, must have made the signal clear. In February 1995, Speedway Motorsports became the first company in its industry to offer shares of stock to the public in a $68 million initial public offering (IPO). Wheeler, named president and chief operating officer of Speedway Motorsports upon its formation, explained the decision to take the company public in a March 30, 1997 interview with the *St Louis Post-Dispatch:* "What we saw was that NASCAR was heading into a strong power curve. We felt there would be a 10–12-year period of strong growth and we needed the capital to take advantage of it." Speedway Motorsports stock debuted at $18 per share, unleashing the acquisitive ambitions of Smith and marking the beginning of a frenetic period of growth for the company.

Speedway Motorsports' IPO touched off a trend in the industry, as Smith's fellow competitors followed his lead into the public spotlight. Within a year, Dover Downs Entertainment, Grand Prix Association of Long Beach, and Penske Motorsports had all gone public. One other company began life as a publicly traded concern in 1996: Daytona Beach, Florida's International Speedway Corporation, Smith's closest rival. The rivalry between Speedway Motorsports and International Speedway was an intriguing one, a battle that was competitive yet one that necessitated a display of diplomacy by each company. The same family that founded and controlled International Speedway also founded and controlled NASCAR, the organization that bestowed the all-important Winston Cup

Key Dates:

1959: O. Bruton Smith begins development of Charlotte Motor Speedway.
1961: Charlotte Motor Speedway declares bankruptcy.
1975: Smith regains control of Charlotte Motor Speedway and is named chief executive officer.
1990: Atlanta Motor Speedway is acquired.
1992: Smith develops the Legends Car Racing Circuit.
1994: Speedway Motorsports is formed and incorporated in December.
1996: Bristol Motor Speedway and Sears Point Raceway are acquired.
1997: Texas Motor Speedway opens and hosts largest sporting event in Texas history.
1999: Las Vegas Motor Speedway is acquired; naming rights to Charlotte Motor Speedway are sold to Lowe's Companies Inc.

events to racetrack operators and upon whose beneficence Smith's fortunes rested. The France family was careful to avoid any inference of favoritism between NASCAR and International Speedway. (Bill France served as International Speedway's chief executive officer and as NASCAR's president.) However, the relationship between the two companies had an undeniable effect on the personality of International Speedway, creating a company whose strategy stood in sharp contrast to the strategy pursued by Speedway Motorsports. Speedway Motorsports was a risk-taking company, assuming an aggressive and ambitious posture that it inherited from Smith. International Speedway, on the other hand, inherited the legacy of NASCAR, making the company far more cautious and conservative in its expansion strategy. Accordingly, Speedway Motorsports was apt to build a 150,000-seat facility in a large market, banking on drawing a capacity crowd, while International Speedway erected smaller facilities in smaller markets, preferring to nurture stock car racing's development before erecting a massive stadium. Wheeler, in a June 28, 1999 interview with *Knight-Ridder/Tribune Business News,* explained the differences between the two companies succinctly, remarking, "Our first priority is to build a company, and theirs is to build a sport."

1995 IPO, Further Expansion

The differences between Speedway Motorsports and its closest rival were readily discernible after Smith took the company public in 1995. With the proceeds from the IPO, Smith was able to actualize his vision and hotly pursue the $2-billion business that stock car racing represented by the mid-1990s. In 1996, Speedway Motorsports acquired two racing facilities, Bristol Motor Speedway, located in Bristol, Tennessee, in January, and Sears Point Raceway, located near San Francisco, in November. The following year, the company furthered its reputation as the industry's most ambitious racetrack operator by completing the construction of Texas Motor Speedway, a $250 million facility that seated 150,000 spectators, twice the capacity of the new racetracks International Speedway was building at the time. Some observers were shocked by Smith's audacity in building a massive complex in uncharted territory for stock car racing, but the popularity of the sport and the increasing revenue it was generating bore out the construction of the Fort Worth, Texas, stadium. By the late 1990s, stock car racing was the fastest-growing sport, as well as the largest spectator sport, in the country. The Winston Cup Series races drew more than 6.1 million spectators in 1997, excluding the 123 million viewers who watched the races on television. Each Winston Cup race generated between $60 million and $80 million in revenue, attracting crowds ranging between 100,000 and 150,000. Sales of NASCAR-licensed products hurtled toward $900 million, drastically more than the $80 million collected from merchandise sales in 1990. During this meteoric upward swing, Speedway Motorsports had increased its total seating capacity from 176,000 in 1993 to 551,000 by 1998, fueling a more than threefold increase in ticket revenues. Smith, whose racetracks hosted nine of the 35 Winston Cup Series events in 1997, had positioned Speedway Motorsports to take advantage of the sport's enormous growth, astutely remaining one step ahead of the popularity that surprised some of stock car racing's onlookers. Speedway Motorsports stood atop its industry as the largest racetrack owner in the United States, eclipsing the stature of International Speedway and the industry's third-ranking contender, Penske Motorsports.

In 1999, Smith pressed ahead with expansion and reached another precedent-setting agreement that galvanized his reputation as an industry pioneer. With attendance figures up 91 percent from the total recorded in 1990, Smith inaugurated 1999 by acquiring Las Vegas Motor Speedway in January. Smith paid $215 million for the facility, eclipsing the $200-million bid offered by International Speedway, which had been confident that the Nevada racetrack would be theirs. In March 1999, International Speedway looked on in surprise again when Smith's company announced a first in stock car racing's history. He sold the naming rights to his flagship CMS facility to home improvement retailer Lowe's Companies Inc. For the right to rename CMS "Lowe's Motor Speedway" and to secure exclusive home improvement category marketing rights at Speedway Motorsports six speedways, the retailer paid Smith's company $35 million for a ten-year agreement. The naming rights agreement sent a shockwave throughout the industry, but just as Smith appeared to be loping toward the 21st century with all competitors safely in the distance, the historically conservative International Speedway made its most aggressive move ever. The announcement by the France family-controlled company set the stage for stock car racing's biggest battle in the decade ahead.

In May 1999, International Speedway revealed it was acquiring the industry's third largest racetrack owner, Penske Motorsports. The $623 million deal delivered a decided blow to Smith's Speedway Motorsports, unseating his company from the number one position in the industry. Perhaps more profound were the implications of the transaction, which greatly enlarged International Speedway's geographic coverage into markets both large and small. As Smith endeavored to secure two Winston Cup Series events at each of his speedways, industry pundits, following the merger of International Speedway and Penske Motorsports, were projecting that the sport's future was not in a cluster of events held at a small number of facilities but in thinning out the schedule of NASCAR-sanctioned events to cover a greater geographic area. Taking this perspective into consideration, International Speedway stood better poised to receive the riches bred by NASCAR-sanctioned events, but few doubted Smith's resolve in offering his riposte to International Speedway's usurpation in the decade ahead.

Principal Subsidiaries

Atlanta Motor Speedway, Inc.; Bristol Motor Speedway, Inc.; Charlotte Motor Speedway, Inc.; Las Vegas Motor Speedway LLC; SPR Acquisition Corporation d/b/a Sears Point Raceway; Texas Motor Speedway, Inc.; Speedway Systems LLC d/b/a Finish Line Events; 600 Racing, Inc.; INEX Corporation; The Speedway Club, Inc.; Oil-Chem Research Corporation; Speedway Funding Corporation; Sonoma Funding Corporation.

Principal Competitors

International Speedway Corporation; Reynard Motorsport, Inc.; Dover Downs Entertainment, Inc.

Further Reading

Alm, Richard, "Texas Motor Speedway Owner Sells Naming Rights to North Carolina Track," *Knight-Ridder/Tribune Business News,* February 10, 1999.

"Lowe's Secures Naming Rights to Charlotte Speedway," *Do-It-Yourself Retailing,* March 1999, p. 23.

Macur, Juliet, "Charlotte, N.C.-Based Speedway Company Races to No. 1 in Industry," *Knight-Ridder/Tribune Business News,* June 28, 1999.

Neelakantan, Shailaja, "Racing for Dollars," *Forbes,* December 16, 1996, p. 14.

"New NASCAR Has Fewer Track Owners," *St. Louis Post-Dispatch,* March 30, 1997, p. 13F.

"Numbers Reflect NASCAR's Growth," *Knight-Ridder/Tribune Business News,* April 6, 1998.

"Speedway Motorsports Inc.," *Discount Store News,* March 8, 1999, p. 29.

"Speedway Motorsports Signs Sponsorship Deal," *Amusement Business,* March 8, 1999, p. 4.

Spiegal, Peter, "Life in the Fast Lane," *Forbes,* November 1, 1999, p. 86.

Taylor, Lisa, "Motor Speedway May Move Up Plans for Industrial Park," *Dallas Business Journal,* March 19, 1999, p. 5.

Veverka, Amber, "Concord, N.C.-Based Speedway Firm Sees Deals for Texas, Atlanta Tracks," *Knight-Ridder/Tribune Business News,* February 9, 1999.

—Jeffrey L. Covell

Subway

325 Bic Drive
Milford, Connecticut 06460
U.S.A.
Telephone: (203) 877-4281
Fax: (203) 876-6695
Web site: http://www.subway.com

Wholly Owned Subsidiary of Doctor's Associates Inc.
Incorporated: 1965 as Pete's Super Submarines
Employees: 730
Sales: $3.5 billion (1999 est.)
NAIC: 722211 Restaurants, Fast Food

The 1999 ad campaign for Doctor's Associates Inc., the franchiser of the Subway chain, proclaims, ''Subway, the way a sandwich should be.'' Apparently, millions around the world concur. With more than 14,085 Subway outlets in 73 countries (nearly 12,000 in the United States alone) and in such exotic locations as the Bahamas, Bolivia, Cyprus, Iceland, Paraguay, Russia, and Venezuela, Fred Deluca and Peter Buck's collaboration has become the largest and most successful submarine sandwich franchise in the world. As the second largest international restaurant chain behind McDonald's, Subway touts its menu as a healthy alternative to fast food and has captured a significant share of the market with fresh low-fat sandwiches and several other signature made-to-order subs.

Evolution of a Sub Sandwich: 1960s–70s

Fred DeLuca was born in Brooklyn in the late 1940s, a time when Harry S. Truman was president, Arthur Miller's *Death of a Salesman* had won a Pulitzer Prize for drama, and Rodgers and Hammerstein's *South Pacific* was a hit on Broadway. Although there were not many ways a kid his age could earn money in the 1950s, DeLuca did—returning two-cent bottles found around the neighborhood, in his case, the Bronx housing projects where his family was living. The family moved upstate to Schenectady, and young Fred delivered newspapers, gradually increasing his clientele until his route covered some 400 patrons on Sundays. Originally planning to study premed in college, DeLuca was faced with the daunting challenge of raising tuition money. It was 1965 and DeLuca was 17.

Concentrating on his immediate future, he worked in a hardware store, earning little cash ($1.25 per hour) but possessing plenty of ambition. He was looking for another job, something paying more than minimum wage. While attending a summer barbecue, DeLuca struck up a conversation with family friend Dr. Peter Buck. Buck was a nuclear physicist, and he talked about a popular sandwich shop near his hometown the community had come to embrace. Buck wondered aloud if DeLuca should open a shop serving submarine sandwiches, a food item gaining considerable popularity. Over the next four hours, the two drew up a business plan; with a $1,000 start-up loan from Buck, the two became partners.

DeLuca moved quickly, looking for a location the very next day. On August 25, 1965, Pete's Super Submarines opened in Bridgeport, Connecticut, serving fresh made-to-order sandwiches, with a choice of toppings and condiments, though oddly, without lettuce (it appeared on the menu later). The shop location was not ideal, but was only a short distance from the hardware store where DeLuca had worked. There was little fanfare and few customers, but Buck and DeLuca met regularly in the latter's family home, discussing strategy over homemade pasta. The new enterprise, however, did not stop DeLuca from beginning his freshman year at the University of Bridgeport in September (he later graduated in 1971 with a B.S. in psychology). Juggling his studies and the sandwich shop, weeks turned into months, and the business never soared as each had hoped. Yet rather than give up, they persevered, and instead of abandoning the partnership, decided on another gambit—to open a second location in 1966. Surely increased visibility and name recognition would steer some of the populace to Pete's Super Submarines. Then they decided to take their gamble a step further, and they opened a third location.

The third time was the charm; the old adage proved right on the money as the third store—in a highly accessible and visible location—began to take off. Not particularly superstitious, DeLuca and Buck did consider ''three'' their lucky number and later emphasized positive numerology in their corporate marketing campaigns. As the business progressed, the partners found the name cumbersome and thought it sounded like ''pizza marine.'' So Pete's Super Submarines was renamed Subway, taken from New York City's early underground railways built

Company Perspectives:

We are committed to customer satisfaction through offering high quality food with exceptional service and good value. We take great pride in serving each other, our customers and our communities. We seek continuous improvement in all that we do. We value a sense of urgency and emphasize an innovative, entrepreneurial approach to business. We expect fairness and mutual respect in all our activities. We know our success depends upon the initiative we take individually and our ability to work as a team.

after the turn of the century. The shop's name was emblazoned in yellow, and the inside decor consisted of faux newspaper articles heralding the new mode of transportation.

In 1974, as the partners approached the tenth year of their alliance, they were supposed to have had 32 submarine shops according to their initial business plan. Instead, they had half this number and decided to explore another option: franchising. DeLuca believed that franchising was the wave of the future, and soon he had convinced a friend to become the first franchisee. The new store opened in upstate Wallingford. The move, though a sound business decision, was a profound risk. The world was experiencing inflation, the dollar had been devalued twice in two years, an energy crisis had forced Americans to cut back on power and fuel usage, and unemployment was on the rise. Yet DeLuca and Buck seemed to have the golden touch; the franchised Subway did well, as did its successors (another 14 or so within the year). Although franchising was an excellent way to expand a business, DeLuca and Buck tinkered with the system for years before finding a formula with which they were completely happy. Yet both had discovered an incontrovertible truth: new business owners needed to invent a product, and then entice an ever growing number of customers. Doing both was demanding, but with franchising, the idea and product were already established so the new business owner simply had to bring in a clientele and keep them happy.

From Nowhere to Everywhere: 1980–94

By 1983 there were 200 Subway shops and DeLuca and Buck discovered one of the largest hurdles was keeping their brand consistent in all locations. This was when the partners decided to have each location bake bread on the premises. As the first fast-food chain to bake bread at each location, Subway's sales steadily increased. The bread became a signature product, with its ingredients and oven time trade secrets. Just two years later, in 1985, after 20 years of partnership, DeLuca and Buck had 596 Subway stores in the United States and abroad; by 1987, the number had more than tripled to 1,810 shops.

Subway's phenomenal growth continued unabated throughout the remainder of the 1980s and into the 1990s. In 1989, there were 4,071 stores; by 1992 there were 7,327. As more and more Subway franchises popped up across the nation as well as outside the United States, the partners had created the ''University of Subway,'' an intensive two-week course at headquarters. Prospective franchisees learned the ins and outs of the Subway business, from the standard decor to bookkeeping, from baking the signature bread to the varied ingredients that made up the chain's popular sandwiches. Another key to Subway's ongoing expansion was innovation and taking convenience a step further than its competitors. Subway stores began appearing in unusual locations, catering to consumers where they might not expect a sandwich shop—at convenience stores and truck stops. These ''nontraditional'' locations were a hit with traveling consumers and by 1993 some 50 such shops dotted the nation, with more on the way. Although these uniquely placed shops were a tiny fraction of Subway's 8,450 locations worldwide, the nontraditional shops thrived and would come to make up a fifth of the company's global sales in coming years.

In 1994 Subway was nearing the 10,000 mark and DeLuca was determined to take on the world's largest fast-food chain, McDonald's Corporation. Although Subway was aggressively targeting the leader, the burger giant, founded in 1948, had nearly 20 years on the upstart Subway. No slough to ingenuity, McDonald's had stores in such nontraditional locations as Wal-Mart stores and Chevron and Amoco gas stations. A key to the success of both chains was consistency: customers counted on McDonald's decor and menu to be virtually the same from town to town; the same was true of Subway. Each chain, of course, made menu concessions in some countries—for Subway it was no pork products in areas with large Muslim populations; lots of salmon at the Norway shop; chicken salad with curry in British Subways; chicken satay with peanut sauce in Australian locations.

A Global Leader: 1995–98

By 1995 Subway had sales of nearly $2.6 billion and 11,420 locations. DeLuca and Buck became increasingly active in charity, giving to a variety of groups including the Girl Scouts of America, Habitat for Humanity, Junior Achievement, the Muscular Dystrophy Association, the Yale-New Haven Children's Hospital, and many others. The company also held several business associations (Better Business Bureau of Western Connecticut, the Connecticut Restaurant Association, the International Franchise Association, the Milford Chamber of Commerce) and even turned to environmental issues. In this vein, Subway introduced the Chocolate Brazil Nut cookie this year, chock full of Brazilian nuts harvested from the Peruvian rainforests, which in turn employed some 250 people and helped keep the rainforest alive.

In Subway's history, 1996 turned out to be a stellar year—the company's revenues increased nearly 25 percent to $3.2 billion, an incredible financial spurt by any standard. Part of the leap had come from further expansion to 12,516 locations, much of it in nontraditional locations. This was backed up by the numbers in 1997, when nontraditional shops reached 2,700, or about 20 percent of the chain's locations. The company had explored a myriad of unusual possibilities, including railway and bus stations, airports, casinos, amusement parks, arenas, hospitals, museums, and department stores. Subway shops in high schools, colleges, and universities were especially successful for both the company and the schools, as students stopped leaving campuses for lunch, bringing profits and jobs back into these establishments. Yet another major coup had been the exclusive agreement with NEXCOM (Naval Exchange Commission) to put Subway stores on naval bases worldwide.

Key Dates:

1965: Partners Fred DeLuca and Dr. Peter Buck open Pete's Super Submarines.
1974: First Subway franchise opens in Wallingford, Connecticut.
1984: First international Subway opens in Bahrain, Saudi Arabia.
1995: Company celebrates 30th anniversary by opening 11,000th Subway.
1999: Subway's 14,000th store opens.

Further civic involvement came in the form of Micro Investment Lending Enterprise (MILE), founded by DeLuca in 1997 to provide small business loans to budding entrepreneurs. The MILE organization opened several chapters in Connecticut, hoped to spread throughout the United States, and created a web site called www.mile.org. In late 1997 and early 1998, numerology was back in Subway lore. Stories circulated about the chain's luck with the number 13, and the many fortunate combinations of seven and six. Not only had Subway gone over the 13,000 mark in 1997, but *Total Food Service* magazine of Greenwich, Connecticut, composed a list of factoids touting Subway's good luck. Beginning with DeLuca's birth on the third of October, there were a myriad of interesting and goofy figures revolving around six, seven, and 13: the menu's seven six-inch subs with six grams of fat or less; three international locations opened on the 13th of the month (Guam, September 13, 1989; South Korea, July 13, 1991; Morocco, December 13, 1997); 13 optional toppings for any sandwich; and consumers ate more than 13 million pounds of steak and almost 13 million pounds of roast beef for the year.

By the fall of 1998, Subway had more than 13,229 shops worldwide and initiated a family-oriented advertising campaign to bring parents and kids into the stores. The company teamed up with Nickelodeon and its popular children's show ''Blue's Clues'' for a Kids' Pak toy tied to the animated television show. Coining the term ''Mutual Agreement,'' an agreement between parent and child to eat better meals, Subway hoped to capitalize on parents' quests for healthier alternatives to deep fried chicken parts and french fries or greasy hamburgers. Just as Subway had touted low-fat sandwiches for health-conscious adults, the Mutual Agreement was designed to capture the ten-and-under age group. Although sales for 1998 did not climb significantly ($3.4 billion, up from $3.3 billion the year before), Subway was still in solid financial shape.

1999 and Beyond

Still targeting McDonald's in 1999, which had more than 25,000 locations worldwide and 40 percent of the U.S. fast-food market, Subway had managed to overtake Burger King as the second largest international restaurant chain, the latter having just less than 11,000 stores (although it remained the number two burger chain). To maintain its second-tier berth and expand further, Subway introduced its own brand of bottled water, a 16.9-fluid ounce container with the slogan ''Refreshing a Thirsty World'' on the label, and stepped up national advertising. Its advertising campaigns had proved quite effective in the past, and the company itself had become a cultural icon. Subway shops were featured in major motion pictures (*Lethal Weapon, Ace Ventura—When Nature Calls, Ransom, Kissing a Fool,* and others) and popular television shows (the WB's huge hit ''Felicity,'' among others), as well as on the Internet with its own frequently visited web site featuring an interactive game, contests, employment applications, franchise information, an entertainment guide (reviews of music, TV, movies, video games), restaurant locator, menu and nutrition information, and special promotions on Subway products.

As the new century approached, Subway's development plans were impressive: to have opened 950 shops annually until 2005, including new locations in India, Germany, and Scotland; and, eventually, to have Subway shops in every country in the world. Subway was still chasing McDonald's as the industry's fast-food leader, but in the submarine sandwich marketplace both Blimpie (ranked second to Subway) and Quizno's (ranked third) were gaining ground. Although the New York-based Blimpie International had 2,000 shops by the end of 1999 and the Denver-based Quizno's Corporation had only 600 in the United States, Canada, and Japan, each chain had ambitious plans mirroring those of Subway—to expand and conquer in 2000 and beyond. In addition, there was the entry into the market of another specialty sandwich chain, Schlotzky's Inc., an Austin-based company. Schlotzsky's was nearing 800 deli stores in 1999 and, though it did not consider its ''sub'' sandwiches the success of the company, which experienced 40 percent growth from 1998 to 1999, was certainly eating into Subway's bottom line.

Yet perhaps the biggest question plaguing DeLuca and Buck was speculation about whether the privately owned company would ever go public. The response was generally the same—not an unequivocal denial, but a carefully evasive statement. ''We think that going public could take the focus off developing the business for our franchisees,'' was what DeLuca told a reporter for the Winston-Salem (N.C.) *Journal* in 1997. But this was nothing business analysts and consultants had not heard before; anything was possible.

Principal Competitors

McDonald's Corporation; Tricon Global Restaurants, Inc.; Blimpie International Inc.; Schlotzsky's Inc.; The Quizno's Corporation.

Further Reading

''*Entrepreneur* Magazine Names Subway Restaurants in Franchise 500, DeLuca Cites Company Goals,'' *PR Newswire,* December 16, 1999.
''Franchise Success Secrets,'' *Successful Franchising,* June 1998.
Kuhn, Susan, ''#13 Lucky for Subway Restaurants and Its Customer 7/6 Campaign Proves to Be a Winner,'' *Total Food Service,* February 1998.
Marshall, Charlee, ''Six Grams of Fat Still Adds Up to a Good Tasting Sub,'' *Index-Journal* (Greenwood, S.C.), January 28, 1999.
McQuilkin, Steve, ''Subway Founder Shares Recipe for Success,'' *Journal* (Winston-Salem, N.C.), November 12, 1997.
Morse, Dan, ''School Cafeterias Are Enrolling As Fast-Food Franchisees,'' *Wall Street Journal,* July 28, 1998.

—Nelson Rhodes

TearDrop Golf Company

1080 Lousons Road
Union, New Jersey 07083
U.S.A.
Telephone: (908) 688-4445
Toll Free: (800) 803-7767
Fax: (908) 688-5444
Web site: http://www.teardropgolf.com

Public Company
Incorporated: 1992 as TearDrop Putter Corporation
Employees: 246
Sales: $60.7 million (1998)
Stock Exchanges: NASDAQ
Ticker Symbol: TDRP
NAIC: 33992 Sporting & Athletic Goods Manufacturing

TearDrop Golf Company designs and manufactures a variety of golf clubs and equipment, including putters, irons, woods, and wedges. Included in TearDrop's family of brands are Armour, RAM, and Zebra. The company is also the sole North American distributor of Walter Genuin golf shoes, one of the largest European makers of golf shoes and apparel. TearDrop is the owner of the TearDrop Professional Golf Tour, a tour for aspiring professional golf players, and it sponsors a number of professional players, including Fred Couples and Steve Jones.

Puttering Along: 1993–95

TearDrop Putter Corporation was established in Hilton Head, South Carolina, in 1992 by Fred Hochman. The company originally manufactured only putters. The company's putters featured a rolled face, and this patented technology made TearDrop putters unique compared with rival putters, which generally had flat faces. The rolled-face putters were designed to prevent the bouncing and skidding that often resulted from flat-faced putters and to produce a smoother roll and increased accuracy.

Over the following three years, TearDrop introduced six more putters, all featuring the rolled-face technology. In early 1996 the company changed its name to TearDrop Golf Company to reflect its diversification strategy and introduced a line of wedges. The signature putter was well received by the golf community and was used by golfers on the Professional Golf Association (PGA) Tour, the Nike Tour, and the PGA Senior Tour by the mid-1990s. The putter was ranked in the top ten on the PGA Tour and the PGA Senior Tour in 1995 for the number of victories and top ten finishes achieved by golfers who used it.

The success of the putter led to increased sales for the manufacturer, with revenues growing from $780,000 in 1994 to a promising $1.06 million in 1995. For 1994 the net loss was $550,000; a year later losses reached $540,000. Not all was rosy at TearDrop, however, and by mid-1996 the company had accumulated about $1.5 million in debt, and TearDrop was treacherously close to shutting down.

Major Changes and Accelerated Growth in the Mid-1990s

As TearDrop teetered on the brink of failure, Rudy Slucker searched for something to occupy his free time. Slucker, a successful and wealthy businessman who had retired in 1990 at the age of 40, had not taken up golf until 1992. Although Slucker had little knowledge of the golf business, he invested in TearDrop in 1995 at the request of friend and fellow Hilton Head homeowner Fred Hochman. In 1996 Hochman informed Slucker that TearDrop might close because of financial problems. Slucker said in *Interview,* "It didn't take me long to tell Fred I would buy it. I thought I could make something out of it and besides, I needed something to do."

Slucker may not have known much about golf, but he knew about business. In 1974 Slucker began working at the Atlas Group, an importer and distributor of hardware items and hand tools. Slucker eventually purchased the company and built its sales from $1.2 million in 1974 to about $50 million by 1987. Slucker acquired and sold about 15 businesses over the course of 27 years and had been owner or part-owner of New York's Beacon Theatre, various hockey and minor league baseball teams, Suburban Dessert Shops of New Jersey, Ambassador Optical of Philadelphia, and Major League Fitness health clubs of New Jersey. In 1990 Slucker sold Atlas for an undisclosed sum and retired, devoting his energy to travel and charitable causes.

Company Perspectives:

TearDrop Golf will be recognized by our customer and the consumer as the leading provider of high quality golf equipment and accessories. We will strengthen our leadership position in high quality golf products through an increased commitment to innovation by providing all golfers with high performing products and providing our customers with the best possible service. TearDrop Golf will continue its commitment to the future of golf by providing aspiring players an opportunity to prepare for the sport's highest level of competition through the TearDrop Professional Golf Tour.

After acquiring TearDrop from Hochman in September 1996, Slucker immediately implemented an aggressive turnaround strategy. Slucker invested $1 million of his own money into the company but realized the need for additional capital. TearDrop's IPO was completed on December 20, 1996 and raised $5.5 million. The proceeds were then used to pare down debt, finance an extensive advertising and marketing campaign, and pay for professional player endorsements, all of which were considered crucial for saving the company. Despite such efforts, TearDrop still faced an uphill battle, as the golf equipment industry had experienced only small gains in the mid-1990s, with the large companies gobbling up the majority of market share.

TearDrop roared full-steam ahead into 1997, starting the year off with the launch of an advertising and marketing campaign that included television infomercials, as well as television spots and print ads. The company aimed to increase brand awareness and boost its reputation and image as a manufacturer of high-quality golf clubs, and advertising was considered a key tool for accomplishing such a goal. TearDrop's first infomercial featured legendary athlete Jim Palmer and Brett Ogle, a two-time winner of the PGA, demonstrating the advantages of the TearDrop putter. The company's infomercial, which aired on such channels as Fox Sports Network, the Learning Channel, Turner Broadcasting Station, Discovery, and the Golf Channel, was well received, encouraging the company to air it on additional networks and in Asian markets, including Japan, beginning in April.

In February TearDrop announced it would be the exclusive sponsor of ''TearDrop Putt of the Week'' on the Golf Channel. The weekly feature showcased the best putts of the week from all golf tours. ''We have previously stated that our objective is to become a leading supplier of high quality specialty clubs by utilizing an aggressive marketing strategy,'' Slucker explained in a prepared statement. ''This strategic feature on the Golf Channel, in conjunction with our infomercial, brings us one step closer to achieving that goal.'' In April TearDrop announced it would sponsor the ''MCI Heritage Classic Golf Report,'' a one-hour program featuring the highlights of the MCI Heritage Classic tournament. The show had a possible audience of approximately 50,000 households.

Along with its new advertising campaign, TearDrop began to sign on numerous professional golfers to act as company spokespersons. In February the company announced that it had secured a number of golfers, including Omar Uresti, Bobby Mitchell, Pat Bates, and P.J. Cowan as spokespersons. The golfers agreed to use the TearDrop putter on their tours, and many also wore golf apparel emblazoned with the TearDrop logo. A month later TearDrop signed Charles Coody, a player on the Senior PGA Tour, as well as Shane Bertsch, Jim Estes, John ''Jumbo'' Elliott, Esteban Toledo, and Karl Zoller. In early April the company signed three more players—Mike Swartz and Rick Stallings, both players on the Nike and PGA tours, and Todd Gleaton, who played on the Nike and Hooters Tournaments. Many of TearDrop's signed players performed well, thereby enhancing TearDrop's image and upping exposure. Omar Uresti secured a third place finish at the Bay Hill Invitational in Orlando, Florida, in March. A month later John ''Jumbo'' Elliott won the Nike Tour's Alabama Classic, and Pat Bates and P.J. Cowan finished in the top ten. Also in April Esteban Toledo secured a first place finish at the Benson & Hedges Open.

TearDrop's efforts paid off, and the company reported that sales for the first quarter ended March 31, 1997, reflected a 102 percent jump over the corresponding period in 1996. Still, net losses increased as well, from $235,000 during the first quarter of 1996 to about $699,000 for the first quarter of 1997. The company attributed the losses to increased expenses associated with its goal to increase brand awareness. TearDrop continued to make strides to meet this goal and posted several successes in the following months: in June TearDrop was chosen as the official putter for the Golden Bear Tour, a developmental tour for up-and-coming golf players, and the NGA/Hooters Tour. In addition, the company was featured on the television series ''The New Competitors,'' which aired on the CNBC Network in June, and TearDrop was voted best putter for 1997–98 by the Golf Industry Association (GIA).

Growth Through Acquisitions in the Late 1990s

After moving its headquarters from Hilton Head to central New Jersey in September 1997, TearDrop bought the assets of Pro Golf Promotions, LLC. The purchase included the Powerbilt Golf Tour, a developmental tour for aspiring professional golfers. The tour was renamed ''The TearDrop Professional Golf Tour.'' In November TearDrop stunned the golf industry by acquiring Tommy Armour Golf Co. from U.S. Industries Inc. for about $24.8 million. Morton Grove, Illinois-based Armour, a well-known and well-respected golf brand, manufactured full sets of woods and irons. Started in 1910 as the Burke Golf Company, Armour was one of the oldest golf equipment manufacturers in the United States. The company achieved significant recognition in the 1980s with the introduction of its 845s line of irons. Armour sold more than 600,000 sets of these irons and secured a spot as one of the prominent businesses in the golf industry. The 1990s presented greater challenges, however, and by the time TearDrop purchased Armour, it was in financial straits. Although Armour had sales of about $45 million a year in the mid-1990s, significantly more than TearDrop, which had 1996 sales of $800,000, Armour had not earned a profit in some years. In addition, Armour's sales had remained flat, while its main competitors had enjoyed increasing revenues. Armour had few noteworthy endorsement contracts, and attempts to launch new lines of golf clubs had failed. TearDrop hoped to capitalize on Armour's strong heritage, and the acquisition boosted TearDrop's offerings to cover a full line of golf clubs. Armour redesigned and relaunched its 845s series in the fall of 1997, and

Key Dates:

1992: TearDrop Putter Corporation is founded.
1995: Rudy Slucker invests in TearDrop.
1996: Company name changes to TearDrop Golf Company. Rudy Slucker assumes controlling interest and becomes president and CEO. TearDrop incorporates and goes public.
1997: TearDrop launches marketing and advertising campaign. Company acquires Tommy Armour Golf Company, RAM Golf Corporation, and Pro Golf Promotions, LLC.

TearDrop planned to take advantage of the line's popularity to accelerate company growth.

TearDrop surprised the golf industry once again in December when it announced the acquisition of RAM Golf Corporation, another well-known yet struggling golf company. The 50-year-old RAM manufactured premium irons, woods, wedges, and putters under such brand names as RAM and Zebra. TearDrop purchased the company for about $10 million in stock and cash. RAM, Tommy Armour, and TearDrop operations were consolidated into Armour's Morton Grove, Illinois facilities.

TearDrop entered 1998 as a much larger company and continued its aggressive effort to secure endorsement contracts. The Armour purchase helped TearDrop sign PGA Tour player Tommy Tolles to play 845s irons, and TearDrop also signed Larry Ziegler, a Senior PGA Tour player. In May 1998 Ziegler won the St. Luke's Classic, his first victory in six years. Ziegler attributed his win to his TearDrop putter, explaining in a company statement, "Much of my success in this event was due to my confidence with my putting. My new TearDrop Putter enabled me to control my speed better than I ever have. It's simply better than my old flat-face putter." TearDrop scored additional wins in 1998 when it signed Steve Jones, a former U.S. Open Champion, and Fred Couples, a celebrated professional golfer and top-ranked money-winner, to act as company and product spokespersons.

Over the first four months of 1998 TearDrop's stock increased 500 percent, as the company posted its first-ever profitable quarter on sales of $25 million. In the spring of 1998 TearDrop added to its roster of golf events by acquiring the California Golf Tour, a developmental tour for aspiring PGA players that included 27 events in California and Nevada. TearDrop also added the 1998 Crown Royal Open to the TearDrop Professional Golf Tour, which consisted of 44 events, and organized the TearDrop Golf Tour, a minor league golf tour that included 75 events. In November the company landed a multiyear agreement with the Golf Channel to televise highlights and other news from the TearDrop Professional Golf Tour on a bimonthly, half-hour program.

Also in 1998 TearDrop became the exclusive North American distributor of Genuin Golf & Dress of America, Inc.'s golf footwear line. Walter Genuin golf shoes typically were sold in high-end retail stores and golf shops, and TearDrop hoped its contract with Genuin would increase its presence and access to such merchants. In December TearDrop sealed an agreement with Internet retailer Value America to sell TearDrop golf clubs through the Value America Internet store.

For fiscal 1998, TearDrop reported sales of $60.7 million, compared with $9.6 million in fiscal 1997. Net losses for the year declined from $9.1 million in 1997 to $6.3 million. If, however, TearDrop, Armour, and RAM operations had been combined for the full year, losses would have reached $42.9 million. Nearly a quarter of TearDrop's revenues were from sales made through Sam's Clubs. Rudy Slucker was hopeful as the company entered 1999, and he wrote in the TearDrop annual report, "Thanks to the dedication of our employees and our shareholder support we were able to make our business grow to unprecedented levels. We anticipate even greater growth, more new product introductions, marquis PGA Tour player signings and if our growth continues at its current pace, profitability in 1999."

The year 1999 was one of ups and downs for TearDrop as the company endeavored to boost sales and recognition. In June the *Robb Report* magazine ranked TearDrop putters as the best putters in its "Best of the Best" annual feature. Walter Genuin golf shoes also were named as the best quality golf footwear. TearDrop-sponsored players continued to perform well using the company's golf products, and throughout the year TearDrop golf clubs gained popularity; by the end of 1999 TearDrop was the fourth-ranked golf putter manufacturer and the fifth-ranked iron maker in the United States in terms of sales.

Continuing with its expansion effort, TearDrop formed a joint venture with Kindai Golf Company of Japan in May 1999. The venture, named TearDrop Japan, marketed and distributed TearDrop's host of golf products, as well as Walter Genuin products, in Japan, the world's second largest golf market. In the summer TearDrop introduced the new Tommy Armour 845 evo line of irons, promoted by the company as the "first true replacement of the 845s irons." The evo line quickly gained in popularity, and by November six PGA players were using the clubs in competition. TearDrop announced that more than 30 PGA players and 35 Nike Tour players had ordered sets. The line was voted "Best New Product Introduction" by the Ontario Professional Golfer's Association.

TearDrop was not without challenges in 1999. Despite the increasing popularity of golf—according to Kon-Lin Research & Analysis Corp., U.S. retail sales of golf clubs were estimated to grow from $1.7 billion in 1994 to about $2.3 billion by 2000 and to nearly $3.0 billion by 2005—golf club sales dropped ten percent in 1998, and many golf companies suffered sales losses. A study by the National Golf Foundation found that participation rates were relatively flat through the 1990s, at about 26.5 million golfers in the United States, because as new players entered the sport, just as many players exited the game. As a result of poor industry conditions, TearDrop's sales suffered as well, and for the six months ended June 30, 1999, the company's sales declined 16 percent, from $44.57 million during the same period in 1998 to $37.59 million. Net income of $2.46 million for the first half of 1998 became a net loss of $2.33 million for the first half of 1999, and it appeared that TearDrop would not meet its November deadline to pay off $21 million in debt. The company, which had estimated that sales in 1999 would reach $90 million, revised its projections to about

$65–$70 million. TearDrop pared back advertising efforts and began discounting its products to encourage sales. Analyst Casey Alexander of Gilford Securities Inc. commented on TearDrop's situation in *Crain's Chicago Business* in August, "The company is highly leveraged now in an extremely competitive industry. . . . They can't afford for too many things to go wrong. As far as I'm concerned, they're walking a tightrope."

In September TearDrop announced that it had failed to meet NASDAQ Small Cap Market listing requirements and was requesting a hearing before the NASDAQ Listing Qualification Panel to ask for an extension. NASDAQ required companies to have $2 million in net assets, fiscal year net income of $500,000, or market capitalization of $35 million. Fortunately for TearDrop, the company was approved for a $30 million line of credit from Textron Inc.'s Textron Financial Corp. in October, and third quarter sales were hopeful. Sales for the third quarter reached $14.3 million, up from $13 million in the same period of 1998. Net income rose as well, from $372,000 during the third quarter of 1998 to $416,000. TearDrop indicated that each of its product divisions enjoyed growth, with demand for new products on the rise.

Despite TearDrop's financial struggles, the company remained confident about its future. TearDrop planned to continue investing in research and development to provide the latest technological developments to golfers, and the company's success with Tommy Armour 845 evo irons offered hope for success to come. Rudy Slucker intended to turn TearDrop into a profitable company and announced in a company statement, "The entire sales and marketing team is truly looking forward to the new millennium as the year 2000 holds great potential for TearDrop."

Principal Subsidiaries

Tommy Armour Golf Company; RAM Golf Corporation; TearDrop Professional Golf Tour; TearDrop Canada; TearDrop Japan (nonmajority stake).

Principal Competitors

Fortune Brands Inc.; Callaway Golf Co.; Karsten Manufacturing Corporation; Taylor Made Golf Company.

Further Reading

Avril, Tom, "Puttering Around N.J. Growing Golf-Club Maker Left the Links of Hilton Head for the Garden State," *Star-Ledger* (Newark, N.J.), November 28, 1997, p. 55.

D'Amato, Gary, "High-tech Putters Changing the Face of Golf," *Milwaukee Journal Sentinel,* April 13, 1997, p. 1.

"FORE! Golf Companies Facing Tough Market," *Going Public: The IPO Reporter,* January 6, 1997.

"Golf Industry Takes a Wicked Slice," *Palm Beach Post,* February 2, 1999, p. 1C.

Henning, Lynn, "Who Is This Guy? Slucker Owns TearDrop, Armour, Ram Yet Remains Virtually Unknown in Golf," *Golfweek,* January 31, 1998, p. 42f.

Murphy, H. Lee, "Armour Golf Teams with Small Player: NJ's TearDrop Wins Bidding for Lagging Local Firm," *Crain's Chicago Business,* November 10, 1997, p. 50.

——, "Debt Deadline: It's Tee Time for TearDrop," *Crain's Chicago Business,* August 16, 1999, p. 4.

Pike, Steve, "Who the Heck Is Rudy Slucker?," *Golf World,* January 30, 1998, p. 44.

Rebello, Stephen, "Irons Man: How Upstart Golf Mogul Rudy Slucker Stormed the Clubhouse," *Success,* August 1, 1998, p. 28.

"Ten Minutes with . . . ," *Interview,* January/February 1998, p. 24f.

—Mariko Fujinaka

Tibbett & Britten Group plc

Ross House
Windmill Hill
Enfield
Middlesex EN2 6SB
United Kingdom
Telephone: +44 181 3679955
Fax: +44 181 3667042
Web site: http://www.tibbett-britten.com

Public Company
Incorporated: 1958 as Tibbett & Britten
Employees: 30,000
Sales: £1.14 billion (US$1.89 billion) (1998)
Stock Exchanges: London
Ticker Symbol: TBG
NAIC: 541614 Transportation Management Consulting Services; 493110 Warehousing and Storage, General Merchandise; 488999 All Other Support Activities for Transportation; 541614 Logistics Management Consulting Services

Fast-moving Tibbett & Britten Group plc is one of the world's leading logistics companies offering warehousing, distribution, and logistical support services, including ''pre-retailing'' services. Market leader in the United Kingdom, Canada, and South Africa, Tibbett & Britten has also captured strong shares in the United States, European, African, Middle Eastern, and Far Eastern markets. Tibbett & Britten's more than 30,000 employees operate in 25 countries, with a focus on the ''fast-moving consumer goods'' (FMCG) segment. Building on its original specialty as a clothing transporter, Tibbett & Britten's primary business comes from the food, consumer goods, clothing and textile, and automobile and light van transportation sectors. The company offers more than 400 warehousing facilities providing some 2.8 million square meters. Tibbett & Britten's fleet of more than 8,500 vehicles operates almost entirely under its clients' colors, spanning the range of major retailers and manufacturers, including Asda, Brooks Brothers, C&A, Marks and Spencer, Black & Decker, Colgate-Palmolive, Compaq, Next, Nestlé, Nissan, Sainsbury, Sears, Wal-Mart, and Reebok. Over 90 percent of the company's business comes from long-term and short-term contracts. In addition to its client-oriented logistics services, Tibbett & Britten is also a major European multi-modal (road and rail) logistics provider. Tibbett & Britten continues to be led by chairman John Harvey, who joined the company in 1969 and has been the chief architect of its growth. Since the mid-1980s, Tibbett & Britten has posted a 25 percent compounded annual growth record; since the beginning of the 1990s, Tibbett & Britten's annual revenues have multiplied by nearly five times.

Origins in the 1950s

John Tibbett began making deliveries in the 1950s, and by the middle of the decade had begun to specialize in transporting clothing from London's East End garment district to retailers in the city's West End. Tibbett's clothing specialty led him to pioneer new methods of transporting garments. Instead of the traditional method of placing clothing in boxes for transport—which required that the clothing not only be taken out of the boxes again but also often that they be ironed for retail presentation—Tibbett outfitted his tiny fleet of trucks to carry the clothing on hangers. By eliminating the need for boxes, Tibbett also enabled his retailer clients to save on storage space—releasing more of their stores for selling space. The savings in cost and time enabled Tibbett to win a loyal clientele. By 1958, Tibbett had been joined by Frank Britten, and the partners incorporated the company as Tibbett & Britten.

Tibbett & Britten remained a small affair, operating out of a converted house in Leytonstone. While the company began to take on new employees, and expand its fleet to ten vehicles by the end of the 1960s, for much of the decade it was forced to rent out a room on the upper floor of the house, using this rent money to pay the company's utilities bills. When the company took on its first storage contract, however, its days as landlord were ended. The company began a steady expansion through the 1960s, winning a contract to provide logistics services to a chain of retail fashion shops. Tibbett & Britten opened a new depot in London's Docklands district, as the company built up its fleet of trucks.

Company Perspectives:

Tibbett & Britten Group's objective is to develop in partnership with its clients and consolidate itself as an internationally acknowledged leader in supply chain management by translating experience and skills across territorial and product sector boundaries.

During this time, Tibbett & Britten had met up with John Harvey, then chief of Unilever's U.K.-based distribution division, SPD, located nearby. By the end of the 1960s, Tibbett & Britten was looking to expand its operations. In order to finance its expansion, Harvey arranged for Unilever, through SPD, together with Dutch transporter Van Gend & Loos (VGL), to each buy 37.5 percent of Tibbett & Britten, while Tibbett & Britten held on to the remaining 25 percent. The SPD/VGL purchase—meant to diversify Unilever's distribution business beyond its core grocery operations—enabled Tibbett & Britten not only to expand its operations, but also to become a more professionally organized business.

By the 1970s, Tibbett & Britten had moved to new headquarters, in Tottenham (its Docklands headquarters had been a garden shed next to the main depot). Strong investment from its new partners enabled the company to expand rapidly during the decades, opening a number of new depots and warehouses, and to take on larger scale contracts from a wider range of customers. Before long, Tibbett & Britten had established itself as a nationally based company, and the first to offer nationwide hanging garment distribution. The company then reformed itself into two divisions, National, and International, which initially focused on allowing the company to enter continental European markets. Both divisions remained specialized on clothing and textile distribution.

Management Buyout in the 1980s

A big boost for the company came when it won a contract to take on distribution work for Marks & Spencer in 1973. The contract, which named Tibbett & Britten as the retailers' exclusive distributor of hanging mens' garments, was extended in 1978, to cover womens' garments as well, placing Tibbett & Britten as the exclusive distributor of the famed British retailer's hanging garment stock. Between 1978 and 1981, the Marks and Spencer contract enabled Tibbett & Britten's revenues to double, and by 1982, the Marks & Spencer contract provided more than 50 percent of Tibbett & Britten's annual sales of £24 million.

Marks & Spencer soon asked Tibbett & Britten to take over all of its hanging garment distribution for its stores and its suppliers, and to build a dedicated depot and distribution network to service this contract. Tibbett & Britten agreed, and in January 1983 the company launched a third division, Transcare, dedicated to its Marks & Spencer business. Establishment of Transcare involved an extensive reorganization on Tibbett & Britten's part, including the opening of new depots, investment in new machinery and handling equipment, and the expansion of the company's fleet of tractor trailers. The investment proved a heavy one, particularly as it came during the economic downswing that marked the early years of the 1980s, and Tibbett & Britten soon found its profits under pressure. By 1983, the company faced a net loss of nearly £800,000.

Tibbett & Britten faced a different transformation in the same year as the Transcare launch. Unilever made the decision to exit its transport operations in 1983; in that year, SPD and VGL decided to end their investment in the Tibbett & Britten partnership. SPD Chairman John Harvey was given the opportunity to lead Tibbett & Britten's management in a management buyout. The buyout was accomplished in December 1984.

Harvey moved first to consolidate the company's clothing distribution operations, reducing expenses in order to bring the company back into profitability. Tibbett & Britten next turned to an analysis of its future expansion. During the company's partnership with VGL and SPD, Tibbett & Britten had not only gained a great deal of investment in technology and operating systems, but had also built up a strong management team with a diversified distribution background. The company determined to put that experience to work, opening out its operations to the wider FMCG market. While the company's Marks and Spencer contract continued to grow, including the design, construction, and operation of a regional distribution center for the retailer in Essex, Tibbett & Britten reorganized to put into place the infrastructure for its diversification into other distribution markets. By 1984, Tibbett & Britten once again showed net profits on the year.

The company established two new divisions in 1986. The first, Dartford Securities Ltd., was established in order to extend its Marks and Spencer business, with new large-scale multi-product warehouses. After opening the first regional distribution center in 1986, the company added two more in 1990 and a fourth in 1991. A second division, Retail Consolidation Services, was created to service the company's other contract clients, built around an IBM-dedicated central warehouse in Milton Keynes, and quickly adding a distribution center in Whitwood, acquired from Unilever. That acquisition also gave the company a seven-year contract to stock and distribute the toiletry and personal care product line of Elida Gibbs. This contract, renewed in 1994, provided the basis of the company's further expansion in this product category.

In order to fund these investments, Tibbett & Britten took a listing on the London stock exchange in 1986. The public offering marked the start of a long period of expansion, which saw the company grow from a base of less than 1,500 employees and sales of just over £32 million in the mid-1980s, to a leading international company of some 20,000 employees and annual sales of more than £1.1 billion at the end of the 1990s.

Expansion in the 1990s

Tibbett & Britten was aided by the changing nature of the retail business. Under pressure from a difficult economic climate and from tightening competition, as well as spiraling real estate costs, retailers also confronted a changing consumer landscape as well. Consumer purchases turned more and more toward so-called ''lifestyle'' purchases, with a resulting new volatility in trends and fashions. Retailers in turn reduced back

Key Dates:

1958: Company incorporates as Tibbett & Britten.
1969: Company acquired by SPD (Unilever) and Van Gend & Loos.
1973: Wins contract with Marks and Spencer.
1978: Marks and Spencer contract is extended.
1984: John Harvey leads management buyout.
1986: Company is listed on London Stock Exchange.
1990: Tibbett & Britten begins international expansion.
1995: Company enters U.S. logistics market.

stock, introducing just-in-time delivery practices that required tighter ordering and delivery coordination. At the same time, the growing number of major and globally operating retail chains demanded internationally based distribution systems. Rather than investing in adapting their own distribution divisions to this new market reality, retailers turned to specialized third parties to handle their logistics needs. Tibbett & Britten found itself well-placed to attract this new wave of clients.

The company continued to invest in new facilities, while diversifying its operations to include distribution of new product types and new logistics services. Tibbett & Britten also began making acquisitions, adding the pre-retailing services—such as tagging and labeling, etc.—of International Garment Services Ltd. and two 100,000-square-foot Woolworth distribution centers (subsequently contracted back to Woolworth Corporation) in 1988. The following year saw the signing on of a number of new major clients, including Colgate-Palmolive, Black & Decker, and supermarketers Asda and Sainsbury. In September 1989, Tibbett & Britten acquired Lowfield Distribution, with its seven grocery-oriented distribution sites. This purchase was followed by the company's entry into the North American market, with the establishment of its Transcare Inc. Canadian subsidiary in Toronto.

Into the 1990s, the company continued to make strategic acquisitions of both distribution companies and customer-owned distribution facilities. For example, the company took over Digital Corp.'s U.K. warehousing, stock, and logistics operations. In Canada, the company renamed its subsidiary operations there as Tibbett & Britten Group Canada Inc. (TBGC), taking on the logistics assets and operations of both Robinsons Department Store and Chesebrough-Ponds. Tibbett & Britten also contracted with Talbot Stores as that company launched its own Canada operations. Back home, the company's garment contracts, other than its Marks and Spencer business, were regrouped under the brand name Fashion Logistics.

The acquisition of Silcock in 1992 brought Tibbett & Britten into the automotive transport business. Silcock had been founded in the early 1920s by two employees of the Ford Motor Company, who hit on the idea of delivering that company's Model Ts in their spare time. By the mid-1920s, the pair had set up the U.K.'s first dedicated auto distribution business, with operations in the United Kingdom, France, Spain, Belgium, and Portugal; Silcock's relation with Ford would continue through the rest of the century. In order to fund the Silcock acquisition, at a price of £31.3 million, Tibbett & Britten performed a one-for-five exchange of stock, worth just under £33 million. By then, Tibbett & Britten's annual sales had grown to £231.75 million.

Reflecting the company's steady growth, Tibbett & Britten reorganized in 1993, forming three major operating divisions, Tibbett & Britten Ltd., containing its U.K. business; Tibbett & Britten International Ltd., for all its non-automotive international business; and Silcock Express Holdings Ltd., for the company's U.K. and international car and light vehicle operations. Tibbett & Britten continued its organic growth, opening storage and distribution facilities for its clients, with new additions such as Warner Brothers' Studio Stores and VAG, the Volkswagen, Audio, Skoda and SEAT parts provider. As Tibbett & Britten stepped up its European operations, including acquiring in 1994 Toleman, an automobile distributor focused on Ford imports, it also expanded into South Africa, while deepening its operations in Canada—particularly with winning a warehousing and distribution contract from Wal-Mart, the first time the retailer had ever outsourced for its distribution needs. The Wal-Mart contract, initially only for one year, continued to be extended through the second half of the decade, including a 1998 contract to create a multi-facility network for Wal-Mart's Canada operations, as well as an extension of the contract to provide logistics support for Wal-Mart's entry into Germany.

Entry into the United States market came in 1995, with the extension of the TBGC subsidiary to include all of North America, and the launch of startup operations for Brooks Brothers in New Jersey and Philips in Memphis, Tennessee. The company also made a number of significant acquisitions, including the purchase of Dutch publisher VNU's distribution arm, Metra Media Transport, in the Netherlands and the purchase, for £12 million, of Unilever's TKL refrigerated traffic distribution wing in Austria. In that year, Tibbett & Britten once again restructured, forming the company into two major divisions: Textiles & Clothing and Consumer Products.

Although Tibbett & Britten continued to look for strategic acquisitions, the company's strong growth remained largely organic, with expansion spurred by the winning of new contracts and clients. New contracts in 1997 included the takeover of a 170-acre, 1.8 million-square-foot grocery distribution center in California, reputedly the world's largest grocery-dedicated warehousing site. A new acquisition in 1998, of Causse Walon, the leading national automotive carrier in France, added £58 million to Tibbett & Britten's annual sales, which in that year hit the £1 billion mark. In 1999, the company acquired California-based EFL Transportation, an apparel distribution provider to clothing retailers, including Gap, marking the company's entry into the U.S. apparel market. Also in 1999, Tibbett & Britten acquired Remijsen, adding grocery distribution to the company's Netherlands operations. As one of the world's only companies wholly dedicated to providing logistics and logistics support services, Tibbett & Britten looked forward to smooth roads in the 21st century.

Principal Subsidiaries

Dartford Securities Ltd.; Fashion Logistics Ltd.; Transcare Distribution Ltd.; Hi-Tech Logistics Ltd.; Axial Ltd; Tibbett & Britten Austria GmbH (95%); Axial SA (Belgium); Tibbett &

Britten Group Canada Inc.; Axis Logistics Inc. (Canada); Matrix Logistics Services Ltd.; (Canada); Summit Logistics Inc. (Canada); SWO Distribution Centres Ltd. (Canada); Tibbett & Britten Clef SA (France); Axial SA (France); Causee Walon SA (France); Tibbett & Britten Group (Ireland) Ltd.; Neptune Freight Ltd (Ireland); Tibbett & Britten Kenya Ltd.; South China Warehousing (Hong Kong) Ltd (75%); Tibbett & Britten International Holdings BV (Netherlands); Metra Media Transport BV (Netherlands); Armadis Armazenagem e Distribuiçao Lda (Portugal); SA Warehousing Services Pty Ltd. (South Africa); Tibbett & Britten España SL; Silcock Holdings SL (Spain); Tibbett & Britten Group North America Inc. (U.S.A.); Compass Logistics Inc. (U.S.A.); Galaxy Logistics Inc. (U.S.A.); Matrix Logistics Inc. (U.S.A.); Summit Logistics Inc. (U.S.A.).

Principal Competitors

Consolidated Delivery & Logistics, Inc.; Roadway Express, Inc.; U.S. Delivery Systems, Inc.; ICTS International N.V.; Target Logistics, Inc.; Universal Express Inc.

Further Reading

Murray, John, "Tibbett Strengthens Ties to Ford Delivery Network," *Independent*, March 30, 1994.

Stevenson, Tom, "Logistical Hitch at Tibbett," *Independent*, March 28, 1996, p. 22.

"Tibbett & Britten," *Independent*, September 16, 1999, p. 21.

—M.L. Cohen

Tokyu Department Store Co., Ltd.

241, Dogenzaka 2-chome
Shibuyaku, Tokyo 150
Japan
Telephone: (81) 3-34773111
Fax: (811) 3-34967200
Web site: http://www.tokyu-depart.co.jp

Public Subsidiary of Tokyu Group
Incorporated: 1919 as Shirokiya Gofukuten Co., Ltd.
Employees: 3,633
Sales: ¥48.75 billion (US$4.09 billion) (1999)
Stock Exchanges: Tokyo
NAIC: 45211 Department Stores

Tokyu Department Store Co., Ltd. operates a chain of department stores in Japan and is the core of the retail and distribution division of the Tokyu Group. With a flagship department store in Shibuya, Tokyo, Tokyu runs 15 stores in Japan, primarily situated in the Tokyo and Yokohama region. The company is also involved in real estate, food processing, the bakery business, information services, and other retail operations. Because of poor economic conditions in Japan in the late 1990s, Tokyu is focusing on diversification and innovation and plans to invest in the increasingly popular suburban shopping malls.

From Drapes to Railways: Early 1900s

Tokyu Department Store's most venerable antecedent dates back to the 17th century. This ancestor was a drapers' shop, Shirokiya, founded in 1662 by Hikotaro Omura in the Nihonbashi area of Tokyo, or Edo as the city was then called. In 1919 this business was incorporated as the Shirokiya Drapery Shop Co., Ltd. Four years later, the store, like most others in Tokyo, was devastated by fire following the Great Kanto Earthquake. Operating under the new trading name of Shirokiya Co., Ltd., the company redeveloped the old site to create a new and more up-to-date store, which opened in June 1933.

The evolution of Shirokiya constitutes one strand of the Tokyu Department Store's history. The other principal strand began in the 1930s, a boom period for Japanese department stores. At this time Tokyo's suburbs were growing rapidly, and railway lines were stretching out from the center to serve them. The railway companies often used the land adjacent to their commuter stations to build department stores, which they financed with money from their transport activities. One of the earliest railway companies to spot this opportunity was the Tokyo Yokohama Electric Railways Co., Ltd., owned by entrepreneur Keita Gotoh's Tokyo Corporation. In 1934 the Tokyo Yokohama Electric Railways Co. opened Toyoko Department Store, the first department store to be sited at a railway station; "Toyoko" was a portmanteau word formed from "Tokyo" and "Yokohama."

After World War II the Allied occupying forces pursued a policy of dismantling the large combines or *zaibatsu,* which in the Allies' opinion had contributed to Japan's entry into the war. Many Tokyu operations were reconstituted as semi-independent companies. One such company, Toyoko Kogyo, assumed control of Tokyu's department store business in 1948, shortly afterwards becoming known as Toyoko Department Store Co., Ltd.

Another company originating in 1948 and later affiliated with Tokyu Department Store was Tokyu Foods. Forty years after its foundation, Tokyu Foods became a significant manufacturer and retailer of bakery goods, operating 140 bakeries in Japan and elsewhere under the name "St-Germain," also selling delicatessen-style meats. Tokyu Foods also built up several restaurant chains. Tokyu Department Store's other important food-manufacturing affiliate, Gold Pak, whose award-winning products were all based on fresh fruit and vegetable juices, began trading in 1966.

Boom Times in the 1940s and 1950s

After the immediate postwar hardships, Japan's prosperity grew rapidly. Department stores flourished because they offered convenient one-stop shopping; from being primarily dry-goods suppliers before the war, they now came to supply everything from food to consumer durables. They also catered to the westernization of Japanese tastes by bringing in imports in a way that

Company Perspectives:

Beauty is the criterion that the Tokyu Group will use to guide us into the coming age. The beauty we pursue arises from harmony among individuals, society and nature to move the hearts of all, spanning nations and generations. We at the Tokyu Group are putting all our energy into achieving our goal of creating a sound, healthy, and beautiful living environment that moves the spirit. We want to play our part in building a harmonious and compassionate society, where each individual can live a happy and fulfilling life. ''Toward a Beautiful Age'' represents the Tokyu Group's resolve to keep striving toward that ideal, and our commitment to take the lead in creating a beautiful living environment for all.

smaller retailers could not afford to do. Department stores were typically situated at railway stations, as were Toyoko's stores.

It was against this promising background that Toyoko Department Store opened its Ikebukuro store in 1950, which was to close after only 14 years of trading. In 1951 the company inaugurated Tokyo's first shopping arcade under the name Toyoko Norengai. The west wing of the main Toyoko store was also extended during the early 1950s.

The two strands of Tokyu Department Store's history came together in the late 1950s. Shirokiya Co. joined the Tokyu group of companies in 1956. Two years later, after a period of intensive modernization and expansion of the Shirokiya main store, Shirokiya and Toyoko Department Store merged, adopting the name Toyoko Co., Ltd. The company took an initial step towards globalization with the creation of Shirokiya Incorporated in 1959. In the same year, this new affiliate opened Tokyu's first overseas store, the Hawaii Shirokiya in the Ala Moana Shopping Center. Over the years Shirokiya Incorporated opened another three stores in Hawaii, two of them in shopping centers and one in a hotel. That Shirokiya became a valued part of Hawaiian life was indicated by the fact that the city of Honolulu designated October 15, 1989, as ''Shirokiya Day'' in honor of the original store's 30th anniversary.

Continued Growth in the 1960s and 1970s

On the domestic front, the early 1960s found department stores facing unprecedented demand for household goods such as televisions and washing machines. However, the stores were also presented with growing competition from the newly arrived supermarkets and superstores which, sited away from town centers as they tended to be, could often provide shoppers with a more relaxed environment and lower-priced goods. Despite this competition, Toyoko continued to grow, both through acquisition and through construction of attractive new stores. In 1966 Toyoko formed a joint venture with Nagano Maruzen, which in 1970 would change its name to the Nagano Tokyu Department Store Ltd.

The company adopted its current name of Tokyu Department Store Co., Ltd. in 1967, the year in which it opened a new main store in Shibuya at one of Tokyo's largest railway stations. Both this and the original Toyoko Store nearby were to undergo an important expansion program in the late 1960s. Also in 1967, the 300-year old Shirokiya shop changed its name to the Nihonbashi Tokyu Department Store. Its advantageous site, adjacent to the intersection of three subway lines and in an important shopping and business district, continued to make it one of Tokyu's busiest enterprises.

The 1973 oil shock precipitated a period of stagnation in the department-store sector. In spite of this, the 1970s were notable for the opening of several new Tokyu stores. In 1973 came the new Sapporo Tokyu Department Store, situated across the road from Sapporo Station in Hokkaido. This was the first Tokyu store to open outside the capital, and Tokyu made a point of staffing it locally to ensure a strong rapport with shoppers and a thorough understanding of their preferences. Initially a company in its own right, Sapporo Tokyu Department Store merged with Tokyu Department Store in 1978.

The Kichijoji store opened in 1974 at the Japan Railways Kichijoji Station in Musashino City, Tokyo. In 1980 the Machida Tokyu Department Store Co. began trading; it became part of the Tokyu Department Store Co. in 1989. Machida was one of Tokyo's most rapidly growing residential suburbs, and the store offered mainly sporting and leisure equipment to local shoppers.

During the 1970s and 1980s there was a trend toward specialization among Japanese department stores. A store catered to specific groups of customers, such as newly married women or teenagers. In 1979 Tokyu Department Store affiliate T.M.D. opened Shibuyu 109, a center aimed at the fashion-conscious woman and which by the 1990s contained 93 separate shops. Its success sparked off a series of similar enterprises, including the KOHRINBO 109 in Kanazawa, opened in 1985; One-Oh-Nine, opened in 1986; and 1092, opened in 1987.

Expansion and Diversification in the 1980s

In 1990 Tokyu launched the first of a new style of fashion store, 1 2 3 (pronounced ''un deux trois'') in Shibuya. Among the boutiques it comprised was Trans Continents, an outlet for Tokyu affiliate Millennium Japan Ltd., also founded in 1990 as a retailer of fashion clothing and accessories. This exemplified Tokyu's participation in the trend for Japanese retailers to develop private-label fashion products, appealing to consumers in the way that designer-labeled goods do, but undercutting designer-label prices.

In the 1980s Tokyu added energetically to its overseas interests, starting with the opening of the Hong Kong Tokyu store in 1980 when it became the principal tenant of the then recently completed New World Center in Kowloon on the Chinese mainland. Then came stores in Bangkok and Thailand in 1985, and in Singapore in 1987. In each case Tokyu made a point of integrating itself into the local community—the slogan of the Singapore store was ''Born and Raised in Singapore''—while offering shoppers a taste of Japanese courtesy and quality. Outside Asia, the OK Gift Shop 109 opened in Auckland, New Zealand, in 1990.

As well as opening new stores, Tokyu expanded overseas through acquisition. It bought the Dragon Seed Co. Ltd., a Hong

Key Dates:

1662: Shirokiya, a drapery shop, is founded in Tokyo.
1919: Shirokiya incorporates as Shirokiya Gofukuten Co., Ltd.
1934: Tokyo Yokohama Electric Railways Co. opens the first Toyoko Department Store.
1948: Toyoko Department Store Co., Ltd. forms.
1951: Toyoko opens Tokyo's first shopping arcade.
1958: Toyoko Department Store and Shirokiya merge and form Toyoko Co., Ltd.
1959: Company establishes Shirokiya Inc. in Hawaii.
1967: Toyoko changes its name to Tokyu Department Store Co., Ltd.
1967: Company opens a new store in Shibuya.
1973: Tokyu opens its first store outside Tokyo, in Sapporo.
1989: Tokyu completes the building of the Bunkamura cultural center in Tokyo.
1993: Restructuring plan announced to strengthen the company's operations includes reducing workforce by about 20 percent.
1999: 330-year-old Nihonbashi store closes.

Kong department store company, in 1988 from investment company First Pacific. With Dragon Seed, Tokyu gained a valuable building in the central area of Hong Kong Island, as well as a ten-store chain. Tokyu bought an equity participation in the Ever Green Department Store Corporation of Taiwan in 1990.

Tokyu's overseas operations were not confined to its retail outlets. International buying operations and joint ventures became increasingly important. Tokyu acquired the monopoly for Jim Thompson Thai silk in 1985, opening a Jim Thompson boutique in its main store. In 1988 it formed an alliance with Williams-Sonoma, a U.S. catalog sales company, to establish Williams-Sonoma Japan. Williams-Sonoma specialties included household goods and furnishings.

Overseas buying was not exclusively a quest for exotica. Like many of its competitors, Tokyu Department Store sought to reduce its unit costs through imports and adopted a ''develop and import'' system whereby it joined forces with local interests to produce goods for sale initially in the local marketplace and, when a sufficiently high standard had been attained, for import to Japan. Goods imported in this way included knitwear from China, clothing from Hong Kong, and fruit from Thailand.

The 1980s was a period of recovery in the Japanese consumer market. Tokyu's expansion in the 1970s had left it well placed to benefit despite continued fierce competition from supermarkets. New Tokyu department stores continued to open. The Kitami Tokyu began trading in 1982 and the Komoro Tokyu store in Nagano prefecture, part of the Nagano Tokyu Department Store Co., began trading the following year, as did the Tama Plaza Tokyu department store. The Tama Plaza Shopping Center, constructed by Tokyu Corporation, was adjacent to Tama Plaza station in Yokohama, and the department store was its principal occupant. The Tama Plaza Tokyu Department Store Co. became the Seinan Tokyu Department Store Co. in 1989, though the store itself continued to be known as Tama Plaza.

Remodeling of stores was a keynote of Tokyu's activities throughout the 1980s. In 1984 it celebrated the 50th anniversary of the opening of Toyoko Department Store with a radical remodeling of the main store in Shibuya. By then the store contained a range of specialty shops under one roof. The Shibuya store's food department in the basement was greatly extended in 1990. The Toyoko store was refitted in 1985 and 1986. This, too, housed a mall of specialty shops, including concessions such as Benetton and the first Williams-Sonoma Japan retail outlet, which opened in 1988. The store's exterior was renovated in 1989.

Outside Tokyo, too, shops were constantly being restyled to keep abreast of consumer preferences. The Nagano Tokyu store was extended in 1986 and a new annex called Cherchez was added, making this the largest urban department store in the Nagano prefecture.

In 1988 the Kichijoji store was redecorated, and the Sapporo store embarked on an extension and renewal program. Thanks to the opening of a new subway line, the store's food floor in the basement was now directly connected to Sapporo station. The Nihonbashi store, too, underwent a dramatic transformation, reopening complete with La Plasis, a huge customer service mall offering postal, travel, and other facilities. The renovated store also boasted a greatly expanded women's clothing department. A couple of years later the Nihonbashi store was crowned with the imaginative addition of a rooftop golf school.

During the 1970s and 1980s the Japanese department store sector, which had previously dominated the retail industry in terms of both sales and profitability, began to lag behind the supermarket companies with their out-of-town superstores. This tendency was attributed partly to the supermarkets' faster conversion to information technology. In 1988, however, Tokyu introduced a Point of Sale (POS) system to all its department stores to automate stock control and keep track of local customer preferences.

Tokyu was also innovative in finding ways to woo the shopper back from the superstores. In February 1987, for instance, the *Economist* reported that four Tokyu stores had introduced door-to-door sales teams of housewives selling on commission. This personal approach was so successful that several other department stores quickly followed suit.

Japanese stores tried to lure shoppers through their own doors by helping to improve the area of the city in which they operated; for example, an adjunct of the Toyoko Store renovation in 1985 was a project to improve and promote the whole street in cooperation with local government. This form of competition became known as the ''Commercial Block War.''

Tokyu played a major role in the revitalization of the Shibuya area, where its headquarters and largest stores were situated. Perhaps Tokyu's most spectacular contribution was the Bunkamura, or Tokyu Culture Village. A cooperative venture between a number of Tokyu companies, it involved the construction of a large complex, including art gallery, concert hall, and theater. It opened in 1989 on a site adjacent to Tokyu's main store, and the *Japan Company Handbook* soon reported that takings at the main store were shooting up under the influence of the Bunkamura.

Facing New Challenges in the Early 1990s

In the early 1990s, healthy turnover of goods such as jewelry and fine art reflected the luxurious ambience which Tokyu endeavored to project in its stores and malls. New stores continued to open, usually in the proximity of stations. In 1990, for instance, Nagano Tokyu Department Store Co., Ltd. opened its Nagano Tokyu Life Store at the Japan Railways Kita-Nagano Station. Tokyu also pursued an active policy of expansion in and beyond the Pacific Rim area. There were four Hawaii stores and one each in Hong Kong, Bangkok, and Singapore, as well as a further six representative offices worldwide by the early 1990s. A second Thai store opened in 1993.

Tokyu Department Store was one of the most important of the Tokyu Group, a complex group of businesses of which Tokyu Corporation was the nucleus. These companies, of which there were nearly 400, were divided into four main groups: retailing and distribution; development; transportation; and recreation and leisure. Tokyu Department Store was the nucleus of the retailing and distribution group, which represented almost 40 percent of the Tokyu Group's total sales in 1990. The retailing and distribution group also comprised a supermarket chain and the Tokyu Store Chain, with more than 100 stores in the greater Tokyo area. Like the department stores, most of these adjoined the Tokyu Corporation's railway lines. Tokyu also operated specialty stores such as Tokyu Time Co., started in 1965 to sell and repair watches, and Sports Tokyu Co., started in 1970. Both of these were affiliates of Tokyu Department Store Co., while a number of other specialty stores, such as Top Shoes, were more closely linked with the Tokyu Store Chain Co. All these specialty stores were available for inclusion in Tokyu Department Store's shopping malls.

The slogan of the Tokyu Group was ''Creating a well-balanced life for the 21st century.'' This aspiration was reflected in Tokyu Department Store's community and lifestyle-oriented approach to its customers. The stores did not simply try to sell individual products and services; they offered lectures, cultural events, and educational programs to the public to reinforce the sales message and at the same time improve the quality of life. The stores used local staff to emphasize that the business was rooted in the customer community.

Writing in an August 1990 *Business JAPAN,* in his capacity as chairman of the Japan Department Stores Association, Tokyu Department Store's president, Mamoru Miura, discussed legislative changes and warned that Japan was about to encounter an ''increasingly sinister'' economic environment with labor shortages, rising interest rates, and unstable stock and foreign exchange markets. He identified the internationalization of the marketplace and the need for better information management as the two main challenges facing the department store industry in the coming decade. In contrast, analyst Ken Egusa of Morgan Stanley & Co. predicted continued growth and success for Japanese department stores in the 1990s. Egusa told *HFD-The Weekly Home Furnishings Newspaper:* ''The 1990s will see consumer demand remaining firm and the marketplace as a whole will be driven, starting in the mid-1990s, during the period when the first and second baby boomers will become full members of the labor force.'' Egusa also indicated that changes in the Large-Scale Retail Store Law would open up opportunities for larger stores and shopping outlets in suburban areas.

Soon after these predictions were made, Japan's economy began to deteriorate, creating difficult conditions for Tokyu and other Japanese retailers. For the fiscal year that ended January 31, 1992, Tokyu indicated that though sales grew 8.2 percent over the previous year, its pretax profit declined 18 percent. The higher-end merchandise that consumers so readily sought in the late 1980s and early 1990s became less desirable as people tightened their spending budgets, and Tokyu's marketing expenses and management costs grew more quickly than sales. Tokyu fared no better the following year, and pretax profit slid 27 percent. Net profit was affected by a new land tax, which required Tokyu to pay ¥670 million in land taxes alone.

As a result of slumping revenues, Tokyu devised a three-year restructuring plan in 1993 to strengthen the company's operations. As part of the restructuring, Tokyu announced plans to reduce its workforce by about 20 percent, about 1,000 jobs, over a three-year period. Tokyu planned to accomplish the task by refraining from hiring new recruits, including high school and university graduates, in spring as was traditionally done, as well as through attrition.

Increasing Challenges in the Late 1990s

Tokyu experienced a brief respite in 1995 as consumer spending picked up slightly. The company reported a net profit of ¥1.84 billion for fiscal year 1996, and during the first half of 1996 sales rose 1.1 percent over the same period a year earlier. Increased sales promotions and extended store hours in the Tokyo region helped generate revenues. Tokyu announced that clothing sales increased 1.8 percent and food sales rose 1.5 percent.

Despite increased revenues, Tokyu noted that sales were still relatively weak and complete recovery could not be anticipated in the near future. Indeed, Tokyu's upturn was brief—the company announced pretax profit for 1997 of ¥1.7 billion, a drop of 32.8 percent from 1996. Tokyu blamed continued slow personal consumption as well as the weather; an unseasonably warm winter resulted in poor clothing sales, and stores failed to meet sales targets in December and January.

To battle the poor economic conditions, Tokyu endeavored to better serve its clientele, hoping its efforts might translate into improved sales. After a five-year moratorium, Tokyu announced it would hire about 100 new employees beginning in the spring of 1998. The company believed introducing a younger employee to its personnel would create a better age balance. New recruits were also needed to accommodate Tokyu's extended hours. Though the Large-Scale Retail Store Law recommended that department stores take a minimum of 24 holidays per year, many ailing department stores believed offering more hours was the key to increasing sales. Tokyu hoped to decrease its holiday closures from 22 to 18 days at three stores in the Tokyo metropolitan area beginning in the summer of 1998.

In addition to the sluggish economy, Tokyu had suburban shopping centers to blame for its struggles. Once the ultimate destination for shoppers, urban department stores began to lose customers to shopping malls and superstores that cropped up in the suburbs. The convenience of suburban shopping appealed to the increasingly car-oriented shopper, and statistics indicated that suburban shopping was not a fluke. The *Asian Wall Street Journal* reported that between 1985 and 1994, the market share of six superstore chains increased from 4.6 percent to 5.3 percent in the overall retail industry. The market share of eight major department store chains, however, dropped from 2.9 percent to 2.6 percent. While most of the major department store operators shunned expansion into suburbs, Tokyu hoped to capitalize on the new trend and began making plans to open stores in suburban shopping centers. The company announced plans to build a shopping mall in the Tokyo suburb of Kohoku New Town with a Tokyu Department Store as a key retailer.

Hard times continued for Tokyu as the economic recession persisted. In 1998, after ten years in Japan, Williams-Sonoma announced it would end its joint venture with Tokyu. Slow expansion—there were 15 Williams-Sonoma stores in Japan—was believed to be one of the reasons for the break. Tokyu posted its first pretax loss since 1949 and sales fell 12 percent for the six-month period ending July 1998, spurring the company to develop a five-year restructuring plan. The plan called for the liquidation or sale of most of its international subsidiaries, including the Hong Kong operations, Merchandising Development USA Inc., a real estate company in the United States, and some operations in Thailand. Tokyu also announced it would close the Nihonbashi store. The Nihonbashi store was the third largest of Tokyu's department stores in terms of sales and contributed about 11 percent of Tokyu's revenues in fiscal 1998. The company also planned to eliminate about 900 jobs by 2002, many through voluntary early retirement.

The closure of the Nihonbashi store was significant news in Japan. The store, which had existed for more than 330 years, held a month-long closing sale in January 1999 that generated unprecedented sales. On the sale's first day on January 2, the store reached record sales of ¥739 million. On the final day of business about 160,000 consumers visited the store. January sales reached a total of ¥16.5 billion, about half of the store's total 1998 sales. In September Tokyu indicated it had found a buyer for the Nihonbashi building; Mitsui Fudosan Co. planned to convert the store into a high-rise office building, with stores on the lower levels.

Though Tokyu shed unprofitable businesses to streamline operations, earnings continued to be bleak throughout 1999. Sales in fiscal 1999 dropped 6.3 percent, and during the first half of 1999 the company reported an unconsolidated pretax loss of ¥713 million, nearly double its year-earlier loss of ¥361 million. Net losses also increased, from ¥1.04 billion during the first half of 1998 to ¥5.07 billion in 1999. Closure of the Nihonbashi store contributed to poor sales, which fell 14 percent. Tokyu hoped to offset losses with the sale of the Nihonbashi building.

In April 1999 Mamoru Miura stepped down from his post as chairman to signal his responsibility in Tokyu's poor performance. Miura had previously resigned his role as president in 1992 and assumed the chairmanship when Tokyu suffered large losses in investments. Tokyu predicted it would continue to rack up losses and forecast an after-tax loss of ¥2.9 billion for fiscal 2000. With the company's efforts to pare down overhead and its openness to take risks—plans to develop suburban shopping centers and to explore the community antenna television (CAT) industry continued—Tokyu appeared armed for the coming millennium.

Principal Subsidiaries

Sapporo Plaza Co., Ltd.; Tokyu Foods Co., Ltd.; Yokohama Tokyu Department Store Co., Ltd.; Gold Pack Co., Ltd. (66.67%); Nagano Tokyu Department Store Co., Ltd. (45.64%); Kitami Tokyu Department Store Co., Ltd. (98.24%); Millennium Japan Ltd. (60%); Seinan Tokyu Department Store Co.; Toyoko Bussan Co., Ltd.; T.M.D. Co., Ltd.; Shibuya-Chikagai Co., Ltd. (66.67%); Tokyu Time Co., Ltd.; Estate Service Co., Ltd.

Principal Competitors

Mycal Corporation; Seiyu Ltd.; Takashimaya Co.; Hankyu Department Stores Inc.; Jusco Co.; Mitsukoshi Ltd.

Further Reading

Diamond's Japan Business Directory 1991, Tokyo: Diamond Lead Co., Ltd., 1991.

"Doorsteps, the New Point of Sale," *Economist*, February 28, 1987.

Gilbert, Les, "Analyst Looks at Japan, 1990s Style," *HFD—The Weekly Home Furnishings Newspaper,* April 9, 1990, p. 14.

"Japan's Department Stores Report Dismal Earnings," *Asian Wall Street Journal,* April 26, 1993, p. 4.

Miura, Mamoru, "Department Stores Must Act As Integrated Life Industries," *Business Japan*, August, 1990.

Ostrom, Douglas, "Consumer Spending in the Dumps, Poised to Get Worse," *JEI Report,* October 2, 1998.

Retail Distribution in Japan, Tokyo: Dodwell Marketing Consultants, 1988.

Shirouzu, Norihiko, "In Retailing, Risk Takers May Be Japan's Safest Bets," *Asian Wall Street Journal,* September 26, 1997, p. 15.

"Tokyu Department Store Expects Loss of $141.5 Million for the Year," *Asian Wall Street Journal,* January 26, 1998, p. 4.

"Tokyu Dept. Store to Close Major Tokyo Retail Outlet," *Japan Economic Newswire,* September 16, 1998.

"Tokyu Dept. Store to End 330-Year History with a Bang," *Japan Economic Newswire,* January 25, 1999.

—Alison Classe
—updated by Mariko Fujinaka

Towers Perrin

335 Madison Avenue
New York, New York 10017-4605
U.S.A.
Telephone: (212) 309-3400
Toll Free: (800) 665-1080
Fax: (212) 309-0975
Web site: http://www.towers.com

Private Company
Incorporated: 1934 as Towers, Perrin, Forster & Crosby, Inc.
Employees: 8,400
Sales: $1.23 billion (1998)
NAIC: 541611 Administrative Management & General Management Consulting Services

Towers Perrin is one of the world's largest management consultant firms, serving about 10,000 clients, among them some 65 percent of the world's largest companies. It has more than 70 offices in 24 countries. The company operates in five fields: human resources and general management consulting; employee benefit services; health industry consulting; reinsurance; and financial services and risk management. The firm is owned by its executives and other principal employees.

Reinsurance and Benefits Specialist: 1934–82

Charles Perrin was a partner in a Kansas City, Missouri insurance underwriting firm that formed an association with Philadelphia's Brown, Crosby & Co. in 1919. The two firms combined in 1923, with the merger also including Henry W. Brown & Co., which dated back to 1871. Perrin became a partner in 1930, along with John A. Towers, a Kansas City colleague who managed the reinsurance department. The founding of Towers, Perrin, Forster & Crosby, Inc. (TPF&C) in 1934 also brought in as partners Arthur Crosby, H. Pratt Weaver, and Walter Chase, all partners of the predecessor company. H. Walter Forster, the other founding partner, brought a new focus to the firm as an expert on both fire prevention and pension planning. Forster, who has been called ''the father of pension planning,'' was president from 1938 to 1949, and Perrin was board chairman during this period.

TPF&C inherited blue-chip corporate clients such as General Foods, International Harvester, and Union Carbide Corporation, and it acquired others such as Monsanto Co. The adoption of New Deal federal legislation such as Social Security and minimum wage laws kept the employee consulting unit busy, while the reinsurance division was active among Lloyd's of London syndicates. (A wholly owned subsidiary dealing with reinsurance, John D. Pryce & Co., was absorbed by its parent in 1952.) TPF&C added offices in Chicago in 1946 and New York in 1949. By 1950 its sales volume had grown ninefold since its inception. The firm opened its first international office in Montreal in 1956. During the 1960s it acquired companies, opened more offices, and expanded its services to include compensation and organization consulting.

Quentin I. Smith, Jr., a former insurance salesman, joined the company in 1957 and rose to become its president in 1971, when revenue came to $12 million. Under Smith's leadership the firm moved its headquarters to New York in 1975 and continued to grow by acquisition. Interviewed by *Business Week* in 1979, Smith said TPF&C was adding experts in more fields because ''We realized that a compensation plan must fit in with a total business plan and so we started adding specialists in strategic planning, marketing, and the like.'' In 1982 the firm ranked sixth among the nation's consulting companies in size, with annual revenue of $120 million.

Acquisitions and Growth in the 1980s

A vital TPF&C acquisition was that of Cresap, McCormick and Paget (CM&P) in 1982. Founded in 1946, CM&P had annual revenue of only about $15 million at the time of the merger but enjoyed a prestigious reputation, predominantly in corporate strategies, human resources, and information processing. It became a division of the parent firm and by 1987 had made five acquisitions of its own, reaching annual sales of $65 million and adding to its roster of clients General Electric Co. and the World Bank. Cresap was flexible in taking assignments,

Company Perspectives:

Building Relationships . . . Producing Results. That simple phrase sums up our view of the qualities that make Towers Perrin an excellent consulting firm. We believe it also expresses the kind of firm we are and the kind of consultants who work for us. In many ways, it also describes our clients: they tend to be organizations in the forefront of their industries. Organizations with effective leadership and a desire to find the best possible partners to help them manage their business effectively and competitively. For those organizations and others like them, we are that partner.

willing to take a piecemeal rather than a total approach. It teamed its consultants with the client's managers to come up with solutions rather than simply handing down a report that the client was then expected to accept and implement. CM&P added a consulting unit for manufacturing in 1988.

Even more important was TPF&C's 1986 acquisition of Tillinghast, Nelson & Warren Inc., the nation's largest independent risk management consultant. The merger created the world's largest staff of professional actuaries, according to an executive at Atlanta-based Tillinghast. TPF&C annexed Tillinghast's benefits unit but preserved the Tillinghast name for risk management consulting and for life and casualty actuarial practice. (TPF&C's own risk management operation was assigned to Tillinghast.) The amalgamation added $58 million to TPF&G's 1985 revenue of $272 million. In terms of sector, employee benefits consulting now accounted for 58 percent of the combined sum; insurance consulting (nonrisk management) for 16 percent; compensation consulting, 13 percent; general management consulting, 12 percent; and risk management consulting, one percent.

Spurred by rising employee benefit costs and new federal laws and regulations, TPF&C accumulated revenue of $465 million in 1987, reaching fourth place in overall consulting income. The benefits business, a consulting expert told John A. Byrne of *Business Week,* is ''like an annuity. It comes around every year, just like Christmas, and every year it gets bigger. It's a business few in consulting enjoy.'' The firm name was shortened to Towers Perrin in 1987. Smith retired at the end of the year and was succeeded as chairman and chief executive officer by James A. Kielley. His goal was to make the company one of the world's two leading providers of management advice to top executives.

Mixed Results in the 1990s

The ensuing years were not good ones for Towers Perrin, although by the end of 1990 the company had more than 60 offices serving more than 8,000 clients. An absence of new federal laws and rules affecting benefit plans, plus a poor national economy and the maturing of the industry, made it harder than before for consultants to find new clients. Towers Perrin's revenue actually dipped from $714 million in 1990 to $686 million in 1991, resulting in a ten percent staff reduction that year and a 2.5 percent cut in its general management and compensation consulting employees the following year. An internal reorganization resulted in some unprofitable projects and led to an unusual number of resignations for a firm known for low turnover.

Towers Perrin continued to look for new business, however. In late 1992 the firm formed a health policy group to help clients prepare for potential changes in medical programs by the incoming Clinton administration. Its health and welfare practice experienced more growth—greater than ten percent—than any other area of its business in 1992. Towers Perrin also introduced Flex Planner, an interactive software program designed to help clients' employees make better-informed choices about their benefit needs, and Ben Val, software allowing employers to make quantitative comparisons between their benefit programs and those of other companies.

Towers Perrin also sought to draw into its fold Buck Consultants Inc., a rival firm one-fourth its size. Combined, the two companies would have been able to pass William M. Mercer Cos. Inc. to become the world's largest benefits consultant. But Buck surprised Towers Perrin in 1994 by offering to buy its bigger competitor for cash and stock. Towers Perrin quickly turned down the offer.

Towers Perrin established a workplace diversity unit in 1992, when it acquired Atlanta-based Diversity Consultants Inc. But it suffered bad publicity and confirmed cynics' opinions about management consultants when the *Wall Street Journal* published an article in 1997 reporting that the firm had offered practically identical workplace diversity recommendations to two different companies. The article went on to say that seven of the 11 other diversity reports provided to clients between late 1994 and late 1996 were also almost identical in their recommendations. After many hours of interviews with managers, employee surveys, and review of company documents, Towers Perrin's consultants produced, according to the newspaper, action plans replicating nearly all of Towers Perrin's basic strategies and tactics. A co-leader of the unit, speaking to Douglas A. Blackmon of the *Journal,* replied, ''That's just one piece of paper and then the real work begins. You're not seeing what we do to work with the president [of the company] to change the market strategy.''

Towers Perrin still ranked second among employee benefits consultants in 1997 and was seventh among actuarial firms. That year it acquired Partners Consulting Group, a healthcare adviser. In 1998 it added Tandem International, a Canadian management consulting firm, and Miller Howard Consulting Group, an Atlanta-based change management firm. It had acquired Kinsley Lord, a leading British change management firm, in 1995. Towers Perrin was appointed investment consultant to Singapore's monetary authority in 1999.

Towers Perrin in 1999

Towers Perrin's human resources and general management consulting unit was offering services in four broad categories in 1999: business strategy, in which the firm often was called upon to help define, clarify, or implement business strategy on an organizational, business unit, or functional level; organizational strategy, which it said called for evaluating every component process through the filter of business strategy to make sure that

Key Dates:

1934: Founding of Towers, Perrin, Forster & Crosby.
1950: TPF&C has grown ninefold in sales since its founding.
1982: Company acquires Cresap, McCormick and Paget.
1986: Acquisition of Tillinghast, Nelson & Warren.
1987: Company name is shortened to Towers Perrin.
1997: Towers Perrin ranks second in size among employee benefit consultants and seventh among actuarial firms.

strategy, structure, and processes were closely interwoven; people strategy, which called for understanding the roles people play in each business situation and making investments in people appropriate to those roles; and change management, intended to help firms learn how to embrace rather than resist change and to implement practices and processes that keep people engaged, productive, and focused on business results.

Towers Perrin's employee benefit services fell into three broad categories: benefit strategy, plan management, and benefit administration. The health industry consulting unit was serving health systems, physician organizations, insurers, and health plans in every U.S. market.

Tillinghast-Towers Perrin was providing management consulting to the financial services industry worldwide. This field of consulting was divided into financial services, property/casualty insurance, risk management, and health insurance. Towers Perrin Reinsurance was providing reinsurance intermediary services and consulting expertise that focused on the creative blending of traditional and nontraditional risk transfer vehicles. Towers Perrin also was offering an array of publications on topics relevant to its activities, many of them in the form of newsletters.

Principal Divisions

Tillinghast-Towers Perrin; Towers Perrin; Towers Perrin Reinsurance Co.

Principal Competitors

Booz Allen & Hamilton Inc.; McKinsey and Company Inc.; Mercer Consulting Group Inc.; Moritz Inc.

Further Reading

Blackmon, Douglas O., "Consultants' Advice on Diversity Was Anything But Diverse," *Wall Street Journal,* March 11, 1997, pp. A1, A16.

Byrne, John A., "A Specialist Slips into Big-League Consulting," *Business Week,* July 27, 1987, pp. 73, 76.

"Charles Perrin," in *National Cyclopedia of Biography,* Volume 56, Clifton, N.J.: James T. White & Co., 1975, p. 320.

Fletcher, Meg, "Merger Strengthens Tillinghast, TPF&C," *Business Insurance,* May 19, 1986, pp. 3, 29.

"H. Walter Forster, Business Counselor," *New York Times,* May 24, 1968, p. 47.

"John Alden Towers, Insurance Official," *New York Times,* November 20, 1956, p. 37.

"The New Shape of Management Consulting," *Business Week,* May 21, 1979, pp. 100–01.

"Towers Perrin Buys Cresap, McCormick, Also a Consulting Firm," *Wall Street Journal,* October 13, 1982, p. 14.

Woolsey, Christine, "Buck's Offer Falls Flat," *Business Insurance,* April 11, 1994, pp. 1, 45.

——, "For Benefit Consultants, Stalled Global Economy Results in Second Year of Slim Revenue Growth," *Business Insurance,* December 21, 1992, p. 11.

—Robert Halasz

TRC Companies, Inc.

5 Waterside Crossing
Windsor, Connecticut 06095
U.S.A.
Telephone: (860) 289-8631
Fax: (860) 298-6380
Web site: http://www.trcec.com

Public Company
Incorporated: 1969 as Travelers Research Corporation
Employees: 650
Sales: $78.22 million (1999)
Stock Exchanges: New York
Ticker Symbol: TRR
NAIC: 541620 Environmental Consulting Services; 541330 Engineering Consulting Services

TRC Companies, Inc. is one of the oldest and largest environmental engineering and consulting companies in the United States, begun just as such sweeping anti-pollution laws as the Clean Air Act and Clean Water Act were being passed by Congress. With regional offices in 20 U.S. cities as well as Lima, Peru, and Santiago, Chile, TRC offers a wide range of environmental services, from cleanup of Superfund sites to archaeological assessment. TRC and its five subsidiaries focus on air pollution control, solid and hazardous waste management, risk assessment, and natural and cultural resource management. TRC was the first air pollution engineering company to be listed on the New York Stock Exchange. The company's client base includes 300 companies in the *Fortune* 500. Federal government contracts account for about 20 percent of the company's work.

Origins: 1960s–70s

TRC has its roots in the Travelers Insurance Company of Hartford, Connecticut, which became concerned about environmentally related problems as it began to lose money on severe storm damage claims and noticed a shortage of weather forecasting facilities. They established two weather- and industrial hygiene-oriented research services in the 1950s, which in the early 1960s evolved into the Travelers Research Center, Inc.

By 1969, the research center went through another change, splitting into two new groups: a nonprofit, independent research organization, the Center for the Environment and Man, which focused on such fields as population growth, and the subsidiary Travelers Research Corporation, which concentrated on applied research and services. Within two years, however, Travelers decided to divest itself of its research arms. Management decided that Travelers Research Corporation would dissolve, and the Center for the Environment and Man would retain its assets and then affiliate with the University of Connecticut. However, 22 members of the Environmental Quality and Waste Management Department protested the move to academia, opting to remain in a profit-oriented organization serving governmental and industrial clients. With Traveler's approval, this small group struck out on its own as TRC—The Research Corporation of New England.

In an effort to locate capital, TRC became a subsidiary of VAST, Inc., an oceanographic research firm, headquartered in Boothbay Harbor, Maine, until VAST went bankrupt in 1974.

From the beginning, TRC grappled with how much work to pursue with the government. "We started with the mandate of serving industry," chief consulting scientist Richard A. Duffee, one of the founders of TRC, told *Inc.* magazine reporter Craig R. Waters in a long profile of the company published in 1984. "We wanted to be free of auditing, of government interference . . . and we preferred working with industry."

Buffeted by Politics: 1970s–80s

But TRC soon discovered, whether its clients were industry- or government-based, the political winds in Washington would shape the company's bottom line. From the Clean Air Act of 1969 through Superfund legislation in 1980, the five largest pieces of environmental legislation in U.S. history were passed in little more than a decade.

"It was a euphoric time when many companies concluded that what they had to sell, the client had to buy. . . . The government was a major forcing factor," recalled Vincent A. Rocco, who was president and later CEO and chairman of TRC from 1979 to 1997, in the *Inc.* article.

Company Perspectives:

TRC is a national environmental services company of more than 650 professionals with expertise in all areas of air quality and hazardous waste management, regulatory compliance and permitting, water resources engineering, air pollution engineering, risk assessment, and environmental liability consulting.

TRC is a multidisciplinary environmental consulting and engineering firm with proven experience. For over 30 years, we have been solving problems associated with regulatory and liability issues. The quality of our work has earned TRC a repeat business of over 80%. TRC's national network of offices allows us to respond quickly and effectively.

During the 1970s, TRC built up its client base, expanding air pollution and waste management services to help companies comply with the numerous new environmental regulations. The company prospered: TRC began with $600,000 in public utility contracts deeded to it by Travelers. A decade later it had annual revenues of $6.5 million, the bulk of which came through government contracts.

However, the flush times came to an abrupt halt after the election of President Ronald Reagan in 1980. No new environmental laws were passed, and enforcement of existing regulations grew more lax. Suddenly, there was less need for the company's services—either by industry or government. Revenues dropped from $9 million in 1980 to $7 million in 1984.

By the mid-1980s, however, more government money was being earmarked for environmental problems, such as acid rain, and TRC bounced back. The company enlarged its hazardous waste staff and began to expand a high-tech toxics measurement division.

In 1983, TRC became one of the few firms in the country to use mobile air testing equipment called the Trace Atmospheric Gas Analyzer, or TAGA. Mounted in two vans, TAGA was used to pinpoint pollutants inside office buildings as well as at hazardous waste sites. With the advent of TAGA, TRC's stock briefly more than doubled, and the *Boston Globe* designated the company as the fifth best-performing New England stock of 1983.

Through the rest of the 1980s and into the 1990s, the company continued to grow, adding subsidiaries, expanding into the global market, and working in such new fields as environmental database development. But success had its price tag, and the wild swings of the environmental market throughout the 1990s kept TRC on its toes.

The Tumultuous 1990s

TRC saw steady growth in revenue in the first half of the decade, from $51 million in 1991 to a record $93 million in 1995. This record growth came at a time when other environmental services firms were having a difficult time raising sales and profits. According to a 1993 *Chemical Week* article, the hazardous waste remediation industry was hit hard by the recession in the early 1990s as companies cut back on hiring outside firms to haul waste offsite for disposal and started incinerating it themselves.

In the article, Rocco looked ahead for ways the industry could prosper: "The timely issues for the next decade are process related—efficiency and pollution prevention," he said.

According to TRC's 1995 annual report, "The environmental services market in the United Sates is changing dramatically. The 'roar' of the environmental industry heard in the 1980s has been significantly muffled during the 1990s. Just five years ago, the environmental services industry was riding the crest of a steep growth curve that exceeded 15 percent per year. Those who claimed that the business was 'recession proof' have been proven wrong in the 1990s. Today the industry is facing increasingly fierce competition, overcapacity in many market segments, eroding profit margins and uncertainty from a new Congress with new priorities."

The report went on to say that "companies who were smart enough to prepare for the changes and quick enough off the mark to respond to new market needs" would nonetheless succeed, concluding: "we are happy to report that TRC is one of those forward thinking, quick-acting companies and therefore we continue to experience growth and profitability."

The early 1990s saw numerous new initiatives and acquisitions for TRC. In 1992, TRC acquired North American Weather Consultants, one of the oldest private meteorological consulting firms in the country, which worked in a variety of fields from cloud seeding to air quality measurement to long-range precipitation forecasts.

In 1994 TRC bought Irvine, California-based Environmental Solutions, Inc., the company's largest acquisition to date. The addition of Environmental Solutions allowed TRC to move into designing and building municipal and hazardous waste landfills and perform site cleanup work.

That year, TRC also acquired Mariah Associates, Inc. The company, begun in 1976, had offices in Laramie, Wyoming; Albuquerque, New Mexico; El Paso, Texas; and Austin, Texas. Mariah served industrial and governmental clients throughout the western United States. Projects ranged from fossil fuel extraction to power transmission to waste management.

TRC's acquisition of Garrow Associates, headquartered in Atlanta, Georgia, added professional cultural resource management to TRC's roster of services. Working throughout the United States and the Caribbean, TRC Garrow performed archaeology and historic preservation studies, along with protected species surveys and wetland evaluations. TRC Garrow had branch offices in Nashville, Tennessee, and Chapel Hill, North Carolina.

In 1996, TRC entered the global market by forming the first U.S. public-private partnership in Poland's post-communist history, a company called PATKO, S.A., with two of Poland's environmental funding agencies. PATKO was chartered by the Polish government to facilitate the importation of U.S. environmental technology and services into the Polish market. TRC worked on both air pollution and industrial water and wastewater plants there.

Key Dates:

1969: Travelers Research Corporation is spun off as a subsidiary of Travelers Insurance Company.
1971: Travelers Research Corporation dissolves, with its engineering and technical consulting services arm reforming as TRC–The Research Corporation of New England.
1979: Vincent Rocco is appointed president of TRC.
1983: TRC becomes one of the few firms in the country to use mobile air testing equipment called the Trace Atmospheric Gas Analyzer, or TAGA.
1992: TRC acquires North American Weather Consultants and Raymond Keyes Associates.
1994: TRC buys Environmental Solutions, Inc. and Mariah Associates, Inc.
1996: TRC enters the global market by forming the first U.S. public-private partnership in Poland's history.
1997: Vincent Rocco resigns and Richard Ellison becomes TRC president and CEO.

During the period, TRC also faced a legal challenge. In 1993, TRC paid $2.4 million to settle allegations that tests at toxic waste sites performed by a subsidiary, MetaTrace, for the U.S. Environmental Protection Agency (EPA) and for the Defense Department were done improperly. According to *American Metal Market*, MetaTrace, which went out of business in the early 1990s, had also previously pled guilty to making false certifications to the EPA. The company paid a $423,000 fine for this criminal charge.

The economic problems plaguing other environmental services firms soon caught up to TRC. TRC had been a little too hasty in painting a rosy future in its 1995 annual report. The next year, its revenues shrank by more than $16 million.

According to a 1996 interview in *Wall Street Transcript Digest*, Rocco said that the environmental consulting and engineering market was ''flat to down'' over prior years. ''Most of the stocks in the environmental sector, particularly the consulting/engineering sector, are at all-time lows,'' the digest reported. Rocco said that there was ''a lack of definition by either party on their environmental initiatives, no new regulations and a real lack of focus in enforcing existing regulations.''

Through the late 1990s, TRC worked to recoup its losses and to remediate its own internal problems. In 1997, longtime Chairman and CEO Vincent Rocco resigned along with TRC President Bruce Cowen. Their resignations came during an investigation about stock options that Rocco and Cowen exercised, and that TRC's board had not authorized. Richard Ellison, who had served for 13 years as president of TRC Environmental Solutions, was named president and CEO.

The company soon bounced back, winning in 1998 a bid for a five-year, $10 million contract with the Federal Aviation Administration for performing environmental investigations and the preparation of remedial designs at FAA's William J. Hughes Technical Center, a research and development facility in Atlantic City, New Jersey.

That year, TRC also pioneered the concept of environmental liability transfer, taking over responsibility for the parties originally held liable for cleanup of Superfund and less contaminated sites. Traditionally, cleanup of Superfund sites could drag on for years as lawsuit after lawsuit was filed over liability for cleanup costs. TRC dubbed its innovative program Exit Strategy.

In 1999, TRC began cleanup of Maine's largest Superfund site, the Portland-Bangor Waste Oil site. TRC assumed the liability of nearly 400 of the major companies in the case, many of whom sent their used motor oil to the dump.

A 1998 *Wall Street Journal* article called the project a ''radical experiment.'' According to the article, the basic cleanup costs were between $10 million and $15 million, but the actual numbers had not been released. The article quoted EPA Administrator Carol Browner on the project, saying it ''sounds like good old American ingenuity to me.''

TRC's work on the project was backed up by a $30 million insurance policy from American International Group. The policy provided protection against unexpected cost increases due to newly discovered contamination or changed conditions.

In a 1999 company press release, Mike Salmon, TRC's senior vice-president responsible for the Exit Strategy program, said that, ''The potentially responsible parties pay a lower overall cost and receive a full release of their liability without litigation. . . . Most importantly, the community will have the site closed much quicker. We plan to have the basic remediation work completed by the end of 2000.''

In October 1999, TRC announced the award of another Exit Strategy project. The $47 million project, contracted with Duke Energy Field Services, would restore 14 natural gas plants and more than 350 ancillary facilities. Year-end also saw a number of other new projects and acquisitions by the company.

In January 1999, TRC acquired Alton Geoscience, which was headquartered adjacent to TRC's largest West Coast office, in Irvine, California. Alton's main activities included site investigations, remediation, and monitoring services for major oil and pipeline companies.

In April 1999, TRC acquired New Jersey-based Vectre Corporation, expanding TRC's brownfields remediation work. Brownfields sites are previously used industrial properties that have not been redeveloped because of concerns about liabilities associated with contamination.

In June, TRC went on to buy A & H Engineers, a transportation consulting and engineering firm headquartered in New York City. ''Together with our recent acquisition of Vectre Corporation in northern New Jersey, TRC has completed its 1999 goal to establish a solid and comprehensive platform to support substantial public and private sector growth in the New York/New Jersey area,'' CEO and President Richard Ellison said in a press release.

To ensure the company would be a player in the Information Age, TRC acquired a start-up environmental compliance software firm, DMR Data, Include, based in New York. DMR's software enabled users to file pollution discharge reports electronically.

The company's 1999 annual report made a few projections for the company's future. A letter from Ellison to shareholders predicted that the company's greatest fiscal 2000 growth would occur with the startup of several new Exit Strategy projects. Ellison predicted ''triple digit'' growth in the field. However, he said growth in environmental services ''will be modest as a reflection of the maturity of the business, although growth in energy deregulatory areas may be substantial.''

Long-term growth in information management was also expected to be high, he said. The company planned to focus on the Sun Belt and West Coast, where ''projected population growth rates will require the continuous development of infrastructure.''

Principal Subsidiaries

TRC Environmental Corporation; TRC Environmental Solutions, Inc.; TRC Garrow Associates; TRC Mariah Associates; TRC North American Weather Consultants; TRC Raymond Keyes Associates.

Principal Competitors

CH2M Hill Ltd.; Dames & Moore, Inc.; EMCON; Environmental Elements; Environmental Resources Management; Harding Lawson Associates Group, Inc.; ICF Kaiser International, Inc.; IDM Environmental; IT Group; Roy F. Weston; Safety-Kleen Corp.; Thermo Terra Tech; Thermo Retec; Waste Management, Inc.

Further Reading

''CEO Interview, Vincent A. Rocco, Chairman and CEO, Discusses the Outlook for TRC,'' *Wall Street Transcript Digest,* September 9, 1996.

Fialka, John J., ''Maine Experiment May Point the Way to Ending Tangle of Litigation Around U.S. Superfund Law,'' *Wall Street Journal,* April 29, 1998.

Mullin, Rick, ''New Direction on Hazwaste,'' *Chemical Week,* January 20, 1993, p. 26.

''TRC Pays $2.4 Million to Settle Toxic Waste Allegations Dispute,'' *American Metal Market,* September 14, 1993, p. 4.

Waters, Craig R., ''When Uncle Sam Sneezes: Environmental Consulting Firm Survives the Whim of Washington,'' *Inc.,* May 1984, p. 127.

—Barbara Ruben

Treasure Chest Advertising Company, Inc.

250 West Pratt, 18th Floor
Baltimore, Maryland 21201
U.S.A.
Telephone: (410) 528-9800
Fax: (410) 528-9288
Web site: http://www.tcadvertising.com

Wholly Owned Subsidiary of Big Flower Holdings, Inc.
Incorporated: 1997
Employees: 5,000
Sales: $1.1 billion (1998)
NAIC: 323110 Commercial Lithographic Printing; 541860 Direct Mail Advertising

Treasure Chest Advertising Company, Inc. (TC Advertising), is the leading supplier in the United States of advertising inserts, newspaper supplements, and other advertising products and services for publishers and advertisers. With more than 20 production facilities located across the United States, TC Advertising produces more than 20 billion ad inserts every year and serves nearly 700 major clients nationwide. Its major markets include general retail, drugstore, grocery, home improvement, and specialty retail. TC Advertising also prints TV magazines, special supplements, Sunday magazines, and Sunday comics that newspapers use to build circulation. As a subsidiary of Big Flower Holdings, Inc., TC Advertising works with other Big Flower companies to provide clients with a complete range of advertising solutions and communications services.

Rapid Growth: 1967–93

Founded in 1967, Treasure Chest Advertising Company, Inc., began in Glendora, California, as a small weekly shopper called the *Treasure Chest of Values.* It was started by two brothers, Paul and Bob Milhous, who bought a used printing press to publish the retail advertising circular. By 1974 revenues were $20 million. During the year the company purchased its first printing press, and from 1974 to 1989 the company grew rapidly. Sales reached $100 million in 1980.

By 1988 TC Advertising had captured 14 percent of the $3.5 billion commercial printing business in the United States. The company's strategy was to locate its production plants near major markets, in order to better service retailers and provide them with a faster turnaround.

While the firm was national in scope, it was more focused on the western United States. Three of its printing plants were located in California, and the firm's market share exceeded 20 percent in the West. In addition to circulars, it printed supplements such as Sunday comics and television magazines for publications such as the *Los Angeles Times* and the *Baltimore Sun.*

A major factor in the company's success was how it managed new printing technologies. It was quick to adopt electronics, using automated printing processes and computer-controlled inking systems. In addition, the firm pioneered new formats for advertising circulars.

In 1989 the company launched the Quality Improvement Process (QIP), which was based on the philosophy of quality management pioneer Dr. W. Edwards Deming. The QIP program formalized TC Advertising's commitment to continuous improvement. It enabled the company to maintain the highest standards and to educate its employees and customers about the latest techniques in print production and advertising.

In 1989 sales passed the half-billion mark, rising to around $550 million. The company owned 15 printing facilities and was the largest printer of retail advertising circulars in the United States. It had 3,400 employees and 25 sales offices.

Expansion Under Big Flower: 1993–99

In 1993 TC Advertising's revenues were $761 million. That year it was acquired by Big Flower Holdings, Inc., then known as Big Flower Press Holdings, Inc. As part of Big Flower, TC Advertising benefited from collaboration with its affiliated companies, Laser Tech Color, Webcraft, Inc., and Columbine JDS.

Company Perspectives:

TC Advertising is the nation's leader in producing high impact targetable advertising insert programs and circulation building products such as Sunday comics, TV magazines, Sunday magazines, and special supplements. With our electronic prepess capabilities and comprehensive products and services, we develop effective and powerful advertising inserts. TC Advertising delivers the vast resources of one of the world's largest offset printers. Our substantial coast-to-coast production capacity gives customers cost savings resulting from considerable efficiencies of scale, fast turnaround times even with the largest orders and tightest deadlines, consistently high quality even on multi-plant runs due to the uniformity of systems, and dependable upgraded materials.

Key Dates:

1967: Paul and Bob Milhous start a weekly shopper called *Treasure Chest of Values* in Glendora, California.
1974: The company purchases its first new printing press.
1980: Revenues reach $100 million.
1989: Revenues surpass $500 million.
1993: Company is acquired by Big Flower Holdings, Inc., then known as Big Flower Press Holdings, Inc.
1995: TC Advertising moves its executive offices from Glendora to Baltimore, Maryland.
1999: Big Flower stockholders approve the merger of Big Flower with BFH Merger Corp., an affiliate of Thomas H. Lee Company and Evercore Capital Partners LP.

Laser Tech Color, also known as The LTC Group, was an industry leader in supplying outsourced, digital premedia, content management, and multimedia and Internet services.

Webcraft, Inc. was a market leader in direct marketing services, including highly personalized direct mail, database management, commercial games, and fragrance samplers. Columbine JDS, finally, offered a variety of automation systems for electronic media advertising. It was a leading provider of computer-based systems that managed the placement of broadcast advertisements, programming material, and sales information data for television stations, radio stations, broadcast and cable networks, and direct broadcast satellite services.

TC Advertising expanded in 1994 with the strategic acquisitions of both Retail Graphics, headquartered in Dallas, Texas, and KTB Associates, located in Saugerties, New York. The acquisition gave TC Advertising a total of 17 printing plants, three of which were from the Retail Graphics acquisition. Retail Graphics had an estimated $91.8 million in sales in 1993.

Toward the end of 1995 TC Advertising moved its executive offices from Glendora to Baltimore, Maryland. The move brought TC Advertising closer to the majority of its customers and plants, as well as nearer to its parent company, which was headquartered in New York City. Revenues for fiscal 1995 (ending June 30) were nearly $900 million, nearly doubling over the previous two years.

Big Flower continued to make acquisitions on behalf of its operating companies. In October 1996, Printco, Inc., in Greenville, Michigan, joined the TC Advertising family. In October 1997, Riverside County Publishing Company (RCPC) in Riverside, California, and First Western Graphics in San Leandro, California, were acquired. With two printing facilities, RCPC added to TC Advertising's production capacity on the West Coast. The company was an experienced printer of advertising inserts for retailers and had revenues of approximately $130 million.

In 1995 TC Advertising began developing its proprietary Target Reach marketing solution tool in association with ReachAmerica, Inc., a software development and database marketing company. Target Reach was a proprietary database information system that enabled advertisers to customize their insert advertising to match the demographic characteristics of more than 20,000 newspaper delivery zones in the top 300 markets in the United States. Target Reach was launched in 1997, and in 1998 Big Flower acquired ReachAmerica, Inc. Through Target Reach, TC Advertising was able to combine sophisticated database marketing techniques with the ability to produce full-color, high-impact advertising inserts.

The acquisition of Reach America, Inc., added to TC Advertising's resources through software development and database marketing. Advertising solutions offered by TC Advertising began with identifying and locating the optimal target audience and ended with the delivery of high-impact advertising and marketing materials into the customers' hands.

Another new program that ReachAmerica brought to TC Advertising was Newspaper MarketReach, which enabled newspaper sales representatives to better serve local businesses through advertising and direct-mail services. Newspaper MarketReach offered complete end-to-end marketing solutions for both publishers and advertisers.

In 1999 TC Advertising's parent, Big Flower Holdings, Inc., began exploring ways to recapitalize. In June it announced that it had reached an agreement with Thomas H. Lee Co., a Boston-based private equity firm, and Evercore Partners, a provider of strategic and financial advisory services. Under the terms of the agreement, a new entity, BFH Merger Corporation, was to be formed by Lee and Evercore for the purpose of recapitalizing Big Flower at $1.9 billion. The agreement was approved by shareholders in November 1999.

TC Advertising's capabilities were further expanded when Big Flower acquired AdOut, a provider of newspaper outsourcing capabilities, in August 1999. Based in Van Nuys, California, AdOut was the largest newspaper advertising production company in the United States. It had expertise in designing and producing retail and classified display ads for newspapers and advertisers. It was the first and only company to successfully outsource the advertising prepress workflow of multiple metropolitan newspapers. The acquisition expanded AdOut's access to newspaper clients and gave TC Advertising the chance to offer a broader range of advertising solutions.

Positioned for the Future

In October 1999 the sales office and production plant in Salt Lake City, Utah, moved into a new facility that doubled press capacity to more than 100,000 square feet with seven presses. The facility also included an in-house digital photography studio operated by The LTC Group. In addition to printing, the company's services included consumer and media research, electronic premedia, freight and transportation, and database marketing. The company was positioned to take advantage of the growth in Internet advertising and electronic commerce, having invested in at least one Internet advertising agency and offering a program, SecureTran Virtual Retailing, to deliver secure, high-volume Internet transactions to retailers.

Principal Competitors

Quebecor Printing (USA) Corp.; R.R. Donnelley & Sons Co.; Schawk Inc.

Further Reading

Henderson, Barry. ''KC's Treasure Chest Printer Buys Dallas Printer,'' *Kansas City Business Journal,* August 5, 1994, p. 18.

Jacobs, Chip. ''Treasure Chest: Printer Captures Nation's Newspaper Insert Niche,'' *Los Angeles Business Journal,* February 5, 1990, p. S42.

''Treasure Chest Advertising Inc.,'' *Baltimore Business Journal,* January 26, 1996, p. S25.

—David P. Bianco

Tri Valley Growers

12667 Alcosta Boulevard
San Ramon, California 94583
U.S.A.
Telephone: (925) 327-6400
Fax: (925) 327-6986
Web site: http://www.trivalleygrowers.com

Cooperative Company
Incorporated: 1932 as Tri Valley Packing Association
Employees: 11,000
Sales: $782 million (1998)
NAIC: 311421 Fruit and Vegetable Canning (pt)

Tri Valley Growers is a leading U.S. food processor. Owned by its 500 member-growers, Tri Valley produces over 50 percent of the nation's canned peaches, 20 percent of its canned olives, and ten percent of its canned tomatoes. In addition to making its own private-label brands of canned fruits and vegetables, Tri Valley sells its goods under a variety of well-recognized brand names, such as S&W Fine Foods, Libby's, Oberti Olives, Redpack Tomatoes, Tuttorosso Tomatoes, and Sacramento Tomato Juice. The company runs eight plants in California, as well as one in New Jersey, and sells its canned goods to supermarkets, foodservice companies, and the government. Tri Valley Growers came into existence after the 1963 merger between two large California fruit and vegetable cooperatives: Tri Valley Packing Association and Turlock Cooperative Growers.

Tri Valley Packing Association: 1932–63

Tri Valley Packing Association (TVPA) was founded in 1932 by George Pfarr. A peach farmer, Pfarr was shaken by the plummeting prices of his key crop during the Great Depression and the devastation it wrought on the agricultural industry. (The price for yellow clingstone peaches dropped from $80 a ton to $6.50 a ton between 1929 and 1932). Pfarr's goal was to enable individual farmers like himself to withstand the vicissitudes of the market. If fruit and vegetable growers were able to band together and cooperate in the sale and marketing of their products, they could better protect themselves from the bust and boom cycles of the commodities market, command more favorable prices from suppliers, and access a greater pool of resources. As his first step towards making his ideal a reality, Pfarr purchased the fruit and vegetable canning plants of the Armour Packing Company in Visalia, Modesto, and San Jose, California, in 1931. After incorporating TVPA, Pfarr became general manager of the San Jose facility. To ensure harmony among the grower-members, all products were included in one pool—instead of operating separate pools for each commodity. After overhead costs were paid at the end of production, the net income was divided among all pool members. This system ensured that the producers of one crop could not dominate the co-op. At the close of 1932, TVPA had 89 grower-members.

TVPA survived the Depression, and experienced rapid growth during World War II. Demand for TVPA's canned fruits and vegetables was constant during the war years, as the federal government—needing to supply fruits and vegetables to the armed forces abroad—became a key customer. (At this time, canning was the only way to preserve these otherwise perishable goods). While wartime demand proved to be a boon to TVPA and the overall canning industry, other circumstances of that period posed significant challenges to canners' economic success. Profit margins were limited by the price ceilings the government imposed on canned goods and vegetables (as well as on a slew of other products). Moreover, labor shortages caused payroll costs to skyrocket. A substantial percentage of working men were shipped overseas to fight the Axis powers, and those workers who remained at home could command a hefty hourly wage. TVPA addressed these problems by using increased mechanization to reduce the number of employees it needed. For instance, the company worked to develop an effective pear ripening system, and a peach pitter that would speed the processing of fruit.

The prosperous postwar years brought their own challenges as well. The population of San Jose and the California Bay Area boomed. Between 1940 and 1950, San Jose's population rose from 68,457 to 95,280. As residential areas expanded, TVPA came under increasing pressure to make sure its processing plants could safely and comfortably coexist with its new neigh-

Company Perspectives:

Tri Valley Growers' vision is to make it economically beneficial for the independent and family farmer and rancher to remain in the agricultural business. Moving growers up the food chain closer to the customer and enabling them to realize a fair share for their efforts.

bors. Waste disposal (especially of cull fruit) became a major concern.

The nature of the canned food industry had also changed in the postwar era, driven primarily by the emergence of regional and then national supermarket chains. While producers like TVPA had previously been able to sell their goods to a few local brokers and buyers (with whom the processors had cultivated personal relationships), the rise of grocery store chains necessitated a much more aggressive marketing and distribution system. As supermarket chains expanded over ever widening geographical areas, companies such as TVPA had to meet the needs of regional markets. The development of the interstate highway system meant that supermarkets could buy their canned goods from one (often geographically distant) producer. The result was that canning companies' transportation costs escalated, as they trucked their merchandise to far-away outposts. The dominance of supermarket chains also spurred canning companies to produce a wider range of products. TVPA's "ability to supply a diversity of products was becoming a competitive necessity," according to *Tri Valley Growers: 50 Years of Survival and Growth.*

TVPA responded to these pressures in several ways. In 1954, the company addressed the problem of product variety with the addition of several new canned products, including tomatoes, tomato juice, sweet potatoes, asparagus, freestone peaches, boysenberries, and mustard and turnip greens. In 1956, TVPA acquired the Aron Canning Company near Stockton, California, which allowed TVPA to expand its operations and also to enter into the burgeoning tomato paste sector. (Although tomatoes had once been considered an insignificant crop, their harvest and price soared in the 1950s.) The company also stepped up its marketing efforts—especially in the essential Los Angeles area—to increase its visibility among both consumers and supermarkets.

Turlock Cooperative Growers: 1929–63

Tri Valley Growers' other progenitor, Turlock Cooperative Growers (TCG), was founded by five growers motivated by concerns and ambitions similar to Pfarr's. Initially, TCG served only as a marketing agency for its grower-members, but in 1934 the cooperative began packing its own fruit after it acquired the McHenry Station in Modesto, California. Buffeted by the same tectonic shifts as TVPA and other California food processors, TCG had the additional challenge of running a multiple pool payout system, which added to the friction between members. As the company's morale dipped in the late 1950s, TCG converted to a single pool system in 1957. One year later, the company acquired the Morpak Preserving Company in Stockton, California. With this purchase, Turlock decisively entered the production of tomato paste—Morpak had produced 41 percent of all tomato paste in the state.

The Formation of Tri Valley Growers

Although both TVPA and TCG had survived the tumultuous changes of the postwar decade, the canning business became more competitive in the early 1960s. Larger processors could cut better dealers with suppliers, such as can manufacturers and sugar producers, and smaller canners were being forced out of business as the industry consolidated. The board members of both TVPA and TCG began to contemplate a merger between the two cooperatives as a solution to the industry's fierce competition. As a TVPA board member stated in a leaflet circulated among his colleagues, "[The] concentration forces independents to expand or merge in order to survive." Talks between the two companies began in 1962, and in 1963 TVPA and TCG agreed to merge their member pools. In an effort to preserve the identity of each corporation, the name Tri Valley Growers was adopted for the cooperative that emerged from the union. The new entity could claim $45 million in annual sales (TVPA had generated about $29 million in revenue in 1962, while TCG had taken in approximately $19 million that year) and, more importantly, was a much more commanding presence in the fruit and vegetable processing industry.

Tri Valley acted quickly to capitalize on its new power. In 1964, Tri Valley formed a joint venture with another California fruit and vegetable cooperative—California Canners and Growers (Cal Can)—in order to reduce the total overhead costs of the cans that were essential to both companies' business. To do so, Tri Valley and Cal Can launched CT Supply Company—a can manufacturing plant in Modesto. Both companies were expected to realize significant savings from this bit of vertical integration. As industry-wide consolidation continued apace, Tri Valley also acquired the Oberti Olive Company in 1965.

In 1966, Tri Valley made the bold decision to transfer its primary canning operations from San Jose to Modesto. The population of the Bay Area had continued to grow at a rapid rate, with San Jose's population alone doubling between 1950 and 1960. Waste management continued to plague Tri Valley, making a move to a more rural area an attractive option. Even more importantly, most of Tri Valley's member-growers had long since relocated their farms to the less populated San Joaquin Valley in central California. "It was felt that transportation costs could be cut down by placing the food processing plants nearer to the production areas," explained *Tri Valley Growers: 50 Years of Survival and Growth.*

The relocation was a massive undertaking. Plant 7, as the new facility was named, cost an estimated $15 million to build, and caused a great deal of upheaval. A part of the move to Modesto was to be the simultaneous closing of Tri Valley's outdated, urban processing facilities and the incorporation of their multiple functions under one roof. But in addition to the logistical nightmare this task presented—shutting down operations and physically moving essential pieces of each plant's equipment to Modesto—the consolidation took its toll on Tri Valley's employees. Merging the four facilities into one created

Key Dates:

1929: Turlock Cooperative Growers (TCG) is formed.
1932: Tri Valley Packing Association (TVPA) is incorporated.
1963: TVPA and TCG merge to form Tri Valley Growers.
1966: Tri Valley Growers begins construction of Plant 7 in Modesto as it implements a major relocation of its primary canning operations.
1978: Tri Valley acquires S&W Fine Foods.
1995: Joe Famalette becomes Tri Valley's president and chief executive officer.
1996: Tri Valley offers stock to its grower-members.
1998: Company reports worst loss in its history.

management redundancies. As a result, some senior employees at individual plants were demoted at Plant 7.

The 1970s and 1980s

After withstanding the upheaval of relocation, Tri Valley faced new obstacles. Returns for member-growers were dismal in 1969, 1970, and 1971 because of labor strikes, high interest rates, and general chaos stemming from the move. Just as the proverbial ''light at the end of the tunnel'' emerged in 1971—with Plant 7 reaching full production capacity—the overall canned goods industry slid into what would become a two-decades-long slump. During this period, consolidation continued to exact its toll on fruit and vegetable processors. Between 1970 and 1985, the number of fruit canners decreased from about 70 to seven. Tri Valley responded to the rampant consolidation by trying to expand its own presence in the marketplace. In 1976 the company purchased two canneries owned by the Joan of Arc Company in Turlock, California. Tri Valley then acquired S&W Fine Foods, a manufacturer and distributor of premium quality fruits and vegetables in 1978. S&W, whose origins dated back to 1896, offered Tri Valley a formidable distribution network in the western United States, as well as in select markets in the Midwest, New York, and New England. Tri Valley operated S&W as a wholly owned subsidiary. In 1983, Tri Valley also bought California Canners and Growers, the second largest canning cooperative in the state.

Despite these efforts, however, Tri Valley—like its rivals—was plagued by increased competition from the cheap canned fruit imports that were flooding onto the U.S. market from countries such as Greece, Chile, and Argentina. Even more devastating to Tri Valley was the changing tastes of consumers. Canned food consumption steadily declined throughout the 1970s and 1980s. ''Canned food is considered old fashioned,'' an industry analyst told the *San Francisco Chronicle* on September 25, 1989. While canning had once been the only way to preserve (and quickly prepare) fruits and vegetables, the widespread use of the microwave in the 1970s made frozen foods popular. Moreover, spurred on by the trend toward increased health consciousness in the 1970s and 1980s, consumers eschewed syrup-packed fruit in favor of fresh produce. Between 1982 and 1989, U.S. consumption of fresh fruits and vegetables rose on average 2.5 percent a year, while purchases of canned produce dropped 1.5 percent during the same period.

Trying to adapt to this shift, Tri Valley began offering more healthy canned choices. The company introduced fruit packed in ''its own juices'' instead of heavy syrup, and also spiced up some of its products, rolling out concepts such as S&W Cajun Stewed Tomatoes. In 1984, Tri Valley joined a four-year industry-wide public relations campaign aimed at dispelling the false belief that canned produce was less nutritious.

The 1990s and Beyond

The prolonged canned foods decline came to a halt in the early 1990s, as U.S. consumption of canned fruits and vegetables steadied. In particular, Tri Valley benefited from the increased demand for canned produce caused by the Gulf War in 1991. In 1995, Tri Valley's board sought to boost the company's sales and profits, and appointed Joe Famalette as its new president and chief executive officer. Although Tri Valley's chairman of the board crowed to the *Modesto Bee* that ''Joe Famalette [was] clearly the kind of visionary we were seeking,'' his hiring became a controversial decision. Famalette made it his mission to ''focus more on [Tri Valley's] core competencies of marketing, growing, and processing food products,'' as he told the February 12, 1997, Modesto Bee. In January 1996, he consolidated S&W into Tri Valley's operations, cutting 60 jobs but generating $5 million in sales. Tri Valley next announced in October of that year that it would fire an additional 65 employees by moving the company's customer service operations from San Ramon, California, to Modesto. In 1997, Tri Valley also sold off its trucking division.

However, the most widespread change occurred in 1996 when Tri Valley issued stock to its 530 member-growers in an attempt to raise capital. Growers received shares of stock instead of cash from the cooperative's pooling system. ''The biggest problem cooperatives face is capital, being as fluid as a public company,'' one member-grower told the *Modesto Bee* on August 3, 1996. ''This will help us compete with [huge food companies such as] ConAgra [and] Del Monte. . . .'' Another key strategic shift took place in 1997, when Tri Valley embarked on a joint venture with Cirio, an Italian food processor. In an effort to address a nagging trade imbalance (exports of produce had been declining for years—by 1992, the United States was the smallest fruit exporter in the world), the arrangement empowered Tri Valley to market Cirio's products in the U.S., Canada, and Mexico, while Cirio would sell Tri Valley's canned goods in Italy.

But this spate of restructuring had disastrous results. Despite booming agricultural yields in the San Joaquin Valley, Tri Valley reported a loss of $53 million for the fiscal year 1998. Accusations flew that Famalette had deliberately concealed the company's losses. In August 1998, Famalette resigned, and was replaced by Jeff Shaw. Although Tri Valley had to face its substantial losses, the company retained considerable advantages. Not only did the company control over one half of the market for processed peaches, pears, and apricots, it also maintained a 20 percent share of the market for olives and ten percent of the processed tomato business. ''I'm not here to change things that don't need to be changed,'' Shaw announced in a Tri

Valley press release. ''I'm here to get the company focused back on our customer and employees. . . .''

Principal Competitors

Del Monte Foods Company; Dole Food Company, Inc.; Pro-Fac Cooperative, Inc.; Chiquita Brands International, Inc.; ConAgra, Inc.; Diageo plc; H.J. Heinz Company; Seneca Foods Corporation.

Further Reading

Beckett, Jamie, ''Decline of California Canners,'' *San Francisco Chronicle,* September 25, 1989.

Estrada, Richard, ''California's Tri Valley Growers Takes Back-to-Basics Approach,'' *Modesto Bee,* September 14, 1998.

——, ''Top Executive at California's Valley Growers Departs,'' *Modesto Bee,* August 8, 1988.

——, ''Tri Valley Growers Go Public, Privately,'' *Modesto Bee,* August 3, 1996.

——, ''TVG to Sell Trucking Division,'' *Modesto Bee,* February 12, 1997.

Schacht, Harry, ''Canned Fruit Industry Under Pressure,'' *San Francisco Chronicle,* November 3, 1992.

Tri Valley Growers: 50 Years of Survival and Growth, San Ramon: Tri Valley Growers, 1983.

''TVG Timeline,'' *Modesto Bee,* August 7, 1998.

Watson, Lloyd, ''New Chief for State's Top Canning Co-op,'' *San Francisco Chronicle,* May 24, 1985.

—Rebecca Stanfel

Unilever

Unilever PLC
P.O. Box 68
Unilever House
Blackfriars
London EC4P 4BQ
United Kingdom
Telephone: (0171) 822-5252
Fax: (0171) 822-5951
Web site: http://www.unilever.com

Unilever N.V.
Weena 455
P.O. Box 760
3000 DK Rotterdam
The Netherlands
Telephone: (10) 217-4000
Fax: (10) 217-4798

Public Company
Incorporated: 1929 as Unilever Limited and Unilever N.V.
Employees: 265,000
Sales: £27.09 billion (US$44.90 billion) (1998)
Stock Exchanges: Amsterdam London New York Paris Frankfurt Brussels Zurich Luxembourg Vienna
Ticker Symbol: UN
NAIC: 311223 Other Oilseed Processing; 311225 Fats & Oils Refining & Blending; 311411 Frozen Fruit, Juice, & Vegetable Processing; 311412 Frozen Specialty Food Manufacturing; 311421 Fruit & Vegetable Canning; 311520 Ice Cream & Frozen Dessert Manufacturing; 311712 Fresh & Frozen Seafood Processing; 311920 Coffee & Tea Manufacturing; 311941 Mayonnaise, Dressing, & Other Prepared Sauce Manufacturing; 311942 Spice & Extract Manufacturing; 312111 Soft Drink Manufacturing; 325611 Soap & Other Detergent Manufacturing; 325620 Toilet Preparation Manufacturing

If the adage ''two heads are better than one'' applies to business, then certainly Unilever is a prime example. The food and consumer products giant actually has two parent companies: Unilever PLC, based in the United Kingdom, and Unilever N.V., based in The Netherlands. The two companies, which operate virtually as a single corporation, are run by a single group of directors and are linked by a number of agreements. Unilever considers itself the second largest consumer goods firm in the world, trailing only Philip Morris Companies Inc., and produces numerous brand name foods, cleaning products, and personal care items. About 52 percent of revenues are generated in the foods sector; brands include Imperial and Promise margarines, Lipton tea, Ragú foods, Lawry's seasonings, Breyers ice cream, and Birds Eye and Gorton's frozen foods. One-quarter of sales come from the personal care area; brands include Caress and Dove soap, Pears and Pond's skin care products, Degree, Fabergé, and Sure deodorants, Suave and Salon Selectives hair care items, Close-Up, Mentadent, and Pepsodent oral care products, and Calvin Klein, Elizabeth Arden, and Elizabeth Taylor prestige fragrances—as well as such miscellaneous brands as Q-Tips and Vaseline. Unilever's third major sector is that of cleaning products, which is responsible for about 22 percent of turnover; brands include Wisk and All laundry detergents, Snuggle and Final Touch fabric softeners, and Sunlight dish detergents, and this area also includes the company's line of institutional cleaning products. Unilever maintains production facilities in 88 countries and sells its products in an additional 70. About 47 percent of revenues originate in Europe, 21 percent in North America, 14 percent in the Asia-Pacific region, 12 percent in Latin America, and six percent in Africa and the Middle East.

Soap and Margarine Origins

William Hesketh Lever, later Lord Leverhulme, was born in Bolton, England, in 1851. The founder of Lever Brothers, Lever had a personality that combined ''the rationality of the business man with the restless ambitions of the explorer,'' according to Unilever historian Charles Wilson.

During the depression of the 1880s, Lever, then a salesman for his father's wholesale grocery business, recognized the advantages of not only selling, but also manufacturing, soap, a noncyclical necessity item. His father, James Lever, initially was opposed to the idea, believing that they should remain grocers, not manufacturers. He softened, however, in the face of his son's determination. In 1885 William established a soap factory in Warrington as a branch of the family grocery business. Within a short time Lever was selling his soap throughout

Company Perspectives:

Our purpose in Unilever is to meet the everyday needs of people—everywhere—to anticipate the aspirations of our consumers and customers and to respond creatively and competitively with branded products and services which raise the quality of life.

Our deep roots in local cultures and markets around the world are our unparalleled inheritance and the foundation for our future growth. We will bring our wealth of knowledge and international expertise to the service of local consumers—a truly multi-local multinational.

Our long term success requires a total commitment to exceptional standards of performance and productivity, to working together effectively and to a willingness to embrace new ideas and learn continuously.

We believe that to succeed requires the highest standards of corporate behaviour towards our employees, consumers and the societies and world in which we live.

This is Unilever's road to sustainable, profitable growth for our business and long-term value creation for our shareholders and employees.

the United Kingdom, as well as in continental Europe, North America, Australia, and South Africa.

William also began a tradition that lasted well into the 20th century—that of producing all its raw components. Lever Brothers, a vertically integrated company, grew to include milling operations used to crush seeds into vegetable oil for margarine as well as packaging and transporting businesses for all of its products, which then included Lux, Lifebuoy, Rinso, and Sunlight soaps.

In 1914, as the German Navy began to threaten the delivery of food imports—particularly Danish butter and Dutch margarine—to Britain, the British government asked William Lever to produce margarine. He eagerly accepted the opportunity, believing that the margarine business would be compatible with the soap business because the products both required oils and fats as raw materials. Lever Brothers' successful diversification, however, now put the company in competition with Jurgens and Van den Bergh, two leading Dutch margarine companies.

1920s: The Birth of Unilever

Jurgens and Van den Bergh both began commercial production of margarine in 1872. Fierce competitors for the remainder of the century, Van den Bergh and Jurgens decided in 1908 to pool their interests in an effort to make the best of the poor economic situation that existed in most of the world. Competition in the margarine industry had intensified, fueled by an increasing number of smaller firms, which were exporting their products and lowering their prices to get a piece of the market. Van den Bergh eliminated the potential for problems such as double taxation—which arose from its interests in both Holland and the United Kingdom—by creating and incorporating two parent companies for itself, one in Holland and one in England. In 1920 Jurgens and Van de Bergh decided there was strength in numbers and joined with another margarine manufacturer, Schicht, in Bohemia. In 1927 the three companies, borrowing the ideal of a dual structure from Van de Bergh, formed Margarine Union Limited, a group of Dutch firms with interests in England, and Margarine Unie N.V., located in Holland.

Through the middle and late 1920s, the oil and fat trades continued to grow. Although the activities of Margarine Unie and Margarine Union were focused on edible fats (margarine), the companies had held soap interests throughout Europe for years. Similarly, although Lever Brothers had produced margarine since World War I, its focus was soap. After two years of discussion, the companies decided that an ''alliance wasted less of everybody's substance than hostility'' and merged on September 2, 1929.

As it does today, the newly formed Unilever consisted of two holding companies: Unilever Limited, previously Margarine Union; and Unilever N.V., formerly Margarine Unie. The new organization included an equalization agreement to assure equal profits for shareholders of both companies, as well as identically structured boards. Unilever's parent companies were actually holding companies supervising the operations of hundreds of manufacturing and trading firms worldwide. The end result of the merger was a company that bought and processed more than a third of the world's commercial oils and fats and traded more products in more places than any other company in the world. Its manufacturing activities—which included detergents and toilet preparations, margarine and edible fats, food products, and oil milling and auxiliary businesses—were joined by a need for similar raw and refined materials, such as coconut, palm, cottonseed, and soybean oil, as well as whale oil and animal fats.

1930s: Surviving the Great Depression

The Great Depression, which struck not long after the new company was formed, affected every aspect of Unilever's multifaceted operation: its raw material companies faced price decreases of 30 to 40 percent in the first year alone; cattle cake, sold as a product of its oil mills, suffered with the decline of the agricultural industry; margarine and other edible fats were affected by damaging competition as the price of butter plummeted; and the company's retail grocery and fish shops saw declining sales.

As prices and profits around the world threatened to collapse, Unilever had to act quickly to build up an efficient system of control. The ''special committee'' was established in September of 1930 to do that. Operating as a board of directors over the two boards the company already had, the special committee was designed to balance Dutch and British interests and act as an inner cabinet for the organization. It also began administering two committees established to deal with Unilever's world affairs: a continental committee to handle businesses in Europe, and an overseas committee to supervise business elsewhere.

A new generation of management led Unilever through the 1930s: Francis D'Arcy Cooper, who had been chairman of Lever Brothers since William Lever's death in 1925; Georg Schicht, the former chairman of Schicht Company; and Paul Rijkens, who succeeded Anton Jurgens as chairman of Jurgens

Key Dates:

1872: Two Dutch firms, Jurgens and Van den Bergh, begin commercial production of margarine.
1885: William Hesketh Lever establishes soap factory in Warrington, marking the beginnings of Lever Brothers.
1908: Jurgens and Van den Bergh pool their interests.
1914: Lever begins producing margarine at the request of the British government.
1927: Jurgens and Van den Bergh create dual-structured Margarine Union Limited and Margarine Unie N.V.
1929: Margarine Union/Margarine Unie merges with Lever Brothers to create Unilever, with dual Anglo-Dutch structure.
1930: Special committee is established as a board of directors over the British and Dutch Unilever holding companies.
1937: Reorganization equalizes the assets of the Dutch and the British groups of Unilever; Thomas J. Lipton Company, U.S. manufacturer of tea, is acquired.
1944: The U.S. toothpaste brand Pepsodent is acquired.
1957: Company acquires U.K. frozen foods maker Birds Eye.
1961: U.S. ice cream novelty maker Good Humor is acquired.
1984: Buying spree begins that will last until 1988 and result in about 80 companies being acquired; Brooke Bond, the leading European tea company, is acquired through hostile takeover.
1986: Company acquires Chesebrough-Pond's, its largest purchase to date.
1989: The acquisition of three companies, including Fabergé Inc., makes the company a major player in the world perfume and cosmetics industry.
1994: The launch of a new laundry detergent in Europe turns into a public relations disaster when tests reveal that it can damage clothes under certain conditions.
1996: Fundamental management reorganization is launched, including the replacing of the special committee with a seven-member executive committee.
1997: Specialty chemicals operations are sold to Imperial Chemical Industries PLC for about US$8 billion.
1999: Company announces that it will eliminate about 1,200 of its brands to focus on around 400 regionally or globally powerful brands.

in 1933. It was Cooper who seemed to lead the efforts to turn the various companies that comprised Unilever into one Anglo-Dutch team. It was also Cooper who convinced the board of the necessity for a reorganization in 1937, when the relationship between the profit-earning capacities of the Dutch and British companies found itself reversed.

Originally, about two-thirds of Unilever's profits were earned by the Dutch group and one-third by the British group. By 1937, however, because of increasing trade conflicts in Europe, particularly in Germany, the situation had reversed. By selling the Lever company's assets outside Great Britain, including Lever Brothers Company in the United States, to the Dutch arm of Unilever, the assets of the two groups were redistributed so that they would be nearly equal in volume and profits, which had always been the objective of the two parent companies.

Before 1945 the oils and fats industries had progressed fairly smoothly. The only major industry breakthroughs were the discovery of the hydrogenation process just before World War I, which enabled manufacturers to turn oils into hard fats, and the possibility of adding vitamins to margarine in the 1920s, which created an opportunity for new health-related product claims. But it was not until the end of World War II that the industry in general, including Unilever, began to recognize the important relationship between marketing and research. Meantime, Unilever expanded its U.S. operations through two important acquisitions: Thomas J. Lipton Company, manufacturer of tea (1937), and the Pepsodent brand of toothpaste (1944).

Postwar Era: Adapting to New Markets and Technology

Although Unilever's growth until the mid-1940s was a result of expanded product lines and plant capacities, its greatest achievements between 1945 and 1965 were its adaptation to new markets and technology. The decade following World War II was a period of recovery, culminating by the early 1950s in rapid economic growth in much of the Western world. Until 1955 demand continued to rise and competition was not a major issue. Afterward, however, profit margins dropped, competition in Europe and North America sharpened, and success was less assured. Unilever's strategy was to acquire companies in new areas, particularly food and chemical manufacturers. Among the postwar acquisitions were U.K. frozen foods maker Birds Eye (1957) and U.S. ice cream novelty maker Good Humor (1961).

Before the formation of Unilever, Lever Brothers had coped with overseas expansion by purchasing two factories in the United States, one in Boston and one in Philadelphia. Following World War II, Unilever found that it lacked the scientific resources needed to compete with U.S. companies in research and development. Previously, key concerns for the soap industry revolved around color, scent, lather, and how well the products adapted to changing fabrics. Following the war—to the dismay of Unilever and its U.S. subsidiary, Lever Brothers Company—development efforts in the United States succeeded in creating a nonsoap, synthetic detergent powder (Procter & Gamble Company's Tide), which had superior cleaning powers and did not form insoluble deposits in plumbing systems in hard water. The disappointment spurred Unilever to value research as highly as marketing and sales. Lever Brothers had three detergent plants in production by 1950 but remained behind in the industry for some time.

Because the primary ingredients of the new detergents were petrochemicals, Unilever now found itself involved in chemical technology. In the synthetic detergent market, each geographic area required a different kind of product depending on the way consumers washed their clothes and the type of water available to them. The new detergents gave rise to new problems, however: the foam that detergents left in sewage systems and rivers had become a major issue by the late 1950s. As a result, by 1965 Unilever had introduced biodegradable products in the United States, the United Kingdom, and West Germany.

Throughout the postwar era, Unilever continued to invest in research and research facilities. One of its major establishments—the Port Sunlight facility in Cheshire that William Lever had founded in the 1920s—researched detergents, chemicals, and timber. In Bedfordshire, the Colworth House facility continued research efforts in food preservation, animal nutrition, and health problems associated with toothpaste, shampoo, and other personal products. By 1965 the company had 11 major research establishments throughout the world, including laboratories in Continental Europe, the United Kingdom, the United States, and India.

One example of how Unilever effectively answered market demands was its continuing research in margarine. When first developed, margarine was simply a substitute for the butter that was in short supply during wartime. But when butter once again became plentiful, the product needed to offer other advantages to the consumer. Research focused on methods to improve the quality of margarine—such as making it easier to spread, more flavorful, and more nutritious. This was the primary emphasis at Unilever's Vlaardingen laboratory. By enhancing techniques used to refine soybean oil, the company succeeded in improving the raw materials available for margarine production while at the same time achieving vast savings, since soybean oil itself was inexpensive.

The advent of the European Economic Community, or Common Market, also created new opportunities for Unilever. The company held several conferences throughout the 1960s to discuss strategies for dealing with marketing, factory location, tariffs, cartels, and transport issues created by the Common Market. Of particular importance was the need to determine the best places for production under changing economic conditions. Since the late 19th century, when the companies that comprised Unilever had set up factories in other European countries to avoid tariff restrictions, Unilever's products had been manufactured wherever it was most economical. Under the Common Market, many of the tariff restrictions that had spawned the multinational facilities were eliminated, giving the company an opportunity to consolidate operations and concentrate production in lower-cost countries.

1980s: Restructuring and Major Acquisitions

In the 1980s Unilever undertook a massive restructuring. The company sold most of its service and ancillary businesses, such as transport, packaging, advertising, and other services that were readily available on the market, and went on a buying spree, snapping up some 80 companies between 1984 and 1988. The restructuring was designed to concentrate the company in "those businesses that we properly understand, in which we have critical mass, and where we believe we have a strong, competitive future," Unilever PLC Chairman M.R. Angus told *Management Today* in 1988. Specifically, Unilever's core businesses were detergents, foods, toiletries, and specialty chemicals.

In addition to increasing profitability in core areas, restructuring also helped Unilever execute its biggest acquisition to date, that of Chesebrough-Pond's in the United States in 1986. A company with sales of nearly $3 billion, Chesebrough owned such brands as Vaseline Intensive Care, Pond's Cold Cream, and Ragú spaghetti sauce. The acquisition allowed Unilever to fill out its international personal products business, particularly in the United States, where Unilever saw a higher profit potential.

During the 1980s Unilever's detergent products posted a 50 percent growth in operating profit, while food products grew at a faster than normal rate. In the United States, plans to take on longtime rival Procter & Gamble were successful in 1984, when Unilever's Wisk moved P&G's Cheer out of the number two spot in the laundry detergent market. In Europe, Unilever in 1984 completed its first hostile takeover attempt in 15 years, acquiring the British company Brooke Bond, the leading European tea company, for £376 million. Brooke Bond complemented Unilever's Lipton brand, the leader in the United States. Two years later, the company launched Wisk in the United Kingdom, as well as Breeze, its first soap powder introduced in the United Kingdom since the debut of Surf more than 30 years before.

In 1989 Unilever became a major player in the world's perfume and cosmetic industry through three more acquisitions. It obtained Shering-Plough's perfume business in Europe; the Calvin Klein business from Minnetonka, Inc.; and, by far the largest purchase of the three, Fabergé Inc., the American producer of Chloe, Lagerfeld, and Fendi perfumes, for $1.55 billion. The upper-end cosmetics market was a high-margin business, and Unilever planned to step up marketing of its new products to raise sales.

Positioning for the 21st Century

As it entered the 1990s, Unilever had virtually completed reorganizing its European business to better compete within the evolving single market in that region. In 1991 the company further refined its operations by selling the last of its packaging businesses and by making provisions for the eventual sales of the majority of its agribusinesses.

Unilever's flexible management structure and diverse product range were integral to its survival in the rapidly changing international market. In a 1992 *Harvard Business Review* article, Chairman and CEO Floris A. Maljers explained Unilever's management structure: "The very nature of our products required proximity to local markets; economies of scale in certain functions justify a number of head-office departments; and the need to benefit from everybody's creativity and experience makes a sophisticated means of transferring information across our organization highly desirable. All of these factors led to our present structure: a matrix of individual managers around the world who nonetheless share a common vision and understanding of corporate strategy."

Despite poor performances by some of its subsidiaries and recessions in Europe and North America, Unilever's broad product range led to overall profit increases in both 1990 and 1991. In 1990 Unilever made substantial inroads into the newly opened markets created by the unification of Germany. The company began producing its Rama margarine at a former East German state plant in Chermnitz, established a task force to select sites for 23 Nordsee fish stores, and began distributing ice cream and frozen novelties to retailers in eastern Germany.

In 1991 Unilever continued to battle with rival Procter & Gamble over the newly opened markets of the former Soviet Union. Unilever purchased an 80 percent stake in the Polish detergent firm Pollena Bydgoscz for $20 million, changing the name to Lever Polska, the first laundry detergent manufacturer to be privatized in Poland. The company earmarked approximately $24 million for product line expansions, including a fabric conditioner and household cleaning products. Also in 1991 Michael Perry was named the U.K. cochairman of Unilever.

Profits in Unilever's personal products division were down 11 percent in 1991, due to sluggish markets in the United States and only moderate growth in European markets. Unilever's newly purchased Elizabeth Arden and Calvin Klein, however, posted strong growth, supported by strong retailer relationships and $24 million in advertising expenditures. Such growth occurred despite an overall drop in department store cosmetic sales of nine percent from 1987 to 1992. In 1992, though, Elizabeth Arden profits began slipping, prompting the resignation of Joseph F. Ronchetti, Arden's CEO since 1978. Unilever underwent further restructuring of its personal products division, creating a prestigious subdivision geared toward introducing Calvin Klein and Elizabeth Arden into overseas markets.

Unilever's fastest growing market in the early 1990s was in Asia. Although Unilever had been operating in Asia since its earliest days, the company was just beginning to tap into the region's newly acquired wealth. Asian sales of personal products, detergent, and packaged foods were growing more than twice as fast as sales in the United States and Europe. By 1992 Unilever was composed of some 500 companies conducting business in 75 different countries.

Unilever continued to make acquisitions in the mid-1990s, completing more than 100 purchases between 1992 and 1996, more than half of which were in foods. In 1993 Unilever gained the number one position in the U.S. ice cream market through the completion of two acquisitions. The company paid $155 million to Empire of Carolina Inc. for the Klondike and Popsicle brands, and about $215 million for the ice cream business of Philip Morris's Kraft General Foods unit, which included the Sealtest and Breyers brands. The acquired brands were merged with the Good Humor line within Good Humor Breyers Ice Cream Company, a subsidiary based in Green Bay, Wisconsin. Also in 1993 Unilever launched a restructuring, taking a US$750 million charge against earnings to close or consolidate 60 plants and lay off 7,500 employees.

One the largest acquisitions of this period was the 1996 takeover of Chicago-based Helene Curtis Industries Inc., manufacturer and marketer of personal care products, primarily shampoo and conditioners, hand and body lotions, and deodorants and antiperspirants. Purchased for about $770 million, Helene Curtis's portfolio included such brands as Suave, Finesse, and Salon Selectives. Another significant 1996 acquisition was that of Northbrook, Illinois-based Diversey Corporation, a maker of institutional chemical cleansers and sanitizers, and Unilever's first foray into the industrial cleaning sector.

Unilever and Procter & Gamble (P&G) began battling again in 1994, this time for supremacy in the European detergent sector. Unilever aggressively went after P&G's market-leading brand, Ariel, with a new soap marketed under the names Persil Power, Omo Power, and Skip Power. Unilever spent $175 million developing the product and another $292 million marketing it during 1994. The product included a manganese complex molecule that Unilever claimed cleaned clothes better at lower temperatures than rival products. P&G conducted tests on Persil Power, however, which indicated that the detergent resulted in abnormal wear after as few as 15 washings. When P&G publicized its findings, Unilever sued the company for slander. But the suit was quickly withdrawn after Unilever admitted that the detergent did indeed contain a flaw—a flaw that had not been uncovered in the prelaunch testing—and could damage clothes when exposed to a particular combination of dyes. Unilever reformulated the product, but not before it had turned into a public relations nightmare. In the end, the Power formula was abandoned entirely and Unilever, therefore, took a £57 million write-off in its 1994 accounts.

According to Andrew Lorenz, writing in the July 1996 issue of *Management Today,* the Persil Power debacle served as a catalyst for a fundamental management reorganization. On September 1, 1996, the three-person special committee that had run Unilever since its formation in 1929 was replaced by a seven-member executive committee composed of the chairmen of Unilever N.V. and Unilever PLC and five high-ranking Unilever executives. At the same time the company did away with a complex two-tiered management structure that included both worldwide product management groups and regional management groups. In their place was created a single team of 14 business presidents, with each president responsible for a portion of the European operations (e.g., the food and beverage Europe group), a portion of the North American operations (e.g., the home and personal care North America group), or a region of the rest of the world (Africa, Latin America, etc.). As was typical of the time, this streamlining was aimed at improving decision-making by pushing authority down to a lower level. Along with this major reorganization came a change in the chairmanships, with Niall FitzGerald replacing Michael Perry as U.K. cochairman; an Irishman, FitzGerald became the first non-English, non-Dutch to serve as cochairman, and he also reached the post despite having been in charge of Unilever's detergent operations during the Persil Power debacle. Continuing on the Dutch side was Morris Tabaksblat, who had replaced Maljers as Dutch cochairman in 1994.

In the late 1990s FitzGerald and Tabaksblat oversaw a comprehensive review of Unilever's wide-ranging businesses in an effort to focus on the strongest core areas: ice cream, margarines, tea-based beverages, detergents, personal soaps, skin care products, and prestige fragrances. Several other areas were identified as ''developing'' core areas: frozen foods, culinary products (sauces and side dishes), hair care products, oral care products, deodorants, household care products, and industrial cleaning products. Businesses outside of these areas were candidates for disposal. In 1996 the company sold its mass-market cosmetics business, its few remaining animal feed operations, some oil-processing units, and a U.K. franchiser of Caterpillar Inc. heavy equipment. Unilever completed its largest disposal the following year, selling its specialty chemicals business to Imperial Chemical Industries PLC for about US$8 billion. The sale resulted in a net profit of US$4.55 billion, part of which cleared Unilever's US$2.78 billion in debt; the proceeds also contributed to a war chest that expanded to US$9.6 billion. The company made one large purchase in 1997, the US$930 million acquisition of Kibon S.A. Indústrias Alimenticia, the number one ice cream maker in Brazil. In 1998 Unilever sold its Plant Breeding International Cambridge Limited unit to Monsanto for about US$525 million. Unilever also sold off its Nordsee fast-food fish chain in the late 1990s.

In early 1999 Unilever spent a large portion of its war chest on a special dividend to shareholders of £5 billion (US$8.1 billion). In July of that year Tabaksblat retired and was replaced as Dutch cochairman by Antony Burgmans. Two months later Unilever announced that it would eliminate about 1,200 of its brands to focus on around 400 regionally or globally powerful brands—a group that accounted for almost 90 percent of 1998 revenue. This sweeping overhaul of the product portfolio was aimed at increasing annual growth rates from four percent to six to eight percent and at eventually reaping annual savings of £1 billion.

Unilever ended the 20th century with a strategic plan that included a focus on top brands within core market sectors and an emphasis on growth within developing countries. Although it was facing considerable competitive pressures in various markets around the world—particularly from Procter & Gamble—Unilever was clearly no longer the risk-averse, staid organization of the past. The whirlwind events of the late 1990s seemed destined to position the company as one of the most formidable global consumer products companies of the 21st century.

Principal Subsidiaries

Eskimo-Iglo Ges.m.b.H (Austria); sterreichische Unilever Ges.m.b.H (Austria); Austria Frost Nahrungsmittel Ges m.b.H; Unilever Belgium N.V.; Unilever _R s. ro. (Czech Republic); Unilever Danmark A/S (Denmark); Suomen Unilever Oy (Finland); Astra-Calvé S.A. (France; 99%); Boursin S.A. (France; 99%); Choky S.A. (France; 99%); Cogesal S.A. (France; 99%); Elida Fabergé S.A. (France; 99%); Fralib S.A. (France; 99%); Frigedoc S.A. (France; 99%); Lever S.A. (France; 99%); Relais d'or-Miko S.A. (France; 99%); Unilever France S.A. (99%); Deutsche Unilever GmbH (Germany); DiverseyLever GmbH (Germany); Fritz Homann Lebensmittelwerke GmbH (Germany); Frozen Fish International GmbH (Germany); HPC Deutschland GmbH (Germany); Langnese-Iglo GmbH (Germany); Meistermarken-Werke GmbH (Germany); Spezialfabrik für Back—und Grossküchenbedarf (Germany); Union Deutsche Lebensmittelwerke GmbH (Germany); 'Elais' Oleaginous Products A.E. (Greece; 51%); Unilever Hellas A.E.B.E. (Greece); Unilever Magyarország Beruházási Kft (Hungary); Lever Fabergé Ireland Ltd.; Lyons Tea Ireland Ltd.; Van den Bergh Foods Ltd. (Ireland); W & C McDonnell Ltd. (Ireland); Unilever Italia SpA (Italy); Sagit SpA (Italy); DiverseyLever B.V. (Netherlands); Iglo-Ola B.V. (Netherlands); Lever Fabergé—Europe Sourcing Unit Bodegraven BV (Netherlands); Lever Fabergé Nederland BV (Netherlands); Loders Croklaan B.V. (Netherlands); Mora B.V. (Netherlands); Unilever Nederland B.V. (Netherlands); UniMills B.V. (Netherlands); Van den Bergh Nederland B.V. (Netherlands); Unilever Polska S.A. (Poland; 99%); IgloOlá—Distribuiçao de Gelados e de Ultracongelado, Lda. (Portugal; 74%); LeverElida-Distribuiçao de Produtos de Limpenza E Higiene Pessoal, Lda. (Portugal; 60%); Unilever Romania (99%); Unilever SNG (Russia); Unilever Slovensko spol.sr.o. (Slovakia); Agra S.A. (Spain); Frigo S.A. (Spain; 99%); Frudesa S.A. (Spain); Unilever España S.A. (Spain); DiverseyLever AB (Sweden); GB Glace AB (Sweden); Lever Fabergé AB (Sweden); Unilever Sverige AB (Sweden); Van den Bergh Foods AB (Sweden); DiverseyLever A.G. (Switzerland); Lever Fabergé A.G. (Switzerland); Lever Fabergé A.G. (Switzerland); Lipton-Sais (Switzerland); Pierrot-Lusso A.G. (Switzerland); Meina Holding A.G. (Switzerland); Sunlight A.G. (Switzerland); Unilever Cosmetics International S.A. (Switzerland); Unilever (Schweiz) A.G. (Switzerland); Birds Eye Wall's Ltd. (U.K.); Calvin Klein Cosmetics (UK) Ltd.; DiverseyLever Ltd. (U.K.); Elida Fabergé Ltd. (U.K.); Elizabeth Arden Ltd. (U.K.); Lever Brothers Ltd. (U.K.); Lipton Ltd. (U.K.); Unilever UK Central Resources Ltd.; Unilever UK Holdings Ltd.; Unipath Ltd. (U.K.); Van den Bergh Foods Ltd. (U.K.); UL Canada Inc; Unilever Canada Limited; Calvin Klein Cosmetics Company (U.S.A.); DiverseyLever Inc. (U.S.A.); Elizabeth Arden Co. (U.S.A.); Good Humor Breyers Ice Cream Company (U.S.A.); Gorton's (U.S.A.); Lipton (U.S.A.); Unilever Capital Corporation (U.S.A.); Unilever Home & Personal Care USA; Unilever United States, Inc; Blohorn S.A. (Côte d'Ivoire; 90%); Compagnie des Margarines, Savons et Cosmétiques au Zäire s.a.r.l. (Democratic Republic of Congo); Plantations et Huileries du Congo (Democratic Republic of Congo; 76%); Unilever Gulf Free Zone Establishment (Dubai); Fine Foods Egypt SAE (60%); Lever Egypt SAE; Unilever Ghana Ltd. (67%); Glidat Strauss Ltd. (Israel; 50%); Lever Israel Ltd.; Brooke Bond Kenya Ltd. (88%); East Africa Industries Ltd. (Kenya; 61%); Lever Brothers (Malawi) Ltd.; Lever Maroc S.A. (Morocco); Lever Brothers Nigeria PLC (50%); Binzagr Lever Ltd. (Saudi Arabia; 49%); Binzagr Lipton Ltd. (Saudi Arabia; 49%); Binzagr Wall's Ltd. (Saudi Arabia; 49%); Lever Arabia Ltd. (Saudi Arabia; 49%); Unilever South Africa (Pty.) Ltd.; Brooke Bond Tanzania Ltd.; Lever Elida Temizlik ve Kisisel Bakim Ürünleri Sanayi Ve Ticaret A.S. (Turkey; 82%); Unikom Sanayi ve Ticaret A.S. (Turkey); Unilever Sanayi ve Ticaret Türk A.S. (Turkey); Unilever Tüketim Ürünleri Satis Pazarlama ve Ticaret A.S. (Turkey); Unilever Uganda Ltd.; Lever Brothers Zambia Limited; Lever Brothers (Private) Ltd. (Zimbabwe); Unilever Australia Ltd.; Lever Brothers Bangladesh Ltd. (61%); Guangdong Lipton Foods Company Ltd. (China; 60%); Hefei Lever Detergent Co. Ltd. (China; 70%); Shanghai Elida Co. Ltd. (China; 90%); Shanghai Lever Company Ltd. (China; 54%); Shanghai Pond's Co. Ltd. (China; 50%); Shanghai Van den Bergh Foods Ltd. (China; 50%); Unilever (China) Ltd.; Unilever (Shanghai) Company Ltd. (China); Unilever (Shanghai) Toothpaste Company Ltd. (China; 60%); Wall's (China) Company Ltd. (97%); ZhangJiaKou Unilever Detergent Co., Ltd. (China; 70%); Unilever Hong Kong Ltd. (China S.A.R.); Hindustan Lever Ltd. (India); P.T. Unilever Indonesia; Nippon Lever B.V. (Japan); Lever Brothers Ltd. (Japan); Unilever (Malaysia) Holdings Sdn. Bhd. (70%); Pamol Plantations Sdn. Bhd. (Malaysia); Unilever New Zealand Ltd.; Lever Brothers Pakistan Ltd. (69%); Unilever Philippines Inc; Unilever Singapore Private Ltd.; Unilever Korea (South Korea); Unilever Ceylon

Ltd. (Sri Lanka); Unilever Taiwan Ltd.; Unilever Thai Holdings Ltd. (Thailand); Lever VISO (Vietnam; 66%); Lever HASO (Vietnam; 66%); Unilever de Argentina S.A.; Quimbol Lever S.A. (Bolivia); Indústrias Gessy Lever Ltda. (Brazil); Kibon S.A. Indústrias Alimenticia (Brazil; 99%); Lever Chile S.A.; Unilever Andina (Colombia) SA; Industrias Unisola S.A. (El Salvador; 60%); Anderson Clayton & Co S.A. (Mexico); Pond's de Mexico S.A. de C.V.; Unilever Becumij N.V. (Netherlands Antilles); Unilever Capsa del Paraguay S.A.; Industrias Pacocha S.A. (Peru; 72%); Lever Brothers West Indies Ltd. (Trinidad & Tobago; 50%); Sudy Lever S.A. (Uruguay); Unilever Andina S.A. (Venezuela).

Principal Operating Units

Africa; Central Asia & Middle East; China; East Asia Pacific; Latin America; DiverseyLever; Food & Beverages—Europe; Ice Cream & Frozen Foods—Europe; Home & Personal Care—Europe; Central & Eastern Europe; Foods—North America; Home & Personal Care—North America.

Principal Competitors

Alberto-Culver Company; Amway Corporation; Avon Products, Inc.; Beiersdorf AG; Ben & Jerry's Homemade, Inc.; Bestfoods; Campbell Soup Company; The Clorox Company; The Coca-Cola Company; Colgate-Palmolive Company; ConAgra, Inc.; Dairy Farmers of America; Groupe Danone; Del Monte Foods Company; The Dial Corporation; The Estée Lauder Companies Inc.; The Gillette Company; Hormel Foods Corporation; Johnson & Johnson; Kraft Foods, Inc.; L'Oréal; LVMH Moet Hennessy Louis Vuitton SA; Mars, Inc.; Nabisco Holdings Corp.; Nestlé S.A.; The Pillsbury Company; The Procter & Gamble Company; Reckitt & Colman plc; Revlon, Inc.; Sara Lee Corporation; S.C. Johnson & Son, Inc.; Shiseido Company, Limited; Unigate PLC.

Further Reading

Beck, Ernest, "Unilever to Cut More Than 1,000 Brands," *Wall Street Journal,* September 22, 1999, p. A17.

"Britain's Most Admired Companies," *Economist,* October 17, 1992.

Davidson, Andrew, "The Davidson Interview: Niall FitzGerald," *Management Today,* November 1997, pp. 50, 52, 54.

——, "The Davidson Interview: Sir Michael Perry," *Management Today,* May 1995, pp. 50–52, 54.

Deveny, Kathleen, and Gabriella Stern, "Lever Brothers Regroups in Wake of Market-Share Losses in 1993," *Wall Street Journal,* April 5, 1994, p. B11.

Dubey, Suman, "Unilever Seeks to Lap Up Bulk of India's Small, Fast-Growing Ice-Cream Market," *Wall Street Journal,* September 9, 1994, p. B6.

Dwyer, Paula, and others, "Unilever's Struggle for Growth," *Business Week,* July 4, 1994, pp. 54–56.

Fieldhouse, D.K., *Unilever Overseas: The Anatomy of a Multinational, 1895–1965,* London: Croom Helm, 1978.

Foster, Geoffrey, "Making Scents Make Sense," *Management Today,* June 1994, pp. 46–49.

Gibson, Richard, and Sara Calian, "Unilever to Acquire Helene Curtis," *Wall Street Journal,* February 15, 1996, pp. A3, A4.

Heller, Robert, "Slipping Up En Route to the Top," *Management Today,* February 1996, p. 21.

Hwang, Suein L., "Unilever to Acquire Ice Cream Business Owned by Kraft Unit of Philip Morris," *Wall Street Journal,* September 9, 1993, p. A4.

Ilgenfritz, Stefanie, "Unilever Joins Liquid Soap Fight, Forcing Competitors to Scramble," *Wall Street Journal,* August 26, 1993, p. B8.

"In Search of Alchemy," *Economist,* February 15, 1997, pp. 60–61.

Kripalani, Manjeet, "Unilever's Jewel: It May Be the Best-Run Outfit in India," *Business Week,* April 26, 1999, p. 114E2.

Levy, Liz, "Unilever Axes Fabergé Firm," *Marketing,* November 2, 1989.

Lipin, Steven, "Unilever to Sell Specialty-Chemicals Unit to ICI of the U.K. for About $8 Billion," *Wall Street Journal,* May 7, 1997, p. A3.

Lorenz, Andrew, "Unilever Changes Its Formula," *Management Today,* July 1996, pp. 44, 46–48.

Maljers, Floris A., "Inside Unilever: The Revolving Transnational Company," *Harvard Business Review,* September/October 1992.

"Munching on Change: Unilever's Food Business," *Economist,* January 6, 1996, p. 48.

Mussey, Dagmar, "Heading Back East: Unilever Knows Way into Reunited Germany," *Advertising Age,* December 30, 1990.

Nayyar, Seema, "Unilever Makes Power Move on Arden," *Adweek's Marketing Week,* June 22, 1992.

Neff, Jack, "P&G and Unilever's Giant Headaches," *Advertising Age,* May 24, 1999, pp. 22–24, 26, 28.

Orr, Deborah, "A Giant Reawakens: Even Unilever, Which Sells $130 Million in Products a Day, Can Lose Sight of Its Customers," *Forbes,* January 25, 1999, p. 52.

Parker-Pope, Tara, "Unilever Plans a Long-Overdue Pruning," *Wall Street Journal,* September 3, 1996, p. A13.

Reader, W.J., *Fifty Years of Unilever, 1930–1980,* London: Heinemann, 1980.

Reed, Stanley, "Unilever Finally Knows Where It's Going: East," *Business Week* (international ed.), May 4, 1998, p. 18.

Rohwedder, Cacilie, "Detergent Wars Bubble Over in Europe: Unilever, P&G Campaigns Become Dirty Business," *Wall Street Journal,* November 18, 1994, p. B7A.

——, "Unilever's Co-Chief Faces Bumpy Road, Maps Course for Major Growth in Asia," *Wall Street Journal,* May 6, 1994, p. B5B.

Wilson, Charles, *The History of Unilever,* 3 vols., London: Cassell & Company, 1970.

Zinn, Laura, "Beauty and the Beastliness," *Business Week,* June 29, 1992.

—Maura Troester
—updated by David E. Salamie

United Natural Foods, Inc.

260 Lake Road
Dayville, Connecticut 06241
U.S.A.
Telephone: (860) 779-2800
Fax: (860) 779-2811

Public Company
Incorporated: 1977 as Cornucopia Natural Foods, Inc.
Employees: 2,600
Sales: $857 million (fiscal 1999)
Stock Exchanges: NASDAQ
Ticker Symbol: UNFI
NAIC: 42211 General Line Grocery Wholesalers

United Natural Foods, Inc. is the leader of only two nationwide distributors of natural foods and related products. Originally known as Cornucopia Natural Foods, Inc., the company has expanded through strong internal growth, acquisitions, and mergers; it is the only publicly traded distributor of natural and organic foods. United Natural has over 6,500 customers—including independent retailers, natural superchains, conventional supermarkets, and restaurants—located in 46 states. The company is the primary supplier to a majority of its customers, offering them a mix of more than 26,000 high-quality national, regional, and private-label natural products. These products include groceries and general merchandise, nutritional supplements, bulk and foodservice products, perishables and frozen foods, and personal care items. For over ten years United Natural has been the primary distributor to the two largest natural superchains: Whole Foods Markets, Inc. and Wild Oats Markets, Inc. To complement its distributorship, the company also owns and operates the National Retail Group (NRG), which consists of 11 retail stores selling natural products in the eastern United States. The company has organized its 12 distribution operations into four principal units: United Natural Foods in the Eastern Region (previously Cornucopia Natural Foods, Inc. and Stow Mills, Inc.); Rainbow Natural Foods, Inc. in the Central Region; Mountain People's Warehouse Incorporated in the Western Region; and Albert's Organics, Inc., serving select markets throughout the United States. For the 1999 fiscal year ending July 31, 1999, United Natural generated net sales and operating income of $857 million and $26.8 million, respectively. Compared to the net sales and operating income of fiscal 1994, these numbers represent compound annual growth rates of 20 percent and 26.1 percent, respectively. On June 29, 1999 Standard & Poor's added United Natural Foods to the S&P SmallCap 600 Index.

The 1970s: Going Back to Nature for Business

The 1970s could be seen as a time of search for relevance between "the world that had been" and "the world that was becoming." Entrepreneurs made and sold tofu; they raised and marketed herbs as well as organic and natural foods. Yoga gained popularity as a calming form of exercise. According to Elaine Lipson's comment in the February 1999 issue of *Natural Foods Merchandiser*, in 1979 the editorial staff of that periodical used typewriters to chronicle the growth of the natural products world. There were no fax machines, web sites, or compact/digital-video discs and players. The period of transition between the rebellions of the 1960s and the excesses of the 1980s, Lipson wrote, was a "perfect breeding ground for natural products visionaries ready to blend alternative lifestyles with business potential."

One of these visionaries was Norman A. Cloutier, who founded Cornucopia Natural Foods, Inc. (Cornucopia) in Coventry, Rhode Island. From 1977 to 1978 he operated Cornucopia as a retail store for natural foods. In 1979, however, Cloutier changed his focus from retailing to the distribution of natural foods and related products. Although most natural products were food products—which included organic foods—the natural products industry encompassed a number of other categories, such as nutritional and herbal supplements, toiletries and personal care items, naturally based cosmetics, natural/homeopathic medicines, and naturally based cleaning agents.

As a matter of fact, by changing from retailing to distribution, Cloutier zeroed in on an emerging need in the rapidly expanding natural products industry. Suppliers of natural products found it difficult to meet the demands of an increasing number of retail

Company Perspectives:

We believe that we are well positioned to provide value-added distribution services to our customers at attractive prices while also providing superior customer service. In addition to our volume purchasing power advantage, a critical component of our position as a low-cost provider is our management of warehouse and distribution costs, primarily as a result of utilizing larger distribution centers within each of our geographic regions and integrating our facilities through our nationwide interregional logistics network. In addition, we have made significant investments in transportation equipment and information technology to enable us to serve our customers.

outlets; they relied on distributors to reach a fragmented customer base and to provide information on consumer preferences at the retail level. Retailers wanted more frequent deliveries, greater product selection, higher fill rates, more information on product movement, and specialized programs—such as financing information, merchandising assistance, marketing support, and assistance in consumer education. Cloutier envisioned the possibility of meeting these needs through a national natural products distribution business that would provide the sourcing, purchasing, warehousing, marketing, and transportation of natural products from suppliers to retailers.

Launching a National Presence: 1980–95

At first, Cornucopia grew by acquiring other distributors of a variety of natural foods and related products. For example, in 1985 the company purchased two distributors to strengthen its position in the New England market and to establish distribution in the mid-Atlantic states: Harvest Provisions, Inc. of Boston, and Earthly Organics, Inc. of Philadelphia. Cornucopia also acquired two specialty suppliers of natural products. In 1987 the company bought Natural Food Systems, Inc.—a distributor of seafood and owner of the ''Natural Sea'' brand; in 1990, Cornucopia acquired certain assets of BGS Distributing, Inc.—a regional distributor and manufacturer of vitamins and the holder of distribution rights to several additional product lines. Furthermore, in 1991 the company made its way into the southeastern United States by opening a distribution center in Georgia.

Then, in 1993, Cornucopia added retailing to its distributor operations by forming the Natural Retail Group with the intention of acquiring retailers of natural products. The NRG strategy consisted of buying independent stores but keeping the former owners to run the stores. By April 1995 Cornucopia owned and operated eight natural food stores located in Connecticut, Florida, Maryland, Massachusetts, and New York. The company believed that these stores received a number of advantages: Cornucopia provided its financial strength and marketing expertise, economies of scale resulting from group purchases, and access to a wider selection of products. The NRG retail stores offered products in each of Cornucopia's six main distributor categories as well as produce, meat, poultry, fresh seafoods, baked goods, and other prepared foods. In addition, NRG provided consumer education through informational brochures, promotional flyers, seminars, workshops, cooking classes, and product samplings.

On the other hand, benefits also accrued to the parent company, which was both the owner of, and distributor to, its retail stores. Cornucopia controlled the purchases made by these stores; increased the distribution and marketing of its private label products; and stayed in touch with the retail marketplace. Furthermore, in these NRG stores, the company could test and evaluate consumer reaction to select products before offering them to a broader, national customer base.

Having established itself in the eastern United States, in May 1995 Cornucopia reached across the country to purchase Seattle, Washington-based Nutrasource, Inc.—a distributor of natural products in the Pacific Northwest region—and in July acquired Denver-based Rainbow Natural Foods, Inc. (Rainbow)—the largest distributor of natural products in the Rocky Mountains and the Plains areas.

1996–99: Stabilizing a National Presence

Cornucopia buttressed its entry into the West in 1996 when it completed a merger with Auburn, California-based Mountain People's Warehouse, Incorporated—the largest distributor of natural products in the western portion of the United States—to form a new company: United Natural Foods, Inc. Cloutier had succeeded in crossing the country with his company. On the other hand, Michael S. Funk—founder and president of Mountain People's—thought the merger broadened ''Mountain People's buying power and enabled the company to offer more services and a wider selection of natural foods and products,'' according to the April 20, 1996 issue of the *Sacramento Bee.* United now had five distribution centers strategically located in the states of California, Colorado, Connecticut, Georgia, and Washington as well as two satellite staging facilities in Florida and Pennsylvania. The company was well positioned to offer nationwide distribution services: namely, next-day delivery service to a majority of its active customers and multiple deliveries each week to its largest customers. Cornucopia now could better coordinate its inventory management with regional purchasing patterns and realize significant operating efficiencies. The company also was able to eliminate geographic overlaps in distribution; integrate administrative, finance, and accounting functions; expand marketing and customer-service programs; and upgrade information systems.

United Natural, however, did not centralize the making of decisions for the majority of its purchasing, pricing, sales, and marketing. These managerial activities remained at the regional level in order to expedite response to the preferences of regional and local customers. Each of the three 1996 regional operators (Cornucopia, Rainbow, and Mountain People's) were better suited to make these decisions because they had extensive knowledge of the local and regional taste preferences in their particular marketplace and could provide products to accommodate local trends. By the end of fiscal 1995, the company's net sales had risen to $283.32 million, compared to $124.37 million at the end of fiscal 1992. United Natural filed an Initial Public Offering on September 4, 1996 and began to trade its stock on the NASDAQ under the ticker symbol UNFI on November 1, 1996.

Key Dates:

1977: Norman A. Cloutier founds Cornucopia Natural Foods, Inc., a retail store for natural foods, in Coventry, Rhode Island.
1979: Cloutier shifts focus of Cornucopia from retailing to distribution of natural foods and related products.
1980: Cornucopia initiates period of aggressive expansion in northeastern and mid-Atlantic states; The Organic Food Production Association of America is founded to create industrywide guidelines.
1989: ''60 Minutes'' reports on the carcinogenic properties of Alar, a chemical used widely in apple growing; demand for organic foods skyrockets.
1991: Company expands into southeastern United States by opening a distribution center in Georgia.
1993: Cloutier forms National Retail Group to acquire and operate retail outlets of natural products.
1995: Company acquires a distributorship in Pacific northeast region and another in Rocky Mountains and Plains areas.
1996: Cornucopia merges with California-based Mountain People's Warehouse and incorporates as United Natural Foods, Inc.; company begins to trade its stock on NASDAQ under the symbol UNFI.
1997: Company merges with New Hampshire-based Stow Mill, Inc., becomes the nation's leading distributor of natural foods and related products.
1999: Company consolidates systems and operations of its eastern region.
2000: United Foods restructures management.

The company's private label products addressed the preferences of customers wanting products not offered by other suppliers. For instance, in 1997 United Natural launched an organic infant food product called Organic Baby. In the February 1997 issue of *Natural Foods Merchandiser,* Emily Esterson commented that sales in baby food were declining because ''baby boomers' children were past baby-food age.'' In most natural products stores, the only available organic baby food was that of Earth's Best, owned by Pittsburgh-based H.J. Heinz. United Natural was interested in expanding to serve innovative, highly specialized niche markets. Other private label products included Clear Spring Waters, Farmer's Pride eggs, Guardian vitamins and supplements, Natural Sea fish products, and Gourmet Artisan pasta and oils. Each year United Natural studied both existing and anticipated consumer preferences in order to evaluate more than 10,000 new products in the natural, organic, ethnic, gourmet, and specialty areas. The company purchased products from approximately 1,800 suppliers and also sourced products from suppliers throughout Europe, Asia, South America, Africa, and Australia.

United Natural reached its goal of being the nation's largest distributor of natural foods and related products in November 1997 when it completed a merger with Chesterfield, New Hampshire-based Stow Mills, Inc., a distributor of natural foods and related products in New England, New York State, the mid-Atlantic states, and the Midwest. According to Emily Esterson's article ''United Adds Stow, Strengthens Midwest Region,'' in the August 1997 issue of *National Foods Merchandiser*, Stow had sales of $208 million for fiscal 1996 and distributed 12,000 products to stores in the Northeast, the Midwest, and the mid-Atlantic regions. The merger ''filled gaps in United Natural's services by adding warehouses in New Hampshire and Pennsylvania, plus a Chicago facility that Stow Mills acquired when it bought Rainbow Distributing in 1996,'' Esterson wrote.

Cloutier also pointed out that Stow brought additional natural products expertise to the company because ''Stow is a well-established, sophisticated operation with experienced and talented staff. There is no shortage of good ideas in the industry, but what separates the successful from the unsuccessful is organizations with the expertise to execute plans,'' said Cloutier. Furthermore, he noted that ''despite the growth of the company and concerted efforts to reach conventional grocers, United remained loyal to independent retailers, which made up approximately 60 percent of the company's sales.'' According to the June 30, 1997 issue of *Sacramento Business Journal,* United Natural President and Vice-Chairman Funk commented that by 1997 the natural foods industry was increasing by 15 percent a year and that conventional supermarkets were selling more and more natural foods products. ''More people are aware of diet and how it affects our health and are into self-healing,'' Funk said, and added that an aging population would fuel continued growth of the industry.

In February 1998 United Natural acquired Hershey Import Co., Inc., a business specializing in the international trading, roasting, and packaging of nuts, seeds, dried fruits, and snack items. In September of the same year United Natural bought Albert's Organics Inc., a company specializing in the purchase, sale, and distribution of produce and other perishable items. Albert's was the country's largest organic produce wholesaler, according to the March 17, 1997 issue of *Business News New Jersey*. Since 1985 United Natural had successfully completed 20 acquisitions and/or mergers of distributors, suppliers, and retail stores. The company's net sales increased to $728.9 million for fiscal 1998, compared to $634.8 million for fiscal 1997.

1999–2000: Reorganizing for a New Millennium

United Natural became a primary source of supply to a diverse base of customers having significantly varied needs. To meet these needs the company distributed over 26,000 products consisting of national brands, regional brands, and private label brands. The company held distribution rights to more than 1,000 nationally known products. Over 800 regional brand products were distributed to consumers in specific geographic regions. United Natural's decentralized purchasing practices enabled regional buyers familiar with consumer demands in their respective regions to offer products of special appeal to these regional consumers.

During fiscal 1999, after an operations and logistics study, United Natural found that $3.4 million could be saved in the northeast region if the company operated two warehouses instead of three in that area. Consequently, the business of the Chesterfield, New Hampshire-based warehouse of Stow Mills was integrated into the Dayville, Connecticut facility and into the expanded New Oxford, Pennsylvania warehouse. Continuing problems and expenses related to the consolidation resulted in lower sales, lower gross margins, and higher operating expenses in the East for the first quarter of fiscal 2000. Furthermore, Chairman and CEO Norman Cloutier resigned for personal reasons, and top management had to be restructured. Michael S. Funk, United's vice-chairman and president, was elected to succeed Cloutier as CEO. Thomas B. Simone was elected chairman of the board, where he had served since 1996; he was president and CEO of Simone & Associates, a consulting company for healthcare and natural products investment.

The change of management came at a time when sales of natural foods were still spiraling upward. According to industry analyst David Wanetick—who chaired the 1999 Natural Foods Industry Conference—sales of natural products continued to grow because of increased accessibility. ''While there were fewer than 90 natural products stores in 1990 with more than 5,000 square feet,'' Wanetick told *Natural Food Merchandiser,* he expected ''the number of these stores to reach 1,000 by the year 2000.'' Wanetick commented that another factor propelling sales of natural foods was Americans' increased health consciousness: ''Millions of American adults are now watching their fat intake and monitoring their dietary cholesterol,'' he explained. Among other trends beneficial to the natural foods industry, Wanetick noted, were the fact that rising costs of healthcare led more people to take better care of their health and that gourmet cooks advocated the use of natural products to ensure better taste. Yet, ''despite all these growth drivers, natural foods have barely penetrated their markets. Since natural foods account for only 2.5 percent of the total food market, natural goods still have a great deal of potential,'' Wanetick emphasized.

Indeed, as the 20th century drew to a close, mainstream customers ''were moving in unprecedented numbers into the natural products channel,'' according to trends in the natural marketplace reported in the December 1999 issue of *Natural Foods Merchandiser.* Uppermost in the minds of these consumers was ''the concept of 'whole health'—an aggregation of many different lifestyle and shopping choices into a self-directed program of healthful living.'' From its earliest days of operation under predecessor Cornucopia Natural Foods, United Natural had seen the business potential of a focus on natural foods and related products. Because of the company's remarkable past performance and of growing consumer awareness of ''whole health,'' it was possible to assume that the difficulties United Natural experienced during the first quarter of fiscal 2000 were a temporary setback and that the company would continue to prosper.

Principal Subsidiaries

Albert's Organics, Inc.; GEM Acquisition Corporation; The Health Hut, Inc.; Hershey Imports, Inc.; Mother Earth, Inc.; Mountain People's Warehouse Incorporated; Natural Retail Group, Inc.; Nature's Finest, Inc.; Nutrasource, Inc.; Rainbow Natural Foods, Inc.; Stow Mills, Inc.

Principal Competitors

Tree of Life Distribution, Inc.; Blooming Prairie Cooperative Warehouse; Nature's Best, Inc.; Northeast Cooperative.

Further Reading

''Creating Healthy Business,'' *Sacramento Bee (California)*, April 20, 1996.

Esterson, Emily, ''United Adds Stow, Strengthens Midwest Region,'' *Natural Foods Merchandiser*, August 1997.

Granato, Heather, ''The Changing Distribution of Natural Foods,'' *Organic and Natural News*, November 1999.

''Healthy Deals,'' *Business News New Jersey*, September 28, 1998, p. 3.

Johnson, Kelly, ''Merger Propels Food Firm to Top,'' *Sacramento Business Journal*, June 30, 1997, pp. 1–2.

Lipson, Elaine, ''Humble Beginnings Become Big Business,'' *Natural Foods Merchandiser*, February 1999.

Plank, Dave, ''Healthy Food Viewed As Key Lifestyle Choice,'' *Natural Foods Merchandiser*, December 1999.

Wanetick, David, [Speech at Natural Foods Industry Conference], November 15, 1999.

Wells, Danny, ''20 Years . . . and Still Going,'' *Natural Foods Merchandiser*, February 1999.

—Gloria A. Lemieux

The Valspar Corporation

The Valspar Corporation

1101 Third Street South
Minneapolis, Minnesota 55415
U.S.A.
Telephone: (612) 332-7371
Fax: (612) 375-7723
Web site: http://www.valspar.com

Public Company
Incorporated: 1832 as Valentine and Company
Employees: 3,800
Sales: $1.16 billion (1998)
Stock Exchanges: New York
Ticker Symbol: VAL
NAIC: 325510 Paint and Coating Manufacturing; 325211 Plastics Material and Resin Manufacturing

The Valspar Corporation is the fifth largest North American manufacturer of paints and coatings, a business it has engaged in for nearly two centuries. Its sterling reputation was built on the Valspar varnish, which was unveiled in 1906 as the first coating for wood that retained its clear finish when exposed to water. Nonetheless, until formative mergers with Rockcote Paint Company in 1960 and Minnesota Paints, Inc. in 1970, Valspar was a relatively small manufacturer with limited possibilities for growth. During the last three decades of the 20th century, however, it rose to *Fortune* 500 status and Wall Street favor through an aggressive acquisition campaign in which dozens of smaller paint and coatings companies entered the Valspar fold.

The company is divided into four large business segments—Consumer Paints, with 34 percent of sales; Packaging Coatings, 28 percent; Industrial Coatings, 24 percent; and Special Products, 14 percent—which provide balance and diversity to counteract the business cycle. Perhaps its greatest potential lies in packaging coatings for the food and beverage industry, a business it dramatically embraced in 1984 with the $100 million purchase of Mobil Corporation's coatings division and then expanded still further in 1998 with the acquisition of Dexter Corporation; Valspar currently ranks number one in this industry worldwide, with a market share of between 35 and 40 percent. The company operates 32 manufacturing plants in the United States, Canada, Mexico, France, Norway, the United Kingdom, Australia, China, and Singapore; has licensing arrangements throughout the world; and markets such consumer brands as Colony, Enterprise, Laura Ashley, Magicolor, Plasti-Kote, and Valspar. In the mid-1990s Valspar began an aggressive international expansion, which quickly increased its overseas sales from three percent to nearly 20 percent of overall sales.

19th-Century Origins

In 1820 two businessmen in Cambridge, Massachusetts, began the first commercial production of varnishes in the United States, a business that was to become Valspar's forte for more than a century. Fourteen years earlier, on Boston's Broad Street, Samuel Tuck opened a paint dealership that led directly to the formation of Valspar. Tuck's business, Paint and Color, changed names and hands several times during the next 50 years. With Augustine Stimson's assumption of the Broad Street business and Lawson Valentine's incorporation of Boston varnish manufacturer Valentine and Company in 1832, the formation of Valspar was made possible. These two businesses soon merged to become Stimson & Valentine. In 1855 Otis Merriam joined Stimson & Valentine as the other principal owner; Merriam, interestingly, had for the previous six years been associated with the original varnish plant in Cambridge. Although popularly known as ''varnish manufacturers,'' these men also conducted an import and retail trade in paints, oils, glass, and beeswax. Around 1860 Valentine's brother, Henry, joined the firm. By 1866, both Stimson and Merriam had retired and left the Valentine brothers the sole partners in the business, which was then renamed Valentine & Company.

Shortly thereafter, Lawson Valentine made a singularly important decision: he hired a chemist at a time when there were fewer than 100 such specialists in the country; this was a first for the American varnish industry. More important than the creation of the position, however, was the candidate selected for the job. That person was Charles Homer, brother of famed New England artist Winslow Homer and an expert craftsman in the mixing of varnishes. According to the *Valspar History,* he ''made varnishes so perfect they could be poured from the can to the back or side of

Company Perspectives:

Valspar's mission is to be the recognized leader in the coatings industry. This leadership will be achieved through the commitment of all employees to Valspar's three Principles of Total Quality: meeting customer requirements; continuous improvement; total employee involvement.

a carriage. . . . Varnishes that flow out smoothly and evenly, dry perfectly.'' Following Lawson's relocation of the business to New York City in 1870, the same year in which the firm acquired Minnesota Linseed Oil Paint Company, Valentine & Company began to specialize in vehicle finishing varnishes that were competitive with widely prized English varnishes. At the time, the company operated a West Coast office with Whittier, Fuller & Company (later renamed W.P. Fuller & Company) as its representative. In 1878 Valentine & Company entered the Midwest market via a Chicago branch office. Four years later Henry Valentine succeeded his brother as president and the company renewed its Boston ties by reopening a plant there. By the turn of the century, Valentine & Company had established additional operations in Pennsylvania as well as Paris, and had won dozens of international medals for its high-quality varnishes.

Early 20th Century: Valspar Varnish

Lawson Valentine's grandson, L. Valentine Pulsifer, joined the company in 1903 after receiving his degree in chemistry from Harvard University. Working under Homer, Pulsifer was allowed to conduct experiments to discover why varnishes always turned white when exposed to water. From Homer's standpoint, the experiments would be edifying, though not otherwise profitable; Pulsifer believed, however, that the formula for a clear varnish existed—it simply had yet to be discovered. Three years later Pulsifer produced Valspar, the first clear varnish ever; factory production began within two years, accompanied by promotional stunts designed to highlight the product's unique features. The first such exhibition involved a boiling water test at the Grand Rapids Furniture Show in 1908. The following year, at the New York Motor Boat Show, Valspar and eight of the best competing brands were applied to a submarine in alternating stripes; the vessel was then submerged and ''gradually took on the appearance of a sea-going zebra, as the other varnishes whitened and Valspar remained clear.''

For the next few decades the company rode on the coattails of Valspar, supported by a strong national advertising campaign during the 1920s that made the product a household word with the tagline ''the varnish that won't turn white.'' Pulsifer's invention, by virtue of its unparalleled appearance, durability, and ease of application, became a willing participant in a number of historic events. These included Admiral Robert Peary's expedition to the North Pole in 1909, U.S. involvement in World War I, and Charles Lindbergh's nonstop solo flight from New York to Paris in 1927; in each of these cases, Valspar finishes were employed as a protective coating on exposed wood surfaces. The varnishing of airplanes, in particular, became synonymous with Valspar during this period. The unveiling of new products and the acquisition of other paint and varnish manufacturers helped Valentine & Company to successfully weather the Great Depression. Among the new products were Super Valspar, Four-Hour Valspar, Val-Oil Clear, Valenite Clear, Valenite Enamels, Three V Floor Varnish, and French Formula Enamel; and among the acquired paint and varnish manufacturers were Con-Ferro Paint and Varnish Company and Detroit-Graphite Company (both acquired in 1930) and Edward Smith & Company (acquired in 1938).

Formative Mergers: Rockcote (1960), Minnesota Paints (1970)

Prior to the stock market crash, in 1927 the seed for another important predecessor to the Valspar Corporation was planted. It was in this year that Ralph J. Baudhuin entered the paint business as a salesman. Within a short time, he helped found the Baudhuin-Anderson Company in Rockford, Illinois. In 1932, the same year that Valentine & Company began to operate as a subsidiary of the newly formed Valspar Corporation, Baudhuin-Anderson became Rockford Paint Manufacturing Company. Four years later, after Ralph Baudhuin had gained sole ownership of the Illinois firm, Rockford Paint was renamed Rockcote Paint Company. During the 1950s Rockcote formed two important subsidiaries. The first, Color Corporation of America, was created to license and sell color systems and related equipment to paint manufacturers; the second, Midwest Synthetics, was formed to develop synthetic resins and resin-based varnishes. Like Valspar, Rockcote also grew by steady acquisitions during this period. By 1958, Baudhuin had taken special notice of Valspar; two years later, he succeeded in merging Rockcote with the old-line firm, then headquartered in Ardmore, Pennsylvania, and consolidated headquarters in Rockford.

Under the direction of the Baudhuin brothers, Ralph and F.J., the 1960s represented a heavy period of growth for Valspar. From the time of the merger until the end of the decade, the company averaged almost two acquisitions per year. Among the businesses purchased were Norco Plastics of Milwaukee, McMurtry Manufacturing of Denver, Keystone Paint and Varnish of Brooklyn, and the Trade Sales Division of Mobil Corporation. Fittingly, the company inaugurated the 1970s with even more phenomenal growth, this time through a historic merger. In June 1970, privately held Minnesota Paints, Inc. of Minneapolis, with annual sales of $24 million, merged with Valspar, with annual sales of $27 million; once again, Valspar's headquarters changed, this time to Minneapolis. The deal came at a propitious time, for the old Valspar had suffered a loss of $148,500 while Minnesota Paints had posted a gain of $200,000. Furthermore, Minnesota Paints boasted a strong, cash-heavy financial position to support further acquisitions. In the first fiscal year following the merger, earnings were $226,000 on revenues of $47.6 million. Within two years, Valspar's earnings had grown to $1.53 million and it was again ready to expand. The consecutive acquisitions of Phelan Faust Paint, Speed-O-Lac Chemical, Conchemco's Detroit Chemical Coatings, Elliott Paint and Varnish, and Conchemco's Coatings Division increased initial annual revenues by another $74 million during the decade.

1980s and Early 1990s: Acquisitions Continue

Overseeing much of this expansion was C. Angus Wurtele, former president of Minnesota Paints and chairman of Valspar

Key Dates:

1806: Samuel Tuck opens a Boston paint dealership called Paint and Color, which is later acquired by Augustine Stimson.
1820: First commercial production of varnishes in the United States begins in Cambridge, Massachusetts.
1832: Valentine and Company, a varnish manufacturer, is incorporated in Boston by Lawson Valentine, and soon merges with Paint and Color to become Stimson & Valentine.
1866: Valentine and his brother, Henry, become sole partners in the business, renaming it Valentine & Company.
1870: Company relocates to New York City and acquires Minnesota Linseed Oil Paint Company.
1882: Henry Valentine succeeds his brother as president.
1903: Chemist L. Valentine Pulsifer, grandson of Lawson Valentine, joins company.
1906: Pulsifer develops Valspar, the first clear varnish.
1932: Valentine & Company begins operating as a subsidiary of newly formed Valspar Corporation.
1960: Valspar merges with Rockcote Paint Company, with new headquarters in Rockford, Illinois.
1970: Valspar merges with Minnesota Paints, Inc., with new headquarters in Minneapolis.
1973: C. Angus Wurtele becomes company chairman.
1984: Mobil Corporation's chemical coatings business is acquired for $100 million.
1990: Sales approach $650 million.
1994: Company acquires Cargill Inc.'s resin products division, combines it with part of existing resin business, and spins it off to shareholders as McWhorter Technologies, Inc.
1995: Richard Rompala becomes CEO, then chairman in 1998.
1996: Two-stage acquisition of the Coates Coatings unit of TOTAL S.A. is begun and is completed in 1997.
1997: Sales reach $1 billion.
1999: Purchase of the packaging coatings business of Dexter Corporation vaults Valspar into the number one position worldwide in packaging coatings.

starting in 1973. At the time of Wurtele's succession approximately 60 percent of Valspar's sales came from its consumer business; the remainder came from industrial coatings. This alignment changed dramatically in the 1980s following the $100 million purchase of Mobil's chemical coatings business in 1984. Among those setting the stage for this acquisition, unprecedented both in size and nature, was Mike Meyers, who reported in June 1984 that "in the last 10 years Valspar's net profits have soared 13-fold, while sales have tripled. However, its formula for prosperity may be about to face a severe test, when Valspar in August is expected to complete the most ambitious acquisition in its history." For Valspar the test was unusually challenging, but not severe.

In effect, the company more than doubled in size through a bargain purchase: 1983 revenues for Valspar were $161 million while revenues for the Mobil division were around $180 million. Valspar's profit margin, at six percent, had been leading the industry, while Mobil's coatings margin lagged at just three percent. When Wurtele was asked by Meyers why Mobil was willing to sell, he responded that the Mobil division represented "less than half of 1 percent of the total corporation." In others words, Mobil, with such a minute investment, could well afford to let the business go and Valspar, with such an established track record in the industry, could ill afford to pass it by. Virtually overnight, the deal elevated Valspar from the tenth to the fifth largest coatings company in North America. In addition, it gave the manufacturer ready access to potentially high-margin markets, including packaging coatings and industrial metal finishes, which it had previously been unable to capitalize on. By 1986, Valspar had successfully integrated the Mobil operations, thereby proving its adeptness at acquiring even the largest paint and chemical plants and instituting means for improving efficiency and profitability. The buy-low, raise-efficiency strategy remained particularly effective for the company, for the tactic tended to postpone costly new construction and allow for a greater investment in research and development.

To achieve its standing objective of remaining among the top three participants within any of the markets it sought, Valspar prudently divested itself of plants and businesses in the 1980s and early 1990s. Yet, for much the same reason, Valspar acquisitions still continued apace. In 1987 Enterprise Paint Companies, maker of Enterprise Paint and the Federal floor care line, was purchased for $60 million. In July 1989 the McCloskey Corporation, with $42 million in sales, was acquired. The purchase was especially significant for the growth of Valspar's resin business, conducted through its McWhorter Inc. subsidiary. In October 1990 the company acquired certain assets of DeSoto, Inc., which had combined revenues of approximately $45 million. This purchase strengthened the company's market-leading packaging coatings group, and elevated it to a leader in coil and extrusion coatings for the construction industry.

Following the much smaller purchases of container coatings and powder coatings businesses, Valspar acquired Hi-Tek Polymers, Inc., from Rhône Poulenc in May 1991. The Hi-Tek purchase was among the key factors in Valspar's 18 percent increase in packaging coatings sales for 1992. During that year, the company spent a record $19.6 million on such capital improvements as a new resin manufacturing plant, a new consumer coatings research facility, and various capacity enhancements. In addition, nearly $25 million was spent on research and development and quality process training.

In May 1993 the company announced a definitive agreement to acquire Cargill Inc.'s resin products division, which had $190 million in revenues for the year ended May 31, 1992. By contrast, Valspar's resin sales then ranged somewhere between $60 million and $85 million. This deal would have moved Valspar into the number two position in the resin industry, trailing Reichhold Chemicals, but it would not be consummated as an outright acquisition. The Federal Trade Commission investigated the acquisition and concluded that the deal would result in Valspar holding too great a share of the resin market in the Midwest. Rather than abandoning the endeavor, Valspar went ahead with the purchase, a $76 million in cash deal concluded in February 1994, and divided the combined resin operations into two separate companies: McWhorter Technologies, Inc. and Engineered Polymer Solutions, Inc. McWhorter, the larger of the two entities, was then spun off to Valspar shareholders in April 1994. McWhorter began its life as an independent public company with all of the resin assets and plants of Cargill plus three of Valspar's resin plants. What Valspar gained from this complicated deal was new technology for its own coatings business.

Mid-to-Late 1990s and Beyond

During 1994 Richard Rompala was brought in as the new president, becoming CEO the following year, and chairman in 1998. The key to hiring Rompala was his experience running global coatings and specialty chemicals businesses at competitor PPG Industries, Inc. Through the mid-1990s, Valspar remained an essentially North American-oriented firm. Only three percent of revenues came from overseas. Under Rompala's leadership, the company would dramatically increase this figure to nearly 20 percent by decade's end, forming joint ventures in China, Hong Kong, Brazil, South Africa, and Mexico and making a number of acquisitions.

A number of these moves were centered within Valspar's packaging coatings unit. In 1996 and 1997 Valspar completed a two-stage acquisition of the Coates Coatings unit of TOTAL S.A., which included packaging coatings and metal decorating inks operations in the United Kingdom, France, Norway, Germany, Spain, Australia, Hong Kong, and China. During 1998 the company purchased Anzol Pty. Ltd., a maker of packaging and industrial coatings and resins based in Australia, and made what was likely its largest acquisition to date, that of the packaging coatings business of Dexter Corporation. The operations acquired from Dexter—which were particularly strong in Europe—had 1997 revenues of $208 million, vaulting Valspar into the number one position worldwide in packaging coatings with a global market share of between 35 and 40 percent. Valspar's consumer unit, meantime, also expanded internationally, through the 1998 acquisition of Plasti-Kote Co., Inc., a maker of consumer aerosol and specialty paint products in the United Kingdom and Scandinavia.

If track records mean anything, Valspar would continue to outperform most of its competitors well into the 21st century, despite rising materials costs and other potential setbacks. With revenues increasing by double-digit percentages in 1997 and 1998, the company was well on its way toward reaching its goal of $2 billion in revenues by 2001. Recurrent market share gains, 24 consecutive years of earnings growth, steady return on equity of more than 20 percent, and 21 consecutive years of dividend increases all pointed to Valspar's preeminence as a perennially exciting company in a longstanding and often overlooked industry.

Principal Subsidiaries

Engineered Polymer Solutions, Inc.; Plasti-Kote Co., Inc.; Valspar Coatings Finance Corporation; Valspar Finance Corporation; Valspar Inc. (Canada); Valspar Refinish, Inc.; The Valspar (Australia) Corporation Pty Limited; The Valspar (H.K.) Corporation Limited (Hong Kong); The Valspar (Singapore) Corporation Pte Ltd; The Valspar (UK) Holding Corporation, Limited.

Principal Operating Units

Consumer Group; Packaging Group; Industrial Group; Special Products.

Principal Competitors

Akzo Nobel N.V.; BASF AG; Benjamin Moore & Co.; E.I. du Pont de Nemours and Company; Ferro Corporation; H.B. Fuller Company; Imperial Chemical Industries PLC; Kelly-Moore Paint Company, Inc.; McWhorter Technologies, Inc.; NL Industries, Inc.; PPG Industries, Inc.; RPM, Inc.; Sherwin-Williams Company.

Further Reading

Autry, Ret, "Valspar," *Fortune,* July 16, 1990, p. 75.

Byrne, Harlan S., "Valspar Corp.: A Paint Maker Makes Headway Against Rising Material Prices," *Barron's,* May 8, 1989, pp. 57–58.

Cahill, William, "Fresh Coat: Industrial Business Is New Focus for Valspar," *Barron's,* August 4, 1986, pp. 39–40.

Carlson, Scott, "Smart Acquisitions Brush Up Valspar," *Pioneer Press and Dispatch,* July 17, 1989.

Cottrill, Ken, "Strategies for World Domination," *Journal of Business Strategy,* May/June 1998, pp. 36–40.

Fattah, Hassan, "Valspar Paints a Brighter Picture," *Chemical Week,* February 12, 1997, p. 36.

Feyder, Susan, "Valspar Earnings Paint Pretty Picture," *Minneapolis Star Tribune,* February 19, 1990, pp. 1D, 6D.

Kiesche, Elizabeth S., "Valspar Settles with FTC over Cargill Resins Acquisition," *Chemical Week,* November 3, 1993, p. 9.

Meyers, Mike, "Valspar Formula Facing Its Biggest Test," *Minneapolis Star and Tribune,* June 18, 1984, pp. 1M, 4M.

160 Years of Valspar History: 1806–1966, Minneapolis: Valspar Corporation, 1966.

——, "Valspar Announces Plan to Buy Cargill Division," *Minneapolis Star Tribune,* May 21, 1993, p. 3D.

——, "Valspar Plans to Buy Global Packaging Coatings Maker," *Minneapolis Star Tribune,* August 26, 1998, p. 1D.

Plishner, Emily S., "Valspar Plan Calls for Going Global," *Chemical Week,* April 15, 1992, p. 21.

Scheraga, Dan, "Sovereign to Buy Valspar's Flexible Packaging Coatings," *Chemical Market Reporter,* April 5, 1999, p. 31.

Tevlin, Jon, "Valspar Seeks Keys to Competence," *Minneapolis Star Tribune,* June 7, 1998, p. 1D.

"Valspar Acquiring Total's Coates Unit," *Chemical Marketing Reporter,* March 4, 1996, p. 9.

"Valspar Winds Up Last Steps to Consolidate Operations," *Corporate Report Minnesota,* April 1973, p. 11.

Walden, Gene, "Valspar Corp.," *The 100 Best Stocks to Own in America,* 2nd ed., Chicago: Dearborn Financial Publishing, 1991.

Weinberg, Neil, "Compound Growth," *Forbes,* January 2, 1995, p. 135.

Weintraub, Adam, "Valspar Buys into Global Markets," *Minneapolis/St. Paul CityBusiness,* July 5, 1999.

Westervelt, Robert, "Valspar Nabs Dexter's Packaging Coatings," *Chemical Week,* August 26, 1998, p. 16.

—Jay P. Pederson
—updated by David E. Salamie

Veeco Instruments Inc.

Terminal Drive
Plainview, New York 11803
U.S.A.
Telephone: (516) 349-8300
Fax: (516) 349-9079
Web site: http://www.veeco.com

Public Company
Incorporated: 1990
Employees: 767
Sales: $206.8 million (1998)
Stock Exchanges: NASDAQ
Ticker Symbol: VECO
NAIC: 334413 Semiconductor and Related Device Manufacturing; 334515 Instrument Manufacturing for Measuring and Testing Electricity and Electrical Signals; 333295 Semiconductor Machinery Manufacturing

Veeco Instruments Inc. manufactures precision equipment for the data storage and semiconductor industries, dividing its business into two segments: metrology and process equipment. Veeco Instruments' high-technology tools and systems are used to manufacture, test, and measure thin-film magnetic heads for computer disk drives and are also used as integral components of silicon wafer fabrication. The company operates manufacturing and engineering facilities in New York, California, and Arizona, which are supported by a worldwide sales and service network comprising offices in the United States, Europe, Japan, and the Pacific Rim. Metrology instruments account for 61 percent of the company's total sales.

Origins

Veeco Instruments' founding in 1945 places the company as one of the earliest competitors in the semiconductor equipment business. Although the name and the business of the company endured without interruption throughout the remainder of the century, there was a distinct difference between the Veeco Instruments of the 1940s and the company that bore the same name a half century later. The post-World War II Veeco Instruments developed into a multifaceted company that by the 1980s comprised three divisions: Lambda Group, Veeco Automation Group, and Veeco Instrument Group. Of the three divisions, Lambda Group ranked as the largest, representing the kernel of the company's operations. Lambda Group operated as a supplier of switching and linear power supplies to the commercial, industrial, and military markets, generating nearly $160 million of Veeco Instruments' $200 million in annual sales during the late 1980s. Rounding out the company's operations were the much smaller divisions: Veeco Automation Group, a manufacturer of flexible automated semiconductor automation systems; and Veeco Instrument Group, which produced test instrumentation, including leak detection systems and surface measurement equipment, primarily for microprocessor applications. The company was structured as such until events triggered by Veeco Instruments' acquisition by another company led to profound changes.

In 1988 Unitech plc, a U.K.-based company, acquired Veeco Instruments. The acquisition ended Veeco Instruments' existence as a publicly held concern and marked the beginning of what would be a short-term marriage between the two entities. Unitech, whose primary business was in connectors and power supplies, was chiefly, and perhaps solely, interested in the power supplies business operated by Veeco Instruments, represented by the company's Lambda Group. Veeco Automation Group and Veeco Instrument Group were deemed incidental businesses, consumed by Unitech merely as a means to gain control over the more pertinent Lambda Group. Any questions about the longevity of the relationship between the peripheral Veeco Instruments divisions and their new parent company were answered a year after the Unitech acquisition, when a longtime Veeco Instruments executive proposed a resolution that would calve Veeco Instrument Group from Veeco Instruments Inc. and free Unitech from its involvement in the test instrumentation business.

1990 Management-Led Buyout

Edward H. Braun offered to buy Veeco Instrument Group from Unitech, announcing his intentions in late 1989. Braun had

Company Perspectives:

Veeco will continue to pursue our corporate strategy, which is focused on expanding our product lines to be the leading full service metrology and process equipment "one-stop" supplier to data storage manufacturers, and developing emerging applications for our metrology equipment in the semiconductor industry. Key elements of this strategy include: Providing our data storage and semiconductor customers with technical expertise and equipment to improve the quality of their products and reduce the time it takes to bring their new products to market; Capitalizing on our technology expertise and working closely with our customers to develop next generation products; Pursuing strategic mergers and acquisitions to provide our customers with a broad range of complementary products and technologies; Identifying important trends in technology in order to capitalize on areas of high growth; Utilizing our global sales and service network to provide world class support to our customers for existing and future products.

joined Veeco Instruments 23 years earlier, starting as a regional/ sales engineer in 1966. In the years to follow, Braun occupied a number of positions, including director of marketing, director of operations, and general manager, gradually working his way up Veeco Instruments' managerial ladder. By the time of his proposed, management-led buyout of the Veeco Instrument division, Braun had culminated his climb by earning promotion to the joint titles of executive vice-president and chief operating officer of Veeco Instruments. Behind him, Braun had a group of fellow managers supporting the buyout and the financial resources of Hambro International, a venture capital firm that agreed to invest in the buyout. At the time of the proposal, the Veeco Instrument division, in the fiscal year ending September 1989, had generated $42 million in sales, averaging 14 percent growth during the preceding five years. Roughly half of the division's sales was derived from domestic business. The other 50 percent of sales was generated by overseas business, primarily from Europe, where the division had maintained a presence for the previous 20 years through sales and service offices in England, France, and West Germany. A smaller proportion of overseas revenues were obtained from the Far East through a sales and service subsidiary in Japan named Veeco KK, established only after years of efforts by Veeco Instruments executives.

Unitech and the Braun-led management group agreed on the purchase price of $29.2 million, clearing the path for the consummation of the transaction in early 1990. Included within the deal were two New York-based manufacturing operations, Vacuum Products in Plainview and UPA Technology in Syosset, as well as Sloan Technology, located in Santa Barbara, California. These facilities and Veeco Instrument's worldwide workforce of 400 employees constituted the division's new, independent corporate existence. Concurrent with the finalization of the deal, the Veeco Instrument division adopted the corporate title of Veeco Instruments Inc., while the Unitech-controlled operations that had previously existed as the identically named Veeco Instruments Inc. were renamed Lambda Electronics, Inc.

Independence from Unitech came at a price that quickly engulfed the Braun-led company in debt. Although Veeco Instruments was profitable after its first year of business, interest expense negated the $2 million the company posted in operating income, leading to a $1.2 million net loss for the year. From its inaugural year as an independent, privately held concern, the annual net losses continued, setting an alarming trend. Despite registering a profit in two of the next three years, the company racked up successive net losses of $3.8 million, $1.6 million, and $410,000 between 1991 and 1993. The dismal financial figures stemmed from the $29.2 million buyout in early 1990, which left Veeco Instruments saddled with $23.7 million of debt as it attempted to stanch the mounting losses in 1994. During the first nine months of 1994, the company turned a financial corner by generating income in excess of its interest expense for the period, but Braun and his management team were not satisfied. For the promising results to continue, the company needed to reduce its debt, so Braun decided to take Veeco Instruments public and filed for an initial public offering (IPO) of stock in late 1994. The IPO netted the company $27.5 million, enabling it to reduce its debt and to greatly increase its chances of achieving consistent, long-term profitability.

During Veeco Instruments' troubled start, cost-cutting measures and consolidation significantly reduced the size of the company. Manufacturing operations in New York were consolidated into one facility, while the company's workforce was trimmed nearly in half. The four-year downsizing period stood in sharp contrast to the ambition and confidence the company exuded following its IPO, a corporate event that touched off an era of expansion that greatly increased Veeco Instruments' stature during the latter half of the 1990s. Concurrent with Veeco Instruments' public debut, there were two notable aspects of the company's business that pointed to a promising future in the data storage and semiconductor markets. Veeco Instruments' largest customer, disk-drive manufacturer Seagate Technology, was driving the company's growth in the data storage market, increasing its orders at an encouraging rate. Seagate, which primarily purchased ion beam etching equipment from Veeco Instruments, accounted for nearly a third of Veeco Instruments' total sales in 1994, a dramatic increase from the less than nine percent the disk-drive maker contributed in 1992. Also buoying hopes for the future was an agreement with IBM naming Veeco Instruments as the exclusive worldwide sales and marketing representative for the SXM Workstation, an atomic force microscope used in surface measurement by semiconductor and data storage manufacturers.

Veeco Instruments' prospects for the 1990s were also boosted by the rapid pace of technological advancement in its market segments, which called for a greater need for the type of high-precision instruments manufactured by the company. The fabrication of semiconductor devices involved a complex series of process steps that were categorized into three procedures—deposition, photolithography, and etching—which were repeated several times during the fabrication process. As technology advanced, spurred by the increasing miniaturization of microelectronic components, the number of manufacturing steps that required greater use of precise etching and deposition equipment also increased, translating into a greater dependence on companies such as Veeco Instruments. The animated pace of technological advancement also factored in Veeco Instruments'

Key Dates:

1990: Braun leads buyout of Veeco Instrument Group from British parent, Unitech.
1994: Initial public offering is completed, greatly reducing debt.
1997: Wyko Corp. and Media & Magnetics Applications are acquired.
1998: The purchase of Digital Instruments, Inc. increases presence in metrology market.
1999: Definitive merger agreements are signed with OptiMag Inc. and Ion Tech, Inc.

data storage business, measured by the increasing capacity of disk drives. Disk drive capacity was largely determined by the capability of magnetic recording heads, which read and write signals onto hard disks. During Veeco Instruments' post-IPO years, most magnetic heads being produced were inductive, but during the late 1990s new designs utilizing magneto resistive (MR) and giant magneto resistive (GMR) heads emerged, allowing for greater areal densities capable of storing exponentially more data. The transition in technology eventually forced Braun to alter the composition of Veeco Instruments, but before that moment arrived, he set about doing what he previously had lacked the resources to accomplish: expanding Veeco Instruments through acquisitions.

Vibrant Growth During the Late 1990s

The company's first financial report as a publicly held concern demonstrated encouraging progress. Veeco Instruments recorded its first full year of profitability since the 1990 buyout, posting $1.5 million in net income. Annual sales, subsequently, began to rise resolutely, swelling from roughly $40 million to $90 million by 1996. After 1996, Braun and his colleagues directed their efforts toward identifying suitable acquisition targets, intent on fleshing out Veeco Instruments' product lines to create a ''one-stop-shopping'' company for semiconductor and data storage manufacturers. In March 1997, the company announced two pending acquisitions that were expected to increase annual sales to $200 million by 1998. Braun signed an agreement to acquire Media & Magnetics Applications, which had developed a state-of-the-art MR/GMR deposition technology coveted by Veeco. Media & Magnetics Applications was a division of Materials Research Corp., a U.S. equipment subsidiary of Sony Corporation. Braun also signed an agreement to acquire Tucson, Arizona-based Wyko Corp., the addition of which extended Veeco Instruments' existing surface metrology product line to include automated, non-contact optical testing systems. Completed later in 1997, the acquisition of Wyko lent Veeco Instruments' strength in optical interferometric measurement systems for its semiconductor and data storage customers.

The addition of both the Media & Magnetics Applications division and Wyko Corp. in the same year proved to be a burdensome task for Braun and his senior executives, pushing the company past ''the critical mass point for size and financial stability,'' according to the February 16, 1998 issue of *Electronic News.* Compounding the strain suffered by the company were technology-related problems arising in each of Veeco Instruments' market segments. Both the data storage and semiconductor markets were caught in a technology transition at the end of 1997, which contributed to a precipitous drop in the company's stock price. From a high of $73.62 in September 1997, Veeco Instruments' stock price plunged to $18.12 in December 1997, prompting Braun to take action. His response was another acquisition, the purchase of Digital Instruments, Inc. in 1998.

Santa Barbara, California-based Digital Instruments operated as a manufacturer of high-precision measurement products. Braun agreed to acquire the company in February 1998, attracted by the complementary relationship between its expertise and the atomic force microscope products represented by Veeco Instruments' agreement with IBM. Further, the $150 million acquisition of Digital Instruments helped Veeco Instruments maneuver out of its downturn by stepping up its involvement in metrology. Braun noted as much in his February 16, 1998 interview with *Electronic News,* candidly remarking, ''Suddenly, we are more a metrology company.'' Following the completion of the transaction, metrology revenue accounted for $150 million of Veeco Instruments' $240 million in overall revenues.

Veeco Instruments announced two more acquisitions before the end of the 1990s, endeavoring to broaden its product line as the company neared its tenth anniversary as an independent concern. In October, Braun further strengthened the company's metrology business by signing a definitive merger agreement with OptiMag, Inc., a supplier of automated optical defect inspection and process control equipment for the data storage thin film magnetic head industry. On the same day the OptiMag agreement was signed, Braun signed a definitive merger agreement with Ion Tech, Inc., a $20-million-in sales supplier of ion beam deposition systems used to manufacture filters critical to extending ''bandwidth'' of fiber optic telecommunication networks. Aside from bolstering Veeco Instruments' process equipment business segment, the addition of Ion Tech ushered Veeco Instruments into a new market, optical telecommunications, which was expected to be a high-growth market. Roughly two weeks after the merger agreements were signed, the company announced its financial results for the first nine months of 1999. The figures were encouraging, perhaps signaling that the difficulties of 1998 had been put to rest. Sales for the period reached a record high of $170 million, but more impressive was the 109 percent increase recorded in the company's net income, which soared to $17.1 million. With these financial results fueling optimism at the company's Plainview, New York headquarters, Veeco Instruments prepared for the 21st century and its second decade of independence.

Principal Subsidiaries

Sloan Technology Corporation; Veeco Instruments S.A. (France); Elvion S.A. (France); Veeco Instruments GmbH (Germany); Veeco Instruments Limited (U.K.); Nihon Veeco K.K. (Japan); Wyko Corporation; Veeco Real Estate, Inc.; Robin Hill Properties, Inc. Digital Instruments (UK) Limited.

Principal Competitors

ADE Corporation; Zygo Corporation; Commonwealth Scientific Corporation; CMI International; KLA Tencor; Applied Materials, Inc.; Hitachi, Ltd.; Varian Associates, Inc.

Further Reading

Bradley, Gale, ''Veeco Acquiring Wyko, MRC Unit,'' *Electronic News,* March 24, 1997, p. 10.

''Debt Drags Down Veeco Net; IPO Proceeds Will Help,'' *Electronic News,* November 21, 1994, p. 48.

Fasca, Chad, ''Metrology Ups Veeco Book-Bill,'' *Electronic News,* June 8, 1998, p. 42.

——, ''Veeco Deals for Digital Instruments,'' *Electronic News,* February 16, 1998, p. 1.

Haber, Carol, ''Gear Makers Post Gains,'' *Electronic News,* August 9, 1999, p. 28.

Kontzamanys, Gregory, ''Management to Purchase Veeco Group,'' *LI Business News,* November 27, 1989, p. 1.

McClenahen, John S., ''Global Averaging: Protection Against Business Downturns,'' *Industry Week,* February 15, 1988, p. 30.

''Pricing Veeco,'' *Electronic News,* February 8, 1999, p. 12.

''Veeco Acquires Elamex' Share of Optimag,'' *PR Newswire,* October 18, 1999, p. 1905.

''Veeco Instruments, Inc.,'' *Electronic News,* December 14, 1998, p. 26.

''Veeco Net Down in 4Q,'' *Electronic News,* February 15, 1999, p. 6.

''Veeco Shows 1st Results; 4Q, 1994 Net, Sales Rise,'' *Electronic News,* February 20, 1995, p. 8.

''Wheeling and Dealing,'' *Electronic News,* August 2, 1999, p. 4.

Wyatt, John, ''She Knows How to Pick IPOs,'' *Fortune,* November 27, 1995, p. 211.

—Jeffrey L. Covell

Virgin Group

120 Campden Hill Road
London W8 7AR
United Kingdom
Telephone: (0171) 229-1282
Fax: (0171) 727-8200
Web site: http://www.virgin.com

Private Company
Founded: 1973 as Virgin Records
Employees: 24,000
Sales: £3 billion (US$5 billion) (1999 est.)
NAIC: 312111 Soft Drink Manufacturing; 446120 Cosmetics, Beauty Supplies, and Perfume Stores; 451220 Prerecorded Tape, Compact Disc, and Record Stores; 453998 All Other Miscellaneous Store Retailers (Except Tobacco Stores); 454110 Electronic Shopping and Mail-Order Houses; 481111 Scheduled Passenger Air Transportation; 482111 Line-Haul Railroads; 511130 Book Publishers; 512131 Motion Picture Theaters (Except Drive-Ins); 512220 Integrated Record Production/Distribution; 512230 Music Publishers; 513112 Radio Stations; 514191 On-Line Information Services; 523999 Miscellaneous Financial Investment Activities; 524113 Direct Life Insurance Carriers; 551112 Offices of Other Holding Companies; 561520 Tour Operators; 721110 Hotels (Except Casino Hotels) and Motels

Virgin Group is a diversified grouping of more than 200 privately held companies. The largest of these are Virgin Atlantic Airways, the number two airline in the United Kingdom; Virgin Holidays, a vacation tour operator; Virgin Rail, the second largest U.K. train operator; the Virgin Retail Group, which operates numerous Virgin Megastores, a retail concept featuring videos, music CDs, and computer games; and Virgin Direct, which offers financial services. Other Virgin businesses include beverage maker Virgin Cola, a record label, book and music publishing operations, hotels, an Internet service provider, movie theaters, a radio station, cosmetics and bridal retailing concepts, and a line of clothing. Holding this disparate group of companies together is the combination of Richard Branson and the Virgin brand name. British entrepreneur Branson dropped out of boarding school at the age of 17, in 1967, to start his own magazine. That venture was an immediate success, establishing the foundation for what would become a multibillion-dollar conglomerate during the 1990s. Along the way, Branson would attain cult status in his home country—the result of his business exploits, quests for adventure, and unique personal style. The Virgin brand had meantime become, according to the company, one of the top 50 brands in the world by the late 1990s; a poll of British consumers at that time showed that 96 percent had heard of Virgin.

Pre-Virgin Undertakings

Branson's entrepreneurial bent emerged during his childhood. "The fact that we never had any money was a very good thing," explained Branson's mother, Eve, in the November 1987 issue of *Inc.* Eve Branson went on to suggest that her son "wanted to help the family." A friend cited Branson's love for sports and competition as another major ingredient of his success; "He likes playing the game for the sake of playing the game. He competes hard because he enjoys the competition," noted Simon Draper in the *Inc.* article.

Although Branson loved sports as a youngster, he was forced to rechannel that energy following a serious knee injury. He decided, instead, to focus on establishing a business. Branson embarked on his first venture, in fact, when he was around 11 years old, planting 1,000 seedlings, which he hoped to eventually sell as Christmas trees. When rabbits ate the seedlings, Branson tried a different scheme a year later. His plan this time was to breed and sell a type of small, highly reproductive parrot. That effort fell through when, according to Branson, rats ate the parrots; Branson's mother, however, contended that she released the birds.

Branson was undaunted by early failures. With the same enthusiasm that would characterize his entry into new endeavors as an adult, he initiated his first major success at the age

Company Perspectives:

"Virgin is about doing things that really work, not just looking the part. We are passionate about running our businesses as well as we can, which means treating our customers with respect, giving them good value and high quality and making the whole process as much fun as it can be." —*Richard Branson, Chairman*

of 15 when he started a magazine called *Student.* His parents reportedly were under the impression that Branson had been working on a simple school newspaper, but they learned that he intended to launch a magazine for the general public after he traveled to London to sell advertising space. Branson's father, Edward, had his doubts, but he did not want to quash his son's excitement. Besides, Edward reasoned, Richard only had £100 (about US$150) to his name, and it would be good for him to learn a lesson about the difficulty of making it on his own.

From Record Seller to Record Label: 1970–83

To the surprise of his parents, Branson sold 50,000 copies of the first issue of *Student,* which was produced in January 1968. In fact, the venture was so successful that Branson dropped out of school when he was 17 to run his business full time. Soon thereafter, in 1970, he launched his second major undertaking, a company called Virgin. Virgin started out as a mail-order record company. A new law had just been passed that allowed people to sell records at discounted prices, and Branson was among the first to take advantage. Like his magazine, Branson's new company was an immediate success. Sales skyrocketed, and Branson scrambled to find workers to keep up with the tremendous order load. When a postal strike crushed the mail-order endeavor, the resilient Branson responded by changing his strategy. In 1971 he opened a small, discount record shop that was also a hit. A string of Virgin Record stores followed.

Early setbacks, such as the postal strike, were representative of the great obstacles that Branson would be forced to overcome in Britain's antibusiness climate of the 1970s and even 1980s. Indeed, during the 1970s the country was mired in economic malaise. Tax rates on unearned income were as high as 98 percent, and labor strikes such as the one that nearly destroyed Virgin were the norm. Furthermore, a general disdain for entrepreneurs and "new money" permeated the business and social environment, making it more difficult for would-be capitalists to get their ideas off the ground. A mid-1980s survey, for example, showed that 29 percent of the executives in the United Kingdom viewed business owners as having the lowest status in the country, while only 13 percent thought they had the highest status.

Nevertheless, Britain's political, social, and economic environments were perfect for Branson; a rebel by nature, he loved a good challenge and enjoyed bucking convention. That characteristic was most conspicuously evidenced by the name that he chose for his company. He used Virgin to signify his lack of knowledge about the businesses into which he entered. While convention demanded that entrepreneurs have experience in the ventures they began, Branson elected to enter businesses that interested him, regardless of his background; he would ask questions and invent his own route to success. Having no preconceived ideas about an industry, he was able to identify unnecessary hurdles that his competitors took for granted, as well as to recognize hidden opportunities.

Branson demonstrated his unique style again when he entered the recording business in 1973. By then, the 23-year-old entrepreneur was becoming bored with his publishing and record store endeavors. Still, he was fascinated by the recording business and wanted to take a crack at running his own studio. Snubbed by the British financial establishment, Branson was able to get friends and relatives to contribute start-up capital for the project. The first act he signed was an unknown artist named Mike Oldfield. They cut a unique album, Virgin Record's first, titled *Tubular Bells.* The record sold five million copies, became one of the biggest selling albums of the decade, and was used as the soundtrack for the movie blockbuster *The Exorcist.*

While Branson enjoyed success with Virgin Records during the mid-1970s, by the end of the decade the company was trying to shake its image as an outmoded "hippie" label. To that end, Branson signed a popular band known as the Sex Pistols. A crude, irreverent, hard-core punk band with a flair for the obscene, the Sex Pistols had become popular during the mid-1970s and were credited with spawning the entire hard-core punk movement. Branson had tried unsuccessfully to sign the band before. Then, in 1976, the Pistols were dumped by the company that held their recording contract, following a particularly offensive display by the band on national television.

Although another company was quick to sign the Pistols, within hours of signing that contract the band trashed that firm's offices and found themselves once again in need of a sponsor. Then, in 1977, Branson moved in to sign a band that would bring the youth market back to Virgin with a vengeance. Under Virgin, the Pistols continued to shock the world—some of their songs were even banned by the British Broadcasting Company (BBC)—and thereby helped Virgin achieve notoriety in the industry. More importantly, though, the Pistols attracted other major talent to Virgin's studios. Steve Winwood, Boy George, Phil Collins, Genesis, and the Rolling Stones all signed onto the Virgin roster.

Virgin Atlantic and Other Risky Endeavors: 1984–89

Branson's burgeoning operations prospered during the early 1980s. Still, the entrepreneur was restless and continued to seek new opportunities. In 1984 he came across another industry that interested him and about which he knew relatively little: the airline industry. Critics effectively laughed off Branson's proposal to begin providing long-haul air service between the United States and London. Nevertheless, he purchased a Boeing 747 and began flying people back and forth between London and New Jersey, offering improved service and unique features. Virgin Atlantic Airways wowed observers by posting a profit in its second year. "It's not so divorced from the music business," Branson pointed out in the November 14, 1988, *Forbes,* noting that "if people are traveling for ten hours, they want to be entertained."

Key Dates:

1968: Richard Branson produces the first issue of *Student* magazine.
1970: Branson forms a firm called Virgin, which begins as a mail-order record company.
1973: Branson forms record label Virgin Records.
1977: Virgin Records signs the Sex Pistols to a recording contract.
1984: Virgin Atlantic Airways is founded; first hotel interest is acquired.
1985: Virgin Holidays, a tour operator, is formed; Virgin Group is created.
1986: Virgin Group PLC is taken public through a $56 million stock offering.
1988: Virgin Group is taken private again through a management buyout; first Virgin Megastore is opened in Sydney, Australia.
1991: Virgin Publishing is formed; Virgin Group generates estimated sales of more than $2 billion.
1992: Virgin Records is sold to Thorn EMI plc for £510 million (US$957 million).
1993: Virgin Radio, the first national commercial rock station in the United Kingdom, is launched; Virgin Atlantic wins libel settlement of £610,000 from British Airways relating to ''dirty tricks'' campaign.
1994: Company enters the soda market with the formation of Virgin Cola Company Ltd.
1995: Virgin Direct is created, representing the group's entrance into financial services.
1996: Euro Belgian Airlines, a low-cost, short-haul airline, is acquired and renamed Virgin Express.
1997: Virgin Rail Group is formed, following the acquisition of two aging, poorly maintained rail lines.

Entertainment was, indeed, an important element of Virgin Atlantic's success during the 1980s and early 1990s. Passengers were entertained with videos and, in some cases, live performances from mimes or musicians such as cellist Julian Lloyd Webber. In addition, first-class travelers enjoyed such perks as roundtrip limousine service to and from the airport. Furthermore, Branson kept expenses low by growing his airline slowly and focusing on low costs and high profit margins. By 1988, the airline consisted of only two planes, but was boasting the highest occupancy rate and greatest profit margins in the industry. Virgin Atlantic expanded during the early 1990s to include routes to several U.S. cities as well as Tokyo, Hong Kong, and Greece.

By 1985, Branson's Virgin companies were generating a hefty $25 million in profits from more than $225 million in sales. His holdings included a string of 60 retail stores, a budding videocassette and television operation, the recording studio, and the airline. They also included a luxury hotel in Deya, Mallorca, which had been acquired in 1984 and was the forerunner of Virgin Hotels, which was formed in 1988 and consisted of hotels in the United Kingdom and the Caribbean. In 1985 Branson also formed Virgin Holidays, a tour operator specializing in the U.S. East and West Coasts. Hungry for expansion capital, Branson formed Virgin Group PLC in 1985, which consisted of all of his holdings except the airline company and some miscellaneous businesses. He put the airline and the other ventures, which included a night club business and airfreight operations, into a separate company called Voyager Ltd.

Branson took Virgin Group PLC public in a 1986 stock offering that generated more than $56 million. In typical Branson style, the offering was promoted through a media blitz that included a television commercial with a pinstriped executive dancing on his desk and the ad slogan: ''From the rock market to the stock market.'' By 1987, Virgin Group PLC's sales had risen to more than $230 million; when combined with sales at Virgin Atlantic, Branson's companies were pulling in over $350 million annually. Interestingly, following the October 1987 stock market crash, Branson took the company private again in 1988 through a management buyout, restructured his companies, and sold 25 percent of his Virgin Music Group for $170 million. Also in 1988 the first Virgin Megastore was opened in Sydney, Australia, selling music CDs, videos, and computer games under one roof.

Virgin's success during the 1970s and 1980s was a tribute to Branson's unusual management style, which was a radical departure from corporate norms at the time. Branson abandoned the traditional suit and tie in favor of a sweater and slacks. In addition, he operated his unwieldy holding company from the bow of his private barge, relying on telephones, fax machines, and a personal secretary to keep him in touch with his managers. The barge, named Duende, was located in the industrial Regents Canal. Branson's logic behind his remote office was that it gave his subordinates, spread out in more than 25 London buildings, greater autonomy. ''People always want to deal with the top person in a building,'' he explained in the November 1987 *Inc.*, ''so somebody besides me takes complete responsibility. He becomes chairman of that company . . . and I can be left to push the group forward into new areas.''

Indeed, one of Branson's greatest virtues was his ability to delegate authority and allow managers to take control of the pet projects that he conceived and started. He relied heavily on a small group of hand-picked executives that he could trust. Allowing them to operate their divisions with minimal interference, Branson also offered them high-value incentives based on performance. For example, distant relative Simon Draper ran the profitable music division. He joined Virgin in 1971 after emigrating from South Africa, and had become a multimillionaire by the late 1980s.

Another of Branson's innovative techniques involved breaking his operations up into multiple units, rather than allowing them to grow into large, less personal organizations: he had broken his record enterprise into five separate companies by the late 1980s, each of which concentrated on different bands and artists. His collection of companies had swelled to an assemblage of more than 100 loosely connected enterprises by the late 1980s, each of which was run by a small, streamlined staff. Importantly, he encouraged his employees to innovate and take risks without the fear of failure. ''You fail if you don't try things,'' Branson explained in the November 1991 *Florida Trend.* ''If you run a company based on fear, then you're not going to get the best out of people. They won't make bold decisions. They won't make any decisions,'' he stated.

Another important, and perhaps the most intriguing, aspect of Branson's leadership was his penchant for peril. His wild, sometimes daredevil stunts earned him a reputation in Britain and the United States as an adventurer and risk-taker. His first publicized stunt was a speed boat crossing of the Atlantic Ocean. The previous speed record of 30 hours was held by an American boat, and when a sailor told Branson that the record could be beat, Branson became hooked on the idea. In 1985, Branson set out in a speedboat that struck submerged debris just three hours short of finishing. Predictably, Branson tried again in 1986 and succeeded in setting a new world record.

Branson's second major stunt was a 1987 attempt to cross the Atlantic in a hot air balloon. He combined the adventure with a public relations effort to market his airline, which included television documentaries that aired both before and after the flight. The project was riddled with mishaps: Branson spiraled out of control on his first parachute jump and was barely rescued, mid-air, by his instructor. The televised misadventure sent Virgin Group's stock price tumbling the day after it was broadcast. Although the harrowing balloon trip succeeded in getting Branson and his copilot across the Atlantic in less than two days, the passenger capsule failed to disengage from the balloon when it landed, and Branson nearly died in the Irish Sea.

Despite such brushes with death, Branson's exploits succeeded in boosting Virgin's image and improving the Virgin Group's bottom line. Branson even decided to start a new company that manufactured balloons, provided balloon flight training, and sold balloon vacations. Branson secured rights to fly over the Taj Mahal and the Pyramids. In addition, he wanted the venture to design and build small balloon airships that would carry observers up for traffic reports, or simply for entertainment, at a fraction of the price that a helicopter operator would charge.

At the same time that Branson was risking his life over the Atlantic, he continued to grow his Virgin Group at an astonishing rate. During the late 1980s, Virgin was reporting over $1 billion in annual sales and was comprised of more than 150 different companies operating in 20 countries. Going into the 1990s, Branson was overseeing holdings related to broadcasting, entertainment, air travel, real estate development, publishing, and other industries. His original Virgin Records enterprise alone had branched into 14 different companies.

The Ever-Expanding Virgin Brand: 1990s

The giant, privately held Virgin Group generated estimated sales of more than $2 billion in 1991, and the 41-year-old Branson continued to deal. He signed pop star Janet Jackson, for example, in a contract valued at $30 million, and was rapidly expanding his Virgin Atlantic airline operations. He also purchased an airline company in Florida. In fact, the buy reflected the company's increasing emphasis on the U.S. market, particularly in Florida, beginning in the early 1990s. Branson planned to build a 40,000-square-foot Virgin Megastore there, as he had at 20 other international locations, and was considering making Florida the home office for Virgin Records. In 1990 Virgin and Japanese retailer Marui created a 50–50 joint venture to operate Virgin Megastores in Japan. Back in Britain, Branson relocated his barge-based office to a three-story Victorian villa backing up to London's Holland Park; he also formed Virgin Publishing by merging WH Allen plc, Allison & Busby, and Virgin Books into a single U.K. book publishing firm.

Branson's office move reflected the immense growth and complexity of Virgin Group. Despite his monstrous financial gains, however, the entrepreneur was generally respected by his fellow capitalist-wary countrymen—he was even selected as the third most popular Brit in a late 1980s poll. ''People can recognize him in a very English sort of sense of fair play and decency and modesty and good manners,'' explained Mick Brown in an *Inc.* article. ''He's that unusual combination, really, of all the things that people expect success and money to corrupt out of people,'' Brown wrote. Backing that assertion was the fact that Branson drove a 1959 Bristol automobile, for which he paid $5,900, and continued to wear casual clothing.

Virgin Group expanded during the early 1990s, despite a global economic downturn that started in the United States and spread to Europe. Branson diminished his holdings significantly when he sold Virgin Records to Thorn EMI plc for £510 million (US$957 million) early in 1992, evidencing his intent to focus on his airline operations. He also further expanded his retail operations. Late in 1992, for example, Virgin announced a joint venture with Florida tycoon and entrepreneur H. Wayne Huizenga of Blockbuster Video. The two decided to combine their knowledge of record store and video store retailing to run Virgin Megastores in the United States, the first of which opened in December 1992 in Los Angeles.

Among other innovative ventures during the early 1990s, Branson fired up an airline charter service connecting Key West and Orlando, using refurbished DC-3 planes and requiring the flight attendants to wear 1940s attire. In 1993 Virgin launched an AM radio station aimed at music listeners in the 25- to 44-year-old group—the first national commercial rock station in the United Kingdom. That same year, Virgin Atlantic Airways won a libel settlement of £610,000 from British Airways Plc relating to an ongoing campaign of ''dirty tricks'' perpetrated by BA against the upstart airline. Among the deeds BA was alleged to have undertaken were the interception of Virgin customers in airport terminals, the theft of Virgin customer lists from the company's computers, and the spreading of false rumors, such as ones claiming that Virgin was on the brink of bankruptcy. A related US$1 billion suit brought in the United States was dismissed for lack of evidence in late 1999, but Virgin Atlantic announced that it intended to appeal the ruling.

In addition to building new businesses, Branson continued to seek adventure. Noteworthy was his hair-raising attempt to cross the Pacific Ocean in a balloon. The craft floated into the jet stream and was blown into the Yukon territory in Canada. After crashing on a frozen lake, Branson was tracked by radar and rescued before he froze to death. Later in the 1990s, Branson failed in three attempts to make the first round-the-world flight in a balloon, a feat finally accomplished by others late in the decade.

During the mid-to-late 1990s, the Virgin Group was particularly active building up its travel-related businesses. In 1994

Virgin Atlantic commenced service from Heathrow to Hong Kong, then added Manchester-Orlando, Heathrow-Washington, D.C., and Heathrow-Johannesburg flights in 1996. That same year Virgin acquired Euro Belgian Airlines for £38 million. Renamed Virgin Express, the low-cost, short-haul airline offered flights from Brussels to Madrid, Barcelona, Rome, Milan, Vienna, and Nice. In 1997 the Virgin Rail Group was formed following the acquisition of two aging, poorly maintained rail lines as part of the privatization of British Rail. Within two years Branson had secured £4 billion in private sector financing in order to completely overhaul the lines by 2001–02, including the introduction of high-speed (140 m.p.h.) titling trains.

Meanwhile, a host of deals were struck and new ventures launched in other areas. Most of the new initiatives were attempts to leverage the increasingly recognized Virgin brand into new areas; they also typically involved partners outside of Virgin putting up most of the equity, while Branson contributed the Virgin brand and agreed to manage the venture in return for a controlling stake. In late 1994 the Virgin Group joined with Canadian private label soda maker Cott Corp. to form the Virgin Cola Company Ltd. and attempt to go head-to-head with two of the world's top brands: Coke and Pepsi. Virgin in January 1998 bought out Cott's interest in the venture, which had gained only a negligible share of the market. In March 1995 Virgin entered the personal financial services arena through the formation of Virgin Direct, which began offering investors shares in a new U.K. mutual fund and initiated sales of life insurance through telemarketing. Virgin Direct saw Branson teaming with Australian Mutual Provident and the Royal Bank of Scotland. Also in 1995 Virgin acquired MGM Cinemas, the largest movie theater operator in the United Kingdom; it soon sold a number of the chain's smaller cinemas to concentrate on multiplexes. In late 1999, however, Virgin announced that it would sell its cinema interests in Britain and Ireland to Vivendi of France. The group continued to operate a Virgin Cinemas Japan unit, and announced, also in late 1999, that it would spend up to US$200 million to develop 20 multiplexes in Japan by the early 21st century; a number of Virgin multiplexes in the United States were also under consideration.

Other late 1990s ventures were the 1996 launchings of a new record label called V2 Music, an Internet service provider called Virgin Net, and a chain of bridal retail stores dubbed Virgin Bride. The following year came the debut of Virgin Vie, a cosmetics retail store. In 1998 the Virgin Clothing Collection—a line of men's and women's wear, footwear, and accessories aimed at 18- to 35-year-olds—made its debut in U.K. retailers and department stores. Virgin Sun was also launched in 1998 and marked Virgin Holidays' first foray into short-haul vacation tours. Endeavors planned for the early 21st century included a major Australian airline, the marketing of mobile telephone products, the selling of music over the Internet, and even commercial space travel under the name Virgin Galactic Airways (the last planned for 2007). With the ever expanding roster of Virgin-branded endeavors, it was clear that Branson was serious when he told *Business Week* in late 1998, "I want Virgin to be as well-known around the world as Coca-Cola."

Principal Subsidiaries

Virgin Travel Group; Virgin Atlantic Airways; Virgin Holidays; Virgin Entertainment Group (70%); Virgin Retail Group; V Entertainment Group; Ginger Media Group (20%); Virgin Express Holdings PLC (50.1%); Virgin Hotels Group; Virgin Direct Limited (50%); Virgin Direct Personal Finance Limited (25%); Victory Corporation PLC (49%); Virgin Rail Group (41%); V2 Records (66%); Virgin Net (51%).

Principal Competitors

AMR Corporation; Compagnie Nationale Air France; Airtours plc; Bertelsmann AG; British Airways Plc; Cadbury Schweppes plc; The Coca-Cola Company; EMI Group plc; Japan Airlines Company, Ltd.; KLM Royal Dutch Airlines; Deutsche Lufthansa AG; MTS, Incorporated; Marriott International, Inc.; The News Corporation Limited; Pearson plc; PepsiCo, Inc.; The Rank Group PLC; The Seagram Company Ltd.; Sony Corporation; Starwood Hotels & Resorts Worldwide, Inc.; Thomson Travel Group plc; Time Warner Inc.; UAL Corporation; Viacom Inc.; The Walt Disney Company.

Further Reading

Amory, Edward Heathcoat, "Is Branson Falling?," *Spectator,* February 21, 1998, pp. 11–12.

Angelo, Bonnie, "Many Times a Virgin," *Time,* June 24, 1996, pp. 51–54.

Beale, Claire, "Virgin Turns the Dial," *Marketing,* April 29, 1993, p. 22.

"Behind Branson," *Economist,* February 21, 1998, pp. 63–66.

Benson, Diane, "Think Small to Score Big," *Florida Trend,* November 1991, p. 19.

Branson, Richard, *Losing My Virginity: How I've Had Fun and Made a Fortune Doing Business My Way,* New York: Times Business, 1998, 488 p.

Brent, Paul, "Virgin Tunes in to Canada: British Retail Group Plans Chain of Music Stores," *Financial Post,* November 10, 1994, p. 1.

Dearlove, Des, *Business the Richard Branson Way: Ten Secrets of the World's Greatest Brand Builder,* New York: Amacom, 1999, 172 p.

Downer, Leslie, "Branson's American Invasion," *Fortune,* December 9, 1996, pp. 32+.

Fabrikant, Geraldine, "Of All That He Sells, He Sells Himself Best," *New York Times,* June 1, 1997, sec. 3, p. 1.

Flynn, Julia, et al., "Then Came Branson," *Business Week* (international ed.), October 26, 1998, pp. 116+.

Ford, Jonathan, "Branson May Feel the Heat If Cash Flow Sun Sets on His Empire," *Financial Times,* August 13, 1998, p. 24.

Fuhrman, Peter, "Brand-Name Branson," *Forbes,* January 2, 1995, p. 41.

Fuhrman, Peter, and Peter Newcomb, "A British Original," *Forbes,* December 9, 1991, p. 43.

Gubernick, Lisa, "If at First You Don't Succeed . . . ," *Forbes,* November 14, 1988, p. 82.

"How the West Was Won," *Panorama,* December 1998, pp. 10–13.

Jackson, Tim, *Virgin King: Inside Richard Branson's Business Empire,* London: HarperCollins, 1994, 383 p.

Kets de Vries, Manfred F.R., and Elizabeth Florent-Treacy, *The New Global Leaders: Richard Branson, Percy Barnevik, and David Simon,* San Francisco: Jossey-Bass, 1999, 188 p.

Larson, Erik, "Then Came Branson," *Inc.,* November 1987, p. 84.

"The Long Haul from Survivor to Contender," *Financial Times,* August 13, 1998, p. 25.

"Name That Opens the Deal Doors," *Financial Times,* August 13, 1998, p. 24.

Rivlin, Richard, and Michael Skapinker, "Virgin Plans £1.2bn IPO After Continental Deal Fails," *Financial Times,* April 17, 1999, p. 1.

Sambrook, Clara, ''Virgin/IMP's Freeway Drive,'' *Marketing,* March 22, 1990, p. 15.

Sheff, David, ''Richard Branson: The Interview,'' *Forbes* (ASAP), February 24, 1997, p. S94.

Smith, Alison, ''A Genius for Publicity,'' *Financial Times,* August 4, 1997, p. 11.

Stackel, I.M., ''An Interview with Richard Branson,'' *South Florida Business Journal,* January 22, 1993, p. A9.

Wada, Isae, ''Soulful Music, Boxer Underwear, Champagne Liven Up 'V' Debut,'' *Travel Weekly,* May 23, 1994, p. 78.

''What's in a Name?,'' *Economist,* January 11, 1997, pp. 62–63.

Willman, John, ''Virgin Fans the Cola War Flames—Again,'' *Financial Times,* February 19, 1998, p. 22.

Wingfield, Nick, ''Virgin Group Joins Competitive Fray: Online Music Sales,'' *Wall Street Journal,* May 3, 1999, p. B6.

Wolmar, Christian, ''Can Branson Get Back on Track?,'' *New Statesman,* November 7, 1997, pp. 12–14.

Wright, Robert, ''Dispelling the Myth That Hides Behind Everyone's Bearded Friend,'' *Financial Times,* May 27, 1998, p. 23.

Zuckerman, Laurence, ''Virgin's Chief Battling Law on Ownership of U.S. Airlines,'' *New York Times,* June 17, 1998, p. D1.

—Dave Mote
—updated by David E. Salamie

Vitesse Semiconductor Corporation

741 Calle Plano
Camarillo, California 93012
U.S.A.
Telephone: (805) 388-3700
Fax: (805) 389-7188
Web site: http://www.vitesse.com

Public Company
Incorporated: 1984 as Vitesse Electronics Corporation
Employees: 650
Sales: $281.5 million (1999)
Stock Exchanges: NASDAQ
Ticker Symbol: VTSS
NAIC: 334413 Semiconductor and Related Device Manufacturing

Vitesse Semiconductor Corporation is an integrated circuit, or chip, manufacturer with a difference: its ICs are made from gallium arsenide (GaAs) instead of silicon and can handle transmissions up to 10 Gb/s (gigabits per second). The performance advantages of GaAs over silicon are based on the fact that electrons travel five to six times faster in GaAs than in silicon. Vitesse pioneered the volume manufacturing of GaAs and eventually began to produce competitively priced ICs that offered superior performance over silicon devices. After a decade of unprofitability, Vitesse became profitable in 1995 with rapidly growing demand from the telecommunications and data communications industries for more bandwidth and faster speeds.

Struggling with New Technology: 1984–87

The company was established in 1984 in Camarillo, California, as Vitesse Electronics Corporation, by a group of engineers from Rockwell International Corporation who had been working on making digital circuits with a new material called gallium arsenide. They formed Vitesse to develop cost-effective digital gallium arsenide integrated circuits (ICs) for the high-performance electronics market.

Initial funding of $30 million came from Norton Company, a manufacturer based in Worcester, Massachusetts. Approximately $18 million went toward developing GaAs technology, and $12 million to design the architecture for a supermini-computer. The computer project was eventually shelved, as the company lost its focus by trying to do too much.

From 1984 to 1988 Vitesse trailed its competitors in getting contracts for GaAs products. The military fueled the development of GaAs technology by awarding large multimillion-dollar contracts. The military favored GaAs's ability to withstand heavy doses of radiation, absorb high temperatures, and operate at high speeds while using a small amount of power. GaAs products were considered ideal for military applications such as missiles, aircraft, satellites, and microwave communications. Most of the military's contracts went to Vitesse's three competitors—GigaBit Logic, Harris Microwave, and TriQuint Semiconductor—as well as to several aerospace companies.

In 1985 Vitesse engineers developed a plan to pursue a commercial market for GaAs outside of aerospace and defense. Louis Tomasetta, one of Vitesse's cofounders and a former director of gallium arsenide development at Rockwell International, told *Electronic Business,* "We looked at the market and realized we had to compete in the silicon world." GaAs was not only a faster material than silicon, but GaAs chips also required less power to operate.

Vitesse realized its first revenues in June 1986. Its chips were about six months late in getting to market, and analysts charged that the company was booking orders it could not deliver. Vitesse needed more capital to continue its work, but Norton was unable and unwilling to provide it. Other venture capitalists were uninterested in Vitesse's computer project, but the GaAs technology attracted one important investor, Pierre Lamond.

Pursuing GaAs Technology Under New Ownership: 1987–91

Lamond was a venture capitalist with Sequoia Capital and a founder of National Semiconductor Corporation. With Lamond's backing, Sequoia became the lead investor in a $10

Company Perspectives:

The name Vitesse, French for speed, expresses what our company epitomizes: the pursuit of ever faster integrated circuits for high-bandwidth, high-performance communications systems. Today, virtually every long distance call passes, at some point, through a Vitesse IC. Most of the world's telecom systems use Vitesse 2.5 Gb/s chips. We play a critical role in the superhighway; we lead the industry in gigabit datacom and 10 Gb/s telecom ICs. Perhaps, most important, we are cost effective. We believe advancing the technology isn't meaningful unless it's feasible.

million secondary round of financing in early 1987, and the company was reorganized to focus on developing GaAs chip technology. Lamond became chairman of the board of Vitesse in February 1987, when the company was incorporated as Vitesse Semiconductor Corporation, a successor to Vitesse Electronics Corporation. Louis Tomasetta was named president and CEO. Tomasetta had been in charge of integrated circuits at Vitesse Electronics and was a Ph.D. graduate of the Massachusetts Institute of Technology.

From 1987 on, Vitesse concentrated on the commercial market for GaAs chips to support LSI (Large Scale Integrated) and, later, VSLI (Very Large Scale Integrated) technologies. The company's goal was to have 70 percent of its customers in industrial and computer markets, with the remainder in military and aerospace.

Vitesse developed the first 2.5 Gb/s (gigabit per second) telecommunications IC in 1987. By March 1988 it had a current order backlog of $1 million and annual revenues of about $3 million. The company was shipping high-speed static RAMs and high-density gate arrays.

As of early 1988 there were about 200 companies in Europe, Japan, and the United States buying GaAs for use in future hardware products. If computer system engineers could design gallium arsenide chips with TTL (transistor-transistor logic) memory circuits and ECL (emitter-coupled logic) gate arrays onto an integrated circuit board, the resulting computer system would operate three times faster than its silicon-based counterpart. The computer would be smaller, use less power, and run cooler.

By early 1988 Vitesse was building about 1,000 GaAs wafers a month in its 45,000-square-foot Camarillo fabrication facility, and could build 5,000 a month on demand. A breakthrough in building GaAs chips came when Vitesse stopped using gold, which was causing temperature instability when the chip's density was increased, and reverted to traditional methods used in building silicon-based semiconductors. This enabled Vitesse to build denser GaAs and to achieve yields high enough to meet demand.

In 1990 Vitesse was the only company in the United States using GaAs to build digital VLSI circuits. It was the leading supplier of 1.0 Gb/s physical layer ICs. The company had 125 employees, about three-quarters of them engineers. The value of the firm's stock had tripled in the past three years, and stock options were used to lure talented engineers.

In May 1990 Vitesse signed a technology agreement with Advanced Micro Devices (AMD) to jointly develop high-speed data communication ICs using gallium arsenide technology. At the time, gallium arsenide chips typically cost five times more than silicon chips. It was already foreseen that gallium arsenide chips would be used in fiber-optic communication systems and possibly in ISDNs (integrated services digital networks). Both cost and technology were preventing more widespread use of gallium arsenide ICs in commercial applications. At the time, the telecommunications and data communications industry was migrating toward gigabit-speed connections between computers, which would require the faster speeds of gallium arsenide technology.

Continuing Losses: 1991–94

For its fiscal year ending September 30, 1991, Vitesse reported a loss of $2.9 million on sales of $23.7 million. The firm had yet to show a profit for a complete fiscal year, although it was marginally profitable for three quarters of fiscal 1991, following a large loss in the first quarter.

Vitesse completed its initial public offering in December 1991 and was listed on the NASDAQ market. Some 3.2 million shares were offered at $9 each. By February 1992 the stock was trading at $18 per share and had reached a high of $21. For the first quarter ending December 31, 1991, the company reported a profit of $268,000 on revenues of $8 million. Analysts were recommending the stock, expecting Vitesse to ride the GaAs wave in the 1990s and noting its strong management team. Having achieved critical mass, the company was seen as ready to enter a stage of rapid growth, with revenues and earnings expected to increase markedly in the years following the IPO.

The company's prospectus revealed that it was encountering inventory control problems and low yields as it attempted to move into volume production of its GaAs circuits. Low yields, in which too many of the manufactured chips are defective, were blamed on the large number of different products the firm manufactured in limited volume as well as the relative immaturity of the firm's H-GaAs (high integration digital gallium arsenide) process technology. In order for the firm to succeed, substantial improvements in yields would be required, as the low yields were causing shipment delays.

In 1992 Vitesse accelerated its hiring and was aggressively seeking at least a dozen new electronics engineers. The additional personnel were needed to help in the firm's expansion into the workstation and microcomputer markets and to sustain its growth. It marked a shift for Vitesse from development to mainstream manufacturing. The firm had about 280 employees at the time.

Although Vitesse wanted to supply its chips to the telecommunications market, the market was not ready yet; therefore, the company focused on the supercomputer market. One supercomputer customer, Convex, accounted for 47 percent of Vitesse's revenues in fiscal 1992. However, the supercomputer industry was collapsing. For 1993, Vitesse's revenues declined 38 percent to $17.7 million, and the company lost $19 million. The

Key Dates:

1984: Vitesse Electronics Corporation is founded by a group of engineers to develop gallium arsenide (GaAs) integrated circuits (ICs).
1987: Company reorganizes, changes name to Vitesse Semiconductor Corporation, and refocuses on GaAs.
1991: Vitesse raises $30 million with its initial public offering.
1995: Company reports its first profitable year as communications markets begin to require faster speeds.
1999: Company reports a record net income of $70 million on sales of $281.5 million.

losses continued in 1994, and the company's stock nosedived to about one-third of its value since the IPO. The firm cut back and laid off about 30 percent of its staff, while remaining employees took a ten percent pay cut for six months.

Market niches began to open for Vitesse around 1994. Vitesse had built a demonstration chip for a new telecommunications standard called SONET, which was being pushed by Bellcore, the research consortium of the Regional Bell Operating Companies (RBOCs). As the telecommunications market evolved, it required greater bandwidth (i.e., speed), which Vitesse's GaAs technology could deliver. By the end of 1994, telecommunications companies were building products to the SONET standard. From the beginning of 1995, Vitesse's revenues began to grow, and by the end of 1998 the telecommunications sector accounted for 51 percent of the company's revenue, with data communications accounting for 23 percent and automated test equipment (ATE) contributing 26 percent.

Explosion in Telecommunications and Data Communications: 1995–99

After reporting a net loss of $4 million for fiscal 1994, revenues picked up in 1995, and the company reported net income of $1.5 million. Its markets were growing, and the company improved its manufacturing processes. By this time, GaAs semiconductors were being used in telecommunications to boost the performance of fiber-optic networks. The chips added capacity to a telecommunications network without having to add additional fiber.

In spite of some semiconductor industry instability in 1996, Vitesse reported record revenues of $59.5 million, up 71 percent from fiscal 1995. Net income was $12.6 million, up from $1.5 million in 1995. The company had nearly 300 employees and a record backlog of $36 million.

Vitesse's market niches—telecommunications, data communications, and automated test equipment (ATE)—were exploding. Internet growth required upgrades to telecommunications networks. Large companies were creating larger computer networks and transferring more data than ever before. High-tech companies needed faster ways to test their products.

Toward the end of 1996 Vitesse raised $108 million for new plant construction through a secondary stock offering at around $36 a share. The company began construction of a new $70 million fabrication facility in Colorado Springs. The facility was needed to keep up with increasing demand from the fast-growing telecommunications market. The plant was completed in 1997 and began production in early 1998. This facility was the only one using six-inch GaAs wafers to produce a large volume of high speed, low power gigabit ICs.

At the end of fiscal 1997, the company had 430 employees. One analyst quoted in *Business Journal-Portland* said, ''Vitesse is definitely the No. 1 player in the telecommunications industry.'' Its high-speed circuits could move information at speeds of up to ten gigabytes per second. Vitesse claimed to have 50 percent of the 2.5 Gb/s SONET/SDH communications IC market. Revenues were $105 million, nearly double sales for fiscal 1996.

Vitesse continued to ride the wave of strong demand for more bandwidth and higher speeds from the communications markets in 1998 and 1999. For fiscal 1998 ending September 30, revenues were $175 million, and net income rose to $53 million. Revenues climbed to $281.5 million in fiscal 1999, due in part to three acquisitions, and net income reached $69.9 million. Communications markets represented 80 percent of revenues, with ATE contributing 20 percent. Tomasetta noted that the Internet was driving sales of communications products, while the ATE market was lagging due to an industry-wide downturn. The company's stock price surpassed its $51 target set by analysts, and the company announced a stock split for October 1999.

Vitesse completed three acquisitions in 1998 and 1999. In December 1998 it acquired Vermont Scientific Technologies, Inc., which specialized in chip design. A second chip design firm, Serano Systems Corp. of Colorado Springs, was acquired in January 1999. The third and largest acquisition was XaQti (pronounced ''Shakti''), a supplier of Internet network processors, for $65 million. The XaQti acquisition was a continuation of Vitesse's product expansion into higher layers of network processing. It would enable the company to offer customers a more complete solution and more extensive chipsets. According to Tomasetta, ''We believe that this acquisition positions Vitesse as a major player in high-end switching and processing.''

Outlook

Vitesse's telecommunications products supported increasing the speed of each transmission channel and the transmission of multiple channels on a single fiber. Faster standards of transmission represented a natural application of Vitesse's high-performance and cost-effective GaAs ICs.

Vitesse planned to expand its product line from making chips for the physical layer of the SONET standard, which represented a potential market of about $1 billion, to making chips for other functions such as switching, processing, and interconnection across the backplane. These other areas represented a combined potential market of about $3 billion. Essentially, Vitesse had integrated four SONET functions into two chips, thus doubling their revenue per port while cutting costs for customers. Eventually, Vitesse planned to integrate all the SONET functions into one chip.

Vitesse had also begun to offer some CMOS (silicon) chip designs in addition to its GaAs products. Its goal was to have 20 percent of its revenues from CMOS products and the rest from GaAs by 2001.

To meet the requirements of suppliers to Internet data networking systems, Vitesse had expanded its line of products for high-performance switch and router applications. The acquisition of XaQti brought active-flow processor technology to Vitesse, forming the core of the packet processing components. These products enabled the construction of universal network system platforms for user-driven customization of networks.

In the area of data communications, Vitesse Fibre Channel ICs allowed for the very fast transfer of large volumes of data in Storage Area Networks (SANs), JBOD (Just a Bunch of Disks) and RAID subsystems, and peripheral devices. These Gigabit Ethernet products increased the bandwidth of local area network (LAN) backbones to 1.25Bg/s. The entire line of Vitesse Fibre Channel ICs focused on eliminating bandwidth bottlenecks in SANs, monitoring vital statistics within the system, and supplanting SCSI devices in the fastest networks.

Vitesse also had a history of expertise in the ATE market. The company supplied all of the major U.S. ATE vendors and was rapidly expanding into the Japanese ATE market. With its strong ATE system level expertise and the high-integration, low-power properties of GaAs, Vitesse's H-GaAs technology was quickly replacing ECL and BiCMOS in the ATE marketplace.

Internationally, Vitesse supplied Japanese manufacturers of telecommunications and ATE equipment as well as system manufacturers in Singapore, Hong Kong, China, and other Pacific Rim countries. It also had expanding operations in Europe to supply telecom and datacom equipment vendors with low-cost, high bandwidth, low power ICs.

Principal Subsidiaries

Vitesse Semiconductor GmbH (Germany); Vitesse Semiconductor, S.r.l. (Italy); Vitesse Semiconductor Japan Corporation.

Principal Competitors

Texas Instruments Incorporated; National Semiconductor Corporation; TriQuint Semiconductor Inc.; Applied Micro Circuits Corp.

Further Reading

Bean, Joanna, "California Semiconductor Firm Builds Plant in Colorado Springs," *Knight-Ridder/Tribune Business News,* May 8, 1997.

——, "California-Based Vitesse Semiconductor Hits its Stride," *Knight-Ridder/Tribune Business News,* November 25, 1996.

Deagon, Brian, "A Start-Up That's Stepping on the Commercial GaAs," *Electronic Business,* March 1, 1988, p. 90.

DeTar, Jim, "Vitesse Takes IC Road Less Traveled," *Electronic News,* October 5, 1998, p. 16.

Goldman, James S., "AMD, Vitesse Sign Joint Agreement to Make Speedier Chips," *Business Journal-San Jose,* May 14, 1990, p. 10.

Harbert, Tam, "The Little Company That Could," *Electronic Business,* April 1999, p. 63.

Kreck, Dolores, "Vitesse Semi Garners Buy Recommendations," *Electronic News,* February 17, 1992, p. 23.

Magee, Harriett, "Vitesse Semiconductor Accelerates Hiring," *EDN,* May 14, 1992, p. 32.

McMillan, Dan, "Vitesse Semiconductor Opens Local Design Center," *Business Journal-Portland,* October 31, 1997, p. 16.

Ristelhueber, Robert, "Vitesse Snagged by Low Yields," *Electronic News,* February 17, 1992, p. 23.

"Vitesse Acquires XaQti for $65m," *Electronic News,* May 31, 1999, p. 10.

"Vitesse Nearly Doubles Revenues," *Electronic News,* January 11, 1999, p. 43.

"Vitesse Results Climb," *Electronic News,* April 19, 1999, p. 50.

"Vitesse Semiconductor Corp.," *EDN,* January 11, 1990, p. 56.

"Vitesse Semiconductor—VTSS," *CDA-Investment Insiders' Chronicle,* February 15, 1999, p. 12.

"Vitesse Semiconductor—VTSS," *CDA-Investment Insiders' Chronicle,* September 9, 1996, p. 3.

"Vitesse Vaults," *Electronic News,* July 13, 1998, p. 78.

—David P. Bianco

Volkswagen Aktiengesellschaft

Berliner Ring 1
D-38436 Wolfsburg
Germany
Telephone: (5361) 9-0
Fax: (5361) 9-2 82 82
Web site: http://www.volkswagen.de

Public Company
Incorporated: 1938 as Volkswagenwerk GmbH
Employees: 297,916
Sales: DM 134.24 billion (US$80.55 billion) (1998)
Stock Exchanges: Berlin Bremen Düsseldorf Frankfurt Hamburg Hanover München Stuttgart Basle Geneva Zürich Antwerp Brussels Luxembourg Amsterdam London Paris Tokyo Madrid Barcelona Bilbao Valencia Milan
NAIC: 336111 Automobile Manufacturing; 336112 Light Truck and Utility Vehicle Manufacturing; 421110 Automobile and Other Motor Vehicle Wholesalers; 522291 Consumer Lending; 532111 Passenger Cars Rental; 532112 Passenger Cars Leasing; 331419 Primary Smelting and Refining of Nonferrous Metal (Except Copper and Aluminum)

Volkswagen Aktiengesellschaft, a company born in the shadow of Nazism, rose to become the world's third largest automobile company. It produced 4.6 million vehicles annually in the late 1990s to control 11.5 percent of the global market. Volkswagen has long been the industry leader in Germany, and it claimed the top position in European sales with a 17 percent market share. But the company also led the trend among automakers to locate production facilities in emerging international markets such as China, Eastern Europe, and Latin America; it also held substantial shares of the passenger car market in these regions: 13.3 percent in Eastern Europe, 30.2 percent in Brazil, 17.2 percent in Argentina, and 56 percent in China. In addition to its flagship make, Volkswagen also produces vehicles under several other names, including Audi, Bentley, Bugatti, Lamborghini, Rolls-Royce, Seat, and Skoda. Volkswagen, which is 18 percent owned by the German state of Lower Saxony, is involved in consumer lending and leasing and car rental through its Financial Services Division; it also holds a 35 percent interest in Israel-based Dead Sea Magnesium Ltd., which produces and distributes magnesium, the lightest metallic mineral and a potential 21st century vehicle design material.

Nazi Era Origins

Volkswagen was founded in 1937 as Gezuvor—Gesellschaft zur Vorbereitung des deutschen Volkswagen GmbH (the Company for the Development of the German Volkswagen); its name was changed the following year, when it was incorporated as Volkswagenwerk GmbH. It embodied the dreams of two men: Ferdinand Porsche and Adolf Hitler. Porsche, an engineer, had designed powerful luxury automobiles for Austro-Daimler, but had been dreaming of a small, low-priced car for the ordinary consumer since the early 1920s. Porsche had tried in vain to find financiers for his venture. Always interested in technical innovation, Porsche had designed a rear-engine, air-cooled vehicle with independent suspension. The radical design had to be perfected, however, and Porsche's first sponsor had little patience for torsion bars that exploded under pressure and engines that malfunctioned after a few miles.

Porsche's meeting with Hitler in 1934 changed everything. By 1938 his roundish, odd-looking car had become the center of a plan to build an ideal worker's city, and a factory was started at Wolfsburg. During the war, however, the Volkswagen plant produced vehicles for the German military, largely with the slave labor of prisoners. By the end of the war the factory had been virtually destroyed by bombing. Hitler's ''people's car'' never materialized.

The Volkswagen factory was operated by the British occupation forces from 1945 to 1949. The company became the focus of an effort to rebuild the German auto industry, and within a decade Volkswagen was producing half of Germany's automobiles. Ironically, it was the British administrators of Volkswagen who started the production of passenger rather than military vehicles, and thus made the dream of the people's car a reality.

Postwar Era and the Beetle

The company came under the control of the German federal government and the state of Lower Saxony in 1949. The man the

Company Perspectives:

The Volkswagen Group offers an unparalleled range of vehicles. Over 50 different automobile models from a range of nine international marques provide a diversity, the likes of which can be found nowhere else in the world and one which serves to accommodate the increasing individuality of customer demand in ever more fragmented markets. A truly comprehensive selection of vehicles, individualised through body design and elegance, but also through technology, safety features and quality. Today's range spans everything from subcompact cars with an accent on economical three-cylinder engines to luxury limousines that meet the highest of demands on performance and prestige; from family convertibles to exclusive sports cars; from small vans to mid-weight lorries. The one thing all vehicle marques and models have in common is the pursuit of perfection—an objective expressed not only in features such as driving pleasure, safety, fuel economy, effective ecology and competitive prices, but likewise in the achievement of the best of quality. This claim to perfection is also translated to external, visible-body design, such as exceptionally thin body gaps on doors and hoods or a guarantee against corrosion covering twelve years.

British selected to head the company, Heinz Nordhoff, was largely responsible for Volkswagen's impressive recovery and the conversion of a reminder of Nazi aspirations into the most popular car ever built. His success was the more surprising given that he was no fan of Volkswagen prior to his arrival there. Nordhoff, an engineer, had been employed by the Adam Opel Company, owned by General Motors, before and during the war. Opel management resented Hitler's Volkswagen because they were hoping to develop a similar automobile of their own.

Unlike Porsche, it was not Nordhoff's skill as an engineer (though he was responsible for innovations) but his managerial ability that made such a contribution to the success of Volkswagen. (Porsche was unable to take part in the realization of his dream; his health was ruined by nearly two years spent in a French prison on charges of war crimes for which he was later acquitted. Porsche died in 1951.) Nordhoff was able to assemble around him a talented team of executives, and he inspired his sometimes despairing and hungry workers. He actually slept in the factory for six months, and instituted the quite novel practice of addressing the workforce on a regular basis. Nordhoff, however, also gained a reputation for being autocratic and even arrogant, perhaps due to his unrelenting managerial approach.

Success came slowly, particularly in the United States. Nordhoff sorely needed U.S. dollars, but his first trip to the United States in 1949 was a failure, and only 330 Volkswagens were sold there in 1950. The car's Nazi associations continued to haunt it. Though American interest in foreign cars grew during the mid-1950s, it was really not until 1959, when the firm of Doyle Dane Bernbach took over the advertising for the car, that it began to appeal to large numbers of Americans. Doyle Dane Bernbach coined the name ''Beetle'' for the Volkswagen. In a series of award-winning advertisements, the ad agency took what had been the car's drawbacks and turned them into selling points with such slogans as ''Think Small'' and ''Ugly Is Only Skin-Deep.'' Even the car's apparently invariable design from year to year was exploited, with an advertisement that had no photography at all and claimed there was nothing new to display about the more recent models. Changes were made internally, however, and the Volkswagen became renowned for its durability. The Beetle eventually had a record production run of over 40 years, during which over 20 million cars were produced, making it the best-selling car in the world. During the 1960s, the Volkswagen Beetle became a counterculture symbol in the United States and helped imports to gain an important foothold in the American market for the first time. Another 1960s icon, the Volkswagen microbus, had made its debut in the mid-1950s.

In 1960 Volkswagen was partly privatized, with the sale of 60 percent of its stock to the public. The remaining 40 percent of the stock was divided evenly between the German government and the government of Lower Saxony. A foundation was also established to promote research in science and technology, and it received all dividends paid to the two governments. These measures settled the disagreement between the federal government and Lower Saxony over the ownership of the company. Nordhoff was glad to have an end to the question, but he did not benefit directly since he and other Volkswagen executives in high income brackets were not eligible to purchase stock under the terms of the sale. At the same time of privatization, the company's name was changed to Volkswagenwerk AG.

In 1965 the company acquired Auto Union GmbH from Daimler-Benz, thereby gaining the Audi make. Nordhoff died in 1968 following a brief illness; Kurt Lotz took over as Volkswagen chairman. Annual production of the Beetle peaked that year at 400,000 units, and by the early 1970s the Beetle was finally regarded as outdated. In 1974 Volkswagen was brought to the brink of bankruptcy. Diminishing sales, rising labor costs, increasing competition from Japanese automakers, and the end of fixed exchange rates had all contributed to the dramatic decline. New models were introduced, but they suffered from a poor reputation.

Ups and Downs in the 1980s and Early 1990s

A development program was instituted to create a successor to the Rabbit, the company's major automobile after the Beetle. Meanwhile in 1981 Volkswagen's U.S. workforce was cut from 10,000 to 6,000, and a plant in Michigan was sold to Chrysler. In 1983 the company lost $144 million in the United States alone. Meantime, in April 1982 Carl H. Hahn, who had worked under Heinz Nordhoff, took over as company chairman.

When the new Golf was finally unveiled, it looked very much like the Rabbit but had a larger engine, more interior space, and better overall performance. The changes paid off: sales rose 25 percent in 1985, profits doubled, and Volkswagen became the leading European auto manufacturer. The Golf GTI was named ''Car of the Year'' by *Motor Trend* in 1985. In the luxury car market, sales of the Audi were up 50 percent for a second straight record year. Even more remarkable was that sales of the Jetta, a model costing about $1,000 more than the

Key Dates:

1937: Company is founded as the Company for the Development of the German Volkswagen.
1938: Company is incorporated under the new name, Volkswagenwerk GmbH.
1945: British occupation forces begin operation of the Volkswagen factory.
1949: Company comes under the control of the German federal government and the state of Lower Saxony; British select Heinz Nordhoff to head the company.
1959: The name ''Beetle'' is coined for the Volkswagen.
1960: Company is partly privatized, with the sale of 60 percent of its stock to the public; remaining 40 percent of the stock is divided evenly between the German government and the government of Lower Saxony; company name is changed to Volkswagenwerk AG.
1965: Company acquires Auto Union GmbH, thereby gaining the Audi make.
1968: Nordhoff dies and is replaced as chairman by Kurt Lotz; annual production of the Beetle peaks at 400,000 units.
1982: Carl C. Hahn takes over as company chairman.
1985: Company changes its name to Volkswagen Aktiengesellschaft.
1986: Majority interest in Spain's Sociedad Española de Automobiles del Turismo S.A. (SEAT) is acquired.
1990: Company gains full control of SEAT.
1991: Company spends US$6 billion to acquire a 31 percent interest in Czech automaker Skoda.
1993: Ferdinand Piëch, grandson of founder Ferdinand Porsche, is named chairman.
1996: The VW Passat is launched.
1998: The New Beetle is launched in the United States; company acquires the Bentley, Bugatti, Lamborghini, and Rolls-Royce brands.
1999: The 100 millionth Volkswagen vehicle is produced.

Golf, jumped 120 percent. Also in 1985, the company changed its name to Volkswagen Aktiengesellschaft.

From the company's point of view, it was significant that the gap between Volkswagen and the competition had been narrowed. It used to be that German cars cost 20 percent more than their Japanese rivals, but the base price of the Golf eventually went below those of competing vehicles from Honda and Toyota. These gains were due in part to Volkswagen's policy of automating its factories. The company spent $194 million on its Halle 54 at the Wolfsburg factory (the largest single automobile factory in the world), where 25 percent of final assembly was performed by robots. The automation provided a time savings of 20 percent.

Not everything looked promising for Volkswagen, however. The company recalled 77,000 Golf and GTI models because the innovative high-density polycarbonate fuel tank which fit under the rear seat and over the axle failed to meet crash test requirements. The cost of the recall ran as high as $18 million. Additionally, 18,000 Vanagons and Campers were recalled for a potential problem with the latches on their sliding doors. Finally, the New York attorney general and two consumer groups asked the Transportation Department to recall 200,000 Audi 5000s, claiming that the cars could suddenly accelerate when shifted out of the park position. Volkswagen maintained that the accidents reported were the result of driver error, but it also replaced some damaged cars or paid repair costs.

In 1986 the company sold Royal Business Machines, one of its office equipment subsidiaries, and purchased a 75 percent interest in Spain's Sociedad Española de Automobiles del Turismo S.A. (SEAT), which had been a money-losing venture. The Spanish government agreed to absorb the company's $1 billion debt and to provide a cash infusion of $114 million. With SEAT, Volkswagen held about 25 percent of the Spanish car market. Volkswagen gained full control of SEAT in 1990.

Volkswagen made agreements with East Germany and China for the production of 300,000 and 100,000 automobile engines, respectively, with options for Volkswagen to buy back some of the engines to help alleviate its capacity problems. The company also negotiated with the Soviet Union to build an engine plant and entered into a licensing agreement with Nissan for the production of kits to build Nissan Santanas. Meanwhile, the company continued its Golf design, but its Scirocco sports model, introduced in the early 1980s, was slated for phase-out and ceased production in 1992.

Volkswagen chairman Hahn's strategy for Volkswagen's resurgence, though it included cost-cutting measures, essentially involved the expenditure of vast sums to build or acquire production facilities and thereby broaden the company's geographic scope. Capital spending, which had been increasing gradually during the latter half of the 1980s, picked up pace, reaching prodigious proportions by the beginning of the 1990s. Hahn spent US$3.3 billion to increase production capacity at a plant in Zwikau in eastern Germany, plowed an additional US$3.3 billion into SEAT, and invested a massive US$6 billion to acquire a 31 percent interest in the Czechoslovakian Skoda automobile company in 1991—all part of an enormous US$34 billion capital spending program set to take place in the first half of the 1990s. A cost-reduction plan initiated in 1987 had saved, by this point, US$2.6 billion, but the expenditures far outweighed the savings. Hahn, whose retirement was scheduled to begin in 1991, was given a two-year extension to oversee the denouement of his bold and costly plan.

Mid-to-Late 1990s: Piëch-Engineered Turnaround

Hahn, however, was gone by the following year, forced to resign at year-end 1992 after presiding over Volkswagen's rise from fourth to first place in European market share during his decade-long tenure. Despite this laudable success, Hahn's strategy had proven too ambitious. Volkswagen's U.S. operations continued to cede market share to Japanese and U.S. car manufacturers and the profit margins realized from sales elsewhere were alarmingly low. The person partly responsible for Hahn's ouster and also selected to replace him was Ferdinand Piëch, grandson of Volkswagen's founder Ferdinand Porsche. Piëch had served as the top development manager at Audi during the 1980s, then became its chairman in 1988. He rose through the ranks to gain overall control of Volkswagen in January 1993, a company he described to *Automotive News* as "a duck grown too fat to fly."

To trim the excess fat from Volkswagen, Piëch announced he would cut 12,500 of Volkswagen's 127,000 German jobs by 1998 and initiate substantial restructuring of all company operations in an effort to save Volkswagen more than US$5 billion, the figure he calculated would enable the company to avoid a loss for the year. Although substantial changes were effected, financial loss was not avoided, and Volkswagen recorded a DM 1.94 billion (US$1.15 billion) loss for 1993, abetted by poor performances of the company's North American operations, Audi AG, and SEAT.

Volkswagen returned to modest profitability in 1994, then profits rose steadily through 1998, when they reached DM 2.24 billion (US$1.35 billion). Revenues grew prodigiously as well, increasing from DM 76.59 billion (US$44.05 billion) to DM 134.24 billion (US$80.55 billion) during this period. Piëch engineered this tremendous turnaround with a strong focus on cost cutting and a reenergized lineup of models. On the cost-cutting front, Piëch managed to pry away from General Motors that company's relentless cost-cutter, José Ignacio López de Arriortúa, in March 1993. López, as he had at GM, moved to change Volkswagen's relationships with its suppliers to the company's advantage. He also took the lead on the construction of a new assembly plant in Resende, Brazil, where production began in 1996. At Resende, Volkswagen began building trucks and buses through a radical scheme in which suppliers did much of the assembly work, creating an even closer relationship between automaker and supplier and in theory a more efficient factory.

López's stay at Volkswagen proved to be a short one, however, after GM accused him of stealing confidential company documents, including plans for future Opel models, and taking them with him to VW. GM subsequently sued Volkswagen over the allegations, and criminal probes were begun in both the United States and Germany. The GM-VW feud culminated with López's November 1996 resignation from VW, his indictment on charges of industrial espionage by German prosecutors one month later, and the announcement in January 1997 of a settlement between the two auto giants whereby Volkswagen agreed to pay the U.S. carmaker $100 million.

Meanwhile, Piëch was implementing a key strategy intended to keep down production costs—producing all of the company's cars, from low- to high-end, from one of a handful of platforms. A platform included the chassis, transmission, and other components; the parts of a car that differentiate it in the eye of a customer—the body shape, steering wheel, seats, engine, etc.—could all be tailored for the specific brand and make. Whereas Volkswagen used 16 platforms in the early 1990s, Piëch had managed by the late 1990s to whittle that down to four for the main company brands: VW, Audi, Seat, and Skoda. This strategy was credited with saving Volkswagen billions of dollars during this period.

Under Piëch's leadership, Volkswagen also revitalized its product development. The VW Polo made its debut in 1994, the VW Passat was launched in mid-1996, and the fourth generation of the Golf was introduced to the public in August 1997. Perhaps the most important debut came in January 1998, when the New Beetle was launched in the United States to great fanfare. The nostalgic model helped jumpstart sales in the United States, where Volkswagen's share of the passenger car market increased from 5.2 percent in 1997 to 7.7 percent in 1998. The company delivered nearly 268,000 units to the United States in 1998, compared to just 50,000 in 1993. Also debuting in 1998 was the VW Lupo, a car featuring an economical three-cylinder engine and marking the company's entry into the subcompact segment.

Another goal of Piëch's was to take Volkswagen upmarket. Rather than taking the more time-consuming route of building a new high-end make, Piëch went the acquisition route. In July 1998 the company acquired the Rolls-Royce and Bentley Motor Cars Group from Vickers P.L.C. for US$640 million. Volkswagen thereby gained the rights to the luxury Bentley brand but the use of the Rolls-Royce was to be only a temporary one, through the end of 2002, when that brand was slated to be taken over by BMW. By September 1998 Volkswagen made several other high-end purchases: Lamborghini, the Italian sports car maker, for about US$110 million; Bugatti, another Italian producer of sports cars; and Cosworth, British maker of specialty engines, which was bought for US$178 million from Vickers Engineering plc.

There were several other important or potentially important developments in the late 1990s. In anticipation of magnesium, the lightest metallic mineral, becoming an important automotive design material, Volkswagen in 1996 acquired a 35 percent interest in Israel-based Dead Sea Magnesium Ltd., a producer, processor, and distributor of the mineral. Also in 1996 came the publication in Germany of a book titled *Volkswagen and Its Workers in the Third Reich.* Commissioned by the company ten years earlier, the 1,005-page book brought back into the light Volkswagen's close association with top Nazis and its use of Jewish concentration camp inmates and Russian prisoners of war at its Wolfsburg plant, where they worked under horrible conditions. Authors Hans Mommsen and Manfred Grieger also contended that workers were sometimes beaten, occasionally to death. In September 1998 Volkswagen announced that it was establishing a DM 20 million (US$12 million) "humanitarian aid" fund to compensate people—the survivors, at least—who were forced to work at the plant. In January 1998, the European Commission fined Volkswagen US$106.2 million for blocking Italian dealers in the early 1990s from selling to citizens of Germany and Austria who were seeking to gain from the cheap lira. Then in 1999 Volkswagen faced another European Commission probe into an alleged price-fixing cartel centering on the Passat model within VW's network of dealers in Germany. Also in 1999, Volkswagen offered to buy the 30 percent of Skoda it did not already own for US$229 million.

In September 1999 Volkswagen produced the 100 millionth vehicle in its 50-plus-year history, becoming the first European automaker to reach this lofty mark. The company had strengthened its position as Europe's number one auto company in the 1990s, and stood at the dawn of the 21st century as number three in the industry worldwide, trailing only General Motors and Ford. But a new number four company, DaimlerChrysler AG—formed in 1998 from the merger of Daimler-Benz and Chrysler Corporation—was sure to be a more formidable competitor in Europe and elsewhere. With increased competition predicted in the global auto industry during the early 21st century, Volkswagen appeared to have less options in regard to workforce reductions or shifting production overseas because of the 18 percent stake in the company still held by the German state of Lower Saxony. Analysts also questioned the company's decision to invest US$745 million to develop a new luxury car under the Volkswagen brand; the car was slated for production in 2001 and would compete directly against Mercedes-Benz and BMW. Even the move to platform sharing—which had saved billions of dollars—had its critics, who contended that it could lead to brand cannibalization; a November 22, 1999, *Business Week* article summarized this potential problem: "Buyers are starting to wonder why they should pay $25,000 for an Audi A6 when it looks suspiciously like a $16,000 Volkswagen Passat." There was finally the question of a successor to Piëch, who was expected to retire in 2002 and whose dictatorial management style may have purged Volkswagen of independent-thinking senior managers.

Principal Subsidiaries

Audi AG (98.99%); Volkswagen Sachsen GmbH; Volkswagen Bruxelles S.A. (Belgium); Volkswagen-Sarajevo d.o.o. (Bosnia-Herzegovina; 58%); Rolls-Royce & Bentley Motor Cars Ltd. (U.K.); Cosworth Technology Ltd. (U.K.); Automobili Lamborghini S.p.A. (Italy); Volkswagen-Poznan Sp. zo. o. (Poland); AutoEuropa - Automóveis Lda. (Portugal); Seat, S.A. (Spain); Volkswagen Navarra, S.A. (Spain); Gearbox del Prat, S.A. (Spain); Volkswagen Slovakia, a.s.; Skoda Auto a.s. (Czech Republic; 70%); Audi Hungária Motor Kft. (Hungary); Volkswagen Argentina S.A.; Volkswagen do Brasil Ltda. (Brazil); Volkswagen de México S.A. de C.V.; Volkswagen of South Africa (Pty.) Ltd.; Cosworth Technology Inc. (U.S.A.); Shanghai-Volkswagen Automotive Company Ltd. (China; 50%); FAW-Volkswagen Automotive Company Ltd. (China; 40%).

Principal Competitors

Bayerische Motoren Werke AG; Daewoo Group; DaimlerChrysler AG; Fiat S.p.A.; Ford Motor Company; General Motors Corporation; Honda Motor Co., Ltd.; Hyundai Motor Company; Isuzu Motors Limited; Kia Motors Corporation; Mazda Motor Corporation; Mitsubishi Motors Corporation; Nissan Motor Co., Ltd.; PSA Peugeot Citroen S.A.; Renault S.A.; Saab Automobile AB; Suzuki Motor Corporation; Toyota Motor Corporation.

Further Reading

Choi, Audrey, "European Auto Makers Show Signs of Bouncing Back; Cost Cutting and Shift Toward Less-Expensive Cars Brighten Outlook," *Wall Street Journal,* September 15, 1994, p. B4.

Coleman, Brian, "VW Chairman Douses Sector's Merger Craze," *Wall Street Journal,* March 26, 1999.

Ewing, Jack, Kathleen Kerwin, and Karen Nickel Anhalt, "VW: Spinning Its Wheels?," *Business Week* (intl. ed.), November 22, 1999, p. 20.

Feast, Richard, "Cutting Cost at VW," *Automotive Industries,* September 1993, p. 37.

Flint, Jerry, "Eastward Ho," *Forbes,* November 26, 1990, p. 291.

Flint, Robert, "VW Envisions China As a Base for Asia Exports," *Wall Street Journal,* September 6, 1996.

Guyon, Janet, "Getting the Bugs Out at VW," *Fortune,* March 29, 1999, pp. 96+.

——, "Volkswagen's Big New Headache," *Fortune,* June 8, 1998, p. 144.

Hopfinger, K.B., *The Volkswagen Story,* 3rd ed., Cambridge, Mass.: Robert Bentley, 1971.

Kahn, Joseph, "Departure of VW's China Unit Head Reveals Flaws in a Rare Success Story," *Wall Street Journal,* April 18, 1997, p. A15.

Klebnikov, Paul, "Bringing Back the Beetle," *Forbes,* April 7, 1997, p. 42.

Kurylko, Diana T., "Lopez Sees VW Return to U.S. Glory of the '70s," *Automotive News,* March 29, 1994, p. 8.

Maling, Nick, "Driving Ambition," *Marketing Week,* March 4, 1999, pp. 26–29.

Miller, Scott, "Europe's Auto Market Takes on American Look," *Wall Street Journal,* September 13, 1999, pp. A33, A38.

——, "VW Sows Confusion with Common Pattern for Models," *Wall Street Journal,* October 25, 1999, pp. A25, A38.

Mitchener, Brandon, "VW's Bid to Face Wartime Past Produces Damning Book Instead," *Wall Street Journal,* November 7, 1996, p. A19.

Naughton, Keith, and Karen Lowry Miller, "From the New Beetle to—a VW Pickup?," *Business Week,* August 9, 1999, p. 37.

Nelson, Walter H., *Small Wonder: The Amazing Story of the Volkswagen,* Boston: Little Brown, 1965, 271 p.; new ed. published as *Small Wonder: The Amazing Story of the Volkswagen Beetle,* Cambridge, Mass.: Robert Bentley, 1998, 378 p.

"The People's Car," *Economist,* March 7, 1992, p. 74.

Sawyer, Arlena, "VW Merges U.S., Canada Units," *Automotive News,* August 8, 1994, p. 1.

Stern, Gabriella, "VW's U.S. Comeback Rides on Restyled Beetle," *Wall Street Journal,* May 6, 1997, p. B1.

Stowe, Robert, "Hard Day's Night: Volkswagen Is Coming Back," *Financial World,* January 30, 1996, p. 48.

Templeman, John, "Carl Hahn's High-Octane Growth Plan for VW," *Business Week,* March 18, 1991, p. 46.

Vlasic, Bill, "Beetlemania to the Rescue," *Business Week,* January 12, 1998, p. 46.

Volkswagen Writes History, Wolfsburg, Germany: Volkswagen AG, [1998].

Winestock, Geoff, "Volkswagen Faces European Probe into Price Fixing," *Wall Street Journal,* September 20, 1999, p. A25.

Woodruff, David, "VW's Factory of the Future," *Business Week,* October 7, 1996, p. 52.

Woodruff, David, and Kathleen Kerwin, "Can Volkswagen Ride Out the Storm?," *Business Week,* November 25, 1996, p. 34.

Woodruff, David, and Keith Naughton, "Hard-Driving Boss: Ferdinand Piëch Is Determined to Make Volkswagen into a Global Force," *Business Week,* October 5, 1998, p. 82.

Woodruff, David, David Lindorff, and Elisabeth Malkin, "VW Is Back, but for How Long?," *Business Week* (intl. ed.), February 26, 1996, pp. 22+.

—Jeffrey L. Covell
—updated by David E. Salamie

Wenner Media, Inc.

1290 Avenue of the Americas, 2nd Floor
New York, New York 10104
U.S.A.
Telephone: (212) 484-1616
Fax: (212) 484-1713
Web site: http://www.usmagazine.com/html/wenner.html

Private Company
Incorporated: 1967 as Straight Arrow Publishers, Inc.
Employees: 350
Sales: $253.5 million (1998)
NAIC: 511120 Periodical Publishers

Wenner Media, Inc. is the owner of *Rolling Stone, US,* and *Men's Journal* magazines. The company was founded in 1967 as Straight Arrow Publishers, Inc. by Jann Wenner and a small group of investors. The San Francisco-based company's initial publication was *Rolling Stone* magazine, which became known as the voice of the late 1960s "Woodstock" generation. Straight Arrow formed a book division in 1971 and purchased or founded a number of other magazines over the years, though these efforts have not been as successful as *Rolling Stone.* Since the company's move to New York City in 1977, *Rolling Stone* has become more glossy, more celebrity-driven, and more profitable, and has successfully focused its energies on wooing younger generations of readers. The company has also produced radio and television programs, in addition to its publishing activities.

1960s Origins

Jann S. Wenner was born (as Jan) in 1946 in New York City. While he was still an infant, his family moved to the San Francisco Bay area, where his father started a baby food manufacturing company. Over the next few years, as Wenner Baby Formulas, Inc. grew into a profitable business, Wenner's parents divorced when he was in his early teens, and he spent most of his high school years at a boarding school near Los Angeles. He had begun writing articles for the school paper, and he continued to pursue this interest when he entered college at Berkeley in 1963. By the middle of his sophomore year he was writing a music column there under the pen name Mr. Jones, which was taken from a Bob Dylan song.

The San Francisco Bay area, home to many of the founders of the 1950s Beat movement, had spawned a new generation of young nonconformists by the mid-1960s, the hippies. At one of the first hippie dance concerts, in October 1965, Jann Wenner met *San Francisco Chronicle* music critic Ralph J. Gleason. The two became friends, and after Wenner had unsuccessfully tried to get a writing job outside of San Francisco, Gleason offered to recommend him for a position at the newly formed *Sunday Ramparts* magazine. When the spinoff of the left-leaning *Ramparts* folded after a few months, the ambitious 21-year-old decided to start his own magazine.

Borrowing $7,500 from a group of investors that consisted of family and friends (issuing one share of stock per dollar invested), Wenner founded Straight Arrow Publishers, Inc. to produce a new biweekly music magazine that would be called *Rolling Stone.* Gleason gave the magazine its name, which was taken from the title of a classic blues song (which had also inspired a group of British musicians, as well as Bob Dylan). The new publication relied heavily on volunteer labor, as well as donated furniture and rent-free office space in the loft above its printing company. A distinctive logo was designed by legendary psychedelic poster artist Rick Griffin.

The first issue of *Rolling Stone* rolled off the presses in October 1967, with Beatle John Lennon on the cover. Sales of the early issues were modest, and there was much competition for the attention of the masses of young people who had come to San Francisco during the "Summer of Love" that year. *Rolling Stone* offered something different from other hippie publications, however, with reporting on music being its primary purpose. The writing was also more journalistic and the design cleaner, thanks to Wenner's sanctioned borrowing of the style and paste-up sheets of *Sunday Ramparts.* During its first year, the publication grew in professionalism and reputation. Wenner scored a major coup in October 1968 when he published photos of Beatle Lennon and his wife Yoko Ono in the nude (taken from the cover of their controversial *Two Virgins* record album), and sold out several printings of the issue. *Rolling Stone*

Key Dates:

1967: Jann Wenner founds Straight Arrow Publishers, Inc. and starts *Rolling Stone* magazine.
1971: Straight Arrow Books division is formed to publish *Lennon Remembers.*
1977: Straight Arrow moves to New York City.
1985: Company purchases 25 percent of *US* magazine; Rolling Stone-inspired film *Perfect* is released.
1989: Remaining 75 percent of *US* is acquired.
1991: *Men's Journal* is founded.
1993: *Family Life* is introduced; company's name changes to Wenner Media, Inc.
1995: Wenner's personal life makes gossip columns; *Family Life* magazine is divested.
1996: *Rolling Stone* launches web site.
1998: Alliance with JAMTV to add features to web site is announced.

was losing money, however, and more funding was needed to keep the magazine afloat.

Seeking More Investors; Starting New Magazines

In the fall of 1968 Wenner located several new investors who quickly infused $40,000 into Straight Arrow. In early 1969, with additional funding from rocker Mick Jagger, the company began to publish *British Rolling Stone,* but sales did not meet expectations and it was soon folded. In May Wenner purchased an entertainment magazine, *New York Scenes,* for ten percent of Straight Arrow's stock. This was another misfire, and publication was suspended after a number of months in the red. In 1970, at the same time that the company was moving to new offices, still another new magazine, *Earth Times,* was started. The environmentalism-themed publication was also unsuccessful, and was abandoned after four issues.

Rolling Stone, however, was booming, and Wenner snagged another major John Lennon scoop by publishing his first interview on the Beatles' breakup, which offered caustic criticism of his former bandmates. The two-part interview sold through several printings and provided the impetus to launch Straight Arrow Books the following year, when the interview was published as *Lennon Remembers* (though against the musician's wishes). Despite this success, and the magazine's increasing acclaim, fiscal 1970 saw the company $250,000 in the red, and Wenner again sought outside financing. He found Max Palevsky, a wealthy ex-computer engineer, who put up $200,000 in a deal which would give him increasing quantities of stock each year the company continued to lose money.

Perhaps spurred on by this arrangement, Wenner tightened ship and Straight Arrow racked up its best year ever, earning a reported $400,000 in 1971. The early 1970s saw *Rolling Stone* turning out some of its finest issues to date, with cover photos by renowned rock photographer Annie Leibovitz and provocative articles by a new series of writers, including Joe Eszterhas, Ben Fong-Torres, Joe Klein, Howard Kohn, and ''Gonzo journalist'' Hunter S. Thompson. Music pieces came from such noted contributors as Greil Marcus, Jon Landau, David Marsh, Langdon Winner, and Lester Bangs. Thompson's unconventional coverage of the 1972 McGovern presidential campaign was a media sensation and resulted in increased sales for each issue it was featured in. *Rolling Stone* also published a number of important investigative articles that explored such topics as the death of nuclear energy whistle-blower Karen Silkwood and the ordeal of kidnapped heiress Patty Hearst.

Jann Wenner, though recognized for his brilliance as an editor, was possessed of both a mercurial personality and, according to author Robert Draper, healthy appetites for cocaine and vodka, which sometimes made the lives of his employees difficult. More than a few writers and editors at *Rolling Stone* burned out over the years, or were fired by Wenner after they had clashed with him.

In 1974 Rolling Stone opened a Washington Bureau, for the purpose of increasing the magazine's political content, but the operation soon proved too expensive and was shut down. A planned offshoot magazine, *Politics,* never reached print. The magazine also shifted its format from the quarter-folded newsprint configuration it had started with to a flat-folded, center-stapled style with four-color covers. This new size enabled the addition of more pages, which gave more space for advertising, thus raising revenues. New staffers were hired to focus on increasing the magazine's advertising content, and ad sales grew by 50 percent in both 1974 and 1975.

1977: Move to New York

With the importance of San Francisco to rock music's cutting edge now mostly a fading memory, and with the entertainment world increasingly dominated by New York-based companies and performers, Wenner made the decision in 1977 to head East. Leaving behind a number of staffers (some of whom would work for the magazine's San Francisco bureau), and a headquarters that cost a mere $6,000 in annual rent, Wenner found a location on Madison Avenue that he fitted with a sleek new interior. The new offices cost a reported $330,000 a year.

Wenner decided to celebrate his company's first decade in business by putting together a television special. The end result was a disappointment, as many big stars dropped out of the cast and the slickness of the show seemed to run counter to the magazine's image. A series of Rolling Stone radio programs were also now being produced, and Wenner began to explore the possibility of getting involved in film production. A new publication, *Outside,* was launched, though it did not seem to catch on initially and was sold after a year. The adventure sports and mountaineering magazine, retooled by its new owners, later found its audience and became a major success. Rolling Stone Press was formed in 1978, as a new book publishing arm that superseded the dormant Straight Arrow Books.

In 1979 Jann Wenner was hired by French publisher David Filipacchi to edit the floundering *Look* magazine. Wenner, whose hands-on involvement at *Rolling Stone* had waxed and waned over the years while a succession of editors handled the day-to-day details of publishing, plunged into the new assignment with gusto. Within two issues he had turned the unprofitable magazine around and put it into the black. Despite this success, Filipacchi suddenly shut down the publication and rejected Wenner's purchase offer.

The beginning of the 1980s saw *Rolling Stone's* advertising revenues declining. As the conservative Reagan era took hold, the magazine that for many defined the 1960s counterculture was forced to change with the times. *Rolling Stone's* focus began to shift toward movie and television celebrities, with music and political reporting sometimes taking a back seat. In 1981 the magazine converted to an all-slick-paper format, dropping the newsprint which it had used since 1967. Further moves to court advertisers were made, including the use of frequent supplement sections. Straight Arrow Publishers also started a sister magazine, *Record,* which focused solely on music. It lasted until 1985. Another spinoff, *Rolling Stone College Papers,* was a financial debacle for the company and was quickly abandoned.

Milestones in the 1980s

The year 1985 saw the realization of one of Wenner's dreams when he participated in the making of a Hollywood motion picture about a *Rolling Stone* type magazine. Cast as an editor to John Travolta's reporter, he received favorable notices for his first acting role. The movie itself, *Perfect,* was less well-received and was a major box office bomb, despite getting a big push from *Rolling Stone.*

The company recorded several other high points in 1985, including *Rolling Stone* topping one million in circulation, an important milestone in the magazine business. Wenner and his wife, Jane, also purchased back most of the outstanding shares of Straight Arrow Publishers, and the company sponsored an advertising campaign called ''Perception/Reality'' which successfully persuaded advertisers to view the magazine's readers as clean-cut yuppies rather than aging hippies. Ad revenues grew over the next several years as a result, with major companies that had never before advertised in the publication signing on with *Rolling Stone.*

The company also purchased 25 percent ownership of *US* magazine, a money-losing celebrity magazine that had been founded by the New York Times Co. in 1977. The fortunes of *US* did not turn around as quickly as was anticipated, and Wenner later admitted its situation had been worse than he knew when he invested in it. In 1989 the company purchased the remaining 75 percent of *US*, and in 1991 it was converted from a biweekly into a monthly, with editorial content now reflecting Wenner's desire to make it ''the next *Vanity Fair.*''

In 1986 Straight Arrow started *Marketing Through Music,* a newsletter which was intended to help advertisers get their messages to music fans by such means as the sponsorship of concert tours. It lasted for three years. *Rolling Stone* itself was getting more and more cozy with advertisers, publishing frequent theme issues that attracted ads from companies whose wares related to the central concept.

New Magazines for the 1990s

In 1991 yet another new magazine was rolled out, this one modeled on *Outside,* the one that got away. *Men's Journal* started out as a semiannual, then went bimonthly, then monthly in its second year. In 1993 the company also founded *Family Life.* This newest effort was intended to appeal to baby boomers who were raising families. Late in 1993 Straight Arrow Publishers changed its name to Wenner Media, Inc. The company's headquarters had moved by this time to New York's Rockefeller Center.

The year 1994 saw *US* reportedly nearing its first money-making year ever, while *Rolling Stone* circulation hit 1.2 million. *Men's Journal* and *Family Life* were less successful, but the company continued to show faith in their eventual profitability. In the summer Wenner Media announced deals with other companies to use the *Rolling Stone* and *Family Life* names to sell recordings and to produce a television program for a home shopping channel.

In early 1995 Wenner's personal life hit the news when his romantic relationship with a Calvin Klein staffer, 20 years his junior, was revealed. Jann and Jane Wenner remained married, however, and continued to jointly control Wenner Media. Shortly after the story hit the press, the company sold *Family Life* to Hachette Filipacchi, though the deal had been in the works for some time.

In the summer of 1995 Wenner announced that *Rolling Stone* would be expanding its coverage of new artists. Though the magazine had periodically made this effort over the years, it still seemed to favor baby boomer heroes over new performers. Now the surging growth of monthly competitor Spin was cutting into the *Rolling Stone* readership and ad sales, and Wenner fought back by hiring the editor of the music magazine Request to make improvements in this area. *Rolling Stone* also went online during the year, with a version of the magazine accessible on Compuserve. A year later the magazine put up its own web site, which joined forces in 1998 with JAMTV (subsequently known as Tunes.com) to offer music and video downloads and other specialized features.

As the 1990s drew to a close, Wenner Media's publications seemed to be cross-pollinating. *Rolling Stone* and *US* both began to increasingly emphasize stories on fashion and hot young celebrities, typically accompanied by lavish photo shoots. *Men's Journal* was also sporting greater coverage of fashion and was running more stories on personal health and celebrity profiles as well.

In 1999 the company announced plans to shift the *US* publication schedule from monthly to weekly. The move was a response to several market forces, including the success of Time, Inc.'s *Entertainment Weekly* and *People* magazines. Wenner expressed his intention to keep *US* ''celebrity-friendly'' in contrast with the more gossipy character of its competitors. He explained to the *New York Times:* ''We will be nice to celebrities. A lot of my friends are in the entertainment business.''

The privately owned Wenner Media, with a third of a century in the publishing industry, had come a long way from its origins in ''Summer of Love'' San Francisco. Since the company had moved to New York City, flagship publication *Rolling Stone* had become more focused and slicker, losing much of its original identity but growing more consistent and profitable in the process. Wenner was committed to making *US* and *Men's Journal* equally successful and had the organization and vision to pull it off, if it could be accomplished in the ultra-competitive marketplace of the late 1990s.

Principal Divisions

Men's Journal; *Rolling Stone*; *US.*

Principal Competitors

Advance Publications, Inc.; Dennis Publishing; Hachette Filipacchi Magazines, Inc.; The Hearst Corporation; Miller Publishing Group; Rodale, Inc.; Stern Publishing; Time Warner, Inc.; VNU N.V.

Further Reading

Adams, Mark, ''*Stone* Changes Its Tune,'' *Mediaweek*, July 17, 1995, p. 4.

Bounds, Wendy, ''Wenner Media Inc. Hires Outsider Berg for *Rolling Stone,* Other Magazines,'' *The Wall Street Journal*, April 9, 1999, p. B6.

Case, Tony, ''When Does Gossip Become News?,'' *Editor & Publisher*, March 18, 1995, p. 9.

Draper, Robert, *Rolling Stone Magazine: The Uncensored History*, New York: Doubleday, 1990.

Granatstein, Lisa, ''RS Rolls out Fresher Look,'' *Mediaweek*, August 10, 1998, p. 6.

Huhn, Mary, ''The Arrow Never Rests,'' *Mediaweek*, July 19, 1993, p. 10.

Kerwin, Ann Marie, ''Understanding *US*,'' *Inside Media*, May 29, 1996, p. 44.

Kuczynski, Alex, ''Striking Back at the Empire,'' *New York Times*, September 27, 1999, p. 1.

Negus, Beth, ''Wenner's Circulation Trifecta,'' *Direct*, October 1, 1995, p. 64.

Reece, Doug, ''*Rolling Stone*, JAMTV Join Web Forces; Collaboration Revamps Magazine's Internet Site,'' *Billboard*, March 7, 1998, p. 48.

Reilly, Patrick M., ''A Rolling Stone: Jann Wenner's Rift with Wife Shakes up His Publishing Empire,'' *Wall Street Journal*, March 3, 1995, p. A1.

Silber, Tony, ''Straight Arrow Takes a Flier on *US*,'' *Folio*, August 1, 1991, p. 43.

Veronsky, Frank, ''Casting New Stones: Not Content to Own His Piece of the Rock Market, Jann Wenner Ambitiously Expands His Media Horizons,'' *Adweek*, February 28, 1994, p. 10.

Warner, Melanie, ''A Younger, Hipper *US*,'' *Inside Media*, May 11, 1994, p. 62.

''Wenner's Manly Move: Straight Arrow to Defy Recession with New Magazine,'' *Advertising Age*, November 25, 1991.

—Frank Uhle

Weyco Group, Incorporated

P.O. Box 1188
Milwaukee, Wisconsin 53201
U.S.A.
Telephone: (414) 908-1600
Fax: (414) 908-1601

Public Company
Incorporated: 1892 as W.R.P. Shoe Company
Employees: 525
Sales: $127.1 million (1998)
Stock Exchanges: NASDAQ
Ticker Symbol: WEYS
NAIC: 316213 Men's Footwear (Except Athletic) Manufacturing; 44821 Shoe Stores; 533110 Brand Name Licensing

Weyco Group, Incorporated is a major manufacturer, purchaser, and marketer of men's and boy's footwear, including mid-priced leather dress shoes and lower-priced casual footwear made from synthetic materials and leather. Weyco Group sells its products to more than 8,000 shoe, clothing, and department stores. Its top brands include Nunn Bush, Brass Boot, and Stacy Adams. The company manages 151 leased departments in men's clothing and department stores nationwide, and operates, through Nunn Bush, 47 company-owned retail stores. It licenses the Stacy Adams name—known by Swing Dancers for the two-tone Dayton Wingtip—for men's clothing and accessories. The Florsheim family—descendants of the founder of footwear giant Florsheim Group—controls 53 percent of Weyco Group's voting power.

Weyco was founded in 1892 by three Appleton, Wisconsin men who formed a partnership known as the W.R.P. Shoe Company, offering retail shoes regionally. By 1895 two of the partners had sold their shares of the business to two brothers. The business was moved to Chippewa Falls, a thriving lumber town in northern Wisconsin. The site was laid out with a retail store on the lower level and a handcrafted shoemaking workshop upstairs. The company catered to workers in the logging industry by providing tough, well-crafted shoes and boots made of quality materials.

Frank Weyenberg, a young man with an eighth grade education, entered the business in 1897 at the age of 15. Three years after becoming a partner, Frank Weyenberg took a trip to Milwaukee to seek help from then Mayor David Rose. The young entrepreneur was interested in building a factory to accommodate expansion. By that time (1900), shoe production had grown to 300 pairs per day. The business was soon relocated from Chippewa Falls to 122 Reed Street in Milwaukee. In Frank Weyenberg's words, "I figured the tanneries were here (Milwaukee) and also we were close to our market." The energetic Frank Weyenberg served as assistant superintendent of the factory, general manager, and traveling salesman.

The company gradually increased production but experienced financial difficulties when it switched to more automated technologies. During this period the two brothers in the partnership became disillusioned and sold out to Frank Weyenberg and his father, Franklin. The company was reorganized from a partnership to an incorporated entity, the Weyenberg Shoe Manufacturing Company, in 1906, with the 24-year-old Frank positioned as company president. A new plant was constructed on Brown Street in Milwaukee in 1910, and additional operations were added in Beaver Dam (1913) and Portage (1918). An office and shipping center were added across the street from the Brown Street plant. Although the company continued to struggle between the years of 1908 and 1920, the company grew from producing 600 to over 8,000 pairs of shoes per day.

Combat Boots for World War I

At the onset of World War I, Frank Weyenberg served on the War Production Board and sold liberty bonds. His company manufactured combat boots for that effort. Recognized as an ambitious man, Frank entered into a business partnership with his golfing partner and organized the Simplex Shoe Manufacturing Company to make children's shoes, justifying the formation of the company because "we couldn't get any money for our scraps [from shoemaking]." He also organized the United Fertilizer Company in 1919. Then when Weyenberg decided that the company was paying too much for shoe cartons, he organized the Manufacturers Box Company, and when he needed chemical supplies, he formed the Manufacturers Chemi-

Company Perspectives:

"The company aims to establish and maintain an Institution and a Name founded on justice and right that will live through generations and will stand as a monument, a credit to the efforts of the men [and women] who made it, to give the world a good product, to stay among the leaders of the industry, and above all to make friends of our business associates—and to gather about us men [and women] whose ambitions are high, and who are equipped in all ways to help us carry on the work we have in hand, and attain the good for which we are striving." –Franklin L. Weyenberg, Weyco president, 1906–64

cal Supply. These were profitable operations, structured as co-operatives, with various shoe companies sharing ownership and reaping the benefits from producing lower-cost supplies.

The period following the end of the war was very difficult financially, but the company survived it and the ensuing Great Depression. Weyenberg applied for a listing in the New York Curb Exchange (later named the American Stock Exchange) in 1937, listing 300,000 outstanding shares of its common stock. The Weyenberg Shoe Company had expanded to include additional operations in Milwaukee, Beaver Dam, Portage, and Hartford, Wisconsin, and Ludington, Michigan. By this time, Weyenberg had become the largest shoe manufacturing company in the city of Milwaukee, producing over 10,000 pairs of shoes per day.

World War II-Era Transition

The company made a transition from producing logging-type shoes and boots to concentrating on the production of fine men's dress shoes. Following the transition, net sales soon climbed to over $8 million. Factories that produced other lines of shoes were closed, including the Ludington plant, which made work shoes (closed in 1942), and the Hartford Plant, which manufactured children's shoes and women's casual shoes (closed in 1953).

By 1964, net sales had grown to over $20 million, and Frank Weyenberg sold $750,000 worth of his stock to Thomas W. Florsheim, who had been associated with a family operated Chicago shoe manufacturing business, the Florsheim Shoe Company. Florsheim became the Weyenberg Shoe Manufacturing Company president and Frank Weyenberg acted as chairman of the board. At that time, the two men issued the following statement outlining their objectives: "We have had a change of management this year to insure continuity in our company. Along with our new, young management team, we are continuing the process of styling up our merchandise, reorganizing our sales approach, updating our facilities and streamlining our procedures. We hope all of this will mean larger profits and bigger sales in 1965." The company was producing a broad line of men's fashion dress shoes and a very selective line of men's work shoes and boots. The company ranked 15th nationally, in dollar sales, among more than 1,000 domestic shoe manufacturers. Management decided to apply for a listing on the New York Stock Exchange in 1965. Frank Weyenberg lived to see his company become a major presence in the fashion shoe industry. He remained on the board of directors until his death in 1976. Shortly thereafter, the company adopted the name Weyco Group, Incorporated, to better reflect the company's increasingly diverse family of shoes.

Foreign purchases of shoes and components became vital to Weyco as competitive pressures increased in the marketplace. The company responded to the necessity for a diversified, broadly priced line of shoes, acquiring the Nunn Bush Shoe Company to supplement its wholesale business. Weyco also assumed ownership of factories in Milwaukee and Edgerton, Wisconsin, in addition to 150 retail and leased outlets. The company opened a factory for manufacturing hand-sewn shoes in Portage, Wisconsin, and acquired Adler Shoe Shops, a retailer of men's shoes based in New York. The Houston, Texas-based Morgan-Hayes, Incorporated, was added the following year. Factories were opened in Waterloo, Wisconsin; Dundalk, Ireland; and Vincenza, Italy. The Stacy-Adams Shoe Company, after more than a century in business, became part of Weyco in 1971. Weyco management wanted more exposure for its Stacy Adams fashion footwear line, which was developed into a major fashion line after signing licensing agreements with hosiery and tailored-clothing leaders. The company chose Lanier Clothes of Atlanta, Georgia, for its apparel licensee and Chatsworth, California-based Keepers International, for hosiery.

Changing Shoe Trends: 1990s

Beginning in the late 1980s, the Stacy Adams line of fashion footwear began adopting the whimsical "retro look" borrowed from styles popular in the 20s, 30s, and 40s. Young Swing dancing consumers, in particular, sported vintage clothing and sought spats, black-and-white wingtips, and oxfords to coordinate with their apparel. An average 200,000 pairs of the Weyco retro-styled shoes were being sold annually, substantially boosting company profits. While many fashion companies compromised these styles by using materials different from the originals, some companies produced footwear using real leather, threads, and colors copied diligently from the past. According to Barbara Schneider-Levy of *Footwear News,* "As men's footwear looks backward while moving ahead . . . retro looks reminiscent of *The Untouchables* and *Top Hat* are showing up in modern fashion terms. However, there are some authentics in the market today, such as the cap-toe boot and oxford called the Madison, circa 1915, from the Stacy Adams line. . .".

Weyco was hit hard when May Department Stores, the company that leased shoe departments in its stores to Weyco, terminated the arrangement, resulting in a drop of 15 percent in profits and ten percent in earnings. Despite that, other factors in the market promised to compensate for the setback, which may have been part of the impetus for company insiders proposing to take the company private. Medium- and lower-priced shoes were selling more than the high-priced ones, just as trends were shifting from athletic footwear to casual shoes, translating into very favorable conditions for Weyco. Company insiders wanted to buy out the minority public stockholders who controlled 43 percent of the votes for $50 million, or $34 per share. The company was debt-free with cash reserves of $27 million. It had overfunded pensions and undervalued inventories. Analysts es-

Key Dates:

1892: W.R.P. Shoe Company was founded.
1905: Partnership is dissolved and company is incorporated a year later as Weyenberg Shoe Manufacturing Company.
1916: Company produces combat boots for soldiers in World War I.
1920: Production exceeds 8,000 pairs of shoes per day.
1937: IPO is completed with the New York Curb Exchange (American Stock Exchange).
1942–53: Company closes selected plants due to new types of products.
1964: Thomas Florsheim buys into Weyenberg Company, becoming president.
1965: Company is listed on the New York Stock Exchange.
1970: Company launches a decade of acquisitions.
1976: Present name is adopted.
1994: Proposal by management to take company private is defeated.
1998: Brand exposure expands via licensing agreements.

timated that Weyco shares were actually worth closer to $43 a share, more than 25 percent over what the insiders were offering. Marcia Berss reported in *Forbes* that Wisconsin law required Weyco Chairman Thomas Florsheim and his group to get approval from half the minority shareholders before it could take the company private, reporting ''The group vowed not to sell if its bid was rejected—turning the bid into a take-it-or-leave-it deal.''

Outraged at what they believed was Weyco management's attempt to buy the company at an undervalued price, Alan Kahn, former president of New York City money management firm Kahn Brothers & Company, and Quest Advisory Group, another New York money manager that held Weyco stock, rallied successfully against the bid. Kahn's daughter Amanda also filed two separate suits against the company. Alan Kahn was known for filing lawsuits against company managers and investment bankers that he perceived were not carrying out their fiduciary duty to best represent shareholders. The company responded cooperatively, and volunteered a shareholder list that the Kahns used to send a letter explaining Alan Kahn's opposition to the proposed deal. Kahn made the point that he and others believed the proposal by Weyco managers represented an abuse of the super-voting rights shareholders had granted insiders in 1987 as an antitakeover measure. To some it appeared that managers were pulling their own hostile takeover—hostile to outside shareholders. In the end, Weyco managers announced that they were withdrawing their offer to buy the company, following indications that they were compromising shareholder support, and considering the effects of a long litigation process.

In their defense, Weyco management said that its bid was based on the analysis of two major investment banking firms: Bear, Stearns & Company, New York City, and Kemper Securities Inc., Chicago. According to Rich Kirchen of the *Business Journal—Milwaukee,* ''Management believed its offer—which at the time represented an all-time high for Weyco stock—gave shareholders a profitable way to exit an illiquid stock.''

Repercussions of the failed buyout proposal appeared on the ballot for the following Weyco annual meeting. The Quest Advisory Corporation proposed that Weyco eliminate the super-voting Class B stock that was issued as an anti-hostile takeover measure—and reestablish a single class of common stock.

Late in 1997 Weyco began construction on a $13 million warehouse and distribution center, locating it on a 12-acre parcel near its roots and its workers. Thomas Florsheim commented that, ''One of our biggest assets is our people,'' adding ''we have extremely low turnover, so we don't want to lose our work force.'' A larger, more modern headquarters was also intended for the site. With production climbing—from 1991 to 1996, the number of pairs of shoes shipped by the company rose from 3.4 million to five million—Weyco facilities were overflowing. The company's only manufacturing facility remained in Beaver Dam, also the site of a large warehouse, which it planned to shut down after the new warehouse in Milwaukee became operational. The shutdown meant job losses for approximately 50 employees.

Company managers anticipated additional growth in the fashion-casual market, the fastest-growing area of the casual market. In 1999, Weyco doubled its advertising budget in order to build the SAO brand of shoes. They targeted the hip-hop culture by placing advertisements in music magazines such as *Vibe, The Source, Blaze,* and *Rap Pages.* According to *Footwear News,* ''The full-page ads have an 'edgy, urban feel to them,' said Florsheim, with the 'centerpiece' shoes appearing in street locales. Weyco is marketing SAO as its own brand, though with subtle links to its parent, Stacy Adams, on boxes and sole plugs.'' Stylish oxfords, boots, and sandals were targeting the 18- to 24-year-old urban streetwear market.

After getting its feet wet with other licensing agreements, Weyco entered into further agreements with Jimmy Sales, New York, to manufacture, market, and distribute Stacy Adams' men's neckwear. Through department and specialty stores, ties and handkerchiefs were marketed for the sophisticated urban consumer. The company began considering additional licensing agreements to include hats, belts, and clothing, but wanted to move carefully in choosing the right partners. In an effort to leverage the strength of the Stacy Adams brand beyond footwear, Weyco chose to enter into a licensing agreement with Dorfman Pacific of Stockton, California, to manufacture and market a collection of Stacy Adams headwear. The company also collaborated with Aquarius Ltd. of St. Louis, to manufacture and market belts and small leather goods.

Encouraged by strong sales, the company confidently approached the new millennium. By the third quarter of 1999, sales had increased seven percent over 1998 third quarter results. Weyco's wholesale division showed a seven percent increase in sales, driven primarily by the Stacy Adams line. Looking ahead, the company intended to continue focusing on its wholesale business.

Principal Subsidiaries

Nunn Bush Shoe Company; Stacy Adams Shoe Company.

Principal Competitors

Brown Group, Inc.; Florsheim Shoe Company; Phillips-Van Heusen Corporation.

Further Reading

Berss, Marcia, "If the Shoe Fits . . . ," *Forbes*, November 7, 1994, p. 12.

——, "Waiting for the Other Shoe to Drop," *Forbes*, June 20, 1994, p. 48.

Dries, Michael, "With 'Shoes all Over the Place,' Weyco Begins Expansion," *Business Journal—Milwaukee*, December 19, 1997, p. 6.

Kirchen, Richard, "Capitalist Crusader Thwarted Weyco Manager's Buyout Bid," *Business Journal—Milwaukee*, July 30, 1994, p. 7.

——, "Weyco Shareholders Seek to Boost Stock," *Business Journal—Milwaukee*, September 24, 1994, p. 9.

"News Digest," *Footwear News*, May 10, 1999, p. 18.

Rieger, Nancy, "Weyco Nixes Plan to Go Private," *Footwear News*, August 1, 1994, p. 41.

Schneider-Levy, Barbara, "Fine and Dandy," *Footwear News*, May 8, 1995, p. 12.

——, "Thread Count: Targeting Young, Urban Men, Stacy Adams Has Extended Its Brand by Licensing Clothing and Hosiery Lines," *Footwear News*, August 10, 1998, p. 64.

"Shoe Maker to Close Beaver Dam, Wisconsin, Warehouse," *Knight-Ridder/Tribune Business News*, June 11, 1999, p. OKRB99162178.

"Weyco Gains 200 Percent in First Quarter," *Footwear News*, May 4, 1992, p. 31.

"Weyco Group Inc. (Special Supplement—Hot Shots)," *Business Journal—Milwaukee*, July 30, 1990, p. X14.

"Weyco Pumps Up Volume for SAO Advertisements," *Footwear News*, February 1, 1999, p. 16.

—Terri Mozzone

World Wrestling Federation Entertainment, Inc.

1241 East Main Street
Stamford, Connecticut 06902
U.S.A.
Telephone: (203) 352-8600
Fax: (203) 359-5151
Web site: http://www.wwf.com

Public Company
Incorporated: 1963 as World Wide Wrestling Federation
Employees: 386
Sales: $251.5 million (1999)
Stock Exchanges: NASDAQ
Ticker Symbol: WWFE
NAIC: 71132 Promoters of Performing Arts, Sports, and Similar Events Without Facilities; 71119 Other Performing Arts Companies

World Wrestling Federation Entertainment, Inc., known to millions of fans worldwide as the WWF, promotes and produces the unique spectacle of professional wrestling. The company's activities spread far and wide, touching on all aspects of an industry that generates well in excess of $1 billion annually. WWF produces roughly 200 live events a year, 12 pay-per-view programs a year, and two cable television programs. The company licenses its wrestling personalities for an enormous array of merchandise, publishes two magazines, *RAW* and *WWF,* and sells home videos and compact discs. WWF events are broadcast to 120 countries and translated into 11 languages.

1960s Origins

Vincent K. McMahon, Jr., represented the third generation of McMahons to earn its living by promoting professional wrestling. His grandfather, Jesse McMahon, established the trend, foregoing his career as a boxing promoter during the 1940s to try his hand at performing the same function for professional wrestling. Jesse McMahon's son, Vincent McMahon, joined his father in the business during the 1950s, when the popularity of professional wrestling was on the rise. Vincent McMahon formed his own promotion company in 1963, naming the enterprise the World Wide Wrestling Federation. The global implication of the company's name belied the realities of the professional wrestling business, which was composed of a patchwork of promoters who were geographically segregated. Far from worldwide, the World Wide Wrestling Federation operated within well-defined boundaries, promoting professional wrestling matches in northeastern cities of the United States.

Although the company's territory was restricted, it embraced heavily populated metropolitan areas, including New York City and Philadelphia. Popular wrestlers such as Gorgeous George had helped professional wrestling gain a loyal following among television viewers during the early years of television. However, not long after McMahon formed the World Wide Wrestling Federation, the half-sport, half-entertainment attraction began to lose its appeal. It was during the business downturn in the late 1960s and early 1970s that the third generation of McMahons entered the professional wrestling promotion business. Vincent K. McMahon, Jr., a pioneer in a decades-old business, entirely transformed the world of professional wrestling.

In a business that was a hybrid of sports and entertainment, McMahon excelled by being half-innovator, half-renegade. His unquestionable marketing skills may have surprised some, considering his less-than-exemplary past, but his iconoclasm probably struck longtime acquaintances as the natural progression of a troubled childhood. As a child, McMahon was exceedingly disruptive in school. Eventually, authorities were forced to present him with one of two alternatives: enroll in a state reform school or in a military academy. McMahon opted for the latter, becoming the first cadet in the history of the Waynesboro, Virginia, Fishburne Military School to be court-martialed. McMahon's academic career only moderately improved after his truncated stay at Fishburne. He spent five years attending college, all the while petitioning professors to raise his grades while attending summer school each of the five years. After college, McMahon tried to make his mark in sales, hawking paper cups and adding machines before deciding to join his father in the promotion of professional wrestling. From his undistinguished background, McMahon emerged to create one of the most successful marketing organizations in the country.

Company Perspectives:

Our objectives are to broaden our leadership position in the creation, production and promotion of our form of televised and live entertainment events and to leverage our technical and operating skills to pursue complementary entertainment-based business opportunities. Some of the key elements of our strategy are to: continue to produce high quality branded programming, live events and consumer products for worldwide distribution; expand our existing television and pay-per-view distribution relationships and develop broader distribution arrangements for our branded programming worldwide; increase the licensing and direct sale of our branded products through our distribution channels; grow our Internet operations to further promote our brand and to develop additional sources of revenue; form strategic relationships with other media and entertainment companies to further promote our brand and our products; create new forms of entertainment and brands that complement our existing businesses, including the development of new television programming that will extend beyond our current programming, all of which will appeal to our targeted demographic market; and develop branded location-based entertainment businesses directly or through licensing agreements, joint ventures or other arrangements.

In 1971, McMahon began working for his father's organization, shuttling throughout the Northeast promoting local shows and serving as an announcer at the matches. A 6'3'' amateur bodybuilder, McMahon fit the mold of a wrestler, but it was never his inclination to blend into the world of professional wrestling. As he had during his years as a schoolboy, McMahon wanted to be a disruptive force. He worked for the company (which dropped the word ''Wide'' from its title in 1979) for nearly a decade, before acquiring WWF in 1982 from his ailing father.

Taking Charge, 1982

With full control over the organization, McMahon was able to express his renegade side and shape the company into a formidable force, the likes of which had never been seen in the business. The difference between McMahon and other promoters was his disregard for the traditions of professional wrestling. He ignored the geographical boundaries that divided the industry and began buying out regional promoters, emerging as a consolidator bent on amalgamating the smaller tours into a national company. Along with the territory he gained from other promoters, McMahon also took other promoters' top wrestling personalities, including a fellow amateur bodybuilder named Terry Bollea. Bollea, whom McMahon lured away from a Minneapolis promoter in 1983, wrestled under the name Hulk Hogan, the most popular professional wrestling star of the 1980s. To provide greater exposure to his motley collection of wrestlers, McMahon purchased time on local television stations to air WWF's matches, hoping to stimulate interest in a spectacle whose popularity had been on the wane for nearly 15 years. Nothing contributed more to WWF's startling success, however, than an industry-shaking announcement McMahon made during the early 1980s. He acknowledged that the winners of professional wrestling matches were predetermined, sparking furor among other promoters and some fans. Aside from freeing WWF from state regulations, which was particularly important in light of the company's aggressive geographic expansion, McMahon's concession pushed professional wrestling headlong into the realm of show business. No longer forced to masquerade as a legitimate sport, professional wrestling could embrace the concept of entertainment wholeheartedly and throw away the trappings of bleak gymnasiums for something more akin to Las Vegas.

Presenting wrestling as pure entertainment unleashed McMahon's marketing talents, transforming WWF's live events into bawdy extravaganzas that titillated crowds. In the scripts that governed the live events, McMahon developed and accentuated rivalries between his wrestlers, creating story lines that carried the actions of one event to their denouement in later events. Marketing, brash and glitzy in its tone, was suffusive and highly effective, transforming the image of such wrestlers as André the Giant, the Iron Sheik, and Hulk Hogan into superheroes or detestable villains. In essence, McMahon amplified the intensity of everything under his control, making Titan Sports, Inc., the company he created in 1982, and WWF, the wholly-owned subsidiary of Titan Sports, a rousing success a few short years after leadership was passed from father to son.

By 1987, McMahon no longer had to pay television stations to broadcast WWF's matches; advertisers were more than willing to sponsor his version of professional wrestling. WWF sold $80 million worth of tickets to live shows in 1987, including the proceeds from the more than 93,000 fans who attended Wrestlemania III in Pontiac, Michigan's Silverdome, which set the attendance record for an indoor event in the United States. Beyond ticket sales, there were a handful of other revenue sources, including merchandise sold at the live shows, television advertising sales, programs, videos, albums, and the three percent licensing fee awarded to WWF for the $170 million in sales racked up by retailers selling items such as professional wrestling lunch boxes and caricature action figures. Accounting for all revenue, *Forbes* magazine, which, tellingly, had taken interest in McMahon's sprawling enterprise, estimated Titan Sports was grossing $145 million in sales annually. WWF, and with it professional wrestling, had become a business phenomenon. WWF distributed four of the top-selling sports videos on the market, besting Jane Fonda's workout video, and produced five television shows internally, three of which were syndicated nationally. Further, pay-per-view cable television had emerged as a potentially lucrative source of revenue. Wrestlemania IV was held at a much smaller venue than the Silverdome, yet grossed a record $30 million thanks to the one million pay-per-view customers who paid $15 per household to watch the event. McMahon, who oversaw all aspects of the WWF marketing machine, was worth in excess of $100 million, having catapulted into the country's business elite in roughly five years.

As the popularity of professional wrestling exploded, it developed into much more than an arena show. National television syndication, pay-per-view television events, and licensing deals for everything from action figures to wrestling-themed air fresheners were indicative of a booming business whose boundaries were stretching beyond precedent. WWF's core audience of children and teens expanded to embrace more and more

Key Dates:

1963: World Wide Wrestling Federation is formed.
1982: Vincent K. McMahon acquires his father's company.
1983: Hulk Hogan, wrestling for a Minneapolis promoter, is signed by WWF.
1987: More than 93,000 fans attend Wrestlemania III; annual ticket sales reach $80 million.
1988: Ted Turner forms rival WCW.
1991: Popular appeal of professional wrestling begins to wane; WWF is rocked by scandals.
1996: WWF stages a comeback; attendance and television ratings soar.
1999: Initial public offering of stock is completed.

adults, blue-collar and white-collar alike. Celebrities such as Sylvester Stallone, Madonna, and Cyndi Lauper began making appearances, performing as referees and timekeepers and, more importantly, helping professional wrestling become a mainstream phenomenon. With a fan base increasing by the droves and steady streams of revenue filling its coffers, WWF basked in the glow of the popularity it had created. However, the company did not stand by itself for long.

Attracted by the enormous financial potential of professional wrestling, media mogul Ted Turner decided he wanted a stake in the business. In 1988, he created World Championship Wrestling (WCW), forming a formidable rival to WWF. Backed by Turner's sizeable fortune and TNT and TBS, the two cable television networks owned by Turner, WCW enjoyed an easy and swift entry into the business, securing a sizeable market presence almost overnight. Wrestlers were easy to come by in the frenzy sweeping the country, as WWF and WCW hired ''almost anyone off the street,'' according to John Wendt, director of the MBA sports and entertainment program at the University of St. Thomas. ''If you're big, mean, and ugly,'' Wendt continued in his May 12, 1997 interview with *Marketing News,* ''you're a world wrestler.'' The emergence of too many unknown wrestlers in the ring, however, delivered a crippling blow to the popularity of professional wrestling. By the end of the 1980s, the flamboyant world created by McMahon had begun to turn stale.

WWF Struggles Through the Early 1990s

The overabundance of unknown wrestlers was just part of the problem affecting WWF. Licensing had proliferated out of control and marketing had grown too pervasive, saturating the appeal of Hulk Hogan and his cohorts to a detrimental extent. Ironically, the same overblown aggrandizement of professional wrestling that fueled its meteoric rise led to its downfall by the beginning of the 1990s, as the hype surrounding the entertainment spectacle eventually suffocated its popularity. By the early 1990s, the celebrities that had once circled the wrestling ring of WWF events were nowhere to be found, fleeing the scene of what was rapidly becoming perceived as a joke. A substantial portion of the fans went with them, causing attendance at live events to fall and television ratings to slip as well.

To make matters worse for McMahon, Titan Sports was the object of scandal during the early 1990s. Federal charges were lodged against McMahon and WWF's parent company for homosexual harassment and illegal steroid use, further deteriorating professional wrestling's image. McMahon and Titan Sports were acquitted of both charges, but damage had already been done, damage that made WWF vulnerable in Turner's mind. In another ironic twist that drew WWF downward, Turner took the opportunity presented to him to do what McMahon had done to regional promoters during the early 1980s. The WCW chief began luring WWF star wrestlers into his organization, including Randy Savage, Rowdy Roddy Piper, and, to complete the circle of events, Hulk Hogan.

Lawsuits and counter-lawsuits between WWF and WCW ensued, providing a litigious backdrop to professional wrestling's waning market appeal. Hobbled by the highly publicized scandals and the departure of some its most popular personalities, WWF lost ground to WCW, but McMahon was ready for another fight. He and his management team made pervasive changes to all facets of the company's operation. Methods governing staffing, licensing, touring, and marketing were altered, and marketing representatives were sent into the field. ''We wanted to get back to grassroots efforts,'' explained WWF's senior vice-president of event booking and operations to *Amusement Business* in a May 13, 1996 interview. Licensing was approached more methodically, with the company choosing its licensees after careful examination. Outside the United States, where WWF had registered considerable success in England and Germany in particular, the company was mindful of oversaturating markets. Company officials emphasized cultivating followings in new markets instead, leading to WWF tours in India, Kuwait, and South Africa during the mid-1990s.

As the company tightened its control over operations, pursuing a general strategy of reigning in corporate functions that had careened during the late 1980s, McMahon amplified the scripted performances of WWF live events. To differentiate WWF from WCW, McMahon stepped up the violence and sexual innuendo contained in WWF shows, casting WWF as the edgier alternative to the tamer WCW. Matches between wrestling personalities were presented as parts within larger plots, following story lines that grew darker and more elaborate in style and content. The live events became chapters in a never-ending saga pitting factions of wrestlers against one another, each victimized by betrayals that spawned endless subplots. In WWF's two-hour television program, 36 minutes of airtime was devoted to wrestling, with the remainder focusing on soap-opera-style feuds and ''behind-the-scenes'' intrigue. The response from the public left little doubt as to the effectiveness of McMahon's changes. Attendance figures rose, highlighted by the highest gross ever for a WWF event at Madison Square Garden in 1996, and television ratings climbed upwards, with WWF eclipsing the figures reported by WCW in each category.

Late 1990s: WWF's Comeback Complete

By the mid-1990s professional wrestling had proven the problems of the early 1990s were only temporary. By the end of the decade, professional wrestling exuded more strength than it had at its peak in the late 1980s. Personalities such as Stone Cold Steve Austin and the Undertaker performed in front of capacity crowds, while WWF programming, which aired in 120 countries in 11 languages, earned record ratings and attracted a different ilk of sponsors. During the 1980s, professional wrestling drew sponsorship deals generally from snack food companies and automotive products makers; however, by the late 1990s the broadening of WWF's fan base attracted more distinguished sponsors, such as Warner Bros., Hasbro, Proctor & Gamble Co., Western Union, and the U.S. Army. The celebrities had returned as well, no longer fearing the stigma that had prompted their departure earlier in the decade. In 1998, two of the National Basketball Association's most popular players, Karl Malone and Dennis Rodman, battled against one another in the ring, the same year a former WWF wrestler, Jesse ''the Body'' Ventura, was elected governor of Minnesota. In terms of revenue-generating capability, professional wrestling demonstrated remarkable prowess. The cornucopia of merchandise, ranging from toys and temporary tattoos to hot sauces, constituted a business valued in excess of $1 billion annually.

As McMahon prepared to lead WWF into the 21st century, his objectives were not limited to beating back the advances of rival WCW. Considering the popular appeal of the more than 200 live events staged by WWF annually and the company's consistent ranking as the highest-rated program on cable television, McMahon could entertain the prospect of mounting an assault against the purveyors of legitimate sport: the National Basketball Association, the National Football League, and Major League Baseball. In one of the last developments of the 1990s, McMahon renamed Titan Sports ''World Wrestling Federation Entertainment, Inc.'' and took the company public. The debut of the ''WWFE'' ticker symbol on the NASDAQ exchange in October 1999 marked the beginning of a new era in the company's history, one that promised to stir the emotions of professional wrestling fans in the years ahead.

Principal Subsidiaries

World Wrestling Federation; World Wrestling Productions.

Principal Competitors

World Championship Wrestling; National Football League; National Basketball Association; National Hockey League.

Further Reading

Authers, John, ''Wrestling Elbows Its Way into Big Money,'' *Financial Times,* May 31, 1999, p. 4.

Brown, Rich, ''WWF Tries Out New Holds.'' *Broadcasting & Cable,* September 2, 1996, p. 50.

Chamish, Barry, ''WWF Riding Wave of Popularity in Israel,'' *Amusement Business,* January 17, 1994, p. 12.

Collins, James, ''Lords of the Ring,'' *Time,* June 29, 1998, p. 66.

Fisher, Eric, ''World Wrestling Federation Parent Mulls Public Offering,'' *Knight-Ridder/Tribune Business News,* May 20, 1999.

Fromm, Emily, ''Good, Clean Entertainment,'' *ADWEEK Eastern Edition,* January 25, 1999, p. 3.

Jensen, Jeff, ''Wrestling Goes Mainstream, Draws Big Ratings, Sponsors,'' *Advertising Age,* August 17, 1998, p. 3.

Katz, Richard, ''Grappling with Success,'' *Variety,* June 14, 1999, p. 17.

Melvin, Mary Kay, ''WWF Officials: This Year's Grosses Prove the Lull Is Over,'' *Amusement Business,* May 13, 1996, p. 10.

Palmeri, Christopher, '' 'We Want to Be Like Disney,' '' *Forbes,* October 17, 1988, p. 133.

''Ring Masters,'' *Economist (US),* August 12, 1995, p. 74.

Rosellini, Lynn, ''Lords of the Ring,'' *U.S. News & World Report,* May 17, 1999, p. 52.

Schmuckler, Eric, ''Steel-Cage Legal Wrangle,'' *MEDIAWEEK,* March 1, 1993, p. 20.

Shermach, Kelly, ''Wrestling on a Peak; Keeps One Eye on Valley,'' *Marketing News,* May 12, 1997, p. 24.

Stanley, T.L., ''Grapplin' for Dollars,'' *Brandweek,* April 19, 1999, p. 48.

''Titan Sports Inc., The Owner of the World Wrestling Federation, Has Acquired the Debbie Reynolds Hotel and Casino in Las Vegas,'' *Broadcasting & Cable,* August 10, 1998, p. 80.

Trigoboff, Dan, ''Wrestling with the Competition,'' *Broadcasting & Cable,* August 12, 1997, p. 76.

—Jeffrey L. Covell

Young's Market Company, LLC

2164 N. Batavia Street
Orange, California 92865
U.S.A.
Telephone: (714) 283-4933
Fax: (714) 283-6175
Web site: http://www.youngsmkt.com

Wholly Owned Subsidiary of Young's Holdings, Inc.
Incorporated: 1906
Employees: 1,700
Sales: $1.1 billion (1999)
NAIC: 42281 Beer and Ale Wholesalers; 42282 Wine and Distilled Alcoholic Beverage Wholesalers

Young's Market Company, LLC is one of the largest wholesalers and distributors of beer, wine, and distilled spirits in the United States. With branch offices in Los Angeles, San Diego, Stockton, Santa Rosa, Eureka, Bakersfield, and Fresno, the company's market territory includes most of California. Its presence is strongest, however, in the southern California/Los Angeles area. Young's Market also operates in the state of Hawaii through a subsidiary called Better Brands, which has branch offices on several of the islands. The company is the sole distributor of most of its brands.

1888–1930: Building a Food Retail Empire

In 1888, John G. Young, founder of Young's Market Company, opened a small food retail store in downtown Los Angeles. When his fledgling business began to grow, Young's four younger brothers joined him in the venture. In 1906, the five Young brothers incorporated their business as Young's Market Company and opened their first joint store at 9th and Main Street in Los Angeles. Four years later, the company opened its first manufacturing plant to produce several of its own food lines, including salad dressings, mayonnaise, corned beef, and sausage products. It also established a facility in a nearby building for receiving fish and seafood.

In 1925, the Young brothers opened a luxurious new store on the corner of 7th Street and Union Avenue. The store, which also served as the Young's Market Company headquarters, was to become a landmark in downtown Los Angeles and an important part of the city's heritage. Built in an Italian Renaissance Revival style, the store's decor featured tile mosaics and friezes. Inside, affluent shoppers could find such gourmet offerings as chocolates made on-site, Young's own line of coffees, and a delicatessen that claimed to offer anything in the world. Young's Market quickly became the caterer of choice for Los Angeles, concocting elaborate wedding cakes for prominent area weddings and supplying William Randolph Hearst with food for his ranch. The company's delivery trucks made deliveries twice each day to many parts of the city.

In 1925, with their flagship store thriving, the Young brothers began opening a chain of what they called "neighborhood" retail stores. The company spent the next several years growing its chain, expanding as far south as San Diego and as far north as Santa Maria. In 1934, Young's opened its first supermarket. The store, named Thriftimart Cash and Carry, was geared less toward the company's traditional gourmet fare and more toward standard grocery products. Four more Thriftimarts soon followed. In 1937, however, the Young brothers sold the five-store chain of supermarkets to Fitzsimmons Markets.

1930s: Post-Prohibition

While the Youngs were working on their Thriftimart chain, a momentous change was taking place in the United States. With the end of Prohibition in 1933, the federal government's ban on alcohol sales was lifted. Retailers immediately jumped into action, providing a thirsty public with drinks that had been illegal for 13 years; Young's Market was in the vanguard of the new liquor business that was quickly forming. The company began wholesaling liquor, while at the same time maintaining its retail grocery business. In 1934, it turned its San Diego store into a combination wholesale and retail food and liquor operation.

As a liquor wholesaler, Young's took an approach slightly different from that of its competitors. At the time, wine and liquor brands were carried by several different distributors, usually with no territorial exclusivity. This meant that competing distributors often carried the same brands. Young's, however, sought exclusive rights to the labels it carried. The com-

Company Perspectives:

The Corporate Mission of Young's Market Company is to be the premier spirits and wine distributor in the United States by diligently marketing and selling our portfolio of brands and by providing the most effective and efficient customer service in the industry.

pany also aligned itself closely with smaller, independent distillers. This approach led to several beneficial and long-lasting alliances with brands such as Bacardi rum and Christian Brothers brandy.

One of the company's most notable successes was the introduction of the José Cuervo tequila line in the United States. The José Cuervo relationship was established by one of Young's new salesmen—Vernon Underwood. At the time, most Americans were unfamiliar with the strange-tasting Mexican liquor. Underwood, who had become acquainted with the drink during his college years at the University of Arizona at Tucson, was sure that it could be a good seller in the United States. He managed to convince both Young and the head of the Cuervo distillery, and Young's obtained U.S. distribution rights from Cuervo.

Tequila might not have become as popular as it did, however, without some further help from Underwood and Young's Market's advertising agency. The main obstacle to popularizing tequila was finding a way to drink it. In Mexico, the traditional method of tequila drinking involved licking salt from the back of the hand, gulping the liquor, and then sucking on a lime. It seemed unlikely, however, that this routine was going to catch on in the United States, and sales of the drink were slow. At that time, however, a Los Angeles restaurant suddenly started ordering five cases of tequila at a time, and Underwood decided to pay a visit to the restaurant's bar to investigate what was behind the increased sales. What he found was the margarita—a new tequila drink invented by the restaurant's head bartender. Young's ad agency used the drink as a springboard for a new tequila campaign, which proved very successful. Sales of Cuervo took off, eventually attaining such popularity that Young's sold the national distribution rights, retaining distribution only in its own territory.

The successful introduction of José Cuervo was to be only the first of Underwood's many contributions to Young's Market. Eventually, he married company founder John Young's daughter, Adrienne, and assumed an increasingly significant role in the business, becoming general manager and chief financial officer.

1940s–70s: Exclusively Wholesale

Since Young's had begun wholesaling liquor in the early 1930s, it had dealt with increasing conflict between the wholesale and retail sides of its business. Some of its wholesale customers were unhappy about doing business with a company that was competing directly against them on the retail level. In 1940, when Young's acquired a Dr Pepper franchise, it appeared that the time had come to choose between retail and wholesale. The company decided to give up its retail segment and focus exclusively on wholesaling wine, spirits, and food. It quickly set about selling its chain of neighborhood stores, which by that time numbered 60. In May 1940, the company closed the doors of its famous headquarters store at 7th and Union.

With a newly defined focus, Young's Market expanded its liquor business in the 1950s, opening branch operations in Long Beach and Rialto, California. The company also built a new headquarters at 500 S. Central Avenue in Los Angeles and moved its meat and food processing segments into a new facility just down the street.

In 1963, Young's Market President William G. Young died. He was replaced by Vernon Underwood, John Young's son-in-law and the company's general manager. One year later, the company established its first subsidiary wine and spirits wholesale business, which was named the William George Company. The new subsidiary opened its first wholesale branch operation in Anaheim, California, in 1967.

Also in 1967, Young's Market first forayed outside its native California with the acquisition of two Hawaii-based liquor wholesale firms. The companies—Cereal and Fruit Products and Better Brands Ltd.—were located in Honolulu. One year after the acquisition, the companies expanded their operations by opening a branch office in Kahului, Maui. A second Hawaii branch operation was opened in 1972, in the community of Hilo. In 1975, Young's added a food wholesaling operation to its growing Hawaii liquor business. The company—Young's Meat and Provisions—was based in Honolulu and provided service to all of the islands.

In the meantime, Young's also was exploring new domestic expansion and diversification possibilities. In 1968, the company became a vintner as well as a distributor when it purchased the Buena Vista Winery in Sonoma, California. A year later, Young's acquired 700 acres of land overlooking the San Francisco Bay to use as a new vineyard for the 100-year-old winery. Buena Vista's vineyard was a part of the Carneros viticultural region, which was characterized by its shallow, dense soil, cool summers, and mild winters. The climate conditions in the Carneros region allowed for longer growing seasons and produced grapes with distinct flavors.

In 1976, with its vineyards thriving, Young's added a new, state-of-the-art fermenting winery to the Buena Vista Winery. Just three years later, the company sold the vineyards and winery to the A. Racke GmbH & Co. of Germany, a family-owned wine and spirits business, which had been founded in 1855.

1980s: Steady Expansion

Young's started off the 1980s with more expansion. In 1980, the company's Hawaiian subsidiaries, Better Brands and Cereal and Fruit, established a third wholesale branch, on the island of Kauai. Back home in Los Angeles, the company opened a warehouse operation in Orange County to service chain stores carrying liquor and wines. In addition, Young's Specialty Foods Division, which carried gourmet and natural food items, moved into an expanded space in Cerritos. The division moved to an even larger facility in just three years, because of increasing business and a growing product line.

Key Dates:

1888: John Young opens his first retail food store in downtown Los Angeles.
1906: Young's Market Company is incorporated.
1925: Young's Market opens its famous headquarters store in Los Angeles.
1927: Young's begins to build a chain of "neighborhood" stores.
1933: Young's begins wholesaling wine and spirits.
1940: The company decides to focus exclusively on wholesaling and begins selling its chain of neighborhood stores.
1963: Vernon Underwood, Sr., becomes president of Young's Market Company.
1967: Young's acquires Better Brands and Cereal and Fruit Products subsidiaries.
1968: Young's purchases the Buena Vista Winery.
1979: Buena Vista Winery is sold.
1990: The Underwood family buys out all remaining stockholders of Young's Market, becoming the company's sole owners.
1994: Young's Market moves its headquarters from Los Angeles to Orange, California.
1997: Charles Andrews becomes president and CEO of the company.

By the mid-1980s, Young's distributorship covered virtually the southern two-thirds of California, stretching as far north as Santa Clara. In 1985, the company inched a bit further north when it acquired a wholesale liquor distributorship in Union City and Santa Rosa. The distributorship—Rathjen Wines and Spirits—was absorbed into Young's and renamed Young's Market Company.

In 1988, Vernon Underwood retired from the business he had helped build for more than 50 years. Having served as the company's CEO and chairman of the board since 1974, he was named chairman emeritus upon his retirement. He was succeeded as chairman and CEO by his son, Vernon Underwood, Jr. The younger Underwood, like his father, had spent his entire career in the family business, starting as a warehouse worker in 1955. He had served as the company's president since 1975.

1990s: Underwood Buyout

Although Young's Market had always been controlled and managed by descendants of the founding Young brothers, the company had acquired a handful of outside investors in its 100-plus years of existence. In 1990, however, the Underwood family bought out the other shareholders, purchasing 37,500 shares at $3,500 per share, and assumed full ownership.

After the buyout, the Underwoods set about making some changes in the business. Perhaps most significantly, the company tightened its focus on the wine and spirits business, shedding its wholesale food distribution divisions. Young's meat distribution business, which was purchased by Con-Agra, and its seafood business, which was purchased by Hunt Bros., accounted for a combined $100 million in sales.

Another of the Underwoods' major changes was the relocation of the company's headquarters. In 1994, Young's moved from downtown Los Angeles to a newly built, 210,000-square-foot facility in Orange, California. According to Underwood, the relocation put Young's closer to more customers and closer to one of its biggest suppliers. Also in 1994, Young's Market reached $1 billion in sales.

In 1997, Young's Market entered into a strategic alliance with Sunbelt Beverage Corporation. Sunbelt was a large liquor distributor with operations in Florida, Maryland, Arizona, Pennsylvania, and South Carolina and affiliated companies in New York, Connecticut, and Washington, D.C. This alliance made Young's a part of the largest distribution network in the United States. Shortly after becoming a part of Sunbelt Beverage, Young's appointed Charles Andrews as its president and CEO. Andrews had served previously as the president and CEO of Sunbelt Beverage.

Looking to the Future

Since reaching the billion-dollar mark in 1994, Young's Market had posted only modest gains in sales; in 1999, the company's sales totaled $1.1 billion. This was due in part to relatively flat sales of wines and spirits industrywide. Consumption of wines had reached a peak, and then a plateau, in the 1980s. Meanwhile, sales of distilled spirits decreased for several years before finally stabilizing in the late 1990s. Because Young's revenues depended entirely upon sales of alcoholic beverages, the company's future performance was inextricably tied to that industry's market conditions.

Principal Subsidiaries

Better Brands Ltd.

Principal Competitors

National Distributing Company, Inc.; Southern Wine & Spirits of America; Charmer Industries, Inc.; Clare Rose, Inc.; Jaydor Corporation; Johnson Brother Wholesale Liquor Company; Paterno Imports Ltd.; Peerless Importers Inc.; Sunbelt Beverage Corporation; Wirtz Corporation.

Further Reading

Britton, Charles, "Young's Market: Food Industry Innovator," *Southern California Business,* December 1, 1985, p. 7.
Klayman, Gary, "In High Spirits: Family Firm Takes New Approach to Its Old Business," *Orange County Business Journal,* October 2, 1995, p. 1.
Wilson, Daniel, "A Fresh Look at Young's Market Co.," *Wines & Vines,* May 1, 1994, p. 37.

—Shawna Brynildssen

INDEX TO COMPANIES

Index to Companies

Listings in this index are arranged in alphabetical order under the company name. Company names beginning with a letter or proper name such as Eli Lilly & Co. will be found under the first letter of the company name. Definite articles (The, Le, La) are ignored for alphabetical purposes as are forms of incorporation that precede the company name (AB, NV). Company names printed in bold type have full, historical essays on the page numbers appearing in bold. Updates to entries that appeared in earlier volumes are signified by the notation **(upd.)**. Company names in light type are references within an essay to that company, not full historical essays. This index is cumulative with volume numbers printed in bold type.

INDEX TO INDUSTRIES

Index to Industries

ACCOUNTING

ADVERTISING & OTHER BUSINESS SERVICES

AEROSPACE

AIRLINES

AUTOMOTIVE

BEVERAGES

BIOTECHNOLOGY

CHEMICALS

CONGLOMERATES

CONSTRUCTION

CONTAINERS

DRUGS/PHARMACEUTICALS

ELECTRICAL & ELECTRONICS

ENGINEERING & MANAGEMENT SERVICES

ENTERTAINMENT & LEISURE

FINANCIAL SERVICES: BANKS

FINANCIAL SERVICES: NON-BANKS

FOOD PRODUCTS

FOOD SERVICES & RETAILERS

HEALTH & PERSONAL CARE PRODUCTS

HEALTH CARE SERVICES

HOTELS

INFORMATION TECHNOLOGY

INSURANCE

LEGAL SERVICES

MANUFACTURING

MATERIALS

MINING & METALS

PAPER & FORESTRY

PERSONAL SERVICES

PETROLEUM

PUBLISHING & PRINTING

REAL ESTATE

RETAIL & WHOLESALE

RUBBER & TIRE

TELECOMMUNICATIONS

TEXTILES & APPAREL

TOBACCO

TRANSPORT SERVICES

UTILITIES

WASTE SERVICES

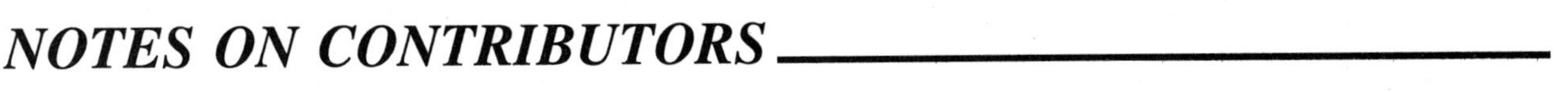

NOTES ON CONTRIBUTORS

Notes on Contributors

BIANCO, David P. Freelance writer.

BRYNILDSSEN, Shawna. Freelance writer and editor based in Bloomington, Indiana.

COHEN, M. L. Novelist and freelance writer living in Paris.

COVELL, Jeffrey L. Freelance writer and corporate history contractor.

FUJINAKA, Mariko. Freelance writer and editor living in Paso Robles, California.

HALASZ, Robert. Former editor in chief of *World Progress* and *Funk & Wagnalls New Encyclopedia Yearbook*; author, *The U.S. Marines* (Millbrook Press, 1993).

INGRAM, Frederick C. South Carolina-based business writer who has contributed to *GSA Business, Appalachian Trailway News,* the *Encyclopedia of Business,* the *Encyclopedia of Global Industries,* the *Encyclopedia of Consumer Brands,* and other regional and trade publications.

LEMIEUX, Gloria. Freelance writer and editor living in Nashua, New Hampshire.

MALLETT, Daryl F. Freelance writer and editor; actor; contributing editor and series editor at The Borgo Press; series editor of SFRA Press's *Studies in Science Fiction, Fantasy and Horror*; associate editor of Gryphon Publications and for *Other Worlds Magazine*; founder and owner of Angel Enterprises, Jacob's Ladder Books, and Dustbunny Productions.

MEDEIROS, Kimbally A. Florida-based freelance writer.

MOZZONE, Terri. Minneapolis-based freelance writer specializing in corporate profiles.

RHODES, Nelson. Freelance editor, writer, and consultant in the Chicago area.

RUBEN, Barbara. Washington, D.C.-area freelance writer.

SALAMIE, David E. Part-owner of InfoWorks Development Group, a reference publication development and editorial services company.

STANFEL, Rebecca. Freelance writer living in Helena, Montana.

UHLE, Frank. Ann Arbor-based freelance writer; movie projectionist, disc jockey, and staff member of *Psychotronic Video* magazine.

WALDEN, David M. Freelance writer and historian in Salt Lake City; adjunct history instructor at Salt Lake City Community College.

WERNICK, Ellen D. Freelance writer and editor.

WOODWARD, A. Freelance writer.